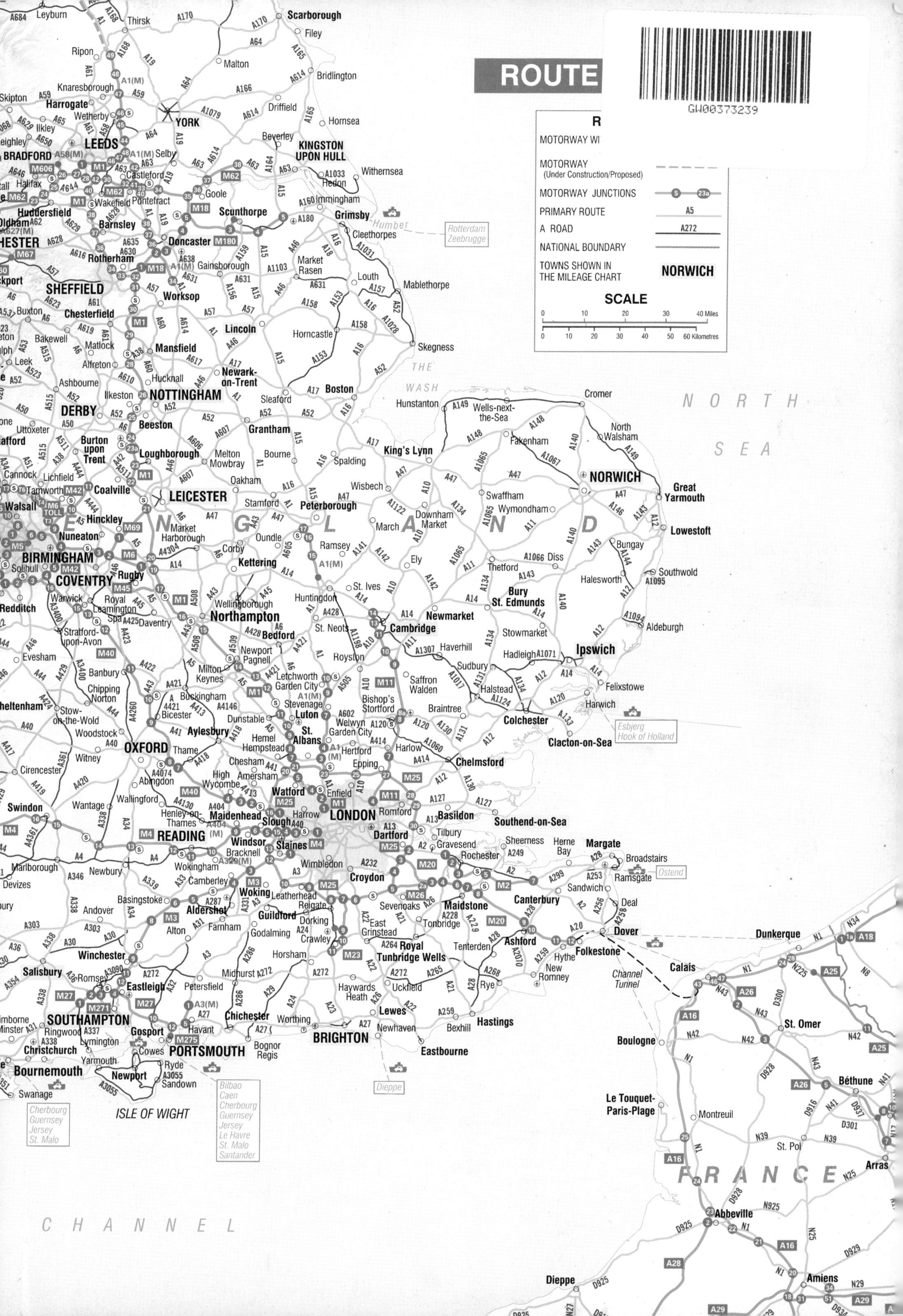

ROUTE
GW00373239
MOTORWAY WI
MOTORWAY (Under Construction/Proposed)
MOTORWAY JUNCTIONS
PRIMARY ROUTE
A ROAD
NATIONAL BOUNDARY
TOWNS SHOWN IN THE MILEAGE CHART
NORWICH
SCALE
0 10 20 30 40 Miles
0 10 20 30 40 50 60 Kilometres
NORTH SEA
ENGLAND
FRANCE
CHANNEL
THE WASH
ISLE OF WIGHT
Channel Tunnel
Rotterdam Zeebrugge
Esbjerg Hook of Holland
Ostend
Dieppe
Bilbao Caen Cherbourg Guernsey Jersey Le Havre St. Malo Santander
Cherbourg Guernsey Jersey St. Malo
LONDON
BIRMINGHAM
LEEDS
SHEFFIELD
NOTTINGHAM
LEICESTER
COVENTRY
DERBY
OXFORD
READING
SOUTHAMPTON
PORTSMOUTH
BRIGHTON
KINGSTON UPON HULL
YORK
Scarborough
Norwich
Cambridge
Ipswich
Colchester
Dover
Canterbury
Calais
Boulogne
Dunkerque
Abbeville
Amiens
Arras

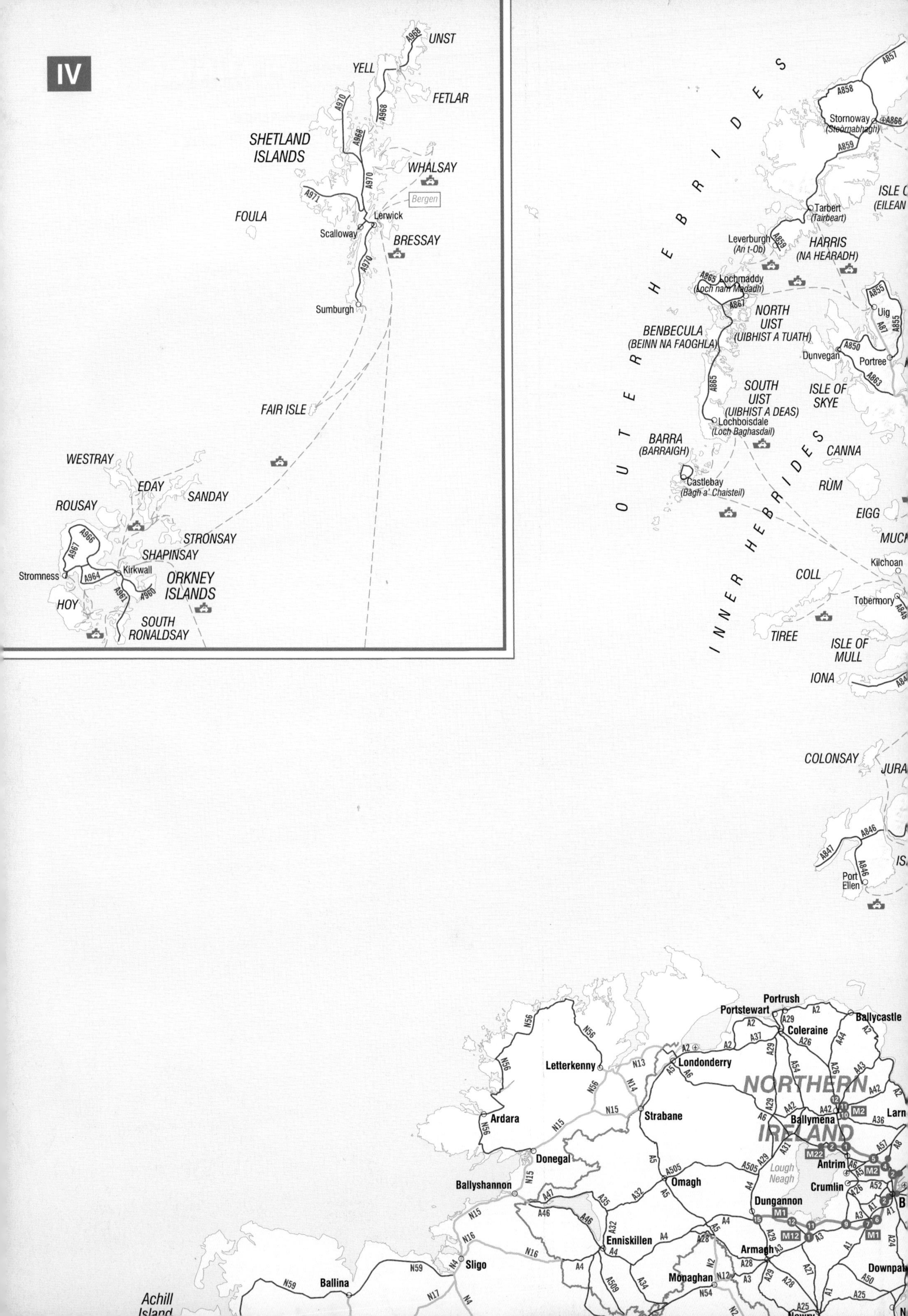
IV
UNST
YELL
FETLAR
SHETLAND ISLANDS
WHALSAY
Bergen
FOULA
Lerwick
Scalloway
BRESSAY
Sumburgh
FAIR ISLE
WESTRAY
EDAY
SANDAY
ROUSAY
STRONSAY
SHAPINSAY
Kirkwall
Stromness
ORKNEY ISLANDS
HOY
SOUTH RONALDSAY
A968
A970
A966
A971
A967
A964
A961
A960
OUTER HEBRIDES
INNER HEBRIDES
Stornoway (Steòrnabhagh)
Tarbert (Tairbeart)
Leverburgh (An t-Ob)
HARRIS (NA HEARADH)
Lochmaddy (Loch nam Madadh)
NORTH UIST (UIBHIST A TUATH)
BENBECULA (BEINN NA FAOGHLA)
SOUTH UIST (UIBHIST A DEAS)
Lochboisdale (Loch Baghasdail)
BARRA (BARRAIGH)
Castlebay (Bàgh a' Chaisteil)
Uig
Dunvegan
Portree
ISLE OF SKYE
CANNA
RÙM
EIGG
Kilchoan
COLL
Tobermory
TIREE
ISLE OF MULL
IONA
COLONSAY
Port Ellen
A857
A858
A866
A859
A865
A867
A855
A87
A850
A863
A846
A847
Portrush
Portstewart
Coleraine
Ballycastle
Londonderry
Letterkenny
NORTHERN IRELAND
Strabane
Ballymena
Ardara
Antrim
Lough Neagh
Donegal
Omagh
Crumlin
Ballyshannon
Dungannon
Enniskillen
Armagh
Sligo
Monaghan
Ballina
Achill Island
N56
N13
N14
N15
N16
N59
N17
N4
N2
N12
N54
A2
A29
A37
A26
A44
A43
A42
A5
A6
A54
M2
M22
A36
A57
A505
A31
A4
A32
A35
A46
A47
A509
A34
A28
A3
A27
M1
M12
A1
A52
A24
A50
A25

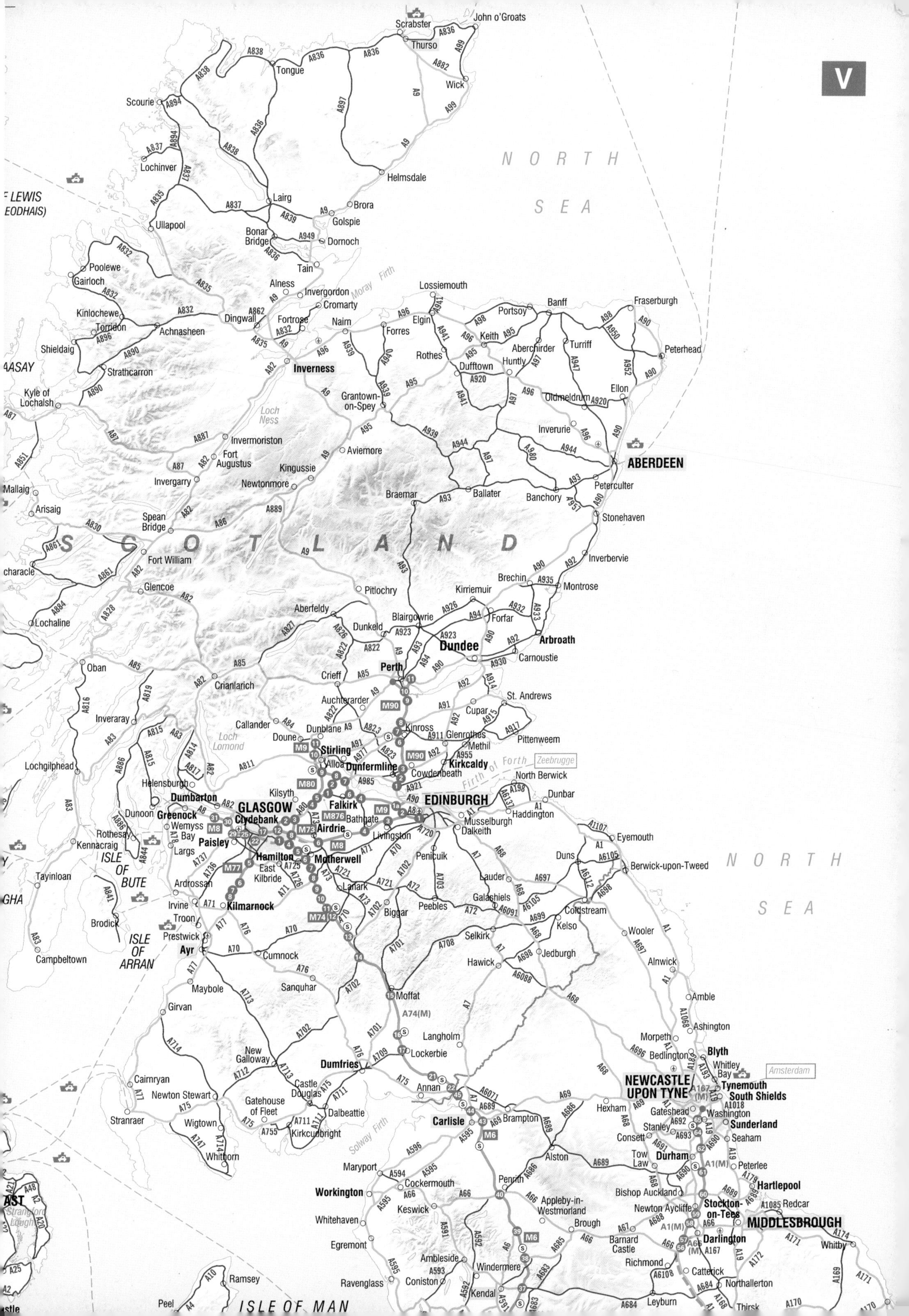

SCOTLAND

NORTH SEA

ISLE OF LEWIS (EODHAIS)

John o'Groats · Scrabster · Thurso · Wick · Tongue · Scourie · Lochinver · Helmsdale · Lairg · Brora · Golspie · Dornoch · Bonar Bridge · Tain · Ullapool · Poolewe · Gairloch · Alness · Invergordon · Cromarty · Lossiemouth · Portsoy · Banff · Fraserburgh · Kinlochewe · Dingwall · Fortrose · Nairn · Forres · Elgin · Keith · Aberchirder · Turriff · Peterhead · Torridon · Achnasheen · Inverness · Rothes · Dufftown · Huntly · Oldmeldrum · Ellon · Shieldaig · Strathcarron · Grantown-on-Spey · Inverurie · RAASAY · Kyle of Lochalsh · Invermoriston · Aviemore · ABERDEEN · Fort Augustus · Kingussie · Petercutter · Mallaig · Invergarry · Newtonmore · Braemar · Ballater · Banchory · Arisaig · Spean Bridge · Stonehaven · characle · Fort William · Pitlochry · Kirriemuir · Brechin · Montrose · Inverbervie · Glencoe · Aberfeldy · Blairgowrie · Forfar · Lochaline · Dunkeld · Dundee · Arbroath · Oban · Crianlarich · Crieff · Perth · Carnoustie · Inveraray · Auchterarder · St. Andrews · Callander · Dunblane · Kinross · Cupar · Pittenweem · Lochgilphead · Doune · Stirling · Glenrothes · Methil · Alloa · Dunfermline · Kirkcaldy · Helensburgh · Cowdenbeath · North Berwick · Zeebrugge · Dumbarton · GLASGOW · Falkirk · EDINBURGH · Dunbar · Greenock · Clydebank · Airdrie · Bathgate · Musselburgh · Haddington · Wemyss Bay · Paisley · Livingston · Dalkeith · Eyemouth · Rothesay · Largs · Hamilton · Motherwell · Penicuik · Kennacraig · ISLE OF BUTE · East Kilbride · Lanark · Lauder · Duns · Berwick-upon-Tweed · Tayinloan · Ardrossan · Biggar · Peebles · Galashiels · Coldstream · Irvine · Kilmarnock · Selkirk · Kelso · Wooler · Troon · Prestwick · Hawick · Jedburgh · Alnwick · Brodick · Ayr · Cumnock · ISLE OF ARRAN · Maybole · Sanquhar · Moffat · Amble · Campbeltown · Girvan · Langholm · Ashington · Morpeth · Bedlington · Blyth · New Galloway · Lockerbie · Whitley Bay · Amsterdam · Cairnryan · Dumfries · Annan · NEWCASTLE UPON TYNE · Tynemouth · Newton Stewart · Castle Douglas · Hexham · Gateshead · South Shields · Stranraer · Wigton · Dalbeattie · Carlisle · Brampton · Stanley · Sunderland · Whithorn · Kirkcudbright · Consett · Seaham · Solway Firth · Maryport · Alston · Tow Law · Durham · Peterlee · AST · Cockermouth · Penrith · Bishop Auckland · Hartlepool · Workington · Keswick · Appleby-in-Westmorland · Newton Aycliffe · Stockton-on-Tees · Redcar · Whitehaven · Brough · Darlington · MIDDLESBROUGH · Egremont · Ambleside · Barnard Castle · Richmond · Whitby · Ravenglass · Coniston · Windermere · Catterick · Northallerton · Kendal · Leyburn · Thirsk · ISLE OF MAN · Peel · Ramsey · Castle

Mileage Chart and Journey Times

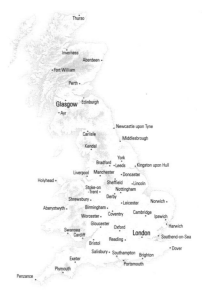

This chart shows the distance in miles and journey time between two cities or towns in Great Britain. Each route has been calculated using a combination of motorways, primary routes and other major roads. This is normally the quickest, though not always the shortest route.

Average journey times are calculated whilst driving at the maximum speed limit. These times are approximate and do not include traffic congestion or convenience breaks.

To find the distance and journey time between two cities or towns, follow a horizontal line and vertical column until they meet each other.

For example, the 285 mile journey from London to Penzance is approximately 4 hours and 59 minutes.

Britain

Journey times

	Aberdeen	Aberystwyth	Ayr	Birmingham	Bradford	Brighton	Bristol	Cambridge	Cardiff	Carlisle	Coventry	Derby	Doncaster	Dover	Edinburgh	Exeter	Fort William	Glasgow	Gloucester	Harwich	Holyhead	Inverness	Ipswich	Kendal	Kingston upon Hull	Leeds	Leicester	Lincoln	Liverpool	Manchester	Middlesbrough	Newcastle upon Tyne	Norwich	Nottingham	Oxford	Penzance	Perth	Plymouth	Portsmouth	Reading	Salisbury	Sheffield	Shrewsbury	Southampton	Southend-on-Sea	Stoke-on-Trent	Swansea	Thurso	Worcester	York	London
Aberdeen		8:21	3:31	7:13	6:28	9:56	8:26	8:15	8:55	4:08	7:27	7:09	6:25	10:16	2:39	9:38	3:38	2:50	7:55	9:32	7:41	2:30	9:08	4:55	6:51	6:16	7:40	7:07	6:13	6:01	5:16	4:39	9:18	7:14	8:18	11:22	1:48	10:16	9:33	8:57	9:21	6:42	7:07	9:25	9:22	6:28	9:31	4:52	7:35	6:07	9:03
Aberystwyth	471		6:34	2:34	3:27	5:21	2:44	4:00	2:29	4:24	2:52	2:56	3:45	5:41	6:20	3:51	8:13	5:53	2:34	5:17	2:29	8:39	4:53	3:40	4:20	3:29	3:18	4:11	2:39	2:54	4:34	5:07	5:03	3:17	3:43	5:35	6:41	4:29	4:27	3:50	4:01	3:41	1:47	4:18	4:56	2:48	1:48	11:00	2:19	4:00	4:28
Ayr	181	324		5:28	4:28	8:11	6:42	6:31	7:10	2:24	5:43	5:25	4:41	8:32	1:48	7:54	3:03	0:48	6:11	7:48	5:56	3:51	7:24	3:10	5:06	4:32	5:55	5:22	4:29	4:16	3:56	3:28	7:34	5:29	6:34	9:37	1:53	8:31	7:49	7:13	7:37	4:57	5:23	7:40	7:37	4:43	7:46	6:12	5:50	4:22	7:16
Birmingham	423	114	272		2:15	3:04	1:41	1:43	2:09	3:16	0:36	1:01	1:40	3:25	5:12	2:53	7:05	4:45	1:10	3:01	2:59	7:31	2:37	2:32	2:21	2:05	1:01	1:55	1:49	1:46	2:55	3:28	2:46	1:08	1:27	4:36	5:33	3:30	2:42	2:06	2:39	1:36	0:59	2:33	2:39	1:02	2:44	9:52	0:49	2:21	2:11
Bradford	377	159	196	124		4:30	3:34	2:43	4:03	2:17	2:19	1:34	0:53	4:37	4:17	4:46	6:06	3:46	3:03	4:01	2:49	6:31	3:37	1:32	1:18	0:28	2:02	1:35	1:22	0:57	1:32	2:06	3:46	1:37	3:05	6:29	4:33	5:24	4:20	3:44	4:18	1:00	2:15	4:12	3:50	1:36	4:38	8:52	2:42	0:59	3:32
Brighton	596	258	441	169	263		2:49	2:09	3:26	6:00	2:42	3:15	3:53	1:53	7:53	3:41	9:49	7:29	2:47	2:19	5:39	10:14	2:20	5:15	4:35	4:19	2:57	3:43	4:32	4:29	5:08	5:42	3:05	3:21	1:58	5:24	8:16	4:18	1:14	1:39	1:54	3:49	3:45	1:35	1:41	3:45	4:01	12:35	3:07	4:35	1:27
Bristol	505	122	375	88	215	129		3:02	0:56	4:31	1:44	2:21	2:59	3:18	6:27	1:37	8:20	6:00	0:47	3:27	4:13	8:45	3:28	3:46	3:41	3:25	2:17	3:11	3:03	3:01	4:15	4:48	3:58	2:28	1:30	3:20	6:48	2:14	2:03	1:26	1:37	2:56	2:14	1:54	2:58	2:17	1:30	11:07	1:07	3:41	2:07
Cambridge	487	198	366	102	156	117	167		3:28	4:20	1:30	1:52	2:03	2:06	6:04	4:11	8:09	5:49	2:29	1:28	4:20	8:35	1:04	3:56	2:37	2:34	1:25	1:47	3:12	3:10	3:19	3:52	1:13	1:41	1:55	5:54	6:37	4:49	2:34	1:51	2:47	2:15	2:26	2:35	1:19	2:26	4:03	10:56	2:08	2:45	1:17
Cardiff	525	106	377	106	233	168	42	201		4:58	2:15	2:48	3:27	3:54	6:54	2:02	8:47	6:27	1:16	4:03	4:23	9:13	4:03	4:14	4:09	3:53	2:46	3:39	3:31	3:28	4:42	5:16	4:31	2:55	2:05	3:46	7:15	2:40	2:38	2:01	2:12	3:23	2:24	2:29	3:33	2:44	0:53	11:34	1:35	4:09	2:43
Carlisle	229	232	89	183	107	345	286	256	288		3:30	3:12	2:28	6:19	2:08	5:41	4:01	1:41	3:58	5:35	3:44	4:27	5:11	0:58	2:54	2:19	3:43	3:10	2:16	2:04	1:44	1:15	5:21	3:17	4:21	7:25	2:29	6:19	5:36	5:00	5:24	2:45	3:10	5:28	5:25	2:31	5:34	6:48	3:38	2:10	5:07
Coventry	442	134	297	18	124	157	102	84	129	200		1:03	1:41	3:05	5:29	2:55	7:22	5:02	1:12	2:49	3:13	7:48	2:21	2:49	2:23	2:06	0:45	1:39	2:06	2:03	2:56	3:30	2:31	1:09	1:04	4:38	5:50	3:32	2:19	1:43	2:17	1:37	1:18	2:11	2:20	1:19	2:49	10:09	0:56	2:22	1:53
Derby	418	137	269	41	88	188	134	99	159	180	43		0:57	3:33	4:58	3:31	7:02	4:42	1:48	3:09	2:52	7:27	2:45	2:28	1:39	1:23	0:49	1:24	1:45	1:42	2:13	2:46	2:55	0:33	1:51	5:14	5:29	4:08	3:06	2:30	3:04	0:54	1:21	2:58	2:48	0:53	3:22	9:49	1:27	1:39	2:19
Doncaster	371	192	239	95	40	232	184	117	210	150	94	57		3:58	4:13	4:12	6:19	3:59	2:30	3:21	3:17	6:44	2:57	2:16	0:56	0:43	1:27	0:55	1:48	1:25	1:28	2:02	3:07	1:02	2:30	5:56	4:46	4:50	3:45	3:09	3:43	0:30	2:13	3:36	3:11	1:44	4:04	9:05	2:09	0:54	2:57
Dover	620	315	477	195	284	81	194	118	233	393	180	208	244		7:56	4:14	10:08	7:48	3:16	2:16	5:59	10:34	2:17	5:35	4:29	4:26	3:14	3:40	4:52	4:49	5:11	5:45	3:02	3:34	2:27	5:57	8:36	4:51	2:23	2:08	2:50	4:06	4:05	2:38	1:37	4:05	4:29	12:55	3:36	4:38	1:34
Edinburgh	126	340	75	284	198	466	377	326	379	91	303	266	212	444		7:38	3:01	1:05	5:55	7:20	5:41	3:02	6:56	2:55	4:38	4:04	5:26	4:54	4:13	4:00	3:00	2:23	7:06	5:01	6:18	9:21	1:02	8:16	7:33	6:57	7:21	4:29	5:07	7:25	7:09	4:28	7:30	5:24	5:34	3:54	6:57
Exeter	581	199	425	161	282	170	75	323	107	336	166	213	257	244	439		9:31	7:11	1:58	4:36	5:24	9:56	4:37	4:57	4:52	4:36	3:28	4:22	4:14	4:12	5:26	5:59	5:07	3:39	2:46	1:54	7:59	0:53	2:38	2:43	1:55	4:07	3:25	2:27	4:02	3:28	2:37	12:18	2:18	4:52	3:16
Fort William	159	430	136	391	305	568	478	456	486	198	415	387	345	591	131	549		2:26	7:49	9:26	7:35	1:32	9:02	4:49	6:44	6:10	7:34	7:00	6:07	5:54	5:34	5:06	9:12	7:07	8:12	11:15	2:09	10:10	9:27	8:51	9:15	6:35	7:01	9:19	9:16	6:22	9:24	4:04	7:28	6:01	8:56
Glasgow	146	322	36	291	203	468	378	355	384	96	313	282	245	491	46	449	100		5:28	7:05	5:13	3:08	6:41	2:28	4:23	3:49	5:12	4:39	3:46	3:33	3:13	2:45	6:51	4:46	5:51	8:54	1:10	7:48	7:06	6:30	6:54	4:14	4:40	6:57	6:55	4:01	7:03	5:29	5:07	3:40	6:36
Gloucester	473	109	317	53	171	152	35	132	53	228	59	93	149	189	331	107	435	324		3:25	3:42	8:14	3:22	3:15	3:10	2:54	1:46	2:39	2:32	2:29	3:43	4:17	3:31	1:56	1:11	3:39	6:16	2:33	2:00	1:24	1:42	2:24	1:42	1:52	2:56	1:45	1:49	10:35	0:36	3:10	2:05
Harwich	568	258	411	170	224	130	203	64	234	323	152	167	185	129	397	262	524	419	171		5:38	9:53	0:42	5:13	3:55	3:52	2:43	3:05	4:30	4:28	4:37	5:10	1:32	2:59	2:26	6:20	7:55	5:14	2:49	2:17	3:12	3:33	3:44	3:01	1:09	3:44	4:38	12:14	3:26	4:03	1:42
Holyhead	452	96	315	151	158	330	204	252	209	226	167	156	169	358	316	279	423	323	189	331		7:58	5:16	2:59	3:39	2:49	3:23	3:52	1:53	2:13	3:53	4:26	5:25	3:15	4:06	7:06	6:00	6:00	5:21	4:45	5:05	3:06	2:10	5:12	5:18	2:11	4:33	10:19	3:19	3:19	4:47
Inverness	105	492	198	449	353	620	536	490	558	260	458	421	369	601	157	607	63	162	496	554	481		9:27	5:14	7:10	6:35	7:59	7:26	6:32	6:20	5:41	5:04	9:37	7:33	8:37	11:41	2:10	10:35	9:52	9:16	9:40	7:01	7:26	9:44	9:41	6:47	9:50	2:31	7:54	6:26	9:21
Ipswich	538	268	420	156	210	125	206	54	240	311	138	155	171	127	381	264	510	409	177	21	307	538		4:50	3:31	3:28	2:20	2:41	4:06	4:04	4:13	4:46	1:08	2:35	2:27	6:21	7:31	5:15	2:50	2:18	3:13	3:09	3:20	3:02	1:10	3:20	4:39	11:50	3:02	3:39	1:43
Kendal	280	182	139	151	62	324	235	215	232	50	170	136	99	344	141	307	248	146	200	279	180	310	268		2:44	1:53	3:02	3:00	1:36	1:23	1:38	1:59	5:00	2:54	3:41	6:44	3:13	5:38	4:56	4:20	4:44	2:22	2:30	4:47	4:53	1:50	4:53	7:32	2:57	2:04	4:22
Kingston upon Hull	398	235	255	139	68	243	228	134	239	165	123	94	37	254	230	290	367	255	195	204	218	387	189	127		1:08	2:08	0:58	2:13	1:49	1:54	2:27	3:18	1:43	3:10	6:36	5:12	5:30	4:25	3:49	4:23	1:11	2:53	4:17	3:43	2:25	4:44	9:31	2:49	1:02	3:39
Leeds	359	171	198	119	9	256	209	144	226	111	117	74	32	275	190	279	309	208	167	217	162	345	197	72	60		1:53	1:25	1:23	0:58	1:20	1:53	3:37	1:27	2:55	6:21	4:38	5:15	4:10	3:34	4:08	0:50	2:16	4:02	3:40	1:37	4:29	8:57	2:34	0:46	3:23
Leicester	445	155	294	43	99	163	118	70	140	214	24	30	73	183	282	189	412	312	83	146	182	431	125	166	98	97		1:16	2:17	2:14	2:42	3:15	2:27	0:46	1:32	5:11	6:01	4:05	2:47	2:11	2:45	1:23	1:43	2:39	2:29	1:24	3:20	10:20	1:25	2:08	2:01
Lincoln	411	208	249	87	80	207	170	88	192	178	76	53	41	206	247	241	376	274	135	152	204	402	124	140	46	72	52		2:31	2:02	2:11	2:44	2:20	0:59	2:28	6:07	5:29	5:01	3:43	3:07	3:41	1:07	2:33	3:34	2:54	2:10	4:16	9:48	2:21	1:35	2:51
Liverpool	354	120	199	99	67	267	180	179	169	110	113	90	89	294	201	240	308	213	142	265	95	370	236	75	126	73	110	118		0:48	2:28	3:01	4:16	2:10	2:56	6:00	4:33	4:54	4:11	3:35	3:59	1:52	1:25	4:03	4:09	1:06	3:48	8:53	2:13	1:54	3:39
Manchester	349	128	204	87	37	252	167	159	188	117	99	58	51	273	208	239	315	215	132	230	120	363	211	72	96	42	95	87	34		2:03	2:36	4:12	1:51	2:52	5:55	4:22	4:49	4:07	3:30	3:55	1:14	1:41	3:58	4:04	1:01	4:04	8:41	2:08	1:29	3:37
Middlesbrough	289	233	181	174	69	316	265	196	287	92	175	130	84	316	147	337	279	192	230	266	226	306	253	77	88	64	154	127	134	106		0:55	4:20	2:15	3:43	7:09	3:40	6:03	4:58	4:22	4:56	1:43	3:20	4:50	4:24	2:40	5:17	8:02	3:22	1:05	4:12
Newcastle upon Tyne	252	266	146	209	98	345	300	232	312	58	209	165	115	350	104	369	237	153	263	297	257	263	287	88	130	96	188	153	167	136	40		4:54	2:49	4:17	7:43	3:03	6:37	5:32	4:56	5:30	2:17	3:54	5:24	4:58	3:14	5:51	7:25	3:56	1:43	4:46
Norwich	536	270	348	163	185	174	234	62	256	280	142	146	142	169	351	284	478	378	193	72	289	505	44	249	145	178	112	103	222	177	221	252		2:44	2:58	6:51	7:40	5:45	3:31	2:48	3:43	3:18	3:29	3:32	2:00	3:28	5:06	11:59	3:10	3:48	2:13
Nottingham	416	155	267	54	78	191	140	84	165	188	52	15	48	210	256	218	386	286	108	165	177	410	140	141	92	72	27	37	107	68	128	159	118		1:57	5:23	5:34	4:17	3:12	2:36	3:10	0:57	1:44	3:04	2:49	1:18	3:31	9:53	1:36	1:42	2:25
Oxford	497	151	335	68	167	106	73	92	106	267	57	101	138	142	358	151	465	365	47	134	208	515	128	223	175	162	76	123	168	157	218	253	159	104		4:30	6:40	3:24	1:28	0:45	1:25	2:25	2:08	1:19	1:56	2:09	2:40	10:59	1:31	3:10	1:15
Penzance	688	301	552	269	394	279	184	343	218	463	278	316	369	355	551	109	663	561	217	374	388	715	375	419	412	391	310	359	353	344	449	481	393	323	261		9:43	1:41	4:22	4:27	3:39	5:51	5:09	4:11	5:46	5:12	4:20	14:02	4:02	6:36	4:59
Perth	86	366	85	336	245	509	412	370	422	134	346	309	254	485	43	487	103	59	362	439	360	113	424	184	273	233	326	290	244	254	191	148	394	299	404	598		8:37	7:54	7:18	7:42	5:03	5:28	7:46	7:43	4:49	7:52	4:30	5:55	4:28	7:24
Plymouth	619	232	461	203	325	206	111	274	159	372	209	254	300	286	485	43	592	490	150	305	322	648	305	348	326	323	231	284	299	281	379	412	327	255	193	75	529		3:16	3:20	2:32	4:44	4:02	3:04	4:39	4:05	3:14	12:55	2:55	5:29	3:54
Portsmouth	579	231	440	147	274	50	95	132	138	357	132	184	231	137	448	127	555	455	114	161	303	603	158	308	268	245	166	209	254	237	315	360	200	191	83	235	486	170		1:18	0:52	3:39	3:23	0:32	2:11	3:23	3:13	12:13	2:20	4:25	1:39
Reading	538	180	399	103	213	79	77	90	112	309	90	138	184	115	402	141	506	406	75	129	264	554	126	263	209	207	113	168	193	197	264	295	152	129	25	251	445	184	60		1:22	3:01	2:45	1:09	1:46	2:45	2:37	11:35	1:44	3:47	0:56
Salisbury	538	178	383	121	245	82	53	140	101	312	113	159	207	158	400	91	510	408	73	177	262	569	177	265	251	230	132	187	213	208	287	318	200	162	65	201	443	132	43	57		3:37	3:09	0:40	2:37	3:12	2:47	12:02	2:02	4:22	1:52
Sheffield	390	173	235	79	40	225	163	121	193	154	75	35	21	268	230	245	352	250	139	185	164	387	176	102	66	33	68	46	74	40	102	133	144	37	137	361	273	293	228	160	203		2:08	3:32	3:22	1:40	3:59	9:22	2:04	1:11	2:53
Shrewsbury	419	73	260	47	100	216	116	140	107	171	64	67	114	249	262	175	369	267	77	215	104	424	195	125	163	102	79	123	59	67	166	203	196	86	105	286	309	218	195	147	150	85		3:16	3:22	1:04	2:45	9:46	1:23	2:46	2:53
Southampton	564	213	401	128	235	64	75	129	122	330	114	167	201	150	433	106	528	426	98	157	287	590	162	276	249	230	136	189	235	215	288	320	190	162	66	217	476	149	20	47	23	206	175		2:26	3:15	3:05	12:05	2:12	4:16	1:40
Southend-on-Sea	549	258	431	152	220	85	177	64	211	342	129	168	185	89	395	226	548	438	152	57	303	549	57	283	200	213	139	156	255	225	262	299	99	160	105	337	439	269	117	98	132	197	173	126		3:21	4:09	12:02	3:03	3:51	1:07
Stoke-on-Trent	381	108	243	47	75	217	127	137	140	150	64	36	74	236	241	202	348	248	95	201	122	410	179	121	117	78	55	87	56	36	142	173	171	55	118	311	287	241	201	147	168	50	35	183	199		3:18	9:08	1:23	2:09	2:53
Swansea	529	76	368	124	220	209	80	236	41	279	150	184	244	264	370	154	477	375	91	279	172	578	279	249	262	229	174	226	168	187	293	323	286	178	144	266	446	196	175	147	136	202	124	159	245	159		12:11	2:10	4:44	3:18
Thurso	212	584	304	557	461	728	644	589	640	352	552	529	475	706	262	715	169	268	604	657	589	108	654	402	492	453	544	510	463	471	410	367	613	519	621	823	220	758	709	662	664	506	523	682	659	502	631		10:15	8:47	11:43
Worcester	448	96	309	29	135	162	62	119	73	220	46	68	124	197	306	136	418	311	28	168	151	480	174	169	166	146	72	118	108	101	203	229	180	85	57	244	350	177	146	95	101	103	49	124	150	65	97	572		2:49	2:24
York	345	193	201	129	34	269	227	151	237	116	129	84	33	269	187	289	314	214	181	232	185	344	200	81	38	24	108	76	96	65	48	83	176	84	174	400	230	331	257	217	244	54	132	244	214	114	268	450	164		3:39
London	537	228	440	118	203	53	118	61	151	309	97	129	171	76	403	179	511	404	116	86	277	562	82	263	214	195	103	155	211	209	251	283	117	128	59	285	451	216	84	41	92	166	161	82	43	161	187	669	136	211	

Distance in miles

Scale to Map Pages

1:220,594 = 3.5 miles to 1 inch (2.54 cm) / 2.2 km to 1 cm

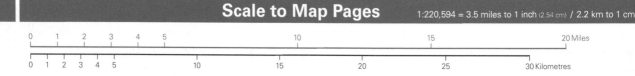

Motorway
Autoroute
Autobahn — M1

Motorway Under Construction
Autoroute en construction
Autobahn im Bau

Motorway Proposed
Autoroute prévue
Geplante Autobahn

Motorway Junctions with Numbers
Unlimited Interchange 4
Limited Interchange 5

Autoroute échangeur numéroté
Echangeur complet
Echangeur partiel

Autobahnanschlußstelle mit Nummer
Unbeschränkter Fahrtrichtungswechsel
Beschränkter Fahrtrichtungswechsel

Motorway Service Area (with fuel station)
with access from one carriageway only

Aire de services d'autoroute (avec station service)
accessible d'un seul côté

Rastplatz oder Raststätte (mit tankstelle)
Einbahn

Major Road Service Areas (with fuel station) with 24 hour facilities
Primary Route S Class A Road S

Aire de services sur route prioritaire (avec station service) Ouverte 24h sur 24
Route à grande circulation   Route de type A

Raststätte (mit tankstelle) Durchgehend geöffnet
Hauptverkehrsstraße   A- Straße

Truckstop (selection of) T
Sélection d'aire pour poids lourds
Auswahl von Fernfahrerrastplatz

Primary Route A41
Route à grande circulation
Hauptverkehrsstraße

Primary Route Junction with Number 5
Echangeur numéroté
Hauptverkehrsstraßenkreuzung mit Nummer

Primary Route Destination DOVER
Route prioritaire, direction
Hauptverkehrsstraße Richtung

Dual Carriageways (A & B roads)
Route à double chaussées séparées (route A & B)
Zweispurige Schnellstraße (A- und B- Straßen)

Class A Road A129
Route de type A
A-Straße

Class B Road B177
Route de type B
B-Straße

Narrow Major Road (passing places)
Route prioritaire étroite (possibilité de dépassement)
Schmale Hauptverkehrsstraße (mit Überholmöglichkeit)

Major Roads Under Construction
Route prioritaire en construction
Hauptverkehrsstraße im Bau

Major Roads Proposed
Route prioritaire prévue
Geplante Hauptverkehrsstaße

Safety Cameras with Speed Limits
Single Camera 30
Multiple Cameras located along road 50
Single & Multiple Variable Speed Cameras V V

Radars de contrôle de vitesse
Radar simple
Radars multiples situés le long de la route
Radars simples et multiples de contrôle de vitesse variable

Sicherheitskameras mit Tempolimit
Einzelne Kamera
Mehrere Kameras entlang der Straße
Einzelne und mehrere Kameras für variables Tempolimit

Fuel Station
Station service
Tankstelle

Gradient 1:5 (20%) **& steeper**
(ascent in direction of arrow)
Pente égale ou supérieure à 20% (dans le sens de la montée)
20% Steigung und steiler (in Pfeilrichtung)

Toll TOLL
Barrière de péage
Gebührenpflichtig

Mileage between markers 8
Distence en miles entre les flèches
Strecke zwischen Markierungen in Meilen

Railway and Station
Voie ferrée et gare
Eisenbahnlinie und Bahnhof

Level Crossing and Tunnel
Passage à niveau et tunnel
Bahnübergang und Tunnel

River or Canal
Rivière ou canal
Fluß oder Kanal

County or Unitary Authority Boundary
Limite de comté ou de division administrative
Grafschafts- oder Verwaltungsbezirksgrenze

National Boundary
Frontière nationale
Landesgrenze

Built-up Area
Agglomération
Geschlossene Ortschaft

Village or Hamlet
Village ou hameau
Dorf oder Weiler

Wooded Area
Zone boisée
Waldgebiet

Spot Height in Feet • 813
Altitude (en pieds)
Höhe in Fuß

Relief above 400' (122m)
Relief par estompage au-dessus de 400' (122m)
Reliefschattierung über 400' (122m)

National Grid Reference (kilometres) 100
Coordonnées géographiques nationales (Kilomètres)
Nationale geographische Koordinaten (Kilometer)

Page Continuation
Suite à la page indiquée
Seitenfortsetzung 48

Area covered by Main Route map MAIN ROUTE 180
Répartition des cartes des principaux axes routiers
Von Karten mit Hauptverkehrsstrecken

Area covered by Town Plan SEE PAGE 194
Ville ayant un plan à la page indiquée
Von Karten mit Stadtplänen erfaßter Bereich

Tourist Information Information Touristeninformationen ℹ

Airport ✈
Aéroport
Flughafen

Airfield ✈
Terrain d'aviation
Flugplatz

Heliport
Héliport
Hubschrauberlandeplatz

Battle Site and Date ✕ 1066
Champ de bataille et date
Schlachtfeld und Datum

Castle (open to public)
Château (ouvert au public)
Schloß / Burg (für die Öffentlichkeit zugänglich)

Castle with Garden (open to public)
Château avec parc (ouvert au public)
Schloß mit Garten (für die Öffentlichkeit zugänglich)

Cathedral, Abbey, Church, Friary, Priory ✝
Cathédrale, abbaye, église, monastère, prieuré
Kathedrale, Abtei, Kirche, Mönchskloster, Kloster

Country Park
Parc régional
Landschaftspark

Ferry (vehicular, sea)
(vehicular, river)
(foot only)

Bac (véhicules, mer)
(véhicules, rivière)
(piétons)

Fähre (auto, meer)
(auto, fluß)
(nur für Personen)

Garden (open to public) ✿
Jardin (ouvert au public)
Garten (für die Öffentlichkeit zugänglich)

Golf Course (9 hole) ⛳9 (18 hole) ⛳18
Terrain de golf (9 trous) (18 trous)
Golfplatz (9 Löcher) (18 Löcher)

Historic Building (open to public)
Monument historique (ouvert au public)
Historisches Gebäude (für die Öffentlichkeit zugänglich)

Historic Building with Garden (open to public)
Monument historique avec jardin (ouvert au public)
Historisches Gebäude mit Garten (für die Öffentlichkeit zugänglich)

Horse Racecourse
Hippodrome
Pferderennbahn

Lighthouse
Phare
Leuchtturm

Motor Racing Circuit
Circuit Automobile
Automobilrennbahn

Museum, Art Gallery
Musée
Museum, Galerie

National Park
Parc national
Nationalpark

National Trust Property
(open) NT
(restricted opening) NT
(National Trust for Scotland) NTS NTS

National Trust Property
(ouvert)
(heures d'ouverture)
(National Trust for Scotland)

National Trust- Eigentum
(geöffnet)
(beschränkte Öffnungszeit)
(National Trust for Scotland)

Nature Reserve or Bird Sanctuary
Réserve naturelle botanique ou ornithologique
Natur- oder Vogelschutzgebiet

Nature Trail or Forest Walk
Chemin forestier, piste verte
Naturpfad oder Waldweg

Place of Interest Monument •
Site, curiosité
Sehenswürdigkeit

Picnic Site
Lieu pour pique-nique
Picknickplatz

Railway, Steam or Narrow Gauge
Chemin de fer, à vapeur ou à voie étroite
Eisenbahn, Dampf- oder Schmalspurbahn

Theme Park
Centre de loisirs
Vergnügungspark

Tourist Information Centre ℹ
Syndicat d'initiative
Information

Viewpoint (360 degrees) (180 degrees)
Vue panoramique (360 degrés) (180 degrés)
Aussichtspunkt (360 Grade) (180 Grade)

Visitor Information Centre ℹ
Centre d'information touristique
Besucherzentrum

Wildlife Park
Réserve de faune
Wildpark

Windmill
Moulin à vent
Windmühle

Zoo or Safari Park
Parc ou réserve zoologique
Zoo oder Safari-Park

Please note: symbols have been enlarged for clarity

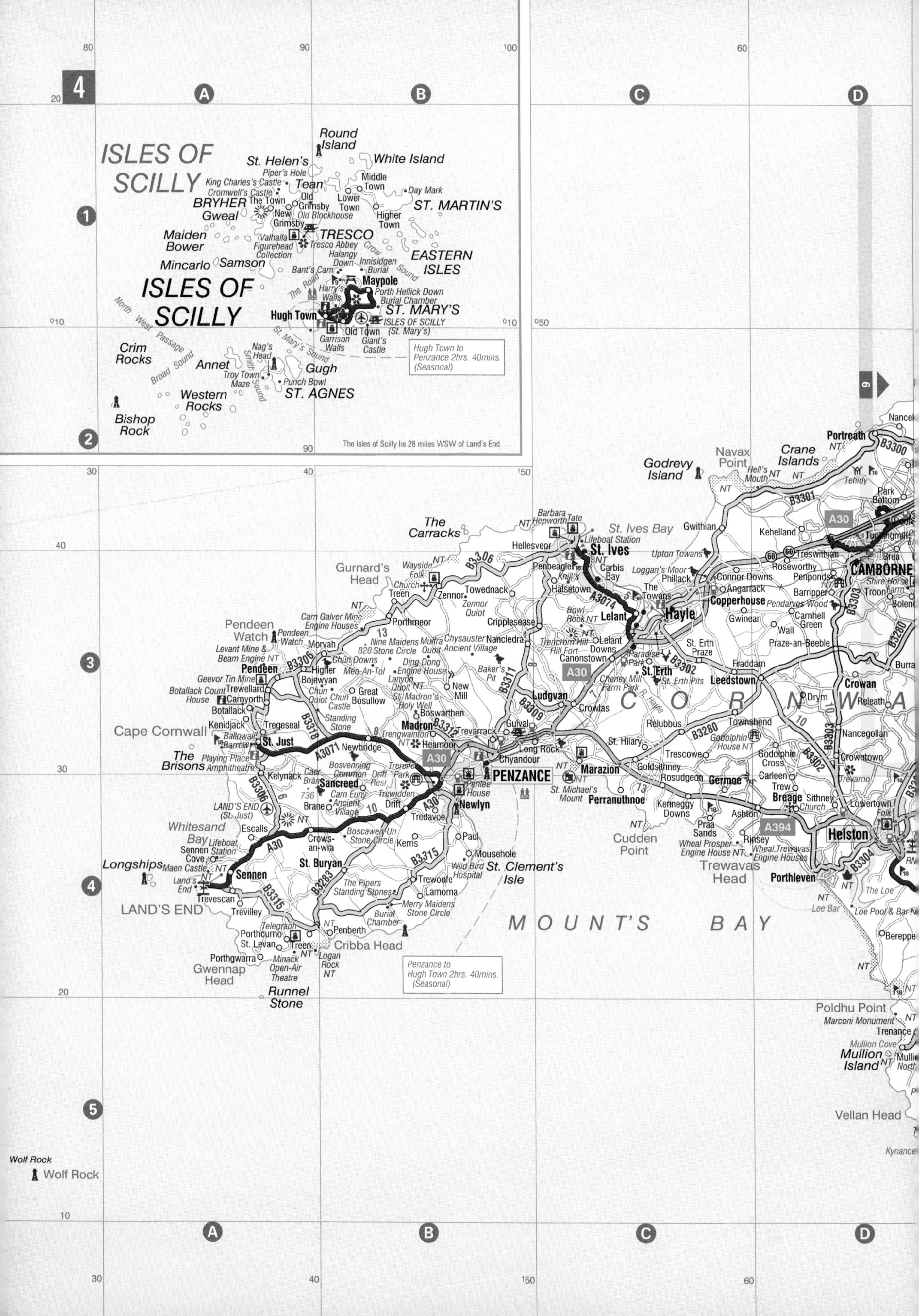

4
ISLES OF SCILLY
Round Island
St. Helen's
White Island
Piper's Hole
King Charles's Castle
Tean
Middle Town
Day Mark
Cromwell's Castle
BRYHER
The Town
Old Grimsby
Lower Town
ST. MARTIN'S
Gweal
New Grimsby
Old Blockhouse
Higher Town
Maiden Bower
Valhalla Figurehead Collection
TRESCO
Tresco Abbey
Crow Sound
Mincarlo
Samson
Halangy Down
Innisidgen Burial
EASTERN ISLES
ISLES OF SCILLY
Bant's Carn
Maypole
Porth Hellick Down Burial Chamber
The Road
Harry's Walls
North West Passage
Hugh Town
ST. MARY'S
ISLES OF SCILLY (St. Mary's)
Garrison Walls
Old Town
Giant's Castle
Crim Rocks
Nag's Head
St. Mary's Sound
Hugh Town to Penzance 2hrs. 40mins. (Seasonal)
Broad Sound
Annet
Gugh
Troy Town Maze
Smith Sound
Punch Bowl
ST. AGNES
Western Rocks
Bishop Rock
The Isles of Scilly lie 28 miles WSW of Land's End
Godrevy Island
Navax Point
Crane Islands
Portreath
Hell's Mouth
Tehidy
Park Bottom
Gwithian
Kehelland
The Carracks
Barbara Hepworth
Tate
St. Ives Bay
Lifeboat Station
Hellesveor
St. Ives
Upton Towans
Treswithian
Gurnard's Head
Wayside Folk
Carbis Bay
Loggan's Moor
Roseworthy
CAMBORNE
Church
Treen
Zennor
Towednack
Penbeagle
Knill's
Halsetown
Phillack
Connor Downs
Angarrack
Penponds
Barripper
Shire Horse Farm
Troon
Zennor Quoit
The Towans
Copperhouse
Pendarves Wood
Carn Galver Mine Engine Houses
Porthmeor
Cripplesease
Lelant
Hayle
Gwinear
Carnhell Green
Pendeen Watch
Nine Maidens
Mulfra Quoit
828 Stone Circle
Chysauster Ancient Village
Nancledra
Trencrom Hill Fort
Lelant Downs
Wall
Levant Mine & Beam Engine
Morvah
Chun Downs
Ding Dong Engine House
Canonstown
Paradise Park
St. Erth Praze
Praze-an-Beeble
Pendeen
Higher Bojewyan
Men-An-Tol
Baker's Pit
St. Erth
Fraddam
Geevor Tin Mine
Lanyon Quoit
Cheney Mill Farm Park
St. Erth Pits
Leedstown
Crowan
Botallack Count House
Trewellard
Carnyorth
Chun Quoit
Chun Castle
Great Bosullow
Madron's Holy Well
New Mill
Ludgvan
Crowlas
CORNWALL
Drym
Releath
Botallack
Standing Stone
Boswarthen
Relubbus
Townshend
Cape Cornwall
Kenidjack
Tregeseal
Madron
Trengwainton
Trevarrack
Gulval
Godolphin House
Nancegollan
Ballowall Barrow
St. Just
Newbridge
Heamoor
Long Rock
St. Hilary
Trescowe
Godolphin Cross
Crowntown
The Brisons
Playing Place Amphitheatre
Bosvenning Common
Trereife Park
Chyandour
Marazion
Goldsithney
Carleen
Kelynack
Caer Brân
Drift Resr.
PENZANCE
Rosudgeon
Germoe
Trew
Trevarno
Sancreed
Carn Euny Ancient Village
Trewidden
Penlee House
St. Michael's Mount
Perranuthnoe
Kenneggy Downs
Breage
Sithney
Lowertown
LAND'S END (St. Just)
Brane
Drift
Newlyn
Church
Folk
Whitesand Bay
Escalls
Tredavoe
Praa Sands
Ashton
A394
Helston
Lifeboat Station
Crows-an-wra
Boscawen-Un Stone Circle
Kerris
Paul
Cudden Point
Rinsey
Sennen Cove
Mousehole
Wheal Prosper Engine House
Wheal Trewavas Engine Houses
Longships
Maen Castle
Sennen
St. Buryan
Wild Bird Hospital
St. Clement's Isle
Trewavas Head
Porthleven
Land's End
Trewoofe
The Pipers Standing Stones
Lamorna
The Loe
Trevescan
Merry Maidens Stone Circle
Loe Bar
LAND'S END
Trevilley
Burial Chamber
MOUNT'S BAY
Telegraph
Penberth
Porthcurno
St. Levan
Treen
Cribba Head
Porthgwarra
Minack Open-Air Theatre
Logan Rock
Bereppe
Gwennap Head
Penzance to Hugh Town 2hrs. 40mins. (Seasonal)
Runnel Stone
Poldhu Point
Marconi Monument
Trenance
Mullion Cove
Mullion Island
Vellan Head
Wolf Rock
Wolf Rock

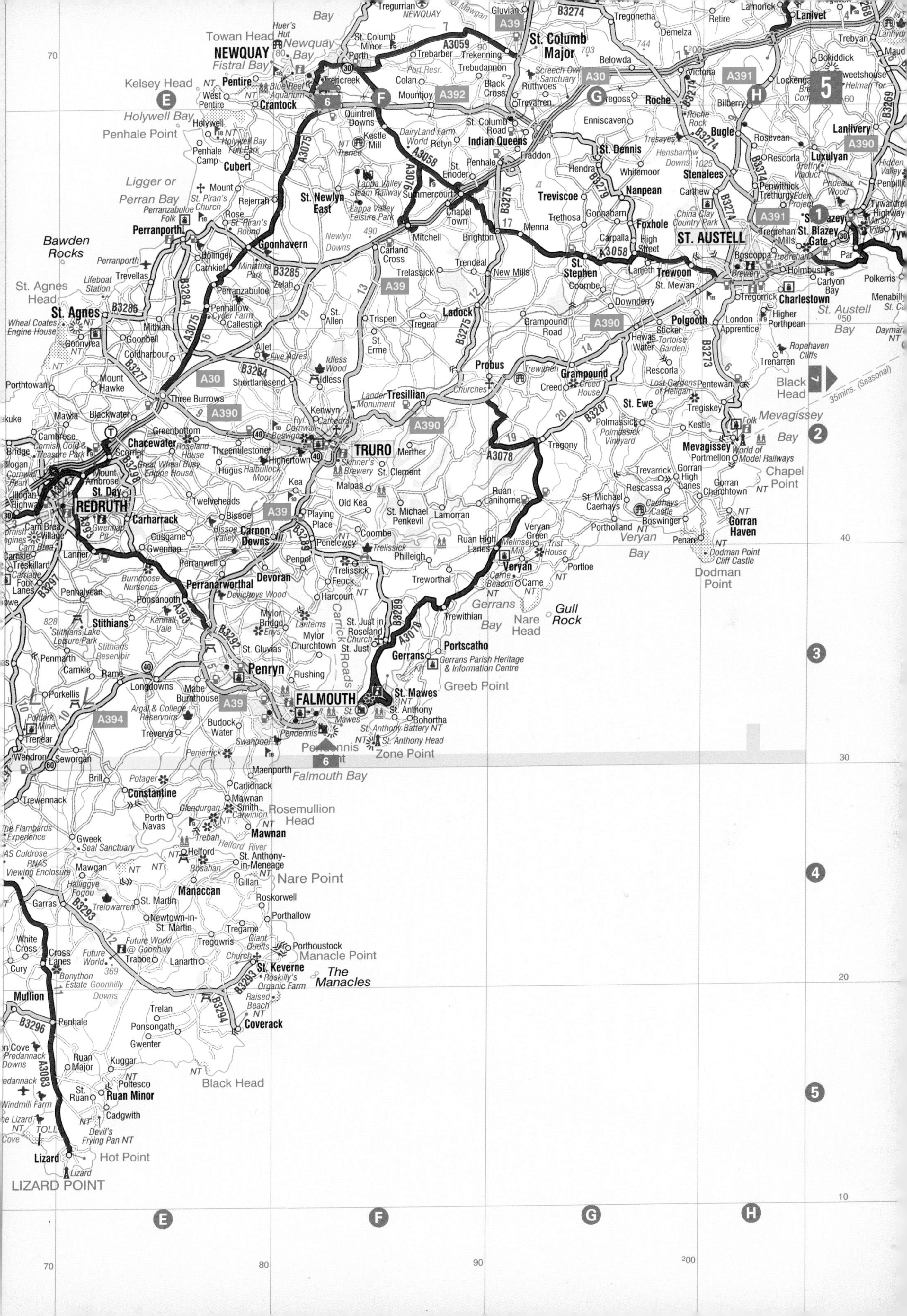
Tregurrian
NEWQUAY
Gluvian
B3274
Lamorick
Lanivet
Bay
Huer's Hut
Towan Head
Newquay Bay
St. Columb Minor
A3059
Trekenning
St. Columb Major
Tregonetha
Demelza
Retire
Trebyan
NEWQUAY
Fistral Bay
Porth
Trebarber
Trebudannon
Belowda
Victoria
Bokiddick
Kelsey Head
Pentire
Blue Reef Aquarium
Trencreek
Port Resr.
Colan
Black Cross
Screech Owl Sanctuary
Ruthvoes
A30
A391
Lockengate
5
West Pentire
Crantock
Mountjoy
A392
Trevarren
Tregoss
Roche
Bilberry
Holywell Bay
Quintrell Downs
Kestle Mill
DairyLand Farm World
Retyn
St. Columb Road
Indian Queens
Enniscaven
Roche Rock
Bugle
Lanlivery
Penhale Point
Holywell
Holywell Bay Fun Park
Trerice
Fraddon
St. Dennis
Tresayes
Hensbarrow Downs
Rosevean
A390
Penhale Camp
Cubert
A3058
A3076
St. Enoder
Penhale
Hendra
Whitemoor
Stenalees
Rescorla
Luxulyan
Treffry Viaduct
Ligger or Perran Bay
Mount
St. Piran's Church
Rejerrah
St. Newlyn East
Lappa Valley Steam Railway
Summercourt
Treviscoe
Nanpean
Carthew
Penwithick
Trethurgy
Eden Project
Prideaux Wood
Tywardreath
Highway
Perranzabuloe Folk
Rose
St. Piran's Round
Lappa Valley Leisure Park
Chapel Town
B3275
Trethosa
Gonnabarn
China Clay Country Park
A391
St. Blazey
Perranporth
Goonhavern
Newlyn Downs
Mitchell
Brighton
Menna
Carpalla
Foxhole
High Street
ST. AUSTELL
Tregrehan Mills
St. Blazey Gate
Par
Bawden Rocks
Bolingey
Carland Cross
Trendeal
St. Stephen
A3058
Lanjeth
Trewoon
Boscoppa
Tregrehan
Perranporth
Carnkief
Miniatura Park
B3285
Trelassick
New Mills
Coombe
St. Mewan
Holmbush
Carlyon Bay
Polkerris
St. Agnes Head
Lifeboat Station
Trevellas
Zelah
A39
Menabilly
Perranzabuloe
Downderry
Tregorrick
Charlestown
St. Agnes
B3286
Penhallow Cyder Farm
Callestick
St. Allen
Trispen
Tregear
Ladock
Grampound Road
A390
Polgooth
Sticker
London Apprentice
Higher Porthpean
St. Austell Bay
Wheal Coates Engine House
Mithian
St. Erme
Hewas Water
Tortoise Garden
Goonbell
Goonvrea
Coldharbour
Allet
Five Acres
Idless Wood
B3273
Ropehaven Cliffs
Trenarren
B3277
A30
B3284
Shortlanesend
Idless
Probus
Trewithen
Grampound
Creed House
Creed
Rescorla
Lost Gardens of Heligan
Pentewan
Black Head
Porthtowan
Mount Hawke
Three Burrows
Lander Monument
Tresillian
Churches
35mins. (Seasonal)
Mawla
Blackwater
A390
Kenwyn
Cathedral
A390
B3287
St. Ewe
Tregiskey
Greenbottom
Ryl. Cornwall Bosvigo
A3078
Polmassick
Polmassick Vineyard
Kestle
Folk
Mevagissey
Cambrose
Cornish Gold & Treasure Park
Chacewater
Roseland House
Threemilestone
TRURO
Merther
Tregony
Mevagissey Bay
Scorrier
Great Wheal Busy Engine House
Highertown
Skinner's Brewery
St. Clement
World of Model Railways
Portmellon
Mount Ambrose
Hugus
Halbullock Moor
Malpas
Trevarrick
Gorran High Lanes
Chapel Point
St. Day
Kea
Rescassa
Gorran Churchtown
REDRUTH
Twelveheads
Old Kea
Ruan Lanihorne
St. Michael Caerhays
Caerhays Castle
Carharrack
Bissoe
A39
Playing Place
St. Michael Penkevil
Lamorran
Boswinger
Gorran Haven
Carn Brea Village
Gwennap Pit
Bissoe Valley
Carnon Downs
Coombe
Veryan Green
Portholland
Veryan Bay
Cusgarne
Gwennap
Penelewey
Trelissick
Ruan High Lanes
Melinsey Mill
Trist House
Penare
Dodman Point Cliff Castle
Lanner
Perranwell
Penpol
Philleigh
Veryan
Portloe
Dodman Point
Treskillard
Devoran
Trelissick
Feock
Treworthal
Carne Beacon
Carne
Four Lanes
Burncoose Nurseries
Perranarworthal
Devichoys Wood
Harcourt
Gerrans Bay
Gull Rock
Nare Head
Penhalvean
Ponsanooth
Mylor Bridge
Enys
Lanterns
St. Just in Roseland
A3078
B3289
Trewithian
Stithians
Kennall Vale
Stithians Lake Leisure Park
B3292
St. Gluvias
Mylor Churchtown
Carrick Roads
St. Just
Portscatho
Stithians Reservoir
Gerrans
Gerrans Parish Heritage & Information Centre
Penmarth
Carnkie
Rame
Longdowns
Mabe Burnthouse
Penryn
Flushing
Greeb Point
Porkellis
FALMOUTH
St. Mawes
St. Anthony
Bohortha
Argal & College Reservoirs
A39
A394
Poldark Mine
Treverva
Budock Water
Pendennis
St. Anthony Battery NT
Trenear
Swanpool
St. Anthony Head
Wendron
Seworgan
Penjerrick
Pendennis Point
Zone Point
Brill
Potager
Maenporth
Falmouth Bay
Constantine
Carlidnack
Trewennack
Glendurgan
Mawnan Smith
Carwinion
Rosemullion Head
Porth Navas
The Flambards Experience
Gweek
Seal Sanctuary
Trebah
Helford River
Mawnan
RNAS Culdrose
RNAS Viewing Enclosure
Helford
St. Anthony-in-Meneage
Bosahan
Mawgan
Gillan
Nare Point
Halliggye Fogou
Manaccan
Garras
B3293
Trelowarren
St. Martin
Roskorwell
Newtown-in-St. Martin
Porthallow
Tregarne
White Cross
Future World @ Goonhilly
Tregowris
Giant Quoits
Porthoustock
Cross Lanes
Future World
Traboe
Lanarth
Church
Manacle Point
Cury
Bonython Estate
Goonhilly Downs
St. Keverne
Roskilly's Organic Farm
The Manacles
Mullion
Raised Beach
Trelan
B3296
Penhale
Ponsongath
B3294
Coverack
Gwenter
Poldhu Cove
Predannack Downs
Ruan Major
Kuggar
A3083
Poltesco
Black Head
St. Ruan
Ruan Minor
Windmill Farm
Cadgwith
The Lizard
TOLL
Devil's Frying Pan NT
Lizard
Hot Point
Lizard
LIZARD POINT
E
F
G
H
1
2
3
4
5
7
70
80
90
200
40
30
20
10

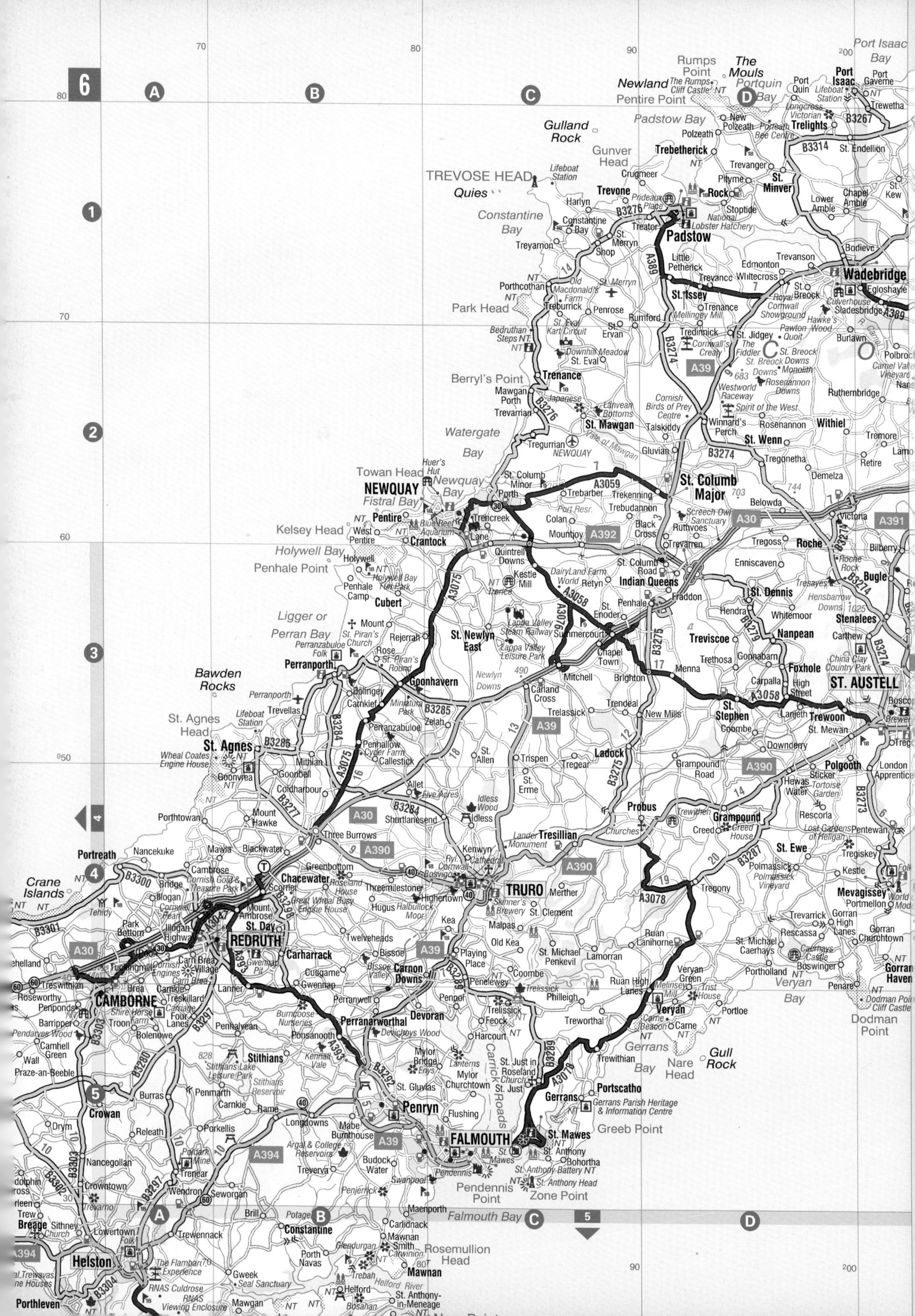

6
70
80
90
200
A
B
C
D
1
2
3
4
5
Port Isaac Bay
Rumps Point
The Mouls
Newland
The Rumps Cliff Castle NT
Pentire Point
Portquin Bay
Port Quin
Port Isaac
Port Gaverne
Trewetha
Padstow Bay
New Polzeath
Polzeath
Trelights
B3267
Gulland Rock
Gunver Head
Trebetherick
B3314
St. Endellion
TREVOSE HEAD
Lifeboat Station
Quies
Crugmeer
Trevanger
Trevone
Rock
St. Minver
Chapel Amble
St. Kew
Lower Amble
Constantine Bay
Harlyn
Prideaux Place
Stoptide
National Lobster Hatchery
B3276
Treator
Padstow
Treyarnon
St. Merryn
Shop
A389
Little Petherick
Edmonton
Trevanson
Whitecross
Bodieve
Wadebridge
Egloshayle
Porthcothan
Old Macdonald's Farm
St. Merryn
St. Issey
Trevance
Royal Cornwall Showground
St. Breock
Culverhouse
Sladesbridge
Park Head
Treburrick
Penrose
Rumford
Trenance
Mellingey Mill
Hawke's Wood
Bedruthan Steps NT
St. Eval Kart Circuit
St. Ervan
Tredinnick
St. Jidgey
Pawton Quoit
Burlawn
Downhill Meadow
St. Eval
B3274
Cornwall's Crealy
The Fiddler
St. Breock Downs
St. Breock Downs Monolith
Polbrock
Camel Valley Vineyard
A39
Berryl's Point
Trenance
Westworld Raceway
Rosenannon Downs
Mawgan Porth
Japanese
Lanvean Bottoms
Cornish Birds of Prey Centre
Ruthernbridge
Trevarrian
B3276
St. Mawgan
Talskiddy
Spirit of the West
Winnard's Perch
Rosenannon
Withiel
Watergate Bay
Tregurrian
NEWQUAY
Vale of Mawgan
Gluvian
St. Wenn
Tremore
B3274
Tregonetha
Retire
Towan Head
Huer's Hut
Newquay Bay
St. Columb Minor
A3059
St. Columb Major
Demelza
NEWQUAY
Fistral Bay
Porth
Trebarber
Trekenning
Trebudannon
Belowda
Pentire
Blue Reef Aquarium
Trencreek
Port Resr.
Screech Owl Sanctuary
A30
Victoria
A391
Kelsey Head
West Pentire
Crantock
Lane
Colan
Ruthvoes
Black Cross
Mountjoy
A392
Trevarren
Tregoss
Roche
Bilberry
Holywell Bay
Quintrell Downs
Roche Rock
Penhale Point
Holywell
Kestle Mill
St. Columb Road
Enniscaven
Bugle
Holywell Bay Fun Park
DairyLand Farm World
Retyn
Indian Queens
Tresayes
Penhale Camp
Cubert
NT Trerice
A3058
St. Dennis
Fraddon
Hensbarrow Downs
Ligger or Perran Bay
A3075
Penhale
St. Enoder
Hendra
Whitemoor
Stenalees
Mount
St. Piran's Church
Lappa Valley Steam Railway
Summercourt
Treviscoe
Nanpean
Carthew
Rejerrah
St. Newlyn East
Perranzabuloe Folk
Rose
St. Piran's Round
Lappa Valley Leisure Park
Chapel Town
B3275
Trethosa
Gonnabarn
China Clay Country Park
Perranporth
Bawden Rocks
Goonhavern
Mitchell
Brighton
Menna
Foxhole
Carpalla
High Street
ST. AUSTELL
Perranporth
Newlyn Downs
Trevellas
Bolingey
Carnkief
Miniature Park
Carland Cross
B3285
Trelassick
Trendeal
New Mills
St. Stephen
A3058
Lanjeth
Trewoon
St. Agnes Head
Lifeboat Station
Zelah
Coombe
St. Mewan
Perranzabuloe
A39
St. Agnes
B3286
B3284
Pennhallow Cyder Farm
Callestick
Downderry
Wheal Coates Engine House
Mithian
St. Allen
Trispen
Tregear
Ladock
Grampound Road
A390
Polgooth
London Apprentice
Goonvrea
Goonbell
St. Erme
Sticker
Hewas Water
Tortoise Garden
Coldharbour
Allet
Five Acres
B3273
Mount Hawke
B3277
Idless Wood
Probus
Trewithen
Grampound
Rescorla
Porthtowan
A30
B3284
Shortlanesend
Idless
Creed
Creed House
Pentewan
Lost Gardens of Heligan
Three Burrows
Lander Monument
Tresillian
Churches
Portreath
Nancekuke
Mawla
Blackwater
A390
Kenwyn
Cathedral
A390
St. Ewe
Tregiskey
Crane Islands
Cambrose
Cornish Gold & Treasure Park
Chacewater
Greenbottom
Roseland House
Ryl. Cornwall
Bosvigo
B3287
Polmassick
Polmassick Vineyard
Kestle
Illogan
Scorrier
Threemilestone
TRURO
Merther
A3078
Tregony
Mevagissey
Portmellon
Tehidy
Great Wheal Busy Engine House
Higher Town
Skinner's Brewery
St. Clement
Park Bottom
Mount Ambrose
Hugus
Halbullock Moor
Trevarrick
Gorran High Lanes
Illogan Highway
St. Day
Kea
Malpas
Ruan Lanihorne
Rescassa
Gorran Churchtown
B3301
REDRUTH
Carharrack
Twelveheads
A39
Old Kea
St. Michael Caerhays
A30
Carn Brea Village
Gwennap Pit
Bissoe
Playing Place
St. Michael Penkevil
Lamorran
Caerhays Castle
Gorran Haven
Tuckingmill
Cornish Engines
Carn Brea
Cusgarne
Bissoe Valley
Carnon Downs
Coombe
Veryan Green
Boswinger
Treswithian
Brea
Carnkie
Gwennap
Trelissick
Ruan High Lanes
Melinsey Mill
Trist House
Portholland
Veryan Bay
Penare
Roseworthy
CAMBORNE
Treskillard
Lanner
Perranwell
Penelewey
Penpol
Philleigh
Veryan
Dodman Point Cliff Castle
Penponds
Shire Horse Farm
Four Lanes
Burncoose Nurseries
Perranarworthal
Devoran
Trelissick
Feock
Treworthal
Carne Beacon
Carne
Portloe
Dodman Point
Barripper
Troon
Bolenowe
Penhalvean
Ponsanooth
Devichoys Wood
Harcourt
Pendarves Wood
Stithians
Kennall Vale
Mylor Bridge
Enys
Lanterns
St. Just in Roseland
Church
Trewithian
Gerrans Bay
Nare Head
Gull Rock
Carnhell Green
Stithians Lake Leisure Park
Mylor Churchtown
St. Just
Praze-an-Beeble
Stithians Reservoir
B3292
St. Gluvias
B3280
Burras
Penmarth
Carnkie
Rame
Penryn
Portscatho
Gerrans
Gerrans Parish Heritage & Information Centre
Crowan
Longdowns
Mabe Burnthouse
Flushing
Carrick Roads
Drym
Releath
Porkellis
A394
Argal & College Reservoirs
FALMOUTH
St. Mawes
St. Mawes
Greeb Point
Poldark Mine
Trenear
Nancegollan
Treverva
Budock Water
Pendennis
St. Anthony
Bohortha
St. Anthony Battery NT
St. Anthony Head
Crowntown
Swanpool
Pendennis Point
Zone Point
Wendron
Seworgan
Penjerrick
Trevarno
Brill
Potager
Maenporth
Falmouth Bay
Breage
Sithney
Constantine
Carlidnack
Lowertown
Trewennack
Mawnan Smith
Rosemullion Head
Carwinion
Glendurgan
Helston
Porth Navas
The Flambards Experience
Trebah
Mawnan
Gweek
Seal Sanctuary
Helford River
RNAS Culdrose
Helford
St. Anthony-in-Meneage
Porthleven
RNAS Viewing Enclosure
Mawgan
Bosahan
B3304
B3297
B3303
B3302
A3047
A393
B3298
B3289
A3078
A3076
A3075

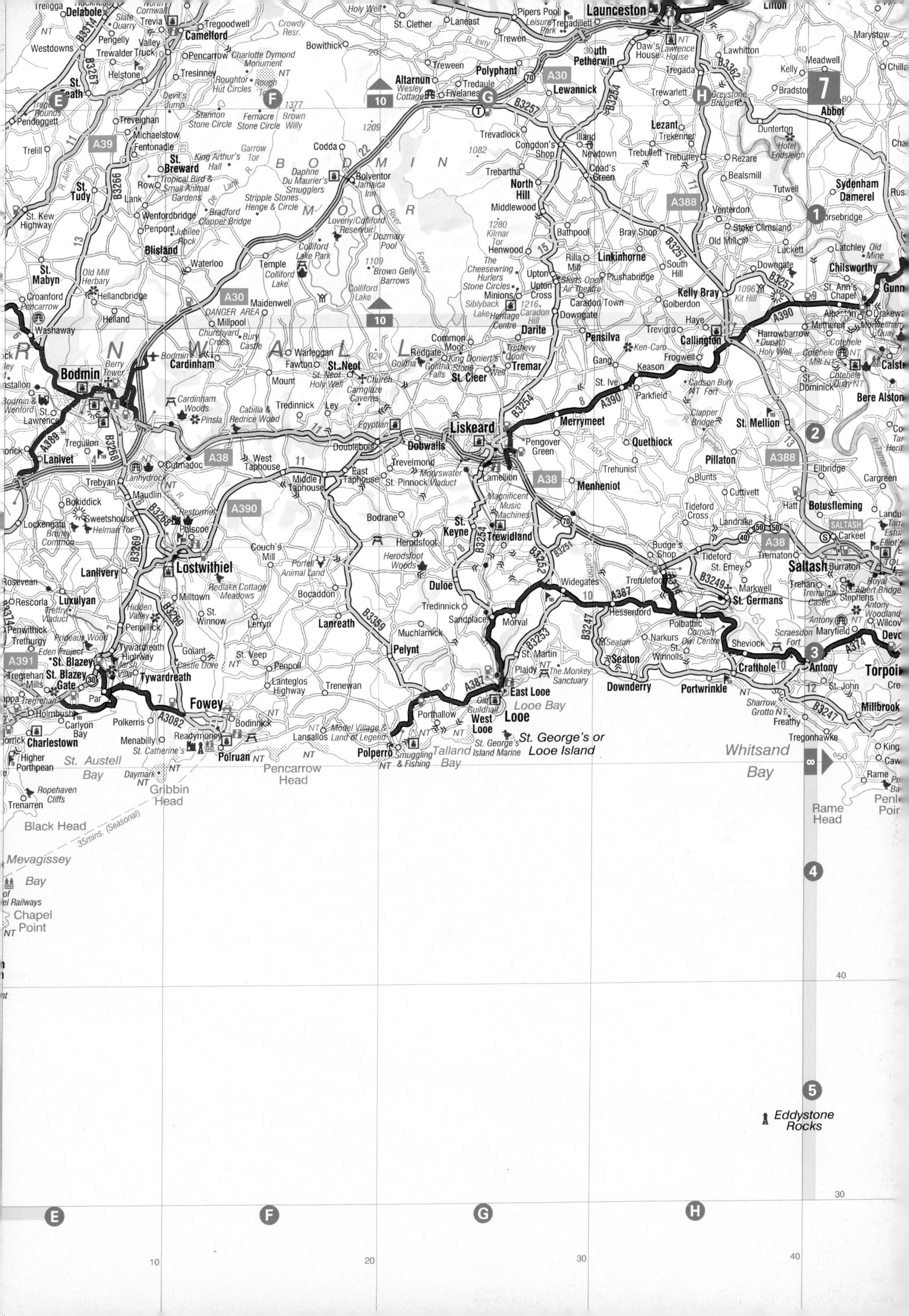

Delabole
Camelford
Tregoodwell
Crowdy Resr.
Holy Well
St. Clether
Laneast
Pipers Pool
Launceston
Tregadillett
Westdowns
Pengelly
Valley Truckle
Trewalder
Helstone
Pencarrow
Charlotte Dymond Monument
Tresinney
Roughtor Hut Circles
Bowithick
Trewen
South Petherwin
Daw's House
Lawrence House
Lawhitton
Marystow
Meadwell
Kelly
Bradstone
St. Teath
Devil's Jump
Stannon Stone Circle
Fernacre Stone Circle
Rough Tor
Brown Willy
Altarnun
Wesley Cottage
Treween
Polyphant
Tredaule
Fivelanes
A30
Lewannick
Trewarlett
Tregada
Greystone Bridge
Abbot
Pendoggett
Treveighan
Michaelstow
Fentonadle
Trelill
A39
St. Breward
King Arthur's Hall
Garrow Tor
Codda
Bolventor
Jamaica Inn
Daphne Du Maurier's Smugglers
B O D M I N
M O O R
Trevadlock
Congdon's Shop
Illand
Newtown
Lezant
Trekenner
Trebullett
Treburley
Rezare
Dunterton
Hotel Endsleigh
Bealsmill
Tutwell
Sydenham Damerel
Trebartha
North Hill
Middlewood
Coad's Green
A388
Venterdon
Horsebridge
Stoke Climsland
St. Tudy
Row
Tropical Bird & Small Animal Gardens
Lank
Stripple Stones Henge & Circle
Loveny/Colliford Reservoir
Dozmary Pool
St. Kew Highway
Wenfordbridge
Bradford Clapper Bridge
Penpont
Jubilee Rock
Kilmar Tor
Henwood
Bathpool
Bray Shop
Rilla Mill
Linkinhorne
Old Mill
Luckett
Latchley
Old Mine
Blisland
Waterloo
Temple
Colliford Lake Park
Colliford Lake
Brown Gelly Barrows
The Cheesewring
Hurlers Stone Circles
Minions
Upton
Upton Cross
Sterts Open Air Theatre
Plushabridge
South Hill
Downgate
Chilsworthy
St. Mabyn
Old Mill Herbary
Hellandbridge
Croanford
Pencarrow
Washaway
Helland
Maidenwell
DANGER AREA
Millpool
Churchyard Cross
Bury Castle
Siblyback Lake
Heritage Centre
Caradon Hill
Caradon Town
Golberdon
Kelly Bray
Kit Hill
St. Ann's Chapel
Gunnislake
Drakewalls
Metherell
Albaston
Haye
Darite
Trevigro
Callington
Harrowbarrow
Dupath Holy Well
Cotehele
Calstock
C O R N W A L L
Bodmin
Berry Tower
Cardinham
Warleggan
Fawton
St. Neot
St. Neot Holy Well
Church
Common Moor
Redgate
Golitha Falls
King Doniert's Stone
Trethevy Quoit
Tremar
St. Cleer
Pensilva
Ken-Caro
Gang
Keason
Frogwell
St. Ive
Parkfield
Cadson Bury Fort
St. Dominick
Bere Alston
Lanhydrock
Cardinham Woods
Pinsla
Cabilla & Redrice Wood
Mount
Tredinnick
Ley
Carnglaze Caverns
Liskeard
Merrymeet
Clapper Bridge
St. Mellion
Bodmin & Wenford
St. Lawrence
Lanivet
Tregullon
Cutmadoc
West Taphouse
Doublebois
Egyptian
Dobwalls
A38
Pengover Green
Quethiock
Pillaton
Ellbridge
Cargreen
Trebyan
Middle Taphouse
East Taphouse
Trevelmond
Moorswater Viaduct
St. Pinnock
Lamellion
Trehunist
Menheniot
Blunts
Cuttivett
Bokiddick
Maudlin
Restormel
A390
Magnificent Music Machines
Tideford Cross
Hatt
Botusfleming
Landulph
Sweetshouse
Helman Tor
Lockengate
Breney Common
Polscoe
Bodrane
St. Keyne
Trewidland
Landrake
SALTASH
Carkeel
Herodsfoot
Couch's Mill
Budge's Shop
Tideford
Trematon
Lanlivery
Lostwithiel
Porfell Animal Land
Herodsfoot Woods
Trerulefoot
St. Erney
Saltash
Burraton
Rosevean
Redlake Cottage Meadows
Duloe
Widegates
Markwell
Trehan
Royal Albert Bridge
Rescorla
Luxulyan
Milltown
Bocaddon
Tredinnick
A387
St. Germans
Trematon Castle
St. Stephens
Treffry Viaduct
Hidden Valley
St. Winnow
Lanreath
Sandplace
Hessenford
Polbathic
Antony Woodland
Wilcove
Penwithick
Penpillick
Lerryn
Muchlarnick
Morval
Cornish Owl Centre
Narkurs
Screasdon Fort
Maryfield
Trethurgy
Prideaux Wood
Eden Project
Tywardreath Highway
Golant
Pelynt
St. Martin
Seaton
St. Winnolls
Sheviock
Antony
Torpoint
A391
St. Blazey
Marsh Villa
Castle Dore
St. Veep
Penpoll
Plaidy
The Monkey Sanctuary
Downderry
Crafthole
Tregrehan Mills
St. Blazey Gate
Tywardreath
Lanteglos Highway
Trenewan
East Looe
Portwrinkle
St. John
Par
Fowey
Looe Bay
Sharrow Grotto
Millbrook
Holmbush
Carlyon Bay
Polkerris
Bodinnick
Porthallow
West Looe
Looe
Freathy
Charlestown
Menabilly
Readymoney
Model Village & Land of Legend
Lansallos
St. George's or Looe Island
Tregonhawke
St. Catherine's
Polruan
Polperro
Smuggling & Fishing
Talland Bay
St. George's Island Marine
Whitsand Bay
Higher Porthpean
St. Austell Bay
Daymark
Pencarrow Head
Rame
Ropehaven Cliffs
Trenarren
Gribbin Head
Rame Head
Black Head
35mins. (Seasonal)
Mevagissey Bay
Chapel Point
Eddystone Rocks
E
F
G
H
10
20
30
40

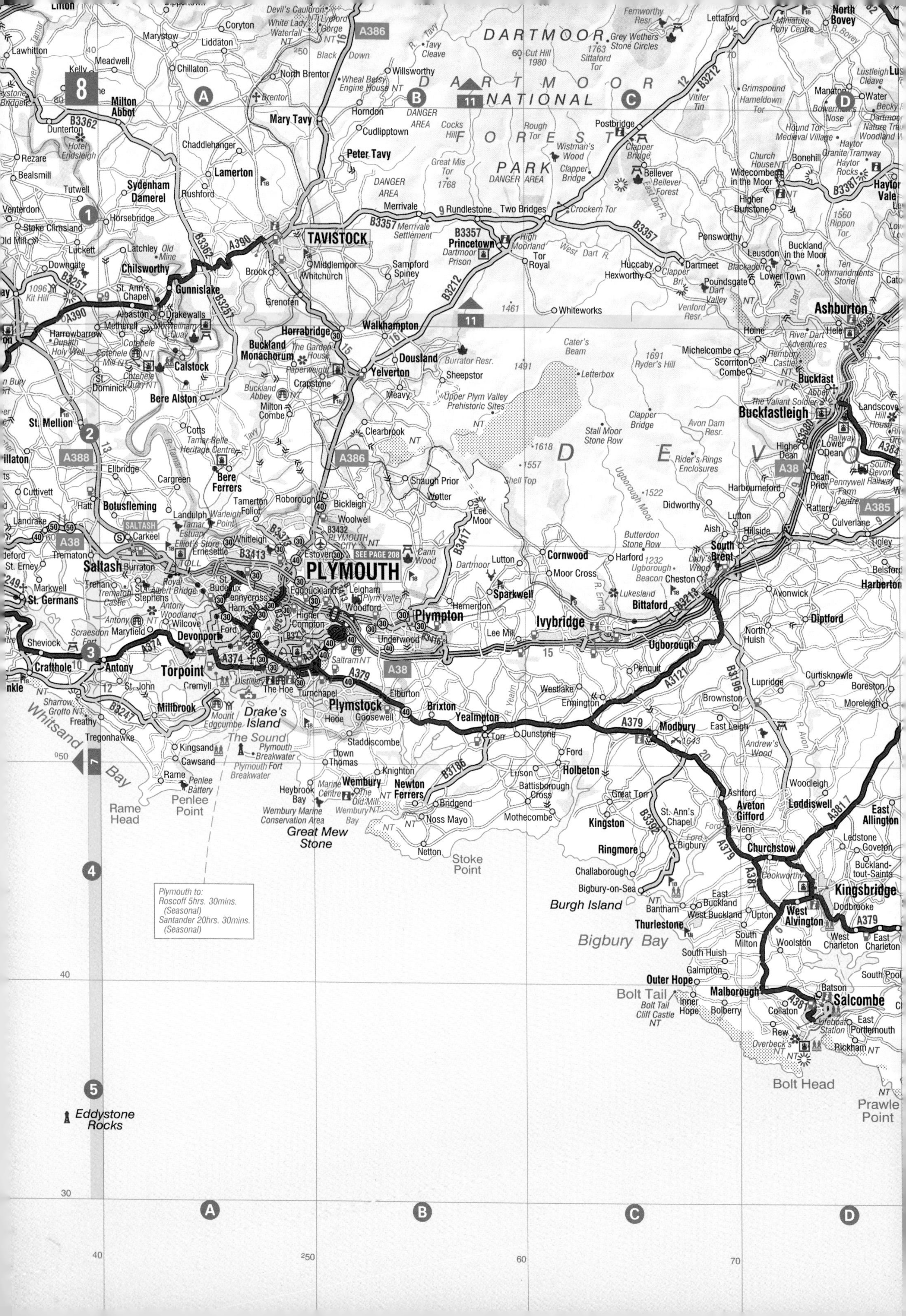
8
PLYMOUTH
TAVISTOCK
DARTMOOR
DARTMOOR NATIONAL FOREST PARK
DEVON
SEE PAGE 208
Saltash
Torpoint
Devonport
Plympton
Plymstock
Ivybridge
Buckfastleigh
Ashburton
Kingsbridge
Salcombe
Modbury
Yealmpton
Princetown
Gunnislake
Calstock
Bere Alston
Bere Ferrers
St. Germans
Millbrook
Drake's Island
The Sound
Plymouth Breakwater
Rame Head
Penlee Point
Whitsand Bay
Great Mew Stone
Stoke Point
Burgh Island
Bigbury Bay
Bolt Tail
Bolt Head
Prawle Point
Eddystone Rocks
Plymouth to:
Roscoff 5hrs. 30mins. (Seasonal)
Santander 20hrs. 30mins. (Seasonal)
A
B
C
D
1
2
3
4
5
7
11

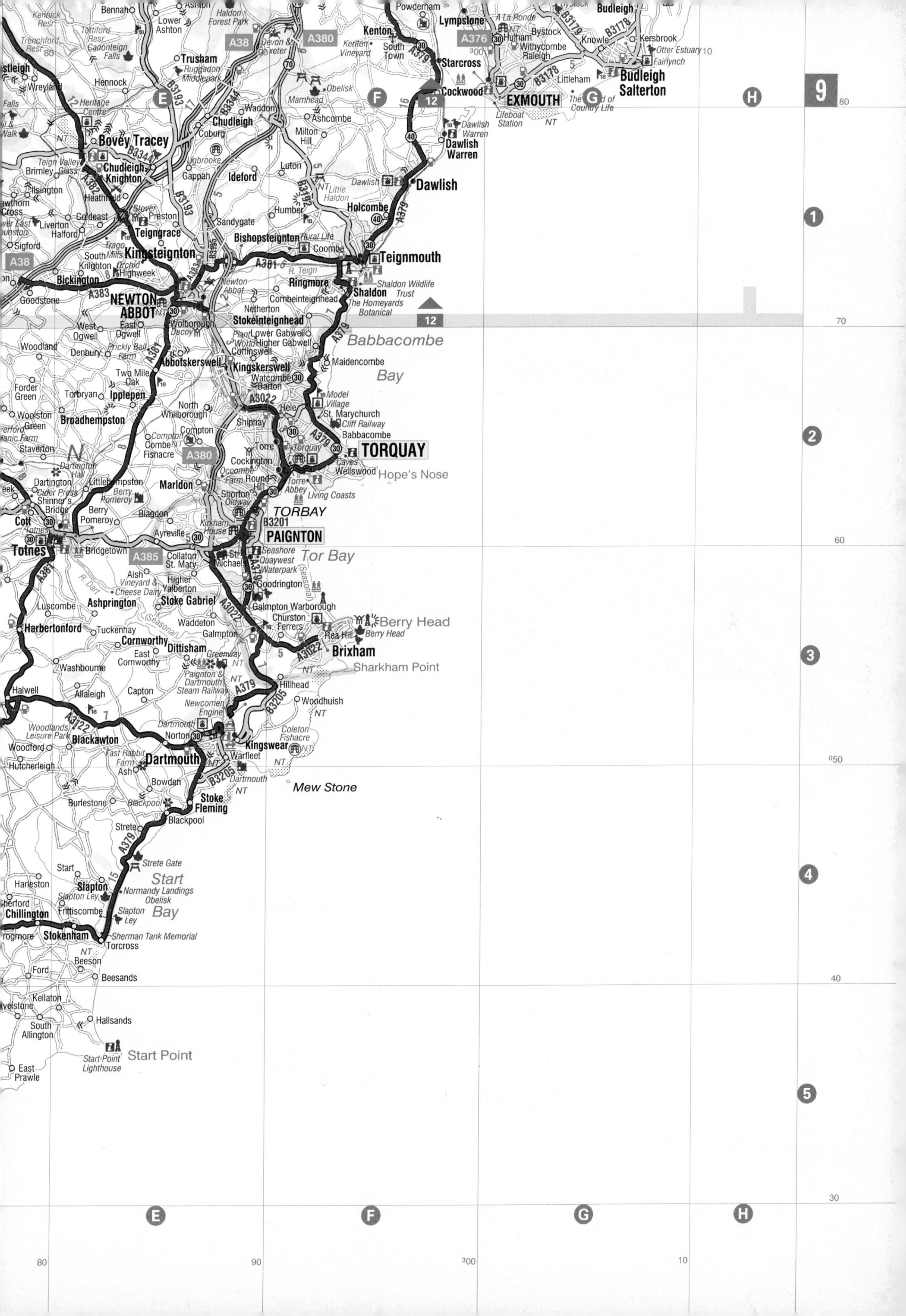
9
Bennah
Lower Ashton
Haldon Forest Park
Kennick Resr
Tottiford Resr
Trenchford Resr
Canonteign Falls
A38
Devon & Exeter
A380
Kenton
Kenton Vineyard
South Town
Powderham
Lympstone
A La Ronde
Bystock
Budleigh
Knowle
Kersbrook
Otter Estuary
Fairlynch
A376
Hulham
Withycombe Raleigh
Littleham
Budleigh Salterton
Starcross
Cockwood
EXMOUTH
The World of Country Life
Lifeboat Station
Trusham
Ruggadon Middlepark
Hennock
Wreyland
Heritage Centre
Obelisk
Mamhead
Ashcombe
Waddon
Chudleigh
Coburg
Bovey Tracey
Teign Valley Glass
Brimley
Chudleigh Knighton
Ilsington
Heathfield
Ugbrooke
Gappah
Ideford
Luton
Milton Hill
Little Haldon
Dawlish Warren
Dawlish
Holcombe
Sandygate
Humber
Bishopsteignton
Rural Life
Coombe
Teignmouth
Colleast
Liverton
Halford
Sigford
Stover
Preston
Teigngrace
Kingsteignton
South Knighton
Orchid
Highweek
Bickington
Goodstone
NEWTON ABBOT
Newton Abbot
Netherton
Ringmore
Combeinteignhead
Shaldon
Shaldon Wildlife Trust
The Homeyards Botanical
Stokeinteignhead
Wolborough
Decoy
East Ogwell
West Ogwell
Woodland
Denbury
Prickly Ball Farm
Lower Gabwell
Higher Gabwell
Plant World
Coffinswell
Babbacombe
Maidencombe
Bay
Abbotskerswell
Kingskerswell
Watcombe
Barton
Two Mile Oak
Forder Green
Torbryan
Ipplepen
North Whilborough
Model Village
St. Marychurch
Cliff Railway
Babbacombe
Hele
Woolston Green
Broadhempston
Shiphay
Compton
Compton Combe
Fishacre
Staverton
Torre
Torquay
TORQUAY
Cockington
Occombe Farm
Round Hill
Torre Abbey
Caves
Wellswood
Hope's Nose
Living Coasts
Dartington Hall
Dartington
Littlehempston
Berry Pomeroy
Marldon
Shorton
Oldway
Cider Press
Shinner's Bridge
TORBAY
Cott
Blagdon
Kirkham House
B3201
PAIGNTON
Totnes
Bridgetown
Ayreville
A385
Collaton St. Mary
St. Michaels
Seashore
Quaywest
Waterpark
Tor Bay
Aish
Vineyard & Cheese Dairy
Higher Yalberton
Goodrington
Luscombe
Ashprington
Stoke Gabriel
Galmpton Warborough
Waddeton
Churston Ferrers
Berry Head
Harbertonford
Tuckenhay
Cornworthy
Galmpton
Dittisham
Greenway
Rea Hill
Brixham
East Cornworthy
Washbourne
Sharkham Point
Paignton & Dartmouth Steam Railway
Hillhead
Halwell
Allaleigh
Capton
Newcomen Engine
Woodhuish
Woodlands Leisure Park
Blackawton
Dartmouth
Norton
Coleton Fishacre
Kingswear
Woodford
Fast Rabbit Farm
Warfleet
Hutcherleigh
Ash
Dartmouth
Bowden
Mew Stone
Burlestone
Blackpool
Stoke Fleming
Blackpool
Strete
Strete Gate
Start
Start Bay
Harleston
Slapton
Slapton Ley
Normandy Landings Obelisk
Chillington
Frittiscombe
Slapton Ley
Stokenham
Sherman Tank Memorial
Torcross
Beeson
Ford
Beesands
Kellaton
South Allington
Hallsands
Start Point
Start Point Lighthouse
East Prawle
E
F
G
H
1
2
3
4
5
80
70
60
50
40
30
80
90
300
10

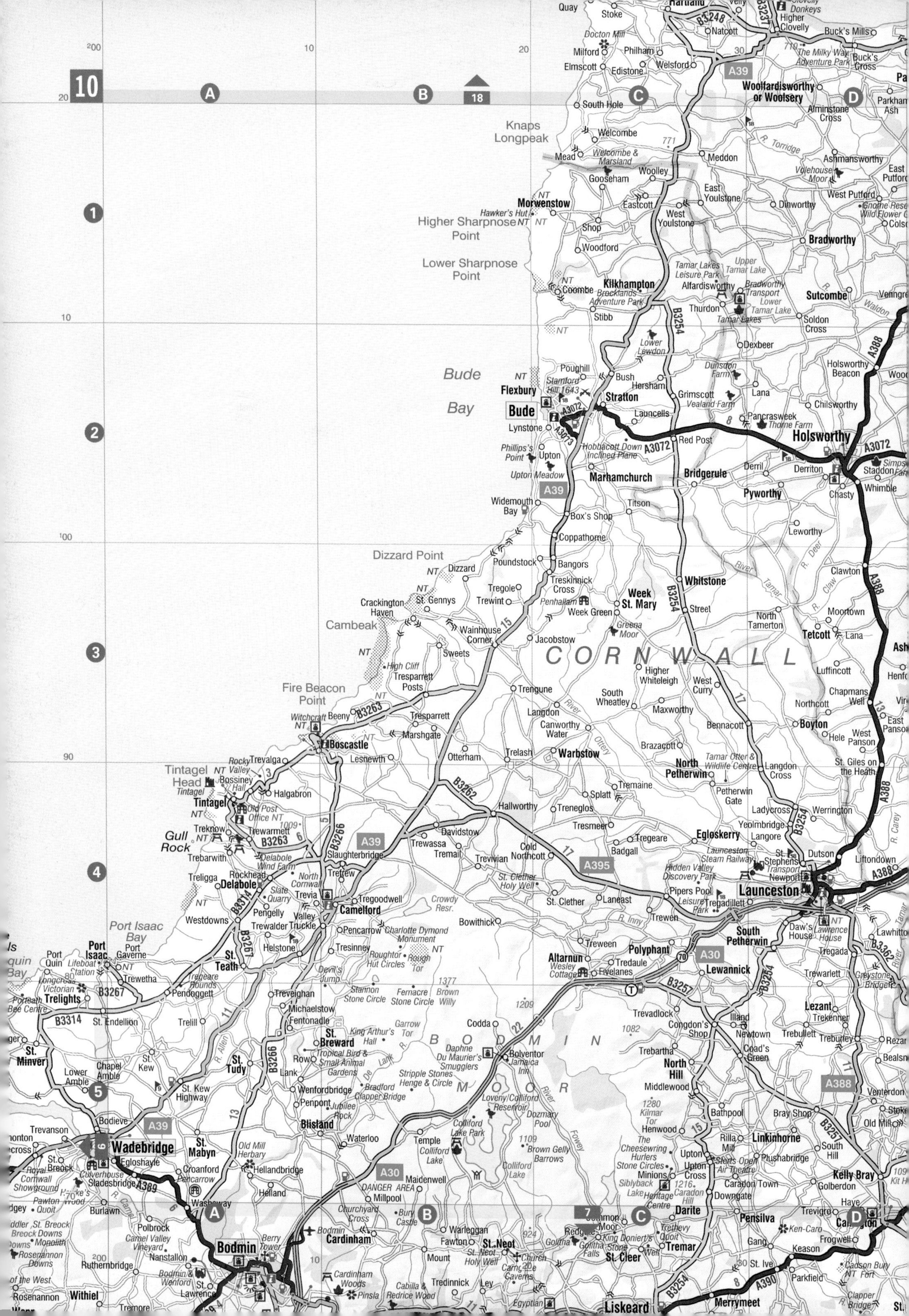

10
A
B
C
D
18
7
1
2
3
4
5
CORNWALL
BODMIN MOOR
Bude Bay
Quay
Stoke
Hartland
Higher Clovelly
Clovelly Donkeys
B3248
B3237
Natcott
Buck's Mills
The Milky Way Adventure Park
Buck's Cross
Doctor Mill
Milford
Philham
Elmscott
Edistone
Welsford
A39
Woolfardisworthy or Woolsery
Alminstone Cross
Parkham Ash
South Hole
Knaps Longpeak
Welcombe
Welcombe & Marsland
Mead
771
Meddon
R. Torridge
Ashmansworthy
Gooseham
Woolley
Volehouse Moor
East Putford
Morwenstow
Hawker's Hut
Eastcott
East Youlstone
West Youlstone
Dinworthy
West Putford
Higher Sharpnose Point
Shop
Woodford
Bradworthy
Lower Sharpnose Point
Tamar Lakes Leisure Park
Upper Tamar Lake
Kilkhampton
Alfardisworthy
Bradworthy Transport
Coombe
Brocklands Adventure Park
Thurdon
Lower Tamar Lake
Tamar Lakes
Sutcombe
Stibb
Soldon Cross
B3254
Dexbeer
Lower Lewdon
Holsworthy Beacon
A388
Poughill
Stamford Hill 1643
Bush
Hersham
Dunsdon Farm
Flexbury
Stratton
Grimscott
Vealand Farm
Lana
Bude
A3072
Launcells
Pancrasweek
Thorne Farm
Chilsworthy
Lynstone
A3073
Red Post
Holsworthy
Phillips's Point
Hobbacott Down Inclined Plane
Upton
Derril
Derriton
Upton Meadow
Marhamchurch
Bridgerule
Chasty
Whimble
Pyworthy
Widemouth Bay
Titson
Box's Shop
Leworthy
Coppathorne
Dizzard Point
Dizzard
Poundstock
Bangors
R. Deer
Clawton
Treskinnick Cross
Tregole
Whitstone
Crackington Haven
St. Gennys
Trewint
Penhallam
Week St. Mary
Week Green
Street
Moortown
Cambeak
Wainhouse Corner
Greena Moor
North Tamerton
Tetcott
Lana
Jacobstow
Sweets
High Cliff
Higher Whiteleigh
Luffincott
Tresparrett Posts
Fire Beacon Point
Trengune
West Curry
South Wheatley
Chapmans Well
Northcott
Beeny
B3263
Langdon
Maxworthy
Witchcraft
Tresparrett
Canworthy Water
Bennacott
Boyton
Hele
West Panson
Boscastle
Marshgate
Brazacott
Lesnewth
Otterham
Trelash
Warbstow
Tamar Otter & Wildlife Centre
Langdon Cross
Rocky Valley
Trevalga
North Petherwin
St. Giles on the Heath
Tintagel Head
Bossiney
Tremaine
Petherwin Gate
Halgabron
B3262
Splatt
Tintagel
Old Post Office NT
Hallworthy
Treneglos
Ladycross
Werrington
Treknow
Trewarmett
Tresmeer
Yeolmbridge
Gull Rock
Davidstow
Tregeare
Egloskerry
Langore
Trewassa
Tremail
Badgall
Launceston Steam Railway
Dutson
Trebarwith
Delabole Wind Farm
Slaughterbridge
Cold Northcott
A395
Hidden Valley Discovery Park
Liftondown
Treligga
Rockhead
Tretrew
Trevivian
St. Clether Holy Well
Launceston
Delabole
North Cornwall
Slate Quarry
Trevia
Camelford
Tregoodwell
Crowdy Resr.
St. Clether
Laneast
Pipers Pool
Tregadillett
Leisure Park
Pengelly
Trewalder
Truckle
Trewen
Westdowns
B3314
Bowithick
R. Inny
Port Isaac Bay
Pencarrow
Charlotte Dymond Monument
South Petherwin
Daw's House
Lawrence House
Helstone
B3267
Tregada
Port Isaac
Port Gaverne
Tresinney
Roughtor Hut Circles
Rough Tor
Treween
Polyphant
Port Quin
Lifeboat Station
St. Teath
Altarnun
Tredaule
A30
Lewannick
Trewarlett
Trewetha
Devil's Jump
Wesley Cottage
Fivelanes
Greystone Bridge
Victorian Trelights
Tregeare Rounds
Pendoggett
Treveighan
Stannon Stone Circle
Fernacre Stone Circle
1377 Brown Willy
B3257
Lezant
Trekenner
Porteath Bee Centre
Michaelstow
1209
Trevadlock
B3314
St. Endellion
Trelill
Fentonadle
Garrow Tor
Codda
Illand
Congdon's Shop
Newtown
Trebullett
Treburley
St. Breward
King Arthur's Hall
1082
St. Minver
Tropical Bird & Small Animal Gardens
Daphne Du Maurier's Smugglers
Bolventor
Jamaica Inn
Trebartha
Coad's Green
Rezare
St. Kew
St. Tudy
North Hill
Beals
Lower Amble
Chapel Amble
B3266
Row
Stripple Stones Henge & Circle
Middlewood
Lank
Bradford Clapper Bridge
1280 Kilmar Tor
A388
Venterdon
St. Kew Highway
Wenfordbridge
Penpont
Jubilee Rock
Loveny/Colliford Reservoir
Dozmary Pool
Bathpool
Bray Shop
Stoke
Bodieve
Blisland
Colliford Lake Park
Henwood
Rilla Mill
Linkinhorne
Old Mill
Trevanson
A39
Wadebridge
St. Mabyn
Old Mill Herbary
Waterloo
Temple
1109
Brown Gelly Barrows
The Cheesewring
Hurlers Stone Circles
Upton
Upton Cross
Sterts Open Air Theatre
South Hill
Colliford Lake
Plushabridge
St. Breock
Egloshayle
Croanford
Pencarrow
Hellandbridge
Minions
Caradon Town
Kelly Bray
Royal Cornwall Showground
Sladesbridge
A389
Maidenwell
Sibleyback Lake
1216 Caradon Hill
Golberdon
Helland
DANGER AREA
Millpool
Heritage Centre
Downgate
Haye
Pawton Quoit
Burlawn
Washaway
Churchyard Cross
Bury Castle
Darite
Trevigro
Callington
St. Breock Downs Monolith
Polbrock
Camel Valley Vineyard
Bodmin
Cardinham
Warleggan
Redgate
Common Moor
Trethevy Quoit
Pensilva
Ken-Caro
Frogwell
Rosenannon Downs
Nanstallon
Berry Tower
Fawton
St. Neot
Golitha Falls
King Doniert's Stone
St. Cleer
Tremar
Gang
Keason
Ruthernbridge
Mount
St. Neot Holy Well
Carnglaze Caverns
St. Ive
Cadson Bury NT Fort
Bodmin & Wenford
St. Lawrence
Cardinham Woods
Parkfield
Withiel
Rosenannon
Tremore
Pinsla
Cabilla & Redrice Wood
Trednnick
Ley
Egyptian
Liskeard
A390
Merrymeet
Clapper Bridge
NT

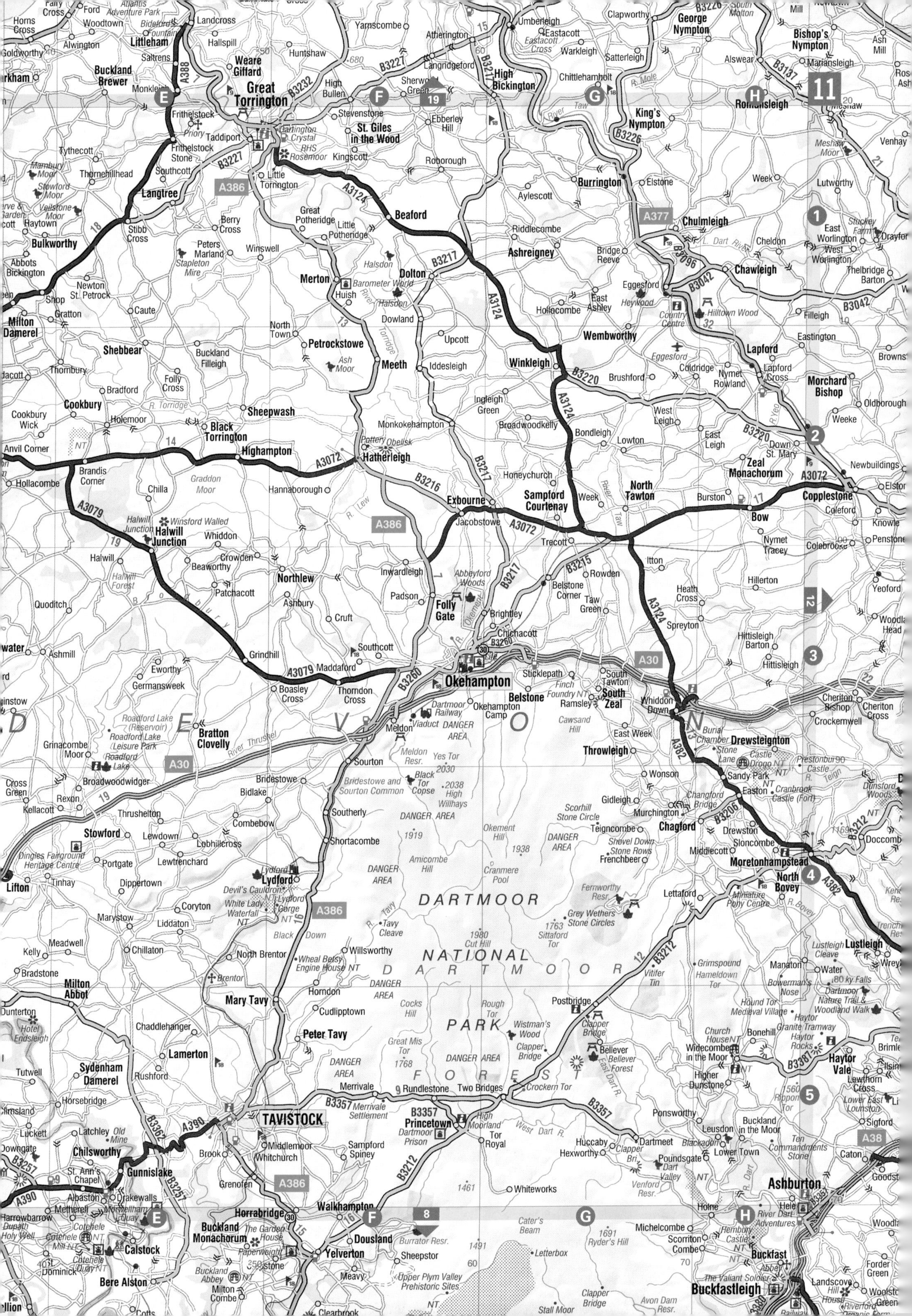

11
Horns Cross
Ford
Woodtown
Landcross
Yarnscombe
Umberleigh
Clapworthy
George Nympton
Bishop's Nympton
Alwington
Littleham
Hallspill
Eastacott
Atherington
Warkleigh
Satterleigh
Alswear
Marianslelgh
Ash Mill
Saltrens
Weare Giffard
Huntshaw
Langridgeford
High Bickington
Chittlehamholt
Buckland Brewer
Monkleigh
Great Torrington
High Bullen
Sherwood Green
Romansleigh
Meshaw
Frithelstock
Stevenstone
St. Giles in the Wood
Ebberley Hill
King's Nympton
Taddiport
Dartington Crystal
RHS Rosemoor
Kingscott
Venhay
Tythecott
Frithelstock Stone
Roborough
Thornehillhead
Southcott
Little Torrington
Burrington
Elstone
Week
Lutworthy
Langtree
Aylescott
Great Potheridge
Little Potheridge
Beaford
Chulmleigh
Berry Cross
Stibb Cross
Haytown
Riddlecombe
East Worlington
Peters Marland
Winswell
Ashreigney
Bridge Reeve
Cheldon
West Worlington
Bulkworthy
Stapleton Mire
Halsdon
Thelbridge Barton
Abbots Bickington
Merton
Barometer World
Dolton
Chawleigh
Newton St. Petrock
Huish
Eggesford
Heywood
Hilltown Wood
Shop
East Ashley
Hollocombe
Country Centre
Filleigh
Milton Damerel
Gratton
Caute
Dowland
North Town
Upcott
Wembworthy
Eastington
Petrockstowe
Lapford
Shebbear
Buckland Filleigh
Ash Moor
Meeth
Iddesleigh
Winkleigh
Coldridge
Nymet Rowland
Lapford Cross
Brownst
Thornbury
Brushford
Morchard Bishop
Folly Cross
Bradford
Ingleigh Green
Oldborough
Cookbury
Sheepwash
West Leigh
Weeke
Cookbury Wick
Holemoor
Black Torrington
Monkokehampton
Broadwoodkelly
Bondleigh
Lowton
East Leigh
Down St. Mary
Anvil Corner
Highampton
Hatherleigh
Zeal Monachorum
Newbuildings
Brandis Corner
Hollacombe
Graddon Moor
Chilla
Hannaborough
Honeychurch
Sampford Courtenay
North Tawton
Burston
Copplestone
Coleford
Exbourne
Jacobstowe
Week
Bow
Knowle
Halwill Junction
Winsford Walled
Whiddon
Trecott
Nymet Tracey
Colebrooke
Penstone
Halwill
Crowden
Beaworthy
Northlew
Inwardleigh
Itton
Rowden
Hillerton
Yeoford
Halwill Forest
Patchacott
Abbeyford Woods
Belstone Corner
Heath Cross
Quoditch
Ashbury
Padson
Folly Gate
Taw Green
Spreyton
Woodla Head
Cruft
Brightley
Chichacott
Hittisleigh Barton
Ashmill
Grindhill
Southcott
Hittisleigh
Eworthy
Maddaford
Okehampton
Sticklepath
South Tawton
Germansweek
Boasley Cross
Thorndon Cross
Belstone
Finch Foundry
South Zeal
Ramsley
Whiddon Down
Cheriton Bishop
Cheriton Cross
Dartmoor Railway
Okehampton Camp
Crockernwell
Roadford Lake (Reservoir)
Roadford Lake Leisure Park
Bratton Clovelly
Meldon
Viaduct
DANGER AREA
Cawsand Hill
East Week
Burial Chamber
Drewsteignton
Grinacombe Moor
Meldon Resr.
Throwleigh
Stone Lane
Castle Drogo
Prestonbury Castle
Sourton
Yes Tor 2030
Broadwoodwidger
Bridestowe
Black Tor Copse
2038 High Willhays
Wonson
Sandy Park
Bridestowe and Sourton Common
Cross Green
Rexon
Bidlake
Easton
Cranbrook Castle (Fort)
Dunsford Woods
Gidleigh
Changford Bridge
Kellacott
Thrushelton
Southerly
Scorhill Stone Circle
Murchington
Chagford
Combebow
DANGER AREA
Okement Hill
Teigncombe
Drewston
Stowford
Lewdown
1919
1938
Shovel Down Stone Rows
Sloncombe
Doccomb
Shortacombe
Lobhillcross
Lewtrenchard
Amicombe Hill
Frenchbeer
Middlecott
Moretonhampstead
Dingles Fairground Heritage Centre
Portgate
Lydford
Cranmere Pool
North Bovey
Lifton
Tinhay
Dippertown
Devil's Cauldron
DANGER AREA
Fernworthy Resr.
Lettaford
Miniature Pony Centre
Coryton
White Lady Waterfall
Lydford Gorge
DARTMOOR
Grey Wethers Stone Circles
Marystow
Liddaton
Tavy Cleave
1763 Sittaford Tor
Meadwell
Black Down
1980 Cut Hill
Lustleigh Cleave
Lustleigh
Kelly
Chillaton
North Brentor
Willsworthy
NATIONAL
Grimspound
Manaton
Water
Wrey
Bradstone
Wheal Betsy Engine House
DARTMOOR
Vitifer Tin
Hameldown Tor
Becky Falls
Milton Abbot
Brentor
DANGER AREA
Horndon
Bowerman's Nose
Dartmoor Nature Trail & Woodland Walk
Dunterton
Mary Tavy
Cocks Hill
Rough Tor
Postbridge
Hound Tor Medieval Village
Haytor
Hotel Endsleigh
Cudlipptown
PARK
Clapper Bridge
Wistman's Wood
Haytor Granite Tramway
Chaddlehanger
Peter Tavy
Great Mis Tor 1768
Bellever
Bellever Forest
Church House
Bonehill
Haytor Rocks
Lamerton
Clapper Bridge
Widecombe in the Moor
Haytor Vale
Sydenham Damerel
DANGER AREA
FOREST
Higher Dunstone
Tutwell
Rushford
Lewthorn Cross
Merrivale
Rundlestone
Two Bridges
Crockern Tor
Horsebridge
Merrivale Settlement
Princetown
Dartmoor Prison
High Moorland
Tor Royal
West Dart R.
1560 Rippon Tor
Lower East Lounston
Gimsland
TAVISTOCK
Ponsworthy
Buckland in the Moor
Sigford
Luckett
Latchley
Old Mine
Middlemoor
Sampford Spiney
Leusdon
Ten Commandments Stone
Chilsworthy
Brook
Whitchurch
Dartmeet
Hexworthy
Huccaby
Clapper Bri.
Poundsgate
Lower Town
Caton
Downgate
Gunnislake
St. Ann's Chapel
Grenofen
Dart Valley
Venford Resr.
Ashburton
Goodst
Albaston
Drakewalls
1461
Whiteworks
Harrowbarrow
Metherell
Morwellham Quay
Horrabridge
Walkhampton
Cater's Beam
Holne
Hele
River Dart Adventures
Woodla
Dupath Holy Well
Cotehele
Buckland Monachorum
The Garden House
Dousland
Burrator Resr.
1691 Ryder's Hill
Michelcombe
Hembury Castle
Calstock
Yelverton
Sheepstor
1491
Scorriton
Combe
Buckfast
Forder Green
St. Dominick
Cotehele Quay
Paperweight
Buckland Abbey
Meavy
Letterbox
Abbey
Landscove
Bere Alston
Upper Plym Valley Prehistoric Sites
The Valiant Soldier
Buckfastleigh
Woolsto
Milton Combe
Clapper Bridge
Avon Dam Resr.
Stall Moor
Riverford
Clearbrook
Cotts
A388
A386
A3124
A377
B3227
B3232
B3217
B3226
B3137
B3096
B3042
B3220
A3072
B3216
A3079
B3215
A30
B3260
A382
B3206
B3212
B3357
B3387
A38
A390
B3362
B3257
B3380
D E V O N

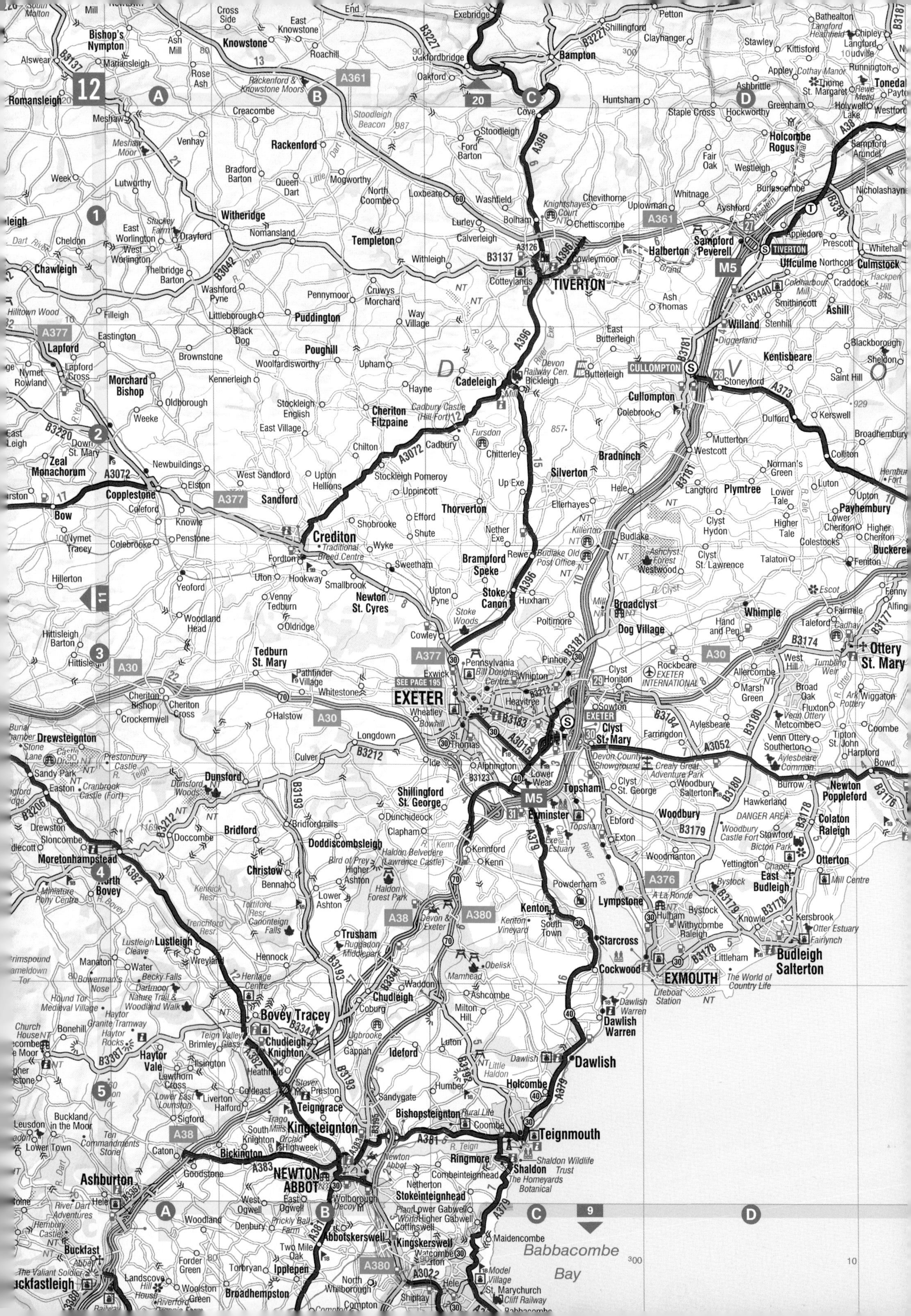

12
20
9
11
EXETER
TIVERTON
CREDITON
EXMOUTH
NEWTON ABBOT
Teignmouth
Dawlish
Bovey Tracey
Kingsteignton
Cullompton
Budleigh Salterton
Ottery St. Mary
Topsham
Crediton
Bampton
Witheridge
Chawleigh
Copplestone
Bow
Moretonhampstead
Ashburton
Buckfastleigh
Starcross
Kenton
Lympstone
Sidmouth
Babbacombe Bay
SEE PAGE 195
M5
A30
A38
A377
A396
A361
A380
A376
A3072
A373

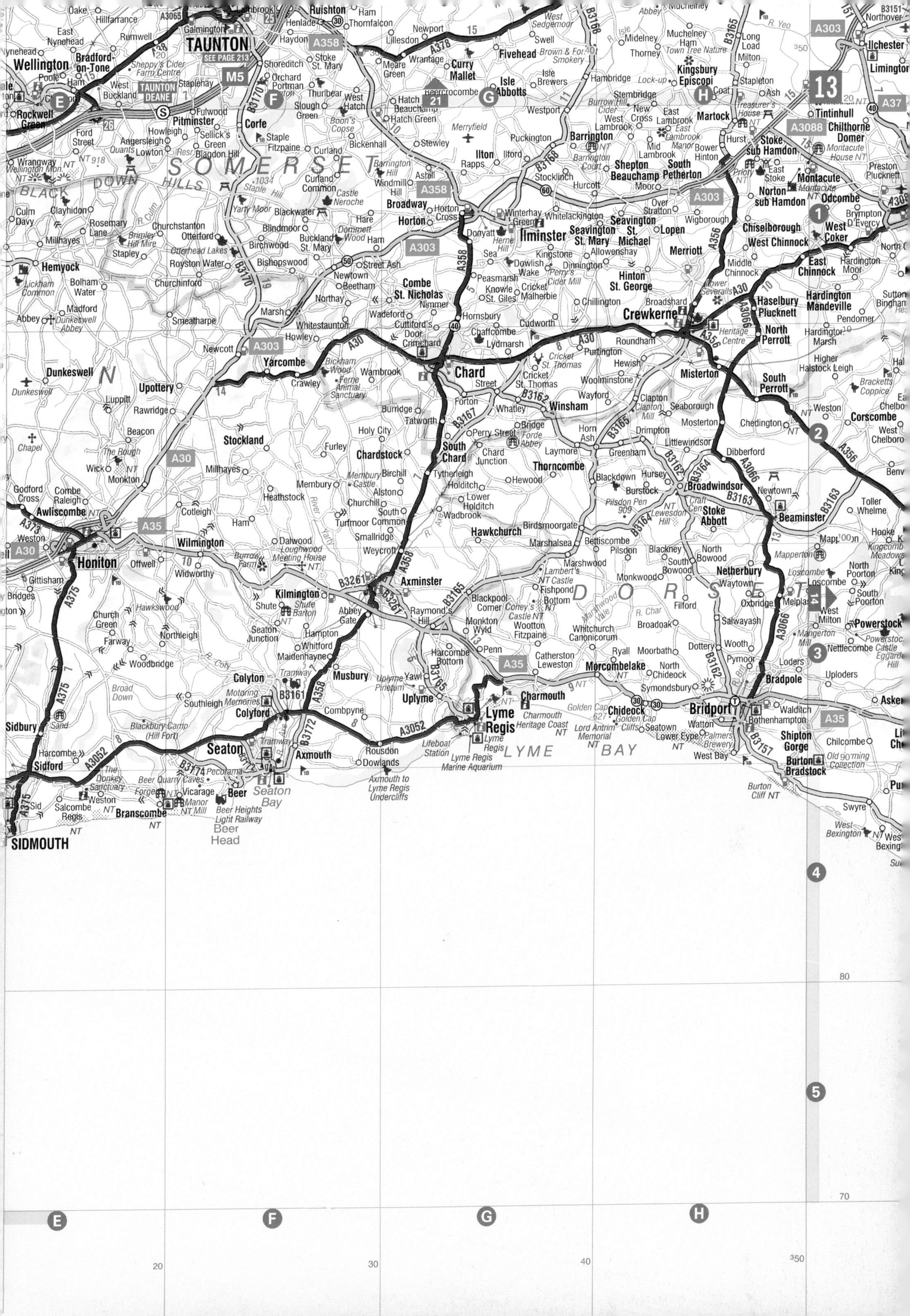

TAUNTON
SEE PAGE 213
M5
TAUNTON DEANE
Wellington
Bradford-on-Tone
Rockwell Green
Sheppy's Cider Farm Centre
Oake
Hillfarrance
Rumwell
Galmington
Lambrook
Ruishton
Ham
Henlade
Thornfalcon
Haydon
Stoke St. Mary
Shoreditch
Orchard Portman
Staplehay
Pitminster
Fulwood
Corfe
Howleigh
Sellick's Green
Angersleigh
Lowton
Blagdon Hill
West Buckland
Staple Fitzpaine
Curland
Thurlbear
Slough Green
West Hatch
Hatch Beauchamp
Hatch Green
Bickenhall
Stewley
Lillesdon
Newport
Meare Green
Wrantage
Curry Mallet
Beercrocombe
Fivehead
Isle Abbotts
Isle Brewers
Swell
West Sedgemoor
Midelney
Thorney
Muchelney
Muchelney Ham
Town Tree Nature
Kingsbury Episcopi
Long Load
Milton
Stapleton
Ash
Ilchester
Limington
Tintinhull
Chilthorne Domer
Martock
Hurst
Stoke sub Hamdon
Montacute
Montacute House NT
Preston Plucknett
Norton sub Hamdon
Odcombe
Brympton D'Evercy
West Coker
East Chinnock
Hardington Moor
Chiselborough
West Chinnock
Middle Chinnock
Haselbury Plucknett
Hardington Mandeville
Pendomer
North Perrott
Hardington Marsh
Higher Halstock Leigh
South Perrott
Corscombe
Weston
Chedington
West Chelborough
Benville
Toller Whelme
Beaminster
Newtown
Mapperton
Hooke
North Poorton
South Poorton
Loscombe
Melplash
West Milton
Powerstock
Mangerton
Netherbury
Waytown
Oxbridge
Salwayash
Netttlecombe
Loders
Uploders
Bradpole
Askerswell
Walditch
Bothenhampton
Shipton Gorge
Chilcombe
Burton Bradstock
Swyre
West Bexington
Burton Cliff NT
Bridport
West Bay
Lower Eype
Watton
Symondsbury
Chideock
Seatown
Golden Cap
Charmouth
Charmouth Heritage Coast NT
Lyme Regis
LYME BAY
Lyme Regis Marine Aquarium
Uplyme
Rousdon
Dowlands
Axmouth to Lyme Regis Undercliffs
Axmouth
Seaton
Seaton Bay
Beer
Beer Head
Branscombe
Salcombe Regis
Weston
SIDMOUTH
Sidford
Sidbury
Harcombe
Colyton
Colyford
Musbury
Combpyne
Axminster
Kilmington
Shute
Shute Barton
Hampton
Whitford
Maidenhayne
Seaton Junction
Northleigh
Farway
Church Green
Southleigh
Woodbridge
Honiton
Awliscombe
Combe Raleigh
Gittisham
Offwell
Widworthy
Wilmington
Dalwood
Loughwood Meeting House NT
Cotleigh
Stockland
Membury
Chardstock
Holy City
Furley
Tytherleigh
Holditch
Wadbrook
Hawkchurch
Birdsmoorgate
Marshalsea
Bettiscombe
Pilsdon
Pilsdon Pen
Marshwood
Monkwood
Fishpond Bottom
Lambert's Castle NT
Wootton Fitzpaine
Whitchurch Canonicorum
Ryall
Moorbath
Morcombelake
North Chideock
Dottery
Wooth
Pymore
Broadoak
Filford
Blackney
South Bowood
North Bowood
Stoke Abbott
Broadwindsor
Blackdown
Burstock
Drimpton
Greenham
Mosterton
Misterton
Crewkerne
Winsham
Clapton
Seaborough
Thorncombe
Hewood
Chard Junction
Forde Abbey
Perry Street
South Chard
Chard
Tatworth
Forton
Whatley
Cricket St. Thomas
Wayford
Woolminstone
Hewish
Purtington
Roundham
Cudworth
Chaffcombe
Lydmarsh
Hornsbury
Cuttiford's Door
Crimchard
Wadeford
Combe St. Nicholas
Whitestaunton
Howley
Yarcombe
Wambrook
Crawley
Upottery
Dunkeswell
Luppitt
Rawridge
Beacon
Hemyock
Culmstock
Clayhidon
Churchstanton
Otterford
Blackwater
Buckland St. Mary
Broadway
Horton
Ilminster
Donyatt
Dowlish Wake
Kingstone
Allowenshay
Dinnington
Hinton St. George
Merriott
Lopen
Seavington St. Mary
Seavington St. Michael
Shepton Beauchamp
South Petherton
Barrington
Puckington
Ilton
Stocklinch
Hurcott
Whitelackington
Westport
Hambridge
Stembridge
East Lambrook
West Lambrook
Mid Lambrook
Bower Hinton
Over Stratton
Wigborough
S O M E R S E T
D O R S E T
BLACK DOWN HILLS
A303
A358
A30
A35
A3052
A375
A3066
A356
A37
A3088
13
14
E
F
G
H
20
30
40
350
70
80

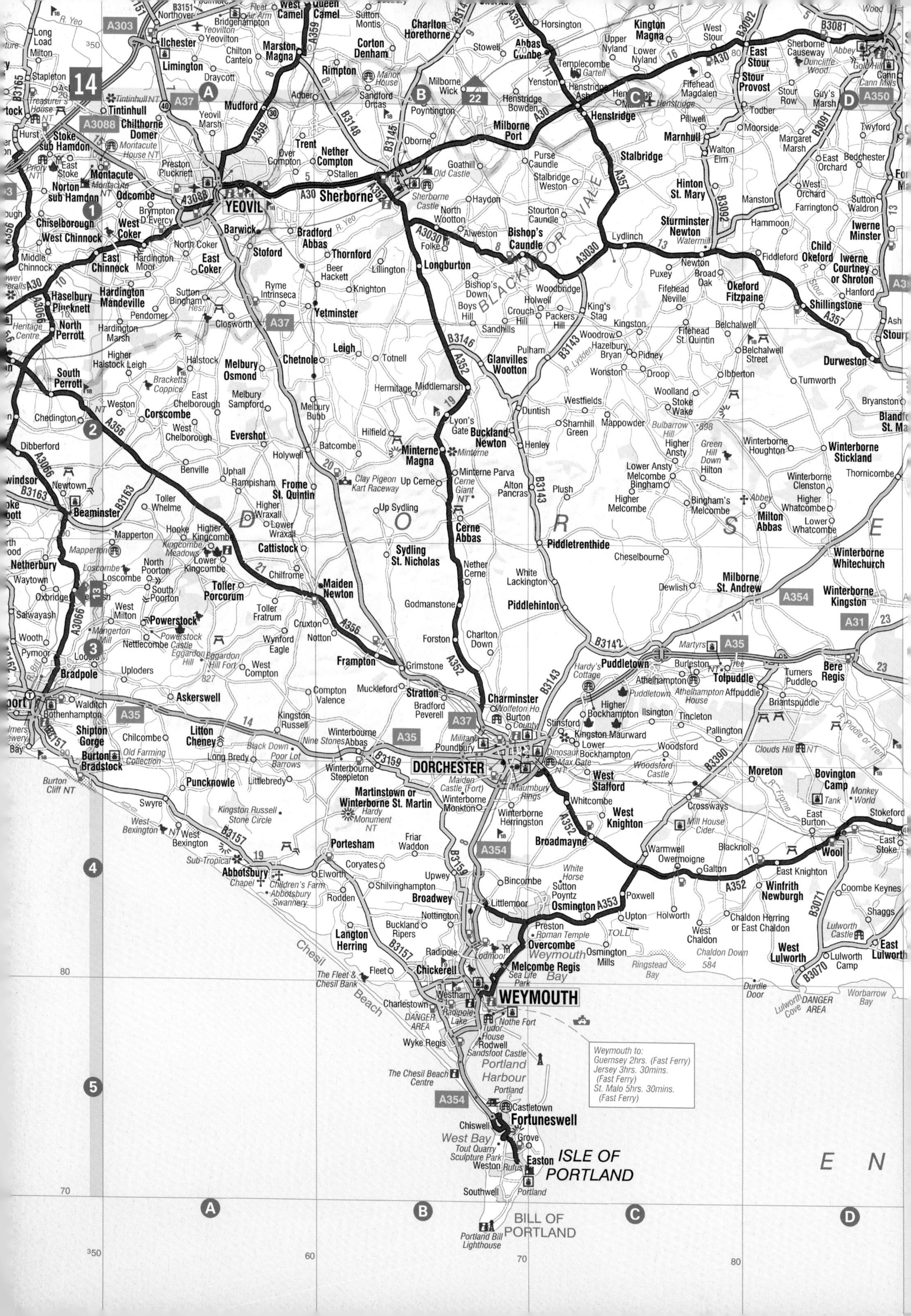

14
A303
Ilchester
Yeovilton
Limington
Marston Magna
Queen Camel
West Camel
Sutton Montis
Charlton Horethorne
Corton Denham
Rimpton
Horsington
Kington Magna
West Stour
Abbas Combe
Upper Nyland
Lower Nyland
Templecombe
East Stour
Stour Provost
Sherborne Causeway
Yenston
Henstridge Ash
Henstridge
Fifehead Magdalen
Todber
Stour Row
Guy's Marsh
A350
A37
A3088
Tintinhull
Chilthorne Domer
Mudford
Yeovil Marsh
Adber
Sandford Orcas
Poyntington
Milborne Wick
Henstridge Bowden
Milborne Port
Pillwell
Marnhull
Moorside
Margaret Marsh
Twyford
Stoke sub Hamdon
East Stoke
Montacute
Norton sub Hamdon
Odcombe
Preston Plucknett
Over Compton
Trent
Nether Compton
Stallen
Oborne
Goathill
Old Castle
Purse Caundle
Stalbridge
Stalbridge Weston
Walton Elm
Hinton St. Mary
East Orchard
Bedchester
West Orchard
YEOVIL
Sherborne
Sherborne Castle
Haydon
North Wootton
Stourton Caundle
Manston
Sutton Waldron
Farrington
Chiselborough
West Chinnock
West Coker
Brympton D'Evercy
Barwick
Bradford Abbas
Alweston
Bishop's Caundle
BLACKMOOR VALE
Sturminster Newton
Hammoon
Iwerne Minster
Middle Chinnock
East Chinnock
Hardington Moor
North Coker
East Coker
Stoford
Thornford
Folke
Longburton
Lydlinch
Fiddleford
Child Okeford
Iwerne Courtney or Shroton
Haselbury Plucknett
Hardington Mandeville
Sutton Bingham
Ryme Intrinseca
Beer Hackett
Lillington
Knighton
Bishop's Down
Woodbridge
Puxey
Newton
Broad Oak
Okeford Fitzpaine
Hanford
Fifehead Neville
North Perrott
Pendomer
Closworth
Yetminster
Boys Hill
Holwell
Crouch Hill
Packers Hill
King's Stag
Shillingstone
Hardington Marsh
Sandhills
Kingston
Fifehead St. Quintin
Belchalwell
Higher Halstock Leigh
Halstock
Melbury Osmond
Chetnole
Leigh
Totnell
Glanvilles Wootton
Pulham
Woodrow
Hazelbury Bryan
Pidney
Belchalwell Street
Durweston
South Perrott
Brackett's Coppice
Hermitage
Middlemarsh
Wonston
Droop
Ibberton
Turnworth
Chedington
Weston
East Chelborough
Corscombe
Melbury Sampford
Melbury Bubb
Duntish
Westfields
Woolland
Stoke Wake
Bryanston
West Chelborough
Evershot
Hilfield
Lyon's Gate
Buckland Newton
Sharnhill Green
Mappowder
Bulbarrow Hill
Dibberford
Batcombe
Minterne Magna
Henley
Higher Ansty
Green Hill Down
Winterborne Houghton
Winterborne Stickland
Benville
Uphall
Holywell
Minterne Parva
Lower Ansty
Melcombe Bingham
Hilton
Thornicombe
Windsor
Newtown
Rampisham
Frome St. Quintin
Clay Pigeon Kart Raceway
Up Cerne
Cerne Giant
Alton Pancras
Plush
Winterborne Clenston
B3163
Toller Whelme
Higher Wraxall
Lower Wraxall
Up Sydling
Higher Melcombe
Bingham's Melcombe
Abbey
Higher Whatcombe
Beaminster
Cerne Abbas
Milton Abbas
Lower Whatcombe
Mapperton
Hooke
Higher Kingcombe
Kingcombe Meadows
Cattistock
Sydling St. Nicholas
Piddletrenthide
Cheselbourne
Winterborne Whitechurch
Netherbury
Loscombe
North Poorton
Lower Kingcombe
Chilfrome
Nether Cerne
White Lackington
Waytown
Oxbridge
South Poorton
Toller Porcorum
Maiden Newton
Dewlish
Milborne St. Andrew
Winterborne Kingston
Salwayash
West Milton
Toller Fratrum
Godmanstone
Piddlehinton
A354
A31
Wooth
Powerstock
Powerstock Castle
Mangerton Mill
Cruxton
Notton
Pymoor
Nettlecombe
Eggardon Hill
Eggardon Hill Fort
Wynford Eagle
Forston
Charlton Down
Martyrs
A35
Loders
Uploders
West Compton
Frampton
Grimstone
B3142
Puddletown
Burleston
Tolpuddle
Turners Puddle
Bere Regis
Bradpole
Hardy's Cottage
Athelhampton
Athelhampton House
Affpuddle
Bridport
Walditch
Askerswell
Compton Valence
Muckleford
Stratton
Charminster
Wolfeton Ho.
Higher Bockhampton
Ilsington
Tincleton
Briantspuddle
Bothenhampton
Kingston Russell
Bradford Peverell
Burton
Stinsford
Kingston Maurward
Pallington
Shipton Gorge
Chilcombe
Litton Cheney
Winterbourne Abbas
Nine Stones
Poundbury
Lower Bockhampton
Woodsford
Clouds Hill
Burton Bradstock
Old Farming Collection
Black Down
Poor Lot Barrows
Long Bredy
B3159
DORCHESTER
Max Gate
Woodsford Castle
B3390
Moreton
Bovington Camp
Monkey World
Burton Cliff
Puncknowle
Littlebredy
Winterbourne Steepleton
Martinstown or Winterbourne St. Martin
Maiden Castle (Fort)
Maumbury Rings
West Stafford
Tank
Winterborne Monkton
Whitcombe
West Knighton
Crossways
East Burton
Stokeford
Swyre
Kingston Russell Stone Circle
Hardy Monument
Winterborne Herringston
Mill House Cider
West Bexington
Friar Waddon
Broadmayne
Warmwell
Owermoigne
Blacknoll
Wool
East Stoke
B3157
Sub-Tropical
Portesham
A354
Abbotsbury
Chapel
Children's Farm
Abbotsbury Swannery
Elworth
Coryates
Upwey
Bincombe
White Horse
Sutton Poyntz
Galton
East Knighton
Shilvinghampton
Rodden
Broadwey
Littlemoor
Osmington
A353
Poxwell
Winfrith Newburgh
Coombe Keynes
Buckland Ripers
Nottington
Preston
Roman Temple
Upton
Holworth
Chaldon Herring or East Chaldon
West Chaldon
Shaggs
Langton Herring
Overcombe
Weymouth Bay
Osmington Mills
Lulworth Castle
West Lulworth
East Lulworth
Chaldon Down
Chesil Beach
Radipole
Fleet
Chickerell
The Fleet & Chesil Bank
Lodmoor
Melcombe Regis
Sea Life Park
Ringstead Bay
Lulworth Camp
B3070
Durdle Door
WEYMOUTH
Westham
Charlestown
DANGER AREA
Radipole Lake
Nothe Fort
Tudor House
Lulworth Cove
Worbarrow Bay
Wyke Regis
Rodwell
Sandsfoot Castle
Portland Harbour
Weymouth to:
Guernsey 2hrs. (Fast Ferry)
Jersey 3hrs. 30mins. (Fast Ferry)
St. Malo 5hrs. 30mins. (Fast Ferry)
The Chesil Beach Centre
Portland
Castletown
Chiswell
Fortuneswell
West Bay
Grove
Tout Quarry Sculpture Park
Easton
ISLE OF PORTLAND
Weston
Rufus
Southwell
BILL OF PORTLAND
Portland Bill Lighthouse
D O R S E T
E N
A B C D
1 2 3 4 5
350 60 70 80

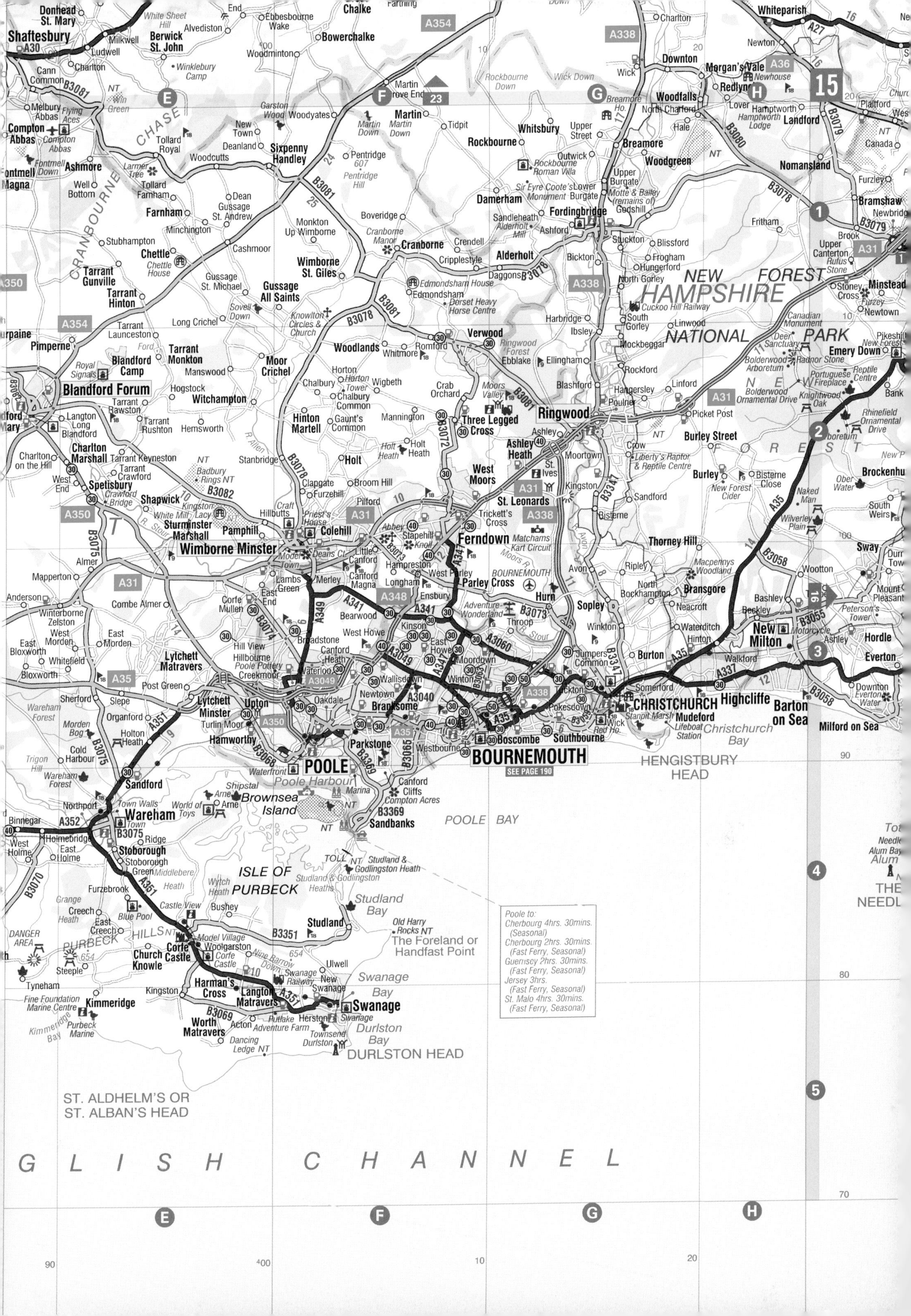

Donhead St. Mary
Shaftesbury
A30
Milkwell
Ludwell
Berwick St. John
White Sheet Hill
Alvediston
Ebbesbourne Wake
Chalke
Bowerchalke
Woodminton
A354
A338
Charlton
Whiteparish
A27
Newton
Downton
Cann Common
B3081
Winklebury Camp
Martin Drove End
23
Rockbourne Down
Wick Down
Wick
Morgan's Vale
A36
Newhouse
Redlynch
15
Melbury Abbas
Flying Aces
Win Green
Compton Abbas
CRANBORNE CHASE
Tollard Royal
New Town
Deanland
Garston Wood
Woodyates
Martin Down
Martin
Tidpit
Sixpenny Handley
Whitsbury
Upper Street
Breamore Ho.
Breamore
Woodfalls
North Charford
Hale
Lover
Hamptworth
Hamptworth Lodge
Landford
Plaitford
B3079
B3080
Canada
Fontmell Down
Fontmell Magna
Ashmore
Larmer Tree
Woodcutts
Pentridge
607
Pentridge Hill
Rockbourne
Outwick
Rockbourne Roman Villa
Woodgreen
Nomansland
Well Bottom
Tollard Farnham
Dean
Gussage St. Andrew
B3081
Sir Eyre Coote's Monument
Lower Burgate
Upper Burgate
Motte & Bailey (remains of)
Godshill
B3078
Furzley
Bramshaw
Newbridge
Farnham
Minchington
Monkton Up Wimborne
Boveridge
Damerham
Sandleheath
Alderholt Mill
Ashford
Fordingbridge
Fritham
1
Brook
B3079
Stubhampton
Chettle
Chettle House
Cashmoor
Cranborne Manor
Cranborne
Crendell
Cripplestyle
Alderholt
Daggons
B3078
Stuckton
Blissford
Frogham
Hungerford
Bickton
Upper Canterton
A31
Rufus Stone
Tarrant Gunville
Tarrant Hinton
Gussage St. Michael
Gussage All Saints
Wimborne St. Giles
Edmondsham House
Edmondsham
Dorset Heavy Horse Centre
A338
North Gorley
NEW FOREST
HAMPSHIRE
Stoney Cross
Minstead
Furzey
Newtown
A350
A354
Tarrant Launceston
Long Crichel
Sovell Down
Knowlton Circles & Church
B3078
Verwood
Harbridge
Ibsley
Cuckoo Hill Railway
South Gorley
Linwood
NATIONAL PARK
Canadian Monument
Pikeshill
New Forest
Pimperne
Ford
Tarrant Monkton
Moor Crichel
Woodlands
Whitmore
Romford
Ringwood Forest
Ebblake
Ellingham
Mockbeggar
Deer Sanctuary
Emery Down
Royal Signals
Blandford Camp
Manswood
Horton
Horton Tower
Wigbeth
Crab Orchard
Moors Valley
B3081
Blashford
Rockford
Bolderwood Arboretum
Radnor Stone
Reptile Centre
Portuguese Fireplace
Blandford Forum
Hogstock
Chalbury
Chalbury Common
Hangersley
Poulner
Linford
A31
Bolderwood Ornamental Drive
Knightwood Oak
Bank
Tarrant Rawston
Witchampton
Hinton Martell
Gaunt's Common
Mannington
B3072
Three Legged Cross
Ringwood
Picket Post
Langton Long Blandford
Tarrant Rushton
Hemsworth
Ashley
Rhinefield Ornamental Drive
Arboretum
Charlton Marshall
Tarrant Keyneston
R. Allen
Holt Heath
Holt
Ashley Heath
Moortown
Crow
Burley Street
FOREST
2
Charlton on the Hill
Tarrant Crawford
Badbury Rings NT
Stanbridge
B3078
West Moors
St. Ives
Liberty's Raptor & Reptile Centre
New Pr.
West End
Spetisbury
Crawford Bridge
Shapwick
B3082
Kingston Lacy NT
White Mill
Clapgate
Furzehill
Broom Hill
Kingston
Burley
Bisterne Close
New Forest Cider
Ober Water
Brockenhurst
A350
Sturminster Marshall
R. Stour
Craft Centre
Hillbutts
Pilford
A31
St. Leonards
Trickett's Cross
A338
Sandford
B3347
Bisterne
Naked Man
A35
South Weirs
Wilverley Plain
Priest's House
Pamphill
Wimborne Minster
Colehill
Abbey
Stapehill Knoll
Ferndown
Matchams Kart Circuit
Thorney Hill
Sway
B3075
Model Town
Deans Ct
Little Canford
B3073
A347
Moors R.
BOURNEMOUTH
Avon
Ripley
Macpennys Woodland
B3058
Wootton
Almer
Mapperton
A31
Lambs Green
Merley
Canford Magna
Hampreston
West Parley
Parley Cross
Hurn
North Bockhampton
Bransgore
Mount Pleasant
Anderson
Combe Almer
Corfe Mullen
East End
A349
A341
Longham
A348
Ensbury
Adventure Wonderland
B3073
Sopley
Neacroft
Bashley
Beckley
B3055
Peterson's Tower
Winterborne Zelston
West Morden
East Morden
B3074
Bearwood
A341
Kinson
East Howe
Throop
R. Stour
Winkton
Waterditch
Hinton
New Milton
Motorcycle
Ashley
Hordle
East Bloxworth
Whitefield
Bloxworth
Lytchett Matravers
Hill View
Broadstone
Canford Heath
West Howe
A3049
A3060
A347
Moordown
Jumpers Common
B3347
Burton
A35
Walkford
3
Everton
Hillbourne
Poole Pottery
Creekmoor
Waterloo
A3049
Wallisdown
Winton
B3063
Tuckton
Somerford
A337
Highcliffe
Downton
Everton Water
Wareham Forest
Sherford
Slepe
Post Green
Lytchett Minster
Upton
Oakdale
Newtown
A3040
Branksome
A338
Pokesdown
CHRISTCHURCH
Stanpit Marsh
Mudeford
Barton on Sea
B3058
Milford on Sea
A35
A351
Organford
Turlin Moor
A350
Hamworthy
B3068
Parkstone
A35
B3065
Westbourne
Boscombe
Southbourne
Red Ho.
Wick
Lifeboat Station
Christchurch Bay
Morden Bog
Holton Heath
Cold Harbour
B3075
Trigon Hill
Waterfront
POOLE
B3369
BOURNEMOUTH
SEE PAGE 190
HENGISTBURY HEAD
90
Wareham Forest
Sandford
Shipstal
Poole Harbour
Marina
Canford Cliffs
Compton Acres
Northport
Town Walls
World of Toys
Arne
Brownsea Island
B3369
Sandbanks
POOLE BAY
Binnegar
A352
Wareham
Town
B3075
Ridge
NT
Holmebridge
West Holme
East Holme
Stoborough
Stoborough Green
Middlebere Heath
TOLL
Studland & Godlingston Heath
ISLE OF PURBECK
Studland & Godlingston Heaths
Needles
Alum Bay
4
THE NEEDLES
B3070
Furzebrook
Grange Heath
Creech
A351
Castle View
Wytch Heath
Bushey
Studland Bay
Blue Pool
East Creech
Studland
Old Harry Rocks NT
Poole to:
Cherbourg 4hrs. 30mins. (Seasonal)
Cherbourg 2hrs. 30mins. (Fast Ferry, Seasonal)
Guernsey 2hrs. 30mins. (Fast Ferry, Seasonal)
Jersey 3hrs. (Fast Ferry, Seasonal)
St. Malo 4hrs. 30mins. (Fast Ferry, Seasonal)
DANGER AREA
PURBECK HILLS
654
B3351
The Foreland or Handfast Point
Model Village
Woolgarston
Corfe Castle
Church Knowle
Steeple
Nine Barrow Down
654
Ulwell
Swanage Railway
New Swanage
Swanage Bay
Tyneham
Kingston
Harman's Cross
Langton Matravers
A351
Swanage
80
Fine Foundation Marine Centre
Kimmeridge
Kimmeridge Bay
Purbeck Marine
B3069
Worth Matravers
Acton
Putlake Adventure Farm
Herston
Townsend
Durlston
Durlston Bay
DURLSTON HEAD
Dancing Ledge NT
5
ST. ALDHELM'S OR ST. ALBAN'S HEAD
GLISH CHANNEL
70
E
F
G
H
90
400
10
20

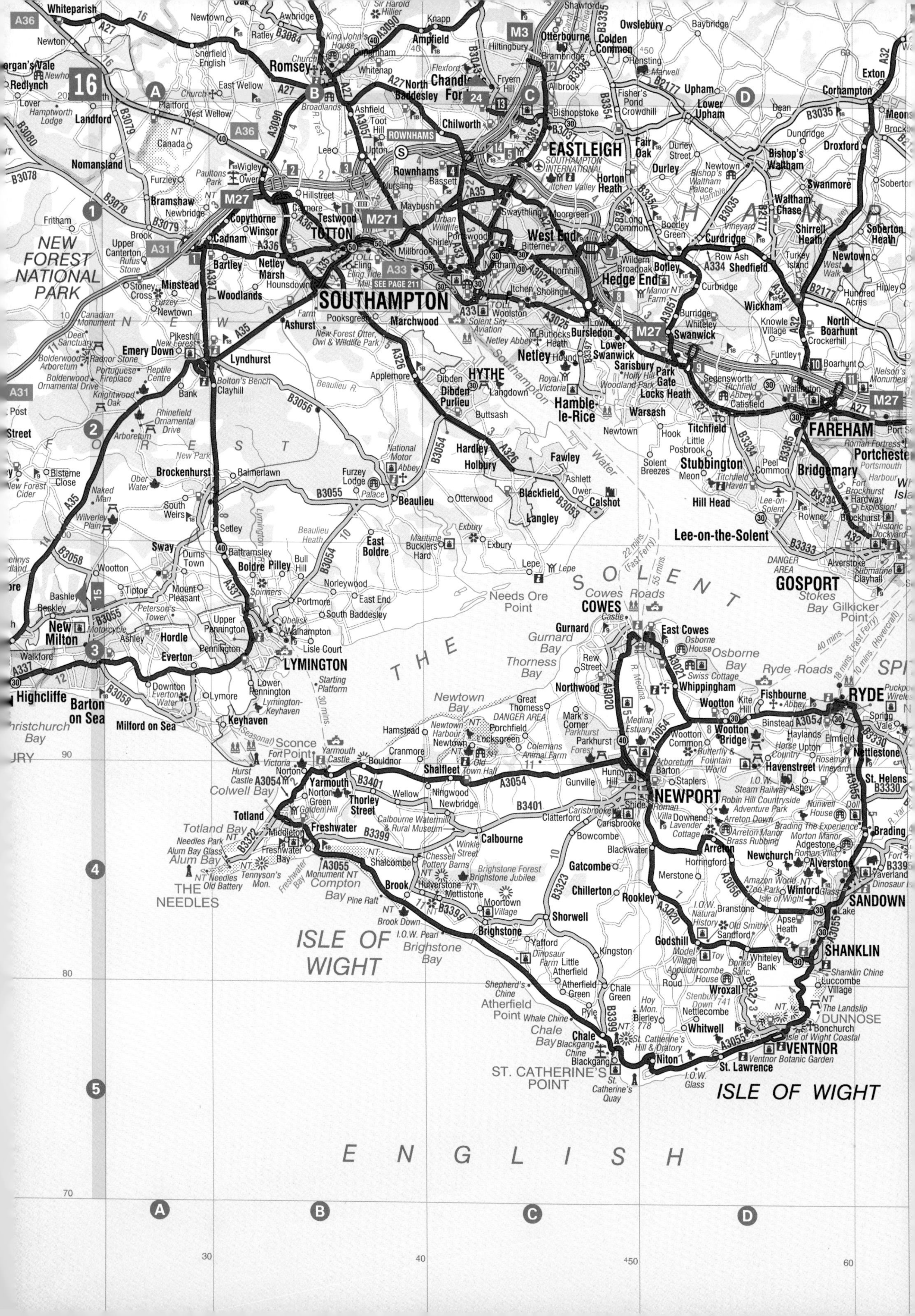

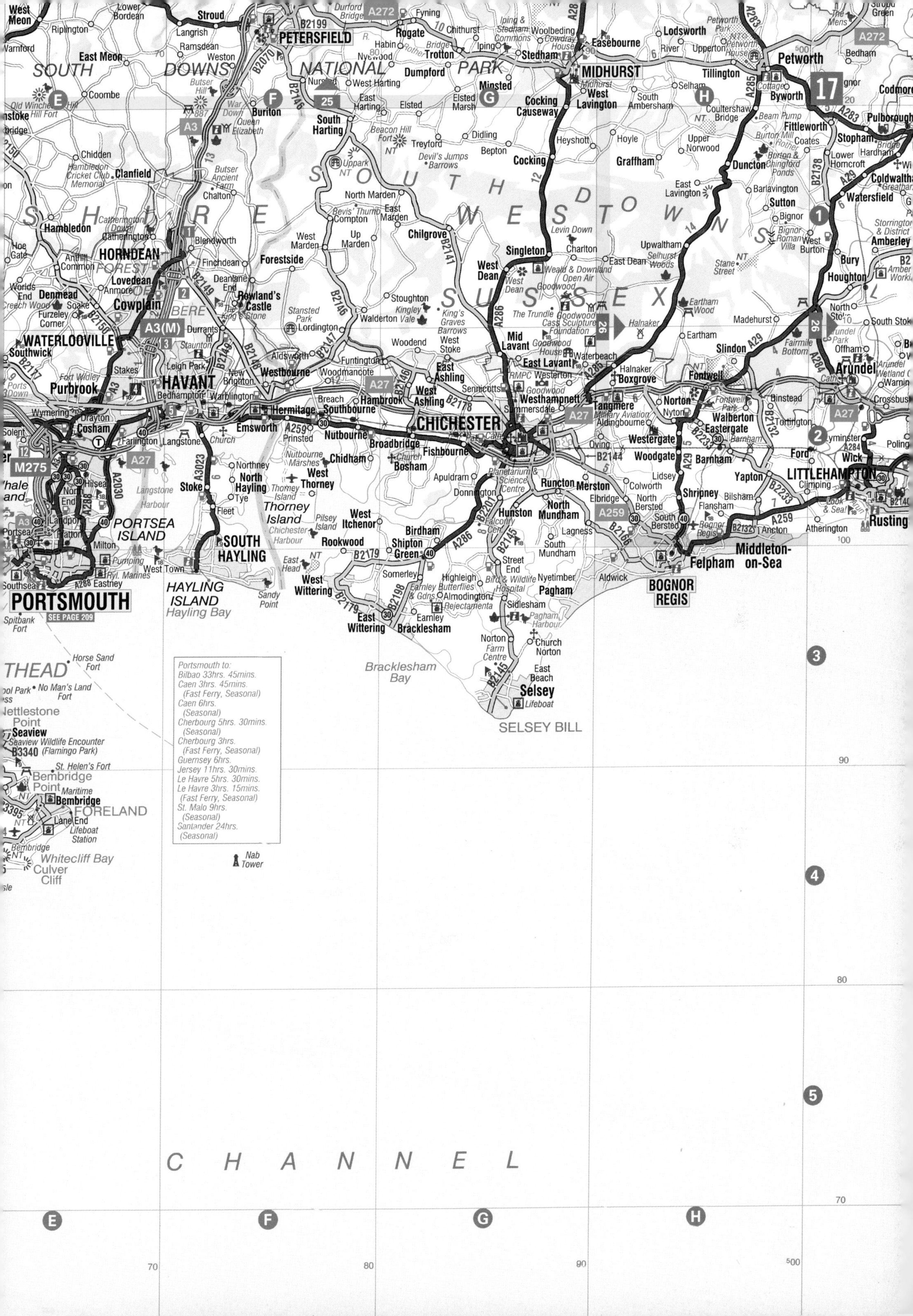

West Meon
Lower Bordean
Stroud
Langrish
Ramsdean
Weston
Ripplington
East Meon
SOUTH
DOWNS
NATIONAL
PARK
PETERSFIELD
B2199
Durford Bridge
A272
Fyning
Rogate
Chithurst
Iping & Stedham Commons
Woolbeding
Cowdray House
Easebourne
Lodsworth
River
Upperton
Petworth Park
Petworth House
Petworth
Bedham
A272
Habin
Trotton
Nyewood
Iping
Stedham
MIDHURST
Dumpford
Minsted
West Harting
Nursted
East Harting
Elsted
Elsted Marsh
South Harting
Cocking Causeway
West Lavington
South Ambersham
Selham
Tillington
Coultershaw Bridge
Byworth
17
Codmore
Pulborough
Coombe
Butser Hill
War Down
Queen Elizabeth
Buriton
Old Winchester Hill
Hill Fort
A3
Beacon Hill Fort
Treyford
Didling
Devil's Jumps Barrows
Bepton
Cocking
Heyshott
Hoyle
Graffham
Upper Norwood
Beam Pump
Burton Mill
Fittleworth
Coates
Stopham Bridge
Hardham
Lower Horncroft
Coldwaltham
Greatham
Watersfield
Chidden
Hambledon Cricket Club Memorial
Clanfield
Butser Ancient Farm
Chalton
Uppark
North Marden
East Marden
Bevis' Thumb
Compton
Duncton
Burton & Chingford Ponds
East Lavington
Barlavington
Sutton
Bignor
Bignor Roman Villa
West Burton
Storrington & District
Amberley
Bury
Houghton
Hambledon
Catherington Down
Catherington
Blendworth
Horndean
Hoe Gate
Anthill Common
Finchdean
Forestside
West Marden
Up Marden
Chilgrove
B2141
Levin Down
Charlton
Singleton
West Dean
Weald & Downland Open Air
East Dean
Upwaltham
Selhurst Woods
Stane Street
Lovedean
Anmore
Deanlane End
Rowland's Castle
Worlds End
Denmead
Creech Wood
Soake
Furzeley Corner
Cowplain
FOREST OF BERE
Stansted Park
Lordington
Stoughton
Kingley Vale
Walderton
King's Graves Barrows
Goodwood
The Trundle
Goodwood Cass Sculpture Foundation
Halnaker
Eartham Wood
Eartham
Madehurst
North Stoke
South Stoke
WATERLOOVILLE
Southwick
A3(M)
Durrants
Staunton
Aldsworth
Funtington
Woodend
West Stoke
East Ashling
Mid Lavant
Goodwood House
Waterbeach
East Lavant
Slindon
Fairmile Bottom
Arundel Park
Offham
Arundel
Arundel Wetland Centre
Warningcamp
Fort Widley
Purbrook
Stakes
Leigh Park
HAVANT
New Brighton
Westbourne
Woodmancote
A27
West Ashling
Hambrook
Sennicotts
RMPC
Westerton
Westhampnett
Halnaker
Boxgrove
Fontwell
Fontwell Park
Norton
Nyton
Walberton
Binstead
Tortington
Crossbush
Wymering
Drayton
Cosham
Bedhampton
Warblington
Breach
Hermitage
Southbourne
Emsworth
Farlington
Langstone
Church
Prinsted
Nutbourne
Broadbridge
CHICHESTER
Fishbourne
Summersdale
Tangmere Military Aviation
Aldingbourne
Westergate
Woodgate
Eastergate
Barnham
Lyminster
Ford
Wick
Poling
LITTLEHAMPTON
Climping
M275
Hilsea
North End
Langstone Harbour
Northney
North Hayling
Tye
Nutbourne Marshes
Chidham
West Thorney
Thorney Island
Bosham
Apuldram
Donnington
Planetarium & Science Centre
Runcton
Merston
Colworth
Lidsey
Shripney
Bilsham
Yapton
Stoke
Fleet
PORTSEA ISLAND
Landport
Portsea
Fratton
Milton
Pumping
Ryl. Marines
Southsea
Eastney
SOUTH HAYLING
West Town
Pilsey Island
Chichester Harbour
West Itchenor
Rookwood
Birdham
Shipton Green
Hunston
Falconry Centre
North Mundham
Lagness
South Mundham
Street End
Elbridge
North Bersted
South Bersted
Bognor Regis
Flansham
Atherington
Ancton
Rustington
Middleton-on-Sea
Felpham
BOGNOR REGIS
Aldwick
Nyetimber
Pagham
Pagham Harbour
Sidlesham
Bird & Wildlife Hospital
Highleigh
Earnley Butterflies & Gdns
Almodington
Rejectamenta
Earnley
Somerley
East Head
West Wittering
East Wittering
Bracklesham
Sandy Point
PORTSMOUTH

SEE PAGE 209

HAYLING ISLAND
Hayling Bay
Spitbank Fort
Norton
Farm Centre
Church Norton
East Beach
Selsey
Lifeboat
Bracklesham Bay
SELSEY BILL
THEAD
Horse Sand Fort
No Man's Land Fort
Nettlestone Point
Seaview
Seaview Wildlife Encounter (Flamingo Park)
B3340
St. Helen's Fort
Bembridge Point
Maritime
Bembridge
FORELAND
Lane End
Lifeboat Station
Whitecliff Bay
Culver Cliff
Nab Tower
Portsmouth to:
Bilbao 33hrs. 45mins.
Caen 3hrs. 45mins.
(Fast Ferry, Seasonal)
Caen 6hrs.
(Seasonal)
Cherbourg 5hrs. 30mins.
(Seasonal)
Cherbourg 3hrs.
(Fast Ferry, Seasonal)
Guernsey 6hrs.
Jersey 11hrs. 30mins.
Le Havre 5hrs. 30mins.
Le Havre 3hrs. 15mins.
(Fast Ferry, Seasonal)
St. Malo 9hrs.
(Seasonal)
Santander 24hrs.
(Seasonal)
CHANNEL
E
F
G
H
1
2
3
4
5
70
80
90
500
100

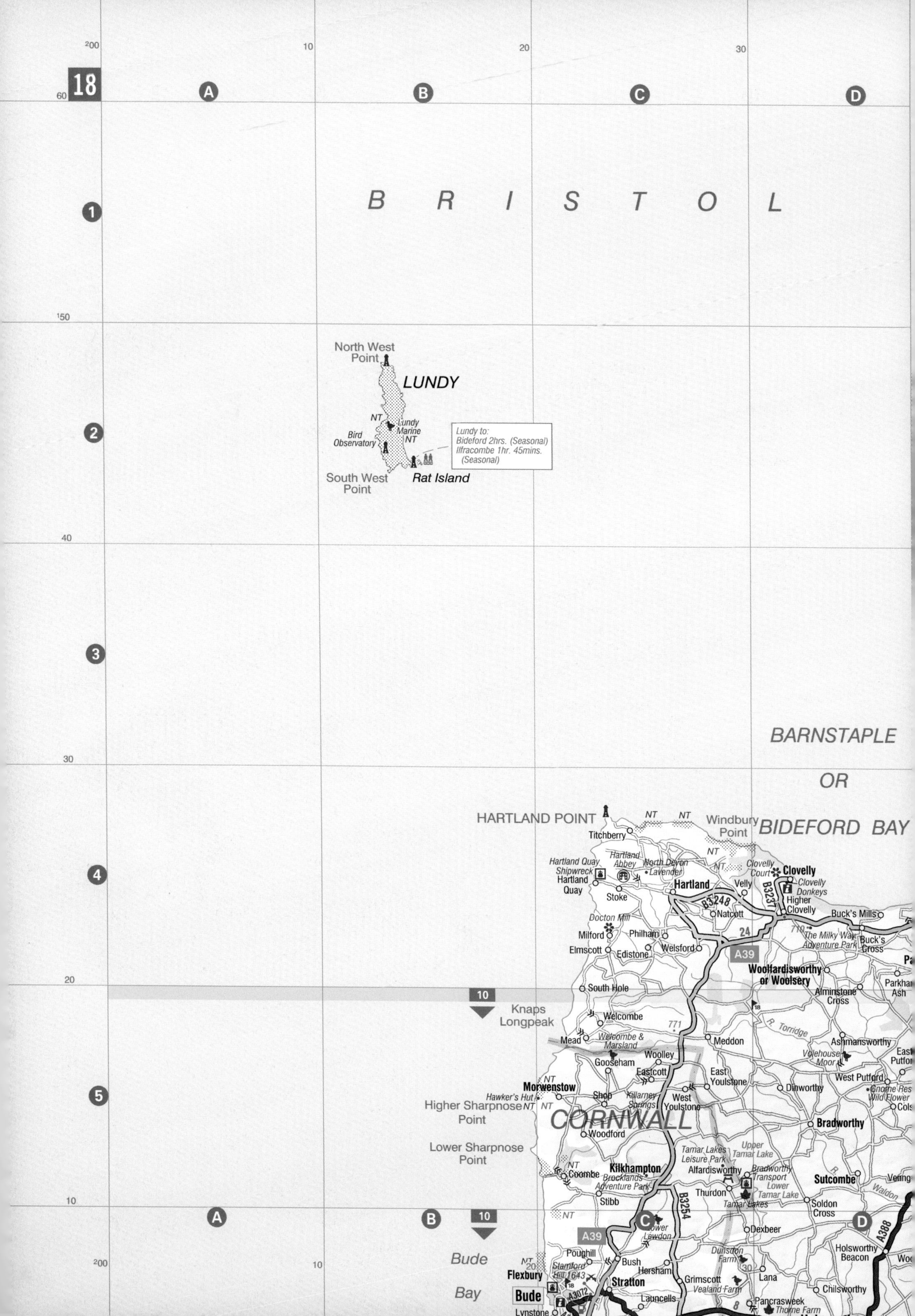

60

A   **B**   **C**   **D**

1

B R I S T O L

150

2

North West Point

LUNDY

NT

Bird Observatory

Lundy Marine NT

Lundy to:
Bideford 2hrs. (Seasonal)
Ilfracombe 1hr. 45mins. (Seasonal)

South West Point

Rat Island

40

3

30

BARNSTAPLE

OR

HARTLAND POINT   NT   NT   Windbury Point   *BIDEFORD BAY*

Titchberry

4

Hartland Quay   Hartland Abbey   North Devon   NT   Clovelly Court   Clovelly
Shipwreck   *Lavender*   Clovelly Donkeys
Hartland Quay   Hartland   Velly   Higher Clovelly
Stoke   B3248   B3237   Buck's Mills
Docton Mill   Natcott   24   710   The Milky Way   Buck's
Milford   Philham   A39   Adventure Park   Cross
Elmscott   Edistone   Welsford   **Woolfardisworthy**   **Pa**
                    or Woolsery

20

South Hole   18   Alminstone   Parkham
                       Cross   Ash

10   Knaps Longpeak   Welcome   771   R. Torridge   Ashmansworthy

Mead   Welcombe & Marsland   Woolley   Meddon   Volehouse Moor   East Putford
             Gooseham   Eastcott   East   West Putford

Morwenstow   NT   Shop   Killarney   Youlstone   Dinworthy   Gnome Res
Hawker's Hut   Springs   West   Wild Flower   Cols

5 Higher Sharpnose   NT   Youlstone
Point   Woodford   **Bradworthy**

CORNWALL

Lower Sharpnose   Tamar Lakes   Upper Tamar Lake
Point   Leisure Park   Bradworthy
         NT   Brocklands   Alfardisworthy   Transport   **Sutcombe**
        Coombe   **Kilkhampton**   Adventure Park   Thurdon   Lower   Veng
                Stibb   B3254   Tamar Lakes   Soldon

10   NT   Cross
                  A39   Lower   Dexbeer   **D**

200   10

Bude Bay   Poughill   Bush   Hersham   Dunsdon Farm   Holsworthy Beacon   Wo

NT   Stamford Hill 1643   Grimscott   30   Lana   Chilsworthy

Flexbury   18   **Stratton**   Vealand Farm   Pancrasweek

Bude   A3072   Launcells   8   Thorne Farm

Lynstone

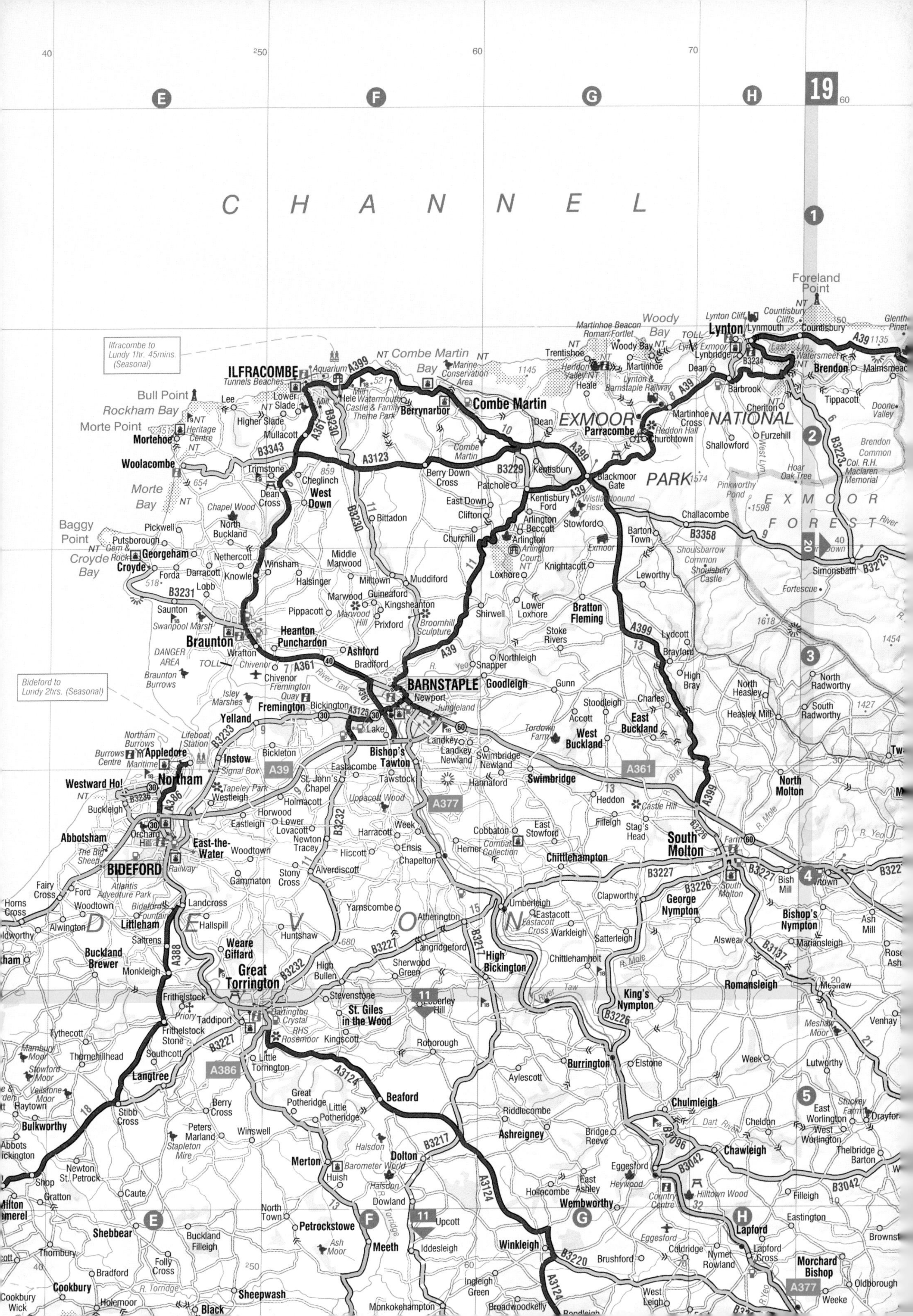

19
E
F
G
H
C H A N N E L
D E V O N
Foreland Point
Woody Bay
Lynton
Lynmouth
Countisbury
Lynbridge
Brendon
Malmsmead
Tippacott
Doone Valley
Martinhoe Beacon Roman Fortlet
Trentishoe
Heddon Valley
Martinhoe
Heale
Lynton & Barnstaple Railway
Dean
Barbrook
Cheriton
Martinhoe Cross
EXMOOR NATIONAL PARK
Parracombe
Heddon Hall
Churchtown
Shallowford
Furzehill
Brendon Common
Col. R.H. Maclaren Memorial
Hoar Oak Tree
EXMOOR FOREST
Pinkworthy Pond
Ilfracombe to Lundy 1hr. 45mins. (Seasonal)
ILFRACOMBE
Tunnels Beaches
Aquarium
Combe Martin Bay
Marine Conservation Area
Combe Martin
Bull Point
Rockham Bay
Morte Point
Mortehoe
Heritage Centre
Lee
Lower Slade
Higher Slade
Mullacott
Hele
Watermouth Castle & Family Theme Park
Berrynarbor
Woolacombe
Morte Bay
Trimstone
Dean Cross
Cheglinch
West Down
Berry Down Cross
Patchole
Kentisbury
Blackmoor Gate
Kentisbury Ford
Wistlandpound Resr
Challacombe
Barton Town
Shoulsbarrow Common
Shoulsbury Castle
Simonsbath
Fortescue
Baggy Point
Putsborough
Georgeham
Croyde Bay
Croyde
Pickwell
North Buckland
Chapel Wood
Nethercott
Forda
Darracott
Knowle
Winsham
Middle Marwood
Halsinger
Milltown
Muddiford
Bittadon
East Down
Clifton
Churchill
Arlington
Arlington Beccott
Arlington Court
Stowford
Exmoor
Knightacott
Loxhore
Lobb
Saunton
Swanpool Marsh
Braunton
Wrafton
Chivenor
Marwood
Guineaford
Kingsheanton
Pippacott
Marwood Hill
Prixford
Broomhill Sculpture
Shirwell
Lower Loxhore
Bratton Fleming
Leworthy
Stoke Rivers
Lydcott
Brayford
High Bray
Heanton Punchardon
Ashford
Bradiford
Northleigh
Snapper
Goodleigh
DANGER AREA
Braunton Burrows
Bideford to Lundy 2hrs. (Seasonal)
Isley Marshes
Fremington Quay
Fremington
BARNSTAPLE
Newport
Jungleland
Gunn
Stoodleigh
Charles
Accott
East Buckland
West Buckland
Tordown Farm
North Heasley
Heasley Mill
North Radworthy
South Radworthy
Yelland
Bickington
Lake
Bishop's Tawton
Landkey
Landkey Newland
Swimbridge
Swimbridge Newland
Northam Burrows
Lifeboat Station
Burrows Centre
Appledore
Maritime
Instow
Bickleton
Eastacombe
St. John's Chapel
Tawstock
Hannaford
Swimbridge
Heddon
Castle Hill
North Molton
Westward Ho!
Northam
Signal Box
Tapeley Park
Westleigh
Holmacott
Uppacott Wood
Buckleigh
Horwood
Lower Lovacott
Eastleigh
Week
Filleigh
Stag's Head
South Molton
Abbotsham
The Big Sheep
Orchard Hill
East-the-Water
Woodtown
Newton Tracey
Harracott
Ensis
Cobbaton
Combat Collection
East Stowford
Herner
Chapelton
Hiscott
BIDEFORD
Railway
Gammaton
Stony Cross
Alverdiscott
Chittlehampton
Bish Mill
Fairy Cross
Ford
Atlantis Adventure Park
Horns Cross
Woodtown
Landcross
Bideford Fountain
Yarnscombe
Umberleigh
Eastacott
Clapworthy
George Nympton
Bishop's Nympton
Alwington
Littleham
Hallspill
Atherington
Warkleigh
Satterleigh
Ash Mill
Saltrens
Weare Giffard
Huntshaw
Langridgeford
Alswear
Mariansleigh
Buckland Brewer
Monkleigh
Great Torrington
High Bullen
Sherwood Green
High Bickington
Chittlehamholt
Romansleigh
Meshaw
Frithelstock
Priory
Stevenstone
St. Giles in the Wood
Ebberley Hill
King's Nympton
Taddiport
Dartington Crystal
RHS Rosemoor
Kingscott
Meshaw Moor
Venhay
Tythecott
Frithelstock Stone
Southcott
Little Torrington
Roborough
Thornehillhead
Langtree
Burrington
Elstone
Week
Lutworthy
Aylescott
Beaford
Great Potheridge
Little Potheridge
Stibb Cross
Berry Cross
Riddlecombe
Ashreigney
Chulmleigh
East Worlington
West Worlington
Stuckey Farm
Drayford
Cheldon
Haytown
Bulkworthy
Peters Marland
Stapleton Mire
Winswell
Halsdon
Dolton
Bridge Reeve
Chawleigh
Thelbridge Barton
Merton
Barometer World
Huish
Eggesford
Heywood
East Ashley
Hollocombe
Country Centre
Hilltown Wood
Filleigh
Newton St. Petrock
Shop
Gratton
Caute
Halsdon
Dowland
Wembworthy
North Town
Petrockstowe
Upcott
Eastington
Lapford
Shebbear
Buckland Filleigh
Ash Moor
Meeth
Iddesleigh
Winkleigh
Eggesford
Coldridge
Nymet Rowland
Lapford Cross
Morchard Bishop
Brownston
Thornbury
Folly Cross
Brushford
Oldborough
Bradford
R. Torridge
Ingleigh Green
West Leigh
Weeke
Cookbury
Holemoor
Black
Sheepwash
Monkokehampton
Broadwoodkelly
A39
A399
A361
A3123
A3125
A377
A386
A388
A3124
B3343
B3230
B3229
B3358
B3223
B3231
B3233
B3232
B3227
B3226
B3217
B3137
B3096
B3042
B3220
B3234

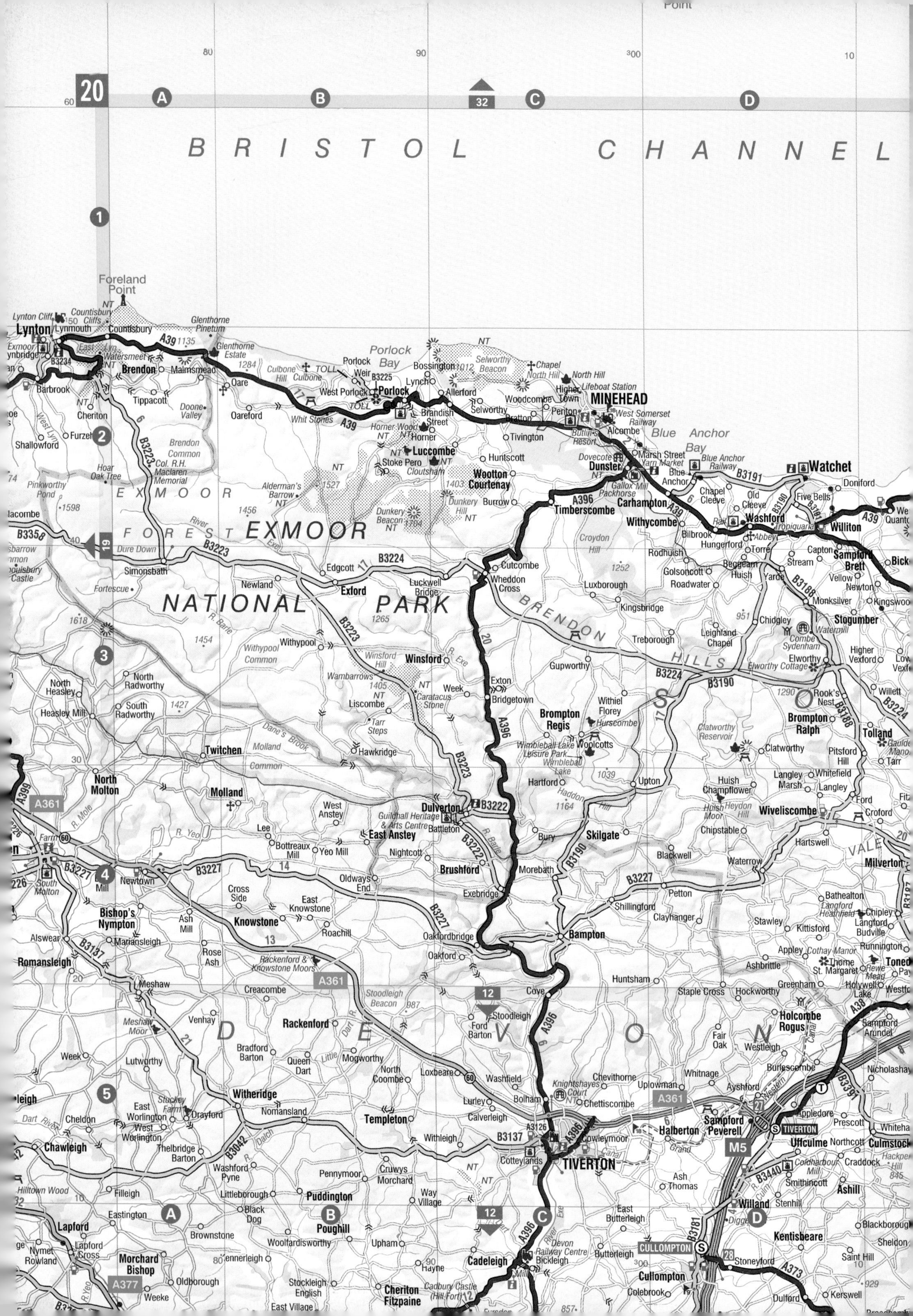
BRISTOL CHANNEL
EXMOOR NATIONAL PARK
EXMOOR FOREST
BRENDON HILLS
DEVON
Lynton
Lynmouth
Countisbury
Foreland Point
Brendon
Porlock
Porlock Bay
Minehead
Blue Anchor Bay
Dunster
Watchet
Williton
Wootton Courtenay
Timberscombe
Carhampton
Withycombe
Exford
Simonsbath
Winsford
Withypool
Dulverton
Brompton Regis
Wiveliscombe
Milverton
North Molton
Molland
Twitchen
Bampton
Bishop's Nympton
Knowstone
Romansleigh
Witheridge
Rackenford
Chawleigh
Templeton
Tiverton
Halberton
Sampford Peverell
Uffculme
Willand
Cullompton
Lapford
Morchard Bishop
Puddington
Poughill
Cadeleigh
Cheriton Fitzpaine
Kentisbeare
Holcombe Rogus
Tolland
Stogumber
Sampford Brett
Brompton Ralph
Skilgate
Brushford
Exebridge
Oakfordbridge
A39
A396
A361
A373
A377
A399
M5
B3223
B3224
B3190
B3191
B3188
B3227
B3222
B3137
B3042
B3181
B3440
B3391
B3234
B3358
32
19
12

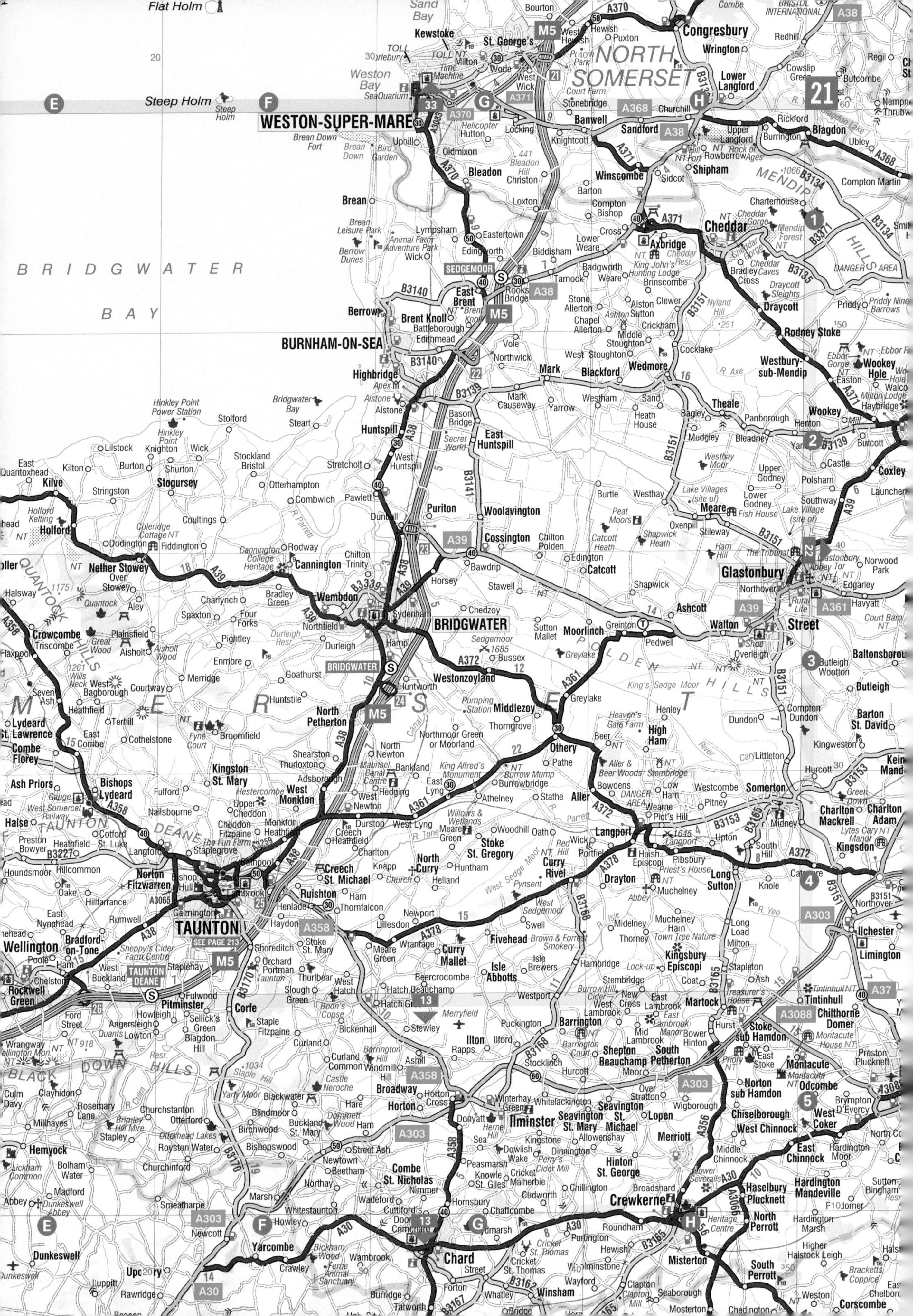

Flat Holm
Sand Bay
Bourton
A370
Hewish
Congresbury
BRISTOL INTERNATIONAL
A38
Kewstoke
M5
West Hewish
Puxton
Redhill
St. George's
NORTH SOMERSET
Wrington
Regil
Milton
Worle
Time Machine
Cowslip Green
Butcombe
Weston Bay
West Wick
Court Farm
Lower Langford
21
SeaQuarium
33
A371
Stonebridge
Churchill
E
Steep Holm
F
G
A370
A368
H
Rickford
Nempnett Thrubwell
WESTON-SUPER-MARE
Banwell
Sandford
A38
Upper Langford
Burrington
Blagdon
Brean Down Fort
Uphill
A3033
Helicopter Museum
Hutton
Locking
Knightcott
Rowberrow
Ubley
Brean Down
Bird Garden
Oldmixon
Bleadon Hill
Winscombe
Sidcot
Shipham
A368
Bleadon
Christon
MENDIP
Compton Martin
Barton
B3134
Brean
Loxton
Compton Bishop
Charterhouse
Cheddar Gorge
Brean Leisure Park
Lympsham
A371
Cheddar
Mendip Forest
1
HILLS
Animal Farm Adventure Park
Eastertown
Cross
Axbridge
B3371
Berrow Dunes
Wick
Edingworth
Biddisham
Lower Weare
Cheddar Resr
King John's Hunting Lodge
Bradley Cross
Cheddar Caves
B3135
DANGER AREA
B R I D G W A T E R
SEDGEMOOR
Badgworth
Tarnock
Weare
Brinscombe
Draycott Sleights
B3140
East Brent
Rooks Bridge
A38
Stone Allerton
Alston Sutton
Clewer
B3151
Nyland Hill
Draycott
Priddy
Priddy Nine Barrows
B A Y
Berrow
Brent Knoll
M5
Ashton
Chapel Allerton
Crickham
Rodney Stoke
Battleborough
Middle Stoughton
Edithmead
Vole
Cocklake
Ebbor Gorge
Wookey Hole
BURNHAM-ON-SEA
Northwick
West
Stoughton
Wedmore
Westbury-sub-Mendip
B3140
Mark
Blackford
R. Axe
Easton
Highbridge
22
Apex Park
B3139
A371
Milton Lodge
Hinkley Point Power Station
Bridgwater Bay
Alstone
Mark Causeway
Westham
Sand
Theale
Haybridge
Alstone
Bason Bridge
Yarrow
Heath House
Bagley
Panborough
Wookey
Henton
Stolford
Hinkley Point
Steart
Huntspill
East Huntspill
Mudgley
Bleadney
Yarley
2
B3139
Burcott
Lilstock
Knighton
Wick
Secret World
A38
B3151
Westhay Moor
Castle
Coxley
East Quantoxhead
Kilton
Burton
Shurton
Stockland Bristol
Stretcholt
West Huntspill
Upper Godney
Polsham
Kilve
Stogursey
Otterhampton
B3141
Burtle
Westhay
Lake Villages (site of)
Lower Godney
Southway
Launcherley
Stringston
Combwich
Pawlett
Puriton
Woolavington
Peat Moors
Meare
Fish House
Lake Village (site of)
Holford
Kelting
Coultings
Dunball
Oxenpill
Stileway
B3151
A39
Holford
Coleridge Cottage
Dodington
Fiddington
R. Parrett
A39
Cossington
Chilton Polden
Catcott Heath
Shapwick Heath
Ham Hill
The Tribunal
Glastonbury Tor
Norwood Park
Cannington College Heritage
Rodway
Cannington
Chilton Trinity
A38
Bawdrip
Edington
Catcott
Glastonbury
QUANTOCK
Nether Stowey
A39
Horsey
Stawell
Shapwick
Northover
Edgarley
Over Stowey
B3339
A39
Halsway
Quantock
Aley
Charlynch
Bradley Green
Wembdon
Sydenham
Chedzoy
Ashcott
A39
A361
Havyatt
A358
Spaxton
Four Forks
Northfield
BRIDGWATER
Sutton Mallet
Moorlinch
Greinton
Walton
Street
Court Barn
Crowcombe
Great Wood
Plainsfield
Pightley
Durleigh Resr
Hamp
Sedgemoor 1685
Pedwell
Shoe Museum
Triscombe
Aisholt
Aisholt Wood
Durleigh
Bussex
Greylake
Overleigh
3
Butleigh Wootton
Baltonsborough
Flaxpool
Wills Neck
Enmore
BRIDGWATER
A372
POLDEN
Seven Ash
West Bagborough
Courtway
Merridge
Goathurst
Huntworth
Westonzoyland
A361
King's Sedge Moor
HILLS
Butleigh
B3151
Huntstile
Pumping Station
Middlezoy
Greylake
Henley
Lydeard St. Lawrence
Heathfield
Terhill
North Petherton
M5
Heaven's Gate Farm
High Ham
Compton Dundon
Barton St. David
Fyne Court
Broomfield
A38
Thorngrove
Dundon
East Combe
Cothelstone
Northmoor Green or Moorland
Beer
Combe Florey
Shearston
North Newton
Othery
Kingweston
Kingston St. Mary
Thurloxton
Bankland
King Alfred's Monument
Pathe
Aller & Beer Woods
Stembridge
Cary Littleton
Hurcott
Ash Priors
Bishops Lydeard
Maunsel Canal Centre
Burrow Mump
Burrowbridge
Kein Mand
Fulford
Hestercombe
Adsborough
West Monkton
East Lyng
Bowdens
Low Ham
Westcombe
Somerton
Hedging
Athelney
Stathe
Aller
DANGER AREA
Gauge Museum
West Somerset Railway
Upper Cheddon
A358
West Newton
A361
Willows & Wetlands
Wearne
Pitney
Charlton Mackrell
Charlton Adam
Nailsbourne
Halse
TAUNTON DEANE
Cotford St. Luke
Cheddon Fitzpaine
Monkton Heathfield
Creech Heathfield
Durston
West Lyng
Meare Green
Woodhill
Oath
Pict's Hill
B3153
Lytes Cary Manor
Preston Bowyer
Heathfield
The Fun Farm
Staplegrove
Langford
Charlton
Stoke St. Gregory
Red Hill
Langport
Langport
Upton
Kingsdon
B3227
Hillcommon
A38
Bathpool
Knapp
North Curry
Wick
Portfield
Huish Episcopi
Pibsbury
South Hill
A372
Houndsmoor
Norton Fitzwarren
Creech St. Michael
West Sedge Moor
Curry Rivel
A378
Priest's House
Long Sutton
Catsgore
Oake
Bishop's Hull
Lambrook
Helland
Huntham
Pynsent
Drayton
Muchelney
4
Knole
Northover
Hillfarrance
Ruishton
Ham
Abbey
Henlade
Thornfalcon
R. Yeo
A3065
Galmington
25
West Sedgemoor
B3168
A303
East Nynehead
Rumwell
Haydon
Newport
Lillesdon
Swell
Isle
Midelney
Muchelney Ham
Long Load
Ilchester
A38
TAUNTON
A358
15
Fivehead
Brown & Forrest Smokery
Thorney
Town Tree Nature
Wellington
Bradford-on-Tone
Sheppy's Cider Farm Centre
SEE PAGE 213
Shoreditch
Stoke St. Mary
A378
Wrantage
Meare Green
Curry Mallet
Milton
Limington
Poole
Ham
Orchard Portman
Kingsbury Episcopi
Chelston
West Buckland
TAUNTON DEANE
Staplehay
M5
Thurlbear
Beercrocombe
Isle Abbotts
Isle Brewers
Hambridge
Lock-up
Stapleton
Rockwell Green
Fulwood
Pitminster
Corfe
Slough Green
West Hatch
Hatch Beauchamp
Westport
Stembridge
Burrow Hill Cider
Coat
Ash
Tintinhull
A37
Ford Street
Howleigh
Angersleigh
Sellick's Green
Boon's Copse
Hatch Green
13
Merryfield
New Cross
West Lambrook
East Lambrook
Treasurer's House
Martock
Tintinhull
Chilthorne Domer
Wrangway
Quants
Lowton
Staple Fitzpaine
Bickenhall
Stewley
Puckington
Barrington
East Lambrook Manor
Hurst
A3088
Stoke sub Hamdon
Montacute House
Preston Plucknett
Blagdon Hill
Curland
Ilton
Ilford
Rapps
Barrington Court
Mid Lambrook
Bower Hinton
Priory
East Stoke
Montacute
BLACK DOWN HILLS
Staple Hill
Barrington Hill
Curland Common
Windmill Hill
Ashill
A358
B3168
Stocklinch
Shepton Beauchamp
South Petherton
Montacute
Odcombe
Culm Davy
Clayhidon
Castle Neroche
Broadway
Hurcott
Moor
A303
Norton sub Hamdon
Brympton D'Evercy
Rosemary Lane
Churchstanton
Yarty Moor
Blackwater
Hare
Horton
Horton Cross
Winterhay Green
Whitelackington
Over Stratton
Seavington St. Michael
Wigborough
5
West Coker
Millhayes
Otterford
Brimley Hill Mire
Blindmoor
Dommett Wood
Donyatt
Ilminster
Seavington St. Mary
Lopen
Chiselborough
Stapley
Otterhead Lakes
Birchwood
Buckland St. Mary
Ham
A303
Sea
Kingstone
Allowenshay
Merriott
A356
West Chinnock
North Coker
Hemyock
Royston Water
B3170
Bishopswood
Street Ash
Dowlish Wake
Perry's Cider Mill
Dinnington
Middle Chinnock
East Chinnock
Hardington Moor
Lickham Common
Bolham Water
Churchinford
Newtown
Beetham
Combe St. Nicholas
A358
Peasmarsh
Knowle St. Giles
Cricket Malherbie
Hinton St. George
Lower Severalls
A30
Haselbury Plucknett
Hardington Mandeville
Sutton Bingham
Madford
Dunkeswell Abbey
Northay
Nimmer
Cudworth
Chillington
Broadshard
Abbey
Smeatharpe
Marsh
Wadeford
Hornsbury
Crewkerne
A3066
North Perrott
A303
Whitestaunton
Cuttiford's Door
Chaffcombe
Hardington Marsh
E
Newcott
F
Howley
Crimchard
13
G
Cudmarsh
Purtington
Roundham
Heritage Centre
H
Yarcombe
A30
Bickham Wood
A30
Cricket St. Thomas
Hewish
B3165
Higher Halstock Leigh
Dunkeswell
Crawley
Wambrook
Chard
Ferne Animal Sanctuary
Cricket St. Thomas
Whitestone
Misterton
South Perrott
Brackett's Coppice
Upottery
Street
B3162
Wayford
Clapton
Luppitt
A30
Rawridge
Burridge
Forton
Whatley
Winsham
Clapton Mill
Seaborough
Weston
Chelborough
Tatworth
B3167
Mosterton
Chedington
Corscombe

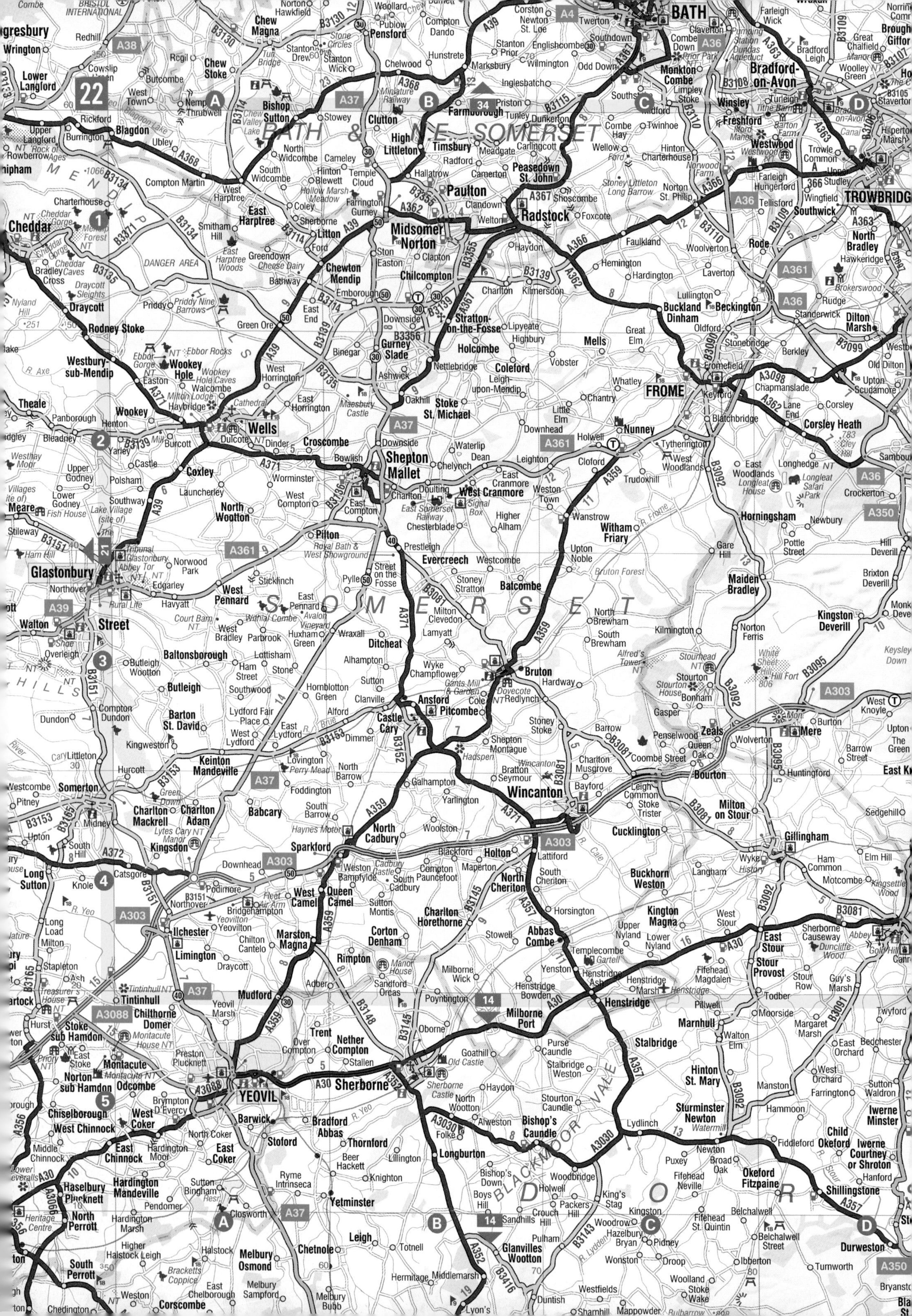
22
BATH & N.E. SOMERSET
SOMERSET
MENDIP HILLS
BLACKMOOR VALE
A
B
C
D
34
21
14
1
2
3
4
5
A38
A37
A39
A4
A36
A368
A367
A362
A361
A366
A371
A359
A303
A350
A357
A30
A3030
A352
A3088
A372
B3151
B3153
B3081
B3092
B3139
B3135
B3134
B3114
B3130
B3355
B3110
B3109
B3098
B3145
B3148
B3143
BATH
Bradford-on-Avon
TROWBRIDGE
Cheddar
Wells
Glastonbury
Street
Shepton Mallet
Midsomer Norton
Radstock
Paulton
Peasedown St. John
FROME
Bruton
Castle Cary
Wincanton
Somerton
Ilchester
YEOVIL
Sherborne
Milborne Port
Henstridge
Gillingham
Mere
Stalbridge
Sturminster Newton
Blagdon
Chew Magna
Pensford
Clutton
Timsbury
Farmborough
Draycott
Rodney Stoke
Westbury-sub-Mendip
Wookey Hole
Wookey
Croscombe
Coxley
North Wootton
Pilton
Evercreech
Batcombe
Nunney
Beckington
Westbury-sub-Mendip
Keinton Mandeville
Babcary
Sparkford
North Cadbury
Queen Camel
West Camel
Marston Magna
Mudford
Tintinhull
Montacute
Stoke sub Hamdon
Martock
Odcombe
West Coker
East Coker
Chiselborough
Yetminster
Bradford Abbas
Longburton
Bishop's Caundle
Marnhull
Templecombe
Horningsham
Maiden Bradley
Kilmington
Zeals
Bourton
Long Sutton
Langport
Kingsdon
Charlton Mackrell
Butleigh
Baltonsborough
Ditcheat
Ansford
Pitcombe
North Cheriton
Holton
Abbas Combe
Rimpton
Corton Denham
Charlton Horethorne
Glanvilles Wootton
Chetnole
Leigh
Melbury Osmond
Corscombe
Hinton St. Mary
Okeford Fitzpaine
Shillingstone
Child Okeford
Iwerne Minster
Durweston

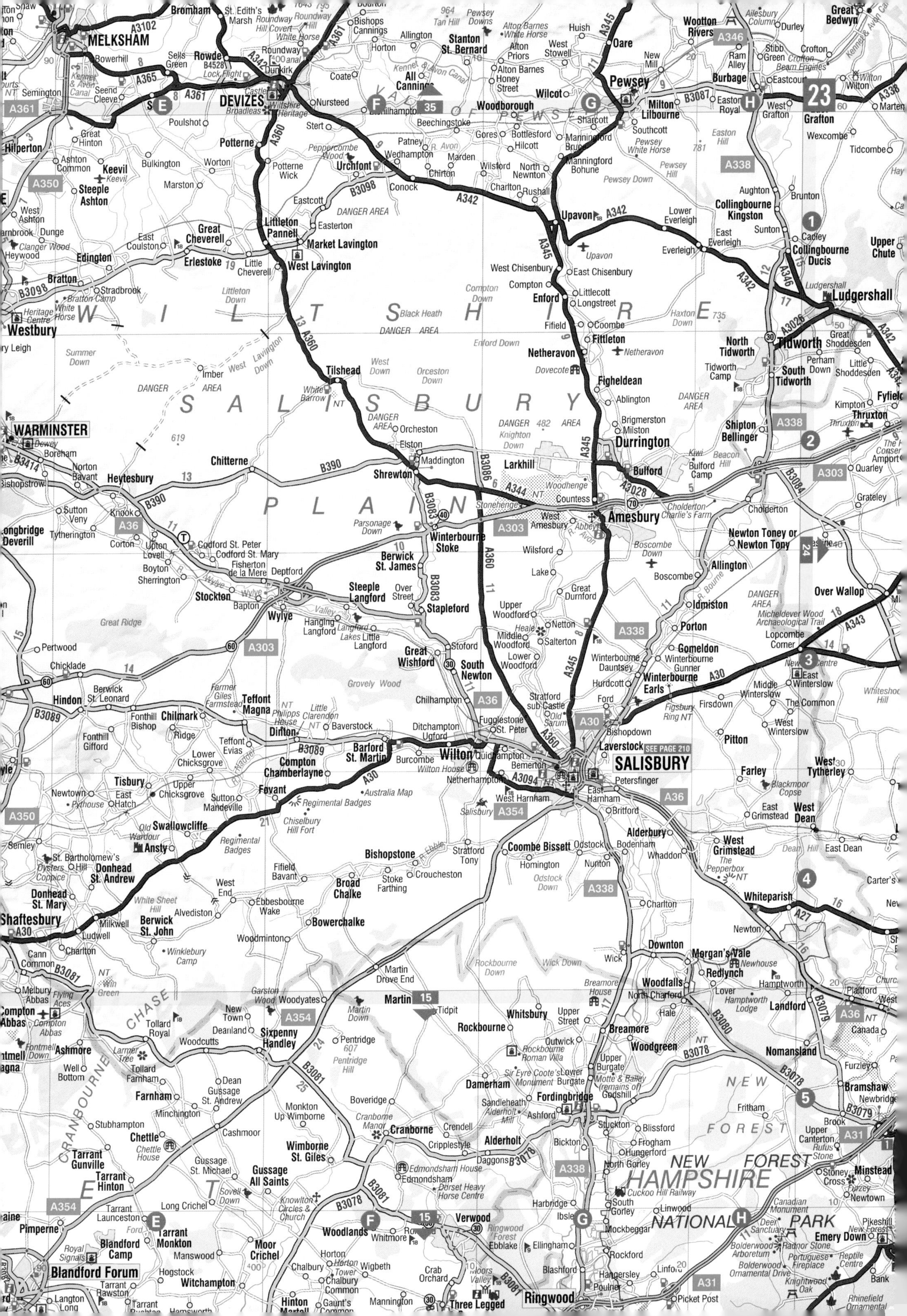

Bromham
St. Edith's Marsh
Roundway Hill Covert
White Horse
Bishops Cannings
Horton
Allington
Stanton St. Bernard
Pewsey Downs
Alton Barnes White Horse
Alton Priors
Alton Barnes
Honey Street
Huish
Oare
West Stowell
New Mill
Wootton Rivers
Aldbourne Column
Durley
Great Bedwyn
Stibb Green
Ram Alley
Crofton
Crofton Beam Engines
Burbage
Eastcourt
Wilton
MELKSHAM
A3102
Bowerhill
Sells Green
Rowde
Lock Flight
Dunkirk
Roundway
Coate
All Cannings
Kennet & Avon Canal
A365
A361
A342
Semington
Seend Cleeve
DEVIZES
Castle
Wiltshire Heritage
Broadleas
Nursteed
Etchilhampton
35
VALE OF PEWSEY
Woodborough
Wilcot
Pewsey
Milton Lilbourne
B3087
Easton Royal
West Grafton
Grafton
23
Marten
Poulshot
Stert
Beechingstoke
Sharcott
Southcott
Pewsey White Horse
Easton Hill
Great Hinton
Potterne
Patney
Gores
Bottlesford
Hilcott
Manningford Bruce
Manningford Bohune
Wexcombe
Tidcombe
Hilperton
A360
Peppercombe Wood
Wedhampton
R. Avon
Marden
Chirton
Wilsford
North Newton
781
Ashton Common
Bulkington
Keevil
Worton
Potterne Wick
Urchfont
Conock
Charlton
Rushall
Pewsey Hill
Pewsey Down
A338
A350
Steeple Ashton
Marston
B3098
A342
Aughton
Brunton
Collingbourne Kingston
Eastcott
DANGER AREA
Upavon
Lower Everleigh
West Ashton
Dunge
Littleton Pannell
Easterton
Sunton
Cadley
Clanger Wood
East Coulston
Great Cheverell
Market Lavington
East Everleigh
Everleigh
Collingbourne Ducis
Upper Chute
Heywood
Edington
Erlestoke
Little Cheverell
West Lavington
A345
Upavon
West Chisenbury
East Chisenbury
Bratton
Stradbrook
Bratton Camp
Littleton Down
Compton Down
Compton
Littlecott
Ludgershall
Heritage Centre
White Horse
Westbury
W I L T S H I R E
Black Heath
Enford
Longstreet
Haxton Down
735
Fifield
Coombe
Tidworth
Great Shoddesden
DANGER AREA
Enford Down
Fittleton
North Tidworth
Summer Down
Imber
West Lavington Down
Tilshead
West Down
Orcheston Down
Netheravon
Tidworth Camp
South Tidworth
Perham Down
Little Shoddesden
Dovecote
Figheldean
DANGER AREA
White Barrow
NT
Ablington
DANGER AREA
Kimpton
Fyfield
Thruxton
S A L I S B U R Y
WARMINSTER
619
DANGER AREA
Orcheston
DANGER 482 AREA
Brigmerston
Milton
Shipton Bellinger
A338
Dewey
Boreham
Elston
Knighton Down
Durrington
Kiwi
Bulford Camp
Beacon Hill
Norton Bavant
Chitterne
B390
Maddington
Larkhill
Bulford
Quarley
Amport
Heytesbury
Shrewton
B3086
A344
Woodhenge
A3028
A303
B3084
Bishopstrow
13
Countess
Cholderton
Charlie's Farm
Grateley
Sutton Veny
Knook
P L A I N
B3083
Stonehenge
A303
West Amesbury
Amesbury
Abbey
Cholderton
Longbridge Deverill
Tytherington
A36
Parsonage Down
Winterbourne Stoke
Boscombe Down
Newton Toney or Newton Tony
24
Corton
Upton Lovell
Codford St. Peter
Codford St. Mary
Wilsford
Allington
Boyton
Fisherton de la Mere
Deptford
Berwick St. James
Lake
Boscombe
Sherrington
Stockton
Steeple Langford
Over Street
Great Durnford
Idmiston
Over Wallop
Bapton
Wylye
Stapleford
Upper Woodford
DANGER AREA
Micheldever Wood Archaeological Trail
Great Ridge
Hanging Langford
Valley
Langford Lakes
Little Langford
Heale
Netton
Middle Woodford
Salterton
A338
Porton
Lopcombe Corner
A343
Pertwood
A303
Stoford
Great Wishford
Lower Woodford
Winterbourne Dauntsey
Gomeldon
Winterbourne Gunner
Chicklade
South Newton
Winterbourne Earls
New Winterslow Centre
East Winterslow
Hindon
Berwick St. Leonard
Farmer Giles Farmstead
Grovely Wood
Hurdcott
A30
Middle Winterslow
Whiteshoot Hill
B3089
Teffont Magna
Chilhampton
A36
Ford
Stratford sub Castle
Figsbury Ring NT
Firsdown
The Common
Fonthill Bishop
Chilmark
Philipps House
Little Clarendon
Baverstock
Fugglestone St. Peter
Old Sarum
A30
Bishopdown
West Winterslow
Fonthill Gifford
Ridge
Teffont Evias
Dinton
B3089
Ditchampton Ugford
Pitton
Laverstock
SEE PAGE 210
Lower Chicksgrove
Compton Chamberlayne
Barford St. Martin
Burcombe
Wilton
Wilton House
Quidhampton
Bemerton
SALISBURY
Petersfinger
Farley
West Tytherley
Tisbury
Upper Chicksgrove
Fovant
Netherhampton
A3094
Blackmoor Copse
Newtown
East Hatch
Pythouse
Sutton Mandeville
Australia Map
Regimental Badges
West Harnham
East Harnham
A36
Britford
East Grimstead
West Dean
A350
A354
Old Wardour
Swallowcliffe
Ansty
Chiselbury Hill Fort
Salisbury
Alderbury
Bodenham
West Grimstead
East Dean
Regimental Badges
Semley
Bishopstone
Stratford Tony
Coombe Bissett
Odstock
Whaddon
Dean Hill
St. Bartholomew's Hill
Donhead St. Andrew
Fifield Bavant
Stoke Farthing
Croucheston
Homington
Nunton
The Pepperbox NT
Carter's
Donhead St. Mary
West End
Broad Chalke
Odstock Down
A338
Whiteparish
White Sheet Hill
Ebbesbourne Wake
Charlton
Shaftesbury
Alvediston
Bowerchalke
A27
Milkwell
Berwick St. John
A30
Ludwell
Woodminton
Newton
Cann Common
Charlton
Winkelbury Camp
Rockbourne Down
Wick Down
Downton
Morgan's Vale
Newhouse
B3081
Martin Drove End
Wick
Redlynch
Melbury Abbas
Flying Aces
Win Green
Garston Wood
Woodyates
Martin
15
Breamore House
Woodfalls
North Charford
Hamptworth
Plaitford
Compton Abbas
Compton Abbas
CHASE
New Town
Tollard Royal
A354
Martin Down
Tidpit
Whitsbury
Upper Street
Hale
Lover
Hamptworth Lodge
Landford
B3079
A36
Canada
Deanland
Sixpenny Handley
Pentridge
Rockbourne
Breamore
B3080
Fontmell Down
Ashmore
Larmer Tree
Woodcutts
607
Pentridge Hill
Outwick
Rockbourne Roman Villa
Woodgreen
B3078
Nomansland
Well Bottom
Tollard Farnham
Upper Burgate
Furzley
Dean
Gussage St. Andrew
B3081
Sir Eyre Coote's Monument
Lower Burgate
Motte & Bailey (remains of)
Damerham
N E W
Bramshaw
Newbridge
Farnham
Minchington
Monkton Up Wimborne
Boveridge
Sandleheath
Alderholt Mill
Fordingbridge
Godshill
Fritham
B3079
CRANBORNE
Stubhampton
Cashmoor
Cranborne Manor
Cranborne
Crendell
Ashford
Stuckton
Blissford
F O R E S T
Brook
Chettle
Chettle House
Wimborne St. Giles
Cripplestyle
Alderholt
Bickton
Frogham
Upper Canterton
A31
Rufus Stone
Tarrant Gunville
Gussage St. Michael
Gussage All Saints
Edmondsham House
Edmondsham
Daggons
B3078
A338
Hungerford
North Gorley
NEW FOREST
HAMPSHIRE
Stoney Cross
Minstead
Furzey
Tarrant Hinton
E
T
Sovell Down
Knowlton Circles & Church
B3081
Dorset Heavy Horse Centre
Cuckoo Hill Railway
South Gorley
Newtown
Long Crichel
B3078
Harbridge
Linwood
Canadian Monument
A354
Tarrant Launceston
Ibsley
Deer Sanctuary
Pimperne
Blandford Camp
Tarrant Monkton
Woodlands
Verwood
Ringwood Forest
Mockbeggar
NATIONAL PARK
Radnor Stone
Pikeshill
New Forest
Emery Down
Royal Signals
Ford
Moor Crichel
Whitmore
Ellingham
Bolderwood Arboretum
Portuguese Fireplace
Reptile Centre
Blandford Forum
Manswood
Horton
Horton Tower
Ebblake
Rockford
Bolderwood Ornamental Drive
Knightwood Oak
Hogstock
Witchampton
Chalbury
Wigbeth
Chalbury Common
Crab Orchard
Moors Valley
B3081
Blashford
Hangersley
Poulner
Linford
A31
Bank
Tarrant Rawston
Langton Long
Tarrant
Hinton
Gaunt's Common
Mannington
Three Legged
Ringwood
Picket Post
Rhinefield Ornamental

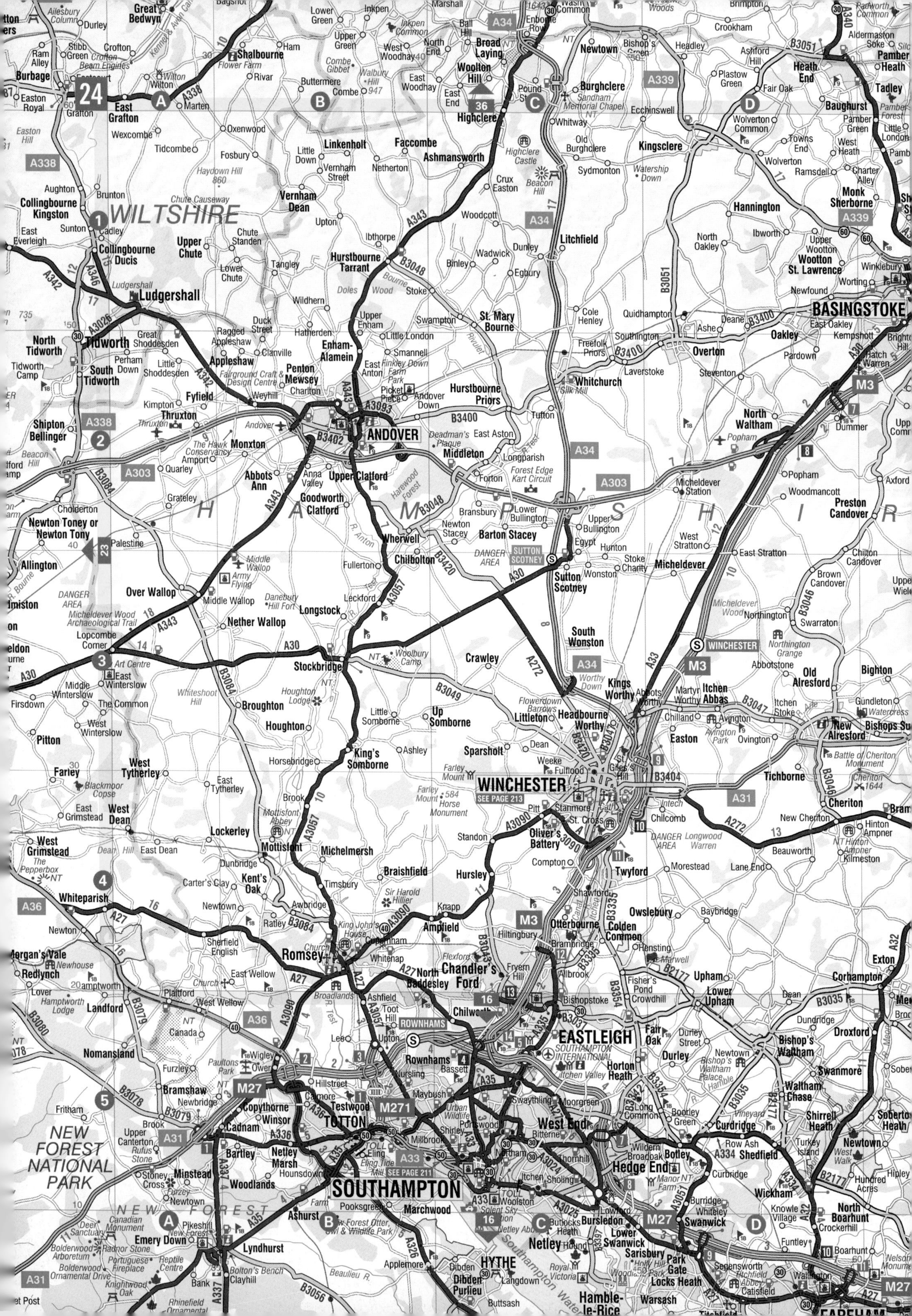

24
WILTSHIRE
Great Bedwyn
Shalbourne
Burbage
East Grafton
Collingbourne Kingston
Collingbourne Ducis
Ludgershall
Tidworth
North Tidworth
South Tidworth
Vernham Dean
Linkenholt
Faccombe
Ashmansworth
Broad Laying
Woolton Hill
Highclere
Burghclere
Newtown
Kingsclere
Baughurst
Tadley
Heath End
Hannington
Monk Sherborne
Wootton St. Lawrence
BASINGSTOKE
Oakley
Overton
Whitchurch
Hurstbourne Tarrant
Hurstbourne Priors
Litchfield
St. Mary Bourne
Enham-Alamein
Penton Mewsey
Appleshaw
Fyfield
Thruxton
Shipton Bellinger
ANDOVER
Upper Clatford
Goodworth Clatford
Abbots Ann
Monxton
Middleton
Longparish
Barton Stacey
Wherwell
Chilbolton
Sutton Scotney
Micheldever
North Waltham
Dummer
Preston Candover
Over Wallop
Nether Wallop
Longstock
Stockbridge
Crawley
South Wonston
Kings Worthy
Headbourne Worthy
Itchen Abbas
New Alresford
Old Alresford
Bighton
WINCHESTER
SEE PAGE 213
Littleton
Sparsholt
Up Somborne
King's Somborne
Houghton
Broughton
West Tytherley
Allington
Pitton
Farley
West Dean
West Grimstead
Lockerley
Mottisfont
Michelmersh
Braishfield
Hursley
Oliver's Battery
Twyford
Tichborne
Cheriton
Owslebury
Otterbourne
Colden Common
Upham
Lower Upham
Corhampton
Exton
Whiteparish
Romsey
Ampfield
North Baddesley
Chandler's Ford
EASTLEIGH
Fair Oak
Durley
Bishop's Waltham
Droxford
Waltham Chase
Swanmore
Shirrell Heath
Shedfield
Wickham
Curdridge
Botley
Hedge End
West End
Horton Heath
Landford
Nomansland
Bramshaw
Copythorne
Cadnam
Netley Marsh
TOTTON
Rownhams
SOUTHAMPTON
SEE PAGE 211
Woodlands
Minstead
Ashurst
Marchwood
Lyndhurst
Emery Down
HYTHE
Dibden Purlieu
Netley
Bursledon
Lower Swanwick
Sarisbury
Park Gate
Locks Heath
Swanwick
Warsash
Hamble-le-Rice
Whiteley
North Boarhunt
NEW FOREST NATIONAL PARK
NEW FOREST
M3
M27
M271
A34
A303
A338
A343
A30
A36
A31
A33
A35
A27
A272
A3057
A3090

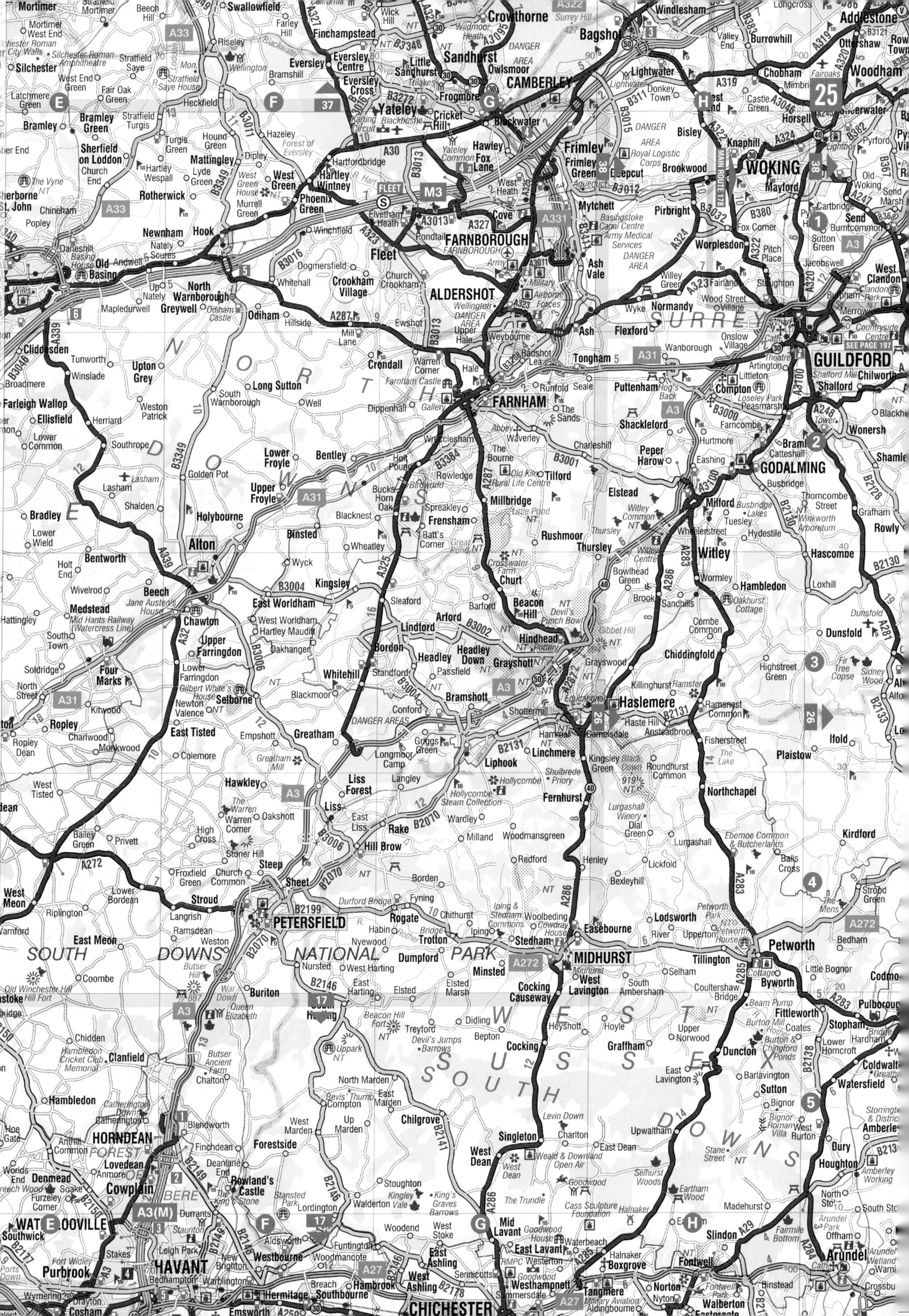

Mortimer
Swallowfield
Finchampstead
Crowthorne
Windlesham
Addlestone
Ottershaw
Bagshot
Sandhurst
Owlsmoor
CAMBERLEY
Chobham
Woodham
Silchester
Stratfield Saye
Eversley
Eversley Centre
Eversley Cross
Little Sandhurst
Yateley
Frogmore
Blackwater
Lightwater
Bisley
Horsell
Latchmere Green
Bramley
Bramley Green
Heckfield
Hazeley
Cricket Hill
Hawley
Fox Lane
Frimley
Frimley Green
Deepcut
Brookwood
Knaphill
WOKING
Mayford
Sherfield on Loddon
Mattingley
Hartley Wintney
West Green
Phoenix Green
FLEET
M3
Elvetham Heath
Cove
FARNBOROUGH
Mytchett
Pirbright
Worplesdon
Sutton Green
Send
Chineham
Rotherwick
Newnham
Hook
Nately Scures
Winchfield
Fleet
Church Crookham
Ash Vale
Basing
Old Basing
North Warnborough
Greywell
Up Nately
Dogmersfield
Crookham Village
ALDERSHOT
Normandy
Wood Street Village
Stoughton
West Clandon
Merrow
Mapledurwell
Odiham
Hillside
Mill Lane
Ewshot
Upper Hale
Weybourne
Badshot Lea
Ash
Flexford
SURREY
Wanborough
Onslow Village
GUILDFORD
Cliddesden
Tunworth
Upton Grey
NORTH DOWNS
Crondall
Warren Corner
Hale
Farnham Castle
Tongham
Runfold
Seale
Puttenham
Compton
Artington
Littleton
Shalford
Chilworth
Winslade
Long Sutton
South Warnborough
Well
Dippenhall
FARNHAM
The Sands
Farleigh Wallop
Ellisfield
Herriard
Weston Patrick
Wrecclesham
Waverley
Shackleford
Peasmarsh
Farncombe
Wonersh
Lower Common
Southrope
Lower Froyle
Bentley
The Bourne
Tilford
Peper Harow
Eashing
GODALMING
Catteshall
Lasham
Shalden
Golden Pot
Upper Froyle
Holt Pound
Rowledge
Millbridge
Elstead
Milford
Busbridge
Thorncombe Street
Bradley
Lower Wield
Holybourne
Bucks Horn Oak
Spreakley
Frensham
Blacknest
Tuesley
Hydestile
Grafham
Rowly
Alton
Binsted
Batt's Corner
Rushmoor
Thursley
Witley
Hascombe
Holt End
Bentworth
Wheatley
Wyck
Churt
Bowlhead Green
Loxhill
Wivelrod
Beech
Kingsley
Sleaford
Beacon Hill
Brook
Sandhills
Hambledon
Medstead
Chawton
East Worldham
West Worldham
Hartley Mauditt
Lindford
Arford
Barford
Hindhead
Combe Common
Dunsfold
Hattingley
South Town
Upper Farringdon
Oakhanger
Bordon
Headley
Headley Down
Grayshott
Grayswood
Chiddingfold
Four Marks
Lower Farringdon
Whitehill
Standford
Passfield
Highstreet Green
North Street
Newton Valence
Selborne
Blackmoor
Bramshott
Killinghurst
Haslemere
Ramsnest Common
Kitwood
Ropley
East Tisted
Empshott
Greatham
Conford
Shottermill
Hammer
Camelsdale
Haste Hill
Anstead Brook
Ifold
Ropley Dean
Charlwood
Monkwood
Colemore
Griggs Green
Longmoor Camp
Liphook
Linchmere
Kingsley Green
Fisherstreet
Plaistow
West Tisted
Hawkley
Liss Forest
Langley
Roundhurst Common
Northchapel
Fernhurst
Liss
East Liss
Rake
Warren Corner
Oakshott
High Cross
Privett
Bailey Green
Hill Brow
Wardley
Milland
Woodmansgreen
Lurgashall
Kirdford
West Meon
Froxfield Green
Church Common
Steep
Sheet
Borden
Redford
Henley
Lickfold
Bexleyhill
Balls Cross
Lower Bordean
Stroud
Ripplington
Langrish
PETERSFIELD
Fyning
Rogate
Chithurst
Woolbeding
Easebourne
Lodsworth
River
Upperton
Strood Green
Warnford
Ramsdean
East Meon
Weston
Habin
Nyewood
Trotton
Iping
Stedham
MIDHURST
Tillington
Petworth
Bedham
SOUTH DOWNS NATIONAL PARK
Nursted
West Harting
Dumpford
Minsted
Selham
Little Bognor
Coombe
Buriton
East Harting
Elsted
Elsted Marsh
Cocking Causeway
West Lavington
South Ambersham
Coultershaw Bridge
Byworth
Fittleworth
Stopham
South Harting
Treyford
Didling
Bepton
Heyshott
Hoyle
Graffham
Upper Norwood
Duncton
Coates
Chidden
Clanfield
Uppark
Cocking
WEST SUSSEX
Chalton
North Marden
East Marden
Compton
East Lavington
Barlavington
Sutton
Bignor
Hambledon
Catherington
Blendworth
HORNDEAN
Up Marden
West Marden
Chilgrove
Levin Down
Charlton
Upwaltham
West Burton
Amberley
Finchdean
Forestside
Singleton
West Dean
East Dean
Bury
Houghton
Denmead
Lovedean
Cowplain
Rowland's Castle
Stoughton
Walderton
Madehurst
North Stoke
Waterlooville
Southwick
Purbrook
HAVANT
Bedhampton
Leigh Park
Durrants
Lordington
Aldsworth
Woodend
West Stoke
Mid Lavant
Eartham
Slindon
Offham
Arundel
Stakes
New Brighton
Westbourne
Funtington
East Ashling
East Lavant
Waterbeach
Halnaker
Boxgrove
Fontwell
Warblington
Hermitage
Southbourne
Emsworth
Hambrook
West Ashling
Westhampnett
Tangmere
Norton
Walberton
Binstead
Crossbush
Drayton
Cosham
CHICHESTER
Aldingbourne
Wymering

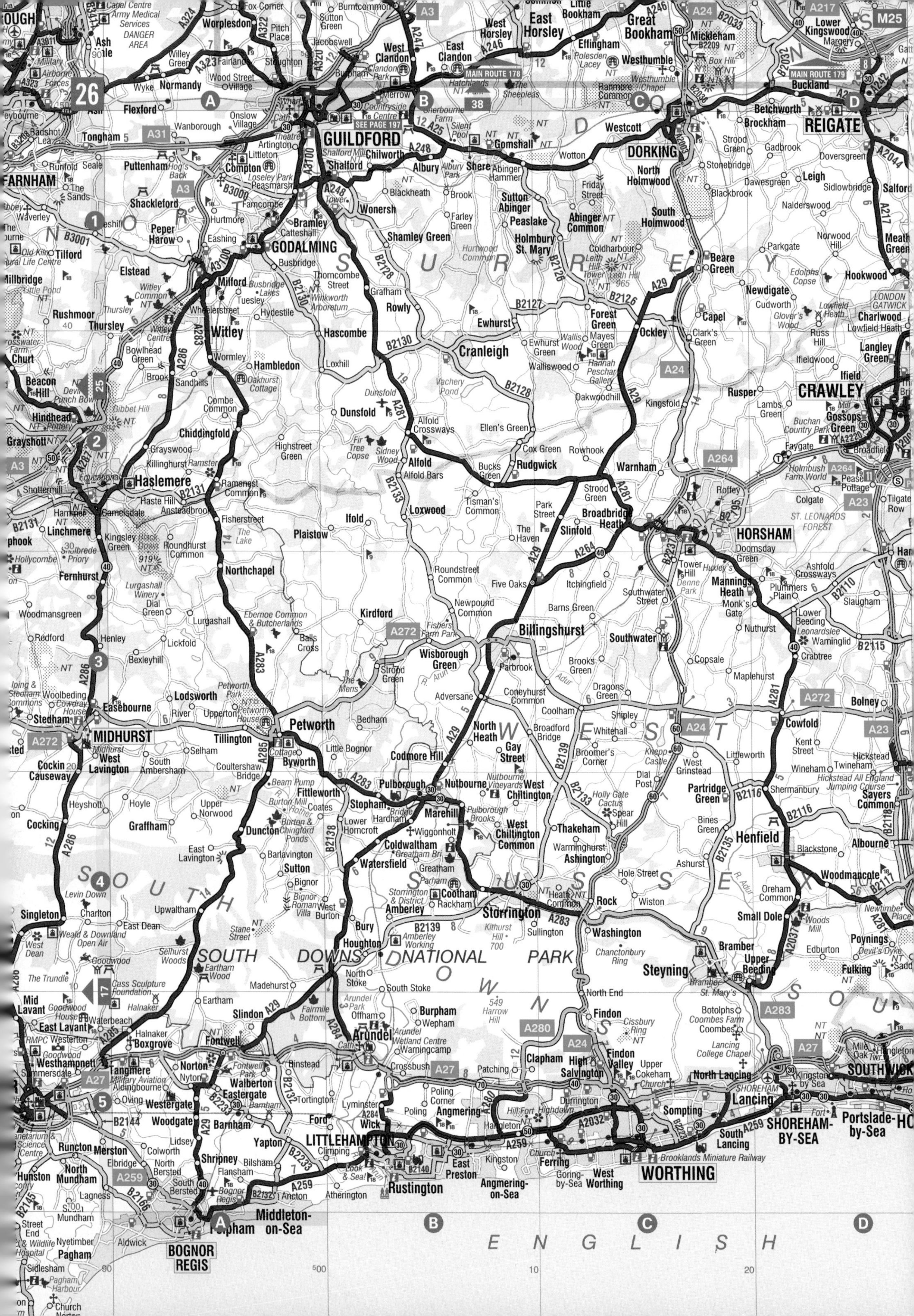

26
MAIN ROUTE 178
MAIN ROUTE 179
38
SEE PAGE 197
M25
A3
A24
A217
Worplesdon
Pitch Place
Sutton Green
Jacobswell
Burntcommon
West Horsley
East Horsley
Little Bookham
Great Bookham
Mickleham
Lower Kingswood
Ash Vale
Normandy
Wood Street Village
Stoughton
West Clandon
East Clandon
Effingham
Westhumble
Box Hill
Wyke
Flexford
Wanborough
Onslow Village
Merrow
Hatchlands
The Sheepleas
Ranmore Common
Buckland
Betchworth
Brockham
REIGATE
Tongham
Artington
GUILDFORD
Chilworth
Gomshall
Westcott
Wotton
DORKING
Strood Green
Gadbrook
Doversgreen
Runfold
Seale
Puttenham
Compton
Shalford
Albury
Shere
Abinger Hammer
North Holmwood
Leigh
Sidlowbridge
Salford
FARNHAM
The Sands
Shackleford
Peasmarsh
Farncombe
Blackheath
Brook
Sutton Abinger
Friday Street
South Holmwood
Blackbrook
Dawesgreen
Nalderswood
Waverley
Hurtmore
Peper Harow
Eashing
Bramley
Catteshall
Wonersh
Farley Green
Peaslake
Abinger Common
Holmbury St. Mary
Shamley Green
Coldharbour
Leith Hill
Norwood Hill
Parkgate
Meath Green
Tilford
Rural Life Centre
GODALMING
Busbridge
Thorncombe Street
Hurtwood Common
SURREY
Beare Green
Edolphs Copse
Hookwood
Millbridge
Elstead
Milford
Tuesley
Winkworth Arboretum
Grafham
Rowly
Newdigate
LONDON GATWICK
Rushmoor
Thursley
Witley Common
Wheelerstreet
Hydestile
Hascombe
Ewhurst
Forest Green
Ockley
Capel
Cudworth
Charlwood
Lowfield Heath
Churt
Witley
Bowlhead Green
Wormley
Hambledon
Loxhill
Cranleigh
Ewhurst Green
Mayes Green
Walliswood
Clark's Green
Russ Hill
Langley Green
Beacon Hill
Brook
Sandhills
Oakhurst Cottage
Vachery Pond
Hannah Peschar Gallery
Oakwoodhill
Kingsfold
Rusper
Ifield
Ifieldwood
CRAWLEY
Hindhead
Devil's Punch Bowl
Gibbet Hill
Combe Common
Dunsfold
Alfold Crossways
Ellen's Green
Lambs Green
Buchan Country Park
Gossops Green
Grayshott
Chiddingfold
Grayswood
Killinghurst
Highstreet Green
Fir Tree Copse
Sidney Wood
Alfold
Cox Green
Rowhook
Faygate
Warnham
Holmbush Farm World
Pease Pottage
Shottermill
Haslemere
Ramsnest Common
Alfold Bars
Bucks Green
Rudgwick
Strood Green
Roffey
Colgate
Tilgate Row
Hammer
Camelsdale
Haste Hill
Anstead Brook
Loxwood
Tisman's Common
Park Street
Broadbridge Heath
HORSHAM
ST. LEONARDS FOREST
Linchmere
Fisherstreet
Ifold
Plaistow
The Haven
Slinfold
Liphook
Kingsley Green
Black Down
Roundhurst Common
Doomsday Green
Hollycombe
Shulbrede Priory
Northchapel
Roundstreet Common
Five Oaks
Itchingfield
Tower Hill
Ashfold Crossways
Fernhurst
Lurgashall Winery
Dial Green
Newpound Common
Southwater Street
Mannings Heath
Plummers Plain
Slaugham
Woodmansgreen
Lurgashall
Ebernoe Common & Butcherlands
Kirdford
Barns Green
Monk's Gate
Lower Beeding
Redford
Henley
Lickfold
Balls Cross
Billingshurst
Southwater
Nuthurst
Leonardslee
Warninglid
Bexleyhill
Wisborough Green
Parbrook
Brooks Green
Copsale
Crabtree
Iping & Stedham Commons
Woolbeding
Cowdray House
Easebourne
Lodsworth
Petworth Park
Strood Green
The Mens
Adversane
Coneyhurst Common
Dragons Green
Maplehurst
Stedham
River
Upperton
Petworth House
Bedham
Coolham
Shipley
Bolney
MIDHURST
Tillington
Petworth
Little Bognor
North Heath
Broadford Bridge
Whitehall
Cowfold
Selham
Codmore Hill
Gay Street
Broomer's Corner
Knepp Castle
West Grinstead
Kent Street
Cocking Causeway
West Lavington
South Ambersham
Coultershaw Bridge
Byworth
Littleworth
Wineham
Twineham
Hickstead
Hickstead All England Jumping Course
Pulborough
Nutbourne
West Chiltington
Dial Post
Partridge Green
Shermanbury
Sayers Common
Heyshott
Hoyle
Upper Norwood
Beam Pump
Fittleworth
Stopham
Coates
Marehill
Hardham
Pulborough Brooks
Thakeham
Holly Gate Cactus
Spear Hill
Henfield
Cocking
Graffham
Duncton
Lower Horncroft
Wiggonholt
West Chiltington Common
Bines Green
Albourne
Burton & Chingford Ponds
Coldwaltham
Greatham
Warminghurst
Ashington
Blackstone
East Lavington
Barlavington
Sutton
Watersfield
Ashurst
Bignor
Bignor Roman Villa
West Burton
Parham
Cootham
Rackham
Storrington
Hole Street
Woodmancote
Oreham Common
SOUTH DOWNS
Levin Down
Charlton
Upwaltham
Amberley
Kithurst Hill
Rock
Wiston
SUSSEX
WEST
Singleton
East Dean
Stane Street
Bury
Sullington
Washington
Small Dole
Woods Mill
Poynings
Devil's Dyke
West Dean
Weald & Downland Open Air
Selhurst Woods
Houghton
Amberley Working
SOUTH DOWNS NATIONAL PARK
Chanctonbury Ring
Bramber
Edburton
Goodwood
Eartham Wood
North Stoke
Steyning
Upper Beeding
Fulking
The Trundle
Cass Sculpture Foundation
Madehurst
South Stoke
Bramber St. Mary's
Mid Lavant
Halnaker
Eartham
Arundel Park
Offham
Burpham
Wepham
549 Harrow Hill
North End
Findon
Cissbury Ring
Botolphs
Coombes Farm
Coombes
East Lavant
Waterbeach
Slindon
Fairmile Bottom
Westerton
Boxgrove
Fontwell
Arundel
Arundel Wetland Centre
Warningcamp
Clapham
High Salvington
Findon Valley
Upper Cokeham
Lancing College Chapel
Mile Oak
Westhampnett
Tangmere
Military Aviation
Norton
Nyton
Fontwell Park
Binstead
Crossbush
Patching
North Lancing
Shoreham
Kingston by Sea
SOUTHWICK
Aldingbourne
Oving
Westergate
Walberton
Eastergate
Barnham
Tortington
Poling Corner
Poling
Angmering
Hill Fort
Highdown
Durrington
Sompting
Lancing
SHOREHAM-BY-SEA
Portslade-by-Sea
Woodgate
Lyminster
Wick
Ford
Hangleton
Lidsey
Yapton
LITTLEHAMPTON
Climping
Church Ferring
Brooklands Miniature Railway
South Lancing
Runcton
Merston
Colworth
Elbridge
North Bersted
Shripney
Flansham
Bilsham
Look & Sea!
East Preston
Kingston
Ferring
Goring-by-Sea
West Worthing
WORTHING
Hunston
North Mundham
South Bersted
Bognor Regis
Ancton
Atherington
Rustington
Angmering-on-Sea
Lagness
Mundham
Street End
Felpham
Middleton-on-Sea
Nyetimber
Pagham
Aldwick
BOGNOR REGIS
Sidlesham
Pagham Harbour
Church Norton
ENGLISH
A
B
C
D
1
2
3
4
5
25
17
500
10
20

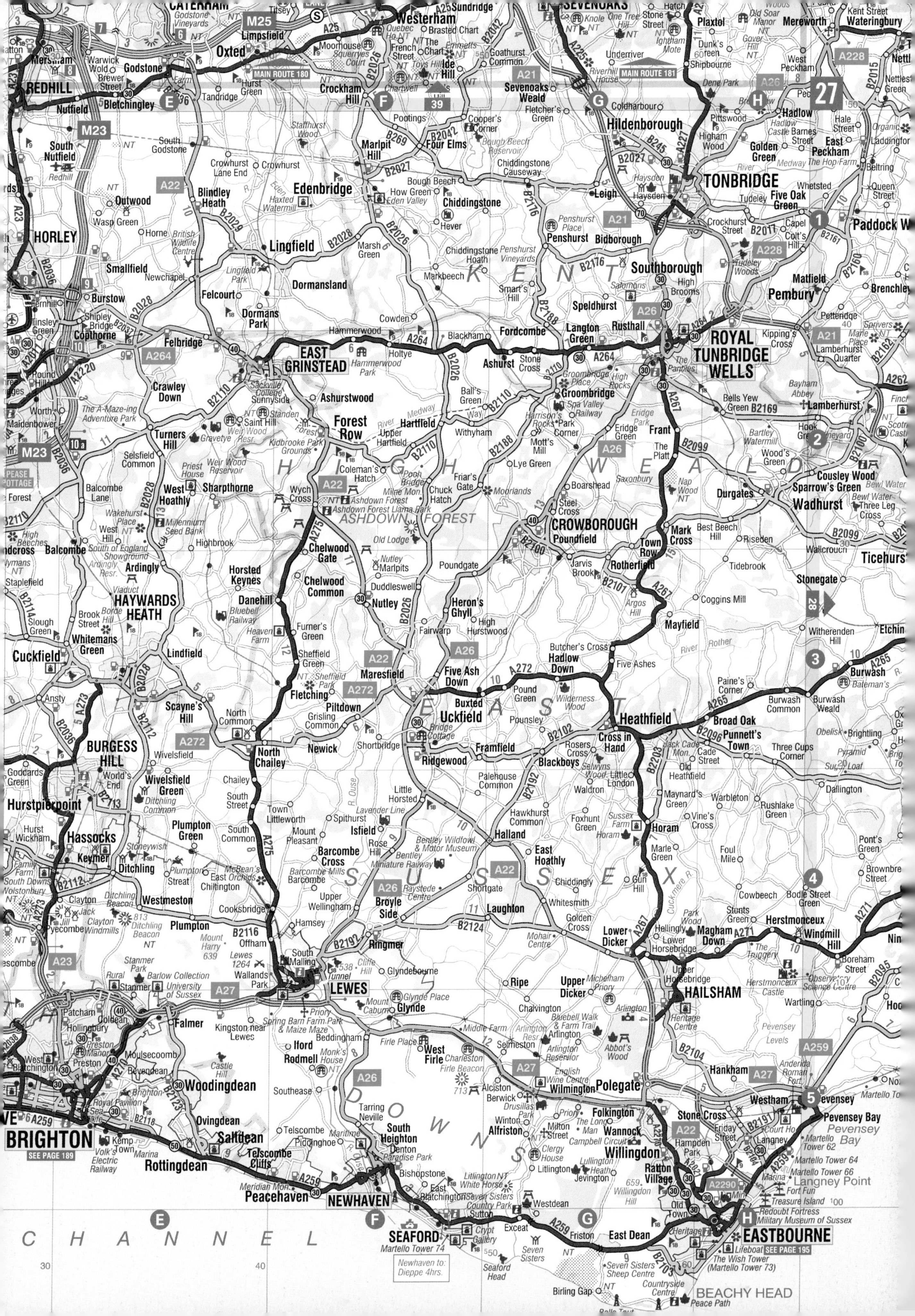

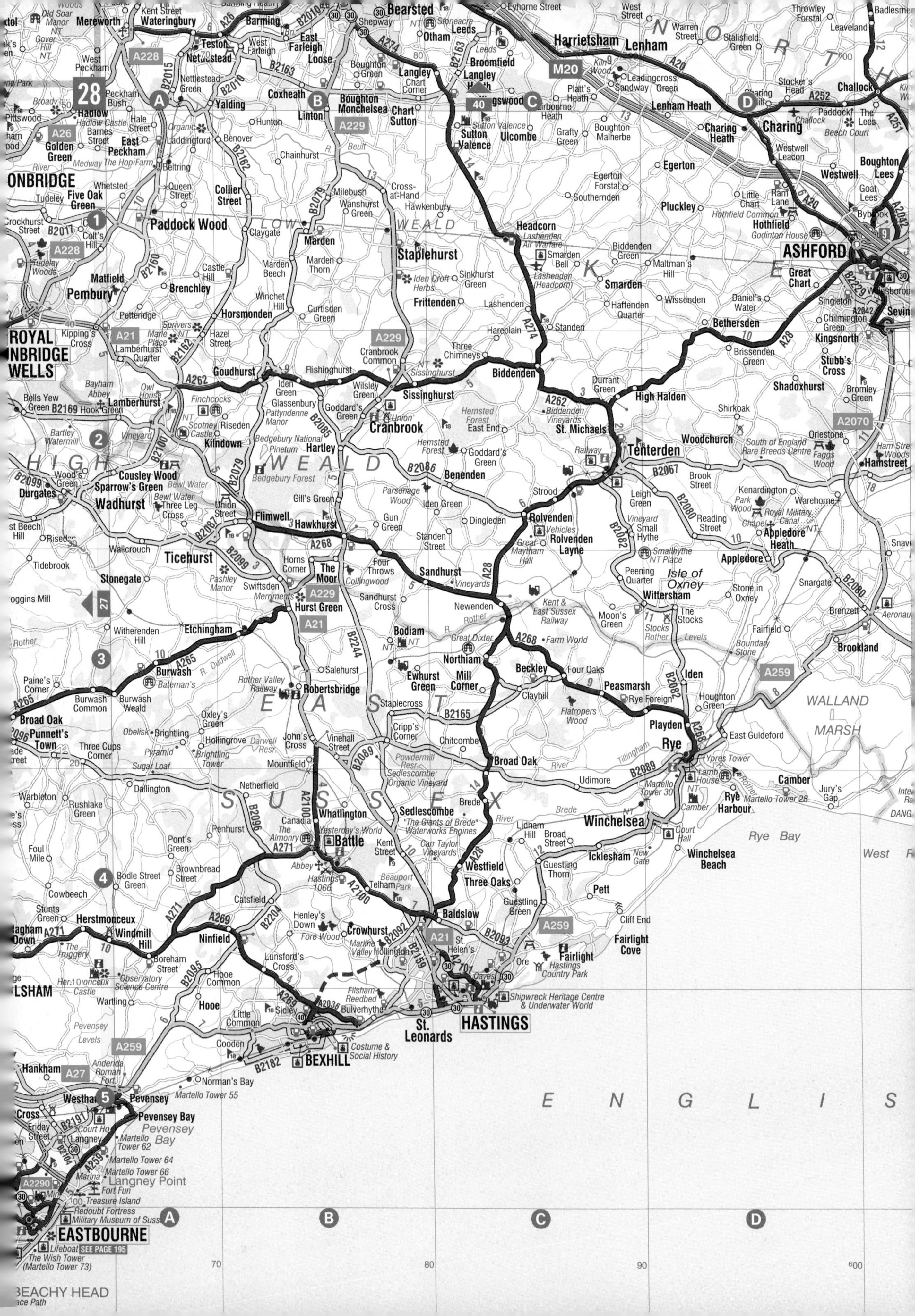

Mereworth
Kent Street
Wateringbury
Barming
Bearsted
Harrietsham
Lenham
Teston
West Farleigh
East Farleigh
Loose
Otham
Leeds
Warren Street
Stalisfield Green
Throwley Forstal
Leaveland
Nettlestead
Nettlestead Green
Boughton Green
Langley
Broomfield
Leadingcross Green
Sandway
Platt's Heath
Stocker's Head
Challock
28
A
B
C
D
Peckham Bush
Hadlow
Yalding
Coxheath
Linton
Boughton Monchelsea
Chart Corner
Chart Sutton
Langley Heath
Kingswood
Fairbourne Heath
Lenham Heath
Charing Heath
Charing
Golden Green
Hale Street
East Peckham
Laddingford
Hunton
Benover
Chainhurst
Sutton Valence
Ulcombe
Grafty Green
Boughton Malherbe
Egerton
Westwell Leacon
Westwell
Boughton Lees
Egerton Forstal
Southernden
Little Chart
Pluckley
Hothfield
ONBRIDGE
Tudeley
Five Oak Green
Whetsted
Queen Street
Collier Street
Milebush
Wanshurst Green
Cross-at-Hand
Hawkenbury
Paddock Wood
Claygate
LOW WEALD
Marden
Staplehurst
Headcorn
Biddenden Green
Maltman's Hill
ASHFORD
Great Chart
Pembury
Matfield
Brenchley
Castle Hill
Marden Beech
Marden Thorn
Sinkhurst Green
Frittenden
Smarden Bell
Smarden
Haffenden Quarter
Wissenden
Daniel's Water
Singleton
Horsmonden
Winchet Hill
Curtisden Green
Lashenden
Standen
Bethersden
Kingsnorth
Chilmington Green
ROYAL TUNBRIDGE WELLS
Kipping's Cross
Lamberhurst Quarter
Hazel Street
Goudhurst
Flishinghurst
Cranbrook Common
Hareplain
Three Chimneys
Biddenden
Brissenden Green
Stubb's Cross
Shadoxhurst
Bayham Abbey
Lamberhurst
Iden Green
Glassenbury
Wilsley Green
Sissinghurst
Durrant Green
High Halden
Shirkoak
Bromley Green
Bells Yew Green
Hook Green
Scotney Castle
Riseden
Kilndown
Goddard's Green
Cranbrook
Hartley
St. Michaels
Tenterden
Woodchurch
Orlestone
Hamstreet
HIGH WEALD
Wadhurst
Cousley Wood
Sparrow's Green
Durgates
Three Leg Cross
Benenden
Brook Street
Leigh Green
Kenardington
Warehorne
Union Street
Flimwell
Hawkhurst
Gill's Green
Iden Green
Dingleden
Rolvenden
Rolvenden Layne
Small Hythe
Reading Street
Appledore Heath
Appledore
Ticehurst
Wallcrouch
Tidebrook
Stonegate
Horns Corner
The Moor
Four Throws
Sandhurst
Standen Street
Peening Quarter
Isle of Oxney
Wittersham
Stone in Oxney
Snargate
Swiftsden
Hurst Green
Sandhurst Cross
Newenden
Moon's Green
The Stocks
Brenzett
Fairfield
Brookland
Etchingham
Witherenden Hill
Bodiam
Great Dixter
Northiam
Burwash
Salehurst
Ewhurst Green
Mill Corner
Beckley
Four Oaks
Peasmarsh
Iden
Robertsbridge
Burwash Common
Burwash Weald
Broad Oak
Punnett's Town
Staplecross
Clayhill
Rye Foreign
Playden
WALLAND MARSH
EAST SUSSEX
Oxley's Green
Brightling
Hollingrove
John's Cross
Vinehall Street
Cripp's Corner
Chitcombe
East Guldeford
Three Cups Corner
Mountfield
Broad Oak
Udimore
Rye
Camber
Jury's Gap
Netherfield
Dallington
Warbleton
Rushlake Green
Penhurst
Whatlington
Sedlescombe
Brede
Winchelsea
Rye Harbour
Rye Bay
Battle
Canada
Kent Street
Lidham Hill
Broad Street
Icklesham
Winchelsea Beach
Foul Mile
Pont's Green
Brownbread Street
Bodle Street Green
Cowbeech
Westfield
Three Oaks
Guestling Thorn
Pett
Catsfield
Telham
Baldslow
Guestling Green
Cliff End
Herstmonceux
Windmill Hill
Ninfield
Henley's Down
Crowhurst
St. Helen's
Fairlight
Fairlight Cove
Boreham Street
Lunsford's Cross
Ore
Hooe Common
Hooe
Wartling
Little Common
Sidley
Bulverhythe
St. Leonards
HASTINGS
Cooden
BEXHILL
Hankham
Norman's Bay
Westham
Pevensey
Pevensey Bay
Langney
Langney Point
EASTBOURNE
SEE PAGE 195
ENGLISH
BEACHY HEAD
70
80
90
600

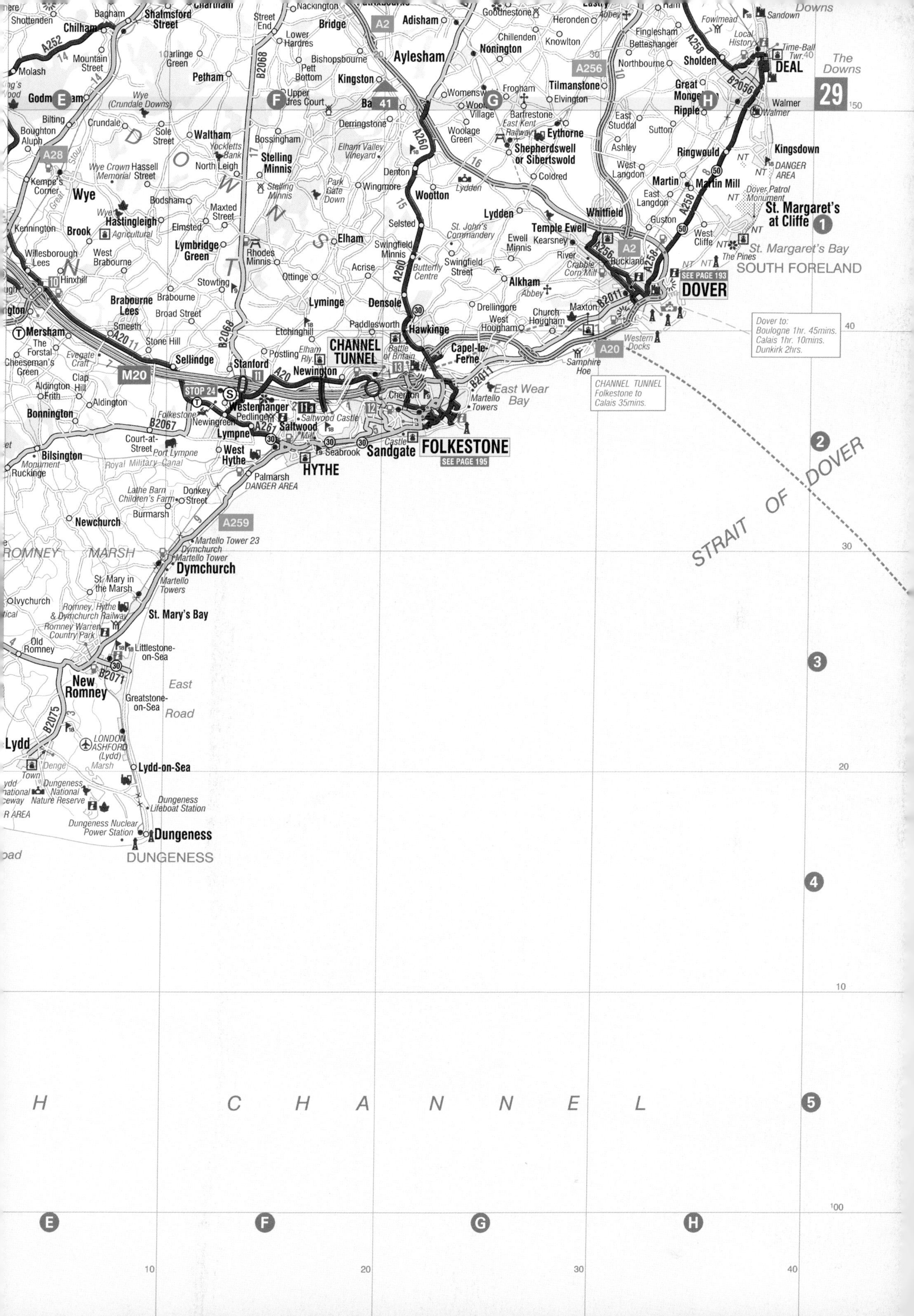
DEAL
DOVER
SEE PAGE 193
FOLKESTONE
SEE PAGE 195
CHANNEL TUNNEL
HYTHE
New Romney
Lydd
Dungeness
DUNGENESS
Dymchurch
St. Mary's Bay
St. Margaret's at Cliffe
SOUTH FORELAND
St. Margaret's Bay
Aylesham
Wye
Sandgate
Capel-le-Ferne
Hawkinge
Lyminge
Elham
Whitfield
Temple Ewell
Shepherdswell or Sibertswold
Eythorne
Ringwould
Kingsdown
Martin Mill
Sholden
Walmer
The Downs
Dover to:
Boulogne 1hr. 45mins.
Calais 1hr. 10mins.
Dunkirk 2hrs.
CHANNEL TUNNEL
Folkestone to
Calais 35mins.
STRAIT OF DOVER
East Wear Bay
East Road
ROMNEY MARSH
H C H A N N E L
M20
A20
A2
A256
A258
A260
A259
A28
A252
B2068
B2067
B2071
B2075
B2011
B2056
Dungeness Nuclear Power Station
Dungeness Lifeboat Station
Dungeness National Nature Reserve
LONDON ASHFORD (Lydd)
Romney, Hythe & Dymchurch Railway
Royal Military Canal
Martello Tower 23
Port Lympne
Saltwood Castle
Samphire Hoe
Western Docks
Dover Patrol Monument
DANGER AREA
Time-Ball Twr.

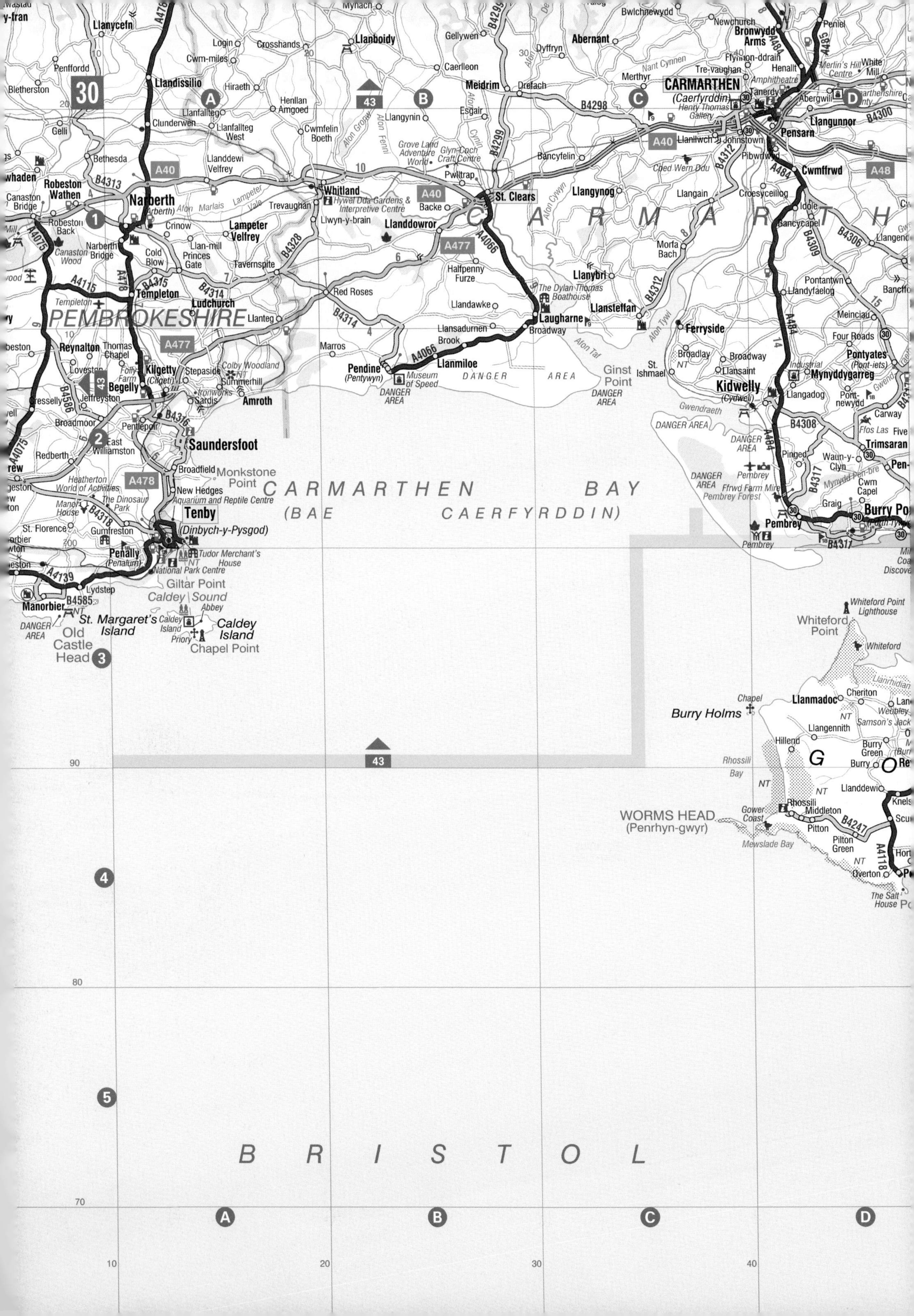

30
43
CARMARTHEN
(Caerfyrddin)
PEMBROKESHIRE
CARMARTHEN BAY
(BAE CAERFYRDDIN)
BRISTOL
Narberth
(Arberth)
Whitland
St. Clears
Laugharne
Pendine
(Pentywyn)
Kidwelly
(Cydweli)
Saundersfoot
Tenby
(Dinbych-y-Pysgod)
Kilgetty
(Cilgeti)
Begelly
Templeton
Llandissilio
Llanboidy
Meidrim
Llansteffan
Ferryside
Pembrey
Burry Port
Caldey Island
St. Margaret's Island
Manorbier
Penally
(Penalun)
Amroth
Llanddowror
Red Roses
Llanmiloe
Llangynog
Cwmffrwd
Llanmadoc
Rhossili
WORMS HEAD
(Penrhyn-gwyr)
Burry Holms
Whiteford Point
Old Castle Head
Giltar Point
Caldey Sound
Chapel Point
Monkstone Point
Ginst Point
DANGER AREA
A40
A477
A478
A4066
A484
A4115
A4075
A4139
A48
B4314
B4328
B4312
B4308
B4317
B4318
B4316
B4585
B4586
B4247
A4118
Carmarthenshire
Museum of Speed
The Dylan Thomas Boathouse
Hywel Dda Gardens & Interpretive Centre
Heatherton World of Activities
Tudor Merchant's House
National Park Centre
Aquarium and Reptile Centre
Ffrwd Farm Mire
Pembrey Forest
Colby Woodland
A
B
C
D
1
2
3
4
5
10
20
30
40
70
80
90

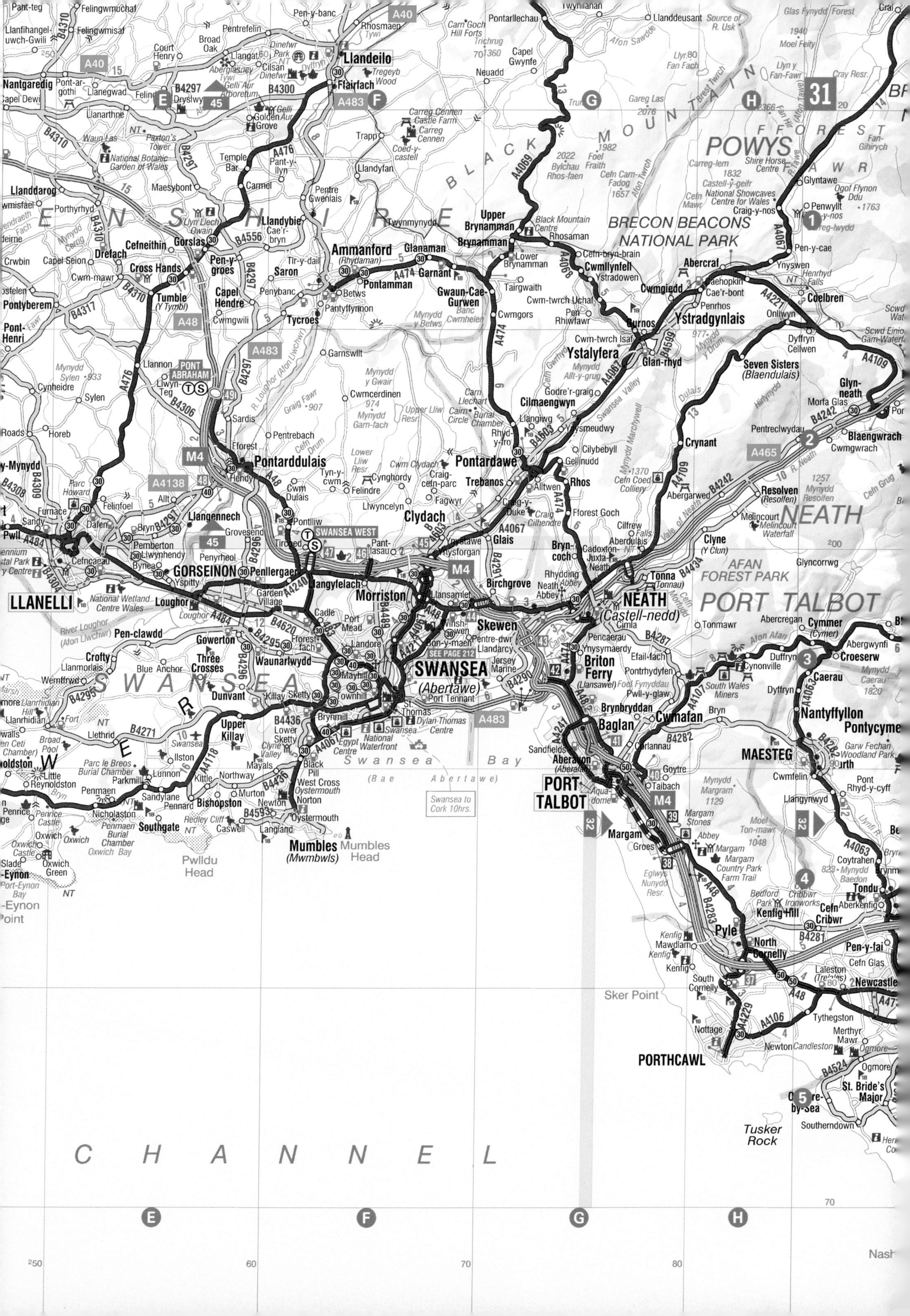

Pant-teg
Felingwmuchaf
Llanfihangel-uwch-Gwili
Felingwmisaf
Pentrefelin
Pen-y-banc
Rhosmaen
A40
Court Henry
Broad Oak
Llangathen
Dinefwr Park
Llandeilo
Nantgaredig
Pont-ar-gothi
Llanegwad
Felindre
Dryslwyn
Cilsan
Ffairfach
Tregeyb Wood
B4297
B4300
A483
Llanarthne
Golden Grove
Carreg Cennen Castle Farm
Carreg Cennen
Trapp
Coed-y-castell
Waun-Las
Paxton's Tower
National Botanic Garden of Wales
Temple Bar
Pant-y-llyn
Llandyfan
Llanddarog
Porthyrhyd
Maesybont
Carmel
Pentre Gwenlais
Drefach
Cefneithin
Gorslas
Llandybie
Cae'r-bryn
Twynmynydd
Crwbin
Capel Seion
Cross Hands
Pen-y-groes
Ammanford
(Rhydaman)
Glanaman
Tir-y-dail
Saron
Cwm-mawr
Pontamman
Garnant
Pontyberem
Tumble
(Y Tymbl)
Capel Hendre
Penybanc
Betws
Pantyffynnon
Tycroes
Cwmgwili
Gwaun-Cae-Gurwen
Pont-Henri
A48
A483
Garnswllt
Mynydd y Betws
Mynydd Sylen
Cynheidre
Sylen
Llannon
PONT ABRAHAM
Llwyn-Teg
Cwmcerdinen
Mynydd y Gwair
Mynydd Garn-fach
Upper Lliw Resr.
Carn Llechart
Cairn Circle
Burial Chamber
Sardis
Pentrebach
Cefn Drum
Horeb
Fforest
Pontarddulais
Hendy
M4
A4138
Lower Lliw Resr.
Cwm Clydach
Pontardawe
Tyn-y-cwm
Cynghordy
Felindre
Craig-cefn-parc
Trebanos
Cwm Dulais
Parc Howard
Felinfoel
Allt
Fagwyr
Llwyncelyn
Clydach
Furnace
Sandy
Dafen
Bryn
Llangennech
Pontlliw
Pwll
Pemberton
Grovesend
Tircoed
SWANSEA WEST
Pant-lasau
Cefncaeau
Llwynhendy
Bynea
Penyrheol
GORSEINON
Penllergaer
Ynysforgan
Ynystawe
Glais
LLANELLI
National Wetland Centre Wales
Loughor
Yspitty
Garden Village
Llangyfelach
Morriston
Llansamlet
Birchgrove
Skewen
River Loughor (Afon Llwchwr)
Pen-clawdd
Gowerton
Cadle
Port Mead
Fforest-fach
Landore
Winsh-wen
Bon-y-maen
Pentre-dwr
Llandarcy
Crofty
Three Crosses
Llanmorlais
Blue Anchor
Waunarlwydd
Jersey Marine
Wernffrwd
SWANSEA
(Abertawe)
Port Tennant
SEE PAGE 212
Dunvant
Killay
Sketty
Mayhill
Townhill
Llanrhidian
Brynmill
St. Thomas
Dylan Thomas Centre
Llethrid
B4271
Upper Killay
B4436
Lower Sketty
Swansea
Egypt Centre
National Waterfront
A483
Broad Pool
Ilston
Clyne Valley
Swansea Bay
(Bae Abertawe)
Parc le Breos Burial Chamber
Parkmill
Lunnon
Kittle
Northway
Mayals
Black Pill
West Cross
Oystermouth
Little Reynoldston
Penmaen
Sandylane
Pennard
Murton
Bishopston
Newton
Norton
Swansea to Cork 10hrs.
Penrice
Penrice Castle
Nicholaston
Southgate
Redley Cliff
Caswell
Langland
Oystermouth
Penmaen Burial Chamber
Oxwich
Oxwich Castle
Oxwich Bay
Mumbles
(Mwmbwls)
Mumbles Head
Pwlldu Head
Slade
Oxwich Green
Port-Eynon Bay
C H A N N E L
Twynllanan
Pontarllechau
Llanddeusant
Source of R. Usk
Glas Fynydd Forest
Carn Goch Hill Forts
Trichrug
Capel Gwynfe
Afon Sawdde
Moel Feity
Llyn y Fan Fach
Llyn y Fan-Fawr
Cray Resr.
Neuadd
Garreg Las
Fan Hir
BLACK MOUNTAIN
POWYS
FFOREST FAWR
Shire Horse Centre
Carreg-lem
Castell-y-geifr
National Showcaves Centre for Wales
Craig-y-nos
Glyntawe
Penwyllt
Ogof Ffynon Ddu
Bylchau Rhos-faen
Foel Fraith
Cefn Carn-Fadog
Upper Brynamman
Black Mountain Centre
Rhosaman
BRECON BEACONS NATIONAL PARK
Brynamman
Lower Brynamman
Cefn-bryn-brain
Cwmllynfell
Ystradowen
Abercraf
Pen-y-cae
Ynyswen
Tairgwaith
Cwm-twrch Uchaf
Cwmgiedd
Caehopkin
Cae'r-bont
Penrhos
Coelbren
Onllwyn
Cwmgors
Pen Rhiwfawr
Gurnos
Ystradgynlais
Dyffryn Cellwen
Cwm-twrch Isaf
Ystalyfera
Glan-rhyd
Seven Sisters
(Blaendulais)
Mynydd Allt-y-grug
Godre'r-graig
Swansea Valley
Glyn-neath
Morfa Glas
Cilmaengwyn
Llangiwg
Ynysmeudwy
Rhyd-y-fro
Pentreclwydau
Blaengwrach
Cwmgwrach
Crynant
A465
Cilybebyll
Gellinudd
Rhos
Alltwen
Cefn Coed Colliery
Resolven
(Resolfen)
Abergarwed
Craig-y-Duke
Fforest Goch
Melincourt
Melincourt Waterfall
NEATH
Cilfrew
Aberdulais Falls
Clyne
(Y Clun)
Bryn-coch
Cadoxton-Juxta-Neath
AFAN FOREST PARK
Glyncorrwg
Rhydding
Neath Abbey
Tonna
(Tonnau)
NEATH
(Castell-nedd)
PORT TALBOT
Tonmawr
Abercregan
Cymmer
(Cymer)
Cimla
Pencaerau
Ynysymaerdy
Efail-fach
Briton Ferry
(Llansawel)
Pontrhydyfen
Foel Fynyddau
Pwll-y-glaw
Duffryn
Cynonville
South Wales Miners
Croeserw
Abergwynfi
Caerau
Dyffryn
Brynbryddan
Cwmafan
Bryn
Nantyffyllon
Baglan
Sandfields
Aberavon
(Aberafan)
Corlannau
Goytre
MAESTEG
Garw Fechan Woodland Park
PORT TALBOT
Taibach
Aquadome
Mynydd Margam
Margam Stones
Cwmfelin
Pont Rhyd-y-cyff
Llangynwyd
Margam
Groes
Abbey
Margam Country Park
Farm Trail
Moel Ton-mawr
Coytrahen
Eglwys Nunydd Resr.
Bedford Park
Cribbwr Ironworks
Kenfig Hill
Cefn Cribwr
Aberkenfig
Tondu
Kenfig
Mawdlam
Pyle
North Cornelly
Pen-y-fai
Cefn Glas
Laleston
(Trelales)
Newcastle
South Cornelly
Sker Point
Tythegston
Nottage
Merthyr Mawr
Newton
Candleston
Ogmore
PORTHCAWL
St. Bride's Major
Ogmore-by-Sea
Southerndown
Tusker Rock
Nash
E
F
G
H
31
32

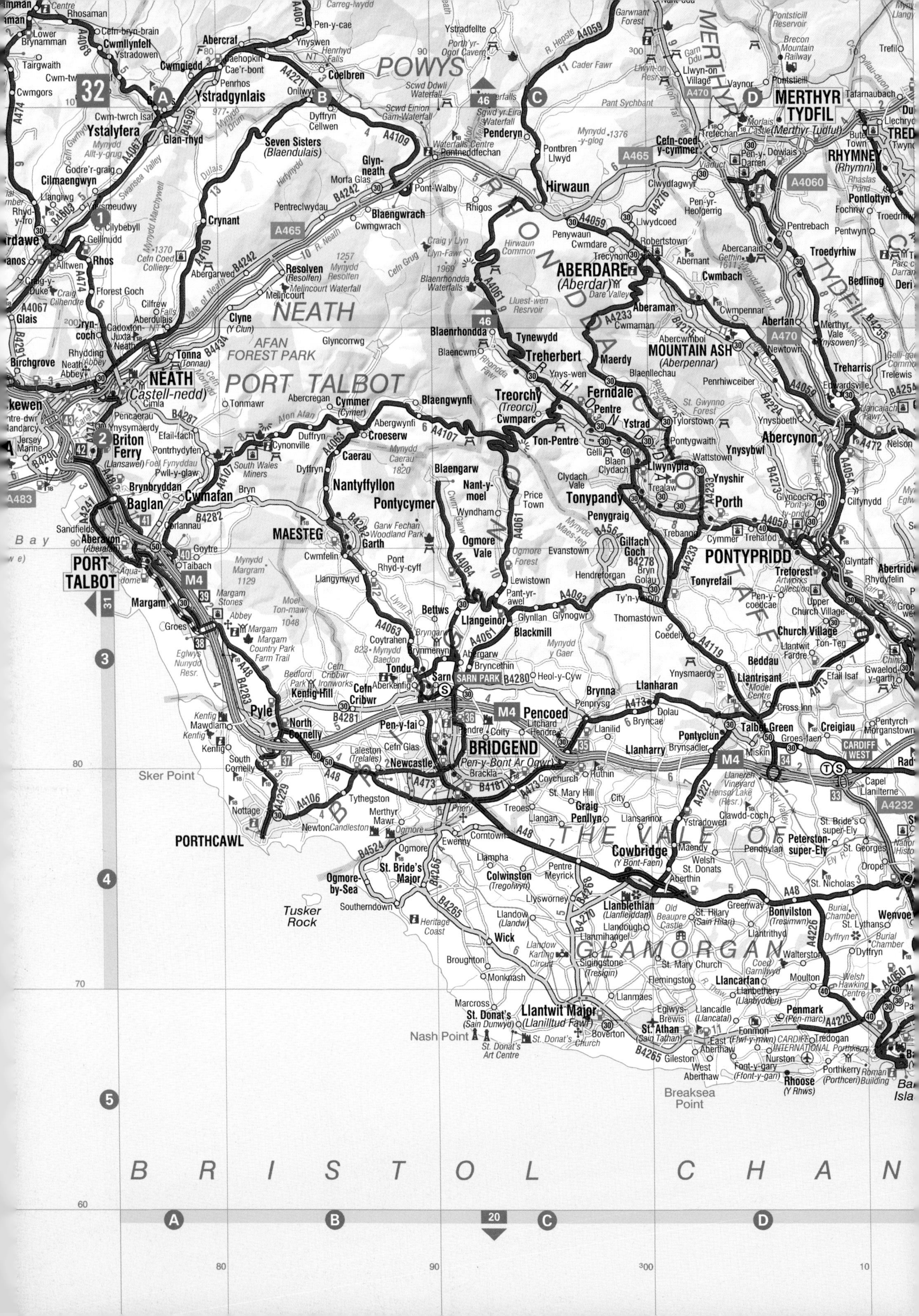

32
POWYS
MERTHYR TYDFIL
RHYMNEY
(Rhymni)
ABERDARE
(Aberdar)
MOUNTAIN ASH
(Aberpennar)
NEATH
(Castell-nedd)
PORT TALBOT
AFAN FOREST PARK
RHONDDA
PONTYPRIDD
BRIDGEND
(Pen-y-Bont Ar Ogwr)
THE VALE OF GLAMORGAN
PORTHCAWL
MAESTEG
Ystradgynlais
Ystalyfera
Abercraf
Coelbren
Seven Sisters
(Blaendulais)
Glyn-neath
Hirwaun
Penderyn
Ystradfellte
Crynant
Resolven
(Resolfen)
Blaengwrach
Pontneddfechan
Rhigos
Treherbert
Treorchy
(Treorci)
Tonypandy
Porth
Ferndale
Ystrad
Pentre
Ton-Pentre
Llwynypia
Abercynon
Aberfan
Treharris
Pontlottyn
Troedyrhiw
Bedlinog
Cwmbach
Aberaman
Robertstown
Penywaun
Llwydcoed
Maerdy
Ynyshir
Ynysybwl
Gilfach Goch
Tonyrefail
Llantrisant
Talbot Green
Pontyclun
Llanharan
Llanharry
Brynna
Pencoed
Beddau
Church Village
Creigiau
Cowbridge
(Y Bont-Faen)
Llantwit Major
(Llanilltud Fawr)
St. Athan
(Sain Tathan)
Rhoose
(Y Rhws)
Penmark
(Pen-marc)
Llancarfan
Bonvilston
(Tresimwn)
Peterston-super-Ely
Colwinston
(Tregolwyn)
Llanblethian
(Llanfleiddan)
St. Bride's Major
Ogmore-by-Sea
Southerndown
Wick
Broughton
Monknash
Marcross
St. Donat's
(Sain Dunwyd)
Nash Point
Tusker Rock
Sker Point
Breaksea Point
Pyle
North Cornelly
South Cornelly
Kenfig
Kenfig Hill
Cefn Cribwr
Tondu
Sarn
SARN PARK
Aberkenfig
Bryncethin
Llangeinor
Blackmill
Ogmore Vale
Nantymoel
Blaengarw
Pontycymer
Garth
Nantyffyllon
Caerau
Cymmer
(Cymer)
Blaengwynfi
Croeserw
Cwmafan
Baglan
Briton Ferry
(Llansawel)
Aberavon
(Aberafan)
Margam
Tonna
(Tonnau)
Clyne
(Y Clun)
Rhos
Alltwen
Cilmaengwyn
Glais
Birchgrove
Skewen
Newcastle
Laleston
Tythegston
Coity
Brackla
Coychurch
Ruthin
St. Mary Hill
Graig Penllyn
Llangan
Treoes
Ewenny
Corntown
Ogmore
Merthyr Mawr
Newton
CARDIFF WEST
CARDIFF INTERNATIONAL
Wenvoe
Dyffryn
St. Nicholas
Welsh St. Donats
Aberthin
M4
A48
A465
A470
A4059
A4061
A4063
A4107
A4119
A4222
A4226
A4232
A4233
A4058
A4054
A4093
A473
A4106
A4229
A4109
A4221
A4067
A474
B4265
B4524
B4270
B4268
B4281
B4280
B4181
46
31
20
BRISTOL CHANNEL
Swansea Bay
A
B
C
D
1
2
3
4
5
60
70
80
90
300
10

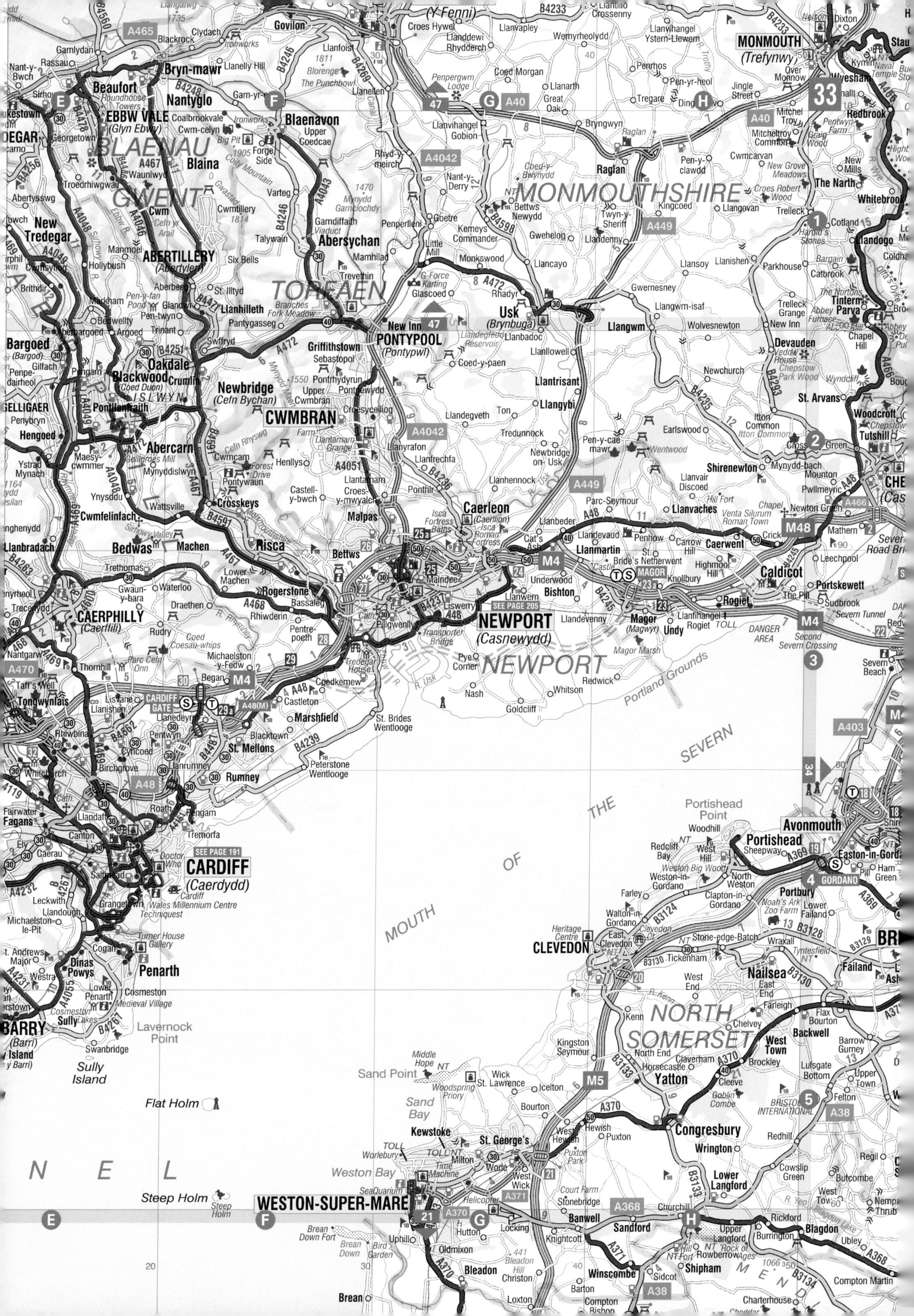

33
34
47
MONMOUTH
(Trefynwy)
MONMOUTHSHIRE
BLAENAU GWENT
TORFAEN
NEWPORT
CARDIFF
(Caerdydd)
SEE PAGE 191
NEWPORT
(Casnewydd)
SEE PAGE 205
CWMBRAN
PONTYPOOL
(Pontypwl)
EBBW VALE
(Glyn Ebwy)
ABERTILLERY
(Abertyleri)
CAERPHILLY
(Caerffili)
BARRY
(Barri)
Penarth
Dinas Powys
Sully
Sully Island
Lavernock Point
Flat Holm
Steep Holm
N E L
SEVERN
THE
OF
MOUTH
Portishead
Portishead Point
Avonmouth
Portbury
CLEVEDON
Nailsea
NORTH SOMERSET
Yatton
Congresbury
WESTON-SUPER-MARE
Weston Bay
Sand Bay
Sand Point
Kewstoke
Worlebury
St. George's
Banwell
Sandford
Churchill
Blagdon
Winscombe
Shipham
Bleadon
Uphill
Brean
Brean Down
Hutton
Locking
Wrington
Backwell
Chepstow
Caldicot
Magor
Undy
Rogiet
Portskewett
Caerwent
Caerleon
Usk
(Brynbuga)
Raglan
Abergavenny (Y Fenni)
Govilon
Blaenavon
Brynmawr
Beaufort
Nantyglo
Blaina
Abersychan
Risca
Rogerstone
Bettws
Malpas
Crosskeys
Abercarn
Newbridge
(Cefn Bychan)
Blackwood
(Coed Duon)
Oakdale
Bargoed
New Tredegar
Hengoed
Bedwas
Machen
Marshfield
St. Mellons
Rumney
Tongwynlais
Whitchurch
Llandaff
Rhiwbina
Llanishen
Lisvane
Tintern Parva
Trelleck
Devauden
St. Arvans
Shirenewton
Llanvaches
Penhow
Llangybi
Llantrisant
Second Severn Crossing
Severn Tunnel
Magor Marsh
Portland Grounds
Goldcliff
Whitson
Redwick
Nash
St. Brides Wentlooge
Peterstone Wentlooge
M4
M48
M5
A48
A40
A449
A4042
A467
A469
A470
A370
A371
A368
A38
A369
A403
A466
A472
E
F
G
H
1
2
3
4
5
20
30

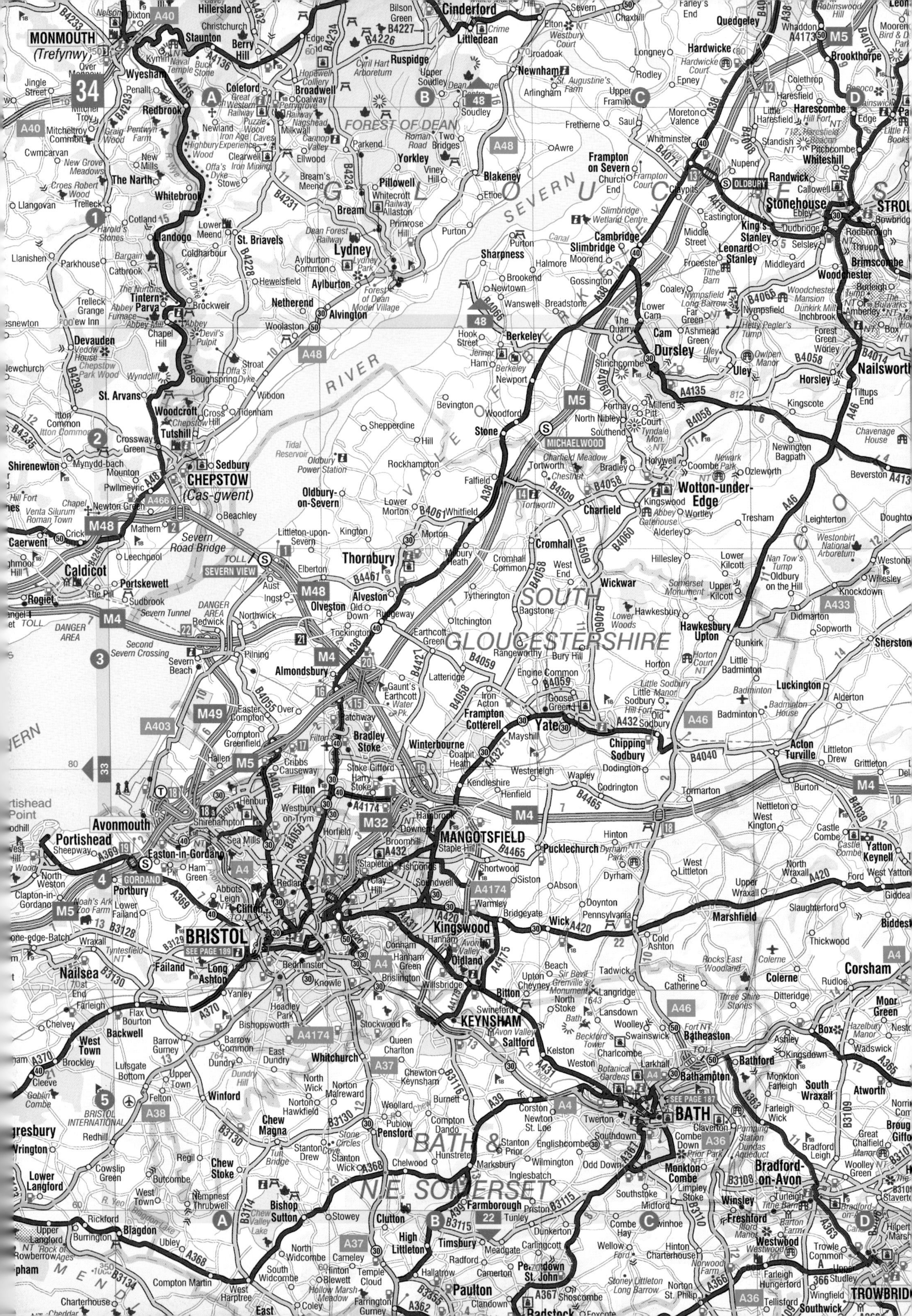

34
MONMOUTH
(Trefynwy)
Cinderford
Littledean
Hillersland
Staunton
Berry Hill
Coleford
Broadwell
Ruspidge
FOREST OF DEAN
Newnham
Quedgeley
Hardwicke
Brookthorpe
M5
48
Redbrook
Yorkley
Blakeney
Parkend
Frampton on Severn
Whitminster
Stonehouse
STROUD
OLDBURY
Whitebrook
Llandogo
St. Briavels
Lydney
Bream
Pillowell
Sharpness
Cambridge
Slimbridge
King's Stanley
Leonard Stanley
SEVERN
Tintern Parva
Alvington
Aylburton
Netherend
Berkeley
Dursley
Cam
Uley
Nailsworth
Woodchester
Devauden
St. Arvans
Woodcroft
Tutshill
CHEPSTOW
(Cas-gwent)
Sedbury
RIVER
Stone
Wotton-under-Edge
Charfield
MICHAELWOOD
VALE OF BERKELEY
Oldbury-on-Severn
Thornbury
Caerwent
Caldicot
Rogiet
Portskewett
SEVERN VIEW
Severn Road Bridge
M48
Wickwar
SOUTH GLOUCESTERSHIRE
Hawkesbury Upton
Alveston
Olveston
Almondsbury
M4
Second Severn Crossing
Severn Beach
Pilning
M49
A403
Bradley Stoke
Yate
Chipping Sodbury
Frampton Cotterell
Winterbourne
Acton Turville
Luckington
Sherston
Filton
M32
MANGOTSFIELD
Pucklechurch
Avonmouth
Portishead
GORDANO
Portbury
Easton-in-Gordano
BRISTOL
SEE PAGE 189
Kingswood
Marshfield
Corsham
Nailsea
Long Ashton
KEYNSHAM
Saltford
Batheaston
BATH
SEE PAGE 187
Bradford-on-Avon
Winsley
Backwell
West Town
Winford
Chew Magna
Whitchurch
Pensford
BATH & N.E. SOMERSET
Chew Stoke
Bishop Sutton
Clutton
High Littleton
Timsbury
Farmborough
Paulton
Peasedown St. John
Radstock
Blagdon
MENDIP
West Harptree
Freshford
Westwood
TROWBRIDGE
22

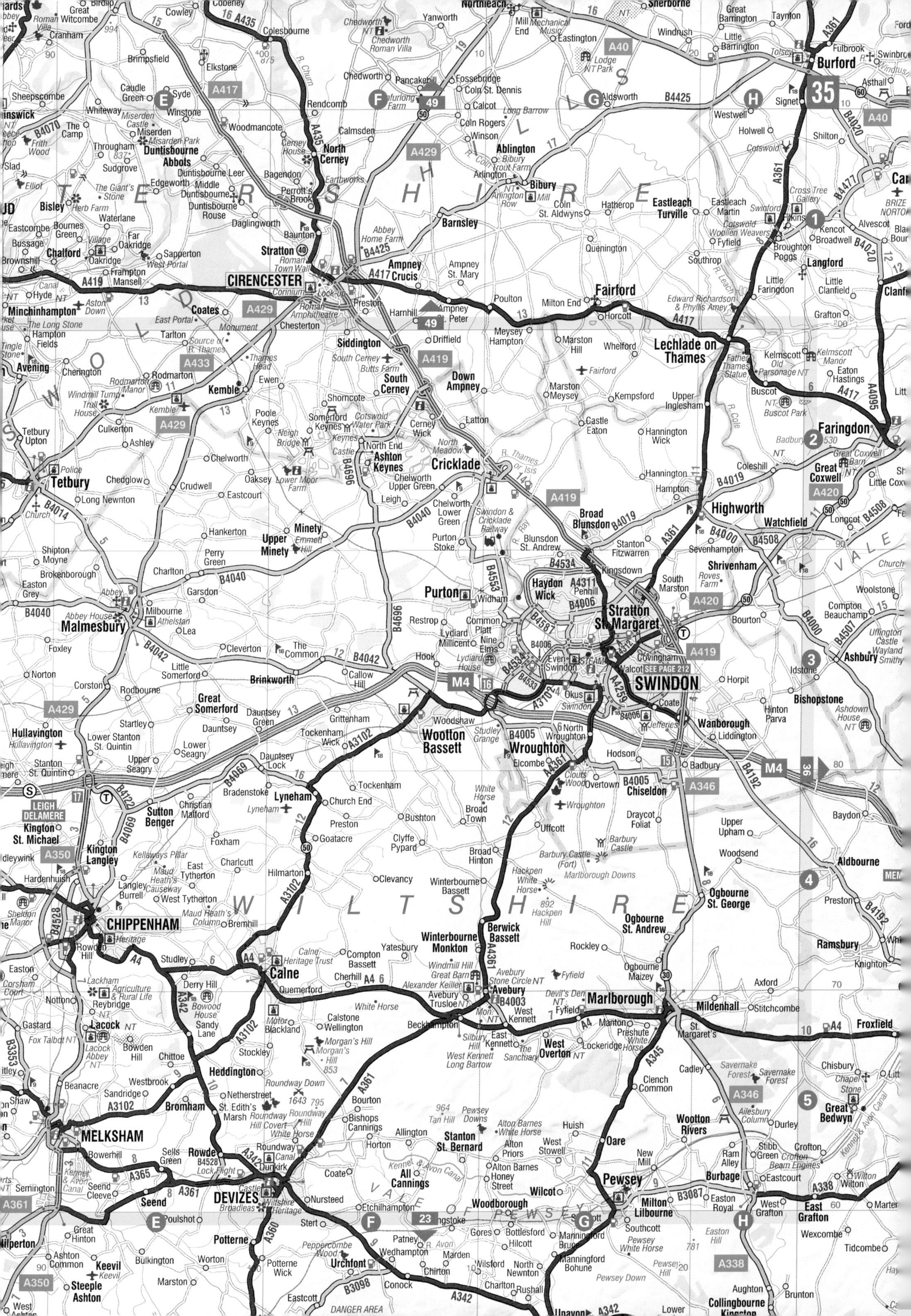

Northleach
Sherborne
Great Barrington
Taynton
Burford
Fulbrook
Swinbrook
Asthall
35
Colesbourne
Cowley
Great Witcombe
Cranham
Chedworth
Chedworth Roman Villa
Yanworth
Mill End
Eastington
Windrush
Little Barrington
A40
A361
A417
A435
A429
A419
A433
A420
A4
M4
Brimpsfield
Elkstone
Syde
Caudle Green
Sheepscombe
Winstone
Whiteway
Miserden
The Camp
Woodmancote
Rendcomb
North Cerney
Calmsden
Pancakehill
Fossebridge
Coln St. Dennis
Calcot
Coln Rogers
Winson
Ablington
Bibury
Arlington
Aldsworth
Westwell
Signet
Holwell
Shilton
Duntisbourne Abbots
Duntisbourne Leer
Duntisbourne Rouse
Middle Duntisbourne
Edgeworth
Bagendon
Perrott's Brook
Bisley
Sudgrove
Waterlane
Daglingworth
Barnsley
Coln St. Aldwyns
Hatherop
Eastleach Turville
Eastleach Martin
Swinford
Filkins
Kencot
Broadwell
Alvescot
Broughton Poggs
Langford
Chalford
Oakridge
Sapperton
Frampton Mansell
Baunton
Stratton
Ampney Crucis
Ampney St. Mary
Quenington
Southrop
Little Faringdon
Little Clanfield
CIRENCESTER
Preston
Harnhill
Ampney St. Peter
Poulton
Milton End
Fairford
Horcott
Grafton
Minchinhampton
Hyde
Coates
Tarlton
Chesterton
Siddington
Driffield
Meysey Hampton
Marston Hill
Whelford
Lechlade on Thames
Kelmscott
Eaton Hastings
Avening
Cherington
Rodmarton
Kemble
Ewen
South Cerney
Down Ampney
Marston Meysey
Kempsford
Upper Inglesham
Buscot
Faringdon
Tetbury Upton
Culkerton
Ashley
Poole Keynes
Somerford Keynes
Shorncote
Cerney Wick
Latton
Castle Eaton
Hannington Wick
Tetbury
Long Newton
Chedglow
Crudwell
Chelworth
Oaksey
Eastcourt
Ashton Keynes
North End
Leigh
Cricklade
Chelworth Upper Green
Chelworth Lower Green
Hannington
Hampton
Coleshill
Great Coxwell
Little Coxwell
Highworth
Watchfield
Longcot
Broad Blunsdon
Blunsdon St. Andrew
Stanton Fitzwarren
Sevenhampton
Shrivenham
Shipton Moyne
Brokenborough
Easton Grey
Hankerton
Perry Green
Charlton
Minety
Upper Minety
Purton Stoke
Purton
Widham
Haydon Wick
Penhill
Kingsdown
South Marston
Woolstone
Compton Beauchamp
Bourton
Garsdon
Malmesbury
Milbourne
Lea
Foxley
Cleverton
The Common
Restrop
Common Platt
Lydiard Millicent
Nine Elms
Stratton St. Margaret
Covingham
Walcot
SEE PAGE 212
SWINDON
Ashbury
Idstone
Bishopstone
Horpit
Norton
Corston
Rodbourne
Little Somerford
Brinkworth
Callow Hill
Hook
Lydiard House
Eastleaze
Even Swindon
Okus
Coate
Hinton Parva
Wanborough
Liddington
Hullavington
Great Somerford
Dauntsey Green
Grittenham
Woodshaw
Wootton Bassett
Studley Grange
Wroughton
North Wroughton
Elcombe
Hodson
Badbury
Lower Stanton St. Quintin
Startley
Dauntsey
Tockenham Wick
Lower Seagry
Upper Seagry
Stanton St. Quintin
Dauntsey Lock
Bradenstoke
Lyneham
Tockenham
Church End
Overtown
Chiseldon
Baydon
LEIGH DELAMERE
Kington St. Michael
Sutton Benger
Christian Malford
Preston
Bushton
White Horse
Broad Town
Draycot Foliat
Upper Upham
Foxham
Goatacre
Clyffe Pypard
Uffcott
Barbury Castle
Woodsend
Aldbourne
Kington Langley
East Tytherton
Charlcutt
Hilmarton
Clevancy
Broad Hinton
Winterbourne Bassett
Hardenhuish
Langley Burrell
Maud Heath's Causeway
West Tytherton
Marlborough Downs
Ogbourne St. George
CHIPPENHAM
Bremhill
Berwick Bassett
Winterbourne Monkton
Ogbourne St. Andrew
Preston
Rowden Hill
Studley
Calne
Compton Bassett
Yatesbury
Cherhill
Rockley
Ogbourne Maizey
Ramsbury
Knighton
Lackham
Derry Hill
Quemerford
Avebury
Avebury Trusloe
Marlborough
Axford
Mildenhall
Stitchcombe
Froxfield
Notton
Reybridge
Bowood House
Sandy Lane
Calstone Wellington
Beckhampton
West Kennett
East Kennett
Fyfield
Manton
Preshute
St. Margaret's
Gastard
Lacock
Bowden Hill
Chittoe
Stockley
Silbury Hill
West Overton
Lockeridge
Chisbury
Beanacre
Heddington
Westbrook
Sandridge
Cadley
Clench Common
Savernake Forest
Shaw
MELKSHAM
Bromham
Netherstreet
St. Edith's Marsh
Bourton
Bishops Cannings
Allington
Stanton St. Bernard
Huish
Wootton Rivers
Great Bedwyn
Durley
Bowerhill
Sells Green
Rowde
Roundway
Horton
Alton Priors
Alton Barnes
Oare
New Mill
Stibb Green
Crofton
Semington
Seend Cleeve
Seend
Coate
All Cannings
Honey Street
Wilcot
Pewsey
Burbage
Eastcourt
Wilton
DEVIZES
Nursteed
Etchilhampton
Woodborough
Milton Lilbourne
Easton Royal
West Grafton
East Grafton
Marten
Poulshot
Stert
Beechingstoke
Gores
Bottlesford
Hilcott
Manningford Bruce
Southcott
Pewsey White Horse
Wexcombe
Tidcombe
Hilperton
Great Hinton
Potterne
Patney
Wedhampton
Marden
Ashton Common
Keevil
Bulkington
Worton
Potterne Wick
Urchfont
Chirton
Wilsford
North Newnton
Manningford Bohune
Pewsey Down
Steeple Ashton
Marston
Conock
Charlton
Rushall
Aughton
Collingbourne Kingston
Brunton
Eastcott
DANGER AREA
Upavon
Lower
W I L T S H I R E
V A L E O F P E W S E Y

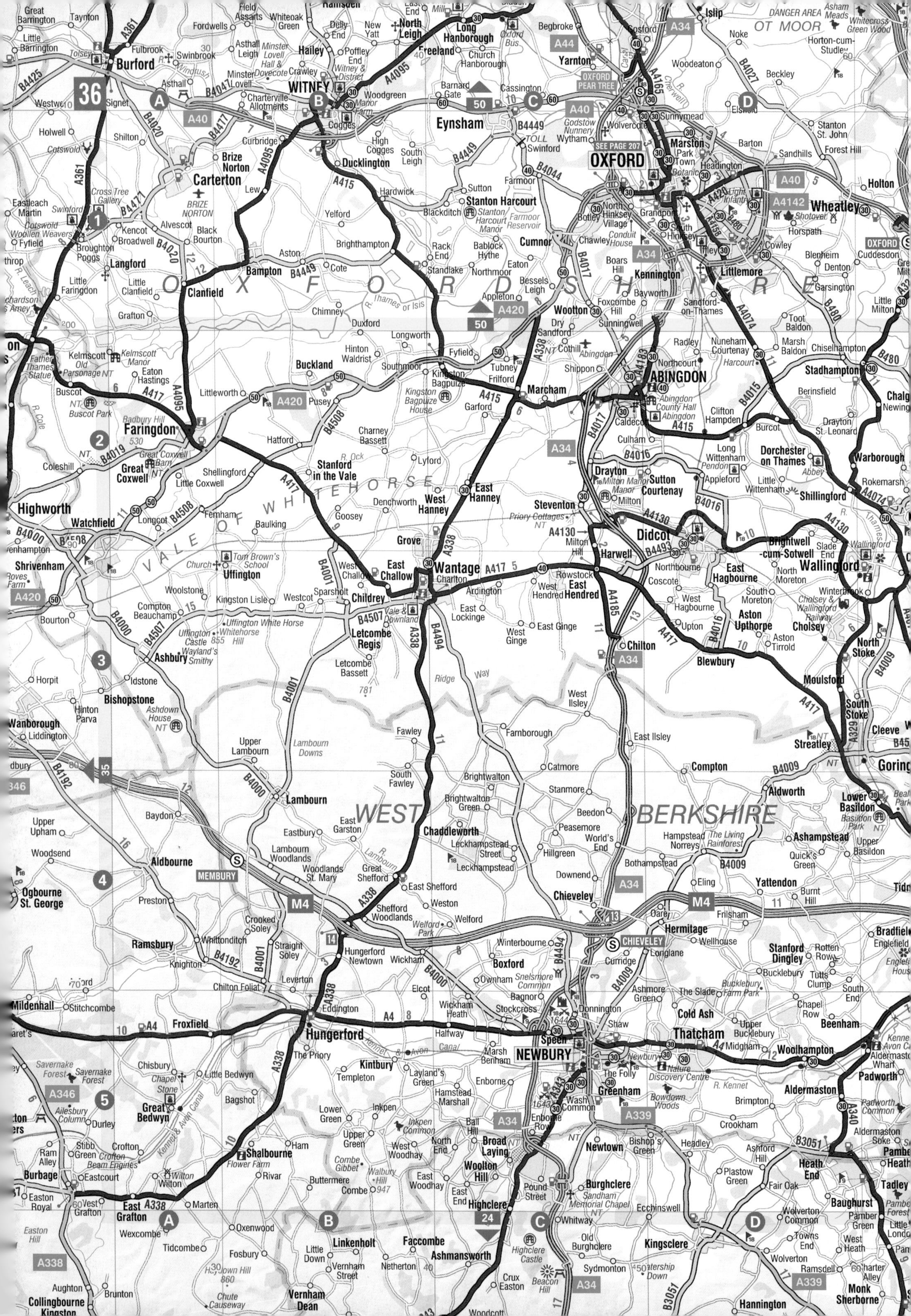
36
35
50
24
A
B
C
D
1
2
3
4
5
Burford
Witney
Carterton
Eynsham
OXFORD
SEE PAGE 207
Wheatley
Abingdon
ABINGDON
Faringdon
Highworth
Shrivenham
Wantage
Didcot
Wallingford
Hungerford
NEWBURY
Thatcham
O X F O R D S H I R E
VALE OF WHITEHORSE
WEST
BERKSHIRE
OT MOOR
Great Barrington
Taynton
Little Barrington
Fulbrook
Swinbrook
Asthall
Signet
Westwell
Holwell
Shilton
Brize Norton
BRIZE NORTON
Alvescot
Black Bourton
Kencot
Broadwell
Broughton Poggs
Langford
Little Faringdon
Little Clanfield
Clanfield
Bampton
Aston
Cote
Grafton
Kelmscott
Kelmscott Manor
Eaton Hastings
Buscot
Buscot Park
Coleshill
Great Coxwell
Little Coxwell
Shellingford
Watchfield
Longcot
Fernham
Baulking
Uffington
Tom Brown's School
Woolstone
Compton Beauchamp
Kingston Lisle
Uffington White Horse
Uffington Castle
Wayland's Smithy
Whitehorse Hill
Ashbury
Bourton
Idstone
Bishopstone
Hinton Parva
Horpit
Wanborough
Liddington
Ashdown House
Upper Lambourn
Lambourn Downs
Lambourn
Eastbury
East Garston
Lambourn Woodlands
Woodlands St. Mary
Great Shefford
East Shefford
Shefford Woodlands
Weston
Welford
Welford Park
Baydon
Aldbourne
Upper Upham
Woodsend
Ogbourne St. George
Preston
Ramsbury
Whittonditch
Crooked Soley
Straight Soley
Knighton
Chilton Foliat
Leverton
MEMBURY
M4
A4
A40
A420
A415
A417
A338
A34
A4095
A4074
A4130
A4185
A339
A343
A346
A329
B4000
B4001
B4009
B4016
B4017
B4019
B4020
B4044
B4047
B4192
B4449
B4494
B4507
B4508
A44
A4142
Minster Lovell
Crawley
Hailey
Ducklington
Curbridge
Cogges
High Cogges
South Leigh
Hardwick
Yelford
Brighthampton
Standlake
Northmoor
Stanton Harcourt
Sutton
Cassington
Yarnton
Begbroke
Long Hanborough
Church Hanborough
Freeland
North Leigh
Swinford
Farmoor
Cumnor
Botley
North Hinksey Village
Wolvercote
Marston
Headington
Kennington
Littlemore
Cowley
Iffley
Sandford-on-Thames
Wootton
Boars Hill
Sunningwell
Appleton
Eaton
Bessels Leigh
Fyfield
Kingston Bagpuize
Tubney
Frilford
Marcham
Garford
Charney Bassett
Lyford
Stanford in the Vale
Hatford
Buckland
Pusey
Longworth
Hinton Waldrist
Southmoor
Littleworth
Goosey
Denchworth
West Hanney
East Hanney
Grove
East Challow
West Challow
Childrey
Sparsholt
Letcombe Regis
Letcombe Bassett
Ardington
East Lockinge
East Hendred
West Hendred
Rowstock
Harwell
Chilton
Steventon
Drayton
Milton
Sutton Courtenay
Culham
Radley
Nuneham Courtenay
Clifton Hampden
Long Wittenham
Little Wittenham
Dorchester on Thames
Warborough
Shillingford
Stadhampton
Chiselhampton
Brightwell-cum-Sotwell
East Hagbourne
West Hagbourne
Blewbury
Aston Upthorpe
Aston Tirrold
Cholsey
Moulsford
North Stoke
South Stoke
Streatley
Goring
Lower Basildon
Compton
Aldworth
West Ilsley
East Ilsley
Farnborough
Fawley
South Fawley
Brightwalton
Chaddleworth
Catmore
Beedon
Chieveley
CHIEVELEY
Hermitage
Curridge
Boxford
Winterbourne
Bagnor
Donnington
Speen
Shaw
Cold Ash
Greenham
Enborne
Kintbury
Inkpen
Shalbourne
Great Bedwyn
Little Bedwyn
Froxfield
Burbage
East Grafton
Highclere
Highclere Castle
Burghclere
Kingsclere
Woolton Hill
Newtown
Aldermaston
Woolhampton
Tadley
Baughurst
Heath End
Linkenholt
Faccombe
Ashmansworth
Vernham Dean
Oxenwood
Fosbury
Tidcombe
Collingbourne Kingston

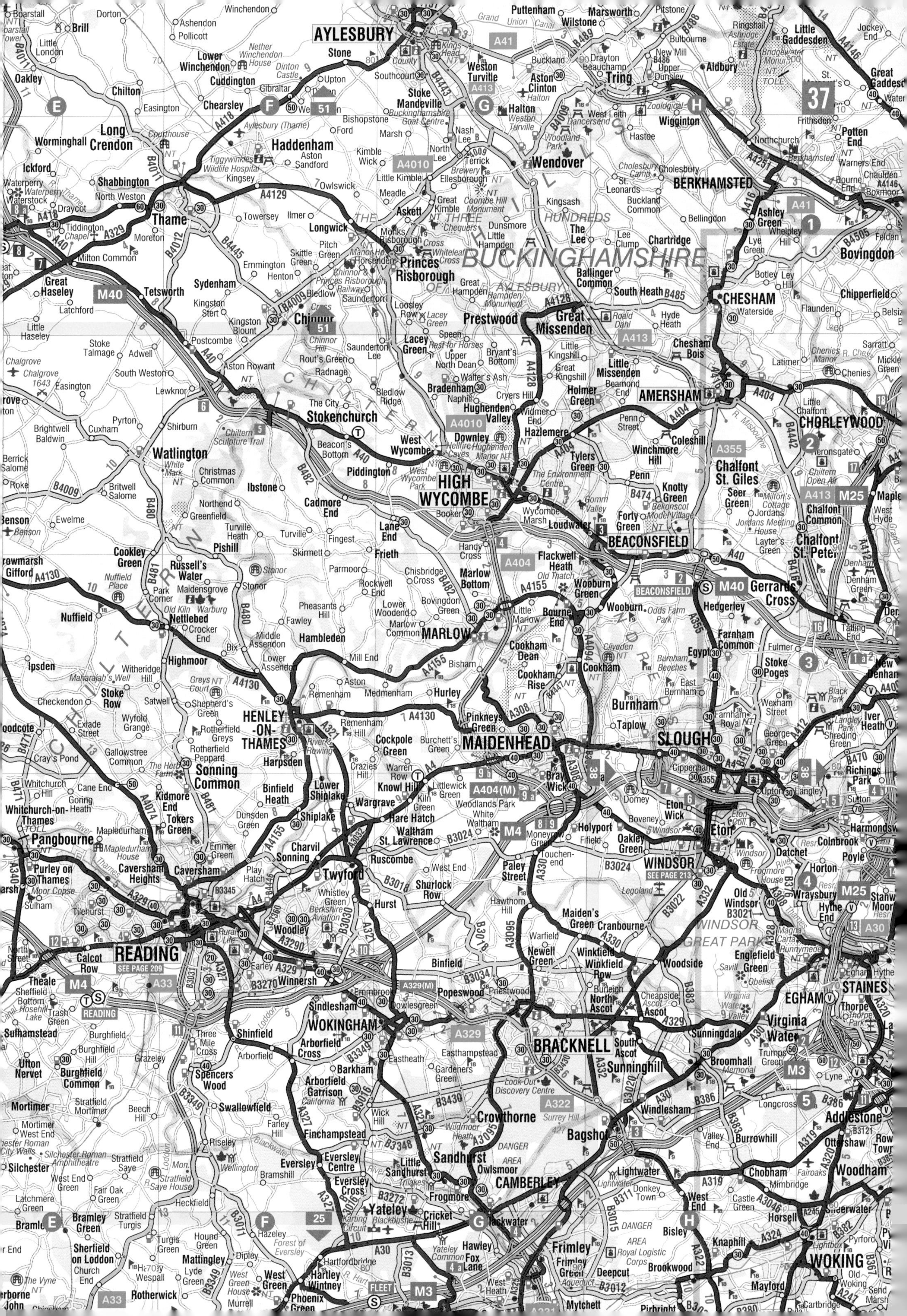

Boarstall
Brill
Dorton
Winchendon
Ashendon
Pollicott
AYLESBURY
Puttenham
Marsworth
Pitstone
Grand Union Canal
Wilstone
Ringshall
Little Gaddesden
Jockey End
Little London
Oakley
Lower Winchendon
Nether Winchendon House
Stone
Dinton Castle
Upton
Cuddington
Gibraltar
Kings Head
County
Southcourt
Weston Turville
Buckland
Aston Clinton
Drayton Beauchamp
New Mill
Bulbourne
Tring
Upper Dunsley
Aldbury
Great Gaddesden
Chilton
Easington
Chearsley
Stoke Mandeville
Buckinghamshire Goat Centre
Halton
Weston Turville
West Leith
Dancersend
Zoological
Wigginton
Hastoe
Frithsden
Potten End
37
Long Crendon
Worminghall
Courthouse
Aylesbury (Thame)
Bishopstone
Ford
Haddenham
Aston Sandford
Marsh
Nash Lee
North Lee
Terrick
Wendover
Woodland Park
Northchurch
Berkhamsted
Warners End
Ickford
Waterperry
Waterstock
Shabbington
North Weston
Draycot
Thame
Tiggywinkles Wildlife Hospital
Kingsey
Kimble Wick
Little Kimble
Ellesborough
Brewery
Coombe Hill Monument
Cholesbury Camp
Cholesbury
St. Leonards
Buckland Common
BERKHAMSTED
Ashley Green
Chaulden
Bourne End
Boxmoor
Owlswick
Meadle
Askett
Great Kimble
THE CHILTERN HUNDREDS
Kingsash
Bellingdon
Whelpley Hill
Bovingdon
Felden
Tiddington
Chapel
Moreton
Towersey
Ilmer
Longwick
Monks Risborough
Whiteleaf Cross
Chequers
Dunsmore
Little Hampden
The Lee
Lee Clump
Chartridge
Lye Green
Milton Common
Great Haseley
Latchford
Tetsworth
Emmington
Henton
Sydenham
Skittle Green
Pitch Green
Manor Ho
Horsenden
Chinnor & Princes Risborough Railway
Princes Risborough
BUCKINGHAMSHIRE
Ballinger Common
Great Hampden
Hampden Monument
VALE OF AYLESBURY
Botley
Ley Hill
CHESHAM
Waterside
Chipperfield
South Heath
Little Haseley
Kingston Stert
Kingston Blount
Bledlow
Saunderton
Chinnor
Loosley Row
Lacey Green
Prestwood
Great Missenden
Roald Dahl
Hyde Heath
Flaunden
Belsize
Stoke Talmage
Adwell
Postcombe
Chinnor Hill
Saunderton Lee
Lacey Green
Speen
Rest for Horses
Upper North Dean
Bryant's Bottom
Little Kingshill
Great Kingshill
Little Missenden
Chesham Bois
Chenies Manor
Sarratt
Latimer
Chenies
Mickle Green
Chalgrove
Chalgrove 1643
South Weston
Aston Rowant
Rout's Green
Radnage
Walter's Ash
Bradenham
Naphill
Cryers Hill
Holmer Green
Beamond End
AMERSHAM
Easington
Lewknor
Bledlow Ridge
The City
Stokenchurch
Hughenden Valley
Widmer End
Penn Street
Little Chalfont
CHORLEYWOOD
Pyrton
Cuxham
Brightwell Baldwin
Shirburn
Chiltern Sculpture Trail
Watlington
White Mark
Beacon's Bottom
West Wycombe
Downley
Hellfire Caves
Hughenden Manor
Hazlemere
Winchmore Hill
Coleshill
Heronsgate
Berrick Salome
Christmas Common
Piddington
HIGH WYCOMBE
Tylers Green
Penn
Chalfont St. Giles
Chiltern Open Air
Roke
Britwell Salome
Ibstone
West Wycombe Park
The Environment Centre
Knotty Green
Seer Green
Milton's Cottage
Maple
Northend
Cadmore End
Booker
Wycombe Marsh
Gomm Valley
Bekonscot Model Village
Forty Green
Jordans
Jordans Meeting House
Chalfont Common
West Hyde
Benson
Ewelme
Greenfield
Turville Heath
Turville
Fingest
Lane End
Loudwater
BEACONSFIELD
Layter's Green
Chalfont St. Peter
Pishill
Skirmett
Frieth
Handy Cross
Flackwell Heath
Old Thatch
Crowmarsh Gifford
Cookley Green
Russell's Water
Stonor
Nuffield Place
Park Corner
Maidensgrove
Parmoor
Rockwell End
Chisbridge Cross
Marlow Bottom
Wooburn Green
BEACONSFIELD
Gerrards Cross
Denham
Denham Green
Nuffield
Old Kiln
Warburg
Nettlebed
Crocker End
Pheasants Hill
Fawley
Lower Woodend
Bovingdon Green
Marlow Common
MARLOW
Little Marlow
Bourne End
Wooburn
Odds Farm Park
Hedgerley
Farnham Common
Tatling End
Ipsden
Middle Assendon
Bix
Hambleden
Mill End
Bisham
Cookham Dean
Cliveden
Burnham Beeches
Egypt
Fulmer
Stoke Poges
New Denham
Witheridge Hill
Maharajah's Well
Highmoor
Greys Court
Lower Assendon
Aston
Remenham
Medmenham
Hurley
Cookham
Cookham Rise
East Burnham
Black Park
Checkendon
Stoke Row
Satwell
Shepherd's Green
HENLEY-ON-THAMES
Remenham Hill
River & Rowing
Pinkneys Green
Burnham
Wexham Street
Iver Heath
Woodcote
Exlade Street
Wyfold Grange
Rotherfield Greys
Rotherfield Peppard
Gallowstree Common
Harpsden
Cockpole Green
Burchett's Green
MAIDENHEAD
Taplow
SLOUGH
Farnham Royal
George Green
Shreding Green
Langley Park
Cray's Pond
The Herb Farm
Sonning Common
Crazies Hill
Warren Row
Knowl Hill
Littlewick Green
Bray Wick
Cippenham
Richings Park
Whitchurch Hill
Cane End
Goring Heath
Kidmore End
Binfield Heath
Lower Shiplake
Shiplake
Wargrave
Kiln Green
Hare Hatch
Woodlands Park
White Waltham
Dorney
Eton Wick
Boveney
Windsor
Upton
Langley
Sutton
Whitchurch-on-Thames
Toll
Mapledurham
Mapledurham House
Tokers Green
Dunsden Green
Waltham St. Lawrence
Holyport
Moneyrow Green
Fifield
Oakley Green
Eton
Harmondsworth
Colnbrook
Pangbourne
Purley on Thames
Moor Copse
Caversham Heights
Caversham
Emmer Green
Charvil
Sonning
Play Hatch
Twyford
Ruscombe
West End
Paley Street
Touchen-end
WINDSOR
SEE PAGE 213
Datchet
Poyle
Horton
Sulham
Tilehurst
Whistley Green
Berkshire Aviation
Hurst
Shurlock Row
Hawthorn Hill
Legoland
Frogmore House
Old Windsor
Wraysbury
Stanwell Moor
Hythe End
WINDSOR GREAT PARK
Magna Carta
Runnymede
North Street
Calcot Row
READING
SEE PAGE 209
Earley
Woodley
Rural Life
Warfield
Newell Green
Maiden's Green
Cranbourne
Winkfield
Winkfield Row
Woodside
Englefield Green
Savill Garden
Obelisk
Egham Hythe
STAINES
Theale
Winnersh
Binfield
Popeswood
Prestwood
Burleigh
North Ascot
Cheapside
Ascot
EGHAM
Thorpe
Thorpe Park
Sheffield Bottom
Hosehill Lake
Trash Green
READING
Sindlesham
Emmbrook
Dowlesgreen
Virginia Water
Virginia Valley
Sulhamstead
Burghfield
Three Mile Cross
Shinfield
WOKINGHAM
Arborfield Cross
Easthampstead
BRACKNELL
South Ascot
Sunninghill
Sunningdale
Trumps Green
Broomhall
Ufton Nervet
Burghfield Hill
Burghfield Common
Grazeley
Arborfield
Spencers Wood
Barkham
Eastheath
Gardeners Green
Look-Out Discovery Centre
Lyne
Mortimer
Stratfield Mortimer
Beech Hill
Swallowfield
Arborfield Garrison
California
Crowthorne
Surrey Hill
Windlesham
Longcross
Addlestone
Mortimer West End
Silchester Roman Amphitheatre
Riseley
Farley Hill
Wick Hill
Finchampstead
Wildmoor Heath
DANGER AREA
Bagshot
Valley End
Burrowhill
Ottershaw
Row Town
Silchester
West End Green
Stratfield Saye
Wellington
Stratfield Saye House
Bramshill
Eversley
Eversley Centre
Little Sandhurst
Sandhurst
Owlsmoor
Lightwater
Chobham
Mimbridge
Fairoaks
Woodham
Latchmere Green
Fair Oak Green
Heckfield
Eversley Cross
Frogmore
CAMBERLEY
Donkey Town
West End
Castle Green
Sheerwater
Bramley
Bramley Green
Stratfield Turgis
Hazeley
Yateley
Cricket Hill
Blackwater
Bisley
Horsell
Pyrford
Sherfield on Loddon
Turgis Green
Hound Green
Forest of Eversley
Hartfordbridge
Hawley
Yateley Common
Fox Lane
Frimley
Royal Logistic Corps
Knaphill
WOKING
Church End
The Vyne
Wespall
Mattingley
Dipley
Lyde Green
West Green House
West Green
Hartley Wintney
R. Hart
FLEET
West Heath
Frimley Green
Deepcut
Brookwood
Mayford
Old Woking
Send Marsh
Sherborne St John
Rotherwick
Murrell
Phoenix Green
Mytchett
Pirbright
Cartbridge
M40
M4
M25
M3
A41
A413
A4010
A4129
A418
A4128
A404
A355
A40
A4155
A4130
A4074
A4
A404(M)
A329
A329(M)
A33
A327
A321
A3095
A322
A30
A332
A330
A308
A412
A4155
B4009
B480
B481
B482
B3024
B3018
B3430
B3348
B3272
B3013

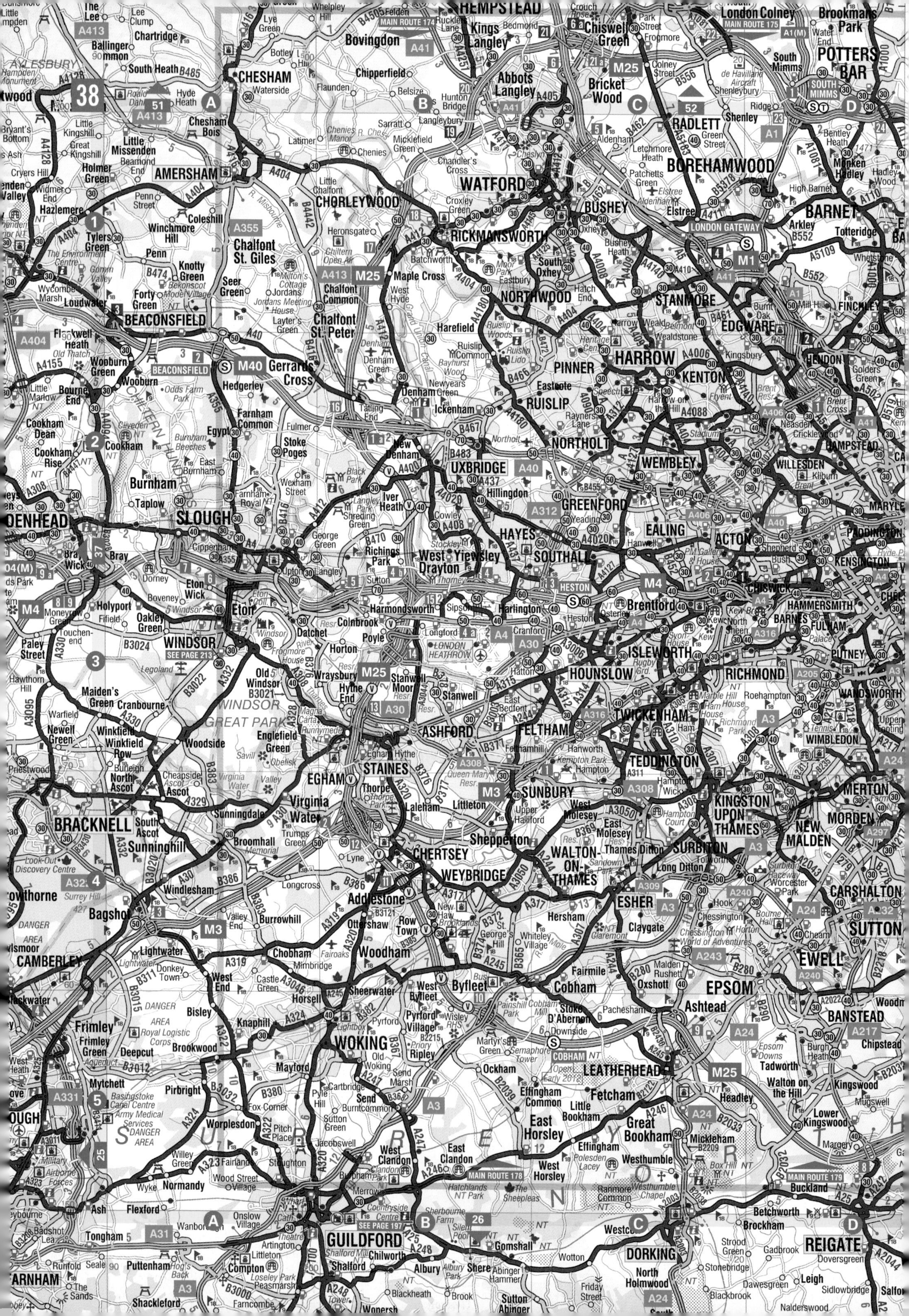
38
HEMPSTEAD
MAIN ROUTE 174
MAIN ROUTE 175
Kings Langley
Bovingdon
Chiswell Green
London Colney
Brookmans Park
POTTERS BAR
South Mimms
Park Street
Frogmore
Colney Street
Abbots Langley
Bricket Wood
Chipperfield
Chartridge
Ballinger Common
South Heath
CHESHAM
Chesham Bois
Hyde Heath
Little Kingshill
Great Kingshill
Little Missenden
Holmer Green
AMERSHAM
Chenies
Latimer
Sarratt
Langleybury
Hunton Bridge
Chandler's Cross
WATFORD
Aldenham
RADLETT
Shenley
Letchmore Heath
Patchetts Green
BOREHAMWOOD
Elstree
BUSHEY
Bushey Heath
Oxhey
South Oxhey
Croxley Green
RICKMANSWORTH
CHORLEYWOOD
Little Chalfont
Heronsgate
Batchworth
Maple Cross
Chalfont St. Giles
Chalfont Common
Chalfont St. Peter
Seer Green
Jordans
Knotty Green
Penn
Tylers Green
Hazlemere
Widmer End
Coleshill
Winchmore Hill
Forty Green
Loudwater
Wycombe Marsh
BEACONSFIELD
Flackwell Heath
Wooburn Green
Wooburn
Bourne End
Little Marlow
Cookham Dean
Cookham
Cookham Rise
Gerrards Cross
Hedgerley
Farnham Common
Fulmer
Stoke Poges
Egypt
Burnham
Taplow
Farnham Royal
Wexham Street
SLOUGH
Bray
Bray Wick
Holyport
Oakley Green
Fifield
Dorney
Boveney
Eton Wick
Eton
WINDSOR
SEE PAGE 213
Datchet
Old Windsor
Horton
Wraysbury
Colnbrook
Poyle
Langley
George Green
Iver Heath
Richings Park
West Drayton
Yiewsley
Denham
Denham Green
New Denham
Tatling End
Harefield
Ruislip Common
Ickenham
UXBRIDGE
Hillingdon
Cowley
NORTHWOOD
Eastbury
Hatch End
STANMORE
EDGWARE
Mill Hill
Burnt Oak
FINCHLEY
BARNET
High Barnet
Arkley
Totteridge
LONDON GATEWAY
PINNER
HARROW
KENTON
Harrow on the Hill
Kingsbury
HENDON
Golders Green
RUISLIP
Eastcote
Rayners Lane
NORTHOLT
WEMBLEY
Neasden
Cricklewood
HAMPSTEAD
WILLESDEN
Kilburn
GREENFORD
Yeading
HAYES
SOUTHALL
EALING
Hanwell
ACTON
Shepherd's Bush
KENSINGTON
CHISWICK
HAMMERSMITH
Brentford
HESTON
Harlington
Harmondsworth
Sipson
Longford
LONDON HEATHROW
Cranford
Osterley
ISLEWORTH
HOUNSLOW
Hatton
Stanwell
Stanwell Moor
Hythe End
RICHMOND
BARNES
FULHAM
PUTNEY
Roehampton
WANDSWORTH
TWICKENHAM
FELTHAM
East Bedfont
Hanworth
ASHFORD
STAINES
EGHAM
Egham Hythe
Englefield Green
WINDSOR GREAT PARK
TEDDINGTON
Hampton
Hampton Wick
WIMBLEDON
KINGSTON UPON THAMES
MERTON
MORDEN
NEW MALDEN
SUNBURY
Upper Halliford
Littleton
Laleham
Thorpe
Virginia Water
Sunningdale
Ascot
North Ascot
Winkfield
Winkfield Row
Woodside
Cranbourne
Maiden's Green
Warfield
Newell Green
Hawthorn Hill
Paley Street
Touchen-end
BRACKNELL
South Ascot
Sunninghill
Broomhall
Trumps Green
Lyne
CHERTSEY
Shepperton
West Molesey
East Molesey
WALTON-ON-THAMES
Thames Ditton
Long Ditton
SURBITON
Tolworth
Worcester Park
CARSHALTON
SUTTON
WEYBRIDGE
Addlestone
Ottershaw
Row Town
New Haw
St. George's Hill
Hersham
ESHER
Claygate
Hook
Chessington
EWELL
Cheam
Crowthorne
Windlesham
Bagshot
Longcross
Burrowhill
Valley End
CAMBERLEY
Lightwater
Donkey Town
West End
Chobham
Castle Green
Woodham
Byfleet
West Byfleet
Sheerwater
Horsell
Bisley
Knaphill
Frimley
Frimley Green
Deepcut
Brookwood
Mytchett
Pirbright
Mayford
WOKING
Pyrford
Pyrford Village
Ripley
Old Woking
Send Marsh
Send
Cartbridge
Burntcommon
Pyle Hill
Sutton Green
Worplesdon
Fox Corner
Pitch Place
Jacobswell
Stoughton
Willey Green
Fairlands
Wood Street Village
Normandy
Wyke
Flexford
Ash
Tongham
Wanborough
Onslow Village
GUILDFORD
SEE PAGE 197
Merrow
West Clandon
East Clandon
Cobham
Fairmile
Oxshott
Stoke D'Abernon
Downside
Ockham
Effingham Common
East Horsley
West Horsley
Little Bookham
Great Bookham
Effingham
Fetcham
LEATHERHEAD
Ashtead
EPSOM
Headley
Mickleham
Westhumble
BANSTEAD
Burgh Heath
Tadworth
Walton on the Hill
Kingswood
Lower Kingswood
Chipstead
MAIN ROUTE 178
MAIN ROUTE 179
Buckland
Betchworth
Brockham
REIGATE
DORKING
Westcott
Wotton
North Holmwood
Gomshall
Shere
Albury
Chilworth
Shalford
Artington
Compton
Puttenham
Seale
FARNHAM
Shackleford
Peasmarsh
Abinger Hammer
Sutton Abinger
Friday Street
Leigh
Strood Green
Gadbrook
M25
M40
M4
M3
M1

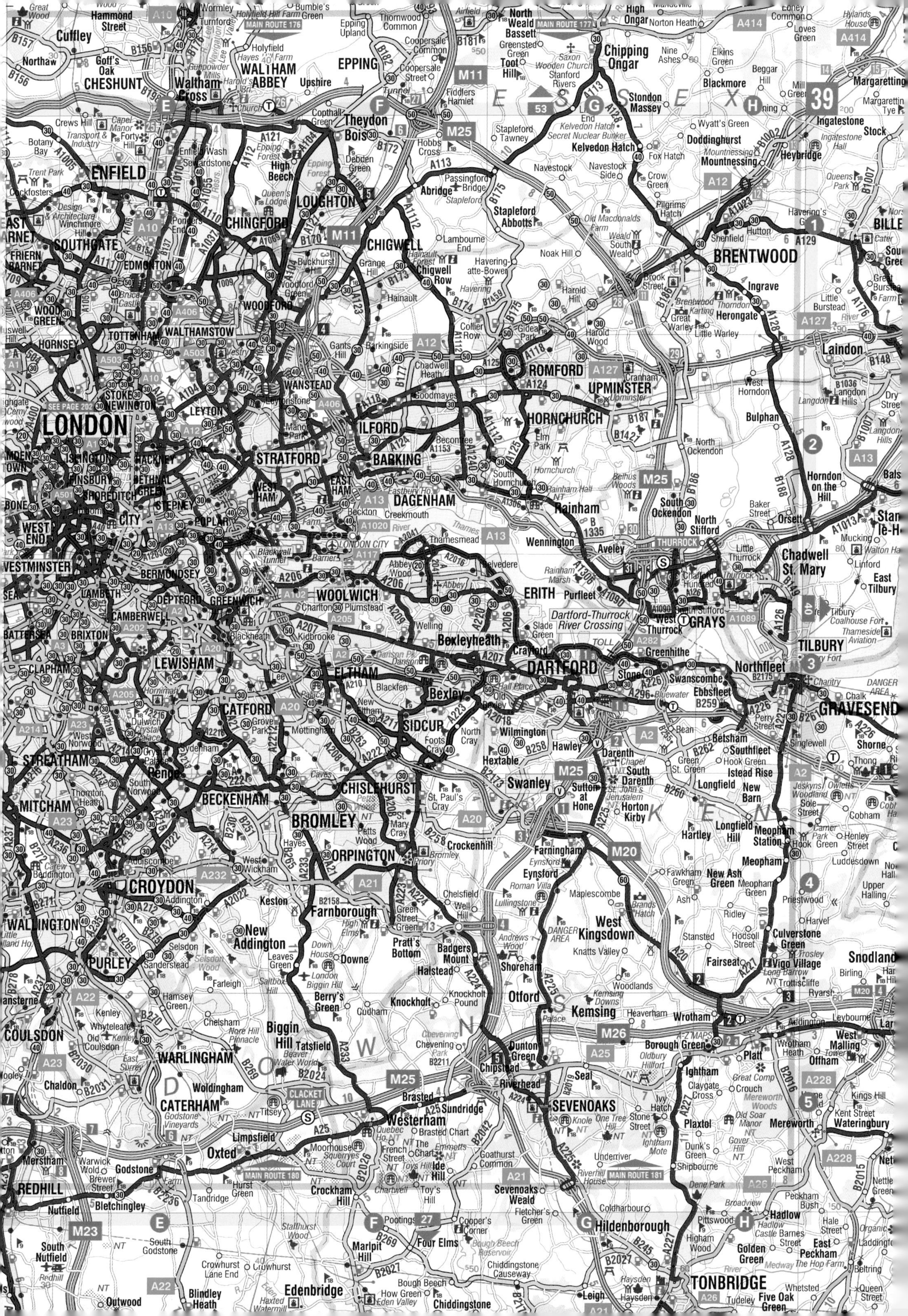
39
MAIN ROUTE 176
MAIN ROUTE 177
MAIN ROUTE 180
MAIN ROUTE 181
SEE PAGE 202
ESSEX
KENT
Great Wood
Hammond Street
Cuffley
Northaw
Goff's Oak
CHESHUNT
Wormley
Turnford
Holyfield Hill Farm
Bumble's Green
Holyfield
Hayes Hill Farm
WALTHAM ABBEY
Waltham Cross
Epping Upland
EPPING
Thornwood Common
Coopersale Common
Coopersale Street
Upshire
North Weald Bassett
Greensted Green
Toot Hill
Saxon Wooden Church
Stanford Rivers
High Ongar
Norton Heath
Chipping Ongar
Nine Ashes
Elkins Green
Blackmore
Beggar Hill
Mill Green
Margaretting
Margaretting Tye
Hylands House
Loves Green
Fiddlers Hamlet
Crews Hill
Capel Manor
Transport & Industry
Forty Hill
Botany Bay
Trent Park
Cockfosters
ENFIELD
Enfield Wash
Sewardstone
Theydon Bois
Copthall Green
High Beech
Epping Forest
Debden Green
Hobbs Cross
Stapleford Tawney
Kelvedon Hatch
Kelvedon Hatch Secret Nuclear Bunker
Stondon Massey
Wyatt's Green
Doddinghurst
Ingatestone
Ingatestone Hall
Stock
Mountnessing
Heybridge
Fox Hatch
Navestock
Navestock Side
Crow Green
Queens Park
Pilgrims Hatch
Passingford Bridge
Abridge
Stapleford
Stapleford Abbotts
LOUGHTON
Queen's Lodge
CHINGFORD
Ponders End
Design & Architecture
Winchmore Hill
SOUTHGATE
FRIERN BARNET
EDMONTON
CHIGWELL
Hainault Forest
Chigwell Row
Lambourne End
Grange Hill
Buckhurst Hill
Woodford Green
WOODFORD
Hainault
Havering-atte-Bower
Noak Hill
Old Macdonalds Farm
Weald South Weald
Shenfield
Hutton
Havering's Grove
BRENTWOOD
Brook Street
Ingrave
Brentwood Karting
Thorndon
Herongate
Great Warley
Little Warley
Little Burstead
Laindon
Harold Hill
Harold Wood
Collier Row
Gidea Park
WOOD GREEN
HORNSEY
TOTTENHAM
WALTHAMSTOW
Gants Hill
Barkingside
Chadwell Heath
ROMFORD
Cranham
UPMINSTER
West Horndon
Langdon Hills
Dry Street
Bulphan
STOKE NEWINGTON
LONDON
LEYTON
Leytonstone
WANSTEAD
Manor Park
ILFORD
Goodmayes
HORNCHURCH
Elm Park
North Ockendon
ISLINGTON
FINSBURY
HACKNEY
BETHNAL GREEN
SHOREDITCH
STRATFORD
WEST HAM
EAST HAM
BARKING
Becontree
DAGENHAM
Eastbury Ho.
South Hornchurch
Rainham Hall
Rainham
Belhus Woods
South Ockendon
North Stifford
Baker Street
Orsett
Horndon on the Hill
STEPNEY
CITY
WEST END
POPLAR
Beckton
Creekmouth
Thames
LONDON CITY
Thamesmead
Wennington
Aveley
THURROCK
Little Thurrock
Chadwell St. Mary
Mucking
Walton Hall
Linford
East Tilbury
WESTMINSTER
BERMONDSEY
Blackwall Tunnel
Barrier
Abbey Wood
Belvedere
Rainham Marsh
Purfleet
ERITH
Chafford Hundred
West Thurrock
GRAYS
South Stifford
Tilbury
Coalhouse Fort
Thameside Aviation
LAMBETH
DEPTFORD
GREENWICH
WOOLWICH
Charlton
Plumstead
CAMBERWELL
BATTERSEA
BRIXTON
Blackheath
Kidbrooke
Welling
Bexleyheath
Slade Green
Dartford-Thurrock River Crossing
TOLL
Greenhithe
Crayford
DARTFORD
Stone
Swanscombe
Bluewater
Ebbsfleet
Northfleet
TILBURY
GRAVESEND
Chantry
DANGER AREA
Chalk
CLAPHAM
LEWISHAM
Lee
Danson Park
ELTHAM
Blackfen
Bexley
Hall Place
Old Bexley
New Eltham
CATFORD
Horniman
Dulwich
Crystal Palace
Grove Park
Mottingham
SIDCUP
Foots Cray
North Cray
Wilmington
Hawley
Darenth
Bean
Betsham
Perry Street
Singlewell
Shorne
Thong
STREATHAM
West Norwood
Sydenham
Penge
South Norwood
Thornton Heath
BECKENHAM
CHISLEHURST
St. Paul's Cray
Hextable
Swanley
Sutton at Hone
Southfleet
Hook Green
Green St. Green
Longfield
Istead Rise
New Barn
Cobham
Jeskyns
Owletts
Sole Street
MITCHAM
Addiscombe
West Wickham
Hayes
BROMLEY
Petts Wood
St. Mary Cray
ORPINGTON
Crockenhill
Farningham
Eynsford
Roman Villa
Horton Kirby
South Darenth
Hartley
Longfield Hill
Meopham Station
Meopham
Camer
Hook Green
Henley Street
Luddesdown
Beddington
Carew
CROYDON
Addington
Keston
Farnborough
Green Street Green
Chelsfield
Well Hill
Lullingstone
Maplescombe
Fawkham Green
New Ash Green
Ash
Meopham Green
Upper Halling
Priestwood
WALLINGTON
New Addington
High Elms
Pratt's Bottom
Badgers Mount
DANGER AREA
West Kingsdown
Brands Hatch
Ridley
Harvel
Stansted
Hodsoll Street
Culverstone Green
Trosley
Vigo Village
Snodland
PURLEY
Sanderstead
Selsdon
Selsdon Wood
Leaves Green
Down House
Downe
Halstead
Andrews Wood
Shoreham
Knatts Valley
Fairseat
Long Barrow
Trottiscliffe
Birling
Ryarsh
Farleigh
London Biggin Hill
Berry's Green
Cudham
Knockholt
Knockholt Pound
Otford
Kemsing
Kemsing Downs
Woodlands
Heaverham
Wrotham
Addington
Leybourne
Hamsey Green
Kenley
Whyteleafe
Chelsham
Nore Hill Pinnacle
Old Coulsdon
COULSDON
Biggin Hill
Tatsfield
Beaver Water World
Chevening
Chevening Park
Dunton Green
Palace
Borough Green
West Malling
Wrotham Heath
Offham
WARLINGHAM
Woldingham
Chaldon
East Surrey
Chipstead
Riverhead
Seal
Oldbury Hillfort
Ightham
Platt
Great Comp
Crouch
Claygate Cross
CATERHAM
Godstone Vineyards
Titsey
CLACKET LANE
Brasted
Sundridge
SEVENOAKS
Knole
One Tree Hill
Stone Street
Ivy Hatch
Ightham Mote
Plaxtol
Old Soar Manor
Mereworth Woods
Mereworth
Kings Hill
Kent Street
Wateringbury
Limpsfield
Westerham
Quebec Ho.
Brasted Chart
The Chart
Emmetts
Oxted
Moorhouse
Squerryes Court
French Street
Toys Hill
Ide Hill
Goathurst Common
Underriver
Riverhill House
Gover Hill
Dunk's Green
Shipbourne
West Peckham
Nettlestead Green
Merstham
Warwick Wold
Godstone
Brewer Street
REDHILL
Bletchingley
Tandridge
Hurst Green
Crockham Hill
Chartwell
Toy's Hill
Sevenoaks Weald
Fletcher's Green
Dene Park
Broadview
Peckham Bush
Nutfield
South Nutfield
South Godstone
Stallhurst Wood
Pootings
Cooper's Corner
Four Elms
Bough Beech Reservoir
Coldharbour
Hildenborough
Pittswood
Hadlow
Hadlow Castle
Barnes Street
Hale Street
East Peckham
The Hop Farm
Golden Green
Higham Wood
Marlpit Hill
Chiddingstone Causeway
Beltring
Redhill
Crowhurst Lane End
Crowhurst
Outwood
Blindley Heath
Edenbridge
Haxted Watermill
How Green
Eden Valley
Bough Beech
Chiddingstone
Leigh
Haysden
TONBRIDGE
Tudeley
Five Oak Green
Whetsted
Queen Street
M11
M25
M20
M26
M23
A10
A12
A13
A414
A127
A128
A129
A2
A20
A21
A22
A23
A25
A26
A227
A228
A232
A406
A1
A503
A1020
A117
A206
A282
A1089
A102
A205
A202
A3
A214
A1090
A226
A296
B2175
B259
B261

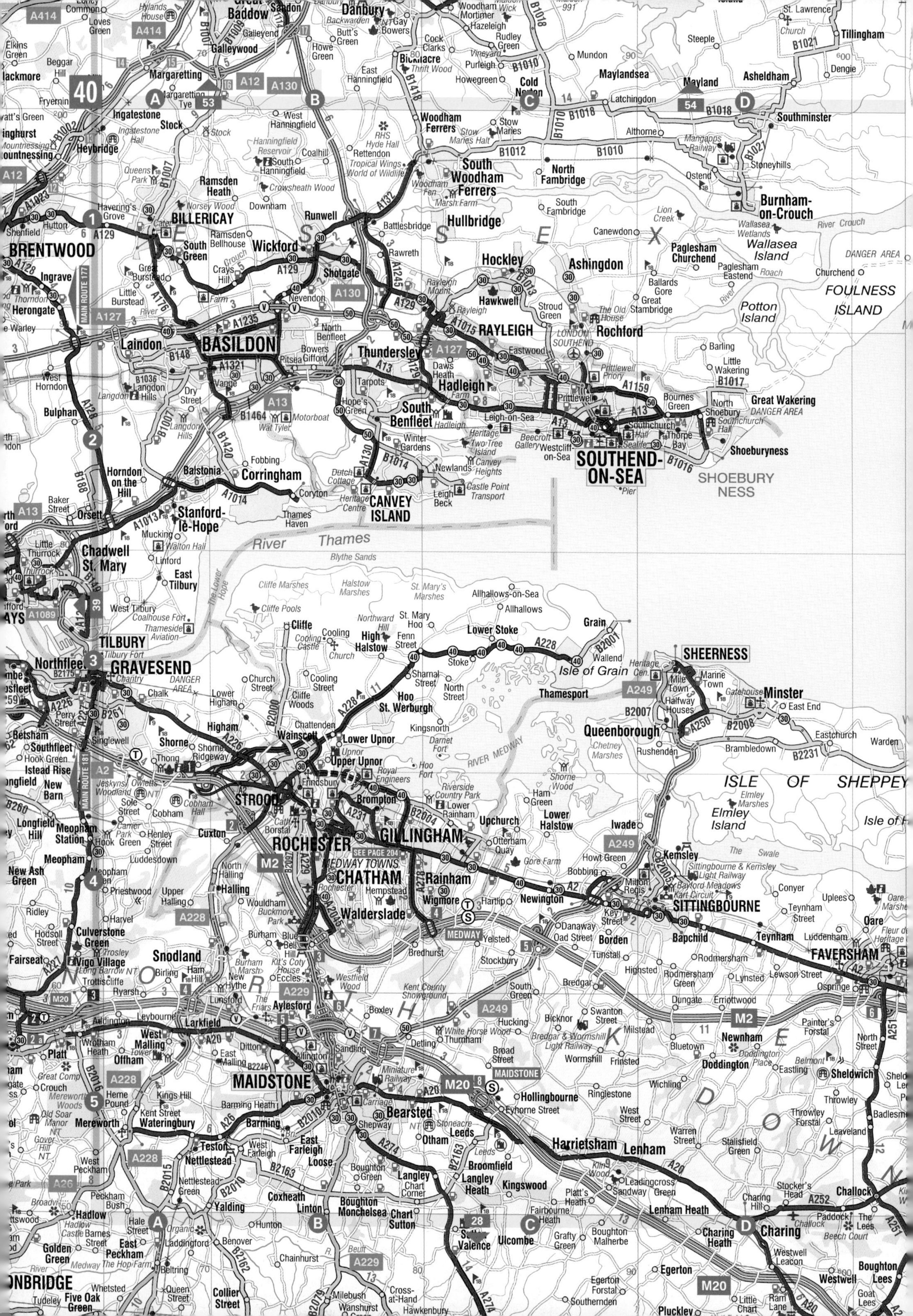

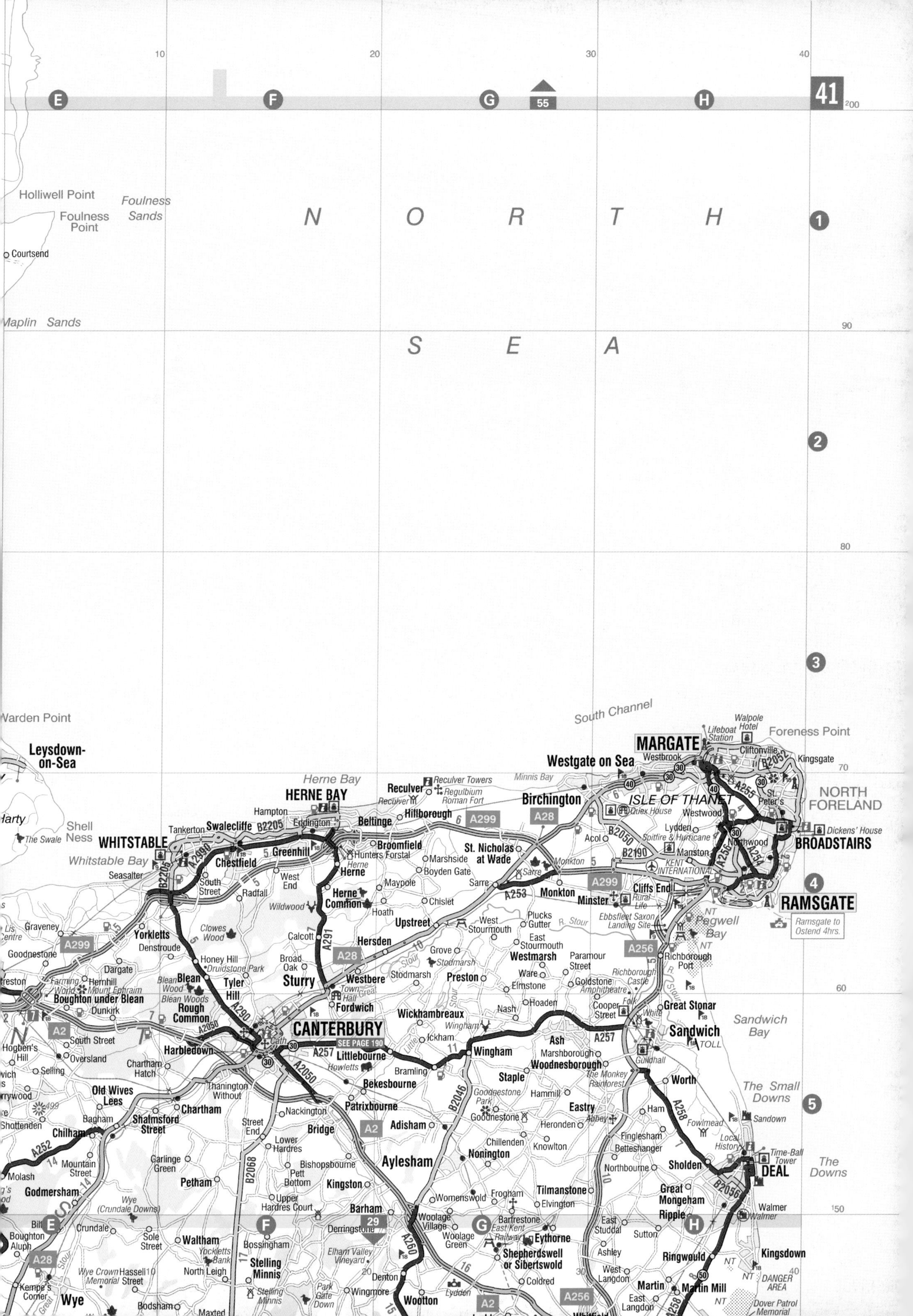

41
NORTH SEA
Holliwell Point
Foulness Point
Foulness Sands
Courtsend
Maplin Sands
Warden Point
Leysdown-on-Sea
South Channel
Foreness Point
MARGATE
Westgate on Sea
Birchington
ISLE OF THANET
NORTH FORELAND
BROADSTAIRS
RAMSGATE
Ramsgate to Ostend 4hrs.
Herne Bay
HERNE BAY
Reculver
WHITSTABLE
Whitstable Bay
Shell Ness
The Swale
CANTERBURY
SEE PAGE 190
Pegwell Bay
Sandwich Bay
Sandwich
The Small Downs
The Downs
DEAL
Walmer
Kingsdown
Aylesham
Wingham
Minster
Monkton
Sturry
Herne
Wye

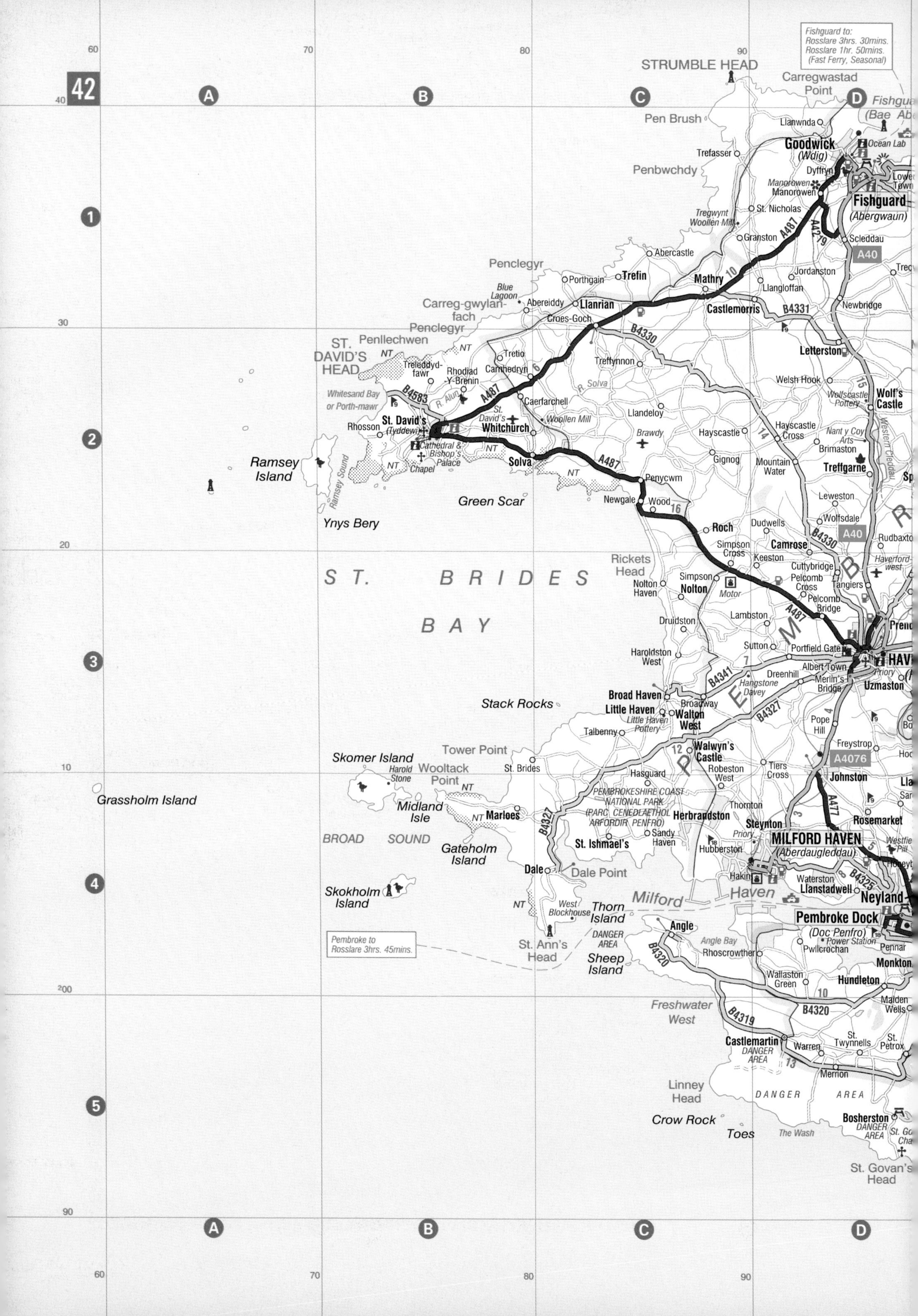
Fishguard to:
Rosslare 3hrs. 30mins.
Rosslare 1hr. 50mins.
(Fast Ferry, Seasonal)
STRUMBLE HEAD
Carregwastad Point
Fishguard (Bae Abergwaun)
Pen Brush
Llanwnda
Goodwick (Wdig)
Ocean Lab
Trefasser
Dyffryn
Penbwchdy
Manorowen
Fishguard (Abergwaun)
St. Nicholas
Tregwynt Woollen Mill
Granston
A487
Scleddau
A40
Abercastle
Penclegyr
Porthgain
Trefin
Mathry
Jordanston
Blue Lagoon
Abereiddy
Llanrian
Llangloffan
Carreg-gwylan-fach
Castlemorris
B4331
Newbridge
Croes-Goch
Penclegyr
ST. DAVID'S HEAD
Penllechwen
B4330
Letterston
Treleddyd-fawr
Tretio
Treffynnon
Rhodiad Y-Brenin
Carnhedryn
Welsh Hook
Whitesand Bay or Porth-mawr
B4583
R. Solva
Wolfscastle Pottery
Wolf's Castle
R. Alun
Caerfarchell
Llandeloy
Rhosson
St. David's (Tyddewi)
St. David's
Whitchurch
Woollen Mill
Brawdy
Hayscastle
Hayscastle Cross
Nant y Coy Arts
Brimaston
Ramsey Island
Cathedral & Bishop's Palace
Chapel
Solva
A487
Gignog
Mountain Water
Treffgarne
Ramsey Sound
Penycwm
Leweston
Green Scar
Newgale
Wood
Wolfsdale
Ynys Bery
Dudwells
Roch
Camrose
Simpson Cross
Keeston
B4330
Rudbaxton
Rickets Head
Cuttybridge
Haverfordwest
ST. BRIDES BAY
Simpson
Pelcomb
Nolton Haven
Nolton
Motor
Pelcomb Cross
Tangiers
Pelcomb Bridge
Druidston
Lambston
Sutton
Portfield Gate
Haroldston West
Albert Town
Dreenhill
Merlin's Bridge
Priory
Uzmaston
B4341
Hangstone Davey
Broad Haven
Stack Rocks
Little Haven
Broadway
Walton West
B4327
Little Haven Pottery
Pope Hill
Talbenny
Skomer Island
Tower Point
Walwyn's Castle
Freystrop
Harold Stone
Wooltack Point
St. Brides
Robeston West
Tiers Cross
A4076
Hasguard
Johnston
Grassholm Island
PEMBROKESHIRE COAST NATIONAL PARK (PARC CENEDLAETHOL ARFORDIR PENFRO)
Midland Isle
Marloes
Herbrandston
Thornton
A477
Rosemarket
B4327
Steynton
Sandy Haven
BROAD SOUND
Gateholm Island
St. Ishmael's
Hubberston
Priory
MILFORD HAVEN (Aberdaugleddau)
Dale
Dale Point
Hakin
Waterston
Llanstadwell
B4325
Neyland
Skokholm Island
West Blockhouse
Thorn Island
Milford Haven
Pembroke Dock (Doc Penfro)
Angle
Power Station
DANGER AREA
Angle Bay
Pennar
Pembroke to Rosslare 3hrs. 45mins.
St. Ann's Head
Sheep Island
B4320
Rhoscrowther
Pwllcrochan
Monkton
Wallaston Green
Hundleton
Freshwater West
B4319
B4320
Maiden Wells
Castlemartin
DANGER AREA
Warren
St. Twynnells
St. Petrox
Merrion
Linney Head
DANGER AREA
Bosherston
DANGER AREA
Crow Rock
Toes
The Wash
St. Govan's Head
NT
A
B
C
D
1
2
3
4
5
60
70
80
90
40
30
20
10
200
90

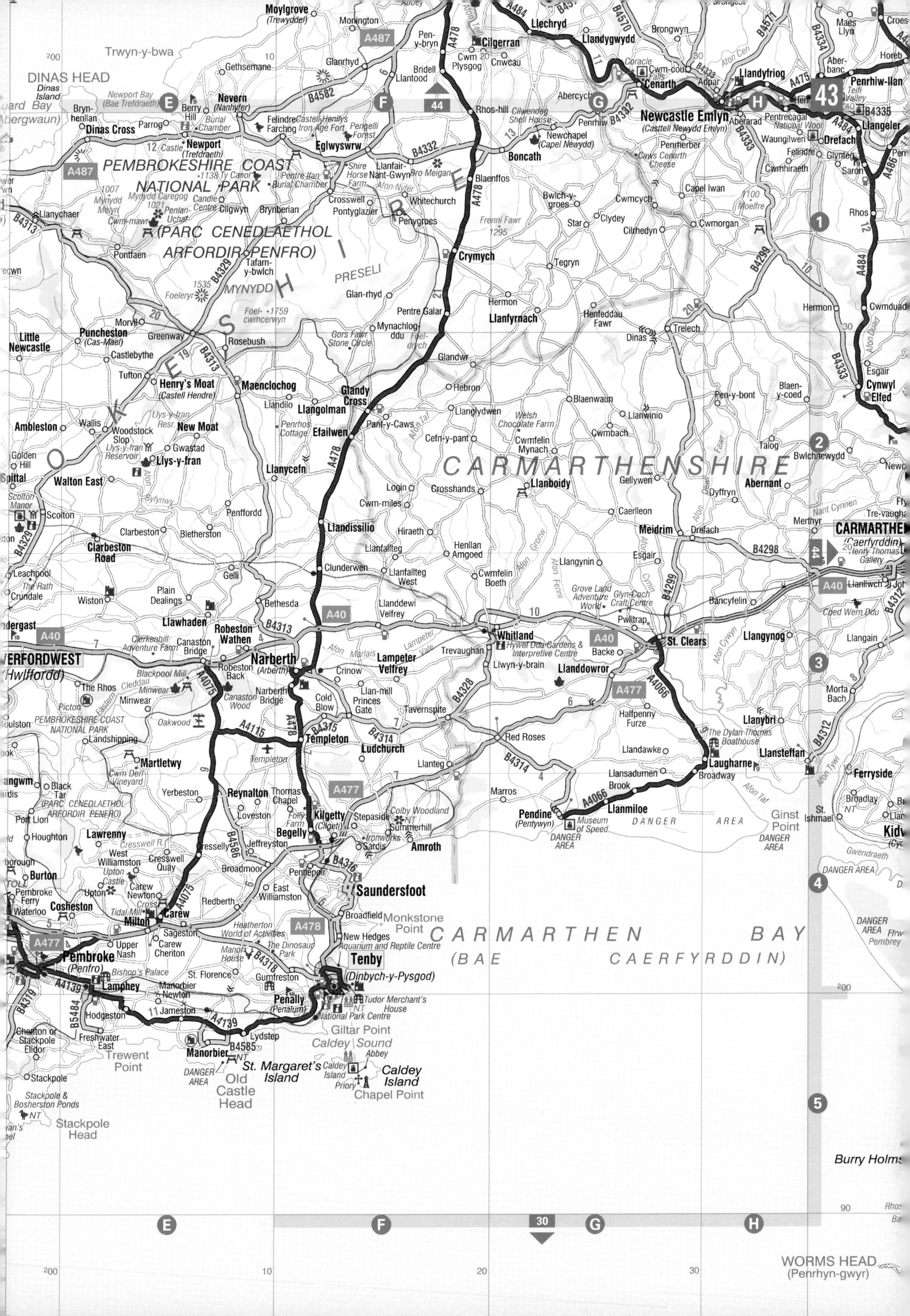
Moylgrove
(Trewyddel)
Monington
A487
Pen-y-bryn
A478
Cilgerran
A484
Llechryd
B4570
Brongwyn
B4571
Maes Llyn
Croes
Trwyn-y-bwa
Cwm Plysgog
Cnwcau
Glanrhyd
Bridell
Llantood
44
Llandygwydd
Coracle
Cwm-cou
Falls
Cenarth
B4333
Adpar
Llandyfriog
Aber-banc
Horeb
Penrhiw-llan
43
Teifi Valley
DINAS HEAD
Dinas Island
Gethsemane
Newport Bay
(Bae Trefdraeth)
E
Berry Hill
Nevern
(Nanhyfer)
Burial Chamber
B4582
F
Rhos-hill
Cilwendeg Shell House
Abercych
G
B4332
Penrhiw
Newcastle Emlyn
(Castell Newydd Emlyn)
Aberarad
H
Pentrecagal
National Wool
B4335
Llangeler
Drefach
Bryn-henllan
Dinas Cross
Parrog
Newport
(Trefdraeth)
Castle
Felindre Farchog
Castell Henllys Iron Age Fort
Pengelli Forest
Eglwyswrw
B4332
Boncath
Newchapel
(Capel Newydd)
Penrherber
Caws Cenarth Cheese
Waungilwen
Felindre
Glynteg
Saron
Cwmhiraeth
PEMBROKESHIRE COAST NATIONAL PARK
(PARC CENEDLAETHOL ARFORDIR PENFRO)
A487
1138 Ty Canol
Mynydd Caregog
Mynydd Melyn
Penlan-Uchaf
Cwm-mawr
Candle Centre
Cilgwyn
Brynberian
Pentre Ifan Burial Chamber
Shire Horse Farm
Llanfair-Nant-Gwyn
Bro Meigan
Afon Nyfer
Blaenffos
Crosswell
Pontyglazier
Whitechurch
Pen-y-groes
Bwlch-y-groes
Cwmcych
Capel Iwan
Moelfre
B4313
Llanychaer
Pontfaen
B4329
Tafarn-y-bwlch
Frenni Fawr
1295
Star
Clydey
Cilrhedyn
Cwmorgan
Rhos
Crymych
PRESELI
MYNYDD
Foeleyrr
1535
Foel-cwmcerwyn
1759
Glan-rhyd
Tegryn
B4299
A484
Hermon
Llanfyrnach
Henfeddau Fawr
Trelech
Dinas
Hermon
Cwmduad
Pentre Galar
Mynachlog-ddu
Gors Fawr Stone Circle
Foel-drych
Afon Duad
B4333
Esgair
Cynwyl Elfed
Little Newcastle
Puncheston
(Cas-Mael)
Greenway
Rosebush
B4313
Castlebythe
Glandwr
Tufton
Henry's Moat
(Castell Hendre)
Maenclochog
Glandy Cross
Hebron
Blaenwaun
Pen-y-bont
Blaen-y-coed
Llandilo
Llangolman
Llanglydwen
Llanwinio
Llys-y-fran Resr.
Ambleston
Wallis
Woodstock Slop
New Moat
Penrhos Cottage
Efailwen
Pant-y-Caws
Afon Taf
Welsh Chocolate Farm
Cwmbach
Cefn-y-pant
Cwmfelin Mynach
Talog
Bwlchnewydd
Llys-y-fran Reservoir
Gwastad
Llys-y-fran
Golden Hill
Spittal
Walton East
Llanycefn
A478
CARMARTHENSHIRE
Llanboidy
Gellywen
Abernant
Login
Crosshands
Scolton Manor
Scolton
Penffordd
Cwm-miles
Dyffryn
Caerlleon
Nant Cynnen
Tre-vaughan
Merthyr
CARMARTHEN
(Caerfyrddin)
Henry Thomas Gallery
Clarbeston
Bletherston
Llandissilio
Hiraeth
Meidrim
Drefach
B4329
Clarbeston Road
Llanfallteg
Henllan Amgoed
Afon Gronw
Esgair
B4298
Leachpool
The Rath
Crundale
Gelli
Clunderwen
Llanfallteg West
Cwmfelin Boeth
Llangynin
Afon Fenni
B4299
A40
Llanllwch
Wiston
Plain Dealings
Bethesda
Llanddewi Velfrey
Grove Land Adventure World
Glyn-Coch Craft Centre
Bancyfelin
Coed Wern Ddu
Llawhaden
A40
10
Pwlltrap
B4312
Haverfordwest
A40
Clerkenhill Adventure Farm
Canaston Bridge
Robeston Wathen
B4313
Whitland
A40
St. Clears
Llangynog
Llangain
HAVERFORDWEST
(Hwlffordd)
Blackpool Mill
Robeston Back
Narberth
(Arberth)
Afon Marlais
Lampeter Velfrey
Lampeter Vale
Trevaughan
Hywel Dda Gardens & Interpretive Centre
Backe
Afon Cywyn
Llwyn-y-brain
Llanddowror
The Rhos
Cleddau
Minwear
A4075
Canaston Wood
Narberth Bridge
Crinow
Cold Blow
Llan-mill
Princes Gate
B4328
A477
A4066
Morfa Bach
Picton
Eastern
Oakwood
A4115
Templeton
B4315
A478
B4314
Tavernspite
Halfpenny Furze
Llanybri
PEMBROKESHIRE COAST NATIONAL PARK
Landshipping
Ludchurch
Red Roses
The Dylan Thomas Boathouse
Llansteffan
B4312
Martletwy
Templeton
Llanteg
Llandawke
Laugharne
Ferryside
Cwm Deri Vineyard
B4314
Afon Tywi
Black Tar
Yerbeston
Reynalton
Thomas Chapel
A477
Marros
Llansadurnen
Broadway
Brook
Afon Taf
Broadlay
(PARC CENEDLAETHOL ARFORDIR PENFRO)
Loveston
Folly Farm
Kilgetty
(Cilgeti)
Stepaside
Colby Woodland
Summerhill
Pendine
(Pentywyn)
A4066
Llanmiloe
Museum of Speed
DANGER AREA
Ginst Point
St. Ishmael
Port Lion
Houghton
Lawrenny
B4586
Begelly
Cresswell R.
Jeffreyston
Cresselly
Ironworks
Sardis
Amroth
DANGER AREA
Kidwelly
West Williamston
Cresswell Quay
Broadmoor
B4316
Upton Castle
Burton
Carew Newton
Pentlepoir
Saundersfoot
Gwendraeth
DANGER AREA
4
Pembroke Ferry
Upton
Cross
East Williamston
Waterloo
Cosheston
Tidal Mill
Carew
A4075
Redberth
Milton
Broadfield
Monkstone Point
DANGER AREA
Pembrey
A477
Sageston
Heatherton World of Activities
A478
New Hedges
Aquarium and Reptile Centre
CARMARTHEN BAY
(BAE CAERFYRDDIN)
Pembroke
(Penfro)
Upper Nash
Carew Cheriton
Manor House
The Dinosaur Park
Tenby
(Dinbych-y-Pysgod)
Bishop's Palace
St. Florence
B4318
Gumfreston
Lamphey
Manorbier Newton
A4139
Penally
(Penalun)
Tudor Merchant's House
National Park Centre
B4319
B5484
Hodgeston
Jameston
A4139
Cheriton or Stackpole Elidor
Freshwater East
Lydstep
Giltar Point
Caldey Sound
Manorbier
B4585
Caldey Abbey
Trewent Point
DANGER AREA
Old Castle Head
St. Margaret's Island
Caldey Island
Priory
Caldey Island
Chapel Point
Stackpole
Stackpole & Bosherston Ponds
Stackpole Head
5
Burry Holms
E
F
30
G
H
WORMS HEAD
(Penrhyn-gwyr)

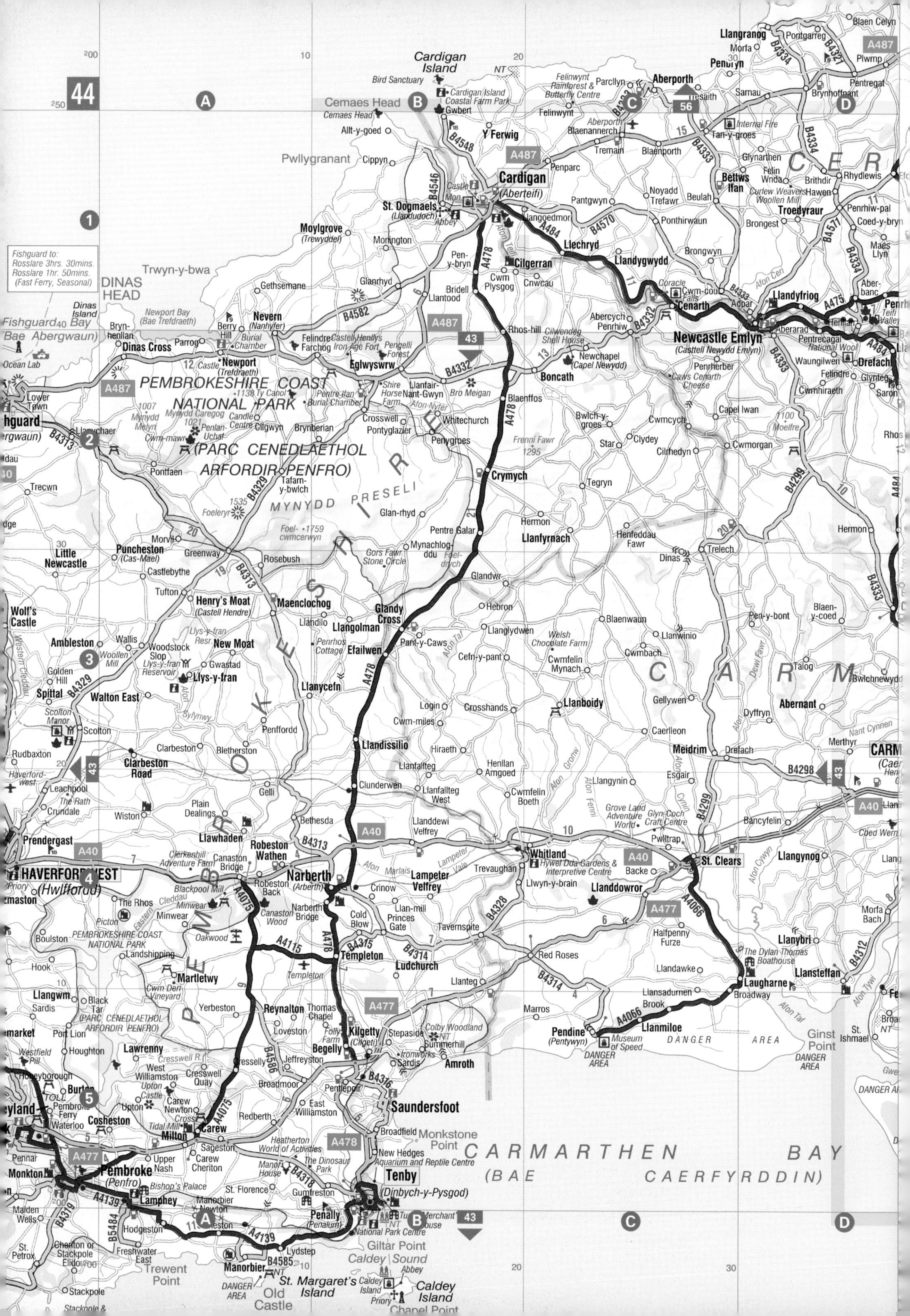
44
Cardigan Island
Bird Sanctuary
Cemaes Head
Cardigan Island Coastal Farm Park
Gwbert
Y Ferwig
Allt-y-goed
Pwllygranant
Cippyn
Cardigan
(Aberteifi)
St. Dogmaels
(Llandudoch)
Moylgrove
(Trewyddel)
Monington
Fishguard to:
Rosslare 3hrs. 30mins.
Rosslare 1hr. 50mins.
(Fast Ferry, Seasonal)
Trwyn-y-bwa
DINAS HEAD
Dinas Island
Fishguard Bay
(Bae Abergwaun)
Ocean Lab
Newport Bay
(Bae Trefdraeth)
Gethsemane
Glanrhyd
Nevern
(Nanhyfer)
Dinas Cross
Parrog
Newport
(Trefdraeth)
Felindre Farchog
Castell Henllys Iron Age Fort
Pengelli Forest
Eglwyswrw
PEMBROKESHIRE COAST NATIONAL PARK
(PARC CENEDLAETHOL ARFORDIR PENFRO)
Lower Town
Llanychaer
Pontfaen
Trecwn
Cilgwyn
Brynberian
Crosswell
Pontyglazier
Whitechurch
Penygroes
Llanfair-Nant-Gwyn
Bro Meigan
Tafarn-y-bwlch
MYNYDD PRESELI
Foeleryr
Glan-rhyd
Pentre Galar
Mynachlog-ddu
Gors Fawr Stone Circle
Foel-cwmcerwyn
Morvil
Greenway
Rosebush
Puncheston
(Cas-Mael)
Little Newcastle
Castlebythe
Tufton
Henry's Moat
(Castell Hendre)
Maenclochog
Llandilo
Llangolman
Glandy Cross
Wolf's Castle
Ambleston
Wallis
Woodstock Slop
New Moat
Gwastad
Llys-y-fran
Llys-y-fran Reservoir
Penrhos Cottage
Efailwen
Pant-y-Caws
Golden Hill
Spittal
Walton East
Llanycefn
Scolton Manor
Scolton
Penffordd
Rudbaxton
Clarbeston
Bletherston
Clarbeston Road
Llandissilio
Haverfordwest
Leachpool
The Rath
Crundale
Gelli
Clunderwen
Plain Dealings
Wiston
Bethesda
Llawhaden
Prendergast
HAVERFORDWEST
(Hwlffordd)
Robeston Wathen
Canaston Bridge
Robeston Back
Narberth
(Arberth)
Clerkenhill Adventure Farm
Blackpool Mill
Minwear
The Rhos
Picton
Canaston Wood
Narberth Bridge
Crinow
Cold Blow
Boulston
PEMBROKESHIRE COAST NATIONAL PARK
Oakwood
Landshipping
Templeton
Martletwy
Cwm Deri Vineyard
Hook
Llangwm
Sardis
Black Tar
(PARC CENEDLAETHOL ARFORDIR PENFRO)
Yerbeston
Reynalton
Thomas Chapel
Loveston
Kilgetty
(Cilgeti)
Begelly
Port Lion
Houghton
Lawrenny
Westfield Pill
West Williamston
Cresswell Quay
Cresselly
Jeffreyston
Honeyborough
Burton
Upton Castle
Carew Newton
Broadmoor
Pentlepoir
East Williamston
Redberth
Pembroke Ferry
Waterloo
Cosheston
Tidal Mill
Milton
Carew
Cross
Sageston
Carew Cheriton
Upper Nash
Heatherton World of Activities
The Dinosaur Park
Manor House
Pennar
Monkton
Pembroke
(Penfro)
Bishop's Palace
Lamphey
St. Florence
Gumfreston
Manorbier Newton
Jameston
Penally
(Penalun)
Hodgeston
Lydstep
Freshwater East
Trewent Point
Manorbier
Malden Wells
St. Petrox
Cheriton or Stackpole Elidor
Stackpole
DANGER AREA
Old Castle
St. Margaret's Island
Caldey Island
Priory
Chapel Point
Caldey Sound
Giltar Point
National Park Centre
Tudor Merchant's House
Tenby
(Dinbych-y-Pysgod)
New Hedges
Aquarium and Reptile Centre
Broadfield
Monkstone Point
Saundersfoot
Stepaside
Colby Woodland
Ironworks
Summerhill
Sardis
Amroth
Folly Farm
CARMARTHEN BAY
(BAE CAERFYRDDIN)
Pendine
(Pentywyn)
Museum of Speed
DANGER AREA
Llanmiloe
Marros
Llanteg
Red Roses
Tavernspite
Llan-mill
Princes Gate
Ludchurch
Lampeter Velfrey
Trevaughan
Whitland
Hywel Dda Gardens & Interpretive Centre
Llwyn-y-brain
Llanddowror
Llanddewi Velfrey
Llanfallteg
Llanfallteg West
Cwmfelin Boeth
Henllan Amgoed
Hiraeth
Cwm-miles
Login
Crosshands
Llanboidy
Cefn-y-pant
Llanglydwen
Hebron
Glandwr
Welsh Chocolate Farm
Cwmfelin Mynach
Blaenwaun
Llanwinio
Cwmbach
Llangynin
Grove Land Adventure World
Glyn-Coch Craft Centre
Pwlltrap
St. Clears
Backe
Halfpenny Furze
Llandawke
The Dylan Thomas Boathouse
Laugharne
Llansadurnen
Brook
Broadway
DANGER AREA
Ginst Point
DANGER AREA
Llansteffan
Llanybri
Morfa Bach
Llangynog
Bancyfelin
Meidrim
Drefach
Esgair
Caerlleon
Gellywen
Dyffryn
Abernant
Talog
Bwlchnewydd
Merthyr
Nant Cynnen
CARM
Pen-y-bont
Blaen-y-coed
Trelech
Dinas
Henfeddau Fawr
Hermon
Llanfyrnach
Tegryn
Hermon
Crymych
Frenni Fawr
Star
Clydey
Cilrhedyn
Cwmorgan
Bwlch-y-groes
Cwmcych
Capel Iwan
Blaenffos
Boncath
Newchapel
(Capel Newydd)
Rhos-hill
Cilwendeg Shell House
Abercych
Penrhiw
Cenarth
Coracle
Cwm-cou
Falls
Adpar
Newcastle Emlyn
(Castell Newydd Emlyn)
Penrherber
Caws Cenarth Cheese
Aberarad
Pentrecagal
National Wool
Waungilwen
Drefach
Felindre
Cwmhiraeth
Glynteg
Saron
Llandyfriog
Henllan
Llechryd
Llandygwydd
Cilgerran
Cwm Plysgog
Cnwcau
Llangoedmor
Pen-y-bryn
Bridell
Llantood
Pentwyn
Pantgwyn
Ponthirwaun
Brongwyn
Noyadd Trefawr
Beulah
Bettws Ifan
Felin Wnda
Brithdir
Curlew Weavers Woollen Mill
Hawen
Troedyraur
Brongest
Rhydlewis
Penrhiw-pal
Coed-y-bryn
Maes Llyn
Aber-banc
Penparc
Tremain
Blaenporth
Blaenannerch
Aberporth
Felinwynt
Felinwynt Rainforest & Butterfly Centre
Parcllyn
Aberporth
Tresaith
Tan-y-groes
Internal Fire
Glynarthen
Sarnau
Brynhoffnant
Pentregat
Penbryn
Llangranog
Morfa
Pontgarreg
Plwmp
Blaen Celyn
CER
A487
A478
A484
A40
A477
A4075
A4115
A4139
A4066
B4548
B4546
B4582
B4332
B4313
B4329
B4570
B4333
B4334
B4321
B4571
B4299
B4298
B4312
B4328
B4314
B4315
B4316
B4318
B4319
B5484
B4585
43
56
Cemaes Head

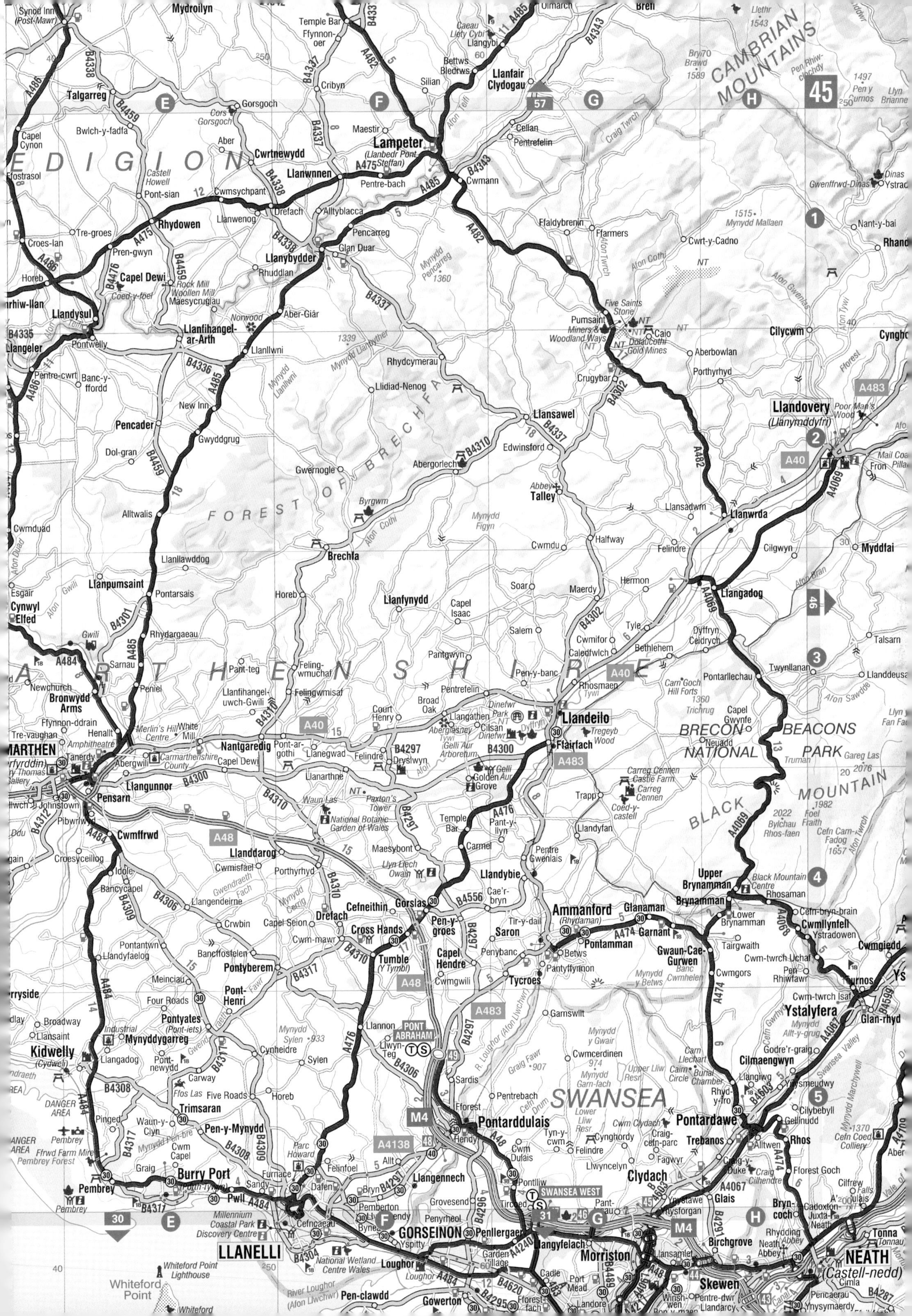

CAMBRIAN MOUNTAINS
45
CEREDIGION
CARMARTHENSHIRE
FOREST OF BRECHFA
BRECON BEACONS NATIONAL PARK
BLACK MOUNTAIN
SWANSEA
Synod Inn (Post-Mawr)
Mydroilyn
Temple Bar
Ffynnon-oer
Cribyn
Caeau Llety Cybi
Llangybi
Bettws Bledrws
Silian
Llanfair Clydogau
Llethr 1543
Bryn Brawd 1589
Pen Rhiw-ciochdy
Peny Garnos
Llyn Brianne
Talgarreg
Gorsgoch
Cors Gorsgoch
Bwlch-y-fadfa
Capel Cynon
Maestir
Lampeter (Llanbedr Pont Steffan)
Cellan
Pentrefelin
Craig Twrch
Aber
Cwrtnewydd
Llanwnnen
Pentre-bach
Cwmann
Ffostrasol
Castell Howell
Pont-sian
Cwmsychpant
Drefach
Alltyblacca
Llanwenog
Rhydowen
Tre-groes
Croes-lan
Pren-gwyn
Pencarreg
Glan Duar
Llanybydder
Mynydd Pencarreg 1360
Ffaldybrenin
Ffarmers
Cwrt-y-Cadno
Mynydd Mallaen
Gwenffrwd-Dinas
Dinas
Ystrad
Nant-y-bai
Rhandirmwyn
Horeb
Capel Dewi
Rock Mill Woollen Mill
Coed-y-foel
Maesycrugiau
Rhuddlan
Llandysul
Norwood
Aber-Giâr
Five Saints Stone
Pumsaint
Miners & Woodland Ways
Dolaucothi Gold Mines
Caio
Cilycwm
Llangeler
Pontwelly
Llanfihangel-ar-Arth
Llanllwni
Mynydd Llanllwni
Mynydd Llanybydder
Rhydcymerau
Aberbowlan
Porthyrhyd
Pentre-cwrt
Banc-y-ffordd
Llidiad-Nenog
Crugybar
Llandovery (Llanymddyfri)
Poor Man's Wood
New Inn
Pencader
Gwyddgrug
Llansawel
Edwinsford
Dol-gran
Gwernogle
Abergorlech
Abbey Talley
Mail Coach Pillar
Fron
Llansadwrn
Llanwrda
Alltwalis
Byrgwm
Mynydd Figyn
Cwmduad
Halfway
Cwmdu
Felindre
Cilgwyn
Myddfai
Llanllawddog
Brechfa
Esgair
Llanpumsaint
Soar
Maerdy
Hermon
Llangadog
Cynwyl Elfed
Pontarsais
Horeb
Llanfynydd
Capel Isaac
Salem
Tyle
Dyffryn Ceidrych
Talsarn
Rhydargaeau
Gwili
Cwmifor
Caledfwlch
Bethlehem
Twynllanan
Llanddeusant
Sarnau
Pant-teg
Feling-wmuchaf
Pantgwyn
Pen-y-banc
Rhosmaen
Pontarllechau
Carn Goch Hill Forts
Trichrug 1360
Capel Gwynfe
Newchurch
Bronwydd Arms
Peniel
Llanfihangel-uwch-Gwili
Felingwmisaf
Pentrefelin
Broad Oak
Court Henry
Llangathen
Aberglasney
Dinefwr Park
Cilsan
Llandeilo
Tregeyb Wood
Ffynnon-ddrain
Tre-vaughan
Henallt
Merlin's Hill Centre
White Mill
Amphitheatre
Carmarthen (Caerfyrddin)
Tanerdy
Abergwili
Carmarthenshire County Museum
Capel Dewi
Nantgaredig
Pont-ar-gothi
Llanegwad
Felindre
Dryslwyn
Gelli Aur Arboretum
Ffairfach
Neuadd
Garreg Las 2076
Trumau
Llangunnor
Pensarn
Llanarthne
Golden Grove
Gelli Aur
Carreg Cennen Castle Farm
Carreg Cennen
Trapp
Coed-y-castell
Johnstown
Paxton's Tower
National Botanic Garden of Wales
Waun Las
Temple Bar
Pant-y-llyn
Llandyfan
2022 Bylchau Rhos-faen
1982 Foel Fraith
Cefn Carn-Fadog 1657
Pibwrlwyd
Cwmffrwd
Maesybont
Carmel
Pentre Gwenlais
Croesyceiliog
Llanddarog
Cwmisfael
Porthyrhyd
Llyn Llech Owain
Llandybie
Upper Brynamman
Black Mountain Centre
Rhosaman
Idole
Bancycapel
Llangendeirne
Gwendraeth Fach
Mynydd Cerrig
Cefneithin
Drefach
Gorslas
Cae'r-bryn
Ammanford (Rhydaman)
Glanaman
Brynamman
Lower Brynamman
Cefn-bryn-brain
Cwmllynfell
Ystradowen
Cwmgiedd
Crwbin
Capel Seion
Cwm-mawr
Cross Hands
Pen-y-groes
Tir-y-dail
Saron
Pontamman
Garnant
Gwaun-Cae-Gurwen
Tairgwaith
Cwm-twrch Uchaf
Pontantwn
Llandyfaelog
Bancffosfelen
Pontyberem
Tumble (Y Tymbl)
Capel Hendre
Penybanc
Betws
Pantyffynnon
Mynydd y Betws
Banc Cwmhelen
Cwmgors
Pen Rhiwfawr
Gurnos
Meinciau
Pont-Henri
Cwmgwili
Tycroes
Cwm-twrch Isaf
Ystalyfera
Glan-rhyd
Four Roads
Pontyates (Pont-iets)
Garnswllt
Mynydd Allt-y-grug
Broadway
Llansaint
Industrial Museum
Mynyddygarreg
Mynydd Sylen 933
Llannon
Pont Abraham
Llwyn-Teg
Mynydd y Gwair
Cwmcerdinen
974 Mynydd Garn-fach
Carn Llechart
Cairn Circle
Burial Chamber
Godre'r-graig
Cilmaengwyn
Kidwelly (Cydweli)
Llangadog
Pont-newydd
Cynheidre
Sylen
Sardis
Graig Fawr 907
Upper Lliw Resr.
Swansea Valley
Carway
Ffos Las
Five Roads
Horeb
Pentrebach
Llanguicke
Rhyd-y-fro
Ynysmeudwy
Mynydd Marchywel
Danger Area
Pinged
Waun-y-Clyn
Trimsaran
Fforest
Pontarddulais
Lower Lliw Resr.
Cwm Clydach
Pontardawe
Gellinudd
Cilybebyll
1370 Cefn Coed Colliery
Pembrey
Ffrwd Farm Mire
Pembrey Forest
Pen-y-Mynydd
Mynydd Pen-bre
Cwm Capel
Parc Howard
Hendy
Tyn-y-cwm
Felindre
Cynghordy
Craig-cefn-parc
Trebanos
Alltwen
Rhos
Graig
Burry Port (Porth Tywyn)
Furnace
Felinfoel
Allt
Llangennech
Cwm Dulais
Llwyncelyn
Fagwyr
Craig-y-Duke
Craig Cilhendre
Fforest Goch
Cilfrew
Pwll
Sandy
Dafen
Bryn
Pontlliw
Swansea West
Clydach
Glais
Bryn-coch
Aberdulais
Cadoxton-Juxta-Neath
Pembrey
Millennium Coastal Park
Discovery Centre
Cefncaeau
Pemberton
Bynea
Llwynhendy
Grovesend
Penyrheol
Tircoed
Pant-lasau
Ynystawe
Ynysforgan
Rhydding
Neath Abbey
Tonna (Tonnau)
Llanelli
Gorseinon
Penllergaer
Llangyfelach
Morriston
Birchgrove
Neath (Castell-nedd)
Whiteford Point Lighthouse
Whiteford Point
National Wetland Centre Wales
Loughor
Ypsitty
Garden Village
Llansamlet
Skewen
Cimla
River Loughor (Afon Llwchwr)
Pen-clawdd
Gowerton
Cadle
Port Mead
Landore
Fforest-fach
Pentre-dwr
Llandarcy
Bon-y-maen
Pencaerau
Ynysymaerdy
Whiteford

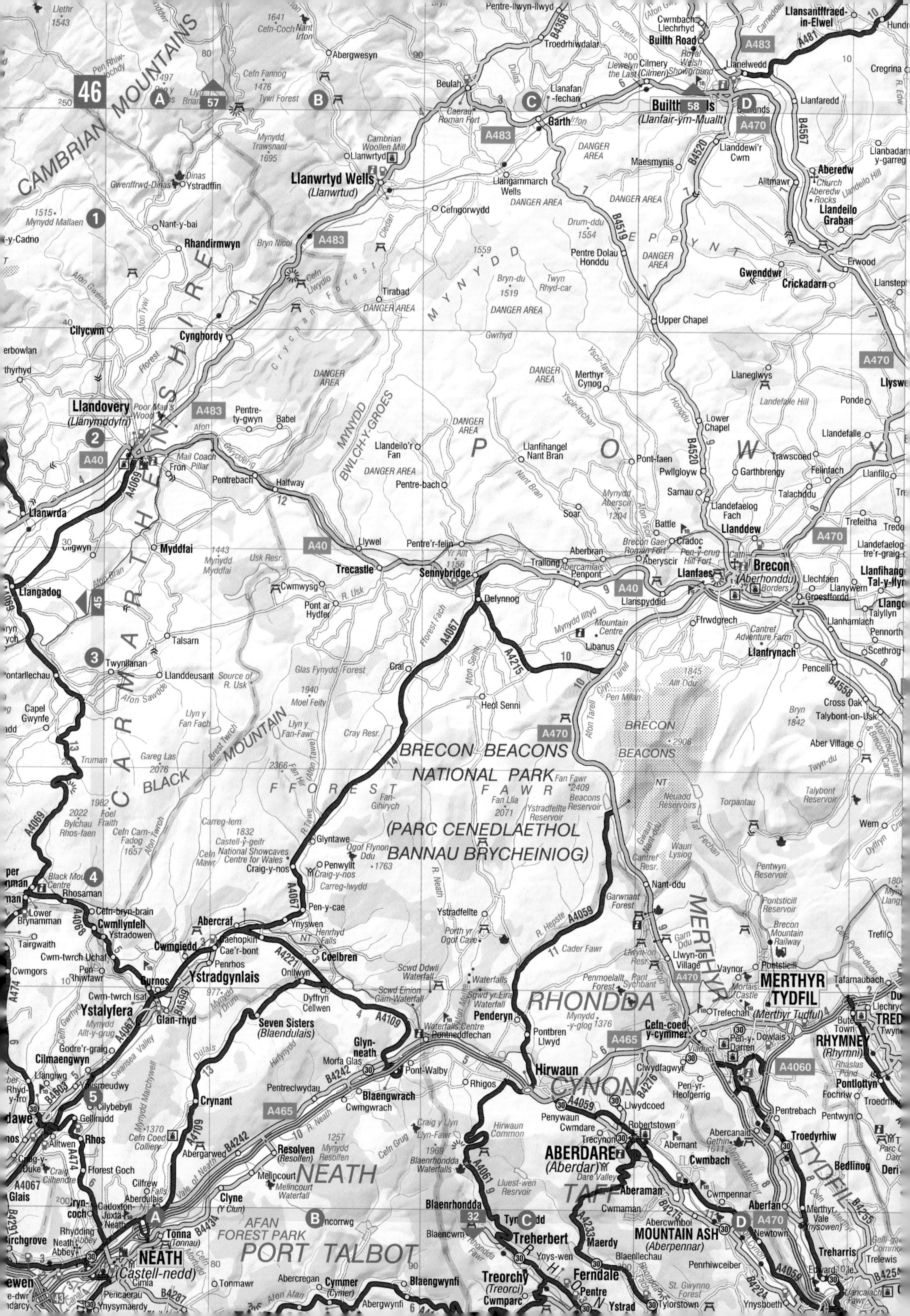
46
CAMBRIAN MOUNTAINS
Llethr 1543
1641 Cefn-Coch
Nant Irfon
Abergwesyn
Pentre-llwyn-llwyd
B4358
Troedrhiwdalar
Cwmbach Llechrhyd
Builth Road
Llansantffraed-in-Elwel
A481
A483
Llanelwedd
Cregrina
Pen Rhiw-ochdy
1497
Llyn Brianne
57
Cefn Fannog 1476
Tywi Forest
Beulah
Caerau Roman Fort
Llanafan-fechan
Llewelyn the Last (Cilmeri)
Cilmery
Royal Welsh Showground
Builth Wells
58
(Llanfair-ym-Muallt)
Llanfaredd
B4567
Garth
A470
Mynydd Trawsnant 1695
Cambrian Woollen Mill
Llanwrtyd
Llangammarch Wells
DANGER AREA
Maesmynis
B4520
Llanddewi'r Cwm
Aberedw
Church
Aberedw Rocks
Llandeilo Graban
Llanbadarn-y-garreg
Llandeilo Hill
Dinas
Gwenffrwd-Dinas
Ystradffin
Llanwrtyd Wells
(Llanwrtud)
Alltmawr
1515 Mynydd Mallaen
Nant-y-bai
Cefngorwydd
Drum-ddu 1554
B4519
E P P Y N T
Rhandirmwyn
Bryn Nicol
A483
Pentre Dolau Honddu
Erwood
Gwenddwr
Crickadarn
Llanstephan
1559
Cefn Llwydlo
Tirabad
M Y N Y D D
Bryn-du 1519
Twyn Rhyd-car
Crychan Forest
Afon Gwenlas
Aton Tywi
Cilycwm
Cynghordy
Upper Chapel
A470
Llyswen
Merthyr Cynog
Yscir-fawr
Yscir-fechan
Llaneglwys
Landefalle Hill
Ponde
Llandovery
(Llanymddyfri)
Poor Man's Wood
A483
Pentre-ty-gwyn
Babel
DANGER AREA
Lower Chapel
Llandefalle
MYNYDD BWLCH-Y-GROES
Llandeilo'r Fan
P
Llanfihangel Nant Bran
O
Pont-faen
W
Y
Trawscoed
Garthbrengy
Felinfach
Llanfilo
A40
A4069
Mail Coach Pillar
Fron
Pentrebach
Halfway
Pentre-bach
Pwllgloyw
Sarnau
Talachddu
Llanwrda
Soar
Mynydd Aberscir 1204
Llandefaelog Fach
Trefeitha
Battle
Llanddew
Cilgwyn
Myddfai
1443 Mynydd Myddfai
Usk Resr.
Llywel
A40
Pentre'r-felin
Yr Allt 1156
Aberbran
Brecon Gaer Roman Fort
Cradoc
Pen-y-crug Hill Fort
A470
Llandefaelog-tre'r-graig
Llangadog
45
Trecastle
Sennybridge
Trallong
Penpont
Aberyscir
Llanfaes
Brecon
(Aberhonddu)
Borders
Llechfaen
Llanfihangel Tal-y-llyn
Llanywern
Groesffordd
Cwmwysg
R. Usk
Pont ar Hydfer
Defynnog
A40
Llanspyddid
Ffrwdgrech
Llanhamlach
Llangorse
Talyllyn
Pennorth
Mynydd Illtyd
Mountain Centre
Libanus
Cantref Adventure Farm
Llanfrynach
Scethrog
Talsarn
Twynllanan
Llanddeusant
Source of R. Usk
Glas Fynydd Forest
Crai
A4067
A4215
Afon Senni
Pencelli
1845 Allt Ddu
Pen Milan
B4558
Cross Oak
Talybont-on-Usk
Bryn 1842
Heol Senni
Capel Gwynfe
Afon Sawdde
1940 Moel Feity
Llyn y Fan Fach
Llyn y Fan-Fawr
Cray Resr.
A470
BRECON
BEACONS
2906
Aber Village
Monmouthshire & Brecon Canal
Twyn-du
C A R M A R T H E N S H I R E
BLACK MOUNTAIN
Garreg Las 2076
Truman
2366 Fan Hir
BRECON BEACONS
NATIONAL PARK
Fan Fawr 2409
Beacons Reservoir
Fan Llia 2071
Ystradfellte Reservoir
NT
Neuadd Reservoirs
Torpantau
Talybont Reservoir
F F O R E S T
F A W R
Fan-Gihirych
1982
2022 Foel Fraith
Bychau Rhos-faen
Cefn Carn-Fadog 1657
Carreg-lem 1832
Castell-y-geifr
National Showcaves Centre for Wales
Cefn Mawr
Glyntawe
Ogof Ffynon Ddu
1763
(PARC CENEDLAETHOL
BANNAU BRYCHEINIOG)
Gwaun Nant-ddu
Waun Lysiog
Taf Fechan
Pentwyn Reservoir
Wern
Dyffryn Crawnon
Black Mountain Centre
Rhosaman
Penwyllt
Craig-y-nos
Carreg-lwydd
R. Neath
Cantref Resr.
Nant-ddu
Garwnant Forest
MERTHYR
Pontsticill Reservoir
Brecon Mountain Railway
Lower Brynamman
Cefn-bryn-brain
A4068
Cwmllynfell
Ystradowen
Abercraf
Pen-y-cae
Ynyswen
Henrhyd Falls
Ystradfellte
Porth yr Ogof Cave
R. Hepste
A4059
Garn Ddu
Llwyn-on Resr.
Llwyn-on Village
Trefil
Tairgwaith
Cwm-twrch Uchaf
Cwmgiedd
Caehopkin
Cae'r-bont
Penrhos
A4221
Coelbren
Sgwd Ddwli Waterfall
Waterfalls
Cader Fawr
Vaynor
Pontsticill
Cwmgors
Pen Rhiwfawr
Gurnos
Ystradgynlais
Onllwyn
Sgwd yr Eira Waterfall
Penmoelallt Forest
Pant Sychbant
A470
Morlais Castle
MERTHYR TYDFIL
Tafarnaubach
A474
Cwm-twrch Isaf
A4067
B4599
977
Dyffryn Cellwen
Scwd Einion Gam Waterfall
RHONDDA
Mynydd-y-glog 1376
Trefechan
(Merthyr Tudful)
Llechryd
Ystalyfera
Mynydd Allt-y-grug
Glan-rhyd
Seven Sisters
(Blaendulais)
A4109
Waterfalls Centre
Pontneddfechan
Penderyn
Pontbren Llwyd
Cefn-coed-y-cymmer
A465
Pen-y-Darren
Dowlais
Bute Town
RHYMNEY
(Rhymni)
Godre'r-graig
Swansea Valley
Dulais
Glyn-neath
Morfa Glas
B4242
Pont-Walby
Rhigos
Hirwaun
Viaduct
Clwydfagwyr
Pen-yr-Heolgerrig
A4060
Rhaslas Pond
Pontlottyn
Cilmaengwyn
Llangiwg
Ynysmeudwy
B4603
Pentreclwydau
Blaengwrach
Cwmgwrach
Hirwaun Common
CYNON
A4059
Llwydcoed
B4276
Fochriw
Troedrhiw
Cilybebyll
Gellinudd
Rhos
Alltwen
Crynant
A465
R. Neath
Craig y Llyn
Llyn-Fawr
1969
Penywaun
Cwmdare
Trecynon
Robertstown
Abernant
Pentrebach
Pentwyn
Abercanaid
Gethin
1611
Troedyrhiw
TYDFIL
Mynydd Marchywell
1370
Cefn Coed Colliery
A4109
Abergarwed
B4242
Resolven
(Resolfen)
1257
Mynydd Resolfen
Cefn Grug
Blaenrhondda Waterfalls
A4061
ABERDARE
(Aberdar)
Dare Valley
Cwmbach
Mynydd Merthyr
Bedlinog
Fforest Goch
A474
A4067
Glais
Cilfrew
Aberdulais
Falls
Vale of Neath
Melincourt
Melincourt Waterfall
NEATH
Lluest-wen Resrvoir
TAFF
Aberaman
Cwmaman
Cwmpennar
Aberfan
A470
Cefn
Merthyr Vale
(Ynysowen)
B4255
Bryn-coch
Cadoxton-Juxta-Neath
Clyne
(Y Clun)
A
B
Blaenrhondda
C
Treherbert
A4233
B4275
Abercwmboi
MOUNTAIN ASH
(Aberpennar)
D
Newtown
Rhydding
Neath Abbey
Tonna
(Tonnau)
B4434
AFAN FOREST PARK
Cwmcorrwg
32
Blaencwm
Rhondda Fawr
Maerdy
Blaenllechau
Penrhiwceiber
Treharris
Trelewis
Birchgrove
NEATH
(Castell-nedd)
PORT TALBOT
Tonmawr
Treorchy
(Treorci)
Ynys-wen
Ferndale
St. Gwynno Forest
A4059
Edwardsville
Abercregan
Cymmer
(Cymer)
Blaengwynfi
Pentre
Cwmparc
Ystrad
Tylorstown
Ynysboeth
B4224
Cimla
Pencaerau
Ynysymaerdy
B4287
Afon Afan
Abergwynfi
Llancaiach Fawr

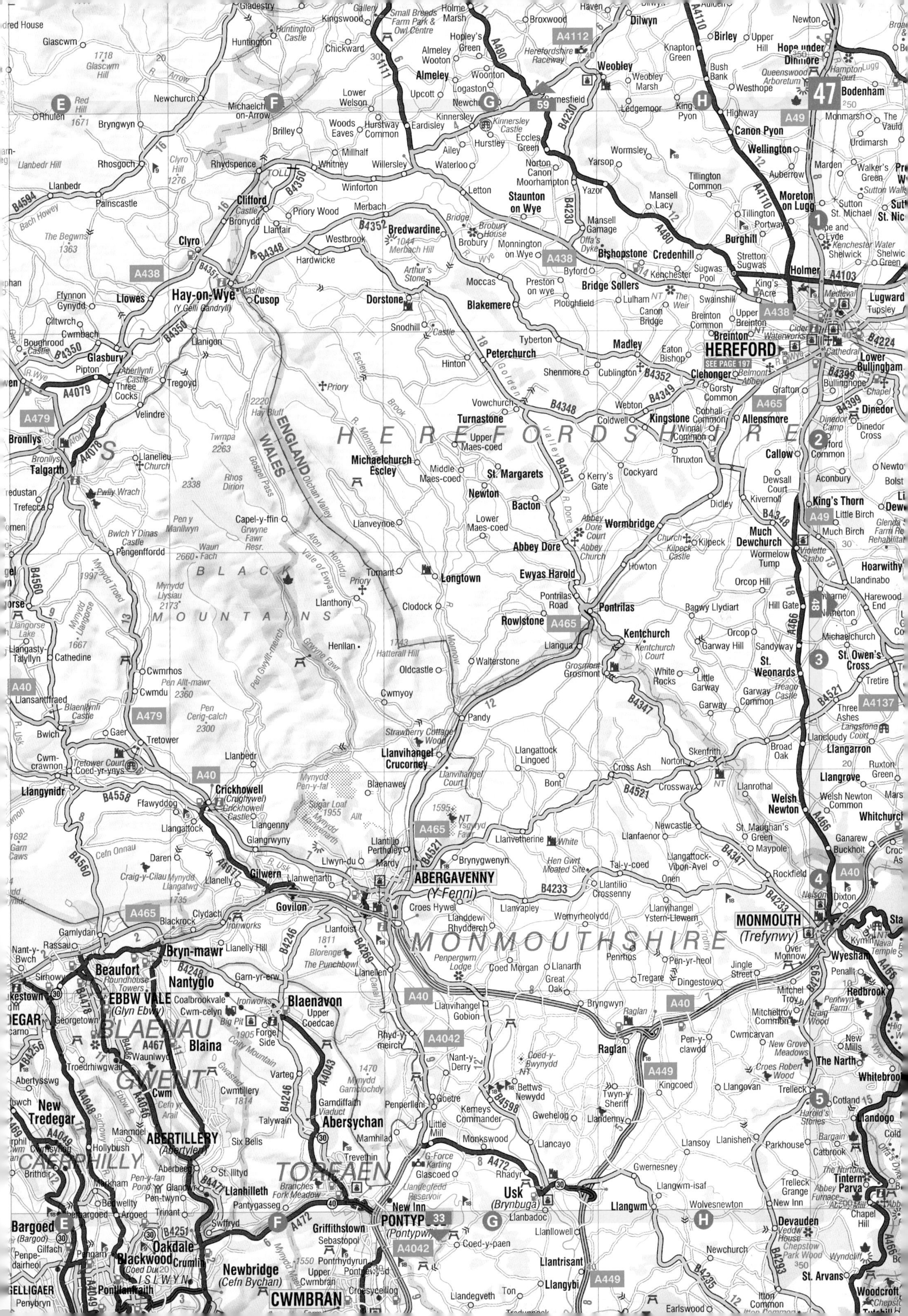

Gladestry
Kingswood
Small Breeds Farm Park & Owl Centre
Holme Marsh
Broxwood
Haven
Dilwyn
A4110
Birley
Upper Hill
Newton
Huntington Castle
Huntington
Chickward
Almeley Wooton
Hopley's Green
A4112
Herefordshire Raceway
Knapton Green
Hope under Dinmore
Glascwm
1718 Glascwm Hill
Almeley
Woonton
Weobley
Weobley Marsh
Bush Bank
Westhope
Queenswood Arboretum
Hampton Court
47
Bodenham
Newchurch
Michaelchurch-on-Arrow
Lower Welson
Upcott
Logaston
Newchurch
59
Garnesfield
Ledgemoor
King's Pyon
Highway
A49
Monmarsh
The Vauld
Red Hill 1671
Rhulen
Bryngwyn
Brilley
Woods Eaves
Hurstway Common
Eardisley
Kinnersley
Kinnersley Castle
Hurstley
Eccles Green
B4230
Canon Pyon
Urdimarsh
Llanbedr Hill
Rhosgoch
Clyro Hill 1276
Rhydspence
Millhalf
Whitney
Willersley
Ailey
Waterloo
Wormsley
Yarsop
Norton Canon
Moorhampton
Wellington
Marden
Walker's Green
Tillington Common
Auberrow
Sutton Walls
Llanbedr
Painscastle
B4594
Bach Howey
B4350
Winforton
Letton
Staunton on Wye
Yazor
Mansell Lacy
Moreton on Lugg
Sutton St. Michael
St. Nicholas
Clifford
Clifford Castle
Bronydd
Priory Wood
Merbach
B4352
Bredwardine
Bridge
Brobury House
Brobury
Mansell Gamage
Offa's Dyke
Tillington
Portway
Burghill
A4110
A480
Lyde
Kenchester Water
Shelwick
The Begwns 1363
Clyro
Llanfair
Westbrook
1044 Merbach Hill
Monnington on Wye
A438
Bishopstone
Credenhill
Stretton Sugwas
Holmer
A4103
Hardwicke
B4348
Arthur's Stone
Moccas
Preston on wye
Byford
Bridge Sollers
Kenchester
Sugwas Pool
King's Acre
Medieval
Lugwardine
A438
B4351
Hay-on-Wye
(Y Gelli Gandryll)
Cusop
Castle
Dorstone
Blakemere
Ploughfield
Lulham
The Weir
Swainshill
Breinton Common
Upper Breinton
Ffynnon Gynydd
Llowes
Ciltwrch
Cwmbach
Snodhill
Castle
Canon Bridge
Tupsley
Boughrood
Glasbury
B4350
Llanigon
Tyberton
Breinton
Cider
Waterworks
Cathedral
B4224
HEREFORD
SEE PAGE 197
Pipton
Aberllynfi Castle
Three Cocks
Tregoyd
Escley
Hinton
Peterchurch
Madley
Eaton Bishop
Shenmore
Cublington
B4352
Clehonger
Belmont Abbey
Lower Bullingham
Bullinghope
A4079
Golden Valley
Priory
Gorsty Common
Grafton
B4399
Chapel
A479
Velindre
2220 Hay Bluff
Brook
Vowchurch
B4348
Webton
B4349
Cobhall Common
Allensmore
A465
Dinedor
Dinedor Camp
Dinedor Cross
Bronllys
A4078
ENGLAND
WALES
Twmpa 2263
H E R E F O R D S H I R E
Turnastone
Upper Maes-coed
Coldwell
Kingstone
Winnal Common
2
Bronllys Castle
Talgarth
Llanelieu Church
Gospel Pass
R. Monnow
Michaelchurch Escley
Middle Maes-coed
St. Margarets
B4347
Kerry's Gate
Cockyard
Thruxton
Callow
Aconbury
Newton
Bolstone
Rhos Dirion
2338
Olchan Valley
Newton
Dewsall Court
Kivernoll
Tredustan
Pwlly Wrach
Bacton
R. Dore
King's Thorn
Trefecca
Lower Maes-coed
Didley
B4348
A49
Little Birch
Much Birch
Pen y Manllwyn
Capel-y-ffin
Grwyne Fawr Resr.
Llanveynoe
Abbey Dore Court
Wormbridge
Church
Kilpeck
Kilpeck Castle
Much Dewchurch
Glenda Farm Rehabilitation
Bwlch Y Dinas Castle
Pengenffordd
2660 Waun Fach
Aton
Honddu
Vale of Ewyas
Abbey Dore
Abbey Church
Wormelow Tump
Violette Szabo
Hoarwithy
B4560
1997
B L A C K
Tumant
Longtown
Ewyas Harold
Howton
Llandinabo
Mynydd Troed
Mynydd Llysiau 2173
Priory
Llanthony
Clodock
Pontrilas Road
Pontrilas
Orcop Hill
Bagwy Llydiart
Hill Gate
48
Harewood End
Langorse
M O U N T A I N S
Rowlstone
A465
Kentchurch
Kentchurch Court
Orcop
Garway Hill
Sandyway
Michaelchurch
Llangorse Lake
Mynydd Llangorse
1667
Llangasty-Talyllyn
Cathedine
Henllan
1743 Hatterall Hill
Llangua
St. Weonards
3
St. Owen's Cross
Pen Gwyllt-meirch
Grwyne Fawr
Oldcastle
Walterstone
Grosmont
White Rocks
Little Garway
Cwmrhos
Pen Allt-mawr 2360
Cwmdu
Garway Common
Treago Castle
Tretire
A40
Llansantffraed
Cwmyoy
B4347
Garway
B4521
Three Ashes
A4137
Blaenllynfi Castle
A479
Pen Cerig-calch 2300
Pandy
Langstone Court
Bwlch
Gaer
Tretower
Strawberry Cottage Wood
Skenfrith
Llancloudy
Llangarron
Broad Oak
Llangattock Lingoed
Norton
Cwm-crawnon
Tretower Court
Coed-yr-ynys
Llanbedr
Llanvihangel Crucorney
Cross Ash
Ruxton Green
A40
Llanvihangel Court
Bont
Crossway
Llanrothal
Llangrove
Llangynidr
Crickhowell
(Crughywel)
Crickhowell Castle
B4558
Ffawyddog
Mynydd Pen-y-fal
Blaenawey
B4521
Welsh Newton
Welsh Newton Common
Whitchurch
Sugar Loaf 1955
Llangattock
Llangenny
1595
A465
Ysgyryd Fawr
Newcastle
Llanfaenor
St. Maughan's Green
Maypole
A466
Garn Caws
Cefn Onnau
Glangrwyney
Llantilio Pertholey
Llanvetherine
White Castle
Ganarew
Buckholt
Daren
Llwyn-du
Mardy
B4521
Brynygwenyn
Hen Gwrt Moated Site
Tal-y-coed
Llangattock-Vibon-Avel
B4347
Rockfield
4
A40
B4560
Craig-y-Cilau
Mynydd Llangatwg
Gilwern
Llanelly
A4077
Llanwenarth
ABERGAVENNY
(Y Fenni)
Llantilio Crossenny
Onen
Dixton
1735
Govilon
Croes Hywel
B4233
Llanvapley
Llanvihangel Ystern-Llewern
B4233
A465
Clydach
Blackrock
Ironworks
Llanddewi Rhydderch
Wernyrheolydd
MONMOUTH
(Trefynwy)
Garnlydan
Llanfoist
1811 Blorenge
B4269
M O N M O U T H S H I R E
Kymin
Naval Temple
Rassau
Nant-y-Bwch
Bryn-mawr
Llanelly Hill
B4246
The Punchbowl
Penpergwm Lodge
Coed Morgan
Llanarth
Penrhos
Pen-yr-heol
Jingle Street
Over Monnow
Wyesham
Beaufort
Roundhouse Towers
Nantyglo
B4248
Garn-yr-erw
Llanellen
Canal
Great Oak
Tregare
Dingestow
Mitchel Troy
Penallt
Redbrook
EBBW VALE
(Glyn Ebwy)
Coalbrookvale
Ironworks
Blaenavon
A40
Llanvihangel Gobion
Bryngwyn
A40
B4293
Pentwyn Farm
Georgetown
Cwm-celyn
Big Pit
Upper Coedcae
Raglan
Mitcheltroy Common
Craig Wood
BLAENAU
A467
Blaina
1905
Forge Side
Coity Mountain
Rhyd-y-meirch
A4042
Cwmcarvan
New Grove Meadows
New Mills
Raglan
Pen-y-clawdd
Gwastad
Waunlwyd
GWENT
Varteg
A4043
1470 Mynydd Garnclochdy
Nant-y-Derry
Coed-y-Bwynydd
A449
The Narth
Troedrhiwgwair
Cwmtillery 1814
Bettws Newydd
Croes Robert Wood
Whitebrook
Abertysswg
B4246
Garndiffaith Viaduct
Penperlleni
Goetre
B4598
Twyn-y-Sheriff
Kingcoed
Llangovan
Trelleck
5
Cotland
New Tredegar
Cwm
A4046
A4048
Sirhowy
Talywain
Abersychan
Kemeys Commander
Gwehelog
Llandenny
Harold's Stones
Llandogo
Manmoel
Little Mill
Hollybush
ABERTILLERY
(Abertyleri)
Six Bells
Mamhilad
Monkswood
Llancayo
Llansoy
Llanishen
Parkhouse
Bargain Wood
Catbrook
CAERPHILLY
Brithdir
Aberbeeg
St. Illtyd
TORFAEN
G-Force Karting
Glascoed
A472
Rhadyr
Gwernesney
The Nurtons
Tintern Parva
Markham
Pen-y-fan Pond
Pen-twyn
Glandwr
B4471
Llanhilleth
Branches Fork Meadow
Llandegfedd Reservoir
Usk
(Brynbuga)
Llangwm-isaf
Trelleck Grange
Abbey Furnace
Bedwellty
Argoed
Trinant
Pantygasseg
New Inn
Llangwm
Wolvesnewton
New Inn
Chapel Hill
Bargoed
(Bargod)
B4251
Swffryd
A472
Griffithstown
PONTYPOOL
Llanbadoc
Devauden
Oakdale
Sebastopol
Pontypwl
A4042
Coed-y-paen
Llanllowell
Veddw House
Chepstow Park Wood
Wyndcliff
Pengam
Gilfach
Penpedairheol
Blackwood
Coed Duon
Crumlin
Newbridge
(Cefn Bychan)
1550 Pontrhydyrun
Upper Cwmbran
Pontnewydd
Llantrisant
Newchurch
St. Arvans
GELLIGAER
Pontllanfraith
I S L W Y N
Croesyceiliog
A449
Llangybi
B4235
Woodcroft
Penybryn
A4049
CWMBRAN
Ton
Llandegveth
Earlswood
Itton Common

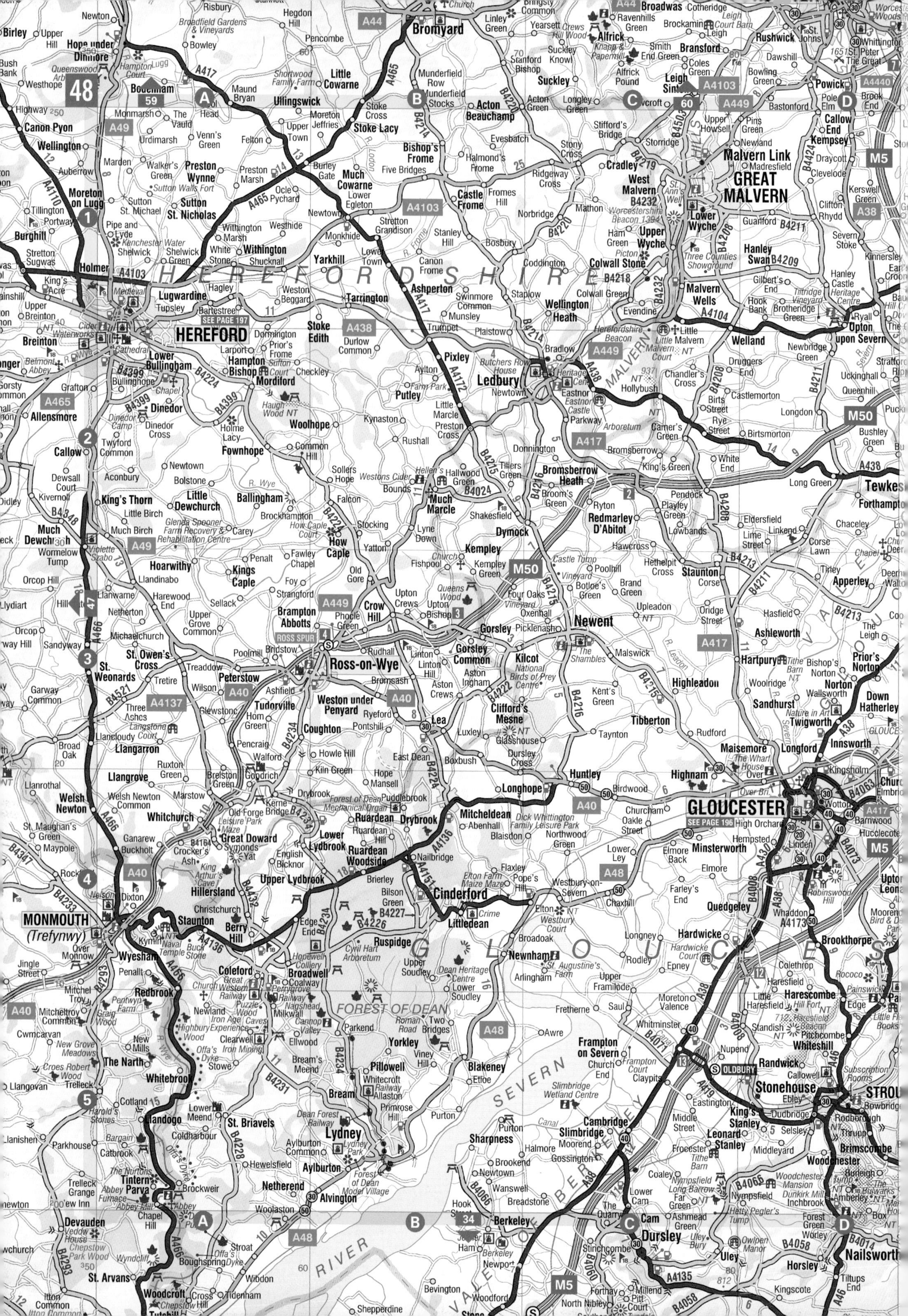

48
59
60
34
A
B
C
D
HEREFORDSHIRE
GLOUCESTERSHIRE
HEREFORD
SEE PAGE 197
GLOUCESTER
SEE PAGE 196
GREAT MALVERN
Malvern Link
Malvern Wells
Ledbury
Bromyard
Ross-on-Wye
ROSS SPUR
Newent
MONMOUTH
(Trefynwy)
Lydney
Cinderford
Coleford
Dursley
Stonehouse
Nailsworth
Tewkesbury
Upton upon Severn
FOREST OF DEAN
RIVER SEVERN
VALE OF BERKELEY
MALVERN HILLS
Berkeley
Sharpness
Newnham
Mitcheldean
Longhope
Huntley
Highnam
Maisemore
Quedgeley
Hardwicke
Brookthorpe
Painswick
Whiteshill
Randwick
Cam
Uley
Tintern Parva
St. Arvans
Chepstow
Woodcroft
Redbrook
Llandogo
St. Briavels
Alvington
Aylburton
Woolaston
Blakeney
Yorkley
Bream
Pillowell
Ruspidge
Ruardean
Drybrook
Lea
Weston under Penyard
Goodrich
Welsh Newton
Llangarron
St. Weonards
Much Dewchurch
Kingstone
Dymock
Kempley
Much Marcle
Putley
Ashperton
Tarrington
Stoke Edith
Mordiford
Fownhope
Withington
Sutton St. Nicholas
Preston Wynne
Moreton on Lugg
Burghill
Canon Pyon
Wellington
Bodenham
Hope under Dinmore
Ullingswick
Little Cowarne
Much Cowarne
Stoke Lacy
Bishop's Frome
Acton Beauchamp
Suckley
Alfrick
Leigh Sinton
Bransford
Powick
Callow End
Kempsey
Cradley
Colwall Stone
Wellington Heath
Bosbury
Castle Frome
A44
A465
A417
A49
A4103
A438
A449
A4172
A40
A4137
A466
A48
A4136
A4151
A38
A46
A4135
A4173
A430
B4215
B4216
B4221
B4224
B4228
B4231
B4234
B4226
B4227
B4066
B4060
B4058
B4008
B4072
M5
M50

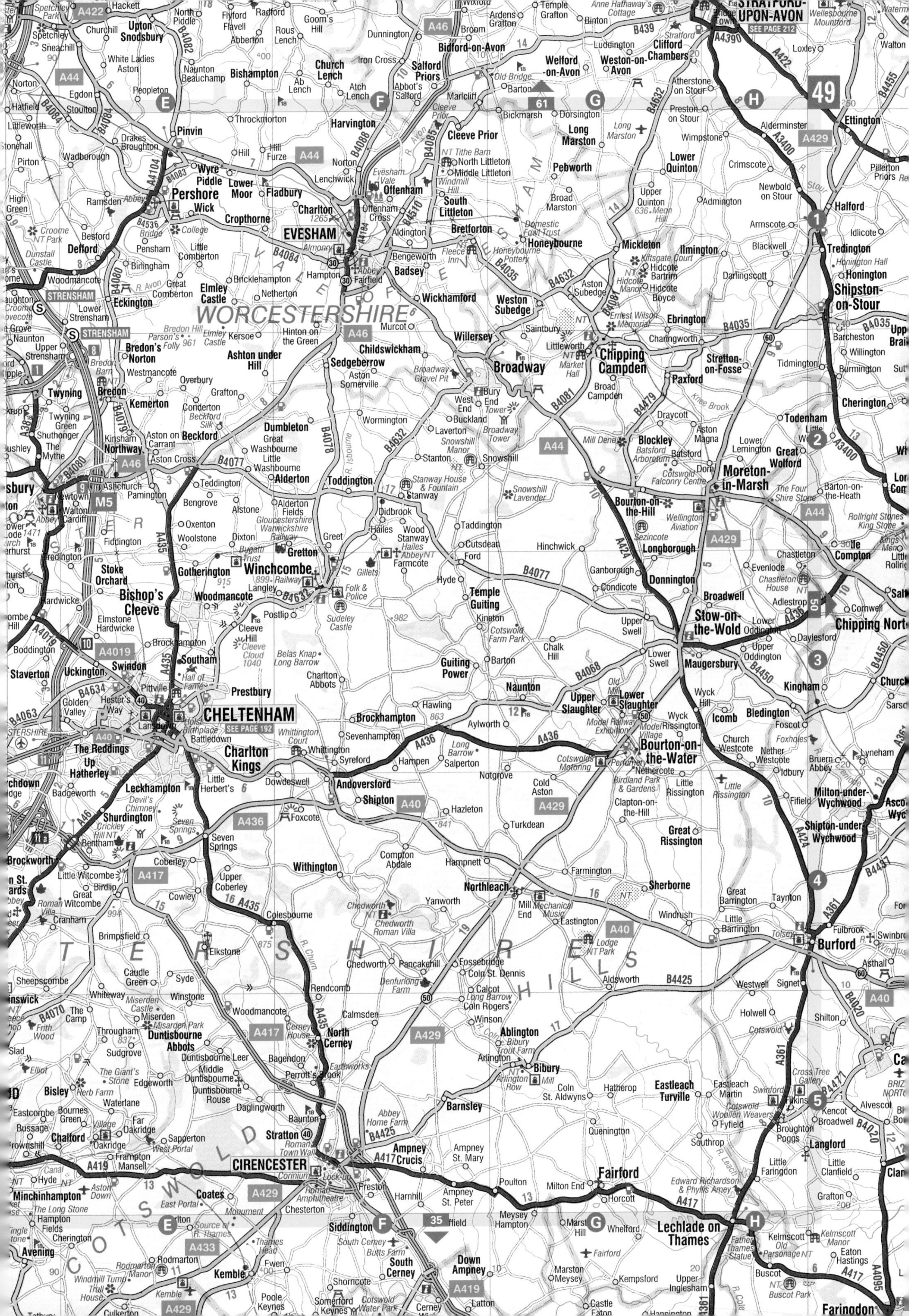
STRATFORD-UPON-AVON
SEE PAGE 212
49
Spetchley
Hackett
North Piddle
Flyford Flavell
Radford
Rous Lench
Goom's Hill
Dunnington
Wixford
Ardens Grafton
Temple Grafton
Binton
Anne Hathaway's Cottage
Broom
Bidford-on-Avon
Luddington
Clifford Chambers
Welford-on-Avon
Weston-on-Avon
Atherstone on Stour
Preston on Stour
Alderminster
Ettington
Loxley
Walton
Wellesbourne Mountford
Churchill
Upton Snodsbury
Abberton
Sneachill
White Ladies Aston
Naunton Beauchamp
Bishampton
Church Lench
Ab Lench
Atch Lench
Iron Cross
Salford Priors
Abbot's Salford
Marlcliff
Old Bridge
Barton
Bickmarsh
Dorsington
Long Marston
Norton
Egdon
Peopleton
Stoulton
Hatfield
Littleworth
Throckmorton
Harvington
Cleeve Prior
NT Tithe Barn
North Littleton
Middle Littleton
Pebworth
Lower Quinton
Upper Quinton
Meon Hill
Wimpstone
Crimscote
Newbold on Stour
Pillerton Priors
Halford
Admington
Armscote
Idlicote
Tredington
Honington Hall
Honington
Shipston-on-Stour
Pinvin
Drakes Broughton
Wadborough
Hill
Hill Furze
Norton
Lenchwick
Evesham Vale
Offenham
Windmill Hill
South Littleton
Wyre Piddle
Lower Moor
Fladbury
Pershore
Wick
Cropthorne
Charlton
Offenham Cross
Bretforton
Domestic Fowl Trust
Honeybourne
Broad Marston
Mickleton
Ilmington
Kiftsgate Court
Hidcote Bartrim
Hidcote Manor
Hidcote Boyce
Blackwell
Darlingscott
High Green
Ramsden
Pirton
Croome NT Park
Besford
Defford
College
Pensham
Little Comberton
Great Comberton
Birlingham
Dunstall Castle
Woodmancote
Eckington
Bricklehampton
Netherton
EVESHAM
Almonry
Aldington
Bengeworth
Badsey
Hampton
Abbey
Fairfield
Wickhamford
Fleece Inn
Honeybourne Pottery
Aston Subedge
Weston Subedge
Ebrington
Ernest Wilson Memorial
Charingworth
WORCESTERSHIRE
VALE OF EVESHAM
STRENSHAM
Lower Strensham
Upper Strensham
Naunton
Bredon Hill
Parson's Folly 961
Elmley Castle
Kersoe
Hinton on the Green
Murcot
Childswickham
Willersey
Saintbury
Littleworth
Chipping Campden
Market Hall
Broad Campden
Stretton-on-Fosse
Paxford
Barcheston
Willington
Tidmington
Burmington
Cherington
Bredon's Norton
Ashton under Hill
Sedgeberrow
Aston Somerville
Broadway
Broadway Gravel Pit
Bredon Barn
Bredon
Westmancote
Overbury
Grafton
Conderton
Beckford Silk
Kemerton
Beckford
Twyning
Twyning Green
Shuthonger
The Mythe
Kinsham
Northway
Aston on Carrant
Aston Cross
Dumbleton
Great Washbourne
Little Washbourne
Alderton
Toddington
Wormington
Laverton
Buckland
Bury End
West End
Broadway Tower
Snowshill Manor
Snowshill
Stanton
Stanway House & Fountain
Stanway
Snowshill Lavender
Kree Brook
Draycott
Aston Magna
Mill Dene
Blockley
Batsford Arboretum
Batsford
Lower Lemington
Todenham
Great Wolford
Little Wolford
Moreton-in-Marsh
Cotswold Falconry Centre
Dorn
The Four Shire Stone
Barton-on-the-Heath
Bourton-on-the-Hill
Wellington Aviation
Sezincote
Longborough
Rollright Stones King Stone
Little Compton
Chastleton
Chastleton House
Evenlode
Ashchurch
Pamington
Teddington
Newtown
Walton Cardiff
Abbey
Bengrove
Alstone
Alderton Fields
Gloucestershire Warwickshire Railway
Didbrook
Wood Stanway
Hailes
Hailes Abbey NT
Farmcote
Taddington
Cutsdean
Ford
Oxenton
Woolstone
Dixton
Fiddington
Tredington
Bugatti Trust
Gretton
Greet
Winchcombe
Gillets
Gotherington
Stoke Orchard
Hardwicke
Bishop's Cleeve
Woodmancote
Langley
Railway
Folk & Police
Sudeley Castle
Postlip
Hyde
Temple Guiting
Kineton
Cotswold Farm Park
Hinchwick
Ganborough
Condicote
Donnington
Broadwell
Adlestrop
Cornwell
Chipping Norton
Stow-on-the-Wold
Upper Swell
Lower Swell
Lower Oddington
Upper Oddington
Daylesford
Maugersbury
Kingham
Elmstone Hardwicke
Boddington
Staverton
Uckington
Swindon
Brockhampton
Southam
Cleeve Hill
Cleeve Cloud 1040
Hall of Fame
Belas Knap Long Barrow
Charlton Abbots
Barton
Guiting Power
Chalk Hill
Upper Slaughter
Lower Slaughter
Naunton
Old Mill
Wyck Hill
Wyck Rissington
Icomb
Bledington
Foscot
Pittville
Hester's Way
Golden Valley
CHELTENHAM
SEE PAGE 192
Holst Birthplace
Prestbury
Hawling
Brockhampton
Sevenhampton
Whittington Court
Whittington
Syreford
Aylworth
Model Railway Exhibition
Model Village
Bourton-on-the-Water
Perfumery
Church Westcote
Nether Westcote
Idbury
Bruern Abbey
Lyneham
The Reddings
Up Hatherley
Lansdown
Battledown
Charlton Kings
Dowdeswell
Andoversford
Shipton
Hampen
Long Barrow
Salperton
Notgrove
Cotswolds Motoring
Nethercote
Birdland Park & Gardens
Cold Aston
Little Rissington
Clapton-on-the-Hill
Milton-under-Wychwood
Fifield
Shipton-under-Wychwood
Churchdown
Badgeworth
Leckhampton
Little Herbert's
Devil's Chimney
Shurdington
Crickley Hill NT
Bentham
Seven Springs
Foxcote
Hazleton
Turkdean
Great Rissington
Brockworth
Coberley
Upper Coberley
Little Witcombe
Great Witcombe
Birdlip
Roman Villa
Cranham
Withington
Compton Abdale
Hampnett
Northleach
Mill End
Mechanical Music
Farmington
Sherborne
Great Barrington
Taynton
Cowley
Colesbourne
Yanworth
Chedworth
Chedworth Roman Villa
Eastington
Windrush
Little Barrington
Tolsey
Burford
Fulbrook
Swinbrook
Brimpsfield
Elkstone
Lodge Park NT
Asthall
Caudle Green
Syde
Chedworth
Pancakehill
Fossebridge
Coln St. Dennis
Aldsworth
Westwell
Signet
Sheepscombe
Whiteway
Winstone
Miserden Castle
Miserden
Denfurlong Farm
Calcot
Long Barrow
Coln Rogers
Rendcomb
Winson
Painswick
The Camp
Frith Wood
Througham
Duntisbourne Abbots
Woodmancote
Calmsden
Ablington
Bibury Trout Farm
Holwell
Shilton
Cotswold
Slad
Sudgrove
Duntisbourne Leer
Cerney House
North Cerney
Bagendon
Earthworks
Arlington
Bibury
Elliot
The Giant's Stone
Middle Duntisbourne
Duntisbourne Rouse
Edgeworth
Perrott's Brook
Arlington Row
Mill
Coln St. Aldwyns
Hatherop
Eastleach Turville
Eastleach Martin
Swinford
Cross Tree Gallery
Filkins
Kencot
Alvescot
Broadwell
Bisley
Herb Farm
Waterlane
Eastcombe
Bournes Green
Daglingworth
Barnsley
Abbey Home Farm
Cotswold Woollen Weavers
Fyfield
Broughton Poggs
Bussage
Village
Oakridge
Far Oakridge
Baunton
Chalford
Sapperton
West Portal
Stratton
Roman Town Wall
Ampney Crucis
Ampney St. Mary
Quenington
Southrop
Langford
Frampton Mansell
CIRENCESTER
Corinium
Lock-up
Roman Amphitheatre
Preston
Little Faringdon
Little Clanfield
Hyde
Minchinhampton
Aston Down
Coates
East Portal
Monument
Chesterton
Harnhill
Ampney St. Peter
Poulton
Milton End
Fairford
Horcott
Edward Richardson & Phyllis Amey
Grafton
The Long Stone
Hampton Fields
Cherington
Tarlton
Source of R. Thames
Siddington
Driffield
Meysey Hampton
Marston Hill
Whelford
Lechlade on Thames
Father Thames Statue
Kelmscott
Kelmscott Manor
Old Parsonage NT
Eaton Hastings
Avening
Rodmarton
Rodmarton Manor
Thames Head
South Cerney
Butts Farm
Fairford
Windmill Tump
Trull House
Ewen
Kemble
South Cerney
Down Ampney
Marston Meysey
Kempsford
Upper Inglesham
Buscot
Buscot Park
Culkerton
Poole Keynes
Shorncote
Somerford Keynes
Cotswold Water Park
Cerney Wick
Latton
Castle Eaton
Hannington
Faringdon
COTSWOLD HILLS
GLOUCESTERSHIRE
61
35
50
M5
A44
A46
A422
A435
A429
A436
A40
A417
A419
A433
A4019
A424
A361
A3400
B4035
B4077
B4632
B4068
B4425
B4450
B4081
B4084

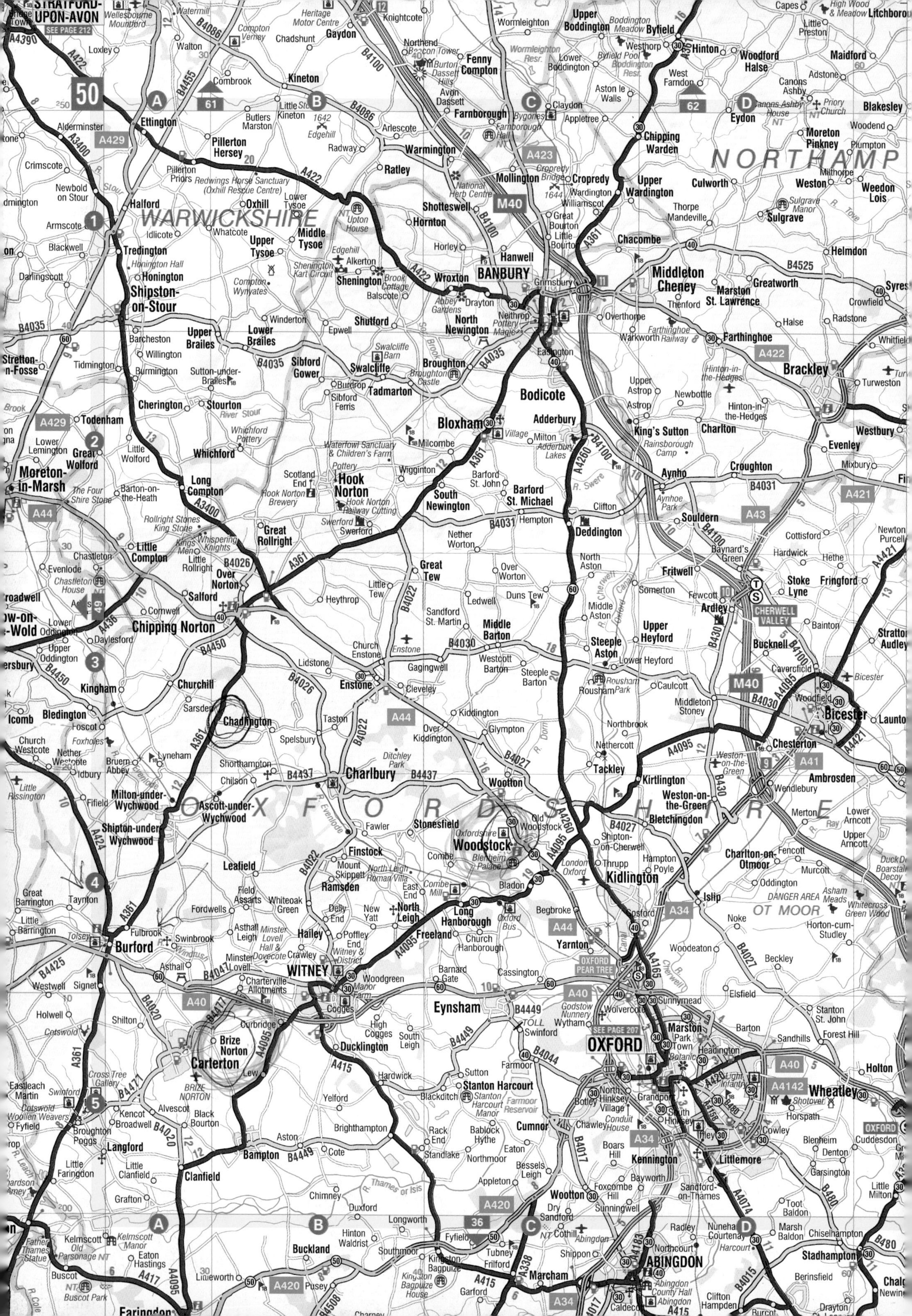

STRATFORD-UPON-AVON
SEE PAGE 212
A4390
Wellesbourne Mountford
Watermill
Compton Verney
Heritage Motor Centre
Gaydon
Chadshunt
Knightcote
Wormleighton
Upper Boddington
Boddington Meadow
Byfield
Capes
High Wood & Meadow
Litchborough
Loxley
Walton
B4086
B4455
Northend
Burton Dassett Hills
Fenny Compton
Wormleighton Resr.
Lower Boddington
Westhorp
Bylield Pool
Boddington Resr.
Hinton
Woodford Halse
Little Preston
Maidford
A422
50
Combrook
Kineton
Little Kineton
B4100
Avon Dassett
Aston le Walls
West Farndon
Adstone
Canons Ashby
Canons Ashby House
Priory Church
Blakesley
A
B
C
D
61
62
1642 Edgehill
Ettington
Butlers Marston
Arlescote
Farnborough
Farnborough Hall
Bygones
Claydon
Appletree
Eydon
Woodend
Alderminster
A3400
A429
Pillerton Hersey
Radway
Warmington
A423
Chipping Warden
Moreton Pinkney
Plumpton
NORTHAMP
Crimscote
Pillerton Priors
Redwings Horse Sanctuary (Oxhill Rescue Centre)
Ratley
Mollington
Cropredy Bridge 1644
Cropredy
Upper Wardington
Culworth
Weston
Weedon Lois
Newbold on Stour
R. Stour
Lower Tysoe
National Herb Centre
Wardington
Williamscot
Sulgrave Manor
Sulgrave
Thorpe Mandeville
Halford
WARWICKSHIRE
Oxhill
Upton House
Shotteswell
M40
Great Bourton
Little Bourton
Armscote
Idlicote
Whatcote
Upper Tysoe
Middle Tysoe
Hornton
Horley
Hanwell
Chacombe
Helmdon
Blackwell
Tredington
Honington Hall
Edgehill
Alkerton
Shenington Kart Circuit
Shenington
Brook Cottage
Balscote
Wroxton
Abbey Gardens
Drayton
BANBURY
Grimsbury
Middleton Cheney
Marston St. Lawrence
Greatworth
B4525
Darlingscott
Honington
Compton Wynyates
Shipston-on-Stour
Winderton
Neithrop
Pottery Magic
Overthorpe
Thenford
Syresham
Crowfield
B4035
Barcheston
Upper Brailes
Lower Brailes
Epwell
Shutford
North Newington
Warkworth
Farthinghoe Railway
Farthinghoe
Halse
Radstone
Whitfield
Stretton-on-Fosse
Tidmington
Willington
Burmington
B4035
Sibford Gower
Swalcliffe Barn
Swalcliffe
Broughton
Broughton Castle
Easington
Hinton-in-the-Hedges
A422
Brackley
Turweston
Sutton-under-Brailes
Burdrop
Sibford Ferris
Tadmarton
Bodicote
Upper Astrop
Newbottle
Astrop
Hinton-in-the-Hedges
Cherington
Stourton
River Stour
Whichford Pottery
Bloxham
Village
Adderbury
A429
Todenham
Lower Lemington
Great Wolford
Little Wolford
Whichford
Waterfowl Sanctuary & Children's Farm
Milcombe
Milton
Adderbury Lakes
King's Sutton
Rainsborough Camp
Charlton
Westbury
Evenley
Moreton-in-Marsh
The Four Shire Stone
Barton-on-the-Heath
Long Compton
Scotland End
Pottery
Hook Norton
Hook Norton Brewery
Wigginton
Barford St. John
Barford St. Michael
B4100
A4260
R. Swere
Aynho
Croughton
Mixbury
A44
A3400
Hook Norton Railway Cutting
Swerford Park
Swerford
South Newington
Clifton
Aynhoe Park
B4031
A421
Rollright Stones King Stone
Kings Men
Whispering Knights
Great Rollright
B4031
Hempton
Deddington
Souldern
A43
Newton Purcell
Chastleton
Little Compton
Little Rollright
A361
Nether Worton
Cottisford
Evenlode
Chastleton House
B4026
Over Norton
Great Tew
North Aston
Hardwick
Hethe
Broadwell
Salford
Little Tew
Over Worton
Fritwell
Baynard's Green
Cornwell
Heythrop
B4022
Ledwell
Duns Tew
Somerton
Fewcott
Stoke Lyne
Fringford
Adlestrop
49
Lower Oddington
Chipping Norton
Sandford St. Martin
Middle Aston
Ardley
CHERWELL VALLEY
Stow-on-the-Wold
A436
Daylesford
Middle Barton
Upper Heyford
Bainton
Stratton Audley
Upper Oddington
B4450
Church Enstone
Enstone
B4030
Westcott Barton
Steeple Aston
Lower Heyford
Bucknell
Caversfield
Bicester
B4450
Kingham
Churchill
Lidstone
Enstone
Gagingwell
Steeple Barton
Rousham Park
Rousham
Caulcott
M40
Middleton Stoney
B4030
A4095
Woodfield
Launton
Icomb
Bledington
Sarsden
Chadlington
B4026
Cleveley
Kiddington
Taston
A44
Over Kiddington
Glympton
Northbrook
Chesterton
Church Westcote
Foscot
Foxholes
Spelsbury
Nethercott
A4095
A41
Nether Westcote
Idbury
Bruern Abbey
Lyneham
Shorthampton
Chilson
Ditchley Park
B4027
Tackley
Weston-on-the-Green
Ambrosden
A4421
Little Rissington
Milton-under-Wychwood
Ascott-under-Wychwood
B4437
Charlbury
B4437
Wootton
Kirtlington
Weston-on-the-Green
Wendlebury
Fifield
OXFORDSHIRE
R. Evenlode
Old Woodstock
A4260
B4027
Bletchingdon
Merton
Lower Arncott
Shipton-under-Wychwood
Fawler
Stonesfield
Oxfordshire
Woodstock
Shipton-on-Cherwell
Upper Arncott
A424
Leafield
Finstock
Mount Skippett
North Leigh Roman Villa
Combe
Blenheim Palace
A4095
Thrupp
Hampton Poyle
Charlton-on-Otmoor
Fencott
Murcott
London Oxford
Kidlington
Ramsden
East End
Combe Mill
Bladon
Oddington
Great Barrington
Taynton
Field Assarts
Whiteoak Green
Delly End
New Yatt
North Leigh
Long Hanborough
Oxford Bus
Begbroke
Islip
DANGER AREA
OT MOOR
Asham Meads
Whitecross Green Wood
Little Barrington
Fordwells
A361
Gosford
A34
Noke
Horton-cum-Studley
Fulbrook
Swinbrook
Asthall Leigh
Minster Lovell Hall & Dovecote
Hailey
Poffley End
Freeland
Church Hanborough
A44
Yarnton
Tolsey
Burford
Windrush
Minster Lovell
Crawley
Witney & District
Woodeaton
A4095
A4165
Beckley
B4425
Asthall
B4047
Charterville Allotments
WITNEY
Woodgreen
Barnard Gate
Cassington
OXFORD PEAR TREE
Westwell
Signet
A40
Manor Farm
A40
Elsfield
Holwell
Cogges
Eynsham
Godstow Nunnery
Wolvercote
Sunnymead
Stanton St. John
Shilton
B4020
A4095
Curbridge
High Cogges
B4449
TOLL
Swinford
Wytham
SEE PAGE 207
Marston
Barton
Forest Hill
Cotswold
Brize Norton
Ducklington
South Leigh
B4449
Park Town
Sandhills
A361
Cross Tree Gallery
Carterton
Lew
OXFORD
Botanic
Headington
Eastleach Martin
BRIZE NORTON
Hardwick
Farmoor
B4044
Light Infantry
A40
Holton
Swinford
B4477
Sutton
Stanton Harcourt
North Hinksey Village
Grandpont
A4142
Wheatley
Cotswold Woollen Weavers
Kencot
Alvescot
Yelford
Blackditch
Stanton Harcourt Manor
Farmoor Reservoir
Botley
Shotover
Horspath
Fyfield
Broadwell
Black Bourton
Brighthampton
Rack End
Bablock Hythe
Cumnor
Chawley
Conduit House
South Hinksey
Iffley
Cowley
OXFORD
Broughton Poggs
B4020
Aston
Standlake
Eaton
Boars Hill
A34
Blenheim
Cuddesdon
Langford
Bampton
B4449
Cote
Northmoor
B4017
Kennington
Littlemore
Denton
Little Faringdon
Little Clanfield
Clanfield
Thames or Isis
Bessels Leigh
Bayworth
Garsington
Chimney
Appleton
Foxcombe Hill
Sandford-on-Thames
A4074
B480
Grafton
Duxford
A420
Wootton
Sunningwell
Toot Baldon
Little Milton
Dry Sandford
Longworth
36
Radley
Nuneham Courtenay
Marsh Baldon
Chiselhampton
Kelmscott
Kelmscott Manor
Hinton Waldrist
Fyfield
Cothill
Abingdon
Harcourt
Old Parsonage
Father Thames Statue
Eaton Hastings
Buckland
Southmoor
Tubney
Frilford
A4183
Northcourt
Stadhampton
B480
Shippon
ABINGDON
Buscot
A417
A4095
Kingston Bagpuize
A415
A338
Marcham
Abingdon County Hall
Berinsfield
Buscot Park
Littleworth
A420
Pusey
Kingston Bagpuize House
Garford
A34
Abingdon
Clifton Hampden
Chalgrove
Faringdon
R. Cole
B4508
Charney
B4017
Caldecot
A415
B4015
Burcot
Drayton
Newington

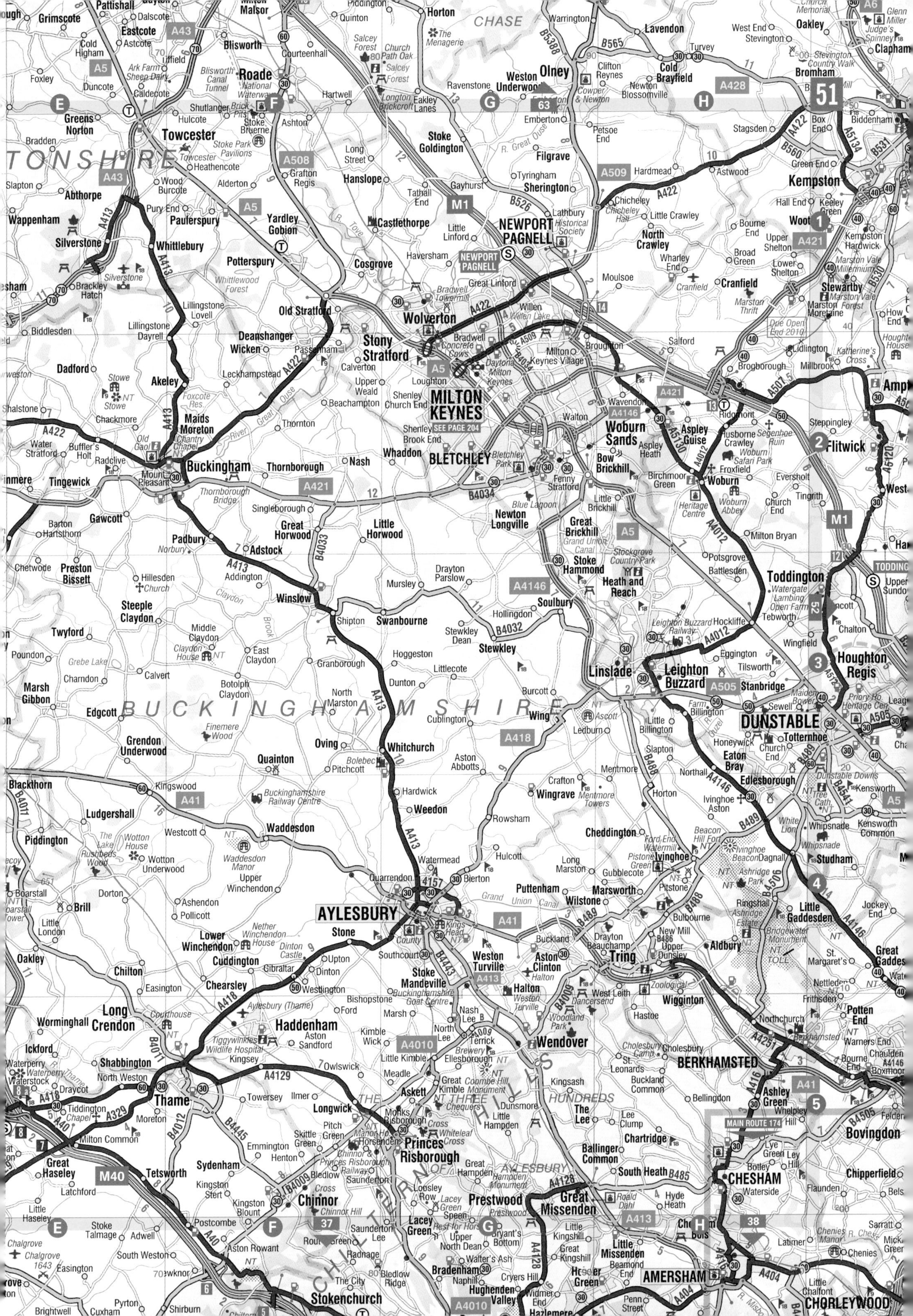

Pattishall
Grimscote
Eastcote
Dalscote
Astcote
Cold Higham
Foxley
Duncote
Milton Malsor
Blisworth
Roade
Courteenhall
Piddington
Quinton
Horton
The Menagerie
Salcey Forest
Church Path Oak
CHASE
Warrington
Lavendon
West End
Stevington
Oakley
Church Memorial
Glenn Miller
Judge's Spinney
Clapham
Stevington Country Walk
Turvey
Cold Brayfield
Clifton Reynes
Newton Blossomville
Bromham
Olney
Weston Underwood
Ravenstone
Cowper & Newton
Emberton
Petsoe End
Hartwell
Ashton
Eakley Lanes
Long Street
Stoke Goldington
Filgrave
Tyringham
Sherington
Gayhurst
Hanslope
Tathall End
Castlethorpe
Little Linford
Haversham
Newport Pagnell
Lathbury
Chicheley
Little Crawley
North Crawley
Bourne End
Upper Shelton
Broad Green
Lower Shelton
Whartey End
Cranfield
Marston Thrift
Stewartby
Marston Moretaine
Moulsoe
Great Linford
Bradwell Towermill
Willen
Willen Lake
Stagsden
Astwood
Hardmead
Box End
Biddenham
Kempston
Green End
Hall End
Keeley Green
Wootton
Kempston Hardwick
Marston Vale Millennium
Marston Vale Forest
How End
Houghton House
Millbrook
Katherine's Cross
Lidlington
Brogborough
Ampthill
Salford
Brick Pits
Stoke Bruerne
Shutlanger
Hulcote
Greens Norton
Bradden
Towcester
Stoke Park Pavilions
Towcester Racecourse
Heathencote
NORTHAMPTONSHIRE
Slapton
Abthorpe
Wood Burcote
Alderton
Grafton Regis
Pury End
Paulerspury
Wappenham
Silverstone
Whittlebury
Yardley Gobion
Potterspury
Whittlewood Forest
Cosgrove
Brackley Hatch
Lillingstone Lovell
Lillingstone Dayrell
Old Stratford
Deanshanger
Wicken
Passenham
Stony Stratford
Calverton
Wolverton
Bradwell
Concrete Cows
Daytona Milton Keynes
Milton Keynes Village
Broughton
Biddlesden
Dadford
Stowe
Akeley
Leckhampstead
Foxcote Res.
Maids Moreton
Chackmore
Shalstone
Upper Weald
Loughton
Shenley Church End
Milton Keynes
See page 204
Beachampton
Thornton
Wavendon
Walton
Woburn Sands
Aspley Heath
Aspley Guise
Ridgmont
Husborne Crawley
Segenhoe Ruin
Steppingley
Flitwick
Water Stratford
Buffler's Holt
Radclive
Old Gaol
Chantry Chapel
Buckingham
Mount Pleasant
Tingewick
Finmere
Thornborough
Thornborough Bridge
Nash
Whaddon
Shenley Brook End
Bletchley
Bletchley Park
Fenny Stratford
Bow Brickhill
Birchmoor Green
Woburn
Woburn Safari Park
Froxfield
Woburn Abbey
Heritage Centre
Eversholt
Tingrith
Church End
Westoning
Little Brickhill
Blue Lagoon
Newton Longville
Singleborough
Great Horwood
Little Horwood
Gawcott
Barton Hartshorn
Padbury
Norbury
Adstock
Great Brickhill
Grand Union Canal
Stockgrove Country Park
Milton Bryan
Harlington
Potsgrove
Battlesden
Toddington
Chetwode
Preston Bissett
Hillesden
Church
Addington
Claydon
Drayton Parslow
Mursley
Stoke Hammond
Heath and Reach
Watergate Lambing Open Farm
Tebworth
Sundon
Chalton
Steeple Claydon
Winslow
Shipton
Swanbourne
Hollingdon
Soulbury
Twyford
Middle Claydon
Claydon House
East Claydon
Stewkley Dean
Stewkley
Leighton Buzzard Railway
Hockliffe
Wingfield
Houghton Regis
Poundon
Grebe Lake
Granborough
Hoggeston
Littlecote
Eggington
Tilsworth
Charndon
Calvert
Botolph Claydon
Dunton
Linslade
Leighton Buzzard
Stanbridge
Marsh Gibbon
North Marston
Burcott
Farm Billington
Sewell
Maiden Bower
Priory Ho Heritage Cen
Dunstable
Edgcott
BUCKINGHAMSHIRE
Cublington
Wing
Ascott
Little Billington
Ledburn
Totternhoe
Honeywick
Church End
Grendon Underwood
Finemere Wood
Oving
Whitchurch
Bolebec
Pitchcott
Aston Abbotts
Slapton
Eaton Bray
Quainton
Mentmore
Northall
Edlesborough
Dunstable Downs
Kensworth
Blackthorn
Kingswood
Buckinghamshire Railway Centre
Hardwick
Crafton
Wingrave
Mentmore Towers
Horton
Ivinghoe Aston
Tree Cath.
Ludgershall
Weedon
Rowsham
Whipsnade
Kensworth Common
Piddington
Westcott
Waddesdon
The Lake
Wotton House
Rushbeds Wood
Wotton Underwood
Waddesdon Manor
Upper Winchendon
Watermead
Hulcott
Cheddington
Ford End Watermill
Long Marston
Pitstone Green
Ivinghoe
Beacon Hill Fort
Ivinghoe Beacon
Dagnall
Studham
Boarstall
Brill
Dorton
Ashendon
Pollicott
Quarrendon
Bierton
Puttenham
Gubblecote
Wilstone
Marsworth
Pitstone
Ashridge Park
Ashridge Estate
Ringshall
Little Gaddesden
Jockey End
Little London
Lower Winchendon
Nether Winchendon House
Aylesbury
Stone
County
Kings Head
Grand Union Canal
Buckland
Drayton Beauchamp
New Mill
Bulbourne
Aldbury
Bridgewater Monument
Great Gaddesden
Oakley
Dinton Castle
Cuddington
Upton
Dinton
Gibraltar
Westlington
Southcourt
Stoke Mandeville
Buckinghamshire Goat Centre
Weston Turville
Aston Clinton
Halton
Tring
Upper Dunsley
Zoological
St. Margaret's
Nettleden
Chilton
Easington
Chearsley
Long Crendon
Worminghall
Courthouse
Haddenham
Aston Sandford
Bishopstone
Ford
Marsh
Nash Lee
North Lee
Weston Turville
Woodland Park
Dancersend
West Leith
Wigginton
Hastoe
Frithsden
Potten End
Northchurch
Berkhamsted
Ickford
Waterperry
Waterstock
Shabbington
North Weston
Tiggywinkles Wildlife Hospital
Kingsey
Kimble Wick
Little Kimble
Terrick
Ellesborough
Brewery
Wendover
Cholesbury Camp
Cholesbury
St. Leonards
Buckland Common
Warners End
Chaulden
Boxmoor
Draycot
Tiddington
Chapel
Thame
Towersey
Moreton
Ilmer
Owlswick
Meadle
Askett
Great Kimble
Coombe Hill Monument
Chequers
Kingsash
Dunsmore
Little Hampden
HUNDREDS
Bellingdon
Ashley Green
Whelpley Hill
Felden
Bovingdon
Milton Common
Great Haseley
Longwick
Pitch Green
Skittle Green
Emmington
Henton
Monks Risborough
Whiteleaf Cross
Princes Risborough
Horsenden
Chinnor & Princes Risborough Railway
Saunderton
Bledlow
The Lee
Lee Clump
Chartridge
Ballinger Common
South Heath
Lye Green
Ley Hill
Botley
Chesham
Waterside
Chipperfield
Flaunden
Latchford
Tetsworth
Sydenham
Kingston Stert
Kingston Blount
Chinnor
Chinnor Hill
Great Hampden
Hampden Monument
AYLESBURY
Prestwood
Great Missenden
Roald Dahl
Hyde Heath
Chenies Manor
Chenies
Sarratt
Little Haseley
Stoke Talmage
Adwell
Postcombe
Aston Rowant
Lacey Green
Loosley Row
Speen
Upper North Dean
Bryant's Bottom
Little Kingshill
Great Kingshill
Little Missenden
Beamond End
Latimer
Chalgrove
Chalgrove 1643
Easington
South Weston
Lewknor
Radnage
Bledlow Ridge
Walter's Ash
Bradenham
Naphill
Cryers Hill
Hughenden Valley
Widmer End
Hazlemere
Holmer Green
Amersham
Penn Street
Little Chalfont
Chorleywood
Pyrton
Cuxham
Brightwell
Shirburn
The City
Stokenchurch
CHILTERN HILLS
Main Route 174
M1
M40
A5
A43
A41
A413
A418
A421
A422
A428
A4146
A505
A509
A4010
51
52
63
37
38

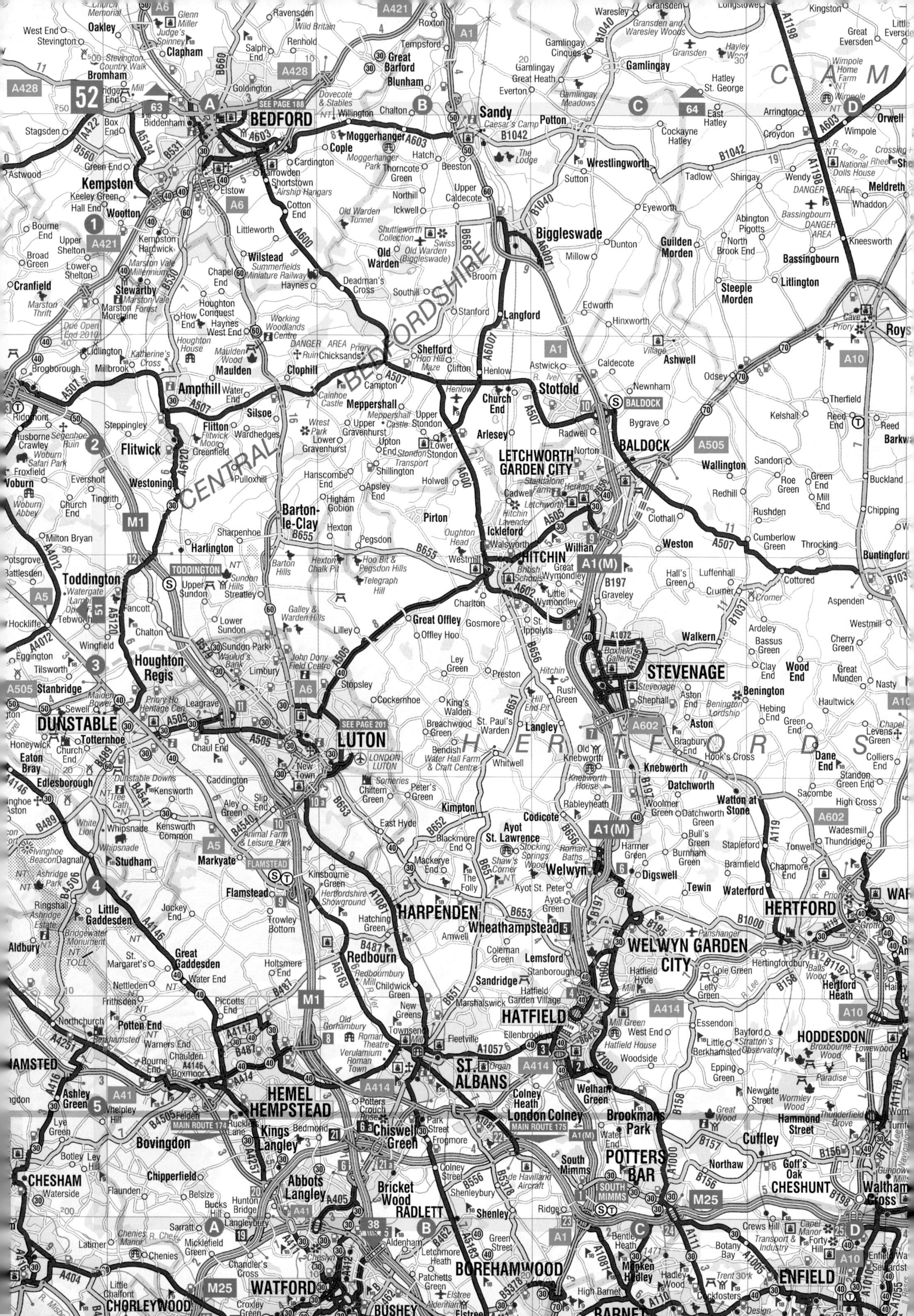

52
63
64
SEE PAGE 188
SEE PAGE 201
MAIN ROUTE 175
BEDFORD
Oakley
Clapham
Bromham
Kempston
Wootton
Cranfield
Stewartby
Ampthill
Flitwick
Woburn
Toddington
Houghton Regis
DUNSTABLE
LUTON
Harlington
Barton-le-Clay
Shefford
Clophill
Maulden
Silsoe
Meppershall
Henlow
Arlesey
Stotfold
Biggleswade
Sandy
Potton
Gamlingay
Great Barford
Blunham
Willington
Moggerhanger
Cople
Cardington
Haynes
Langford
Ashwell
BALDOCK
LETCHWORTH GARDEN CITY
HITCHIN
Ickleford
Pirton
STEVENAGE
Knebworth
Welwyn
WELWYN GARDEN CITY
HATFIELD
HERTFORD
HODDESDON
Cuffley
CHESHUNT
Waltham Cross
ENFIELD
POTTERS BAR
Brookmans Park
London Colney
ST. ALBANS
HARPENDEN
Wheathampstead
Redbourn
HEMEL HEMPSTEAD
Kings Langley
Abbots Langley
Bovingdon
CHESHAM
CHORLEYWOOD
WATFORD
BUSHEY
RADLETT
BOREHAMWOOD
BARNET
Bricket Wood
Chiswell Green
Shenley
South Mimms
Edlesborough
Studham
Markyate
Flamstead
Little Gaddesden
Great Gaddesden
Aldbury
Potten End
Tring
Watton at Stone
Datchworth
Benington
Aston
Codicote
Kimpton
Ayot St. Lawrence
Lemsford
Sandridge
Digswell
Tewin
Waterford
Great Offley
Meldreth
Bassingbourn
Litlington
Steeple Morden
Guilden Morden
Wrestlingworth
Orwell
Wimpole
Whaddon
Buntingford
Chipping
Wallington
Weston
Graveley
Walkern
Wood End
CENTRAL BEDFORDSHIRE
HERTFORDSHIRE
CAM
M1
M25
A1(M)
A1
A6
A5
A505
A507
A600
A10
A414
A41
A602
A421
A428
TODDINGTON
BALDOCK
FLAMSTEAD
SOUTH MIMMS

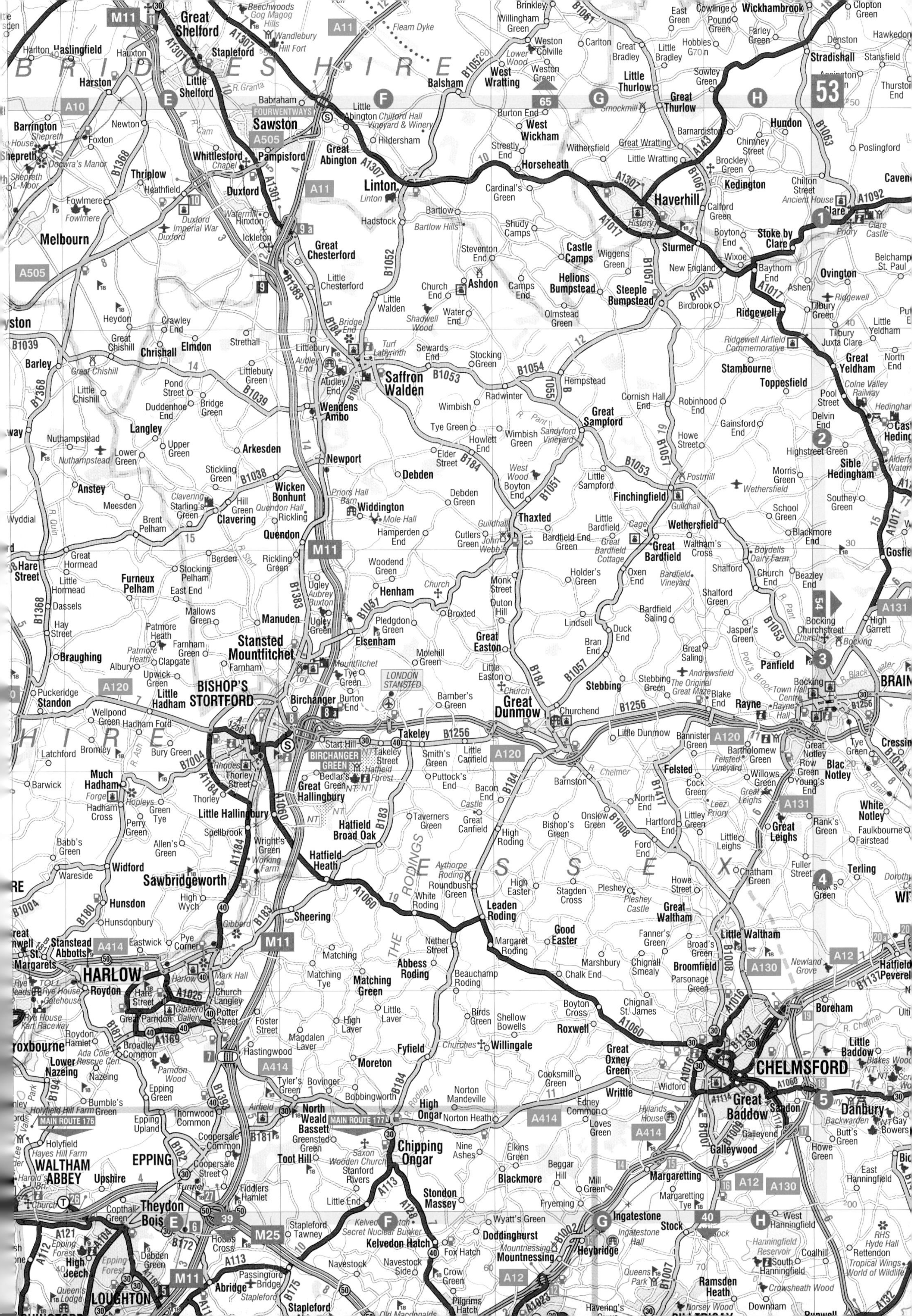
53
65
54
CAMBRIDGESHIRE
ESSEX
Great Shelford
Sawston
Linton
Haverhill
Saffron Walden
Thaxted
Great Dunmow
Bishop's Stortford
Stansted Mountfitchet
Harlow
Epping
Waltham Abbey
Chipping Ongar
Chelmsford
Great Baddow
Braintree
Sawbridgeworth
Loughton
Theydon Bois
Ingatestone
Finchingfield
Wethersfield
Great Bardfield
Steeple Bumpstead
Clare
Stoke by Clare
Melbourne
Royston
Duxford
Great Chesterford
Newport
Great Sampford
Rayne
Felsted
Great Waltham
Broomfield
Writtle
Danbury
Terling
Great Leighs
Abridge
Doddinghurst
Mountnessing
Kelvedon Hatch
Stanstead Abbotts
Hunsdon
Much Hadham
Little Hadham
Braughing
Standon
MAIN ROUTE 176
MAIN ROUTE 177
M11
M25
A120
A12
A414
A1307

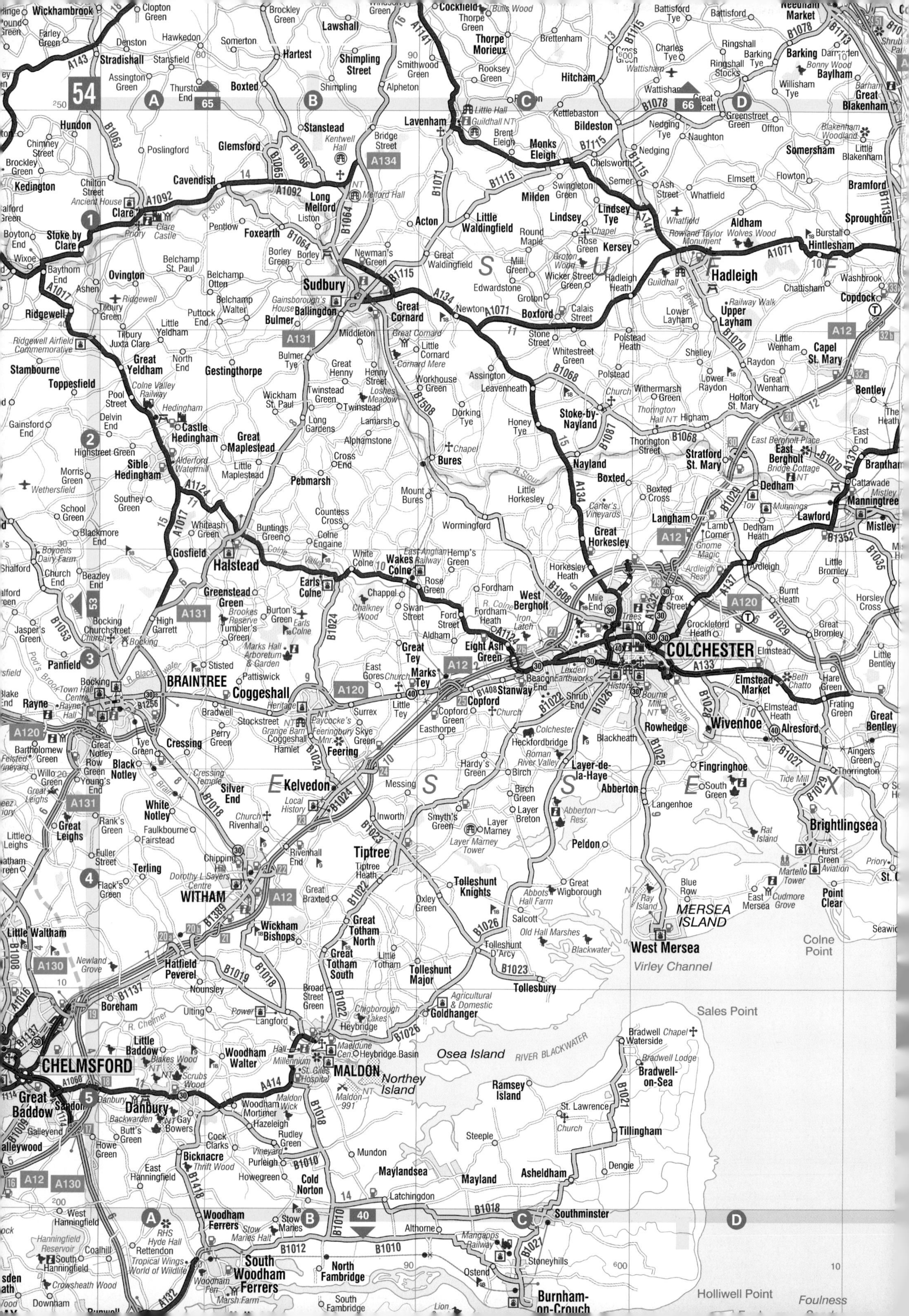

Wickhambrook
Farley Green
Clopton Green
Brockley Green
Lawshall
Cockfield
Bulls Wood
Thorpe Green
Battisford Tye
Battisford
Needham Market
Denston
Hawkedon
Somerton
Hartest
Shimpling Street
Thorpe Morieux
Brettenham
Cross Green
Charles Tye
Ringshall
Barking Tye
Barking
Darmsden
Bonny Wood
Stradishall
Stansfield
Smithwood Green
Rooksey Green
Hitcham
Wattisham
Ringshall Stocks
Baylham
Willisham Tye
Assington Green
Thurston End
Boxted
Shimpling
Alpheton
Barham
Great Blakenham
54
A
65
B
C
66
D
Hundon
Stanstead
Lavenham
Little Hall
Guildhall NT
Kettlebaston
Bildeston
Nedging Tye
Naughton
Greenstreet Green
Offton
Kentwell Hall
Bridge Street
Brent Eleigh
Monks Eleigh
Blakenham Woodland
Chimney Street
Poslingford
Glemsford
A134
Nedging
Somersham
Little Blakenham
Brockley Green
Chelsworth
Flowton
Cavendish
Semer
Elmsett
Kedington
Chilton Street
Ancient House
Clare
Long Melford
Melford Hall
Milden
Swingleton Green
Ash Street
Whatfield
Bramford
Liston
Acton
Lindsey
Lindsey Tye
Whatfield
Sproughton
Pentlow
Foxearth
Little Waldingfield
Aldham
Wolves Wood
Rowland Taylor Monument
Burstall
Boyton End
Stoke by Clare
Clare Castle
Priory
Round Maple
Chapel
Rose Green
Kersey
Hintlesham
Wixoe
Belchamp St. Paul
Borley Green
Borley
Newman's Green
Great Waldingfield
Mill Green
Groton Wood
Hadleigh
Baythorn End
Ashen
Ovington
Belchamp Otten
Sudbury
Gainsborough's House
Ballingdon
Great Cornard
Edwardstone
Wicker Street Green
Hadleigh Heath
Guildhall
Washbrook
Chattisham
Copdock
Ridgewell
Tilbury Green
Belchamp Walter
Newton
Boxford
Groton
Calais Street
Lower Layham
Upper Layham
Railway Walk
Little Yeldham
Puttock End
Bulmer
Middleton
Great Cornard
Little Cornard
Cornard Mere
Stone Street
Whitestreet Green
Polstead Heath
Little Wenham
Capel St. Mary
Tilbury Juxta Clare
A131
Ridgewell Airfield Commemorative
Great Yeldham
North End
Gestingthorpe
Bulmer Tye
Great Henny
Henny Street
Workhouse Green
Assington
Leavenheath
Polstead
Shelley
Raydon
Bentley
Stambourne
Toppesfield
Colne Valley Railway
Wickham St. Paul
Twinstead Green
Twinstead
Loshes Meadow
Dorking Tye
Withermarsh Green
Lower Raydon
Great Wenham
Holton St. Mary
Pool Street
Hedingham
Church
Thorington Hall NT
Higham
Gainsford End
Delvin End
Castle Hedingham
Great Maplestead
Long Gardens
Lamarsh
Honey Tye
Stoke-by-Nayland
Thorington Street
East Bergholt Place
East Bergholt
Bridge Cottage NT
East End
Brantham
Highstreet Green
Sible Hedingham
Alderford Watermill
Little Maplestead
Alphamstone
Cross End
Chapel
Bures
Nayland
Stratford St. Mary
Morris Green
Wethersfield
Pebmarsh
Boxted
Boxted Cross
Dedham
Cattawade
Mistley
Manningtree
Southey Green
Mount Bures
Little Horkesley
Carter's Vineyards
Toy
Munnings
Lawford
School Green
Whiteash Green
Countess Cross
Wormingford
Langham
Lamb Corner
Dedham Heath
Mistley
Blackmore End
Buntings Green
Colne Engaine
Great Horkesley
A12
Gnome Magic
Boyde's Dairy Farm
Gosfield
Halstead
White Colne
Wakes Colne
East Anglian Railway
Hemp's Green
Horkesley Heath
Ardleigh Resr.
Ardleigh
Little Bromley
Shalford
Church End
Beazley End
Earls Colne
Rose Green
Fordham
West Bergholt
Mile End
Fox Street
A120
Burnt Heath
Horsley Cross
Greenstead Green
Burton's Green
Chappel
Chalkney Wood
Swan Street
Ford Street
Fordham Heath
Iron Latch
Trees
Crockleford Heath
Great Bromley
Bocking Churchstreet
High Garrett
Brookes Reserve
Tumbler's Green
Earls Colne
Aldham
Eight Ash Green
Jasper's Green
Bocking
Marks Hall Arboretum & Garden
Great Tey
COLCHESTER
Elmstead
Little Bentley
Panfield
Stisted
East Gores
Church
Marks Tey
Lexden Earthworks
History
Elmstead Market
Beth Chatto
Hare Green
BRAINTREE
Pattiswick
Coggeshall
Heritage
Surrex
Little Tey
Stanway
Beacon End
Shrub End
Bourne Mill NT
Wivenhoe
Frating Green
Great Bentley
Rayne
Town Hall Centre
Rayne Hall
Bradwell
Stockstreet
Paycocke's NT
Grange Barn NT
Feeringbury Mnr.
Skye Green
Copford
Copford Green
Church
Easthorpe
Colchester
Heckfordbridge
Blackheath
Rowhedge
Elmstead Heath
Alresford
Bartholomew Green
Great Notley
Tye Green
Perry Green
Cressing
Coggeshall Hamlet
Feering
Roman River Valley
Layer-de-la-Haye
Fingringhoe
Aingers Green
Thorrington
Felsted Vineyard
Black Notley
Cressing Temple
Kelvedon
Messing
Hardy's Green
Birch
Abberton
South Green
Tide Mill
Willo Green
Young's End
Silver End
Local History
Birch Green
Layer Breton
Abberton Resr.
Langenhoe
Brightlingsea
Great Leighs
White Notley
Church
Rivenhall
Inworth
Smyth's Green
Layer Marney
Layer Marney Tower
Rat Island
Little Leighs
Rank's Green
Faulkbourne
Fairstead
Tiptree
Peldon
Hurst Green
Aviation
Priory
St. O
Fuller Street
Terling
Chipping Hill
Dorothy L Sayers Centre
Rivenhall End
Tiptree Heath
Tolleshunt Knights
Great Wigborough
Blue Row
Martello Tower
Flack's Green
WITHAM
Great Braxted
Oxley Green
Abbots Hall Farm
Ray Island
MERSEA ISLAND
East Mersea
Cudmore Grove
Point Clear
Great Totham North
Salcott
Little Waltham
Wickham Bishops
Old Hall Marshes
Blackwater
West Mersea
Colne Point
Seawick
Newland Grove
Hatfield Peverel
Great Totham South
Little Totham
Tolleshunt D'Arcy
Tolleshunt Major
Virley Channel
Tollesbury
Boreham
Nounsley
Broad Street Green
Agricultural & Domestic
Goldhanger
Sales Point
Ulting
Power
Langford
Chigborough Lakes
Heybridge
Little Baddow
Woodham Walter
Hall
Maeldune Cen.
Heybridge Basin
Osea Island
RIVER BLACKWATER
Bradwell Chapel
Waterside
Bradwell Lodge
Bradwell-on-Sea
CHELMSFORD
Blakes Wood
Scrubs Wood
Millennium
St. Giles Hospital
MALDON
Northey Island
Maldon 991
Ramsey Island
Great Baddow
Sandon
Danbury
Danbury
Backwarden
Gay Bowers
Woodham Mortimer
Maldon Wick
St. Lawrence
Church
Galleywood
Butt's Green
Cock Clarks
Hazeleigh
Rudley Green
Tillingham
Steeple
Howe Green
Bicknacre
Thrift Wood
Vineyard
Purleigh
Mundon
Dengie
East Hanningfield
Howegreen
Cold Norton
Maylandsea
Mayland
Asheldham
A12
A130
Latchingdon
West Hanningfield
Woodham Ferrers
Stow Maries
RHS Hyde Hall
Stow Maries Halt
40
Althorne
Southminster
Hanningfield Reservoir
Coalhill
Rettendon
South Hanningfield
Tropical Wings World of Wildlife
South Woodham Ferrers
North Fambridge
Mangapps Railway
Stoneyhills
Ostend
Crowsheath Wood
Woodham Fen
Marsh Farm
South Fambridge
Burnham-on-Crouch
Holliwell Point
Foulness
Downham
53

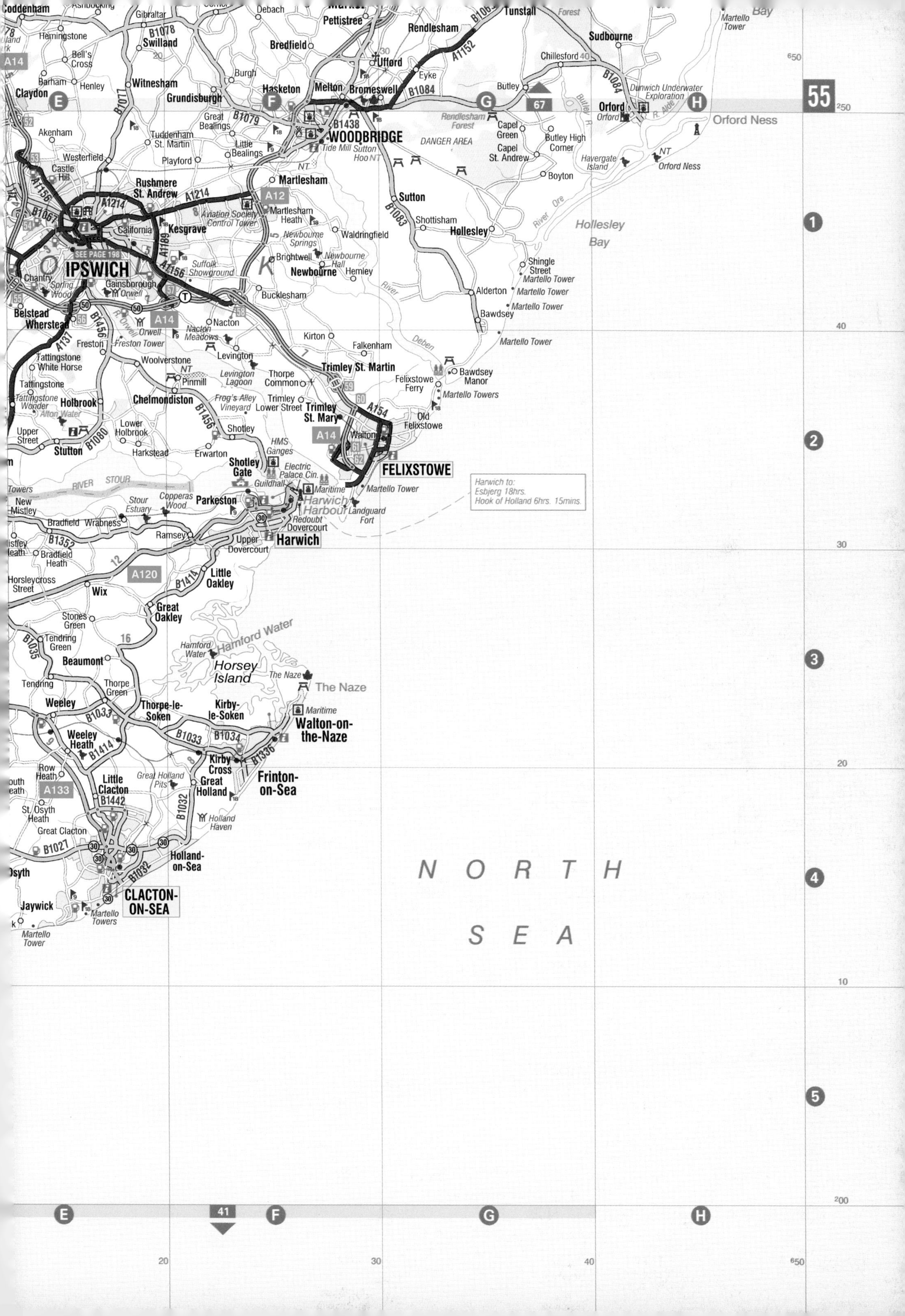

55
IPSWICH
WOODBRIDGE
FELIXSTOWE
Harwich
CLACTON-ON-SEA
Walton-on-the-Naze
Frinton-on-Sea
Holland-on-Sea
Orford Ness
Hollesley Bay
Harwich to:
Esbjerg 18hrs.
Hook of Holland 6hrs. 15mins.
NORTH
SEA
SEE PAGE 198
67
41

10   20   30   40

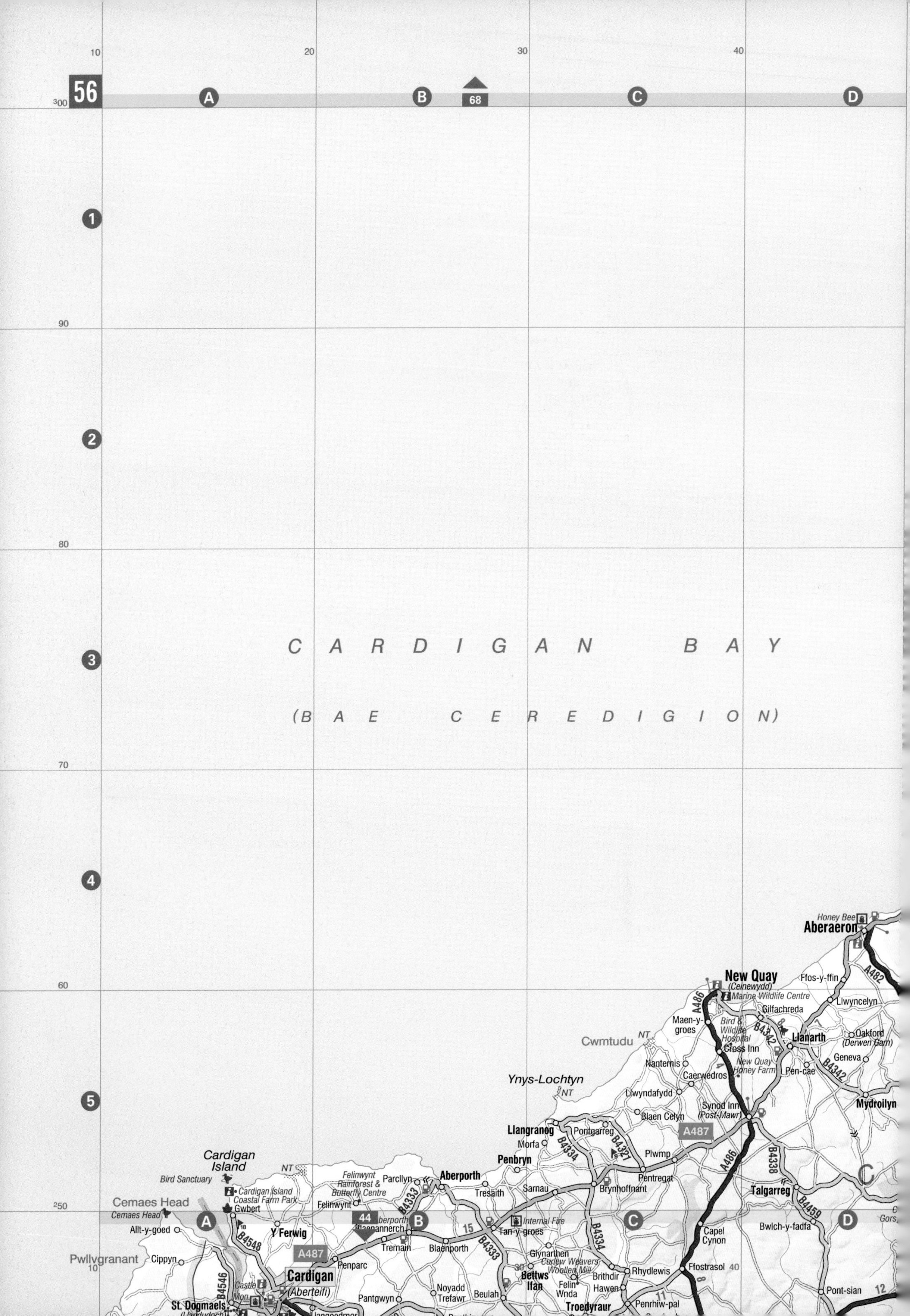

A   B   68   C   D

1

90

2

80

C A R D I G A N   B A Y

3

(B A E   C E R E D I G I O N)

70

4

Honey Bee

Aberaeron

60

Ffos-y-ffin

New Quay
(Ceinewydd)
Marine Wildlife Centre

A486

Gilfachreda

Llwyncelyn

Maen-y-groes

Bird & Wildlife Hospital

Cwmtudu

Cross Inn

Llanarth

Oakford (Derwen Gam)

Geneva

Nanternis

New Quay Honey Farm

Caerwedros

Pen-cae

B4342

Ynys-Lochtyn

NT

Llwyndafydd

Mydroilyn

5

Blaen Celyn

Synod Inn (Post-Mawr)

A487

A486

Llangranog

Pontgarreg

B4334

B4321

Plwmp

B4338

C

Cardigan
Island

Morfa

Penbryn

Pentregat

Bird Sanctuary

NT

Cardigan Island
Coastal Farm Park

Felinwynt
Rainforest &
Butterfly Centre

Parcllyn

Aberporth

Sarnau

Brynhoffnant

Talgarreg

B4459

Cemaes Head

Gwbert

Felinwynt

Tresaith

B4353

Curlew Weavers Woollen Mill

250

Cemaes Head

A

44

aberporth

B

15

Internal Fire

C

D

Gors

Allt-y-goed

B4548

Blaenannerch

Tan-y-groes

Capel Cynon

Bwlch-y-fadfa

Pwllvgranant

Cippyn

A487

Y Ferwig

Tremain

Blaenporth

B4333

B4334

Ffostrasol

40

10

B4546

Penparc

Glynarthen

Cardigan
(Aberteifi)

Pantgwyn

Noyadd
Trefawr

Beulah

**Bettws
Ifan**

Felin
Wnda

Brithdir

Rhydlewis

St. Dogmaels
(Llandudoch)

Castle

Troedyraur

Hawen

Penrhiw-pal

Pont-sian

12

11

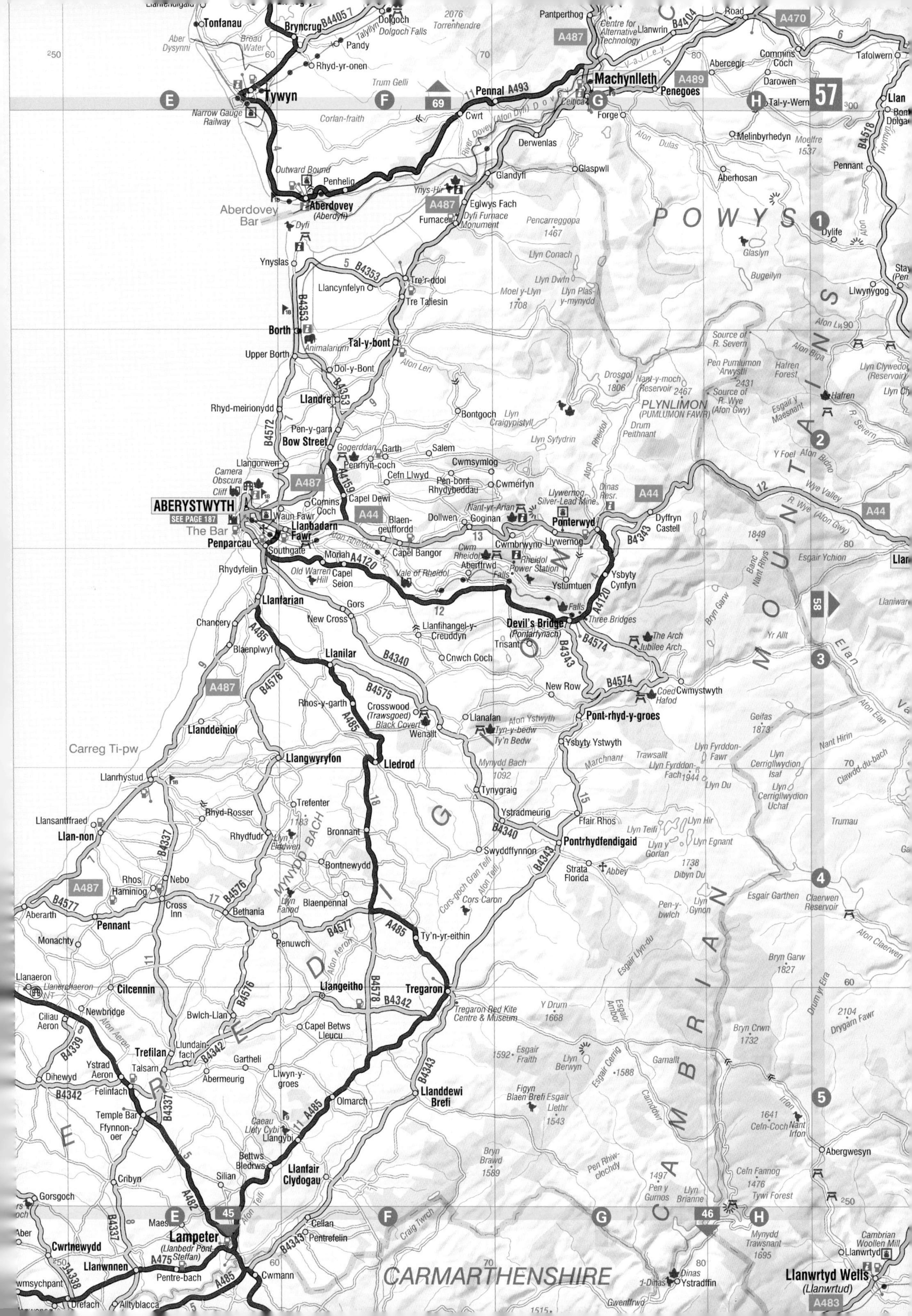

Tonfanau
Bryncrug
B4405
Dolgoch
Dolgoch Falls
Talyllyn
Pandy
2076
Torrenhendre
Pantperthog
Centre for Alternative Technology
Llanwrin
B4404
Road
A470
A487
Aber Dysynni
Broad Water
Rhyd-yr-onen
70
Tafolwern
Commins Coch
Abercegir
Darowen
A489
Machynlleth
Penegoes
57
Tywyn
Narrow Gauge Railway
E
F
Trum Gelli
69
Pennal
A493
Cwrt
G
Forge
H
Tal-y-Wern
Llan
Bont Dolgad
Corlan-fraith
Afon Dulas
Melinbyrhedyn
Moelfre 1537
B4518
Derwenlas
Outward Bound
Penhelig
Glandyfi
Glaspwll
Aberhosan
Pennant
Aberdovey Bar
Aberdovey
(Aberdyfi)
Ynys-Hir
A487
Eglwys Fach
Furnace
Dyfi Furnace Monument
Pencarreggopa 1467
POWYS
Dylife
Dyfi
Glaslyn
Llyn Conach
Ynyslas
B4353
Tre'r-ddol
Llancynfelyn
Tre Taliesin
Llyn Dwfn
Moel y-Llyn 1708
Llyn Plas-y-mynydd
Bugeilyn
Stay
Llwynygog
Borth
Animalarium
Tal-y-bont
Upper Borth
Dol-y-Bont
Afon Leri
Source of R. Severn
Pen Pumlumon Arwystli 2431
Hafren Forest
Llyn Clywedog (Reservoir)
Drosgol 1806
Nant-y-moch Reservoir 2467
Source of R. Wye (Afon Gwy)
Hafren
Llandre
Rhyd-meirionydd
B4572
Bontgoch
Llyn Craigypistyll
PLYNLIMON
(PUMLUMON FAWR)
Drum Peithnant
Esgair y Maesnant
R. Severn
Pen-y-garn
Bow Street
Llyn Syfydrin
Gogerddan
Garth
Salem
Y Foel
Afon Bidno
Llangorwen
Penrhyn-coch
Cwmsymlog
Camera Obscura
Cliff
A487
A4159
Cefn Llwyd
Pen-bont Rhydybeddau
Cwmerfyn
Llywernog Silver-Lead Mine
Dinas Resr.
Wye Valley
ABERYSTWYTH
SEE PAGE 187
Comins Coch
Capel Dewi
A44
Nant-yr-Arian
A44
Waun Fawr
Llanbadarn Fawr
The Bar
Penparcau
Blaen-geuffordd
Dollwen
Goginan
Ponterwyd
Dyffryn Castell
R. Wye (Afon Gwy)
1849
Southgate
Capel Bangor
Cwmbrwyno
Llywernog
B4343
Moriah
A4120
Cwm Rheidol
Aberffrwd
Rheidol Power Station
Esgair Ychion
Rhydyfelin
Old Warren Hill
Capel Seion
Vale of Rheidol
Rheidol Falls
Ystumtuen
Ysbyty Cynfyn
Llanfarian
Gors
Banc Nant Rhys
Bryn Garw
58
Chancery
New Cross
Llanfihangel-y-Creuddyn
Devil's Bridge
(Pontarfynach)
Falls
Three Bridges
Yr Allt
A485
Blaenplwyf
Llanilar
B4340
Cnwch Coch
Trisant
B4574
The Arch
Jubilee Arch
Elan
A487
B4576
B4575
New Row
B4574
Coed Hafod
Cwmystwyth
Rhos-y-garth
Crosswood (Trawsgoed)
Black Covert
Wenallt
Llanafan
Afon Ystwyth
Tyn-y-bedw
Ty'n Bedw
Pont-rhyd-y-groes
Geifas 1873
Afon Elan
Llanddeiniol
Ysbyty Ystwyth
Carreg Ti-pw
Llangwyryfon
Lledrod
Mynydd Bach 1092
Marchnant
Trawsallt
Llyn Fyrddon-Fawr
Llyn Fyrddon-Fach 1944
Llyn Cerrigllwydion Isaf
Nant Hirin
Clawdd-du-bach
Llanrhystud
Tynygraig
Llyn Du
Llyn Cerrigllwydion Uchaf
Trefenter
1183
Rhyd-Rosser
Ystradmeurig
Ffair Rhos
Trumau
Llansantffraed
Llan-non
Rhydfudr
Llyn Eiddwen
Bronnant
B4340
Llyn Teifi
Llyn Hir
Pontrhydfendigaid
Llyn y Gorlan
Llyn Egnant
B4337
MYNYDD BACH
Swyddffynnon
1738
Bontnewydd
Strata Florida
Abbey
Dibyn Du
A487
Rhos
Haminiog
Nebo
Cors-goch Glan Teifi
Afon Teifi
B4343
B4576
Cors Caron
Llyn Gynon
Claerwen Reservoir
Esgair Garthen
Aberarth
B4577
Cross Inn
Bethania
Llyn Fanod
Blaenpennal
Pen-y-bwlch
Pennant
B4577
A485
Ty'n-yr-eithin
Afon Claerwen
Monachty
Penuwch
Afon Aeron
Esgair Llyn-du
Bryn Garw 1827
Llanaeron
Llanerchaeron
Cilcennin
Llangeitho
B4578
Tregaron
Drum yr Eira
B4576
B4342
Tregaron Red Kite Centre & Museum
Y Drum 1668
Esgair Ambor
2104 Drygarn Fawr
Ciliau Aeron
Newbridge
Afon Aeron
Bwlch-Llan
Capel Betws Lleucu
Bryn Crwn 1732
B4339
Trefilan
Lluindain-fach
B4342
Esgair Fraith
1592
Llyn Berwyn
Esgair Cerrig
Ystrad Aeron
Talsarn
Gartheli
Abermeurig
Llwyn-y-groes
1588
Gamallt
Dihewyd
B4342
Felinfach
B4343
Llanddewi Brefi
Figyn Blaen Brefi
Esgair Llethr 1543
Camddwr
Irfon
Temple Bar
Ffynnon-oer
B4337
Olmarch
A485
Caeau Llety Cybi
Llangybi
1641
Cefn-Coch
Nant Irfon
Bettws Bledrws
Llanfair Clydogau
Bryn Brawd 1589
Pen Rhiw-clochdy
Abergwesyn
Cribyn
Silian
1497
Pen y Gurnos
Llyn Brianne
Cefn Fannog 1476
Tywi Forest
Gorsgoch
A482
45
Alon Teifi
Craig Twrch
46
Maesa
Cellan
Pentrefelin
Mynydd Trawsnant 1695
Aber
Cwrtnewydd
Lampeter
(Llanbedr Pont Steffan)
A475
B4343
Cambrian Woollen Mill
Llanwrtyd
Llanwnnen
Pentre-bach
Cwmann
CARMARTHENSHIRE
Dinas
Ystradffin
Llanwrtyd Wells
(Llanwrtud)
Cwmsychpant
B4338
A485
Drefach
Alltyblacca
Gwenffrwd
A483
CAMBRIAN MOUNTAINS
CEREDIGION
1
2
3
4
5

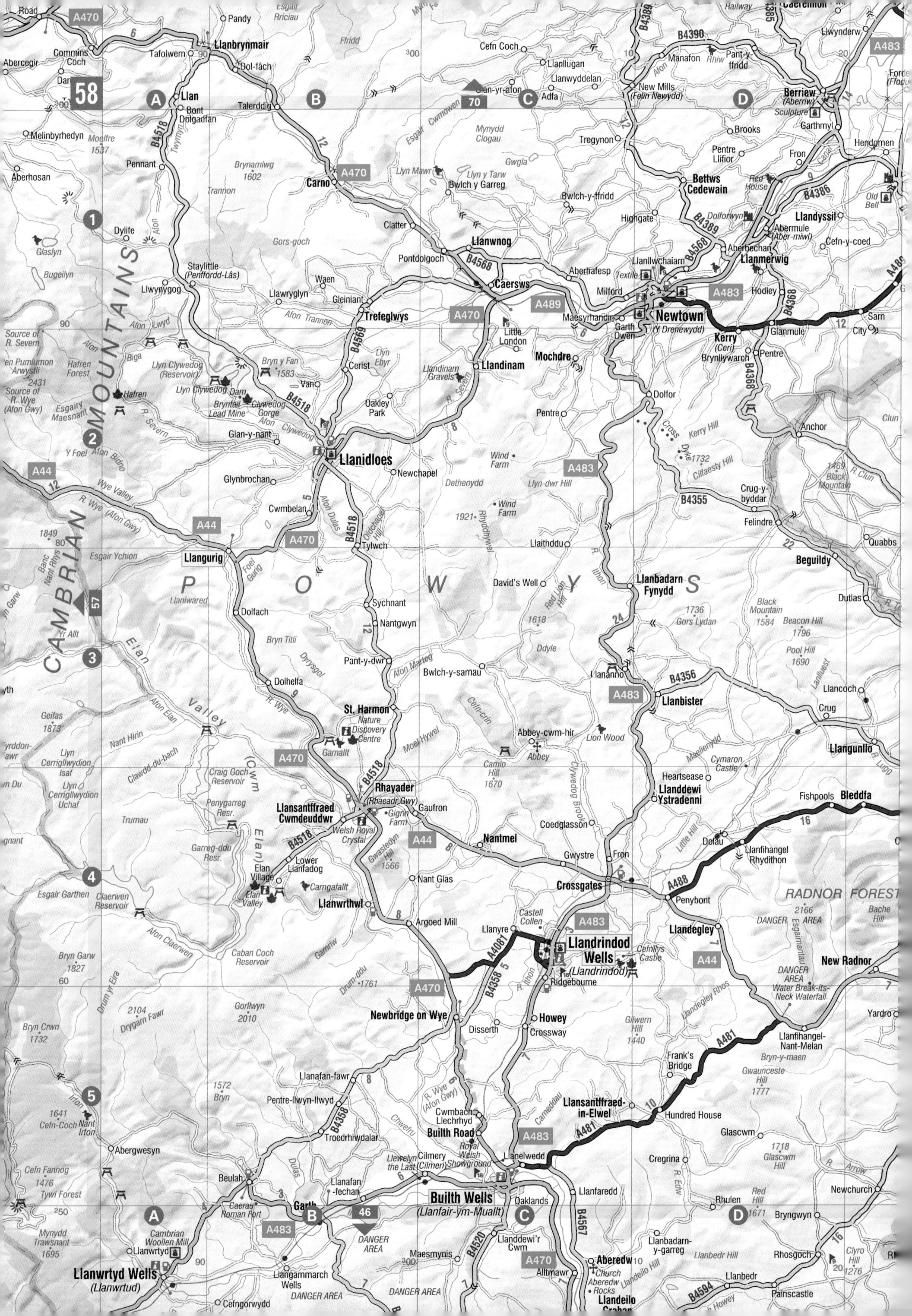
58
A
B
C
D
A470
Llanbrynmair
Pandy
Tafolwern
Commins Coch
Abercegir
Dol-fâch
Llan
Bont Dolgadfan
Talerddig
Melinbyrhedyn
Moelfre 1537
Pennant
Aberhosan
Carno
Brynamlwg 1602
Trannon
Cefn Coch
Llanllugan
Llanwyddelan
Glan-yr-afon
Adfa
70
Mynydd Clogau
Gwgla
Llyn Mawr
Llyn y Tarw
Bwlch y Garreg
Tregynon
New Mills (Felin Newydd)
Manafon
Pant-y-ffridd
B4390
Berriew (Aberriw)
Garthmyl
Brooks
Pentre Llifior
Fron
Hendomen
Bettws Cedewain
Bwlch-y-ffridd
Highgate
Red House
Old Bell
B4386
Llandyssil
Abermule (Aber-miwl)
Cefn-y-coed
Dolforwyn
B4389
Aberbechan
Llanmerwig
Llanllwchaiarn
B4568
Aberhafesp
Textile
Milford
Hodley
B4368
Newtown (Y Drenewydd)
A483
Kerry (Ceri)
Glanmule
Sarn
City
Brynllywarch
Pentre
1
Dylife
Glaslyn
Bugeilyn
Staylittle (Penffordd-Lâs)
Llwynygog
Clatter
Llanwnog
Pontdolgoch
Gors-goch
Caersws
A489
Maesyrhandir
Garth Owen
Waen
Llawryglyn
Gleiniant
Trefeglwys
B4569
Afon Trannon
Little London
Mochdre
Source of R. Severn
Pen Pumlumon Arwystli 2431
Source of R. Wye (Afon Gwy)
Hafren Forest
Hafren
Esgairy Maesnant
Llyn Clywedog (Reservoir)
Bryn y Fan 1583
Llyn Ebyr
Cerist
Van
Llandinam Gravels
Llandinam
Bryntail Lead Mine
Clywedog Gorge
Oakley Park
B4518
Dolfor
Pentre
Cross Dyke
Kerry Hill
1732
Anchor
Clun
2
Glan-y-nant
Llanidloes
Newchapel
Wind Farm
Dethenydd
Llyn-dwr Hill
Cilfaesty Hill
1469 Black Mountain
R. Clun
A44
Y Foel
Glynbrochan
Wye Valley
Cwmbelan
Afon Dulas
Crug-y-byddar
B4355
Felindre
1921
Rhydhywel
CAMBRIAN MOUNTAINS
1849
Esgair Ychion
Llangurig
Tylwch
Llaithddu
Quabbs
Beguildy
P O W Y S
Llaniwared
57
Sychnant
David's Well
Llanbadarn Fynydd
Dutlas
Dolfach
Nantgwyn
1618
1736 Gors Lydan
Black Mountain 1584
Beacon Hill 1796
Yr Allt
Bryn Titli
Ddyle
Pool Hill 1690
3
Elan
Pant-y-dwr
Bwlch-y-sarnau
Llananno
B4356
Llanbister
Llancoch
Dolhelfa
Crug
Geifas 1873
Afon Elan
Elan Valley
St. Harmon
Nature Discovery Centre
Abbey-cwm-hir
Abbey
Lion Wood
Llangunllo
Nant Hirin
Gamallt
Llyn Cerrigllwydion Isaf
Llyn Cerrigllwydion Uchaf
Craig Goch Reservoir
Camlo Hill 1670
Cymaron Castle
Heartsease
Llanddewi Ystradenni
Fishpools
Bleddfa
Penygarreg Resr.
Rhayader (Rhaeadr Gwy)
Llansantffraed Cwmdeuddwr
Gaufron
Gigrin Farm
Welsh Royal Crystal
Coedglasson
Trumau
Garreg-ddu Resr.
Nantmel
Gwystre
Fron
Dolau
Llanfihangel Rhydithon
16
4
Lower Llanfadog
Elan Village
Gwastedyn Hill 1566
Nant Glas
Crossgates
A488
Penybont
RADNOR FOREST
Esgair Garthen
Claerwen Reservoir
Carngafallt
Llanwrthwl
Argoed Mill
Llanyre
Castell Collen
Llandrindod Wells (Llandrindod)
Cefnllys Castle
Llandegley
2166 DANGER AREA
Bache Hill
Afon Claerwen
Bryn Garw 1827
Caban Coch Reservoir
A4081
Drum-ddu 1761
B4358
Ridgebourne
New Radnor
Water Break-its-Neck Waterfall
Drum yr Eira
2104 Drygarn Fawr
Gorllwyn 2010
Newbridge on Wye
Disserth
Howey
Crossway
Gilwern Hill 1440
Llandegley Rhos
Yardro
Bryn Crwn 1732
Llanfihangel-Nant-Melan
Bryn-y-maen
A481
Frank's Bridge
Gwaunceste Hill 1777
5
1641 Cefn-Coch
Nant Irfon
Llanafan-fawr
1572 Bryn
Pentre-llwyn-llwyd
Cwmbach Llechrhyd
Llansantffraed-in-Elwel
Hundred House
Builth Road
Royal Welsh Showground
Glascwm
Abergwesyn
Troedrhiwdalar
Chwefru
Dulas
1718 Glascwm Hill
Cefn Fannog 1476
Tywi Forest
Beulah
Llanafan-fechan
Llewelyn the Last (Cilmeri)
Cilmery
Llanelwedd
Cregrina
Builth Wells (Llanfair-ym-Muallt)
Oaklands
Llanfaredd
R. Edw
B4567
Newchurch
Rhulen
Red Hill 1671
Bryngwyn
Caerau Roman Fort
Garth
46
DANGER AREA
Mynydd Trawsnant 1695
Cambrian Woollen Mill
Llanwrtyd
Llanwrtyd Wells (Llanwrtud)
Llangammarch Wells
B4520
Maesmynis
Llanddewi'r Cwm
Aberedw
Church
Aberedw Rocks
Llanbadarn-y-garreg
Llanbedr Hill
Rhosgoch
Clyro Hill 1276
Alltmawr
Llanbedr
Painscastle
B4594
Cefngorwydd
Llanddeilo Graban

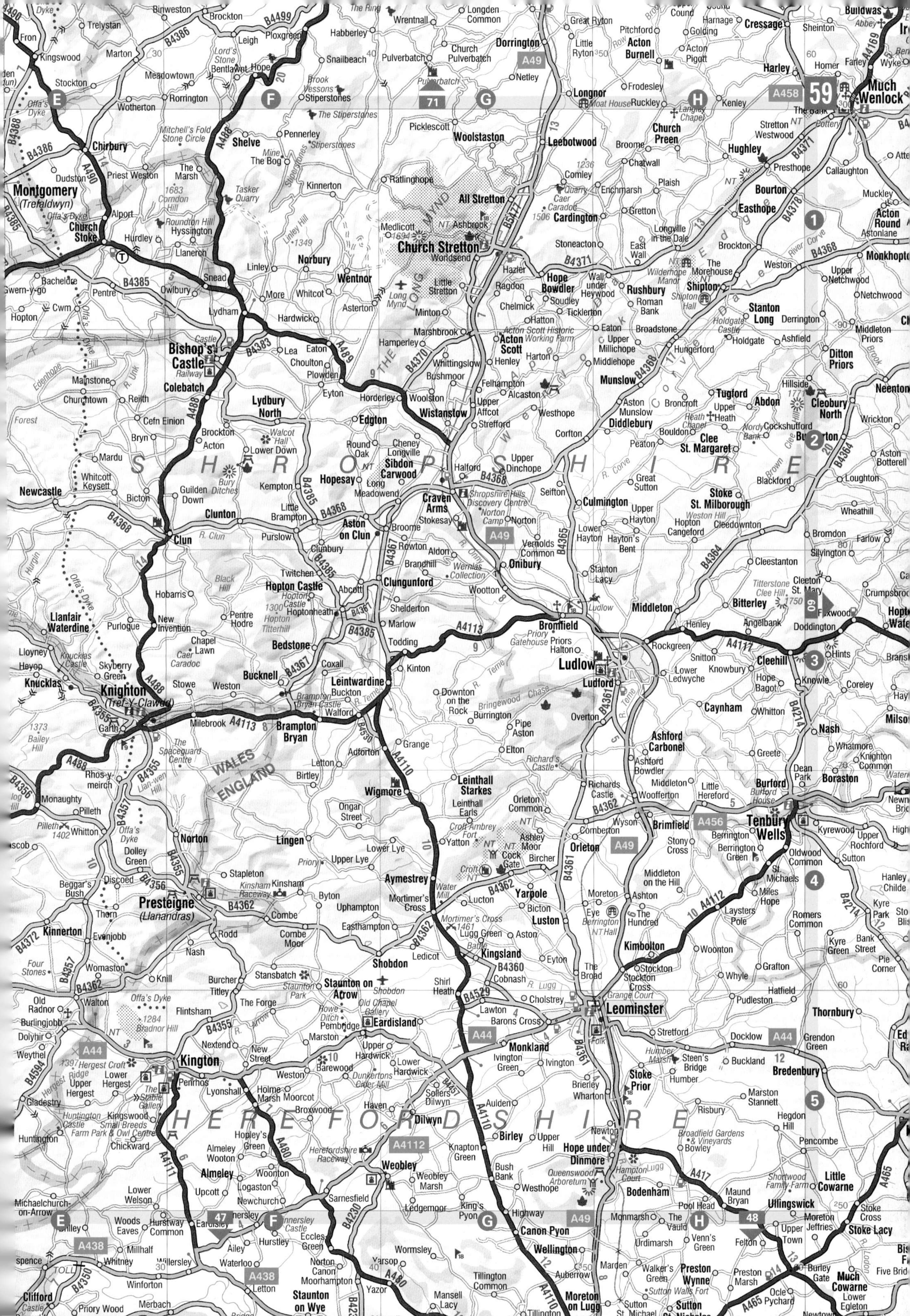

Fron
Kingswood
Trelystan
Binweston
Brockton
Leigh
Ploxgreen
B4499
B4386
Marton
Lord's Stone
Bentlawnt
Hope
Habberley
Snailbeach
Wrentnall
Pulverbatch
Church Pulverbatch
Longden Common
Dorrington
Great Ryton
Little Ryton
Pitchford
Acton Burnell
Cound
Harnage
Golding
Acton Pigott
Cressage
Sheinton
Buildwas
Abbey
Harley
Homer
Farley
Wyke
Much Wenlock
A458
59
Stockton
Meadowtown
Rorrington
Brook Vessons
Stiperstones
The Stiperstones
Pulverbatch
71
Netley
A49
Longnor
Moat House
Frodesley
Ruckley
Langley Chapel
Kenley
The Bank
Offa's Dyke
Wotherton
E
F
G
H
B4388
B4386
Chirbury
Mitchell's Fold Stone Circle
A488
Shelve
Pennerley
Stiperstones
Picklescott
Woolstaston
Leebotwood
Church Preen
Broome
Chatwall
Stretton Westwood
Hughley
Presthope
Callaughton
B4371
Mine
The Bog
Montgomery
(Trefaldwyn)
Offa's Dyke
Dudston
A490
Priest Weston
The Marsh
1683 Corndon Hill
Tasker Quarry
Kinnerton
Ratlinghope
1236 Comley
Quarry
Caer Caradoc
1506
Enchmarsh
Plaish
Bourton
Muckley
Acton Round
Astonlane
Eastope
B4378
Church Stoke
Alport
Roundton Hill
Hyssington
Hurdley
Llanerch
Linley Hill
1349
Medlicott
1694
Long Mynd
NT Ashbrook
All Stretton
Cardington
Gretton
Longville in the Dale
Church Stretton
Worldsend
Stoneacton
East Wall
Brockton
Monkhopton
B4368
B4371
Wilderhope Manor
The Morehouse
Weston
Upper Netchwood
Netchwood
B4385
Bacheldre
Pentre
Owlbury
Snead
Linley
Norbury
Wentnor
Hazler
Hope Bowdler
Wall under Heywood
Rushbury
Roman Bank
Shipton
Shipton Hall
Stanton Long
Derrington
Gwern-y-go
Hopton
Cwm
More
Whitcot
Asterton
Long Mynd
Little Stretton
Ragdon
Chelmick
Soudley
Ticklerton
Lydham
Hardwick
Minton
Hatton
Acton Scott Historic Working Farm
Eaton
Broadstone
Holdgate Castle
Holdgate
Middleton Priors
Bishop's Castle
Castle
Railway
B4383
Lea
Eaton
A489
Choulton
Plowden
Hamperley
Marshbrook
B4370
Whittingslow
Acton Scott
Henley
Harton
Upper Millichope
Middlehope
Hungerford
Ashfield
Ditton Priors
Forest
Edenhope
Mainstone
Churchtown
Reilth
R. Unk
Colebatch
Eyton
Horderley
Woolston
Bushmoor
Wistanstow
Upper Affcot
Strefford
Felhampton
Alcaston
Westhope
Munslow
B4368
Aston Munslow
Broncroft
Tugford
Abdon
Upper Heath
Heath Chapel
Cleobury North
1771
Neenton
Lydbury North
Edgton
Diddlebury
Corfton
Bouldon
Nordy Bank
Cockshutford
Clee St. Margaret
Wrickton
Cefn Einion
Bryn
Brockton
Acton
Walcot Hall
Lower Down
Round Oak
Cheney Longville
Sibdon Carwood
Halford
Upper Dinchope
B4368
Peaton
Mardu
Whitcott Keysett
Bury Ditches
Kempton
Hopesay
Long Meadowend
Shropshire Hills Discovery Centre
Great Sutton
Blackford
Aston Botterell
Loughton
Stoke St. Milborough
Newcastle
Bicton
Guilden Down
Clunton
Little Brampton
B4385
Craven Arms
Norton Camp
Seifton
Culmington
Upper Hayton
Weston Hill
Hopton Cangeford
Cleedownton
Wheathill
B4368
Clun
R. Clun
Purslow
Aston on Clun
Broome
Stokesay
Norton
Lower Hayton
Hayton's Bent
Bromdon
Farlow
Silvington
Hurgin
Offa's Dyke
Clunbury
B4367
Rowton
Aldon
Vernolds Common
A49
Onibury
B4365
Cleestanton
B4364
Twitchen
B4385
Brandhill
Wernlas Collection
Stanton Lacy
Hobarris
Black Hill
Hopton Castle
Abcott
Clungunford
Wootton
Titterstone Clee Hill
Clee St. Mary
750
Crumpsbrook
1300 Hopton Titterhill
Hoptonheath
Shelderton
Middleton
Bitterley
Llanfair Waterdine
Purlogue
New Invention
Pentre Hodre
Marlow
Bromfield
Ludlow
Henley
Angelbank
Foxwood
Doddington
Lloyney
Heyop
Knucklas Castle
Chapel Lawn
Caer Caradoc
Bedstone
Todding
A4113
Priory Gatehouse
Priors Halton
Rockgreen
Snitton
A4117
Cleehill
Hints
Knucklas
Skyborry Green
Knighton
(Tref-Y-Clawdd)
Stowe
Weston
Bucknell
Coxall
Leintwardine
Kinton
Downton on the Rock
Bringewood Chase
Ludlow
Ludford
Lower Ledwyche
Knowbury
Hope Bagot
Knowle
Coreley
B4355
Garth
1373 Bailey Hill
Milebrook
A4113
Brampton Bryan
Brampton Bryan Castle
Buckton
Walford
R. Teme
Burrington
Pipe Aston
Overton
B4361
Caynham
Whitton
B4214
Nash
A488
The Spacequard Centre
WALES
ENGLAND
Adforton
Grange
Elton
Ashford Carbonel
Ashford Bowdler
Greete
Whatmore
Knighton Common
Rhos-y-meirch
B4356
Llan-wen Hill
Letton
Birtley
A4110
Leinthall Starkes
Richard's Castle
Richards Castle
Middleton
Dean Park
Boraston
Monaughty
Pilleth
Wigmore
Leinthall Earls
Orleton Common
Woofferton
Little Hereford
Burford
Burford House
Tenbury Wells
Kyrewood
B4357
Pilleth 1402
Whitton
Offa's Dyke
Ongar Street
Croft Ambrey Fort
Ashley Moor
Comberton
Wyson
Brimfield
A456
Berrington
Upper Rochford
Norton
Lingen
Lower Lye
Yatton
Croft
Cock Gate
Bircher
Orleton
Stony Cross
Berrington Green
Oldwood Common
Sutton
Dolley Green
Discoed
Priory
Upper Lye
Aymestrey
Water Mill
B4362
Yarpole
B4361
Middleton on the Hill
St. Michaels
Hanley Childe
Beggar's Bush
B4356
Stapleton
Kinsham Raceway
Kinsham
Byton
Mortimer's Cross
Lucton
Bicton
Moreton
Ashton
Miles Hope
Kyre Park
Presteigne
(Llanandras)
B4362
Combe
Uphampton
Mortimer's Cross 1461
Luston
Eye
Berrington NT Hall
The Hundred
A4112
Laysters Pole
Romers Common
B4214
Thorn
Kinnerton
Evenjobb
Rodd
Easthampton
Combe Moor
Lugg Green
Aston
Kyre Green
Bank Street
B4372
Four Stones
B4357
Womaston
Nash
Shobdon
Ledicot
Kingsland
Eyton
Kimbolton
Woonton
Pie Corner
Knill
Stansbatch
Staunton Park
Staunton on Arrow
Shobdon
B4360
Cobnash
The Broad
Stockton
Stockton Cross
Whyle
Grafton
B4362
Walton
Burcher
Titley
Offa's Dyke
Old Radnor
Burlingjobb
The Forge
Rowe Ditch
Pembridge
Old Chapel Gallery
Shirl Heath
B4529
Lawton
Barons Cross
R. Lugg
Cholstrey
Grange Court
Leominster
Hatfield
Pudleston
Thornbury
1284 Bradnor Hill
Flintsham
Eardisland
A44
Monkland
B4361
Stretford
Docklow
A44
Grendon Green
Dolyhir
Weythel
B4355
Nextend
Marston
Upper Hardwick
Lower Hardwick
Ivington Green
Ivington
Humber Marsh
Steen's Bridge
Buckland
Bredenbury
1397 Hergest Croft
Hergest Ridge
Upper Hergest
Lower Hergest
Kington
Penrhos
New Street
Weston
Barewood
Dunkertons Cider Mill
Stoke Prior
Humber
B4594
Gladestry
The Stables Gallery
Lyonshall
Holme Marsh
Moorcot
Broxwood
Sollers Dilwyn
B4457
Aulden
Brierley
Wharton
Marston Stannett
Huntington Castle
Kingswood
Small Breeds Farm Park & Owl Centre
HEREFORDSHIRE
Haven
Dilwyn
A4110
Newton
Risbury
Hegdon Hill
Huntington
Chickward
Hopley's Green
A480
Herefordshire Raceway
A4112
Birley
Upper Hill
Broadfield Gardens & Vineyards
Bowley
Pencombe
A4111
Almeley Wooton
Woonton
Knapton Green
Hope under Dinmore
Almeley
Weobley
Weobley Marsh
Bush Bank
Queenswood Arboretum
Hampton Court
A417
Shortwood Family Farm
Little Cowarne
A465
Lower Welson
Upcott
Logaston
Newchurch
Sarnesfield
B4230
Westhope
Bodenham
Maund Bryan
Michaelchurch-on-Arrow
Woods Eaves
Hurstway Common
Ledgemoor
King's Pyon
Highway
Pool Head
Ullingswick
Stoke Cross
Eardisley
Nunnersley Castle
47
48
Monmarsh
The Vauld
Moreton Jeffries
Stoke Lacy
A438
Millhalf
Hurstley
Eccles Green
A49
Canon Pyon
Urdimarsh
Venn's Green
Felton
Upper Town
Whitney
Willersley
Ailey
Waterloo
Wormsley
Wellington
Marden
Walker's Green
Preston Wynne
Preston Marsh
Burley Gate
Much Cowarne
Five Bridges
TOLL
Winforton
A438
Norton Canon
Moorhampton
Yarsop
A480
Tillington Common
Auberrow
Sutton Walls Fort
Clifford
Castle
B4350
Priory Wood
Merbach
Letton
Staunton on Wye
Yazor
Mansell Lacy
A4110
Moreton on Lugg
Sutton St. Michael
Sutton St. Nicholas
Ocle Pychard
Lower Egleton
Newtown
Tillington

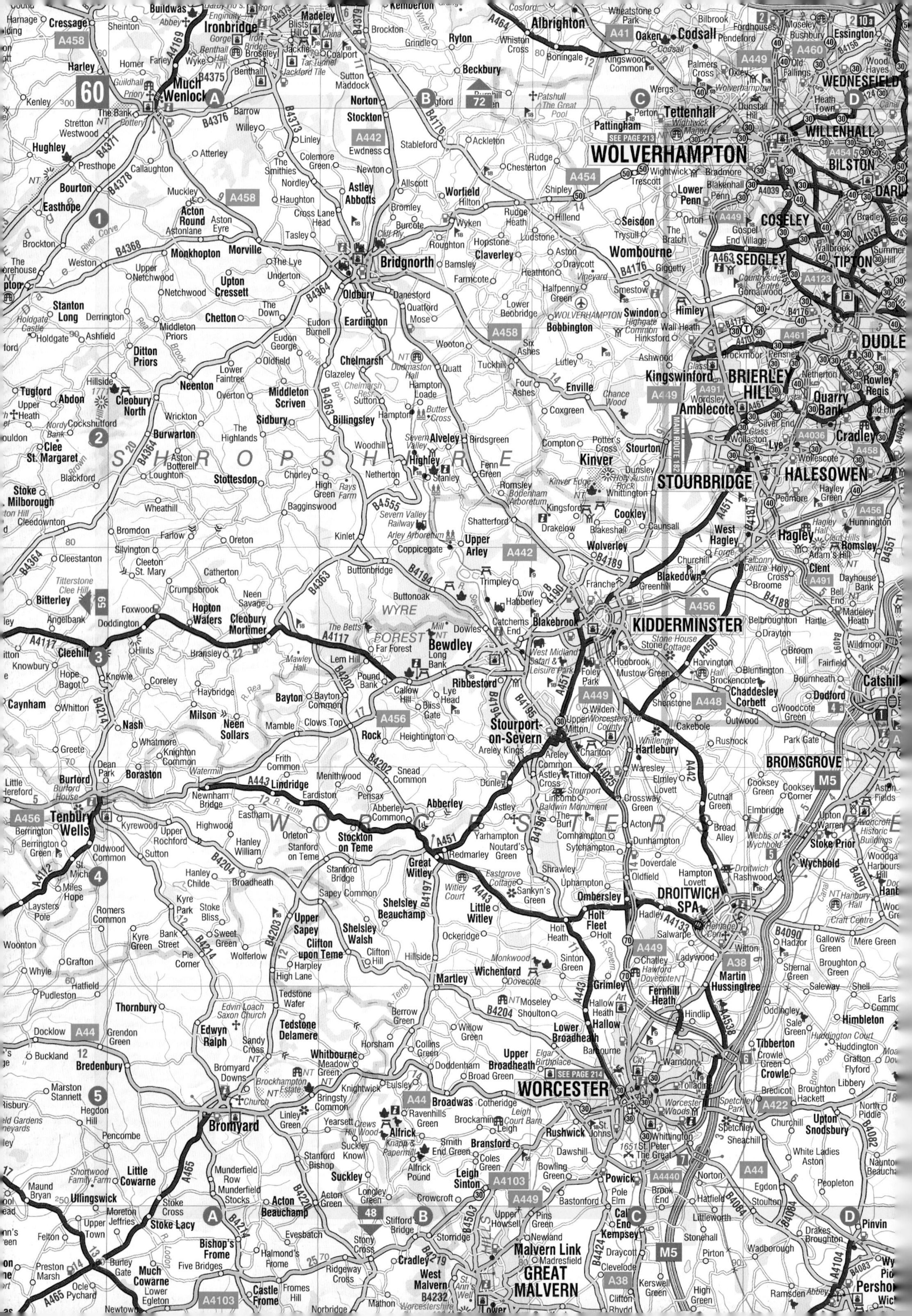

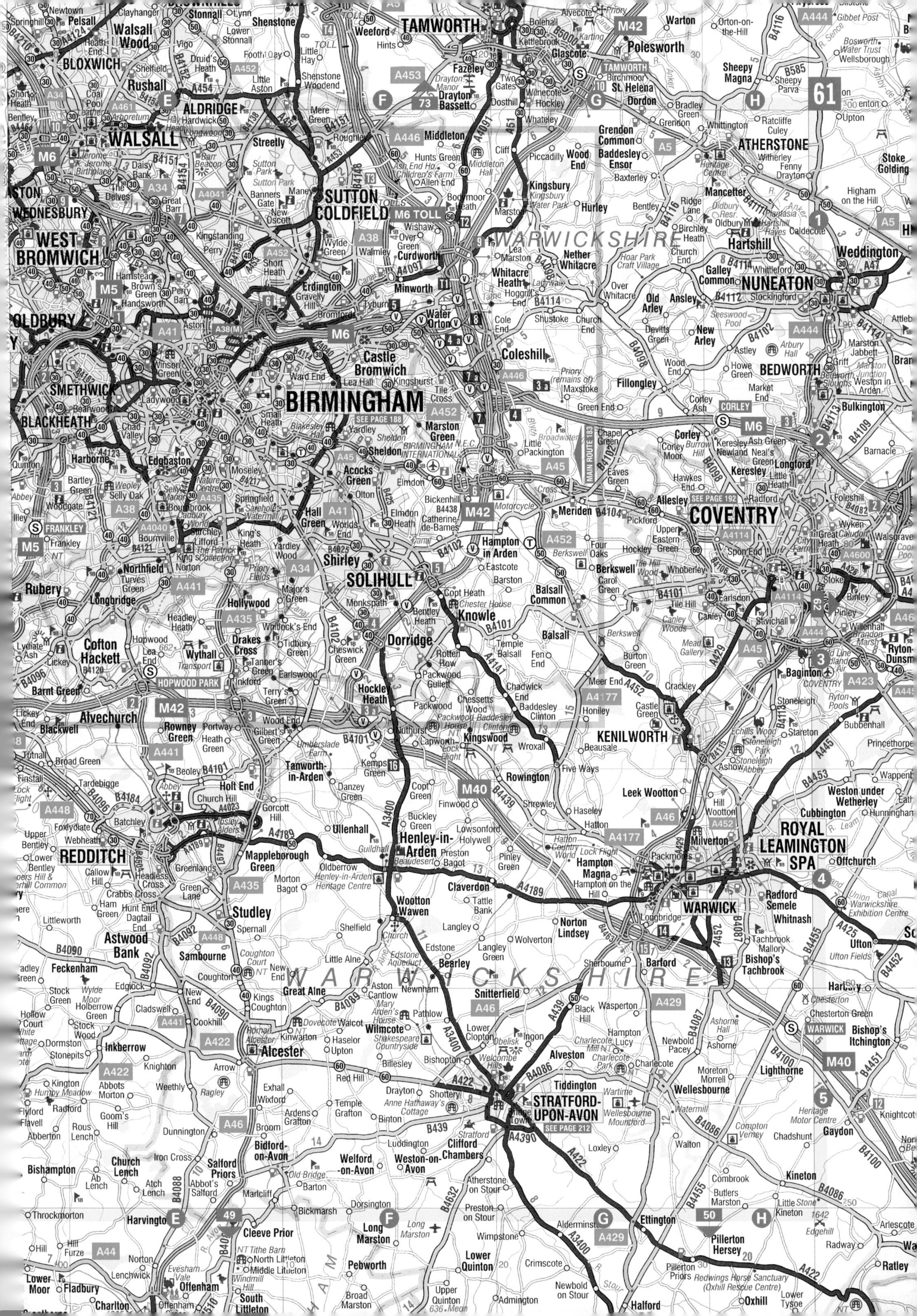

61
TAMWORTH
Polesworth
Atherstone
WALSALL
ALDRIDGE
BLOXWICH
WEDNESBURY
WEST BROMWICH
SUTTON COLDFIELD
OLDBURY
SMETHWICK
BLACKHEATH
BIRMINGHAM
SEE PAGE 188
Castle Bromwich
Coleshill
WARWICKSHIRE
NUNEATON
BEDWORTH
COVENTRY
SEE PAGE 192
SOLIHULL
Knowle
Dorridge
Shirley
Northfield
Rubery
Harborne
Edgbaston
Kingsbury
Meriden
Balsall Common
KENILWORTH
ROYAL LEAMINGTON SPA
WARWICK
Henley-in-Arden
REDDITCH
Alvechurch
Studley
Alcester
Astwood Bank
STRATFORD-UPON-AVON
SEE PAGE 212
Wellesbourne
Kineton
Shipston-on-Stour
Ettington
Pillerton Hersey
Bidford-on-Avon
Cleeve Prior
Long Marston
Offenham
Fladbury
Evesham Vale
Inkberrow
Feckenham
M6
M5
M42
M40
M6 TOLL
MAIN ROUTE 183
A5
A38
A34
A45
A46
A435
A422
A429
A452
A444
A4189
A3400
A439
A441

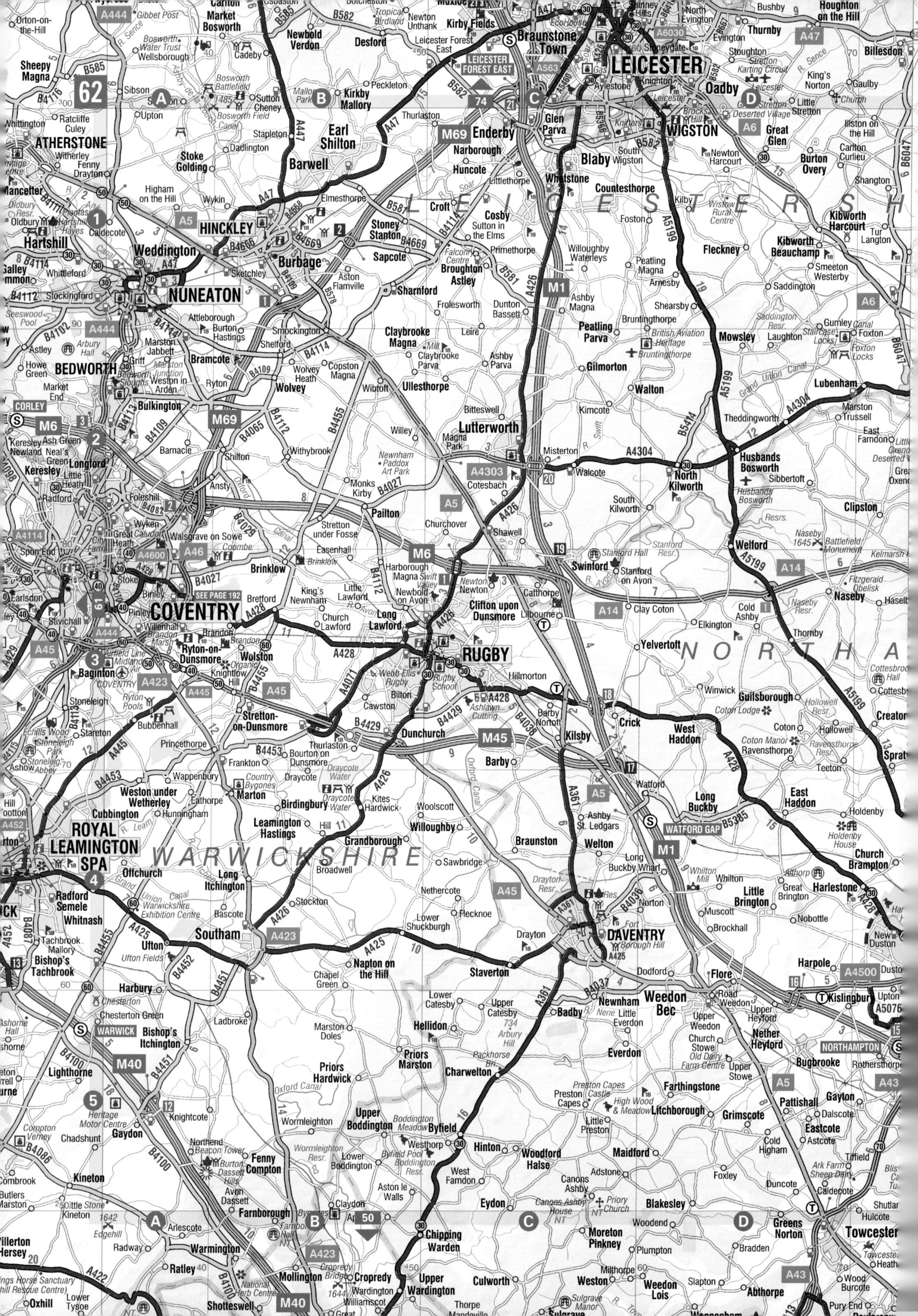

62
74
LEICESTER FOREST EAST
SEE PAGE 192
61
50
A
B
C
D
LEICESTER
Oadby
WIGSTON
Braunstone Town
Leicester Forest East
Kirby Fields
Glen Parva
Blaby
South Wigston
Enderby
Narborough
Huncote
Whetstone
Countesthorpe
Cosby
Croft
Thurlaston
Desford
Newbold Verdon
Market Bosworth
Carlton
Cadeby
Bosworth Battlefield
Sutton Cheney
Kirkby Mallory
Peckleton
Earl Shilton
Barwell
Stoke Golding
Dadlington
Stapleton
Sibson
Upton
Sheepy Magna
Orton-on-the-Hill
Ratcliffe Culey
Witherley
ATHERSTONE
Fenny Drayton
Mancetter
Higham on the Hill
Wykin
HINCKLEY
Burbage
Elmesthorpe
Stoney Stanton
Sapcote
Sharnford
Aston Flamville
Weddington
NUNEATON
Caldecote
Hartshill
Oldbury
Whittleford
Stockingford
Attleborough
Burton Hastings
Marston Jabbett
BEDWORTH
Bramcote
Astley
Bulkington
Weston in Arden
Ryton
Wolvey
Wolvey Heath
Shelford
Smockington
Copston Magna
Wibtoft
Claybrooke Magna
Claybrooke Parva
Frolesworth
Leire
Ullesthorpe
Dunton Bassett
Ashby Parva
Broughton Astley
Primethorpe
Sutton in the Elms
Willoughby Waterleys
Peatling Magna
Arnesby
Ashby Magna
Shearsby
Bruntingthorpe
Peatling Parva
Gilmorton
Walton
Kimcote
Bitteswell
Lutterworth
Magna Park
Misterton
Walcote
North Kilworth
South Kilworth
Husbands Bosworth
Sibbertoft
Theddingworth
Lubenham
Marston Trussell
East Farndon
Mowsley
Laughton
Gumley
Foxton
Saddington
Fleckney
Kibworth Beauchamp
Kibworth Harcourt
Smeeton Westerby
Tur Langton
Shangton
Burton Overy
Carlton Curlieu
Illston on the Hill
Great Glen
Newton Harcourt
Kilby
Foston
Wistow
Stoughton
Thurnby
Bushby
Houghton on the Hill
Billesdon
King's Norton
Gaulby
Little Stretton
Evington
North Evington
Knighton
Aylestone
LEICESTERSHIRE
NORTHA
WARWICKSHIRE
Corley
Keresley
Longford
Little Heath
Radford
Foleshill
Ansty
Shilton
Barnacle
Withybrook
Monks Kirby
Pailton
Stretton under Fosse
Wyken
Walsgrave on Sowe
Great Heath
Spon End
Stoke
Binley
COVENTRY
Earlsdon
Stivichall
Willenhall
Brandon
Ryton-on-Dunsmore
Wolston
Bretford
Brinklow
Easenhall
King's Newnham
Church Lawford
Little Lawford
Long Lawford
Harborough Magna
Newbold on Avon
Newton
Clifton upon Dunsmore
Churchover
Cotesbach
Shawell
Swinford
Stanford on Avon
Catthorpe
Lilbourne
Clay Coton
Elkington
Yelvertoft
Cold Ashby
Naseby
Thornby
Welford
Clipston
RUGBY
Hillmorton
Bilton
Cawston
Dunchurch
Thurlaston
Barby
Barby Nortoft
Kilsby
Crick
West Haddon
Winwick
Guilsborough
Coton
Ravensthorpe
Teeton
Hollowell
Creaton
East Haddon
Holdenby
Long Buckby
Watford
Ashby St. Ledgers
Welton
Braunston
Long Buckby Wharf
Whilton
Little Brington
Great Brington
Harlestone
Church Brampton
Nobottle
New Duston
Harpole
Muscott
Brockhall
Norton
DAVENTRY
Drayton
Staverton
Badby
Newnham
Little Everdon
Everdon
Dodford
Flore
Weedon Bec
Upper Weedon
Church Stowe
Upper Stowe
Upper Heyford
Nether Heyford
Bugbrooke
Kislingbury
Rothersthorpe
Farthingstone
Litchborough
Preston Capes
Little Preston
Maidford
Adstone
Canons Ashby
Woodend
Blakesley
Grimscote
Cold Higham
Pattishall
Gayton
Eastcote
Astcote
Tiffield
Duncote
Foxley
Greens Norton
Towcester
Caldecote
Bradden
Slapton
Abthorpe
Plumpton
Moreton Pinkney
Weston
Weedon Lois
Sulgrave
Culworth
Eydon
Woodford Halse
Hinton
Byfield
Charwelton
Hellidon
Upper Catesby
Lower Catesby
Priors Marston
Priors Hardwick
Marston Doles
Napton on the Hill
Chapel Green
Lower Shuckburgh
Flecknoe
Nethercote
Sawbridge
Willoughby
Woolscott
Grandborough
Kites Hardwick
Birdingbury
Leamington Hastings
Hill
Broadwell
Stockton
Southam
Long Itchington
Bascote
Marton
Eathorpe
Hunningham
Weston under Wetherley
Cubbington
Wappenbury
Princethorpe
Frankton
Bourton on Dunsmore
Draycote
Stretton-on-Dunsmore
Knightlow Hill
Baginton
Bubbenhall
Stoneleigh
Stareton
Ashow
ROYAL LEAMINGTON SPA
Offchurch
Radford Semele
Whitnash
Tachbrook Mallory
Bishop's Tachbrook
Ufton
Harbury
Chesterton Green
Bishop's Itchington
Ladbroke
Lighthorne
Gaydon
Knightcote
Chadshunt
Northend
Fenny Compton
Kineton
Avon Dassett
Farnborough
Arlescote
Warmington
Radway
Ratley
Shotteswell
Mollington
Cropredy
Wardington
Upper Wardington
Claydon
Aston le Walls
Lower Boddington
Upper Boddington
Wormleighton
West Farndon
Chipping Warden
Oxhill
Lower Tysoe
Edgehill
Little Kineton
Butlers Marston
WARWICK
NORTHAMPTON
WATFORD GAP
M1
M6
M69
M45
M40
A5
A14
A45
A46
A47
A423
A426
A428
A4303
A4304
A5199
A6
A43
A361
A4500

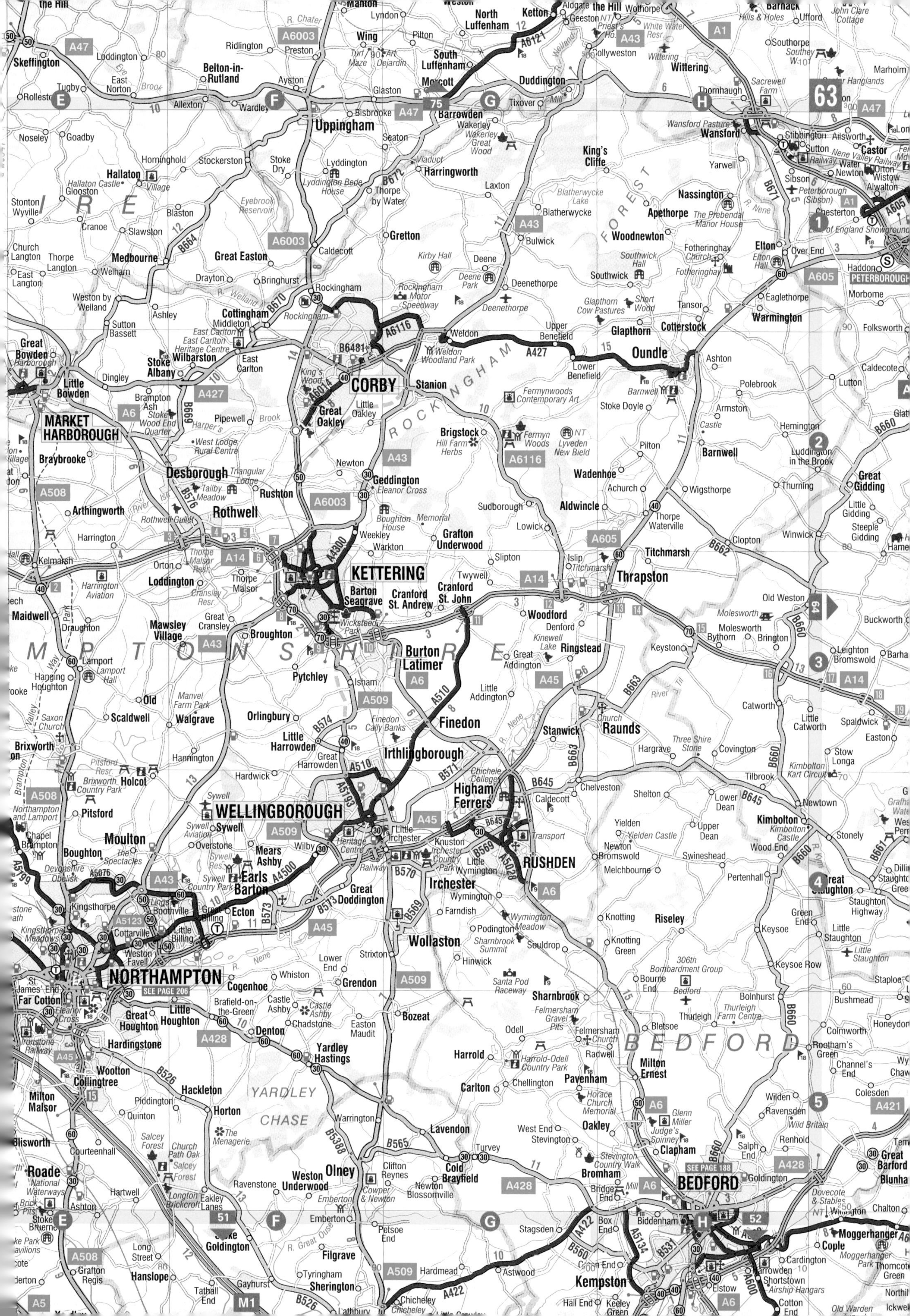

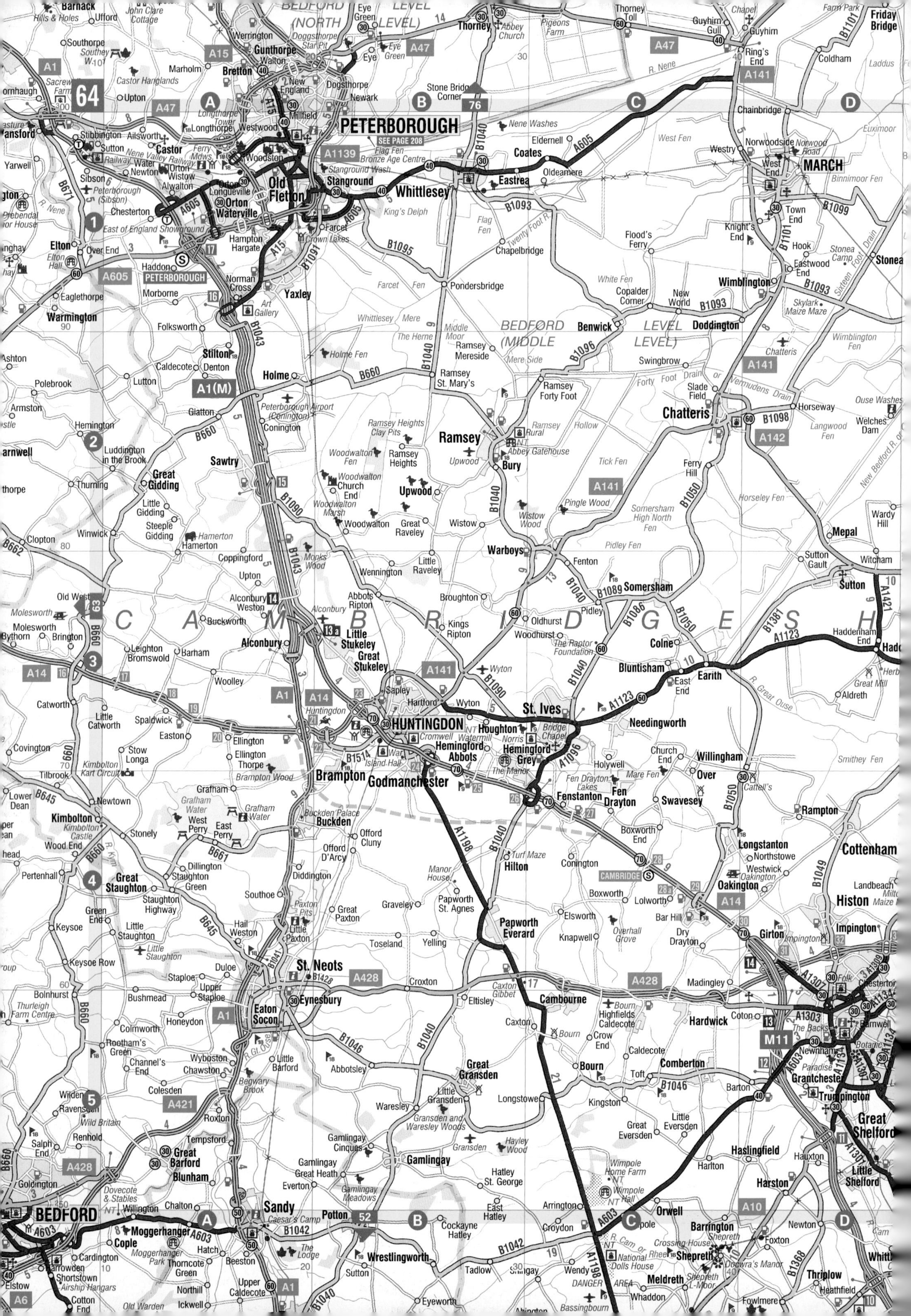

64
76
PETERBOROUGH
SEE PAGE 208
BEDFORD (NORTH LEVEL)
BEDFORD (MIDDLE LEVEL)
CAMBRIDGESHIRE
Barnack
Hills & Holes
John Clare Cottage
Ufford
Werrington
Eye Green
Eye
Thorney
Abbey Church
Thorney Toll
Pigeons Farm
Guyhirn Gull
Guyhirn
Chapel
Ring's End
Farm Park
Friday Bridge
Coldham
Laddus
Southorpe
Southey W.
Gunthorpe
Walton
Marholm
Bretton
New England
Dogsthorpe
Newark
Stone Bridge Corner
R. Nene
Castor Hanglands
Upton
Sacrewell Farm
Thornhaugh
Wansford
Longthorpe
Longthorpe Tower
Westwood
Millfield
Stibbington
Ailsworth
Castor
Sutton
Nene Valley Railway
Ferry Mdws
Woodston
Water Newton
Orton Wistow
Alwalton
Orton Longueville
Orton Waterville
Old Fletton
Stanground
Stanground Wash
Flag Fen Bronze Age Centre
Nene Washes
Eldernell
Coates
Eastrea
Oldeamere
Whittlesey
West Fen
Westry
Norwoodside
Norwood Road
West End
MARCH
Binnimoor Fen
Chainbridge
Euximoor
Yarwell
Sibson
Peterborough (Sibson)
Prebendal Manor House
R. Nene
Chesterton
East of England Showground
Hampton Hargate
Farcet
Crown Lakes
King's Delph
Flag Fen
Twenty Foot R.
Chapelbridge
Flood's Ferry
Town End
Knight's End
Hook
Eastwood End
Stonea Camp
Stonea
Sixteen Foot Drain
Elton
Elton Hall
Overend
Haddon
PETERBOROUGH
Norman Cross
Yaxley
Art Gallery
Farcet Fen
Pondersbridge
White Fen
Copalder Corner
New World
Wimblington
Skylark Maize Maze
Doddington
Eaglethorpe
Morborne
Warmington
Folksworth
Stilton
Caldecote
Denton
Whittlesey Mere
The Herne
Holme Fen
Middle Moor
Ramsey Mereside
Mere Side
Benwick
Swingbrow
Chatteris
Wimblington Fen
Ashton
Polebrook
Lutton
Holme
Ramsey St. Mary's
Ramsey Forty Foot
Forty Foot Drain
Vermudens Drain
Slade Field
Armston
Glatton
Peterborough Airport (Conington)
Conington
Ramsey Heights Clay Pits
Ramsey
Ramsey Rural
Abbey Gatehouse
Hollow
Horseway
Ouse Washes
Welches Dam
Langwood Fen
Hemington
Luddington in the Brook
Sawtry
Woodwalton Fen
Ramsey Heights
Upwood
Bury
Tick Fen
Ferry Hill
New Bedford R. or
Barnwell
Great Gidding
Thurning
Woodwalton Church End
Pingle Wood
Somersham High North Fen
Horseley Fen
Little Gidding
Steeple Gidding
Woodwalton Marsh
Woodwalton
Great Raveley
Wistow
Wistow Wood
Wardy Hill
Mepal
Clopton
Winwick
Hamerton
Coppingford
Monks Wood
Little Raveley
Wennington
Warboys
Pidley Fen
Fenton
Sutton Gault
Witcham
Upton
Abbots Ripton
Broughton
Somersham
Pidley
Sutton
Old Weston
Molesworth
Brington
Bythorn
Alconbury Weston
Buckworth
Alconbury
Kings Ripton
Oldhurst
Woodhurst
The Raptor Foundation
Colne
Haddenham End
Haddenham
Leighton Bromswold
Barham
Alconbury
Little Stukeley
Great Stukeley
Bluntisham
Earith
Herb
Great Mill
Aldreth
Woolley
Sapley
Wyton
R. Great Ouse
Catworth
Little Catworth
Spaldwick
Easton
Hartford
Huntingdon
HUNTINGDON
Houghton
St. Ives
East End
Needingworth
Covington
Stow Longa
Ellington
Ellington Thorpe
Cromwell
Watermill
Norris
Bridge Chapel
Hemingford Abbots
Hemingford Grey
Church End
Willingham
Smithey Fen
Tilbrook
Kimbolton Kart Circuit
Brampton Wood
Island Hall
Brampton
Godmanchester
The Manor
Holywell
Fen Drayton Lakes
Mare Fen
Over
Cattell's
Lower Dean
Newtown
Grafham
Grafham Water
Fenstanton
Fen Drayton
Swavesey
Rampton
Kimbolton
Kimbolton Castle
West Perry
East Perry
Buckden Palace
Buckden
Boxworth End
Longstanton
Northstowe
Cottenham
Stonely
Offord Cluny
Offord D'Arcy
Turf Maze
Hilton
Conington
Westwick
Oakington
Wood End
Pertenhall
Dillington
Great Staughton
Staughton Green
Manor House
Diddington
CAMBRIDGE
Landbeach
Histon
Southoe
Paxton Pits
Great Paxton
Graveley
Papworth St. Agnes
Boxworth
Lolworth
Bar Hill
Green End
Staughton Highway
Keysoe
Little Staughton
Little Paxton
Hail Weston
Papworth Everard
Elsworth
Overhall Grove
Knapwell
Dry Drayton
Girton
Impington
Toseland
Yelling
Keysoe Row
St. Neots
Staploe
Duloe
Upper Staploe
Croxton
Caxton Gibbet
Eltisley
Cambourne
Bourn Highfields
Caldecote
Madingley
Coton
Chesterton
Bolnhurst
Thurleigh Farm Centre
Bushmead
Eaton Socon
Eynesbury
Honeydon
Colmworth
Caxton
Bourn
Crow End
Hardwick
Barnwell
The Backs
Newnham
Botanic
Paradise
Grantchester
Trumpington
Rootham's Green
Channel's End
Wyboston
Chawston
R. Gt. Ouse
Little Barford
Abbotsley
Great Gransden
Caldecote
Bourn
Toft
Comberton
Barton
Colesden
Begwary Brook
Little Gransden
Longstowe
Kingston
Widen
Ravensden
Wild Britain
Roxton
Waresley
Gransden and Waresley Woods
Great Eversden
Little Eversden
Great Shelford
Renhold
Salph End
Tempsford
Great Barford
Blunham
Gamlingay Cinques
Gransden
Hayley Wood
Haslingfield
Harlton
Hauxton
Little Shelford
Goldington
Dovecote & Stables
Gamlingay
Great Heath
Gamlingay Meadows
Everton
Hatley St. George
Wimpole Home Farm
Wimpole Hall
Harston
BEDFORD
Willington
Chalton
Sandy
Caesar's Camp
Potton
East Hatley
Arrington
Orwell
Newton
Moggerhanger
Cople
Cockayne Hatley
Croydon
Barrington
Shepreth
Crossing House
Foxton
Moggerhanger Park
Cardington
Hatch
Thorncote Green
Beeston
The Lodge
Wrestlingworth
Tadlow
Shingay
Wendy
R. Cam or Rhee
National Dolls House
Docwra's Manor
Shepreth L-Moor
Thriplow
Whittlesford
Harrowden
Shortstown
Airship Hangars
Elstow
Northill
Upper Caldecote
Sutton
Meldreth
Heathfield
Cotton End
Old Warden
Ickwell
Eyeworth
DANGER AREA
Whaddon
Bassingbourn
Fowlmere
A
B
C
D
1
2
3
4
5
A1
A1(M)
A6
A14
A15
A47
A141
A142
A421
A428
A603
A605
A1123
A1139
A1198
A1303
A1307
A1421
A10
M11
B660
B1040
B1042
B1043
B1046
B1050
B1086
B1089
B1090
B1091
B1093
B1095
B1096
B1098
B1099
B1101
B1368
B1381
B1049
B1514
B645
B661
B662
B671

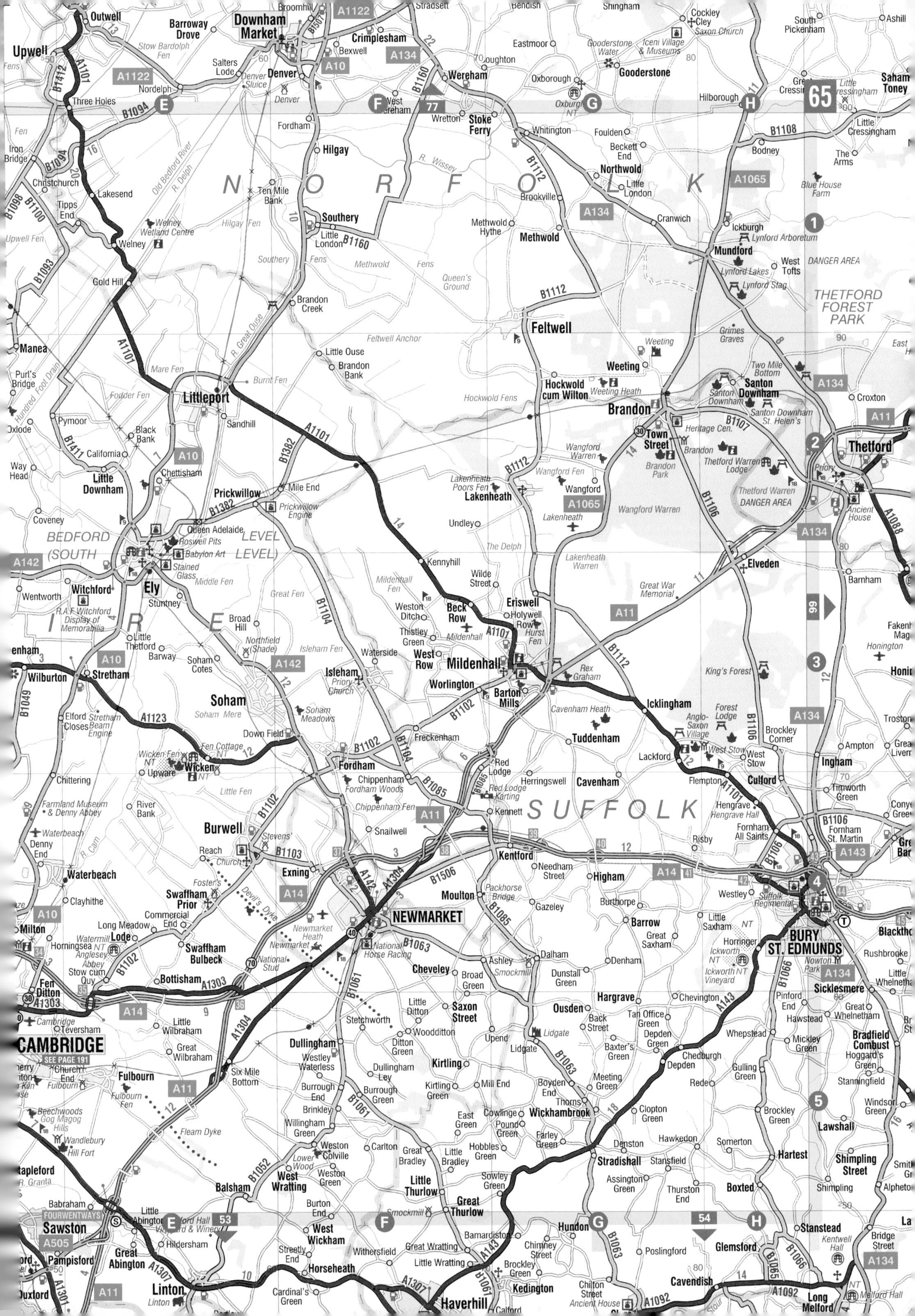

65
Outwell
Upwell
Barroway Drove
Downham Market
Broomhill
A1122
Crimplesham
Bexwell
A134
A10
Denver
Denver Sluice
Salters Lode
Stow Bardolph Fen
Nordelph
A1101
B1412
Three Holes
B1094
Wereham
Eastmoor
Gooderstone Water
Iceni Village & Museums
Gooderstone
Cockley Cley
Saxon Church
South Pickenham
Ashill
Oxborough
Oxburgh NT
Stoke Ferry
Wretton
West Dereham
Fordham
Hilgay
Whitington
Foulden
Beckett End
Northwold
Little London
Hilborough
Little Cressingham
Saham Toney
B1108
Bodney
The Arms
A1065
Blue House Farm
NORFOLK
Christchurch
Lakesend
Ten Mile Bank
Tipps End
Welney
Welney Wetland Centre
Hilgay Fen
Southery
Little London
B1160
Methwold Hythe
Methwold
Brookville
A134
Cranwich
Ickburgh
Lynford Arboretum
Mundford
West Tofts
DANGER AREA
Lynford Lakes
Lynford Stag
THETFORD FOREST PARK
Upwell Fen
Gold Hill
Brandon Creek
Southery Fens
Methwold Fens
Queen's Ground
B1112
Feltwell
Feltwell Anchor
Little Ouse
Brandon Bank
Manea
Purl's Bridge
Hundred Foot Drain
Mare Fen
Burnt Fen
Fodder Fen
Littleport
Sandhill
Hockwold Fens
Hockwold cum Wilton
Weeting Heath
Weeting
Grimes Graves
Two Mile Bottom
Santon
Santon Downham
Santon Downham St. Helen's
A134
Croxton
Brandon
Town Street
Heritage Cen.
B1107
Thetford
A11
Pymoor
Black Bank
California
Little Downham
A10
Chettisham
A1101
B1382
Mile End
Lakenheath Poors Fen
Lakenheath
Wangford Warren
Wangford Fen
Wangford
Brandon Park
Thetford Warren Lodge
Thetford Warren
Priory
Ancient House
A1088
Coveney
Prickwillow
Prickwillow Engine
Queen Adelaide
A1065
Lakenheath
Undley
BEDFORD (SOUTH LEVEL)
Roswell Pits
Babylon Art
Stained Glass
The Delph
Elveden
A142
Ely
Witchford
Wentworth
R.A.F. Witchford Display of Memorabilia
Middle Fen
Stuntney
Kennyhill
Wilde Street
Lakenheath Warren
Great War Memorial
Barnham
Mildenhall Fen
Beck Row
Eriswell
Holywell Row
Hurst Fen
Broad Hill
Great Fen
Weston Ditch
Thistley Green
Little Thetford
Northfield (Shade)
Isleham Fen
West Row
Waterside
Mildenhall
A1101
Fakenham Magna
Honington
Wilburton
Stretham
Barway
Soham Cotes
Isleham
Isleham Priory Church
Worlington
Barton Mills
Rex Graham
B1112
Icklingham
King's Forest
Soham
Soham Mere
B1049
Elford Closes
Stretham Beam Engine
A1123
Down Field
Soham Meadows
B1102
Freckenham
Cavenham Heath
Tuddenham
Anglo-Saxon Village
Forest Lodge
Brockley Corner
A134
Troston
Wicken Fen NT
Fen Cottage
Wicken
Upware
Fordham
Chippenham
Fordham Woods
B1104
Red Lodge
Red Lodge Karting
Herringswell
Cavenham
Lackford
West Stow
Flempton
Culford
Ingham
Ampton
Chittering
Little Fen
Chippenham Fen
Kennett
SUFFOLK
Hengrave
Hengrave Hall
Timworth Green
Farmland Museum & Denny Abbey
River Bank
B1085
A11
Fornham All Saints
B1106
Fornham St. Martin
Waterbeach
Denny End
Burwell
Stevens'
Snailwell
Risby
A143
Reach
Church
B1103
Kentford
Exning
Needham Street
Higham
A14
Foster's
Devil's Dyke
A14
Moulton
B1506
Packhorse Bridge
Burthorpe
Westley
Suffolk Regimental
Swaffham Prior
Waterbeach
Clayhithe
NEWMARKET
Gazeley
Barrow
Little Saxham NT
Commercial End
Newmarket Heath
Great Saxham
BURY ST. EDMUNDS
Blackthorpe
Milton
Long Meadow
Lode
Swaffham Bulbeck
Anglesey Abbey
National Horse Racing
B1063
Ashley
Dalham
Denham
Horringer
Ickworth NT
Ickworth NT Vineyard
Nowton Park
A134
Rushbrooke
Horningsea
Watermill
Stow cum Quy
National Stud
Cheveley
Broad Green
Smockmill
Dunstall Green
B1066
Sicklesmere
Little Whelnetham
Fen Ditton
Bottisham
A1303
Hargrave
Chevington
Pinford End
Great Whelnetham
CAMBRIDGE
SEE PAGE 191
Teversham
A14
Little Wilbraham
Great Wilbraham
Stetchworth
Little Ditton
Saxon Street
Ousden
Back Street
Tan Office Green
Depden Green
Hawstead
Mickley Green
Bradfield Combust
Hoggard's Green
Cherry Hinton
Church End
Fulbourn
Six Mile Bottom
A1304
Dullingham
Westley Waterless
Woodditton
Ditton Green
Kirtling
Upend
Lidgate
Lidgate
Baxter's Green
Chedburgh
Depden
Gulling Green
Whepstead
Stanningfield
Cherry Hinton
Fulbourn Fen
A11
Burrough End
Dullingham Ley
Burrough Green
Kirtling Green
Mill End
Boyden End
Meeting Green
Rede
Brinkley
Thorns
Wickhambrook
Clopton Green
Lawshall
Windsor Green
Beechwoods
Gog Magog Hills
Wandlebury Hill Fort
Fleam Dyke
Willingham Green
East Green
Cowlinge
Pound Green
Farley Green
Brockley Green
Weston Colville
Carlton
Great Bradley
Little Bradley
Hobbles Green
Denston
Hawkedon
Somerton
Hartest
Shimpling Street
Stapleford
R. Granta
Balsham
Lower Wood
West Wratting
Weston Green
Little Thurlow
Sowley Green
Stradishall
Stansfield
Assington Green
Thurston End
Boxted
Shimpling
Alpheton
Babraham
Burton End
Great Thurlow
Smockmill
FOURWENTWAYS
Little Abington
Sawston
A505
Great Abington
Hildersham
West Wickham
Barnardiston
Hundon
Chimney Street
Poslingford
Glemsford
Stanstead
Kentwell Hall
Bridge Street
Pampisford
Streetly End
Withersfield
Great Wratting
Little Wratting
Brockley Green
Kedington
Horseheath
Linton
A1307
Cardinal's Green
Haverhill
Calford
Chilton Street
Ancient House
A1092
Cavendish
Long Melford
Melford Hall
Duxford
A1301
A11

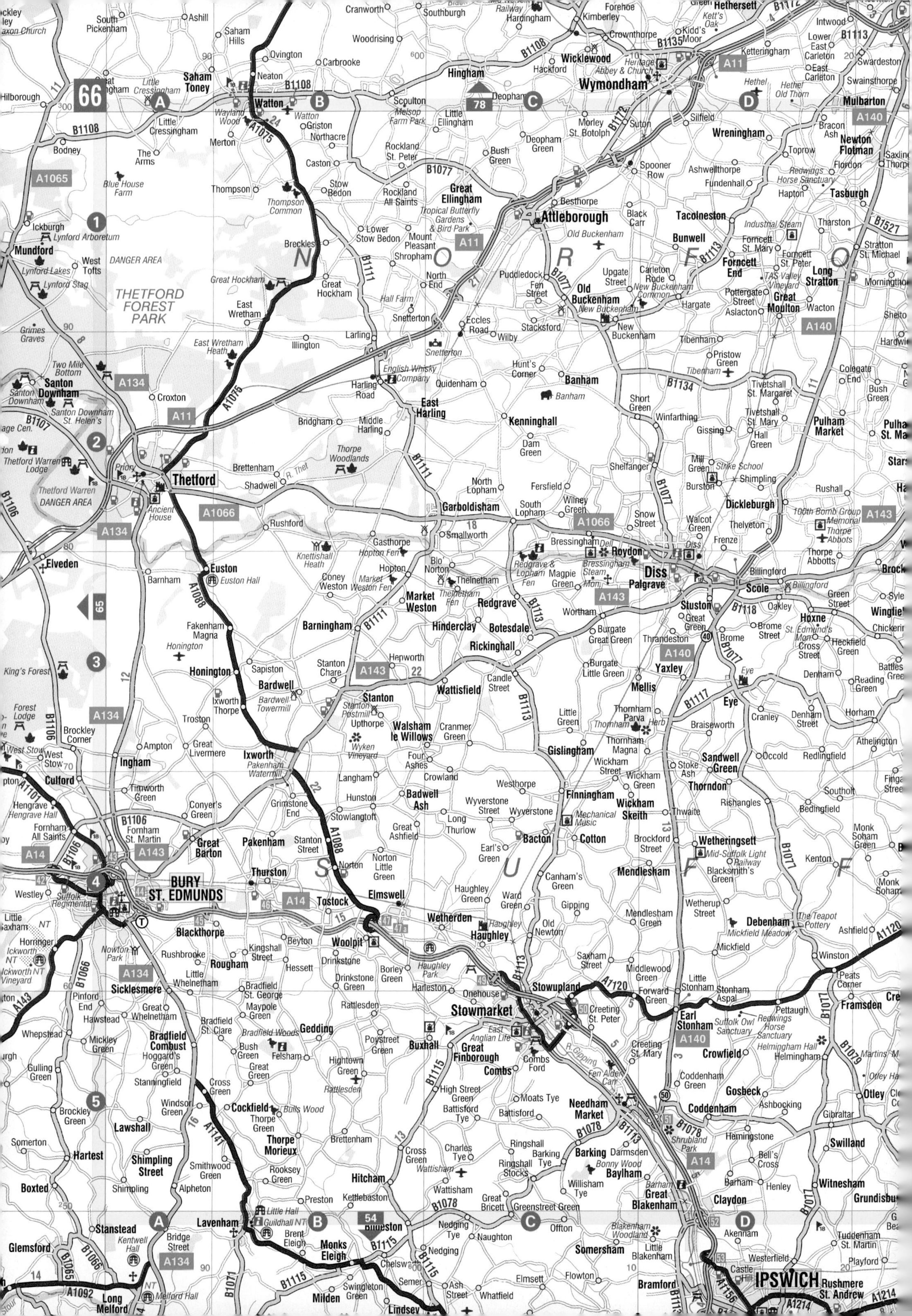
66
A
B
C
D
78
65
54
1
2
3
4
5
NORFOLK
SUFFOLK
South Pickenham
Ashill
Saham Hills
Ovington
Cranworth
Southburgh
Hardingham
Kimberley
Forehoe
Crownthorpe
Kidd's Moor
Kett's Oak
Hethersett
Intwood
Woodrising
Carbrooke
Saham Toney
Watton
Neaton
Wayland Wood
Merton
Griston
Northacre
Little Cressingham
Hilborough
Bodney
The Arms
Scoulton
Melsop Farm Park
Hingham
Deopham
Deopham Green
Little Ellingham
Rockland St. Peter
Caston
Stow Bedon
Rockland All Saints
Great Ellingham
Tropical Butterfly Gardens & Bird Park
Bush Green
Wicklewood
Hackford
Wymondham
Heritage
Abbey & Church
Ketteringham
Lower Carleton
East Carleton
Swardeston
Swainsthorpe
Hethel
Hethel Old Thorn
Mulbarton
Silfield
Morley St. Botolph
Suton
Spooner Row
Wreningham
Ashwellthorpe
Fundenhall
Bracon Ash
Newton Flotman
Toprow
Saxlingham Thorpe
Flordon
Redwings Horse Sanctuary
Hapton
Tasburgh
Besthorpe
Attleborough
Old Buckenham
Black Carr
Tacolneston
Bunwell
Industrial Steam
Tharston
Forncett St. Mary
Forncett St. Peter
Forncett End
Long Stratton
Stratton St. Michael
Morningthorpe
TAS Valley Vineyard
Pottergate Street
Great Moulton
Aslacton
Wacton
Carleton Rode
New Buckenham Common
Upgate Street
Hargate
Old Buckenham
New Buckenham
Puddledock
Fen Street
Stacksford
Eccles Road
Wilby
Snetterton
Hall Farm
North End
Mount Pleasant
Shropham
Lower Stow Bedon
Breckles
Great Hockham
Thompson
Thompson Common
Blue House Farm
Ickburgh
Lynford Arboretum
Mundford
West Tofts
Lynford Lakes
Lynford Stag
DANGER AREA
THETFORD FOREST PARK
Great Hockham
East Wretham
Grimes Graves
East Wretham Heath
Illington
Larling
English Whisky Company
Harling Road
Quidenham
Hunt's Corner
Banham
Tibenham
Pristow Green
Colegate End
Bush Green
Tivetshall St. Margaret
Tivetshall St. Mary
Pulham Market
Pulham St. Mary
Two Mile Bottom
Santon Downham
Santon Downham St. Helen's
Croxton
East Harling
Middle Harling
Bridgham
Kenninghall
Short Green
Winfarthing
Gissing
Hall Green
Dam Green
Thorpe Woodlands
Brettenham
R. Thet
Shadwell
Thetford
Priory
Thetford Warren Lodge
Thetford Warren
Ancient House
North Lopham
Fersfield
Shelfanger
Mill Green
Strike School
Shimpling
Burston
Rushall
Dickleburgh
100th Bomb Group Memorial
Thelveton
Garboldisham
South Lopham
Wilney Green
Snow Street
Walcot Green
Frenze
Thorpe Abbotts
Rushford
Smallworth
Gasthorpe
Hopton Fen
Knettishall Heath
Elveden
Euston
Euston Hall
Barnham
Coney Weston
Market Weston Fen
Hopton
Blo' Norton
Thelnetham
Thelnetham Fen
Redgrave & Lopham Fen
Bressingham
Bressingham Steam
Roydon
Diss
Magpie Green
Palgrave
Billingford
Scole
Oakley
Green Street
Syleham
Wingfield
Market Weston
Redgrave
Wortham
Stuston
Great Green
Brome Street
Brome
Hoxne
St. Edmund's Mon.
Heckfield Green
Cross Street
Chickering
Fakenham Magna
Honington
Barningham
Hinderclay
Botesdale
Rickinghall
Burgate Great Green
Thrandeston
King's Forest
Sapiston
Stanton Chare
Hepworth
Wattisfield
Candle Street
Burgate Little Green
Yaxley
Mellis
Eye
Denham
Reading Green
Battles Green
Bardwell
Bardwell Towermill
Stanton
Stanton Postmill
Upthorpe
Walsham le Willows
Cranmer Green
Little Green
Thornham Parva
Thornham Herb
Braiseworth
Cranley
Denham Street
Horham
Forest Lodge
Ixworth Thorpe
Troston
Brockley Corner
West Stow
Ampton
Great Livermere
Ixworth
Pakenham Watermill
Wyken Vineyard
Four Ashes
Crowland
Gislingham
Thornham Magna
Wickham Street
Stoke Ash
Sandwell Green
Occold
Redlingfield
Athelington
Culford
Ingham
Timworth Green
Langham
Hunston
Westhorpe
Wickham Green
Finningham
Thorndon
Southolt
Bedingfield
Hengrave
Hengrave Hall
Conyer's Green
Grimstone End
Stowlangtoft
Badwell Ash
Wyverstone Street
Wyverstone
Long Thurlow
Wickham Skeith
Thwaite
Rishangles
Fornham All Saints
Fornham St. Martin
Great Barton
Pakenham
Stanton Street
Great Ashfield
Mechanical Music
Cotton
Bacton
Earl's Green
Brockford Street
Wetheringsett
Mid-Suffolk Light Railway
Blacksmith's Green
Kenton
Monk Soham Green
Monk Soham
Westley
Suffolk Regimental
Bury St. Edmunds
Thurston
Norton
Norton Little Green
Elmswell
Tostock
Canham's Green
Mendlesham
Wetherup Street
Debenham
The Teapot Pottery
Mickfield Meadow
Ashfield
Little Saxham
Horringer
Ickworth
Nowton Park
Blackthorpe
Rushbrooke
Kingshall Street
Beyton
Woolpit
Drinkstone
Hessett
Haughley Green
Ward Green
Wetherden
Haughley
Haughley Park
Old Newton
Gipping
Mendlesham Green
Mickfield
Winston
Peats Corner
Rougham
Drinkstone Green
Borley Green
Harleston
Onehouse
Saxham Street
Middlewood Green
Forward Green
Stowupland
Little Stonham
Stonham Aspal
Framsden
Sicklesmere
Little Whelnetham
Bradfield St. George
Maypole Green
Rattlesden
Stowmarket
Creeting St. Peter
Earl Stonham
Suffolk Owl Sanctuary
Redwings Horse Sanctuary
Pettaugh
Pinford End
Hawstead
Great Whelnetham
Bradfield St. Clare
Bradfield Woods
Gedding
Poystreet Green
Buxhall
East Anglian Life
Great Finborough
Combs
Combs Ford
R. Gipping
Creeting St. Mary
Helmingham Hall
Helmingham
Crowfield
Whepstead
Mickley Green
Bradfield Combust
Hoggard's Green
Bush Green
Felsham
Hightown Green
Gulling Green
Stanningfield
Great Green
Rattlesden
Fen Alder Carr
Coddenham Green
Gosbeck
Otley
Cross Green
Windsor Green
High Street Green
Battisford Tye
Moats Tye
Battisford
Needham Market
Coddenham
Ashbocking
Brockley Green
Cockfield
Bulls Wood
Thorpe Green
Thorpe Morieux
Brettenham
Lawshall
Somerton
Hartest
Shimpling Street
Smithwood Green
Rooksey Green
Cross Green
Charles Tye
Wattisham
Ringshall
Ringshall Stocks
Barking Tye
Barking
Darmsden
Bonny Wood
Baylham
Shrubland Park
Hemingstone
Bell's Cross
Swilland
Boxted
Shimpling
Alpheton
Preston
Hitcham
Kettlebaston
Willisham Tye
Great Blakenham
Barham
Henley
Witnesham
Grundisburgh
Claydon
Stanstead
Lavenham
Little Hall
Guildhall NT
Brent Eleigh
Bildeston
Nedging Tye
Naughton
Great Bricett
Greenstreet Green
Offton
Blakenham Woodland
Akenham
Tuddenham St. Martin
Glemsford
Kentwell Hall
Bridge Street
Monks Eleigh
Chelsworth
Nedging
Somersham
Little Blakenham
Westerfield
Playford
Long Melford
Melford Hall
Milden
Swingleton Green
Semer
Ash Street
Whatfield
Elmsett
Flowton
Bramford
Castle Hill
IPSWICH
Rushmere St. Andrew
Lindsey
A11
A14
A134
A140
A143
A1066
A1065
A1075
A1088
A1092
A1101
A1120
A1141
A1156
A1214
B1077
B1078
B1079
B1106
B1107
B1108
B1111
B1113
B1115
B1117
B1118
B1134
B1135
B1172
B1527
B1066
B1065
B1071
B1115
B1113
B1078

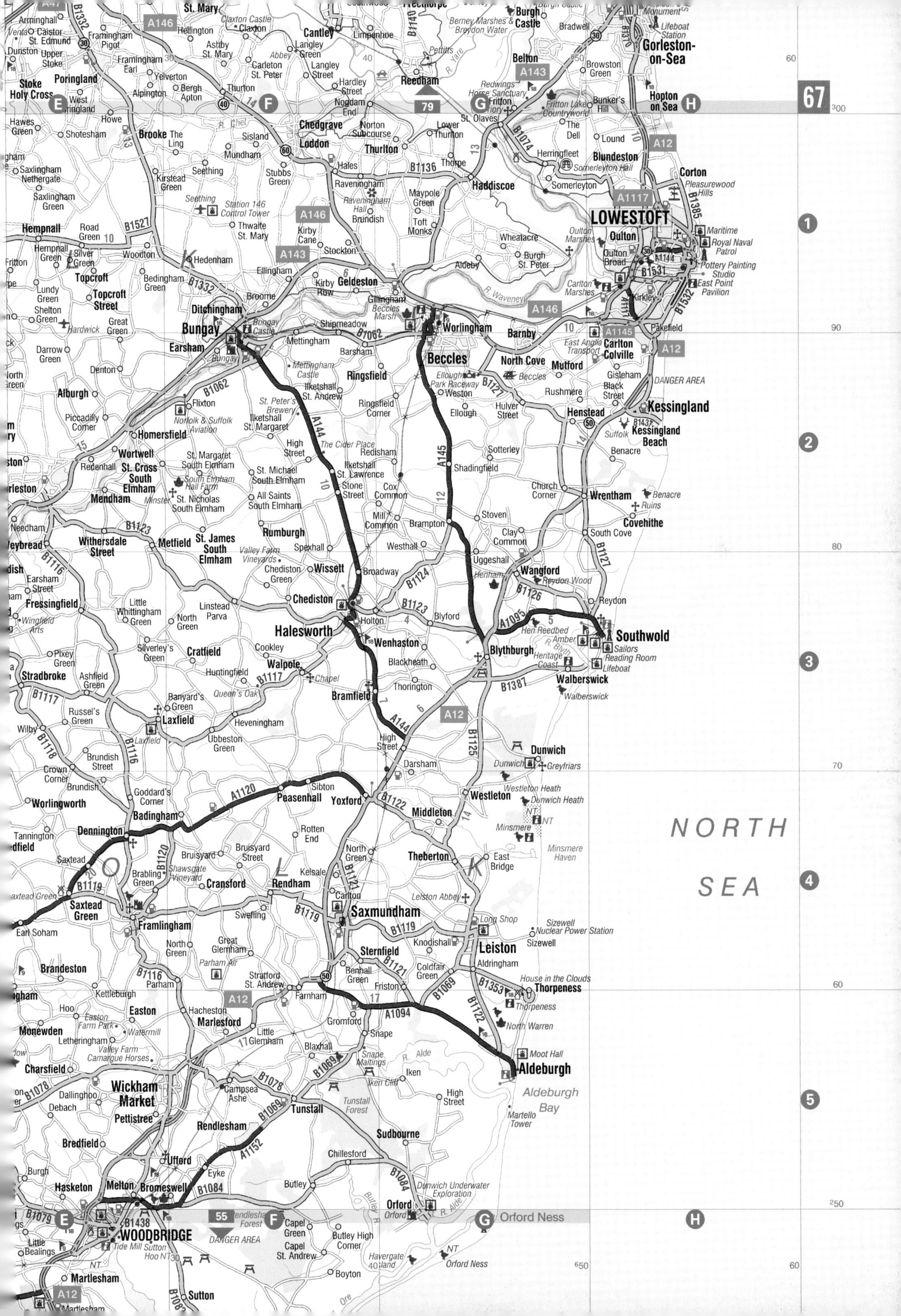

67
St. Mary
Claxton Castle
Claxton
Arminghall
Venta
Caistor St. Edmund
Framingham Pigot
Dunston
Upper Stoke
Framingham Earl
Hellington
Ashby St. Mary
Carleton St. Peter
Cantley
Langley Green
Langley Street
Limpenhoe
Reedham
Pettitts
Berney Marshes & Breydon Water
Burgh Castle
Bradwell
Belton
Browston Green
Redwings Horse Sanctuary
Fritton
Fritton Lake Countryworld
Lifeboat Station
Gorleston-on-Sea
Hopton on Sea
Bunker's Hill
Stoke Holy Cross
Poringland
Yelverton
Alpington
Bergh Apton
Thurton
Hardley Street
Nogdam End
West Poringland
Howe
Hawes Green
Shotesham
Brooke
The Ling
Sisland
Mundham
Chedgrave
Loddon
Norton Subcourse
Thurlton
Lower Thurlton
St. Olaves
The Dell
Lound
Herringfleet
Somerleyton Hall
Blundeston
Somerleyton
Corton
Pleasurewood Hills
Saxlingham Nethergate
Saxlingham Green
Kirstead Green
Seething
Stubbs Green
Hales
Raveningham
Raveningham Hall
Brundish
Maypole Green
Toft Monks
Thorpe
Haddiscoe
Seething
Station 146 Control Tower
Thwaite St. Mary
Kirby Cane
Stockton
Wheatacre
Burgh St. Peter
Aldeby
LOWESTOFT
Oulton
Oulton Marshes
Oulton Broad
Maritime
Royal Naval Patrol
Pottery Painting Studio
East Point Pavilion
Carlton Marshes
Kirkley
Hempnall
Road Green
Hempnall Green
Silver Green
Fritton
Woodton
Hedenham
Topcroft
Topcroft Street
Lundy Green
Shelton Green
Hardwick
Great Green
Bedingham Green
Ellingham
Kirby Row
Geldeston
Gillingham
Beccles Marsh
Broome
Ditchingham
Bungay
Bungay Castle
Earsham
Shipmeadow
Mettingham
Barsham
Worlingham
Barnby
Beccles
North Cove
Mutford
East Anglia Transport
Carlton Colville
Pakefield
Darrow Green
Denton
Mettingham Castle
Ringsfield
Ellough Park Raceway
Weston
Ellough
Gisleham
Black Street
Rushmere
DANGER AREA
Kessingland
Alburgh
Flixton
Ilketshall St. Andrew
Ringsfield Corner
Hulver Street
Henstead
Kessingland Beach
Suffolk
Piccadilly Corner
Norfolk & Suffolk Aviation
Homersfield
St. Peter's Brewery
Ilketshall St. Margaret
High Street
The Cider Place
Redisham
Sotterley
Shadingfield
Benacre
Wortwell
Redenhall
St. Cross South Elmham
St. Margaret South Elmham
South Elmham Hall Farm
St. Michael South Elmham
Ilketshall St. Lawrence
Stone Street
Cox Common
Church Corner
Wrentham
Benacre
Ruins
Covehithe
Mendham
Minster
St. Nicholas South Elmham
All Saints South Elmham
Mill Common
Brampton
Stoven
Clay Common
South Cove
Needham
Withersdale Street
Metfield
St. James South Elmham
Rumburgh
Spexhall
Westhall
Uggeshall
Wangford
Henham
Reydon Wood
Reydon
Valley Farm Vineyards
Chediston Green
Wissett
Broadway
Earsham Street
Fressingfield
Wingfield Arts
Little Whittingham Green
North Green
Linstead Parva
Chediston
Holton
Blyford
Hen Reedbed
Southwold
Sailors Reading Room
Lifeboat
Halesworth
Wenhaston
Blythburgh
Amber
Heritage Coast
Walberswick
Pixey Green
Silverley's Green
Cratfield
Cookley
Walpole
Blackheath
Stradbroke
Ashfield Green
Huntingfield
Chapel
Thorington
Bramfield
Queen's Oak
Banyard's Green
Russel's Green
Laxfield
Heveningham
Wilby
Ubbeston Green
High Street
Dunwich
Greyfriars
Brundish Street
Crown Corner
Brundish
Darsham
Westleton Heath
Dunwich Heath
Goddard's Corner
Sibton
Peasenhall
Yoxford
Westleton
Worlingworth
Badingham
Middleton
Minsmere
NORTH
SEA
Tannington
Dennington
Rotten End
Minsmere Haven
Bruisyard
Bruisyard Street
North Green
Theberton
East Bridge
Saxtead
Shawsgate Vineyard
Brabling Green
Cransford
Kelsale
Rendham
Carlton
Leiston Abbey
Saxtead Green
Framlingham
Swefling
Saxmundham
Long Shop
Sizewell Nuclear Power Station
Sizewell
Earl Soham
North Green
Great Glemham
Sternfield
Knodishall
Leiston
Aldringham
Parham Air
Brandeston
Parham
Stratford St. Andrew
Benhall Green
Coldfair Green
House in the Clouds
Thorpeness
Friston
Kettleburgh
Easton
Hacheston
Farnham
Hoo
Easton Farm Park
Watermill
Marlesford
Gromford
Snape
North Warren
Monewden
Letheringham
Little Glemham
Valley Farm Camargue Horses
Blaxhall
Snape Maltings
Moot Hall
Aldeburgh
Charsfield
Iken
Iken Cliff
Campsea Ashe
Aldeburgh Bay
Dallinghoo
Wickham Market
Tunstall
Tunstall Forest
High Street
Debach
Pettistree
Martello Tower
Rendlesham
Sudbourne
Bredfield
Chillesford
Ufford
Eyke
Burgh
Butley
Dunwich Underwater Exploration
Hasketon
Melton
Bromeswell
Orford
Rendlesham Forest
Orford Ness
Capel Green
Butley High Corner
WOODBRIDGE
DANGER AREA
Little Bealings
Tide Mill
Sutton Hoo
Capel St. Andrew
Havergate Island
Orford Ness
Martlesham
Boyton
Sutton
Ore
Martlesham
A146
A143
A12
A1117
A1145
A144
A145
A1095
A1120
A1094
A1152
B1332
B1140
B1074
B1136
B1527
B1332
B7062
B1062
B1127
B1385
B1531
B1532
B1437
B1123
B1124
B1126
B1116
B1117
B1118
B1387
B1125
B1122
B1120
B1119
B1121
B1069
B1353
B1078
B1084
B1079
B1438
B1083
79
55

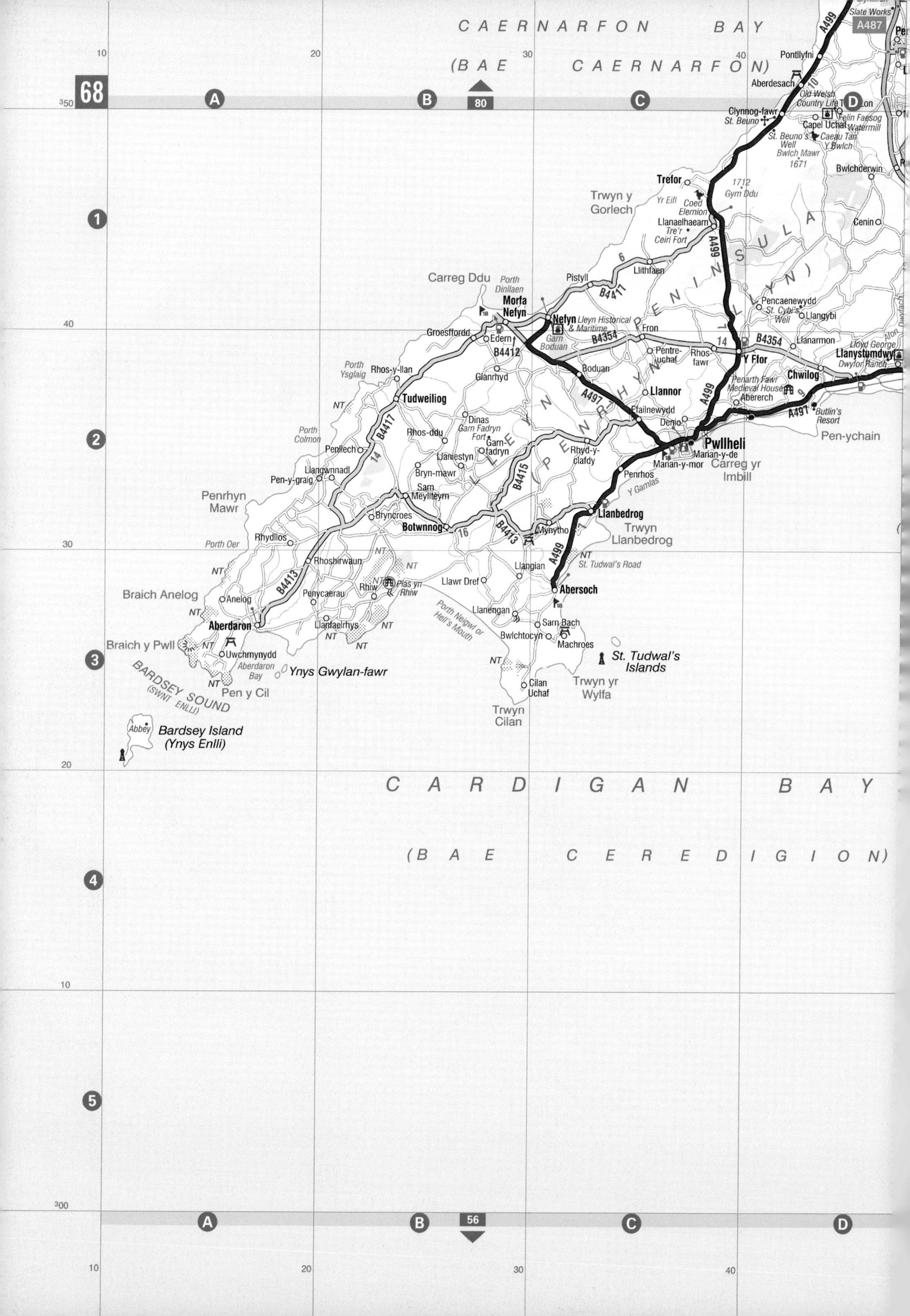

CAERNARFON BAY
(BAE CAERNARFON)

CARDIGAN BAY
(BAE CEREDIGION)

A   B   80   C   D

1

Carreg Ddu
Porth Dinllaen
Morfa Nefyn
Groesffordd   Edern
B4412
Porth Ysglaig   Rhos-y-llan
Glanrhyd
Tudweiliog
B4417
Porth Colmon   Rhos-ddu
Dinas   Garn Fadryn Fort
Penllech   14   Garn Fadryn
Llangwnnadl   Llaniestyn   Garn-Fadryn
Pen-y-graig   Bryn-mawr
Sarn Meyllteyrn
Penrhyn Mawr   Bryncroes
Botwnnog   16
Rhydlios   *Porth Oer*   B4413
Rhoshirwaun   NT
B4413   NT
Braich Anelog   Penycaerau
NT   Anelog   Rhiw   Plas yn Rhiw
NT   Llanfaelrhys
Aberdaron
Braich y Pwll   Uwchmynydd   *Aberdaron Bay*
NT   Pen y Cil

Trefor
Trwyn y Gorlech   Yr Eifl   *1712 Gym Ddu*
Coed Elernion
Llanaelhaearn   Tre'r Ceiri Fort
B4411   6   Pistyll
Liithfaen
Nefyn   *Lleyn Historical & Maritime*   Fron
Garn Boduan   B4354
Boduan   Pentre-uchaf   Rhos-fawr
A497   Llannor   Efailnewydd   Denio
Rhyd-y-clafdy   Pwllheli
Marian-y-de   Carreg yr Imbill
Marian-y-mor
Penrhos   *Y Gamlas*
Llanbedrog   Trwyn Llanbedrog
Mynytho   Llangian   A499   NT   *St. Tudwal's Road*
Llawr Dref   Abersoch
Llanengan
Bwlchtocyn   Sarn Bach
Machroes   St. Tudwal's Islands
Porth Neigwl or Hell's Mouth
NT   Cilan Uchaf   Trwyn yr Wylfa
Trwyn Cilan

L L E Y N   P E N I N S U L A   (P E N   L L Y N)

A499

Pontllyfni
Aberdesach   *Old Welsh Country Life*
Clynnog-fawr   St. Beuno
Capel Uchaf   Felin Faesog Watermill
St. Beuno's Well   Caeau Tan Y Bwlch
Bwlch Mawr 1671   Bwlchderwin
Pencaenewydd   St. Cybi's Well   Llangybi
B4354   Llanarmon
Y Flor   *Lloyd George*   Llanystumdwy   *Dwyfor Ranch*
Penarth Fawr Medieval House   Chwilog
Abererch   A491   Butlin's Resort
Pen-ychain
A487
Slate Works

Ynys Gwylan-fawr

BARDSEY SOUND (SWNT ENLLI)
Abbey Bardsey Island (Ynys Enlli)

2

3

4

5

40

30

20

10

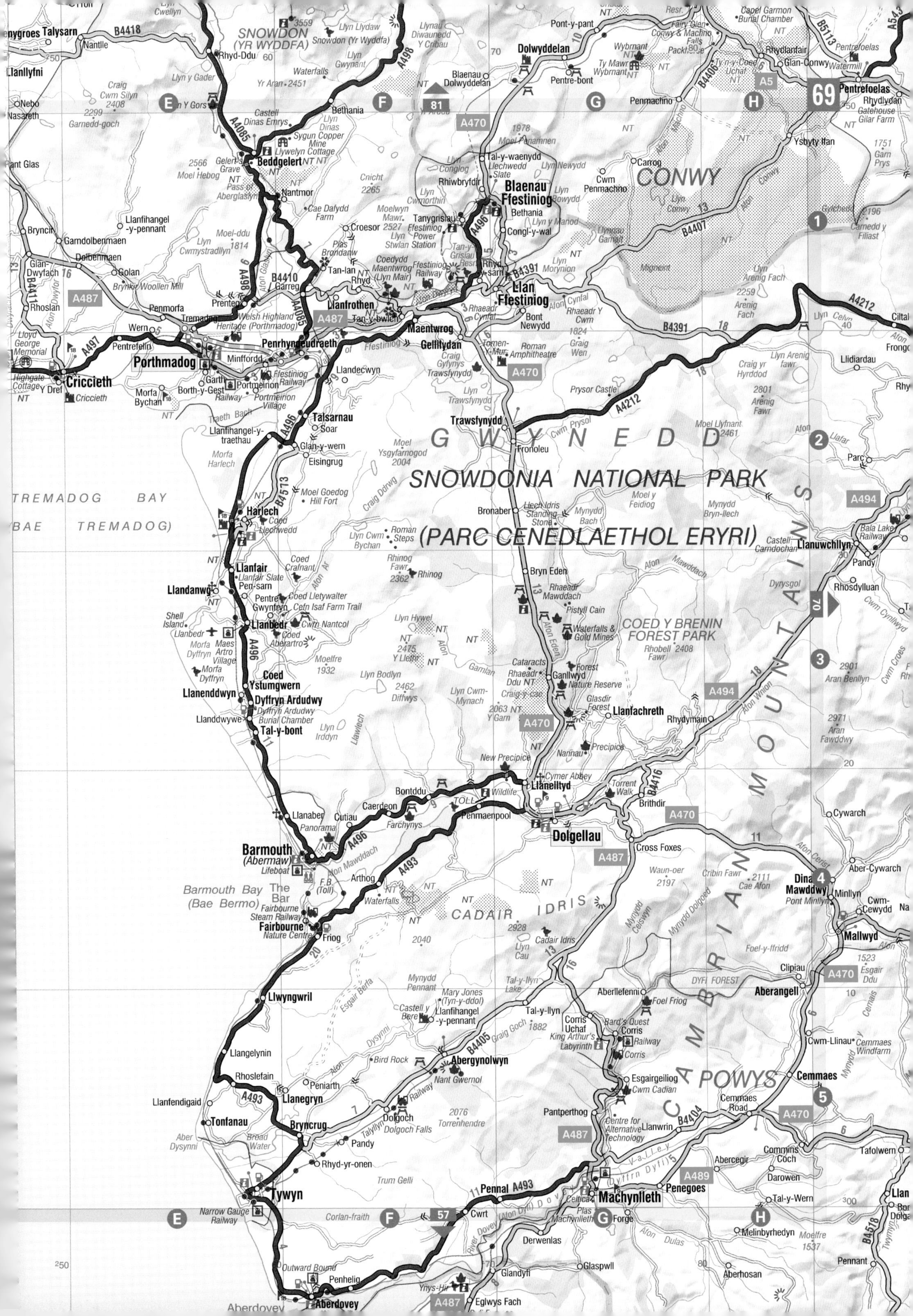

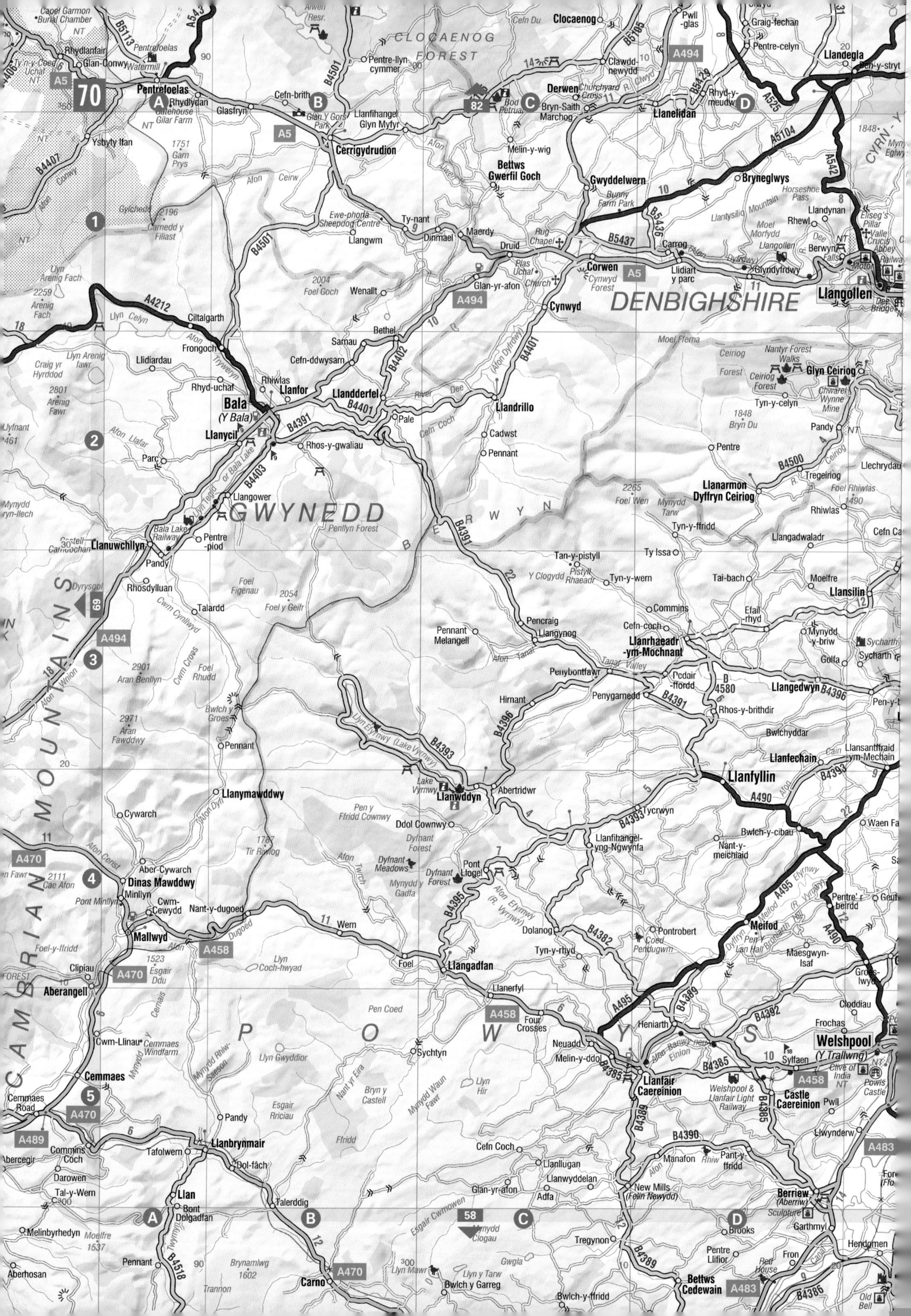

Capel Garmon
Burial Chamber
Rhydlanfair
Glan-Conwy
Watermill
Pentrefoelas
70
A5
Rhydlydan
Gatehouse
Gilar Farm
Glasfryn
Cefn-brith
Glan Y Gors Park
Llanfihangel Glyn Myfyr
Pentre-llyn-cymmer
Alwen Resr.
CLOCAENOG FOREST
Cefn Du
Clocaenog
Clawdd-newydd
Derwen
Churchyard Cross
Bryn-Saith Marchog
Bod Petrual
82
Pwll-glas
A494
Rhyd-y-meudwy
Llanelidan
Graig-fechan
Pentre-celyn
Llandegla
Pen-y-stryt
A525
A5104
A542
Ysbyty Ifan
B4407
1751 Garn Prys
Cerrigydrudion
Melin-y-wig
Bettws Gwerfil Goch
Gwyddelwern
Bunny Farm Park
Bryneglwys
Horseshoe Pass
Llantysilio Mountain
Llandynan
Rhewl
Eliseg's Pillar
Valle Crucis Abbey
Moel Morfydd
Llangollen
Berwyn
Glyndyfrdwy
Carrog
Llidiart y parc
B5437
B5436
Corwen
Cynwyd Forest
Rug Chapel
Plas Uchaf
Church
Druid
Maerdy
Dinmael
Ty-nant
Ewe-phoria Sheepdog Centre
Llangwm
Gylchedd
2196 Carnedd y Filiast
Llyn Arenig Fach
2259 Arenig Fach
B4501
2004 Foel Goch
Wenallt
Glan-yr-afon
A494
Cynwyd
DENBIGHSHIRE
Llangollen
A4212
Llyn Celyn
Ciltalgarth
Frongoch
Llyn Arenig fawr
Craig yr Hyrdded
Llidiardau
2801 Arenig Fawr
Rhyd-uchaf
Rhiwlas
Llanfor
Bala (Y Bala)
Llanycil
Sarnau
Cefn-ddwysarn
Bethel
B4402
Llandderfel
B4401
Pale
River Dee
Llandrillo
Moel Fferna
Nantyr Forest Walks
Ceiriog Forest
Glyn Ceiriog
Chwarel Wynne Mine
Tyn-y-celyn
1848 Bryn Du
Pandy
Afon Llafar
Parc
B4391
Rhos-y-gwaliau
Cefn Coch
Cadwst
Pennant
Pentre
B4500
Tregeiriog
Llechrydau
Llanarmon Dyffryn Ceiriog
Foel Rhiwlas 1490
Rhiwlas
B4403
Llangower
Llyn Tegid or Bala Lake
GWYNEDD
BERWYN
2265 Foel Wen
Mynydd Tarw
Tyn-y-ffridd
Llangadwaladr
Penllyn Forest
Bala Lake Railway
Pentre-piod
Castell Carndochan
Llanuwchllyn
Pandy
Dyrysgol
Rhosdylluan
69
Foel Figenau
2054 Foel y Geifr
Talardd
Cwm Cynllwyd
A494
CAMBRIAN MOUNTAINS
Tan-y-pistyll
Y Clogydd
Pistyll Rhaeadr
Tyn-y-wern
Ty Issa
Tai-bach
Moelfre
Llansilin
Commins
Efail-rhyd
Pencraig
Llangynog
Cefn-coch
Llanrhaeadr-ym-Mochnant
Mynydd-y-briw
Sycharth
Pennant Melangell
Tanat Valley
Golfa
Penybontfawr
Pedair-ffordd
B4580
Llangedwyn
B4396
2901 Aran Benllyn
Cwm Cross
Foel Rhudd
Afon Wnion
Bwlch y Groes
Hirnant
Penygarnedd
Rhos-y-brithdir
Bwlchyddar
2971 Aran Fawddwy
Pennant
Llyn Efyrnwy (Lake Vyrnwy)
B4393
Llansantffraid-ym-Mechain
Llanfechain
Llanfyllin
A490
Llanymawddwy
Lake Vyrnwy
Llanwddyn
Abertridwr
Tycrwyn
Cywarch
Pen y Ffridd Cownwy
Ddol Cownwy
Bwlch-y-cibau
Waen Fach
Llanfihangel-yng-Ngwynfa
Nant-y-meichiaid
A470
Afon Cerist
2111 Cae Afon
Aber-Cywarch
Dinas Mawddwy
1787 Tir Rawlog
Dyfnant Forest
Dyfnant Meadows
Pont Llogel
Mynydd y Gadfa
Afon Twrch
Afon Efyrnwy (R. Vyrnwy)
A495
Pentre'r beirdd
Pont Minllyn
Minllyn
Cwm-Cewydd
Nant-y-dugoed
Wern
B4395
Dolanog
B4382
Pontrobert
Coed Pendugwm
Meifod
Pen Y Lan Hall
Maesgwyn-Isaf
Mallwyd
Foel-y-ffridd
A458
Dugoed
Llyn Coch-hwyad
Foel
Llangadfan
Tyn-y-rhyd
Clipiau
1523 Esgair Ddu
A470
Aberangell
Llanerfyl
Pen Coed
A458
Four Crosses
Cemmaes Windfarm
Cwm-Llinau
POWYS
Heniarth
B4389
B4392
Cloddiau
Frochas
Welshpool (Y Trallwng)
Sylfaen
Clive of India
Powis Castle
Cemmaes
Mynydd Rhiw-Saeson
Llyn Gwyddior
Sychtyn
Nant yr Eira
Bryn y Castell
Mynydd Waun Fawr
Llyn Hir
Neuadd
Melin-y-ddol
Llanfair Caereinion
B4385
Welshpool & Llanfair Light Railway
Castle Caereinion
Pwll
Cemmaes Road
A470
A489
Esgair Rriciau
Pandy
Ffridd
Llwynderw
A483
Abercegir
Commins Coch
Tafolwern
Llanbrynmair
Dol-fâch
Cefn Coch
Llanllugan
B4390
Manafon
Rhiw
Pant-y-ffridd
Darowen
Llanwyddelan
Tal-y-Wern
Llan
Bont Dolgadfan
Talerddig
Glan-yr-afon
Adfa
New Mills (Felin Newydd)
Berriew (Aberriw)
Sculpture
Garthmyl
58
Esgair Cwmowen
Mynydd Clogau
Tregynon
Brooks
Hendomen
Melinbyrhedyn
Moelfre 1537
Pennant
B4518
Brynamlwg 1602
Trannon
Carno
A470
Llyn Mawr
Llyn y Tarw
Gwgla
Bwlch y Garreg
Bwlch-y-ffridd
B4389
Pentre Llifior
Red House
Fron
Bettws Cedewain
A483
B4386
Aberhosan

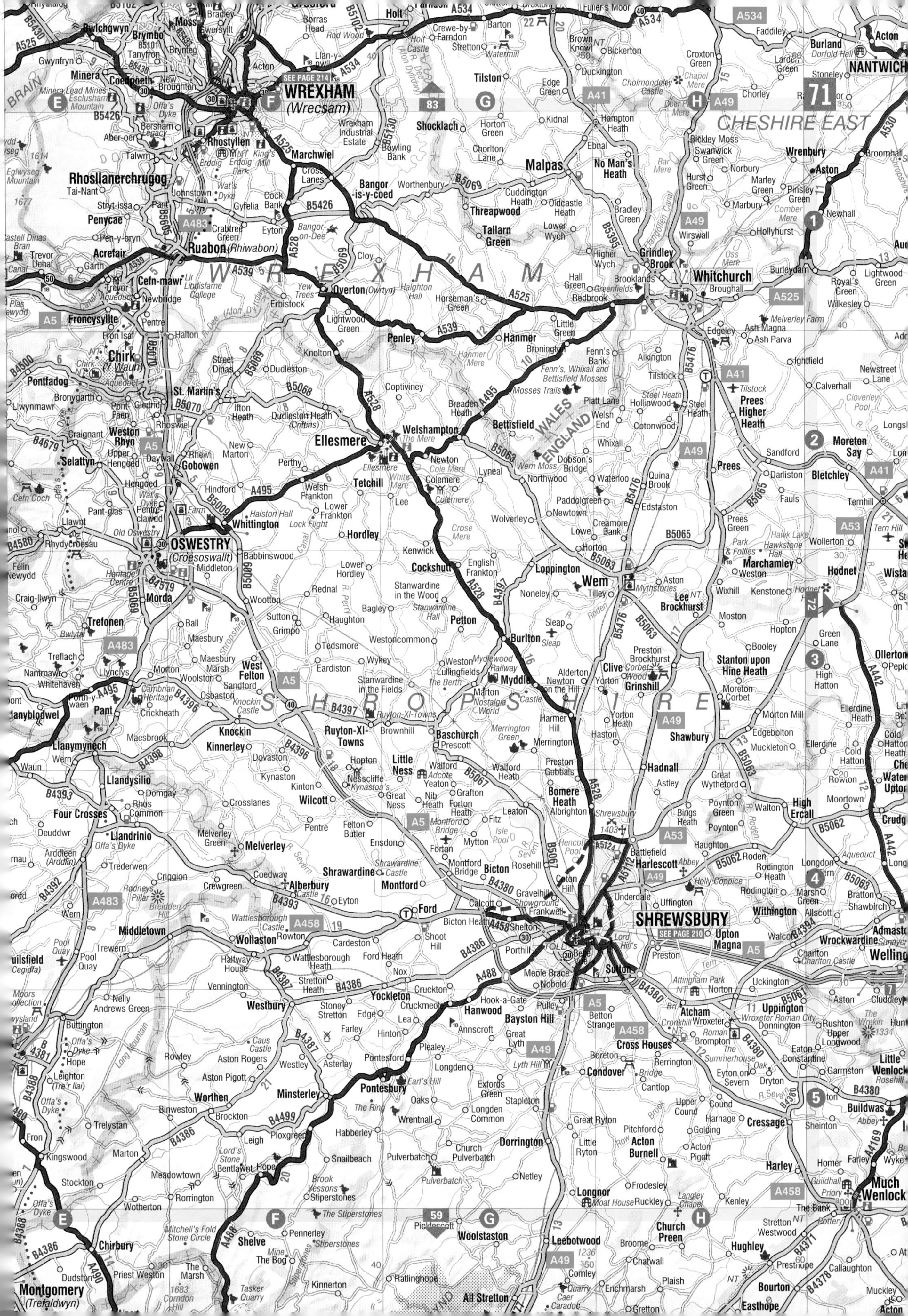

WREXHAM
(Wrecsam)
SEE PAGE 214
71
83
CHESHIRE EAST
NANTWICH
Acton
Burland
Faddiley
A534
Holt
Farndon
Barton
Tilston
Malpas
Shocklach
Bangor-is-y-coed
Marchwiel
Rhosllanerchrugog
Ruabon (Rhiwabon)
Minera
Coedpoeth
Brymbo
Bwlchgwyn
Gresford
Rhostyllen
Penycae
Acrefair
Cefn-mawr
Froncysyllte
Chirk (Y Waun)
Pontfadog
Overton (Owrtyn)
Penley
Hanmer
Whitchurch
Wrenbury
Aston
Newhall
Burleydam
Grindley Brook
Threapwood
Tallarn Green
No Man's Heath
W R E X H A M
WALES
ENGLAND
Ellesmere
Welshampton
Bettisfield
Whixall
Prees
Prees Higher Heath
Moreton Say
Bletchley
Market Drayton
Ternhill
St. Martin's
Weston Rhyn
Selattyn
Gobowen
Whittington
OSWESTRY
(Croesoswallt)
Morda
Trefonen
Tetchill
Hordley
Cockshutt
Loppington
Wem
Lee Brockhurst
Marchamley
Hodnet
72
Petton
Burlton
Myddle
Clive
Grinshill
Stanton upon Hine Heath
Shawbury
West Felton
Pant
Llanymynech
Knockin
Kinnerley
Ruyton-XI-Towns
Baschurch
Little Ness
Wilcott
Hadnall
High Ercall
S H R O P S H I R E
Four Crosses
Llandrinio
Melverley
Alberbury
Shrawardine
Montford
Bicton
Ford
Middletown
Wollaston
Harlescott
Withington
SHREWSBURY
SEE PAGE 210
Upton Magna
Wrockwardine
Wellington
Westbury
Yockleton
Hanwood
Bayston Hill
Atcham
Uppington
Cross Houses
Condover
Minsterley
Pontesbury
Worthen
Dorrington
Acton Burnell
Cressage
Buildwas
Much Wenlock
Harley
Longnor
Church Preen
Hughley
Shelve
Woolstaston
Leebotwood
Chirbury
Montgomery
(Trefaldwyn)
All Stretton
59
Bourton
Easthope
A5
A41
A49
A53
A442
A458
A483
A488
A490
A495
A525
A528
A539

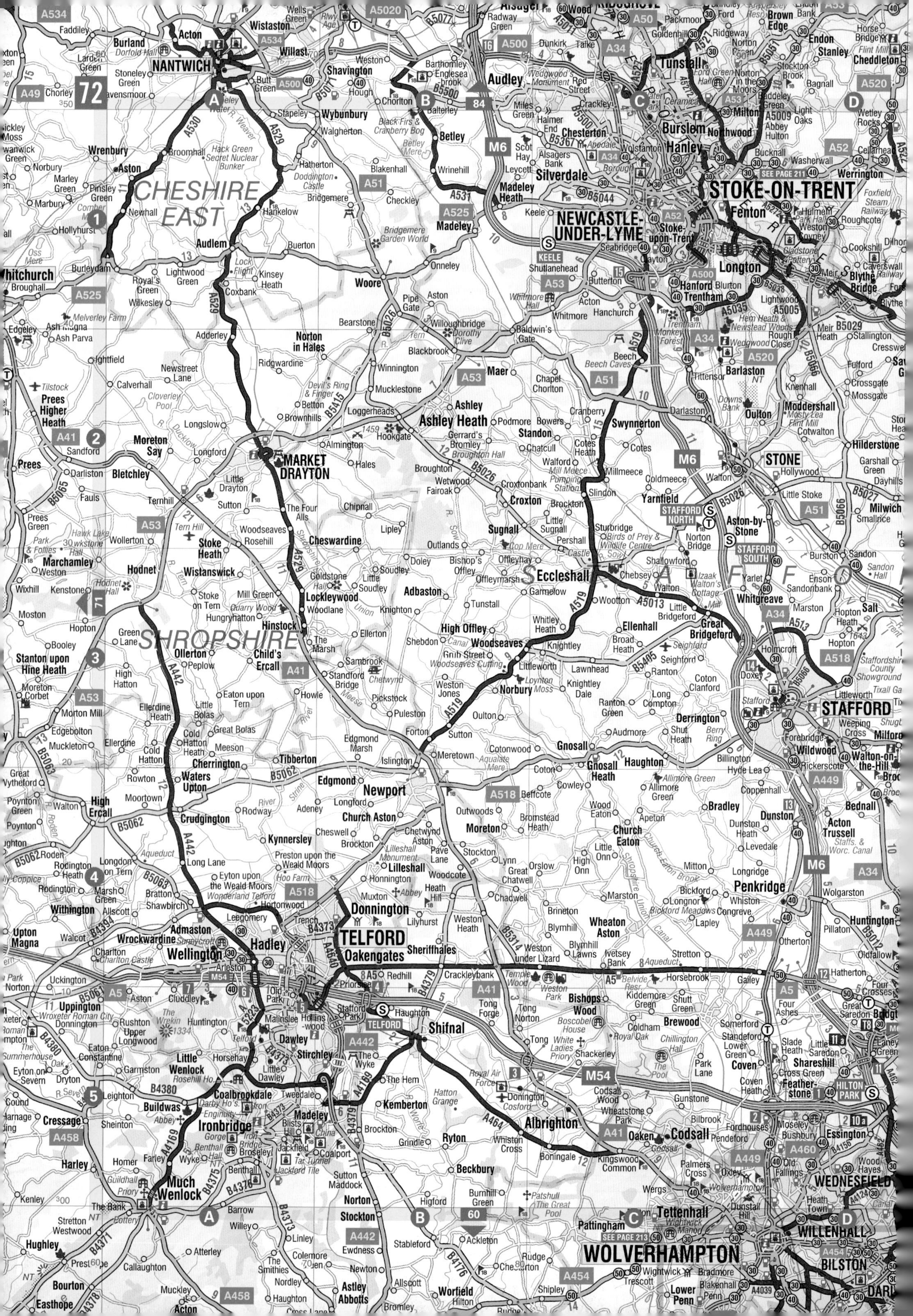

72
NANTWICH
Acton
Wistaston
Willaston
Burland
Faddiley
Stoneley Green
Shavington
Weston
Wybunbury
Audley
Wrenbury
Aston
CHESHIRE EAST
Hack Green Secret Nuclear Bunker
Audlem
Whitchurch
Hankelow
Buerton
Woore
Betley
Madeley
Madeley Heath
Keele
Silverdale
NEWCASTLE-UNDER-LYME
Stoke-upon-Trent
STOKE-ON-TRENT
Burslem
Hanley
Tunstall
Fenton
Longton
Trentham
Chesterton
Norton in Hales
Market Drayton
MARKET DRAYTON
Adderley
Loggerheads
Ashley
Ashley Heath
Maer
Swynnerton
STONE
Cheddleton
Endon
Blythe Bridge
Barlaston
Eccleshall
Prees
Moreton Say
Hodnet
SHROPSHIRE
Cheswardine
Hinstock
Child's Ercall
High Offley
Woodseaves
Norbury
Gnosall
Newport
Stafford
STAFFORD
Haughton
Penkridge
Bradley
Dunston
Great Bridgeford
Yarnfield
Milwich
Hilderstone
High Ercall
Waters Upton
Crudgington
Edgmond
Lilleshall
Donnington
TELFORD
Oakengates
Hadley
Wellington
Shifnal
Dawley
Madeley
Coalbrookdale
Ironbridge
Little Wenlock
Much Wenlock
Buildwas
Albrighton
Codsall
Brewood
Coven
Featherstone
Wheaton Aston
Tettenhall
WOLVERHAMPTON
WEDNESFIELD
WILLENHALL
BILSTON
Pattingham
Worfield
Astley Abbotts
Norton
Stockton
Beckbury
Kemberton
Ryton
Boningale
Oaken
Bishops Wood
Weston Park
Boscobel House
Upton Magna
Withington
Uppington
Cressage
Harley
Hughley
Bourton
Easthope
M6
M54
A53
A41
A51
A34
A442
A464
A518
A519
A529
A5
A49
A458
A454
A449
A500
A50
A52
A520
A525
A530
A4169
B5062
B4380
60
SEE PAGE 211
SEE PAGE 213
71
84

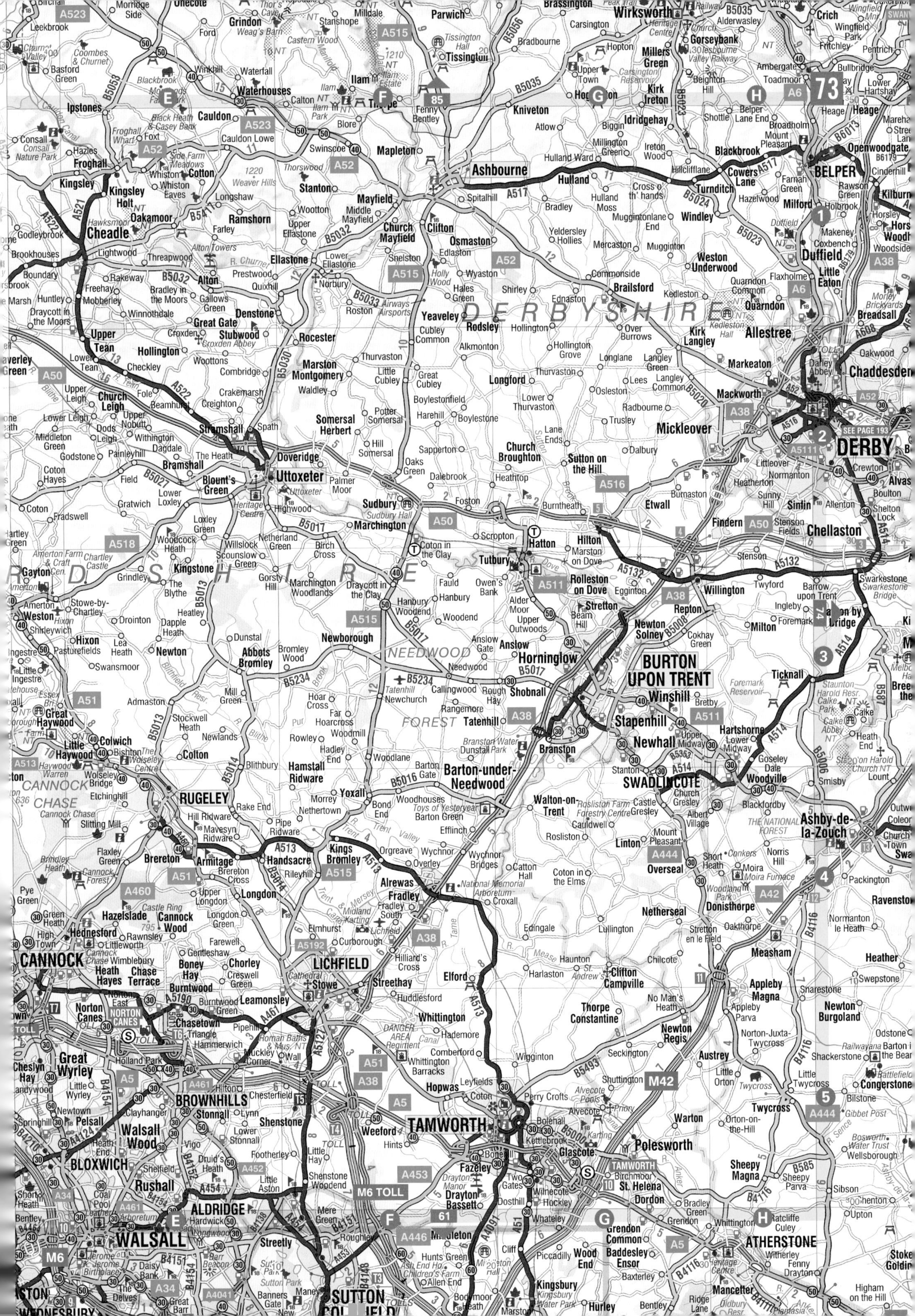

73
74
SEE PAGE 193
DERBYSHIRE
Leekbrook
Ipstones
Cheadle
Kingsley
Froghall
Oakamoor
Alton
Waterhouses
Cauldon
Ilam
Thorpe
Parwich
Tissington
Ashbourne
Mapleton
Mayfield
Clifton
Ellastone
Rocester
Denstone
Upper Tean
Uttoxeter
Doveridge
Sudbury
Marchington
Tutbury
Hatton
Hilton
Etwall
Mickleover
Findern
Willington
Repton
Chellaston
Derby
Allestree
Duffield
Belper
Milford
Kirk Langley
Brailsford
Hulland
Turnditch
Wirksworth
Crich
Heage
Horninglow
Burton upon Trent
Winshill
Stapenhill
Newhall
Branston
Barton-under-Needwood
Swadlincote
Woodville
Ashby-de-la-Zouch
Measham
Overseal
Linton
Rugeley
Colwich
Great Haywood
Little Haywood
Abbots Bromley
Newborough
Yoxall
Kings Bromley
Armitage
Handsacre
Alrewas
Fradley
Lichfield
Elford
Whittington
Hednesford
Cannock
Great Wyrley
Norton Canes
Chasetown
Burntwood
Brownhills
Walsall Wood
Bloxwich
Walsall
Aldridge
Shenstone
Sutton Coldfield
Tamworth
Fazeley
Polesworth
Atherstone
Twycross
Appleby Magna
Newton Burgoland
Congerstone
Kingsbury
Hurley
Wood End
Baddesley Ensor
Grendon
Dordon
Mancetter
NEEDWOOD FOREST
CANNOCK CHASE
M6 TOLL
M42
M6
A38
A50
A52
A515
A513
A5

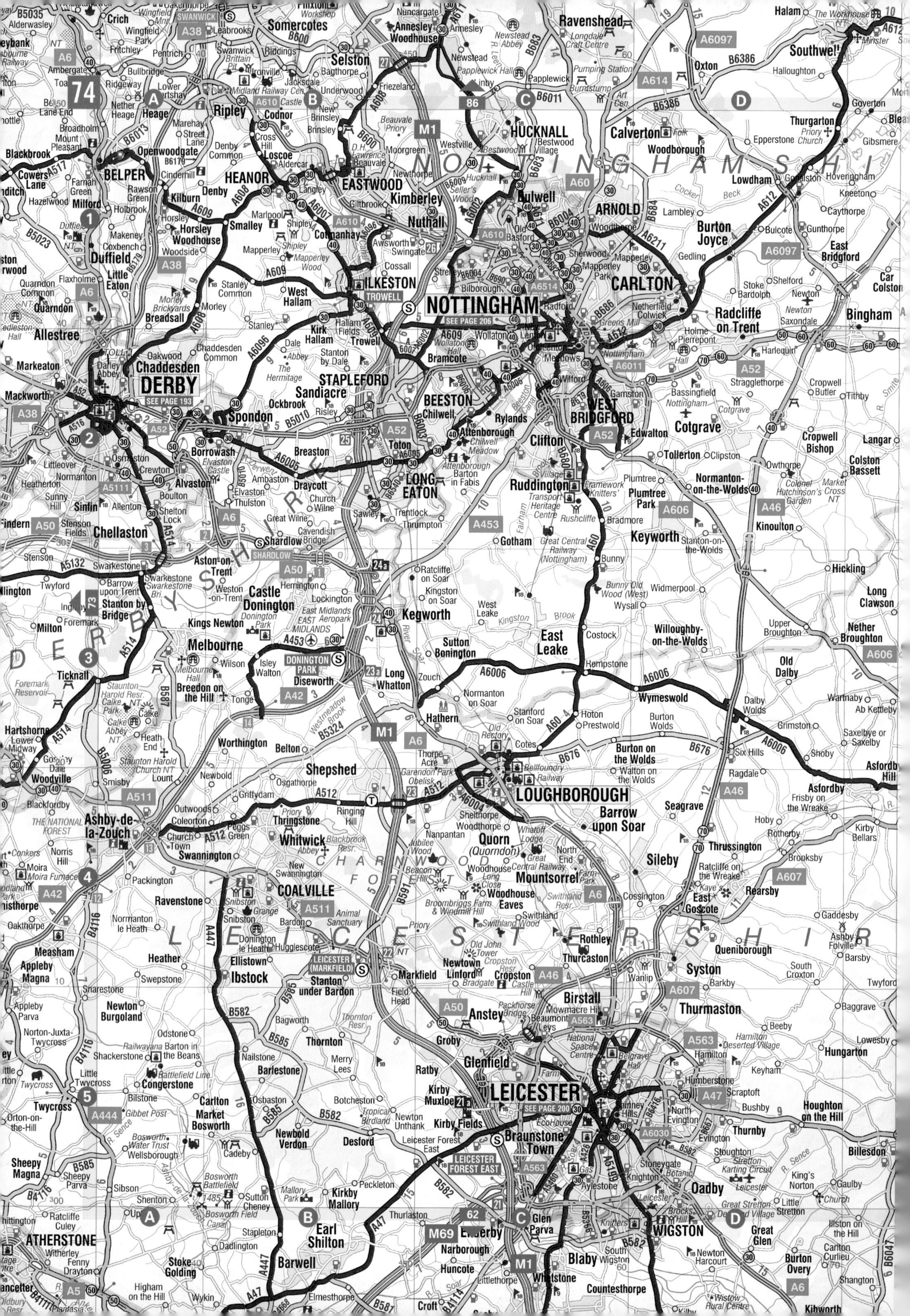

74
86
73
62
A
B
C
D
1
2
3
4
5
Alderwasley
Crich
Wingfield Park
Somercotes
Selston
Annesley Woodhouse
Annesley
Newstead
Ravenshead
Halam
Southwell
Fritchley
Pentrich
Swanwick
Riddings
Jacksdale
Underwood
Bagthorpe
Papplewick
Oxton
Halloughton
Ambergate
Bullbridge
Ridgeway
Lower Hartshay
Heage
Nether Heage
Ripley
Codnor
New Brinsley
Brinsley
Linby
Hucknall
Calverton
Epperstone
Thurgarton
Goverton
Gibsmere
Belper
Openwoodgate
Blackbrook
Cowers Lane
Farnah Green
Hazelwood
Milford
Denby
Heanor
Loscoe
Aldercar
Langley
Eastwood
Kimberley
Nuthall
Bulwell
Bestwood Village
Arnold
Lambley
Woodborough
Lowdham
Gonalston
Hoveringham
Caythorpe
Kneeton
Duffield
Kilburn
Smalley
Horsley Woodhouse
Horsley
Shipley
Cotmanhay
Awsworth
Mapperley
Woodthorpe
Burton Joyce
Bulcote
Gunthorpe
East Bridgford
Little Eaton
Stanley Common
West Hallam
Ilkeston
Trowell
Cossall
Strelley
Bilborough
Sherwood
Mapperley Park
Carlton
Gedling
Stoke Bardolph
Shelford
Newton
Car Colston
Quarndon
Allestree
Breadsall
Morley
Stanley
Kirk Hallam
Hallam Fields
Nottingham
See page 206
Radford
Netherfield
Colwick
Radcliffe on Trent
Holme Pierrepont
Saxondale
Bingham
Derby
See page 193
Chaddesden
Chaddesden Common
Oakwood
Darley Abbey
Markeaton
Mackworth
Dale Abbey
Stanton by Dale
Stapleford
Sandiacre
Bramcote
Wollaton
Lenton
Meadows
Wilford
Gamston
Bassingfield
Harlequin
Cropwell Butler
Tithby
Spondon
Ockbrook
Risley
Beeston
Chilwell
Rylands
Attenborough
Clifton
West Bridgford
Edwalton
Cotgrave
Stragglethorpe
Cropwell Bishop
Langar
Borrowash
Alvaston
Osmaston
Littleover
Normanton
Crewton
Breaston
Draycott
Toton
Long Eaton
Barton in Fabis
Ruddington
Tollerton
Clipston
Plumtree
Plumtree Park
Normanton-on-the-Wolds
Owthorpe
Colston Bassett
Sinfin
Allenton
Boulton
Elvaston
Thulston
Church Wilne
Sawley
Trentlock
Thrumpton
Bradmore
Keyworth
Stanton-on-the-Wolds
Kinoulton
Chellaston
Shelton Lock
Stenson Fields
Great Wilne
Shardlow
Cavendish Bridge
Gotham
Bunny
Swarkestone
Aston-on-Trent
Weston-on-Trent
Castle Donington
Hemington
Lockington
Ratcliffe on Soar
Kingston on Soar
Kegworth
West Leake
East Leake
Widmerpool
Wysall
Hickling
Long Clawson
Twyford
Barrow upon Trent
Stanton by Bridge
Ingleby
Foremark
Milton
Kings Newton
Melbourne
Wilson
Isley Walton
Diseworth
Long Whatton
Sutton Bonington
Costock
Willoughby-on-the-Wolds
Upper Broughton
Nether Broughton
Ticknall
Breedon on the Hill
Tonge
Zouch
Hathern
Normanton on Soar
Rempstone
Wymeswold
Old Dalby
Wartnaby
Ab Kettleby
Calke
Hartshorne
Heath End
Worthington
Belton
Stanford on Soar
Hoton
Prestwold
Burton Wolds
Dalby Wolds
Grimston
Saxelbye or Saxelby
Woodville
Smisby
Lount
Newbold
Shepshed
Osgathorpe
Thorpe Acre
Cotes
Burton on the Wolds
Walton on the Wolds
Six Hills
Shoby
Asfordby
Asfordby Hill
Griffydam
Loughborough
Barrow upon Soar
Seagrave
Ragdale
Frisby on the Wreake
Blackfordby
Ashby-de-la-Zouch
Outwoods
Coleorton
Peggs Green
Thringstone
Ringing Hill
Shelthorpe
Woodthorpe
Nanpantan
Quorn (Quorndon)
Hoby
Rotherby
Kirby Bellars
Church Town
Swannington
Whitwick
New Swannington
Mountsorrel
Sileby
Thrussington
Brooksby
Moira
Norris Hill
Packington
Coalville
Woodhouse
Woodhouse Eaves
Swithland
Cossington
Ratcliffe on the Wreake
Rearsby
Ravenstone
Snibston
East Goscote
Gaddesby
Measham
Normanton le Heath
Bardon
Rothley
Queniborough
Ashby Folville
Barsby
Appleby Magna
Heather
Ellistown
Ibstock
Hugglescote
Donington le Heath
Markfield
Newtown Linford
Cropston
Thurcaston
Wanlip
Syston
South Croxton
Twyford
Swepstone
Snarestone
Stanton under Barden
Field Head
Anstey
Birstall
Barkby
Thurmaston
Appleby Parva
Newton Burgoland
Bagworth
Thornton
Groby
Beaumont Leys
Baggrave
Norton-Juxta-Twycross
Odstone
Barton in the Beans
Shackerstone
Nailstone
Barlestone
Merry Lees
Ratby
Glenfield
Hamilton
Beeby
Lowesby
Hungarton
Keyham
Little Twycross
Congerstone
Kirby Muxloe
Leicester
See page 200
Humberstone
Scraptoft
Twycross
Bilstone
Carlton
Market Bosworth
Osbaston
Botcheston
Newton Unthank
Kirby Fields
Bushby
Houghton on the Hill
Orton-on-the-Hill
Newbold Verdon
Desford
Leicester Forest East
Braunstone Town
North Evington
Thurnby
Evington
Stoughton
Stoneygate
Billesdon
Sheepy Magna
Sheepy Parva
Wellsborough
Cadeby
Knighton
Aylestone
Oadby
King's Norton
Gaulby
Sibson
Shenton
Sutton Cheney
Peckleton
Kirkby Mallory
Little Stretton
Atherstone
Ratcliffe Culey
Upton
Earl Shilton
Thurlaston
Glen Parva
Enderby
Wigston
Great Glen
Illston on the Hill
Witherley
Fenny Drayton
Stapleton
Dadlington
Narborough
Blaby
South Wigston
Newton Harcourt
Carlton Curlieu
Stoke Golding
Barwell
Huncote
Whetstone
Burton Overy
Shangton
Higham on the Hill
Wykin
Elmesthorpe
Croft
Littlethorpe
Countesthorpe
Kibworth
DERBYSHIRE
NOTTINGHAMSHIRE
LEICESTERSHIRE
CHARNWOOD FOREST
M1
M69
A6
A38
A52
A50
A42
A46
A47
A60
A610
A609
A6005
A6006
A511
A512
A453
A444
A563
A607
A606
A612
A614
A6097
A5

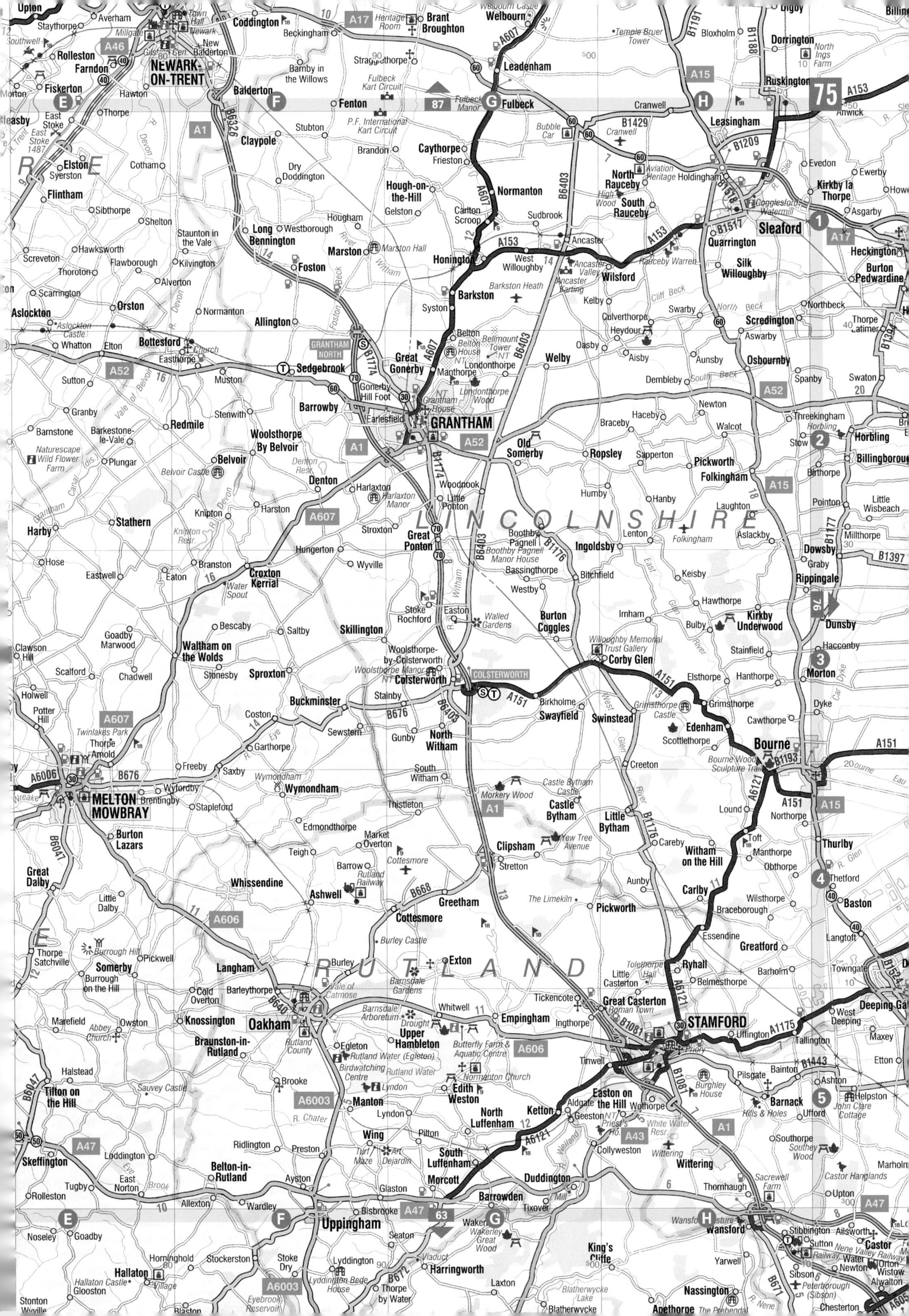

Upton
Averham
Staythorpe
Southwell
Rolleston
Farndon
Fiskerton
Morton
Town Hall
Millgate
Newark
New Balderton
NEWARK-ON-TRENT
Hawton
Thorpe
Balderton
A46
A1
B6326
Coddington
Beckingham
A17
Heritage Room
Brant Broughton
Barnby in the Willows
Stragglethorpe
Fulbeck Kart Circuit
Fenton
P.F. International Kart Circuit
87
Fulbeck Manor
Fulbeck
Welbourn
A607
Leadenham
Temple Bruer Tower
B1191
Bloxholm
B1188
Digby
Dorrington
North Ings Farm
Ruskington
75
A153
Anwick
Cranwell
Leasingham
B1429
B1209
Bubble Car
Aviation Heritage
Holdingham
North Rauceby
South Rauceby
High Wood
Cogglesford Watermill
Sleaford
Evedon
Ewerby
Kirkby la Thorpe
Howell
Asgarby
Quarrington
A17
Heckington
B1517
B1518
A15
Claypole
Stubton
Brandon
Caythorpe
Frieston
Dry Doddington
Cotham
East Stoke
Elston
Syerston
Flintham
Sibthorpe
Shelton
Hough-on-the-Hill
Gelston
Normanton
Carlton Scroop
Sudbrook
Ancaster
B6403
Hougham
Long Bennington
Westborough
Staunton in the Vale
Marston
Marston Hall
Honington
A153
West Willoughby
Ancaster Valley
Ancaster Karting
Wilsford
Rauceby Warren
Silk Willoughby
Burton Pedwardine
Screveton
Hawksworth
Flawborough
Kilvington
Thoroton
Foston
Alverton
Scarrington
Orston
Aslockton
Aslockton Castle
Whatton
Elton
Normanton
Allington
Barkston
Barkston Heath
Syston
Kelby
Culverthorpe
Heydour
Swarby
Scredington
Northbeck
Thorpe Latimer
Aswarby
Aisby
Oasby
Belton
Belton House
Bellmount Tower
Londonthorpe
Welby
Aunsby
Osbournby
Spanby
Swaton
B1394
Bottesford
Church
Easthorpe
GRANTHAM NORTH
Sedgebrook
Great Gonerby
Manthorpe
Londonthorpe Wood
Gonerby Hill Foot
B1174
Sutton
Muston
A52
Barrowby
Earlesfield
Grantham House
GRANTHAM
Dembleby
Newton
Threekingham
Horbling
Stow
Granby
Barnstone
Barkestone-le-Vale
Redmile
Stenwith
Woolsthorpe By Belvoir
Vale of Belvoir
Naturescape Wild Flower Farm
Plungar
Belvoir
Belvoir Castle
Denton Resr.
Denton
Harlaxton
Harlaxton Manor
Old Somerby
Braceby
Haceby
Walcot
Ropsley
Sapperton
Pickworth
Folkingham
Billingborough
Birthorpe
Woodnook
Little Ponton
Humby
Hanby
Laughton
Pointon
Little Wisbeach
Harby
Stathern
Knipton
Knipton Resr.
Harston
A607
Stroxton
Great Ponton
LINCOLNSHIRE
Boothby Pagnell
Boothby Pagnell Manor House
B1176
Ingoldsby
Lenton
Folkingham
Aslackby
Millthorpe
B1177
Dowsby
Graby
B1397
Rippingale
Hose
Eastwell
Eaton
Branston
Croxton Kerrial
Water Spout
Hungerton
Wyville
Bassingthorpe
Westby
Bitchfield
Keisby
Hawthorpe
Stoke Rochford
Easton
Walled Gardens
Burton Coggles
Irnham
Bulby
Kirkby Underwood
Dunsby
76
Clawson Hill
Goadby Marwood
Bescaby
Saltby
Skillington
Waltham on the Wolds
Scalford
Chadwell
Stonesby
Sproxton
Woolsthorpe-by-Colsterworth
Woolsthorpe Manor
Colsterworth
COLSTERWORTH
Willoughby Memorial Trust Gallery
Corby Glen
Stainfield
Hacconby
Morton
Elsthorpe
Hanthorpe
Holwell
Potter Hill
A607
Twinlakes Park
Buckminster
Stainby
B676
Coston
Sewstern
Gunby
North Witham
A151
Birkholme
Swayfield
Swinstead
Grimsthorpe Castle
Grimsthorpe
Edenham
Scottlethorpe
Cawthorpe
Dyke
Bourne
Bourne Wood Sculpture Trail
B1193
A151
Thorpe Arnold
Garthorpe
Freeby
Saxby
Wymondham
South Witham
Creeton
A6006
B676
Wyfordby
Brentingby
MELTON MOWBRAY
Stapleford
Thistleton
Morkery Wood
A1
Castle Bytham
Little Bytham
A6121
Lound
Northorpe
A15
Burton Lazars
B6047
Edmondthorpe
Market Overton
Teigh
Cottesmore
Barrow
Rutland Railway
Clipsham
Stretton
Yew Tree Avenue
Careby
Witham on the Hill
Toft
Manthorpe
Obthorpe
Thurlby
Thetford
Great Dalby
Little Dalby
Whissendine
Ashwell
B668
Greetham
The Limekiln
Pickworth
Aunby
Carlby
Wilsthorpe
Braceborough
Baston
A606
Cottesmore
Burley Castle
Essendine
Greatford
Langtoft
Thorpe Satchville
Burrough Hill
Pickwell
Somerby
Burrough on the Hill
Langham
Cold Overton
RUTLAND
Burley
Exton
Barnsdale Gardens
Tolethorpe Hall
Little Casterton
Ryhall
Belmesthorpe
Barholm
Towngate
Barleythorpe
Vale of Catmose
B640
Oakham
Knossington
Owston
Marefield
Abbey Church
Braunston-in-Rutland
Rutland County
Barnsdale Arboretum
Drought
Upper Hambleton
Whitwell
Empingham
Tickencote
Great Casterton
Roman Town
Ingthorpe
A1
B1081
STAMFORD
Uffington
A1175
Tallington
West Deeping
Deeping Gate
Maxey
Etton
Egleton
Rutland Water (Egleton)
Birdwatching Centre
Rutland Water
Butterfly Farm & Aquatic Centre
Normanton Church
A606
Tinwell
Priory
B1443
Pilsgate
Bainton
Ashton
Burghley House
Barnack
Hills & Holes
Helpston
John Clare Cottage
Ufford
Halstead
Tilton on the Hill
Sauvey Castle
Brooke
A6003
R. Chater
Lyndon
Manton
Edith Weston
North Luffenham
Ketton
Aldgate
Geeston
Easton on the Hill
Wothorpe
Priest's Ho.
White Water Resr.
Wittering
A43
Collyweston
Southorpe
Southey Wood
Marholm
Castor Hanglands
Skeffington
A47
Loddington
Ridlington
Wing
Turf Maze
Art Dejardin
Pilton
Preston
South Luffenham
Morcott
Duddington
Sacrewell Farm
Thornhaugh
Upton
Tugby
East Norton
Rolleston
Allexton
Belton-in-Rutland
Ayston
Wardley
Glaston
Bisbrooke
Barrowden
Tixover
Mill
Wansford
Stibbington
Ailsworth
Castor
Sutton
Nene Valley Railway
Water Newton
Orton
Wistow
Noseley
Goadby
Uppingham
63
Seaton
Wakerley
Wakerley Great Wood
King's Cliffe
Yarwell
Sibson
Peterborough (Sibson)
Alwalton
Hallaton
Hallaton Castle
Glooston
Horninghold
Stockerston
Stoke Dry
Lyddington
Lyddington Bede House
B672
Viaduct
Harringworth
Thorpe by Water
Laxton
Blatherwycke Lake
Blatherwycke
Nassington
Apethorpe
The Prebendal
Chesterton
B671
Eyebrook Reservoir
Blaston
Stonton Wyville
A6003

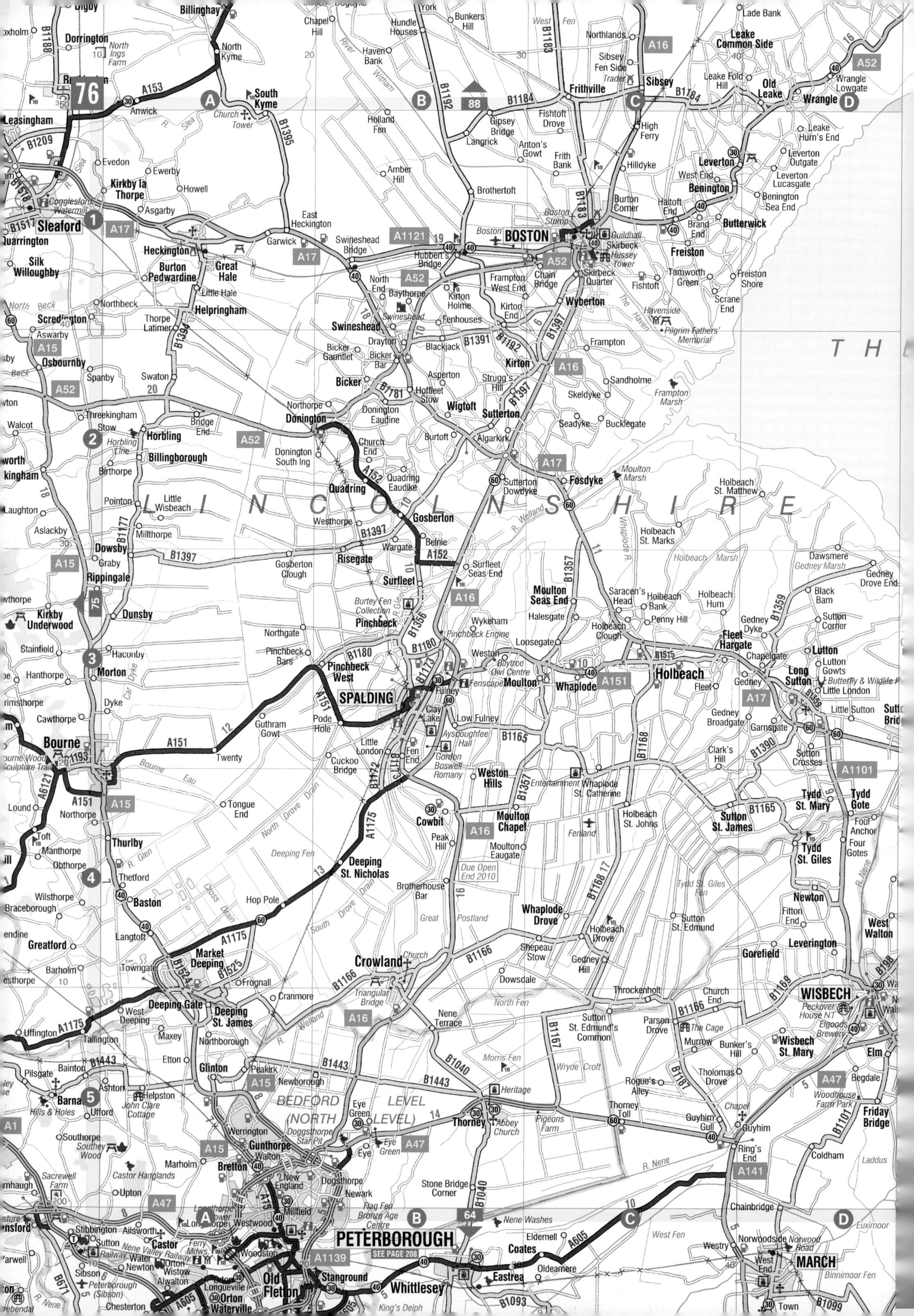

76
88
75
64
SEE PAGE 208
LINCOLNSHIRE
BEDFORD LEVEL (NORTH LEVEL)
Sleaford
Quarrington
Silk Willoughby
Leasingham
Kirkby la Thorpe
Evedon
Ewerby
Howell
Asgarby
Anwick
North Kyme
South Kyme
Billinghay
Dorrington
North Ings Farm
Heckington
Great Hale
Little Hale
Burton Pedwardine
Helpringham
Thorpe Latimer
Scredington
Aswarby
Osbournby
Spanby
Swaton
Threekingham
Stow
Horbling
Billingborough
Birthorpe
Pointon
Little Wisbeach
Millthorpe
Dowsby
Graby
Rippingale
Kirkby Underwood
Dunsby
Hacconby
Morton
Stainfield
Hanthorpe
Dyke
Cawthorpe
Bourne
Twenty
Northorpe
Thurlby
Manthorpe
Obthorpe
Toft
Lound
Thetford
Baston
Wilsthorpe
Braceborough
Greatford
Langtoft
Barholm
Market Deeping
Deeping Gate
Deeping St. James
Frognall
Towngate
West Deeping
Tallington
Uffington
Maxey
Northborough
Etton
Glinton
Peakirk
Newborough
Bainton
Ashton
Helpston
Pilsgate
Barnack
Hills & Holes
Ufford
John Clare Cottage
Southorpe
Southey Wood
Sacrewell Farm
Castor Hanglands
Marholm
Upton
Stibbington
Ailsworth
Castor
Sutton
Nene Valley Railway
Water Newton
Ferry Mdws.
Orton Wistow
Alwalton
Sibson
Peterborough (Sibson)
Chesterton
Orton Longueville
Orton Waterville
Longthorpe
Westwood
Werrington
Gunthorpe
Walton
Bretton
New England
Dogsthorpe
Millfield
Newark
Eye
Eye Green
Doggsthorpe Star Pit
Flag Fen Bronze Age Centre
PETERBOROUGH
Stanground
Old Fletton
Woodston
Whittlesey
King's Delph
Eastrea
Coates
Eldernell
Oldeamere
Nene Washes
Stone Bridge Corner
Thorney
Abbey Church
Thorney Toll
Pigeons Farm
Heritage
Morris Fen
Wryde Croft
Crowland
Triangular Bridge
Cranmore
Nene Terrace
North Fen
Dowsdale
Shepeau Stow
Gedney Hill
Whaplode Drove
Holbeach Drove
Throckenholt
Sutton St. Edmund's Common
Sutton St. Edmund
Parson Drove
The Cage
Murrow
Bunker's Hill
Rogue's Alley
Tholomas Drove
Guyhirn
Guyhirn Gull
Ring's End
Chapel
Church End
Gorefield
Leverington
WISBECH
Peckover House NT
Elgoods Brewery
Wisbech St. Mary
Elm
Begdale
Woodhouse Farm Park
Friday Bridge
Coldham
Laddus
Chainbridge
Westry
Norwoodside
Norwood Road
West End
MARCH
Binnimoor Fen
Town End
Euximoor
West Fen
Newton
Fitton End
West Walton
Tydd St. Giles
Tydd St. Mary
Tydd Gote
Four Anchor
Four Gotes
Sutton St. James
Sutton Crosses
Little Sutton
Long Sutton
Lutton
Lutton Gowts
Butterfly & Wildlife Park
Little London
Garnsgate
Gedney
Gedney Broadgate
Clark's Hill
Chapelgate
Gedney Dyke
Fleet Hargate
Fleet
Holbeach
Holbeach Clough
Holbeach Bank
Penny Hill
Holbeach Hurn
Saracen's Head
Holbeach St. Marks
Holbeach St. Matthew
Holbeach Marsh
Dawsmere
Gedney Drove End
Black Barn
Sutton Corner
Holbeach St. Johns
Whaplode St. Catherine
Whaplode
Moulton
Moulton Seas End
Halesgate
Loosegate
Moulton Chapel
Moulton Eaugate
Fenland
Weston
Weston Hills
Baytree Owl Centre
Fenscape
Cowbit
Peak Hill
Due Open End 2010
Brotherhouse Bar
Great Postland
Deeping St. Nicholas
Deeping Fen
Hop Pole
Tongue End
Guthram Gowt
Pode Hole
Little London
Cuckoo Bridge
Fen End
Gordon Boswell Romany
Ayscoughfee Hall
Clay Lake
Low Fulney
Fulney
SPALDING
Pinchbeck West
Pinchbeck Bars
Northgate
Pinchbeck
Burtey Fen Collection
Pinchbeck Engine
Wykeham
Surfleet
Surfleet Seas End
Gosberton
Gosberton Clough
Risegate
Wargate
Belnie
Westhorpe
Quadring
Quadring Eaudike
Church End
Donington
Donington South Ing
Northorpe
Donington Eaudine
Bicker
Bicker Gauntlet
Bicker Bar
Drayton
Swineshead
Swineshead Bridge
Baythorpe
North End
Hoffleet Stow
Blackjack
Asperton
Wigtoft
Burtoft
Struggs Hill
Sutterton
Algarkirk
Sutterton Dowdyke
Fosdyke
Moulton Marsh
Kirton
Kirton End
Kirton Holme
Fenhouses
Frampton
Frampton West End
Frampton Marsh
Sandholme
Skeldyke
Seadyke
Bucklegate
Wyberton
Chain Bridge
Skirbeck Quarter
Skirbeck
Hussey Tower
Guildhall
BOSTON
Boston Stump
Hubbert's Bridge
Brothertoft
Amber Hill
Holland Fen
Langrick
Gipsey Bridge
Fishtoft Drove
Anton's Gowt
Frith Bank
Frithville
Sibsey
Sibsey Fen Side
Trader
Northlands
West Fen
Chapel Hill
Haven Bank
Hundle Houses
Bunkers Hill
River Witham
Garwick
East Heckington
High Ferry
Hilldyke
Burton Corner
Haltoft End
Brand End
Fishtoft
Freiston
Freiston Shore
Tamworth Green
Scrane End
Havenside
Pilgrim Fathers' Memorial
Butterwick
Benington
Benington Sea End
West End
Leverton
Leverton Outgate
Leverton Lucasgate
Leake Hurn's End
Wrangle
Wrangle Lowgate
Old Leake
Leake Fold Hill
Leake Commonside
Lade Bank
THE

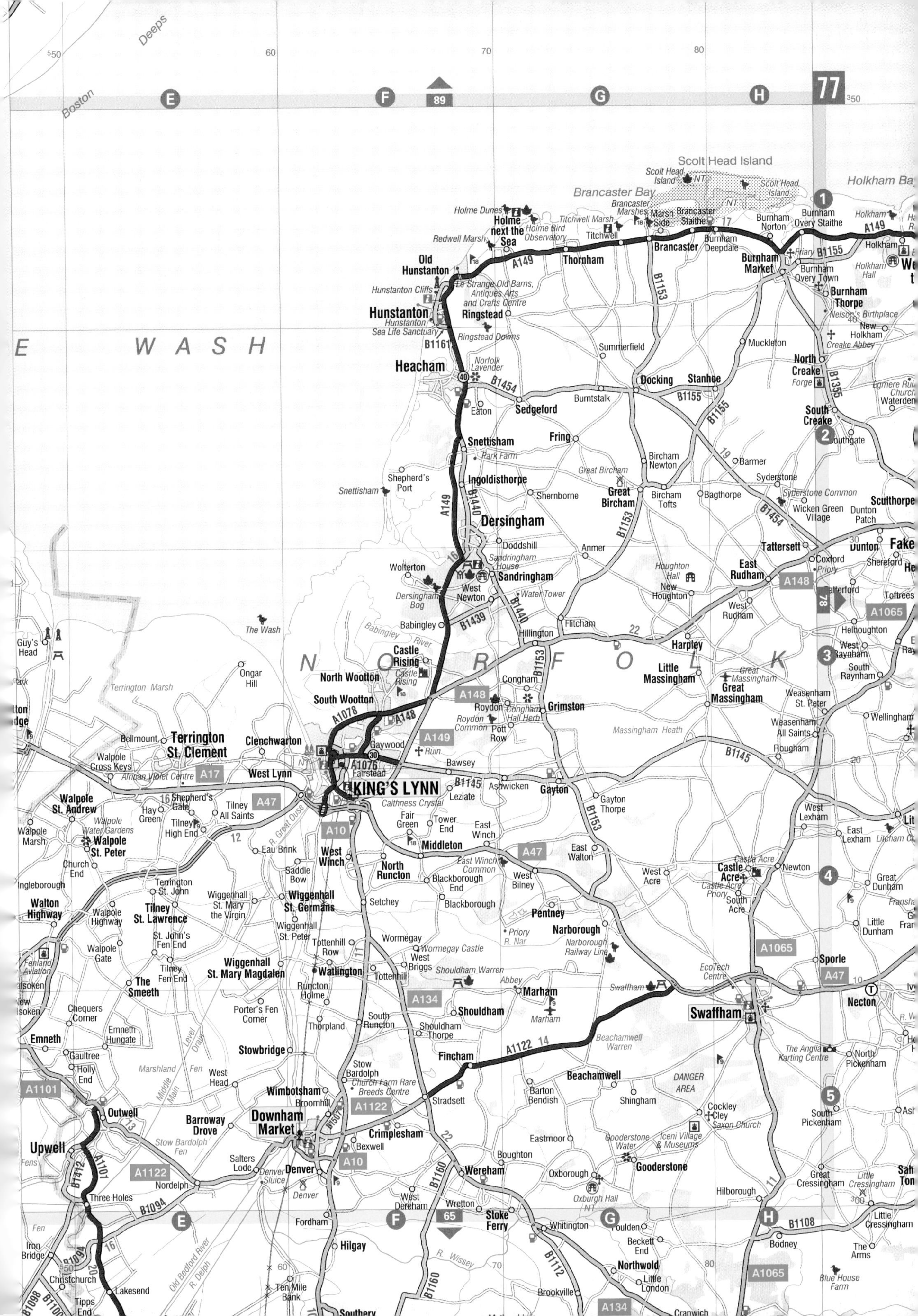
Boston Deeps
89
E
F
G
H
Scolt Head Island
Brancaster Bay
Holkham Bay
Holme Dunes
Holme next the Sea
Holme Bird Observatory
Titchwell Marsh
Titchwell
Brancaster Marshes
Marsh Side
Brancaster Staithe
Burnham Deepdale
Brancaster
Burnham Norton
Burnham Overy Staithe
Burnham Market
Burnham Overy Town
Burnham Thorpe
Nelson's Birthplace
Holkham
Holkham Hall
Redwell Marsh
Old Hunstanton
Hunstanton Cliffs
Le Strange Old Barns, Antiques, Arts and Crafts Centre
Hunstanton
Hunstanton Sea Life Sanctuary
Ringstead
Ringstead Downs
Thornham
THE WASH
Heacham
Norfolk Lavender
Summerfield
Docking
Stanhoe
Muckleton
North Creake
Creake Abbey
New Holkham
Burntstalk
Sedgeford
Eaton
South Creake
Egmere
Waterden
Snettisham
Park Farm
Fring
Bircham Newton
Barmer
Southgate
Shepherd's Port
Snettisham
Ingoldisthorpe
Great Bircham
Shernborne
Bircham Tofts
Bagthorpe
Syderstone
Syderstone Common
Wicken Green Village
Sculthorpe
Dunton Patch
Dersingham
Doddshill
Anmer
Tattersett
Dunton
Fakenham
Coxford Priory
Shereford
Wolferton
Sandringham House
Sandringham
Houghton Hall
New Houghton
East Rudham
West Rudham
Dersingham Bog
West Newton
Water Tower
Tatterford
Toftrees
Babingley
Babingley River
Flitcham
Hillington
Harpley
Helhoughton
The Wash
Castle Rising
North Wootton
South Wootton
Congham
Roydon
Roydon Common
Congham Hall Herbs
Pott Row
Grimston
Little Massingham
Great Massingham
Weasenham St. Peter
Weasenham All Saints
West Raynham
South Raynham
Wellingham
NORFOLK
Guy's Head
Terrington Marsh
Ongar Hill
Massingham Heath
Rougham
Bellmount
Terrington St. Clement
Clenchwarton
Gaywood
Ruin
Bawsey
Walpole Cross Keys
African Violet Centre
West Lynn
Fairstead
KING'S LYNN
Ashwicken
Gayton
Gayton Thorpe
Leziate
Caithness Crystal
Walpole St. Andrew
Walpole Water Gardens
Walpole Marsh
Walpole St. Peter
Shepherd's Gate
Hay Green
Tilney All Saints
Tilney High End
Fair Green
Tower End
East Winch
West Lexham
East Lexham
Church End
Eau Brink
West Winch
Middleton
North Runcton
Saddle Bow
East Winch Common
West Bilney
East Walton
West Acre
Castle Acre
Castle Acre Priory
South Acre
Newton
Great Dunham
Ingleborough
Terrington St. John
Wiggenhall St. Mary the Virgin
Wiggenhall St. Germans
Wiggenhall St. Peter
Blackborough End
Blackborough
Setchey
Pentney
Narborough
Narborough Railway Line
Priory
R. Nar
Little Dunham
Walton Highway
Walpole Highway
Tilney St. Lawrence
St. John's Fen End
Tottenhill Row
Wormegay
Wormegay Castle
West Briggs
Fenland Aviation
Walpole Gate
Tilney Fen End
The Smeeth
Wiggenhall St. Mary Magdalen
Watlington
Tottenhill
Shouldham Warren
Abbey
Marham
Swaffham
EcoTech Centre
Sporle
Runcton Holme
Shouldham
Chequers Corner
Emneth Hungate
Porter's Fen Corner
South Runcton
Thorpland
Shouldham Thorpe
Necton
Emneth
Level Drain
Stowbridge
Fincham
Beachamwell Warren
The Anglia Karting Centre
North Pickenham
Gaultree
Holly End
Marshland
Fen
West Head
Middle Main
Stow Bardolph
Church Farm Rare Breeds Centre
Wimbotsham
Broomhill
Beachamwell
Barton Bendish
Shingham
DANGER AREA
Outwell
Barroway Drove
Downham Market
Crimplesham
Stradsett
Cockley Cley
Saxon Church
South Pickenham
Upwell
Stow Bardolph Fen
Bexwell
Eastmoor
Gooderstone Water
Iceni Village & Museums
Gooderstone
Salters Lode
Denver Sluice
Denver
Boughton
Wereham
Oxborough
Oxburgh Hall
Great Cressingham
Little Cressingham
Nordelph
Three Holes
West Dereham
Wretton
Hilborough
Fordham
Stoke Ferry
Whittington
Foulden
Little Cressingham
Bodney
Fen
Iron Bridge
Beckett End
The Arms
Hilgay
R. Wissey
Northwold
Christchurch
Old Bedford River
R. Delph
Ten Mile Bank
Little London
Blue House Farm
Tipps End
Lakesend
Brookville
Southery
Cranwich
65
78

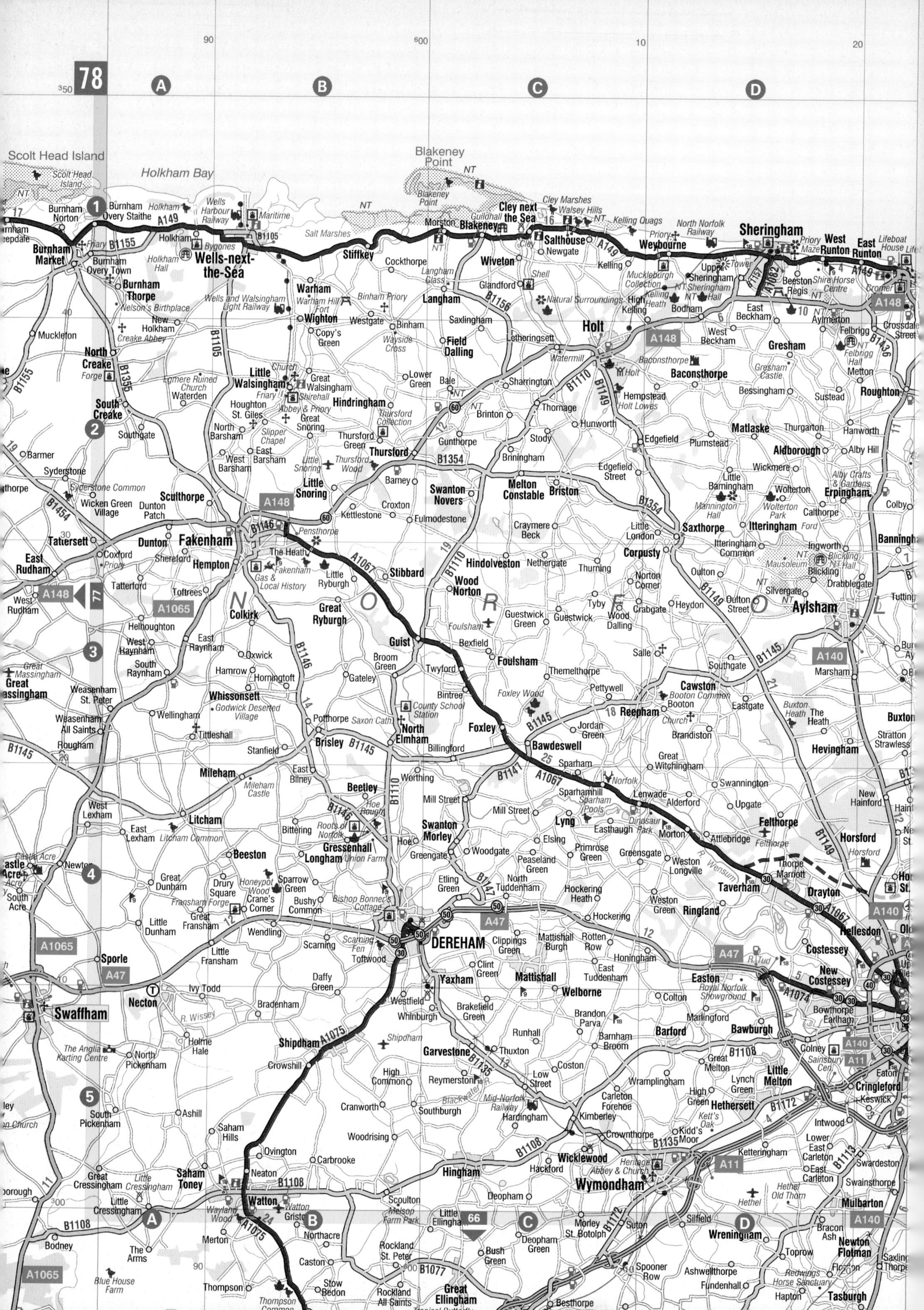

78
A
B
C
D
90
600
10
20
Scolt Head Island
Scolt Head Island
Holkham Bay
Blakeney Point
Blakeney Point
NT
Salt Marshes
Burnham Norton
Burnham Overy Staithe
Holkham
Wells Harbour Railway
Maritime
Wells-next-the-Sea
Burnham Market
Burnham Overy Town
Burnham Thorpe
Nelson's Birthplace
Holkham Hall
Bygones
Stiffkey
Morston
Blakeney
Cley next the Sea
Cley Marshes
Walsey Hills
Kelling Quags
North Norfolk Railway
Sheringham
Priory Maze
West Runton
East Runton
Lifeboat House
Salthouse
Newgate
Weybourne
Kelling
Muckleburgh Collection
Upper Sheringham
Sheringham Hall
Beeston Regis
Shire Horse Centre
Cromer
Cockthorpe
Langham Glass
Langham
Glandford
Shell
Wiveton
Natural Surroundings
Kelling Heath
High Kelling
Bodham
East Beckham
Aylmerton
Felbrigg
Crossdale Street
Warham
Warham Hill Fort
Binham Priory
Wells and Walsingham Light Railway
Wighton
Copy's Green
Westgate
Binham
Wayside Cross
Field Dalling
Saxlingham
Letheringsett
Holt
Watermill
Baconsthorpe
West Beckham
Gresham
Gresham Castle
Felbrigg Hall
Metton
Muckleton
New Holkham
Creake Abbey
North Creake
Forge
Egmere Ruined Church
Waterden
Little Walsingham
Great Walsingham
Friary
Shirehall
Abbey & Priory
Houghton St. Giles
Slipper Chapel
Hindringham
Thursford Collection
Lower Green
Bale
Sharrington
Brinton
Thornage
Hempstead
Holt Lowes
Bessingham
Sustead
Roughton
South Creake
Southgate
North Barsham
West Barsham
East Barsham
Great Snoring
Little Snoring
Thursford Green
Thursford
Thursford Wood
Gunthorpe
Stody
Hunworth
Edgefield
Plumstead
Matlaske
Thurgarton
Hanworth
Aldborough
Alby Hill
Barmer
Syderstone
Syderstone Common
Sculthorpe
Wicken Green Village
Dunton Patch
Barney
Briningham
Melton Constable
Briston
Edgefield Street
Little Barningham
Mannington Hall
Wickmere
Wolterton
Wolterton Park
Alby Crafts & Gardens
Erpingham
Calthorpe
Colby
Swanton Novers
Croxton
Kettlestone
Fulmodestone
Craymere Beck
Little London
Saxthorpe
Itteringham
Itteringham Common
Ingworth
Blickling
Blickling Hall
Mausoleum
Banningham
Tattersett
Coxford Priory
Dunton
Fakenham
Shereford
Hempton
Pensthorpe
The Heath
Fakenham
Gas & Local History
East Rudham
Tatterford
Toftrees
Little Ryburgh
Stibbard
Hindolveston
Nethergate
Thurning
Corpusty
Norton Corner
Oulton
Oulton Street
Drabblegate
Silvergate
Aylsham
Tuttington
West Rudham
Helhoughton
Colkirk
Great Ryburgh
Wood Norton
Guestwick Green
Guestwick
Tyby
Wood Dalling
Crabgate
Heydon
N O R F O L K
West Raynham
East Raynham
Oxwick
Great Massingham
Great Massingham
South Raynham
Hamrow
Horningtoft
Guist
Foulsham
Bexfield
Broom Green
Foulsham
Themelthorpe
Salle
Southgate
Marsham
Weasenham St. Peter
Weasenham All Saints
Whissonsett
Godwick Deserted Village
Wellingham
Tittleshall
Gateley
Twyford
Bintree
County School Station
Foxley Wood
Pettywell
Cawston
Booton Common
Booton
Reepham
Eastgate
Buxton Heath
The Heath
Buxton
Stratton Strawless
Rougham
Potthorpe
Saxon Cath
North Elmham
Brisley
Stanfield
Billingford
Foxley
Bawdeswell
Jordan Green
Church
Brandiston
Hevingham
Mileham
Mileham Castle
East Bilney
Worthing
Sparham
Norfolk
Great Witchingham
Swannington
New Hainford
West Lexham
Litcham
Beetley
Hoe Rough
Mill Street
Mill Street
Sparhamhill
Sparham Pools
Lenwade
Alderford
Upgate
Felthorpe
East Lexham
Litcham Common
Bittering
Roots of Norfolk
Gressenhall
Swanton Morley
Lyng
Elsing
Dinosaur Park
Easthaugh
Morton
Attlebridge
Felthorpe
Horsford
Castle Acre
Newton
Beeston
Longham
Union Farm
Hoe
Greengate
Woodgate
Peaseland Green
Primrose Green
Greensgate
Weston Longville
R. Wensum
Thorpe Marriott
South Acre
Great Dunham
Drury Square
Honeypot Wood
Sparrow Green
Crane's Corner
Bushy Common
Bishop Bonner's Cottage
Etling Green
North Tuddenham
Hockering Heath
Weston Green
Ringland
Taverham
Drayton
Fransham Forge
Great Fransham
Little Dunham
Wendling
Scarning
Scarning Fen
Toftwood
DEREHAM
Clippings Green
Mattishall Burgh
Rotten Row
Hockering
Honingham
Hellesdon
Costessey
Sporle
Little Fransham
Daffy Green
Clint Green
Yaxham
Mattishall
East Tuddenham
Easton
R. Tud
New Costessey
Swaffham
Necton
Ivy Todd
Bradenham
Westfield
Whinburgh
Brakefield Green
Welborne
Royal Norfolk Showground
Colton
Bowthorpe
Earlham
R. Wissey
Holme Hale
Brandon Parva
Marlingford
Barford
Bawburgh
The Anglia Karting Centre
North Pickenham
Shipdham
Shipdham
Garvestone
Thuxton
Runhall
Barnham Broom
Colney
Sainsbury Cen.
Eaton
Crowshill
High Common
Reymerston
Coston
Low Street
Great Melton
Little Melton
Cringleford
Keswick
South Pickenham
Ashill
Cranworth
Southburgh
Blackwater R.
Mid-Norfolk Railway
Hardingham
Wramplingham
Carleton Forehoe
High Green
Lynch Green
Hethersett
Kett's Oak
Intwood
Saham Hills
Woodrising
Kimberley
Crownthorpe
Kidd's Moor
Lower East Carleton
East Carleton
Ovington
Carbrooke
Wicklewood
Ketteringham
Swardeston
Great Cressingham
Little Cressingham
Saham Toney
Neaton
Hingham
Hackford
Heritage Abbey & Church
Wymondham
Swainsthorpe
Little Cressingham
Watton
Watton
Griston
Scoulton
Melsop Farm Park
Deopham
Hethel
Hethel Old Thorn
Mulbarton
Bodney
Wayland Wood
Northacre
Little Ellingham
66
Deopham Green
Morley St. Botolph
Suton
Silfield
Wreningham
Bracon Ash
Newton Flotman
Merton
The Arms
Rockland St. Peter
Bush Green
Toprow
Saxlingham Thorpe
Caston
Spooner Row
Ashwellthorpe
Redwings Horse Sanctuary
Flordon
Blue House Farm
Thompson
Stow Bedon
Rockland All Saints
Great Ellingham
Fundenhall
Hapton
Tasburgh
Thompson Common
Tropical Butterfly Gardens
Besthorpe
Attleborough
Black
Tacolneston
A149
A148
A1067
A1065
A47
A1075
A1082
A140
A1074
A11
B1155
B1105
B1355
B1454
B1145
B1146
B1110
B1354
B1156
B1149
B1147
B1135
B1108
B1172
B1113
B1077
B1436
77

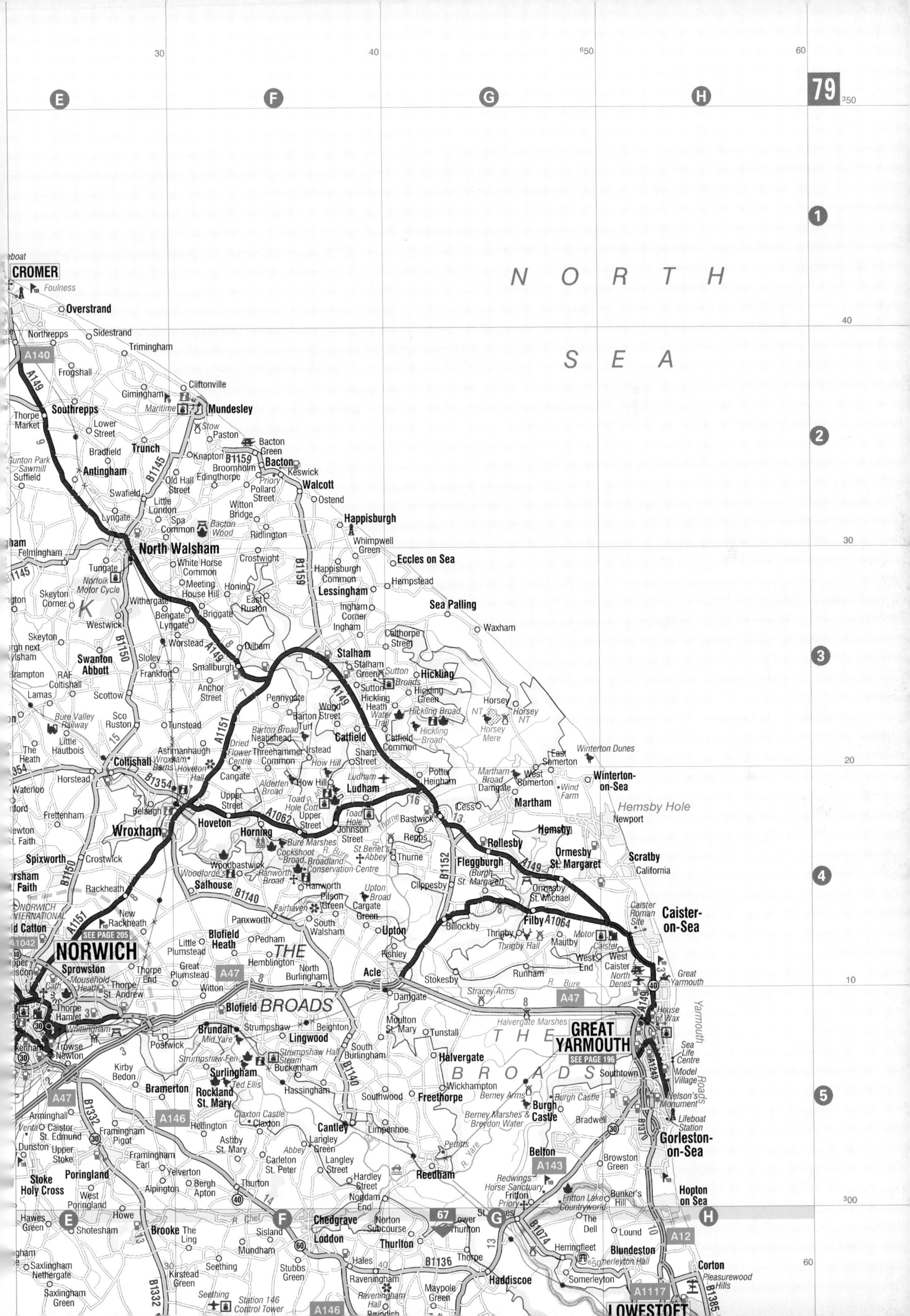
NORTH SEA
CROMER
Overstrand
Northrepps
Sidestrand
Trimingham
Mundesley
Bacton
Walcott
Happisburgh
Eccles on Sea
North Walsham
Sea Palling
Stalham
Hickling
Ludham
Wroxham
Hoveton
Horning
Martham
Hemsby
Winterton-on-Sea
Hemsby Hole
Rollesby
Ormesby St. Margaret
Scratby
Fleggburgh
Caister-on-Sea
Acle
Filby
NORWICH
SEE PAGE 205
BROADS
THE BROADS
GREAT YARMOUTH
SEE PAGE 196
Gorleston-on-Sea
Hopton on Sea
Reedham
Loddon
Chedgrave
Brundall
Blofield
LOWESTOFT
Corton

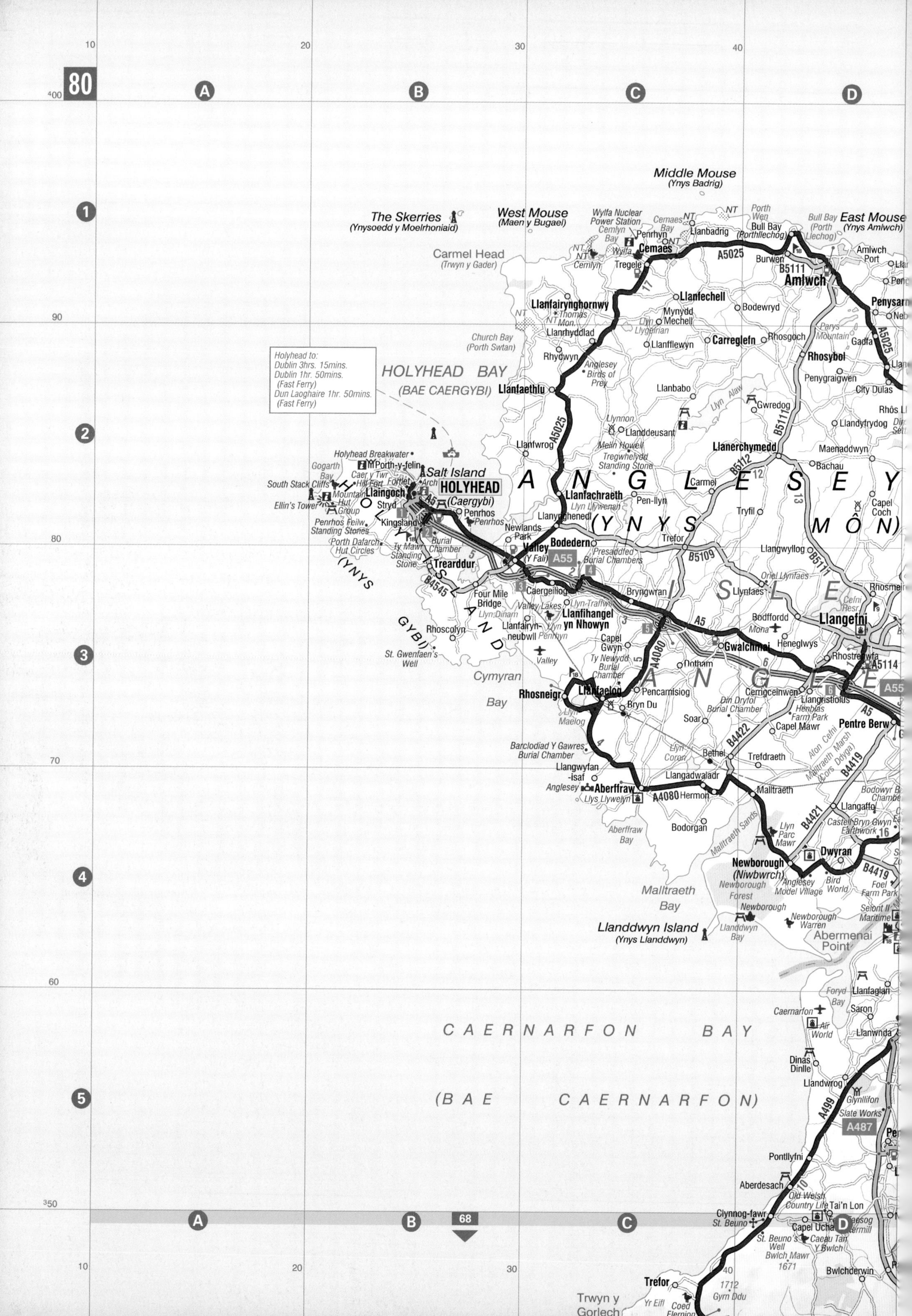
Middle Mouse
(Ynys Badrig)
The Skerries
(Ynysoedd y Moelrhoniaid)
West Mouse
(Maen y Bugael)
East Mouse
(Ynys Amlwch)
Carmel Head
(Trwyn y Gader)
Wylfa Nuclear Power Station
Cemaes
Amlwch
Llanfairynghornwy
Llanfechell
Church Bay
(Porth Swtan)
Holyhead to:
Dublin 3hrs. 15mins.
Dublin 1hr. 50mins.
(Fast Ferry)
Dun Laoghaire 1hr. 50mins.
(Fast Ferry)
HOLYHEAD BAY
(BAE CAERGYBI)
Llanfaethlu
Carreglefn
Rhosybol
Llanerchymedd
Salt Island
HOLYHEAD
(Caergybi)
ANGLESEY
(YNYS MÔN)
HOLY ISLAND
(YNYS GYBI)
Llanfachraeth
Valley
(Y Fali)
Bodedern
Trearddur
Four Mile Bridge
Rhoscolyn
Llanfihangel yn Nhowyn
Bryngwran
Llangefni
Gwalchmai
Cymyran Bay
Rhosneigr
Llanfaelog
Pentre Berw
Aberffraw
Malltraeth
Newborough
(Niwbwrch)
Dwyran
Malltraeth Bay
Llanddwyn Island
(Ynys Llanddwyn)
Abermenai Point
CAERNARFON BAY
(BAE CAERNARFON)
Pontllyfni
Clynnog-fawr
Trefor
Trwyn y Gorlech
A5025
A5
A55
A4080
B4545
A499
A487

68

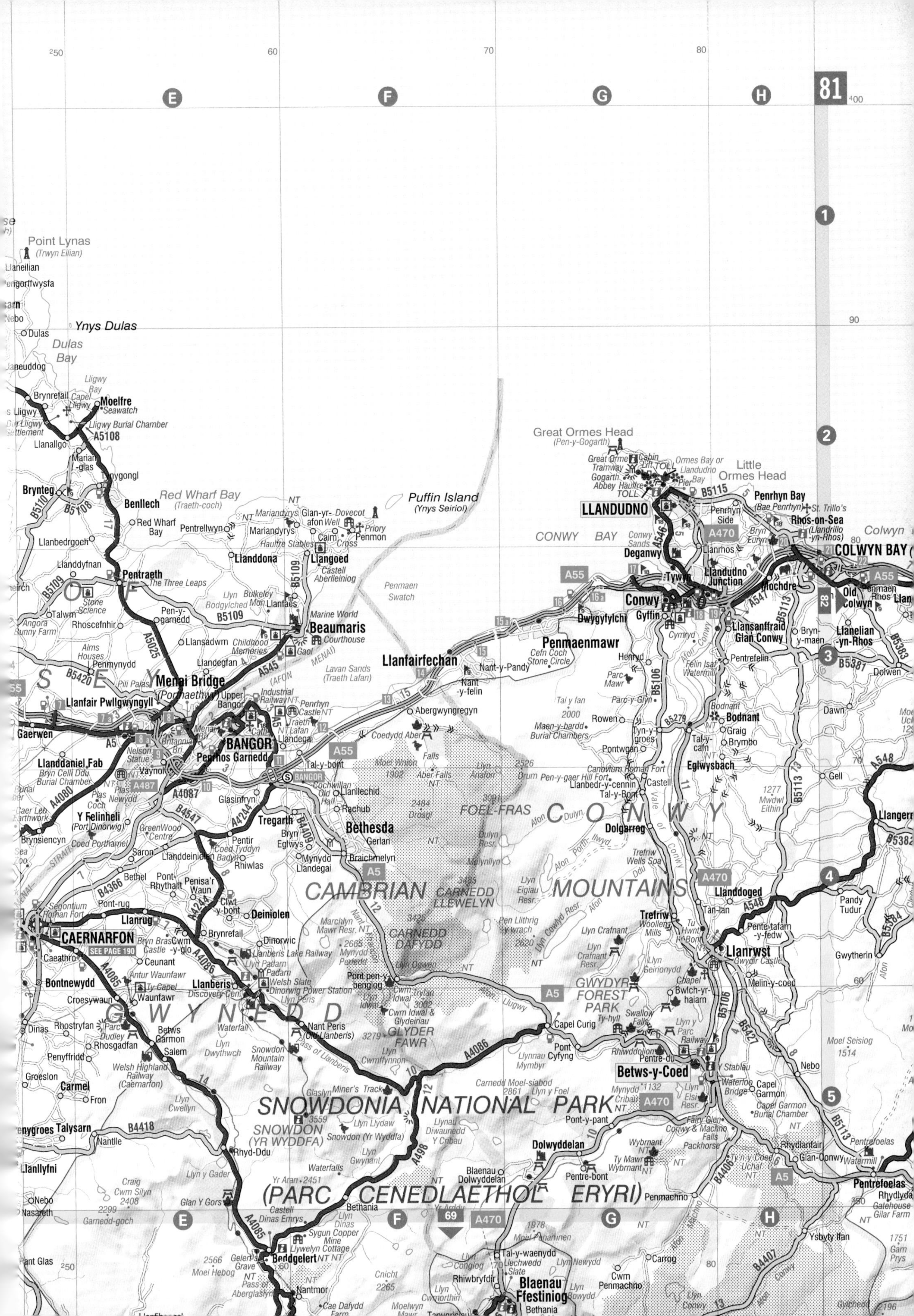
81
E
F
G
H
250
60
70
80
400
90
Point Lynas
(Trwyn Eilian)
Llaneilian
Nebo
Dulas
Ynys Dulas
Dulas Bay
Lligwy Bay
Brynrefail
Moelfre
Seawatch
Lligwy Burial Chamber
Llanallgo
A5108
Marian-glas
Tynygongl
Brynteg
Benllech
Red Wharf Bay
(Traeth-coch)
Red Wharf Bay
Pentrellwyn
Mariandyrys
Glan-yr-afon
Dovecot
Priory
Penmon
Haulfre Stables
Caim
Cross
Puffin Island
(Ynys Seiriol)
Llanddona
Llangoed
Castell Aberlleiniog
Llanbedrgoch
Llanddyfnan
Pentraeth
The Three Leaps
Stone Science
Talwrn
Rhoscefnhir
Pen-y-garnedd
B5109
Llansadwrn
Childhood Memories
Beaumaris
Marine World
Courthouse
Gaol
Penmaen Swatch
Alms Houses
Penmynydd
Llandegfan
A545
Lavan Sands
(Traeth Lafan)
Pili Palas
Menai Bridge
(Porthaethwy)
Upper Bangor
Industrial Railway
Penrhyn Castle
Llanfair Pwllgwyngyll
Gaerwen
Llanddaniel Fab
Bryn Celli Ddu Burial Chamber
Nelson Statue
Vaynol
BANGOR
Penrhos Garnedd
Llandegai
Tal-y-bont
Cochwillan Old Hall
Llanllechid
Rachub
A487
A4087
A4080
Plas Newydd
Plas Coch
Y Felinheli
(Port Dinorwig)
GreenWood Centre
Coed Porthamel
Brynsiencyn
Glasinfryn
Tregarth
Bryn Eglwys
Bethesda
Gerlan
Mynydd Llandegai
Braichmelyn
Pentir
Coed Tyddyn Badyn
Rhiwlas
Llanddeiniolen
Saron
Bethel
Pont-Rhythallt
Penisa'r Waun
B4366
Segontium Roman Fort
Pont-rug
Llanrug
Clwt-y-bont
Deiniolen
Brynrefail
Dinorwic
CAERNARFON
SEE PAGE 190
Caeathro
Bryn Bras Castle
Cwm-y-glo
Ceunant
Llanberis Lake Railway
Llyn Padarn
Padarn
Antur Waunfawr
Ty Capel
Waunfawr
Llanberis
Discovery Cen.
Welsh Slate
Dinorwig Power Station
Llyn Peris
Bontnewydd
Croesywaun
GWYNEDD
Dinas
Rhostryfan
Parc Dudley
Rhosgadfan
Betws Garmon
Salem
Waterfall
Llyn Dwythwch
Snowdon Mountain Railway
Nant Peris
(Old Llanberis)
Pass of Llanberis
Penyffridd
Groeslon
Carmel
Fron
Welsh Highland Railway
(Caernarfon)
Llyn Cwellyn
Talysarn
B4418
Nantlle
Rhyd-Ddu
Llanllyfni
Llyn y Gader
Craig Cwm Silyn
2408
2299
Garnedd-goch
Nebo
Nasareth
Glan Y Gors
Castell Dinas Emrys
A4085
Sygun Copper Mine
Llywelyn Cottage
Beddgelert
Gelert's Grave
Pass of Aberglaslyn
2566
Moel Hebog
Nantmor
Cae Dafydd Farm
Pant Glas
Cnicht
2265
Moelwyn Mawr
Tanygrisiau
Llyn Cwmorthin
Llyn Conglog
Rhiwbryfdir
Blaenau Ffestiniog
Bethania
Tal-y-waenydd
Llechwedd Slate
Llyn Newydd
Moel Penamnen
1978
Llyn Bowydd
Cwm Penmachno
Carrog
Llyn Conwy
B4407
Ysbyty Ifan
Gylchedd
2196
Garn Prys
1751
Bethania
Llyn Dinas
Yr Aran 2451
Waterfalls
Llyn Gwynant
SNOWDON
(YR WYDDFA)
3559
Snowdon (Yr Wyddfa)
Llyn Llydaw
Glaslyn
Miner's Track
SNOWDONIA NATIONAL PARK
(PARC CENEDLAETHOL ERYRI)
A498
Llynau Diwaunedd
Y Cribau
Llyn Cwmffynnon
3279
GLYDER FAWR
Cwm Idwal
Llyn Idwal
Tryfan 3002
Cwm Idwal & Glydeiriau
Pont pen-y-benglog
Llyn Ogwen
Nant Ffrancon
Marchlyn Mawr Resr.
2665
Mynydd Perfedd
CARNEDD DAFYDD
3425
CARNEDD LLEWELYN
3485
CAMBRIAN MOUNTAINS
A5
Moel Wnion
1902
Aber Falls
Falls
Drosgl
2484
FOEL-FRAS
3091
Dulyn Resr.
Melynllyn
Llyn Anafon
Coedydd Aber
Abergwyngregyn
A55
Llanfairfechan
Nant-y-Pandy
Nant-y-felin
Penmaenmawr
Cefn Coch Stone Circle
Dwygyfylchi
Henryd
Parc Mawr
Parc-y-Glyn
Tal y fan
2000
Maen-y-bardd Burial Chambers
Rowen
Tyn-y-groes
Pontwgan
Canovium Roman Fort
Pen-y-gaer Hill Fort
Drum 2526
Llanbedr-y-cennin
Tal-y-Bont
Castell
CONWY
Dolgarrog
Afon Dulyn
Afon Porth-llwyd
Trefriw Wells Spa
Llyn Eigiau Resr.
Llyn Cowlyd Resr.
Pen Llithrig y wrach
2620
Trefriw
Woollen Mills
Llyn Crafnant
Llyn Crafnant Resr.
Llyn Geirionydd
GWYDYR FOREST PARK
Capel Curig
Ty-hyll
Swallow Falls
Pont Cyfyng
Llynnau Mymbyr
A4086
Rhiwddolion
Pentre-du
Betws-y-Coed
Carnedd Moel-siabod
2861
Llyn y Foel
Mynydd Cribau
1132
A470
Pont-y-pant
Dolwyddelan
Wybrnant
Ty Mawr Wybrnant
Pentre-bont
Blaenau Dolwyddelan
Penmachno
Afon Machno
Fairy Glen
Conwy & Machno Falls
Packhorse
Ty-n-y-Coed Uchaf
B4406
Rhydlanfair
Glan-Conwy
Pentrefoelas
Watermill
Rhydlydan
Gatehouse
Gilar Farm
B5113
Capel Garmon
Capel Garmon Burial Chamber
Nebo
Moel Seisiog
1514
Waterloo Bridge
Y Stablau
Llyn Elsi Resr.
Bwlch-yr-haiarn
Chapel
Llyn y Parc
Railway
Melin-y-coed
Llanrwst
Gwydir Castle
Tu Hwnt i'r Bont
Tan-lan
Llanddoged
A548
Pente-tafarn-y-fedw
Gwytherin
Pandy Tudur
B5384
Llangerniew
B5382
Vale of Conwy
A470
Eglwysbach
Bodnant
Graig
Brymbo
Tal-y-cafn
Felin Isaf Watermill
Pentrefelin
Llansanffraid Glan Conwy
Cymryd
Afon Conwy
B5106
B5279
Mwdwl Eithin
1277
Gell
Dawn
A548
Bryn-y-maen
Llanelian-yn-Rhos
B5381
B5383
Dolwen
Old Colwyn
COLWYN BAY
Colwyn
Rhos-on-Sea
(Llandrillo-yn-Rhos)
St. Trillo's
Penrhyn Bay
(Bae Penrhyn)
Penrhyn Side
Bryn Euryn
Mochdre
A547
Llandudno Junction
Llanrhos
Deganwy
Tywyn
Conwy
Gyffin
A546
Conwy Sands
CONWY BAY
LLANDUDNO
B5115
Great Ormes Head
(Pen-y-Gogarth)
Great Orme Tramway
Cabin Lift
TOLL
Gogarth Abbey
Haulfre
Pier
Ormes Bay or Llandudno Bay
Little Ormes Head
Menai Strait
Afon Menai
69
82

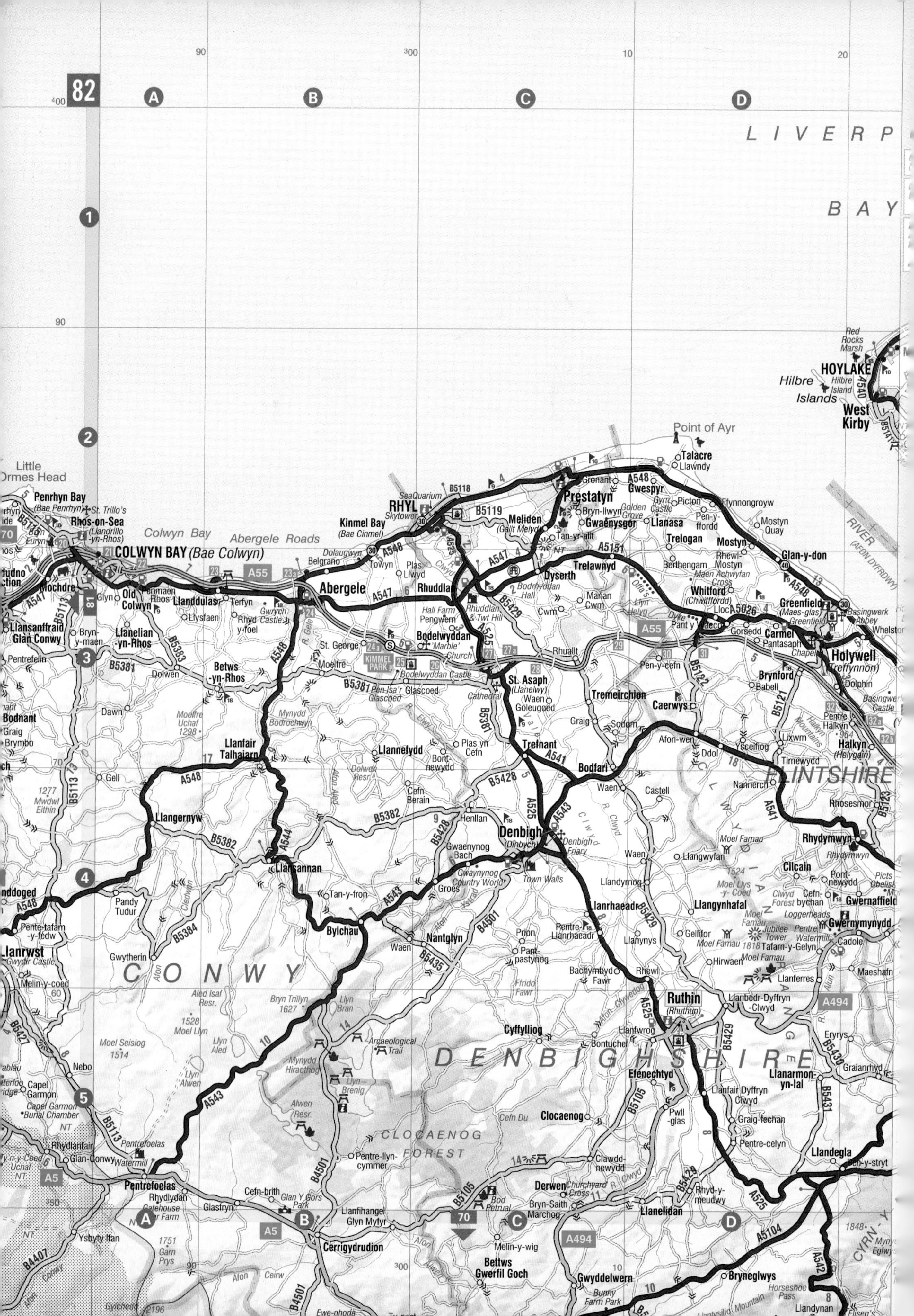
LIVERP
BAY
HOYLAKE
West Kirby
Hilbre Islands
Point of Ayr
Talacre
Prestatyn
RHYL
Kinmel Bay
Colwyn Bay
Abergele Roads
COLWYN BAY (Bae Colwyn)
Rhos-on-Sea
Penrhyn Bay
Little Ormes Head
Abergele
Rhuddlan
Dyserth
Meliden
Gronant
Gwespyr
Mostyn
Glan-y-don
Greenfield
Holywell (Treffynnon)
Whitford
St. Asaph (Llanelwy)
Trefnant
Denbigh (Dinbych)
Llansannan
Llangernyw
Llanfair Talhaiarn
Bylchau
Nantglyn
Henllan
Bodfari
Llanrhaeadr
Ruthin (Rhuthun)
Llanarmon-yn-Ial
Llandegla
Cyffylliog
Clocaenog
Efenechtyd
Derwen
Llanelidan
Bettws Gwerfil Goch
Gwyddelwern
Cerrigydrudion
Pentrefoelas
Llanrwst
Nebo
Halkyn
Cilcain
Rhydymwyn
Gwernymynydd
Caerwys
Tremeirchion
Llangynhafal
Bryneglwys
CONWY
DENBIGHSHIRE
FLINTSHIRE
CLOCAENOG FOREST
Moel Famau
Llyn Brenig
Alwen Resr.
A55
A5
A494
A543
A548
A525
A541
70

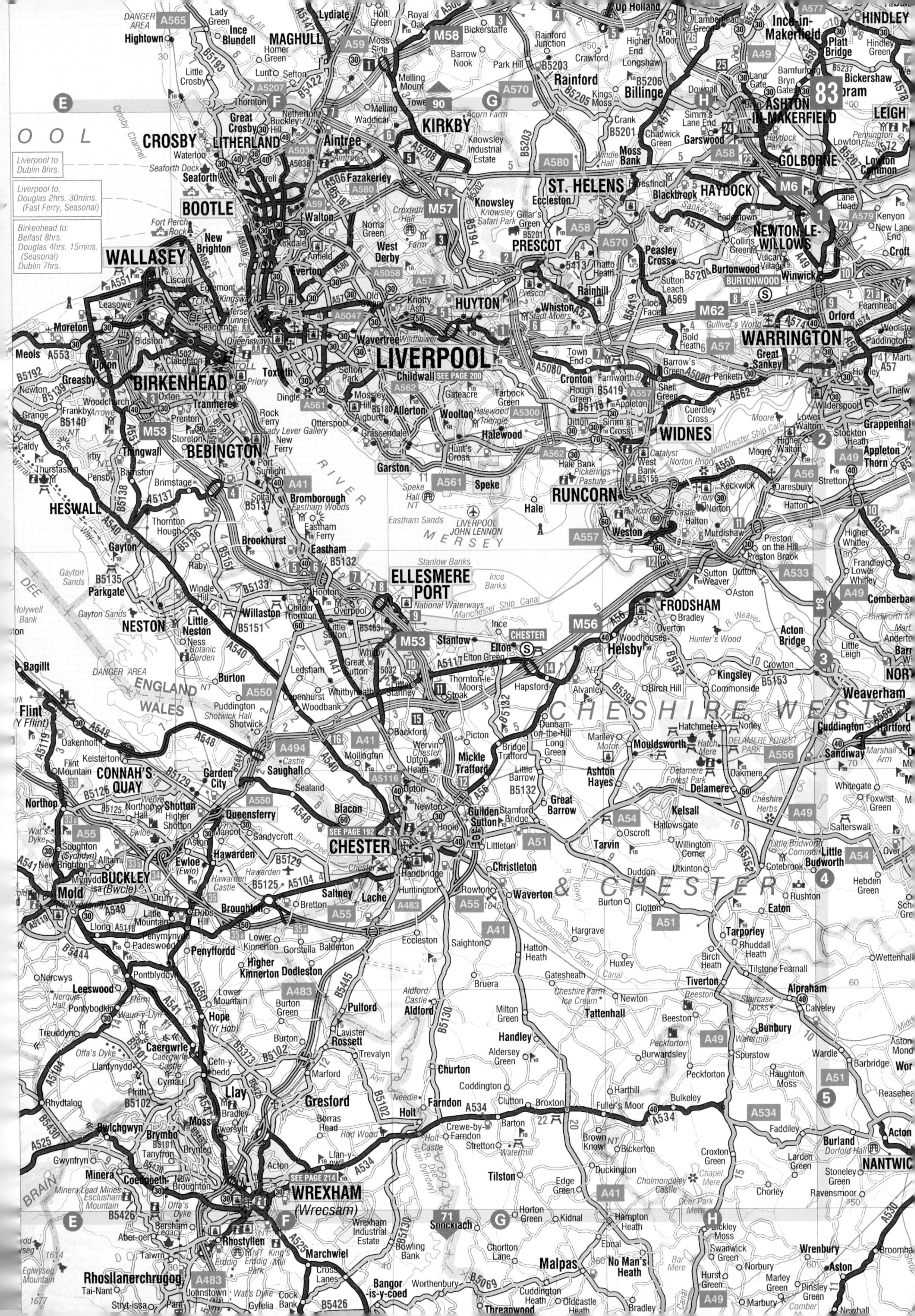

83
DANGER AREA
A565
Hightown
Lady Green
Ince Blundell
MAGHULL
Lydiate
Holt Green
Royal Oak
M58
Bickerstaffe
Up Holland
Lamberhead Green
Ince-in-Makerfield
HINDLEY
Platt Bridge
Hindley Green
Homer Green
Little Crosby
Lunt
Sefton
A59
Moss Side
Barrow Nook
Park Hill
Rainford Junction
Crawford
Higher End
Longshaw
Far Moor
A49
Bamfurlong
Bryn Gates
Bickershaw
Land Gate
A5207
Thornton
Melling Mount
Tower Hill
90
A570
Rainford
Kings Moss
Billinge
Downall Green
ASHTON IN-MAKERFIELD
LEIGH
OOL
Crosby Channel
Great Crosby
Netherton
Buckley Hill
Melling
Waddicar
KIRKBY
Acorn Farm
Knowsley Industrial Estate
Crank
B5201
Chadwick Green
Simm's Lane End
Garswood
Haydock Park
Lowton
Pennington Flash
CROSBY
LITHERLAND
Aintree
Liverpool to Dublin 8hrs.
Waterloo
Seaforth Dock
Seaforth
A5036
A5038
A5208
A580
Windle Hall
Moss Bank
A58
GOLBORNE
Lowton Common
Liverpool to: Douglas 2hrs. 30mins. (Fast Ferry, Seasonal)
Fazakerley
Orrell
ST. HELENS
Haresfinch
Blackbrook
HAYDOCK
M6
BOOTLE
Knowsley
Eccleston
Sankey Canal
Lane Head
Kenyon
Birkenhead to: Belfast 8hrs. Douglas 4hrs. 15mins. (Seasonal) Dublin 7hrs.
Fort Perch Rock
New Brighton
Walton
Croxteth Hall
M57
Knowsley Safari Park
Gillar's Green
A58
Earlestown
NEWTON-LE-WILLOWS
New Lane End
Norris Green
Parr
A572
Collins Green
WALLASEY
Kirkdale
Anfield
West Derby
PRESCOT
A570
Peasley Cross
Vulcan Village
Croft
Liscard
Egremont
Everton
A5058
Thatto Heath
Burtonwood
Winwick
A551
Leasowe
Kingsway
A57
Old Swan
Knotty Ash
HUYTON
Rainhill
Sutton Leach
BURTONWOOD
A569
Clock Face
Whiston
Stadt Moers
Orford
Fearnhead
Moreton
Seacombe
Queensway
A5047
Wavertree
M62
Gulliver's World
Bold Heath
A574
WARRINGTON
Woolston
Paddington
Meols
A553
Bidston
A502
Claughton
Upton
LIVERPOOL
Town End
A57
Great Sankey
Martinscroft
B5192
Greasby
BIRKENHEAD
Toxteth
Priory
Sefton Park
Childwall
SEE PAGE 200
A5080
Cronton
Farnworth
Barrow's Green
Penketh
Houghton Green
Thelwall
Newton
B5138
Oxton
Dingle
Mossley Hill
A562
Gateacre
Tarbock Green
Hough Green
B5419
A557
Shell Green
A562
Wilderspool
Grange
Frankby
Woodchurch
Arrowe
Tranmere
A561
Aigburth
Allerton
Woolton
Halewood Triangle
A5300
B5178
Appleton
Cuerdley Cross
Moore
Lower Walton
Grappenhall
B5140
Prenton
Rock Ferry
Lady Lever Gallery
Otterspool
Grassendale
Halewood
Ditton
Simm's Cross
WIDNES
Manchester Ship Canal
Stockton Heath
M53
Storeton
New Ferry
Hunt's Cross
A562
Hale Bank
Catalyst
Higher Walton
Appleton Thorn
Caldy
Thingwall
BEBINGTON
Port Sunlight
RIVER
Garston
Pickerings Pasture
West Bank
Norton Priory
A558
Moore
A49
Irby
Thurstaston
Pensby
Barnston
Brimstage
A41
Bromborough
A561
Speke
Speke Hall NT
A56
Daresbury
Stretton
RUNCORN
Keckwick
Hale
Norton
Hatton
HESWALL
A5137
Spital
B5137
Eastham Woods
MERSEY
Eastham Sands
LIVERPOOL JOHN LENNON
Runcorn Hill
Castle
Halton
A559
Thornton Hough
Brookhurst
Eastham Ferry
Eastham
Weston
A557
Murdishaw
Higher Whitley
Preston on the Hill
Preston Brook
Gayton
Raby
B5132
Stanlow Banks
Sutton Weaver
Dutton
A533
Frandley
Lower Whitley
Gayton Sands
B5135
Parkgate
B5151
Windle Hill
B5133
Hooton
ELLESMERE PORT
Inca Banks
Aston
A49
Comberbach
DEE
Holywell Bank
Gayton Sands
NESTON
Little Neston
Willaston
Childer Thornton
Overpool
National Waterways
Manchester Ship Canal
FRODSHAM
Bradley
R. Weaver
Budworth Mere
Little Sutton
Ince
CHESTER
M56
Overton
Hunter's Wood
Acton Bridge
Anderton
Ness Botanic Garden
B5463
M53
Stanlow
Woodhouses
Helsby
Barnton
Bagillt
DANGER AREA
Burton
A540
Ledsham
Great Sutton
Whitby
A5032
A5117
Elton Green
Elton
Little Leigh
Crowton
NORTHWICH
ENGLAND
WALES
A550
Capenhurst
Woodbank
Whitby Heath
Little Stanney
Thornton-le-Moors
Stoak
Hapsford
Alvanley
B5393
Birch Hill
Kingsley
Commonside
B5153
Weaverham
Flint (Y Fflint)
Puddington
Shotwick Hall
Shotwick
Backford
Picton
Dunham-on-the-Hill
CHESHIRE WEST
Hatchmere
Norley
Cuddington
Hartford
A548
A5119
Oakenholt
Kelsterton
A548
A494
A41
Mollington
Wervin
Chester Zoo
Mickle Trafford
Bridge Trafford
Long Green
Manley
Mouldsworth
Delamere Forest Park
A556
Sandiway
Marshall's Arm
Flint Mountain
CONNAH'S QUAY
Garden City
B5129
Saughall
Castle
Upton Heath
Little Barrow
Ashton Hayes
Delamere Forest Park
Oakmere
Delamere
Whitegate
Foxwist Green
Northop
B5126
B5125
Northop Hall
Shotton
Higher Shotton
Queensferry
A550
Sealand
A548
Blacon
A5116
Upton
Newton
Hoole
Guilden Sutton
Stamford Bridge
B5132
Great Barrow
A54
Kelsall
Cheshire Herbs
A49
Salterswall
A55
Wat's Dyke
Ewloe
Mancot
Aston
Sandycroft
River Dee
SEE PAGE 192
CHESTER
Littleton
A51
Oscroft
Hallowsgate
Tarvin
Willington Corner
Little Budworth Common
Little Budworth
A54
Over
Soughton (Sychdyn)
A541
New Brighton
Alltami
Ewloe (Ewlo)
Hawarden
B5129
Hawarden Castle
B5125
A5104
Chester
Handbridge
Christleton
Utkinton
Cotebrook
Rushton
Hebden Green
Mynydd Isa
BUCKLEY (Bwcle)
Mold
Drury
Saltney
Lache
Huntington
Rowton
Waverton
& CHESTER
Duddon
Burton
Clotton
Eaton
Bretton
Broughton
A549
A5119
Little Mountain
Dobs Hill
A483
A55
1645
A51
Tarporley
Llong
A5118
Pentre
Penymynydd
Padeswood
Lower Kinnerton
Gorstella
Balderton
Eccleston
Saighton
A41
Hargrave
Rhuddall Heath
B5444
Penyffordd
Higher Kinnerton
Dodleston
Hatton Heath
Birch Heath
Wettenhall
Huxley
Tilstone Fearnall
Nercwys
Pontblyddyn
Gatesheath
Shropshire Union Canal
Leeswood
Nerquis Hall
Pontybodkin
A550
Lower Mountain
A483
Aldford Castle
Aldford
Bruera
Cheshire Farm Ice Cream
Tiverton
Beeston Castle
Alpraham
Calveley
Newton
Staircase Locks
Waun-y-Llyn
Hope (Yr Hob)
Burton Green
B5445
Pulford
Milton Green
Tattenhall
Beeston
Bunbury
Treuddyn
Offa's Dyke
Caergwrle
Caergwrle Castle
B5373
B5102
Burton
Lavister
Rossett
Handley
A49
Peckforton
Wardle
Llanfynydd
Cefn-y-bedd
Cymau
Trevalyn
Marford
Churton
Aldersey Green
Burwardsley
Spurstow
Haughton Moss
Barbridge
Worleston
Ffrith
B5102
Llay
Bradley
Coddington
Peckforton
A51
Rhydtalog
Gresford
Needle
B5102
Farndon
A534
Clutton
Broxton
Harthill
Fuller's Moor
Bulkeley
Reaseheath
Bwlchgwyn
Moss
Gwersyllt
Borras Head
Holt
Crewe-by-Farndon
Barton
A534
Faddiley
Burland
Dorfold Hall
Acton
A525
Brymbo
Tanyfron
Brynteg
Rod Wood
Holt Castle
Stretton
Watermill
Brown Knowl
Bickerton
Croxton Green
Larden Green
NANTWICH
Gwynfryn
Minera
Coedpoeth
New Broughton
Acton
Llan-y-pwll
A534
R. Dee (Afon Dyfrdwy)
Tilston
Duckington
Cholmondeley Castle
Chapel Mere
Stoneley Green
Chorley
Ravensmoor
Minera Lead Mines
Esclusham Mountain
Offa's Dyke
SEE PAGE 214
WREXHAM (Wrecsam)
Edge Green
A41
Deer Park Mere
B5426
Bersham
Legacy
Wrexham Industrial Estate
B5130
71
Shocklach
Horton Green
Kidnal
Hampton Heath
Bickley Moss
A530
Aber-oer
Rhostyllen
Erddig
King's Mills
A525
Bowling Bank
Chorlton Lane
Ebnal
Swanwick Green
Wrenbury
Broomhall
Talwrn
Erddig Park
Marchwiel
Cross Lanes
Malpas
No Man's Heath
Bar Mere
Norbury
Aston
Eglwyseg Mountain
Rhosllanerchrugog
A483
Johnstown
Wat's Dyke
Cock Bank
Bangor-is-y-coed
Worthenbury
B5069
Cuddington Heath
Oldcastle Heath
Hurst Green
Marley Green
Pinsley Green
A49
Tai-Nant
Stryt-issa
Gyfelia
B5426
Threapwood
Bradley
Marbury
Newhall
84

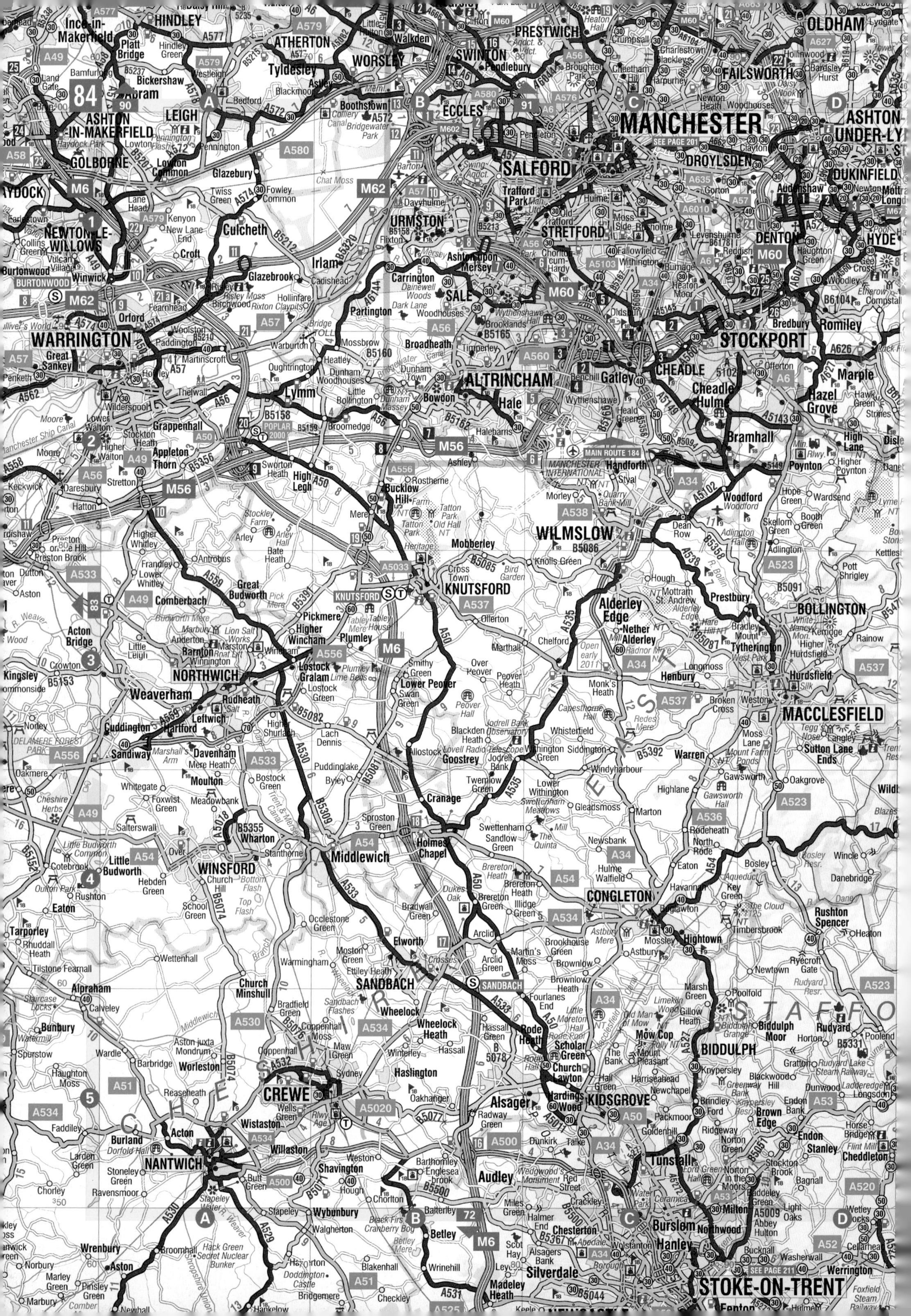
84
90
91
72
83
SEE PAGE 201
SEE PAGE 211
MAIN ROUTE 184
HINDLEY
ATHERTON
WORSLEY
SWINTON
PRESTWICH
OLDHAM
Ince-in-Makerfield
Platt Bridge
Tyldesley
Walkden
Pendlebury
FAILSWORTH
ASHTON-IN-MAKERFIELD
LEIGH
Boothstown
ECCLES
MANCHESTER
ASHTON UNDER-LYNE
DROYLSDEN
SALFORD
GOLBORNE
Lowton Common
Glazebury
Trafford Park
DUKINFIELD
Culcheth
URMSTON
STRETFORD
DENTON
HYDE
NEWTON-LE-WILLOWS
Irlam
Carrington
Ashton upon Mersey
Chorlton-cum-Hardy
Fallowfield
Withington
SALE
Partington
Didsbury
Bredbury
Romiley
WARRINGTON
Great Sankey
Broadheath
Timperley
STOCKPORT
CHEADLE
Gatley
ALTRINCHAM
Marple
Lymm
Hale
Cheadle Hulme
Hazel Grove
Bowdon
Bramhall
Grappenhall
Appleton Thorn
High Legh
Handforth
Poynton
High Lane
MANCHESTER INTERNATIONAL
Bucklow Hill
Tatton Park
Woodford
WILMSLOW
Mobberley
KNUTSFORD
Alderley Edge
Prestbury
BOLLINGTON
Comberbach
Great Budworth
Pickmere
Plumley
Nether Alderley
Tytherington
Rainow
Acton Bridge
Barnton
NORTHWICH
Lostock Gralam
Lower Peover
Over Peover
Henbury
MACCLESFIELD
Weaverham
Rudheath
Cuddington
Hartford
Davenham
Allostock
Goostrey
Jodrell Bank
Warren
Sutton Lane Ends
Sandiway
Moulton
Cranage
Gawsworth
Wharton
Middlewich
Holmes Chapel
WINSFORD
Little Budworth
CONGLETON
Rushton Spencer
Tarporley
Elworth
SANDBACH
Church Minshull
Wheelock
BIDDULPH
Alpraham
Bunbury
Rode Heath
Scholar Green
Church Lawton
KIDSGROVE
CREWE
Haslington
Alsager
Wistaston
Willaston
Acton
NANTWICH
Shavington
Audley
Tunstall
Wybunbury
Betley
Burslem
Hanley
Milton
Silverdale
Madeley Heath
Wrenbury
Aston
STOKE-ON-TRENT
Werrington
Cheddleton
Endon
Brown Edge
Stanley
M6
M60
M62
M56
M602
A580
A556
A534
A500
STAFFO

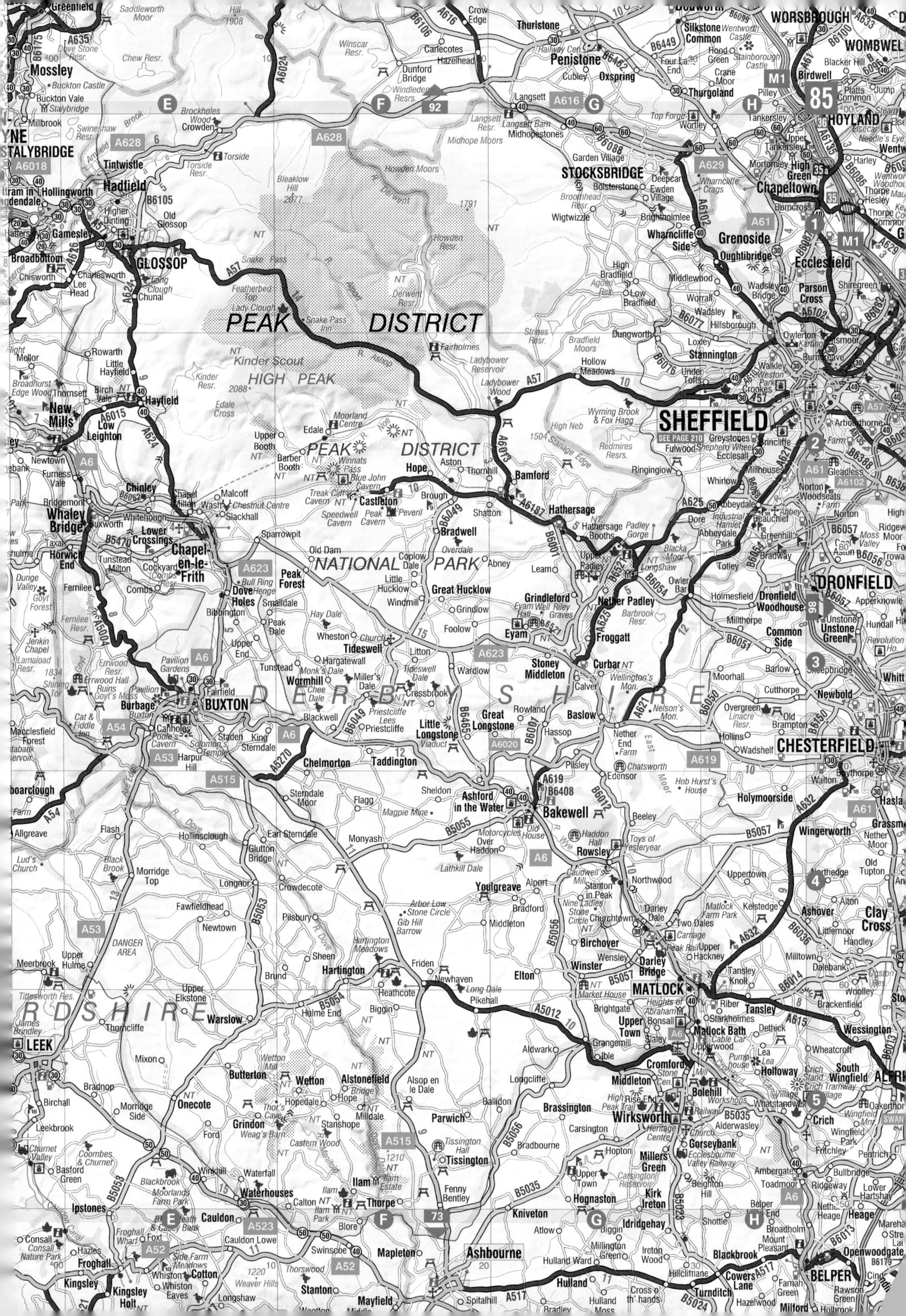
85
92
73
SEE PAGE 210
PEAK DISTRICT
HIGH PEAK
PEAK DISTRICT
NATIONAL PARK
DERBYSHIRE
RDSHIRE
SHEFFIELD
CHESTERFIELD
DRONFIELD
BUXTON
GLOSSOP
MATLOCK
LEEK
BELPER
STOCKSBRIDGE
STALYBRIDGE
WORSBROUGH
WOMBWELL
HOYLAND
Ashbourne
Greenfield
Mossley
Saddleworth Moor
Chew Resr.
Dove Stone Resr.
Buckton Castle
Buckton Vale
Millbrook
Tintwistle
Hadfield
Hollingworth
Gamesley
Broadbottom
Charlesworth
Chisworth
Old Glossop
Torside
Crowden
Brockholes Wood
Bleaklow Hill
Snake Pass
Featherbed Top
Lady Clough
Kinder Scout
Kinder Resr.
Edale Cross
Hayfield
Little Hayfield
Rowarth
Mellor
Birch Vale
Thornsett
New Mills
Low Leighton
Newtown
Furness Vale
Chinley
Bridgemont
Whaley Bridge
Buxworth
Chapel Milton
Lower Crossings
Chapel-en-le-Frith
Horwich End
Taxal
Tunstead Milton
Combs
Dove Holes
Fernilee
Goyt Forest
Errwood Resr.
Burbage
Harpur Hill
Chelmorton
Taddington
Peak Forest
Tideswell
Wormhill
Miller's Dale
Litton
Great Hucklow
Eyam
Stoney Middleton
Hope
Castleton
Edale
Bamford
Hathersage
Ladybower Reservoir
Derwent Resr.
Howden Resr.
Howden Moors
Fairholmes
Penistone
Oxspring
Thurlstone
Langsett
Midhopestones
Thurgoland
Wortley
Deepcar
Grenoside
Chapeltown
Ecclesfield
High Green
Oughtibridge
Wharncliffe Side
Bradfield
Low Bradfield
Dungworth
Stannington
Hillsborough
Crookes
Walkley
Fulwood
Ringinglow
Dore
Totley
Abbeydale
Greenhill
Bradway
Norton
Grindleford
Froggatt
Curbar
Calver
Baslow
Hassop
Great Longstone
Little Longstone
Ashford in the Water
Bakewell
Rowsley
Beeley
Edensor
Chatsworth
Pilsley
Holymoorside
Walton
Wingerworth
Ashover
Clay Cross
Darley Dale
Darley Bridge
Two Dales
Tansley
Riber
Matlock Bath
Cromford
Wirksworth
Middleton
Bolehill
Brassington
Youlgreave
Monyash
Sheldon
Flagg
Earl Sterndale
Longnor
Hartington
Hulme End
Warslow
Onecote
Butterton
Wetton
Alstonefield
Grindon
Waterhouses
Ilam
Thorpe
Tissington
Parwich
Kniveton
Hognaston
Kirk Ireton
Idridgehay
Cauldon
Ipstones
Froghall
Kingsley
Kingsley Holt
Cotton
Stanton
Mayfield
Mapleton
Hulland
Turnditch
Cowers Lane
Crich
South Wingfield
Wessington
Heage
Ambergate
Openwoodgate
A57
A6
A61
A623
A628
A616
A6024
A624
A6187
A625
A621
A619
A632
A615
A515
A5012
A53
A54
A523
A52
A517
M1
B6049
B5056
B5053
B5054
B5035
B5023
B6012
B6001

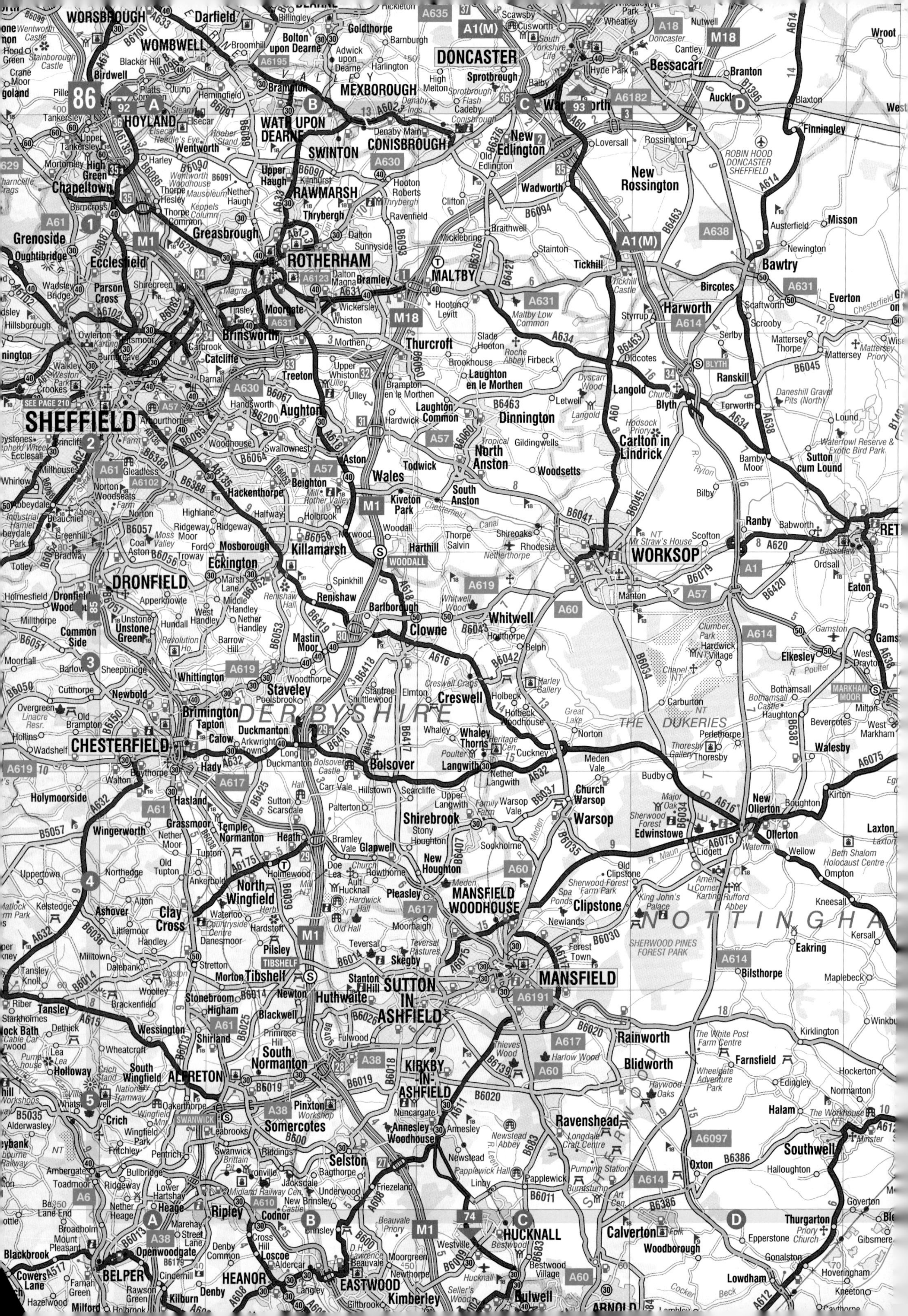
86
88
SEE PAGE 210
WORSBROUGH
Darfield
WOMBWELL
Goldthorpe
Bolton upon Dearne
Adwick upon Dearne
Barnburgh
Harlington
Scawsby
Cusworth
DONCASTER
Sprotbrough
Wheatley
Nutwell
Cantley
Bessacarr
Branton
Auckley
Blaxton
Finningley
Wroot
Birdwell
Hoyland
Elsecar
Jump
Hemingfield
Brampton
WATH UPON DEARNE
MEXBOROUGH
Denaby Main
CONISBROUGH
SWINTON
High Melton
Cadeby
Balby
Warmsworth
New Edlington
Old Edlington
Loversall
Rossington
New Rossington
ROBIN HOOD DONCASTER SHEFFIELD
Tankersley
Chapeltown
Wentworth
Harley
Upper Haugh
Nether Haugh
RAWMARSH
Kilnhurst
Hooton Roberts
Thrybergh
Ravenfield
Clifton
Wadworth
Braithwell
Micklebring
Stainton
Tickhill
Grenoside
Oughtibridge
Ecclesfield
Greasbrough
ROTHERHAM
Dalton
Sunnyside
Dalton Magna
Bramley
MALTBY
Hooton Levitt
Maltby Low Common
Tickhill Castle
Bawtry
Austerfield
Newington
Misson
Wadsley Bridge
Parson Cross
Shiregreen
Tinsley
Moorgate
Wickersley
Whiston
Brinsworth
Catcliffe
Treeton
Thurcroft
Slade Hooton
Roche Abbey
Firbeck
Styrrup
Harworth
Bircotes
Scaftworth
Scrooby
Everton
Serlby
Mattersey
Mattersey Thorpe
Mattersey Priory
Hillsborough
Owlerton
Walkley
Crookes
SHEFFIELD
Darnall
Handsworth
Aughton
Upper Whiston
Ulley
Brampton en le Morthen
Laughton en le Morthen
Laughton Common
Hardwick
Dinnington
Letwell
Langold
Oldcotes
Blyth
Ranskill
Torworth
Daneshill Gravel Pits (North)
Gildingwells
Carlton in Lindrick
Hodsock Priory
Barnby Moor
Sutton cum Lound
Lound
Waterfowl Reserve & Exotic Bird Park
Ecclesall
Millhouses
Gleadless
Woodhouse
Swallownest
Aston
Todwick
North Anston
South Anston
Wales
Kiveton Park
Woodsetts
Beighton
Hackenthorpe
Norton
Woodseats
Beauchief
Abbeydale
Highlane
Ridgeway
Ridgeway Moor
Halfway
Holbrook
Norwood
Killamarsh
Woodall
Harthill
Thorpe Salvin
Shireoaks
Rhodesia
Netherthorpe
Mr Straw's House
Scofton
WORKSOP
Ranby
Babworth
Bassetlaw
Ordsall
Eaton
Greenhill
Coal Aston
Bradway
Mosborough
Eckington
Troway
Ford
Marsh Lane
Totley
DRONFIELD
Dronfield Woodhouse
Apperknowle
Middle Handley
West Handley
Nether Handley
Spinkhill
Renishaw
Renishaw Hall
Barlborough
Clowne
Whitwell
Whitwell Wood
Hodthorpe
Belph
Manton
Clumber Park
Hardwick Village
Gamston
Elkesley
West Drayton
Holmesfield
Millthorpe
Common Side
Unstone
Unstone Green
Hundall
Barrow Hill
Revolution Ho.
Mastin Moor
Woodthorpe
Staveley
Poolsbrook
Shuttlewood
Stanfree
Elmton
Creswell
Creswell Crags
Harley Gallery
Holbeck
Holbeck Woodhouse
Welbeck
Chapel
Carburton
Bothamsall
Bothamsall Castle
Haughton
MARKHAM MOOR
Milton
West Markham
Moorhall
Barlow
Sheepbridge
Whittington
Cutthorpe
Newbold
Overgreen
Linacre Resr.
Old Brampton
Brimington
Tapton
DERBYSHIRE
Duckmanton
Arkwright Town
Calow
Long Duckmanton
Bolsover
Bolsover Castle
Whaley
Whaley Thorns
Heritage Cen.
Langwith
Poulter
Nether Langwith
Cuckney
Norton
Great Lake
THE DUKERIES
Perlethorpe
Thoresby Gallery
Thoresby
Beevercotes
Walesby
Hollins
Wadshelf
CHESTERFIELD
Hady
Walton
Boythorpe
Holymoorside
Hasland
Sutton Scarsdale
Carr Vale
Hillstown
Palterton
Scarcliffe
Upper Langwith
Warsop Vale
Church Warsop
Warsop
Meden Vale
Budby
Major Oak
Sherwood Forest
Edwinstowe
New Ollerton
Ollerton
Boughton
Kirton
Wingerworth
Grassmoor
Temple Normanton
Heath
Bramley Vale
Glapwell
Stony Houghton
Shirebrook
Sookholme
Laxton
Beth Shalom Holocaust Centre
Wellow
Ompton
Nether Moor
Tupton
Old Tupton
Ankerbold
Holmewood
Doe Lea
Rowthorne
Ault Hucknall
Hardwick Hall
Pleasley
New Houghton
MANSFIELD WOODHOUSE
Old Clipstone
Clipstone
Sherwood Forest Farm Park
Spa Ponds
Lidgett
Amen Corner Karting
Rufford Abbey
King John's Palace
Newlands
Forest Town
SHERWOOD PINES FOREST PARK
NOTTINGHAM
Kneesall
Kersall
Eakring
Uppertown
Northedge
North Wingfield
Clay Cross
Ashover
Kelstedge
Alton
Waterloo
Countryside Centre
Littlemoor
Handley
Danesmoor
Hardstoft
Pilsley
Old Hall
Teversal
Teversal Pastures
Moorhaigh
Skegby
Milltown
Dalebank
Stretton
Morton
Tibshelf
Ogston Res.
Tansley Knoll
Woolley
Brackenfield
Stonebroom
Higham
Newton
Huthwaite
Stanton Hill
SUTTON IN ASHFIELD
MANSFIELD
Bilsthorpe
Maplebeck
Riber
Tansley
Starkholmes
Matlock Bath
Cable Car
Dethick
Lea
Holloway
Wessington
Shirland
Blackwell
Primrose Hill
Fulwood
South Normanton
Rainworth
The White Post Farm Centre
Farnsfield
Kirklington
Winkburn
Whatstandwell
Crich
Crich Stand
National Tramway
South Wingfield
ALFRETON
Oakerthorpe
Wingfield Manor
Wingfield Park
Pinxton
Pinxton Workshop
Somercotes
Leabrooks
Swanwick
SWANWICK
Riddings
KIRKBY-IN-ASHFIELD
Annesley
Annesley Woodhouse
Nuncargate
Thieves Wood
Harlow Wood
Blidworth
Haywood Oaks
Wheelgate Adventure Park
Edingley
Hockerton
Normanton
Halam
The Workhouse
Southwell
Minster
Ravenshead
Longdale Craft Centre
Newstead Abbey
Newstead
Papplewick
Papplewick Hall
Pumping Station
Linby
Oxton
Halloughton
Alderwasley
Fritchley
Pentrich
Ambergate
Toadmoor
Bullbridge
Ridgeway
Lower Hartshay
Heage
Nether Heage
Ironville
Midland Railway Cen.
Jacksdale
Underwood
Selston
Bagthorpe
Friezeland
New Brinsley
Brinsley
Codnor
Ripley
Beauvale Priory
Hucknall
HUCKNALL
Calverton
Woodborough
Epperstone
Thurgarton
Thurgarton Priory Church
Goverton
Gibsmere
Bull Lane End
Broadholm
Mount Pleasant
Blackbrook
Openwoodgate
Marehay
Street Lane
Denby Common
Cross Hill
Loscoe
Aldercar
D.H. Lawrence
Moorgreen
Westville
Bestwood
Bestwood Village
Gonalston
Hoveringham
Lowdham
Kneeton
Cowers Lane
BELPER
Farnah Green
Hazelwood
Milford
Holbrook
Cinderhill
Kilburn
Denby
Rawson Green
HEANOR
Langley
EASTWOOD
Newthorpe
Beauvale
Giltbrook
Kimberley
Seller's Wood
Bulwell
ARNOLD
Cocker Beck
Caythorpe
TIBSHELF
WOODALL
BLYTH
NOTTINGHA
M1
M18
A1(M)
A1
A57
A60
A61
A614
A631
A616
A617
A619
A630
A632
A638
A38
A610
A6
A608
A6097
A6075
A6191
A6182
A6123
A6102
A6195
A635
A18
A620
A634
A6075
A612

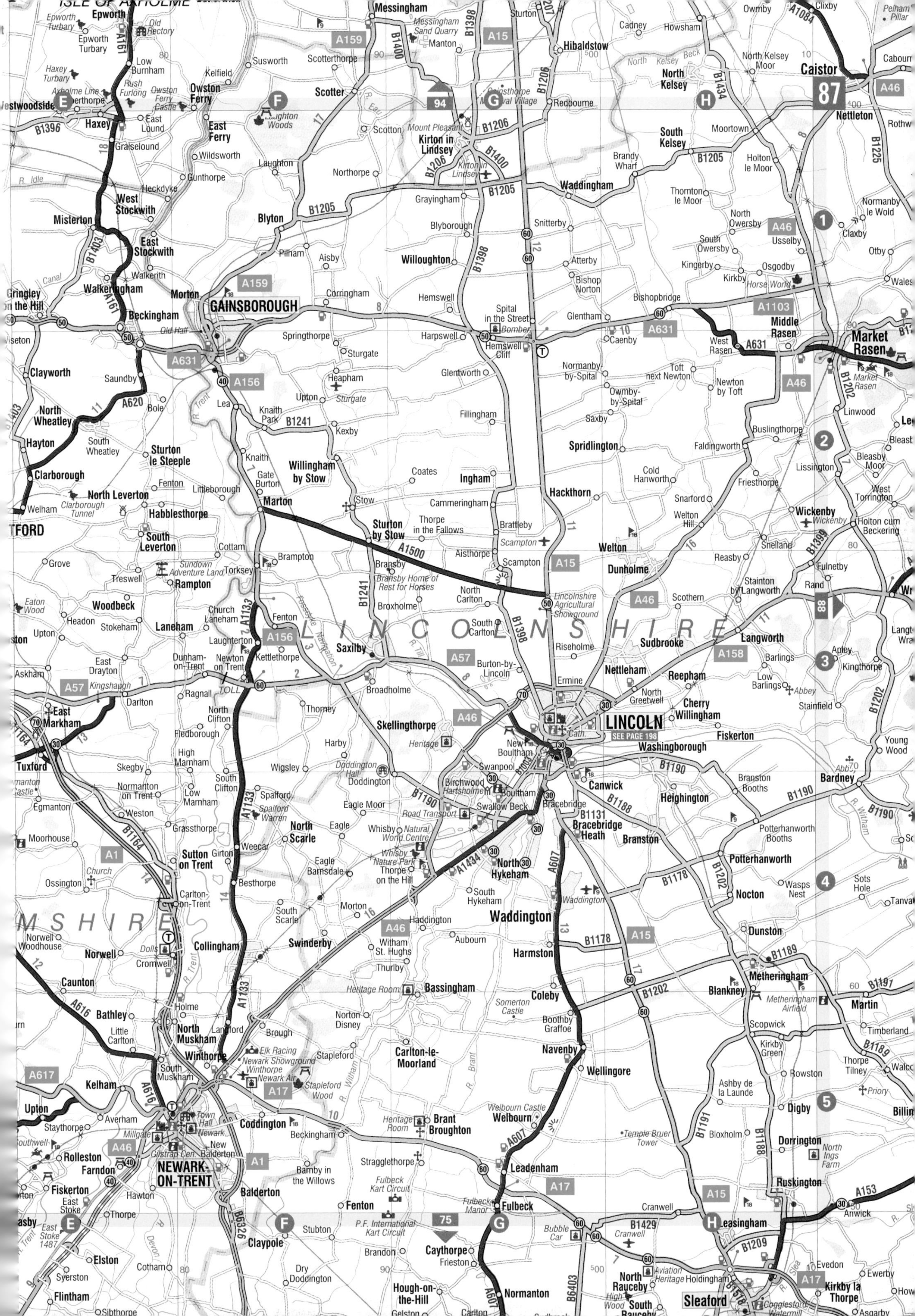

ISLE OF AXHOLME
Epworth
Epworth Turbary
Old Rectory
Messingham
Messingham Sand Quarry
Manton
Sturton
Hibaldstow
Cadney
Howsham
Owmby
Clixby
Pelham Pillar
Caistor
87
Cabourne
A46
Haxey Turbary
Low Burnham
Kelfield
Susworth
Scotterthorpe
A159
A15
B1398
B1400
B1206
North Kelsey Moor
North Kelsey
Kelsey Beck
B1434
A1084
A161
Axholme Line
Rush Furlong
Owston Ferry
Owston Ferry Castle
Scotter
Laughton Woods
Gainsthorpe Medieval Village
Redbourne
Nettleton
Rothwell
Westwoodside
Haxey
East Lound
East Ferry
Scotton
Mount Pleasant
94
Kirton in Lindsey
Kirton in Lindsey
South Kelsey
Moortown
B1225
B1396
Graiselound
Wildsworth
Laughton
Northorpe
Brandy Wharf
B1205
Holton le Moor
R. Idle
Heckdyke
Gunthorpe
Grayingham
Waddingham
Thornton le Moor
Normanby le Wold
West Stockwith
Blyton
Snitterby
North Owersby
Claxby
Misterton
B1205
Blyborough
South Owersby
Usselby
Otby
East Stockwith
Pilham
Aisby
Willoughton
Atterby
Kingerby
Osgodby
B1403
Walkerith
Bishop Norton
Kirkby
Horse World
Walesby
Canal
Walkeringham
Morton
A159
Corringham
Hemswell
Bishopbridge
Gringley on the Hill
Beckingham
GAINSBOROUGH
Spital in the Street
Bomber
Glentham
A1103
Middle Rasen
Market Rasen
Old Hall
Springthorpe
Harpswell
Hemswell Cliff
Caenby
A631
West Rasen
A631
Everton
Clayworth
Sturgate
Normanby-by-Spital
Toft next Newton
Newton by Toft
Market Rasen
A631
Saundby
Heapham
Glentworth
Owmby-by-Spital
A46
B1202
A620
A156
Bole
Lea
Upton
Sturgate
Knaith Park
B1241
Fillingham
Saxby
Linwood
North Wheatley
Kexby
Buslingthorpe
Hayton
South Wheatley
Sturton le Steeple
Willingham by Stow
Spridlington
Faldingworth
Bleasby Moor
Knaith
Gate Burton
Cold Hanworth
Lissington
Clarborough
Fenton
Littleborough
Coates
Ingham
Friesthorpe
North Leverton
Hackthorn
Snarford
West Torrington
Welham
Clarborough Tunnel
Habblesthorpe
Marton
Stow
Cammeringham
Welton Hill
Wickenby
RETFORD
South Leverton
Sturton by Stow
Thorpe in the Fallows
Brattleby
Holton cum Beckering
A1500
Scampton
Welton
Shelland
Cottam
Brampton
Aisthorpe
Scampton
B1399
Grove
Sundown Adventure Land
Torksey
Bransby
Bransby Home of Rest for Horses
Dunholme
Reasby
Fulnetby
Treswell
Rampton
A15
Stainton by Langworth
Rand
Eaton Wood
Woodbeck
Church Laneham
A1133
Broxholme
North Carlton
Lincolnshire Agricultural Showground
A46
Scothern
88
Headon
Stokeham
Laneham
Fenton
Fossdyke Navigation
South Carlton
LINCOLNSHIRE
Sudbrooke
Langworth
Upton
Laughterton
A156
Saxilby
B1398
Riseholme
Apley
Askham
Dunham-on-Trent
Newton on Trent
Kettlethorpe
A57
Burton-by-Lincoln
Nettleham
A158
Barlings
Kingthorpe
East Drayton
Kingshaugh
TOLL
Broadholme
Ermine
Reepham
Low Barlings
Abbey
A57
Ragnall
North Greetwell
Cherry Willingham
Stainfield
East Markham
Darlton
Thorney
LINCOLN
SEE PAGE 198
Markham
North Clifton
Skellingthorpe
A46
Cath.
Fiskerton
Fledborough
Heritage
New Boultham
Washingborough
Young Wood
Tuxford
High Marnham
Harby
Swanpool
B1190
Bardney
Skegby
Doddington Hall
Doddington
Birchwood
Hartsholme
Boultham
Canwick
Branston Booths
Normanton on Trent
South Clifton
Spalford
Bracebridge
B1188
Heighington
B1190
Egmanton
Low Marnham
Spalford Warren
Eagle Moor
B1190
Swallow Beck
B1131
Bracebridge Heath
Weston
Road Transport
Branston
Potterhanworth Booths
Moorhouse
Grassthorpe
A1133
North Scarle
Eagle
Whisby
Natural World Centre
A1
Sutton on Trent
Girton
Weecar
Whisby Nature Park
North Hykeham
A607
B1178
Potterhanworth
B1164
Eagle Barnsdale
Thorpe on the Hill
A1434
B1202
Wasps Nest
Sots Hole
Ossington
Church
Besthorpe
South Hykeham
Waddington
Nocton
Tanvats
Carlton-on-Trent
South Scarle
Morton
Haddington
Waddington
NOTTINGHAMSHIRE
Swinderby
A46
Aubourn
B1178
A15
Dunston
Norwell Woodhouse
Dolls
Collingham
Witham St. Hughs
Harmston
B1189
Norwell
Cromwell
R. Trent
Thurlby
Metheringham
Caunton
A1133
Heritage Room
Bassingham
Somerton Castle
Coleby
B1202
Blankney
Metheringham Airfield
B1191
Martin
A616
Bathley
Holme
Norton Disney
Boothby Graffoe
Scopwick
Timberland
Little Carlton
North Muskham
Langford
Brough
Kirkby Green
B1189
Elk Racing
Newark Showground
Stapleford
Carlton-le-Moorland
Navenby
Thorpe Tilney
Walcott
A617
Winthorpe
Newark Air Museum
R. Brant
Wellingore
Rowston
Kelham
South Muskham
A616
Stapleford Wood
A17
Ashby de la Laundе
Priory
Upton
Averham
Town Hall
Newark
Coddington
R. Witham
Welbourn Castle
Welbourn
Digby
Billinghay
Staythorpe
Millgate
Heritage Room
Brant Broughton
B1191
Blox holme
B1188
Southwell
Rolleston
A46
Gilstrap Cen.
New Balderton
Beckingham
Temple Bruer Tower
Dorrington
North Ings Farm
Farndon
NEWARK-ON-TRENT
A1
Barnby in the Willows
Stragglethorpe
Leadenham
Ruskington
Fiskerton
Hawton
Balderton
Fulbeck Kart Circuit
A17
East Stoke
Thorpe
Fenton
Fulbeck Manor
Fulbeck
Cranwell
A15
A153
Anwick
Bleasby
East Stoke 1487
B6326
P.F. International Kart Circuit
Stubton
75
Bubble Car
B1429
Cranwell
Leasingham
Claypole
Caythorpe
Brandon
Elston
Cotham
Frieston
Dry Doddington
B1209
Evedon
Syerston
Hough-on-the-Hill
Aviation Heritage
North Rauceby
Holdingham
A17
Ewerby
Flintham
A607
Normanton
B6403
High Wood
South Rauceby
Sleaford
B1517
Cogglesford Watermill
Kirkby la Thorpe
Howell
Sibthorpe
Gelston
Carlton
Asgarby

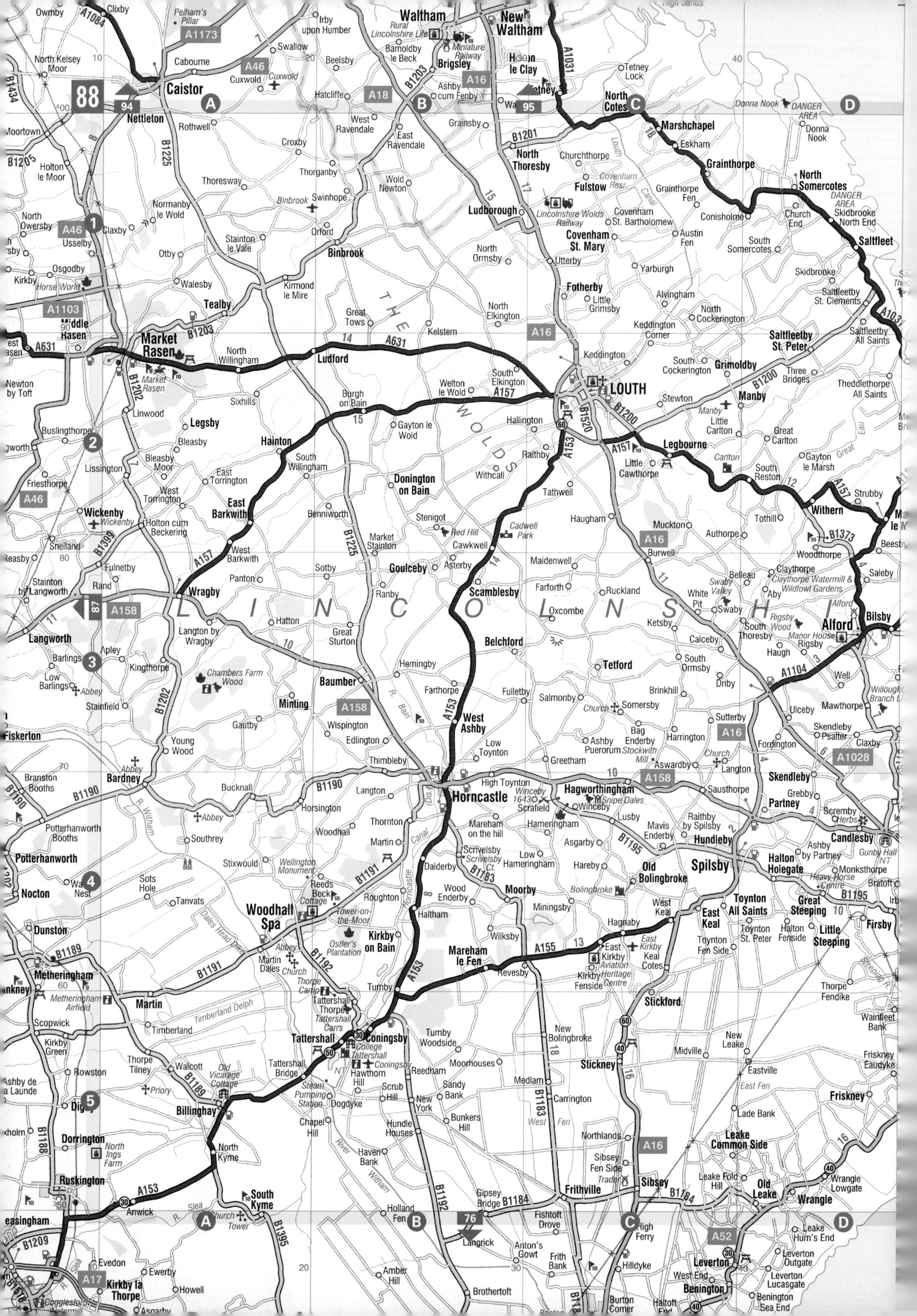

88
94
95
87
76
A
B
C
D
1
2
3
4
5
Ownby
Clixby
A1084
Pelham's Pillar
A1173
Irby upon Humber
Waltham
Rural Lincolnshire Life
New Waltham
Barnoldby le Beck
Miniature Railway
Brigsley
Swallow
Beelsby
North Kelsey Moor
Cabourne
A46
Cuxwold
Caistor
Hatcliffe
A18
B1203
Ashby cum Fenby
A16
Holton le Clay
A1031
Tetney Lock
North Cotes
Donna Nook
DANGER AREA
Donna Nook
B1434
Nettleton
Rothwell
West Ravendale
East Ravendale
Grainsby
B1201
North Thoresby
Churchthorpe
Marshchapel
Eskham
Moortown
B1225
Croxby
Covenham Resr.
Grainthorpe
B1205
Holton le Moor
Thoresway
Thorganby
Wold Newton
Fulstow
Grainthorpe Fen
North Somercotes
Normanby le Wold
Binbrook
Swinhope
Ludborough
Lincolnshire Wolds Railway
Covenham St. Bartholomew
Conisholme
DANGER AREA
Church End
Skidbrooke North End
North Owersby
Claxby
Orford
Covenham St. Mary
Austin Fen
Saltfleet
A46
Usselby
Stainton le Vale
Binbrook
North Ormsby
South Somercotes
Otby
Utterby
Yarburgh
Osgodby
Skidbrooke
Kirkby
Horse World
Walesby
Kirmond le Mire
Fotherby
Little Grimsby
Alvingham
Saltfleetby St. Clements
A1103
Tealby
THE WOLDS
North Elkington
North Cockerington
Middle Rasen
Great Tows
Keddington Corner
A1031
B1203
Kelstern
A16
Saltfleetby All Saints
Market Rasen
A631
Saltfleetby St. Peter
North Willingham
Ludford
Keddington
South Cockerington
Grimoldby
Three Bridges
Market Rasen
South Elkington
Welton le Wold
A157
LOUTH
Theddlethorpe All Saints
Newton by Toft
B1202
Sixhills
Burgh on Bain
Stewton
B1200
Manby
Linwood
Hallington
Little Carlton
Legsby
Gayton le Wold
Great Carlton
Buslingthorpe
Bleasby
Hainton
B1520
A153
Legbourne
Raithby
Little Cawthorpe
Carlton
Gayton le Marsh
Bleasby Moor
South Willingham
Lissington
East Torrington
Donington on Bain
Withcall
South Reston
Friesthorpe
West Torrington
Tathwell
Strubby
A46
East Barkwith
Withern
Wickenby
Benniworth
Haugham
Tothill
Wickenby
Holton cum Beckering
Stenigot
Red Hill
Cadwell Park
Muckton
Authorpe
B1373
Snelland
B1399
West Barkwith
Market Stainton
Cawkwell
A16
Burwell
Woodthorpe
Reasby
A157
Asterby
Maidenwell
Belleau
Claythorpe
Saleby
Fulnetby
Panton
Sotby
Goulceby
Claythorpe Watermill & Wildfowl Gardens
Stainton by Langworth
Rand
Wragby
Ranby
Scamblesby
Farforth
Ruckland
White Pit
Swaby Valley
Aby
A158
LINCOLNSHIRE
Oxcombe
Swaby
Alford
Bilsby
Langworth
Hatton
Ketsby
Rigsby Wood
Langton by Wragby
South Thoresby
Manor House
Belchford
Calceby
Rigsby
Apley
Great Sturton
Barlings
Hemingby
Haugh
Kingthorpe
Tetford
South Ormsby
A1104
Well
Low Barlings
Chambers Farm Wood
Abbey
Baumber
Brinkhill
Driby
Farthorpe
Fulletby
Minting
Salmonby
Stainfield
A158
Somersby
Ulceby
Mawthorpe
B1202
West Ashby
Church
Fiskerton
Gautby
Wispington
Sutterby
Bag Enderby
Skendleby Psalter
Edlington
Harrington
A16
Claxby
Young Wood
Low Toynton
Ashby Puerorum
Stockwith Mill
Fordington
Greetham
Church
A1028
Thimbleby
Aswardby
Langton
Abbey
Bardney
Branston Booths
B1190
Bucknall
B1190
Langton
High Toynton
Winceby 1643
Hagworthingham
A158
Sausthorpe
Skendleby
Horncastle
Snipe Dales
Grebby
B1190
Horsington
Scrafield
Winceby
Partney
Abbey
Lusby
Raithby by Spilsby
Scremby
Mareham on the hill
Hameringham
Potterhanworth Booths
Woodhall
Thornton
Mavis Enderby
Candlesby
Southrey
Martin
Asgarby
Hundleby
Canal
B1195
Potterhanworth
Scrivelsby
Low Hameringham
Spilsby
Ashby by Partney
Gunby Hall NT
Stixwould
Wellington Monument
Scrivelsby Ct.
Hareby
Halton Holegate
Monksthorpe
Heavy Horse Centre
Dalderby
B1183
Old Bolingbroke
Bratoft
Nocton
Sots Hole
Reeds Beck
B1191
Wood Enderby
Moorby
Bolingbroke
Toynton All Saints
Great Steeping
Tanvats
Roughton
Miningsby
West Keal
B1195
Woodhall Spa
Tower-on-the-Moor
Haltham
East Keal
Little Steeping
Firsby
Dunston
Dales Head Dike
Ostler's Plantation
Kirkby on Bain
Wilksby
Hagnaby
Toynton St. Peter
Halton Fenside
B1189
Abbey
Mareham le Fen
A155
East Kirkby
East Kirkby Aviation Heritage Centre
Keal Cotes
Toynton Fen Side
Martin Dales
Church
B1192
A153
Revesby
Metheringham
B1191
Thorpe Camp
Kirkby Fenside
Thorpe Fendike
Metheringham Airfield
Martin
Tumby
Stickford
Tattershall Thorpe
Tattershall Carrs
Timberland Delph
Scopwick
Timberland
Tattershall
Coningsby
Tumby Woodside
New Bolingbroke
Wainfleet Bank
Kirkby Green
New Leake
College
Tattershall
Thorpe Tilney
Tattershall Bridge
Coningsby
Hawthorn Hill
Moorhouses
Midville
Stickney
Friskney Eaudyke
Rowston
Walcott
Old Vicarage Cottage
Reedham
Eastville
Ashby de la Launde
B1189
Priory
Steam Pumping Station
Dogdyke
Scrub Hill
Sandy Bank
Medlam
East Fen
Digby
Billinghay
New York
B1183
Carrington
Friskney
Chapel Hill
Hundle Houses
Bunkers Hill
West Fen
Lade Bank
B1188
Dorrington
North Ings Farm
River Witham
Northlands
A16
Leake Common Side
North Kyme
Haven Bank
Sibsey Fen Side
Trader
Ruskington
South Kyme
B1192
Gipsey Bridge
B1184
Frithville
Sibsey
Leake Fold Hill
Old Leake
Wrangle Lowgate
Wrangle
A153
Anwick
Church Tower
Holland Fen
Fishtoft Drove
High Ferry
A52
Leake Hurn's End
Leasingham
B1395
Langrick
B1209
Evedon
Anton's Gowt
Frith Bank
Hilldyke
Leverton
Leverton Outgate
A17
Ewerby
Amber Hill
West End
Leverton Lucasgate
Kirkby la Thorpe
Howell
Brothertoft
Benington
Benington Sea End
Cogglesford Watermill
Asgarby
Burton Corner
Haltoft End

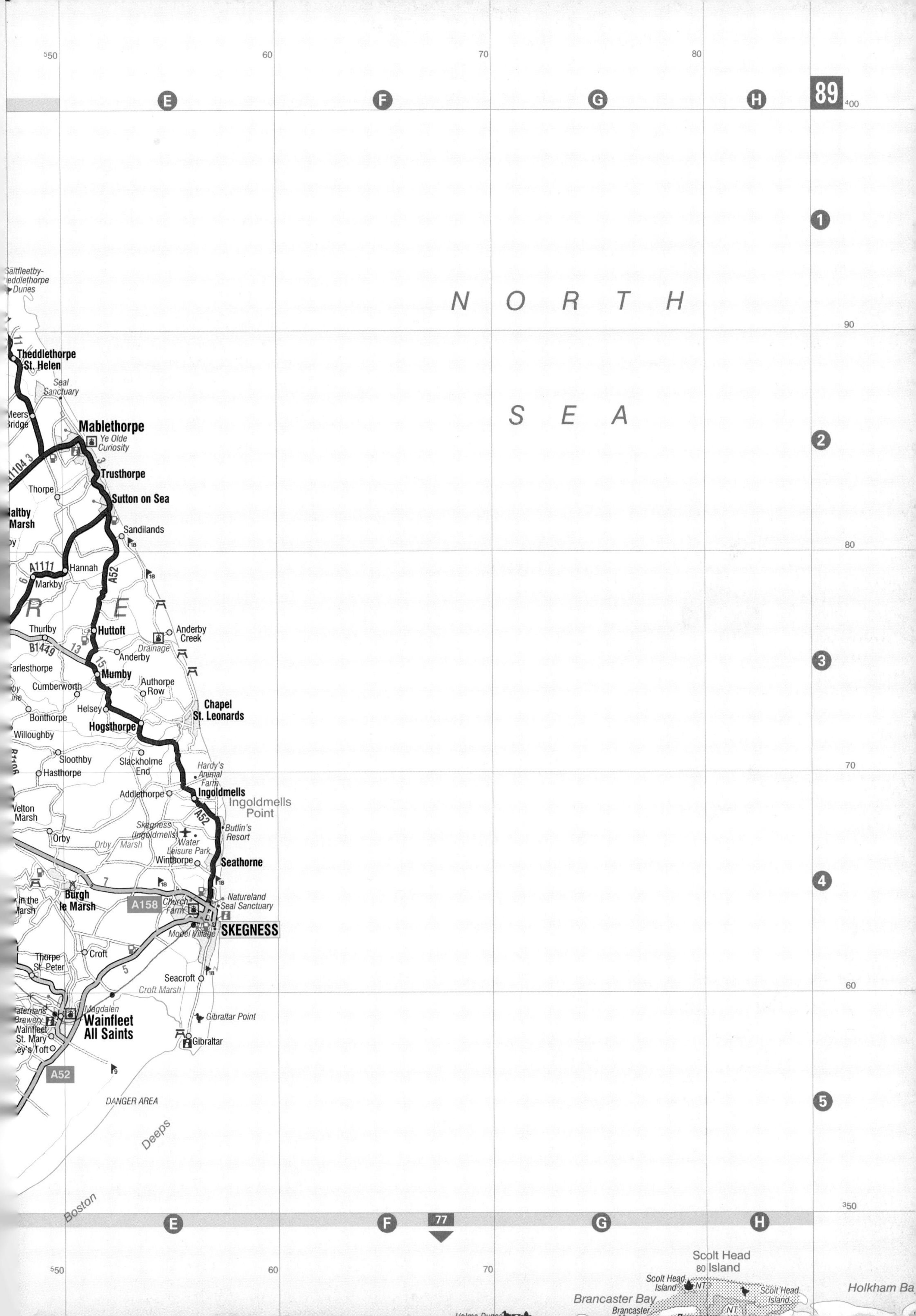

550   60   70   80

1

N O R T H

S E A

90

2

80

Saltfleetby-
Theddlethorpe
▸Dunes

Theddlethorpe
St. Helen

Seal
Sanctuary

Meers
Bridge

Mablethorpe
Ye Olde
Curiosity

A1104 3

Thorpe

Trusthorpe

Maltby
Marsh

Sutton on Sea

A52

Sandilands

A1111   Hannah

Markby

R   E

Thurlby   **Huttoft**   Anderby
Creek

B1449   13   Anderby   Drainage

Charlesthorpe   15   **Mumby**   Authorpe
Row

Cumberworth

ne   Helsey   Chapel
St. Leonards

Bonthorpe   **Hogsthorpe**

Willoughby

B1106   Sloothby   Slackholme
End   Hardy's
Animal
Farm

Hasthorpe

Addlethorpe   **Ingoldmells**

Welton
Marsh   Ingoldmells
Point

Orby   Orby Marsh   A52

Skegness
(Ingoldmells)   Butlin's
Resort

Water
Leisure Park

Winthorpe   **Seathorne**

in the
Marsh   **Burgh
le Marsh**   7   A158   Church
Farm   Natureland
Seal Sanctuary

SKEGNESS

Model Village

Thorpe
St. Peter   Croft   5

Seacroft

Croft Marsh

Bateman's
Brewery

Magdalen
**Wainfleet
All Saints**   Gibraltar Point

Wainfleet
St. Mary   Gibraltar

ey's Toft

A52   9

3

70

4

60

DANGER AREA

5

350

Deeps

Boston

550   60   70

Scolt Head
80 Island

Scolt Head
Island   NT   Scolt Head
Island

Brancaster Bay   NT   Holkham Ba

Brancaster

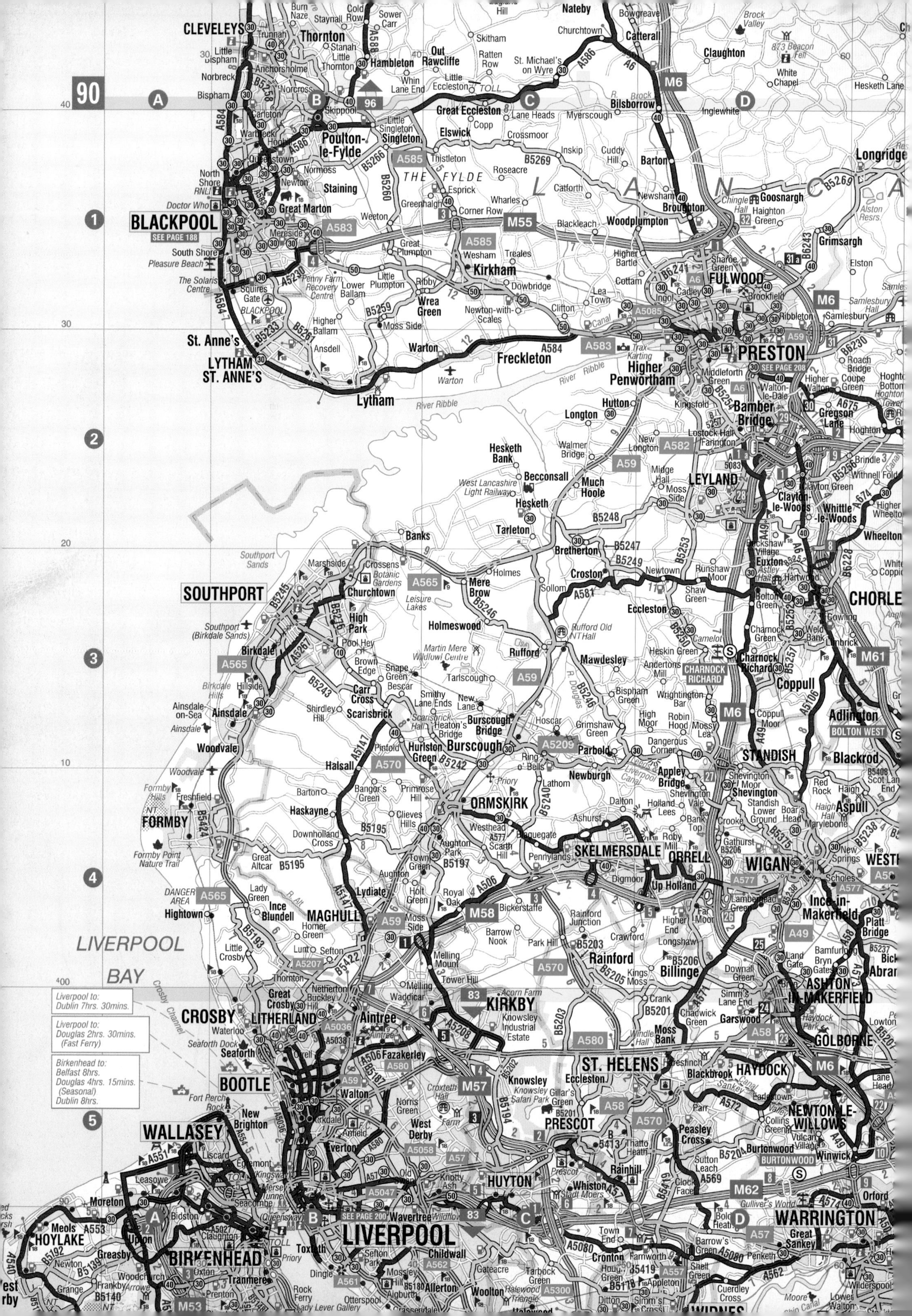

90
CLEVELEYS
Thornton
Hambleton
Out Rawcliffe
Nateby
Catterall
Churchtown
St. Michael's on Wyre
Claughton
Bilsborrow
Great Eccleston
Elswick
Poulton-le-Fylde
Singleton
THE FYLDE
BLACKPOOL
SEE PAGE 188
Staining
Great Marton
Kirkham
Wesham
Wrea Green
Freckleton
Warton
LYTHAM ST. ANNE'S
St. Anne's
Lytham
River Ribble
Longridge
Goosnargh
Grimsargh
Broughton
Woodplumpton
FULWOOD
PRESTON
SEE PAGE 208
Higher Penwortham
Bamber Bridge
Hutton
Longton
Hesketh Bank
Becconsall
Much Hoole
Tarleton
LEYLAND
Clayton-le-Woods
Whittle-le-Woods
Banks
Southport Sands
SOUTHPORT
Churchtown
Crossens
Mere Brow
Holmeswood
Croston
Eccleston
Rufford
Mawdesley
CHORLEY
Coppull
Charnock Richard
Adlington
Birkdale
Ainsdale
Scarisbrick
Burscough
Halsall
Woodvale
FORMBY
Formby Point Nature Trail
ORMSKIRK
Parbold
Newburgh
STANDISH
Shevington
Aspull
SKELMERSDALE
ORRELL
WIGAN
Up Holland
Ince-in-Makerfield
Hightown
Ince Blundell
MAGHULL
Lydiate
Aughton
LIVERPOOL BAY
Billinge
Rainford
ASHTON-IN-MAKERFIELD
CROSBY
LITHERLAND
Aintree
KIRKBY
Knowsley Industrial Estate
GOLBORNE
ST. HELENS
HAYDOCK
BOOTLE
NEWTON-LE-WILLOWS
WALLASEY
New Brighton
Eccleston
PRESCOT
HUYTON
Moreton
Hoylake
BIRKENHEAD
LIVERPOOL
SEE PAGE 200
WARRINGTON
Great Sankey
Childwall
Woolton
Allerton
Toxteth
Wavertree
Liverpool to: Dublin 7hrs. 30mins.
Liverpool to: Douglas 2hrs. 30mins. (Fast Ferry)
Birkenhead to: Belfast 8hrs. Douglas 4hrs. 15mins. (Seasonal) Dublin 8hrs.
M6
M55
M58
M57
M62
M61
M53

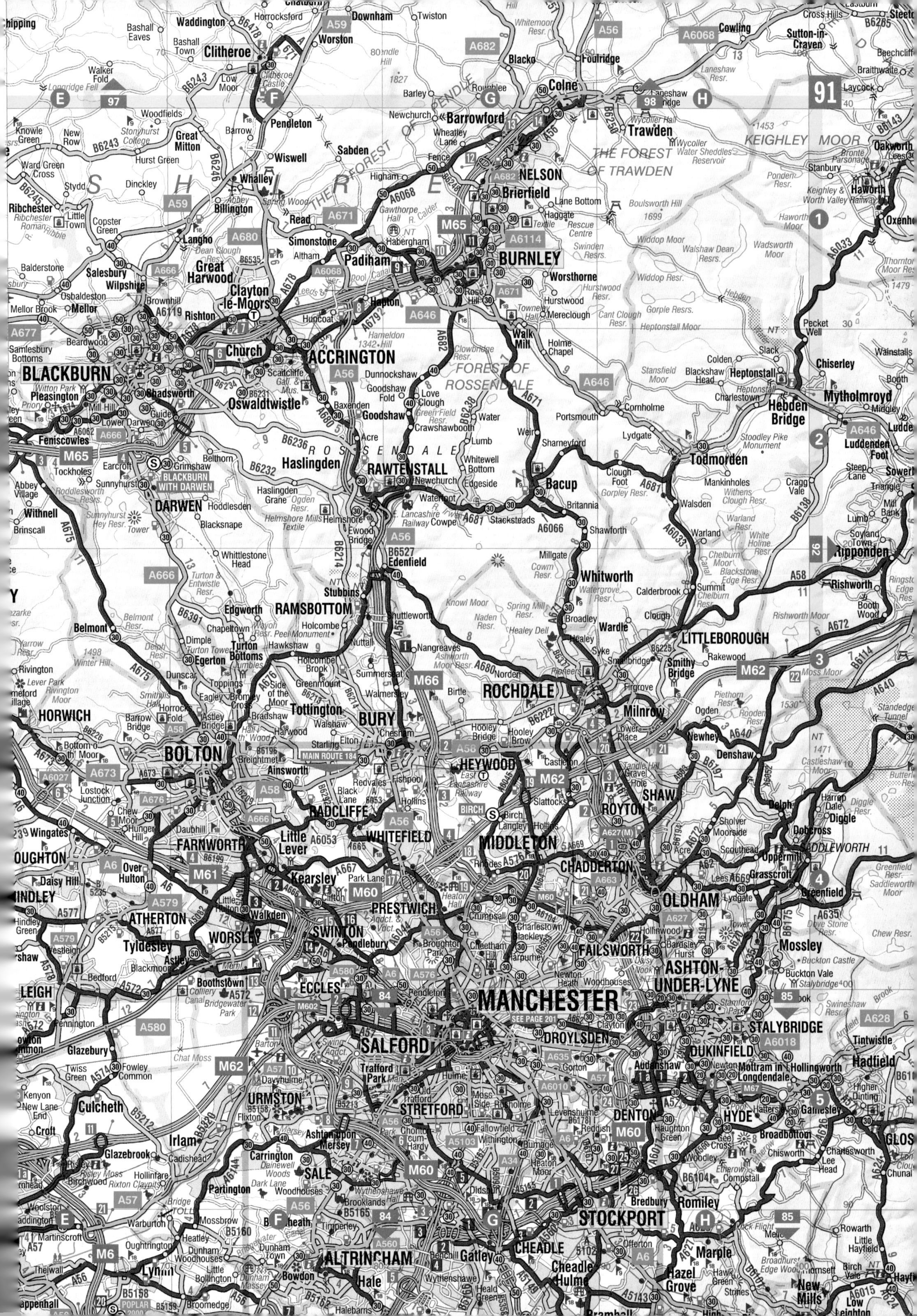

Chipping
Bashall Eaves
Waddington
Horrocksford
Downham
Twiston
Clitheroe
Worston
Whitemoor Resr.
Cowling
Cross Hills
Sutton-in-Craven
Steeton
Walker Fold
Longridge Fell
Low Moor
Clitheroe Castle
Pendle Hill
Blacko
Foulridge
Laneshaw Resr.
Braithwaite
Laycock
97
98
91
Barley
Roughlee
Colne
Laneshaw Bridge
E
F
G
H
Woodfields
Newchurch
Barrowford
Wycoller Hall
Knowle Green
New Row
Stonyhurst College
Great Mitton
Barrow
Pendleton
Wheatley Lane
Trawden
Wycoller
KEIGHLEY MOOR
Oakworth
Hurst Green
Wiswell
Sabden
THE FOREST OF PENDLE
Fence
THE FOREST OF TRAWDEN
Water Sheddles Reservoir
Brontë Parsonage
Ward Green Cross
Stydd
Dinckley
Whalley
Higham
NELSON
Stanbury
Haworth
Ribchester
Little Town
Abbey
Billington
Spring Wood
Brierfield
Lane Bottom
Keighley & Worth Valley Railway
Copster Green
Read
Gawthorpe Hall
Haggate
Boulsworth Hill
Oxenhope
Langho
Simonstone
Habergham
Rescue Centre
Haworth Moor
Dean Clough
Altham
Padiham
BURNLEY
Swinden Resrs.
Widdop Moor
Balderstone
Salesbury
Great Harwood
Walshaw Dean Resrs.
Wadsworth Moor
Thornton Moor Resr.
Wilpshire
Clayton-le-Moors
Worsthorne
Widdop Resr.
Osbaldeston
Brownhill
Hapton
Hurstwood
Hurstwood Resr.
Mellor Brook
Mellor
Rishton
Huncoat
Rose Hill
Towneley Hall
Mereclough
Cant Clough Resr.
Gorple Resrs.
Heptonstall Moor
Pecket Well
Hameldon Hill
Walk Mill
Samlesbury Bottoms
Beardwood
Church
ACCRINGTON
Clowbridge Resr.
Holme Chapel
Slack
Wainstalls
BLACKBURN
Scaitcliffe
Dunnockshaw
FOREST OF ROSSENDALE
Colden
Heptonstall
Chiserley
Witton Park
Shadsworth
Gall. & Mus.
Goodshaw Fold
Love Clough
Stansfield Moor
Blackshaw Head
Booth
Pleasington
Oswaldtwistle
Charlestown
Mytholmroyd
Mill Hill
Baxenden
Green Field Resr.
Hebden Bridge
Midgley
Guide
Goodshaw
Water
Portsmouth
Cornholme
Lower Darwen
Crawshawbooth
Weir
Lydgate
Stoodley Pike Monument
Luddenden Foot
Feniscowles
Acre
Lumb
Sharneyford
M65
Haslingden
ROSSENDALE
Belthorn
Whitewell Bottom
Clough Foot
Todmorden
Steep Lane
Grimshaw
RAWTENSTALL
Bacup
Gorpley Resr.
Mankinholes
Cragg Vale
Tockholes
Earcroft
Newchurch
Edgeside
Withens Clough Resr.
Abbey Village
Sunnyhurst
BLACKBURN WITH DARWEN
Haslingden Grane
Waterfoot
Britannia
Walsden
Roddlesworth Resrs.
Ogden Resr.
DARWEN
Hoddlesden
Helmshore Mills Textile
Helmshore
E. Lancashire Railway
Cowpe
Stacksteads
Withnell
Sunnyhurst Hey Resr.
Tower
Blacksnape
Ewood Bridge
Shawforth
Warland Resr.
Brinscall
Warland
White Holme Resr.
Edenfield
Millgate
Soyland Town
Whittlestone Head
Cowm Resr.
Chelburn Moor
Ripponden
Blackstone Edge Resr.
Turton & Entwistle Resr.
Stubbins
Whitworth
Watergrove Resr.
Calderbrook
Summit
Rishworth
Chelburn Resr.
Edgworth
RAMSBOTTOM
Knowl Moor
Spring Mill Resr.
Booth Wood
Belmont Resr.
Clough
Wayoh Resr.
Holcombe
Peel Monument
Shuttleworth
Naden Resr.
Broadley
Wardle
Rishworth Moor
Belmont
Chapeltown
Healey Dell
Yarrow Resr.
Dimple
Turton Tower
Turton Bottoms
Hawkshaw
Nuttall
Nangreaves
Healey
LITTLEBOROUGH
1498 Winter Hill
Delph Resr.
Egerton
Jumbles
Holcombe Brook
Ashworth Moor Resr.
Norden
Syke
Smallbridge
Rakewood
Smithy Bridge
Rivington
Summerseat
Moss Moor
Lever Park
Rivington Moor
Dunscar
Toppings
Side of the Moor
Greenmount
M66
Pioneers
Firgrove
Piethorn Resr.
Eagley
Bromley Cross
Walmersley
Birtle
ROCHDALE
Milnrow
Standedge Tunnel
HORWICH
Horrocks Fold
Bradshaw
Tottington
Ogden
Rooden Resr.
Barrow Bridge
Astley Bridge
Hall i' th' Wood
Harwood
Walshaw
BURY
Hooley Bridge
Hooley Brow
Lower Place
Newhey
Chesham
Starling
Elton
Castleton
Denshaw
Bottom o' th' Moor
BOLTON
Breightmet
MAIN ROUTE 184
HEYWOOD
Tandle Hill
Gravel Hole
Castleshaw Moor
Ainsworth
Fishpool
East Lancashire Railway
Lostock Junction
Redvales
Black Lane
Slattocks
SHAW
Hollins
Harrop Dale
Diggle
Chew Moor
Hunger Hill
RADCLIFFE
BIRCH
Birch
Langley
ROYTON
Sholver
Moorside
Diggle Resr.
Dobcross
Wingates
Daubhill
Little Lever
WHITEFIELD
MIDDLETON
SADDLEWORTH
FARNWORTH
Rhodes
Scouthead
Uppermill
OUGHTON
Over Hulton
Kearsley
Park Lane
CHADDERTON
Lees
Grasscroft
Greenfield Resr.
Saddleworth Moor
Daisy Hill
M61
Clifton
Heaton Hall
Greenfield
INDLEY
PRESTWICH
Crumpsall
OLDHAM
Lydgate
ATHERTON
Walkden
Little Hulton
Agdct. & Vdct.
Charlestown
Blackley
Hollinwood
Dove Stone Resr.
Hindley Green
SWINTON
Bardsley
Hurst
Chew Resr.
Westleigh
Tyldesley
WORSLEY
Pendlebury
Broughton Park
Cheetham Hill
FAILSWORTH
Mossley
Astley
Harpurhey
Daisy Nook
Buckton Castle
ASHTON-UNDER-LYNE
Buckton Vale
Stalybridge
Blackmoor
Boothstown
Newton Heath
Woodhouses
Bedford
LEIGH
ECCLES
Pendleton
MANCHESTER
SEE PAGE 201
Swineshaw Resr.
Colliery Canal
Bridgewater Park
Stamford Park
85
84
STALYBRIDGE
Pennington
DROYLSDEN
A628
Barton
Swing Aqdct.
SALFORD
Clayton
Tintwistle
Glazebury
Chat Moss
Gorton
DUKINFIELD
Hadfield
Twiss Green
Fowley Common
M62
Trafford Park
Audenshaw
Mottram in Longdendale
Hollingworth
Davyhulme
Old Trafford
Hulme
Moss Side
Rusholme
Higher Dinting
Kenyon
New Lane End
URMSTON
STRETFORD
Levenshulme
DENTON
HYDE
Gamesley
Culcheth
Flixton
Chorlton-cum-Hardy
Fallowfield
Reddish
Haughton Green
Hattersley
Croft
Ashton upon Mersey
Withington
Burnage
M60
Gee Cross
Broadbottom
Irlam
Carrington
Dainewell Woods
Heaton Moor
Woodley
Chisworth
Charlesworth
Glazebrook
Cadishead
SALE
Lee Head
Risley
Risley Moss
Hollinfare
Rixton Claypits
Partington
Dark Lane
Woodhouses
Bredbury
Compstall
Chunal
Birchwood
Romiley
Brooklands
Didsbury
STOCKPORT
Woolston
Bridge
Mossbrow
Broadheath
Timperley
Warburton
Heatley
Rowarth
Little Hayfield
Martinscroft
Oughtrington
Dunham Woodhouses
Dunham Town
ALTRINCHAM
Gatley
CHEADLE
Offerton
Marple
Rock Flight
Mellor
Broadhurst Edge Wood
Thelwall
Lymm
Little Bollington
Dunham Massey
Bowdon
Hale
Wythenshawe
Cheadle Hulme
Hazel Grove
Hawk Green
Strines
Birch Vale
New Mills
Hayfield
Low Leighton
Broomedge
POPLAR 2000
Halebarns
Heald Green
Bramhall
Appenhall

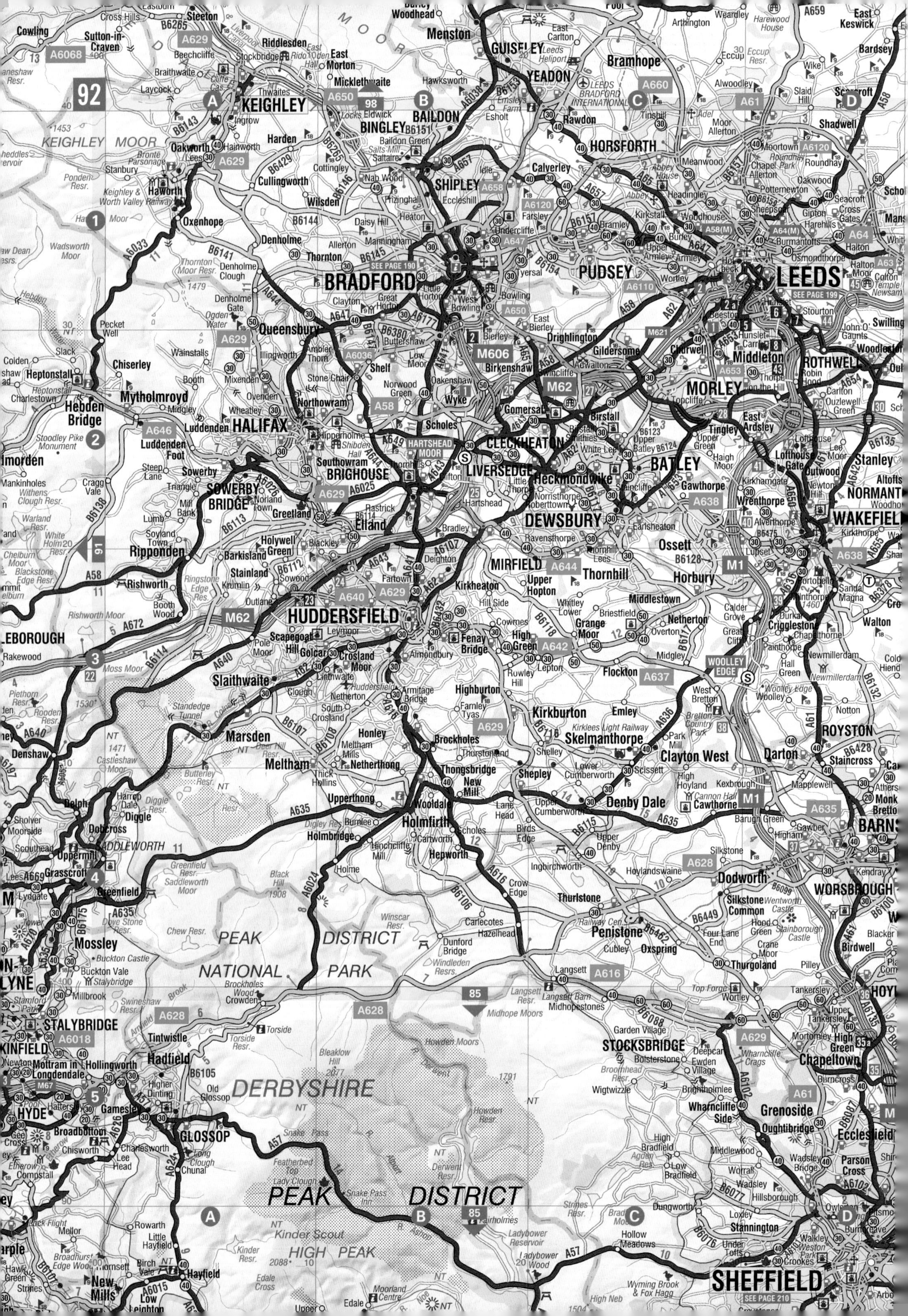

92
98
91
85
SEE PAGE 190
SEE PAGE 199
SEE PAGE 210
KEIGHLEY
KEIGHLEY MOOR
BINGLEY
BAILDON
SHIPLEY
GUISELEY
YEADON
Bramhope
Horsforth
LEEDS BRADFORD INTERNATIONAL
BRADFORD
PUDSEY
LEEDS
Menston
Cowling
Sutton-in-Craven
Steeton
Riddlesden
East Morton
Micklethwaite
Haworth
Oakworth
Oxenhope
Cullingworth
Wilsden
Denholme
Thornton
Queensbury
Harden
Calverley
Farsley
Horsforth
Roundhay
Shadwell
Scarcroft
Bardsey
East Keswick
Harewood House
Wike
Eccup
Alwoodley
ROTHWELL
MORLEY
Middleton
Drighlington
Gildersome
Birkenshaw
CLECKHEATON
Heckmondwike
LIVERSEDGE
BATLEY
DEWSBURY
Ossett
Horbury
WAKEFIELD
Stanley
HALIFAX
Hebden Bridge
Heptonstall
Mytholmroyd
Luddenden
Luddenden Foot
SOWERBY BRIDGE
Sowerby
BRIGHOUSE
Elland
Greetland
Ripponden
Rishworth
Stainland
HUDDERSFIELD
MIRFIELD
Thornhill
Slaithwaite
Marsden
Meltham
Honley
Holmfirth
Kirkburton
Skelmanthorpe
Clayton West
Denby Dale
Darton
ROYSTON
Cawthorne
Dodworth
WORSBROUGH
Penistone
Oxspring
Thurgoland
STOCKSBRIDGE
Chapeltown
Grenoside
Ecclesfield
SHEFFIELD
Stannington
Hillsborough
Loxley
Bradfield
Low Bradfield
High Bradfield
Oughtibridge
Mossley
STALYBRIDGE
Hadfield
Tintwistle
GLOSSOP
HYDE
Hayfield
New Mills
Diggle
Delph
Dobcross
Uppermill
Greenfield
Denshaw
SADDLEWORTH
PEAK DISTRICT NATIONAL PARK
DERBYSHIRE
PEAK DISTRICT
HIGH PEAK
Kinder Scout
Snake Pass
Ladybower Reservoir
Langsett
Midhopestones
Hollow Meadows
Crowden
Holmbridge
HARTSHEAD MOOR
WOOLLEY EDGE
M62
M606
M621
M1
M67
A629
A650
A660
A61
A58
A62
A635
A628
A616
A57
A6024
A646
A6033
A640
A672
A642
A637
A638
A636
A644
A6036
A641
A643
A6025
A6026
A653
A654
A6120
A64
A58(M)
A64(M)
A6110
A647
A6177
A6018
A6015
A6068
B6265
B6429
B6144
B6141
B6145
B6138
B6113
B6114
B6112
B6107
B6108
B6106
B6115
B6117
B6118
B6128
B6123
B6124
B6132
B6099
B6449
B6462
B6088
B6077
B6076
B6105

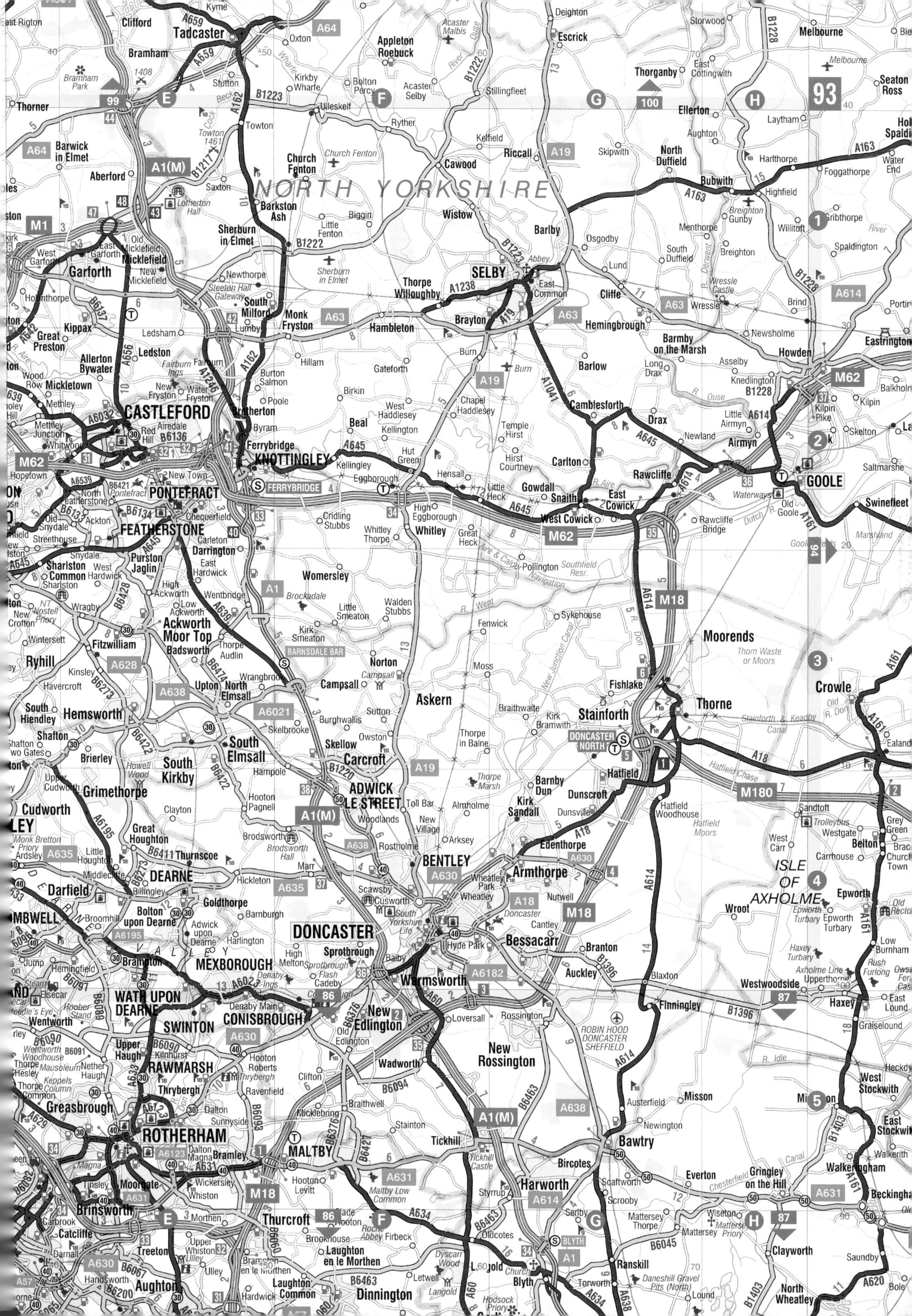
NORTH YORKSHIRE
93
94
99
100
86
87
E
F
G
H
1
2
3
4
5
Tadcaster
Clifford
Kyme
Bramham
Bramham Park
Thorner
Oxton
Appleton Roebuck
Acaster Malbis
Escrick
Deighton
Storwood
Melbourne
Thorganby
East Cottingwith
Seaton Ross
Kirkby Wharfe
Bolton Percy
Acaster Selby
Stillingfleet
Ellerton
Laytham
Stutton
Towton
Towton 1461
Ulleskelf
Ryther
Kelfield
Riccall
Skipwith
North Duffield
Aughton
Harlthorpe
Foggathorpe
Bubwith
Highfield
Barwick in Elmet
Aberford
Church Fenton
Cawood
Saxton
Lotherton Hall
Barkston Ash
Wistow
Barlby
Osgodby
Menthorpe
Breighton
Gunby
Gribthorpe
Willitoft
Spaldington
Sherburn in Elmet
Little Fenton
Biggin
South Duffield
Lund
Wressle Castle
Wressle
Brind
Garforth
West Garforth
East Garforth
Micklefield
Old Micklefield
New Micklefield
Newthorpe
Steeton Hall Gateway
Thorpe Willoughby
SELBY
Selby Abbey
East Common
Cliffe
Hemingbrough
Newsholme
Eastrington
Howden
Hollinthorpe
South Milford
Monk Fryston
Hambleton
Brayton
Kippax
Great Preston
Ledsham
Ledston
Lumby
Barmby on the Marsh
Long Drax
Asselby
Knedlington
Allerton Bywater
Fairburn
Fairburn Ings
Hillam
Burn
Gateforth
Barlow
Burton Salmon
New Fryston
Water Fryston
Poole
Birkin
Chapel Haddlesey
West Haddlesey
Camblesforth
Drax
Little Airmyn
Airmyn
Kilpin
Kilpin Pike
Balkholme
Wood Row
Mickletown
Methley
CASTLEFORD
Airedale
Red Hill
Brotherton
Byram
Beal
Kellington
Temple Hirst
Hirst Courtney
Carlton
Newland
Skelton
Saltmarshe
Methley Junction
Whitwood
Ferrybridge
KNOTTINGLEY
Kellingley
Hut Green
Eggborough
Hensall
Gowdall
Snaith
Rawcliffe
East Cowick
Waterways
GOOLE
Old Goole
Swinefleet
Hopetown
New Town
PONTEFRACT
FERRYBRIDGE
Little Heck
West Cowick
Rawcliffe Bridge
Dutch R.
Marshland
North Featherstone
Old Snydale
Ackton
FEATHERSTONE
Chequerfield
Cridling Stubbs
High Eggborough
Whitley
Whitley Thorpe
Great Heck
Streethouse
Snydale
Carleton
Darrington
Purston Jaglin
Pollington
Southfield Resr.
Aire & Calder Navigation
Goole Fields
Sharlston
Sharlston Common
West Hardwick
East Hardwick
Womersley
Wentbridge
High Ackworth
Low Ackworth
Brockadale
Little Smeaton
Walden Stubbs
R. Went
Sykehouse
Fenwick
Nostell Priory
New Crofton
Wragby
Ackworth Moor Top
Kirk Smeaton
BARNSDALE BAR
Moorends
Thorn Waste or Moors
Wintersett
Fitzwilliam
Thorpe Audlin
Badsworth
Ryhill
Kinsley
Havercroft
Norton
Campsall
Moss
New Junction Canal
Fishlake
Crowle
Upton
North Elmsall
Wrangbrook
Askern
Thorne
Braithwaite
Kirk Bramwith
Stainforth
Old R. Don
Stainforth & Keadby Canal
South Hiendley
Hemsworth
South Elmsall
Skelbrooke
Burghwallis
Sutton
Owston
Skellow
Shafton
Brierley
Howell Wood
South Kirkby
Carcroft
Hampole
Thorpe in Balne
DONCASTER NORTH
Hatfield
Hatfield Chase
Eaton
Upper Cudworth
Grimethorpe
Hooton Pagnell
ADWICK LE STREET
Toll Bar
Thorpe Marsh
Barnby Dun
Dunscroft
Kirk Sandall
Almholme
Dunsville
Hatfield Woodhouse
Hatfield Moors
Sandtoft
Trolleybus
Westgate
Grey Green
Cudworth
Clayton
Woodlands
New Village
Arksey
West Carr
Belton
Carrhouse
Church Town
Monk Bretton
Priory
Ardsley
Great Houghton
Little Houghton
Thurnscoe
Brodsworth
Brodsworth Hall
Rostholme
BENTLEY
Edenthorpe
Armthorpe
ISLE OF AXHOLME
Epworth
Epworth Turbary
Wroot
Middlecliffe
DEARNE
Hickleton
Marr
Scawsby
Cusworth
Wheatley Park
Wheatley
Nutwell
Doncaster
Cantley
Darfield
Billingley
Goldthorpe
Barnburgh
South Yorkshire Life
Bolton upon Dearne
Broomhill
Adwick upon Dearne
Harlington
DONCASTER
Sprotbrough
Hyde Park
Bessacarr
Branton
Low Burnham
Haxey Turbary
Axholme Line
Rush Furlong
Owston
Wombwell
DEARNE VALLEY
Jump
Brampton
Hemingfield
MEXBOROUGH
High Melton
Sprotbrough Flash
Cadeby
Denaby Ings
Balby
Warmsworth
Auckley
Blaxton
Westwoodside
Upperthorpe
Haxey
East Lound
Elsecar
Wentworth
WATH UPON DEARNE
SWINTON
Denaby Main
CONISBROUGH
New Edlington
Old Edlington
Loversall
Rossington
Finningley
ROBIN HOOD DONCASTER SHEFFIELD
Graiseland
Upper Haugh
Kilnhurst
RAWMARSH
Nether Haugh
Thorpe Hesley
Hooton Roberts
Thrybergh
Ravenfield
Clifton
Wadworth
New Rossington
R. Idle
Heckdyke
West Stockwith
Keppels Column
Greasbrough
Dalton
Sunnyside
Braithwell
Micklebring
Stainton
Austerfield
Misson
Newington
East Stockwith
ROTHERHAM
Dalton Magna
Bramley
MALTBY
Tickhill
Tickhill Castle
Bawtry
Walkerith
Walkeringham
Magna
Tinsley
Moorgate
Wickersley
Whiston
Hooton Levitt
Maltby Low Common
Styrrup
Harworth
Bircotes
Scaftworth
Scrooby
Everton
Gringley on the Hill
Beckingham
Brinsworth
Catcliffe
Morthen
Thurcroft
Slade Hooton
Roche Abbey
Firbeck
Oldcotes
Serlby
Mattersey Thorpe
Mattersey
Wiseton
Mattersey Priory
Clayworth
Treeton
Upper Whiston
Brookhouse
Laughton en le Morthen
Dyscarr Wood
BLYTH
Ranskill
Saundby
Ulley
Handsworth
Aughton
Hardwick
Laughton Common
Dinnington
Letwell
Langold
Blyth
Torworth
Daneshill Gravel Pits (North)
Lound
North Wheatley
Bole
Hodsock Priory
M62
M1
M18
M180
A1(M)
A1
A19
A63
A64
A614
A162
A645
A639
A628
A638
A6021
A635
A630
A6195
A6023
A6182
A18
A631
A634
A6123
A614
A163
A161
A1041
A1238
A659
A656
A6032
A6136
A6139
B1223
B1222
B1228
B1217
B1220
B1396
B6045
B6463
B6094
B6376
B6422
B6428
B6474
B6273
B6411
B6097
B6089
B6090
B6091
B6093
B6060
B6067
B6200
B1403

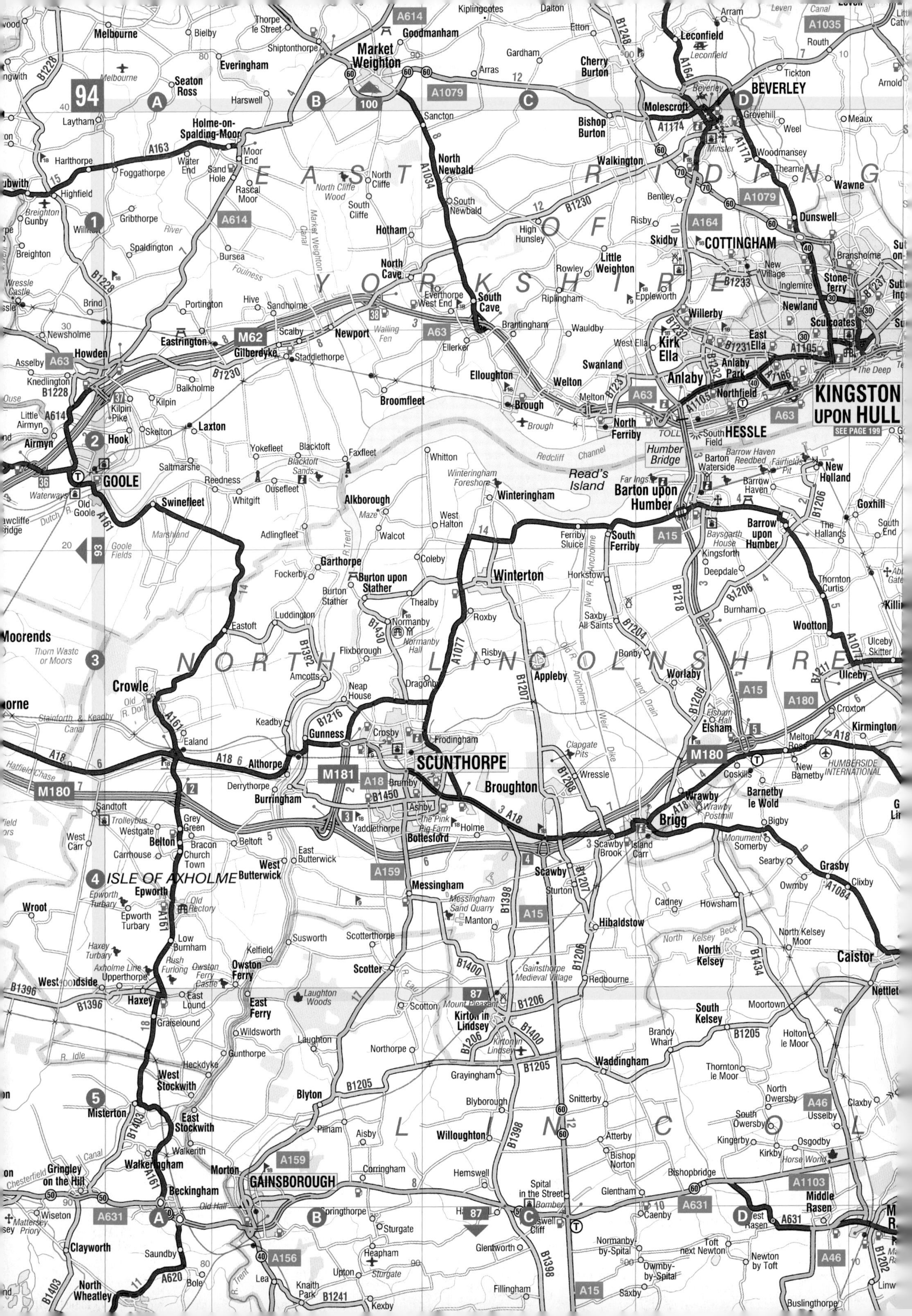
94
93
87
100
A
B
C
D
1
2
3
4
5
Melbourne
Bielby
Thorpe le Street
A614
Kiplingcotes
Dalton
Arram
Leven
Canal
A1035
Goodmanham
Shiptonthorpe
Market Weighton
Etton
B1248
Leconfield
Routh
Everingham
Gardham
Cherry Burton
Arras
A1079
Tickton
Arnold
Seaton Ross
Harswell
Sancton
Bishop Burton
Molescroft
BEVERLEY
Grovehill
Meaux
Laytham
Holme-on-Spalding-Moor
A163
Moor End
Water End
Sand Hole
Foggathorpe
Hartlhorpe
Highfield
Rascal Moor
North Newbald
South Newbald
North Cliffe
North Cliffe Wood
South Cliffe
A1034
Walkington
B1230
A1174
A164
Woodmansey
Weel
Thearne
Wawne
EAST RIDING OF YORKSHIRE
Breighton
Gunby
Willitoft
Gribthorpe
A614
River Foulness
Spaldington
Bursea
Hotham
Market Weighton Canal
High Hunsley
Bentley
Risby
Skidby
COTTINGHAM
A1079
Dunswell
Little Weighton
Rowley
North Cave
Riplingham
Eppleworth
New Village
Bransholme
Inglemire
Stoneferry
Wressle Castle
Brind
Portington
Hive
Sandholme
Everthorpe
West End
South Cave
B1233
Willerby
Newland
Sculcoates
Newsholme
Eastrington
M62
Scalby
Newport
Walling Fen
A63
Brantingham
Wauldby
West Ella
Kirk Ella
East Ella
B1231
A1105
Asselby
Howden
Gilberdyke
Staddlethorpe
Ellerker
Swanland
Anlaby Park
Knedlington
B1228
Balkholme
Elloughton
Welton
Anlaby
A1166
The Deep
Ouse
Little Airmyn
A614
Airmyn
Kilpin
Kilpin Pike
Broomfield
Melton
Northfield
KINGSTON UPON HULL
SEE PAGE 199
Hook
Skelton
Laxton
Brough
North Ferriby
A1105
HESSLE
South Field
TOLL
Yokefleet
Blacktoft
Faxfleet
Whitton
Redcliff Channel
Humber Bridge
Barton Waterside
Barrow Haven Reedbed
Fairfields Pit
New Holland
GOOLE
Saltmarshe
Reedness
Blacktoft Sands
Winteringham Foreshore
Read's Island
Far Ings
Barton upon Humber
Barrow Haven
Waterways
Old Goole
Whitgift
Ousefleet
Winteringham
Swinefleet
Alkborough
Maze
West Halton
Goxhill
Dutch R.
A161
Adlingfleet
Walcot
Ferriby Sluice
South Ferriby
A15
Baysgarth House
Barrow upon Humber
South End
The Hallands
Goole Fields
Marshland
Garthorpe
Coleby
Winterton
Horkstow
Kingsforth
Deepdale
Thornton Curtis
Fockerby
Burton upon Stather
Burton Stather
Thealby
New River Ancholme
B1218
B1206
Burnham
Luddington
Normanby
Normanby Hall
Roxby
Saxby All Saints
B1204
Wootton
Moorends
Eastoft
B1430
B1392
A1077
Ulceby Skitter
Thorn Waste or Moors
Flixborough
Risby
Bonby
NORTH LINCOLNSHIRE
Old R. Ancholme
Land Drain
Worlaby
Ulceby
Amcotts
Dragonby
Appleby
B1207
B1211
A15
A180
Crowle
Neap House
Elsham Hall
Elsham
Croxton
Old R. Don
Stainforth & Keadby Canal
Keadby
B1216
Gunness
Crosby
Frodingham
Weir Dike
Clapgate Pits
Kirmington
A161
Ealand
A18
Melton Ross
HUMBERSIDE INTERNATIONAL
Hatfield Chase
Althorpe
SCUNTHORPE
M180
Coskills
New Barnetby
M181
Derrythorpe
Brumby
Broughton
B1208
Wressle
Barnetby le Wold
Sandtoft
Trolleybus
Burringham
B1450
Ashby
Wrawby
Wrawby Postmill
Brigg
Grey Green
Westgate
Yaddlethorpe
The Pink Pig Farm
Holme
Bigby
West Carr
Belton
Bracon
Church Town
Beltoft
Bottesford
Scawby Brook
Island Carr
Monument
Somerby
Carrhouse
East Butterwick
West Butterwick
Searby
Grasby
Clixby
ISLE OF AXHOLME
A159
Messingham
Scawby
Sturton
Owmby
A1084
Epworth
Old Rectory
Epworth Turbary
Wroot
Messingham Sand Quarry
Manton
B1398
Cadney
Howsham
A15
Hibaldstow
North Kelsey Moor
Haxey Turbary
Low Burnham
Susworth
Scotterthorpe
North Kelsey Beck
North Kelsey
B1434
Caistor
Axholme Line
Kelfield
Rush Furlong
Owston Ferry
Owston Ferry Castle
Scotter
R. Eau
Gainsthorpe Medieval Village
Redbourne
Nettleton
Upperthorpe
Westwoodside
B1396
Haxey
East Lound
East Ferry
Laughton Woods
Scotton
Mount Pleasant
Kirton in Lindsey
B1206
Moortown
South Kelsey
Graiseland
Wildsworth
B1400
Brandy Wharf
B1205
Holton le Moor
R. Idle
Gunthorpe
Laughton
Northorpe
Kirton in Lindsey
Heckdyke
Waddingham
Thornton le Moor
West Stockwith
Grayingham
Blyton
Misterton
North Owersby
Claxby
Blyborough
Snitterby
East Stockwith
Pilham
Aisby
LINCOL
Willoughton
South Owersby
A46
Usselby
Atterby
Kingerby
Osgodby
Walkerith
Kirkby
Horse World
Bishop Norton
Chesterfield Canal
Gringley on the Hill
Walkeringham
Morton
A159
Corringham
Hemswell
Bishopbridge
A1103
Spital in the Street
Glentham
Middle Rasen
Beckingham
GAINSBOROUGH
Bomber
A631
Old Hall
Springthorpe
Caenby
A631
West Rasen
Wiseton
Mattersey Priory
Sturgate
Hemswell Cliff
Glentworth
B1398
Clayworth
Saundby
Normanby-by-Spital
Owmby-by-Spital
Toft next Newton
Newton by Toft
A46
A156
Heapham
Sturgate
A620
Bole
North Wheatley
Lea
Upton
B1403
B1241
Knaith Park
Kexby
Fillingham
A15
Saxby
Buslingthorpe
B1202
Linwood

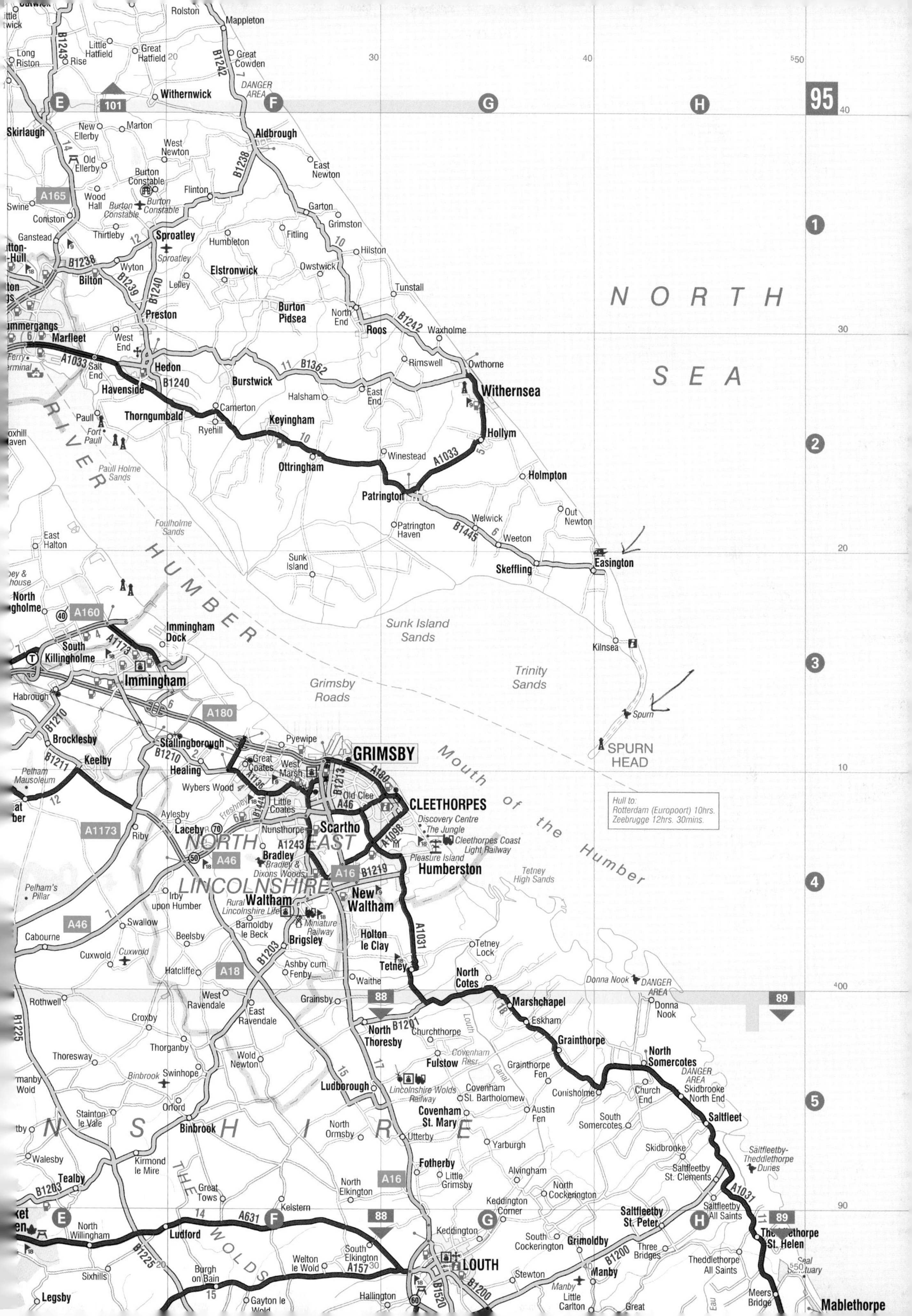
95
NORTH SEA
RIVER HUMBER
Mouth of the Humber
GRIMSBY
CLEETHORPES
Immingham
LOUTH
Withernsea
Hedon
Patrington
Easington
SPURN HEAD
Spurn
Kilnsea
Sunk Island Sands
Trinity Sands
Grimsby Roads
NORTH EAST LINCOLNSHIRE
Hull to:
Rotterdam (Europoort) 10hrs.
Zeebrugge 12hrs. 30mins.
Aldbrough
Roos
Hollym
Holmpton
Skeffling
Keyingham
Ottringham
Thorngumbald
Burstwick
Sproatley
Skirlaugh
Marfleet
Preston
Bilton
Humberston
New Waltham
Waltham
Scartho
Laceby
Healing
Stallingborough
Keelby
Brocklesby
North Thoresby
Marshchapel
Grainthorpe
North Somercotes
Saltfleet
Saltfleetby St. Peter
Tetney
Holton le Clay
Fulstow
Ludborough
Covenham St. Mary
Binbrook
Ludford
Tealby
Manby
Grimoldby
Mablethorpe
Theddlethorpe St. Helen
Cleethorpes Coast Light Railway
Lincolnshire Wolds Railway
DANGER AREA
Donna Nook
101
88
89
A1033
A180
A46
A16
A18
A1173
A160
A631
A157
A1031
B1242
B1362
B1445
B1200
E F G H
1 2 3 4 5

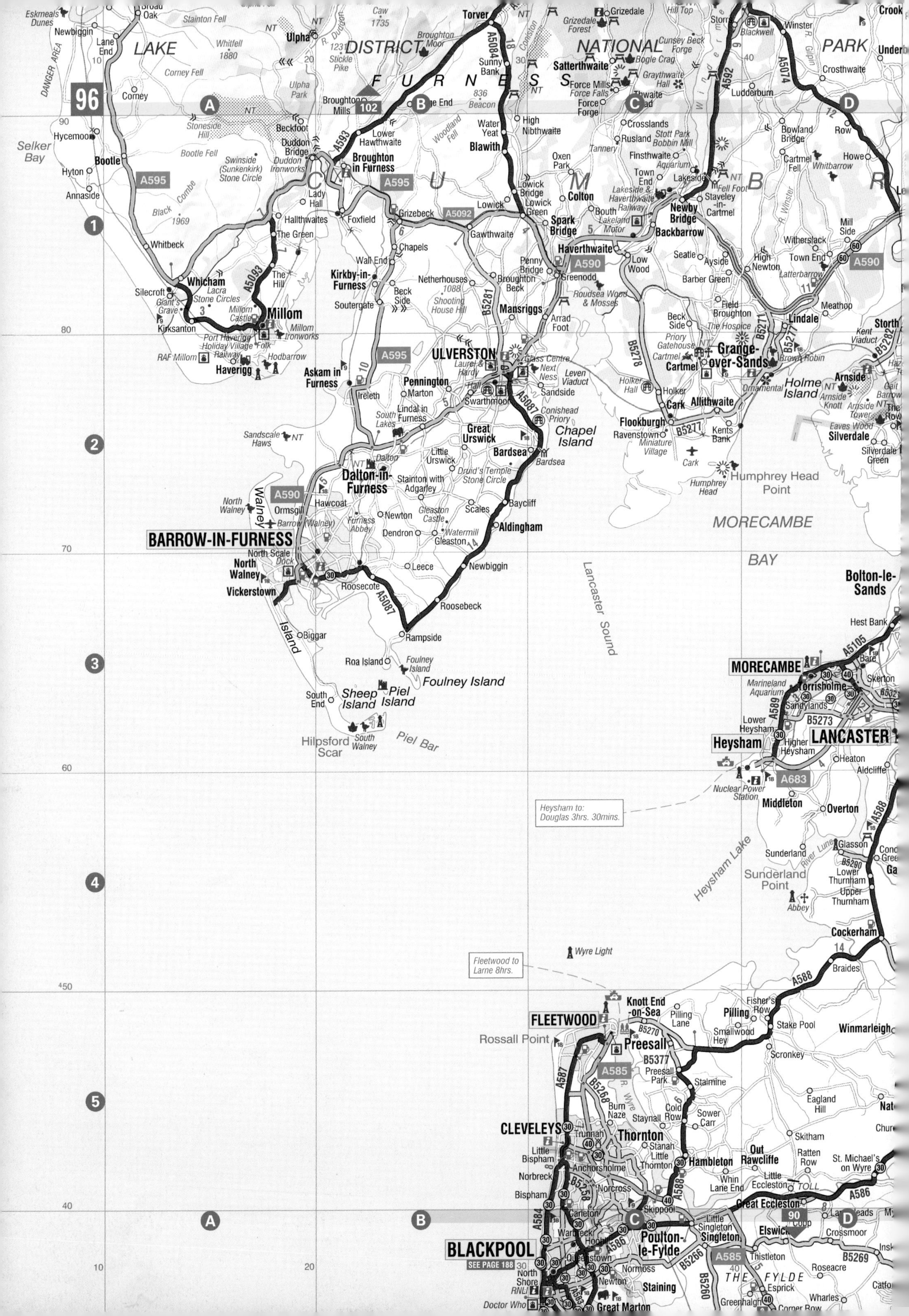

96
LAKE
DISTRICT
NATIONAL
PARK
FURNESS
CUMBRIA
A
B
C
D
1
2
3
4
5
102
90
Selker Bay
Bootle
Hycemoor
Hyton
Annaside
Newbiggin
Eskmeals Dunes
DANGER AREA
Lane End
Corney
Corney Fell
Stainton Fell
Whitfell 1880
Ulpha
Ulpha Park
Stickle Pike
Caw 1735
Broughton Moor
Torver
Coniston
Grizedale
Grizedale Forest
Hill Top
Satterthwaite
Bogle Crag
Cunsey Beck Forge
Graythwaite Hall
Force Mills
Force Falls
Force Forge
Thwaite Head
Storrs
Blackwell
Winster
Crook
Underbarrow
Crosthwaite
Lydderburn
Bowland Bridge
Row
Howe
Cartmel Fell
Whitbarrow
Stoneside Hill
Beckfoot
Duddon Bridge
Duddon Ironworks
Bootle Fell
Swinside (Sunkenkirk) Stone Circle
Broughton Mills
Broughton in Furness
Lower Hawthwaite
Woodland Fell
Water Yeat
Blawith
High Nibthwaite
Crosslands
Rusland
Stott Park Bobbin Mill
Finsthwaite
Aquarium
Oxen Park
Tannery
Town End
Lakeside
Fell Foot
Lakeside & Haverthwaite Railway
Newby Bridge
Staveley-in-Cartmel
Backbarrow
Black Combe 1969
Lady Hall
Foxfield
Grizebeck
Lowick
Lowick Bridge
Lowick Green
Colton
Bouth
Lakeland Motor
Spark Bridge
Haverthwaite
Low Wood
Hallthwaites
The Green
Whitbeck
Chapels
Gawthwaite
Mill Side
Witherslack
Town End
High Newton
Seatle
Ayside
Barber Green
Latterbarrow
Meathop
Lindale
Field Broughton
The Hospice
Beck Side
Priory Gatehouse
Cartmel
Grange-over-Sands
Brown Robin
Kent Viaduct
Storth
Arnside
Arnside Knott
Arnside Tower
Holme Island
Silverdale
Silverdale Green
Eaves Wood
Whicham
Lacra Stone Circles
The Hill
Silecroft
Giant's Grave
Kirksanton
Millom
Millom Castle
Millom Ironworks
Port Haverigg Holiday Village
RAF Millom
Haverigg
Hodbarrow
Wall End
Kirkby-in-Furness
Beck Side
Soutergate
Netherhouses
Shooting House Hill
Broughton Beck
Penny Bridge
Greenodd
Roudsea Wood & Mosses
Mansriggs
Arrad Foot
Askam in Furness
Ireleth
ULVERSTON
Laurel & Hardy
Glass Centre
Next Ness
Leven Viaduct
Sandside
Pennington
Marton
Lindal in Furness
South Lakes
Swarthmoor
Conishead Priory
Chapel Island
Holker Hall
Holker
Cark
Allithwaite
Flookburgh
Ravenstown
Miniature Village
Kents Bank
Humphrey Head
Humphrey Head Point
Sandscale Haws
Dalton
Dalton-in-Furness
Little Urswick
Great Urswick
Bardsea
Druid's Temple Stone Circle
Stainton with Adgarley
North Walney
Walney
A590
Ormsgill
Hawcoat
Barrow (Walney)
Furness Abbey
Newton
Gleaston Castle
Scales
Baycliff
Aldingham
Dendron
Watermill
Gleaston
BARROW-IN-FURNESS
North Scale
Dock
North Walney
Vickerstown
Leece
Newbiggin
Roosecote
Roosebeck
Rampside
Biggar
Walney Island
Lancaster Sound
MORECAMBE
BAY
Bolton-le-Sands
Hest Bank
Bare
Skerton
Roa Island
Foulney Island
Piel Island
Sheep Island
South End
Hilpsford Scar
South Walney
Piel Bar
MORECAMBE
Marineland Aquarium
Torrisholme
Sandylands
LANCASTER
Lower Heysham
Heysham
Higher Heysham
Heaton
Aldcliffe
Nuclear Power Station
Middleton
Overton
Heysham to: Douglas 3hrs. 30mins.
Heysham Lake
Sunderland
Glasson
River Lune
Lower Thurnham
Upper Thurnham
Sunderland Point
Abbey
Cockerham
Braides
Wyre Light
Fleetwood to Larne 8hrs.
Knott End-on-Sea
Pilling Lane
Pilling
Fisher's Row
Stake Pool
Smallwood Hey
Winmarleigh
FLEETWOOD
Rossall Point
Preesall
Scronkey
Preesall Park
Stalmine
Eagland Hill
Burn Naze
Staynall
Cold Row
Sower Carr
Skitham
CLEVELEYS
Trunnah
Thornton
Stanah
Little Thornton
Little Bispham
Hambleton
Out Rawcliffe
Ratten Row
St. Michael's on Wyre
Anchorsholme
Norbreck
Whin Lane End
Little Eccleston
TOLL
Bispham
Norcross
Great Eccleston
Carleton
Skippool
Little Singleton
Singleton
Elswick
Crossmoor
Poulton-le-Fylde
BLACKPOOL
SEE PAGE 188
Warbreck
Hoohill
Queenstown
North Shore
RNLI
Normoss
Staining
Newton
Great Marton
Doctor Who
Thistleton
THE FYLDE
Roseacre
Esprick
Greenhalgh
Wharles
Corner Row
90
A595
A5092
A5084
A593
A5093
A592
A5074
B5281
B5278
B5277
B5271
B5282
A5087
A590
A5105
A589
B5273
A683
A588
B5290
A587
A585
B5268
B5270
B5377
A586
A584
B5266
B5260
B5269
10
20
40
450
60
70
80

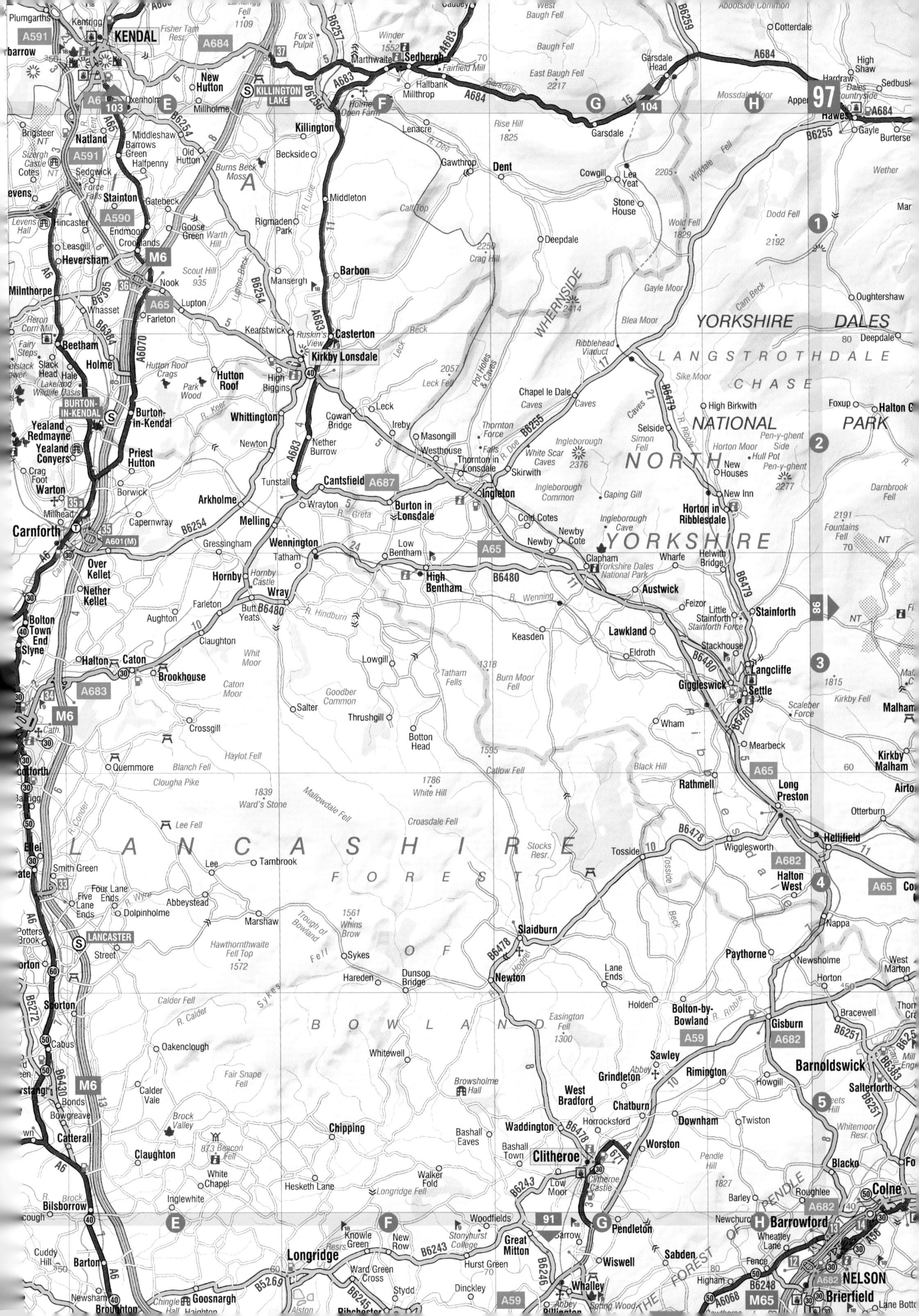

Plumgarths
Kentrigg
KENDAL
A591
A684
Fisher Tarn Resr
Lambrigg Fell 1109
Fox's Pulpit
B6257
Winder 1552
Marthwaite
Sedbergh
A683
West Baugh Fell
Baugh Fell
East Baugh Fell 2217
B6259
Abbotside Common
Cotterdale
Garsdale Head
A684
High Shaw
Hardraw
Dales Countryside
Sedbusk
Appersett
Hawes
97
Mossdale Moor
Gayle
Burtersett
B6255
103
104
E
F
G
H
Oxenholme
New Hutton
Millholme
KILLINGTON LAKE
Hallbank
Millthrop
Fairfield Mill
Garsdale
Holme Open Farm
Killington
Lenacre
Rise Hill 1825
R. Dee
Brigsteer NT
Natland
Middleshaw
Barrows Green
Old Hutton
Halfpenny
Sizergh Castle NT
Cotes
Sedgwick
Force Falls
Beckside
Burns Beck Moss
Gawthrop
Dent
Cowgill
Lea Yeat
Widdale Fell
2205
Wether
Levens
Stainton
Gatebeck
A590
Levens Hall
Hincaster
Endmoor
Goose Green
Warth Hill
Rigmaden Park
Middleton
R. Lune
Calf Top
Stone House
Dodd Fell
Wold Fell 1829
2192
Crooklands
Leasgill
Heversham
M6
Deepdale
Crag Hill 2250
Scout Hill 935
Mansergh
Barbon
Milnthorpe
Nook
B6385
A65
Lupton
Whasset
Farleton
Lupton Beck
B6254
WHERNSIDE 2414
Gayle Moor
Cam Beck
Oughtershaw
Heron Corn Mill
Fairy Steps
Beetham
Kearstwick
Casterton
Ruskin's View
Leck Beck
Blea Moor
YORKSHIRE DALES
Deepdale
Ribblehead Viaduct
LANGSTROTHDALE CHASE
Sike Moor
Slack Head
Hale
Holme
Lakeland Wildlife Oasis
A6070
Hutton Roof Crags
Park Wood
Hutton Roof
Kirkby Lonsdale
High Biggins
2057 Leck Fell
Pot Holes & Caves
Chapel le Dale
Caves
High Birkwith
Foxup
Halton Gill
NATIONAL PARK
BURTON-IN-KENDAL
Burton-in-Kendal
Yealand Redmayne
Yealand Conyers
R. Keer
Whittington
Cowan Bridge
Leck
Ireby
Masongill
Thornton Force
B6255
Selside
Simon Fell
R. Ribble
Pen-y-ghent Side
Crag Foot
Priest Hutton
Newton
Nether Burrow
Westhouse
Falls
Ingleborough 2376
White Scar Caves
NORTH
Horton Moor
New Houses
Hull Pot
Pen-y-ghent 2277
Darnbrook Fell
Warton
Borwick
Tunstall
Thornton in Lonsdale
Skirwith
Ingleborough Common
Gaping Gill
New Inn
Millhead
Arkholme
Cantsfield
A687
Ingleton
Horton in Ribblesdale
Carnforth
Capernwray
Wrayton
Burton in Lonsdale
R. Greta
Cold Cotes
Newby Cote
Newby
Ingleborough Cave
YORKSHIRE
2191 Fountains Fell
A601(M)
Melling
Over Kellet
Gressingham
Wennington
Low Bentham
Tatham
Clapham
Yorkshire Dales National Park
Wharfe
Helwith Bridge
B6479
Nether Kellet
Hornby
Hornby Castle
Wray
High Bentham
B6480
R. Wenning
Austwick
Stainforth
86
Bolton Town End
Farleton
Butt Yeats
R. Hindburn
Feizor
Little Stainforth
Stainforth Force
Slyne
Aughton
Claughton
Keasden
Lawkland
Eldroth
Stackhouse
Halton
Caton
Whit Moor
Lowgill
Tatham Fells
1318
Burn Moor Fell
Langcliffe
Brookhouse
Caton Moor
Goodber Common
Giggleswick
Settle
1815
Kirkby Fell
Malham
A683
Salter
Thrushgill
Scaleber Force
Wham
Crossgill
Botton Head
Cath.
Mearbeck
Quernmore
Blanch Fell
Haylot Fell
1595
Catlow Fell
Black Hill
Kirkby Malham
Clougha Pike
Rathmell
Long Preston
Airton
1839 Ward's Stone
Mallowdale Fell
1786 White Hill
Otterburn
Lee Fell
Croasdale Fell
R. Conder
Stocks Resr.
Hellifield
LANCASHIRE
B6478
Tosside
Wigglesworth
A682
Ellel
Lee
Tarnbrook
FOREST
Halton West
Smith Green
Four Lane Ends
Five Lane Ends
Dolphinholme
R. Wyre
Abbeystead
Trough of Bowland
Marshaw
1561 Whins Brow
Slaidburn
Nappa
LANCASTER
Potters Brook
Street
Hawthornthwaite Fell Top 1572
Sykes Fell
Sykes
OF
Paythorne
Newsholme
West Marton
Hareden
Dunsop Bridge
Newton
R. Hodder
Lane Ends
Horton
Scorton
Calder Fell
R. Calder
BOWLAND
Easington Fell 1300
Holden
Bolton-by-Bowland
R. Ribble
Gisburn
Bracewell
B5272
Cabus
Oakenclough
A59
B6251
Whitewell
Sawley
Abbey
Rimington
Barnoldswick
Fair Snape Fell
B6430
Calder Vale
Browsholme Hall
Grindleton
West Bradford
Howgill
Salterforth
Bonds
Bowgreave
Chatburn
Downham
Twiston
Brock Valley
Chipping
Waddington
Horrocksford
Whitemoor Resr.
Catterall
Claughton
Beacon Fell 873
Bashall Eaves
Bashall Town
Worston
Pendle Hill 1827
Clitheroe
Blacko
White Chapel
Walker Fold
Low Moor
Clitheroe Castle
B6243
Hesketh Lane
Longridge Fell
Inglewhite
R. Brock
Bilsborrow
Barley
Roughlee
Colne
Newchurch
Barrowford
Woodfields
91
Pendleton
Knowle Green
New Row
Stonyhurst College
Great Mitton
Barrow
Wheatley Lane
PENDLE
Cuddy Hill
Barton
Longridge
Resrs
B6243
Hurst Green
Wiswell
Sabden
Fence
Ward Green Cross
B6246
THE FOREST OF PENDLE
Higham
B6248
NELSON
Newsham
Broughton
Chingle Hall
Goosnargh
Haighton
B5269
Alston
Stydd
B6245
Ribchester
Dinckley
A59
Whalley
Abbey
Billington
Spring Wood
A6068
M65
Brierfield
Lane Bottom
1
2
3
4
5

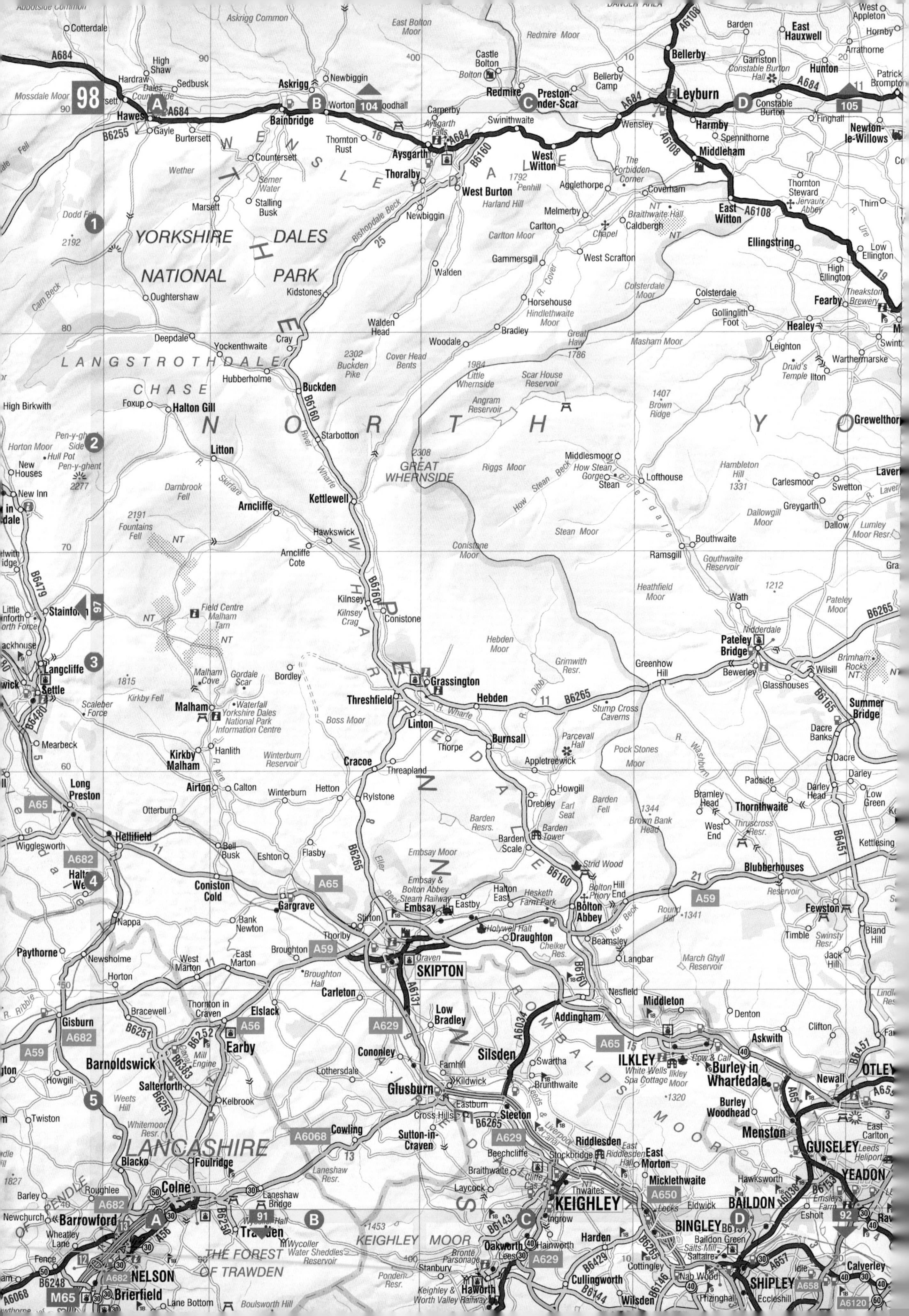

Abbotside Common
Cotterdale
Askrigg Common
East Bolton Moor
DANGER AREA
A6108
Redmire Moor
Barden
East Hauxwell
West Appleton
Hornby
A684
High Shaw
Hardraw
Dales Countryside
Sedbusk
Askrigg
Newbiggin
Castle Bolton
Bolton
Bellerby
Bellerby Camp
Garriston
Constable Burton Hall
Arrathorne
Hunton
Patrick Brompton
Mossdale Moor
98
Hawes
A684
Bainbridge
Worton
104
Woodhall
Carperby
Aysgarth Falls
Redmire
Preston-under-Scar
Leyburn
Constable Burton
105
Finghall
Newton-le-Willows
Gayle
B6255
Burtersett
Thornton Rust
Aysgarth
Swinithwaite
Wensley
Harmby
Spennithorne
Countersett
West Witton
A6108
Middleham
WENSLEYDALE
Wether Fell
Semer Water
Stalling Busk
Marsett
Thoralby
West Burton
B6160
1792 Penhill
Harland Hill
Agglethorpe
The Forbidden Corner
Coverham
Thornton Steward
Jervaulx Abbey
East Witton
A6108
Thirn
Dodd Fell
2192
YORKSHIRE DALES NATIONAL PARK
Bishopdale Beck
Newbiggin
Melmerby
Braithwaite Hall
Carlton
Caldbergh
Carlton Moor
Chapel
Ellingstring
West Scrafton
Gammersgill
Low Ellington
High Ellington
Walden
Cam Beck
Oughtershaw
Kidstones
Horsehouse
Hindlethwaite Moor
Colsterdale Moor
Colsterdale
Gollinglith Foot
Fearby
Theakston Brewery
Healey
Walden Head
Deepdale
Yockenthwaite
Cray
Woodale
Bradley
Great Haw 1786
Masham Moor
Leighton
Swinton
Warthermarske
LANGSTROTHDALE CHASE
2302 Buckden Pike
Cover Head Bents
1984 Little Whernside
Scar House Reservoir
Druid's Temple
Ilton
Hubberholme
Buckden
Angram Reservoir
1407 Brown Ridge
Foxup
Halton Gill
High Birkwith
B6160
NORTH YORKSHIRE
Grewelthorpe
Pen-y-ghent Side
Horton Moor
Hull Pot
Pen-y-ghent 2277
Starbotton
Litton
River Wharfe
2308 GREAT WHERNSIDE
Middlesmoor
How Stean Gorge
Stean
Lofthouse
Riggs Moor
Hambleton Hill 1331
Carlesmoor
Swetton
New Houses
New Inn
Darnbrook Fell
R. Skirfare
Arncliffe
Kettlewell
Stean Moor
Nidderdale
Greygarth
Dallowgill Moor
Dallow
Lumley Moor Resr.
2191 Fountains Fell
NT
Hawkswick
Arncliffe Cote
Coniston Moor
Bouthwaite
Ramsgill
Gouthwaite Reservoir
B6479
Heathfield Moor
1212
Field Centre Malham Tarn
Kilnsey
Kilnsey Crag
B6160
Conistone
Wath
Pateley Moor
Stainforth
97
NT
Langcliffe
Settle
B6480
Scaleber Force
Kirkby Fell
1815
Malham Cove
Gordale Scar
Bordley
Hebden Moor
Grimwith Resr.
Grassington
Nidderdale
Pateley Bridge
Bewerley
Greenhow Hill
Brimham Rocks NT
Wilsill
Glasshouses
Malham
Waterfall
Yorkshire Dales National Park Information Centre
Threshfield
Hebden
B6265
Stump Cross Caverns
Dibb
Linton
R. Wharfe
Boss Moor
Burnsall
Thorpe
Parcevall Hall
B6165
Summer Bridge
Dacre Banks
Dacre
Mearbeck
Hanlith
Kirkby Malham
Winterburn Reservoir
Cracoe
Threapland
Appletreewick
Pock Stones Moor
R. Washburn
Long Preston
Airton
Calton
R. Aire
Winterburn
Hetton
Rylstone
Howgill
Barden Fell
Padside
Darley
Darley Head
Low Green
A65
Otterburn
Drebley
Earl Seat
1344 Brown Bank Head
Bramley Head
Thornthwaite
Thruscross Resr.
West End
Barden Resrs.
Barden Scale
Barden Tower
Hellifield
Wigglesworth
Bell Busk
Eshton
Flasby
Embsay Moor
B6451
Kettlesing
A682
Halton West
Strid Wood
B6160
Blubberhouses
Coniston Cold
A65
Embsay & Bolton Abbey Steam Railway
Halton East
Hesketh Farm Park
Bolton Priory
Hill End
21
A59
Reservoir
Gargrave
Embsay
Eastby
Bolton Abbey
Kex Beck
Round Hill 1341
Fewston
Nappa
Bank Newton
Stirton
Thorlby
Holywell Halt
Draughton
Beamsley
Timble
Swinsty Resr.
Bland Hill
Paythorne
Newsholme
West Marton
East Marton
Broughton
A59
Craven
SKIPTON
Chelker Res.
Langbar
March Ghyll Reservoir
Jack Hill
Horton
Broughton Hall
Carleton
B6160
Nesfield
Middleton
Denton
R. Ribble
Gisburn
A682
Bracewell
Thornton in Craven
Elslack
A56
A629
A6131
Low Bradley
Addingham
A6034
Clifton
A59
B6251
B6252
Earby
Mill Engine
Cononley
Silsden
A65
ILKLEY
White Wells Spa Cottage
Ilkley Moor
Cow & Calf
Burley in Wharfedale
Askwith
B6451
OTLEY
Barnoldswick
B6383
Howgill
Salterforth
Lothersdale
Farnhill
Kildwick
Glusburn
Swartha
Brunthwaite
Newall
Kelbrook
Eastburn
Cross Hills
Steeton
1320
Burley Woodhead
East Carlton
Twiston
Weets Hill
Whitemoor Resr.
A6068
Cowling
Sutton-in-Craven
B6265
A629
Leeds & Liverpool Canal
Riddlesden
East Riddlesden Hall
Menston
GUISELEY
Leeds Heliport
RUMBALDS MOOR
LANCASHIRE
Blacko
Foulridge
Laneshaw Resr.
Beechcliffe
Stockbridge
East Morton
Braithwaite
Cliffe Castle
Thwaites
Micklethwaite
Hawksworth
YEADON
Barley
Roughlee
Colne
A682
Laneshaw Bridge
Laycock
KEIGHLEY
A650
Locks
Eldwick
BAILDON
Esholt
Newchurch
Barrowford
91
Wycoller Hall
Trawden
1453
Ingrow
BINGLEY
Baildon Green
Salts Mill
Saltaire
92
Wheatley Lane
Wycoller
Water Sheddles Reservoir
KEIGHLEY MOOR
Oakworth
Lees
Hainworth
A629
Harden
B6429
Cottingley
Idle
Calverley
Fence
B6248
A682
NELSON
THE FOREST OF TRAWDEN
Brontë Parsonage
Stanbury
Ponden Resr.
Haworth
Cullingworth
Nab Wood
SHIPLEY
A658
Eccleshill
A6120
A6068
M65
Brierfield
Lane Bottom
Boulsworth Hill
Keighley & Worth Valley Railway
B6144
Wilsden
B6146
Frizinghall
A657

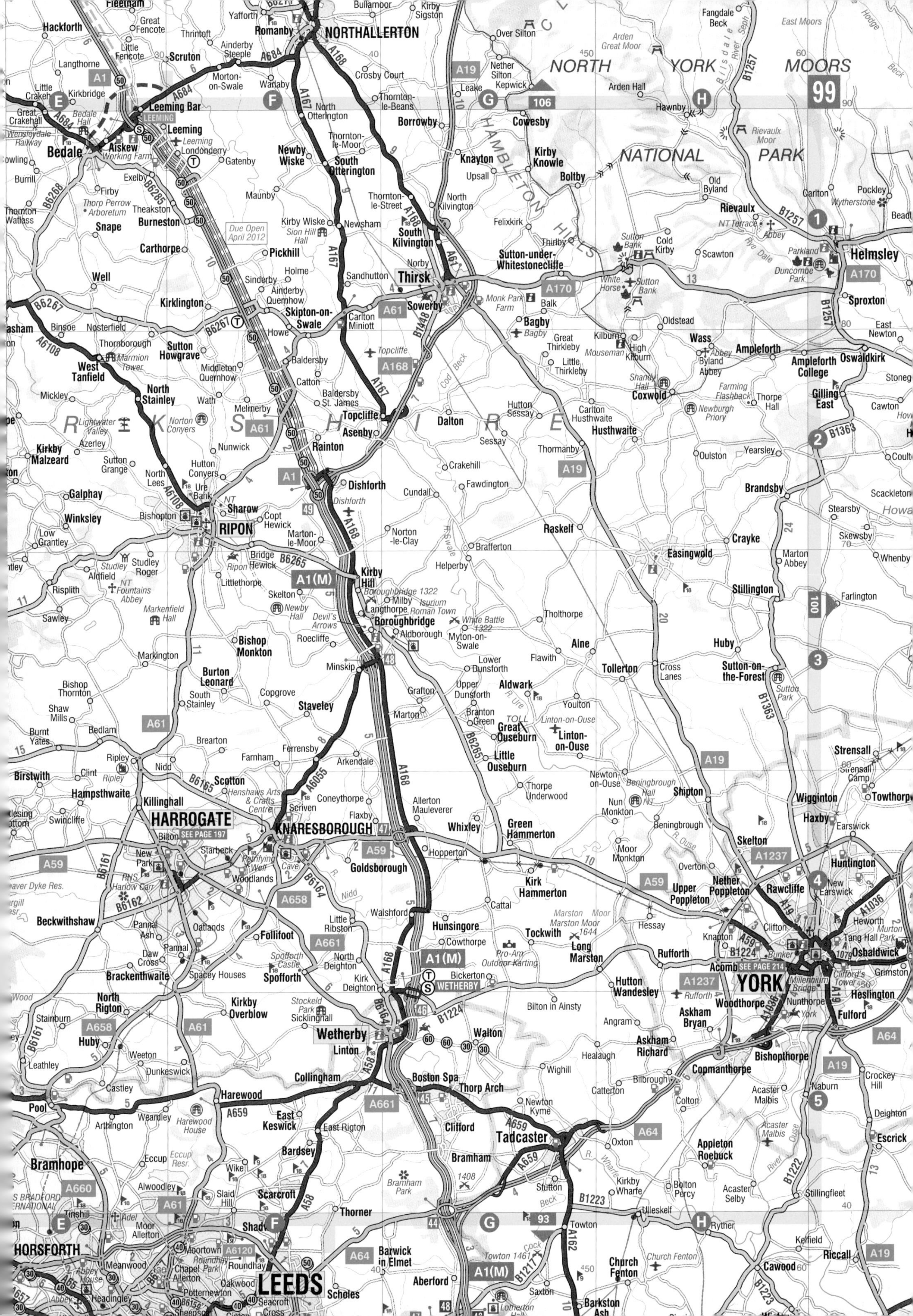

Hackforth
Great Fencote
Little Fencote
Thrintoft
Yafforth
Romanby
Ainderby Steeple
NORTHALLERTON
Bullamoor
Kirby Sigston
Over Silton
Fangdale Beck
East Moors
Arden Great Moor
NORTH YORK MOORS
99
Langthorne
Scruton
Morton-on-Swale
Warlaby
A684
A168
Crosby Court
A19
Nether Silton
Kepwick
Leake
Arden Hall
Bilsdale
B1257
Little Crakehall
Kirkbridge
Great Crakehall
Bedale Hall
Wensleydale Railway
Bedale
A1
Leeming Bar
LEEMING
North Otterington
Thornton-le-Beans
Borrowby
106
Cowesby
Hawnby
Aiskew
Leeming
Londonderry
Gatenby
Newby Wiske
Thornton-le-Moor
South Otterington
Knayton
Upsall
Kirby Knowle
Boltby
HAMBLETON HILLS
NATIONAL PARK
Rievaulx Moor
Burrill
Exelby
Firby
Thorp Perrow Arboretum
Thornton Watlass
Theakston
Burneston
Snape
Maunby
Thornton-le-Street
North Kilvington
Old Byland
Carlton
Pockley
Wytherstone
Rievaulx
NT Terrace
Abbey
Kirby Wiske
Sion Hill Hall
Newsham
South Kilvington
Felixkirk
Thirlby
Sutton Bank
Cold Kirby
Scawton
Parkland
Duncombe Park
Helmsley
Due Open April 2012
Carthorpe
Pickhill
Norby
Thirsk
Sutton-under-Whitestonecliffe
Well
Holme
Sinderby
Ainderby Quernhow
Sandhutton
Sowerby
A61
A170
White Horse
Monk Park Farm
Balk
Bagby
Kirklington
Skipton-on-Swale
Carlton Miniott
Oldstead
Kilburn
Wass
Sproxton
East Newton
Binsoe
Nosterfield
B6267
Thornborough
Marmion Tower
West Tanfield
Sutton Howgrave
Howe
Middleton Quernhow
Baldersby
Topcliffe
A168
Great Thirkleby
Little Thirkleby
Mouseman
High Kilburn
Byland Abbey
Ampleforth
Ampleforth College
Oswaldkirk
Stonegrave
Mickley
North Stainley
Catton
Baldersby St. James
Shandy Hall
Coxwold
Farming Flashback
Thorpe Hall
Gilling East
Cawton
Lightwater Valley
Norton Conyers
Wath
Melmerby
Asenby
Dalton
Hutton Sessay
Carlton Husthwaite
Husthwaite
Newburgh Priory
B1363
Kirkby Malzeard
Azerley
Nunwick
Rainton
Sessay
Thormanby
Oulston
Yearsley
Sutton Grange
North Lees
Hutton Conyers
Crakehill
Fawdington
Ure Bank
Dishforth
Cundall
Brandsby
Scackleton
Galphay
Sharow
Bishopton
RIPON
Copt Hewick
Winksley
Marton-le-Moor
Norton-le-Clay
Raskelf
Stearsby
Crayke
Skewsby
Low Grantley
Brafferton
Easingwold
Marton Abbey
Whenby
Studley Roger
Bridge Hewick
B6265
A1(M)
Kirby Hill
Helperby
Fountains Abbey
Aldfield
Risplith
Littlethorpe
Skelton
Newby Hall
Boroughbridge 1322
Milby
Isurium Roman Town
Langthorpe
Boroughbridge
Aldborough
Stillington
Farlington
100
Sawley
Markenfield Hall
Devil's Arrows
White Battle 1322
Myton-on-Swale
Tholthorpe
Roecliffe
Bishop Monkton
Alne
Huby
Sutton-on-the-Forest
Sutton Park
Markington
Minskip
Lower Dunsforth
Flawith
Tollerton
Cross Lanes
Bishop Thornton
Burton Leonard
South Stainley
Copgrove
Staveley
Grafton
Upper Dunsforth
Aldwark
Youlton
Shaw Mills
Bedlam
Burnt Yates
Marton
Branton Green
Great Ouseburn
Linton-on-Ouse
Little Ouseburn
Brearton
Ferrensby
Farnham
Arkendale
Strensall
Strensall Camp
Ripley
Nidd
Clint
Birstwith
Hampsthwaite
Killinghall
Scotton
Henshaws Arts & Crafts Centre
Coneythorpe
Scriven
Allerton Mauleverer
Thorpe Underwood
Newton-on-Ouse
Beningbrough Hall
Shipton
Nun Monkton
Wigginton
Towthorpe
Haxby
Earswick
HARROGATE
SEE PAGE 197
KNARESBOROUGH
Flaxby
Whixley
Green Hammerton
Beningbrough
Swincliffe
Bilton
Starbeck
Petrifying Well
Cave
A59
Goldsborough
Hopperton
Moor Monkton
Skelton
A1237
Huntington
New Park
Harlow Carr
Woodlands
B6164
Kirk Hammerton
Overton
Nether Poppleton
Upper Poppleton
Rawcliffe
New Earswick
Beaver Dyke Res.
B6162
A658
Cattal
Walshford
Hessay
Clifton
Heworth
Beckwithshaw
Pannal Ash
Oatlands
Follifoot
Little Ribston
Hunsingore
Cowthorpe
Marston Moor
Marston Moor 1644
Tockwith
Long Marston
Knapton
Tang Hall
Murton
Osbaldwick
Pannal
Daw Cross
Spofforth Castle
Spofforth
North Deighton
Kirk Deighton
A661
Pro-Am Outdoor Karting
Rufforth
Acomb
SEE PAGE 214
YORK
Bunker
Clifford's Tower
Millennium Bridge
Grimston
Brackenthwaite
Spacey Houses
Bickerton
WETHERBY
Hutton Wandesley
A1237
Rufforth
Heslington
North Rigton
Kirkby Overblow
Stockeld Park
Sicklinghall
Wetherby
B1224
Bilton in Ainsty
Askham Bryan
Woodthorpe
Nunthorpe
Fulford
Stainburn
Huby
A61
Linton
Walton
Angram
Askham Richard
Healaugh
Bishopthorpe
A64
Leathley
Weeton
Dunkeswick
Collingham
Wighill
Copmanthorpe
Crockey Hill
Castley
Harewood
Boston Spa
Thorp Arch
Catterton
Bilbrough
Acaster Malbis
Naburn
Pool
Weardley
Arthington
Harewood House
A659
East Keswick
East Rigton
Clifford
Newton Kyme
Tadcaster
Colton
Deighton
Bramhope
Eccup
Eccup Resr.
Bardsey
Bramham
Oxton
Appleton Roebuck
Escrick
A660
Alwoodley
Wike
Bramham Park
1408
Kirkby Wharfe
Stutton
Bolton Percy
Acaster Selby
Stillingfleet
Slaid Hill
Scarcroft
A58
B1223
Ulleskelf
Tinshill
Adel
Moor Allerton
Thorner
Shadwell
93
Towton
Ryther
Kelfield
HORSFORTH
Moortown
A6120
Roundhay
Barwick in Elmet
Towton 1461
Cock Beck
Church Fenton
Cawood
Riccall
Meanwood
Chapel Allerton
Roundhay Park
Abbey House
Oakwood
Potternewton
LEEDS
Scholes
Aberford
Saxton
Barkston Ash
Headingley
Seacroft
Cross
Lotherton Hall
A162

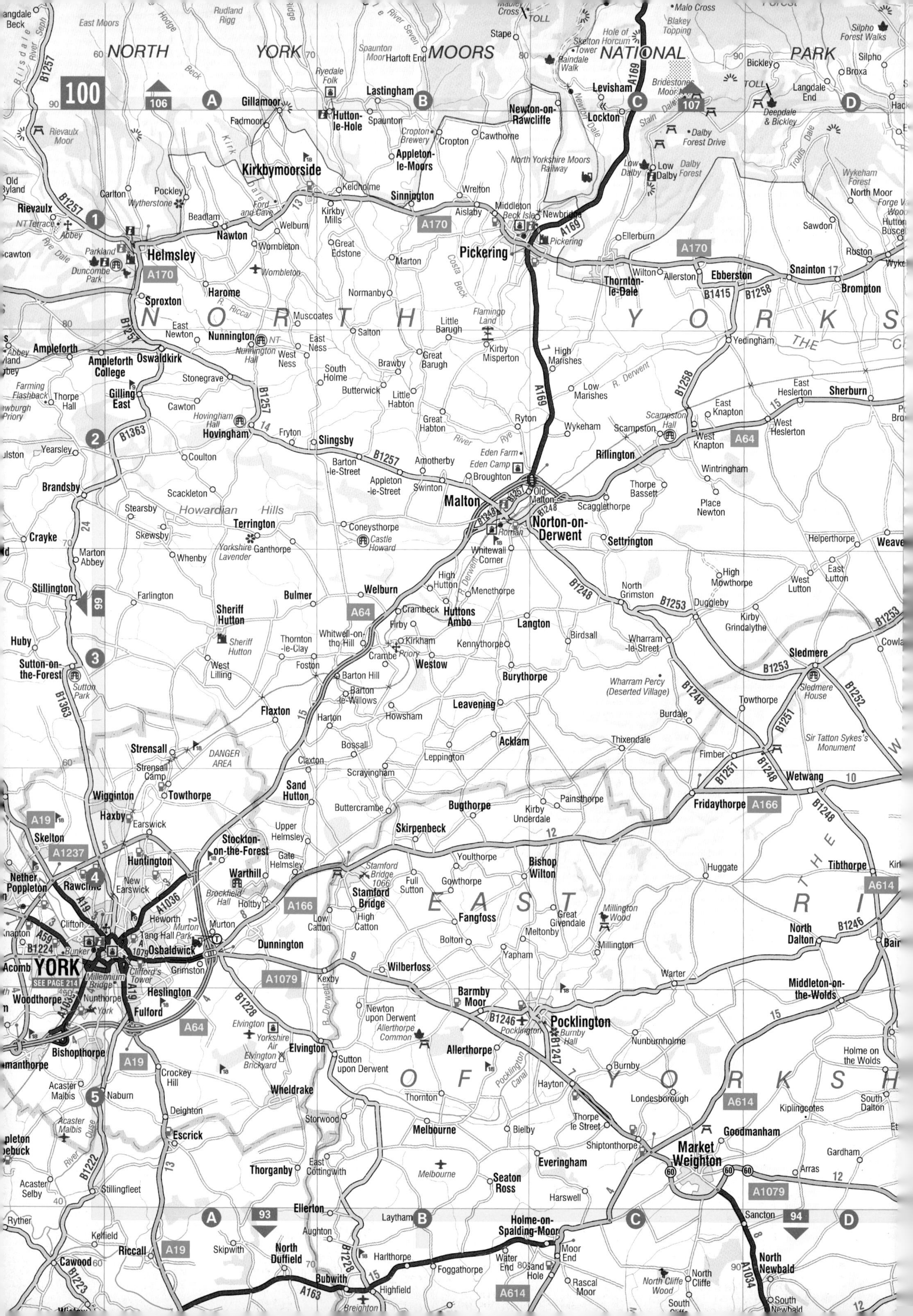
100
NORTH YORK MOORS NATIONAL PARK
106
107
99
93
94
A
B
C
D
1
2
3
4
5
Bilsdale
Beck
East Moors
Rudland Rigg
Hodge Beck
Spaunton Moor
Hartoft End
River Seven
Ryedale Folk
Hutton-le-Hole
Lastingham
Spaunton
Gillamoor
Fadmoor
Rievaulx Moor
Crossy Toll
Stape
Hole of Horcum
Skelton Horcum
Tower
Raindale Walk
Malo Cross
Blakey Topping
Silpho Forest Walks
Silpho
Bickley
Broxa
Langdale End
Deepdale & Bickley
Bridestones Moor
Levisham
Lockton
Newton-on-Rawcliffe
Newton Dale
Stain Dale
Dalby Forest Drive
Troutsdale
Cropton Brewery
Cropton
Cawthorne
Appleton-le-Moors
North Yorkshire Moors Railway
Low Dalby
Dalby Forest
Wykeham Forest
North Moor
Forge Valley Woods
Hutton Buscel
Old Byland
Rievaulx
NT Terrace
Abbey
Carlton
Pockley
Wytherstone
Kirkbymoorside
Keldholme
Sinnington
Wrelton
Middleton
Beck Isle
Newbridge
Aislaby
Kirkby Mills
Beadlam
Nawton
Welburn
Ford and Cave
Scawton
Rye Dale
Parkland
Duncombe Park
Helmsley
Wombleton
Great Edstone
Marton
Pickering
Ellerburn
Sawdon
Ruston
Wykeham
A170
A169
Thornton-le-Dale
Wilton
Allerston
Ebberston
Snainton
Brompton
B1415
B1258
Harome
Sproxton
Normanby
Costa Beck
R. Riccal
NORTH YORKS
East Newton
Nunnington
Nunnington Hall
Muscoates
East Ness
West Ness
Salton
Little Barugh
Flamingo Land
Kirby Misperton
High Marishes
Yedingham
THE
B1257
Abbey
Ampleforth
Ampleforth College
Oswaldkirk
Stonegrave
South Holme
Brawby
Great Barugh
Low Marishes
R. Derwent
East Heslerton
Sherburn
Farming Flashback
Thorpe Hall
Gilling East
Newburgh Priory
Cawton
Butterwick
Little Habton
Great Habton
Ryton
Wykeham
Scampston
Scampston Hall
East Knapton
West Knapton
West Heslerton
A64
Hovingham Hall
Hovingham
Fryton
Slingsby
B1363
Yearsley
Coulton
Barton-le-Street
Appleton-le-Street
Amotherby
Swinton
Eden Farm
Eden Camp
Broughton
Rillington
Wintringham
Brandsby
Scackleton
Howardian Hills
Malton
Old Malton
Thorpe Bassett
Scagglethorpe
Place Newton
Stearsby
Skewsby
Terrington
Coneysthorpe
Castle Howard
Norton-on-Derwent
Roman
Settrington
Helperthorpe
Weaverthorpe
Crayke
Yorkshire Lavender
Ganthorpe
Whitewall Corner
Marton Abbey
Whenby
High Hutton
High Mowthorpe
East Lutton
West Lutton
Stillington
Farlington
Sheriff Hutton
Bulmer
Welburn
Menethorpe
North Grimston
B1248
B1253
Duggleby
Kirby Grindalythe
Crambeck
Huttons Ambo
Langton
Firby
Huby
Thornton-le-Clay
Whitwell-on-the-Hill
Kirkham
Kirkham Priory
Crambe
Kennythorpe
Birdsall
Wharram-le-Street
Sledmere
Cowlam
Sutton-on-the-Forest
Sutton Park
West Lilling
Foston
Westow
Burythorpe
Wharram Percy (Deserted Village)
Sledmere House
B1252
Barton Hill
Barton-le-Willows
Howsham
Leavening
Towthorpe
Flaxton
Harton
Burdale
B1251
Sir Tatton Sykes's Monument
Strensall
DANGER AREA
Strensall Camp
Bossall
Claxton
Scrayingham
Leppington
Acklam
Thixendale
Fimber
Wetwang
Wigginton
Haxby
Towthorpe
Sand Hutton
Buttercrambe
Bugthorpe
Kirby Underdale
Painsthorpe
Fridaythorpe
A166
A19
Skelton
A1237
Earswick
Upper Helmsley
Stockton-on-the-Forest
Skirpenbeck
Huntington
Gate Helmsley
Stamford Bridge 1066
Youlthorpe
Bishop Wilton
Huggate
Tibthorpe
Nether Poppleton
Rawcliffe
New Earswick
Warthill
Full Sutton
Gowthorpe
A614
A1036
Brockfield Hall
Holtby
Stamford Bridge
EAST RIDING OF YORKSHIRE
Clifton
Heworth
Murton Park
Murton
Low Catton
High Catton
Fangfoss
Great Givendale
Millington Wood
Meltonby
Millington
North Dalton
B1246
Bainton
Acomb
A59
B1224
Bunker
Tang Hall Park
A1079
Osbaldwick
Dunnington
Bolton
Yapham
YORK
SEE PAGE 214
Millennium Bridge
Clifford's Tower
Grimston
Kexby
Wilberfoss
Warter
Middleton-on-the-Wolds
Woodthorpe
Nunthorpe
York
Heslington
B1228
R. Derwent
Barmby Moor
Fulford
Newton upon Derwent
Allerthorpe Common
B1246
Pocklington
Burnby Hall
Nunburnholme
Bishopthorpe
Elvington
Yorkshire Air Museum
Elvington Brickyard
Sutton upon Derwent
Allerthorpe
B1247
Pocklington Canal
Burnby
Holme on the Wolds
Copmanthorpe
Crockey Hill
Acaster Malbis
Naburn
Wheldrake
Thornton
Hayton
Londesborough
South Dalton
Kiplingcotes
Deighton
Storwood
Melbourne
Bielby
Thorpe le Street
Goodmanham
Appleton Roebuck
Escrick
Shiptonthorpe
Market Weighton
Gardham
R. Ouse
B1222
Thorganby
East Cottingwith
Everingham
Arras
Acaster Selby
Stillingfleet
Seaton Ross
Harswell
A1079
Ryther
Ellerton
Laytham
Holme-on-Spalding-Moor
Sancton
Kelfield
Aughton
Moor End
North Newbald
Riccall
Skipwith
North Duffield
Harlthorpe
Water End
Sand Hole
Cawood
B1223
Bubwith
Foggathorpe
A163
Highfield
Breighton
Rascal Moor
North Cliffe Wood
North Cliffe
A1034
South Newbald
South Cliffe

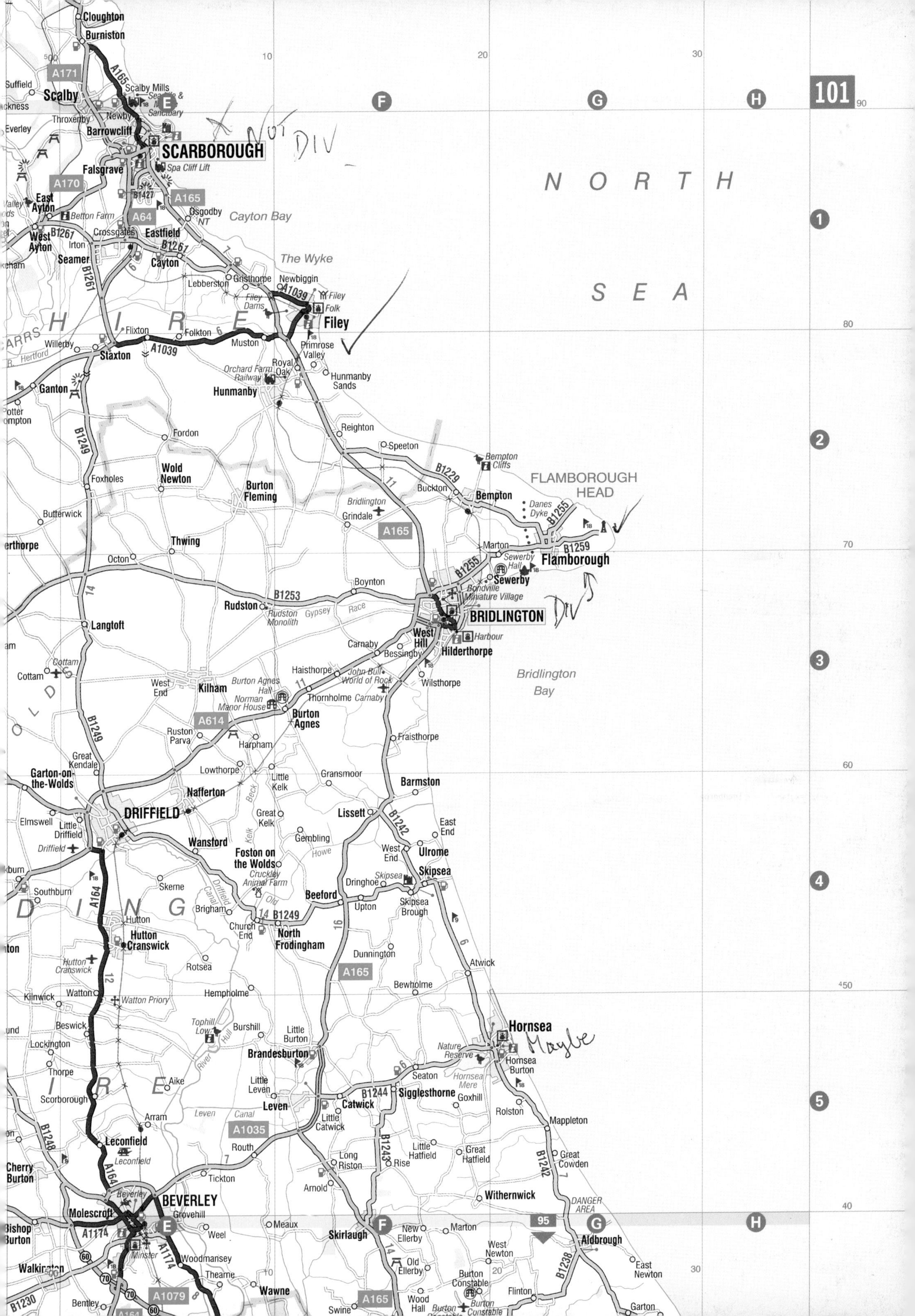
101
NORTH SEA
FLAMBOROUGH HEAD
Cayton Bay
The Wyke
Bridlington Bay
SCARBOROUGH
BRIDLINGTON
DRIFFIELD
BEVERLEY
Filey
Flamborough
Hornsea
Scalby
Cloughton
Burniston
Falsgrave
Eastfield
Cayton
Seamer
Hunmanby
Staxton
Bempton
Sewerby
Nafferton
Kilham
Rudston
Langtoft
Leven
Leconfield
Aldbrough
Skirlaugh
Barmston
Skipsea
Brandesburton
Hutton Cranswick
North Frodingham
Burton Agnes
Burton Fleming
Wold Newton
Thwing
Beeford
Ulrome
Lissett
Wansford
Foston on the Wolds
Garton-on-the-Wolds
Catwick
Sigglesthorne
Withernwick
Molescroft
Woodmansey
Wawne
A165
A64
A170
A171
A1039
A614
A1035
A164
A1174
A1079
B1249
B1253
B1255
B1259
B1229
B1242
B1243
B1244
B1261
B1248
B1238
95
Not DIV
DIV
Maybe

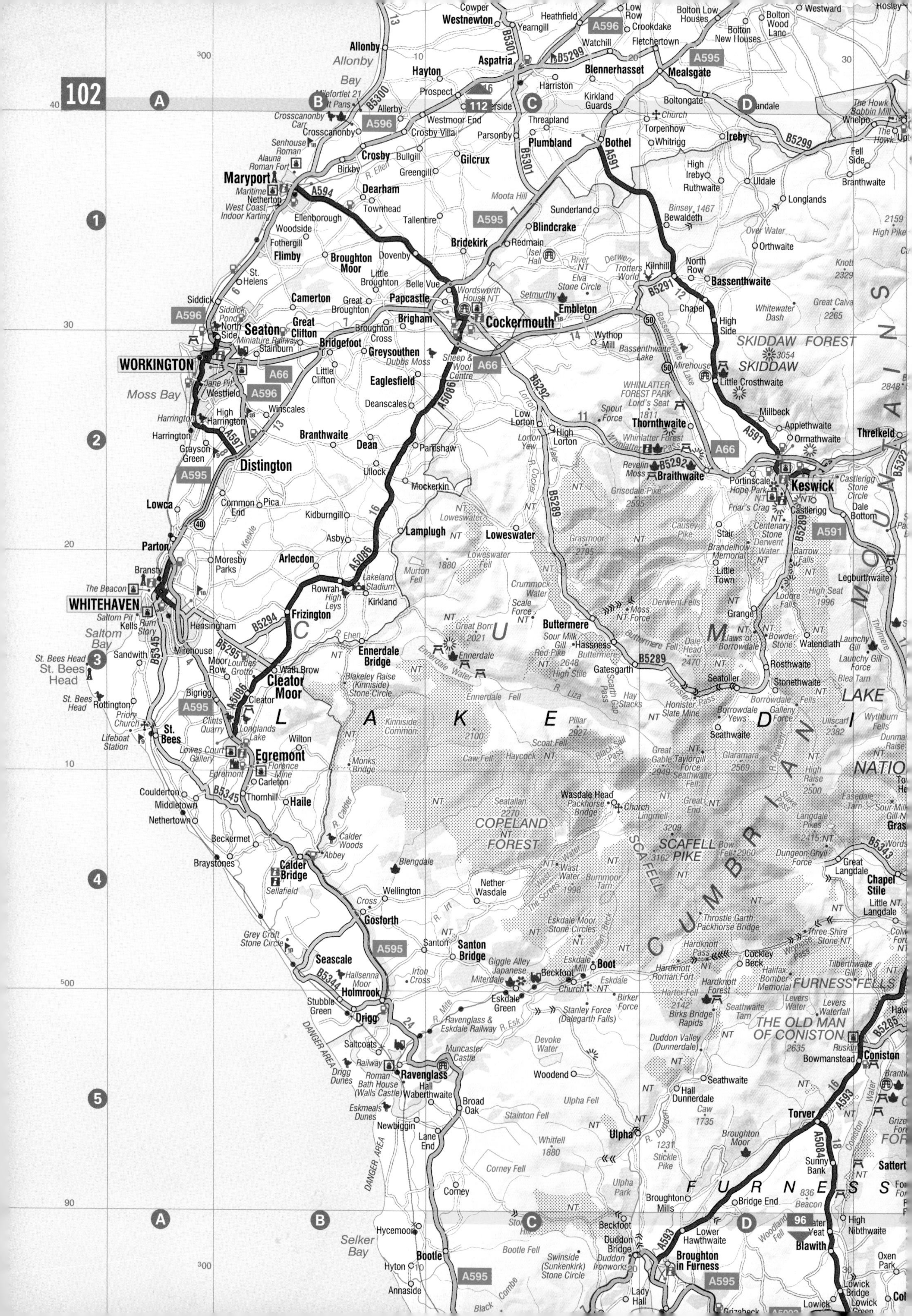

102
A
B
C
D
1
2
3
4
5
Allonby
Allonby Bay
Westnewton
Cowper
Heathfield
Yearngill
Crookdake
Watchill
Fletchertown
Bolton Low Houses
Bolton Wood Lane
Bolton New Houses
Westward
Aspatria
Hayton
Prospect
Blennerhasset
Mealsgate
Harriston
Kirkland Guards
Boltongate
Allerby
Westmoor End
Threapland
Crosby Villa
Parsonby
Plumbland
Bothel
Torpenhow
Whitrigg
Ireby
Crosscanonby
Crosby
Bullgill
Gilcrux
Greengill
Birkby
High Ireby
Ruthwaite
Uldale
Longlands
Maryport
Netherton
West Coast Indoor Karting
Dearham
Townhead
Tallentire
Moota Hill
Sunderland
Blindcrake
Binsey 1467
Bewaldeth
Ellenborough
Woodside
Fothergill
Flimby
Broughton Moor
Dovenby
Little Broughton
Bridekirk
Redmain
Isel Hall
Over Water
Orthwaite
St. Helens
Belle Vue
Papcastle
Camerton
Great Broughton
Wordsworth House NT
Cockermouth
Embleton
Setmurthy
Elva Stone Circle
Trotters World
Kilnhill
North Row
Bassenthwaite
Chapel
High Side
Siddick
Seaton
Great Clifton
Broughton Cross
Brigham
Bridgefoot
Stainburn
Greysouthen
Dubbs Moss
Wythop Mill
Bassenthwaite Lake
Mirehouse
Skiddaw Forest
3054
Skiddaw
Little Crosthwaite
Workington
Moss Bay
Jane Pit
Westfield
Little Clifton
Eaglesfield
Sheep & Wool Centre
Whinlatter Forest Park
Lord's Seat 1811
Winscales
High Harrington
Harrington
Deanscales
Low Lorton
High Lorton
Spout Force
Thornthwaite
Millbeck
Applethwaite
Ormathwaite
Threlkeld
Branthwaite
Dean
Pardshaw
Grayson Green
Distington
Ullock
Mockerkin
Braithwaite
Revelin Moss
Portinscale
Keswick
Castlerigg
Castlerigg Stone Circle
Lowca
Common End
Pica
Kidburngill
Lamplugh
Loweswater
Grisedale Pike 2593
Friar's Crag
Asby
Parton
Moresby Parks
Arlecdon
Grasmoor 2795
Causey Pike
Stair
Brandelhow Memorial
Little Town
Lakeland Stadium
Rowrah
Kirkland
High Leys
Murton Fell
Loweswater Fell
Crummock Water
Scale Force
Legburthwaite
High Seat 1996
Bransty
The Beacon
Whitehaven
Saltom Pit
Kells
Saltom Bay
Hensingham
Frizington
Buttermere
Sour Milk Gill
Red Pike 2648
High Stile
Hassness
Derwent Fells
Moss Force
Grange
Jaws of Borrowdale
Bowder Stone
Watendlath
Launchy Gill
Lodore Falls
St. Bees Head
Sandwith
Mirehouse
Moor Row
Lourdes Grotto
Ennerdale Bridge
Great Borne 2021
Ennerdale
Ennerdale Water
Gatesgarth
Dale Head 2470
Seatoller
Rosthwaite
Stonethwaite
Wath Brow
Cleator Moor
Bigrigg
Cleator
Blakeley Raise (Kinniside) Stone Circle
Ennerdale Fell
Hay Stacks
Scarth Gap Pass
Honister Pass
Honister Slate Mine
Borrowdale Yews
Borrowdale Fells
Seathwaite
Ullscarf 2382
Wythburn Fells
Rottington
Priory Church
St. Bees
Lifeboat Station
Clints Quarry
Longlands Lake
Lowes Court Gallery
Egremont
Florence Mine
Carleton
Wilton
Kinniside Common
2100
Pillar 2921
Scoat Fell
Haycock
Caw Fell
Black Sail Pass
Great Gable 2949
Taylorgill Force
Seathwaite Fell
Glaramara 2569
High Raise 2500
Lake District
Lakes
Cumbrian Mountains
Coulderton
Middletown
Nethertown
Thornhill
Haile
Monks Bridge
Seatallan 2270
Copeland Forest
Wasdale Head
Packhorse Bridge
Church
Lingmell
Great End
Stake Pass
Easedale Tarn
Langdale Pikes
2415
Beckermet
Braystones
Calder Bridge
Sellafield
Calder Abbey
Calder Woods
Blengdale
Scafell Pike 3162
Bow Fell 2960
Scafell 3209
Dungeon Ghyll Force
Great Langdale
Chapel Stile
Little Langdale
Wellington
Nether Wasdale
Wast Water
The Screes
Illgill Head 1998
Burnmoor Tarn
Cross
Gosforth
Grey Croft Stone Circle
Eskdale Moor Stone Circles
Throstle Garth Packhorse Bridge
Three Shire Stone
Santon
Santon Bridge
Seascale
Hallsenna Moor
Irton Cross
Giggle Alley Japanese Garden
Miterdale
Beckfoot
Eskdale Mill
Boot
Whillan Beck
Hardknott Pass
Hardknott Roman Fort
Hardknott Forest
Cockley Beck
Wrynose Pass
Halifax Bomber Memorial
Tilberthwaite Gill
Furness Fells
Holmrook
Stubble Green
Drigg
Eskdale Green
Stanley Force (Dalegarth Falls)
Birker Force
Harter Fell 2142
Birks Bridge Rapids
Seathwaite Tarn
Levers Water
Levers Waterfall
The Old Man of Coniston 2635
Saltcoats
Ravenglass & Eskdale Railway
Danger Area
Drigg Dunes
Roman Bath House (Walls Castle)
Ravenglass
Muncaster Castle
Devoke Water
Duddon Valley (Dunnerdale)
Bowmanstead
Coniston
Ruskin
Hall Waberthwaite
Broad Oak
Woodend
Seathwaite
Hall Dunnerdale
Caw 1735
Eskmeals Dunes
Newbiggin
Lane End
Stainton Fell
Ulpha Fell
Ulpha
Whitfell 1880
Broughton Moor
Torver
Sunny Bank
Stickle Pike 1231
Corney Fell
Corney
Ulpha Park
Broughton Mills
Bridge End
Beacon 836
Furness
Satterthwaite
Hycemoor
Selker Bay
Bootle
Bootle Fell
Swinside (Sunkenkirk) Stone Circle
Beckfoot
Duddon Bridge
Duddon Ironworks
Lower Hawthwaite
Broughton in Furness
Woodland Fell
Water Yeat
Blawith
High Nibthwaite
Oxen Park
Lowick Bridge
Lowick Green
Lowick
Hyton
Annaside
Black Combe
Lady Hall
Grizebeck
Rosley
Sebergham
Bobbin Mill
Whelpo
Fell Side
Branthwaite
High Pike 2159
Knott 2329
Great Calva 2265
Whitewater Dash
Blea Tarn
Dale Bottom
Rivington
112
96
A595
A596
A594
A591
A66
A5086
A597
A593
A5084
A5092
B5300
B5301
B5299
B5291
B5292
B5289
B5294
B5295
B5345
B5344
B5343
B5285
B5322

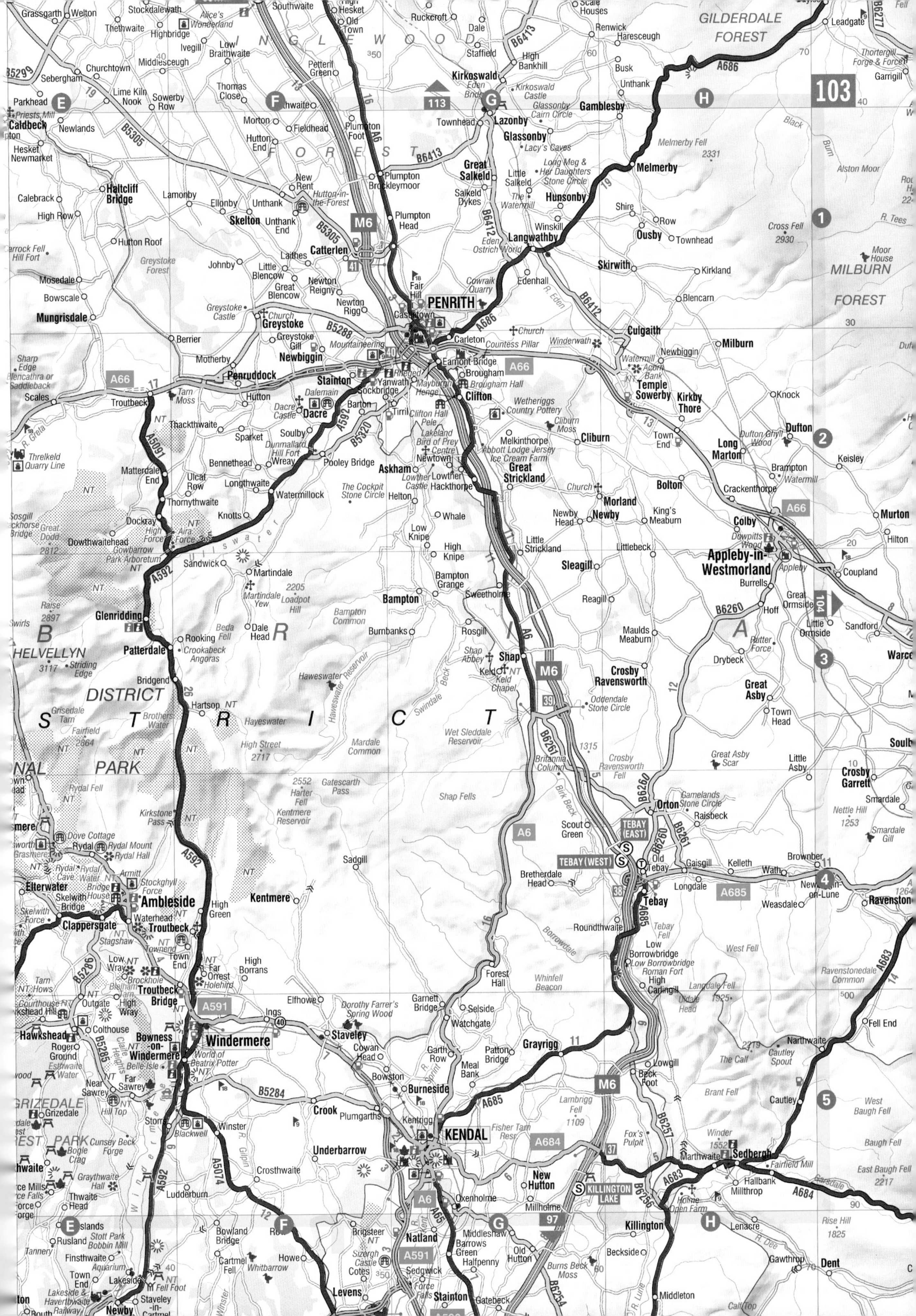

Grassgarth
Welton
Stockdalewath
Alice's Wonderland
Southwaite
High Hesket
Old Town
Ruckcroft
Dale
Scale Houses
Renwick
Haresceugh
GILDERDALE FOREST
Leadgate
B6277
Thethwaite
Highbridge
Ivegill
Low Braithwaite
INGLEWOOD
Staffield
B6413
High Bankhill
Busk
Thortergill Forge & Force
Garrigill
A686
B5299
Sebergham
Churchtown
Middlesceugh
Petteril Green
Kirkoswald
Eden Bridge
Kirkoswald Castle
Unthank
103
Parkhead
E
Priests Mill
Caldbeck
Lime Kiln Nook
Sowerby Row
Thomas Close
F
Thwaite
113
G
Glassonby Cairn Circle
Gamblesby
H
Newlands
B5305
Morton
Fieldhead
Plumpton Foot
A6
Townhead
Lazonby
Black Burn
Hesket Newmarket
Hutton End
FOREST
B6413
Glassonby
Lacy's Caves
Melmerby Fell
2331
Alston Moor
Plumpton
Brockleymoor
Great Salkeld
Long Meg & Her Daughters Stone Circle
Melmerby
New Rent
Hutton-in-the-Forest
Little Salkeld
Haltcliff Bridge
Lamonby
Ellonby
Unthank
Salkeld Dykes
The Watermill
Hunsonby
Calebeck
Skelton
Unthank End
M6
Plumpton Head
Shire
Row
High Row
B6412
Winskill
Ousby
Townhead
Cross Fell
2930
R. Tees
Hutton Roof
Catterlen
Langwathby
Eden Ostrich World
Carrock Fell
Hill Fort
Greystoke Forest
Laithes
Moor House
Johnby
Little Blencow
Skirwith
Kirkland
MILBURN
Mosedale
Great Blencow
Newton Reigny
Fair Hill
Cowraik Quarry
Edenhall
FOREST
Bowscale
Newton Rigg
PENRITH
Castletown
R. Eden
B6412
Blencarn
Mungrisdale
Greystoke Castle
Church
Greystoke
B5288
A686
Church
Culgaith
Berrier
Greystoke Gill
Mountaineering
Carleton
Countess Pillar
Winderwath
Milburn
Motherby
Newbiggin
Eamont Bridge
A66
Watermill
Acorn Bank
Newbiggin
Sharp Edge
Blencathra or Saddleback
A66
Penruddock
Stainton
Rheged
Yanwath
Brougham
Brougham Hall
Temple Sowerby
Kirkby Thore
Scales
Troutbeck
Tarn Moss
Hutton
Dalemain
Sockbridge
Mayburgh Henge
Clifton
Knock
R. Greta
Dacre Castle
Dacre
Barton
Tirril
Clifton Hall Pele
Wetheriggs Country Pottery
Thackthwaite
A5091
A592
B5320
Lakeland Bird of Prey Centre
Cliburn Moss
Dufton Ghyll Wood
Dufton
Threlkeld Quarry Line
Sparket
Soulby
Dunmallard Hill Fort
Melkinthorpe
Abbott Lodge Jersey Ice Cream Farm
Cliburn
Town End
Long Marton
Keisley
Bennethead
Wreay
Pooley Bridge
Askham
Newtown
Great Strickland
Brampton
Brampton Watermill
Matterdale End
Ulcat Row
Longthwaite
The Cockpit Stone Circle
Lowther Castle
Lowther
Hackthorpe
Church
Morland
Bolton
Crackenthorpe
Thornythwaite
Watermillock
Helton
Newby Head
Newby
King's Meaburn
A66
Murton
Sosgill
Knotts
Whale
Colby
Dockray
Aira Force
High Force
Great Dodd
2812
Dowthwaitehead
Gowbarrow Park Arboretum
Low Knipe
Little Strickland
Littlebeck
Dowpitts Wood
Appleby-in-Westmorland
Hilton
Sandwick
Martindale
High Knipe
Sleagill
Appleby
Coupland
Martindale Yew
2205 Loadpot Hill
Bampton Grange
Sweetholme
Reagill
Burrells
Great Ormside
104
Raise
2897
Glenridding
Bampton
Bampton Common
B6260
Hoff
Little Ormside
Sandford
Rooking
Beda Fell
Dale Head
R
Burnbanks
Rosgill
A6
Maulds Meaburn
A
Rutter Force
Patterdale
Crookabeck Angoras
Shap Abbey
Shap
Keld
Keld Chapel
Drybeck
HELVELLYN
3117
Striding Edge
Haweswater
Haweswater Reservoir
M6
Crosby Ravensworth
Great Asby
Bridgend
DISTRICT
Hartsop
Swindale Beck
39
Oddendale Stone Circle
Town Head
Grisedale Tarn
Brothers Water
Hayeswater
S
R
I
C
T
Fairfield
2864
Wet Sleddale Reservoir
B6261
1315
High Street
2717
Mardale Common
Britannia Column
Crosby Ravensworth Fell
Great Asby Scar
Little Asby
Crosby Garrett
NAL
PARK
2552 Harter Fell
Gatescarth Pass
Rydal Fell
Kentmere Reservoir
Shap Fells
Birk Beck
B6260
Orton
Gamelands Stone Circle
Raisbeck
Nettle Hill 1253
Smardale
Kirkstone Pass
A6
Scout Green
TEBAY (EAST)
B6261
Smardale Gill
Dove Cottage
Rydal
Rydal Mount
Rydal Hall
Grasmere
A592
Sadgill
TEBAY (WEST)
Old Tebay
Gaisgill
Kelleth
Brownber
Wath
Rydal Cave
Rydal Water
Armitt
Stockghyll Force
Bretherdale Head
Tebay
Longdale
A685
Newbiggin-on-Lune
Elterwater
Skelwith Bridge
Kentmere
Ambleside
High Green
Weasdale
Ravenstonedale
Skelwith Force
Clappersgate
Waterhead
Troutbeck
Roundthwaite
Tebay Fell
Borrowdale
Stagshaw
Townend
Low Borrowbridge
Low Borrowbridge Roman Fort
West Fell
Tarn Hows
B5286
Low Wray
Town End
High Borrans
Forest Hall
Whinfell Beacon
High Carlingill
Langdale Fell
Uldale Head
Ravenstonedale Common
A683
Brockhole
Holehird
Blelham Tarn
Troutbeck Bridge
Outgate
High Wray
A591
Elfhowe
Dorothy Farrer's Spring Wood
Garnett Bridge
Selside
Courthouse
Hawkshead Hill
Colthouse
Bowness-on-Windermere
Windermere
Ings
Staveley
Watchgate
Fell End
Hawkshead
Roger Ground
B5285
Claife Heights
World of Beatrix Potter
Belle Isle
Cowan Head
Garth Row
Patton Bridge
Grayrigg
Lowgill
Narthwaite
The Calf
Cautley Spout
Esthwaite Water
Near Sawrey
Far Sawrey
Bowston
Meal Bank
Beck Foot
Brant Fell
Cautley
West Baugh Fell
GRIZEDALE
Grizedale
Hill Top
B5284
Burneside
A685
Lambrigg Fell
1109
M6
Crook
Plumgarths
Kentrigg
KENDAL
Fisher Tarn Reservoir
Storrs
Blackwell
Winster
R. Gilpin
A684
Fox's Pulpit
Winder
1552
B6257
Baugh Fell
FOREST PARK
Cunsey Beck Forge
Bogle Crag
Underbarrow
Marthwaite
Sedbergh
Fairfield Mill
East Baugh Fell
2217
Satterthwaite
Grizedale Hall
A5074
Crosthwaite
New Hutton
KILLINGTON LAKE
A683
Hallbank
Millthrop
Force Mills
Force Falls
Thwaite Head
A592
Lutterburn
A6
Oxenholme
Millholme
B6256
Holme Open Farm
A684
Rise Hill
1825
Islands
Rusland
Stott Park Bobbin Mill
Bowland Bridge
Brigsteer
Natland
G
Middleshaw
Barrows Green
Halfpenny
97
Killington
H
Lenacre
R. Dee
Tannery
Finsthwaite
Aquarium
Lakeside
Cartmel Fell
Whitbarrow
Howe
Sizergh Castle
Cotes
A591
Old Hutton
Burns Beck Moss
Beckside
Gawthrop
Dent
Town End
Lakeside & Haverthwaite Railway
Fell Foot
Staveley-in-Cartmel
Newby
Levens
Sedgwick
Force Falls
Stainton
Gatebeck
B6254
R. Lune
Middleton
Calf Top

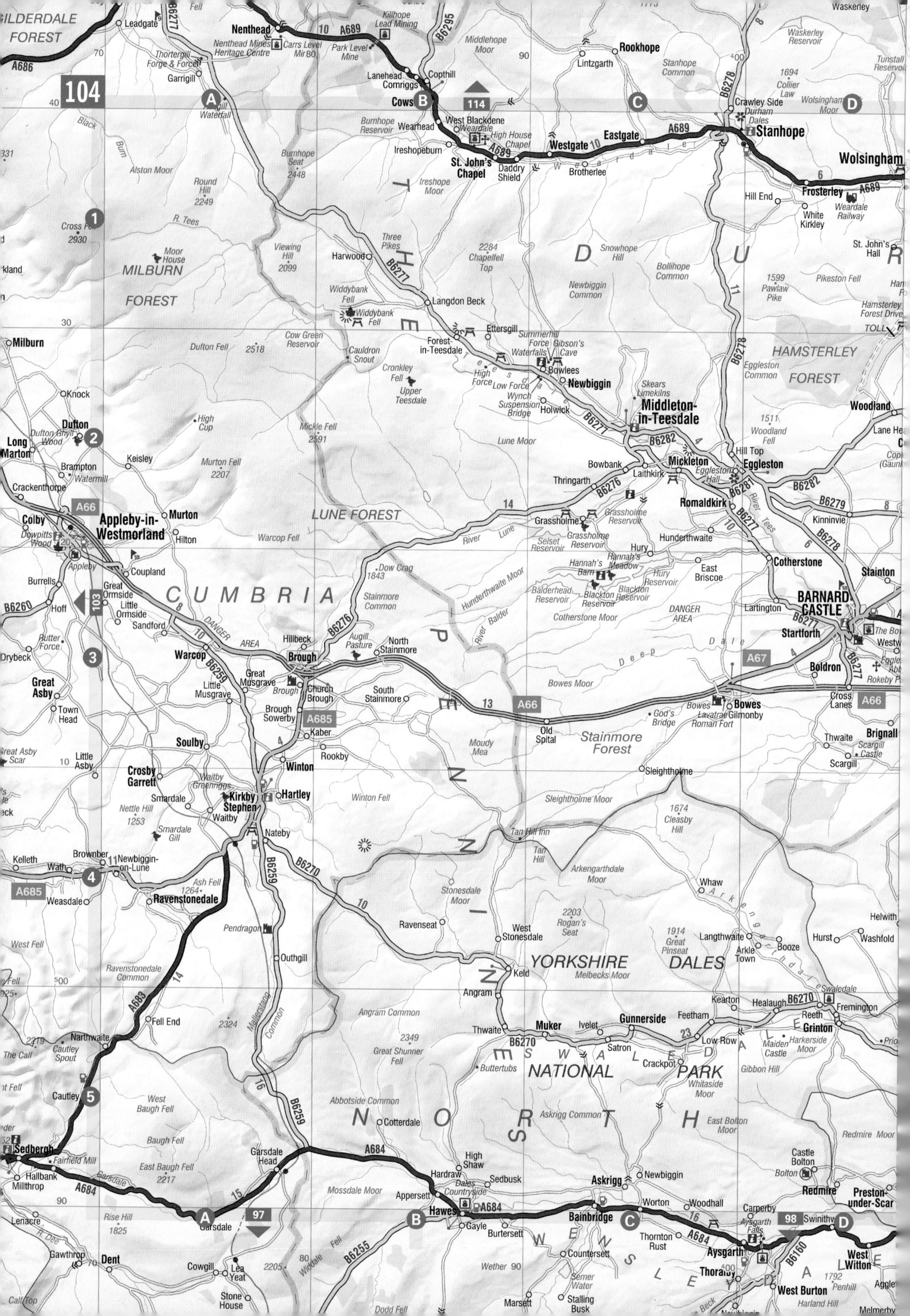
104
114
103
97
98
GILDERDALE
FOREST
A686
Leadgate
B6277
Nenthead
Nenthead Mines Heritage Centre
Carrs Level Mir
Killhope Lead Mining
Park Level Mine
A689
B6295
Middlehope Moor
Rookhope
Waskerley
Waskerley Reservoir
Tunstall Reservoir
Thortergill Forge & Force
Garrigill
Lanehead
Cornriggs
Copthill
Lintzgarth
Stanhope Common
Collier Law
Cows
Crawley Side
Durham Dales
Wolsingham Moor
Waterfall
Black Burn
Burnhope Reservoir
Wearhead
West Blackdene
Weardale
High House Chapel
Westgate
Eastgate
Stanhope
Wolsingham
Alston Moor
Burnhope Seat
2448
Ireshopeburn
St. John's Chapel
Daddry Shield
Brotherlee
Round Hill
2249
Ireshope Moor
Hill End
Frosterley
Weardale Railway
White Kirkley
Cross Fell
2930
R. Tees
Moor House
MILBURN
FOREST
Viewing Hill
2099
Three Pikes
Harwood
2284
Chapelfell Top
Snowhope Hill
Bollihope Common
St. John's Hall
Pawlaw Pike
Pikeston Fell
Hamsterley Forest Drive
Widdybank Fell
Langdon Beck
Newbiggin Common
Milburn
Dufton Fell
2518
Cow Green Reservoir
Cauldron Snout
Ettersgill
Forest-in-Teesdale
Summerhill Force
Gibson's Cave
Waterfalls
Bowlees
High Force
Low Force
Newbiggin
Cronkley Fell
Upper Teesdale
Wynch Suspension Bridge
Holwick
Skears Limekilns
Middleton-in-Teesdale
HAMSTERLEY
FOREST
Eggleston Common
Knock
Dufton
Dufton Ghyll Wood
Long Marton
High Cup
Mickle Fell
2591
Lune Moor
B6282
Woodland
Lane Head
Brampton
Watermill
Keisley
Murton Fell
2207
Bowbank
Mickleton
Hill Top
Eggleston
Eggleston Hall
Thringarth
Laithkirk
B6276
Romaldkirk
B6281
B6279
Crackenthorpe
A66
Colby
Dowpitts Wood
Appleby-in-Westmorland
Murton
Hilton
LUNE FOREST
Warcop Fell
River Lune
Grassholme
Grassholme Reservoir
Selset Reservoir
Hury
Hunderthwaite
Kinninvie
Appleby
Coupland
Burrells
Great Ormside
Little Ormside
Dow Crag
1843
Hunderthwaite Moor
Hannah's Meadow
Balderhead Reservoir
Blackton Reservoir
Hury Reservoir
East Briscoe
Cotherstone
Stainton
B6260
Hoff
CUMBRIA
Stainmore Common
Cotherstone Moor
DANGER AREA
Lartington
BARNARD CASTLE
Sandford
River Balder
Startforth
Rutter Force
Hillbeck
Augill Pasture
North Stainmore
Deep Dale
A67
Drybeck
Warcop
Brough
Boldron
Rokeby Park
Great Asby
Great Musgrave
Little Musgrave
Church Brough
South Stainmore
Bowes Moor
Cross Lanes
Town Head
Brough Sowerby
A685
13
Old Spital
Bowes
Gilmonby
Lavatrae Roman Fort
God's Bridge
Kaber
Stainmore Forest
Thwaite
Brignall
Scargill Castle
Scargill
Great Asby Scar
Little Asby
Soulby
Rookby
Moudy Mea
Winton
Crosby Garrett
Waitby Greenriggs
Hartley
Winton Fell
Sleightholme
Sleightholme Moor
Smardale
Kirkby Stephen
Nettle Hill
1253
Waitby
Smardale Gill
1674
Cleasby Hill
Nateby
Tan Hill Inn
Tan Hill
Kelleth
Brownber
Wath
Newbiggin-on-Lune
B6270
B6259
Arkengarthdale Moor
Ash Fell
1264
Ravenstonedale
Weasdale
Whaw
Arkengarthdale
Stonesdale Moor
2203
Rogan's Seat
Ravenseat
West Stonesdale
Helwith
West Fell
Pendragon
1914
Great Pinseat
Langthwaite
Hurst
Washfold
Outhgill
Arkle Town
Booze
YORKSHIRE
DALES
Ravenstonedale Common
Keld
Melbecks Moor
Swaledale
Angram
Kearton
Healaugh
Fremington
Fell End
Mallerstang Common
Angram Common
Feetham
Reeth
A683
2324
Thwaite
Muker
Ivelet
Gunnerside
Low Row
Grinton
Harkerside Moor
2279
Narthwaite
Cautley Spout
2349
Great Shunner Fell
B6270
Satron
Crackpot
Maiden Castle
The Calf
Buttertubs
SWALEDALE
NATIONAL
PARK
Gibbon Hill
Whitaside Moor
Cautley
West Baugh Fell
Abbotside Common
Askrigg Common
East Bolton Moor
NORTH
Cotterdale
Redmire Moor
Baugh Fell
Sedbergh
Fairfield Mill
Garsdale Head
A684
High Shaw
Castle Bolton
East Baugh Fell
2217
Hardraw
Sedbusk
Askrigg
Newbiggin
Bolton
Redmire
Preston-under-Scar
Hallbank
Millthrop
Garsdale
Mossdale Moor
Dales Countryside
Appersett
Hawes
Gayle
Worton
Woodhall
Carperby
Aysgarth Falls
Swinithwaite
Lenacre
Rise Hill
1825
Burtersett
Bainbridge
Thornton Rust
Aysgarth
West Witton
R. Dee
Gawthrop
Dent
Cowgill
Lea Yeat
2205
Widdale Fell
B6255
Countersett
Semer Water
Thoralby
B6160
1792
Penhill
West Burton
Wether Fell
Marsett
Stalling Busk
Stone House
Calf Top
Dodd Fell
Harland Hill
WENSLEYDALE
PENNINES

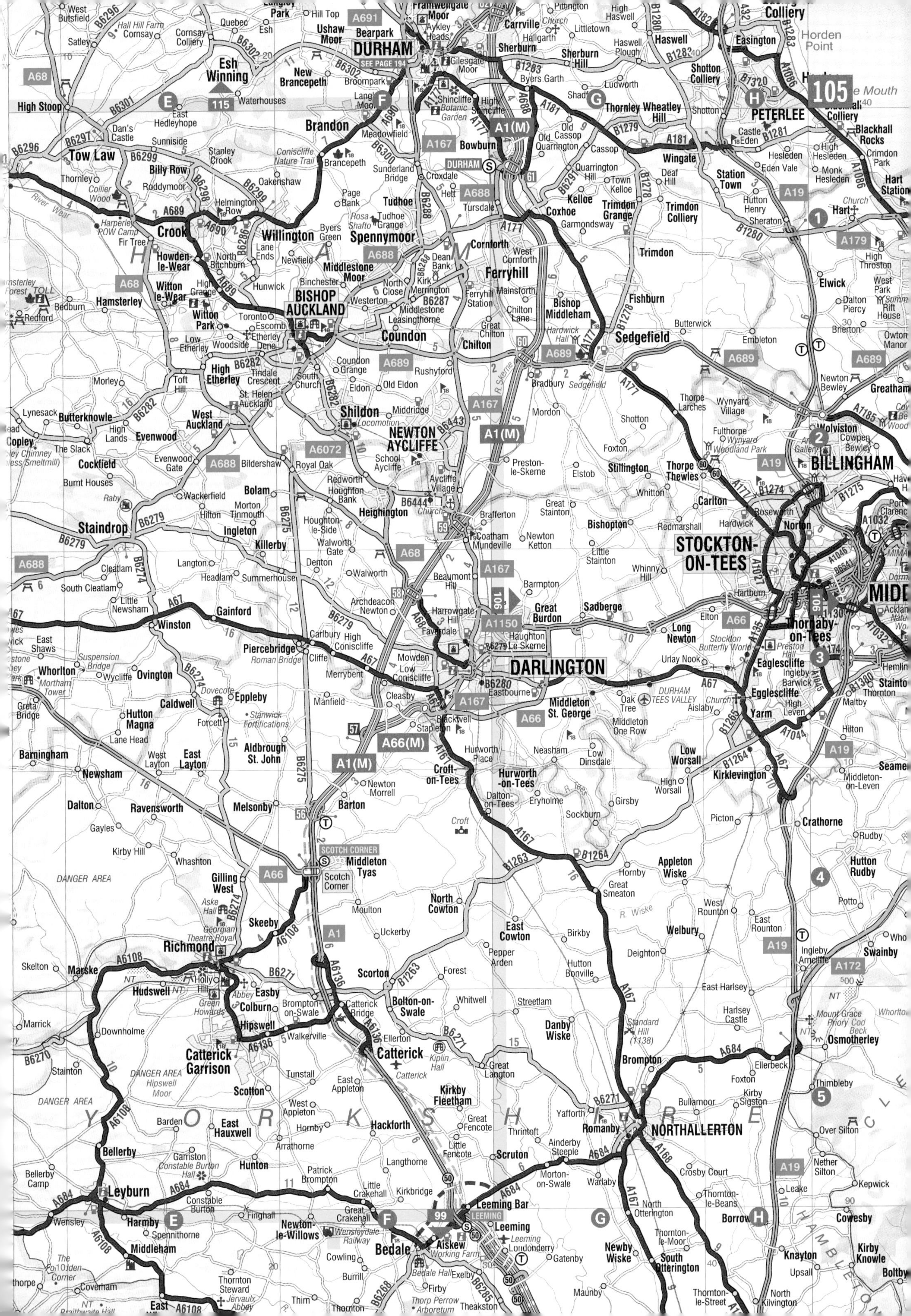

105
DURHAM
SEE PAGE 194
BISHOP AUCKLAND
DARLINGTON
STOCKTON-ON-TEES
BILLINGHAM
PETERLEE
NORTHALLERTON
Richmond
Catterick Garrison
Catterick
Leyburn
Bedale
Leeming Bar
Spennymoor
Newton Aycliffe
Shildon
Sedgefield
Yarm
Thornaby-on-Tees
SCOTCH CORNER
DURHAM TEES VALLEY
106
99
115
Y O R K S H I R E

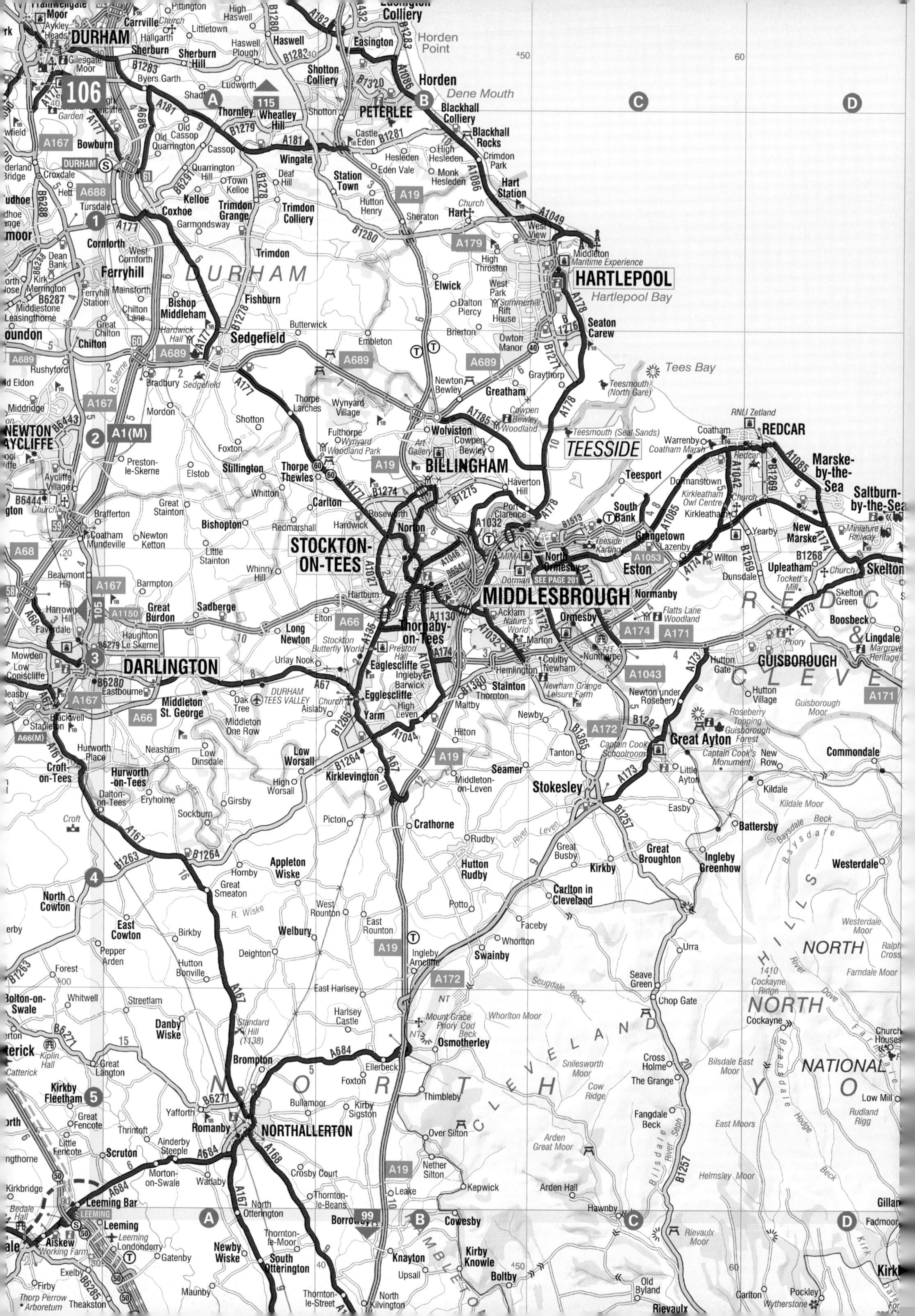
DURHAM
106
Carrville
Pittington
High Haswell
Littletown
Hallgarth
Haswell
Haswell Plough
Easington Colliery
Easington
Horden Point
Horden
Dene Mouth
Sherburn
Sherburn Hill
Gilesgate Moor
Byers Garth
Ludworth
Shadforth
115
Thornley
Wheatley Hill
Shotton Colliery
Shotton
PETERLEE
Blackhall Colliery
Blackhall Rocks
Castle Eden
Old Cassop
Old Quarrington
Cassop
Wingate
Bowburn
Croxdale
Quarrington Hill
Town Kelloe
Deaf Hill
Station Town
Hesleden
High Hesleden
Eden Vale
Monk Hesleden
Crimdon Park
Hart Station
Hett
Tursdale
Kelloe
Coxhoe
Trimdon Grange
Trimdon Colliery
Hutton Henry
Sheraton
Church
Hart
Garmondsway
Trimdon
West View
Middleton
Maritime Experience
HARTLEPOOL
Hartlepool Bay
Cornforth
West Cornforth
DURHAM
Ferryhill
Dean Bank
Kirk Merrington
Ferryhill Station
Mainsforth
Chilton Lane
Middlestone
Leasingthorne
Bishop Middleham
Fishburn
Elwick
High Throston
West Park
Summerhill
Dalton Piercy
Rift House
Seaton Carew
Great Chilton
Chilton
Hardwick Hall
Sedgefield
Butterwick
Embleton
Brierton
Owton Manor
Rushyford
Bradbury
Greatham
Graythorp
Tees Bay
Teesmouth (North Gare)
Newton Bewley
Mordon
Thorpe Larches
Wynyard Village
Middridge
NEWTON AYCLIFFE
Shotton
Fulthorpe
Wynyard Woodland Park
Wolviston
Cowpen Bewley
Cowpen Bewley Woodland
Teesmouth (Seal Sands)
TEESSIDE
RNLI Zetland
Coatham
REDCAR
Warrenby
Coatham Marsh
Foxton
Preston-le-Skerne
Aycliffe Village
Elstob
Stillington
Thorpe Thewles
Art Gallery
BILLINGHAM
Haverton Hill
Teesport
Dormanstown
Kirkleatham Owl Centre
Kirkleatham
Marske-by-the-Sea
Saltburn-by-the-Sea
Whitton
Carlton
Great Stainton
Brafferton
Bishopton
Redmarshall
Hardwick
Norton
Port Clarence
South Bank
Grangetown
Yearby
New Marske
Miniature Railway
Coatham Mundeville
Newton Ketton
Little Stainton
STOCKTON-ON-TEES
Teesside Karting
MIMA
North Ormesby
SEE PAGE 201
Lazenby
Eston
Wilton
Dunsdale
Upleatham
Tockett's Mill
Skelton
Skelton Green
Whinny Hill
Beaumont Hill
Barmpton
Hartburn
MIDDLESBROUGH
Normanby
Flatts Lane Woodland
REDCAR
Great Burdon
Sadberge
Elton
Harrowgate Hill
Faverdale
Long Newton
Acklam
Dorman
Nature's World
Ormesby
Thornaby-on-Tees
Boosbeck
Lingdale
Margrove Heritage
Haughton Le Skerne
Stockton Butterfly World
Preston Hall
Marton
Nunthorpe
Coulby Newham
Hemlington
Priory
Mowden
Low Coniscliffe
DARLINGTON
Urlay Nook
Eaglescliffe
Ingleby Barwick
Hutton Gate
GUISBOROUGH
CLEVE
Eastbourne
DURHAM TEES VALLEY
Oak Tree
Egglescliffe
Aislaby
Stainton
Thornton
Newham Grange Leisure Farm
Newton under Roseberry
Hutton Village
Guisborough Moor
Middleton St. George
Middleton One Row
Yarm
High Leven
Maltby
Newby
Roseberry Topping
Guisborough Forest
Blackwell
Stapleton
Hilton
Great Ayton
Captain Cook Schoolroom
Captain Cook's Monument
Commondale
Hurworth Place
Neasham
Low Dinsdale
Low Worsall
Tanton
Seamer
New Row
Croft-on-Tees
Hurworth-on-Tees
Kirklevington
High Worsall
Middleton-on-Leven
Stokesley
Little Ayton
Kildale
Dalton-on-Tees
Eryholme
Girsby
Kildale Moor
Croft
Sockburn
Picton
Crathorne
Easby
Battersby
Baysdale Beck
Rudby
Great Busby
Great Broughton
Ingleby Greenhow
Westerdale
Appleton Wiske
Hornby
Great Smeaton
Hutton Rudby
Kirkby
North Cowton
Carlton in Cleveland
Potto
West Rounton
East Rounton
Faceby
East Cowton
Birkby
Welbury
Whorlton
Westerdale Moor
Ralph Cross
Pepper Arden
Deighton
Ingleby Arncliffe
Swainby
Urra
NORTH
Forest
Hutton Bonville
Farndale Moor
Bolton-on-Swale
Whitwell
Streetlam
East Harlsey
Seave Green
1410 Cockayne Ridge
Scugdale Beck
Chop Gate
NORTH
Danby Wiske
Harlsey Castle
Mount Grace Priory
Cod Beck
Whorlton Moor
Cockayne
Standard Hill (1138)
Osmotherley
CLEVELAND
Church Houses
Great Langton
Brompton
Ellerbeck
Snilesworth Moor
Cross Holme
Bilsdale East Moor
NATIONAL
Catterick
Kiplin Hall
NORTH
Foxton
The Grange
Cow Ridge
Kirkby Fleetham
Thimbleby
Low Mill
Rudland Rigg
Great Fencote
Yafforth
Bullamoor
Kirby Sigston
Fangdale Beck
East Moors
Thrintoft
Romanby
NORTHALLERTON
Over Silton
Arden Great Moor
Little Fencote
Scruton
Ainderby Steeple
Morton-on-Swale
Warlaby
Crosby Court
Nether Silton
Bilsdale
River Seph
Helmsley Moor
Kirkbridge
Leeming Bar
LEEMING
North Otterington
Thornton-le-Beans
Kepwick
Arden Hall
Gillan
Bedale Hall
Aiskew
Leeming
Leeming Working Farm
Londonderry
Borrowby
99
Cowesby
Hawnby
Rievaulx Moor
Fadmoor
Thornton-le-Moor
Newby Wiske
Knayton
Kirby Knowle
Gatenby
South Otterington
Upsall
Boltby
Exelby
Firby
Thorp Perrow Arboretum
Theakston
Maunby
Thornton-le-Street
North Kilvington
Old Byland
Carlton
Pockley
Wytherstone
Rievaulx

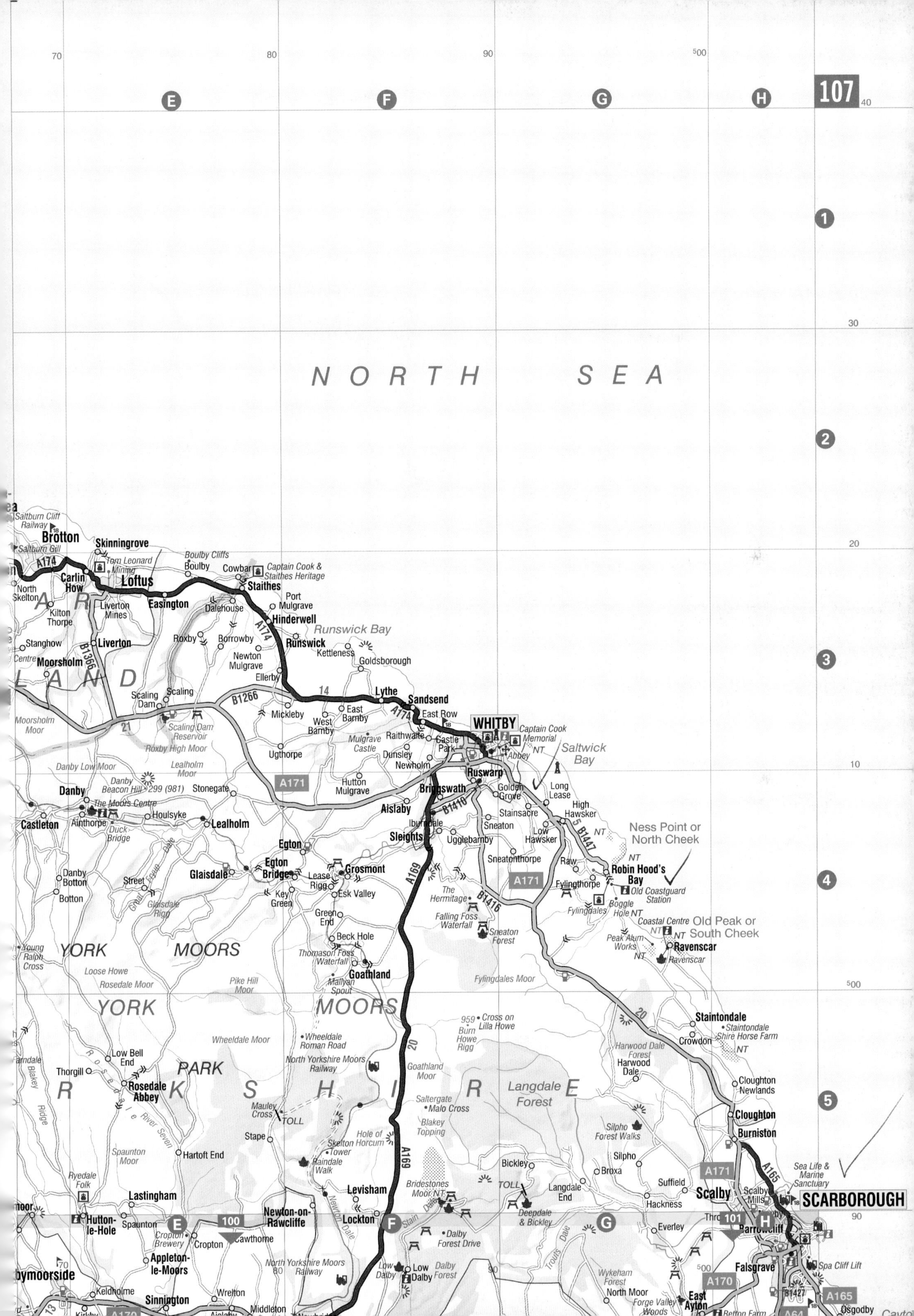
107
E
F
G
H
NORTH SEA
Saltburn Cliff Railway
Brotton
Skinningrove
Tom Leonard Mining
Boulby Cliffs
Boulby
Cowbar
Captain Cook & Staithes Heritage
Staithes
Carlin How
Loftus
North Skelton
Kilton Thorpe
Liverton Mines
Easington
Dalehouse
Port Mulgrave
Hinderwell
Runswick Bay
Runswick
Kettleness
Goldsborough
Stanghow
Liverton
Roxby
Borrowby
Newton Mulgrave
Ellerby
Moorsholm
Scaling Dam
Scaling
Scaling Dam Reservoir
Roxby High Moor
Moorsholm Moor
Mickleby
West Barnby
East Barnby
Lythe
Sandsend
East Row
WHITBY
Captain Cook Memorial
Abbey
Saltwick Bay
Raithwaite
Castle Park
Mulgrave Castle
Dunsley
Newholm
Ugthorpe
Danby Low Moor
Lealholm Moor
Danby
Danby Beacon Hill 299 (981)
Stonegate
The Moors Centre
Castleton
Ainthorpe
Duck Bridge
Houlsyke
Lealholm
Hutton Mulgrave
Aislaby
Ruswarp
Briggswath
Golden Grove
Long Lease
High Hawsker
Stainsacre
Sneaton
Low Hawsker
Ness Point or North Cheek
Iburndale
Sleights
Ugglebarnby
Sneatonthorpe
Raw
Robin Hood's Bay
Old Coastguard Station
Fylingthorpe
Fylingdales
Boggle Hole
Egton
Egton Bridge
Glaisdale
Grosmont
Lease Rigg
Esk Valley
Key Green
Danby Botton
Botton
Street
Glaisdale Rigg
Green End
The Hermitage
Falling Foss Waterfall
Sneaton Forest
Coastal Centre
Old Peak or South Cheek
Peak Alum Works
Ravenscar
Beck Hole
Thomason Foss Waterfall
Goathland
Mallyan Spout
Young Ralph Cross
YORK
MOORS
Loose Howe
Rosedale Moor
Pike Hill Moor
Fylingdales Moor
YORK
MOORS
959 Cross on Lilla Howe
Burn Howe Rigg
Staintondale
Staintondale Shire Horse Farm
Crowdon
Wheeldale Moor
Wheeldale Roman Road
North Yorkshire Moors Railway
Harwood Dale Forest
Harwood Dale
Low Bell End
Thorgill
PARK
Goathland Moor
Cloughton Newlands
Rosedale Abbey
Langdale Forest
Saltergate
Malo Cross
Blakey Topping
Blakey Ridge
River Seven
Maulev Cross
TOLL
Stape
Hole of Horcum
Skelton Tower
Silpho Forest Walks
Cloughton
Burniston
Silpho
Hartoft End
Spaunton Moor
Raindale Walk
Bridestones Moor
Bickley
Broxa
Suffield
Sea Life & Marine Sanctuary
Ryedale Folk
Lastingham
Levisham
TOLL
Langdale End
Hackness
Scalby
Scalby Mills
SCARBOROUGH
Hutton-le-Hole
Spaunton
Newton-on-Rawcliffe
Lockton
Deepdale & Bickley
Everley
Throxenby
Barrowcliff
Cropton Brewery
Cropton
Cawthorne
Dalby Forest Drive
Appleton-le-Moors
North Yorkshire Moors Railway
Low Dalby
Dalby Forest
Troutsdale
Wykeham Forest
North Moor
Falsgrave
Spa Cliff Lift
Kirkbymoorside
Keldholme
Sinnington
Wrelton
Middleton
Forge Valley Woods
East Ayton
Betton Farm
Osgodby
A174
A171
A169
A165
A170
A64
B1266
B1366
B1410
B1416
B1447
B1427
100
101
70
80
90
500
40
30
20
10
1
2
3
4
5

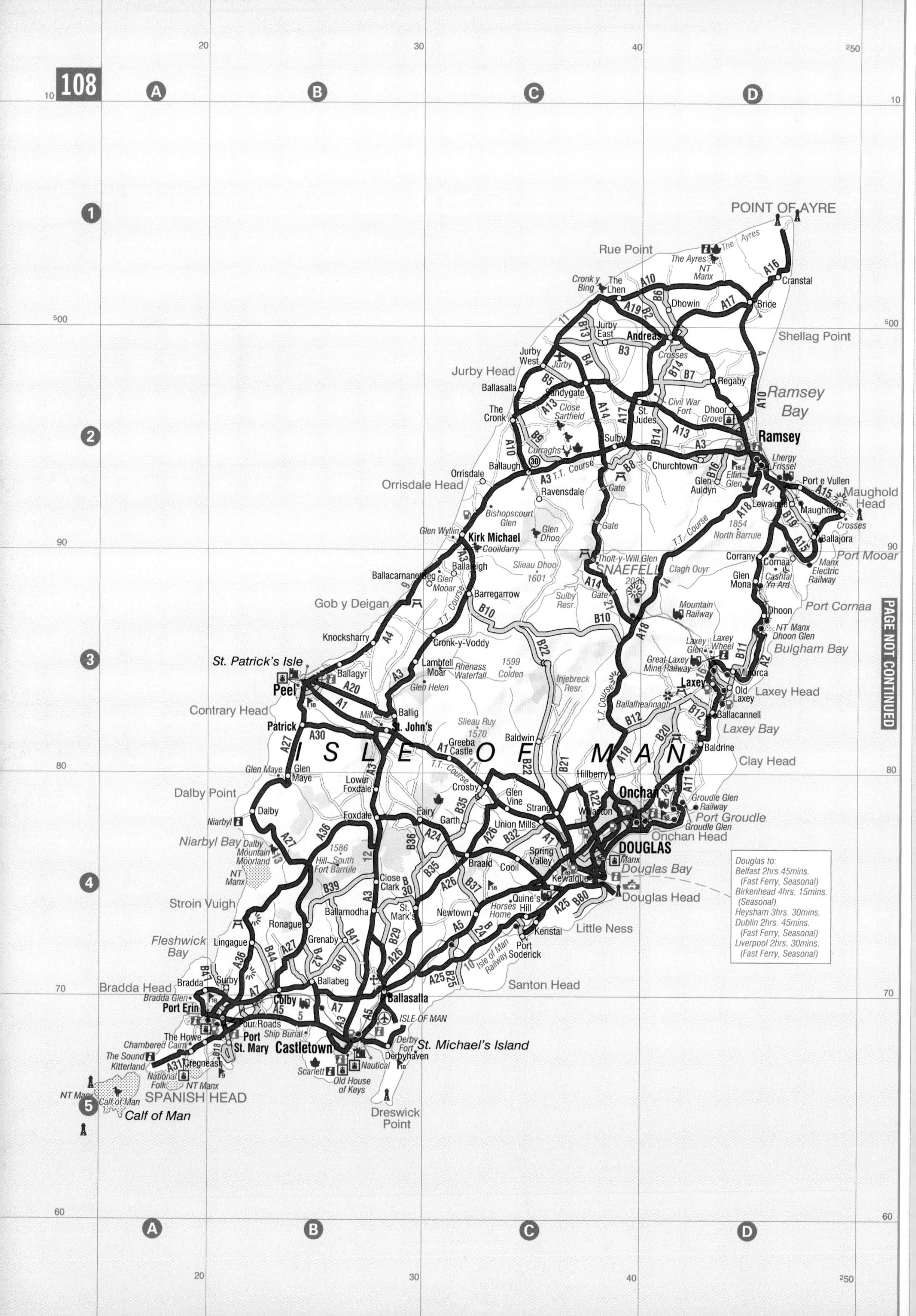

ISLE OF MAN

POINT OF AYRE

Rue Point

The Ayres
NT Manx

Cranstal

Cronk y
Bing

The
Lhen

Dhowin

Bride

Shellag Point

Jurby
East

Andreas

Crosses

Regaby

Ramsey Bay

Jurby West

Jurby Head

Jurby

Ballasalla

Sandygate

St.
Judes

Civil War
Fort

Dhoor
Grove

Ramsey

The Cronk

Close
Sartfield

Sulby

Churchtown

Lhergy
Frissel

Port e Vullen

Orrisdale Head

Orrisdale

Ballaugh

Curraghs

T.T. Course

Gate

Glen
Auldyn

Elfin
Glen

Maughold Head

Maughold

Ravensdale

A3 T.T. Course

Gate

North Barrule

T.T. Course

Corrany

Cornaa

Crosses

Ballajora

Port Mooar

Bishopscourt
Glen

Glen Wyllin

Kirk Michael

Cooildarry

Glen
Dhoo

SNAEFELL
2036

Clagh Ouyr

Glen
Mona

Manx
Electric
Railway

Port Cornaa

Ballaleigh

Slieau Dhoo
1601

Sulby
Resr.

Gate

Mountain
Railway

Dhoon

Ballacarnane beg

Glen
Mooar

Barregarrow

Gob y Deigan

B10

Snaefell

NT Manx
Dhoon Glen

Bulgham Bay

Knocksharry

Cronk-y-Voddy

1599
Colden

Laxey
Glen

Great Laxey
Mine Railway

Laxey
Wheel

Minorca

St. Patrick's Isle

Lambfell
Moar

Rhenass
Waterfall

Injebreck
Resr.

Laxey

Old
Laxey

Laxey Head

Peel

Ballagyr

Glen Helen

Ballaheannagh

Ballacannell

Patrick

Ballig

St. John's

Greeba
Castle

Baldwin

Laxey Bay

Contrary Head

Mill

Slieau Ruy
1570

T.T. Course

Baldrine

Clay Head

ISLE OF MAN

Hillberry

Glen Maye

Glen
Maye

Lower
Foxdale

Crosby

Glen
Vine

Strang

Hillberry

Onchan

Dalby Point

Dalby

Foxdale

Fairy

Garth

Union Mills

Willaston

Groudle Glen
Railway

Port Groudle

Niarbyl

Dalby
Mountain
Moorland

1586
South
Barrule

B36

Braaid

Cooil

Spring
Valley

DOUGLAS

Onchan Head

Niarbyl Bay

NT Manx

Hill
Fort

Close
Clark

Ballamodha

St.
Mark's

Newtown

Quine's
Home

Kewaigue

Manx

Douglas Bay

Stroin Vuigh

Ronague

Grenaby

Horses
Hill

Kerista

Douglas Head

Fleshwick Bay

Lingague

Ballabeg

Port
Soderick

Little Ness

Bradda
Glen

Bradda

Surby

Isle of Man
Railway

Colby

Ballasalla

Santon Head

Bradda Head

Port Erin

Four Roads

A7

ISLE OF MAN

Derby
Fort

St. Michael's Island

The Howe

Port
St. Mary

Ship Burial

Castletown

Derbyhaven

Chambered Cairn

Cregneash

National
Folk

NT Manx

Scarlett

Nautical

The Sound

Kitterland

Old House
of Keys

NT Manx

Calf of Man

SPANISH HEAD

Calf of Man

Dreswick
Point

Douglas to:
Belfast 2hrs.45mins.
(Fast Ferry, Seasonal)
Birkenhead 4hrs. 15mins.
(Seasonal)
Heysham 3hrs. 30mins.
Dublin 2hrs. 45mins.
(Fast Ferry, Seasonal)
Liverpool 2hrs. 30mins.
(Fast Ferry, Seasonal)

PAGE NOT CONTINUED

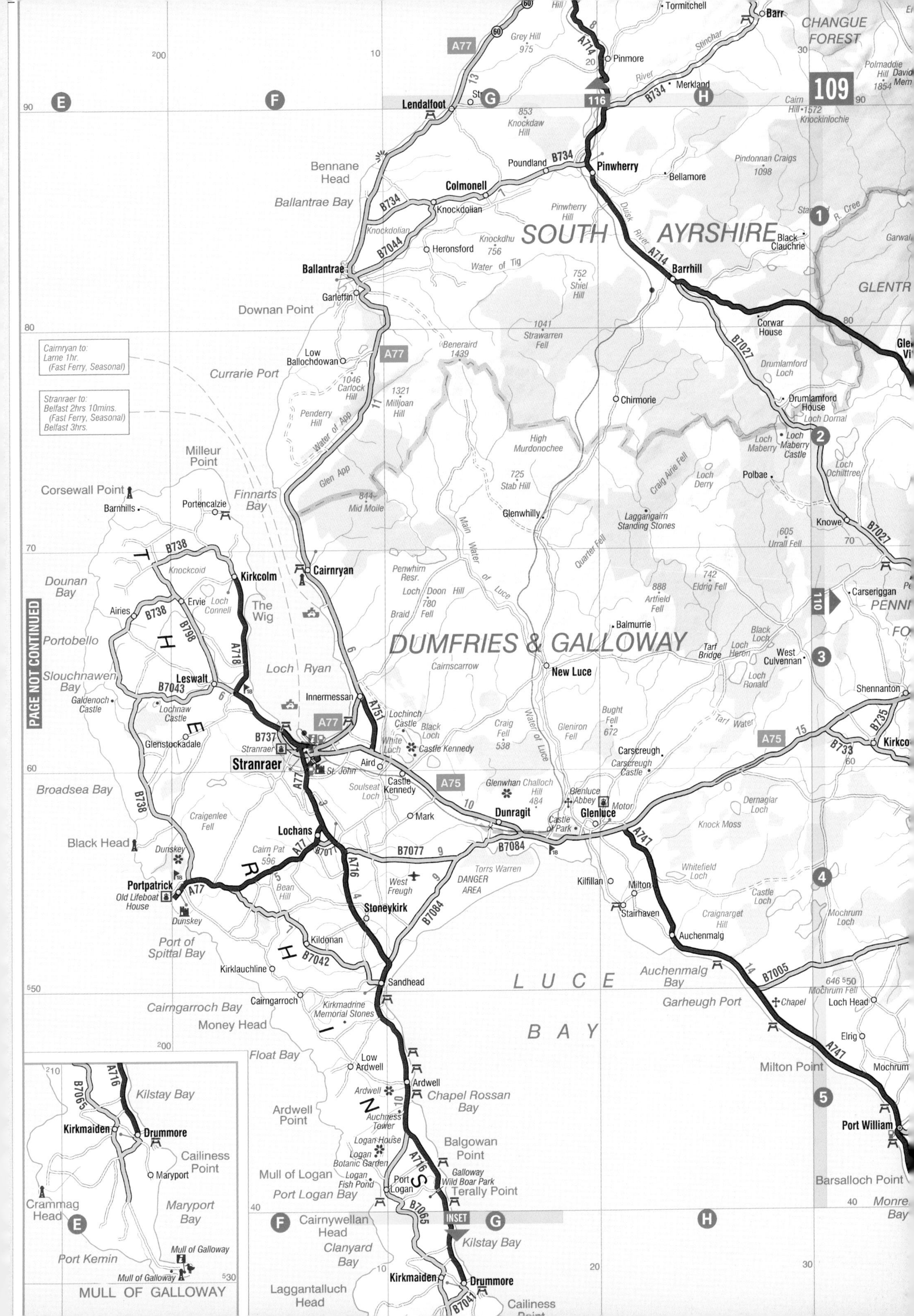

109
SOUTH AYRSHIRE
DUMFRIES & GALLOWAY
THE RHINNS
LUCE BAY
CHANGUE FOREST
PAGE NOT CONTINUED
Cairnryan to:
Larne 1hr.
(Fast Ferry, Seasonal)
Stranraer to:
Belfast 2hrs 10mins.
(Fast Ferry, Seasonal)
Belfast 3hrs.
Stranraer
Cairnryan
Kirkcolm
Leswalt
Portpatrick
Lochans
Stoneykirk
Sandhead
Glenluce
New Luce
Dunragit
Ballantrae
Colmonell
Pinwherry
Barrhill
Lendalfoot
Barr
Pinmore
Port Logan
Ardwell
Drummore
Kirkmaiden
Auchenmalg
Port William
Loch Ryan
Corsewall Point
Black Head
Mull of Logan
Mull of Galloway
MULL OF GALLOWAY
INSET

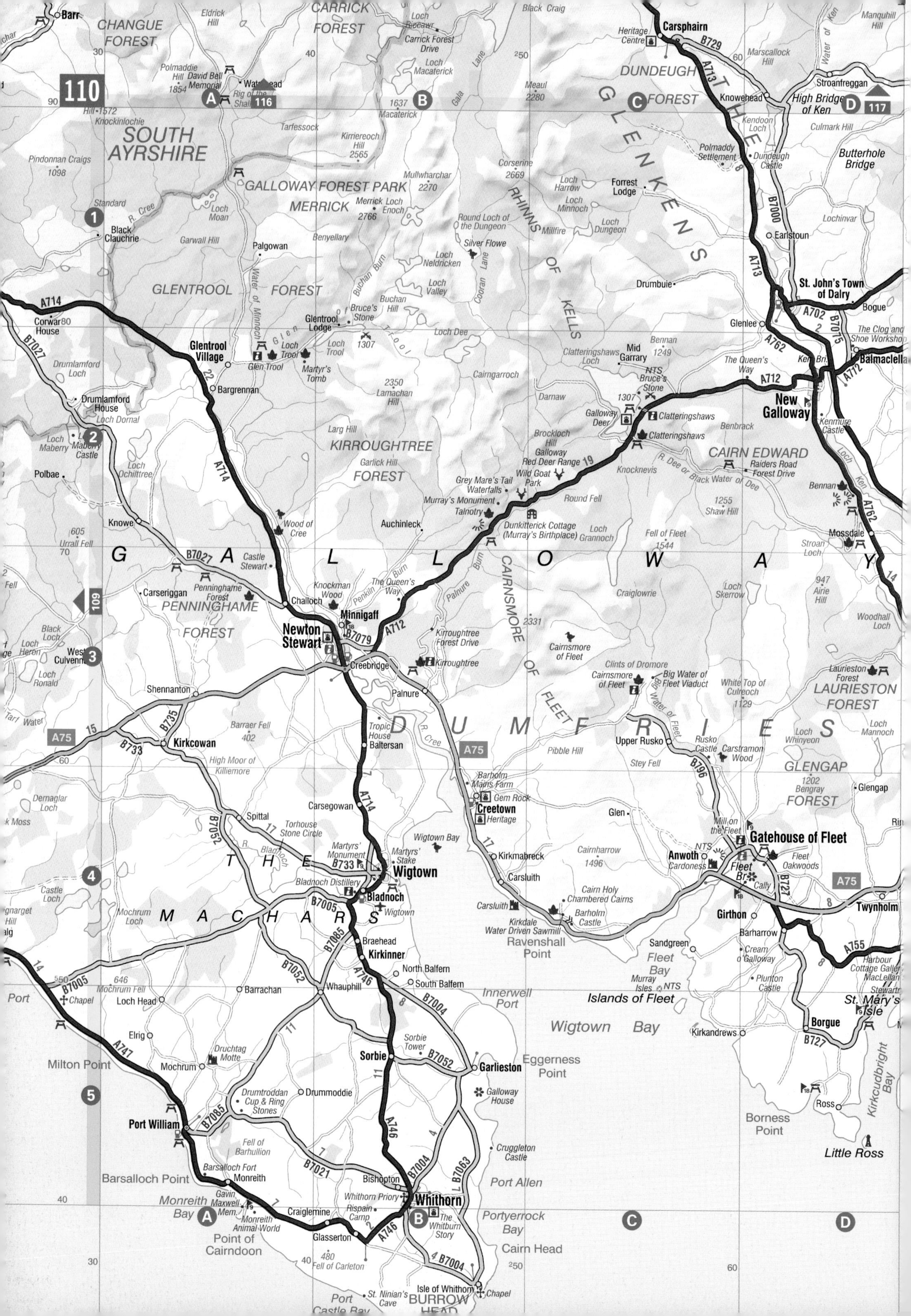
Barr
CHANGUE FOREST
Eldrick Hill
CARRICK FOREST
Loch Riecawr
Carrick Forest Drive
Black Craig
Heritage Centre
Carsphairn
B729
Manquhill Hill
Marscallock Hill
Loch Macaterick
Polmaddie Hill 1854
David Bell Memorial
Waterhead
Rig of the Shalloch
116
Meaul 2280
DUNDEUGH FOREST
Knowehead
Stroanfreggan
High Bridge of Ken
117
Hill 1572
Knockinlochie
Macaterick 1637
Gala Lane
GLENKENS
THE GLENKENS
A713
Culmark Hill
Tarfessock
Kendoon Loch
SOUTH AYRSHIRE
Kirriereoch Hill 2565
Polmaddy Settlement
Dundeugh Castle
Butterhole Bridge
Pindonnan Craigs 1098
Corserine 2669
GALLOWAY FOREST PARK
Mullwharchar 2270
Loch Harrow
Forrest Lodge
MERRICK
Merrick 2766
Loch Enoch
Loch Minnoch
Standard
R. Cree
Loch Moan
RHINNS OF KELLS
B7000
Lochinvar
Black Clauchrie
Round Loch of the Dungeon
Millfire
Loch Dungeon
Earlstoun
Garwall Hill
Benyellary
Silver Flowe
Palgowan
Loch Neldricken
A713
Water of Minnoch
Buchan Burn
Loch Valley
Cooran Lane
GLENTROOL FOREST
Drumbuie
St. John's Town of Dalry
A714
Buchan Hill
Bogue
Corwar House
Bruce's Stone
Glentrool Lodge
Loch Dee
Glenlee
A702
B7075
B7027
Glen Trool
Loch Trool
1307
The Clog and Shoe Workshop
Glentrool Village
Glen Trool
Martyr's Tomb
Clatteringshaws Loch
Mid Garrary
Bennan 1249
The Queen's Way
A762
Ken Bridge
Balmaclellan
Drumlamford Loch
NTS Bruce's Stone
A712
Bargrennan
2350 Lamachan Hill
Cairngarroch
Drumlamford House
Darnaw
1307
New Galloway
Loch Dornal
Galloway Deer
Clatteringshaws
Kenmure Castle
Loch Maberry
Maberry Castle
Larg Hill
Brockloch Hill
Benbrack
KIRROUGHTREE
Clatteringshaws
CAIRN EDWARD
Galloway Red Deer Range
Raiders Road Forest Drive
Polbae
Loch Ochiltree
Garlick Hill
FOREST
R. Dee or Black Water of Dee
Loch Ken
A714
Grey Mare's Tail Waterfalls
Wild Goat Park
Knocknevis
Bennan
Murray's Monument
Talnotry
Round Fell
1255 Shaw Hill
Wood of Cree
Auchinleck
Dunkitterick Cottage (Murray's Birthplace)
Knowe
Loch Grannoch
Fell of Fleet 1544
605 Urrall Fell
Mossdale
A762
GALLOWAY
Stroan Loch
B7027
Castle Stewart
CAIRNSMORE OF FLEET
Palnure Burn
947 Airie Hill
Fell
Carseriggan
Penninghame Forest
Knockman Wood
Penkiln Burn
The Queen's Way
Craiglowrie
Loch Skerrow
109
PENNINGHAME FOREST
Challoch
Minnigaff
2331
Woodhall Loch
Black Loch
Newton Stewart
B7079
A712
Kirroughtree Forest Drive
Loch Heron
West Culvennan
FOREST
Cairnsmore of Fleet
Clints of Dromore
Laurieston Forest
Kirroughtree
Creebridge
Cairnsmore of Fleet
Big Water of Fleet Viaduct
White Top of Culreoch 1129
LAURIESTON FOREST
Loch Ronald
Shennanton
Palnure
Tarf Water
B735
Barraer Fell 402
Tropic House
Baltersan
DUMFRIES
Big Water of Fleet
Loch Mannoch
A75
Kirkcowan
R. Cree
A75
Pibble Hill
Upper Rusko
Rusko Castle
Carstramon Wood
Loch Whinyeon
B733
High Moor of Killiemore
Stey Fell
B796
GLENGAP
Dernaglar Loch
Barholm Mains Farm
Gem Rock
Creetown
Heritage
1202 Bengray
Glengap
FOREST
Moss
Spittal
Carsegowan
A714
Glen
B7052
Torhouse Stone Circle
Wigtown Bay
Mill on the Fleet
Gatehouse of Fleet
R. Bladnoch
Martyrs' Monument
Martyrs' Stake
Kirkmabreck
Cairnharrow 1496
NTS
Anwoth
Cardoness
Fleet Oakwoods
B733
Wigtown
Carsluith
Fleet Br.
Castle Loch
Bladnoch Distillery
Bladnoch
Cairn Holy Chambered Cairns
Cally
B727
A75
Wigtown
Carsluith
Girthon
Twynholm
Mochrum Loch
THE MACHARS
B7005
Barholm Castle
Kirkdale Water Driven Sawmill
B7085
Braehead
Ravenshall Point
Barharrow
Sandgreen
Fleet Bay
Kirkinner
Cream o' Galloway
A755
Harbour Cottage Gallery
MacLellan
B7052
North Balfern
A746
South Balfern
Murray Isles
NTS
Plunton Castle
Port
B7005
Mochrum Fell
Barrachan
Whauphill
Innerwell Port
Islands of Fleet
St. Mary's Isle
Chapel
Loch Head
B7004
Borgue
Wigtown Bay
Elrig
Kirkandrews
B727
Sorbie Tower
Kirkcudbright Bay
A747
Druchtag Motte
Sorbie
B7052
Garlieston
Eggerness Point
Milton Point
Mochrum
Drumtroddan Cup & Ring Stones
Drummoddie
Galloway House
Ross
Port William
B7085
A746
Borness Point
Fell of Barhullion
Cruggleton Castle
Little Ross
B7021
B7004
B7063
Barsalloch Fort
Monreith
Bishopton
Port Allen
Barsalloch Point
Whithorn Priory
Whithorn
Monreith Bay
Gavin Maxwell Mem.
Monreith Animal World
Craiglemine
Rispain Camp
The Whithorn Story
Portyerrock Bay
Point of Cairndoon
Glasserton
A746
Cairn Head
480 Fell of Carleton
B7004
Isle of Whithorn
Chapel
Port Castle Bay
St. Ninian's Cave
BURROW HEAD

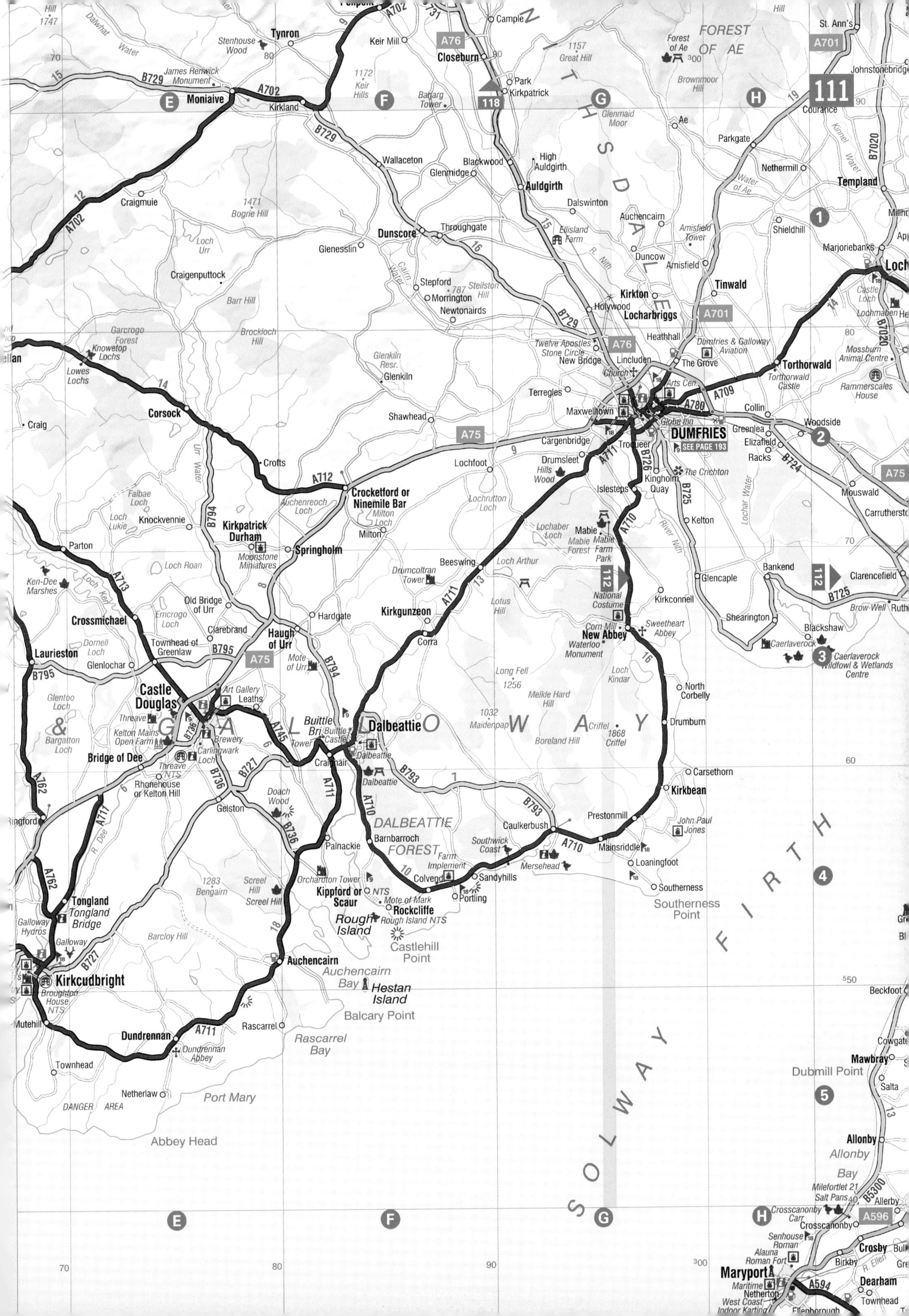

111
112
118
SEE PAGE 193
DUMFRIES
Castle Douglas
Kirkcudbright
Dalbeattie
Moniaive
NITHSDALE
GALLOWAY
SOLWAY FIRTH
FOREST OF AE
DALBEATTIE FOREST
Maryport

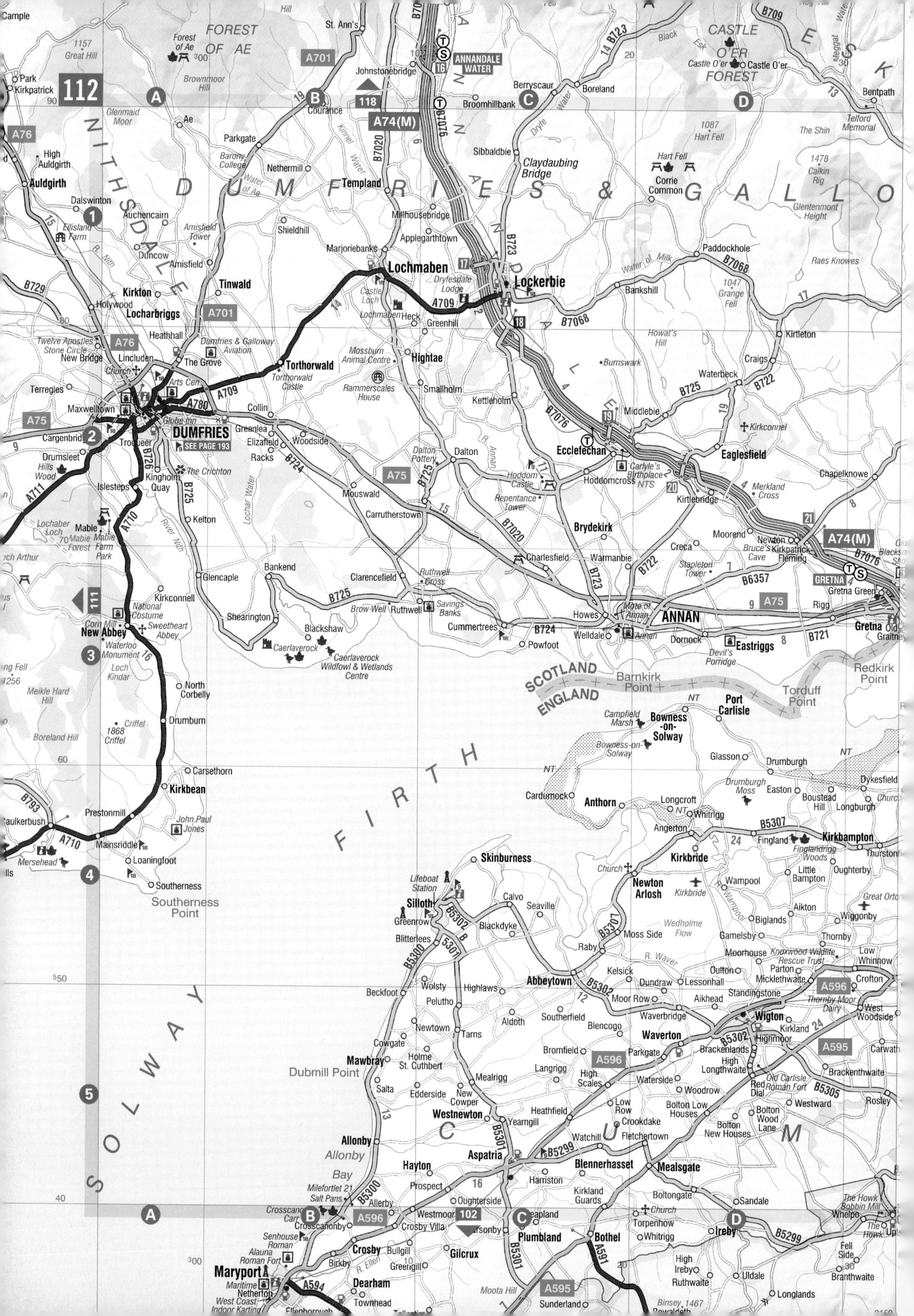

112
111
102
118
Cample
FOREST OF AE
Forest of Ae
1157 Great Hill
Brownmoor Hill
St. Ann's
A701
Johnstonebridge
ANNANDALE WATER
16
Berryscaur
Boreland
Broomhillbank
B7076
CASTLE O'ER FOREST
Castle O'er
Bentpath
B709
B723
Black Esk
Park
Kirkpatrick
Glenmaid Moor
Ae
Courance
A74(M)
Kinnel Water
B7020
Dryfe Water
Telford Memorial
The Shin
1087 Hart Fell
Hart Fell
Corrie Common
1478 Calkin Rig
Glentenmont Height
A76
High Auldgirth
Auldgirth
Parkgate
Barony College
Water of Ae
Nethermill
Templand
Sibbaldbie
Claydaubing Bridge
NITHSDALE
DUMFRIES & GALLOWAY
ESK
Dalswinton
Auchencairn
Ellisland Farm
Amisfield Tower
Shieldhill
Millhousebridge
Applegarthtown
Duncow
Amisfield
R. Nith
Marjoriebanks
Lochmaben
Lockerbie
Paddockhole
Water of Milk
B7068
Raes Knowes
Bankshill
1047 Grange Fell
B729
Kirkton
Holywood
Locharbriggs
Tinwald
Castle Loch
Lochmaben
Heck
Dryfesdale Lodge
A709
17
18
Greenhill
Heathhall
Twelve Apostles Stone Circle
New Bridge
Lincluden
Church
Dumfries & Galloway Aviation
The Grove
Torthorwald
Torthorwald Castle
Mossburn Animal Centre
Hightae
Rammerscales House
Smallholm
Howat's Hill
Burnswark
Kirtleton
Craigs
Waterbeck
B725
B722
Terregles
Arts Cen.
A780
Collin
Kettleholm
Middlebie
Maxwelltown
A75
Cargenbridge
Troqueer
Globe Inn
DUMFRIES
SEE PAGE 193
Greenlea
Elizafield
Racks
Woodside
B724
Dalton Pottery
Dalton
R. Annan
B7076
19
Kirkconnel
Ecclefechan
Carlyle's Birthplace NTS
Eaglesfield
Chapelknowe
Drumsleet
Hills Wood
B726
Kingholm Quay
The Crichton
Mouswald
Hoddom Castle
Hoddomcross
20
Kirtlebridge
Merkland Cross
A711
Islesteps
Carrutherstown
Repentance Tower
Lochar Water
Kelton
River Nith
B7020
Brydekirk
Moorend
Newton
Bruce's Cave
Kirkpatrick Fleming
21
Lochaber Loch
Mabie
Mabie Farm Park
Mabie Forest
A710
Loch Arthur
Bankend
Glencaple
Clarencefield
Ruthwell Cross
Charlesfield
Warmanbie
Creca
Stapleton Tower
B6357
GRETNA
Gretna Green
Kirkconnell
National Costume
Brow Well
Ruthwell
Savings Banks
Shearington
Mote of Annan
Howes
ANNAN
Rigg
Corn Mill
New Abbey
Sweetheart Abbey
Waterloo Monument
Blackshaw
Caerlaverock
Caerlaverock Wildfowl & Wetlands Centre
Cummertrees
Powfoot
Welldale
Dornock
Eastriggs
Devil's Porridge
B721
Gretna
Loch Kindar
Long Fell
Meikle Hard Hill
North Corbelly
Drumburn
Criffel
1868 Criffel
Boreland Hill
SCOTLAND
ENGLAND
Barnkirk Point
Torduff Point
Redkirk Point
Port Carlisle
Campfield Marsh
Bowness-on-Solway
Glasson
Drumburgh
Drumburgh Moss
Easton
Dykesfield
Boustead Hill
Longburgh
Carsethorn
Kirkbean
SOLWAY FIRTH
Cardurnock
Anthorn
Longcroft
Whitrigg
Angerton
B5307
Fingland
Finglandrigg Woods
Kirkbampton
Thurstonfield
B793
Caulkerbush
Prestonmill
John Paul Jones
Mainsriddle
Mersehead
Loaningfoot
Southerness
Southerness Point
Skinburness
Kirkbride
Church
Newton Arlosh
Wampool
Little Bampton
Oughterby
Great Orton
Lifeboat Station
Silloth
Greenrow
Calvo
Seaville
Aikton
Biglands
Wiggonby
Blackdyke
Blitterlees
B5302
B5300
Wedholme Flow
Moss Side
Gamelsby
Thornby
Raby
R. Waver
Moorhouse
Knoxwood Wildlife Rescue Trust
Low Whinnow
Parton
Crofton
Kelsick
Oulton
Micklethwaite
A596
Beckfoot
Wolsty
Highlaws
Abbeytown
Dundraw
Lessonhall
Standingstone
Pelutho
Moor Row
Aikhead
Thornby Moor Dairy
West Woodside
Aldoth
Southerfield
Waverbridge
Wigton
Kirkland
Newtown
Tarns
Blencogo
Waverton
Highmoor
Cowgate
Bromfield
Parkgate
Brackenlands
A595
Carwath
Mawbray
Holme St. Cuthbert
Dubmill Point
Mealrigg
Langrigg
High Scales
High Longthwaite
Brackenthwaite
Old Carlisle Roman Fort
Red Dial
B5305
Salta
Edderside
New Cowper
Waterside
Woodrow
Westward
Rosley
Westnewton
Yearngill
Heathfield
Low Row
Bolton Low Houses
Bolton Wood Lane
Bolton New Houses
Crookdake
Allonby
Allonby Bay
Watchill
Fletchertown
CUMBRIA
B5301
B5299
Hayton
Aspatria
Blennerhasset
Mealsgate
Prospect
Harriston
Milefortlet 21 Salt Pans
Allerby
Oughterside
Kirkland Guards
Boltongate
Sandale
The Howk Bobbin Mill
Whelpo
Crosscanonby Carr
Crosscanonby
Westmoor
Crosby Villa
Arsonby
Plumbland
Bothel
Church
Torpenhow
Whitrigg
Ireby
The Howk
Senhouse Roman Museum
Alauna Roman Fort
Crosby
Bullgill
Gilcrux
Greengill
R. Ellen
Birkby
Maryport
Maritime Museum
Netherton
West Coast Indoor Karting
A594
Dearham
Townhead
Ellenborough
Moota Hill
Sunderland
High Ireby
Ruthwaite
Uldale
Longlands
Fell Side
Branthwaite
Binsey 1467
A591

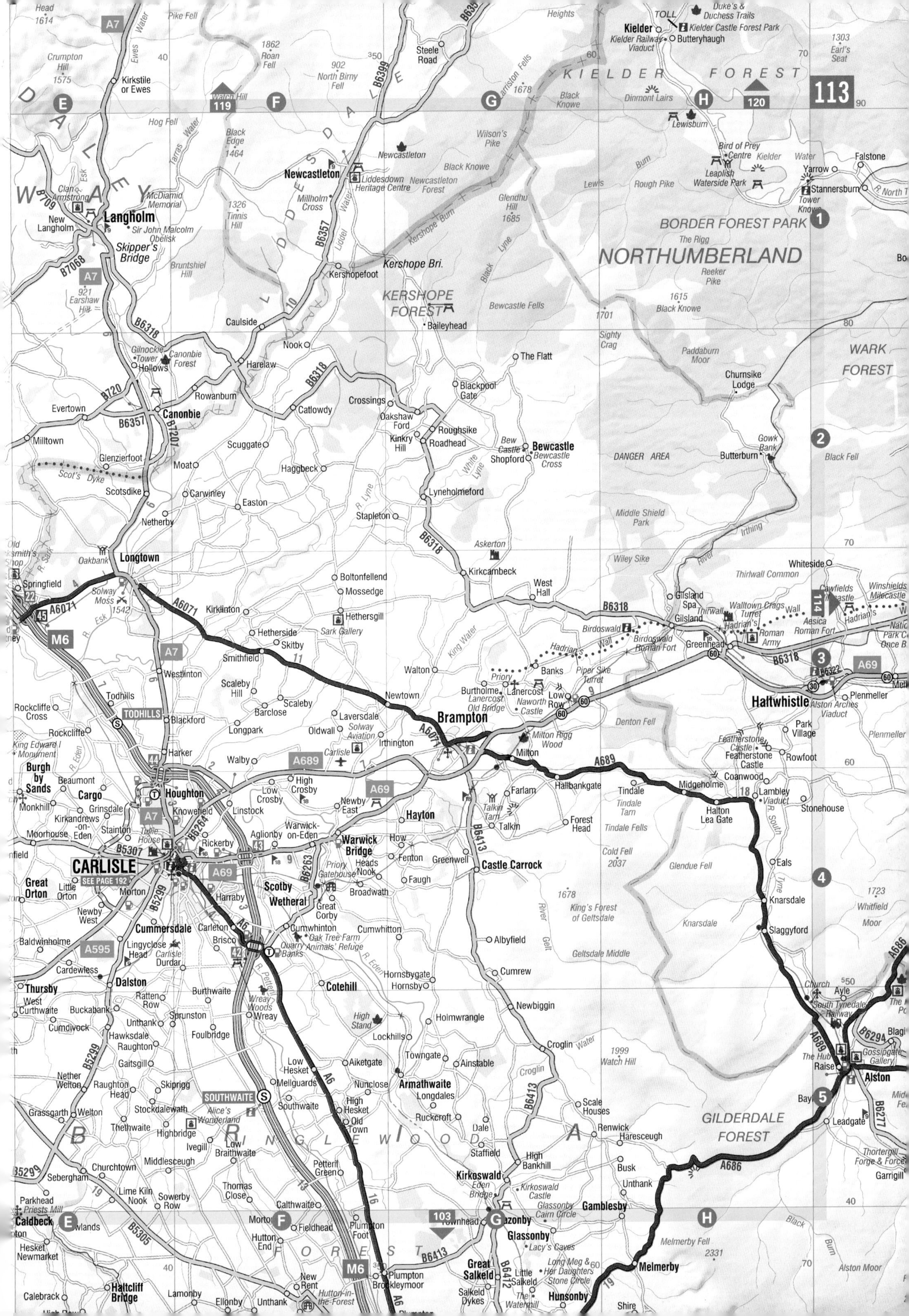
Head
1614
A7
Ewes Water
Pike Fell
40
1862
Roan
Fell
350
902
North Birny
Fell
B6399
Steele
Road
B6357
Heights
Duke's &
Duchess Trails
TOLL
Kielder
Kielder Castle Forest Park
Kielder Railway
Viaduct
Butteryhaugh
60
70
1303
Earl's
Seat
Crumpton
Hill
1575
Kirkstile
or Ewes
Watch Hill
119
E
F
G
Garriston Fells
1678
KIELDER FOREST
Black
Knowe
Dinmont Lairs
H
120
90
DALEY
Hog Fell
Tarras Water
Black
Edge
1464
LIDDESDALE
Wilson's
Pike
Lewisburn
Newcastleton
Newcastleton
Liddesdown
Heritage Centre
Newcastleton
Forest
Black Knowe
Bird of Prey
Centre
Kielder Water
Falstone
Leaplish
Waterside Park
Yarrow
Stannersburn
R. North Tyne
Lewis Burn
Rough Pike
Lewis
WALEY
B709
Clan
Armstrong
R. Esk
McDiamid
Memorial
Langholm
New
Langholm
Sir John Malcolm
Obelisk
Skipper's
Bridge
1326
Tinnis
Hill
Millholm
Cross
Liddel Water
B6357
Kershope Burn
Glendhu
Hill
1685
Black Lyne
Tower
Knowe
1
BORDER FOREST PARK
The Rigg
NORTHUMBERLAND
Bo
B7068
A7
Bruntshiel
Hill
921
Earshaw
Hill
Kershopefoot
Kershope Bri.
KERSHOPE
FOREST
Baileyhead
Bewcastle Fells
Reeker
Pike
1615
Black Knowe
1701
Sighty
Crag
80
WARK
FOREST
Paddaburn
Moor
B6318
Caulside
Nook
Gilnockie
Tower
Hollows
Canonbie
Forest
Harelaw
B6318
The Flatt
Churnsike
Lodge
B720
Evertown
Rowanburn
Canonbie
B6357
B7201
Catlowdy
Crossings
Oakshaw
Ford
Blackpool
Gate
Kinkry
Hill
Roughsike
Roadhead
Milltown
Scuggate
Glenzierfoot
Scot's Dyke
Moat
Haggbeck
Bew
Castle
Shopford
Bewcastle
Bewcastle
Cross
White Lyne
DANGER AREA
Gowk
Bank
Butterburn
2
Black Fell
Scotsdike
Carwinley
Easton
R. Lyne
Lyneholmeford
Netherby
Stapleton
Middle Shield
Park
Irthing
Old
Blacksmith's
Shop
R. Sark
Oakbank
Longtown
B6318
Askerton
Wiley Sike
River
Whiteside
70
Springfield
22
45
A6071
Solway
Moss
1542
Boltonfellend
Mossedge
Kirkcambeck
Thirlwall Common
West
Hall
B6318
Gilsland
Spa
Gilsland
Thirlwall
Walltown Crags
Turret
Cawfields
Milecastle
Winshields
Milecastle
114
Hadrian's Wall
Kirklinton
Hethersgill
Sark Gallery
R. Esk
M6
Hetherside
Skitby
Smithfield
A7
Westlinton
Birdoswald
Birdoswald
Roman Fort
Hadrian's Wall
Greenhead
Roman
Army
Aesica
Roman Fort
National
Park Centre
Once Brewed
King Water
Walton
Priory
Lanercost
Burtholme
Lanercost
Old Bridge
Naworth
Castle
Banks
Piper Sike
Turret
Low
Row
60
B6318
3
B6322
A69
Haltwhistle
Plenmeller
Alston Arches
Viaduct
Todhills
Rockcliffe
Cross
Scaleby
Hill
Scaleby
Barclose
Newtown
Brampton
TODHILLS
Blackford
Longpark
Laversdale
Solway
Aviation
Oldwall
Irthington
A6071
Denton Fell
Milton Rigg
Wood
Park
Village
Featherstone
Castle
Featherstone
Castle
Rowfoot
Plenmeller
Rockcliffe
King Edward I
Monument
R. Eden
Harker
Walby
A689
Carlisle
Milton
A689
60
Burgh
by
Sands
Beaumont
Cargo
Houghton
Low
Crosby
High
Crosby
A69
Newby
East
Farlam
Hallbankgate
Tindale
Tindale
Tarn
Midgeholme
Coanwood
Lambley
Viaduct
18
Halton
Lea Gate
Stonehouse
R. South Tyne
Monkhill
Grinsdale
A7
Knowefield
B6264
Linstock
Hayton
Talkin
Tarn
Talkin
Forest
Head
Tindale Fells
Kirkandrews
-on-
Eden
Stainton
Tullie
House
Moorhouse
Rickerby
Aglionby
43
Warwick-
on-Eden
Warwick
Bridge
How
Fenton
Greenwell
B6413
Cold Fell
2037
Glendue Fell
Eals
Thurstonfield
CARLISLE
SEE PAGE 192
B5307
A69
B6263
Priory
Gatehouse
Heads
Nook
Faugh
Castle Carrock
Great
Orton
Little
Orton
Morton
B5299
Harraby
Scotby
Wetheral
Broadwath
Great
Corby
4
1678
King's Forest
of Geltsdale
River Gelt
Tyne
Knarsdale
Knarsdale
1723
Whitfield
Moor
Newby
West
Cummersdale
Carleton
A6
Cumwhinton
Oak Tree Farm
Cumwhitton
Baldwinholme
A595
Lingyclose
Head
Carlisle
Durdar
Brisco
42
Quarry
Banks
Animals' Refuge
R. Eden
Albyfield
Geltsdale Middle
Slaggyford
A686
Cardewlees
Dalston
R. Petteril
Hornsbygate
Hornsby
Cumrew
Thursby
West
Curthwaite
Buckabank
Ratten
Row
Burthwaite
Wreay
Woods
Wreay
Cotehill
Newbiggin
550
Church
Ayle
South Tynedale
Railway
A689
Unthank
Sprunston
High
Stand
Holmwrangle
Cumdivock
Hawksdale
Raughton
Foulbridge
Lockhills
B6294
Gossipgate
Gallery
Blagill
Gaitsgill
Towngate
Ainstable
Croglin
Croglin Water
1999
Watch Hill
The Hub
Raise
Alston
B5299
Nether
Welton
Raughton
Head
Skiprigg
Low
Hesket
Mellguards
Aiketgate
A6
Nunclose
Armathwaite
Longdales
Croglin
B6413
Bay
5
Grassgarth
Welton
SOUTHWAITE
Stockdalewath
Alice's
Wonderland
Southwaite
High
Hesket
Old
Town
Ruckcroft
Scale
Houses
GILDERDALE
FOREST
Leadgate
B6277
Thethwaite
Highbridge
Ivegill
Low
Braithwaite
INGLEWOOD
Dale
Staffield
Renwick
Haresceugh
Thortergill
Forge & Force
Garrigill
B5299
Churchtown
Middlesceugh
High
Bankhill
Busk
Sebergham
Lime Kiln
Nook
Sowerby
Row
Thomas
Close
Petteril
Green
Kirkoswald
Eden
Bridge
Kirkoswald
Castle
Unthank
A686
40
Parkhead
Priests Mill
Caldbeck
Calthwaite
Glassonby
Cairn Circle
Gamblesby
Morton
Fieldhead
Plumpton
Foot
103
Townhead
Gazonby
Glassonby
Lacy's Caves
Black Burn
Hesket
Newmarket
Hutton
End
FOREST
B6413
Great
Salkeld
B6412
Little
Salkeld
Long Meg &
Her Daughters
Stone Circle
Melmerby Fell
2331
Melmerby
70
Alston Moor
40
M6
Plumpton
Brockleymoor
New
Rent
Hutton-in-
the-Forest
Calebrack
Haltcliff
Bridge
Lamonby
Ellonby
Unthank
Salkeld
Dykes
The
Watermill
Hunsonby
Shire

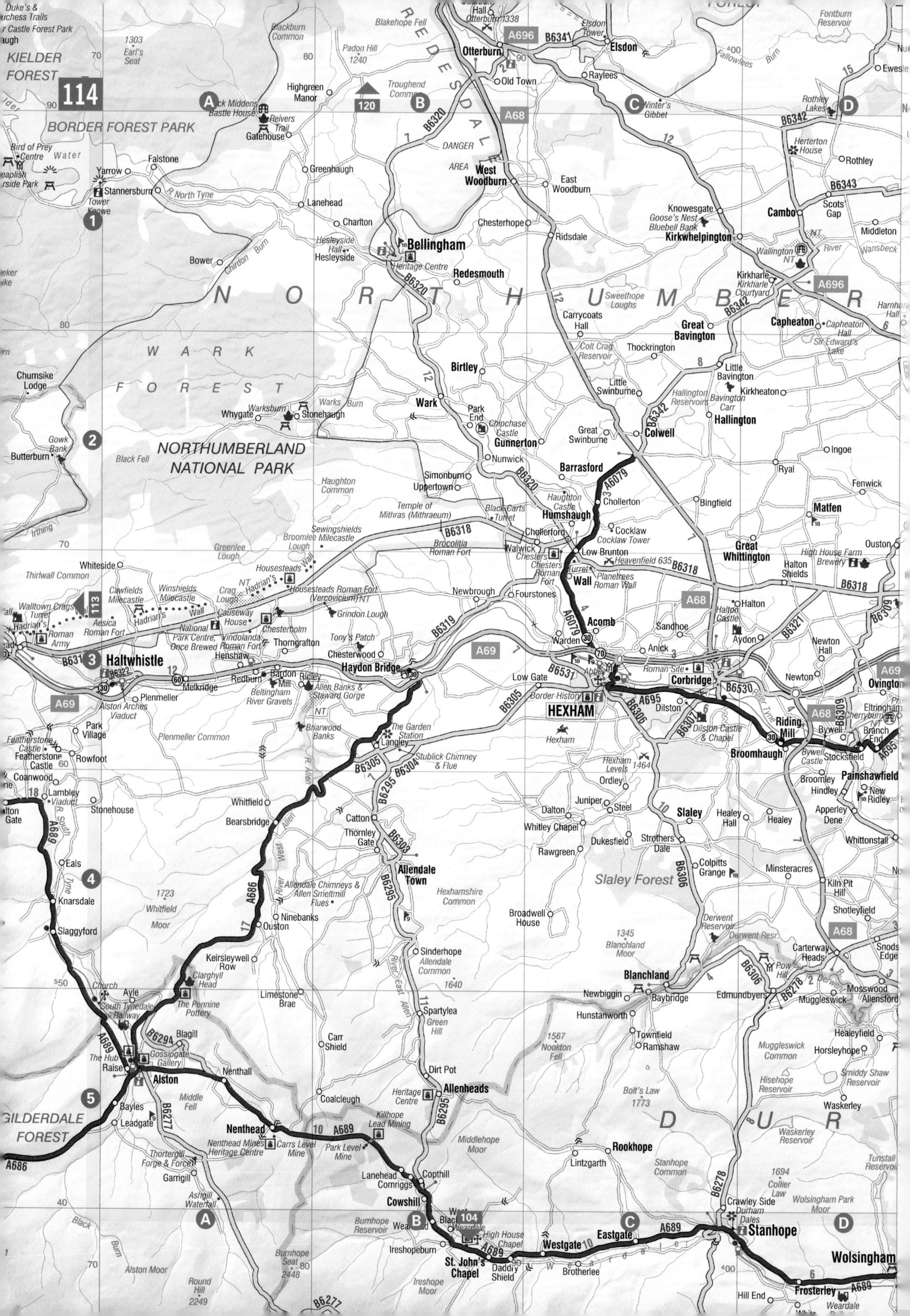
KIELDER FOREST
114
BORDER FOREST PARK
NORTHUMBERLAND NATIONAL PARK
WARK FOREST
NORTHUMBER
REDESDALE
Otterburn
Elsdon
Bellingham
Wark
Barrasford
Humshaugh
Chollerford
Wall
Acomb
HEXHAM
Corbridge
Riding Mill
Haltwhistle
Haydon Bridge
Allendale Town
Allenheads
Alston
Nenthead
Blanchland
Slaley
Slaley Forest
Stanhope
Wolsingham
Westgate
Eastgate
St. John's Chapel
Cowshill
GILDERDALE FOREST
120
113
104
A68
A69
A696
A686
A689
A6079
B6318
B6320
B6306
B6295

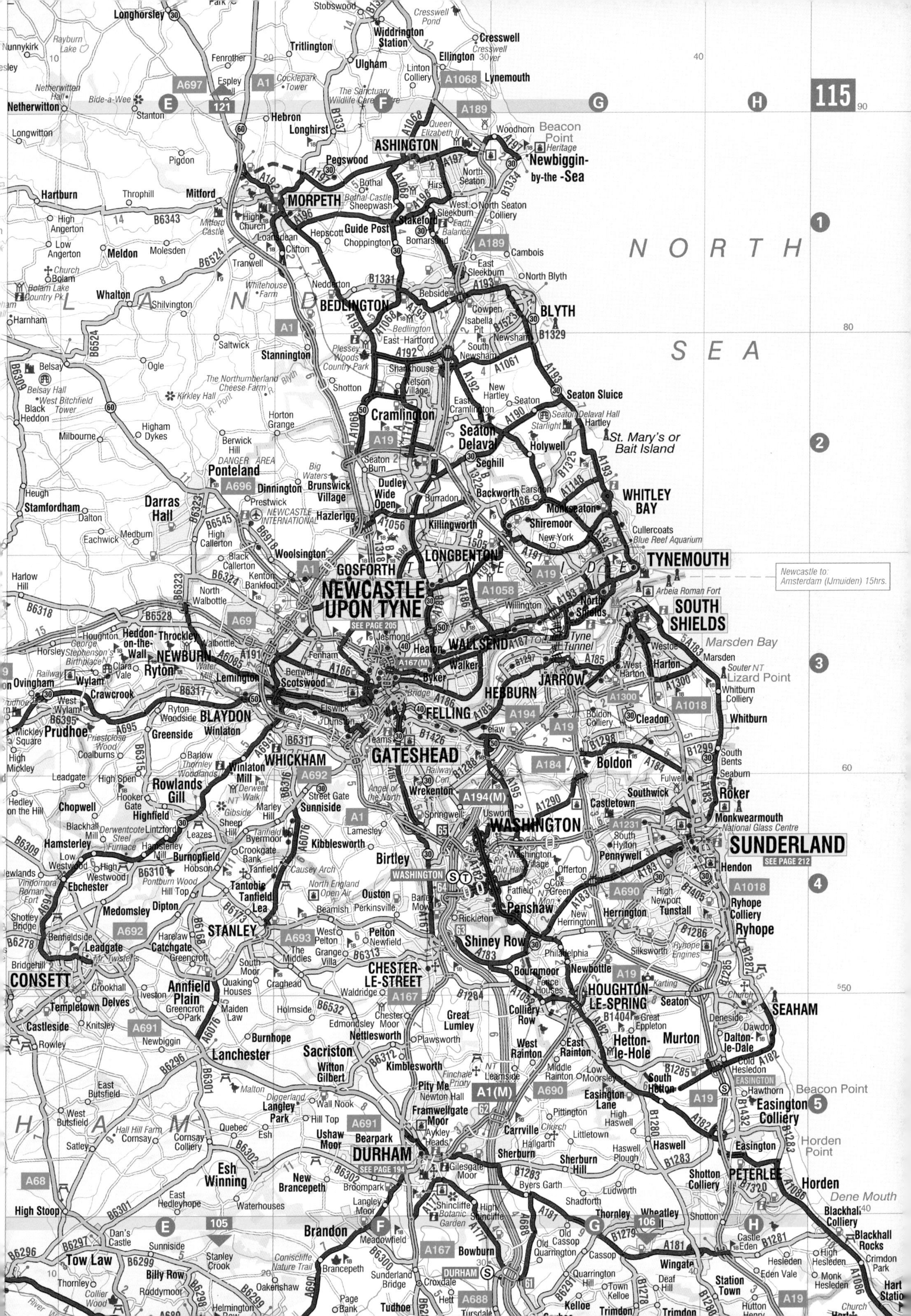
NORTH
SEA
ASHINGTON
MORPETH
Newbiggin-by-the-Sea
BEDLINGTON
BLYTH
Cramlington
Seaton Delaval
Seaton Sluice
St. Mary's or Bait Island
WHITLEY BAY
TYNEMOUTH
Newcastle to: Amsterdam (IJmuiden) 15hrs.
NEWCASTLE UPON TYNE
SEE PAGE 205
GOSFORTH
LONGBENTON
WALLSEND
SOUTH SHIELDS
Marsden Bay
JARROW
HEBBURN
FELLING
GATESHEAD
BLAYDON
WHICKHAM
NEWBURN
Ryton
Prudhoe
Ponteland
Darras Hall
NEWCASTLE INTERNATIONAL
WASHINGTON
SUNDERLAND
SEE PAGE 212
Roker
Boldon
Cleadon
Whitburn
Ryhope
Penshaw
Shiney Row
HOUGHTON-LE-SPRING
CHESTER-LE-STREET
Birtley
STANLEY
CONSETT
Annfield Plain
Lanchester
Sacriston
DURHAM
SEE PAGE 194
Brandon
SEAHAM
Murton
Hetton-le-Hole
Easington Colliery
PETERLEE
Horden
Blackhall Colliery
Tow Law
Esh Winning
Stamfordham
Mitford
Hartburn
Belsay
Lynemouth
Cresswell
Ellington
Widdrington Station
Longhorsley
Netherwitton
Pegswood
Guide Post
Stakeford
Cambois
Hexham
Rowlands Gill
Hamsterley
Ebchester
Bowburn
Wingate
Sherburn
West Rainton
A1
A1(M)
A19
A69
A68
A167
A189
A690
A691
A692
A693
A696
A697
A1058
A1068
A1018
A184
A194
A194(M)
A1300
A1231
E
F
G
H
1
2
3
4
5
105
106
121

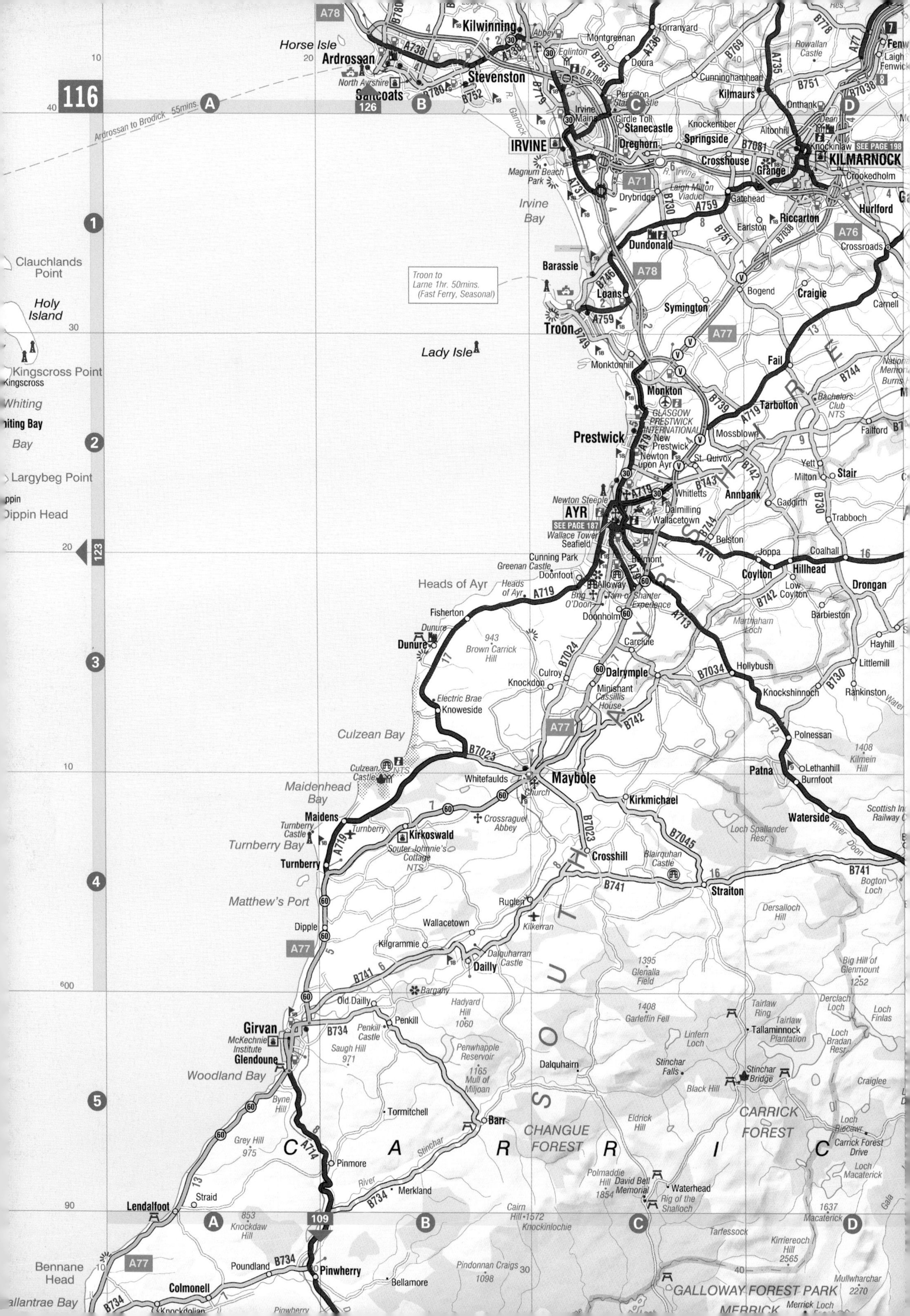
116
123
126
109
Ardrossan to Brodick 55mins.
Troon to Larne 1hr. 50mins. (Fast Ferry, Seasonal)
SEE PAGE 198
SEE PAGE 187
Ardrossan
Saltcoats
Stevenston
Kilwinning
IRVINE
KILMARNOCK
Troon
Prestwick
AYR
Maybole
Girvan
Irvine Bay
Culzean Bay
Maidenhead Bay
Turnberry Bay
Woodland Bay
Horse Isle
Lady Isle
Holy Island
Clauchlands Point
Kingscross Point
Largybeg Point
Dippin Head
Heads of Ayr
Bennane Head
Ballantrae Bay
SOUTH AYRSHIRE
CARRICK
CHANGUE FOREST
CARRICK FOREST
GALLOWAY FOREST PARK
GLASGOW PRESTWICK INTERNATIONAL
Dalrymple
Dailly
Barr
Colmonell
Pinwherry
Lendalfoot
Straiton
Patna
Coylton
Drongan
Hurlford
Tarbolton
Dundonald
Symington
Kirkoswald
Kirkmichael
Crosshill
Turnberry
Maidens
Dunure
Alloway
Monkton

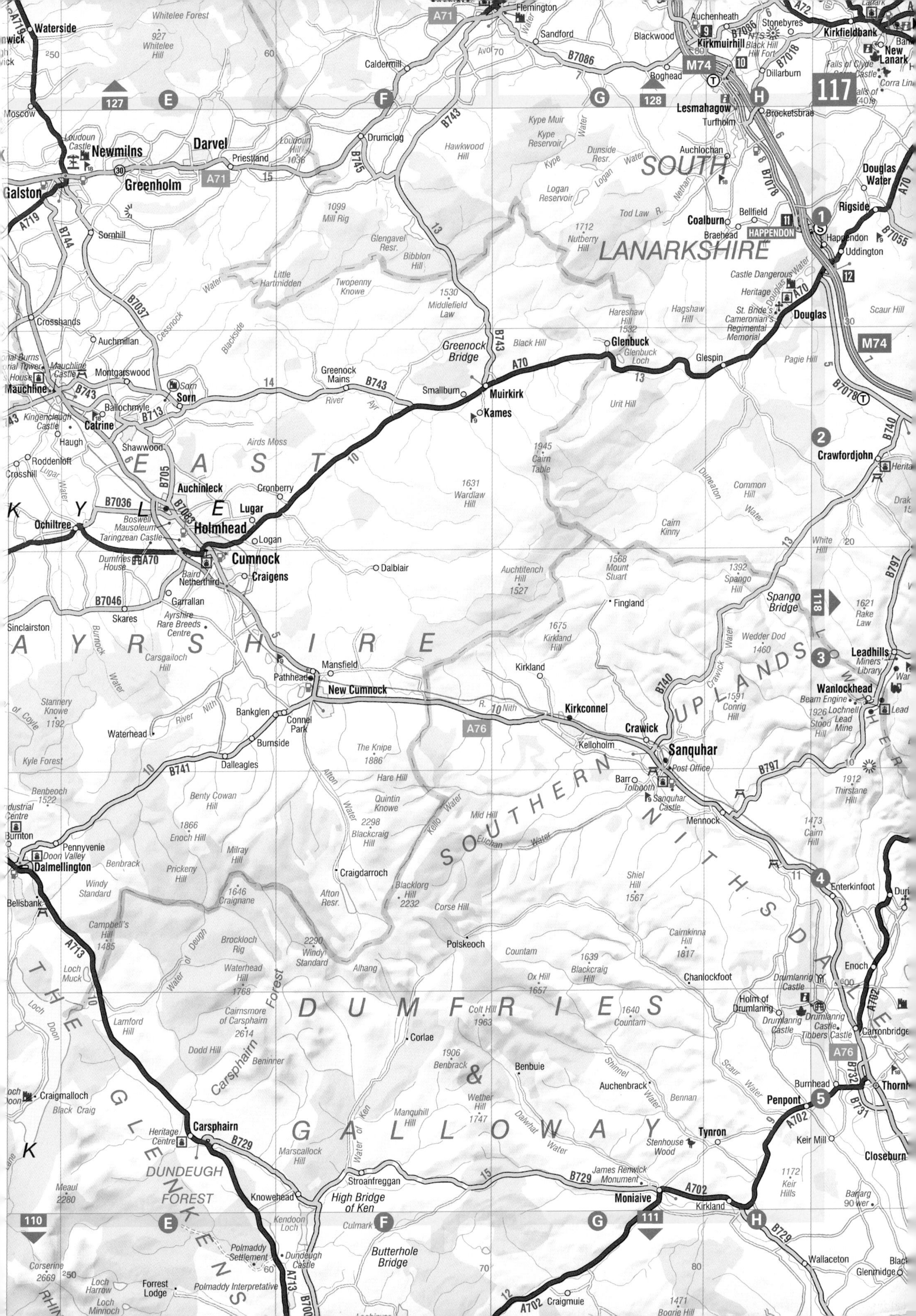

Whitelee Forest
927 Whitelee Hill
Waterside
Flemington
Sandford
Auchenheath
Stonebyres
Kirkfieldbank
New Lanark
Falls of Clyde
Corra Castle
Calderrmill
Blackwood
Kirkmuirhill
Black Hill Hill Fort
Dillarburn
Boghead
M74
117
127
128
E
F
G
H
Moscow
Loudoun Castle
Newmilns
Darvel
Priestland
Drumclog
Loudoun Hill 1036
Hawkwood Hill
Kype Muir
Kype Reservoir
Dunside Resr.
Lesmahagow
Turfholm
Brocketsbrae
Auchlochan
SOUTH
LANARKSHIRE
Douglas Water
Galston
Greenholm
A71
A719
B744
Sornhill
1099 Mill Rig
Glengavel Resr.
Bibblon Hill
Logan Reservoir
Tod Law
1712 Nutberry Hill
Coalburn
Bellfield
Braehead
HAPPENDON
Happendon
Uddington
Rigside
B7055
Little Hartmidden
Twopenny Knowe
1530 Middlefield Law
Castle Dangerous
Heritage
St. Bride's
Cameronian's Regimental Memorial
Douglas
Hagshaw Hill
Hareshaw Hill 1532
Scaur Hill
B7037
Crosshands
Auchmillan
Cessnock
Blackside
Greenock Bridge
Black Hill
Glenbuck
Glenbuck Loch
Glespin
Pagie Hill
Burns House
Mauchline
Mauchline Castle
Montgarswood
Sorn
Greenock Mains
B743
Smallburn
Muirkirk
A70
Kames
Kingencleugh Castle
Ballochmyle
Catrine
B713
River Ayr
Urit Hill
B7078
B740
Haugh
Shawwood
Airds Moss
1945 Cairn Table
Crawfordjohn
Roddenloft
Crosshill
Lugar Water
EAST
B705
Auchinleck
Cronberry
1631 Wardlaw Hill
Duneaton
Common Hill
Water
KYLE
B7036
B7083
Lugar
Ochiltree
Boswell Mausoleum
Taringzean Castle
Holmhead
Logan
Cairn Kinny
White Hill
Dumfries House
Cumnock
Craigens
Baird
Netherthird
Dalblair
1568 Mount Stuart
1392 Spango Hill
Spango Bridge
118
1621 Rake Law
Auchtitench Hill 1527
B7046
Skares
Garrallan
Finglaud
Sinclairston
Ayrshire Rare Breeds Centre
AYRSHIRE
1675 Kirkland Hill
Wedder Dod 1460
Leadhills
Miners' Library
Carsgailoch Hill
Mansfield
Pathhead
Kirkland
New Cumnock
B740
UPLANDS
Wanlockhead
Beam Engine
1591 Conrig Hill
1926 Lochnell Lead Mine
Stood Hill
Stannery Knowe 1192
Bankglen
Connel Park
River Nith
Waterhead
Burnside
R. Nith
Kirkconnel
A76
Crawick
Kelloholm
Sanquhar
Post Office
Kyle Forest
Dalleagles
B741
The Knipe 1886
Hare Hill
SOUTHERN
B797
1912 Thirstane Hill
Benbeoch 1522
Benty Cowan Hill
Quintin Knowe
Barr
Tolbooth
Sanquhar Castle
Mennock
Industrial Centre
Burnton
1866 Enoch Hill
2298 Blackcraig Hill
Afton Water
Kello Water
Mid Hill
Euchan Water
NITHSDALE
1473 Cairn Hill
Pennyvenie
Doon Valley
Dalmellington
Benbrack
Milray Hill
Prickeny Hill
Craigdarroch
Windy Standard
Bellsbank
1646 Craignane
Afton Resr.
Blacklorg Hill 2232
Corse Hill
Shiel Hill 1567
Enterkinfoot
Campbell's Hill 1485
A713
Brockloch Rig
2290 Windy Standard
Polskeoch
Countam
Cairnkinna Hill 1817
Loch Muck
Water of Deugh
Waterhead Hill 1768
Alhang
1639 Blackcraig Hill
Ox Hill 1657
Chanlockfoot
Drumlanrig Castle
Enoch
Carsphairn Forest
DUMFRIES
Colt Hill 1963
1640 Countam
Holm of Drumlanrig
Drumlanrig Castle
Tibbers Castle
Carronbridge
THE GLENKENS
Loch Doon
Lamford Hill
Cairnsmore of Carsphairn 2614
Corlae
A702
Dodd Hill
Beninner
1906 Benbrack
Benbuie
Shinnel Water
Scaur Water
A76
&
Auchenbrack
Bennan
Burnhead
Thornhill
B732
Craigmalloch
Black Craig
Wether Hill 1747
Penpont
B731
Carsphairn
Heritage Centre
B729
GALLOWAY
Manquhill Hill
Water of Ken
Dalwhat Water
Tynron
Stenhouse Wood
Keir Mill
Closeburn
DUNDEUGH FOREST
Marscallock Hill
James Renwick Monument
1172 Keir Hills
Meaul 2280
Stroanfreggan
Moniaive
Kirkland
Barjarg Tower
Knowehead
High Bridge of Ken
110
111
Kendoon Loch
Culmark
Polmaddy Settlement
Butterhole Bridge
Wallaceton
Glenmidge
Corserine 2669
Dundeugh Castle
Loch Harrow
Loch Minnoch
Forrest Lodge
Polmaddy Interpretative
RHINNS
Craigmuie
1471 Bogrie Hill
B700

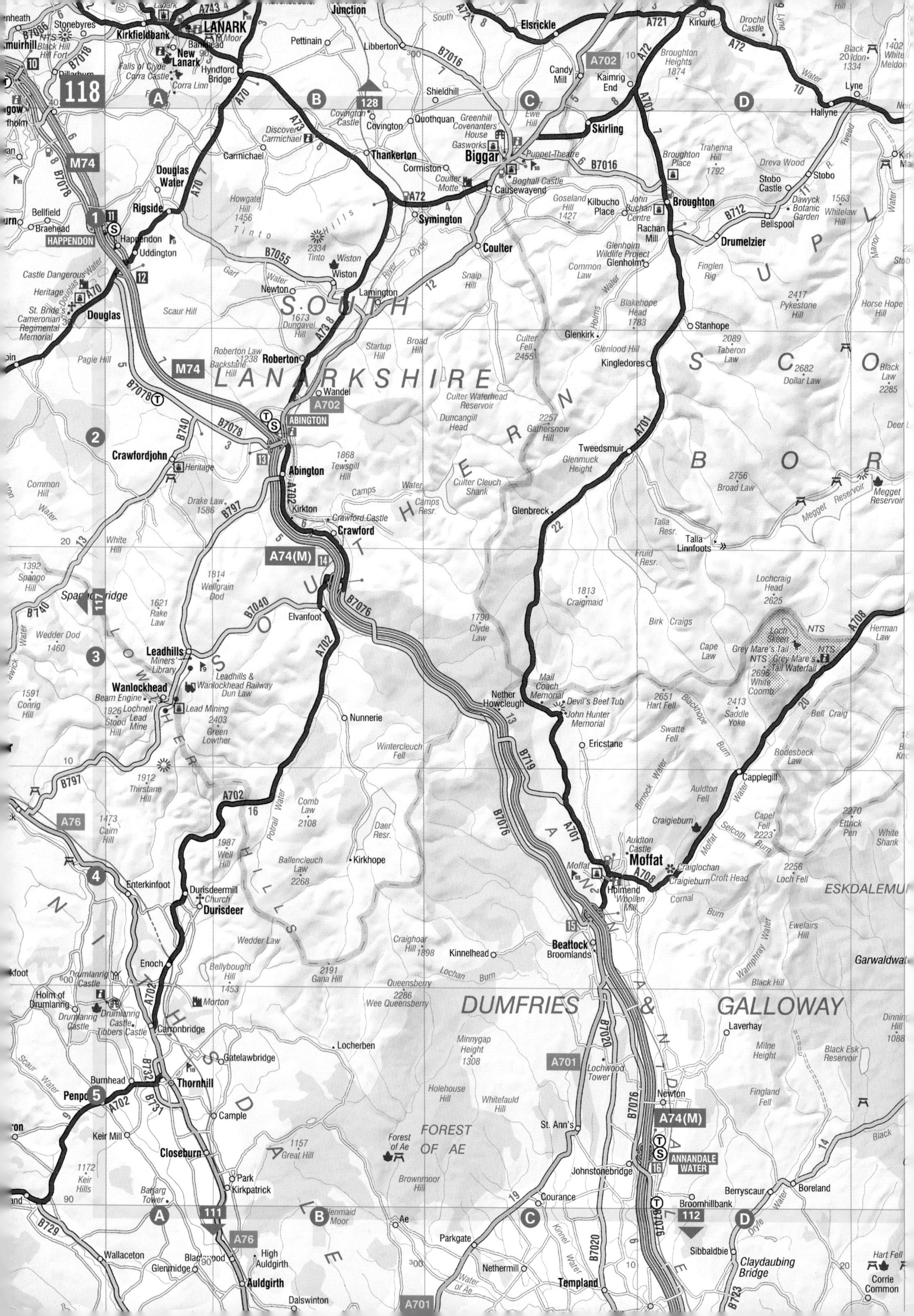

118
128
117
111
112
LANARK
Kirkfieldbank
Stonebyres
New Lanark
Falls of Clyde
Corra Castle
Corra Linn
Hyndford Bridge
Bankhead
Pettinain
Libberton
Junction
Elsrickle
Kirkurd
Drochil Castle
Candy Mill
Kaimrig End
Broughton Heights 1874
Black Meldon 1334
Lyne
Hallyne
Covington Castle
Covington
Quothquan
Shieldhill
Greenhill Covenanters' House
Gasworks
Biggar
Puppet Theatre
Skirling
Discover Carmichael
Carmichael
Thankerton
Cormiston
Coulter Motte
Boghall Castle
Causewayend
Symington
Coulter
Broughton
Broughton Place
Trahenna Hill 1792
Dreva Wood
Stobo
Stobo Castle
Dawyck Botanic Garden
Bellspool
Drumelzier
Goseland Hill 1427
Kilbucho Place
John Buchan Centre
Rachan Mill
Glenholm Wildlife Project
Glenholm
Douglas Water
Rigside
Howgate Hill 1456
Tinto Hills
2334 Tinto
Wiston
Lamington
Newton
River Clyde
Bellfield
Braehead
HAPPENDON
Happendon
Uddington
Castle Dangerous
Heritage
St. Bride's
Cameronian Regimental Memorial
Douglas
Scaur Hill
SOUTH
1673 Dungavel Hill
Roberton
Robertson Law 1238
Backstane Hill
Startup Hill
Broad Hill
Snaip Hill
Common Law
Blakehope Head 1783
Stanhope
Finglen Rig
2417 Pykestone Hill
Horse Hope Hill
Culter Fell 2455
Glenkirk
Glenlood Hill
Kingledores
2089 Taberon Law
2682 Dollar Law
Black Law 2285
Pagie Hill
LANARKSHIRE
Wandel
ABINGTON
Abington
Culter Waterhead Reservoir
Duncangill Head
2257 Gathersnow Hill
Glenmuck Height
Tweedsmuir
Crawfordjohn
Heritage
1868 Tewsgill Hill
Culter Cleuch Shank
Camps Water
Camps Resr.
Common Hill
Drake Law 1586
Kirkton
Crawford Castle
Crawford
Glenbreck
2756 Broad Law
Megget Reservoir
Talla Resr.
Talla Linnfoots
Fruid Resr.
White Hill
1392 Spango Hill
Spango Bridge
1814 Wellgrain Dod
1621 Rake Law
Elvanfoot
1813 Craigmaid
Lochcraig Head 2625
Wedder Dod 1460
Leadhills
Miners' Library
Leadhills & Wanlockhead Railway
Dun Law
1790 Clyde Law
Birk Craigs
Cape Law
Loch Skeen
Grey Mare's Tail
Grey Mare's Tail Waterfall
NTS
Herman Law
Wanlockhead
Beam Engine
Lead Mining
1926 Lochnell Lead Mine
Stood Hill
2403 Green Lowther
1591 Conrig Hill
Nether Howcleugh
Mail Coach Memorial
Devil's Beef Tub
John Hunter Memorial
2651 Hart Fell
2696 White Coomb
2413 Saddle Yoke
Bell Craig
Nunnerie
Ericstane
Swatte Fell
Blackhope Burn
Wintercleuch Fell
Bodesbeck Law
1912 Thirstane Hill
Comb Law 2108
Potrail Water
Capplegill
Auldton Fell
Daer Resr.
Craigieburn
Capel Fell 2223
2270 Ettrick Pen
White Shank
1473 Cairn Hill
1987 Well Hill
Ballencleuch Law 2268
Kirkhope
Auldton Castle
Moffat
Craiglochan
Craigieburn
Croft Head
2256 Loch Fell
ESKDALEMUIR
Enterkinfoot
Durisdeermill
Church
Durisdeer
Holmend
Woollen Mill
Selcoth Burn
Cornal Burn
Ewelairs Hill
Wedder Law
Craighoar Hill 1898
Kinnelhead
Beattock
Broomlands
Wamphray Water
Garwaldwater
Enoch
Bellybought Hill 1453
Drumlanrig Castle
Holm of Drumlanrig
Drumlanrig Castle
Tibbers Castle
Morton
2191 Gana Hill
Lochan Burn
Queensberry 2286
Wee Queensberry
DUMFRIES
&
GALLOWAY
Black Hill
Laverhay
Dinning Hill 1088
Carronbridge
Locherben
Minnygap Height 1308
Milne Height
Black Esk Reservoir
Gatelawbridge
Lochwood Tower
Burnhead
Thornhill
Penpont
Scaur Water
Holehouse Hill
Whitefauld Hill
Newton
Fingland Fell
Keir Mill
Cample
Forest of Ae
FOREST OF AE
St. Ann's
Closeburn
1157 Great Hill
ANNANDALE WATER
Johnstonebridge
1172 Keir Hills
Park
Kirkpatrick
Brownmoor Hill
Berryscaur
Boreland
Barjarg Tower
Courance
Broomhillbank
Glenmaid Moor
Ae
Dryfe Water
Sibbaldbie
Parkgate
Wallaceton
Glenmidge
Blackwood
High Auldgirth
Auldgirth
Nethermill
Kinnel Water
Water of Ae
Templand
Claydaubing Bridge
Hart Fell
Corrie Common
Dalswinton
LOWTHER HILLS
NITHSDALE
ANNANDALE
SOUTHERN UPLANDS
M74
A74(M)
A70
A73
A72
A702
A701
A708
A76
A721
A743
B7078
B740
B797
B7040
B7076
B719
B7020
B7016
B7055
B712
B729
B732
B731
B723

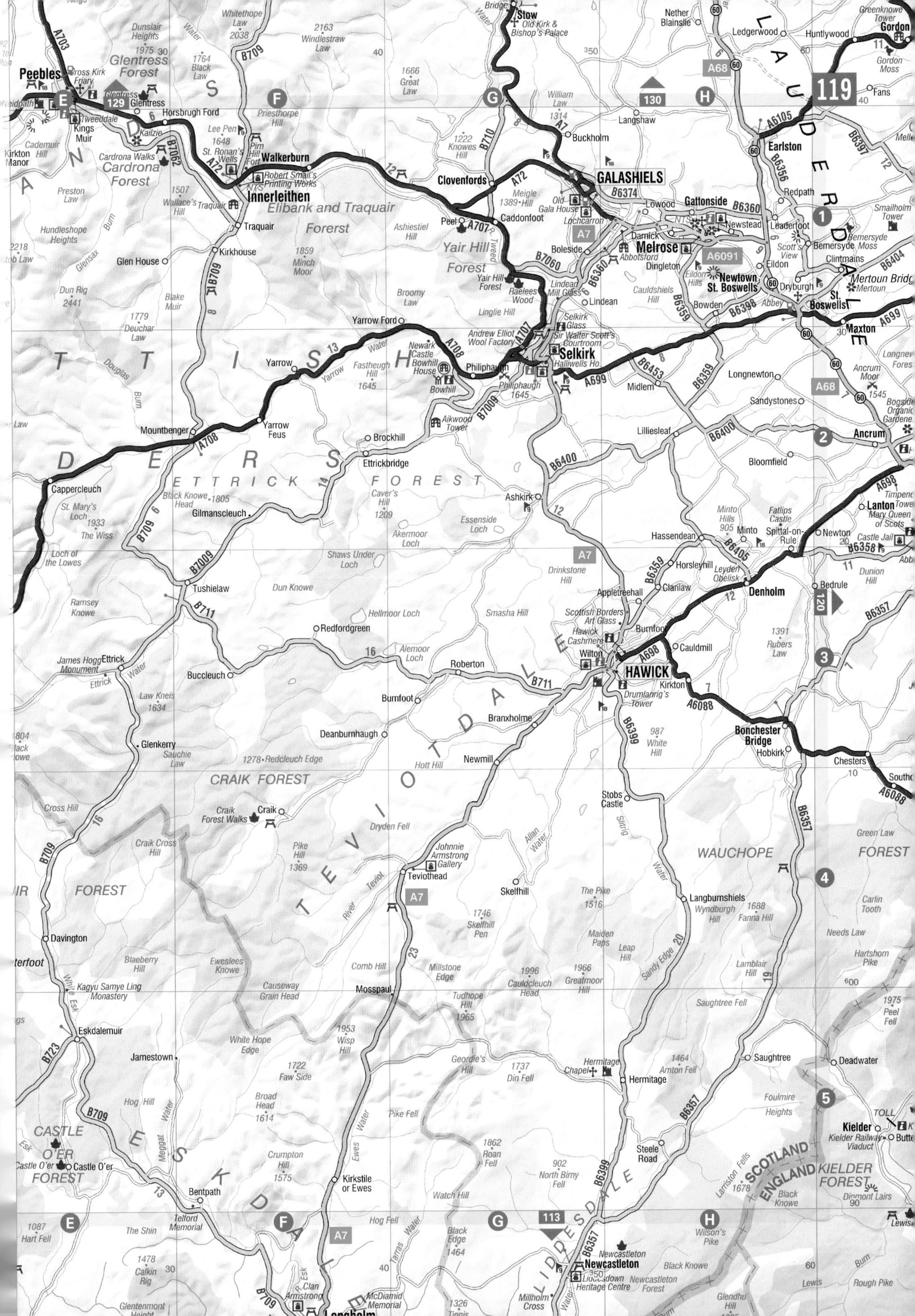

119
129
130
120
113
E
F
G
H
1
2
3
4
5
Peebles
Cross Kirk Friary
Glentress
Glentress Forest
Dunslair Heights
1975
Whitehope Law
2038
Windlestrawa Law
2163
1764 Black Law
1666 Great Law
Kings Muir
Tweeddale
Kailzie
Horsbrugh Ford
Cademuir Hill
Kirkton Manor
Cardrona Walks
Cardrona Forest
Priesthorpe Hill
Lee Pen 1648
St. Ronan's Wells
Pirn Hill Fort
Walkerburn
Robert Smail's Printing Works
Innerleithen
Elibank and Traquair Forerst
Traquair
Preston Law
1507 Wallace's Hill
Hundleshope Heights
Kirkhouse
Glen House
2218
Dun Rig 2441
Blake Muir
1859 Minch Moor
1779 Deuchar Law
Ashiestiel Hill
Yair Hill Forest
Peel
Caddonfoot
Clovenfords
1222 Knowes Hill
Meigle 1389 Hill
Old Gala House
Lochcarron
GALASHIELS
Buckholm
William Law 1314
Langshaw
Stow
Old Kirk & Bishop's Palace
Bridge
Nether Blainslie
Ledgerwood
Huntlywood
Gordon
Gordon Moss
Fans
Greenknowe Tower
Earlston
Redpath
Leaderfoot
Smailholm Tower
Bemersyde
Bemersyde Moss
Scott's View
Gattonside
Lowood
Newstead
Darnick
Melrose
Abbotsford
Dingleton
Eildon
Eildon Hills
Newtown St. Boswells
Dryburgh Abbey
St. Boswells
Clintmains
Mertoun Bridge
Mertoun
Boleside
Lindean Mill Glass
Lindean
Cauldshiels Hill
Bowden
Maxton
Raelees Wood
Yair Hill Forest
Broomy Law
Linglie Hill
Yarrow Ford
Andrew Elliot Wool Factory
Selkirk Glass
Sir Walter Scott's Courtroom
Selkirk
Halliwells Ho.
Newark Castle
Bowhill House
Bowhill
Fastheugh Hill 1645
Philiphaugh
Philiphaugh 1645
Yarrow
Yarrow Feus
Mountbenger
Aikwood Tower
Brockhill
Ettrickbridge
Midlem
Longnewton
Sandystones
Lilliesleaf
Ancrum Moor 1545
Ancrum
Bogside Organic Gardens
Bloomfield
Cappercleuch
St. Mary's Loch
1933 The Wiss
Loch of the Lowes
Black Knowe Head 1805
Gilmanscleuch
ETTRICK FOREST
Caver's Hill 1209
Ashkirk
Essenside Loch
Akermoor Loch
Shaws Under Loch
Minto Hills 905
Minto
Fatlips Castle
Spittal-on-Rule
Lanton
Timpendean Tower
Mary Queen of Scots
Newton
Castle Jail
Hassendean
Horsleyhill
Leyden Obelisk
Denholm
Bedrule
Dunion Hill
Tushielaw
Dun Knowe
Drinkstone Hill
Appletreehall
Clarilaw
Ramsey Knowe
Hellmoor Loch
Smasha Hill
Scottish Borders Art Glass
Hawick Cashmere
Burnfoot
Cauldmill
1391 Rubers Law
Redfordgreen
Alemoor Loch
James Hogg Monument
Ettrick
Buccleuch
Roberton
Wilton
HAWICK
Kirkton
Drumlanrig's Tower
Burnfoot
Law Kneis 1634
Branxholme
Deanburnhaugh
987 White Hill
Bonchester Bridge
Hobkirk
Chesters
Glenkerry
Sauchie Law
1278 Redcleuch Edge
Hott Hill
Newmill
CRAIK FOREST
Stobs Castle
Cross Hill
Craik Forest Walks
Craik
Dryden Fell
Craik Cross Hill
Pike Hill 1369
Johnnie Armstrong Gallery
Teviothead
Allan Water
Slitrig
WAUCHOPE FOREST
Green Law
FOREST
Skelfhill
The Pike 1516
Langburnshiels
Wyndburgh Hill
1688 Fanna Hill
Carlin Tooth
1746 Skelfhill Pen
Maiden Paps
Leap Hill
Needs Law
Hartshorn Pike
Davington
Blaeberry Hill
Eweslees Knowe
Comb Hill
Millstone Edge
1996 Cauldcleuch Head
1966 Greatmoor Hill
Sandy Edge
Lamblair Hill
Kagyu Samye Ling Monastery
Causeway Grain Head
Mosspaul
Tudhope Hill 1965
Saughtree Fell
1975 Peel Fell
Eskdalemuir
1953 Wisp Hill
White Hope Edge
Jamestown
1722 Faw Side
Geordie's Hill
1737 Din Fell
Hermitage Chapel
Hermitage
1464 Arnton Fell
Saughtree
Deadwater
Foulmire Heights
Hog Hill
Broad Head 1614
Pike Fell
Kielder
Kielder Railway Viaduct
CASTLE O'ER FOREST
Castle O'er
Crumpton Hill 1575
1862 Roan Fell
902 North Birny Fell
Steele Road
Larriston Fells
1678
SCOTLAND
ENGLAND
KIELDER FOREST
Black Knowe
Dinmont Lairs
Bentpath
Kirkstile or Ewes
Watch Hill
1087 Hart Fell
The Shin
Telford Memorial
Hog Fell
Black Edge 1464
Wilson's Pike
Newcastleton Forest
Newcastleton
Liddesdown Heritage Centre
Black Knowe
Lewis
Rough Pike
1478 Calkin Rig
Clan Armstrong
McDiarmid Memorial
Langholm
Millholm Cross
Glendhu Hill
1326
Glentenmont
TWEEDDALE
LAUDERDALE
TEVIOTDALE
ESKDALE
LIDDESDALE
ETTRICK
SELKIRKSHIRE
A703
A72
A7
A68
A6105
A6091
A699
A698
A708
A707
A6088
B709
B7062
B710
B6374
B6360
B6356
B6397
B6404
B7060
B6398
B6359
B6453
B6400
B7009
B711
B6405
B6358
B6357
B6399
B723

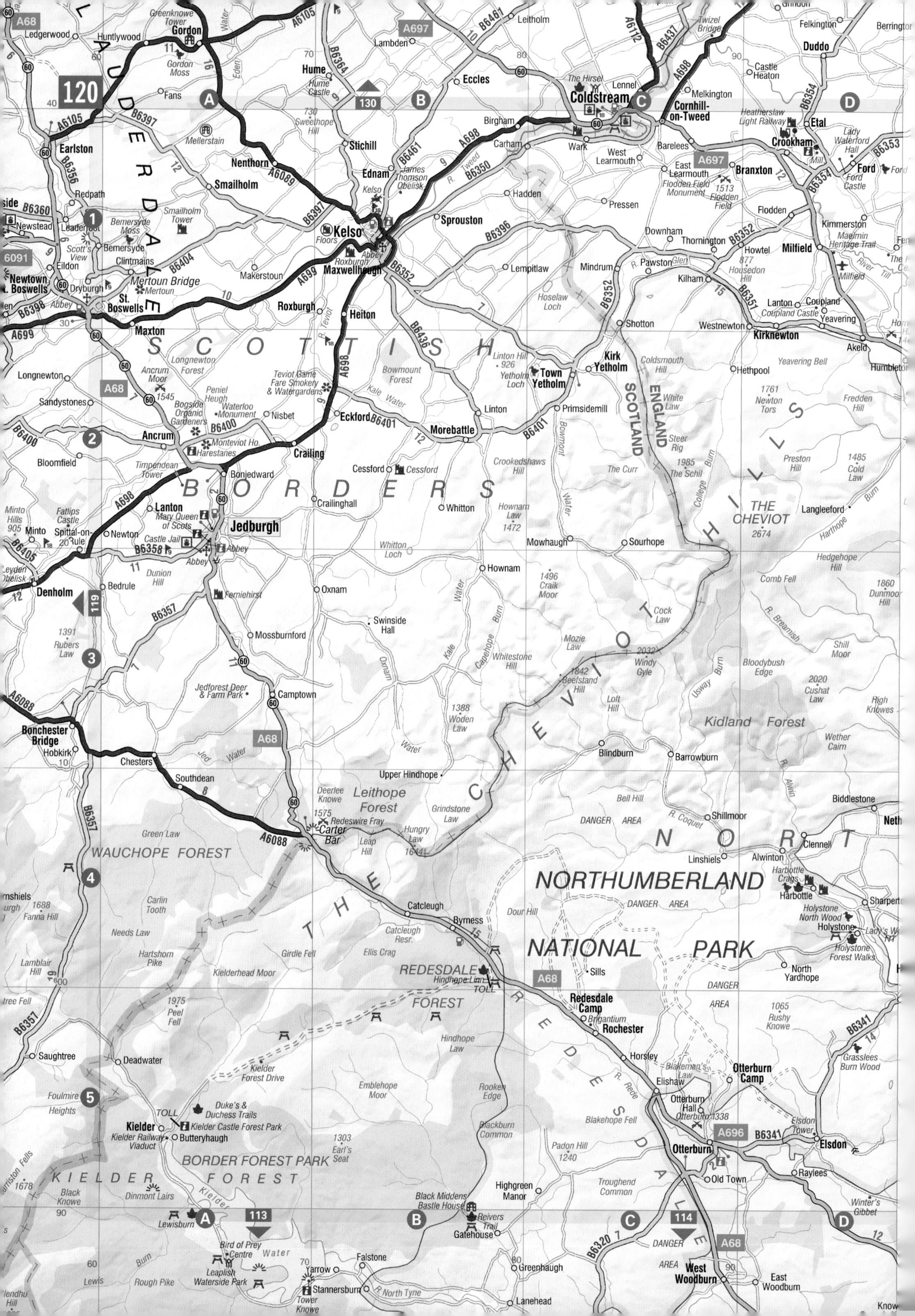
120
A68
Ledgerwood
Huntlywood
Greenknowe Tower
Gordon
Gordon Moss
Fans
A
A6105
Earlston
B6397
Mellerstain
Nenthorn
A6089
B6356
Redpath
B6360
Newstead
Leaderfoot
1
Smailholm
Smailholm Tower
Bemersyde Moss
Bemersyde
Scott's View
Eildon
Clintmains
B6404
Makerstoun
Newtown St. Boswells
Dryburgh
Mertoun Bridge
Mertoun
St. Boswells
Abbey
B6398
A699
Maxton
LAUDERDALE
Hume
Hume Castle
Sweethope Hill
130
B
Lambden
A697
B6364
Leitholm
B6461
Eccles
Stichill
Ednam
James Thomson Obelisk
Kelso
Floors
Abbey
Roxburgh
Maxwellheugh
B6352
Roxburgh
Heiton
R. Teviot
A698
Birgham
Carham
B6350
R. Tweed
Hadden
Sprouston
B6396
Lempitlaw
Hoselaw Loch
The Hirsel
Lennel
Coldstream
C
A6112
B6437
Twizel Bridge
Melkington
Cornhill-on-Tweed
Wark
West Learmouth
Barelees
East Learmouth
Flodden Field Monument
1513 Flodden Field
Pressen
Branxton
Downham
Thornington
B6352
Mindrum
Pawston
Kilham
Shotton
Felkington
Berrington
Duddo
Castle Heaton
D
Heatherslaw Light Railway
Etal
Crookham
Lady Waterford Hall
Mill
B6353
B6354
Ford
Ford Castle
Flodden
Kimmerston
Maelmin Heritage Trail
Milfield
Howtel
Housedon Hill
B6351
River Till
Lanton
Coupland
Coupland Castle
Yeavering
Westnewton
Kirknewton
Akeld
Humbleton
Hethpool
Yeavering Bell
SCOTTISH BORDERS
Longnewton
Longnewton Forest
Ancrum Moor
1545
Peniel Heugh
A68
Sandystones
Bogside Organic Gardeners
Waterloo Monument
Nisbet
Teviot Game Fare Smokery & Watergardens
Bowmount Forest
B6436
Kale Water
Eckford
B6401
Morebattle
Linton
Linton Hill 926
Yetholm Loch
Town Yetholm
Kirk Yetholm
Primsidemill
Coldsmouth Hill
SCOTLAND
ENGLAND
White Law
Steer Rig
1761 Newton Tors
Fredden Hill
2
B6400
Ancrum
Monteviot Ho.
Harestanes
Crailing
Bloomfield
Timpendean Tower
Bonjedward
Cessford
Crailinghall
Whitton
Crookedshaws Hill
Bowmont Water
The Curr
1985 The Schil
College Burn
Preston Hill
1485 Cold Law
Minto Hills 905
Minto
Fatlips Castle
Lanton
Mary Queen of Scots
Jedburgh
Spittal-on-Rule
Newton
Castle Jail
Abbey
B6358
Hownam Law 1472
Mowhaugh
Sourhope
THE CHEVIOT 2674
Langleeford
Harthope Burn
B6405
Leyden Obelisk
Denholm
119
Dunion Hill
Bedrule
Ferniehirst
Oxnam
Whitton Loch
Hownam
1496 Craik Moor
Hedgehope Hill
Comb Fell
1860 Dunmoor Hill
B6357
1391 Rubers Law
3
Mossburnford
Swinside Hall
Oxnam Water
Kale Water
Capehope Burn
Whitestone Hill
Mozie Law
Cock Law
2032 Windy Gyle
1842 Beefstand Hill
R. Breamish
Shill Moor
Bloodybush Edge
Usway Burn
2020 Cushat Law
High Knowes
A6088
Jedforest Deer & Farm Park
Camptown
1388 Woden Law
Loft Hill
Kidland Forest
Wether Cairn
Bonchester Bridge
Hobkirk
Chesters
Jed Water
A68
Blindburn
Barrowburn
Southdean
Upper Hindhope
Deerlee Knowe
Leithope Forest
1575 Redeswire Fray
Carter Bar
Leap Hill
Grindstone Law
Hungry Law 1644
Bell Hill
DANGER AREA
R. Coquet
Shillmoor
Biddlestone
R. Alwin
Green Law
WAUCHOPE FOREST
4
A6088
Linshiels
Alwinton
Clennell
Harbottle Crags
Harbottle
NORTHUMBERLAND NATIONAL PARK
Fanna Hill 1688
Carlin Tooth
Catcleugh
Byrness
Catcleugh Resr.
Dour Hill
Holystone North Wood
Holystone
Lady's Well
Holystone Forest Walks
Sharperton
Needs Law
Hartshorn Pike
Girdle Fell
Ellis Crag
REDESDALE
Hindhope Linn
TOLL
A68
Sills
North Yardhope
Lamblair Hill
Kielderhead Moor
1975 Peel Fell
FOREST
Redesdale Camp
Bremenium
Rochester
1065 Rushy Knowe
B6341
Grasslees Burn Wood
B6357
Saughtree
Deadwater
Kielder Forest Drive
Hindhope Law
Horsley
Blakeman's Law
Otterburn Camp
Foulmire Heights
5
Emblehope Moor
Rooken Edge
R. Rede
Elishaw
Otterburn Hall
Otterburn 1338
Duke's & Duchess Trails
Kielder Castle Forest Park
Kielder
Kielder Railway Viaduct
Butteryhaugh
Blakehope Fell
Blackburn Common
1303 Earl's Seat
Padon Hill 1240
A696
B6341
Elsdon Tower
Elsdon
Otterburn
BORDER FOREST PARK
KIELDER FOREST
1678
Black Knowe
Dinmont Lairs
Highgreen Manor
Troughend Common
Old Town
Raylees
Winter's Gibbet
A
113
Lewisburn
Black Middens Bastle House
Reivers Trail
Gatehouse
B
C
114
D
B6320
DANGER AREA
A68
Bird of Prey Centre
Leaplish Waterside Park
Yarrow
Falstone
Stannersburn
R. North Tyne
Tower Knowe
Greenhaugh
Lanehead
West Woodburn
East Woodburn
Rough Pike
Lewis Burn

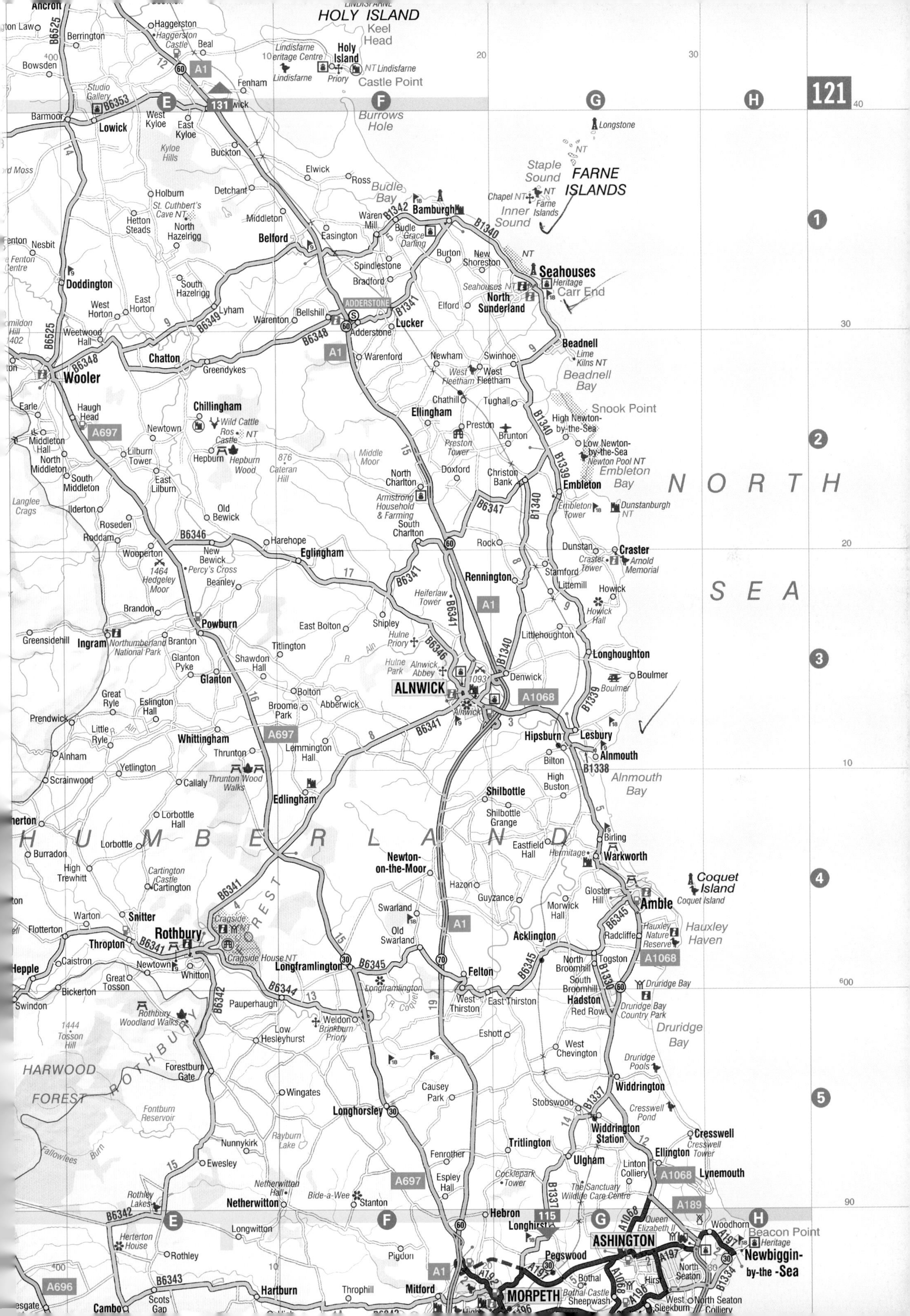

121
HOLY ISLAND
Keel Head
Holy Island
Lindisfarne Heritage Centre
Lindisfarne Priory
NT Lindisfarne Castle
Castle Point
Burrows Hole
Haggerston
Haggerston Castle
Beal
Berrington
Bowsden
Fenham
Barmoor
Lowick
West Kyloe
East Kyloe
Kyloe Hills
Buckton
Studio Gallery
Longstone
Staple Sound
FARNE ISLANDS
Chapel NT
Farne Islands
Inner Sound
Elwick
Ross
Budle Bay
Bamburgh
Waren Mill
Budle
Grace Darling
Holburn
Detchant
St. Cuthbert's Cave NT
Middleton
Hetton Steads
North Hazelrigg
Belford
Easington
Burton
New Shoreston
Seahouses
Seahouses NT
Heritage
Carr End
North Sunderland
Nesbit
Fenton Centre
Doddington
Spindlestone
Bradford
South Hazelrigg
West Horton
East Horton
Lyham
Warenton
Bellshill
ADDERSTONE
Adderstone
Lucker
Elford
Beadnell
Lime Kilns NT
Beadnell Bay
Weetwood Hall
Chatton
Greendykes
Warenford
Newham
Swinhoe
West Fleetham
Wooler
Earle
Haugh Head
Chillingham
Wild Cattle
Ros Castle NT
Chathill
Tughall
Ellingham
Snook Point
High Newton-by-the-Sea
Low Newton-by-the-Sea
Newton Pool NT
Embleton Bay
Preston
Preston Tower
Brunton
Middleton Hall
North Middleton
Newtown
Lilburn Tower
Hepburn
Hepburn Wood
876 Cateran Hill
Middle Moor
South Middleton
East Lilburn
North Charlton
Doxford
Christon Bank
Embleton
NORTH
Langlee Crags
Ilderton
Roseden
Old Bewick
Armstrong Household & Farming
South Charlton
Embleton Tower
Dunstanburgh NT
Roddam
Wooperton
1464 Hedgeley Moor
New Bewick
Percy's Cross
Harehope
Eglingham
Rock
Dunstan
Craster
Craster Tower
Arnold Memorial
Beanley
Rennington
Stamford
Littlemill
Howick
Howick Hall
SEA
Brandon
Heiferlaw Tower
Powburn
East Bolton
Shipley
Greensidehill
Ingram
Northumberland National Park
Branton
Titlington
Hulne Priory
Littlehoughton
Longhoughton
Glanton Pyke
Glanton
Shawdon Hall
Hulne Park
Alnwick Abbey
ALNWICK
Denwick
Boulmer
Great Ryle
Eslington Hall
Bolton
Broome Park
Abberwick
Prendwick
Little Ryle
Whittingham
Hipsburn
Lesbury
Alnmouth
Alnham
Thrunton
Lemmington Hall
Bilton
Scrainwood
Yetlington
Callaly
Thrunton Wood Walks
Edlingham
High Buston
Alnmouth Bay
Shilbottle
Shilbottle Grange
Lorbottle Hall
Lorbottle
Burradon
High Trewhitt
Cartington Castle
Cartington
Newton-on-the-Moor
Eastfield Hall
Hermitage
Birling
Warkworth
Hazon
Guyzance
Coquet Island
Gloster Hill
Amble
Morwick Hall
Warton
Snitter
Swarland
Old Swarland
Flotterton
Thropton
Rothbury
Cragside
Cragside House NT
Acklington
Hauxley
Radcliffe
Nature Reserve
Hauxley Haven
Caistron
Newtown
Whitton
Longframlington
Felton
North Broomhill
Togston
South Broomhill
Druridge Bay
Hepple
Great Tosson
Bickerton
Swindon
Pauperhaugh
West Thirston
East Thirston
Hadston
Red Row
Druridge Bay Country Park
Rothbury Woodland Walks
Weldon
Brinkburn Priory
Low Hesleyhurst
1444 Tosson Hill
Eshott
West Chevington
Druridge Pools
HARWOOD FOREST
Forestburn Gate
Fontburn Reservoir
Wingates
Causey Park
Widdrington
Longhorsley
Stobswood
Cresswell Pond
Widdrington Station
Cresswell
Cresswell Tower
Rayburn Lake
Nunnykirk
Tritlington
Ulgham
Ellington
Fallowlees Burn
Ewesley
Fenrother
Linton Colliery
Lynemouth
Netherwitton Hall
Espley Hall
Cockle Park Tower
The Sanctuary Wildlife Care Centre
Rothley Lakes
Netherwitton
Bide-a-Wee
Stanton
Hebron
Longhirst
ASHINGTON
Queen Elizabeth II
Woodhorn
Beacon Point
Heritage
Newbiggin-by-the-Sea
Herterton House
Longwitton
Rothley
Pigdon
Pegswood
Bothal
North Seaton
Cambo
Scots' Gap
Hartburn
Throphill
Mitford
MORPETH
Bothal Castle
Sheepwash
West Sleekburn
North Seaton Colliery

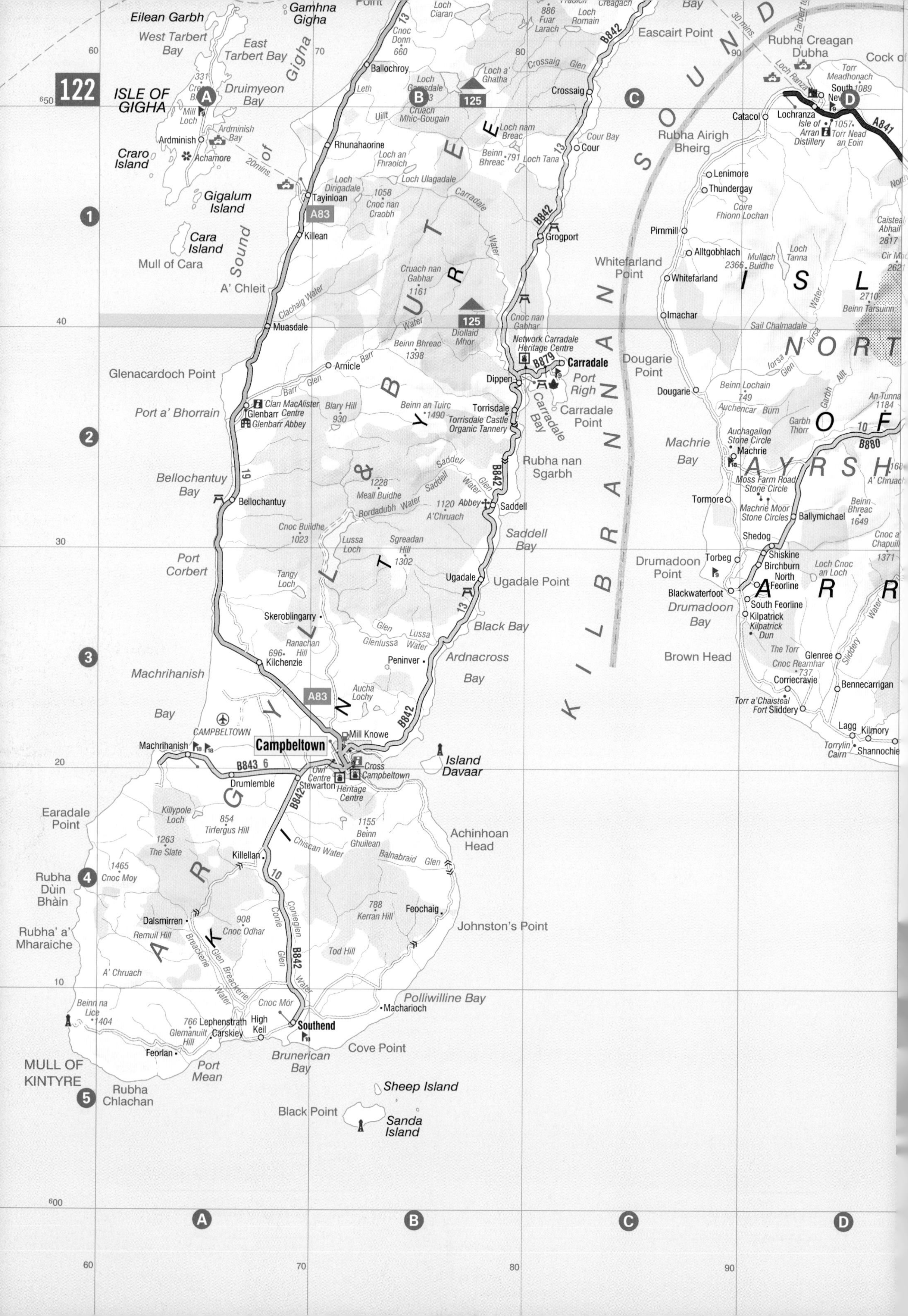
Eilean Garbh
Gamhna Gigha
West Tarbert Bay
East Tarbert Bay
Gigha
ISLE OF GIGHA
Druimyeon Bay
Mill Loch
Ardminish
Ardminish Bay
Craro Island
Achamore
Sound of Gigha
20mins
Gigalum Island
Cara Island
Mull of Cara
A' Chleit
Loch Ciaran
Cnoc Donn 660
Ballochroy
Leth
Loch Garasdale
Cruach Mhic-Gougain
Uillt
Rhunahaorine
Loch an Fhraoich
Loch Dirigadale
Loch Ulagadale
Tayinloan
1058 Cnoc nan Craobh
A83
Killean
Clachaig Water
Muasdale
Arnicle
Barr Glen
Glenacardoch Point
Port a' Bhorrain
Clan MacAlister Centre
Glenbarr
Glenbarr Abbey
Blary Hill 930
Bellochantuy Bay
Bellochantuy
Port Corbert
Cnoc Buidhe 1023
Tangy Loch
Lussa Loch
Skeroblingarry
696 Ranachan Hill
Kilchenzie
Machrihanish Bay
CAMPBELTOWN
Machrihanish
Campbeltown
B843
Drumlemble
Stewarton
Owl Centre
Heritage Centre
Cross
Campbeltown
Mill Knowe
Killypole Loch
854 Tirfergus Hill
1263 The Slate
Earadale Point
1465 Cnoc Moy
Rubha Dùin Bhàin
Killellan
Chiscan Water
1155 Beinn Ghuilean
Balnabraid Glen
Achinhoan Head
Dalsmirren
908 Cnoc Odhar
Remuil Hill
Rubha' a' Mharaiche
Breackerie Water
Glen Breackerie
Conie Glen
Conieglen Water
B842
788 Kerran Hill
Feochaig
Johnston's Point
Tod Hill
A' Chruach
Beinn na Lice 1404
766 Lephenstrath
Glemanuilt Hill
Carskiey
High Keil
Cnoc Mór
Southend
Macharioch
Polliwilline Bay
Feorlan
MULL OF KINTYRE
Port Mean
Brunerican Bay
Cove Point
Rubha Chlachan
Sheep Island
Black Point
Sanda Island
Island Davaar
ARGYLL & BUTE
886 Fuar Larach
Loch Romain
Creagach
Loch a' Ghatha
Crossaig Glen
Crossaig
125
Loch nam Breac
Beinn Bhreac 791
Loch Tana
Cour Bay
Cour
Carradale Water
Grogport
Cruach nan Gabhar 1161
Cnoc nan Gabhar
Water
Diollaid Mhor
Beinn Bhreac 1398
Network Carradale Heritage Centre
B879
Carradale
Dippen
Port Righ
Carradale Bay
Carradale Point
Beinn an Tuirc 1490
Torrisdale
Torrisdale Castle Organic Tannery
Rubha nan Sgarbh
Saddell Water
Saddell Glen
1228 Meall Buidhe
Bordadubh Water
1120 A'Chruach
Abbey
Saddell
Saddell Bay
Sgreadan Hill 1302
Ugadale
Ugadale Point
Black Bay
Glen Lussa
Glenlussa Water
Peninver
Ardnacross Bay
Aucha Lochy
KILBRANNAN SOUND
Bay
Eascairt Point
30 mins
Tarbert
Rubha Creagan Dubha
Cock of
Torr Meadhonach
Loch Ranza
South 1089
Newton
Lochranza
Catacol
Isle of Arran Distillery
1057 Torr Nead an Eoin
A841
Rubha Airigh Bheirg
Lenimore
Thundergay
Coire Fhionn Lochan
North
Caisteal Abhail 2817
Cir Mhor 2621
Pirnmill
Alltgobhlach
Mullach Buidhe 2366
Loch Tanna
Whitefarland Point
Whitefarland
Water
2710 Beinn Tarsuinn
Imachar
Sail Chalmadale
Iorsa Glen
Dougarie Point
Dougarie
Beinn Lochain 749
Auchencar Burn
Garbh Allt
Garbh Thorr
An Tunna 1184
Auchagallon Stone Circle
Machrie
Machrie Bay
B880
A' Chruach
Moss Farm Road Stone Circle
Machrie Moor Stone Circles
Tormore
Ballymichael
Beinn Bhreac 1649
Shedog
Cnoc a Chapuill 1371
Shiskine
Birchburn
Drumadoon Point
Torbeg
Loch Cnoc an Loch
North Feorline
Blackwaterfoot
South Feorline
Drumadoon Bay
Kilpatrick
Kilpatrick Dun
Water
The Torr
Glenree
Sliddery
Brown Head
Cnoc Reamhar 737
Corriecravie
Bennecarrigan
Torr a'Chaisteal Fort
Sliddery
Lagg
Kilmory
Torrylin Cairn
Shannochie
ISLE OF ARRAN
NORTH AYRSHIRE
A B C D
1 2 3 4 5
60 70 80 90
650 40 30 20 10 600

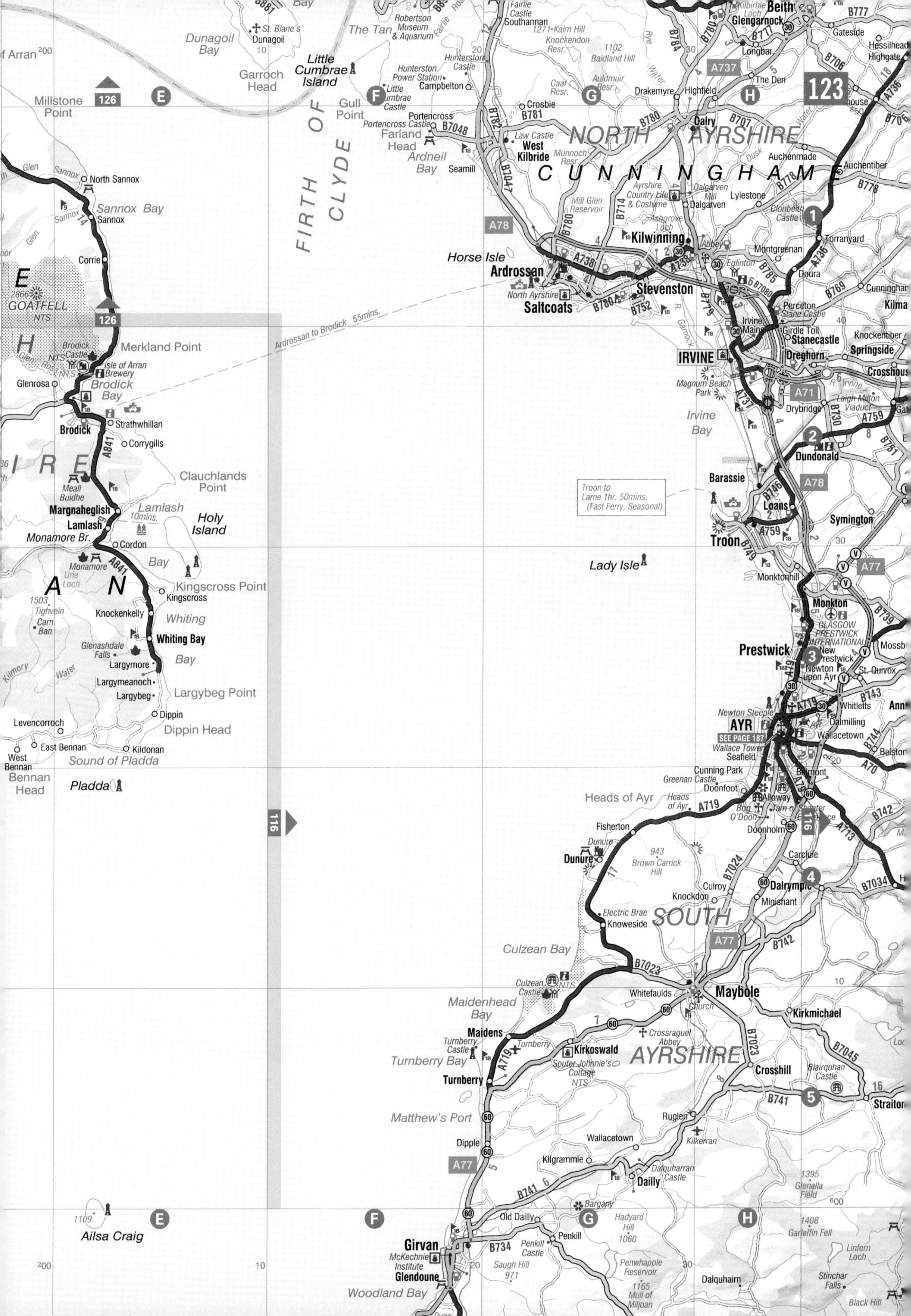

123
NORTH AYRSHIRE
CUNNINGHAME
SOUTH
AYRSHIRE
FIRTH OF CLYDE
ARRAN
GOATFELL
Irvine Bay
Ardrossan
Saltcoats
Stevenston
Kilwinning
IRVINE
Troon
Prestwick
AYR
SEE PAGE 187
Maybole
Girvan
Brodick
Lamlash
Whiting Bay
Holy Island
Pladda
Ailsa Craig
Lady Isle
Horse Isle
Little Cumbrae Island
Troon to Larne 1hr. 50mins. (Fast Ferry, Seasonal)
Ardrossan to Brodick 55mins.
Dalry
Beith
Glengarnock
West Kilbride
Dundonald
Monkton
GLASGOW PRESTWICK INTERNATIONAL
Dalrymple
Kirkoswald
Turnberry
Maidens
Culzean Castle
Dunure
Crosshill
Kirkmichael
Dailly

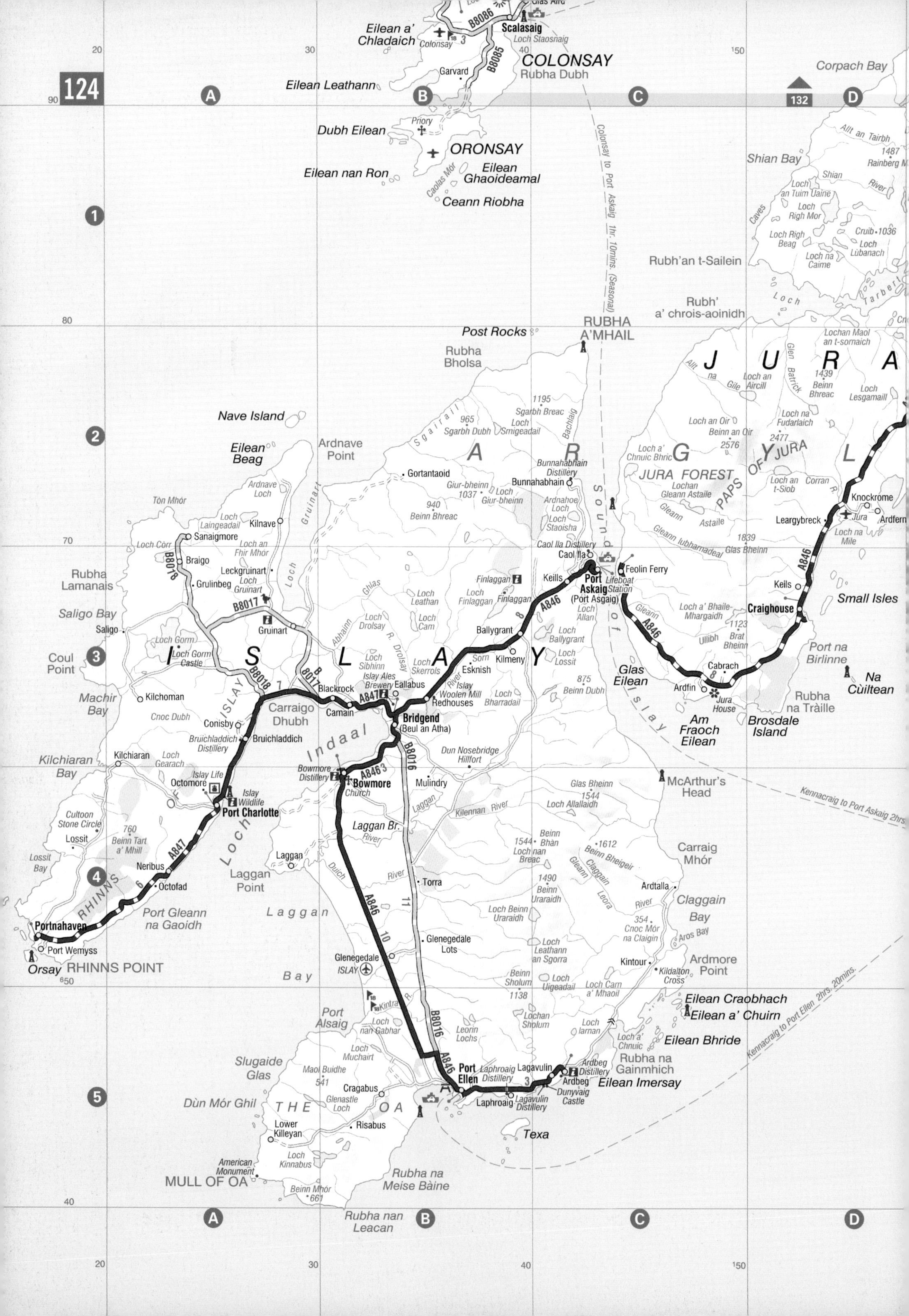
Scalasaig
B8086
Eilean a' Chladaich
Colonsay
Loch Staosnaig
B8085
COLONSAY
Rubha Dubh
Garvard
Eilean Leathann
Corpach Bay
132
Priory
Dubh Eilean
ORONSAY
Eilean nan Ron
Eilean Ghaoideamal
Caolas Mòr
Ceann Riobha
Colonsay to Port Askaig 1hr. 10mins. (Seasonal)
Allt an Tairbh
1487
Rainberg M
Shian Bay
Shian
River
Loch an Tuim Uaine
Loch Righ Mor
Caves
Loch Righ Beag
Cruib 1036
Loch Lùbanach
Loch na Caime
Rubh'an t-Sailein
Rubh' a' chrois-aoinidh
Loch
Tarbert
Post Rocks
RUBHA A'MHAIL
Rubha Bholsa
Lochan Maol an t-sornaich
Glen Batrick
J U R A
Allt na Gile
Loch an Aircill
1439 Beinn Bhreac
Loch Lesgamaill
Nave Island
1195 Sgarbh Breac
Loch Smigeadail
Bachlaig
965 Sgarbh Dubh
Sgairail
Loch na Fudarlaich
Loch an Oir
Beinn an Oir 2576
2477
JURA
Eilean Beag
Ardnave Point
A R G Y L L
Loch a' Chnuic Bhric
PAPS OF
Gortantaoid
Bunnahabhain Distillery
Bunnahabhain
JURA FOREST
Lochan Gleann Astaile
Loch an t-Siob
Corran
Ardnave Loch
Gruinart
Giur-bheinn 1037
Loch Giur-bheinn
Sound of Islay
Knockrome
Tòn Mhór
940 Beinn Bhreac
Ardnahoe Loch
Gleann Astaile
Leargybreck
Jura
Ardfern
Loch Laingeadail
Kilnave
Loch Staoisha
Loch na Mile
Sanaigmore
Loch Còrr
Loch an Fhir Mhòr
Gleann Iubharnadeal
1839 Glas Bheinn
Caol Ila Distillery
Caol Ila
Braigo
B8018
Leckgruinart
Loch Gruinart
Feolin Ferry
Rubha Lamanais
Grulinbeg
Loch
Finlaggan
Keills
Port Askaig
Lifeboat Station
(Port Asgaig)
Keils
Small Isles
B8017
Ghlas
Loch Leathan
Loch Finlaggan
Loch Allan
Gleann
Loch a' Bhaile-Mhargaidh
Craighouse
Saligo Bay
Gruinart
Loch Drolsay
Loch Cam
A846
1123 Brat Bheinn
Saligo
Loch Gorm
Abhainn
Ballygrant
Loch Ballygrant
Ullibh
Coul Point
Loch Gorm Castle
I S L A Y
B8018
Loch Sibhinn
R. Drolsay
Loch Skerrols
Sorn
Esknish
Kilmeny
Loch Lossit
Port na Birlinne
Cabrach
Na Cùiltean
Islay Ales Brewery
Ballabus
Islay Woolen Mill
Redhouses
River
Loch Bharradail
875 Beinn Dubh
Glas Eilean
Ardfin
Jura House
Rubha na Tràille
Machir Bay
Kilchoman
Blackrock
A847
Carraigo Dhubh
Camain
Cnoc Dubh
Conisby
Bridgend
(Beul an Atha)
Am Fraoch Eilean
Brosdale Island
Bruichladdich
Bruichladdich Distillery
Indaal
B8016
Dun Nosebridge Hillfort
Kilchiaran Bay
Kilchiaran
Loch Gearach
Bowmore Distillery
A846
Bowmore
Church
Mulindry
McArthur's Head
Glas Bheinn 1544
Islay Life
Octomore
Islay Wildlife
Port Charlotte
Kilennan River
Loch Allallaidh
Kennacraig to Port Askaig 2hrs
Cultoon Stone Circle
760 Beinn Tart a' Mhill
Laggan
Laggan Br.
River
1544 Beinn Bhàn
1612 Beinn Bheigeir
Loch nan Breac
Carraig Mhòr
Lossit
A847
Loch
Lossit Bay
Laggan
Laggan Point
Duich
River
Torra
Gleann
Claggain
Leora
1490 Beinn Uraraidh
Ardtalla
Neribus
Octofad
RHINNS
OF ISLAY
Claggain Bay
Port Gleann na Gaoidh
Laggan
Loch Beinn Uraraidh
River
354 Cnoc Mòr na Claigin
Aros Bay
Portnahaven
Glenegedale Lots
Port Wemyss
Glenegedale
ISLAY
Loch Leathann an Sgorra
Kintour
Ardmore Point
Orsay
RHINNS POINT
Kildalton Cross
Bay
Beinn Sholum
1138
Loch Uigeadail
Loch Carn a' Mhaoil
Eilean Craobhach
Eilean a' Chuirn
Kennacraig to Port Ellen 2hrs. 20mins.
Kintra
Port Alsaig
Loch nan Gabhar
B8016
Lochan Sholum
Leorin Lochs
Loch Iarnan
Loch a' Chnuic
Eilean Bhride
Slugaide Glas
Loch Muchairt
Maol Buidhe 541
A846
Port Ellen
Laphroaig Distillery
Lagavulin
Ardbeg Distillery
Ardbeg
Rubha na Gainmhich
Eilean Imersay
Cragabus
Dùn Mór Ghil
Glenastle Loch
THE OA
Laphroaig
Lagavulin Distillery
Dunyvaig Castle
Lower Killeyan
Risabus
Texa
Loch Kinnabus
American Monument
Rubha na Meise Bàine
MULL OF OA
Beinn Mhòr 661
Rubha nan Leacan
A B C D
1 2 3 4 5
20 30 40 150
90 80 70 650 40

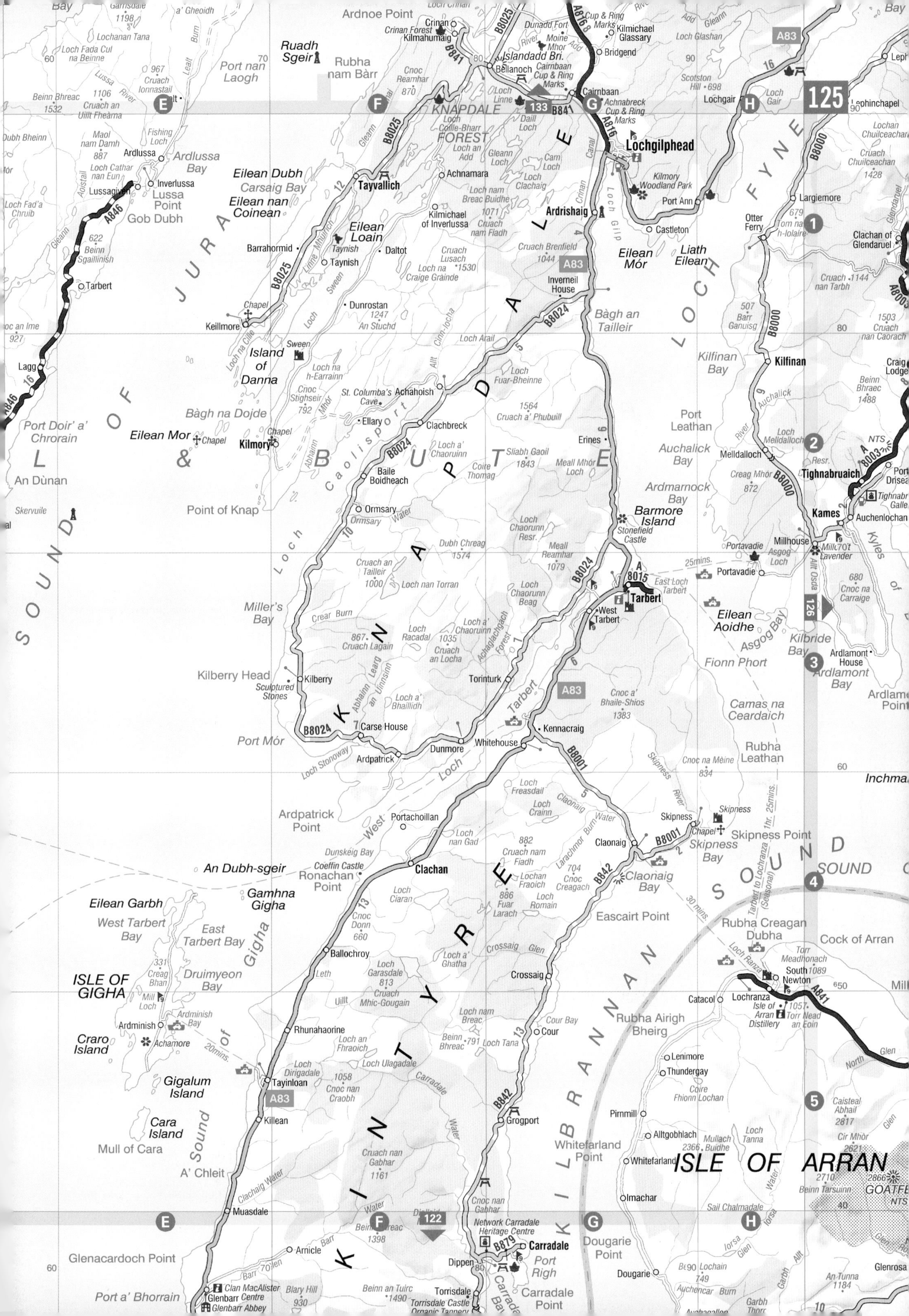

Ardnoe Point
Crinan
Crinan Forest
Kilmahumaig
Ruadh Sgeir
Rubha nam Bàrr
Port nan Laogh
Islandadd Bri.
Bellanoch
Cairnbaan
Kilmichael Glassary
Bridgend
KNAPDALE FOREST
Lochgilphead
Lochgair
Lephinchapel
125
133
Ardlussa
Ardlussa Bay
Inverlussa
Lussa Point
Lussagiven
Gob Dubh
Eilean Dubh
Carsaig Bay
Eilean nan Coinean
Tayvallich
Achnamara
Eilean Loain
Taynish
Daltot
Barrahormid
Kilmichael of Inverlussa
Ardrishaig
Castleton
Port Ann
Eilean Mór
Liath Eilean
Largiemore
Otter Ferry
Clachan of Glendaruel
Tarbert
Keillmore
Dunrostan
Inverneil House
Bàgh an Tailleir
Island of Danna
Sween
Lagg
Achahoish
Ellary
Clachbreck
Kilmory
Eilean Mor
Bàgh na Dojde
Port Doir' a' Chrorain
An Dùnan
Point of Knap
Baile Boidheach
Ormsary
Erines
Kilfinan
Kilfinan Bay
Port Leathan
Auchalick Bay
Melldalloch
Tighnabruaich
Kames
Auchenlochan
Ardmarnock Bay
Barmore Island
Stonefield Castle
Millhouse
Portavadie
Tarbert
West Tarbert
Eilean Aoidhe
Kilbride Bay
Ardlamont House
Ardlamont Bay
Fionn Phort
Miller's Bay
Kilberry Head
Kilberry
Carse House
Torinturk
Port Mór
Dunmore
Ardpatrick
Whitehouse
Kennacraig
Camas na Ceardaich
Rubha Leathan
Ardpatrick Point
Portachoillan
Skipness
Skipness Point
Skipness Bay
Claonaig
Claonaig Bay
An Dubh-sgeir
Ronachan Point
Clachan
Gamhna Gigha
Eilean Garbh
West Tarbert Bay
East Tarbert Bay
ISLE OF GIGHA
Druimyeon Bay
Eascairt Point
Rubha Creagan Dubha
Cock of Arran
Ballochroy
Crossaig
South Newton
Lochranza
Catacol
Ardminish
Craro Island
Achamore
Rhunahaorine
Cour
Rubha Airigh Bheirg
Tayinloan
Gigalum Island
Cara Island
Mull of Cara
Killean
Grogport
Lenimore
Thundergay
Pirnmill
Alltgobhlach
Whitefarland
Whitefarland Point
ISLE OF ARRAN
A' Chleit
Imachar
Muasdale
122
Carradale
Network Carradale Heritage Centre
Port Righ
Dougarie Point
Dougarie
Glenacardoch Point
Arnicle
Dippen
Torrisdale
Carradale Point
Port a' Bhorrain
Clan MacAlister Glenbarr Centre
Glenbarr Abbey
Glenrosa
SOUND OF JURA
LOCH FYNE
KNAPDALE
KINTYRE
KILBRANNAN SOUND
Sound of Gigha

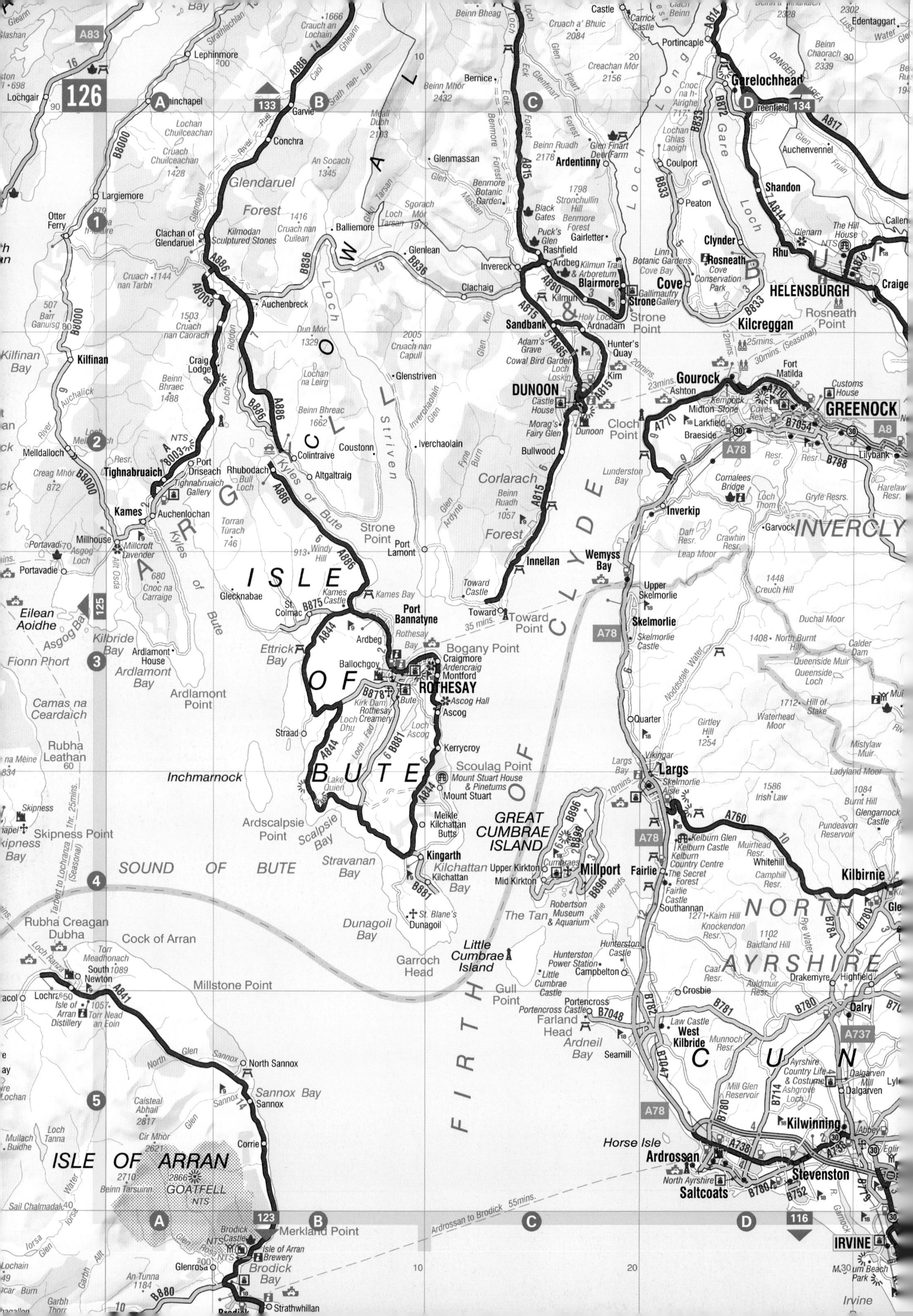

126
133
134
125
123
116
A
B
C
D
1
2
3
4
5
ISLE OF BUTE
COWAL
ARGYLL
FIRTH OF CLYDE
ISLE OF ARRAN
NORTH AYRSHIRE
INVERCLYDE
SOUND OF BUTE
DUNOON
ROTHESAY
GREENOCK
HELENSBURGH
Gourock
Largs
Millport
Tighnabruaich
Kames
Kilfinan
Garelochhead
Shandon
Rhu
Rosneath
Kilcreggan
Cove
Strone
Blairmore
Ardentinny
Sandbank
Hunter's Quay
Kirn
Innellan
Toward Point
Wemyss Bay
Skelmorlie
Inverkip
Fairlie
Kilbirnie
West Kilbride
Ardrossan
Saltcoats
Stevenston
Kilwinning
Dalry
IRVINE
Port Bannatyne
Kingarth
Colintraive
Portavadie
Glendaruel
GREAT CUMBRAE ISLAND
Little Cumbrae Island
Inchmarnock
GOATFELL
Brodick
Corrie
Sannox
North Sannox
Lochranza
Ardrossan to Brodick 55mins.

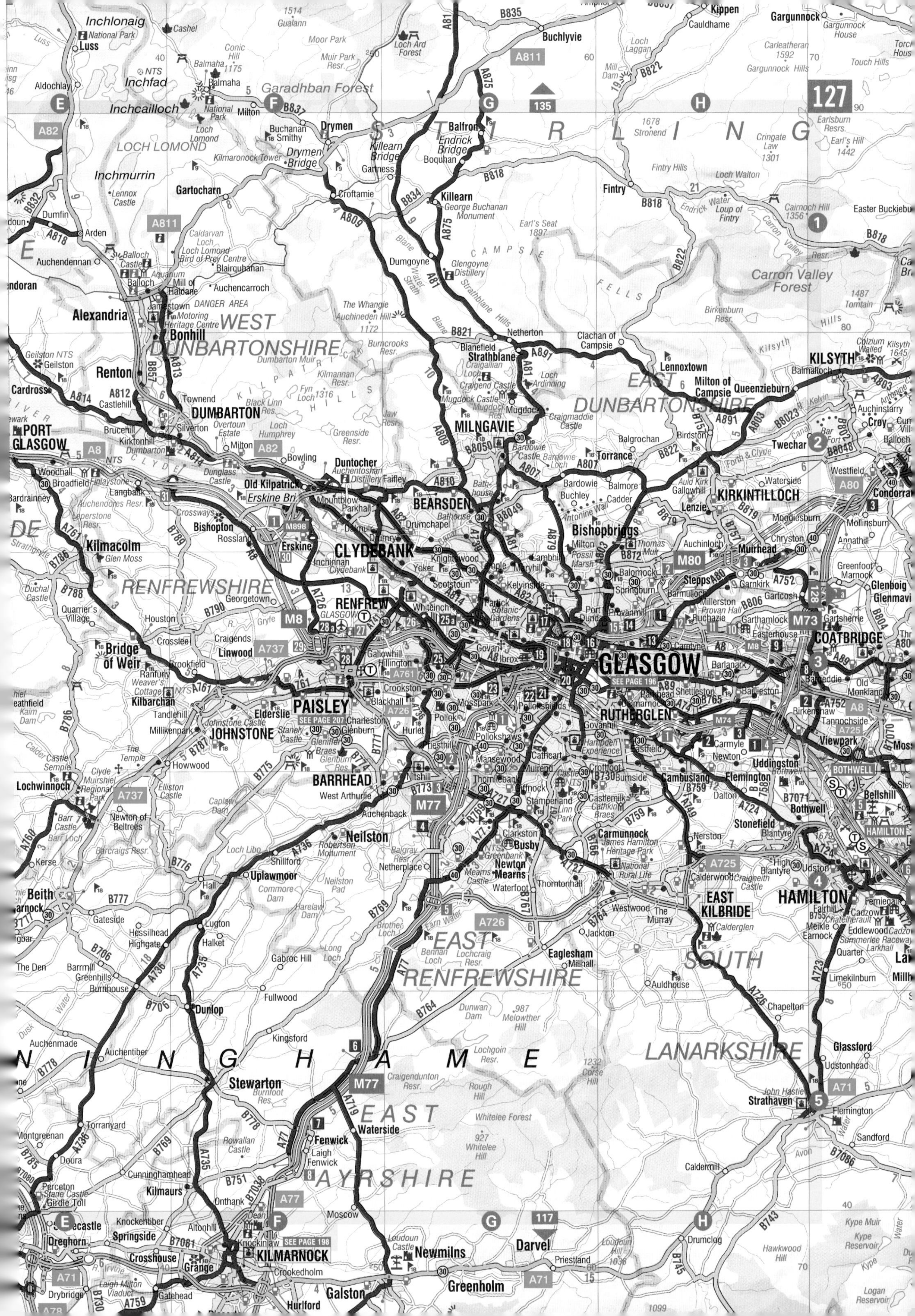
127
135
117
SEE PAGE 196
SEE PAGE 207
SEE PAGE 198
STIRLING
WEST DUNBARTONSHIRE
EAST DUNBARTONSHIRE
RENFREWSHIRE
EAST RENFREWSHIRE
SOUTH LANARKSHIRE
EAST AYRSHIRE
CUNNINGHAME
CAMPSIE FELLS
KILPATRICK HILLS
LOCH LOMOND
GLASGOW
PAISLEY
CLYDEBANK
RENFREW
BEARSDEN
MILNGAVIE
KIRKINTILLOCH
COATBRIDGE
RUTHERGLEN
HAMILTON
EAST KILBRIDE
DUMBARTON
PORT GLASGOW
JOHNSTONE
BARRHEAD
KILMARNOCK
KILSYTH
BOTHWELL
Inchlonaig
Luss
Inchfad
Inchcailloch
Balmaha
Garadhban Forest
Loch Ard Forest
Buchlyvie
Kippen
Gargunnock
Cauldhame
Drymen
Balfron
Killearn
Fintry
Carron Valley Forest
Inchmurrin
Gartocharn
Alexandria
Balloch
Bonhill
Renton
Cardross
Milton of Campsie
Lennoxtown
Queenzieburn
Strathblane
Croy
Twechar
Torrance
Bishopbriggs
Lenzie
Stepps
Muirhead
Moodiesburn
Chryston
Erskine
Bishopton
Kilmacolm
Bridge of Weir
Houston
Linwood
Kilbarchan
Elderslie
Howwood
Lochwinnoch
Beith
Uplawmoor
Neilston
Newton Mearns
Busby
Clarkston
Giffnock
Cambuslang
Uddingston
Bellshill
Blantyre
Stonefield
Lugton
Dunlop
Stewarton
Fenwick
Waterside
Kilmaurs
Dreghorn
Springside
Crosshouse
Newmilns
Darvel
Galston
Greenholm
Strathaven
Glassford
Eaglesham
Hurlford
Drumclog
Auldhouse
Chapelton
Sandford
Flemington
Caldermill
Whitelee Forest
M8
M73
M74
M77
M80
A737
A725
A726
A71
A77
A82
A811

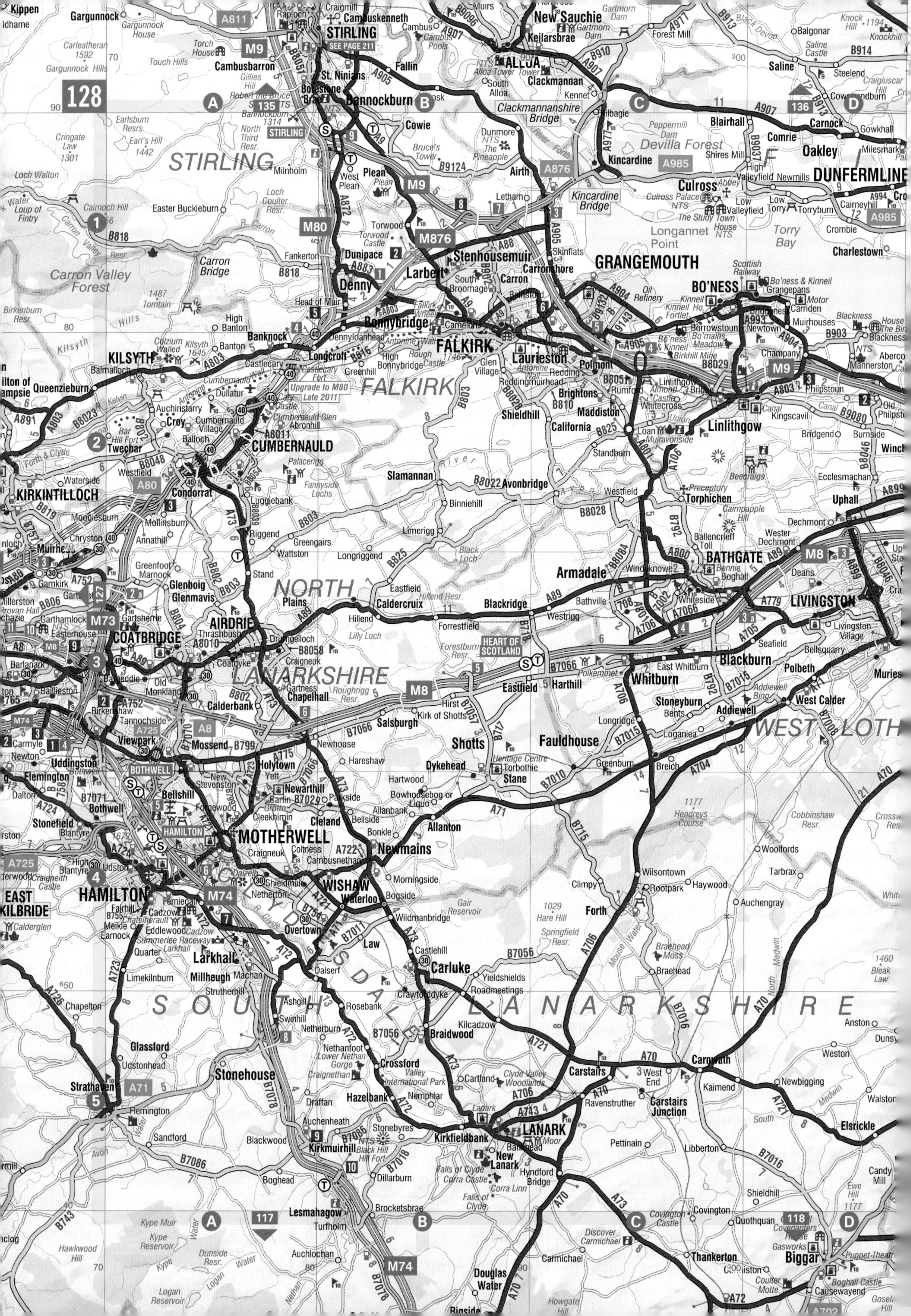
128
STIRLING
SEE PAGE 211
Kippen
Gargunnock
Gargunnock House
Raploch
Craigmill
Cambuskenneth
Cambus
New Sauchie
Keilarsbrae
Alloa
Forest Mill
Balgonar
Saline
Steelend
Carleatheran 1592
Touch Hills
Torch House
Cambusbarron
Fallin
St. Ninians
Clackmannan
Kennet
Bannockburn
Cowie
Clackmannanshire Bridge
Kilbagie
Blairhall
Comrie
Carnock
Oakley
Cowstrandburn
Gowkhall
Milesmark
DUNFERMLINE
Devilla Forest
Shires Mill
Kincardine
Culross
Newmills
High Valleyfield
Low Valleyfield
Low Torry
Torryburn
Cairneyhill
Crombie
Charlestown
Torry Bay
Longannet Point
Kincardine Bridge
Plean
West Plean
Airth
Dunmore
The Pineapple
Letham
Earlsburn Resrs.
Cringate Law 1301
Earl's Hill 1442
North Third Resr.
Milnholm
Loch Walton
Loch Coulter Resr.
Easter Buckieburn
Cairnoch Hill
Carron Valley Forest
Carron Bridge
Fankerton
Torwood
Torwood Castle
Dunipace
Denny
Larbert
Stenhousemuir
Skinflats
Carronshore
GRANGEMOUTH
Carron
South Broomage
BO'NESS
Bo'ness & Kinneil
Grangepans
Carriden
Muirhouses
Blackness
Kinneil
Bridgeness
Newtown
Champany
Borrowstoun
Head of Muir
High Banton
Banton
Banknock
Bonnybridge
Dennyloanhead
Longcroft
Camelon
FALKIRK
Laurieston
Polmont
Redding
Reddingmuirhead
Glen Village
High Bonnybridge
Greenhill
Castlecary
KILSYTH
Queenzieburn
Balmalloch
Dullatur
Upgrade to M80 Late 2011
Brightons
Rumford
Linlithgow Bridge
Linlithgow
Philpstoun
Kingscavil
Bridgend
Burnside
Shieldhill
Maddiston
California
Whitecross
Muiravonside
Auchinstarry
Croy
Cumbernauld Village
Abronhill
Twechar
Balloch
CUMBERNAULD
Westfield
Waterside
KIRKINTILLOCH
Condorrat
Luggiebank
Slamannan
Avonbridge
Binniehill
Westfield
Torphichen
Ecclesmachan
Uphall
Dechmont
Moodiesburn
Mollinsburn
Chryston
Muirhead
Annathill
Riggend
Greengairs
Wattston
Limerigg
Longriggend
Ballencrieff Toll
BATHGATE
Armadale
Windyknowe
Deans
LIVINGSTON
Glenboig
Glenmavis
Stand
Eastfield
Caldercruix
Plains
Blackridge
Bathville
Westrigg
Whiteside
Boghall
NORTH
Garnkirk
AIRDRIE
Hillend
Forrestfield
Livingston Village
Seafield
Bellsquarry
COATBRIDGE
Drumgelloch
Craigneuk
HEART OF SCOTLAND
Whitburn
East Whitburn
Blackburn
Polbeth
Coatdyke
LANARKSHIRE
Eastfield
Harthill
Addiewell
West Calder
Old Monkland
Gartness
Chapelhall
Hirst
Kirk of Shotts
Stoneyburn
Bents
Calderbank
Salsburgh
Shotts
Fauldhouse
Longridge
Loganlea
WEST LOTHIAN
Birkenshaw
Tannochside
Viewpark
Mossend
Newhouse
Uddingston
Carmyle
Holytown
Hareshaw
Dykehead
Torbothie
Stane
Greenburn
Breich
Newton
Flemington
BOTHWELL
New Stevenston
Bellshill
Newarthill
Carfin
Parkside
Hartwood
Bowhousebog or Liquo
Allanbank
Bothwell
Cleland
Bellside
Forgewood
Cleekhimin
Stonefield
Blantyre
HAMILTON
MOTHERWELL
Newmains
Allanton
Bonkle
Craigneuk
Coltness
Cambusnethan
Morningside
Woolfords
Tarbrax
Wilsontown
Rootpark
Haywood
Climpy
Forth
Auchengray
High Blantyre
Udston
WISHAW
Waterloo
Bogside
Shieldmuir
Netherton
EAST KILBRIDE
Ferniegair
Cadzow
Fairhill
Eddlewood
Meikle Earnock
Overtown
Wildmanbridge
Law
Castlehill
Carluke
Yieldshields
Braehead
Quarter
Larkhall
Millheugh
Machan
Limekilnburn
Dalserf
Roadmeetings
Crawforddyke
Struthernill
Ashgill
Rosebank
Chapelton
SOUTH LANARKSHIRE
Swinhill
Netherburn
Kilcadzow
Braidwood
Anston
Dunsyre
Nethanfoot
Glassford
Udstonhead
Stonehouse
Crossford
Carstairs
Carnwath
West End
Weston
Newbigging
Strathaven
Draffan
Hazelbank
Cartland
Nemphlar
Ravenstruther
Carstairs Junction
Kaimend
Walston
Elsrickle
Flemington
Auchenheath
Stonebyres
Kirkfieldbank
LANARK
Sandford
Blackwood
Kirkmuirhill
New Lanark
Hyndford Bridge
Pettinain
Libberton
Candy Mill
Boghead
Dillarburn
Shieldhill
Brocketsbrae
Lesmahagow
Turfholm
Covington
Covington Castle
Quothquan
Kype Muir
Kype Reservoir
Hawkwood Hill
Dunside Resr.
Auchlochan
Discover Carmichael
Carmichael
Thankerton
Biggar
Logan Reservoir
Douglas Water
Howgate Hill
Causewayend
Coulter Motte
117
118
135
136
M9
M80
M876
M73
M8
M74
A8
A71
A70
A73
A72
A706
A725
A985
A876
A811

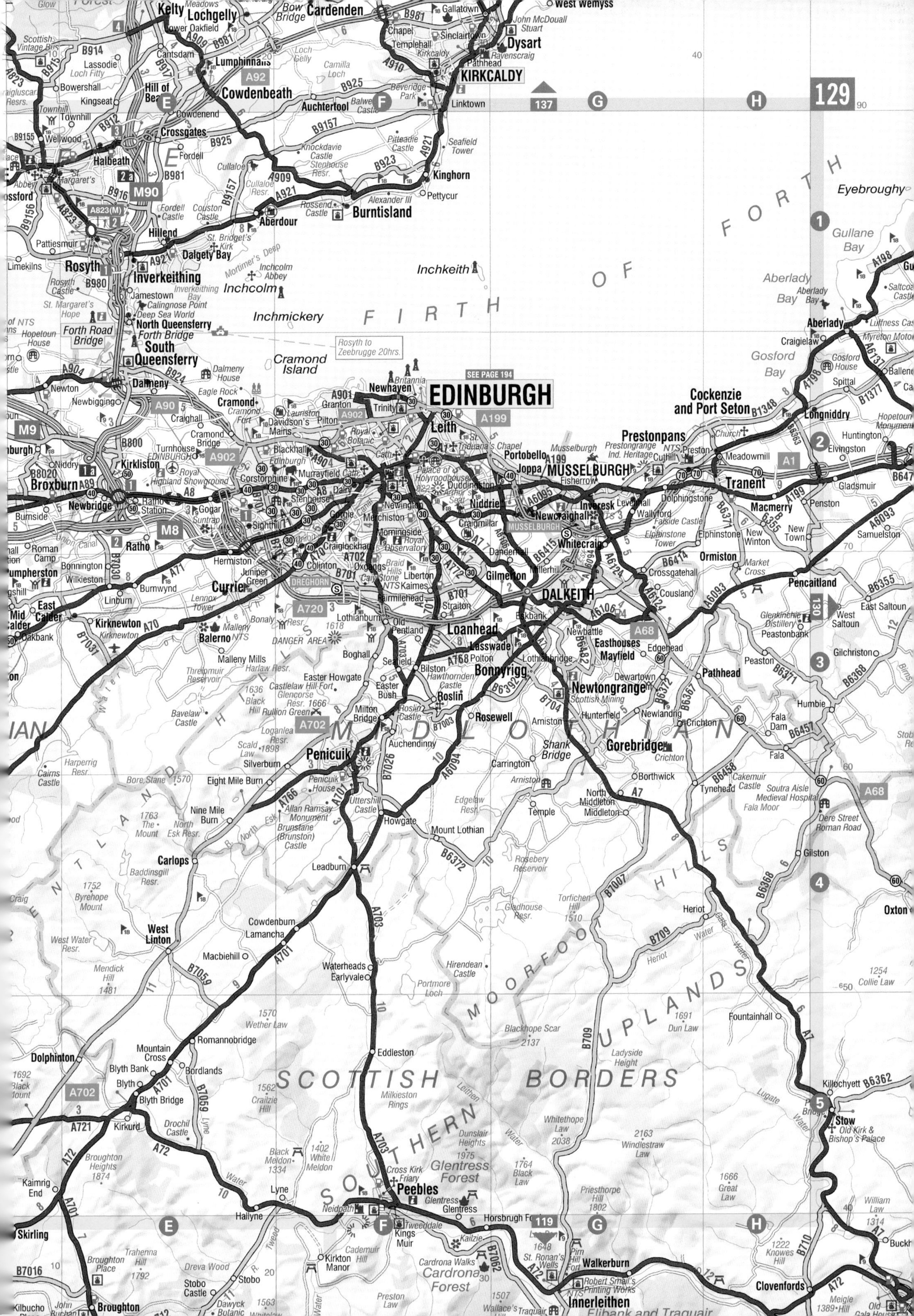
129
137
130
119
SEE PAGE 194
EDINBURGH
FIRTH OF FORTH
MIDLOTHIAN
SCOTTISH BORDERS
SOUTHERN UPLANDS
MOORFOOT HILLS
PENTLAND HILLS
Kelty
Lochgelly
Cardenden
Bow Bridge
Gallatown
West Wemyss
John McDouall Stuart
Dysart
Chapel
Sinclairtown
Templehall
Kirkcaldy
Ravenscraig
Pathhead
KIRKCALDY
Linktown
Lumphinnans
Cowdenbeath
Auchtertool
Balwearie Castle
Beveridge Park
Loch Gelly
Camilla Loch
Hill of Beath
Crossgates
Cowdenend
Halbeath
Fordell
Kingseat
Townhill
Wellwood
Lassodie
Loch Fitty
Bowershall
Cantsdam
Lower Oakfield
Scottish Vintage Bus
St. Margaret's
Abbey
Knockdavie Castle
Stenhouse Resr.
Pitteadie Castle
Seafield Tower
Kinghorn
Pettycur
Alexander III
Burntisland
Rossend Castle
Aberdour
Cullaloe
Cullaloe Resr.
Fordell Castle
Couston Castle
Hillend
Dalgety Bay
St. Bridget's Kirk
Mortimer's Deep
Inchcolm Abbey
Inchcolm
Inchkeith
Inchmickery
Rosyth
Rosyth Castle
Pattiesmuir
Limekilns
Inverkeithing
Inverkeithing Bay
Jamestown
Calingnose Point
Deep Sea World
North Queensferry
Forth Bridge
Forth Road Bridge
St. Margaret's Hope
Hopetoun House
South Queensferry
Rosyth to Zeebrugge 20hrs.
Cramond Island
Dalmeny
Dalmeny House
Newton
Newbigging
Eagle Rock
Cramond
Cramond Fort
Craighall
Lauriston
Davidson's Mains
Granton
Newhaven
Britannia
Trinity
Pilton
Royal Botanic
Leith
Blackhall
Edinburgh Zoo
Murrayfield
Corstorphine
Cramond Bridge
Turnhouse
EDINBURGH
Royal Highland Showground
Kirkliston
Niddry
Broxburn
Newbridge
Ratho Station
Gogar
Suntrap
Sighthill
Burnside
Ratho
Hermiston
Union Canal
Roman Camp
Bonnington
Wilkieston
Pumpherston
Burnwynd
Currie
Juniper Green
Colinton
Craiglockhart
Oxgangs
Braid Hills
Liberton
Kaimes
Fairmilehead
Lenox Tower
Linburn
East Calder
Mid Calder
Oakbank
Kirknewton
Balerno
Malleny
Bonaly
Lothianburn
DANGER AREA
Malleny Mills
Harlaw Resr.
Threipmuir Reservoir
Castlelaw Hill Fort
Glencorse Resr.
Black Hill
Rullion Green
Bavelaw Castle
Loganlea Resr.
Scald Law
Silverburn
Penicuik
Penicuik House
Harperrig Resr.
Cairns Castle
Bore Stane
Eight Mile Burn
Nine Mile Burn
The Mount
North Esk Resr.
Carlops
Baddinsgill Resr.
Byrehope Mount
West Linton
West Water Resr.
Mendick Hill
Macbiehill
Cowdenburn
Lamancha
Dolphinton
Mountain Cross
Romannobridge
Blyth Bank
Blyth
Blyth Bridge
Bordlands
Black Mount
Kirkurd
Drochil Castle
Broughton Heights
Kaimrig End
Skirling
Broughton Place
Trahenna Hill
Dreva Wood
Stobo
Stobo Castle
Dawyck Botanic
Broughton
Kilbucho
Hallyne
Lyne
Whiteholm
Craizie Hill
Black Meldon
White Meldon
Wether Law
Milkieston Rings
Eddleston
Waterheads
Earlyvale
Leadburn
Howgate
Uttershill Castle
Allan Ramsay Monument
Brunstane (Brunston) Castle
Auchendinny
Milton Bridge
Roslin
Roslin Castle
Rosewell
Bilston
Hawthornden Castle
Easter Howgate
Easter Bush
Seafield
Boghall
Old Pentland
Loanhead
Lasswade
Polton
Bonnyrigg
Straiton
Gilmerton
Danderhall
Millerhill
Eskbank
Dalkeith
DALKEITH
Lothianbridge
Newbattle
Easthouses
Mayfield
Newtongrange
Scottish Mining
Arniston
Hunterfield
Gorebridge
Crichton
Newlandrig
Shank Bridge
Carrington
North Middleton
Middleton
Temple
Mount Lothian
Edgelaw Resr.
Rosebery Reservoir
Gladhouse Resr.
Torfichen Hill
Portmore Loch
Hirendean Castle
Blackhope Scar
Ladyside Height
Dunslair Heights
Glentress Forest
Glentress
Cross Kirk
Friary
Peebles
Neidpath
Kings Muir
Tweeddale
Kailzie
Cademuir Hill
Kirkton Manor
Cardrona Walks
Cardrona Forest
Horsburgh Ford
St. Ronan's Wells
Walkerburn
Robert Small's Printing Works
Innerleithen
Traquair
Elibank and Traquair
Preston Law
Priesthorpe Hill
Whitehope Law
Windlestraw Law
Black Law
Great Law
Heriot
Heriot Water
Borthwick
Tyneheads
Cakemuir Castle
Soutra Aisle Medieval Hospital
Fala Moor
Fala
Fala Dam
Humbie
Dere Street Roman Road
Gilston
Oxton
Collie Law
Fountainhall
Dun Law
Killochyett
Stow
Old Kirk & Bishop's Palace
William Law
Knowes Hill
Clovenfords
Meigle Hill
Buckholm
Gala House
Portobello
Joppa
Musselburgh
MUSSELBURGH
Fisherrow
Duddingston
Holyroodhouse
Arthur's Seat
Newington
Merchiston
Morningside
Royal Observatory
Niddrie
Craigmillar
Newcraighall
Inveresk
Levenhall
Wallyford
Whitecraig
Crossgatehall
Cousland
Ormiston
Elphinstone
Elphinstone Tower
Falside Castle
Dolphingstone
Tranent
Prestonpans
Prestongrange Ind. Heritage
Cuthill
Preston
Cockenzie and Port Seton
Meadowmill
Macmerry
Penston
Gladsmuir
New Winton
Market Cross
New Town
Samuelston
Pencaitland
Glenkinchie Distillery
Peastonbank
Peaston
West Saltoun
East Saltoun
Gilchriston
Pathhead
Edgehead
Dewartown
Longniddry
Elvingston
Huntington
Hopetoun Monument
Spittal
Gosford Bay
Gosford House
Craigielaw
Aberlady
Aberlady Bay
Luffness Castle
Myreton Motor
Saltcoats Castle
Gullane Bay
Eyebroughy
Ballencrieff
Wester Hailes
DREGHORN
MUSSELBURGH
Dalmeny

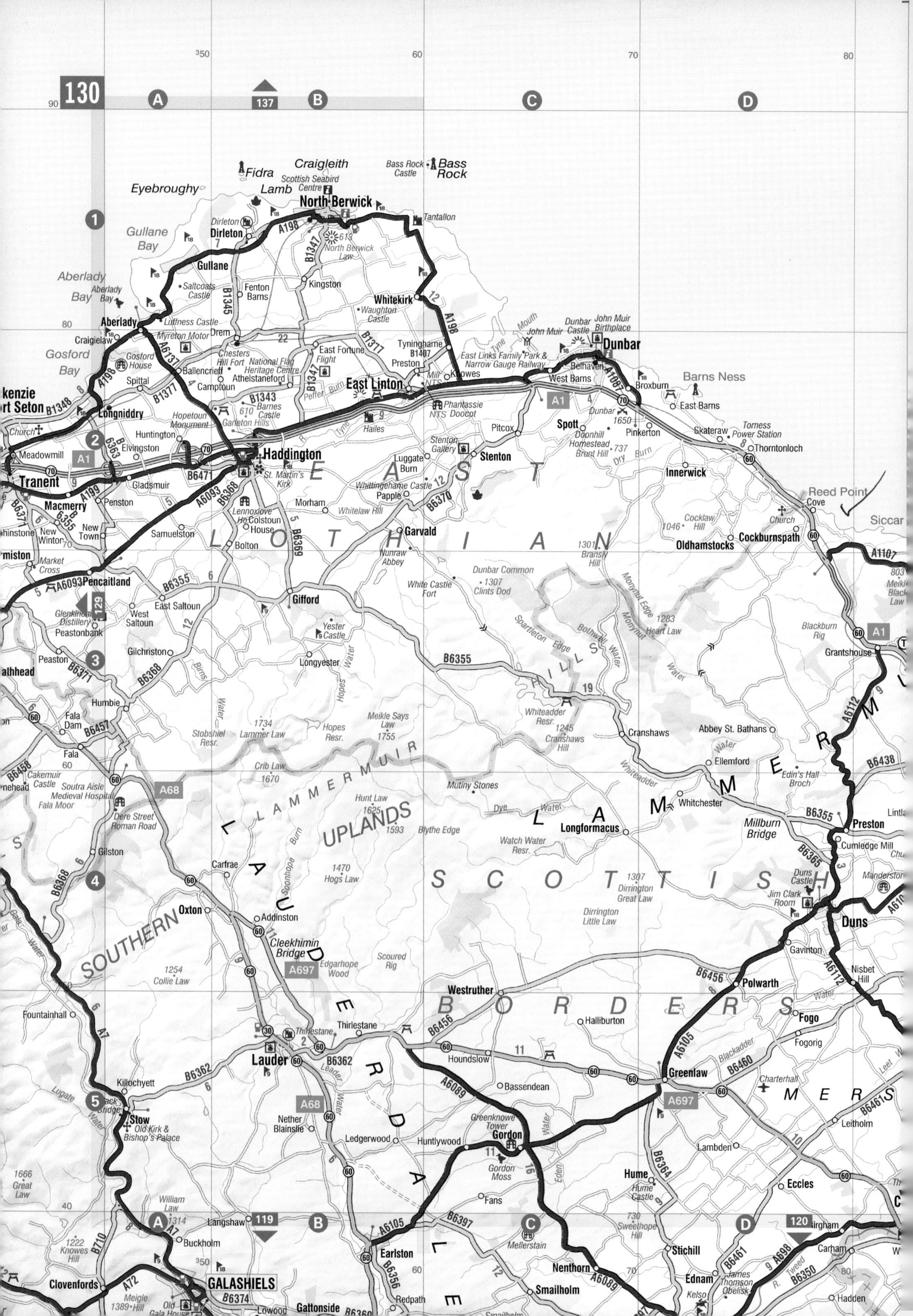

137
129
119
120
North Berwick
Dunbar
Haddington
East Linton
Dirleton
Gullane
Aberlady
Longniddry
Tranent
Macmerry
Pencaitland
Gifford
Garvald
Stenton
Spott
Innerwick
Cockburnspath
Oldhamstocks
Grantshouse
Preston
Duns
Polwarth
Greenlaw
Westruther
Lauder
Stow
Oxton
Gordon
Earlston
GALASHIELS
Clovenfords
Smailholm
Nenthorn
Stichill
Ednam
Hume
Eccles
Fogo
Longformacus
Cranshaws
Abbey St. Bathans
Bass Rock
Fidra
Craigleith
Lamb
Eyebroughy
Gullane Bay
Aberlady Bay
Gosford Bay
Barns Ness
Reed Point
Siccar
EAST LOTHIAN
LAMMERMUIR HILLS
LAMMERMUIR
SOUTHERN UPLANDS
SCOTTISH BORDERS
LAUDERDALE
MERSE

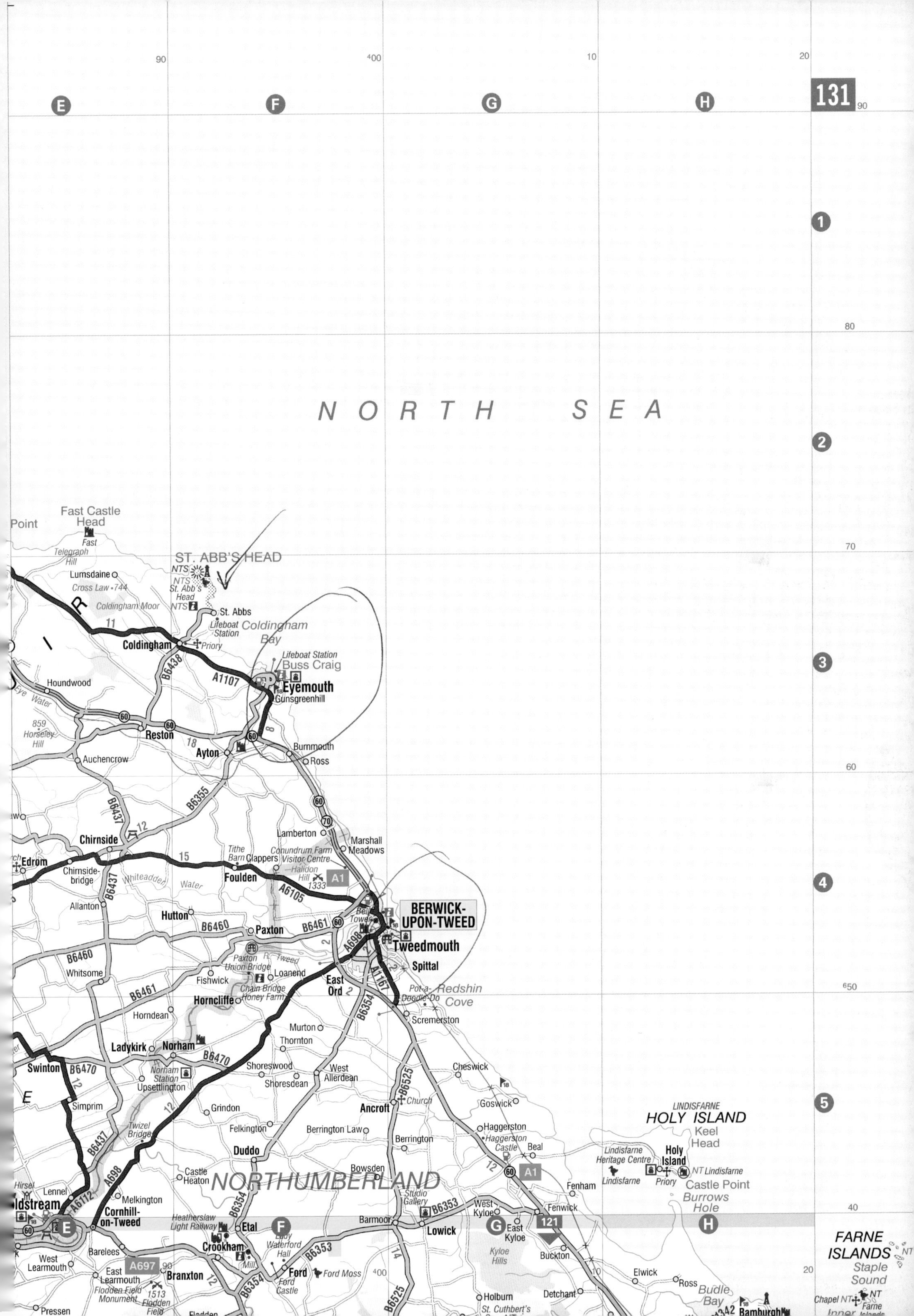

NORTH SEA

Point

Fast Castle Head

Fast Telegraph Hill

Lumsdaine

Cross Law •744

Coldingham Moor

ST. ABB'S HEAD

NTS
NTS
NTS
St. Abb's Head

St. Abbs

Coldingham Bay

11

Coldingham
Priory

B6438

A1107

Houndwood

Lifeboat Station

Lifeboat Station
Buss Craig
Eyemouth
Gunsgreenhill

Eye Water

859
Horseley Hill

60

60

Reston

18

Ayton

Burnmouth
Ross

B6437

12

B6355

60

70

Lamberton

Chirnside

Tithe Barn Clappers

Conundrum Farm
Visitor Centre
Halidon
Hill A1
1333

Marshall
Meadows

Edrom

Chirnside-bridge

15

Foulden

A6105

Allanton

B6437

Whiteadder Water

Hutton

B6460

Paxton

B6461

60

A698

BERWICK-UPON-TWEED

Bell
Tower

Whitsome

B6460

Paxton
Union Bridge

Fishwick

Chain Bridge
Honey Farm

Loanend

Tweedmouth

Spittal

Horncliffe

Horndean

East
Ord 2

Pot-a-
Deedle-Do

Redshin
Cove

B6461

R. Tweed

650

Ladykirk

Norham

Murton
Thornton

Scremerston

Swinton

B6470

Norham
Station
Upsettlington

B6470

Shoreswood

West
Allerdean

Cheswick

B6525

Church

Goswick

Simprim

12

Grindon

Felkington

Ancroft

Haggerston
Haggerston
Castle
Beal

Twizel
Bridge

Berrington Law

Berrington

HOLY ISLAND

LINDISFARNE
HOLY ISLAND
Keel
Head

Duddo

Bowsden

Lindisfarne
Heritage Centre

Holy
Island

Lindisfarne
Priory

NT Lindisfarne
Castle Point
Burrows
Hole

Hirsel
Lennel

Castle
Heaton

Melkington

NORTHUMBERLAND

Studio
Gallery

Lindisfarne

A1

60

Fenham

ldstream

A6112

A698

Cornhill-on-Tweed

Heatherslaw
Light Railway

Etal

Barmoor

B6353

West
Kyloe

Lowick

East
Kyloe

121

Fenwick

Buckton

FARNE
ISLANDS
Staple
Sound

West
Learmouth

60

Crookham

Lady
Waterford
Hall

B6353

Kyloe
Hills

Bareless

Elwick

Ross

Budle
Bay

Chapel NT
Farne
Inner Islands

East
Learmouth

Flodden Field
Monument

A697

90

Branxton

12

Ford

Mill

Ford Moss

1513
Flodden
Field

B6354

400

B6525

Holburn

St. Cuthbert's

Detchant

A2 Bamburgh

Pressen

Fladden

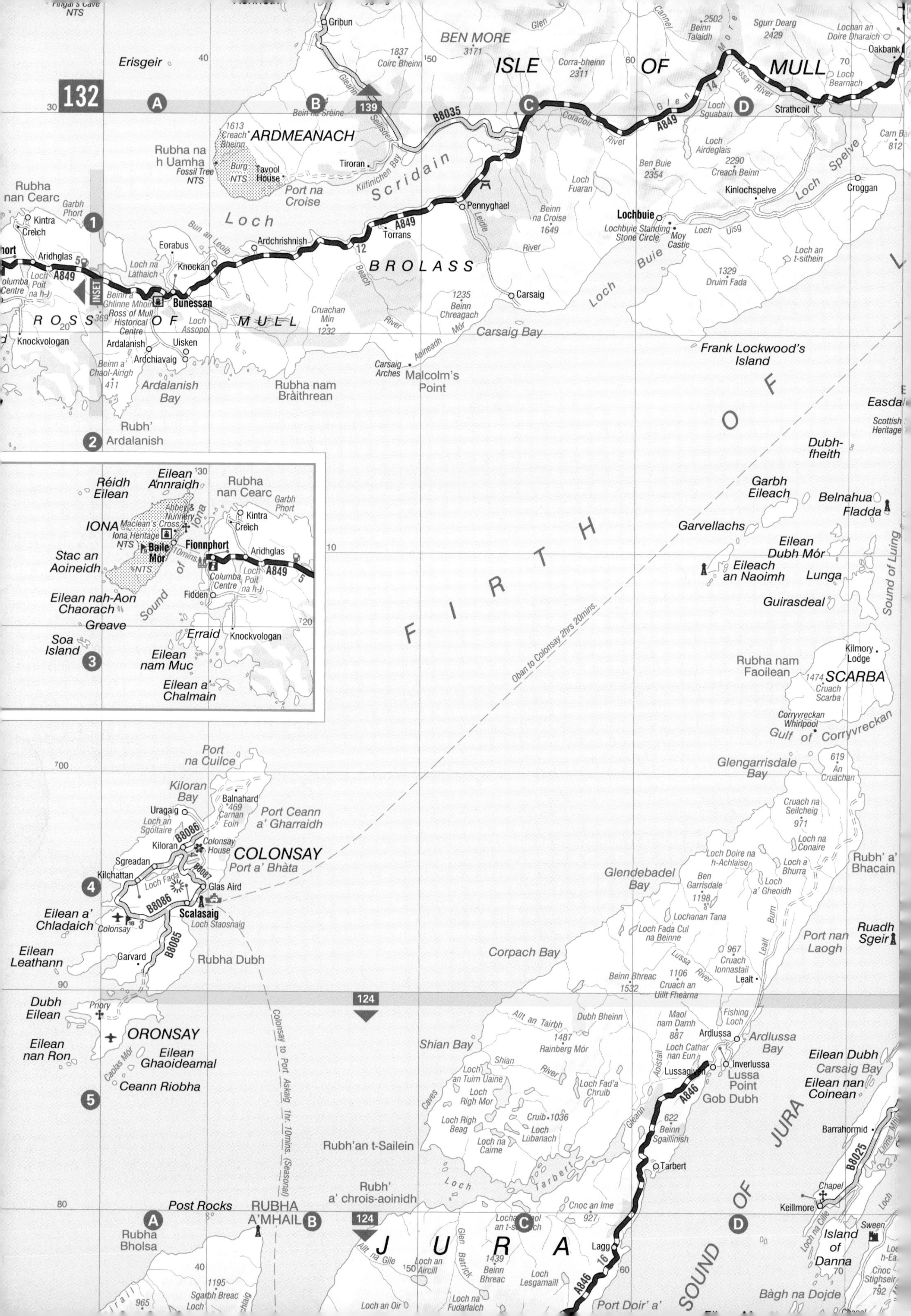
132
139
124
ISLE OF MULL
BEN MORE
ARDMEANACH
BROLASS
ROSS OF MULL
Loch Scridain
Bunessan
Pennyghael
Lochbuie
Kinlochspelve
Croggan
Carsaig
Loch Buie
FIRTH OF LORN
IONA
Baile Mòr
Fionnphort
Sound of Iona
Frank Lockwood's Island
Garvellachs
Eileach an Naoimh
Lunga
SCARBA
Gulf of Corryvreckan
COLONSAY
Scalasaig
Kiloran
ORONSAY
JURA
Ardlussa
Lussagiven
Tarbert
Lagg
Sound of Jura
Island of Danna
Keillmore
Oban to Colonsay 2hrs 20mins.
Colonsay to Port Askaig 1hr. 10mins. (Seasonal)

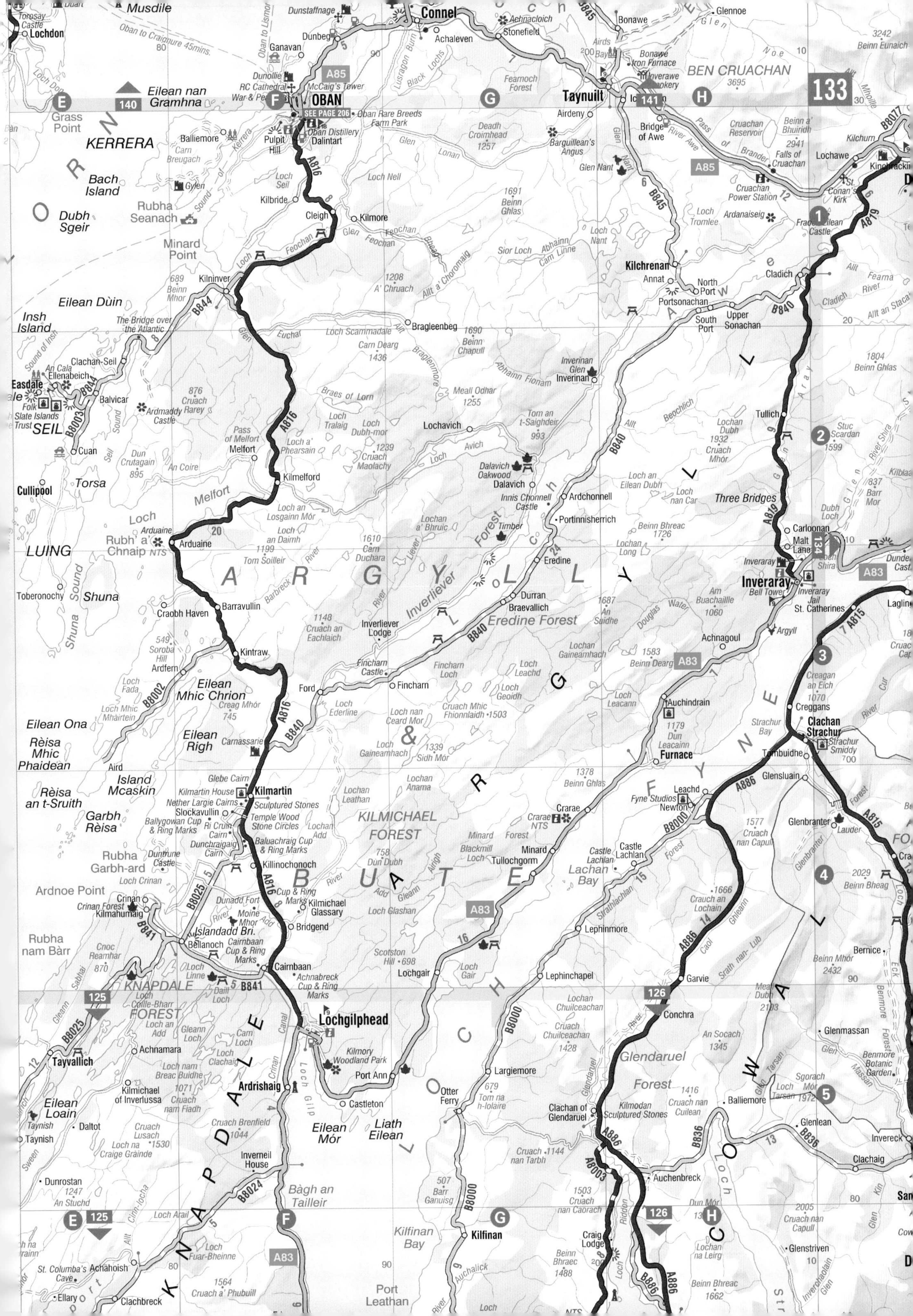

Musdile
Torosay Castle
Lochdon
Oban to Craignure 45mins.
Dunstaffnage
Connel
Achnacloich
Stonefield
Bonawe
Glennoe
Oban to Lismore
Dunbeg
Ganavan
Achaleven
Lusragon Burn
Black Lochs
Airds Bay
Bonawe Iron Furnace
Inverawe Smokery
BEN CRUACHAN
3695
3242
Beinn Eunaich
133
Dunollie
RC Cathedral
McCaig's Tower
War & Peace
A85
Eilean nan Gramhna
140
E
F
OBAN
G
Taynuilt
141
H
Grass Point
SEE PAGE 206
Oban Rare Breeds Farm Park
Fearnoch Forest
Airdeny
KERRERA
Balliemore
Pulpit Hill
Oban Distillery
Dalintart
Deadh Croimhead
1257
Barguillean's Angus
Bridge of Awe
River Awe
Pass of Brander
Cruachan Reservoir
Beinn a' Bhuiridh
2941
Falls of Cruachan
Kilchurn
Lochawe
Kinchrackine
B8077
Carn Breugach
Sound of Kerrera
Glen Lonan
Glen Nant
A85
Bach Island
Gylen
Loch Seil
Loch Nell
B845
Cruachan Power Station
St. Conan's Kirk
Dubh Sgeir
Rubha Seanach
Kilbride
1691
Beinn Ghlas
Loch Tromlee
Ardanaiseig
Cleigh
Kilmore
Glen Feochan
Fraoch Eilean Castle
1
A819
Minard Point
Loch Feochan
Sior Loch
Abhainn Cam Linne
Loch Nant
Kilchrenan
Kilninver
689
Beinn Mhor
1208
A' Chruach
Allt a' Chòromaig
Annat
North Port
Cladich
Portsonachan
Eilean Dùin
B844
Insh Island
The Bridge over the Atlantic
Glen Euchar
Loch Scammadale
Bragleenbeg
1690
Beinn Chapull
South Port
Upper Sonachan
B840
Fearna River
Allt an Stacain
Sound of Insh
Clachan-Seil
Carn Dearg
1436
Abhainn Fionain
Inverinan Glen
Inverinan
1804
Beinn Ghlas
An Cala
Ellenabeich
Easdale
Folk
Slate Islands Trust
B844
Balvicar
876
Cruach Rarey
Ardmaddy Castle
Braes of Lorn
Meall Odhar
1255
Tom an t-Saighdeir
993
Beochlich
SEIL
B8003
Pass of Melfort
Loch Tralaig
Loch Dubh-mor
Lochavich
Lochan Dubh
1932
Cruach Mhòr
Tullich
2
Stuc Scardan
1599
Cuan
Seil Sound
Melfort
Loch a' Phearsain
1239
Cruach Maolachy
Loch Avich
Dalavich Oakwood
Dalavich
B840
Dun Crutagain
895
An Coire
Kilmelford
Loch an Eilean Dubh
Loch nan Car
Three Bridges
837
Barr Mor
Cullipool
Torsa
Loch Melfort
Loch an Losgainn Mòr
Lochan a' Bhruic
Innis Chonnell Castle
Ardchonnell
Portinnisherrich
A819
Dubh Loch
Carloonan
Malt Lane
134
Loch Arduaine
Rubh' a' Chnaip
Arduaine
NTS
20
Loch an Daimh
1610
Carn Duchara
Inverliever Forest
Timber
Beinn Bhreac
1726
Lochan Long
Eredine
Inveraray
River Shira
A83
Dunderave Castle
LUING
1199
Tom Soilleir
Barbreck River
River Liever
Inveraray Bell Tower
Inveraray Jail
St. Catherines
Toberonochy
Shuna Sound
Shuna
ARGYLL
Durran
Braevallich
Eredine Forest
1687
An Suidhe
Am Buachaille
1060
Douglas Water
Lagline
Craobh Haven
Barravullin
1148
Cruach an Eachlaich
Inverliever Lodge
B840
Achnagoul
Argyll
A815
3
549
Soroba Hill
Ardfern
Kintraw
Lochan Gaineamhach
1583
Beinn Dearg
A83
Creagan an Eich
Loch Fada
Eilean Mhic Chrion
Fincharn Castle
Fincharn Loch
Fincharn
Loch Leachd
Loch Geoidh
Auchindrain
1070
Creggans
Loch Mhic Mhàirtein
B8002
Creag Mhòr
745
A816
Ford
Loch Ederline
Loch nan Ceard Mor
Cruach Mhic Fhionnlaidh
1503
Loch Leacann
Strachur Bay
Clachan Strachur
Strachur Smiddy
Eilean Ona
Eilean Righ
Carnassarie
B840
Loch Gaineamhach
1339
Sidh Mor
1179
Dun Leacainn
Furnace
Tombuidhe
700
Rèisa Mhic Phaidean
Aird
Glebe Cairn
Kilmartin House
Kilmartin
Lochan Anama
1378
Beinn Ghlas
A886
Glensluain
Island Mcaskin
Rèisa an t-Sruith
Nether Largie Cairns
Sculptured Stones
Slockavullin
Lochan Leathan
KILMICHAEL FOREST
Crarae
Crarae NTS
Leachd
Fyne Studios
Newton
Glenbranter
Lauder
Garbh Rèisa
Ballygowan Cup & Ring Marks
Ri Cruin Cairn
Temple Wood Stone Circles
Lochan Add
B8000
1577
Cruach nan Capull
A815
Dunchraigaig Cairn
Baluachraig Cup & Ring Marks
Minard Forest
Blackmill Loch
Minard
Tullochgorm
Castle Lachlan
Castle Lachlan
Rubha Garbh-ard
Duntrune Castle
Killinochonoch
758
Dun Dubh
Lachan Bay
Forest
4
2029
Beinn Bheag
Loch Crinan
B8025
River Add
BUTE
Ardnoe Point
Crinan
Crinan Forest
Kilmahumaig
Dunadd Fort
Moine Mhor
Cup & Ring Marks
Kilmichael Glassary
Gleann Airigh
Loch Glashan
A83
Strathlachlan
1666
Crauch an Lochain
Glenbranter
B841
Islandadd Bri.
Bellanoch
Cairnbaan Cup & Ring Marks
Bridgend
Lephinmore
Caol Ghleann
Rubha nam Bàrr
Cnoc Reamhar
870
Loch Linne
Cairnbaan
Achnabreck Cup & Ring Marks
Scotston Hill
698
Lochgair
Loch Gair
Lephinchapel
Garvie
Srath nan- Lub
Beinn Mhor
2432
Bernice
KNAPDALE FOREST
Daill Loch
B841
125
Loch Coille-Bharr
126
Lochan Chuilceachan
Conchra
Meall Dubh
2103
Gleann Sabhail
Loch an Add
Gleann Loch
Cam Loch
Lochgilphead
Crinan Canal
Loch Gilp
B8000
Cruach Chuilceachan
1428
An Socach
1345
Glenmassan
Benmore Forest
Tayvallich
Achnamara
Loch Clachaig
Kilmory Woodland Park
Glendaruel Forest
Glen Massan
Benmore Botanic Garden
Loch nam Breac Buidhe
1071
Cruach nam Fiadh
Port Ann
Largiemore
679
Tom na h-Iolaire
Kilmichael of Inverlussa
Ardrishaig
Castleton
Otter Ferry
1416
Cruach nan Cuilean
Sgorach Mòr
1972
Balliemore
5
Eilean Loain
Taynish
Daltot
Cruach Brenfield
1044
Eilean Mòr
Liath Eilean
Clachan of Glendaruel
Kilmodan Sculptured Stones
Glenlean
B836
Inverchapel
Cruach Lusach
Loch na Craige Grainde
1530
Sween
Inverneil House
Cruach nan Tarbh
1144
A886
A8003
Auchenbreck
Clachaig
Dunrostan
1247
An Stuchd
B8024
Bàgh an Tailleir
507
Barr Ganuisg
1503
Cruach nan Caorach
Dun Mòr
2005
Cruach nan Capull
Loch Arail
Kilfinan Bay
Kilfinan
Craig Lodge
Loch Riddon
Glenstriven
St. Columba's Cave
Achahoish
Loch Fuar-Bheinne
A83
Beinn Bhreac
1488
Lochan na Leirg
1564
Cruach a' Phubuill
Ellary
Clachbreck
Port Leathan
Auchalick
Beinn Bhreac
1662
KNAPDALE
LOCH FYNE
COWAL
LOCH AWE
LORN

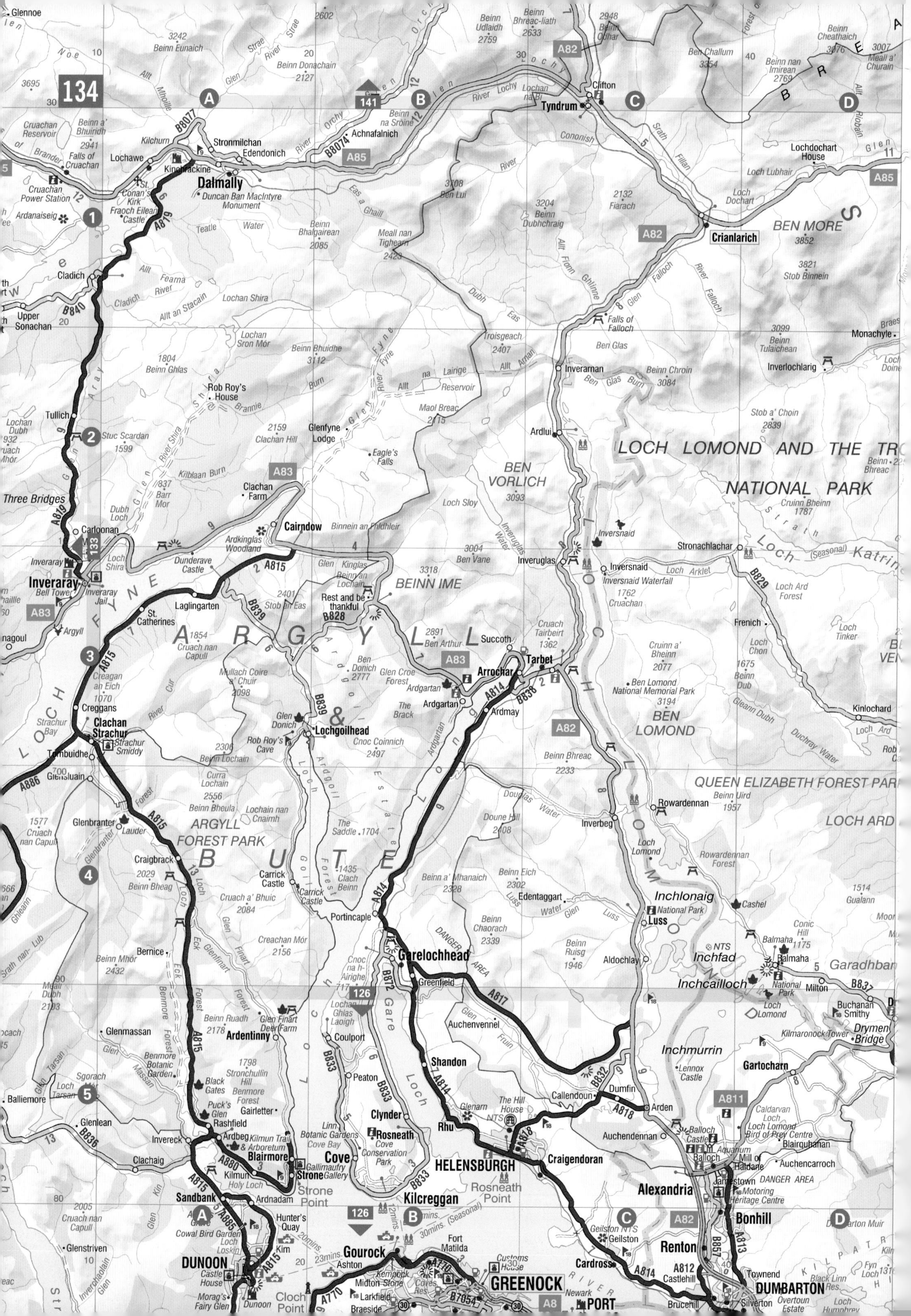
134
141
133
126
A
B
C
D
1
2
3
4
5
Glennoe
Beinn Eunaich
3242
Glen Strae
River Strae
Beinn Donachain
2127
2602
Beinn Udlaidh
2759
Beinn Bhreac-liath
2633
2948
Beinn Odhar
A82
Ben Challum
3354
Beinn Cheathaich
3076
3007
Meall a' Chuirn
Beinn nan Imirean
2769
BREADALBANE
Cruachan Reservoir
Beinn a' Bhuiridh
2941
Falls of Cruachan
Kilchurn
Stronmilchan
Edendonich
Achnafalnich
Beinn na Sròine
B8074
B8077
A85
Lochawe
Kinglrackine
Dalmally
Cruachan Power Station
St. Conan's Kirk
Fraoch Eilean Castle
Duncan Ban MacIntyre Monument
Ardanaiseig
A819
B840
River Lochy
Lochan na Bì
Clifton
Tyndrum
Cononish
Strath Fillan
Lochdochart House
Loch Lubhair
Loch Dochart
Crianlarich
BEN MORE
3852
3821
Stob Binnein
3708
Ben Lui
3204
Beinn Dubhchraig
2132
Fiarach
Eas a' Ghaill
Beinn Bhalgairean
2085
Meall nan Tighearn
2423
Teatle Water
Cladich
Fearna River
Upper Sonachan
Allt an Stacain
Lochan Shira
Lochan Sron Mór
Beinn Bhuidhe
3112
1804
Beinn Ghlas
Rob Roy's House
River Shira
Brannie Burn
Tullich
Stuc Scardan
1599
2159
Clachan Hill
Glenfyne Lodge
Glen Fyne
Lairige Reservoir
Maol Breac
2115
Eagle's Falls
Dubh Eas
Troisgeach
2407
Allt Arnan
Falls of Falloch
Glen Falloch
River Falloch
Ben Glas
Inverarnan
Ben Glas Burn
Beinn Chroin
3084
3099
Beinn Tulaichean
Inverlochlarig
Monachyle
Ardlui
Stob a' Choin
2839
LOCH LOMOND AND THE TROSSACHS NATIONAL PARK
Three Bridges
837
Barr Mor
Kilblaan Burn
A83
Clachan Farm
Cairndow
Binnein an Fhidhleir
BEN VORLICH
3093
Loch Sloy
Cruinn Bheinn
1787
Carloonan
Dubh Loch
Ardkinglas Woodland
Dunderave Castle
Inveraray
Bell Tower
Inveraray Jail
Loch Shira
A815
Glen Kinglas
Beinn an Lochain
3318
BEINN IME
3004
Ben Vane
Inveruglas Water
Inveruglas
Inversnaid
Inversnaid Waterfall
1762
Cruachan
Loch Arklet
Stronachlachar
Loch Katrine
B829
Loch Ard Forest
Laglingarten
St. Catherines
B839
2401
Stob an Eas
Rest and be thankful
B828
ARGYLL
2891
Ben Arthur
Succoth
Cruach Tairbeirt
1362
Tarbet
Arrochar
Frenich
Loch Tinker
Loch Chon
1854
Cruach nan Capull
Mullach Coire a' Chuir
2098
Ben Donich
2777
Glen Croe Forest
Ardgartan
The Brack
A814
B838
Ardmay
Cruinn a' Bheinn
2077
Ben Lomond National Memorial Park
3194
BEN LOMOND
1675
Beinn Dubh
Gleann Dubh
Kinlochard
Loch Ard
Duchray Water
Creagan an Eich
1070
Creggans
Strachur Bay
Clachan Strachur
Strachur Smiddy
Tombuidhe
Glenshuain
A886
Glen Donich
Lochgoilhead
Rob Roy's Cave
Cnoc Coinnich
2497
Beinn Lochain
2306
Curra Lochain
2556
Beinn Bheula
Lochain nan Cnaimh
Beinn Bhreac
2233
Douglas Water
Doune Hill
2408
Rowardennan
Inverbeg
QUEEN ELIZABETH FOREST PARK
Beinn Uird
1957
LOCH ARD
1577
Cruach nan Capull
Glenbranter
Lauder
ARGYLL FOREST PARK
The Saddle
1704
Craigbrack
2029
Beinn Bheag
BUTE
Carrick Castle
1435
Clach Beinn
Loch Lomond
Rowardennan Forest
Beinn a' Mhanaich
2328
Beinn Eich
2302
Edentaggart
Glen Luss
Luss Water
Inchlonaig
National Park
Luss
Cashel
1514
Gualann
Cruach a' Bhuic
2084
Portincaple
Creachan Mór
2156
Beinn Chaorach
2339
DANGER AREA
Beinn Ruisg
1946
Aldochlay
NTS
Inchfad
Inchcailloch
Conic Hill
1175
Balmaha
Garadhban
Milton
B837
Beinn Mhór
2432
Bernice
Glen Finart
Glenfinart Forest
Garelochhead
Greenfield
A817
Cnoc na h-Airighe
717
B872
Gare Loch
Glen Fruin
Auchenvennel
Lochan Ghlas Laoigh
Coulport
Glen Finart Deer Farm
Beinn Ruadh
2178
Ardentinny
Glenmassan
Meall Dubh
2103
Benmore Forest
Benmore Botanic Garden
Black Gates
1798
Stronchullin Hill
Benmore Forest
Puck's Glen
Gairletter
Rashfield
Peaton
B833
Shandon
A814
B832
Dumfin
Callendoun
Arden
A818
Inchmurrin
Lennox Castle
Buchanan Smithy
Kilmaronock Tower
Drymen Bridge
Gartocharn
A811
Sgorach Mor
Loch Tarsan
Balliemore
Glenlean
B836
Invereck
Ardbeg
Kilmun Trail & Arboretum
Blairmore
A880
Kilmun
Holy Loch
Strone
Strone Point
Gallimaufry Gallery
Clachaig
Clynder
Rosneath
Cove Conservation Park
Linn Botanic Gardens
Cove Bay
Cove
Glenarn
The Hill House
Rhu
HELENSBURGH
Craigendoran
Auchendennan
Balloch Castle
Aquarium
Balloch
Mill of Haldane
Caldarvan
Loch Lomond Bird of Prey Centre
Blairquhanan
Auchencarroch
Sandbank
Ardnadam
A885
Hunter's Quay
Kilcreggan
Rosneath Point
Jamestown
DANGER AREA
Motoring Heritage Centre
Alexandria
Bonhill
A813
Gowk Muir
2005
Cruach nan Capull
Cowal Bird Garden
Loch Loskin
Kim
Glenstriven
Inverchaolain Glen
DUNOON
Castle House
Morag's Fairy Glen
Dunoon
Cloch Point
Gourock
Ashton
Kempock Stone
Midton
Larkfield
Braeside
A770
Fort Matilda
Customs House
GREENOCK
B7054
A8
Newark
PORT GLASGOW
RIVER CLYDE
Geilston NTS
Geilston
Renton
A82
Cardross
A814
A812
Castlehill
Bruce Hill
B857
Townend
DUMBARTON
Silverton
Overtoun Estate
Black Linn Res.
Fyn Loch
Loch Humphrey
KILPATRICK HILLS

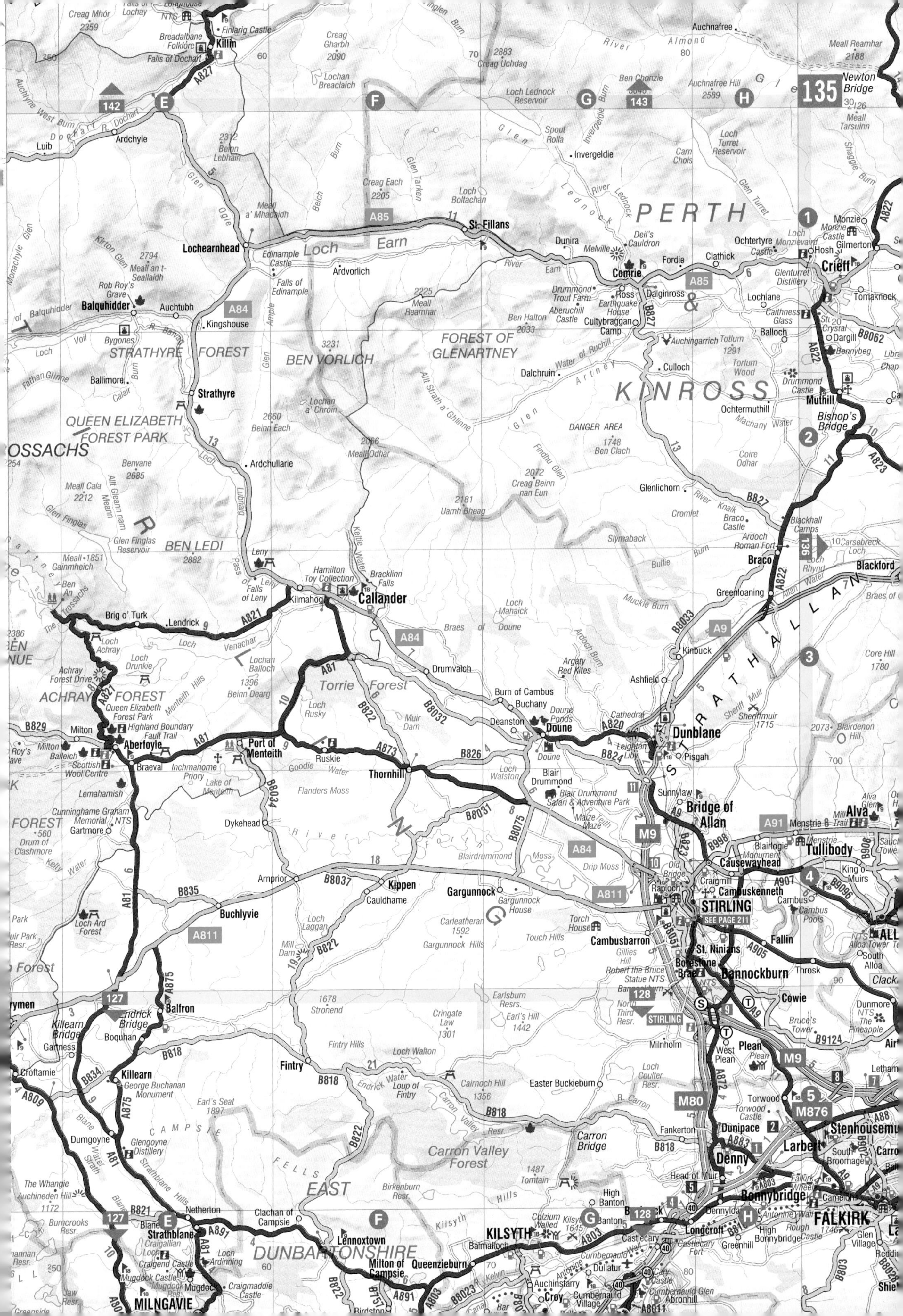
135
Creag Mhór
2359
Killin
Finlarig Castle
Breadalbane Folklore
Falls of Dochart
A827
142
E
Creag Gharbh
2090
Lochan Breaclaich
F
2883
Creag Uchdag
River Almond
Auchnafree
Meall Reamhar
2188
Newton Bridge
Ben Chonzie
Auchnafree Hill
2589
Loch Lednock Reservoir
G
143
H
2126
Meall Tarsuinn
Luib
Ardchyle
Glen Dochart
2312
Beinn Lebhain
Spout Rolla
Invergeldie
Carn Chois
Loch Turret Reservoir
Glen Turret
Shaggie Burn
Glen Tarken
Creag Each
2205
Loch Boltachan
Glen Ogle
Meall a' Mhadaidh
A85
St. Fillans
PERTH
1
Monzie
Monzie Castle
Loch Monzievaird
Ochtertyre Castle
Hosh
Gilmerton
Crieff
Lochearnhead
Edinample Castle
Loch Earn
Ardvorlich
River Earn
Dunira
Deil's Cauldron
Melville
Comrie
Fordie
Clathick
Glenturret Distillery
Falls of Edinample
Drummond Trout Farm
Ross
Earthquake House
Aberuchill Castle
Dalginross
Cultybraggan Camp
B827
Lochlane
Caithness Glass
Tomaknock
Crystal
Dargill
B8062
Balquhidder
Rob Roy's Grave
2794
Meall an t-Seallaidh
Auchtubh
A84
Kingshouse
2225
Meall Reamhar
Ben Halton
2033
Balloch
Bennybeg
Loch Voil
Bygones
STRATHYRE
FOREST
3231
BEN VORLICH
FOREST OF GLENARTNEY
Water of Ruchill
Auchingarrich
Totlum
1291
Torlum Wood
Dalchruin
Culloch
Drummond Castle
Fathan Glinne
Ballimore
Strathyre
Lochan a' Chroin
KINROSS
Muthill
Ochtermuthill
Machany Water
Bishop's Bridge
Glen Artney
QUEEN ELIZABETH FOREST PARK
TROSSACHS
2660
Beinn Each
DANGER AREA
1748
Ben Clach
2
A823
Benvane
2685
Ardchullarie
2066
Meall Odhar
Coire Odhar
Meall Cala
2212
Findhu Glen
2072
Creag Beinn nan Eun
Glenlichorn
River Knaik
Glen Finglas
2181
Uamh Bheag
Cromlet
Braco Castle
B827
Blackhall Camps
Ardoch Roman Fort
Glen Finglas Reservoir
BEN LEDI
2882
Slymaback
Braco
136
Carsebreck Loch
Meall 1851 Gainmheich
Leny
Keltie Water
Bullie
Loch Rhynd
Blackford
Hamilton Toy Collection
Bracklinn Falls
Pass of Leny
Falls of Leny
Kilmahog
Callander
Greenloaning
A822
Allan Water
Braes of Doune
Brig o' Turk
Lendrick
A821
Loch Mahaick
Braes of Doune
Muckle Burn
B8033
A9
Loch Achray
Loch Venachar
A84
Loch Drunkie
Lochan Balloch
Drumvaich
Kinbuck
3
Core Hill
1780
Achray Forest Drive
1396
Beinn Dearg
A81
Torrie Forest
Argaty Red Kites
Ashfield
ACHRAY FOREST
Queen Elizabeth Forest Park
Menteith Hills
Loch Rusky
B822
B8032
Burn of Cambus
Buchany
Doune Ponds
Cathedral
Dunblane
STRATHALLAN
Sheriffmuir
1715
2073
Blairdenon Hill
Highland Boundary Fault Trail
B829
Milton
Aberfoyle
Port of Menteith
Muir Dam
Deanston
Doune
A820
Leighton Library
Pisgah
Milton of Balleich
Scottish Wool Centre
Braeval
Inchmahome Priory
Lake of Menteith
Ruskie
Goodie Water
A873
Thornhill
B826
Loch Watston
Blair Drummond
Blair Drummond Safari & Adventure Park
Sunnylaw
Bridge of Allan
Lemahamish
Flanders Moss
B8034
Cunninghame Graham Memorial NTS
Gartmore
B8031
B8075
M9
A91
Menstrie
Alva
Tullibody
Dykehead
River Forth
Blairdrummond Moss
A84
Drip Moss
B998
Blairlogie
Causewayhead
Arnprior
B8037
Kippen
Cauldhame
Gargunnock
Gargunnock House
A811
Old Bridge
Raploch
Craigmill
Cambuskenneth
STIRLING
SEE PAGE 211
King o' Muirs
Cambus
Cambus Pools
4
B835
Buchlyvie
Loch Laggan
Carleatheran
1592
Gargunnock Hills
Touch Hills
Torch House
Cambusbarron
Gillies Hill
Robert the Bruce Statue NTS
St. Ninians
Fallin
A905
A811
Loch Ard Forest
Mill Dam
B822
Borestone Brae
Bannockburn
Throsk
Alloa Tower
South Alloa
Clackmannan
1678
Stronend
Cringate Law
1301
Earlsburn Resrs.
Earl's Hill
1442
North Third Resr.
128
STIRLING
Cowie
Dunmore
The Pineapple
Bruce's Tower
B9124
127
Endrick Bridge
Balfron
A875
Killearn Bridge
Gartness
Boquhan
Fintry Hills
Loch Walton
Milnholm
West Plean
Plean
M9
B818
Killearn
George Buchanan Monument
Fintry
B818
Endrick Water
Loup of Fintry
Cairnoch Hill
1356
Easter Buckieburn
Loch Coulter Resr.
M80
Torwood
Torwood Castle
5
M876
Croftamie
A809
B834
Earl's Seat
1897
CAMPSIE FELLS
B818
Carron Valley Resr.
Carron Valley Forest
Fankerton
Carron Bridge
B818
Dunipace
Denny
A883
Stenhousemuir
Larbert
South Broomage
Dumgoyne
Glengoyne Distillery
B822
EAST
Birkenburn Resr.
1487
Tomtain
Head of Muir
Falkirk Wheel
A803
Bonnybridge
The Whangie
Auchineden Hill
1172
Strathblane Hills
Netherton
B821
Blanefield
Strathblane
127
E
Clachan of Campsie
Lennoxtown
F
Kilsyth Hills
High Banton
Banton
G
Colzium Walled Garden
Kilsyth
1645
KILSYTH
A803
128
Castlecary
Longcroft
Dennyloanhead
H
Antonine Wall
High Bonnybridge
Rough Castle
FALKIRK
Camelon
Burncrooks Resr.
Craigallian Loch
Craigend Castle
Mugdock Castle
Mugdock
A891
Loch Ardinning
Craigmaddie Castle
DUNBARTONSHIRE
Milton of Campsie
Queenzieburn
Balmalloch
Cumbernauld
Dullatur
Auchinstarry
Croy
Cumbernauld Village
Castle Cary Castle
Cumbernauld Glen
Abronhill
Greenhill
Glen Village
A80
MILNGAVIE
B822
B757
A891
A803
B8023
A8011
B803

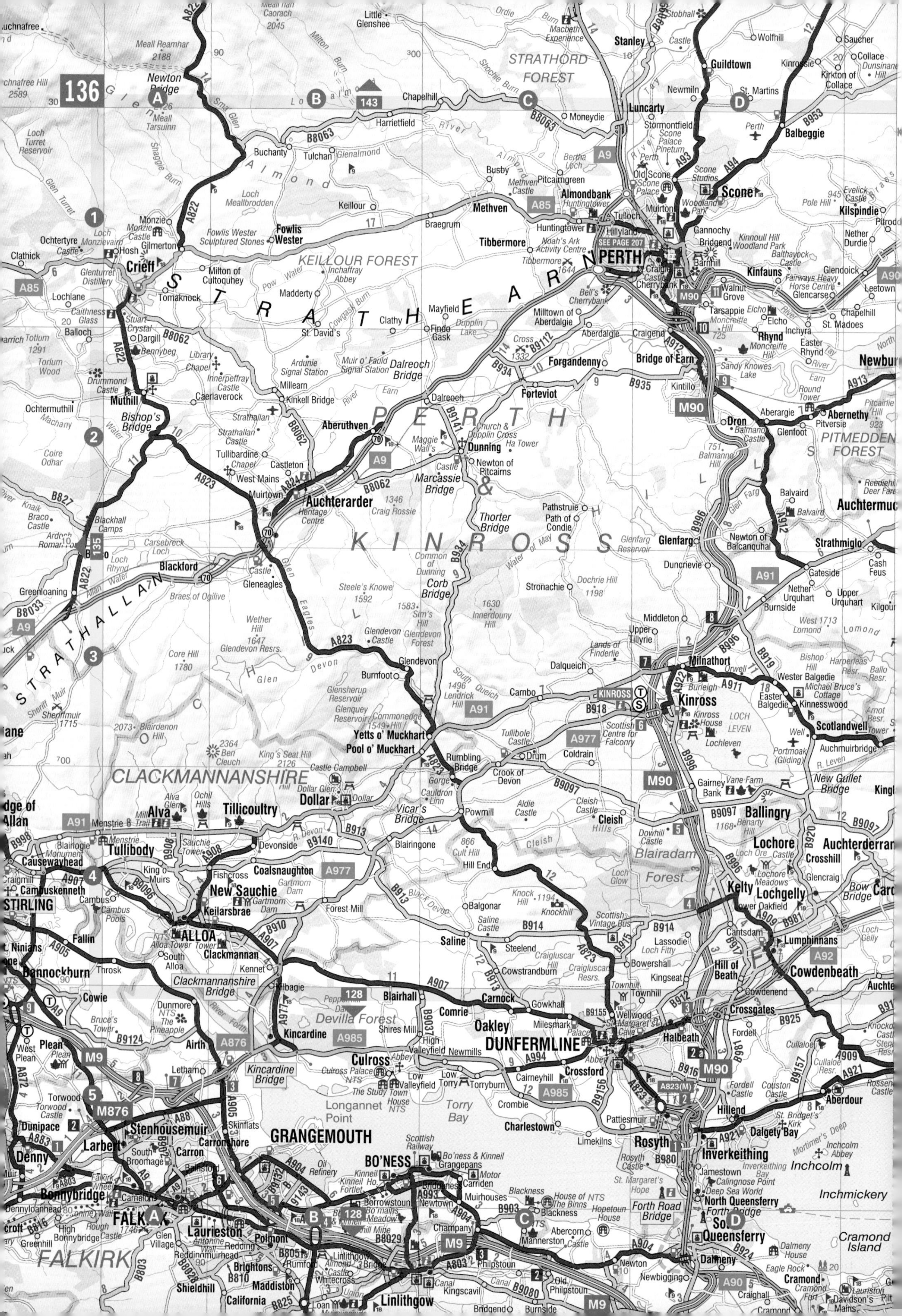

136
143
128
SEE PAGE 207
Little Glenshee
Stanley
Guildtown
Wolfhill
Saucher
Collace
Kinrossie
Kirkton of Collace
Newton Bridge
Meall Tarsuinn
Chapelhill
Harrietfield
Moneydie
STRATHORD FOREST
Luncarty
Stormontfield
Scone Palace Pinetum
St. Martins
Balbeggie
Newmiln
Loch Turret Reservoir
Glen Turret
Buchanty
Tulchan
Glenalmond
Almond
Busby
Methven Castle
Pitcairngreen
Almondbank
Huntingtower
Old Scone
Scone Palace
Scone Studios
Scone
Keillour
Methven
Muirton
Woodland Park
Evelick Castle
Pole Hill
Kilspindie
Monzie
Monzie Castle
Gilmerton
Fowlis Wester Sculptured Stones
Fowlis Wester
Braegrum
Tibbermore
Noah's Ark Activity Centre
Tulloch
Hillyland
PERTH
Gannochy
Bridgend
Kinnoull Hill Woodland Park
Balthayock Castle
Nether Durdie
Ochtertyre Castle
Loch Monzievaird
Hosh
Clathick
Crieff
Glenturret Distillery
KEILLOUR FOREST
Milton of Cultoquhey
Inchaffray Abbey
Craigie
Cherrybank
Bell's Cherrybank
Barnhill
Kinfauns
Fairways Heavy Horse Centre
Glendoick
Glencarse
Walnut Grove
Leetown
Lochlane
Tomaknock
STRATHEARN
Madderty
Mayfield
Clathy
Findo Gask
Dupplin Lake
Milltown of Aberdalgie
Aberdalgie
Craigend
Tarsappie
Elcho
Moncreiffe Hill
Rhynd
Chapelhill
St. Madoes
Inchyra
Caithness Glass
Stuart Crystal
Balloch
Dargill
Bennybeg
Totlum
Torlum Wood
St. David's
Library Chapel
Ardunie Signal Station
Muir o' Fauld Signal Station
Dalreoch Bridge
Cross
Forgandenny
Bridge of Earn
Kintillo
Moncreiffe Hill
Easter Rhynd
Sandy Knowes Lake
Round Tower
Newburgh
Drummond Castle
Innerpeffray Castle
Caerlaverock
Millearn
Kinkell Bridge
Dalreoch
Forteviot
Aberargie
Abernethy
Pitversie
Pitcairlie Hill
Ochtermuthill
Muthill
Bishop's Bridge
Machany Water
Strathallan
Strathallan Castle
Aberuthven
PERTH
Church & Dupplin Cross
Ha Tower
Maggie Wall's
Dunning
Newton of Pitcairns
Dron
Balmanno Castle
Glenfoot
PITMEDDEN FOREST
Coire Odhar
Tullibardine Chapel
Castleton
West Mains
Muirtown
Auchterarder
Heritage Centre
Castle
Marcassie Bridge
&
Balmanno Hill
Reediehill Deer Farm
Balvaird
Auchtermuchty
Knaik
Braco Castle
Ardoch Roman Fort
Blackhall Camps
Craig Rossie
Pathstruie
Path of Condie
Thorter Bridge
KINROSS
Glenfarg
Glenfarg Reservoir
Newton of Balcanqual
Strathmiglo
Carsebreck Loch
Loch Rhynd
Blackford
Gleneagles
Castle
Common of Dunning
Corb Bridge
Water of May
Duncrievie
Gateside
Cash Feus
Greenloaning
STRATHALLAN
Allan Water
Braes of Ogilvie
Steele's Knowe
Innerdouny Hill
Stronachie
Dochrie Hill
Nether Urquhart
Upper Urquhart
Burnside
Kilgour
Wether Hill
Glendevon Resrs.
Sim's Hill
Glendevon Castle
Glendevon Forest
Glen Eagles
Middleton
Upper Tillyrie
West Lomond
Lomond
Core Hill
Glen Devon
Glendevon
Lands of Finderlie
Dalqueich
Milnathort
Orwell
Bishop Hill
Harperleas Resr.
Ballo Resr.
Sheriffmuir
Burnfoot
Lendrick Hill
South Queich
Carnbo
KINROSS
Burleigh
Kinross
Wester Balgedie
Easter Balgedie
Michael Bruce's Cottage
Kinnesswood
Arnot Resr.
Blairdenon Hill
Glensherup Reservoir
Glenquey Reservoir
Commonedge Hill
Yetts o' Muckhart
Pool o' Muckhart
Tullibole Castle
Drum
Scottish Centre for Falconry
Kinross House
LOCH LEVEN
Lochleven
Scotlandwell
Portmoak (Gliding)
Auchmuirbridge
Ben Cleuch
King's Seat Hill
Castle Campbell
Rumbling Bridge
Crook of Devon
Coldrain
R. Leven
CLACKMANNANSHIRE
Dollar Glen
Dollar
Cauldron Linn
Gorge
Vane Farm
Gairney Bank
New Gullet Bridge
Alva Glen
Ochil Hills
Alva
Tillicoultry
Mill Trail
Menstrie
Vicar's Bridge
Powmill
Aldie Castle
Cleish Castle
Cleish
Cleish Hills
Ballingry
Benarty Hill
Bridge of Allan
Blairlogie
Menstrie
Wallace Monument
Causewayhead
Tullibody
Sauchie Tower
Devonside
R. Devon
Blairingone
Cult Hill
Dowhill Castle
Blairadam Forest
Lochore
Loch Ore
Lochore Castle
Lochore Meadows
Auchterderran
Crosshill
Glencraig
Craigmill
Cambuskenneth
Cambus
Cambus Pools
King o' Muirs
Fishcross
Coalsnaughton
Gartmorn Dam
New Sauchie
Keilarsbrae
Hill End
Loch Glow
Kelty
Lochgelly
Lower Oakfield
Bow Bridge
STIRLING
Forest Mill
Balgonar
Knock Hill
Knockhill
Scottish Vintage Bus
Saline
Saline Castle
Steelend
Lassodie
Loch Fitty
Cantsdam
Lumphinnans
Loch Gelly
St. Ninians
Fallin
ALLOA
Alloa Tower
Clackmannan
South Alloa
Kennet
Craigluscar Hill
Craigluscar Resrs.
Cowstrandburn
Bowershall
Kingseat
Hill of Beath
Cowdenbeath
Bannockburn
Throsk
Clackmannanshire Bridge
Kilbagie
Blairhall
Comrie
Carnock
Gowkhall
Townhill
Cowdenend
Cowie
Dunmore
The Pineapple
River Forth
Devilla Forest
Shires Mill
Oakley
Wellwood
Milesmark
St. Margaret's Cave
Crossgates
Bruce's Tower
Airth
Kincardine
High Valleyfield
Newmills
DUNFERMLINE
Abbey
Palace
Halbeath
Fordell
Cullaloe
Cullaloe Resr.
Knockdavie
West Plean
Plean
Letham
Kincardine Bridge
Culross
Culross Palace
Abbey
Low Valleyfield
Low Torry
Torryburn
Cairneyhill
Crossford
Fordell Castle
Couston Castle
Aberdour
Torwood
Torwood Castle
The Study
Town House
Longannet Point
Torry Bay
Crombie
Hillend
Dunipace
Stenhousemuir
Skinflats
Charlestown
Pattiesmuir
St. Bridget's Kirk
Dalgety Bay
Mortimer's Deep
Larbert
Carronshore
Carron
South Broomage
GRANGEMOUTH
Scottish Railway
Limekilns
Rosyth
Inverkeithing
Incholm Abbey
Inchcolm
Denny
Bainsford
Oil Refinery
BO'NESS
Bo'ness & Kinneil
Grangepans
Kinneil
Kinneil Ho.
Fortlet
Motor
Carriden
Rosyth Castle
Jamestown
Inverkeithing Bay
Calingnose Point
Deep Sea World
North Queensferry
Inchmickery
Falkirk Wheel
Bonnybridge
Camelon
Borrowstoun
Bridgeness
Newtown
Muirhouses
Blackness
House of The Binns
Hopetoun House
Forth Road Bridge
Forth Bridge
Dennyloanhead
FALKIRK
Laurieston
Polmont
Bo'mains Meadow
Mill Mine
Champany
Blackness
Abercorn Castle
Mannerston
South Queensferry
Queensferry
Cramond Island
Dalmeny House
High Bonnybridge
Rough Castle
Glen Village
Antonine Wall
Redding
Reddingmuirhead
Brightons
Rumford
Linlithgow Bridge
Almond Castle
Whitecross
Philpstoun
Newton
Dalmeny
Eagle Rock
Cramond
Greenhill
FALKIRK
Shieldhill
Maddiston
California
Union Canal
Linlithgow
Kingscavil
Canal
Old Philpstoun
Newbigging
Craighall
Cramond Fort
Lauriston Castle
Davidson's Mains
Loan
Bridgend
Burnside
Cramond
M9
M90
M876
A9
A85
A91
A977
A985
A876
A92
A90
A823(M)
Tibbermore
Pitmedden

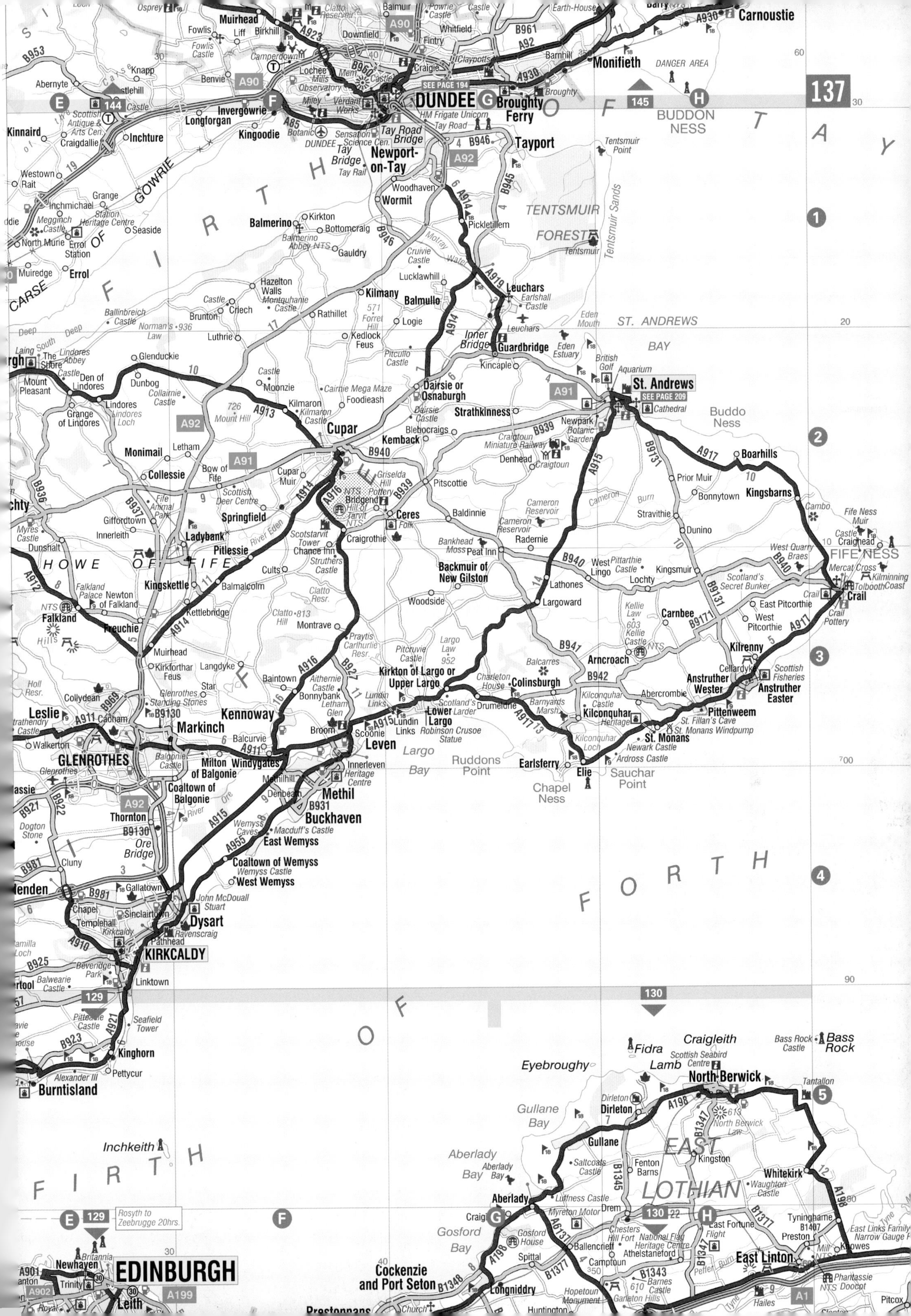

137
Muirhead
Fowlis
Liff
Birkhill
Fowlis Castle
Camperdown
Lochee
Downfield
Whitfield
Fintry
Craigie
Claypotts
Barnhill
Monifieth
Carnoustie
DANGER AREA
Broughty
Broughty Ferry
DUNDEE
SEE PAGE 194
HM Frigate Unicorn
Tay Road
Tay Road Bridge
Sensation Science Cen.
Tay Bridge
Tay Rail
Newport-on-Tay
Tayport
Tentsmuir Point
BUDDON NESS
FIRTH OF TAY
Knapp
Abernyte
Benvie
Invergowrie
Longforgan
Kingoodie
Kinnaird
Craigdallie
Inchture
Scottish Antique & Arts Cen.
Castle
Westown
Rait
Grange
Inchmichael
Megginch Castle
Station Heritage Centre
North Murie
Errol Station
Seaside
Muiredge
Errol
CARSE OF GOWRIE
Woodhaven
Wormit
Balmerino
Kirkton
Bottomcraig
Balmerino Abbey NTS
Gauldry
Pickletillem
TENTSMUIR FOREST
Tentsmuir
Tentsmuir Sands
Motray Water
Cruivie Castle
Lucklawhill
Leuchars
Earlshall Castle
Hazelton Walls
Montquhanie Castle
Kilmany
Balmullo
Castle
Creich
Brunton
Rathillet
Forret Hill
Logie
Ballinbreich Castle
Norman's Law
Luthrie
Kedlock Feus
Eden Mouth
ST. ANDREWS BAY
Inner Bridge
Guardbridge
Eden Estuary
Pitcullo Castle
British Golf
Aquarium
Kincaple
Laing
The Shore
Lindores Abbey
Glenduckie
Dunbog
Den of Lindores
Mount Pleasant
Lindores
Grange of Lindores
Lindores Loch
Collairnie Castle
Mount Hill
Castle
Moonzie
Kilmaron
Kilmaron Castle
Cairnie Mega Maze
Foodieash
Dairsie or Osnaburgh
Dairsie Castle
Strathkinness
St. Andrews
SEE PAGE 209
Cathedral
Buddo Ness
Cupar
Blebocraigs
Kemback
Newpark
Botanic Garden
Craigtoun Miniature Railway
Craigtoun
Denhead
Monimail
Letham
Bow of Fife
Collessie
Cupar Muir
Scottish Deer Centre
Griselda Hill Pottery
Bridgend
Hill of Tarvit NTS
Pitscottie
Boarhills
Prior Muir
Bonnytown
Kingsbarns
Cambo
Fife Ness Muir
Fife Animal Park
Springfield
Ceres
Folk
Baldinnie
Cameron Reservoir
Cameron Burn
Stravithie
Dunino
Giffordtown
Innerleith
Ladybank
Scotstarvit Tower
Chance Inn
Craigrothie
Struthers Castle
Bankhead Moss
Peat Inn
Radernie
West Quarry Braes
Castle
Craighead
FIFE NESS
Mercat Cross
Kilminning Coast
Myres Castle
Dunshalt
HOWE OF FIFE
Pitlessie
River Eden
Cults
Backmuir of New Gilston
West Lingo
Pittarthie Castle
Lochty
Kingsmuir
Scotland's Secret Bunker
Tolbooth
Crail
Crail Pottery
Falkland Palace
Newton of Falkland
Falkland
Kingskettle
Balmalcolm
Clatto Resr.
Woodside
Lathones
Largoward
Kellie Law
Kellie Castle
Carnbee
East Pitcorthie
West Pitcorthie
Freuchie
Kettlebridge
Clatto Hill
Montrave
Praytis
Carlhurlie Resr.
Largo Law
Pitcruvie Castle
Balcarres
Arncroach
Kilrenny
Cellardyke
Scottish Fisheries
Anstruther Wester
Anstruther Easter
Holl Resr.
Muirhead
Kirkforthar Feus
Langdyke
Star
Baintown
Airthernie Castle
Bonnybank
Kirkton of Largo or Upper Largo
Charleton House
Colinsburgh
Kilconquhar Castle
Abercrombie
Pittenweem
Collydean
Glenrothes Standing Stones
Kennoway
Letham Glen
Lundin Links
Scotland's Larder
Drumeldrie
Barnyards Marsh
Kilconquhar
Heritage
St. Fillan's Cave
St. Monans Windpump
St. Monans
Newark Castle
Leslie
Cadham
Markinch
Balcurvie
Broom
Scoonie
Lower Largo
Robinson Crusoe Statue
Leven
Largo Bay
Ruddons Point
Kilconquhar Loch
Earlsferry
Elie
Ardross Castle
Sauchar Point
Walkerton
GLENROTHES
Balgonie Castle
Milton of Balgonie
Windygates
Innerleven
Heritage Centre
Chapel Ness
Glenrothes
Coaltown of Balgonie
Methilhill
Denbeath
Methil
Buckhaven
Thornton
River Ore
Wemyss Caves
Macduff's Castle
East Wemyss
Dogton Stone
Ore Bridge
Cluny
Coaltown of Wemyss
Wemyss Castle
West Wemyss
Galatown
Chapel
Sinclairtown
John McDouall Stuart
Dysart
Templehall
Kirkcaldy
Ravenscraig
Pathhead
KIRKCALDY
Beveridge Park
Balwearie Castle
Linktown
FIRTH OF FORTH
129
130
Pitteadie Castle
Seafield Tower
Kinghorn
Alexander III
Pettycur
Burntisland
Fidra
Craigleith
Bass Rock Castle
Bass Rock
Scottish Seabird Centre
Lamb
Eyebroughy
North Berwick
Tantallon
Dirleton
Gullane Bay
North Berwick Law
Gullane
Inchkeith
Saltcoats Castle
Fenton Barns
EAST LOTHIAN
Kingston
Aberlady Bay
Whitekirk
Waughton Castle
Aberlady
Luffness Castle
Myreton Motor
Drem
Craig
Rosyth to Zeebrugge 20hrs.
Gosford Bay
Gosford House
Chesters Hill Fort
National Flag Heritage Centre
East Fortune Flight
Tyninghame
Preston
East Links Family
Narrow Gauge
Ballencrieff
Athelstaneford
Spittal
Camptoun
East Linton
Knowes
Britannia
Newhaven
EDINBURGH
Trinity
Leith
Cockenzie and Port Seton
Longniddry
Barnes Castle
Garleton Hills
Hopetoun Monument
Phantassie NTS Doocot
Hailes
Prestonpans
Huntington
Pitcox

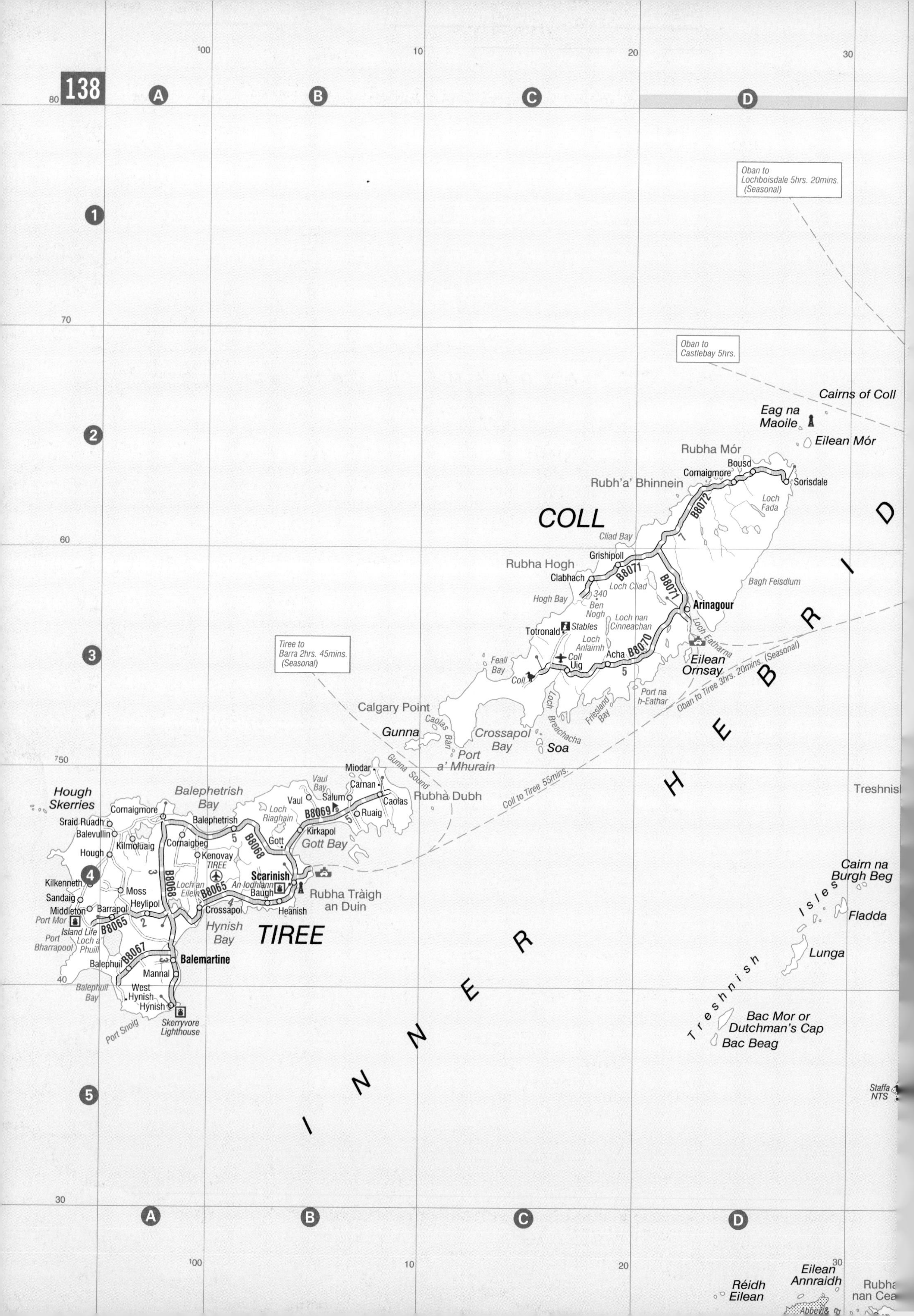

80

100   10   20   30

A   B   C   D

1

70

Oban to
Lochboisdale 5hrs. 20mins.
(Seasonal)

Oban to
Castlebay 5hrs.

Cairns of Coll

Eag na
Maoile

Rubha Mór

Bousd

Cornaigmore   Sorisdale

2   Eilean Mór

Rubh'a' Bhinnein   B8072   Loch
                                              Fada

COLL

Cliad Bay

60   Grishipoll

Rubha Hogh   B8071

Clabhach   *Bagh Feisdlum*

340   B8071

Hogh Bay   Ben   Loch Cliad

Nogh   Loch nan

Cinneachan   **Arinagour**

Totronald   Stables   Loch a' Chatharna

Loch   B8070

Anlaimh

3   *Eilean*

Feall   + Coll   5   *Ornsay*

Bay   Uig   Acha

Coll   Port na

h-Eathar   Oban to Tiree 3hrs. 20mins. (Seasonal)

Tiree to
Barra 2hrs. 45mins.
(Seasonal)

Calgary Point

Gunna   Crossapol   H

Bay

Port   *Soa*   E

a' Mhurain   B

Coll to Tiree 55mins.   R   Treshnish

Miodar   *Rubhà Dubh*

Vaul   Carnan   I

Bay*

750   *Hough   Balephetrish*   Vaul   Salum   B8069   Caolas   D

Skerries   Bay   Loch   Ruaig

Cornaigmore   Riaghain   5   E

Sraid Ruadh   Balephetrish   Kirkapol   S

Balevullin   Cornaigbeg   Gott   *Gott Bay*   *Cairn na*

Kilmoluaig   B8068   *Burgh Beg*

Hough   3   Kenovay   I   *Fladda*

B8068   TIREE   s

4   Kilkenneth   An Iodhlann   Rubha Tràigh   l   *Lunga*

Sandaig   Moss   B8065   **Scarinish**   an Duin   e

Middleton   Barrapol   Heylipol   Baugh   s

Port Mor   2   Crossapol   Heanish

Island Life   B8065   *Hynish*   T

Port   Loch a'   Bay   r

Bharrapool   Loch a'   *TIREE*   e   *Bac Mor or*

Phuill   B8067   s   *Dutchman's Cap*

Balephuil   Mannal   **Balemartine**   h   *Bac Beag*

40

Balephuil   West   n

Bay   Hynish   i

Hynish   s

Port Snoig   *Skerryvore*   h   *Staffa*

Lighthouse   *NTS*

5   I   N   N   E   R   I

s

l

e

s

30

A   B   C   D

100   10   20   30

Réidh   Eilean

Eilean   Annraidh   *Rubha*

nan Cea

Abbey &

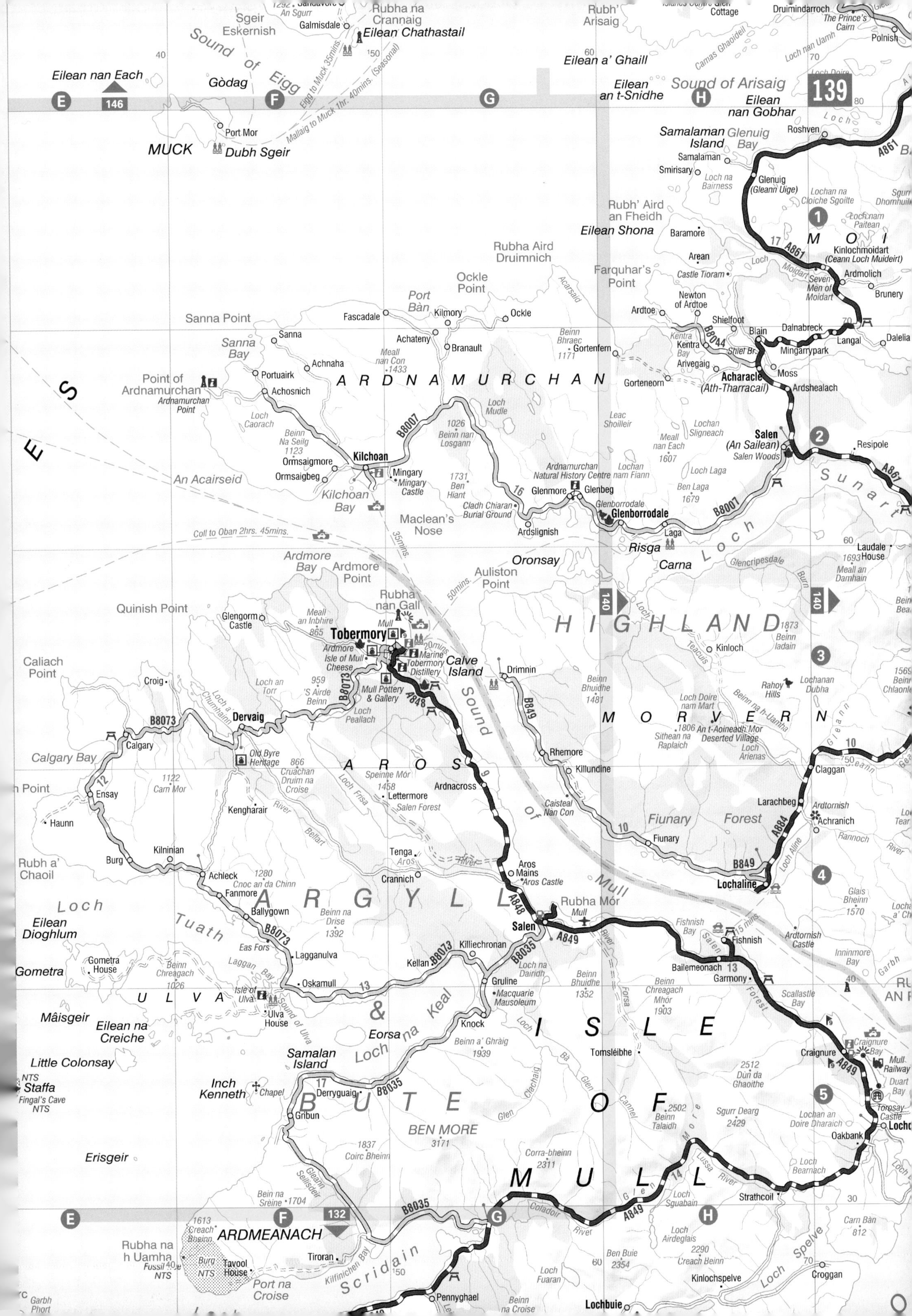

139
Sgeir Eskernish
An Sgurr
Galmisdale
Rubha na Crannaig
Eilean Chathastail
Sound of Eigg
Eigg to Muck 35mins.
Mallaig to Muck 1hr. 40mins. (Seasonal)
Eilean nan Each
146
Gòdag
Port Mor
MUCK
Dubh Sgeir
Rubh' Arisaig
Eilean a' Ghaill
Camas Ghaoideil
Eilean an t-Snidhe
Sound of Arisaig
Eilean nan Gobhar
Cottage
Druimindarroch
The Prince's Cairn
Polnish
Loch nan Uamh
Loch
Roshven
Samalaman Island
Glenuig Bay
Samalaman
Smirisary
Loch na Bairness
Glenuig (Gleann Uige)
Lochan na Cloiche Sgoilte
Sgurr Dhomhuill
Lochan nam Paitean
Rubh' Aird an Fheidh
Eilean Shona
Baramore
M O I
A861
Kinlochmoidart (Ceann Loch Muideirt)
Arean
Castle Tioram
Moidart
Seven Men of Moidart
Ardmolich
Brunery
Rubha Aird Druimnich
Farquhar's Point
Ockle Point
Newton of Ardtoe
Ardtoe
Port Bàn
Kilmory
Ockle
Acarsaid
Shielfoot
Blain
Dalnabreck
Langal
Dalelia
Sanna Point
Fascadale
Sanna
Sanna Bay
Achateny
Branault
Meall nan Con 1433
Beinn Bhraec 1171
Gortenfern
Kentra Bay
Kentra
B8044
Shiel Br.
Mingarrypark
Arivegaig
Moss
Achnaha
Portuairk
Point of Ardnamurchan
Ardnamurchan Point
Achosnich
A R D N A M U R C H A N
Gorteneorn
Acharacle (Ath-Tharracail)
Ardshealach
Loch Mudle
Loch Caorach
B8007
1026 Beinn nan Losgann
Leac Shoilleir
Lochan Sligneach
Meall nan Each 1607
Salen (An Sailean)
Salen Woods
Resipole
Beinn Na Seilg 1123
Kilchoan
Ormsaigmore
Ormsaigbeg
An Acairseid
Mingary
Mingary Castle
Kilchoan Bay
1731 Ben Hiant
Ardnamurchan Natural History Centre
Lochan nam Fiann
Loch Laga
Ben Laga 1679
Sunart
Glenmore
Glenbeg
Cladh Chiaran Burial Ground
Glenborrodale
Glenborrodale
Maclean's Nose
Ardslignish
Laga
Coll to Oban 2hrs. 45mins.
35mins.
Risga
Carna
Loch
Laudale House
1693
Meall an Damhain
Glencripesdale
Burn
Ardmore Bay
Ardmore Point
Oronsay
Auliston Point
50mins.
140
Quinish Point
Glengorm Castle
Meall an Inbhire 865
Rubha nan Gall
Mull
H I G H L A N D
1873 Beinn Iadain
Tobermory
Ardmore
Isle of Mull Cheese
Marine
Tobermory Distillery
20mins
Calve Island
Kinloch
Teacuis
Caliach Point
Croig
Loch an Torr
959 'S Airde Beinn
B8073
Mull Pottery & Gallery
A848
Drimnin
Rahoy Hills
Lochanan Dubha
1569 Beinn Chlaonleac
Beinn Bhuidhe 1481
Loch Doire nam Mart
Beinn na h-Uamha
Loch a' Chumhainn
B8073
Dervaig
Loch Peallach
Sound
B849
M O R V E R N
1806 An t-Aoineadh Mor Deserted Village
Sithean na Raplaich
Loch Arienas
Calgary
Calgary Bay
Old Byre Heritage
866 Cruachan Druim na Croise
A R O S
Speinne Mór 1458
Rhemore
Killundine
Claggan
Point
12
Ensay
1122 Cam Mor
Loch Frisa
Lettermore
Salen Forest
Ardnacross
of
Caisteal Nan Con
Larachbeg
Ardtornish
Achranich
Kengharair
River
Bellart
Fiunary Forest
Funary
A884
Rannoch
Haunn
Kilninian
Tenga
Aros
River
B849
Lochaline
Loch Aline
Rubh a' Chaoil
Burg
Achleck
1280 Cnoc an da Chinn
Crannich
Aros Mains
Aros Castle
Mull
Loch
Fanmore
A R G Y L L
Rubha Mór
Mull
Glais Bheinn 1570
Eilean Dioghlum
Tuath
Ballygown
Beinn na Drise 1392
A848
Salen
A849
Fishnish Bay
15 mins
Fishnish
Ardtornish Castle
B8073
Eas Fors
Killiechronan
B8035
Salen
River
Inninmore Bay
Gometra House
Gometra
Beinn Chreagach 1026
Laggan
Bay
Lagganulva
Kellan
Gruline
Loch na Dairidh
Forsa
Beinn Bhuidhe 1352
Bailemeonach
Garmony
Forest
Scallastle Bay
U L V A
Isle of Ulva
Oskamull
13
Macquarie Mausoleum
Beinn Chreagach Mhòr 1903
Ulva House
Sound of Ulva
&
Keal
Knock
Mâisgeir
Eilean na Creiche
Eorsa
I S L E
Loch na
Beinn a' Ghràig 1939
Tomsléibhe
2512 Dun da Ghaoithe
Craignure
Craignure Bay
A849
Mull Railway
Little Colonsay
Samalan Island
Loch
NTS Staffa
Fingal's Cave NTS
Inch Kenneth
Chapel
17
Derryguaig
B8035
B U T E
O F
Glen Clachaig
Glen Cannel
2502 Beinn Talaidh
Sgurr Dearg 2429
Duart Bay
Torosay Castle
Lochan an Doire Dharaich
Gribun
Glen
BEN MORE 3171
Oakbank
Erisgeir
1837 Coirc Bheinn
Corra-bheinn 2311
Lussa
River
Loch Beannach
M U L L
14
Glen
Strathcoil
Gleann Seilisdeir
Bein na Srèine 1704
Loch Squabain
A849
30
B8035
132
Coladoir
River
1613 Creach Bheinn
ARDMEANACH
Loch Airdeglais
2290 Creach Beinn
Carn Bàn 812
Rubha na h Uamha
Fussil NTS
Burg NTS
Tavool House
Tiroran
Kilfinichen Bay
Scridain
Ben Buie 2354
Loch Fuaran
Kinlochspelve
Loch Spelve
Croggan
Port na Croise
Pennyghael
Beinn na Croise
Lochbuie
Garbh Phort

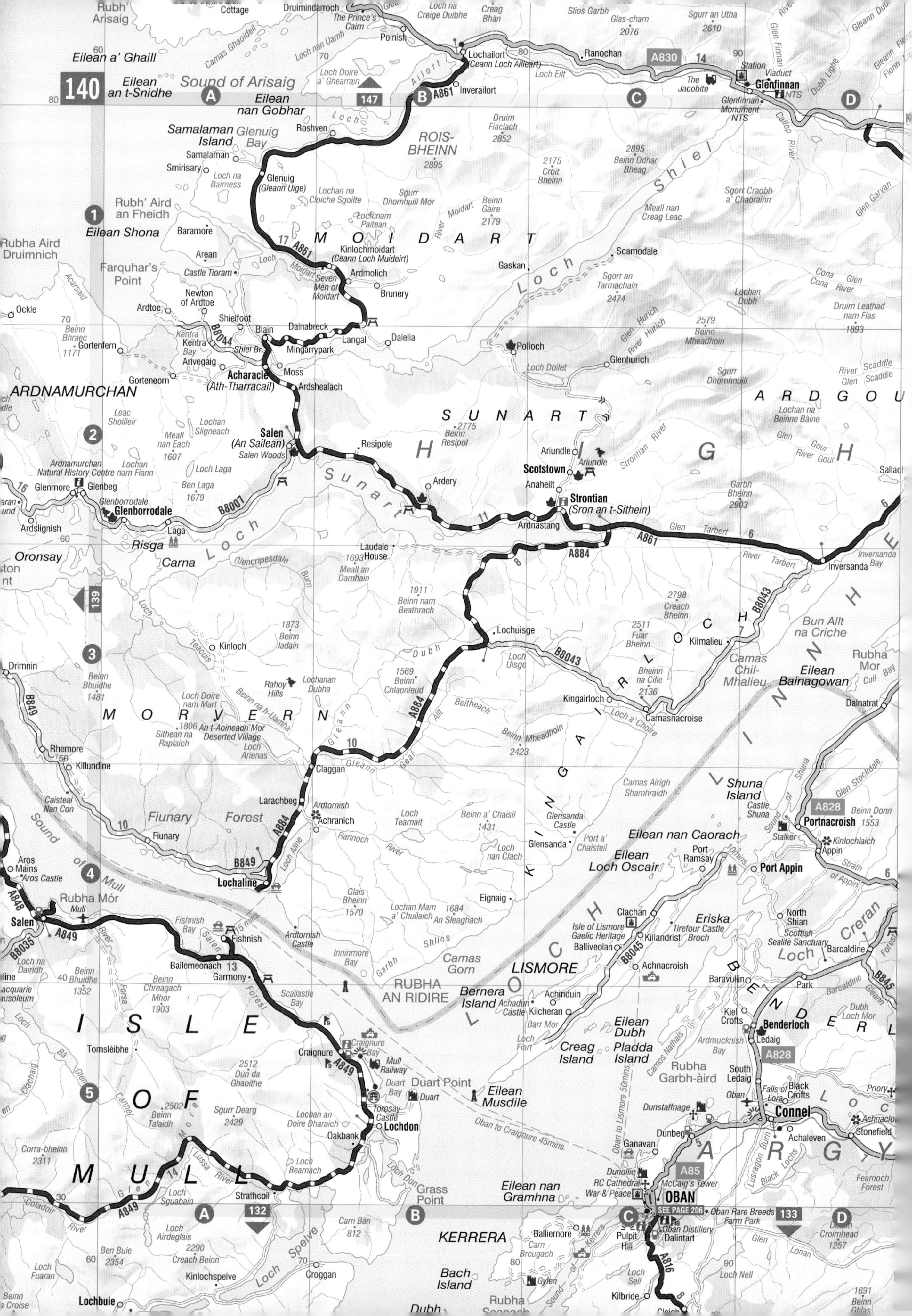

140
Sound of Arisaig
Eilean a' Ghaill
Eilean an t-Snidhe
Eilean nan Gobhar
147
139
132
133
SEE PAGE 206
Lochailort (Ceann Loch Ailleart)
Inverailort
Glenfinnan
Glenfinnan Monument NTS
The Jacobite
Ranochan
Glenuig (Gleann Uige)
Samalaman Island
Glenuig Bay
Roshven
ROIS-BHEINN 2895
MOIDART
Kinlochmoidart (Ceann Loch Muideirt)
Seven Men of Moidart
Loch Shiel
Eilean Shona
Castle Tioram
Dalnabreck
Acharacle (Ath-Tharracail)
ARDNAMURCHAN
Salen (An Sailean)
Resipole
SUNART
Loch Sunart
Polloch
Scotstown
Strontian (Sron an t-Sithein)
Ardnastang
Glenborrodale
Ardnamurchan Natural History Centre
Glenhurich
ARDGOUR
Inversanda
Carna
Oronsay
Risga
Lochuisge
Kingairloch
Camasnacroise
Kilmalieu
MORVERN
Loch Teacuis
Kinloch
Drimnin
Rhemore
Killundine
Claggan
Larachbeg
Achranich
Fiunary
Funary Forest
Lochaline
Ardtornish Castle
Glensanda Castle
Glensanda
KINGAIRLOCH
Loch Linnhe
Shuna Island
Castle Shuna
Portnacroish
Port Appin
Eilean Balnagowan
Eilean nan Caorach
Eilean Loch Oscair
Port Ramsay
LISMORE
Clachan
Isle of Lismore Gaelic Heritage
Balliveolan
Achnacroish
Achinduin
Kilcheran
Bernera Island
RUBHA AN RIDIRE
Eriska
Barcaldine
Benderloch
Ledaig
Connel
Dunstaffnage
Dunbeg
Ganavan
Dunollie
McCaig's Tower
OBAN
Oban Rare Breeds Farm Park
Oban Distillery
Dalintart
Pulpit Hill
KERRERA
Gylen
Eilean Musdile
Duart Point
Duart Castle
Torosay Castle
Craignure
Mull Railway
Lochdon
Oakbank
Grass Point
Strathcoil
Fishnish
Garmony
Ballemeonach
Salen
Aros Castle
Sound of Mull
ISLE OF MULL
Tomsléibhe
Dùn da Ghaoithe 2512
Glen More
Lussa River
Loch Spelve
Croggan
Kinlochspelve
Lochbuie
Oban to Craignure 45mins
Oban to Lismore 50mins
A861
A830
A884
A849
A848
A828
A85
A816
B8043
B8007
B8044
B849
B8045
B8035
B845

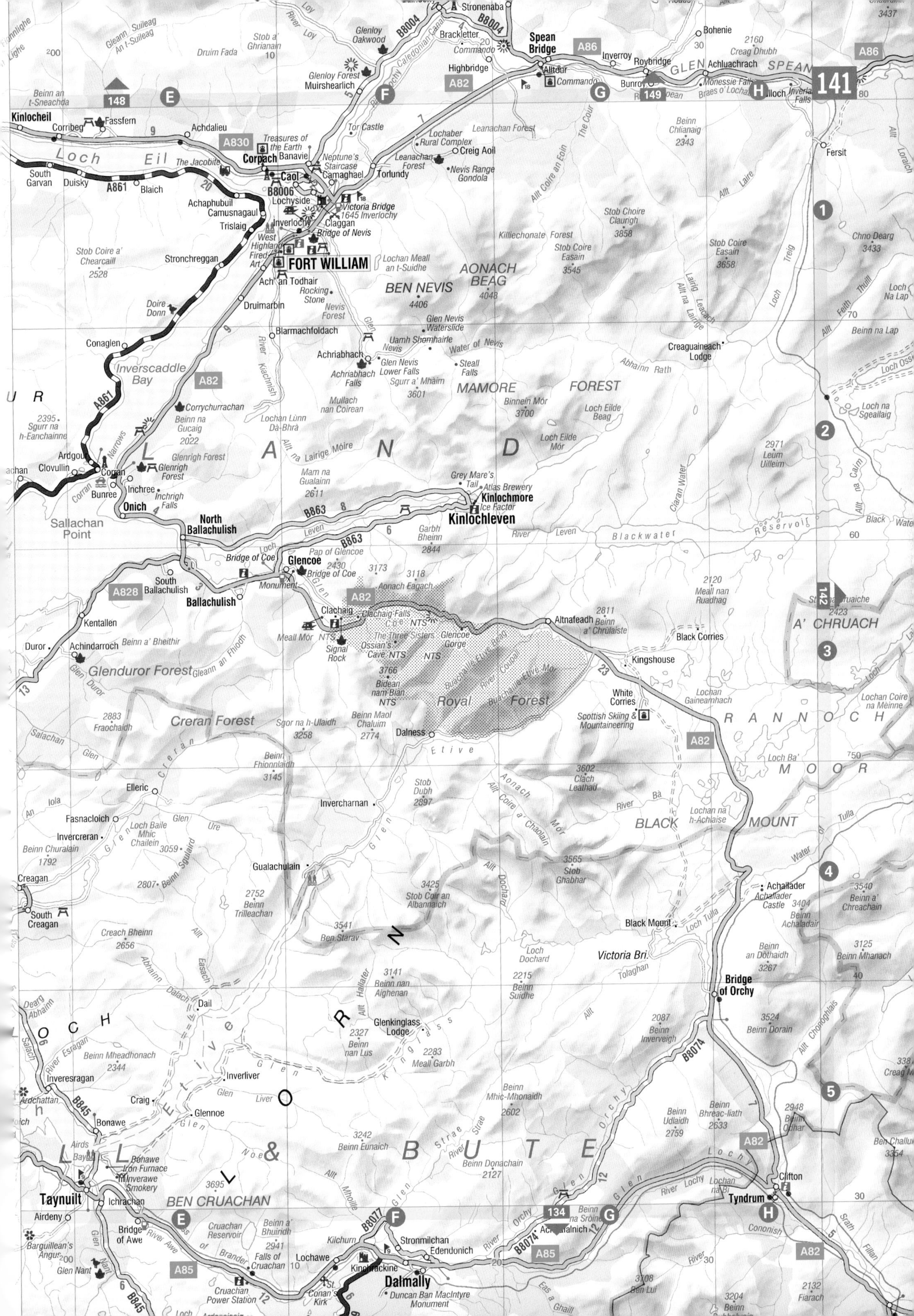
141
Stronenaba
Spean Bridge
A86
Inverroy
Roybridge
Bohenie
Glen Spean
Achluachrach
2160
Creag Dhubh
3437
Glen Loy
River Loy
Glenloy Oakwood
B8004
Brackletter
Commando
Highbridge
A82
Glenloy Forest
Muirshearlich
Caledonian Canal
Alltour
Commando
Bunroy
149
Monessie Falls
Braes o' Lochaber
Inverlair Falls
Stob a' Ghrianain
Druim Fada
Gleann Suileag
An t-Suileag
Beinn an t-Sneachda
148
Kinlocheil
Corribeg
Fassfern
Achdalieu
A830
Loch Eil
Treasures of the Earth
Corpach
Banavie
The Jacobite
Caol
Neptune's Staircase
Camaghael
Torlundy
Tor Castle
Lochaber Rural Complex
Leanachan Forest
Creig Aoil
Nevis Range Gondola
Fersit
Beinn Chlianaig
2343
South Garvan
Duisky
A861
Blaich
B8006
Lochyside
Victoria Bridge
1645 Inverlochy
Achaphubuil
Camusnagaul
Trislaig
Inverlochy
Claggan
Bridge of Nevis
West Highland
Fired Art
FORT WILLIAM
Ach' an Todhair
Stob Coire a' Chearcaill
2528
Stronchreggan
Lochan Meall an t-Suidhe
BEN NEVIS
4406
AONACH BEAG
4048
Killiechonate Forest
Stob Choire Claurigh
3858
Stob Coire Easain
3545
3658
Chno Dearg
3433
Loch Treig
Lairig Leacach
Rocking Stone
Nevis Forest
Doire Donn
Druimarbin
Blarmachfoldach
Glen Nevis Waterslide
Uamh Shomhairle
Water of Nevis
Loch Na Lap
Beinn na Lap
Conaglen
Inverscaddle Bay
River Kiachnish
Achriabhach
Achriabhach Falls
Glen Nevis Lower Falls
Sgurr a' Mhaim
3601
Steall Falls
MAMORE FOREST
Abhainn Rath
Creaguaineach Lodge
Loch Ossian
Binnein Mòr
3700
Loch Eilde Beag
Loch Eilde Mòr
Loch na Sgeallaig
Mullach nan Coirean
Corrychurrachan
2395
Sgurr na h-Eanchainne
Beinn na Gucaig
2022
Lochan Lùnn Dà-Bhrà
Allt na Lairige Mòire
Glenrigh Forest
2971
Leum Uilleim
Ardgour
Clovullin
Corran
Corran Narrows
Glenrigh Forest
Inchree
Inchrigh Falls
Bunree
Onich
Mam na Gualainn
2611
Grey Mare's Tail
Atlas Brewery
Kinlochmore
Ice Factor
Kinlochleven
Ciaran Water
Sallachan Point
North Ballachulish
B863
River Leven
Garbh Bheinn
2844
Blackwater Reservoir
Loch Leven
Bridge of Coe
Glencoe
Pap of Glencoe
2430
3173
3118
Aonach Eagach
2120
Meall nan Ruadhag
142
A' CHRUACH
South Ballachulish
A828
Ballachulish
Monument
Clachaig
Clachaig Falls
Coe
Altnafeadh
2811
Beinn a' Chrùlaiste
Black Corries
Kentallen
Beinn a' Bheithir
Meall Mòr
Signal Rock
The Three Sisters
Glencoe Gorge
Ossian's Cave
Kingshouse
Duror
Achindarroch
Glen Duror
Glendurор Forest
Gleann an Fhiodh
3766
Bidean nam Bian
Buachaille Etive Beag
River Coupall
Buachaille Etive Mòr
Royal Forest
White Corries
Scottish Skiing & Mountaineering
Lochan Gaineamhach
Lochan Coire na Mèinne
RANNOCH MOOR
2883
Fraochaidh
Creran Forest
Sgor na h-Ulaidh
3258
Beinn Maol Chaluim
2774
Dalness
Glen Etive
A82
Salachan Glen
Glen Creran
Beinn Fhionnlaidh
3145
3602
Clach Leathad
Aonach Mòr
Loch Ba'
Elleric
Glen Iola
Fasnacloich
Invercreran
Inverchamnan
Stob Dubh
2897
Allt Coire a' Chaolain
River Bà
Lochan na h-Achlaise
BLACK MOUNT
Water of Tulla
Loch Baile Mhic Chailein
Glen Ure
3059
Beinn Sgulaird
Beinn Churalain
1792
Gualachulain
3565
Stob Ghabhar
Achallader
Achallader Castle
3540
Beinn a' Chreachain
Creagan
2807
2752
Beinn Trilleachan
3425
Stob Coir an Albannaich
Allt Dochard
3404
Beinn Achaladair
South Creagan
Creach Bheinn
2656
Allt Easach
3541
Ben Starav
Black Mount
Loch Tulla
Victoria Bri.
Loch Dochard
Beinn an Dòthaidh
3267
3125
Beinn Mhanach
Abhainn Dalach
Allt Hallater
3141
Beinn nan Aighenan
2215
Beinn Suidhe
Tolaghan
Bridge of Orchy
Dail
Glenkinglass Lodge
3524
Beinn Dorain
Dearg Abhainn
Loch Etive
Allt Chonoghlais
2327
Beinn nan Lus
2283
Meall Garbh
2087
Beinn Inverveigh
B8074
River Esragan
Beinn Mheadhonach
2344
Inveresragan
Ardchattan
Inverliver
Glen Kinglass
Glen Liver
Beinn Mhic-Mhonaidh
2602
Glen Orchy
Beinn Udlaidh
2759
Beinn Bhreac-liath
2633
2948
Beinn Odhar
Ben Challum
3354
B845
Craig
Glennoe
Bonawe
Glen Noe
3242
Beinn Eunaich
Glen Strae
River Strae
ARGYLL & BUTE
Beinn Donachain
2127
A82
Loch Lochy
Airds Bay
Bonawe Iron Furnace
Inverawe Smokery
3695
BEN CRUACHAN
Allt Mhoille
Glen Orchy
River Lochy
Lochan na Bi
Clifton
Tyndrum
Taynuilt
Ichrachan
Airdeny
Bridge of Awe
River Awe
Cruachan Reservoir
Beinn a' Bhuiridh
2941
Falls of Cruachan
B8077
Kilchurn
Stronmilchan
Edendonich
River Orchy
134
Achallalnich
Beinn na Sròine
A85
Cononish
Strath Fillan
Barguillean's Angus
Glen Nant
Pass of Brander
Cruachan Power Station
Lochawe
Kinchrackine
St. Conan's Kirk
Dalmally
Duncan Ban MacIntyre Monument
Eas a Ghaill
River
3708
Ben Lui
3204
2132
Fiarach

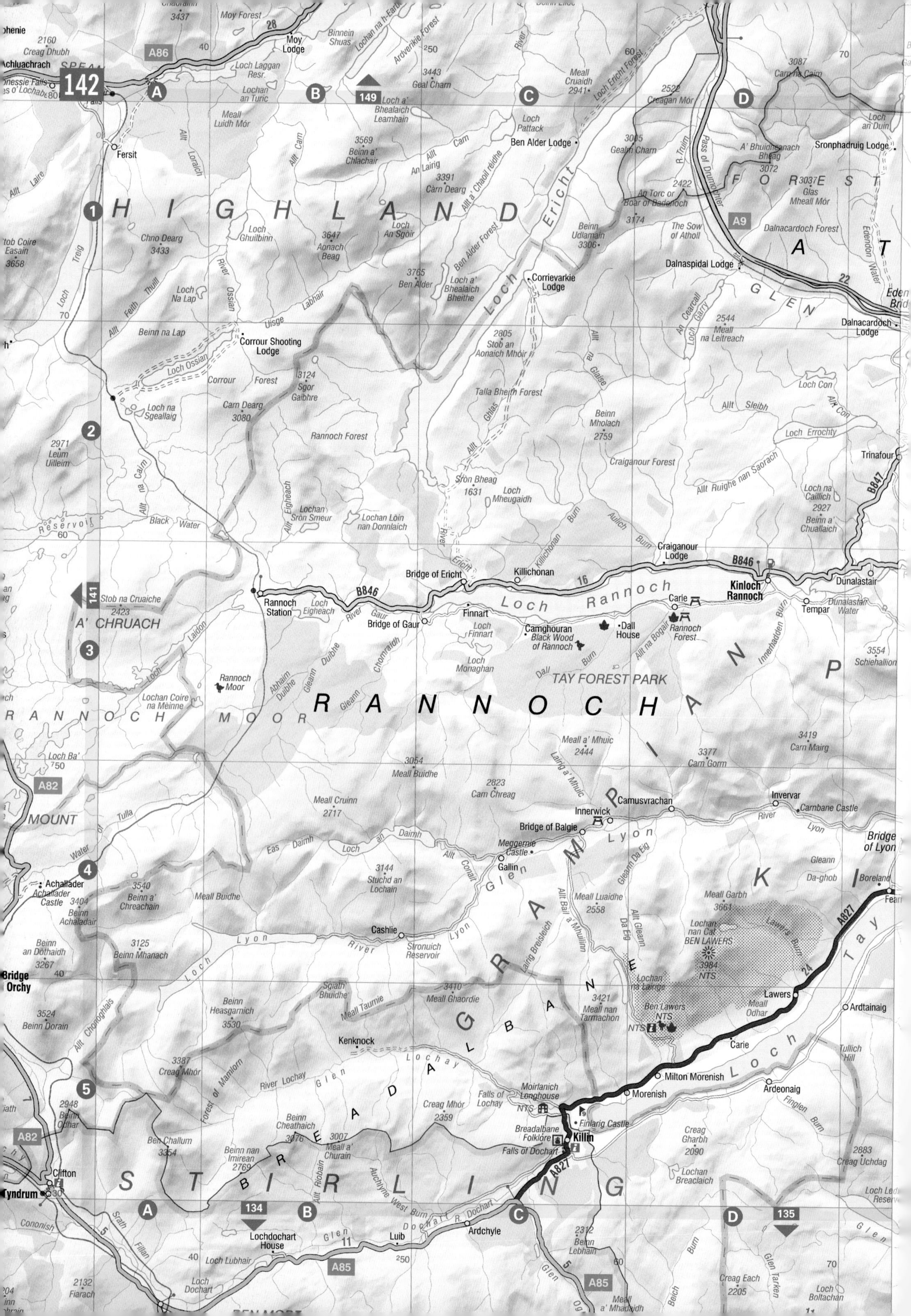
142
149
141
134
135
HIGHLAND
RANNOCH MOOR
RANNOCHAN
GRAMPIAN
BREADALBANE
STIRLING
Moy Forest
Moy Lodge
Loch Laggan Resr.
Lochan an Turic
Meall Luidh Mór
Fersit
Loch a' Bhealaich Leamhain
Geal Charn 3443
Ardverikie Forest
Loch Ericht Forest
Meall Cruaidh 2941
Creagan Mór 2522
Carn na Caim 3087
Loch an Duin
Sronphadruig Lodge
Ben Alder Lodge
Loch Pattack
Beinn a' Chlachair 3569
Carn Dearg 3391
Geal Charn 3005
A' Bhuidheanach Bheag 3072
Glas Mheall Mór 3037
Pass of Drumochter
An Torc or Boar of Badenoch 2422
Chno Dearg 3433
Loch Ghuilbinn
Aonach Beag 3647
Loch An Sgoir
Beinn Udlamain 3306
The Sow of Atholl
Dalnacardoch Forest
Dalnaspidal Lodge
Ben Alder 3765
Ben Alder Forest
Loch a' Bhealaich Bheithe
Corrievarkie Lodge
Loch Na Lap
Beinn na Lap
Corrour Shooting Lodge
Loch Ossian
Corrour Forest
Sgor Gaibhre 3124
Stob an Aonaich Mhóir 2805
Meall na Leitreach 2544
Dalnacardoch Lodge
Loch na Sgeallaig
Carn Dearg 3080
Talla Bheith Forest
Loch Con
Beinn Mholach 2759
Loch Errochty
Leum Uilleim 2971
Rannoch Forest
Craiganour Forest
Trinafour
Sròn Bheag 1631
Loch Mheugaidh
Lochan Sròn Smeur
Lochan Lóin nan Donnlaich
Loch na Caillich 2927
Beinn a' Chuallaich
Black Water
Reservoir
Craiganour Lodge
Bridge of Ericht
Killichonan
Kinloch Rannoch
Dunalastair
Stob na Cruaiche 2423
A' CHRUACH
Rannoch Station
Loch Rannoch
Carie
Tempar
Dunalastair Water
Finnart
Bridge of Gaur
Loch Finnart
Camghouran
Black Wood of Rannoch
Dall House
Rannoch Forest
Loch Monaghan
Schiehallion 3554
Rannoch Moor
TAY FOREST PARK
Lochan Coire na Mèinne
Meall a' Mhuic 2444
Carn Mairg 3419
Carn Gorm 3377
Loch Ba'
Meall Buidhe 3054
Carn Chreag 2823
Meall Cruinn 2717
Camusvrachan
Innerwick
Invervar
Carnbane Castle
Bridge of Balgie
Bridge of Lyon
MOUNT
Meggernie Castle
Gallin
Glen Lyon
Stuchd an Lochain 3144
Achallader
Achallader Castle
Beinn a' Chreachain 3540
Beinn Achaladair 3404
Meall Buidhe
Meall Luaidhe 2558
Meall Garbh 3661
Boreland
Lochan nan Cat
BEN LAWERS 3984 NTS
Cashlie
Stronuich Reservoir
Beinn an Dòthaidh 3267
Beinn Mhanach 3125
Bridge of Orchy
Loch Lyon
Sgiath Bhuidhe
Meall Ghaordie 3410
Lochan na Lairige
Beinn Dorain 3524
Beinn Heasgarnich 3530
Meall nan Tarmachan 3421
Ben Lawers NTS
Lawers
Meall Odhar
Ardtainaig
Kenknock
Carie
Creag Mhór 3387
Forest of Mamlorn
River Lochay
Glen Lochay
Milton Morenish
Morenish
Loch Tay
Tullich Hill
Ardeonaig
Beinn Odhar 2948
Moirlanich Longhouse NTS
Falls of Lochay
Creag Mhór 2359
Finlarig Castle
Beinn Cheathaich 3076
Meall a' Churain 3007
Breadalbane Folklore
Killin
Falls of Dochart
Creag Gharbh 2090
Finglen Burn
Ben Challum 3354
Beinn nan Imirean 2769
Creag Uchdag 2883
Clifton
Tyndrum
Lochan Breaclaich
Loch Lednock Reservoir
Cononish
Strath Fillan
Lochdochart House
Luib
Ardchyle
Glen Dochart
Beinn Leabhain 2312
Loch Lubhair
Loch Dochart
Fiarach 2132
Creag Each 2205
Loch Boltachan
Meall a' Mhadaidh
A86
A82
A9
A85
A827
B846
B847

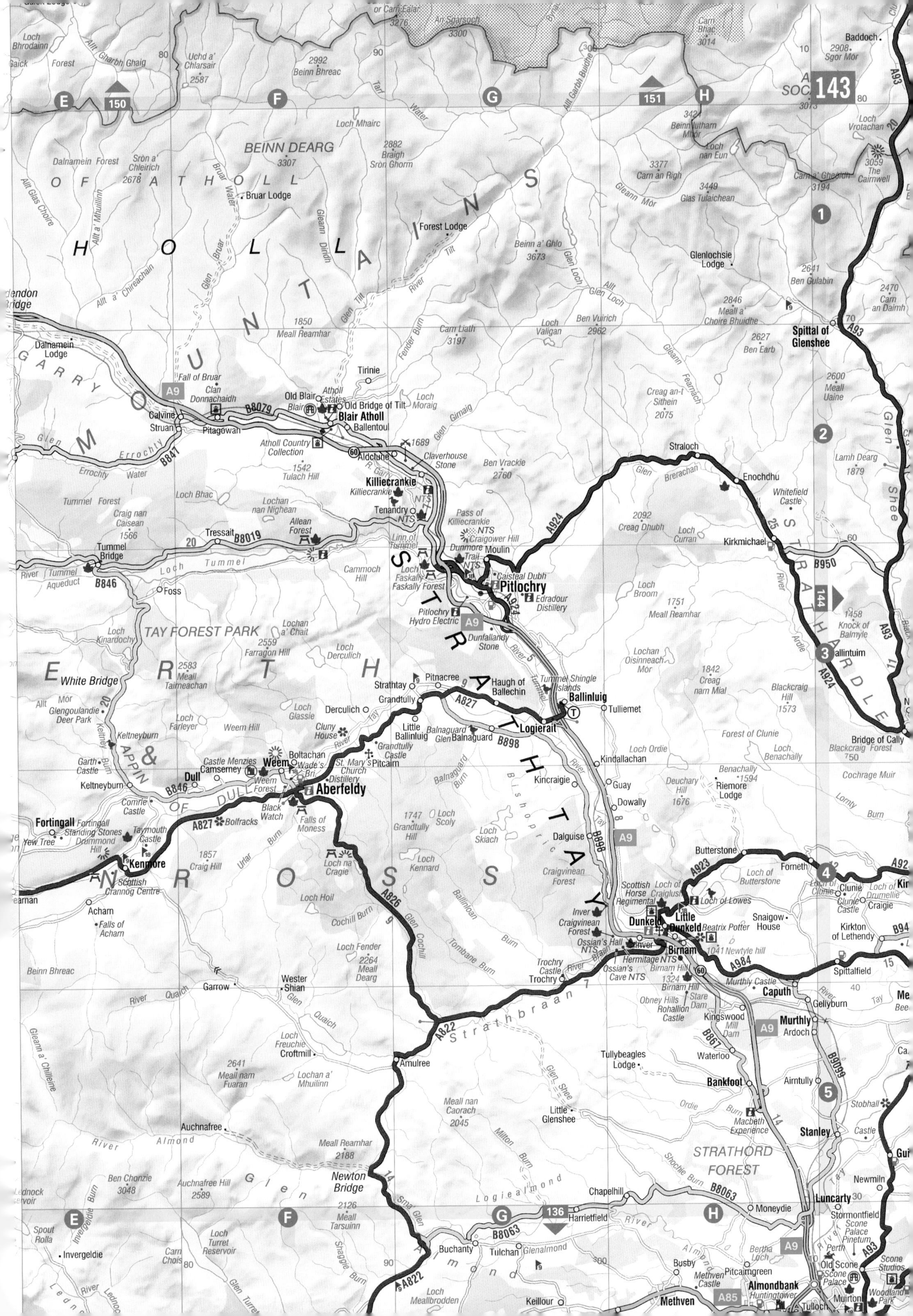
143
144
150
151
136
E
F
G
H
1
2
3
4
5
Loch Bhrodainn
Gaick Forest
Allt Gharbh Ghaig
Uchd a' Chlarsair
2587
2992
Beinn Bhreac
or Carn Ealar
3276
An Sgarsoch
3300
Carn Bhac
3014
Baddoch
2908
Sgor Mor
Tarf Water
Loch Mhairc
Allt Garbh Buidhe
3424
Beinn Iutharn Mhor
Loch nan Eun
Loch Vrotachan
3059
The Cairnwell
Carn a' Gheoidh
3194
BEINN DEARG
3307
2882
Braigh Sròn Ghorm
3377
Carn an Righ
3449
Glas Tulaichean
Gleann Mor
Dalnamein Forest
Sròn a' Chleirich
2678
FOREST OF ATHOLL
Allt Glas Choire
Allt a' Mhuilinn
Bruar Water
Bruar Lodge
Forest Lodge
Beinn a' Ghlo
3673
Glen Loch
Glenlochsie Lodge
2641
Ben Gulabin
2470
Carn an Daimh
THE GRAMPIAN MOUNTAINS
River Tilt
Glen Tilt
Allt a' Chireachain
Glen Bruar
Gleann Diridh
Allt Glen Loch
2846
Meall a' Choire Bhuidhe
Spittal of Glenshee
A93
Dalnamein Lodge
1850
Meall Reamhar
Fender Burn
Carn Liath
3197
Loch Valigan
Ben Vuirich
2962
2627
Ben Earb
Gleann Fearnach
GARRY
Fall of Bruar
Clan Donnachaidh
A9
Tirinie
Old Blair
Atholl Estates
Old Bridge of Tilt
Blair Atholl
Ballentoul
Loch Moraig
Glen Girnaig
Creag an-t Sithein
2075
2600
Meall Uaine
Calvine
Struan
Pitagowan
B8079
Glen Errochty
Errochty Water
B847
Atholl Country Collection
Aldclune
1689
Claverhouse Stone
Ben Vrackie
2760
Straloch
Glen Brerachan
Enochdhu
Lamh Dearg
1879
Glen Shee
1542
Tulach Hill
Killiecrankie
NTS
Loch Bhac
Lochan nan Nighean
Tummel Forest
Craig nan Caisean
1566
Tenandry
Pass of Killiecrankie
Craigower Hill
Allean Forest
Tressait
B8019
A924
2092
Creag Dhubh
Loch Curran
Whitefield Castle
Kirkmichael
B950
STRATHARDLE
Tummel Bridge
Loch Tummel
Linn of Tummel
Dunmore Trail
Moulin
Caisteal Dubh
Pitlochry
Edradour Distillery
River Tummel Aqueduct
B846
Foss
Cammoch Hill
Loch Faskally
Faskally Forest
Loch Broom
1751
Meall Reamhar
1458
Knock of Balmyle
Pitlochry Hydro Electric
TAY FOREST PARK
Lochan a' Chait
Loch Kinardochy
2559
Farragon Hill
Loch Derculich
Dunfallandy Stone
River Tummel
Lochan Oisinneach Mòr
Ballintuim
PERTH
White Bridge
2583
Meall Tairneachan
Strathtay
Pitnacree
Haugh of Ballechin
Tummel Shingle Islands
Ballinluig
Tulliemet
1842
Creag nam Mial
Blackcraig Hill
1573
STRATH TAY
Allt Mòr
Glengoulandie Deer Park
Loch Glassie
Derculich
Grandtully
A827
Logierait
Little Ballinluig
Balnaguard Glen
Balnaguard
B898
Loch Farleyer
Weem Hill
Cluny House
Forest of Clunie
Bridge of Cally
Blackcraig Forest
Keltneyburn
Keltney Burn
Grandtully Castle
St. Mary's Church
Pitcairn
Boltachan
Wade's Bri.
Distillery
Loch Ordie
Kindallachan
Loch Benachally
Benachally
1594
Cochrage Muir
Garth Castle
APPIN
Castle Menzies
Camserney
Weem
Dull
Weem Forest
Aberfeldy
Balnaguard Burn
Kincraigie
Bishopric
Guay
Deuchary Hill
1676
Riemore Lodge
Lornty Burn
Keltneyburn
Comrie Castle
OF DULL
Black Watch
Falls of Moness
1747
Grandtully Hill
Loch Scoly
Dowally
Fortingall
Fortingall Standing Stones
Yew Tree
Taymouth Castle
Drummond Hill
A827
Bolfracks
Urlar Burn
Loch Skiach
Dalguise
B898
Kenmore
1857
Craig Hill
Loch na Craigie
Loch Kennard
Craigvinean Forest
Butterstone
A923
Loch of Butterstone
Forneth
Loch of Clunie
Clunie
Loch of Drumellie
Clunie Castle
Craigie
Scottish Crannog Centre
ROSS
Kenmore
Acharn
Falls of Acharn
Loch Hoil
Cochill Burn
A826
Glen Cochill
Ballinloan Burn
Inver
Craigvinean Forest
Scottish Horse Regimental
Loch of Craiglush
Loch of Lowes
Dunkeld
Little Dunkeld
Beatrix Potter
Snaigow House
Kirkton of Lethendy
Beinn Bhreac
Loch Fender
2264
Meall Dearg
Tombane Burn
Ossian's Hall NTS
Hermitage NTS
Birnam
Birnam Hill
1041 Newtyle hill
A984
Spittalfield
Trochry Castle
Trochry
River Braan
Ossian's Cave NTS
1324
Birnam Hill
Murthly Castle
Caputh
Gellyburn
Garrow
Wester Shian
Glen Quaich
River Quaich
Strathbraan
A822
Obney Hills
Rohallion Castle
Stare Dam
Kingswood
Mill Dam
Murthly
Ardoch
River Tay
Gleann a' Chilleine
Loch Freuchie
Croftmill
Tullybeagles Lodge
Glen Shee
B867
Waterloo
B9099
Amulree
2641
Meall nam Fuaran
Lochan a' Mhuilinn
Meall nan Caorach
2045
Bankfoot
Airntully
Little Glenshee
Ordie Burn
Macbeth Experience
Stobhall
Stanley
Castle
Auchnafree
River Almond
Milton Burn
STRATHORD FOREST
Shochie Burn
Meall Reamhar
2188
Ben Chonzie
3048
Auchnafree Hill
2589
Glen Almond
Newton Bridge
Logiealmond
Chapelhill
B8063
Newmiln
Luncarty
Invergeldie Burn
2126
Meall Tarsuinn
Sma' Glen
Harrietfield
River Almond
Moneydie
Stormontfield
Scone Palace Pinetum
Spout Rolla
Invergeldie
Loch Turret Reservoir
Carn Chois
Shaggie Burn
Buchanty
Tulchan
Glenalmond
B8063
Bertha Loch
Perth
Old Scone
Scone Palace
Scone Studios
A93
River Lednock
A822
Loch Meallbrodden
Keillour
Busby
Methven Castle
Pitcairngreen
Almondbank
Huntingtower
Methven
A85
Tulloch
Muirton
Woodland Park

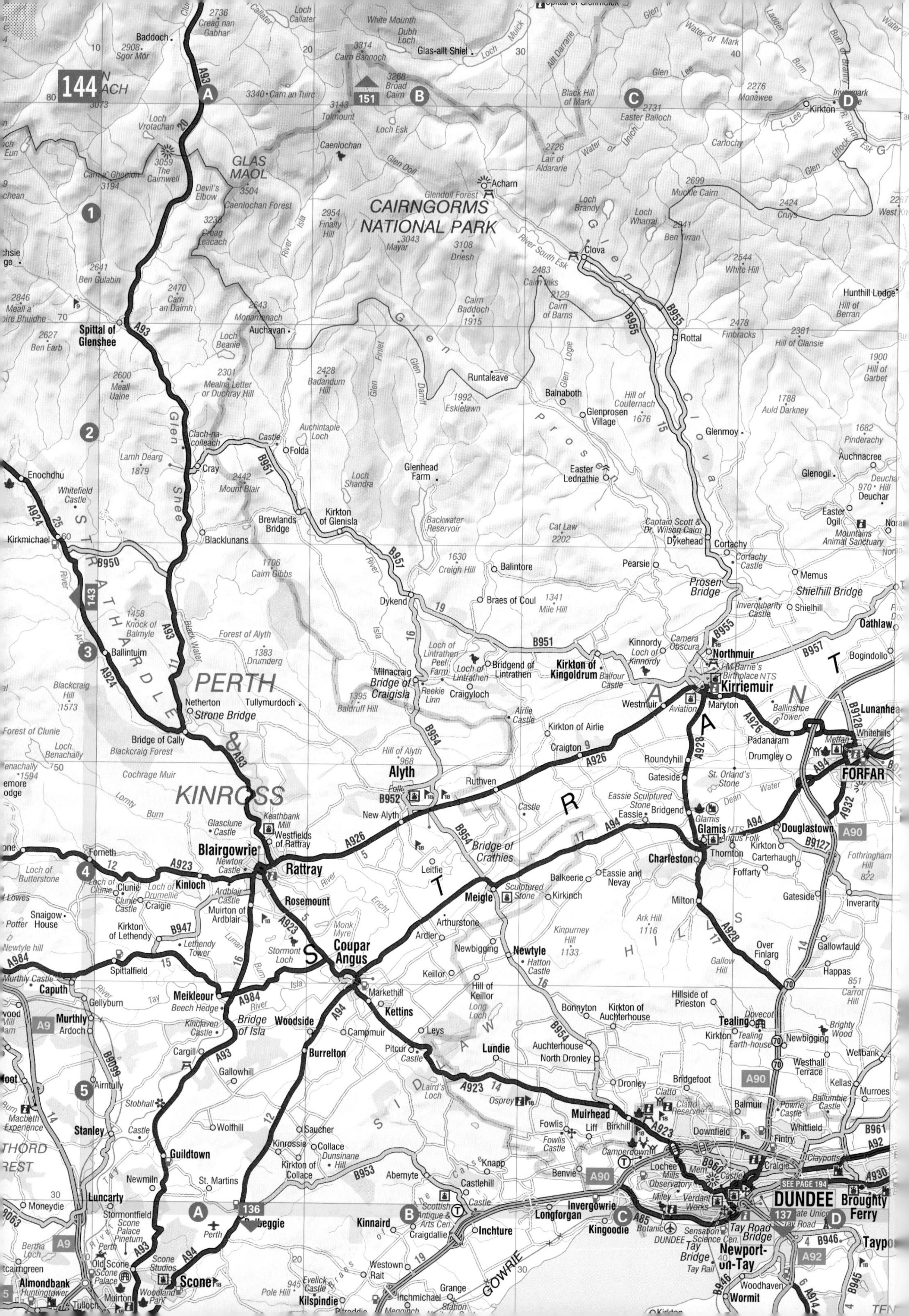

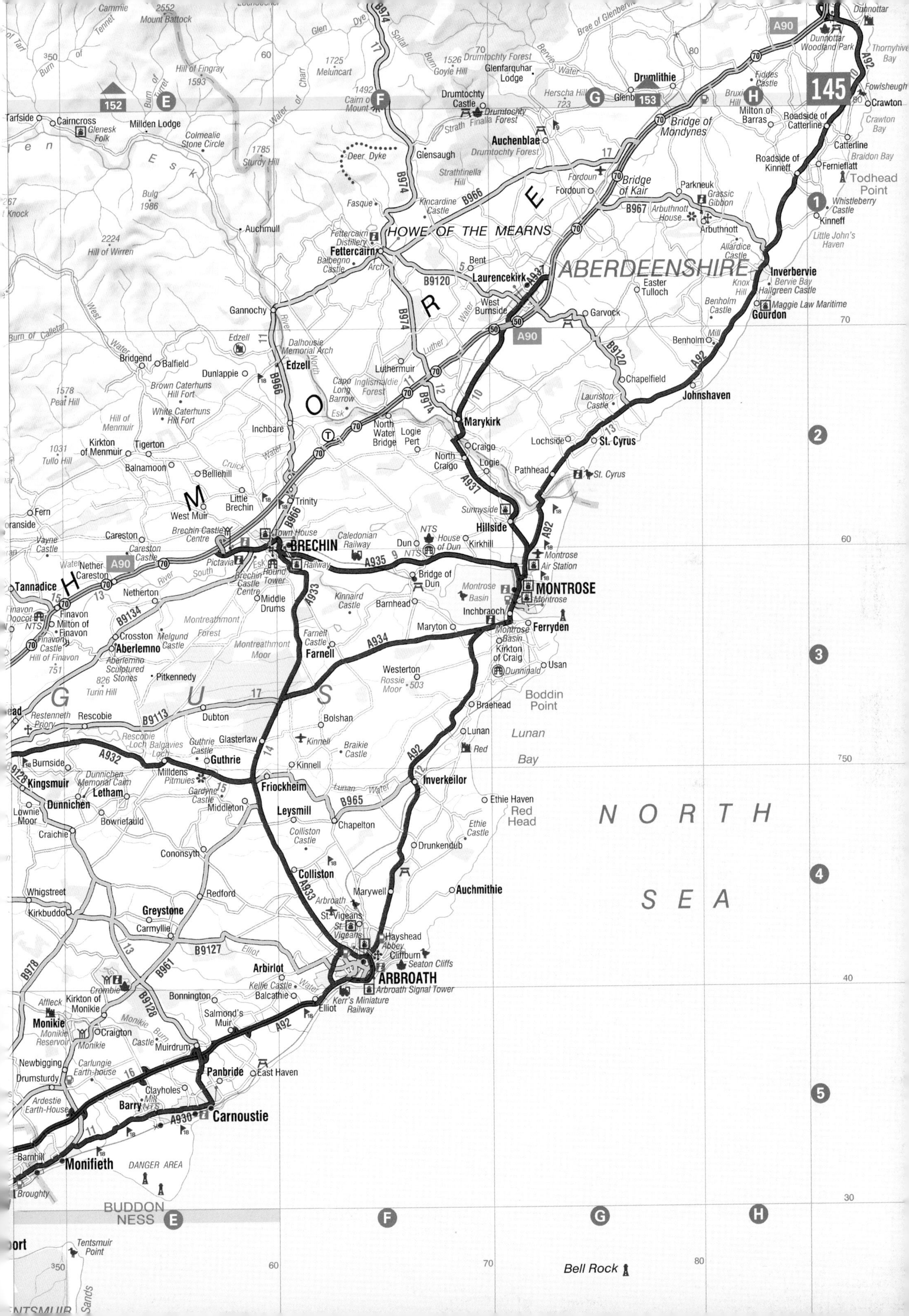

145
Cammie
2552 Mount Battock
Dunnottar
A90
Dunnottar Woodland Park
Thornyhive Bay
Hill of Fingray 1593
1725 Meluncart
1526 Drumtochty Forest
Glenfarquhar Lodge
Drumlithie
Fiddes Castle
A92
Fowlsheugh
Crawton
152
E
1492 Cairn o' Mount
F
Drumtochty Castle
Herscha Hill 723
G
Glenb
153
H
Bruxie Hill
Milton of Barras
Roadside of Catterline
Crawton Bay
Tarfside
Cairncross
Glenesk Folk
Millden Lodge
Colmealie Stone Circle
1785 Sturdy Hill
Deer Dyke
Glensaugh
Drumtochty Forest
Auchenblae
Bridge of Mondynes
Catterline
Braidon Bay
Roadside of Kinneff
Fernieflatt
Todhead Point
Strathfinella Hill
Fordoun
Bridge of Kair
Parkneuk
Grassic Gibbon
1
Whistleberry Castle
Kinneff
Little John's Haven
Bulg 1986
Fasque
Kincardine Castle
B966
B967
Arbuthnott House
Arbuthnott
Auchmull
Fettercairn Distillery
HOWE OF THE MEARNS
Allardice Castle
2224 Hill of Wirren
Fettercairn
Balbegno Castle
Arch
Bent
Laurencekirk
A937
ABERDEENSHIRE
Inverbervie
Bervie Bay
Hallgreen Castle
Easter Tulloch
Knox Hill
Benholm Castle
Maggie Law Maritime
Gourdon
B9120
Gannochy
West Burnside
Garvock
70
A90
Edzell
Dalhousie Memorial Arch
Benholm
Mill
B9120
Bridgend
Balfield
Dunlappie
Edzell
Luthermuir
Chapelfield
1578 Peat Hill
Brown Caterhuns Hill Fort
White Caterhuns Hill Fort
Cairn o' Mount Long Barrow
Inglismaldie Forest
B974
Lauriston Castle
Johnshaven
Hill of Menmuir
Inchbare
North Water Bridge
Logie Pert
Marykirk
2
1031 Tullo Hill
Kirkton of Menmuir
Tigerton
Craigo
North Craigo
Lochside
St. Cyrus
Balnamoon
Belliehill
Logie
Pathhead
St. Cyrus
Little Brechin
Trinity
Fern
West Muir
Sunnyside
Hillside
Careston
Brechin Castle Centre
Town House
BRECHIN
Caledonian Railway
NTS House of Dun
Dun
Kirkhill
60
Vayne Castle
Careston Castle
Nether Careston
Pictavia
Round Tower
Railway
A935
Montrose Air Station
Tannadice
Netherton
Brechin Castle Centre
Bridge of Dun
Montrose Basin
MONTROSE
Montrose
Finavon Doocot
Milton of Finavon
Middle Drums
Kinnaird Castle
Barnhead
Inchbraoch
B9134
Montreathmont Forest
Maryton
Ferryden
Finavon Castle
Crosston
Melgund Castle
Aberlemno
Farnell Castle
A934
Montrose Basin
Hill of Finavon 751
Aberlemno Sculptured Stones
Montreathmont Moor
Farnell
Kirkton of Craig
3
Dunninald
Usan
826 Turin Hill
Pitkennedy
Westerton
Rossie Moor 503
Boddin Point
Braehead
Restenneth Priory
Rescobie
B9113
Dubton
Bolshan
Lunan
Rescobie Loch
Balgavies Loch
Guthrie Castle
Glasterlaw
Kinnell
Braikie Castle
Red Castle
Lunan Bay
750
Burnside
A932
Guthrie
Kinnell
Kingsmuir
Dunnichen Memorial Cairn
Milldens
Pitmuies
Friockheim
Inverkeilor
Dunnichen
Letham
Gardyne Castle
Middleton
B965
Lunan Water
Ethie Haven
Red Head
NORTH
Lownie Moor
Bowriefauld
Leysmill
Chapelton
Ethie Castle
Craichie
Colliston Castle
Drunkendub
Cononsyth
Colliston
4
Whigstreet
Maryweli
Auchmithie
SEA
Kirkbuddo
Redford
A933
Arbroath
Greystone
St. Vigeans
Carmyllie
Hayshead Abbey
B9127
Cliffburn
Seaton Cliffs
B978
B961
Arbirlot
ARBROATH
Kellie Castle
Arbroath Signal Tower
40
Crombie
Affleck
Kirkton of Monikie
B9128
Bonnington
Balcathie
Kerr's Miniature Railway
Monikie
Craigton
Salmond's Muir
Elliot
Monikie Reservoir
Castle
A92
Muirdrum
Newbigging
Carlungie Earth-house
Panbride
East Haven
Drumsturdy
Clayholes
5
Ardestie Earth-House
Mill
Barry
A930
Carnoustie
Barnhill
Monifieth
DANGER AREA
Broughty
BUDDON NESS
E
F
G
H
30
Tentsmuir Point
350
60
70
Bell Rock
80
Sands

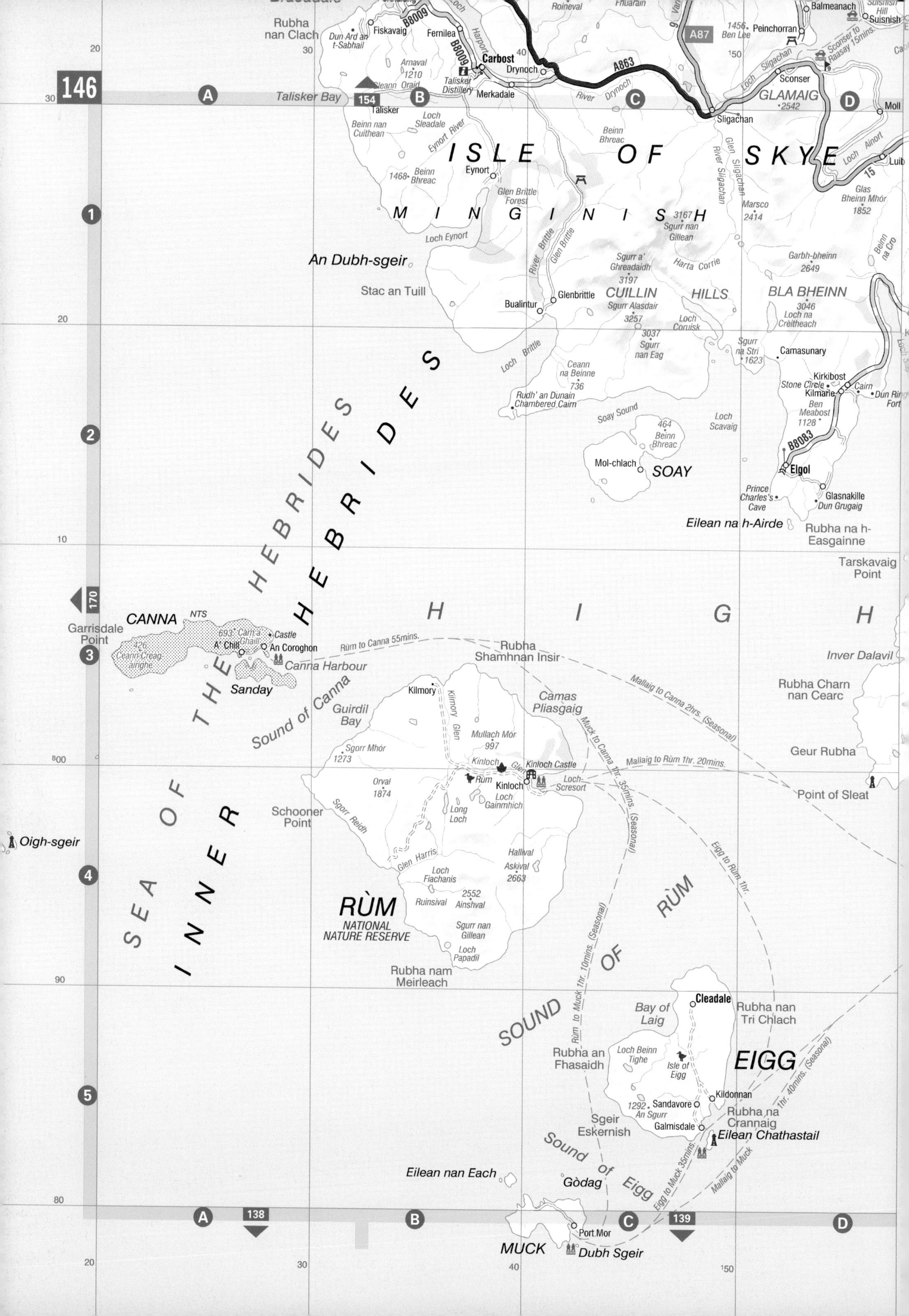

ISLE OF SKYE
MINGINISH
CUILLIN HILLS
BLA BHEINN
GLAMAIG
SOAY
Carbost
Drynoch
Merkadale
Talisker
Talisker Bay
Talisker Distillery
Fiskavaig
Fernilea
Sligachan
Sconser
Peinchorran
Balmeanach
Suisnish
Moll
Luib
Eynort
Glenbrittle
Bualintur
Camasunary
Kirkibost
Kilmarie
Elgol
Glasnakille
Dun Grugaig
Mol-chlach
Loch Eynort
Loch Brittle
Loch Scavaig
Loch Coruisk
Soay Sound
Rubha nan Clach
An Dubh-sgeir
Stac an Tuill
Rudh' an Dunain Chambered Cairn
Prince Charles's Cave
Eilean na h-Airde
Rubha na h-Easgainne
Tarskavaig Point
SEA OF THE HEBRIDES
INNER HEBRIDES
HIGHLAND
CANNA
NTS
Garrisdale Point
A' Chill
An Coroghon
Castle
Canna Harbour
Sanday
Sound of Canna
Rùm to Canna 55mins.
Rubha Shamhnan Insir
Mallaig to Canna 2hrs. (Seasonal)
Mallaig to Rùm 1hr. 20mins.
Muck to Canna 1hr. 35mins. (Seasonal)
Rùm to Muck 1hr. 10mins. (Seasonal)
Eigg to Rùm 1hr.
Eigg to Muck 35mins.
Mallaig to Muck
1hr. 40mins. (Seasonal)
Camas Pliasgaig
Kilmory
Guirdil Bay
Kinloch
Kinloch Castle
Loch Scresort
Schooner Point
Oigh-sgeir
RÙM
NATIONAL NATURE RESERVE
Rubha nam Meirleach
Inver Dalavil
Rubha Charn nan Cearc
Geur Rubha
Point of Sleat
SOUND OF RÙM
Cleadale
Bay of Laig
Rubha nan Tri Chlach
Rubha an Fhasaidh
EIGG
Kildonnan
Sandavore
Galmisdale
Rubha na Crannaig
Eilean Chathastail
Sgeir Eskernish
Sound of Eigg
Eilean nan Each
Gòdag
Port Mor
MUCK
Dubh Sgeir
A87
A863
B8009
B8083
138
139
154
170

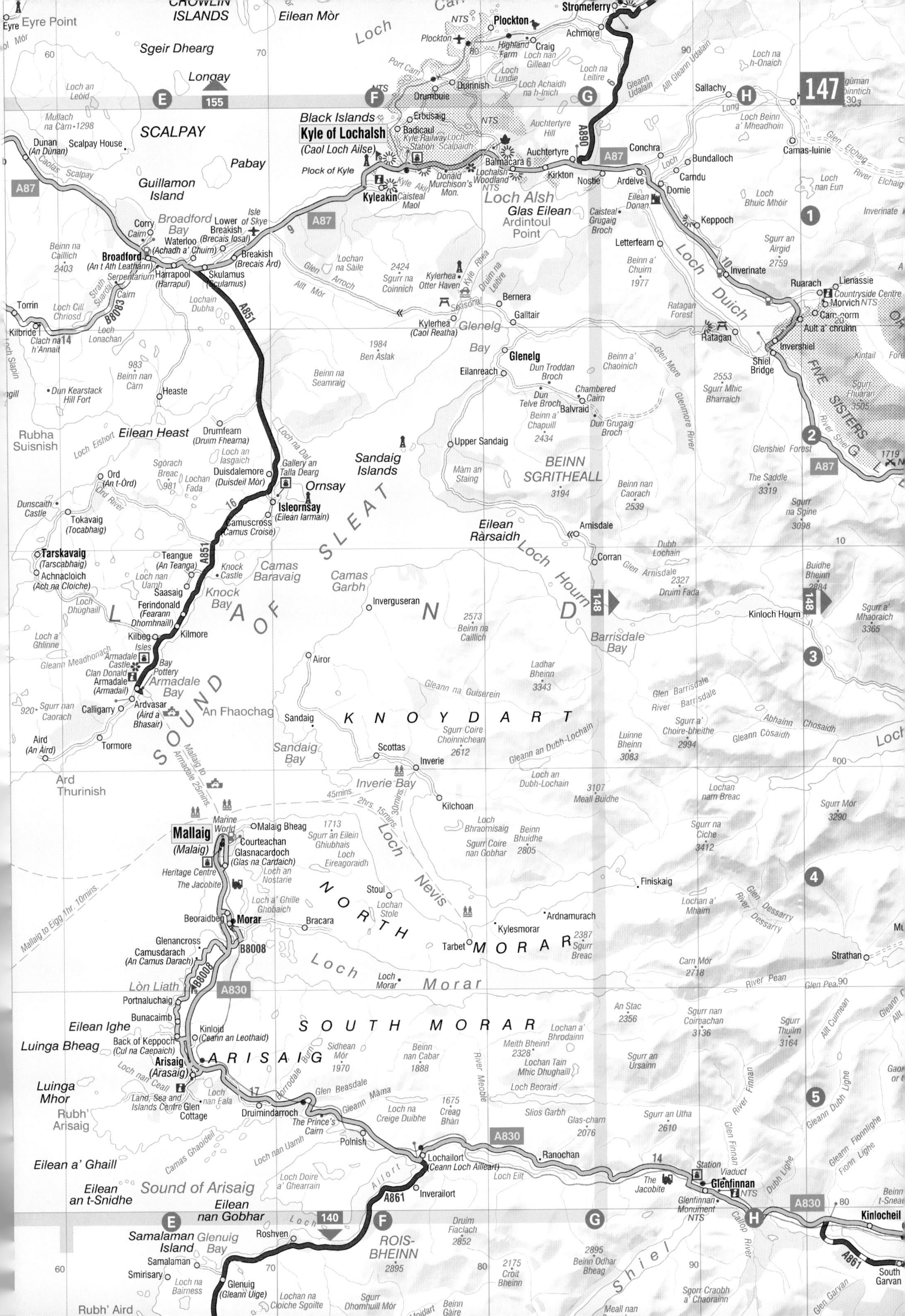

147
CROWLIN ISLANDS
Eyre Point
Eilean Mòr
Sgeir Dhearg
Longay
155
Loch
Stromeferry
Plockton
Achmore
Craig
Highland Farm
Loch nan Gillean
Port Cam
Duirinish
Drumbuie
Loch Lundie
Loch Achaidh na h-Inich
Loch na Leitire
Gleann Udalain
Allt Gleann Udalain
Loch na h-Onaich
Sallachy
SCALPAY
Mullach na Càrn 1298
Loch an Leòid
Black Islands
Erbusaig
Badicaul
Kyle Railway Station
Loch Scalpaidh
Kyle of Lochalsh
(Caol Loch Ailse)
Auchtertyre Hill
Auchtertyre
Balmacara
Conchra
A890
A87
Loch Beinn a' Mheadhoin
Camas-luinie
Glen Elchaig
Dunan (An Dùnan)
Scalpay House
Caolas Scalpay
Pabay
Plock of Kyle
Kyleakin
Kyle Akin
Caisteal Maol
Donald Murchison's Mon.
Lochalsh Woodland
Kirkton
Nostie
Ardelve
Bundalloch
Carndu
Dornie
Eilean Donan
Loch nan Eun
Loch Bhuic Mhòir
Inverinate
Guillamon Island
Broadford Bay
Corry
Cairn
Lower Breakish
Isle of Skye
Waterloo (Brecais Iosal)
Breakish (Brecais Àrd)
Loch Alsh
Glas Eilean
Ardintoul Point
Caisteal Grugaig Broch
Letterfearn
Keppoch
Broadford (An t Ath Leathann)
Beinn na Caillich 2403
Harrapool (Harrapul)
Skulamus (Sculamus)
Serpentarium
Strath Suardal
Lochan na Sàile
Glen Arroch
Allt Mòr
2424 Sgurr na Coinnich
Kylerhea Otter Haven
Kyle Rhea
Druim na Leitire
Beinn a' Chuirn 1977
Loch Duich
Sgurr an Airgid 2759
Ruarach
Lienassie
Countryside Centre
Morvich
Torrin
Loch Cill Chriosd
Lochain Dubha
A851
B8083
Kilbride
Clach na h'Annait
Loch Lonachan
Bernera
Galltair
Kylerhea (Caol Reatha)
Glenelg Bay
Ratagan Forest
Ratagan
Ault a' chruinn
Invershiel
Shiel Bridge
Kintail
FIVE SISTERS
1984 Ben Aslak
983 Beinn nan Càrn
Glenelg
Eilanreach
Dun Troddan Broch
Beinn a' Chaoinich
Glen More
Beinn na Seamraig
Dun Kearstack Hill Fort
Heaste
Dun Telve Broch
Balvraid
Chambered Cairn
Dun Grugaig Broch
Beinn a' Chapuill 2434
2553 Sgurr Mhic Bharraich
Sgurr Fhuaran 3505
Glenmore River
Rubha Suisnish
Eilean Heast
Loch Eishort
Drumfearn (Druim Fhearna)
Loch an Iasgaich
Loch na Dal
Sandaig Islands
Upper Sandaig
Glenshiel Forest
River Shiel
Ord (An t-Òrd)
Sgòrach Breac 981
Lochan Fada
Duisdalemore (Duisdeil Mòr)
Gallery an Talla Dearg
Ornsay
Màm an Staing
BEINN SGRITHEALL 3194
Beinn nan Caorach 2539
The Saddle 3319
Dunscaith Castle
Ord River
Tokavaig (Tocabhaig)
Isleornsay (Eilean Iarmain)
Camuscross (Camus Croise)
Eilean Ràrsaidh
Arnisdale
Sgurr na Sgine 3098
Tarskavaig (Tarscabhaig)
Achnacloich (Ach na Cloiche)
Teangue (An Teanga)
Loch nan Uamh
Knock Castle
Camas Baravaig
Camas Garbh
Corran
Loch Hourn
Dubh Lochain
Glen Arnisdale
2327 Druim Fada
Buidhe Bheinn 2884
Saasaig
Knock Bay
Loch Dhùghaill
Ferindonald (Fearann Dhomhnaill)
SLEAT
LAND OF
Inverguseran
148
Kinloch Hourn
Sgurr a' Mhaoraich 3365
Loch a' Ghlinne
Kilbeg
Kilmore
Isles
2573 Beinn na Caillich
Barrisdale Bay
Gleann Meadhonach
Armadale Castle
Clan Donald
Armadale (Armadail)
Bay Pottery
Armadale Bay
Airor
Ladhar Bheinn 3343
Gleann na Guiserein
920 Sgurr nan Caorach
Calligarry
Ardvasar (Àird a Bhasair)
An Fhaochag
Sandaig
KNOYDART
Sgurr Coire Choinnichean 2612
Glen Barrisdale
River Barrisdale
Sgurr a' Choire-bheithe 2994
Luinne Bheinn 3083
Abhainn Chosaidh
Gleann Cosaidh
Aird (An Àird)
Tormore
SOUND
Sandaig Bay
Scottas
Inverie
Gleann an Dubh-Lochain
Loch an Dubh-Lochain
Ard Thurinish
Mallaig to Armadale 25mins.
Inverie Bay
45mins.
2hrs. 15mins.
30mins.
Kilchoan
3107 Meall Buidhe
Lochan nam Breac
Sgurr Mòr 3290
Mallaig (Malaig)
Marine World
Malaig Bheag
Courteachan
Glasnacardoch (Glas na Cardaich)
Heritage Centre
The Jacobite
1713 Sgurr an Eilein Ghiubhais
Loch Eireagoraidh
Loch an Nostarie
Loch Bhraomisaig
Sgurr Coire nan Gobhar
Beinn Bhuidhe 2805
Sgurr na Ciche 3412
Loch Nevis
Loch a' Ghille Ghobaich
NORTH
Stoul
Lochan Stole
Finiskaig
Lochan a' Mhaim
Glen Dessarry
River Dessarry
Mallaig to Eigg 1hr. 10mins.
Beoraidbeg
Morar
Bracara
Ardnamurach
Kylesmorar
Tarbet
MORAR
2387 Sgurr Breac
Glenancross
Camusdarach (An Camus Darach)
B8008
Loch Morar
Carn Mòr 2718
Strathan
River Pean
Glen Pean
Lòn Liath
A830
Portnaluchaig
Bunacaimb
An Stac 2356
Sgurr nan Coireachan 3136
Sgurr Thuilm 3164
Allt Cuirnean
Eilean Ighe
Kinloid (Ceann an Leothaid)
SOUTH MORAR
Lochan a' Bhrodainn
Luinga Bheag
Back of Keppoch (Cul na Caepaich)
Arisaig (Arasaig)
ARISAIG
Sidhean Mòr 1970
Beinn nan Cabar 1888
Meith Bheinn 2328
River Meoble
Lochan Tain Mhic Dhughaill
Sgurr an Ursainn
Luinga Mhor
Loch nan Ceall
Land, Sea and Islands Centre
Glen Cottage
Loch nan Eala
Borrodale Burn
Glen Beasdale
Loch Beoraid
Rubh' Arisaig
Druimindarroch
The Prince's Cairn
Gleann Màma
Loch na Creige Duibhe
1675 Creag Bhàn
Slios Garbh
Glas-charn 2076
Sgurr an Utha 2610
River Finnan
Gleann Dubh Lighe
Gleann Fionnlighe
Camas Ghaoideil
Polnish
Loch nan Uamh
Eilean a' Ghaill
Lochailort (Ceann Loch Ailleart)
Ranochan
Loch Eilt
Glen Finnan
Station
Viaduct
The Jacobite
Glenfinnan
Dubh Lighe
Fionn Lighe
Eilean an t-Snidhe
Sound of Arisaig
Loch Doire a' Ghearrain
Ailort
A861
Inverailort
Glenfinnan Monument
Beinn t-Sneach
Eilean nan Gobhar
Loch
140
Kinlocheil
Samalaman Island
Glenuig Bay
Roshven
ROIS-BHEINN 2895
Druim Fiaclach 2852
2895 Beinn Odhar Bheag
Callop River
Shiel
Samalaman
Smirisary
2175 Croit Bheinn
Loch na Bairness
Glenuig (Gleann Uige)
Lochan na Cloiche Sgoilte
Sgurr Dhomhuill Mòr
Beinn Gàire
Meall nan
Sgorr Craobh a' Chaorainn
Glen Garvan
South Garvan
Rubh' Aird

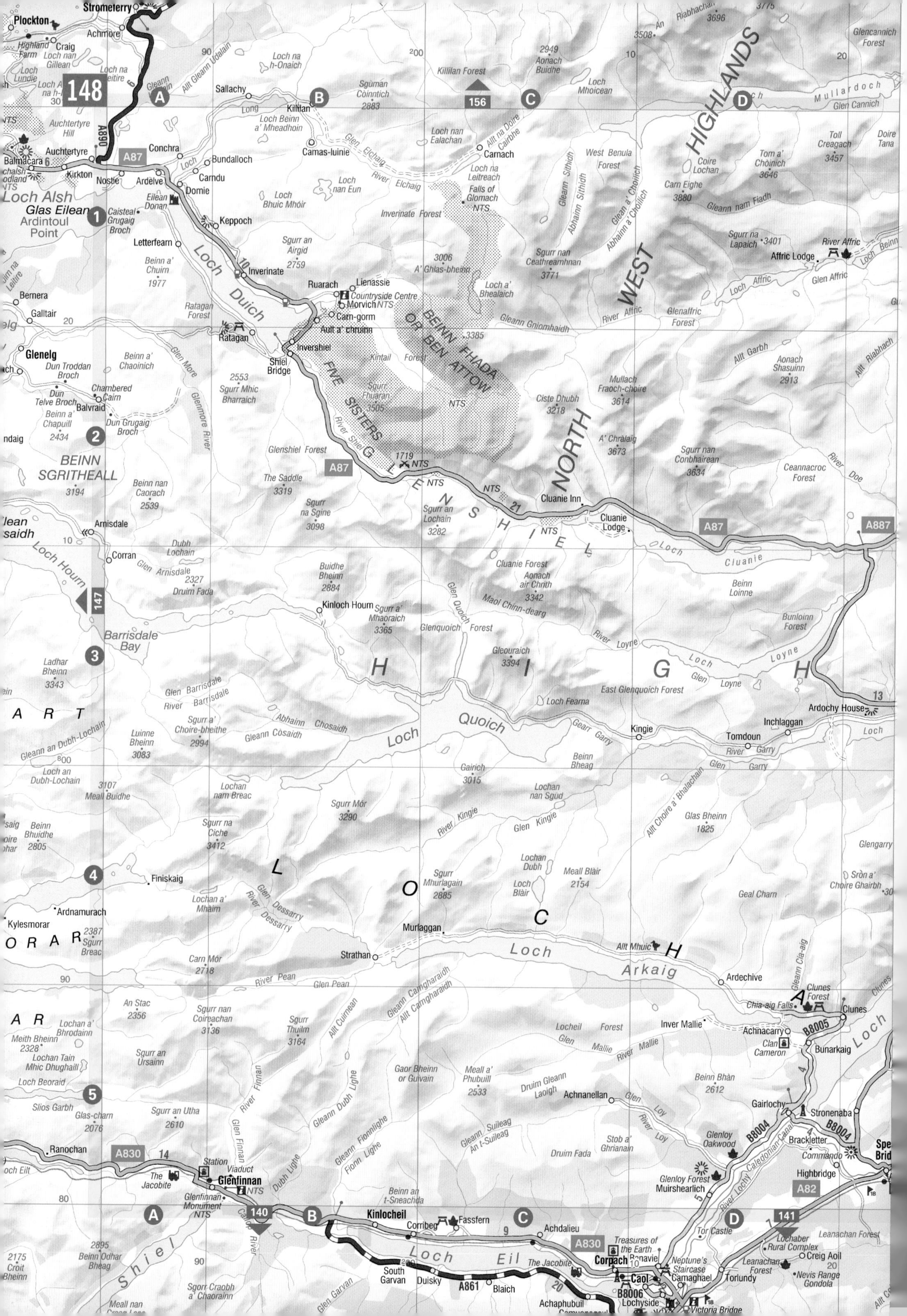
Stromeferry
Plockton
Achmore
148
156
147
140
141
A87
A890
A887
A830
A82
A861
B8004
B8005
B8006
Loch Alsh
Glas Eilean
Ardintoul Point
Kirkton
Nostie
Ardelve
Dornie
Eilean Donan
Conchra
Sallachy
Killilan
Camas-luinie
Carnach
Keppoch
Letterfearn
Inverinate
Loch Duich
Ruarach
Lienassie
Countryside Centre
Morvich
Carn-gorm
Ault a' chruinn
Invershiel
Shiel Bridge
Ratagan
Glenelg
Bernera
Galltair
Balvraid
Dun Grugaig Broch
BEINN SGRITHEALL
FIVE SISTERS
BEINN FHADA OR BEN ATTOW
Kintail Forest
GLEN SHIEL
Cluanie Inn
Cluanie Lodge
Loch Cluanie
NORTH WEST HIGHLANDS
Loch Mullardoch
Glen Cannich
Carn Eighe
Affric Lodge
River Affric
Loch Affric
Glen Affric
Arnisdale
Corran
Loch Hourn
Kinloch Hourn
Barrisdale Bay
Glenquoich Forest
Loch Quoich
Kingie
Tomdoun
Inchlaggan
Ardochy House
River Garry
Glen Garry
Finiskaig
Ardnamurach
Kylesmorar
Murlaggan
Strathan
Loch Arkaig
Ardechive
Clunes
Achnacarry
Bunarkaig
Clan Cameron
Inver Mallie
Achnanellan
Gairlochy
Stronenaba
Brackletter
Commando
Highbridge
Glenloy Forest
Muirshearlich
Ranochan
Glenfinnan
Glenfinnan Monument NTS
The Jacobite
Loch Shiel
Kinlocheil
Corribeg
Fassfern
Achdalieu
Loch Eil
South Garvan
Duisky
Blaich
Corpach
Caol
Banavie
Lochyside
Achaphubuil
Neptune's Staircase
Camaghael
Torlundy
Tor Castle
Victoria Bridge
Leanachan Forest
Lochaber Rural Complex
Creag Aoil
Nevis Range Gondola
LOCH HOURN
LOCHABER

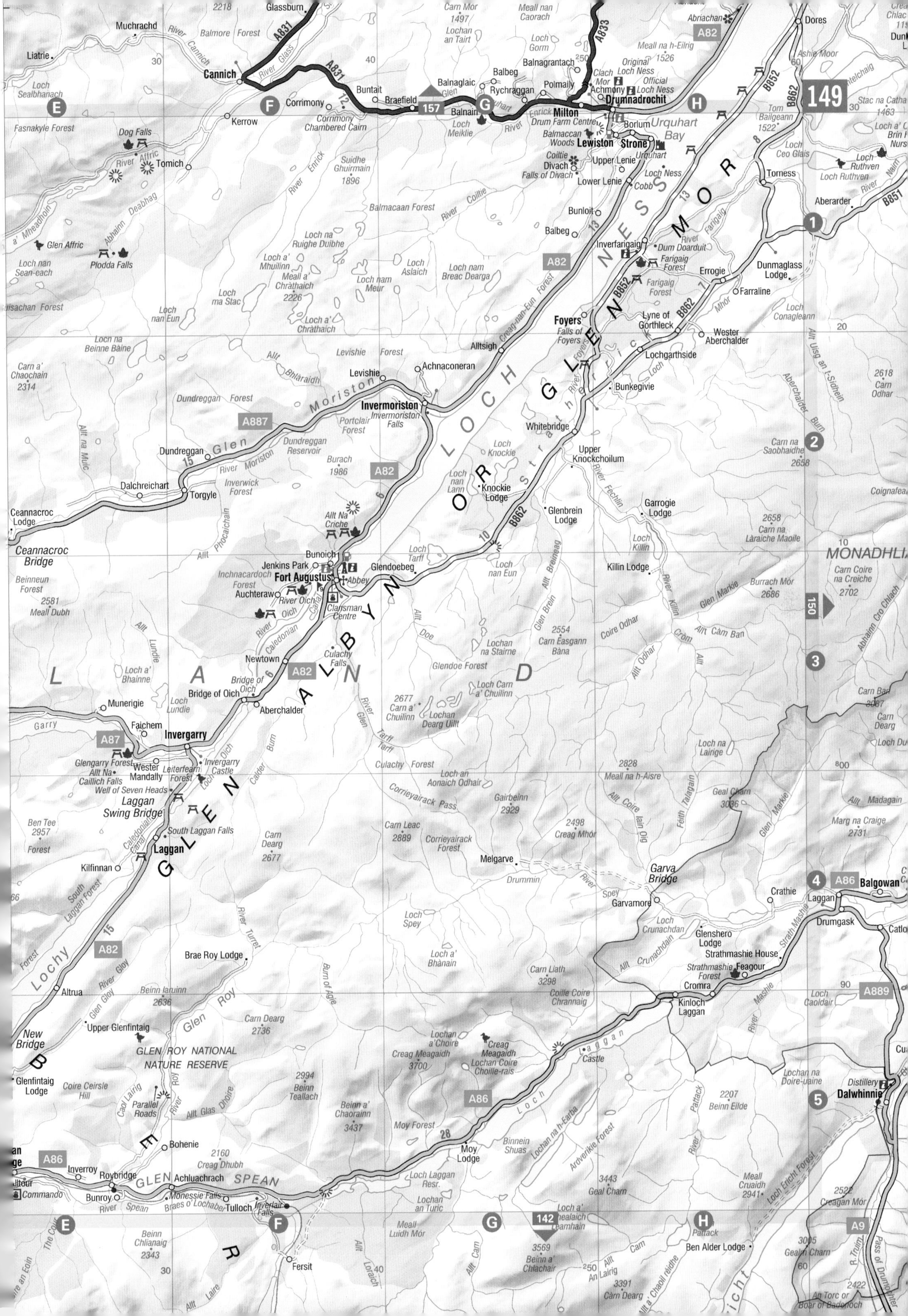
149
150
157
142
Glassburn
Muchrachd
Liatrie
Cannich
Balmore Forest
River Cannich
River Glass
A831
A833
A82
A887
A87
A86
A889
A9
B852
B862
B851
Loch Sealbhanach
Fasnakyle Forest
Dog Falls
Tomich
River Affric
Glen Affric
Plodda Falls
Loch nan Sean-each
Kerrow
Corrimony
Corrimony Chambered Cairn
Buntait
Braefield
Balnaglaic
Balbeg
Rychraggan
Balnain
Loch Meiklie
Polmaily
Milton
Drumnadrochit
Drum Farm Centre
Borlum
Urquhart Bay
Urquhart
Lewiston
Strone
Balmaccan Woods
Coiltie
Divach
Falls of Divach
Upper Lenie
Lower Lenie
Cobb
Bunloit
Balbeg
Abriachan
Dores
Balnagrantach
Clach Mor
Achmony
Original Loch Ness
Official Loch Ness
Meall na h-Eilrig 1526
Carn Mor 1497
Lochan an Tairt
Meall nan Caorach
Loch Gorm
Ashie Moor
Tom Bailgeann 1522
Loch Ceo Glais
Torness
Loch Ruthven
Aberarder
Stac na Catha 1463
Suidhe Ghuirmain 1896
Balmacaan Forest
River Enrick
River Coiltie
Loch na Ruighe Duibhe
Loch a' Mhuilinn
Meall a' Chràthaich 2226
Loch nam Meur
Loch Aslaich
Loch nam Breac Dearga
Loch a' Chràthaich
Loch ma Stac
Loch nan Eun
Inverfarigaig
Dun Dearduil
Farigaig Forest
River Farigaig
Errogie
Dunmaglass Lodge
Farraline
Loch Conagleann
Foyers
Falls of Foyers
Lyne of Gorthleck
Wester Aberchalder
Lochgarthside
Bunkegivie
Alltsigh
Creag-nan-Eun Forest
Achnaconeran
Levishie
Levishie Forest
Allt Bhlàraidh
Carn a' Chaochain 2314
Dundreggan Forest
Glen Moriston
Invermoriston
Invermoriston Falls
Portclair Forest
Dundreggan
Dundreggan Reservoir
River Moriston
Burach 1986
Inverwick Forest
Dalchreichart
Torgyle
Ceannacroc Lodge
Ceannacroc Bridge
Whitebridge
Loch Knockie
Upper Knockchoilum
Loch nan Lann
Knockie Lodge
Glenbrein Lodge
River Fechlin
Garrogie Lodge
Loch Killin
Killin Lodge
2618 Carn Odhar
Carn na Saobhaidhe 2658
Coignafearn
2658 Carn na Làraiche Maoile
MONADHLIATH
Carn Coire na Creiche 2702
Burrach Mòr 2686
Glen Markie
Allt Na Criche
Bunoich
Jenkins Park
Fort Augustus
Abbey
Clansman Centre
Glendoebeg
Loch Tarff
Loch nan Eun
Inchnacardoch Forest
Auchteraw
River Oich
Beinneun Forest
2581 Meall Dubh
Allt Doe
Lochan na Stairne
2554 Carn Easgann Bàna
Coire Odhar
Allt Càm Ban
Culachy Falls
Newtown
Glendoe Forest
Loch Carn a' Chuilinn
2677 Carn a' Chuilinn
Lochan Dearg Uillt
Loch a' Bhainne
Bridge of Oich
Aberchalder
Loch Lundie
Munerigie
Faichem
Invergarry
Garry
Glengarry Forest
Wester Mandally
Allt Na Caillich Falls
Well of Seven Heads
Laggan Swing Bridge
Invergarry Castle
Leiterfearn Forest
Loch Oich
Culachy Forest
Loch an Aonaich Odhair
Corrieyairack Pass
Gairbeinn 2929
Loch na Lairige
2828 Meall na h-Aisre
Geal Charn 3036
Madagain
Marg na Craige 2731
Ben Tee 2957
South Laggan Falls
Laggan
Carn Dearg 2677
Carn Leac 2889
Corrieyairack Forest
2498 Creag Mhòr
Melgarve
Drummin
Garva Bridge
Garvamore
Crathie
Laggan
Balgowan
Drumgask
Kilfinnan
South Laggan Forest
River Turret
Loch Spey
Loch Crunachdan
Glenshero Lodge
Strathmashie House
Strathmashie Forest
Feagour
Brae Roy Lodge
Loch a' Bhànain
Carn Liath 3298
Coille Coire Chrannaig
Cromra
Kinloch Laggan
Loch Caoldair
Altrua
River Gloy
Beinn Iaruinn 2636
Glen Roy
Carn Dearg 2736
Lochan a'Choire
Creag Meagaidh 3700
Creag Meagaidh
Lochan Coire Choille-rais
Laggan Castle
New Bridge
Upper Glenfintaig
GLEN ROY NATIONAL NATURE RESERVE
Glenfintaig Lodge
Coire Ceirsle Hill
Parallel Roads
2994 Beinn Teallach
Beinn a' Chaorainn 3437
Moy Forest
Lochan na Doire-uaine
Distillery
Dalwhinnie
2207 Beinn Eilde
Bohenie
2160 Creag Dhubh
Moy Lodge
Binnein Shuas
Ardverikie Forest
3443 Geal Charn
Meall Cruaidh 2941
Loch Ericht Forest
Inverroy
Roybridge
Achluachrach
GLEN SPEAN
Monessie Falls
Tulloch
Inverlair Falls
Commando
Bunroy
Braes o' Lochaber
Loch Laggan Resr.
Lochan an Turic
Meall Luidh Mòr
Loch a' Bhealaich Leamhain
3569 Beinn a' Chlachair
Pattack
Ben Alder Lodge
2522 Creagan Mòr
3005 Geal Charn
Beinn Chlianaig 2343
Fersit
3391 Carn Dearg
An Torc or Boar of Badenoch
2422
Pass of Drumochter
LOCH NESS
GLEN MOR
GLEN ALBYN
OR
LAND
GLEN
BEN
Strath Errick
Loch Lochy
Lochy Forest
Caledonian Canal

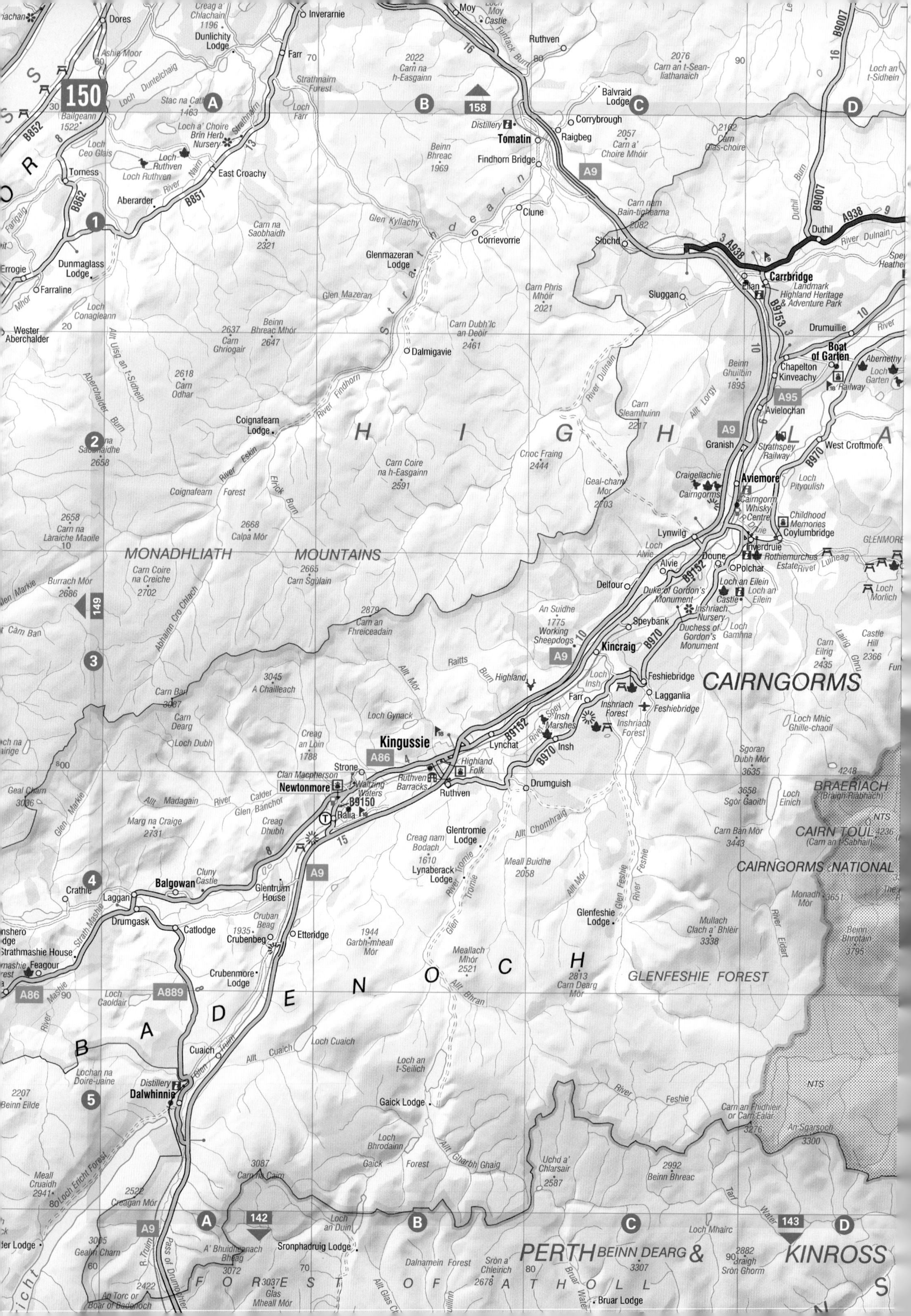
150
158
149
142
143
A
B
C
D
1
2
3
4
5
H I G H L A
MONADHLIATH MOUNTAINS
CAIRNGORMS
BADENOCH
FOREST OF ATHOLL
PERTH & KINROSS
Inverarnie
Dores
Moy
Moy Castle
Ruthven
Dunlichity Lodge
Farr
Strathnairn Forest
Balvraid Lodge
Tomatin
Distillery
Corrybrough
Raigbeg
Findhorn Bridge
Torness
East Croachy
Aberarder
Clune
Corrievorrie
Slochd
Carrbridge
Duthil
Glenmazeran Lodge
Dunmaglass Lodge
Farraline
Wester Aberchalder
Dalmigavie
Sluggan
Landmark Highland Heritage & Adventure Park
Drumuillie
Boat of Garten
Chapelton
Kinveachy
Avielochan
Granish
Aviemore
Coignafearn Lodge
Coignafearn Forest
West Croftmore
Strathspey Railway
Craigellachie
Cairngorm Whisky Centre
Childhood Memories
Coylumbridge
Lynwilg
Inverdruie
Rothiemurchus Estate
Doune
Polchar
Alvie
Delfour
Loch an Eilein Castle
Duke of Gordon's Monument
Inshriach Nursery
Speybank
Kincraig
Feshiebridge
Lagganlia
Kingussie
Lynchat
Highland Folk
Ruthven Barracks
Ruthven
Drumguish
Insh
Insh Marshes
Inshriach Forest
Newtonmore
Clan Macpherson
Waltzing Waters
Strone
Ralia
Glentromie Lodge
Lynaberack Lodge
Balgowan
Cluny Castle
Crathie
Laggan
Glentruim House
Drumgask
Catlodge
Etteridge
Crubenbeg
Crubenmore Lodge
Strathmashie House
Feagour
Glenfeshie Lodge
GLENFESHIE FOREST
BRAERIACH
CAIRN TOUL
CAIRNGORMS NATIONAL
Cuaich
Loch Cuaich
Dalwhinnie
Gaick Lodge
Gaick Forest
Sronphadruig Lodge
Dalnamein Forest
BEINN DEARG
Bruar Lodge
A9
A86
A889
A938
A95
B9007
B852
B862
B851
B9153
B9152
B970
B9150

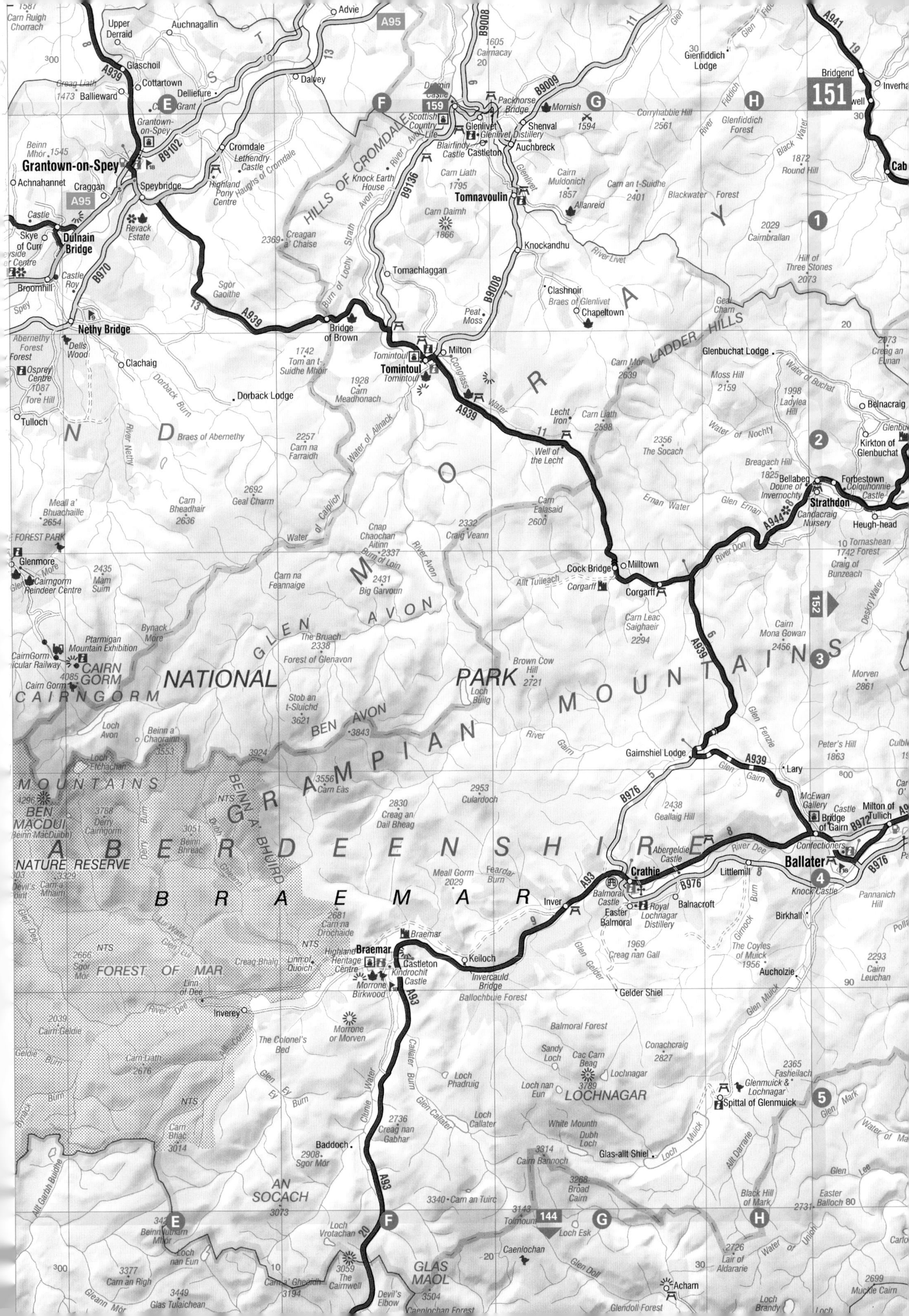

151
159
152
144
Grantown-on-Spey
Nethy Bridge
Dulnain Bridge
Tomintoul
Tomnavoulin
Glenlivet
Cock Bridge
Corgarff
Strathdon
Crathie
Ballater
Braemar
HILLS OF CROMDALE
LADDER HILLS
CAIRNGORM MOUNTAINS
NATIONAL PARK
GRAMPIAN MOUNTAINS
ABERDEENSHIRE
BRAEMAR
GLEN AVON
BEN AVON
BEINN A' BHUIRD
FOREST OF MAR
LOCHNAGAR
AN SOCACH
GLAS MAOL
MORAY
CAIRN GORM
BEN MACDUI
NATURE RESERVE
A939
A95
A93
A944
B9008
B9009
B9136
B9102
B970
B976
B972

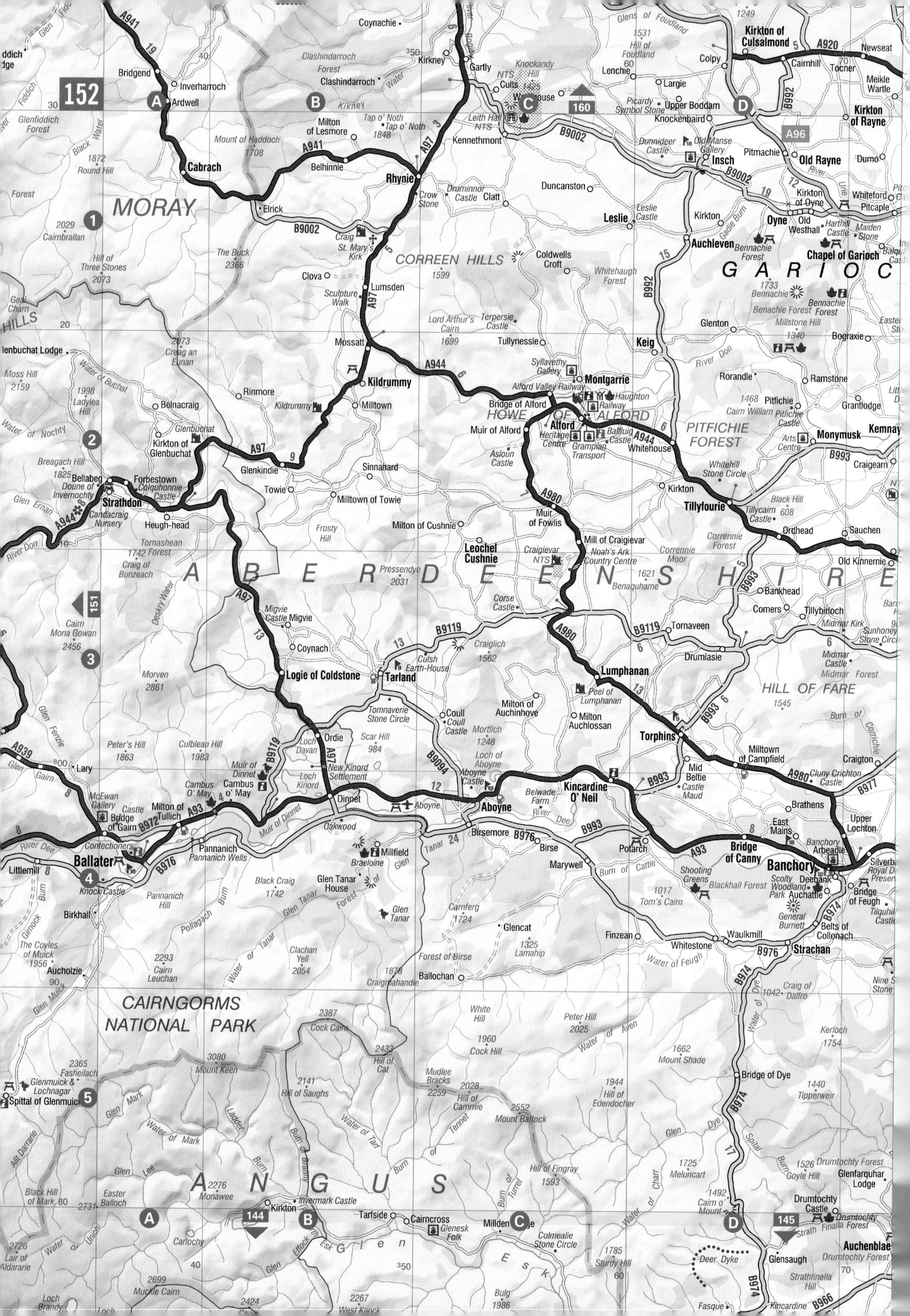
152
160
151
144
145
A
B
C
D
1
2
3
4
5
MORAY
ABERDEENSHIRE
GARIOCH
ANGUS
CAIRNGORMS NATIONAL PARK
CORREEN HILLS
HOWE OF ALFORD
PITFICHIE FOREST
HILL OF FARE
A941
A97
A944
A980
A93
A939
A920
A96
B9002
B992
B993
B9119
B9094
B976
B972
B974
B977
B966
Coynachie
Glens of Foudland
Kirkton of Culsalmond
Newseat
Bridgend
Inverharroch
Ardwell
Clashindarroch Forest
Clashindarroch
Kirkney
Gartly
Knockandy Hill
Cults
Wardhouse
Leith Hall NTS
Kennethmont
Lenchie
Largie
Picardy Symbol Stone
Upper Boddam
Knockenbaird
Colpy
Cairnhill
Tocher
Meikle Wartle
Kirkton of Rayne
Glenfiddich Forest
Milton of Lesmore
Tap o' Noth 1848
Mount of Haddoch 1708
Cabrach
Belhinnie
Rhynie
Crow Stone
Druminnor Castle
Clatt
Dunnideer Castle
Old Manse Gallery
Insch
Pitmachie
Old Rayne
Durno
Duncanston
Leslie
Leslie Castle
Kirkton
Kirkton of Oyne
Oyne
Old Westhall
Harthill Castle
Whiteford
Pitcaple
Maiden Stone
Auchleven
Bennachie Forest
Chapel of Garioch
Round Hill 1872
Elrick
Cairnbrallan 2029
Hill of Three Stones 2073
The Buck 2366
Craig
St. Mary's Kirk
Coldwells Croft
Whitehaugh Forest
Clova
Lumsden
Sculpture Walk
Bennachie 1733
Benachie Forest
Millstone Hill 1340
Glenton
Bograxie
Lord Arthur's Cairn 1699
Terpersie Castle
Tullynessle
Keig
Glenbuchat Lodge
Creag an Eunan 2073
Mossatt
Syllavethy Gallery
Montgarrie
River Don
Rorandle
Ramstone
Moss Hill 2159
Ladylea Hill 1998
Rinmore
Belnacraig
Kildrummy
Milltown
Alford Valley Railway
Haughton
Bridge of Alford
Cairn William 1468
Pitfichie
Pitfichie Castle
Grantlodge
Water of Nochty
Glenbuchat
Kirkton of Glenbuchat
Muir of Alford
Alford
Heritage Centre
Grampian Transport
Balfluig Castle
Whitehouse
Arts Centre
Monymusk
Kemnay
Breagach Hill 1825
Bellabeg
Doune of Invernochty
Forbestown
Colquhonnie Castle
Strathdon
Glenkindie
Asloun Castle
Sinnahard
Towie
Milltown of Towie
Craigearn
Whitehill Stone Circle
Black Hill 608
Tillyfourie
Tillycairn Castle
Candacraig Nursery
Heugh-head
Glen Ernan
Frosty Hill
Milton of Cushnie
Muir of Fowlis
Ordhead
Sauchen
Tornashean Forest 1742
Craig of Bunzeach
Leochel Cushnie
Craigievar NTS
Mill of Craigievar
Noah's Ark Country Centre
Correnie Moor
Correnie Forest
Old Kinnernie
Pressendye 2031
Benaquhame 1621
Bankhead
Comers
Tillybirloch
Midmar Kirk
Sunhoney Stone Circle
Cairn Mona Gowan 2456
Deskry Water
Migvie Castle
Migvie
Corse Castle
Tornaveen
Coynach
Craiglich 1562
Culsh Earth-House
Drumlasie
Midmar Castle
Midmar Forest
Morven 2861
Logie of Coldstone
Tarland
Lumphanan
Peel of Lumphanan
Tomnaverie Stone Circle
Milton of Auchinhove
Milton Auchlossan
Torphins
Glen Fenzie
Coull
Coull Castle
Mortlich 1248
Burn of Corrichie
Peter's Hill 1863
Culblean Hill 1983
Loch Davan
Ordie
Scar Hill 984
Loch of Aboyne
Milltown of Campfield
Craigton
Lary
Muir of Dinnet
Cambus O' May
New Kinord Settlement
Loch Kinord
Aboyne Castle
Mid Beltie
Beltie Castle
Maud
Cluny Crichton Castle
Glen Gairn
McEwan Gallery
Bridge of Gairn
Castle
Milton of Tullich
Dinnet
Aboyne
Kincardine O' Neil
Belwade Farm
Brathens
Upper Lochton
River Dee
Oakwood
Birsemore
Birse
Potarch
East Mains
Bridge of Canny
Banchory
Arbeadie
Silverbank
Ballater
Littlemill
Confectioners
Pannanich
Pannanich Wells
Braeloine
Millfield
Marywell
Burn of Cattie
Shooting Greens
Blackhall Forest
Scolty Woodland Park
Deebank
Auchattie
Bridge of Feugh
Knock Castle
Black Craig 1742
Glen Tanar House
Tom's Cairn 1017
General Burnett
Belts of Collonach
Birkhall
Pannanich Hill
Pollagach Burn
Glen Tanar
Carnferg 1724
Glencat
Finzean
Whitestone
Waulkmill
Strachan
The Coyles of Muick 1956
Cairn Leuchan 2293
Clachan Yell 2054
Lamahip 1325
Forest of Birse
Water of Feugh
Aucholzie
Ballochan
Craigmahandle 1878
Craig of Dalfro 1042
Nine Stone
Glen Muick
White Hill
Peter Hill 2025
Cock Cairn 2387
Cock Hill 1960
Water of Aven
Kerloch 1754
Mount Shade 1662
Fasheilach 2365
Mount Keen 3080
Hill of Cat 2433
Mudlee Bracks 2259
Hill of Cammie 2028
Mount Battock 2552
Hill of Edendocher 1944
Bridge of Dye
Tipperweir 1440
Glenmuick & Lochnagar
Spittal of Glenmuick
Glen Mark
Water of Mark
Hill of Saughs 2141
Water of Tarf
Hill of Fingray 1593
Meluncart 1725
Glen Dye
Goyle Hill 1526
Drumtochty Forest
Glenfarquhar Lodge
Black Hill of Mark 2731
Easter Balloch
Monawee 2276
Glen Lee
Kirkton
Invermark Castle
Tarfside
Cairncross
Glenesk Folk
Millden
Colmealie Stone Circle
Cairn o' Mount 1492
Drumtochty Castle
Strath Finalla Forest
Auchenblae
Carlochy
Lair of Aldararie 2726
Water of Unich
Glen Esk
Sturdy Hill 1785
Deer Dyke
Glensaugh
Strathfinella Hill
Mickle Cairn 2699
Loch Brandy
West Knock 2267
Bulg 1986
Fasque
Kincardine

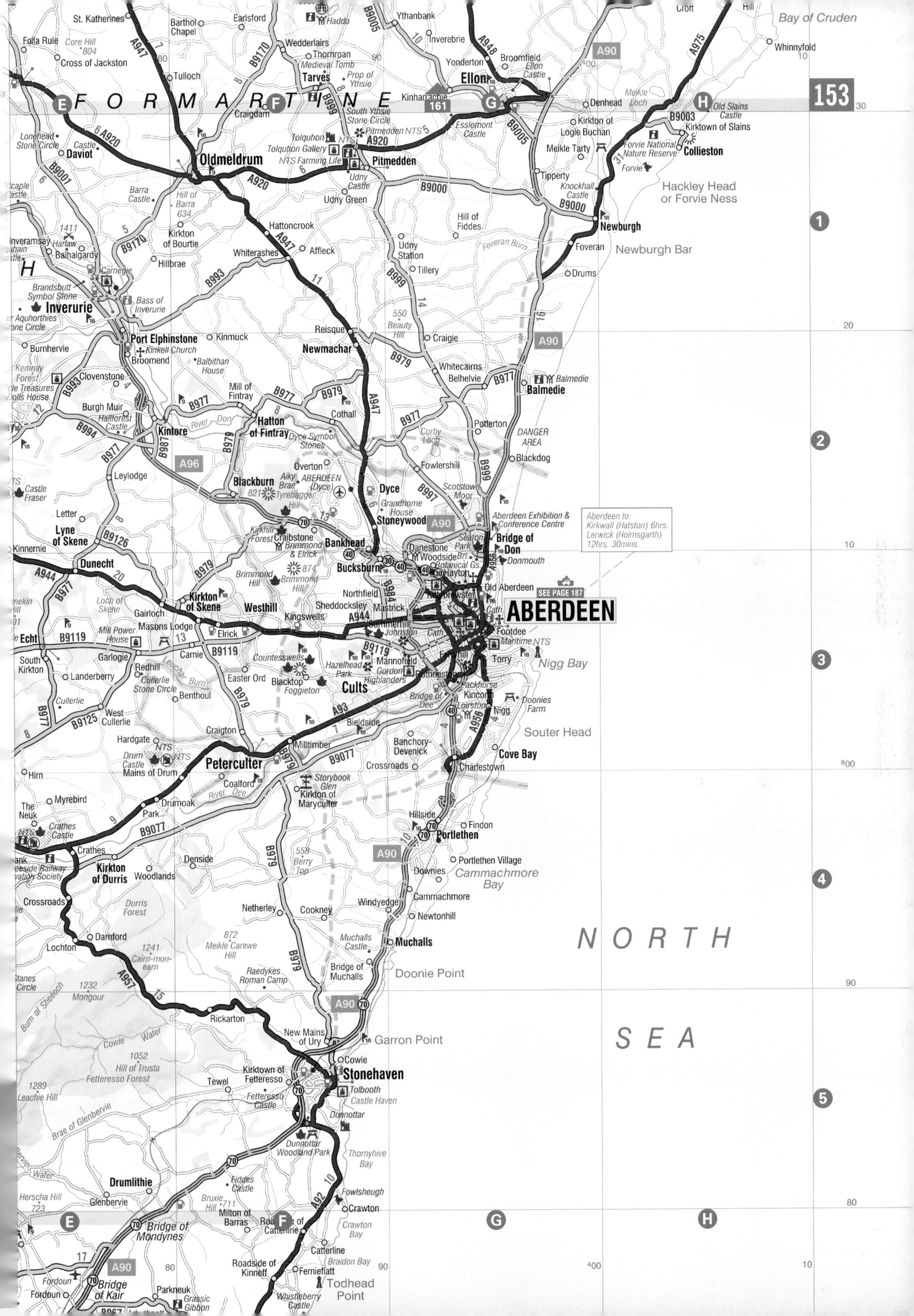

153
Bay of Cruden
Whinnyfold
Ythanbank
Inverebrie
Haddo
St. Katherines
Barthol Chapel
Earlsford
Folla Rule
Core Hill 804
Cross of Jackston
Wedderlairs
Thornroan
Medieval Tomb
Tarves
Prop of Ythsie
Tulloch
Yonderton
Broomfield
Ellon Castle
Ellon
Kinharrachie
FORMARTINE
Craigdam
South Ythsie Stone Circle
Pitmedden NTS
Esslemont Castle
Denhead
Meikle Loch
Old Slains Castle
Kirktown of Slains
Kirkton of Logie Buchan
Forvie National Nature Reserve
Collieston
Forvie
Meikle Tarty
Lonehead Stone Circle
Castle
Daviot
Tolquhon
Tolquhon Gallery
NTS Farming Life
Oldmeldrum
Pitmedden
Udny Castle
Udny Green
Tipperty
Knockhall Castle
Hackley Head or Forvie Ness
Barra Castle
Hill of Barra 634
Kirkton of Bourtie
Hattoncrook
Hill of Fiddes
Newburgh
Inveramsay
Harlaw
Balhalgardy
Hillbrae
Whiterashes
Affleck
Udny Station
Foveran Burn
Foveran
Newburgh Bar
Tillery
Drums
Carnegie
Brandsbutt Symbol Stone
Bass of Inverurie
Inverurie
550 Beauty Hill
Reisque
Port Elphinstone
Kinmuck
Kinkell Church
Broomend
Burnhervie
Newmachar
Craigie
Kemnay Forest
Clovenstone
Balbithan House
Whitecairns
Belhelvie
Balmedie
Mill of Fintray
Cothall
Burgh Muir
Hallforest Castle
Kintore
River Don
Hatton of Fintray
Dyce Symbol Stones
Corby Loch
Potterton
DANGER AREA
Blackdog
Leylodge
Overton
Fowlershill
Blackburn
Aiky Brae
ABERDEEN (Dyce)
Dyce
Scotstown Moor
821 Tyrebagger Hill
Grandhome House
Castle Fraser
Letter
Stoneywood
Aberdeen Exhibition & Conference Centre
Aberdeen to:
Kirkwall (Hatston) 6hrs.
Lerwick (Holmsgarth) 12hrs. 30mins.
Lyne of Skene
Kirkhill Forest
Craibstone
Brimmond & Elrick
Bankhead
Danestone
Woodside
Seaton Park
Bridge of Don
Donmouth
Kinnernie
Dunecht
Bucksburn
Botanical Gs.
Hayton
Brimmond Hill
874 Brimmond Hill
Northfield
Old Aberdeen
SEE PAGE 187
Kirkton of Skene
Loch of Skene
Gairloch
Westhill
Sheddocksley
Mastrick
ABERDEEN
Masons Lodge
Kingswells
Echt
Mill Power House
Elrick
Johnston
Footdee
Maritime NTS
Carnie
South Kirkton
Garlogie
Countesswells
Hazlehead Park
Mannofield
Gordon Highlanders
Torry
Nigg Bay
Redhill
Landerberry
Cullerlie Stone Circle
Easter Ord
Blacktop
Foggieton
Cults
Leuchar Burn
Benthoul
Kincorth
Doonies Farm
Cullerlie
West Cullerlie
Bridge of Dee
Nigg
Bieldside
Souter Head
Craigton
Hardgate
Drum Castle
Mains of Drum
Milltimber
Banchory-Devenick
Cove Bay
Peterculter
Crossroads
Charlestown
Hirn
Coalford
River Dee
Storybook Glen
Kirkton of Maryculter
The Neuk
Myrebird
Drumoak
Park
Crathes Castle
Hillside
Findon
Portlethen
Crathes
Kirkton of Durris
Denside
Woodlands
558 Berry Top
Portlethen Village
Downies
Cammachmore Bay
Cammachmore
Windyedge
Newtonhill
Durris Forest
Netherley
Cookney
Damford
Lochton
872 Meikle Carewe Hill
Muchalls Castle
Muchalls
NORTH SEA
1241 Cairn-mon-earn
Bridge of Muchalls
Doonie Point
Raedykes Roman Camp
1232 Mongour
Burn of Sheeoch
Rickarton
Cowie Water
New Mains of Ury
Garron Point
Cowie
1052 Hill of Trusta
Fetteresso Forest
Kirktown of Fetteresso
Stonehaven
1289 Leachie Hill
Tewel
Tolbooth
Castle Haven
Fetteresso Castle
Dunnottar
Brae of Glenbervie
Dunnottar Woodland Park
Thornyhive Bay
Drumlithie
Fiddes Castle
Fowlsheugh
Hirscha Hill 723
Glenbervie
Bruxie Hill 711
Milton of Barras
Crawton
Crawton Bay
Bridge of Mondynes
Catterline
Braidon Bay
Roadside of Kinneff
Fernieflatt
Todhead Point
Fordoun
Bridge of Kair
Parkneuk
Grassic Gibbon
Whistleberry Castle
A90
A920
A947
A948
A975
A96
A944
A93
A956
A957
A92
B9005
B999
B9170
B9001
B9000
B9003
B993
B977
B979
B994
B987
B9126
B9119
B9125
B9077
B997
B984
1 2 3 4 5
E F G H

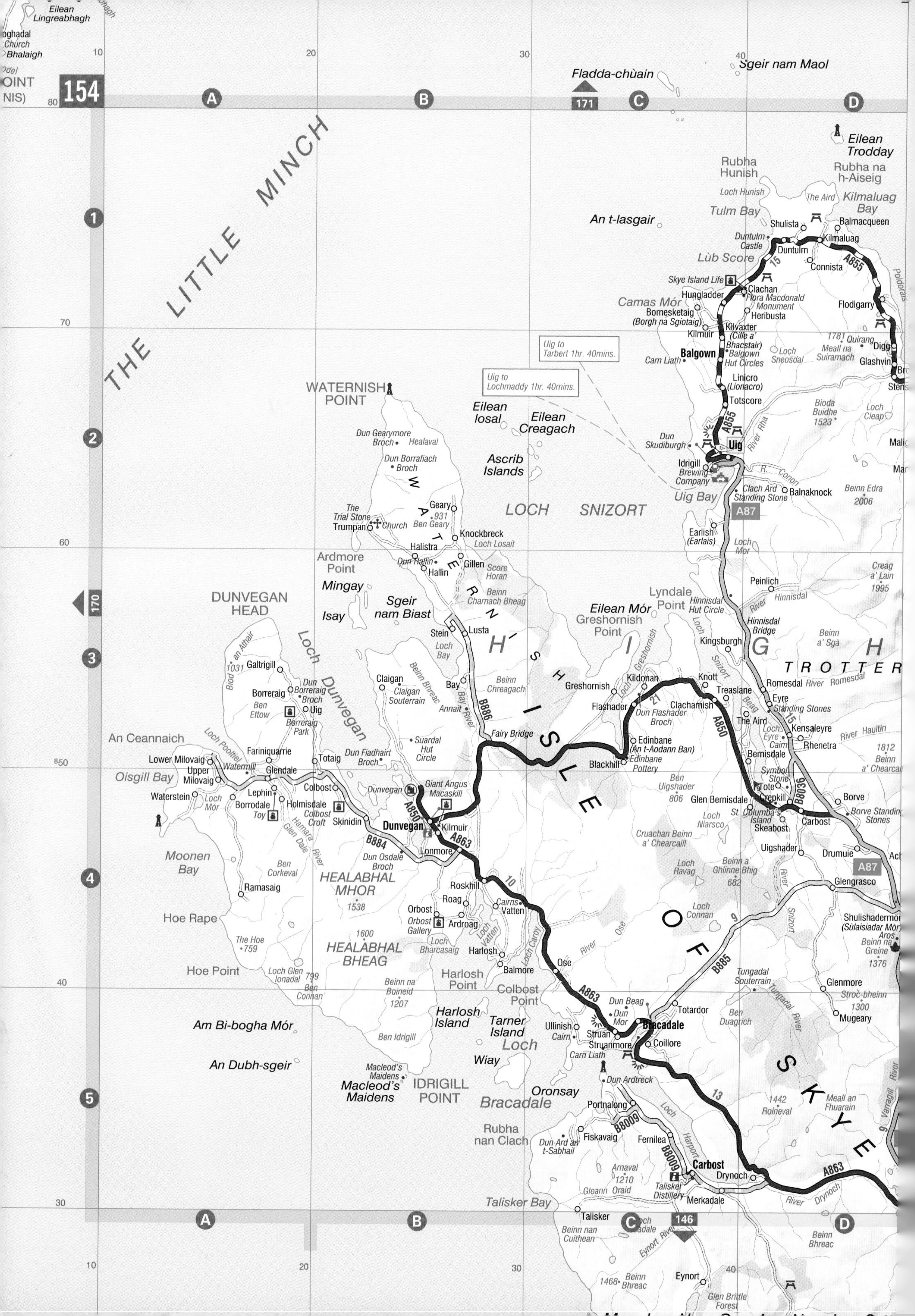

154
Eilean Lingreabhagh
Church
Bhalaigh
10
20
30
40
80
A
B
C
D
Fladda-chùain
171
Sgeir nam Maol
Eilean Trodday
Rubha Hunish
Rubha na h-Aiseig
Loch Hunish
The Aird
Kilmaluag Bay
Tulm Bay
Shulista
Balmacqueen
An t-Iasgair
Duntulm Castle
Duntulm
Kilmaluag
Lùb Score
Connista
A855
Skye Island Life
Clachan
Flora Macdonald Monument
Hungladder
Camas Mór
Bornesketaig (Borgh na Sgiotaig)
Heribusta
Flodigarry
Kilmuir
Kilvaxter (Cille a' Bhacstair)
Balgown Hut Circles
Balgown
Carn Liath
Loch Sneosdal
1781 Quirang
Meall na Suiramach
Digg
Glashvin
Uig to Tarbert 1hr. 40mins.
Uig to Lochmaddy 1hr. 40mins.
THE LITTLE MINCH
1
2
3
4
5
70
60
50
40
30
WATERNISH POINT
Linicro (Lionacro)
Totscore
Bioda Buidhe 1523
Loch Cleap
Eilean Iosal
Eilean Creagach
Dun Gearymore Broch
Healaval
Dun Borrafiach Broch
Ascrib Islands
Dun Skudiburgh
Uig
River Rha
Idrigill Brewing Company
R. Conon
Clach Ard Standing Stone
Balnaknock
Beinn Edra 2006
Uig Bay
A87
LOCH SNIZORT
Geary
931 Ben Geary
The Trial Stone
Trumpan
Church
Knockbreck
Loch Losait
Earlish (Earlais)
Loch Mor
Halistra
Dun Hallin
Hallin
Gillen
Score Horan
Ardmore Point
Mingay
Creag a' Lain 1995
Peinlich
DUNVEGAN HEAD
170
Isay
Sgeir nam Biast
Beinn Charnach Bheag
Eilean Mór
Greshornish Point
Lyndale Point
Hinnisdal Hut Circle
Hinnisdal
River Hinnisdal
Hinnisdal Bridge
Stein
Lusta
Loch Bay
Kingsburgh
Beinn a' Sgà
WATERNISH
TROTTERNISH
ISLE OF SKYE
Loch Dunvegan
Loch Greshornish
Loch Snizort
1031
Biod an Athair
Galtrigill
Dun Borreraig Broch
Borreraig
Ben Ettow
Uig
Borreraig Park
Claigan
Claigan Souterrain
Beinn Bhreac
Bay
Bay River
Annait
B886
Beinn Chreagach
Greshornish
Kildonan
Knott
Treaslane
Romesdal
River Romesdal
Flashader
Dun Flashader Broch
Clachamish
Eyre
Standing Stones
The Aird
A850
21
An Ceannaich
Loch Pooltiel
Fariniquarrie
Suardal Hut Circle
Fairy Bridge
Edinbane (An t-Aodann Ban)
Edinbane Pottery
Blackhill
Loch Eyre
Cairn
Kensaleyre
Rhenetra
River Haultin
1812 Beinn a' Chearcall
Lower Milovaig
Upper Milovaig
Watermill
Glendale
Totaig
Dun Fiadhairt Broch
Bernisdale
Oisgill Bay
Waterstein
Loch Mór
Lephin
Borrodale
Holmisdale
Colbost
Toy
Colbost Croft
Skinidin
Dunvegan
Giant Angus Macaskill
Kilmuir
Ben Uigshader 806
Glen Bernisdale
Symbol Stone
Tote
Crepkill
B8036
Borve
Borve Standing Stones
St. Columba's Island
Skeabost
Carbost
Loch Niarsco
Hamara River
Glen Dale
B884
Lonmore
A863
Moonen Bay
Ben Corkeval
Dun Osdale Broch
HEALABHAL MHOR
1538
Cruachan Beinn a' Chearcaill
Uigshader
Drumuie
Loch Ravag
Beinn a' Ghlinne Bhig 682
Ramasaig
Roskhill
Roag
10
Cairns
Vatten
Glengrasco
Hoe Rape
Orbost
Orbost Gallery
Ardroag
Loch Vatten
Loch Connan
Shulishadermor (Sùlaisiadar Mòr)
Aros
Beinn na Greine 1376
The Hoe 759
1600
HEALABHAL BHEAG
Loch Bharcasaig
Harlosh
Balmore
Loch Caroy
Ose
River Ose
9
B885
Hoe Point
Loch Glen Ionadal
799 Ben Connan
Beinn na Boineid 1207
Harlosh Point
Colbost Point
Tungadal Souterrain
Tungadal River
Glenmore
Stroc-bheinn 1300
Mugeary
Am Bi-bogha Mór
Harlosh Island
Tarner Island
Dun Beag
Dun Mor
Bracadale
Totardor
Ben Duagrich
Ullinish Cairn
Struan
Struanmore
Coillore
Ben Idrigill
Loch
Wiay
An Dubh-sgeir
Carn Liath
Macleod's Maidens
IDRIGILL POINT
Oronsay
Dun Ardtreck
13
1442 Roineval
Meall an Fhuarain
Bracadale
Portnalong
Loch Harport
B8009
Rubha nan Clach
Dun Ard an t-Sabhail
Fiskavaig
Fernilea
Carbost
Drynoch
A863
Arnaval 1210
Gleann Oraid
Talisker Distillery
Merkadale
River Drynoch
Talisker Bay
Talisker
146
Eynort River
Beinn nan Cuithean
Beinn Bhreac
1468 Beinn Bhreac
Eynort
Glen Brittle Forest

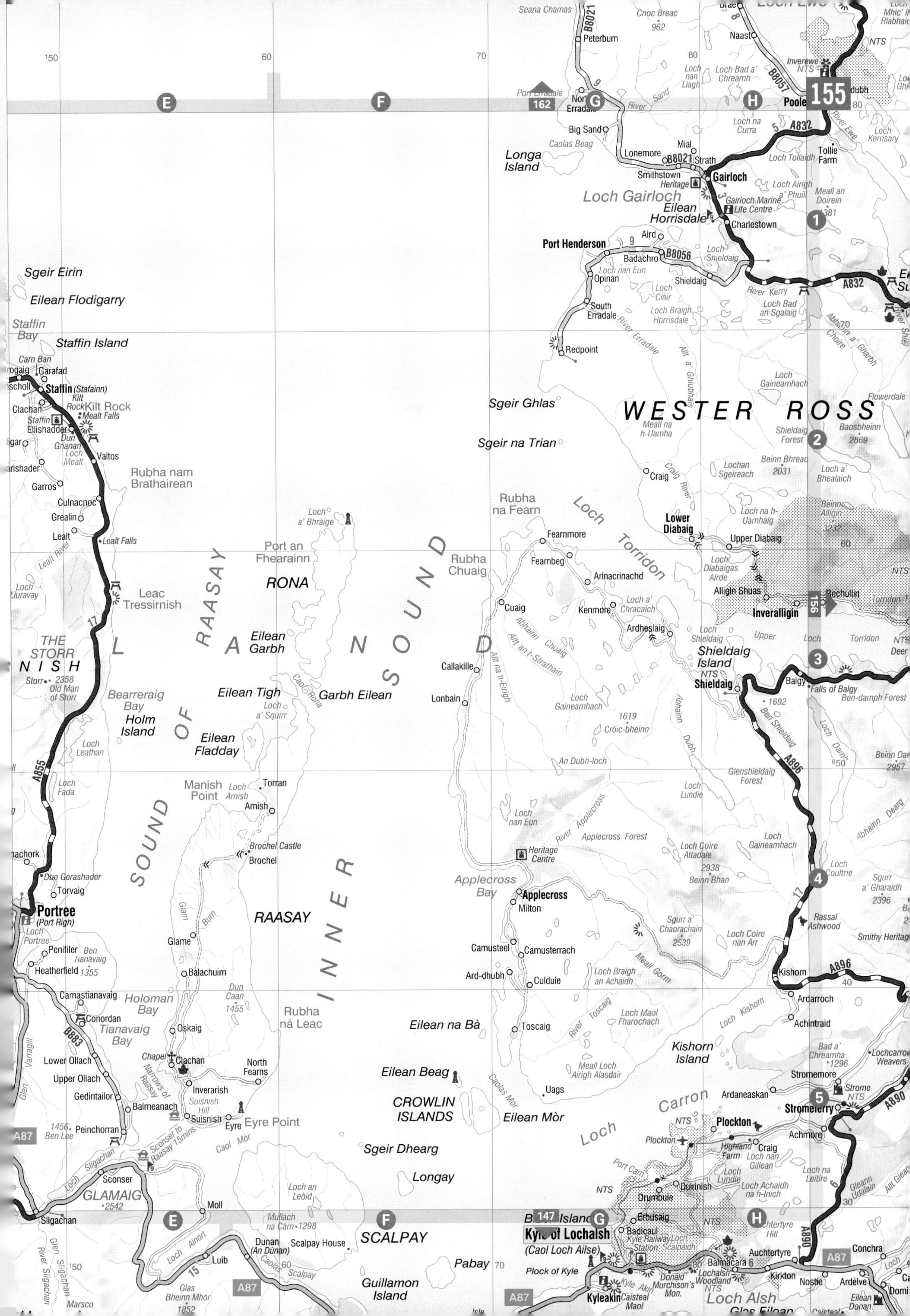

155
156
162
147
WESTER ROSS
Loch Gairloch
Gairloch
Poolewe
Inverewe NTS
Naast
Peterburn
North Erradale
Big Sand
Longa Island
Lonemore
Strath
Smithstown
Charlestown
Eilean Horrisdale
Port Henderson
Badachro
Aird
Opinan
South Erradale
Shieldaig
Redpoint
Sgeir Eirin
Eilean Flodigarry
Staffin Bay
Staffin Island
Staffin (Stafainn)
Kilt Rock
Mealt Falls
Ellishadder
Valtos
Rubha nam Brathairean
Garros
Culnacnoc
Grealin
Lealt
Lealt Falls
Leac Tressirnish
THE STORR
Old Man of Storr
Bearreraig Bay
Holm Island
Sgeir Ghlas
Sgeir na Trian
Rubha na Fearn
Loch Torridon
Fearnmore
Fearnbeg
Arinacrinachd
Cuaig
Kenmore
Ardheslaig
Lower Diabaig
Upper Diabaig
Alligin Shuas
Inveralligin
Rechullin
Shieldaig Island
Balgy
Falls of Balgy
Ben-damph Forest
Beinn Alligin 3232
Baosbheinn 2869
Beinn Bhreac 2031
Craig
Port an Fhearainn
RONA
RAASAY
SOUND OF RAASAY
INNER SOUND
Eilean Garbh
Eilean Tigh
Garbh Eilean
Eilean Fladday
Rubha Chuaig
Callakille
Lonbain
Manish Point
Torran
Arnish
Brochel Castle
Brochel
Applecross Bay
Applecross
Heritage Centre
Milton
Camusteel
Camusterrach
Ard-dhubh
Culduie
Toscaig
Portree (Port Righ)
Torvaig
Penifiler
Heatherfield
Camastianavaig
Holoman Bay
Conordan
Tianavaig Bay
Lower Ollach
Upper Ollach
Gedintailor
Balmeanach
Peinchorran
Glame
Balachuirn
Dun Caan 1455
Oskaig
Clachan
Inverarish
Suisnish
Eyre
Eyre Point
North Fearns
Rubha na Leac
Eilean na Bà
Eilean Beag
CROWLIN ISLANDS
Eilean Mòr
Sgeir Dhearg
Longay
Kishorn Island
Kishorn
Ardarroch
Achintraid
Stromemore
Ardaneaskan
Strome
Stromeferry
Plockton
Achmore
Duirinish
Drumbuie
Erbusaig
Badicaul
Kyle of Lochalsh (Caol Loch Ailse)
Plock of Kyle
Kyleakin
Balmacara
Auchtertyre
Kirkton
Nostie
Ardelve
Conchra
Loch Alsh
Loch Carron
Sconser
Sligachan
GLAMAIG 2542
Moll
Luib
SCALPAY
Scalpay House
Dunan (An Dùnan)
Pabay
Guillamon Island
Glas Bheinn Mhòr 1852
Marsco
A832
A896
A890
A87
A855
B8021
B8056
B8057
B883

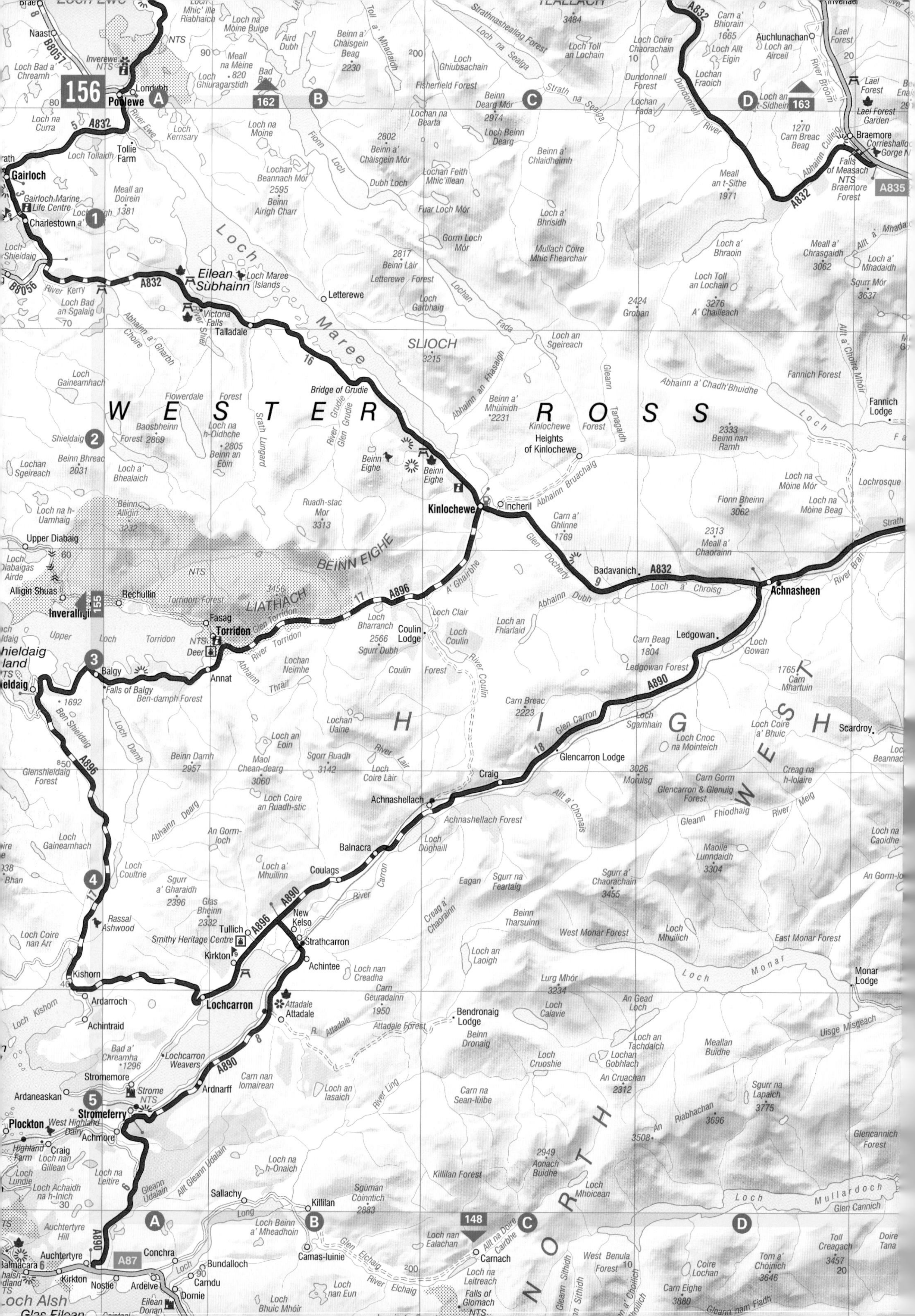

156
162
163
155
148
Poolewe
Inverewe NTS
Naast
Londubh
Gairloch
Gairloch Marine Life Centre
Charlestown
Tollie Farm
Eilean Sùbhainn
Loch Maree Islands
Victoria Falls
Talladale
Letterewe
Loch Maree
Fisherfield Forest
Letterewe Forest
Strathnasheallag Forest
Dundonnell Forest
Auchlunachan
Lael Forest
Lael Forest Garden
Braemore
Corrieshalloch Gorge NNR
Falls of Measach NTS
Braemore Forest
Slioch 3215
Bridge of Grudie
Flowerdale Forest
WESTER ROSS
Kinlochewe Forest
Heights of Kinlochewe
Fannich Forest
Fannich Lodge
Lochrosque
Beinn Eighe
Kinlochewe
Incheril
Badavanich
Achnasheen
Loch a' Chroisg
Upper Diabaig
Alligin Shuas
Inveralligin
Rechullin
Torridon Forest
Liathach
Beinn Eighe
Fasag
Torridon
Deer
Annat
Balgy
Falls of Balgy
Ben-damph Forest
Coulin Lodge
Coulin Forest
Loch Clair
Loch Coulin
Ledgowan
Ledgowan Forest
Glen Carron
Glencarron Lodge
Scardroy
Craig
Achnashellach
Achnashellach Forest
Glencarron & Glenuig Forest
HIGHLAND
NORTH WEST
Balnacra
Coulags
New Kelso
Strathcarron
Tullich
Smithy Heritage Centre
Kirkton
Achintee
Rassal Ashwood
Kishorn
Ardarroch
Achintraid
Lochcarron
Attadale
Bendronaig Lodge
Attadale Forest
West Monar Forest
East Monar Forest
Loch Monar
Monar Lodge
Lochcarron Weavers
Stromemore
Strome NTS
Ardaneaskan
Ardnarff
Stromeferry
Plockton
West Highland Dairy
Achmore
Craig
Highland Farm
Killilan Forest
Sallachy
Killilan
Camas-luinie
Carnach
Loch Mullardoch
Glen Cannich
Glencannich Forest
West Benula Forest
Auchtertyre
Balmacara
Conchra
Bundalloch
Carndu
Dornie
Kirkton
Nostie
Ardelve
Eilean Donan
Falls of Glomach NTS
Loch Alsh
A832
A835
A896
A890
A87
B8057
B8056

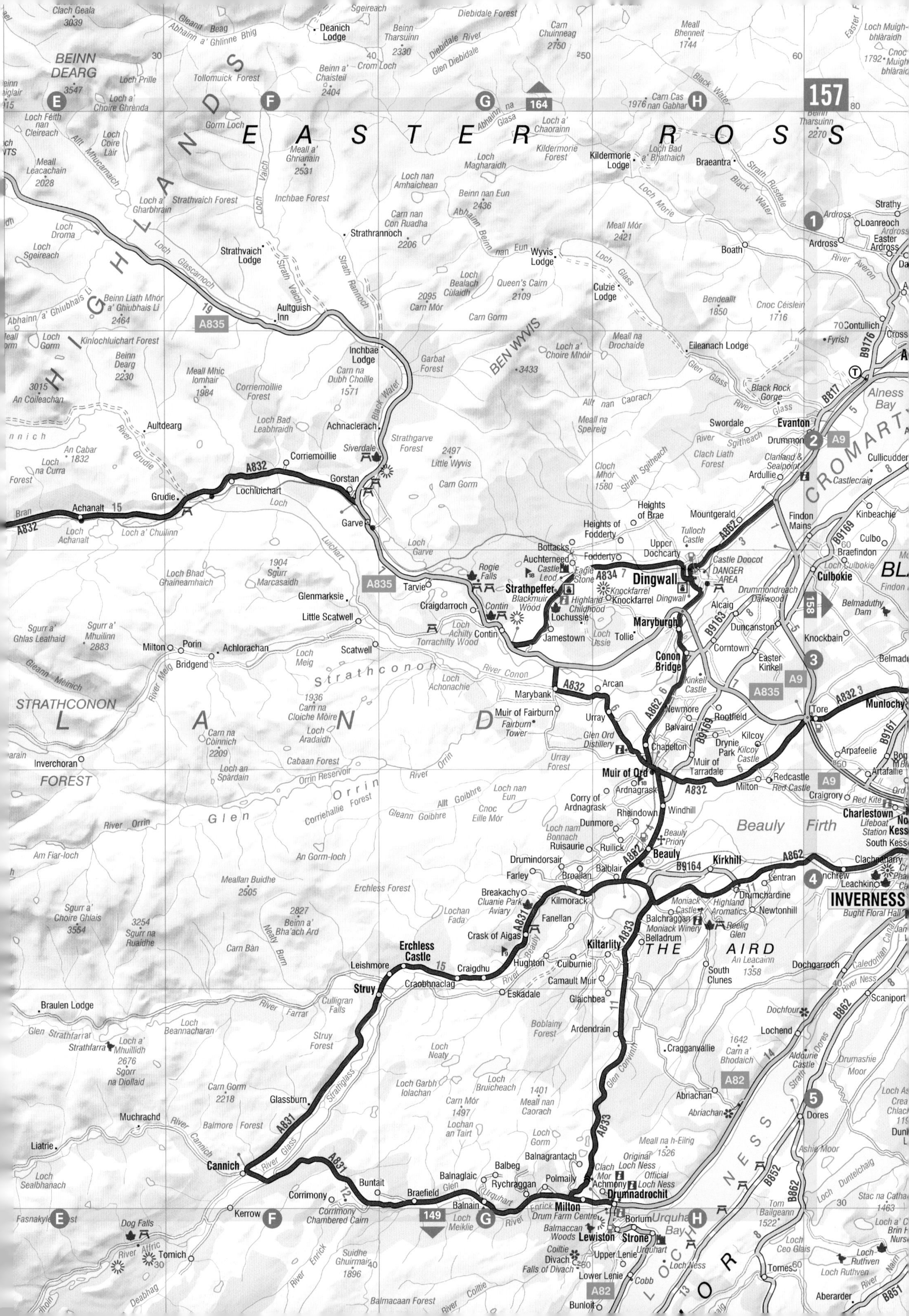

157
164
149
158
EASTER ROSS
HIGHLANDS
LAND
FOREST
STRATHCONON
CROMARTY
BEAULY FIRTH
THE AIRD
LOCH NESS
INVERNESS
Clach Geala 3039
Gleann Beag
Abhainn a' Ghlinne Bhig
Sgeireach
Deanich Lodge
Diebidale Forest
Beinn Tharsuinn 2330
Diebidale River
Glen Diebidale
Carn Chuinneag 2750
Meall Bhenneit 1744
Loch Muigh-bhlàraidh
1792 Cnoc Muigh-bhlàraidh
BEINN DEARG 3547
Loch Prille
Tollomuick Forest
Beinn a' Chaisteil 2404
Crom Loch
Black Water
Carn Cas nan Gabhar 1976
Beinn Tharsuinn 2270
Loch a' Choire Ghrànda
Loch Féith nan Cleireach
Gorm Loch
Abhainn na Glasa
Loch a' Chaorainn
Kildermorie Forest
Kildermorie Lodge
Loch Bad a' Bhathaich
Braeantra
Strath Rusdale
Loch Coire Lair
Allt Mhucarnaich
Meall Leacachain 2028
Meall a' Ghrianain 2531
Loch Vaich
Loch Magharaidh
Loch nan Amhaichean
Inchbae Forest
Beinn nan Eun 2436
Loch Morie
Black Water
Strathy
Ardross
Loanreoch
Easter Ardross
Loch a' Gharbhrain
Strathvaich Forest
Carn nan Con Ruadha 2206
Abhainn Beinn nan Eun
Meall Mór 2421
Loch Droma
Strathrannoch
Wyvis Lodge
Loch Glass
Boath
River Averon
Loch Sgeireach
Loch Glascarnoch
Strathvaich Lodge
Strath Vaich
Strath Rannoch
Loch Bealach Cùlaidh
Queen's Cairn 2109
Culzie Lodge
Bendeallt 1650
Cnoc Céislein 1716
Abhainn a' Ghiubhais Li
Beinn Liath Mhór a' Ghiubhais Li 2464
Aultguish Inn
2095 Carn Mór
Carn Gorm
A835
Loch Gorm
Kinlochluichart Forest
Inchbae Lodge
BEN WYVIS 3433
Meall na Drochaide
Loch a' Choire Mhóir
Eileanach Lodge
Contullich
Fyrish
B9176
B817
Beinn Dearg 2230
Meall Mhic Iomhair 1984
Corriemoillie Forest
Carn na Dubh Choille 1571
Garbat Forest
Glen Glass
Black Rock Gorge
Alness Bay
3015 An Coileachan
Loch Bad Leabhraidh
Allt nan Caorach
Aultdearg
River Grudie
Achnaclerach
Meall na Speireig
Swordale
Evanton
Drummond
A9
An Cabar 1832
Loch na Curra
Siverdale
Strathgarve Forest
2497 Little Wyvis
River Sgitheach
Clach Liath Forest
Clanland & Sealpoint
Cullicudden
Corriemoillie
A832
Lochluichart
Gorstan
Carn Gorm
Cloch Mhór 1580
Strath Sgitheach
Ardullie
Castlecraig
Grudie
Achanalt
Loch Luichart
Garve
Heights of Brae
Mountgerald
Findon Mains
Kinbeachie
Loch Achanalt
Loch a' Chuilinn
Loch Garve
Heights of Fodderty
Tulloch Castle
B9169
Culbo
Bottacks
Auchterneed
Castle Leod
Eagle Stone
Fodderty
Upper Dochcarty
Castle Doocot
DANGER AREA
Braefindon
Culbokie
Loch Bhad Ghaineamhaich
1904 Sgurr Marcasaidh
Rogie Falls
Strathpeffer
A834
Dingwall
Knockfarrel
Highland Childhood
Drummondreach Oakwood
Findon
Belmaduthy Dam
Tarvie
Glenmarksie
Craigdarroch
Contin
Blackmuir Wood
Lochussie
Alcaig
Little Scatwell
Maryburgh
B9163
Duncanston
Knockbain
Sgurr a' Ghlas Leathaid
Sgurr a' Mhuilinn 2883
Loch Achilty
Torrachilty Wood
Jamestown
Loch Ussie
Tollie
Corntown
Milton
Porin
Achlorachan
Bridgend
Loch Meig
Scatwell
Conon Bridge
Easter Kinkell
Belmaduthy
River Meig
Gleann Meinich
Strathconon
River Conon
Loch Achonachie
Kinkell Castle
A835
A832
Arcan
Marybank
1936 Carn na Cloiche Móire
Muir of Fairburn
Fairburn Tower
Urray
A862
Newmore
Rootfield
Tore
Munlochy
Carn na Coinnich 2209
Loch Aradaidh
Balvaird
Drynie Park
Kilcoy
Kilcoy Castle
Arpafeelie
B9161
Inverchoran
Loch an Spàrdain
Cabaan Forest
Glen Ord Distillery
Chapelton
Urray Forest
Orrin Reservoir
River Orrin
Muir of Ord
Muir of Tarradale
Redcastle
Red Castle
Artafallie
Glen Orrin
Corriehallie Forest
Allt Goibhre
Loch nan Eun
Ardnagrask
Milton
Craigrory
Red Kite
Charlestown
Lifeboat Station
Corry of Ardnagrask
Rheindown
Windhill
River Orrin
Gleann Goibhre
Cnoc Eille Mór
Dunmore
Loch nam Bonnach
Ruisaurie
Beauly Priory
Ruilick
South Kessock
Am Fiar-loch
An Gorm-loch
Drumindorsair
Beauly
Kirkhill
B9164
Clachnaharry
Meallan Buidhe 2505
Farley
Broallan
Balblair
Lentran
Inchrew
Leachkin
Erchless Forest
Breakachy
Cluanie Park Aviary
Kilmorack
Moniack Castle
Highland Aromatics
Drumchardine
Newtonhill
Bught Floral Hall
Sgurr a' Choire Ghlais 3554
3254 Sgurr na Ruaidhe
2827 Beinn a' Bha'ach Ard
Lochan Fada
Fanellan
Balchraggan
Moniack Winery
Reelig Glen
Neaty Burn
Carn Bàn
Crask of Aigas
A831
Belladrum
Erchless Castle
Kiltarlity
A833
An Leacainn 1358
Leishmore
Craigdhu
Hughton
Culburnie
South Clunes
Dochgarroch
Caledonian Canal
Struy
Craobhnaclag
Camault Muir
River Beauly
Eskadale
Glaichbea
River Ness
Scaniport
Braulen Lodge
River Farrar
Culligran Falls
Loch Beannacharan
Dochfour
B862
Glen Strathfarrar
Strathfarrar
Loch a' Mhuillidh 2676
Sgurr na Diollaid
Struy Forest
Boblainy Forest
Ardendrain
Lochend
Loch Neaty
Cragganvallie
1642 Carn a' Bhodaich
Aldourie Castle
Drumashie Moor
Loch Garbh Iolachan
Loch Bruicheach
Carn Gorm 2218
Carn Mór 1497
1401 Meall nan Caorach
Glen Convinth
Abriachan
A82
Glassburn
Strathglass
Lochan an Tairt
Dores
Muchrachd
River Cannich
Balmore Forest
Loch Gorm
Liatrie
Meall na h-Eilig 1526
Ashie Moor
Loch Sealbhanach
Cannich
River Glass
Balnagrantach
Clach Mor
Original Loch Ness
Official Loch Ness
Balbeg
Rychraggan
Polmaily
Achmony
Drumnadrochit
Buntait
Balnaglaic
Glen Urquhart
Loch Duntelchaig
Stac na Cathaig 1463
Corrimony
Braefield
Corrimony Chambered Cairn
Kerrow
Balnain
Loch Meiklie
River Enrick
Milton
Drum Farm Centre
Borlum
Urquhart Bay
Tom Bailgeann 1522
Fasnakyle
Dog Falls
Balmaccan Woods
Lewiston
Strone
Urquhart Castle
Loch Ceo Glais
Loch Ruthven
River Affric
Tomich
Sgurr Ghuirmain 1896
Coiltie
Divach
Falls of Divach
Upper Lenie
Lower Lenie
Cobb
Tomes
Aberarder
B851
B852
Deabhag
Balmacaan Forest
River Coiltie
Bunloit

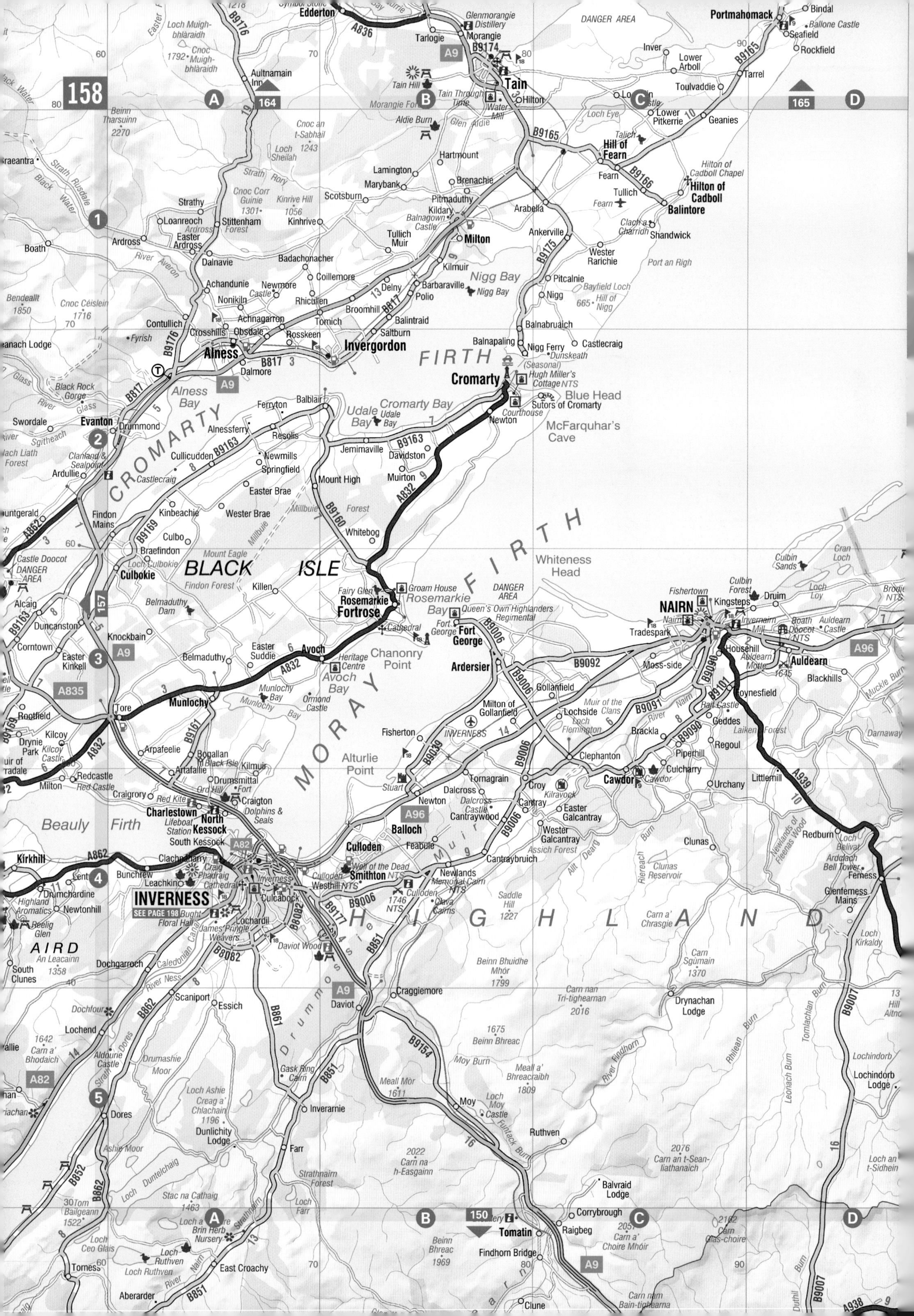

158
164
165
157
150
A
B
C
D
1
2
3
4
5
Edderton
Glenmorangie Distillery
Morangie
Tarlogie
B9174
A9
A836
B9176
Loch Muigh-bhlàraidh
Cnoc Muigh-bhlàraidh
Aultnamain Inn
Tain Hill
Tain
Tain Through Time
Hilton
Water Mill
Morangie Forest
Aldie Burn
Glen Aldie
DANGER AREA
Portmahomack
Bindal
Ballone Castle
Seafield
Rockfield
Inver
Lower Arboll
Tarrel
Toulvaddie
B9165
Lower Pitkerrie
Geanies
Loch Eye
Hill of Fearn
Talich
Fearn
B9166
Tullich
Hilton of Cadboll Chapel
Hilton of Cadboll
Balintore
Shandwick
Clach a' Charridh
Port an Righ
Beinn Tharsuinn
Cnoc an t-Sabhail
Loch Sheilah
Strath Rory
Hartmount
Lamington
Marybank
Brenachie
Scotsburn
Pitmaduthy
Kildary
Balnagown Castle
Milton
Arabella
Ankerville
B9175
Wester Rarichie
Cnoc Corr Guinie
Kinrive Hill
Kinkhrive
Strathy
Loanreoch
Stittenham
Ardross Forest
Ardross
Easter Ardross
Boath
River Averon
Dalnavie
Tullich Muir
Badachonacher
Coillemore
Kilmuir
Nigg Bay
Pitcalnie
Bayfield Loch
Hill of Nigg
Nigg
Achandunie
Newmore Castle
Nonikiln
Rhicullen
Delny
Barbaraville
Polio
Broomhill
B817
Balintraid
Tomich
Achnagarron
Saltburn
Balnabruaich
Balnapaling
Nigg Ferry
Castlecraig
Dunskeath
Bendeallt
Cnoc Céislein
Contullich
Fyrish
Crosshills
Obsdale
Rosskeen
Invergordon
Alness
Dalmore
FIRTH
Cromarty
Hugh Miller's Cottage NTS
Blue Head
Sutors of Cromarty
Courthouse
Newton
McFarquhar's Cave
Black Rock Gorge
Alness Bay
Glass
River Glass
Swordale
Evanton
Drummond
Ferryton
Balblair
Udale Bay
Cromarty Bay
Alnessferry
Resolis
Jemimaville
B9163
Davidston
Cullicudden
Newmills
Springfield
Castlecraig
Clanland & Sealpoint
Ardullie
Mount High
Muirton
A832
Easter Brae
Wester Brae
Millbuie Forest
B9160
Kinbeachie
Findon Mains
A862
Culbo
Whitebog
Braefindon
Castle Doocot
CROMARTY
MORAY FIRTH
Whiteness Head
Mount Eagle
Loch Culbokie
Culbokie
BLACK ISLE
Findon Forest
Killen
Fairy Glen
Groam House
Rosemarkie
Fortrose
Rosemarkie Bay
DANGER AREA
Queen's Own Highlanders Regimental
Fort George
Cathedral
Alcaig
Duncanston
Belmaduthy Dam
Knockbain
Corntown
Easter Kinkell
A835
Belmaduthy
Easter Suddie
Avoch
Heritage Centre
Avoch Bay
Chanonry Point
Ardersier
Tore
Munlochy
Munlochy Bay
Ormond Castle
MORAY
Rootfield
Kilcoy
Drynie Park
Kilcoy Castle
Muir of Ord
Redcastle
Red Castle
Milton
B9161
Arpafeelie
Bogallan
Artafallie
Kilmuir
Drumsmittal
Ord Hill Fort
Red Kite
Craigrory
Craigton
Dolphins & Seals
Charlestown
North Kessock
Lifeboat Station
South Kessock
Beauly Firth
Alturlie Point
Fisherton
Stuart
Kirkhill
A862
Clachnaharry
Craig Phadraig
Bunchrew
Leachkin
Cathedral
Lentran
Drumchardine
Highland Aromatics
Newtonhill
Reelig Glen
INVERNESS
SEE PAGE 198
Bught Floral Hall
Culcabock
Lochardil
James Pringle Weavers
Caledonian Canal
B8082
AIRD
An Leacainn
South Clunes
Dochgarroch
Daviot Wood
B9177
Drummossie Muir
B851
River Ness
Scaniport
Essich
Dochfour
Lochend
Aldourie Castle
Drumashie Moor
Carn a' Bhodaich
A82
Loch Ashie
Creag a' Chlachain
Dunlichity Lodge
Dores
Ashie Moor
Loch Duntelchaig
Stac na Cathaig
B852
B862
Tom Bailgeann
Loch a' Chlaidh
Brin Herb Nursery
Loch Ceo Glais
Loch Ruthven
Torness
East Croachy
Aberarder
River Nairn
Strathnairn
Gask Ring Cairn
Inverarnie
B861
Farr
Strathnairn Forest
Loch Farr
Daviot
A9
Craggiemore
B9154
Meall Mòr
Moy Burn
Moy
Loch Moy
Moy Castle
Funtack Burn
Carn na h-Easgainn
Tomatin
Beinn Bhreac
Findhorn Bridge
Clune
Culloden
Smithton
Westhill
Well of the Dead
B9006
Culloden NTS
Clava Cairns
Newlands
Memorial Cairn
Balloch
Feabuie
A96
Newton
Dalcross
Dalcross Castle
Cantraywood
Tornagrain
INVERNESS
Cantray
Croy
Kilravock
Easter Galcantray
Wester Galcantray
Assich Forest
Cantraybruich
Allt Dearg
Saddle Hill
HIGHLAND
Beinn Bhuidhe Mhòr
Carn nan Tri-tighearnan
Beinn Bhreac
Meall a' Bhreacraibh
River Findhorn
Ruthven
Carn an t-Sean-liathanaich
Balvraid Lodge
Corrybrough
Raigbeg
Carn a' Choire Mhòir
Carn Glas-choire
Carn nam Bain-tighearna
B9039
Milton of Gollanfield
Gollanfield
B9092
Moss-side
Lochside
Loch Flemington
Muir of the Clans
Clephanton
B9091
River Nairn
Brackla
B9090
Cawdor
Culcharry
Piperhill
Urchany
Regoul
Geddes
Rait Castle
B9101
Laiken Forest
Littlemill
A939
Clunas
Clunas Reservoir
Rireach Burn
Carn a' Chrasgie
Carn Sgumain
Drynachan Lodge
NAIRN
Fishertown
Kingsteps
Nairn
Tradespark
Househill
Auldearn Motte
Auldearn
Boath Doocot NTS
Auldearn Castle
Blackhills
Boynesfield
Culbin Forest
Culbin Sands
Druim
Loch Loy
Cran Loch
Darnaway
Muckle Burn
A96
Redburn
Loch Belivat
Ardclach Bell Tower
Ferness
Glenferness Mains
Newlands of Fleenas Wood
Loch Kirkaldy
B9007
Hill of Aitnoch
Tomlachan Burn
Rhilean Burn
Leonach Burn
Lochindorb
Lochindorb Lodge
Loch an t-Sidhein
Dulnain Burn
Duthil Burn
A938

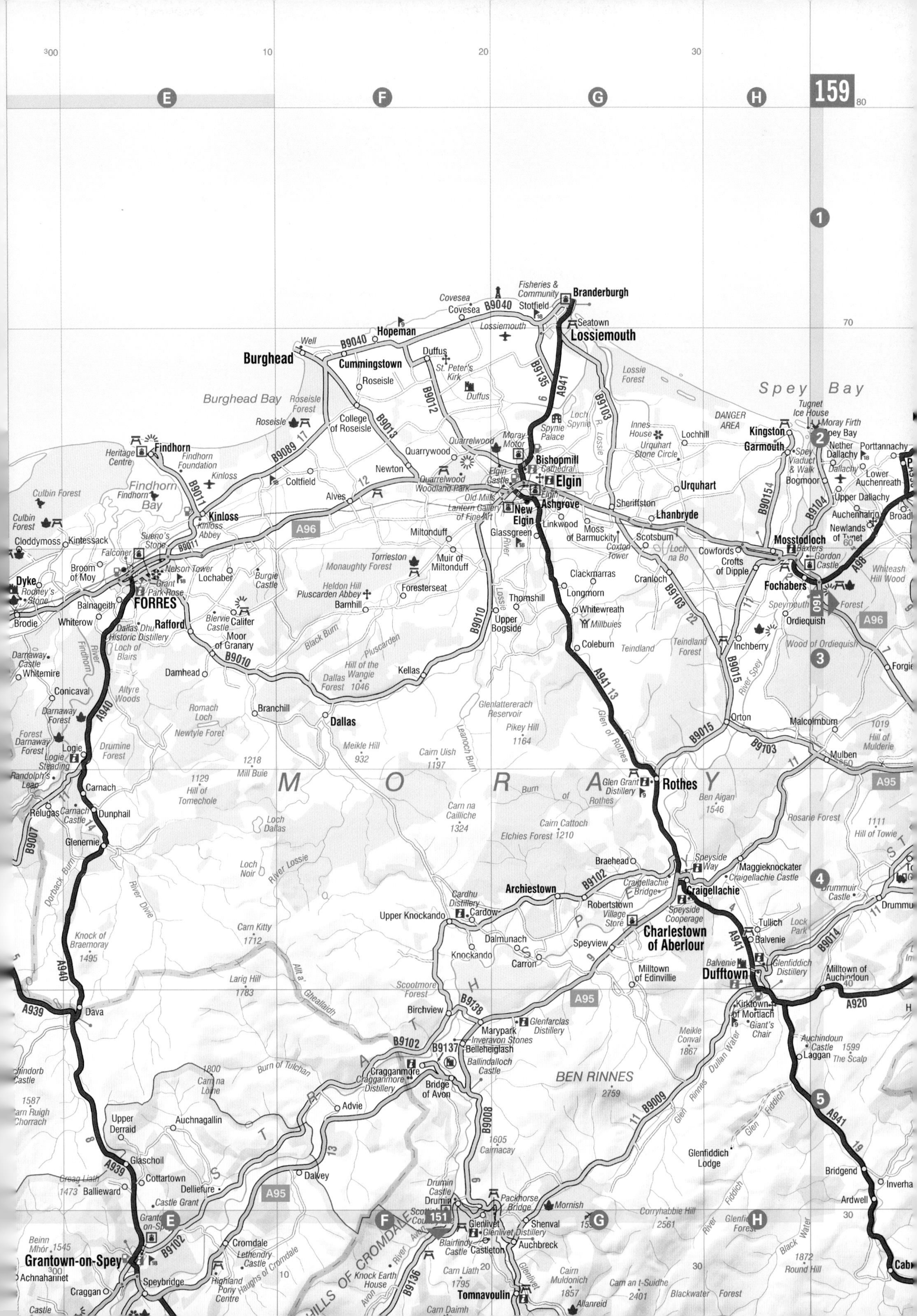
E
F
G
H
1
2
3
4
5
Spey Bay
Burghead Bay
Covesea
Fisheries & Community
Branderburgh
Stotfield
Seatown
Lossiemouth
Hopeman
Well
Burghead
Cummingstown
Duffus
St. Peter's Kirk
Roseisle
Roseisle Forest
College of Roseisle
Lossie Forest
Loch Spynie
Spynie Palace
Innes House
Urquhart Stone Circle
Lochhill
DANGER AREA
Tugnet Ice House
Moray Firth
Kingston
Garmouth
Spey Viaduct & Walk
Nether Dallachy
Porttannachy
Dallachy
Lower Auchenreath
Bogmoor
Upper Dallachy
Auchenhalrig
Newlands of Tynet
Findhorn
Heritage Centre
Findhorn Foundation
Kinloss
Findhorn Bay
Culbin Forest
Kinloss Abbey
Quarrywood
Quarrelwood
Moray Motor
Bishopmill
Elgin
Elgin Castle
Elgin Cathedral
Newton
Quarrelwood Woodland Park
Coltfield
Alves
Old Mills
Lantern Gallery of Fine Art
New Elgin
Ashgrove
Linkwood
Urquhart
Sheriffston
Lhanbryde
Moss of Barmuckity
Coxton Tower
Scotsburn
Loch na Bo
Mosstodloch
Baxters
Cowfords
Crofts of Dipple
Gordon Castle
Fochabers
Whiteash Hill Wood
Cloddymoss
Kintessack
Dyke
Rodney's Stone
Sueno's Stone
Falconer
Broom of Moy
Nelson Tower
Grant Park
Rose
FORRES
Lochaber
Burgie Castle
Torrieston
Monaughty Forest
Milton Duff
Muir of Miltonduff
Glassgreen
Heldon Hill
Pluscarden Abbey
Foresterseat
Barnhill
Clackmarras
Longmorn
Cranloch
Speymouth
Forest
Ordiequish
Wood of Ordiequish
Brodie
Bainageith
Whiterow
Dallas Dhu Historic Distillery
Rafford
Blervie Castle
Califer
Moor of Granary
Thornshill
Upper Bogside
Whitewreath
Millbuies
Coleburn
Teindland
Teindland Forest
Inchberry
River Spey
Forgie
Darnaway Castle
Whitemire
Loch of Blairs
Damhead
Black Burn
Pluscarden
Hill of the Wangie 1046
Dallas Forest
Kellas
Conicaval
Altyre Woods
Romach Loch
Newtyle Forest
Branchill
Dallas
Glenlatterach Reservoir
Pikey Hill 1164
Glen of Rothes
Orton
Malcolmburn
Hill of Mulderie
Darnaway Forest
Forest Darnaway Forest
Logie
Logie Steading
Drumine Forest
Meikle Hill 932
Cairn Uish 1197
Leanoch Burn
Mulben
Randolph's Leap
Carnach
1129 Hill of Tomechole
1218 Mill Buie
MORAY
Burn of Rothes
Glen Grant Distillery
Rothes
Ben Aigan 1546
Relugas
Carnach Castle
Dunphail
Loch Dallas
Carn na Cailliche 1324
Cairn Cattoch
Elchies Forest 1210
Rosarie Forest
Hill of Towie
Glenernie
Loch Noir
River Lossie
Braehead
Speyside Way
Maggieknockater
Craigellachie Castle
Drummuir Castle
Dorback Burn
River Divie
Cardhu Distillery
Cardow
Archiestown
Craigellachie Bridge
Craigellachie
Robertstown
Village Store
Speyside Cooperage
Tullich
Lock Park
Balvenie
Knock of Braemoray 1495
Carn Kitty 1712
Upper Knockando
Dalmunach
Knockando
Carron
Speyview
Charlestown of Aberlour
Balvenie
Glenfiddich Distillery
Dufftown
Milltown of Edinvillie
Milltown of Auchindoun
Larig Hill 1783
Allt a' Ghealláich
Scootmore Forest
Dava
Birchview
Marypark
Glenfarclas Distillery
Inveravon Stones
Kirktown of Mortlach
Giant's Chair
Belleheiglash
Meikle Conval 1867
Auchindoun Castle
1599 The Scalp
Laggan
Lochindorb Castle
Burn of Tulchan
1800 Carn na Loine
Cragganmore
Cragganmore Distillery
Ballindalloch Castle
Bridge of Avon
BEN RINNES 2759
Dullan Water
Glen Rinnes
Glen Fiddich
1587 Carn Ruigh Chorrach
Upper Derraid
Auchnagallin
Advie
Glenfiddich Lodge
Bridgend
Inverharnie
Glaschoil
Creag Liath 1473
Cottartown
Balliewards
Dellefure
Dalvey
1605 Carnacay
Drumin Castle
Drumin
Packhorse Bridge
Mornish
Ardwell
Castle Grant
Grantown-on-Spey
Beinn Mhór 1545
Cromdale
Lethendry Castle
Scottish Council
Glenlivet
Glenlivet Distillery
Shenval
Corryhabbie Hill 2561
Glenfiddich Forest
Black Water
Auchbreck
Blairfindy Castle
Castleton
HILLS OF CROMDALE
Haughs of Cromdale
Highland Pony Centre
Achnahannet
Speybridge
Craggan
Knock Earth House
Carn Liath 1795
Tomnavoulin
Cairn Muldonich 1857
Carn an t-Suidhe 2401
Blackwater Forest
1872 Round Hill
Allanreird
Carn Daimh
Cabrach
A96
A941
A940
A939
A95
A98
A920
B9040
B9089
B9013
B9012
B9135
B9103
B9011
B9010
B9015
B90154
B9104
B9102
B9138
B9137
B9008
B9009
B9007
B9014
B9136
B9703
160
151

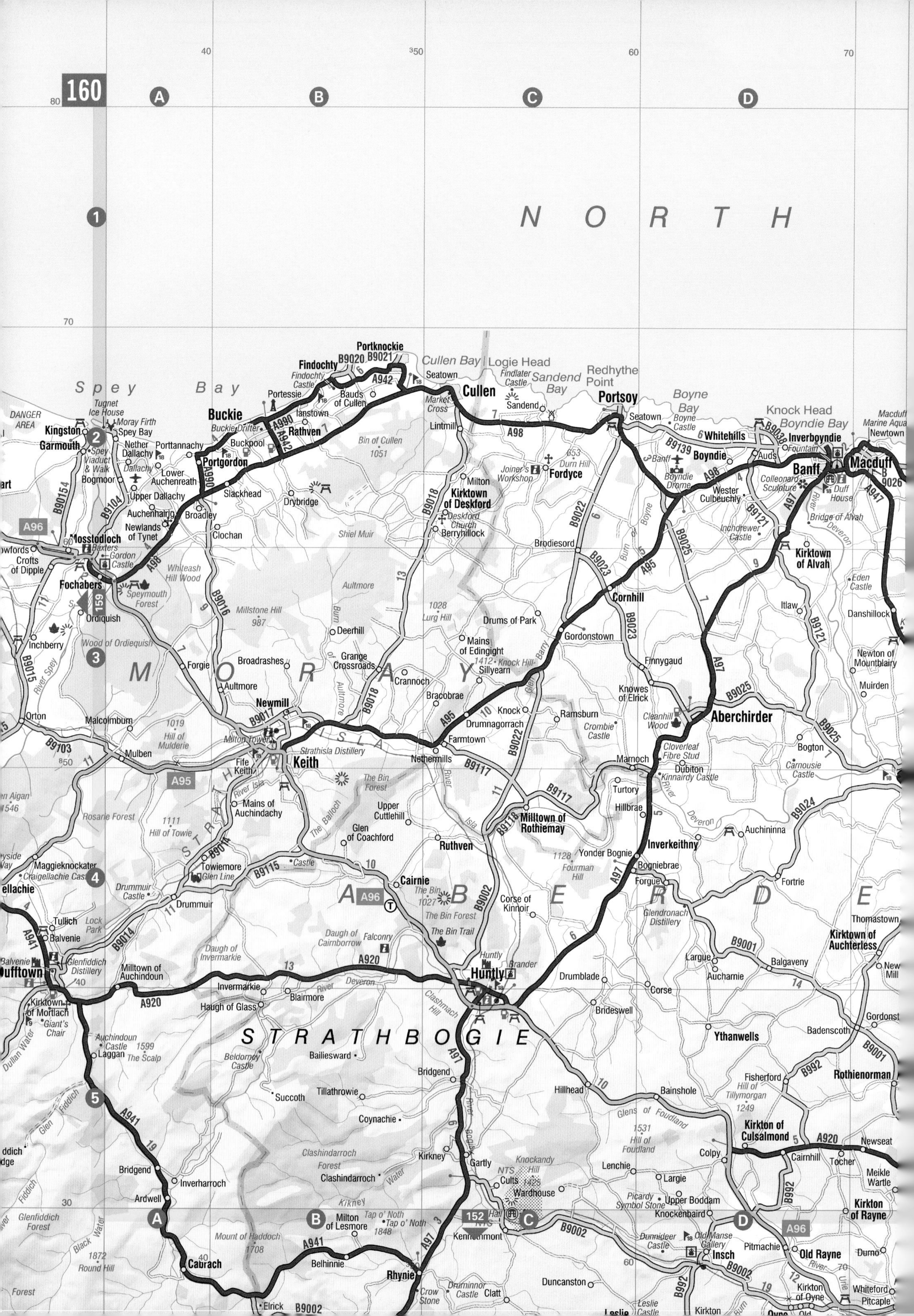

160
A
B
C
D
1
2
3
4
5
40
350
60
70
80
N O R T H
Spey Bay
Tugnet Ice House
DANGER AREA
Kingston
Garmouth
Moray Firth Spey Bay
Spey Viaduct & Walk
Nether Dallachy
Dallachy
Porttannachy
Lower Auchenreath
Bogmoor
Upper Dallachy
Auchenhalrig
Newlands of Tynet
Buckie
Buckie Drifter
Buckpool
Portgordon
Slackhead
Broadley
Clochan
Drybridge
Portessie
Findochty
Findochty Castle
Portknockie
B9020
B9021
A942
A990
Bauds of Cullen
Ianstown
Rathven
Bin of Cullen 1051
Cullen Bay
Logie Head
Findlater Castle
Seatown
Cullen
Market Cross
Lintmill
Sandend Bay
Sandend
Redhythe Point
Portsoy
Seatown
Boyne Bay
Boyne Castle
Knock Head
Boyndie Bay
Whitehills
Inverboyndie
Fountain
Macduff
Macduff Marine Aquarium
Newtown
Banff
Boyndie
Banff
Boyndie Drome
Auds
Colleonard Sculpture
Duff House
Wester Culbeuchly
Inchdrewer Castle
Bridge of Alvah
Kirktown of Alvah
Eden Castle
Itlaw
Danshillock
Newton of Mountblairy
Muirden
A98
B9139
B9038
B9121
A947
B9026
A97
River Deveron
Milton
Kirktown of Deskford
Deskford Church
Berryhillock
Joiner's Workshop
Fordyce
653 Durn Hill
B9018
Brodiesord
B9022
B9023
A95
Burn of Boyne
B9025
Cornhill
Gordonstown
Finnygaud
Knowes of Elrick
Aberchirder
Cleanhill Wood
B9025
Bogton
Carnousie Castle
Marnoch
Cloverleaf Fibre Stud
Dubiton
Kinnairdy Castle
Turtory
Hillbrae
B9024
Auchininna
Inverkeithny
Fortrie
Mosstodloch
Baxters
Gordon Castle
Fochabers
A96
A98
Crofts of Dipple
Whiteash Hill Wood
Speymouth Forest
Shiel Muir
Aultmore
159
Ordiquish
Inchberry
Wood of Ordiequish
B9015
River Spey
B9154
B9104
B9016
Millstone Hill 987
Burn of Aultmore
Deerhill
1028 Lurg Hill
Drums of Park
Mains of Edingight
1412 Knock Hill
Sillyearn
M O R A Y
Forgie
Aultmore
Broadrashes
Grange Crossroads
Crannoch
Bracobrae
Orton
Malcolmburn
1019 Hill of Mulderie
Newmill
B9017
Milton Tower
Keith
Fife Keith
Strathisla Distillery
Isla
Knock
Drumnagorrach
Ramsburn
Crombie Castle
Farmtown
Nethermills
B9117
River Isla
B9103
Mulben
A95
The Bin Forest
Mains of Auchindachy
Upper Cuttlehill
Milltown of Rothiemay
B9118
Rosarie Forest
1111 Hill of Towie
The Balloch
Glen of Coachford
Ruthven
1128 Fourman Hill
Yonder Bognie
Bogniebrae
Forgue
Glendronach Distillery
Maggieknockater
Craigellachie Castle
Towiemore
Glen Line
B9014
B9115
Castle
Cairnie
The Bin 1027
The Bin Forest
The Bin Trail
A96
B9002
Corse of Kinnoir
A B E R D E E N
Thomastown
Kirktown of Auchterless
Drummuir Castle
Drummuir
Tullich
Balvenie
Lock Park
Daugh of Cairnborrow
Falconry
Daugh of Invermarkie
Huntly
Brander
B9001
Largue
Auchamie
Balgaveny
New Mill
Balvenie
Dufftown
Glenfiddich Distillery
Milltown of Auchindoun
A920
Invermarkie
Blairmore
River Deveron
Haugh of Glass
Clashmach Hill
Drumblade
Corse
Brideswell
Gordonstown
Badenscoth
Kirktown of Mortlach
Giant's Chair
Dullan Water
Auchindoun Castle
1599 The Scalp
Laggan
S T R A T H B O G I E
Ythanwells
Beldorney Castle
Bailiesward
Bridgend
A97
Hillhead
Bainshole
Fisherford
Hill of Tillymorgan 1249
B992
Rothienorman
B9001
Succoth
Tillathrowie
Glens of Foudland
1531 Hill of Foudland
Coynachie
Kirkton of Culsalmond
A920
Newseat
A941
Glen Fiddich
Clashindarroch Forest
Clashindarroch
Kirkney Water
Kirkney
Gartly
Knockandy Hill
NTS
Colpy
Cairnhill
Tocher
Meikle Wartle
Bridgend
Inverharroch
Cults
1423
Wardhouse
Lenchie
Largie
Ardwell
Picardy Symbol Stone
Upper Boddam
Knockenbaird
Kirkton of Rayne
Glenfiddich Forest
Milton of Lesmore
Tap o' Noth
1848
152
Hall
Kennethmont
B9002
Dunnideer Castle
Old Manse Gallery
Insch
Pitmachie
Old Rayne
Durno
A96
Black Water
1872 Round Hill
Mount of Haddoch 1708
Cabrach
A941
Belhinnie
Rhynie
Duncanston
B9002
River Urie
Forest
Crow Stone
Druminnor Castle
Clatt
Elrick
B9002
Leslie Castle
Leslie
Kirkton
Kirkton of Oyne
Whiteford
Pitcaple
Oyne

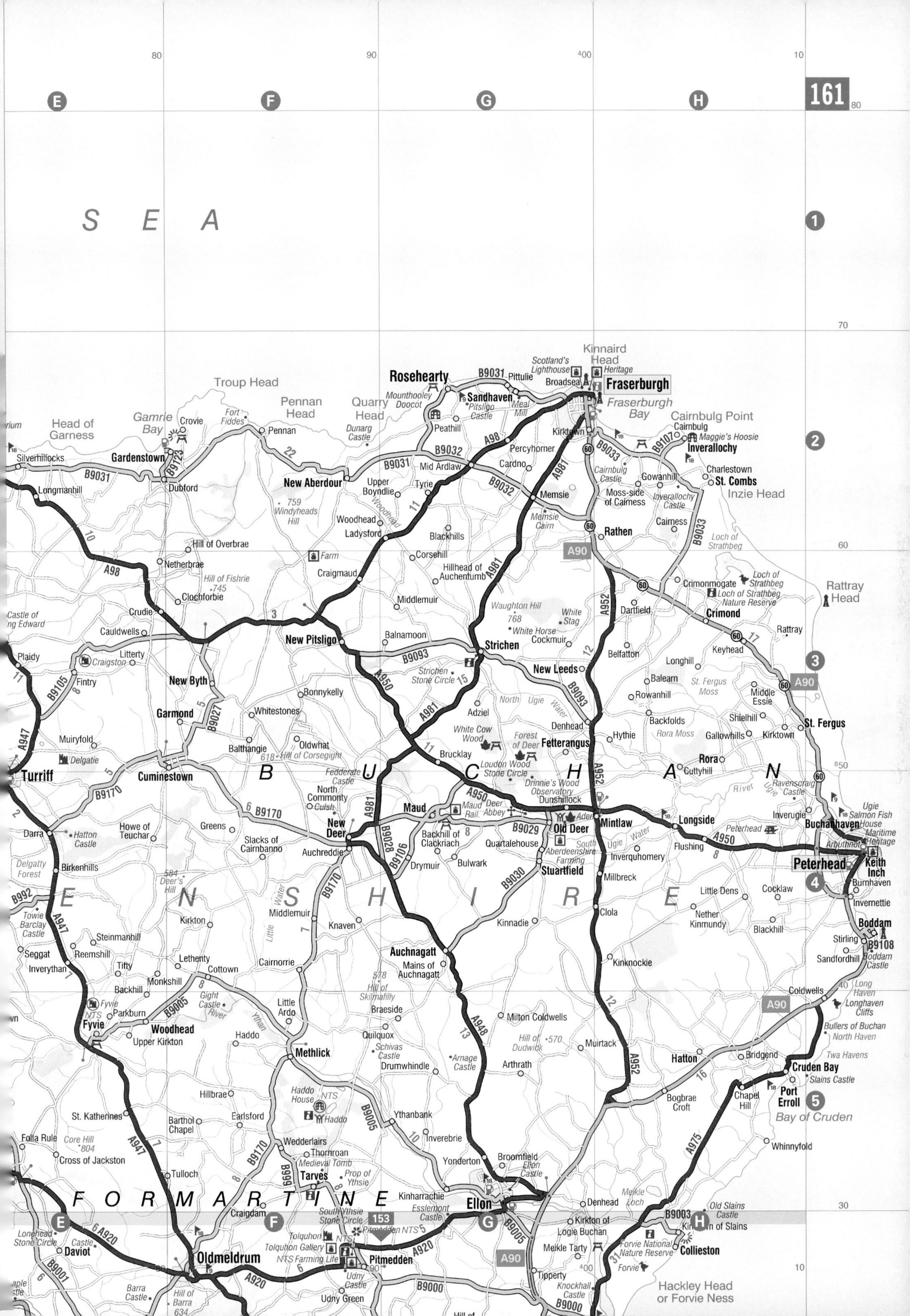

SEA
Troup Head
Pennan Head
Quarry Head
Head of Garness
Gamrie Bay
Rosehearty
Sandhaven
Fraserburgh
Fraserburgh Bay
Kinnaird Head
Scotland's Lighthouse
Heritage
Broadsea
Pittulie
Mounthooley Doocot
Pitsligo Castle
Meal Mill
Cairnbulg Point
Cairnbulg
Maggie's Hoosie
Inverallochy
Charlestown
St. Combs
Inzie Head
Crovie
Fort Fiddes
Pennan
Dunarg Castle
Peathill
Silverhillocks
Gardenstown
Dubford
New Aberdour
Upper Boyndlie
Tyrie
Mid Ardlaw
Percyhorner
Cardno
Kirktown
Memsie
Memsie Cairn
Cairnbulg Castle
Gowanhill
Moss-side of Cairness
Inverallochy Castle
Cairness
Rathen
Loch of Strathbeg
Longmanhill
759 Windyheads Hill
Woodhead
Ladysford
Blackhills
Hill of Overbrae
Farm
Corsehill
Netherbrae
Craigmaud
Hillhead of Auchentumb
Hill of Fishrie 745
Clochforbie
Middlemuir
Waughton Hill 768
White Stag
White Horse
Cockmuir
Dartfield
Crimonmogate
Loch of Strathbeg Nature Reserve
Crimond
Rattray Head
Rattray
Keyhead
Crudie
Cauldwells
New Pitsligo
Balnamoon
Strichen
Belfatton
Longhill
Castle of King Edward
Plaidy
Litterty
Craigston
Fintry
New Byth
Strichen Stone Circle
New Leeds
Balearn
St. Fergus Moss
Middle Essie
Rowanhill
Bonnykelly
Garmond
Whitestones
Adziel
North Ugie Water
Denhead
Hythie
Backfolds
Rora Moss
Shielhill
Gallowhills
Kirktown
St. Fergus
Muiryfold
Delgatie
Balthangie
Oldwhat
618 Hill of Corsegight
White Cow Wood
Forest of Deer
Fetterangus
Bruckley
Loudon Wood Stone Circle
Rora
Cuttyhill
Turriff
Cuminestown
BUCHAN
Fedderate Castle
North Commonty
Culsh
Maud
Maud Rail.
Deer Abbey
Drinnie's Wood Observatory
Dunshillock
River Ugie
Ravenscraig Castle
Inverugie
Ugie Salmon Fish House
Buchanhaven
Maritime Heritage
Arbuthnot
Peterhead
Keith Inch
Howe of Teuchar
Greens
Slacks of Cairnbanno
New Deer
Auchreddie
Backhill of Clackriach
Drymuir
Bulwark
Quartalehouse
Aden
Old Deer
Mintlaw
South Aberdeenshire Farming
Stuartfield
Longside
Peterhead
Flushing
Ugie Water
Inverquhomery
Darra
Hatton Castle
Birkenhills
Delgatty Forest
584 Deer's Hill
Millbreck
Burnhaven
Invernettie
ABERDEENSHIRE
Towie Barclay Castle
Kirkton
Middlemuir
Little Water
Knaven
Kinnadie
Clola
Little Dens
Nether Kinmundy
Cocklaw
Boddam
Blackhill
Steinmanhill
Seggat
Reemshill
Inverythan
Tifty
Lethenty
Cottown
Cairnorrie
Auchnagatt
Mains of Auchnagatt
Kinknockie
Stirling
Sandfordhill
Boddam Castle
578 Hill of Skilmafilly
Backhill
Monkshill
Fyvie
NTS
Parkburn
Gight Castle
River Ythan
Little Ardo
Braeside
Milton Coldwells
Coldwells
Long Haven
Longhaven Cliffs
Fyvie
Woodhead
Upper Kirkton
Haddo
Quilquox
Schivas Castle
Methlick
Drumwhindle
Arnage Castle
Hill of Dudwick 570
Muirtack
Bullers of Buchan
North Haven
Twa Havens
Hatton
Bridgend
Cruden Bay
Slains Castle
Arthrath
Port Erroll
Bay of Cruden
Hillbrae
Haddo House NTS
Haddo
Bogbrae Croft
Chapel Hill
St. Katherines
Earlsford
Barthol Chapel
Ythanbank
Inverebrie
Folla Rule
Core Hill 804
Cross of Jackston
Wedderlairs
Thornroan Medieval Tomb
Whinnyfold
Tulloch
Tarves
Prop of Ythsie
Yonderton
Broomfield
Ellon Castle
FORMARTINE
Kinharrachie
Esslemont Castle
Ellon
Meikle Loch
Denhead
Old Slains Castle
Kirkton of Slains
Craigdam
South Ythsie Stone Circle
Pitmedden NTS
Kirkton of Logie Buchan
Lonehead Stone Circle
Castle
Daviot
Tolquhon
Tolquhon Gallery
NTS Farming Life
Pitmedden
Meikle Tarty
Forvie National Nature Reserve
Collieston
Forvie
Oldmeldrum
Udny Castle
Tipperty
Knockhall Castle
Hackley Head or Forvie Ness
Barra Castle
Hill of Barra 634
Udny Green
153

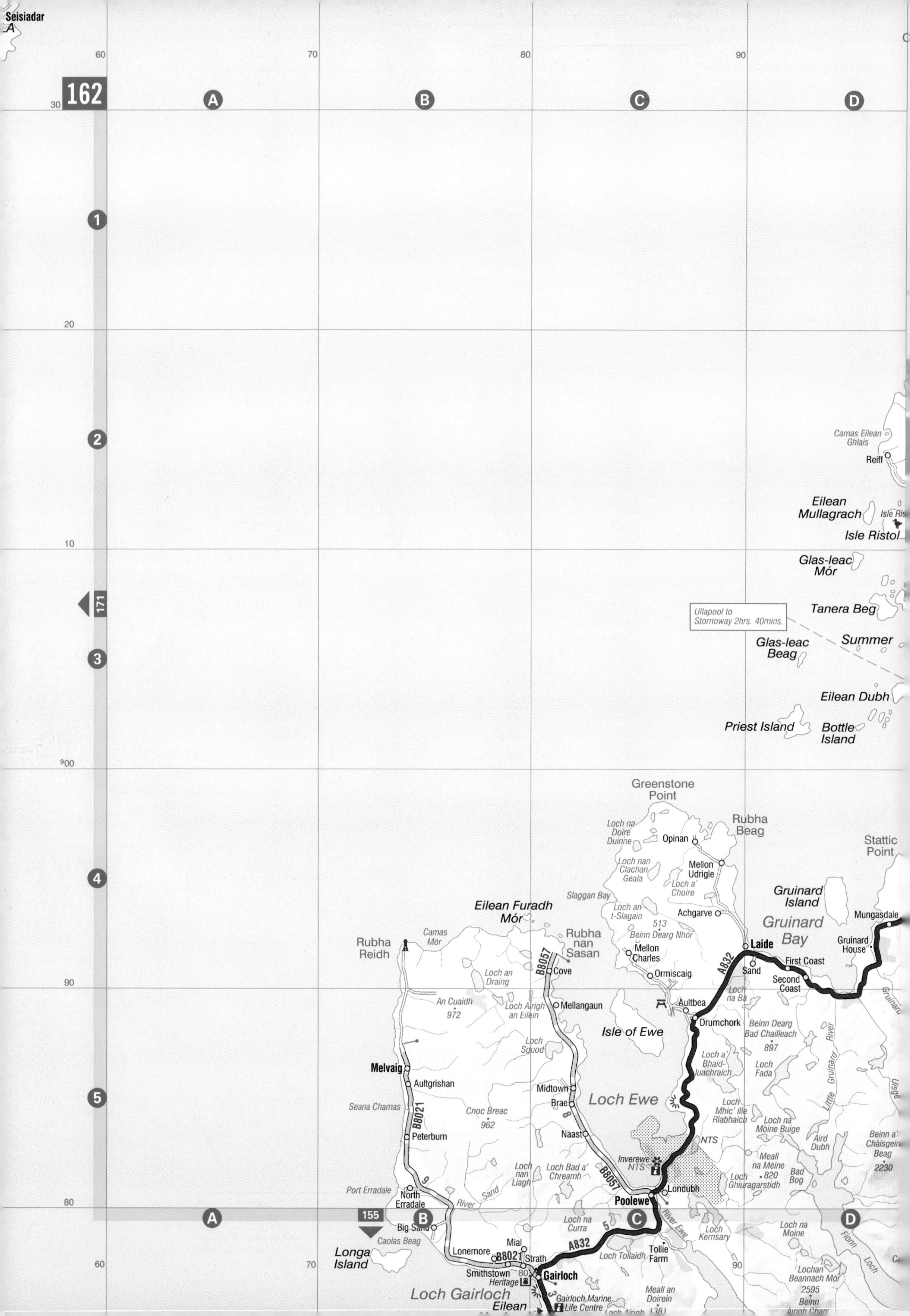

Seisiadar
A

60   70   80   90

Ⓐ   Ⓑ   Ⓒ   Ⓓ

30

20

❶

10

20

171

❷

10

Reiff

Camas Eilean Ghlais

Eilean Mullagrach   Isle Ris

Isle Ristol

Glas-leac Mór

Ullapool to
Stornoway 2hrs. 40mins.

Tanera Beg

Summer

❸

900

Glas-leac Beag

Eilean Dubh

Priest Island   Bottle Island

Greenstone Point

Rubha Beag

Stattic Point

Loch na Doire Duinne

Opinan

Mellon Udrigle

❹

Loch nan Clachan Geala

Gruinard Island

Mungasdale

Loch a' Choire

Slaggan Bay

Achgarve

Gruinard Bay

90

Eilean Furadh Mór

Loch an t-Slagain

513
Beinn Dearg Nhòr

Mellon Charles

Laide

Gruinard House

Rubha Reidh

Camas Mór

Rubha nan Sasan

B8057

Cove

Ormiscaig

First Coast

Sand   Second Coast

A832

Loch na Bà

Loch Airigh an Eilein

Mellangaun

Aultbea

Little Gruinard River

An Cuaidh
972

Isle of Ewe

Drumchork

Beinn Dearg Bad Chailleach
897

Gruinard River

Loch Sguod

Loch a' Bhaid-luachraich

Loch Fada

Melvaig

Aultgrishan

Cnoc Breac
962

Midtown

Brae

Loch Ewe

Loch Mhic' ille Riabhaich

Loch na Mòine Buige

Aird Dubh

Beinn a' Chàisgein Beag
2230

❺

B8021

Seana Chamas

Naast

NTS

Meall na Mèine
820

Bad Bog

Loch Ghiuragarstidh

Peterburn

Inverewe
NTS

Londubh

Loch na Mòine

Loch Bad a' Chreamh

B8057

B8057

Loch Kernsary

Port Erradale

North Erradale

9

River Sand

Loch nan Liagh

Poolewe

5

River Ewe

80

155

Ⓐ

60

Ⓑ

Big Sand

70

A832

Loch na Curra

Ⓒ

Tollie Farm

Loch na Mòine

Ⓓ

90

Lochan Beannach Mór
2595

Longa Island

Caolas Beag

Lonemore

Mial

B8021

Strath

80

Smithstown
Heritage

Gairloch

Loch Tollaidh

Meall an Doirein

Beinn Airigh Charr

Loch Gairloch

Eilean

Gairloch Marine
Life Centre

3

Loch Airigh

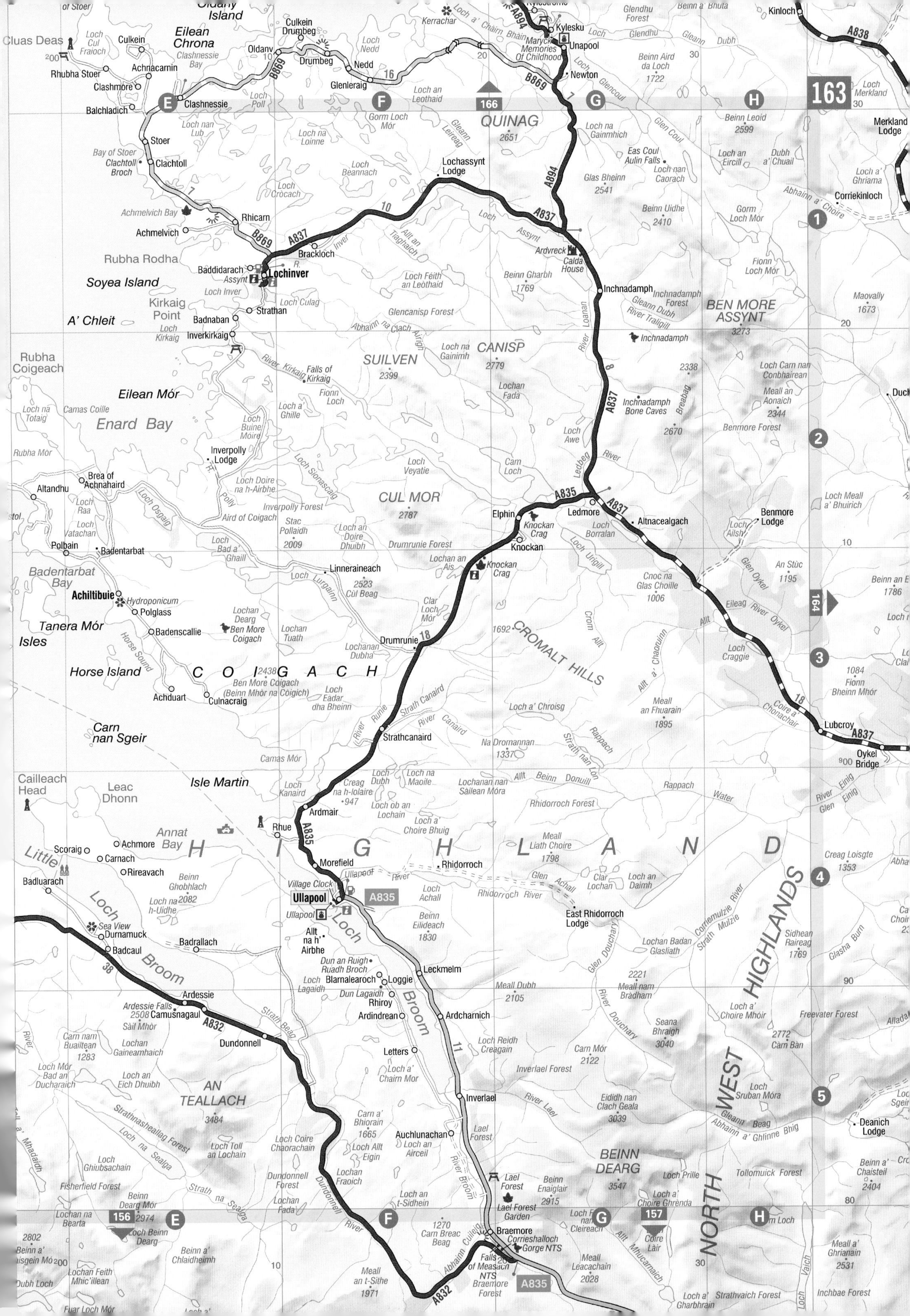

163
166
164
156
157
Lochinver
Ullapool
Achiltibuie
QUINAG
CANISP
SUILVEN
CUL MOR
BEN MORE ASSYNT
CROMALT HILLS
COIGACH
HIGHLAND
NORTH WEST HIGHLANDS
AN TEALLACH
BEINN DEARG
Enard Bay
Loch Broom
Little Loch Broom
Kylesku
Unapool
Inchnadamph
Ledmore
Elphin
Knockan
Drumrunie
Strathcanaird
Ardmair
Rhue
Morefield
Leckmelm
Ardcharnich
Inverlael
Braemore
Dundonnell
Lubcroy
Oykel Bridge
Altnacealgach
Stoer
Clachtoll
Clashnessie
Drumbeg
Nedd
Glenleraig
Rhicarn
Achmelvich
Strathan
Inverkirkaig
Polbain
Badentarbat
Polglass
Badenscallie
Achduart
Culnacraig
Scoraig
Achmore
Carnach
Badluarach
Durnamuck
Badcaul
Badrallach
Ardessie
Camusnagaul
Letters
Auchlunachan
Rhidorroch
East Rhidorroch Lodge
Deanich Lodge
Benmore Lodge
Merkland Lodge
Kinloch
A835
A837
A832
A894
A838
B869

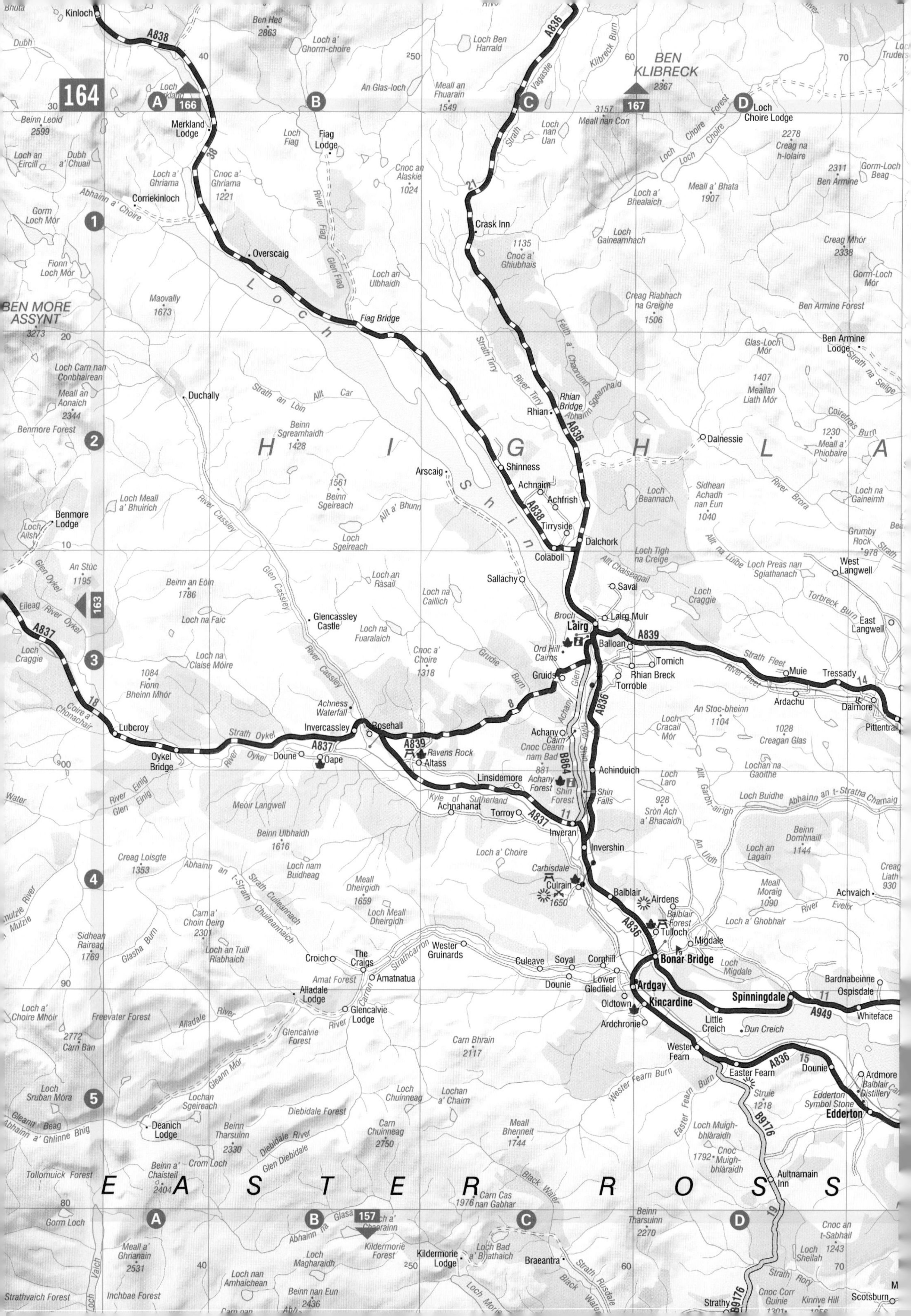

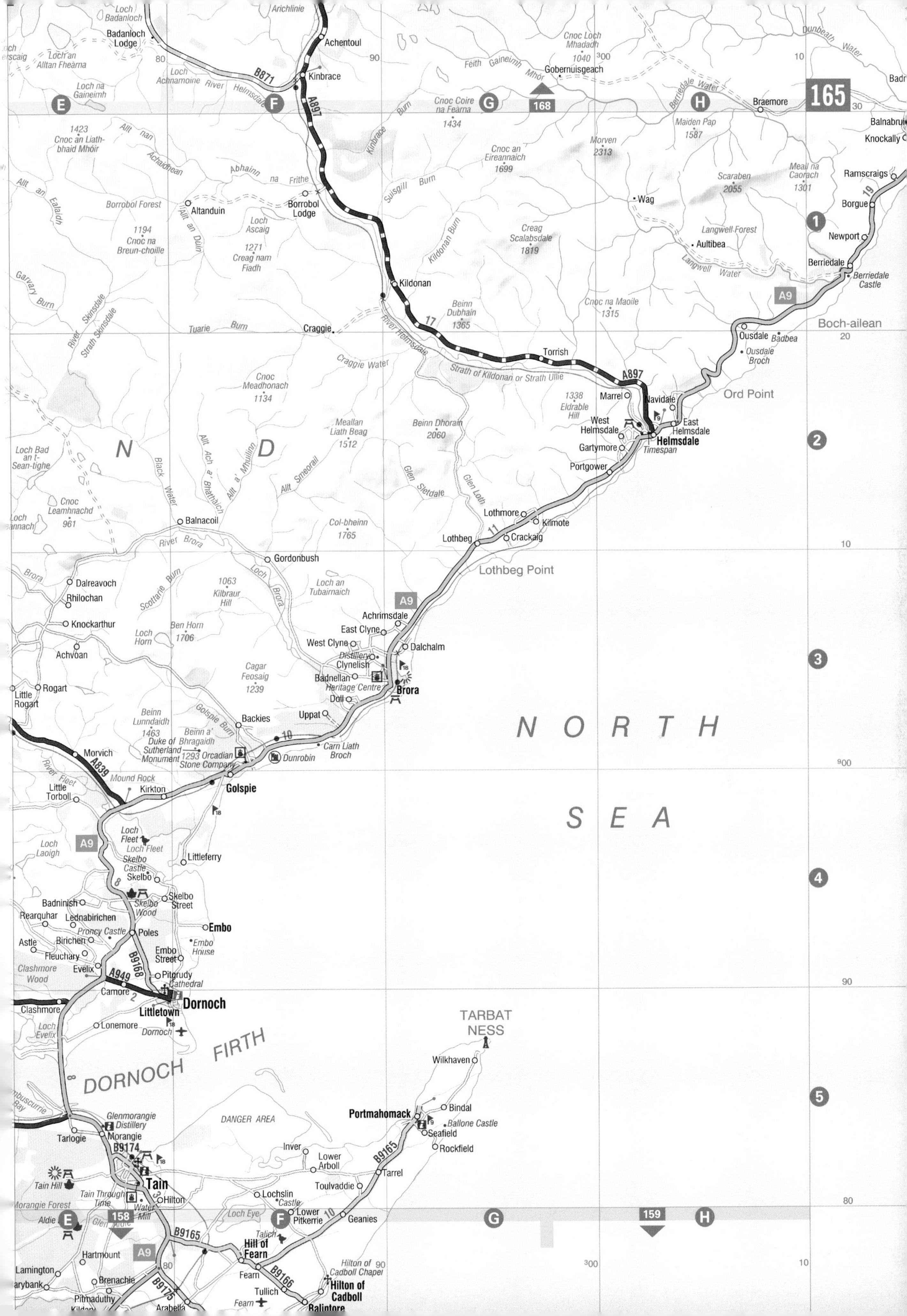
165
168
159
158
NORTH SEA
DORNOCH FIRTH
TARBAT NESS
Helmsdale
Brora
Golspie
Dornoch
Tain
Portmahomack
Kinbrace
Achentoul
Kildonan
Borrobol Lodge
Altanduin
Craggie
Torrish
Marrel
Navidale
West Helmsdale
East Helmsdale
Gartymore
Portgower
Lothmore
Kilmote
Lothbeg
Crackaig
Lothbeg Point
Ord Point
Ousdale
Badbea
Berriedale
Berriedale Castle
Newport
Borgue
Ramscraigs
Knockally
Balnabruich
Braemore
Wag
Aultibea
Gobernuisgeach
Balnacoil
Gordonbush
Dalreavoch
Rhilochan
Knockarthur
Achvoan
Rogart
Little Rogart
Achrimsdale
East Clyne
West Clyne
Dalchalm
Clynelish
Badnellan
Doll
Uppat
Backies
Morvich
Kirkton
Little Torboll
Littleferry
Skelbo
Skelbo Street
Embo
Embo Street
Pitgrudy
Poles
Badninish
Rearquhar
Lednabirichen
Astle
Birichen
Fleuchary
Evelix
Camore
Clashmore
Littletown
Lonemore
Wilkhaven
Bindal
Seafield
Rockfield
Inver
Lower Arboll
Tarrel
Toulvaddie
Lochslin
Lower Pitkerrie
Geanies
Hilton
Tarlogie
Morangie
Hartmount
Lamington
Brenachie
Pitmaduthy
Arabella
Hill of Fearn
Fearn
Tullich
Hilton of Cadboll
Balintore
A9
A897
A839
A949
B871
B9168
B9174
B9165
B9166
B9175
Boch-ailean
Badanloch Lodge
Loch Badanloch
Arichlinie
Strath of Kildonan or Strath Ullie
Morven 2313
Scaraben 2055
Maiden Pap 1587
Langwell Forest
Borrobol Forest
Carn Liath Broch
Dunrobin
Orcadian Stone Company
Duke of Sutherland Monument
Mound Rock
Loch Fleet
Skelbo Castle
Skelbo Wood
Proncy Castle
Embo House
Cathedral
Dornoch
Glenmorangie Distillery
Tain Hill
Tain Through Time
Water Mill
Ballone Castle
Lochslin Castle
Talich
Fearn
Hilton of Cadboll Chapel
DANGER AREA
Heritage Centre
Distillery
Timespan
E F G H
1 2 3 4 5

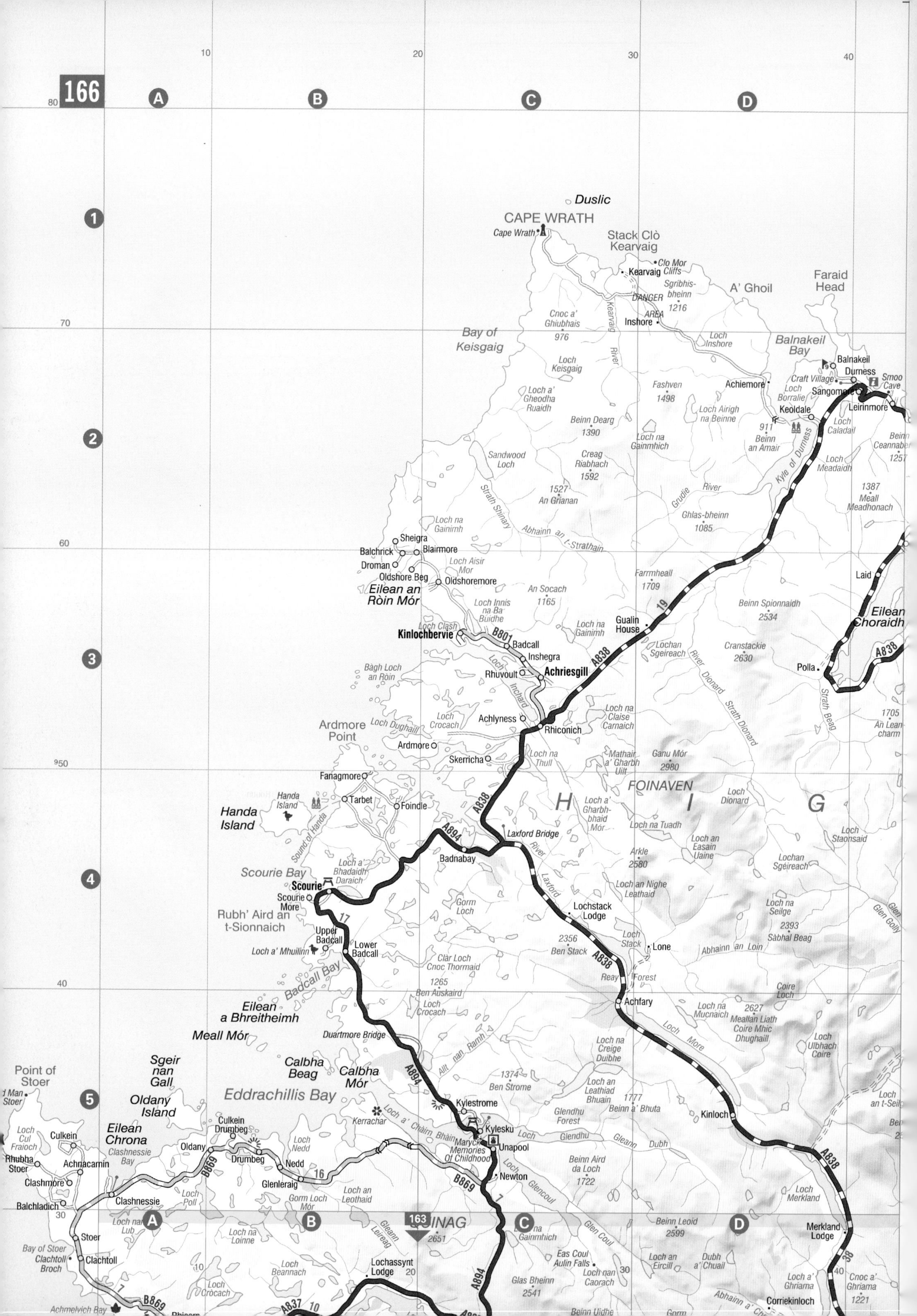

A
B
C
D
1
2
3
4
5
10
20
30
40
80
70
60
50
40
Duslic
CAPE WRATH
Cape Wrath
Stack Clò Kearvaig
Clo Mor Cliffs
Kearvaig
Sgribhis-bheinn 1216
DANGER AREA
A' Ghoil
Faraid Head
Inshore
Bay of Keisgaig
Cnoc a' Ghiubhais 976
Kearvaig River
Loch Inshore
Balnakeil Bay
Balnakeil
Durness
Smoo Cave
Craft Village
Loch Borralie
Sangomore
Leirinmore
Loch Keisgaig
Fashven 1498
Achiemore
Loch a' Gheodha Ruaidh
Loch Airigh na Beinne
Keoldale
911 Beinn an Amair
Loch Caladail
Beinn Ceannabeinne 1257
Beinn Dearg 1390
Loch na Gainmhich
Creag Riabhach 1592
Sandwood Loch
Kyle of Durness
Loch Meadaidh
Grudie River
1387 Meall Meadhonach
1527 An Grianan
Strath Shinary
Glhas-bheinn 1085
Loch na Gainimh
Abhainn an t-Strathain
Sheigra
Balchrick
Blairmore
Droman
Loch Aisir Mor
Oldshore Beg
Oldshoremore
Eilean an Ròin Mór
Farrmheall 1709
An Socach 1165
Laid
Loch Innis na Ba Buidhe
Beinn Spionnaidh 2534
Eilean Choraidh
Loch Clash
Kinlochbervie
B801
Badcall
Inshegra
Loch na Gainimh
Gualin House
Lochan Sgeireach
Cranstackie 2630
A838
Bàgh Loch an Ròin
Loch Inchard
Rhuvoult
Achriesgill
River Dionard
Polla
Strath Dionard
Strath Beag
Loch Dughaill
Loch Crocach
Achlyness
Rhiconich
Loch na Claise Carnaich
1705 An Lean-charm
Ardmore Point
Ardmore
Skerricha
Loch na Thull
Mathair a' Gharbh Uilt
Ganu Mór 2980
Fanagmore
FOINAVEN
H I G
Handa Island
Tarbet
Foindle
Loch a' Gharbh-bhaid Mór
Loch Dionard
Sound of Handa
Laxford Bridge
Loch na Tuadh
A894
Badnabay
River Laxford
Arkle 2580
Loch an Easain Uaine
Loch Staonsaid
Scourie Bay
Loch a' Bhadaidh Daraich
Lochan Sgeireach
Scourie
Scourie More
Loch an Nighe Leathaid
Gorm Loch
Lochstack Lodge
Loch na Seilge
Rubh' Aird an t-Sionnaich
2393 Sàbhal Beag
Glen Golly
Upper Badcall
Lower Badcall
Loch a' Mhuilinn
2356 Ben Stack
Loch Stack
Lone
Abhainn an Loin
Badcall Bay
Clàr Loch
Cnoc Thormaid
Reay Forest
1265 Ben Auskaird
Coire Loch
Eilean a Bhreitheimh
Loch Crocach
Achfary
Loch na Mucnaich
2627 Meallan Liath Coire Mhic Dhughaill
Meall Mór
Duartmore Bridge
Loch More
Loch na Creige Duibhe
Loch Ulbhach Coire
Point of Stoer
Sgeir nan Gall
Calbha Beag
Calbha Mór
Allt nan Ramh
1374 Ben Strome
Loch an Leathiad Bhuain
1777 Beinn a' Bhuta
Loch an t-Seilg
Oldany Island
Eddrachillis Bay
Kylestrome
Kinloch
Kerrachar
Loch a' Chàirn Bhàin
Kylesku
Glendhu Forest
Loch Glendhu
Gleann Dubh
Eilean Chrona
Culkein Drumbeg
Loch Cul Fraioch
Culkein
Loch Nedd
Maryck Memories Of Childhood
Unapool
Rhubha Stoer
Achnacarnin
Clashnessie Bay
Oldany
Drumbeg
Nedd
Clashmore
B869
Glenleraig
16
Newton
Beinn Aird da Loch 1722
Loch Glencoul
Balchladich
Clashnessie
Loch Poll
Gorm Loch Mór
Loch an Leothaid
Loch Merkland
Loch nan Lub
163
QUINAG
2651
Gleann Leireag
Loch na Gainmhich
Glen Coul
Beinn Leoid 2599
Merkland Lodge
Stoer
Loch na Loinne
Bay of Stoer
Clachtoll Broch
Clachtoll
Loch Beannach
Lochassynt Lodge
Eas Coul Aulin Falls
Loch nan Caorach
Loch an Eircill
Dubh a' Chuail
Loch a' Ghriama
Cnoc a' Ghriama 1221
Loch Cròcach
Glas Bheinn 2541
Corriekinloch
Achmelvich Bay
A837
Beinn Uidhe
Gorm
Abhainn a' Ch
A838

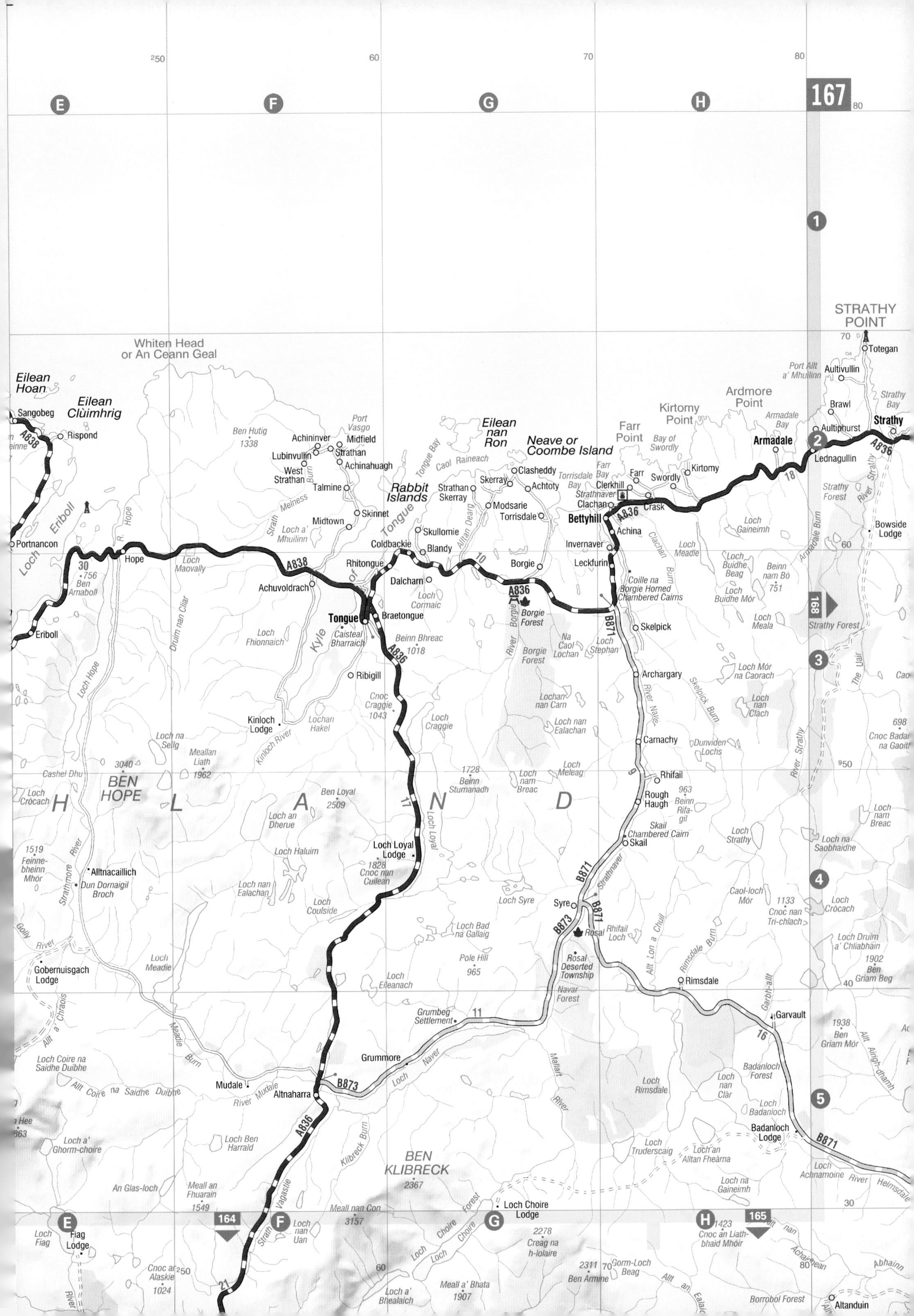
E
F
G
H
1
2
3
4
5
STRATHY POINT
Totegan
Port Allt a' Mhuilinn
Aultivullin
Strathy Bay
Brawl
Strathy
Aultiphurst
Armadale Bay
Ardmore Point
Kirtomy Point
Farr Point
Bay of Swordly
Armadale
Lednagullin
A836
Kirtomy
Swordly
Farr
Farr Bay
Torrisdale Bay
Clerkhill
Strathnaver
Clachan
Crask
Bettyhill
Achina
Invernaver
Leckfurin
Borgie
Whiten Head or An Ceann Geal
Eilean Hoan
Eilean Clùimhrig
Sangobeg
Rispond
A838
Ben Hutig 1338
Port Vasgo
Achininver
Midfield
Lubinvullin
Strathan
Achinahaugh
West Strathan
Talmine
Skinnet
Midtown
Strath Melness
Loch a' Mhuilinn
Eilean nan Ron
Neave or Coombe Island
Caol Raineach
Tongue Bay
Rabbit Islands
Strathan Skerray
Skerray
Clasheddy
Achtoty
Modsarie
Torrisdale
Skullomie
Coldbackie
Blandy
Rhitongue
Dalcharn
Loch Cormaic
Achuvoldrach
Tongue
Braetongue
Caisteal Bharraich
Kyle of Tongue
Beinn Bhreac 1018
Ribigill
Portnancon
Loch Eriboll
Hope
Loch Maovally
Ben Arnaboll 756
Eriboll
Loch Hope
Druim nan Cliar
Loch Fhionnaich
Borgie Forest
Na Caol Lochan
Loch Stephan
Coille na Borgie Horned Chambered Cairns
Skelpick
Archargary
River Naver
Skelpick Burn
Loch Mòr na Caorach
Loch nan Clach
Loch Gaineimh
Loch Meadie
Loch Buidhe Beag
Beinn nam Bò 751
Loch Buidhe Mòr
Loch Meala
Strathy Forest
Bowside Lodge
168
Armadale Burn
River Strathy
The Uair
Cnoc Craggie 1043
Loch Craggie
Lochan nan Carn
Loch nan Ealachan
Kinloch Lodge
Kinloch River
Lochan Hakel
Loch na Seilg
Meallan Liath 1962
3040
BEN HOPE
Cashel Dhu
Loch Crocach
H
L
A
N
D
Ben Loyal 2509
1728 Beinn Stumanadh
Loch nam Breac
Loch Meleag
Carnachy
Dunviden Lochs
Rhifail
Rough Haugh
963 Beinn Rifa-gil
Skail Chambered Cairn
Skail
Loch Strathy
Loch nam Breac
Loch na Saobhaidhe
698 Cnoc Badar na Gaoith
Loch an Dherue
Loch Haluim
Loch Loyal Lodge
Loch Loyal
1828 Cnoc nan Cuilean
1519 Feinne-bheinn Mhòr
Strathmore River
Alltnacaillich
Dun Dornaigil Broch
Loch nan Ealachan
Loch Coulside
Loch Syre
Syre
Strathnaver
B871
B873
Rosal
Rhifail Loch
Caol-loch Mòr
1133 Cnoc nan Tri-chlach
Loch Crocach
Loch Druim a' Chliabhain
1902 Ben Griam Beg
Loch Bad na Gallaig
Pole Hill 965
Rosal Deserted Township
Allt Lon a Chuil
Rimsdale Burn
Rimsdale
Golly River
Gobernuisgach Lodge
Loch Meadie
Loch Eileanach
Navar Forest
Garbh-allt
Garvault
1938 Ben Griam Mòr
Allt Airigh-dhamh
Grumbeg Settlement
Allt a' Chraois
Meadie Burn
Loch Coire na Saidhe Duibhe
Allt Coire na Saidhe Duibhe
Grummore
Loch Naver
Mallart River
Loch Rimsdale
Badanloch Forest
Loch nan Clàr
Loch Badanloch
Badanloch Lodge
Mudale
River Mudale
Altnaharra
Hee 863
Loch a' Ghorm-choire
Loch Ben Harrald
Kilbreck Burn
BEN KLIBRECK 2367
Loch Truderscaig
Loch an Alltan Fheàrna
Loch Achnamoine
River Helmsdale
An Glas-loch
Meall an Fhuarain 1549
Strath Vagastie
Meall nan Con 3157
Loch Choire Forest
Loch Choire Lodge
Loch na Gaineimh
164
165
Loch Fiag
Fiag Lodge
Loch nan Uan
Loch Choire
2278 Creag na h-Iolaire
1423 Cnoc an Liath-bhaid Mhòir
Allt nan Achaidhean
Abhainn
Cnoc an Alaskie 1024
River
Loch a' Bhealaich
Meall a' Bhata 1907
2311 Ben Armine
Gorm-Loch Beag
Allt an Ealaich
Borrobol Forest
Altanduin
250
60
70
80
50
40
30

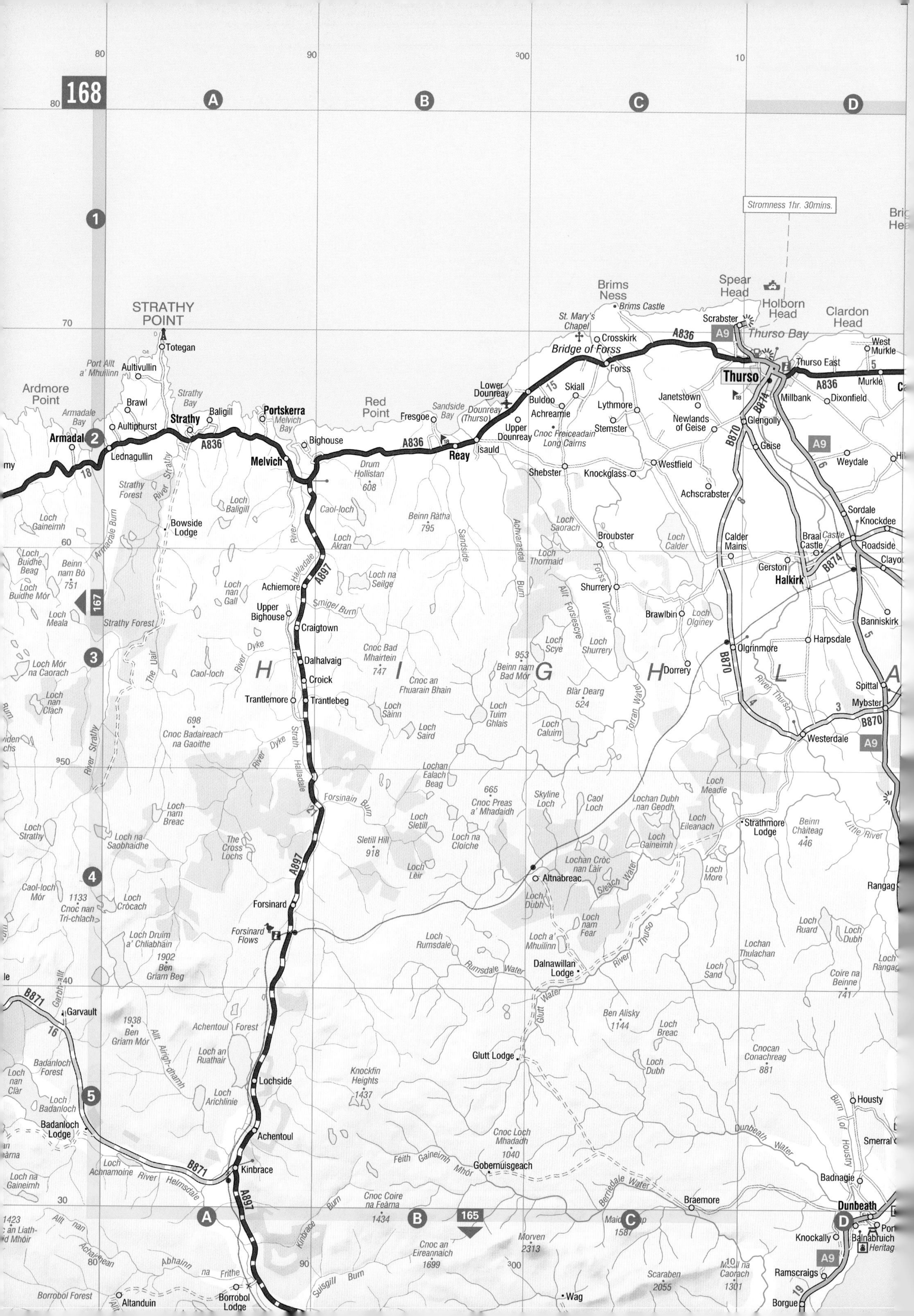
STRATHY POINT
Totegan
Port Allt a' Mhuilinn
Aultivullin
Ardmore Point
Armadale Bay
Brawl
Strathy Bay
Strathy
Baligill
Portskerra
Melvich Bay
Aultiphurst
Armadale
Lednagullin
A836
Melvich
Bighouse
Red Point
Fresgoe
Sandside Bay
Dounreay (Thurso)
Lower Dounreay
Reay
Isauld
Upper Dounrey
Brims Ness
Brims Castle
St. Mary's Chapel
Crosskirk
Bridge of Forss
Forss
Buldoo
Skiall
Achreamie
Lythmore
Cnoc Freiceadain Long Cairns
Stemster
Spear Head
Holborn Head
Scrabster
Thurso Bay
Stromness 1hr. 30mins.
Clardon Head
West Murkle
Thurso
Thurso East
Murkle
Millbank
Dixonfield
Janetstown
Newlands of Geise
Glengolly
Geise
Weydale
Westfield
Shebster
Knockglass
Achscrabster
Strathy Forest
River Strathy
Loch Baligill
Bowside Lodge
Drum Hollistan 608
Caol-loch
Loch Akran
Beinn Ràtha 795
Sandside
Achvarasdal Burn
Loch Saorach
Broubster
Loch Calder
Calder Mains
Sordale
Knockdee
Braal Castle
Roadside
Gerston
Halkirk
Clayoc
Loch Thormaid
Loch Gaineimh
Loch Buidhe Beag
Beinn nam Bò 751
Loch Buidhe Mòr
Loch Meala
Armadale Burn
Loch nan Gall
Achiemore
Halladale River
A897
Loch na Seilge
Upper Bighouse
Smigel Burn
Craigtown
Forss Water
Allt Forsiescye
Shurrery
Brawlbin
Loch Olginey
Banniskirk
Harpsdale
Olgrinmore
B870
B874
Loch Scye
Loch Shurrery
Dorrery
Loch Mòr na Caorach
Dalhalvaig
Croick
Cnoc Bad Mhairtein 747
Cnoc an Fhuarain Bhain
Beinn nam Bad Mòr 953
Blàr Dearg 524
River Thurso
Spittal
Mybster
Westerdale
A9
Loch nan Clàch
The Uair
River Dyke
Caol-loch
Trantlemore
Trantlebeg
Loch Sàinn
Loch Tuim Ghlais
Torran Water
Loch Calum
698
Cnoc Badaireach na Gaoithe
Loch Saird
Strath Halladale
Lochan Ealach Beag
665 Cnoc Preas a' Mhadaidh
Skyline Loch
Caol Loch
Lochan Dubh nan Geodh
Loch Meadie
Forsinain Burn
Loch nam Breac
Loch Sletill
Sletill Hill 918
Loch na Cloiche
Loch Eileanach
Strathmore Lodge
Beinn Chàiteag 446
Little River
Loch Strathy
Loch na Saobhaidhe
The Cross Lochs
Loch Lèir
Loch Gaineimh
Lochan Cròc nan Làir
Altnabreac
Sleach Water
Loch More
Rangag
Caol-loch Mòr
1133 Cnoc nan Tri-chlach
Loch Cròcach
Forsinard
Loch Dubh
Loch nam Fear
Forsinard Flows
Loch Druim a' Chliabhain
1902 Ben Griam Beg
Loch Rumsdale
Loch a' Mhuilinn
Rumsdale Water
Dalnawillan Lodge
Lochan Thulachan
Loch Ruard
Loch Dubh
Loch Sand
Coire na Beinne 741
Loch Rangag
B871
Garvault
Glutt Water
Ben Alisky 1144
Loch Breac
1938 Ben Griam Mòr
Achentoul Forest
Allt Airigh-dhamh
Loch an Ruathair
Cnocan Conachreag 881
Glutt Lodge
Loch Dubh
Badanloch Forest
Loch nan Clàr
Lochside
Knockfin Heights 1437
Loch Arichlinie
Loch Badanloch
Houtsy
Burn of Houstry
Badanloch Lodge
Achentoul
Cnoc Loch Mhadadh 1040
Dunbeath Water
Smerral
Loch Achnamoine
River Helmsdale
Kinbrace
Fèith Gaineimh Mhòr
Gobernuisgeach
Badnagie
Loch na Gaineimh
Berriedale Water
Braemore
Dunbeath
1423 Cnoc an Liath-bhaid Mhòir
Allt nan Ach'-Fhean
Kinbrace Burn
Cnoc Coire na Fearna 1434
165
Maiden Pap 1587
Knockally
Balnabruich
Heritage
Cnoc an Eireannaich 1699
Morven 2313
Abhainn na Frithe
Suisgill Burn
Scaraben 2055
Meall na Caorach 1301
Ramscaigs
Borrobol Forest
Altanduin
Borrobol Lodge
Wag
Borgue
167
H I G H L A
A B C D
1 2 3 4 5
80 90 300 10
70 60 950 40 30

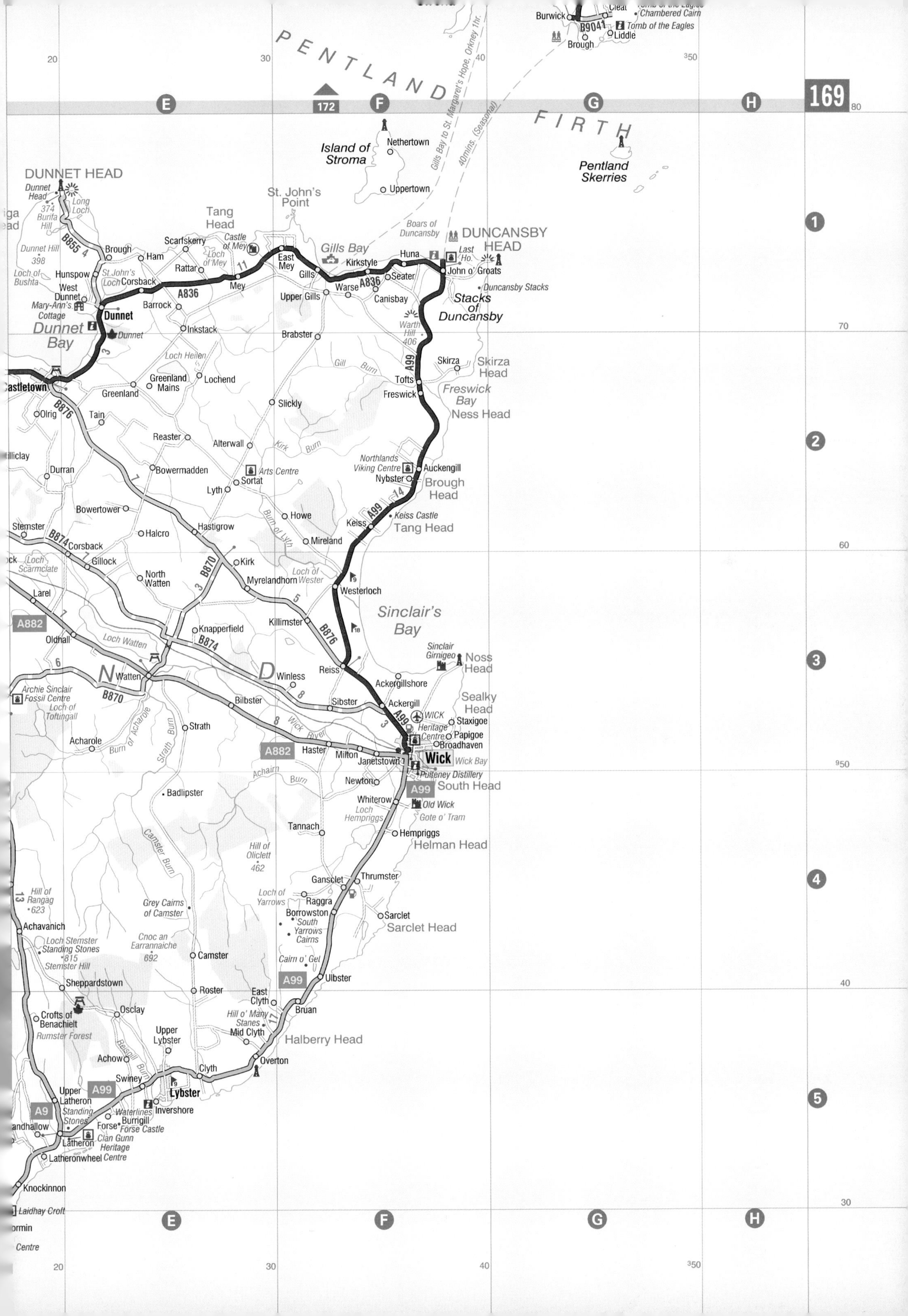
PENTLAND FIRTH
Island of Stroma
Nethertown
Uppertown
Pentland Skerries
DUNNET HEAD
St. John's Point
Tang Head
Gills Bay
DUNCANSBY HEAD
John o' Groats
Stacks of Duncansby
Dunnet
Dunnet Bay
Castletown
Skirza Head
Freswick Bay
Ness Head
Brough Head
Tang Head
Sinclair's Bay
Noss Head
Sealky Head
Wick
Wick Bay
South Head
Helman Head
Sarclet Head
Halberry Head
Lybster
Watten
Burwick
Brough
Liddle
Tomb of the Eagles
Castle of Mey
Mey
Keiss
Westerloch
Reiss
Ackergillshore
Ackergill
Staxigoe
Papigoe
Broadhaven
Thrumster
Ulbster
Bruan
Clyth
Latheron
Latheronwheel
Knockinnon
A99
A836
A882
A9
B876
B874
B870
B855
B9041
172

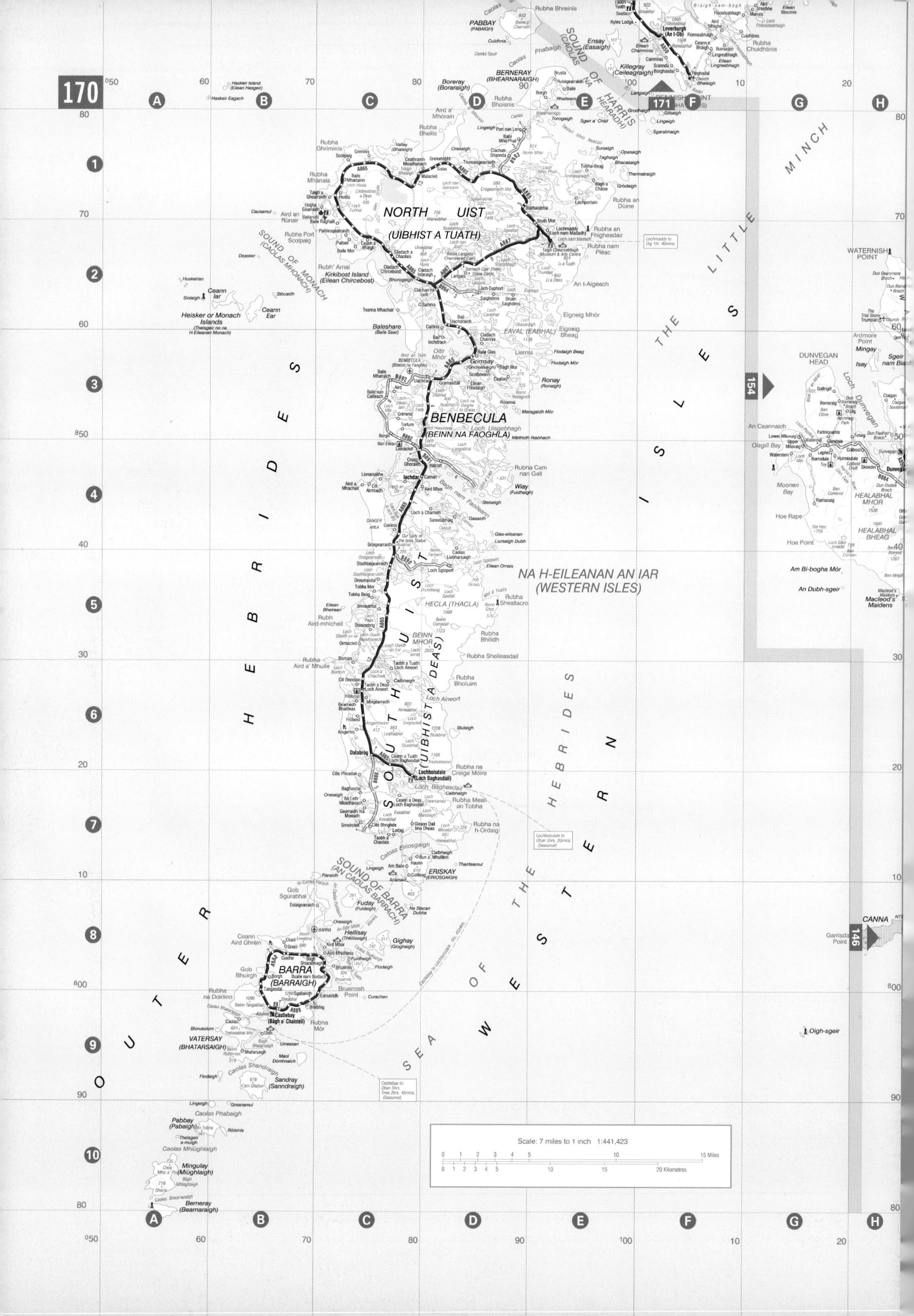

NORTH UIST
(UIBHIST A TUATH)
BENBECULA
(BEINN NA FAOGHLA)
SOUTH UIST
(UIBHIST A DEAS)
BARRA
(BARRAIGH)
NA H-EILEANAN AN IAR
(WESTERN ISLES)
OUTER HEBRIDES
THE LITTLE MINCH
SEA OF THE HEBRIDES
WESTERN ISLES
SOUND OF HARRIS
(CAOLAS NA HEARADH)
SOUND OF MONACH
(CAOLAS MHONACH)
SOUND OF BARRA
(AN CAOLAS BARRACH)
PABBAY
(PABAIGH)
BERNERAY
(BHEARNARAIGH)
Boreray
(Boraraigh)
Ensay
(Easaigh)
Killegray
(Ceilleagraigh)
Leverburgh
(An t-Ob)
Rubha Bhreinis
Heisker or Monach Islands
(Theisgeir no na H-Eileanan Monach)
Ceann Iar
Ceann Ear
Haskeir Island
(Eilean Hasgeir)
Haskeir Eagach
Causamul
Rubha Ghriminis
Rubha Mhanais
Rubha Port Scolpaig
Rubh' Arnal
Kirkibost Island
(Eilean Chirceboist)
Lochmaddy
(Loch nam Madadh)
Rubha an Fhigheadair
Rubha nam Pleac
Rubha an Dùine
An t-Algeach
Eigneig Mhòr
Eigneig Bheag
EAVAL (EABHAL)
Baleshare
(Baile Sear)
Grimsay
(Griomasaigh)
Ronay
(Ronaigh)
Liernis
Flodaigh Beag
Flodaigh Mòr
Oitir Mhòr
Rubha Cam nan Gall
Wiay
(Fuidhaigh)
HECLA (THACLA)
BEINN MHOR
Rubha Sheallacro
Rubha Bhìlidh
Rubha Sheileasdail
Rubha Bholuim
Loch Aineort
Stulaigh
Rubha Aird a' Mhuile
Dalabrog
Lochboisdale
(Loch Baghasdail)
Loch Baghasdail
Rubha na Creige Moire
Rubha Meall an Tobha
Rubha na h-Ordaig
Caolas Eiriosgaigh
ERISKAY
(EIRIOSGAIGH)
Fuday
(Fuideigh)
Hellisay
(Theiliseigh)
Gighay
(Gioghaigh)
Gob Sgùrabhal
Ceann Aird Ghrèin
Gob Bhuirgh
Rubha na Doirlinn
Bruernish Point
Castlebay
(Bàgh a' Chaisteil)
Rubha Mòr
VATERSAY
(BHATARSAIGH)
Sandray
(Sanndraigh)
Caolas Shandraigh
Pabbay
(Pabaigh)
Caolas Phabaigh
Caolas Mhiùghlaigh
Mingulay
(Miùghlaigh)
Berneray
(Bearnaraigh)
WATERNISH POINT
DUNVEGAN HEAD
Loch Dunvegan
Ardmore Point
Mingay
Isay
Sgeir nam Biast
An Ceannaich
Oisgill Bay
Moonen Bay
HEALABHAL MHOR
HEALABHAL BHEAG
Hoe Rape
Hoe Point
Am Bi-bogha Mòr
An Dubh-sgeir
Macleod's Maidens
CANNA
Garrisdale Point
Oigh-sgeir
171
154
146
Scale: 7 miles to 1 inch 1:441,423
0 1 2 3 4 5 10 15 Miles
0 1 2 3 4 5 10 15 20 Kilometres

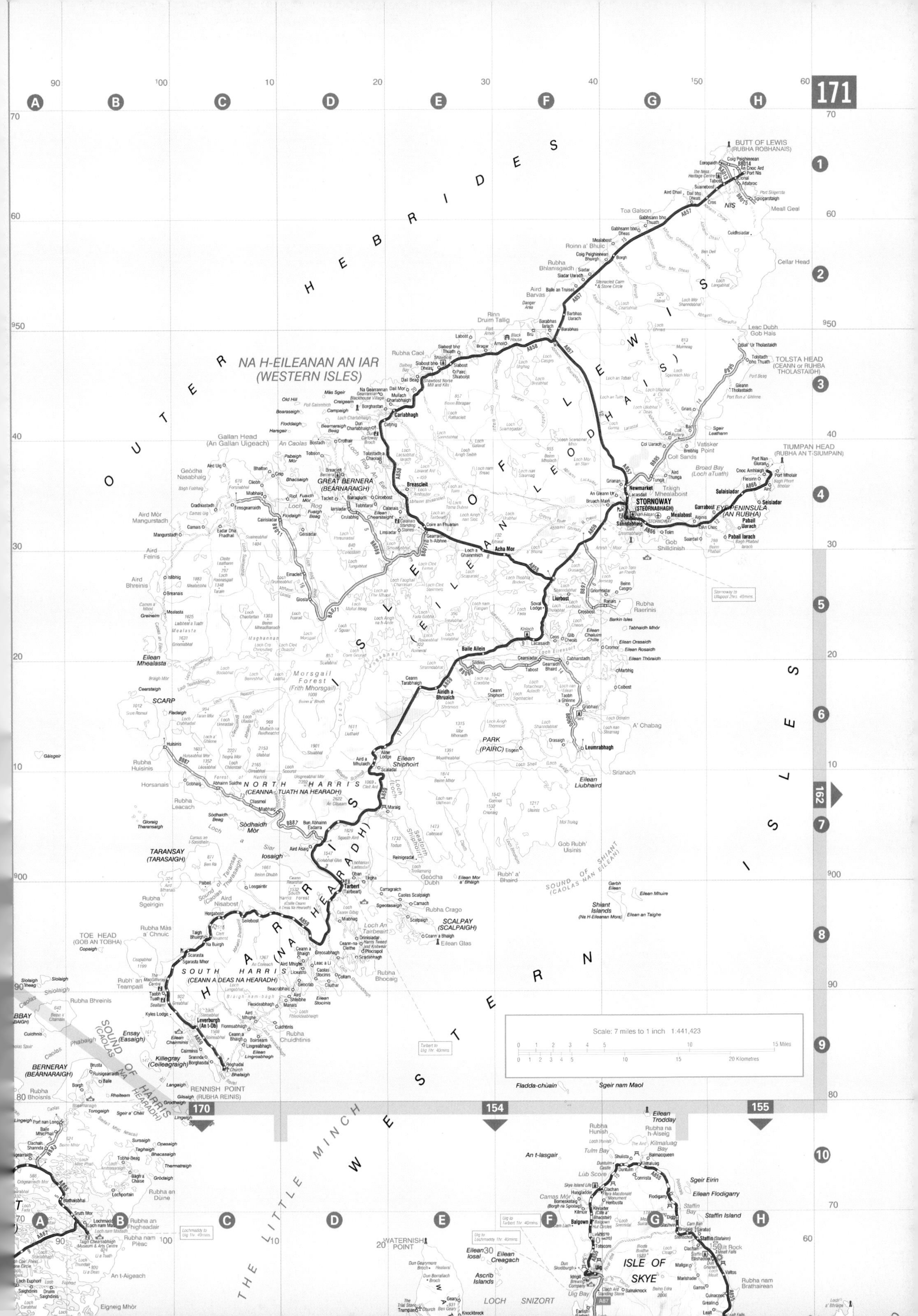

171
OUTER HEBRIDES
NA H-EILEANAN AN IAR (WESTERN ISLES)
BUTT OF LEWIS (RUBHA ROBHANAIS)
NIS
Cellar Head
TOLSTA HEAD (CEANN or RUBHA THOLASTAIDH)
TIUMPAN HEAD (RUBHA AN T-SIUMPAIN)
EYE PENINSULA (AN RUBHA)
Broad Bay (Loch aTuath)
STORNOWAY (STEORNABHAGH)
Newmarket
Carlabhagh
GREAT BERNERA (BEARNARAIGH)
Gallan Head (An Gallan Uigeach)
Aird Mòr Mangurstadh
ISLE OF LEWIS (EILEAN LEODHAIS)
Acha Mor
Liurbost
Baile Ailein
Morsgail Forest (Frith Mhorsgail)
PARK (PAIRC)
Eilean Liubhaird
Srianach
NORTH HARRIS (CEANNA TUATH NA HEARADH)
Eilean Shiphoirt
Loch Shiphoirt
Eilean Mhealasta
SCARP
Rubha Huisinis
Horsanais
Rubha Leacach
Sòdhaidh Mòr
TARANSAY (TARASAIGH)
Tarbert (Tairbeart)
SCALPAY (SCALPAIGH)
Rubha Crago
Eilean Glas
SOUND OF SHIANT (CAOLAS NAN EILEAN)
Shiant Islands (Na H-Eileanan Mora)
HARRIS (NA HEARADH)
SOUTH HARRIS (CEANN A DEAS NA HEARADH)
TOE HEAD (GOB AN TOBHA)
Leverburgh (An t-Ob)
Rubha Chuidhtinis
Killegray (Ceileagraigh)
Ensay (Easaigh)
RENNISH POINT (RUBHA REINIS)
SOUND OF HARRIS (CAOLAS NA HEARADH)
BERNERAY (BEÀRNARAIGH)
Rubha Bhoisnis
Fladda-chùain
Sgeir nam Maol
Scale: 7 miles to 1 inch 1:441,423
15 Miles
20 Kilometres
170
154
155
162
THE LITTLE MINCH
Eilean Trodday
Rubha Hunish
Rubha na h-Aiseig
Kilmaluag Bay
An t-Iasgair
Tulm Bay
Duntulm
Staffin Bay
Staffin Island
Eilean Flodigarry
Sgeir Eirin
WATERNISH POINT
Eilean Iosal
Eilean Creagach
Ascrib Islands
LOCH SNIZORT
ISLE OF SKYE
Uig
Uig Bay
Rubha nam Brathairean
Rubha an Dùine
Rubha an Fhigheadair
Rubha nam Pleac
An t-Aigeach
Eigneig Mhòr

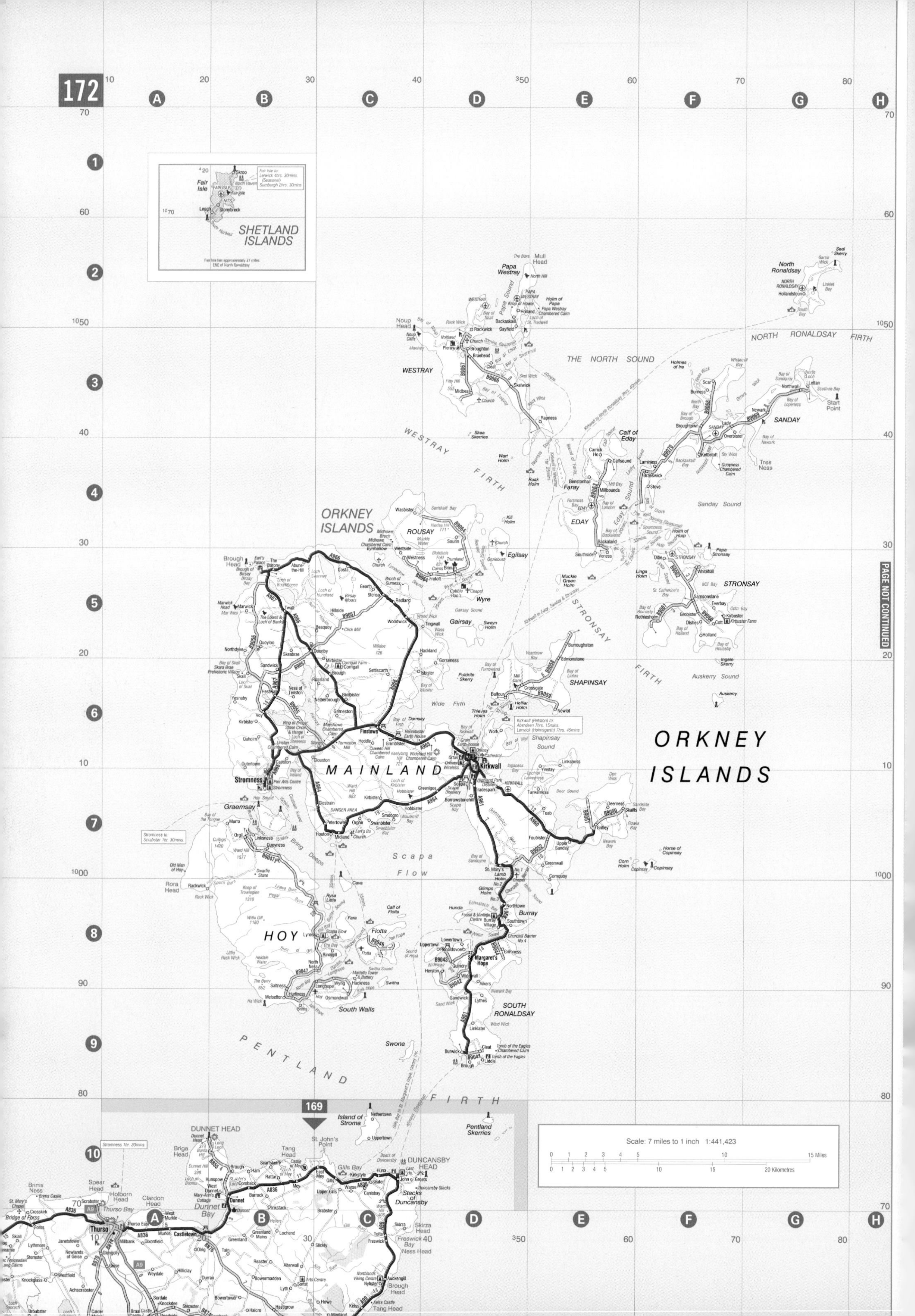

172
ORKNEY ISLANDS
SHETLAND ISLANDS
Fair Isle
Skroo
North Haven
Stonybreck
Leogh
South Harbour
Fair Isle to: Lerwick 4hrs. 30mins. (Seasonal) Sumburgh 2hrs. 30mins
Fair Isle lies approximately 27 miles ENE of North Ronaldsay
North Ronaldsay
Seal Skerry
Hollandstoun
NORTH RONALDSAY FIRTH
Papa Westray
Mull Head
North Hill
Holm of Papa
Noup Head
WESTRAY
Rackwick
Pierowall
Broughton
Midbea
THE NORTH SOUND
WESTRAY FIRTH
Calf of Eday
Carrick Ho
Calfsound
Faray
EDAY
Backaland
Sanday Sound
SANDAY
Start Point
Tres Ness
Lady
Kettletoft
Stove
Rapness
Wart Holm
Rusk Holm
ORKNEY ISLANDS
ROUSAY
Wasbister
Sourin
Egilsay
Wyre
Gairsay
STRONSAY
Papa Stronsay
Whitehall
Linga Holm
Holland
Auskerry
Auskerry Sound
STRONSAY FIRTH
Muckle Green Holm
SHAPINSAY
Balfour
Burroughston
Helliar Holm
Shapinsay Sound
Wide Firth
Brough Head
Marwick Head
Marwick
Twatt
Dounby
Finstown
Kirkwall
MAINLAND
Stromness
Graemsay
Hoy Sound
Orphir
Houton
Scapa Flow
Deerness
Skaills
Horse of Copinsay
Copinsay
Corn Holm
Cava
Fara
Flotta
HOY
Lyness
North Ness
Rora Head
Rackwick
Melsetter
Brims
South Walls
Swona
Burray
St Mary's
St Margaret's Hope
SOUTH RONALDSAY
Burwick
Brough
PENTLAND FIRTH
Pentland Skerries
Island of Stroma
169
St. John's Point
DUNCANSBY HEAD
Stacks of Duncansby
DUNNET HEAD
Dunnet Bay
Dunnet
Brough
Gills Bay
John o' Groats
Canisbay
Mey
Castletown
Thurso
Scrabster
Holborn Head
Clardon Head
Brims Ness
Thurso Bay
Bridge of Forss
Skirza Head
Freswick Bay
Ness Head
Keiss
Tang Head
Stromness to: Scrabster 1hr. 30mins.
Kirkwall (Hatston) to: Aberdeen 7hrs. 15mins. Lerwick (Holmsgarth) 7hrs. 45mins.
Scale: 7 miles to 1 inch 1:441,423
0 1 2 3 4 5 10 15 Miles
0 1 2 3 4 5 10 15 20 Kilometres
PAGE NOT CONTINUED

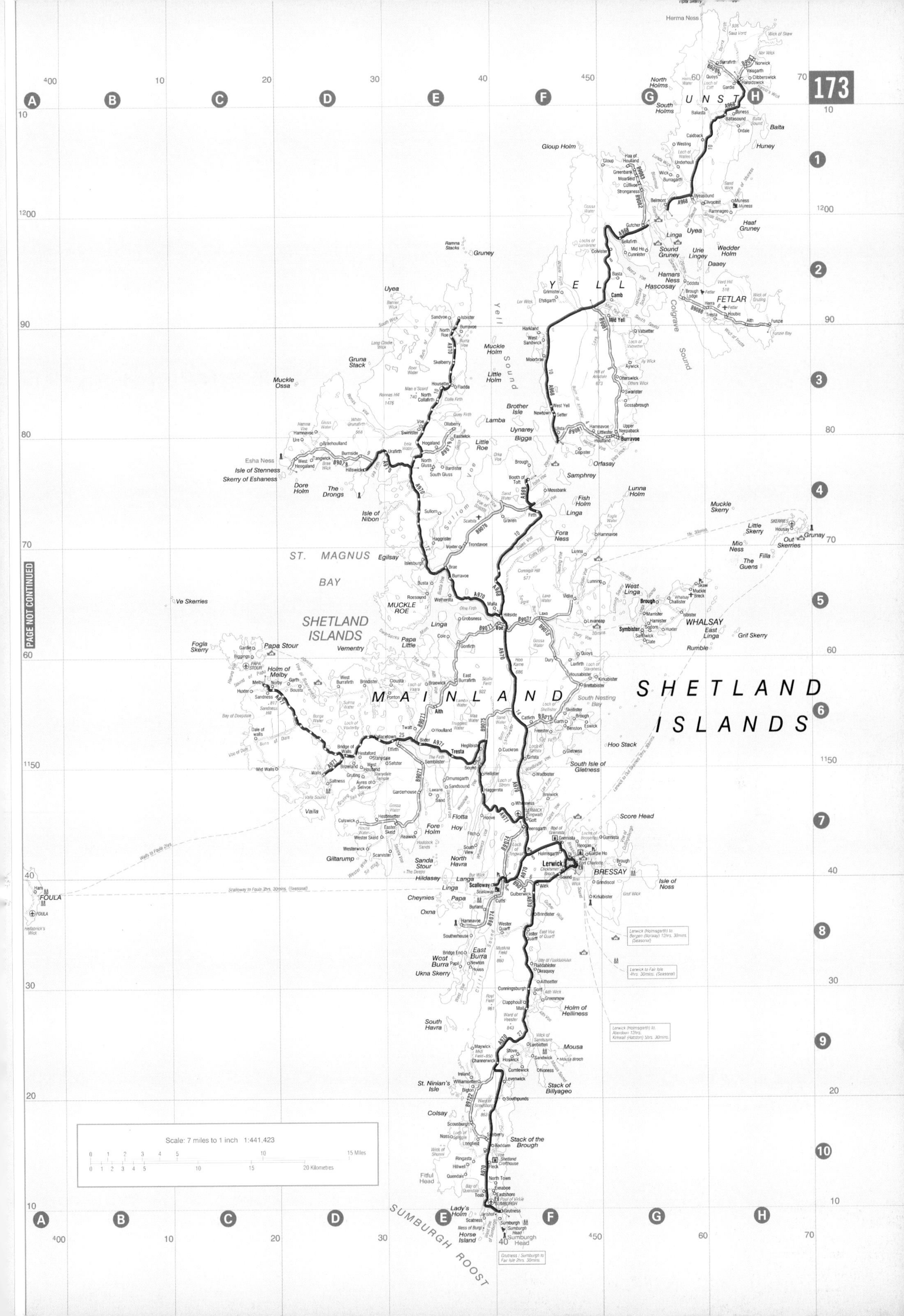
173
PAGE NOT CONTINUED
SHETLAND ISLANDS
SHETLAND ISLANDS
MAINLAND
UNST
YELL
FETLAR
WHALSAY
BRESSAY
FOULA
ST. MAGNUS BAY
MUCKLE ROE
SUMBURGH ROOST
Herma Ness
North Holms
South Holms
Balta
Huney
Gloup Holm
Uyea
Haaf Gruney
Wedder Holm
Linga
Sound Gruney
Urie Lingey
Daaey
Hamars Ness
Hascosay
Colgrave Sound
Yell Sound
Gruney
Ramna Stacks
Uyea
Gruna Stack
Muckle Ossa
Muckle Holm
Little Holm
Brother Isle
Lamba
Uynarey
Bigga
Little Roe
Samphrey
Orfasay
Esha Ness
Isle of Stenness
Skerry of Eshaness
Dore Holm
The Drongs
Isle of Nibon
Fish Holm
Lunna Holm
Muckle Skerry
Little Skerry
Out Skerries
Mio Ness
Fora Ness
Linga
Filla
The Guens
Egilsay
Ve Skerries
West Linga
East Linga
Grif Skerry
Rumble
Fogla Skerry
Papa Stour
Holm of Melby
Vementry
Papa Little
Linga
South Nesting Bay
Hoo Stack
South Isle of Gletness
Vaila
Score Head
Isle of Noss
Flotta
Fore Holm
Hoy
Sanda Stour
North Havra
Giltarump
Hildasay
Langa
Linga
Cheynies
Papa
Oxna
Lerwick
Scalloway
East Burra
West Burra
Ukna Skerry
Holm of Helliness
South Havra
Mousa
St. Ninian's Isle
Stack of Billyageo
Colsay
Stack of the Brough
Fitful Head
Lady's Holm
Horse Island
Sumburgh Head
Scale: 7 miles to 1 inch 1:441,423
0 1 2 3 4 5 10 15 Miles
0 1 2 3 4 5 10 15 20 Kilometres
A B C D E F G H
400 10 20 30 40 450 60 70
1 2 3 4 5 6 7 8 9 10

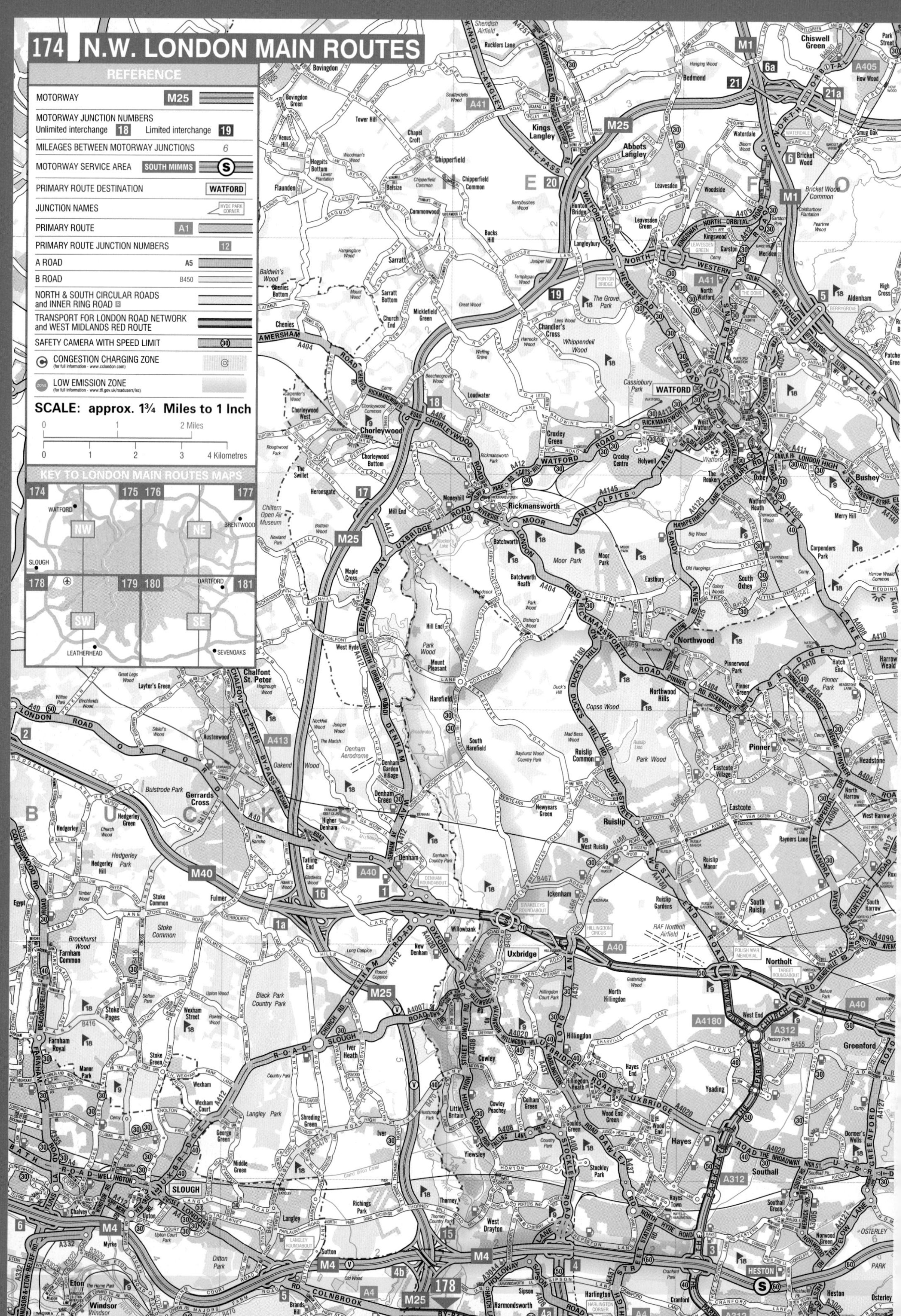
REFERENCE
MOTORWAY M25
MOTORWAY JUNCTION NUMBERS
Unlimited interchange 18 Limited interchange 19
MILEAGES BETWEEN MOTORWAY JUNCTIONS 6
MOTORWAY SERVICE AREA SOUTH MIMMS S
PRIMARY ROUTE DESTINATION WATFORD
JUNCTION NAMES HYDE PARK CORNER
PRIMARY ROUTE A1
PRIMARY ROUTE JUNCTION NUMBERS 12
A ROAD A5
B ROAD B450
NORTH & SOUTH CIRCULAR ROADS and INNER RING ROAD
TRANSPORT FOR LONDON ROAD NETWORK and WEST MIDLANDS RED ROUTE
SAFETY CAMERA WITH SPEED LIMIT 30
CONGESTION CHARGING ZONE
(for full information - www.cclondon.com)
LOW EMISSION ZONE
(for full information - www.tfl.gov.uk/roadusers/lez)
SCALE: approx. 1¾ Miles to 1 Inch
0 1 2 Miles
0 1 2 3 4 Kilometres
KEY TO LONDON MAIN ROUTES MAPS
174 175 176 177
WATFORD NW NE BRENTWOOD
SLOUGH
178 179 180 181
DARTFORD
SW SE
LEATHERHEAD SEVENOAKS
Bovingdon
Chipperfield
Kings Langley
Abbots Langley
Chiswell Green
Bedmond
Watford
WATFORD
Bushey
Rickmansworth
Chorleywood
Chenies
Sarratt
Croxley Green
Moor Park
Northwood
Pinner
Harefield
Ruislip
Eastcote
Ickenham
Uxbridge
Northolt
Hillingdon
Hayes
Southall
Yeading
Greenford
West Drayton
Yiewsley
Cowley
Harmondsworth
Harlington
Heston
Cranford
Slough
SLOUGH
Langley
Iver
Gerrards Cross
Denham
Chalfont St. Peter
Farnham Royal
Stoke Poges
Windsor
Eton
Datchet
M25
M40
M4
M1
A40
A41
A4
A312
A4180
178

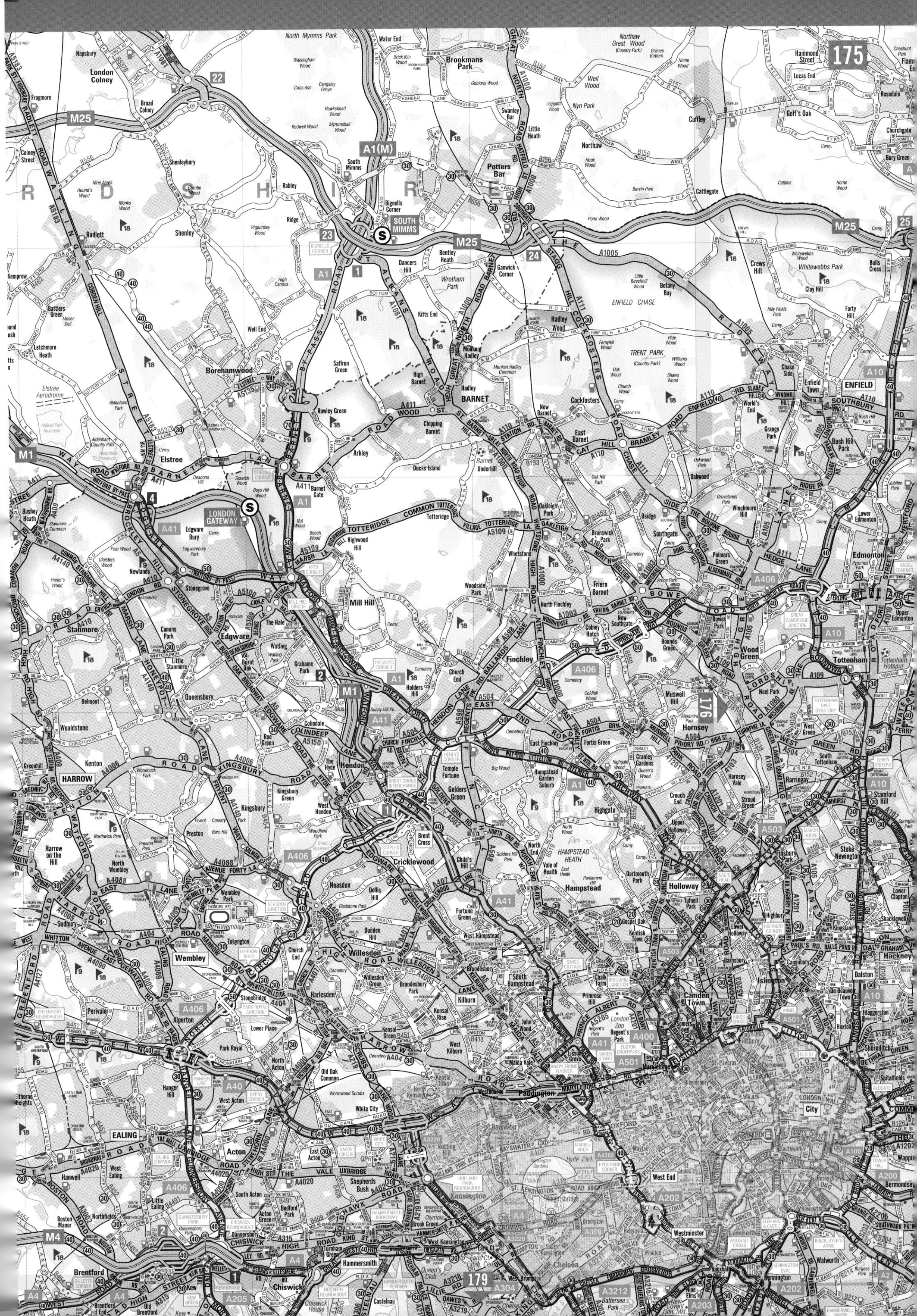

175
176
179
M25
M1
M4
A1(M)
A1
A41
A406
A10
A40
A4
A503
A501
A400
A202
A205
A304
A3212
A203
A2
North Mymms Park
Water End
Brookmans Park
Northaw Great Wood (Country Park)
Hammond Street
Cheshunt
Lucas End
Rosedale
Goff's Oak
Cuffley
Napsbury
London Colney
Frogmore
Broad Colney
Colney Street
Shenleybury
Shenley
Radlett
South Mimms
Potters Bar
Little Heath
Northaw
Cattlegate
Bignells Corner
SOUTH MIMMS
Ridge
Rabley
Dancers Hill
Bentley Heath
Ganwick Corner
Wrotham Park
Kitts End
Hadley Wood
ENFIELD CHASE
TRENT PARK (Country Park)
Botany Bay
Crews Hill
Whitewebbs Park
Clay Hill
Bulls Cross
Forty Hill
Chase Side
Enfield Town
ENFIELD
Borehamwood
Elstree Aerodrome
Letchmore Heath
Well End
Saffron Green
High Barnet
Monken Hadley
BARNET
Rowley Green
Chipping Barnet
Arkley
New Barnet
Cockfosters
East Barnet
World's End
Grange Park
Bush Hill Park
Southbury
Elstree
Ducks Island
Underhill
Oakwood
Oakleigh Park
Osidge
Southgate
Winchmore Hill
Lower Edmonton
Bushey Heath
Edgware Bury
LONDON GATEWAY
Totteridge
Highwood Hill
Whetstone
Brunswick Park
Palmers Green
Edmonton
Stanmore
Newlands
Stonegrove
Mill Hill
Woodside Park
Friern Barnet
North Finchley
New Southgate
Bowes Park
Upper Edmonton
Canons Park
Edgware
The Hale
Colney Hatch
Bounds Green
Wood Green
Tottenham
Little Stanmore
Burnt Oak
Watling Park
Grahame Park
Finchley
Church End
Muswell Hill
Belmont
Queensbury
Colindale
Holders Hill
East Finchley
Fortis Green
Hornsey
West Green
Wealdstone
Roe Green
The Hyde
Hendon
Temple Fortune
Cranley Gardens
South Tottenham
Kenton
HARROW
Kingsbury
Hampstead Garden Suburb
Crouch End
Harringay
Stamford Hill
Kingsbury Green
West Hendon
Golders Green
Highgate
Hornsey Vale
Stroud Green
Harrow on the Hill
Preston
Brent Cross
Cricklewood
Child's Hill
Upper Holloway
North End
Vale of Health
HAMPSTEAD HEATH
Finsbury Park
Stoke Newington
North Wembley
Neasden
Dollis Hill
Hampstead
Dartmouth Park
Holloway
Wembley Park
Fortune Green
Tufnell Park
Sudbury
Wembley
Tokyngton
Dudden Hill
West Hampstead
Kentish Town
Highbury
Church End
Willesden
Brondesbury
South Hampstead
Chalk Farm
Camden Town
Islington
Canonbury
Dalston
Hackney
Perivale
Alperton
Stonebridge
Harlesden
Willesden Green
Brondesbury Park
Kilburn
Primrose Hill
Lower Place
Kensal Rise
Kensal Green
Park Royal
North Acton
West Kilburn
Maida Vale
St. John's Wood
Regent's Park
London Zoo
Marylebone
Haggerston
Hoxton
Shoreditch
Old Oak Common
Hanger Hill
Wormwood Scrubs
White City
Paddington
Spitalfields
City
West Acton
EALING
Acton
Notting Hill
Bayswater
Hyde Park
East Acton
West End
West Ealing
Hanwell
Shepherds Bush
Kensington
South Acton
Little Ealing
Northfields
Boston Manor
Bedford Park
Knightsbridge
Westminster
Brompton
Lambeth
Bermondsey
Gunnersbury
Chiswick
Hammersmith
Turnham Green
Olympia
West Kensington
Chelsea
Pimlico
Walworth
Brentford
Kennington
Old Brentford
Castelnau
West Brompton
Battersea Park
Nine Elms
Vauxhall
Kew

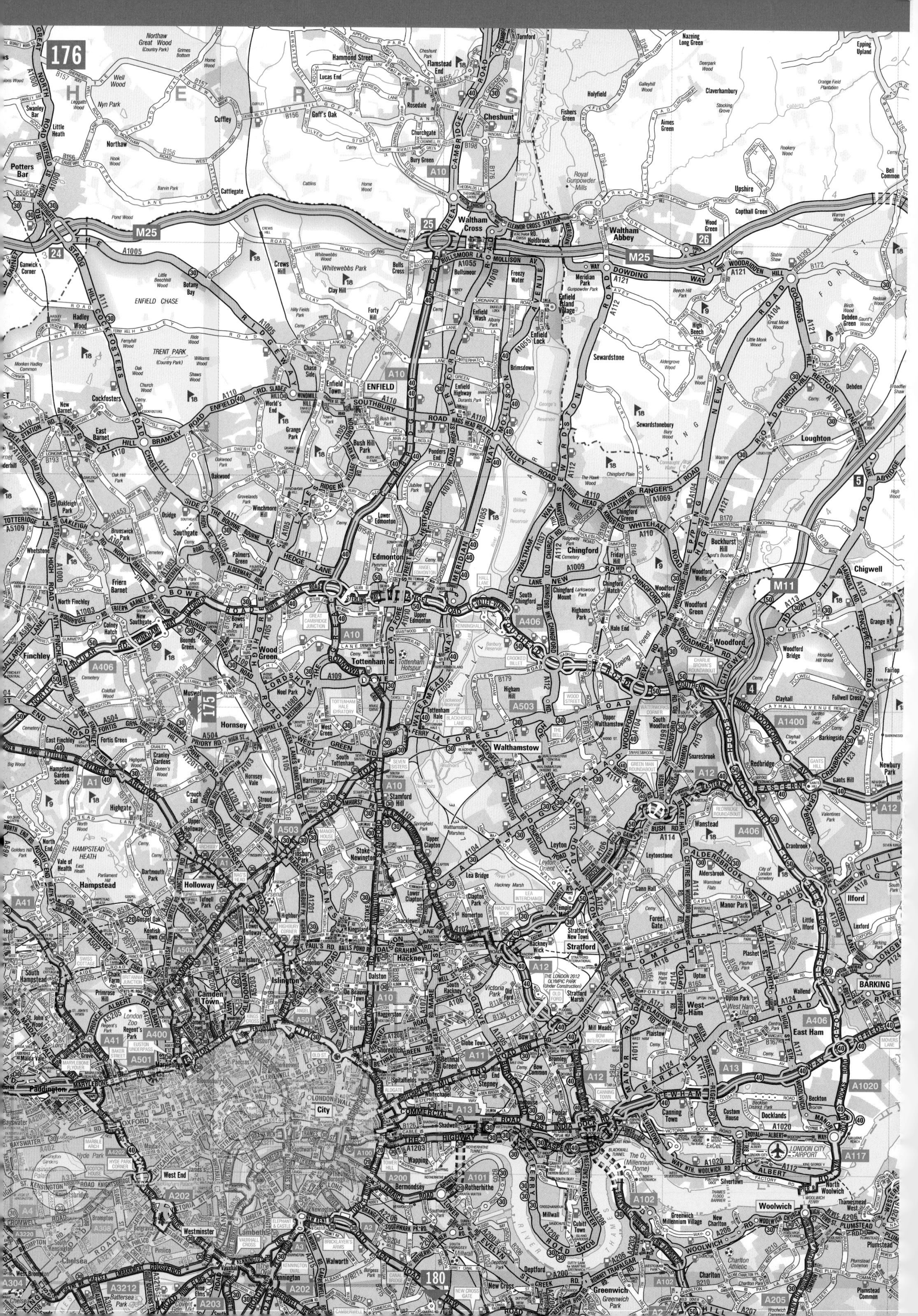
176
175
180
Northaw Great Wood (Country Park)
Potters Bar
Little Heath
Northaw
Cuffley
Hammond Street
Lucas End
Goff's Oak
Flamstead End
Rosedale
Churchgate
Cheshunt
Turnford
Nazeing Long Green
Epping Upland
Holyfield
Claverhambury
Fishers Green
Aimes Green
Royal Gunpowder Mills
Upshire
Copthall Green
Bell Common
Waltham Cross
Waltham Abbey
Holdbrook
M25
Ganwick Corner
Crews Hill
Botany Bay
Bulls Cross
Bullsmoor
Freezy Water
Whitewebbs Park
Clay Hill
ENFIELD CHASE
Hadley Wood
Forty Hill
Enfield Wash
Enfield Island Village
Enfield Lock
TRENT PARK (Country Park)
Chase Side
Enfield Town
ENFIELD
Southbury
Brimsdown
Sewardstone
High Beech
Debden Green
Debden
Loughton
Sewardstonebury
Cockfosters
New Barnet
East Barnet
World's End
Grange Park
Bush Hill Park
Enfield Highway
Ponders End
Oakwood
Winchmore Hill
Lower Edmonton
Edmonton
Chingford
Buckhurst Hill
Chigwell
M11
Totteridge
Oakleigh Park
Whetstone
Osidge
Southgate
Palmers Green
Friern Barnet
North Finchley
New Southgate
Colney Hatch
Bowes Park
Bounds Green
Wood Green
Upper Edmonton
Tottenham
South Chingford
Chingford Mount
Highams Park
Hale End
Woodford Green
Woodford
Woodford Bridge
Grange Hill
Fairlop
Finchley
East Finchley
Muswell Hill
Hornsey
Noel Park
Tottenham Hale
Higham Hill
Walthamstow
Upper Walthamstow
South Woodford
Snaresbrook
Redbridge
Clayhall
Barkingside
Gants Hill
Newbury Park
Hampstead Garden Suburb
Fortis Green
Crouch End
Stroud Green
Harringay
South Tottenham
Stamford Hill
Highgate
Upper Holloway
Stoke Newington
Upper Clapton
Leyton
Leytonstone
Wanstead
Aldersbrook
Cranbrook
Ilford
North End
HAMPSTEAD HEATH
Vale of Health
Hampstead
Dartmouth Park
Holloway
Tufnell Park
Finsbury Park
Highbury
Lower Clapton
Clapton Park
Lea Bridge
Hackney Marsh
Homerton
Temple Mills
Cann Hall
Forest Gate
Manor Park
Little Ilford
Loxford
Gospel Oak
Kentish Town
Lower Holloway
Barnsbury
Kingsland
Dalston
Hackney
Hackney Wick
Stratford
Stratford New Town
South Hampstead
Chalk Farm
Primrose Hill
Camden Town
Islington
Canonbury
De Beauvoir Town
South Hackney
Victoria Park
Old Ford
Stratford Marsh
Upton
Plashet
West Ham
East Ham
Wallend
BARKING
Regent's Park
St. John's Wood
Somers Town
Haggerston
Hoxton
Globe Town
Bow
Mill Meads
Plaistow
Marylebone
Paddington
Bethnal Green
Shoreditch
Spitalfields
Mile End
Stepney
Bow Common
Bromley
Whitechapel
City
Limehouse
Poplar
Canning Town
Custom House
Docklands
Beckton
Bayswater
Mayfair
Hyde Park
West End
Shadwell
Wapping
Rotherhithe
Millwall
Cubitt Town
The O2 (Millennium Dome)
LONDON CITY AIRPORT
Silvertown
North Woolwich
Woolwich
Knightsbridge
Bermondsey
Westminster
Lambeth
Brompton
South Kensington
Belgravia
Pimlico
Walworth
Deptford
Greenwich Millennium Village
New Charlton
Thamesmead West
Plumstead
Plumstead Common
Chelsea
Kennington
Vauxhall
Nine Elms
Battersea Park
West Brompton
New Cross
Greenwich
Charlton
Shooters Hill

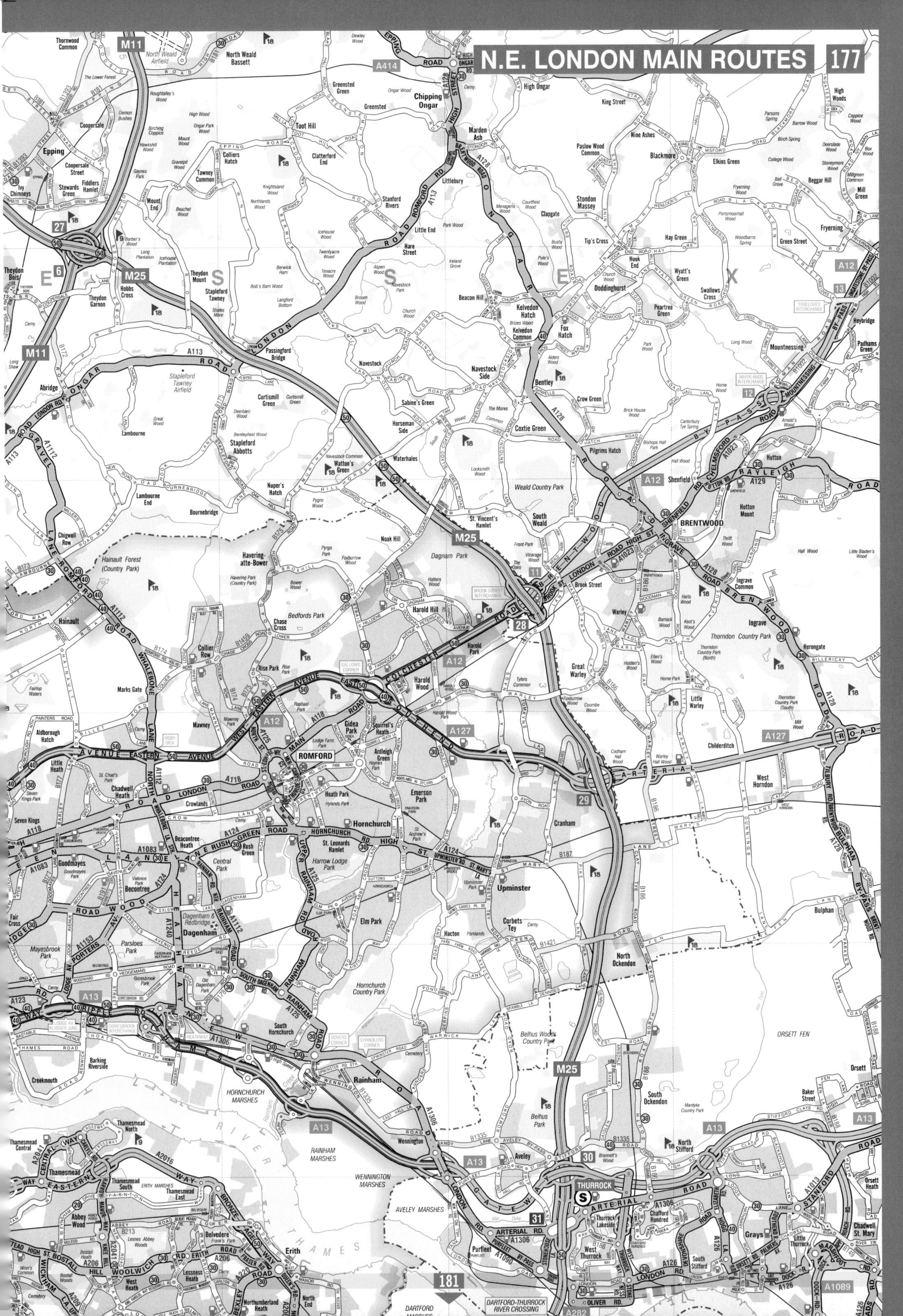

N.E. LONDON MAIN ROUTES
177
Thornwood Common
M11
North Weald Airfield
North Weald Bassett
A414
ONGAR
Chipping Ongar
Greensted Green
Greensted
Toot Hill
High Ongar
King Street
Marden Ash
Epping
Coopersale
Coopersale Street
Ivy Chimneys
Stewards Green
Fiddlers Hamlet
Colliers Hatch
Tawney Common
Clatterford End
Nine Ashes
Paslow Wood Common
Blackmore
Elkins Green
High Woods
Mount End
Stanford Rivers
Littlebury
Stondon Massey
Clapgate
Beggar Hill
Mill Green
Little End
Hare Street
Tip's Cross
Hay Green
Green Street
Fryerning
Theydon Bois
Theydon Mount
Hobbs Cross
M25
Stapleford Tawney
Hook End
Wyatt's Green
Swallows Cross
A12
Theydon Garnon
Beacon Hill
Kelvedon Hatch
Kelvedon Common
Doddinghurst
Peartree Green
Fox Hatch
Heybridge
Padhams Green
Mountnessing
M11
Passingford Bridge
A113
Stapleford Tawney Airfield
Navestock
Navestock Side
Abridge
Curtismill Green
Bentley
Crow Green
Sabine's Green
Horseman Side
Coxtie Green
Lambourne
Stapleford Abbotts
Watton's Green
Waterhales
Pilgrims Hatch
Shenfield
Hutton
Weald Country Park
Lambourne End
Bournebridge
Nuper's Hatch
South Weald
St. Vincent's Hamlet
BRENTWOOD
Hutton Mount
Chigwell Row
Hainault Forest (Country Park)
Havering-atte-Bower
Noak Hill
Dagnam Park
Brook Street
Ingrave Common
Ingrave
Hainault
Bedfords Park
Harold Hill
Chase Cross
Collier Row
Rise Park
Harold Park
Warley
Thorndon Country Park
Herongate
Marks Gate
Harold Wood
Great Warley
Tylers Common
Little Warley
Mawney
Gidea Park
Squirrel's Heath
A127
Aldborough Hatch
Ardleigh Green
Childerditch
ROMFORD
Little Heath
Chadwell Heath
Crowlands
Heath Park
Emerson Park
West Horndon
Seven Kings
Hornchurch
Cranham
Beacontree Heath
Rush Green
St. Leonards Hamlet
Goodmayes
Central Park
Harrow Lodge Park
Upminster
Becontree
Elm Park
Corbets Tey
Bulphan
Dagenham
Parsloes Park
Hacton
North Ockendon
Mayesbrook Park
Hornchurch Country Park
Fair Cross
A13
Belhus Woods Country Park
ORSETT FEN
South Hornchurch
Barking Riverside
Creekmouth
HORNCHURCH MARSHES
Rainham
Orsett
Baker Street
South Ockendon
North Stifford
Belhus Park
Thamesmead North
Thamesmead Central
Thamesmead
RAINHAM MARSHES
Wennington
Aveley
WENNINGTON MARSHES
Thamesmead South
Thamesmead East
THURROCK
Chafford Hundred
Thurrock Lakeside
AVELEY MARSHES
Abbey Wood
Belvedere
Grays
Little Thurrock
Chadwell St. Mary
Orsett Heath
Purfleet
West Thurrock
South Stifford
Erith
RIVER THAMES
West Heath
Lessness Heath
Bostall Woods
North End
Northumberland Heath
181
DARTFORD-THURROCK RIVER CROSSING
DARTFORD MARSHES

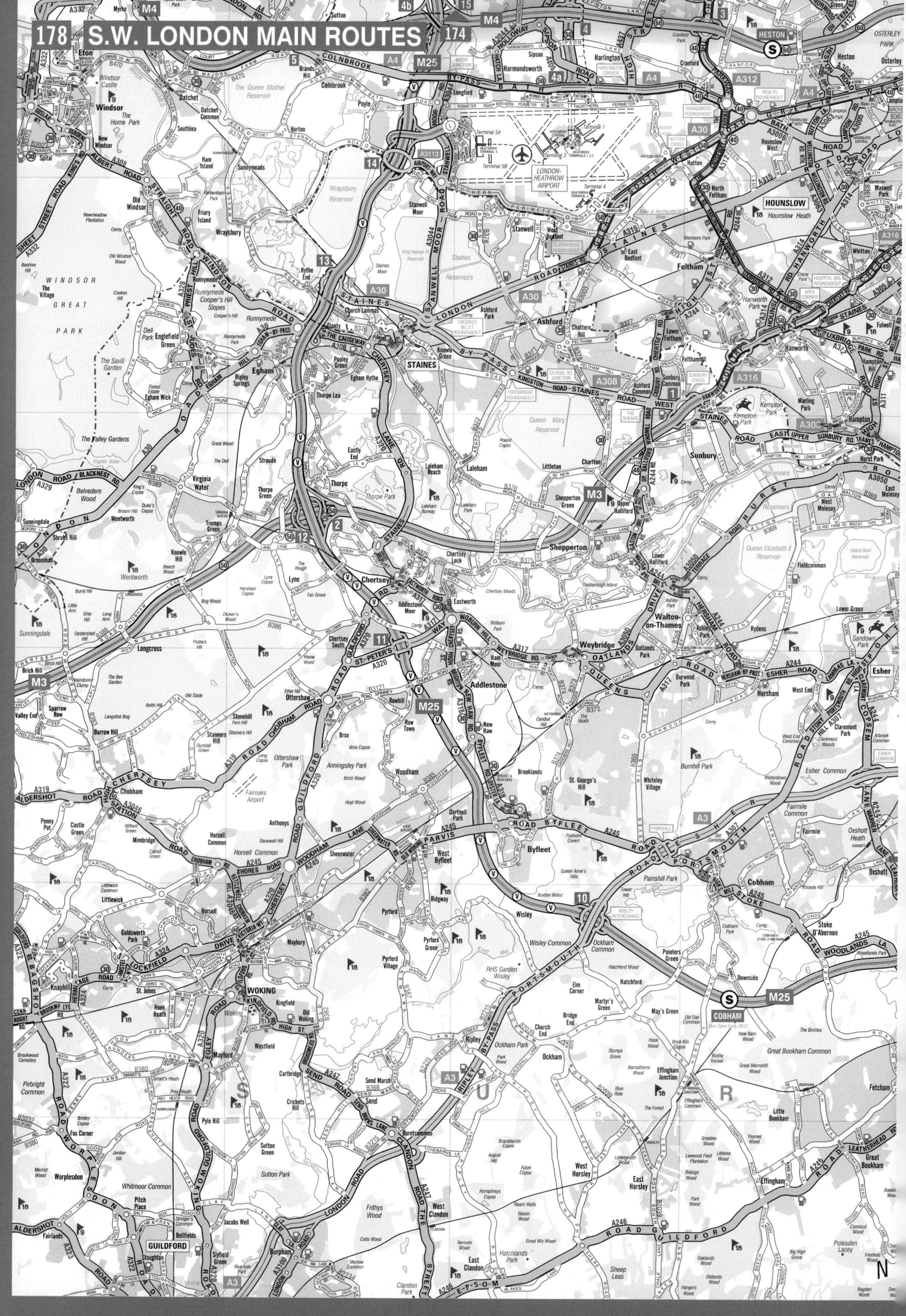
174
Windsor
Eton
Datchet
Colnbrook
Harmondsworth
Heston
Hounslow
London-Heathrow Airport
Stanwell
Ashford
Feltham
Staines
Egham
Virginia Water
Chertsey
Laleham
Shepperton
Sunbury
Hampton
Walton-on-Thames
Weybridge
Addlestone
Esher
Byfleet
Cobham
Woking
Ripley
Ockham
Guildford
Great Bookham
Fetcham
Windsor Great Park
Queen Mary Reservoir
Wisley Common
Horsell Common
Whitmoor Common
Thorpe Park
Kempton Park
Sandown Park
RHS Garden Wisley
Chobham
Ottershaw
Pyrford
Send
Effingham
East Horsley
West Horsley
West Clandon
East Clandon

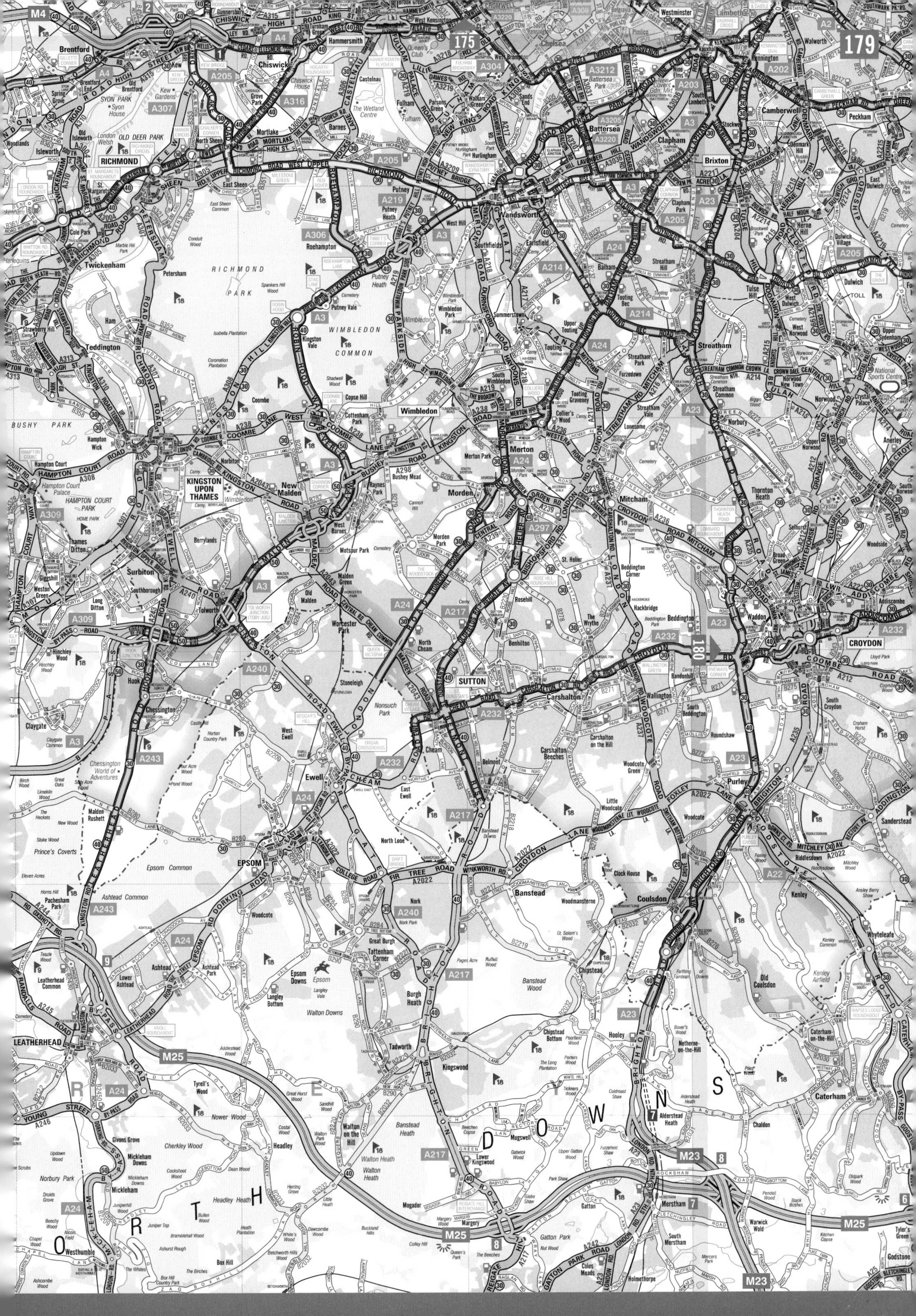175
179
180
Brentford
Chiswick
Hammersmith
Fulham
Chelsea
Westminster
Lambeth
Vauxhall
Kennington
Walworth
Camberwell
Peckham
Battersea
Clapham
Brixton
Putney
Barnes
Mortlake
Kew
RICHMOND
Isleworth
Twickenham
Teddington
Sheen
East Sheen
RICHMOND PARK
Roehampton
Wandsworth
Southfields
Earlsfield
Balham
Streatham
Tooting
Dulwich
Herne Hill
WIMBLEDON COMMON
Wimbledon
Merton
Morden
Mitcham
Norbury
Norwood
Crystal Palace
Anerley
Thornton Heath
Selhurst
BUSHY PARK
Hampton Wick
Hampton Court
HAMPTON COURT PARK
KINGSTON UPON THAMES
Norbiton
New Malden
Surbiton
Thames Ditton
Tolworth
Worcester Park
Stoneleigh
Ewell
SUTTON
Cheam
Carshalton
Wallington
Beddington
Waddon
CROYDON
South Croydon
Purley
Coulsdon
Kenley
Whyteleafe
Caterham
Chessington
Hook
Claygate
EPSOM
Epsom Common
Ashtead
Banstead
Tadworth
Kingswood
Chipstead
Hooley
Merstham
LEATHERHEAD
Mickleham
Headley
Walton on the Hill
Box Hill
Westhumble
NORTH DOWNS
M4
M25
M23
A3
A23
A24
A217
A232
A240
A243

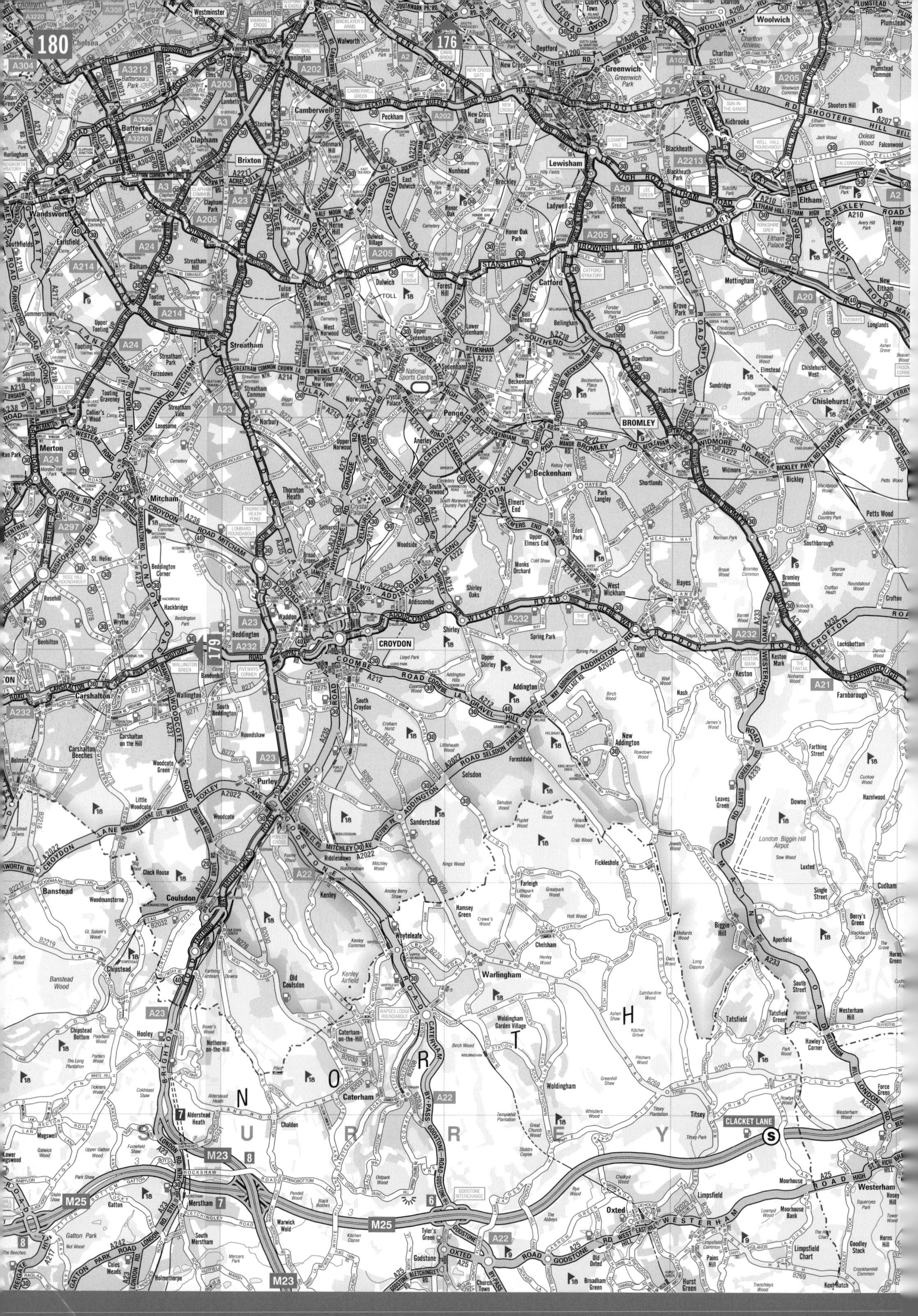
180
176
179
Westminster
Chelsea
Lambeth
Walworth
Kennington
Millwall
Deptford
Greenwich
Woolwich
Plumstead
Charlton
Battersea
Clapham
Camberwell
Peckham
New Cross
Blackheath
Kidbrooke
Shooters Hill
Brixton
Lewisham
Wandsworth
Nunhead
East Dulwich
Brockley
Hither Green
Eltham
Ladywell
Honor Oak
Balham
Streatham Hill
Dulwich
Forest Hill
Catford
Mottingham
Tooting Bec
Tulse Hill
West Dulwich
Summerstown
Upper Tooting
West Norwood
Upper Sydenham
Lower Sydenham
Bellingham
Grove Park
Tooting
Streatham
Sydenham
National Sports Centre
Crystal Palace
Penge
Downham
Plaistow
Sundridge
Chislehurst
Norwood
New Beckenham
Colliers Wood
Norbury
Anerley
Upper Norwood
BROMLEY
Widmore
Merton
Beckenham
Shortlands
Bickley
Thornton Heath
South Norwood
Elmers End
Park Langley
Mitcham
Petts Wood
Eden Park
Woodside
Upper Elmers End
Southborough
St. Helier
Selhurst
Monks Orchard
Hayes
Beddington Corner
Shirley Oaks
West Wickham
Bromley Common
Rosehill
Hackbridge
Addiscombe
The Wrythe
Waddon
Shirley
Beddington
CROYDON
Locksbottom
Benhilton
Upper Shirley
Coney Hall
Keston Mark
Keston
Addington
Carshalton
Wallington
Bandonhill
South Beddington
Nash
Farnborough
South Croydon
Roundshaw
Carshalton Beeches
Carshalton on the Hill
Forestdale
New Addington
Farthing Street
Woodcote Green
Selsdon
Purley
Leaves Green
Downe
Little Woodcote
Woodcote
Sanderstead
London Biggin Hill Airport
Riddlesdown
Fickleshole
Luxted
Clock House
Kenley
Farleigh
Cudham
Banstead
Woodmansterne
Coulsdon
Hamsey Green
Single Street
Whyteleafe
Chelsham
Biggin Hill
Berry's Green
Aperfield
Chipstead
Old Coulsdon
Kenley Airfield
Warlingham
Banstead Wood
South Street
Hooley
Woldingham Garden Village
Tatsfield
Westerham Hill
Chipstead Bottom
Netherne-on-the-Hill
Caterham-on-the-Hill
Hawley's Corner
Woldingham
Caterham
Alderstead Heath
Chaldon
Titsey
CLACKET LANE
Force Green
NORTH
SURREY
Mugswell
Merstham
South Merstham
Limpsfield
Moorhouse
Westerham
Gatton
Gatton Park
Oxted
Tyler's Green
Godstone
Old Oxted
Limpsfield Chart
Goodley Stock
Coles Meads
Holmethorpe
Broadham Green
Hurst Green
Church Town
Kent Hatch
M25
M23
A22
A23
A232
A21
A20
A2
A205
A24
A214
A3
A202
A3212
A3220
A3205
A203
A236
A297
A212
A222
A233
GODSTONE INTERCHANGE
WAPSES LODGE ROUNDABOUT

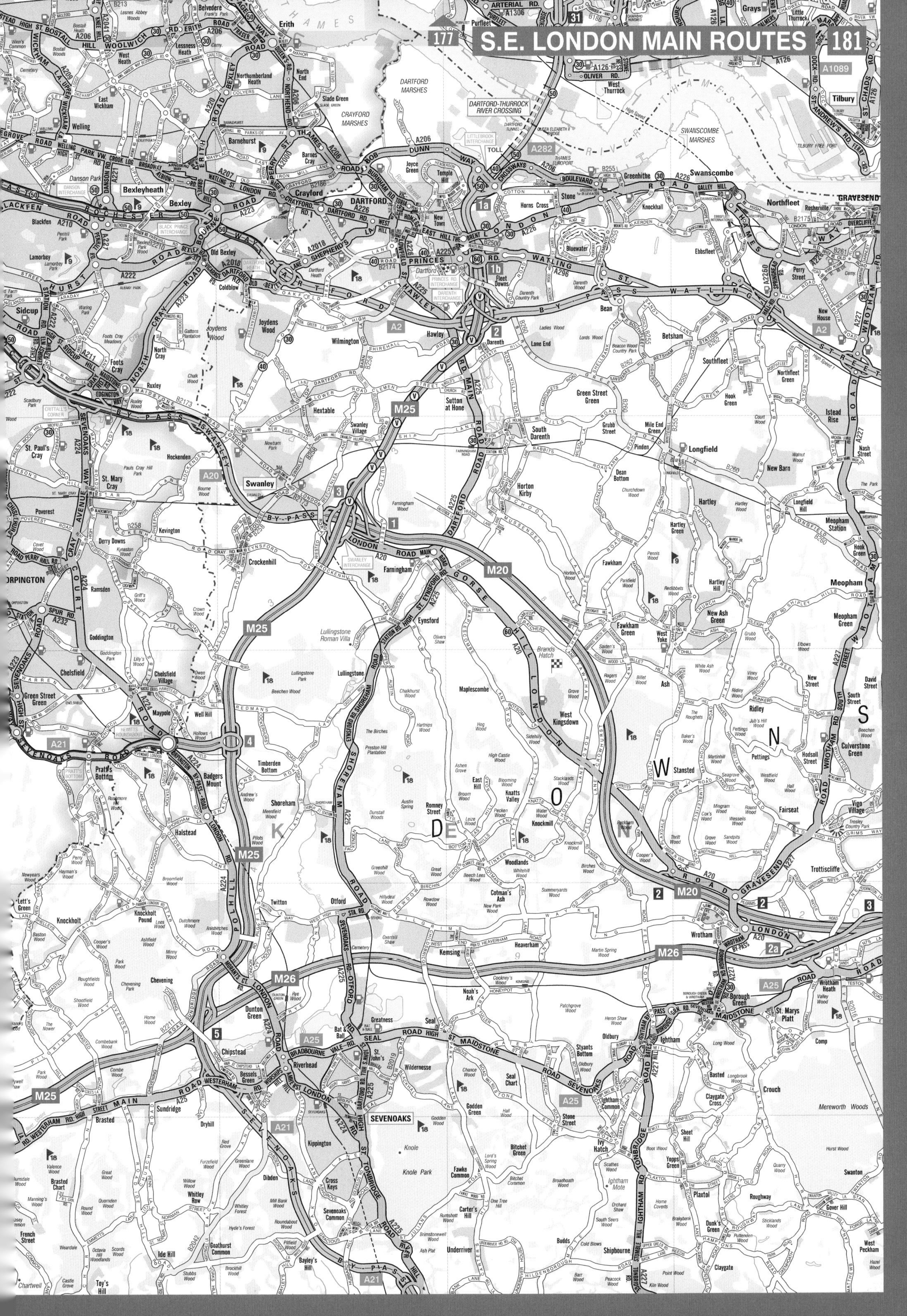
177
S.E. LONDON MAIN ROUTES
181
DARTFORD
SWANLEY
SEVENOAKS
MAIDSTONE
Gravesend
Bexleyheath
Sidcup
Orpington
Crayford
Erith
Tilbury
Northfleet
Swanscombe
Greenhithe
Longfield
Meopham
West Kingsdown
Eynsford
Farningham
Shoreham
Otford
Kemsing
Wrotham
Borough Green
Ightham
Riverhead
Chipstead
Brasted
Sundridge
Halstead
Knockholt
Chevening
Dunton Green
Seal
Plaxtol
Shipbourne
Underriver
Ide Hill
Westerham
DARTFORD-THURROCK RIVER CROSSING
Bluewater
Brands Hatch
M25
M20
M26
A2
A20
A21
A25
A282
K E N T
D O W N S

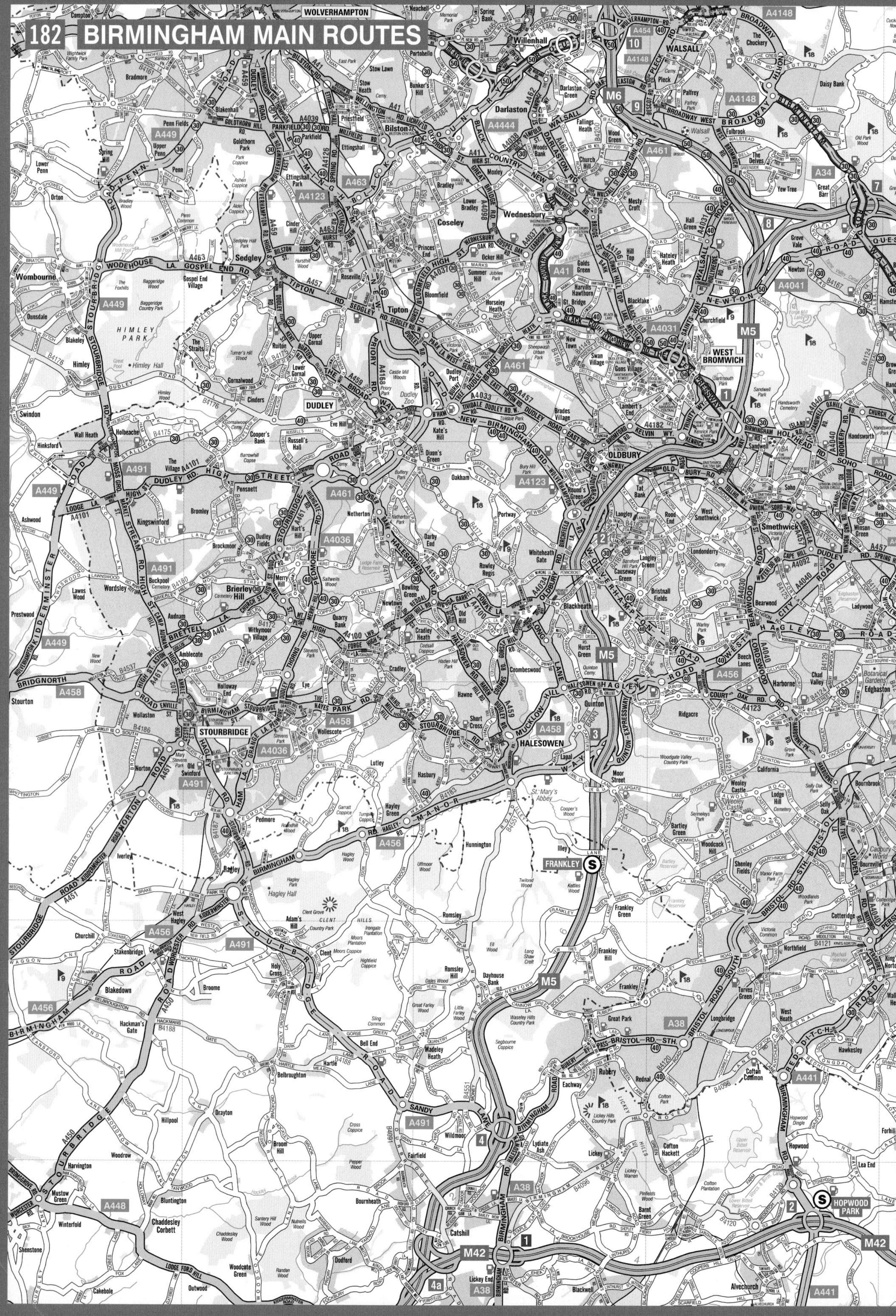
WOLVERHAMPTON
Willenhall
WALSALL
Bilston
Darlaston
Wednesbury
Coseley
Sedgley
Tipton
Wombourne
HIMLEY PARK
Himley Hall
DUDLEY
WEST BROMWICH
OLDBURY
Smethwick
Kingswinford
Brierley Hill
Netherton
Rowley Regis
Blackheath
Cradley
Halesowen
HALESOWEN
STOURBRIDGE
Wollaston
Hagley
Hagley Hall
Romsley
FRANKLEY
Quinton
Harborne
Edgbaston
Selly Oak
Bournville
Northfield
Longbridge
Rubery
Rednal
Lickey
Catshill
Blakedown
Belbroughton
Chaddesley Corbett
Alvechurch
HOPWOOD PARK
M5
M6
M42
A449
A491
A456
A458
A461
A4123
A4036
A38
A441
A448
A4041
A4148
A461
A4031
A41
A34
A457
A4040
A459
A4444
A463
A4123
A491

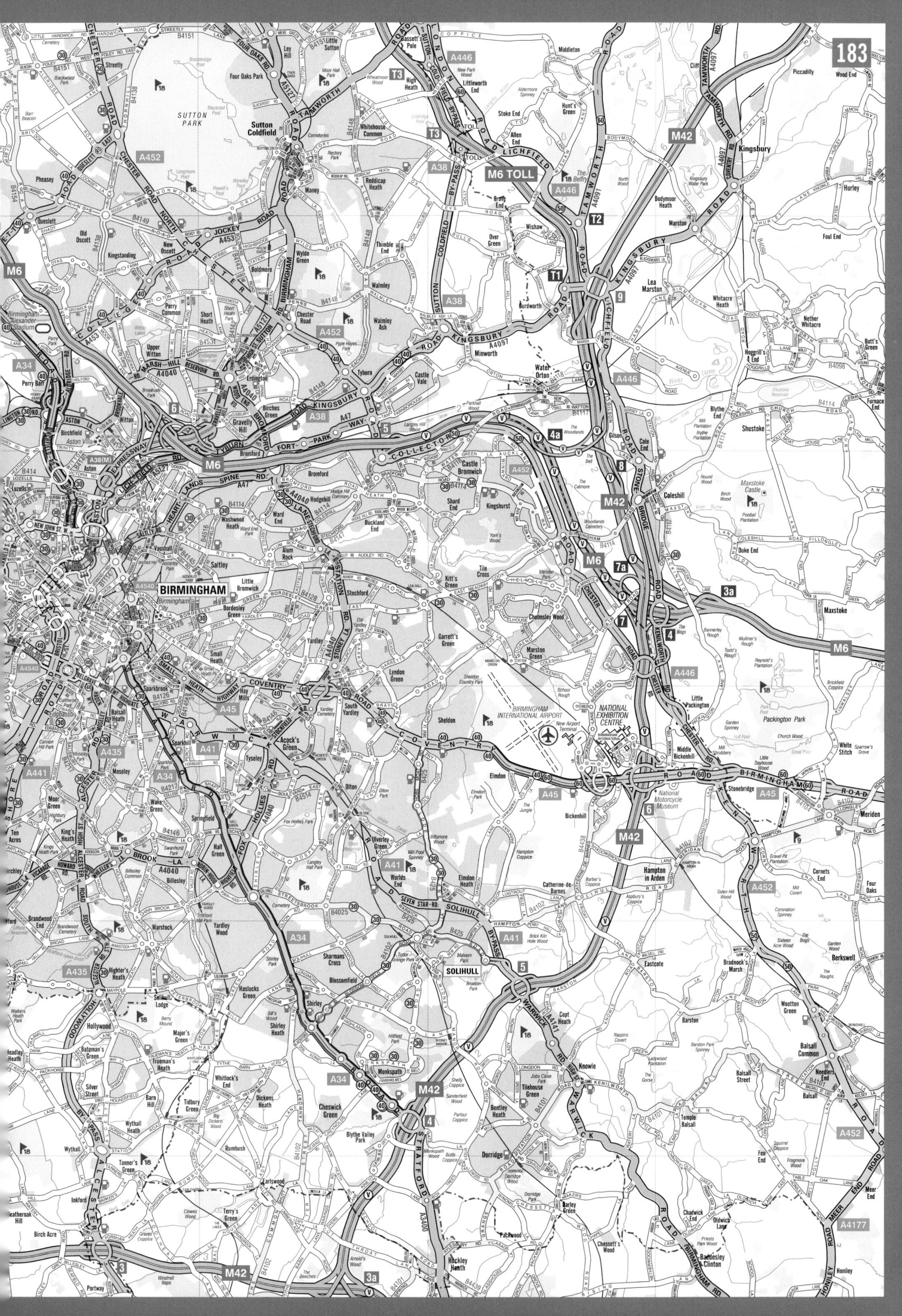

Little Sutton
Bassett Pole
Middleton
Piccadilly
Wood End
Four Oaks Park
Ley Hill
High Heath
Littleworth End
Stoke End
Hunt's Green
Cliff
SUTTON PARK
Sutton Coldfield
Whitehouse Common
Allen End
Kingsbury
M6 TOLL
Pheasey
Reddicap Heath
Maney
Grove End
Bodymoor Heath
Hurley
Queslett
Old Oscott
Kingstanding
New Oscott
Thimble End
Over Green
Wishaw
Marston
Foul End
Wylde Green
Boldmere
Walmley
Lea Marston
Whitacre Heath
Nether Whitacre
Perry Common
Short Heath
Chester Road
Walmley Ash
Bodymoor
Minworth
Hoggrill's End
Bott's Green
Upper Witton
Erdington
Tyburn
Castle Vale
Water Orton
Perry Barr
Witton
Birches Green
Gravelly Hill
Aston Villa
Aston
Bromford
Blythe End
Shustoke
Furnace End
Lozells
Castle Bromwich
Cole End
Coleshill
Maxstoke Castle
Washwood Heath
Ward End
Hodgehill
Shard End
Kingshurst
Buckland End
Vauxhall
Saltley
Alum Rock
Tile Cross
Duke End
BIRMINGHAM
Little Bromwich
Stechford
Kitt's Green
Chelmsley Wood
Maxstoke
Bordesley Green
Yardley
Garrett's Green
Marston Green
Small Heath
Lyndon Green
Sparkbrook
Hay Mills
South Yardley
BIRMINGHAM INTERNATIONAL AIRPORT
NATIONAL EXHIBITION CENTRE
Little Packington
Packington Park
Edgbaston
Balsall Heath
Sparkhill
Acock's Green
Sheldon
Middle Bickenhill
White Stitch
Moseley
Tyseley
Olton
Elmdon
Stonebridge
Meriden
Moor Green
Wake Green
Springfield
Bickenhill
Ten Acres
King's Heath
Hall Green
Ulverley Green
Worlds End
Hampton in Arden
Cornets End
Four Oaks
Billesley
Elmdon Heath
Catherine-de-Barnes
Brandwood End
Warstock
Yardley Wood
Sharmans Cross
SOLIHULL
Eastcote
Bradnock's Marsh
Berkswell
Highter's Heath
Blossomfield
Solihull Lodge
Haslocks Green
Shirley
Shirley Heath
Copt Heath
Barston
Wootton Green
Hollywood
Major's Green
Balsall Common
Bateman's Green
Trueman's Heath
Knowle
Balsall Street
Whitlock's End
Monkspath
Silver Street
Barn Hill
Tidbury Green
Dickens Heath
Cheswick Green
Tilehouse Green
Bentley Heath
Temple Balsall
Balsall
Wythall Heath
Rumbush
Blythe Valley Park
Wythall
Tanner's Green
Dorridge
Fen End
Earlswood
Barley Green
Chadwick End
Meer End
Inkford
Terry's Green
Packwood
Chessett's Wood
Oldwich Lane
Birch Acre
Hockley Heath
Baddesley Clinton
Portway
Honiley
M6
M42
A446
A452
A38
A34
A45
A41
A435
A441
A4177

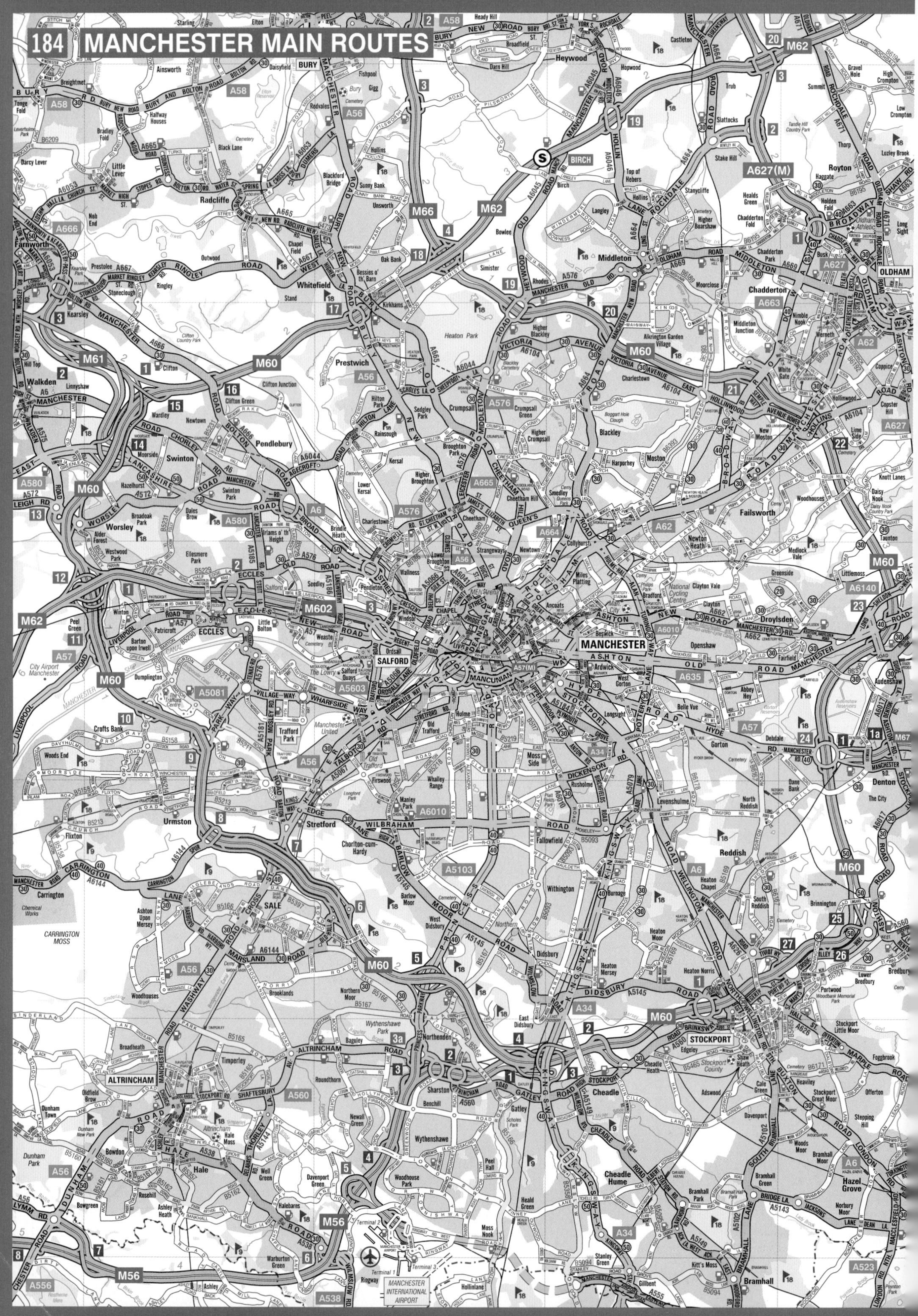
BURY
Heywood
Castleton
Radcliffe
Whitefield
Prestwich
Middleton
Royton
OLDHAM
Chadderton
Failsworth
Walkden
Swinton
Pendlebury
Worsley
Eccles
SALFORD
MANCHESTER
Droylsden
Denton
Stretford
Urmston
SALE
Altrincham
ALTRINCHAM
Hale
Bowdon
Cheadle
Cheadle Hume
STOCKPORT
Bramhall
Hazel Grove
Reddish
Gorton
Openshaw
Levenshulme
Rusholme
Moss Side
Hulme
Withington
Didsbury
Fallowfield
Burnage
Chorlton-cum-Hardy
Northenden
Wythenshawe
Gatley
Heald Green
Timperley
Carrington
Flixton
Farnworth
Kearsley
Crumpsall
Blackley
Moston
Newton Heath
Clayton
Ardwick
Heaton Park
Trafford Park
MANCHESTER INTERNATIONAL AIRPORT
Heaton Chapel
Heaton Moor
Heaton Mersey
Heaton Norris
Edgeley
Woodhouses
Partington
Ashton Upon Mersey
Brooklands
M60
M62
M61
M66
M602
M56
A627(M)
A57(M)
A56
A6
A34
A57
A62
A580
A5103

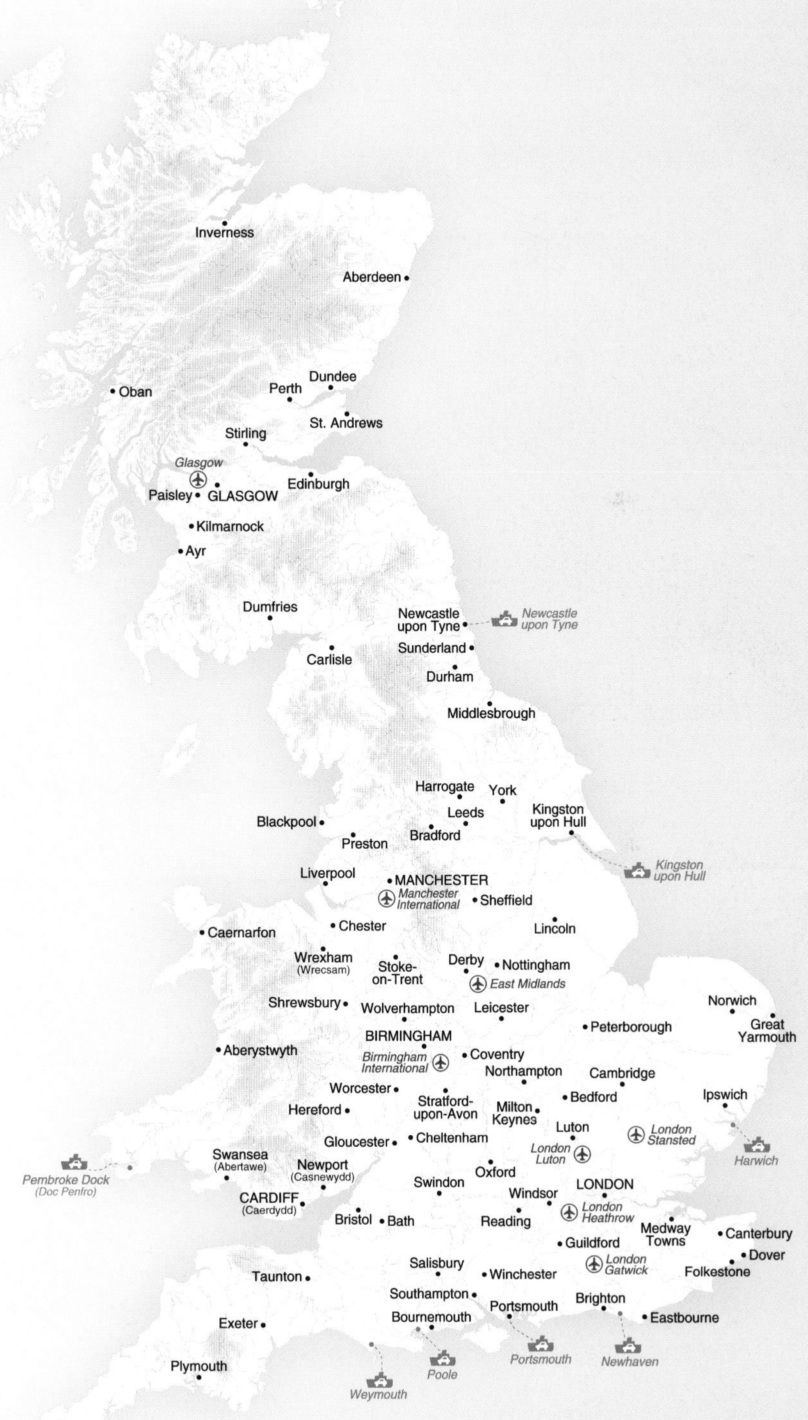

Motorway
Autoroute
Autobahn

Motorway Under Construction
Autoroute en construction
Autobahn im Bau

Motorway Proposed
Autoroute prévue
Geplante Autobahn

Motorway Junctions with Numbers
Unlimited Interchange
Limited Interchange

Autoroute échangeur numéroté
Echangeur complet
Echangeur partiel

Autobahnanschlußstelle mit Nummer
Unbeschränkter Fahrtrichtungswechsel
Beschränkter Fahrtrichtungswechsel

Primary Route
Route à grande circulation
Hauptverkehrsstraße

Dual Carriageways (A & B roads)
Route à double chaussées séparées (route A & B)
Zweispurige Schnellstraße (A- und B- Straßen)

Class A Road
Route de type A
A-Straße

Class B Road
Route de type B
B-Straße

Major Roads Under Construction
Route prioritaire en construction
Hauptverkehrsstaße im Bau

Major Roads Proposed
Route prioritaire prévue
Geplante Hauptverkehrsstaße

Minor Roads
Route secondaire
Nebenstraße

Safety Camera
Radars de contrôle de vitesse
Sicherheitskamera

Restricted Access
Accès réglementé
Beschränkte Zufahrt

Pedestrianized Road & Main Footway
Rue piétonne et chemin réservé aux piétons
Fußgängerstraße und Fußweg

One Way Streets
Sens unique
Einbahnstraße

Fuel Station
Station service
Tankstelle

Toll
Barrière de péage
Gebührenpflichtig

Railway & Station
Voie ferrée et gare
Eisenbahnlinie und Bahnhof

Underground / Metro & DLR Station
Station de métro et DLR
U-Bahnstation und DLR-Station

Level Crossing & Tunnel
Passage à niveau et tunnel
Bahnübergang und Tunnel

Tram Stop & One Way Tram Stop
Arrêt de tramway
Straßenbahnhaltestelle

Built-up Area
Agglomération
Geschloßene Ortschaft

Abbey, Cathedral, Priory etc
Abbaye, cathédrale, prieuré etc
Abtei, Kathedrale, Kloster usw

Airport
Aéroport
Flughafen

Bus Station
Gare routière
Bushaltestelle

Car Park (selection of)
Sélection de parkings
Auswahl von Parkplatz

Church
Eglise
Kirche

City Wall
Murs d'enceinte
Stadtmauer

Congestion Charging Zone
Zone de péage urbain
City-Maut Zone

Ferry (vehicular)
(foot only)

Bac (véhicules)
(piétons)

Fähre (autos)
(nur für Personen)

Golf Course
Terrain de golf
Golfplatz

Heliport
Héliport
Hubschrauberlandeplatz

Hospital
Hôpital
Krankenhaus

Lighthouse
Phare
Leuchtturm

Market
Marché
Markt

National Trust Property
(open)
(restricted opening)
(National Trust for Scotland)
National Trust Property
(ouvert)
(heures d'ouverture)
(National Trust for Scotland)
National Trust- Eigentum
(geöffnet)
(beschränkte Öffnungszeit)
(National Trust for Scotland)

Park & Ride
Parking relais
Auswahl von Parkplatz

Place of Interest
Curiosité
Sehenswürdigkeit

Police Station
Commissariat de police
Polizeirevier

Post Office
Bureau de poste
Postamt

Shopping Area (main street & precinct)
Quartier commerçant (rue et zone principales)
Einkaufsviertel (hauptgeschäftsstraße, fußgängerzone)

Shopmobility
Shopmobility
Shopmobility

Toilet
Toilettes
Toilette

Tourist Information Centre
Syndicat d'initiative
Information

Viewpoint
Vue panoramique
Aussichtspunkt

Visitor Information Centre
Centre d'information touristique
Besucherzentrum

Please note: symbols have been enlarged for clarity

ABERDEEN

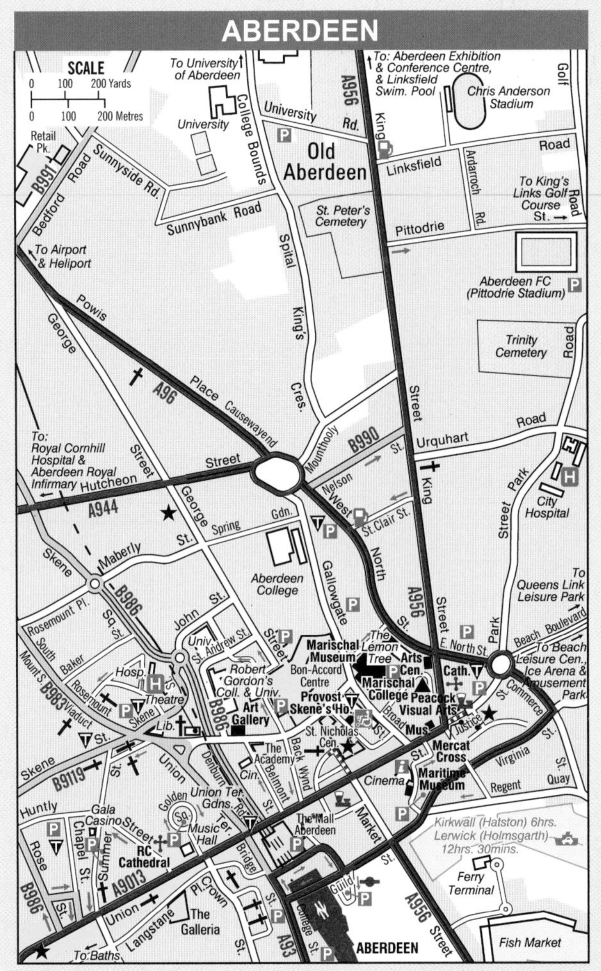
SCALE
0 100 200 Yards
0 100 200 Metres
To University of Aberdeen
To: Aberdeen Exhibition & Conference Centre, & Linksfield Swim. Pool
Chris Anderson Stadium
Golf
Retail Pk.
University
College Bounds
University Rd.
Old Aberdeen
Linksfield
Road
Sunnyside Rd.
Bedford Road
B991
Sunnybank Road
St. Peter's Cemetery
Ardarroch Rd.
To King's Links Golf Course
Pittodrie
To Airport & Heliport
Aberdeen FC (Pittodrie Stadium)
Powis
George
Spital
King's
Cres.
Trinity Cemetery
Road
A96
Place
Causewayend
Street
King
A956
To: Royal Cornhill Hospital & Aberdeen Royal Infirmary
Hutcheon
Street
B990
Urquhart
Road
A944
Mounthooly
Nelson
West
North
St.Clair St.
King
City Hospital
Park
Street
Skene
Maberly
George
Spring
Gdn.
Aberdeen College
Gallowgate
To Queens Link Leisure Park
Rosemount Pl.
B986
John St.
Sq. St.
South
Baker
Univ.
St. Andrew St.
Marischal Museum
The Lemon Tree
Arts Cen.
E. North St.
Cath.
Beach Boulevard
To Beach Leisure Cen., Ice Arena & Amusement Park
Hosp.
Robert Gordon's Coll. & Univ.
Bon-Accord Centre
Marischal College
Peacock Visual Arts
Mount St.
B983
Rosemount Viaduct
Theatre
Skene
Lib.
B986
Art Gallery
Provost Skene's Ho.
St. Nicholas Cen.
Broad
Mus.
Justice
Commerce
Mercat Cross
Maritime Museum
Cinema
Virginia
Regent
Quay
Skene
B9119
Union
The Academy
Belmont
Back Wynd
Huntly
Gala Casino
Golden Sq.
Union Ter. Gdns.
Music Hall
Street
The Mall Aberdeen
Market
St.
Kirkwall (Hatston) 6hrs.
Lerwick (Holmsgarth) 12hrs. 30mins.
Ferry Terminal
Rose
Chapel St.
Summer
RC Cathedral
A9013
Bridge
Crown
Guild
B986
St.
Union
Langstane Pl.
The Galleria
College St.
A93
ABERDEEN
A956
Street
Fish Market
To: Baths

ABERYSTWYTH

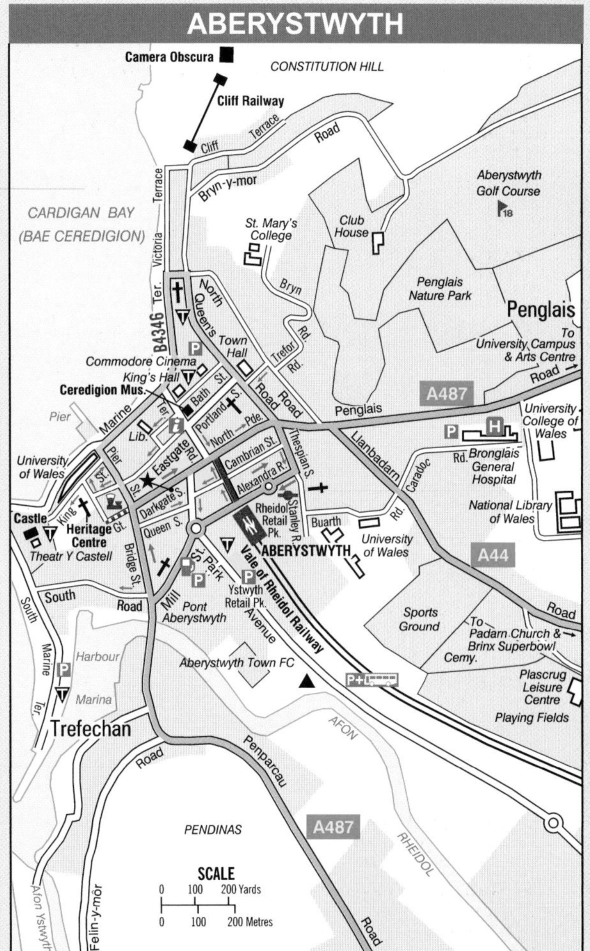
Camera Obscura
CONSTITUTION HILL
Cliff Railway
Cliff
Terrace
Road
Bryn-y-mor
Aberystwyth Golf Course
CARDIGAN BAY
(BAE CEREDIGION)
Victoria
Terrace
St. Mary's College
Club House
Penglais Nature Park
Bryn
B4346
Ter.
North
Queens
Rd.
Town Hall
Trefor
Rd.
Penglais
To University Campus & Arts Centre
Commodore Cinema
King's Hall
Ceredigion Mus.
Bath St.
A487
Road
Penglais
Pier
Marine
Ter.
Lib.
Portland St.
North Pde.
Road
Thespian S.
Llanbadarn
University College of Wales
University of Wales
Pier
St.
Eastgate
Cambrian St.
Alexandra R.
Caradoc
Rd.
Bronglais General Hospital
Castle
Heritage Centre
King's
Gl.
Darkgate S.
Queen S.
Rheidol Retail Pk.
Stanley R.
Buarth
Rd.
National Library of Wales
Theatr Y Castell
Vale of Rheidol Railway
ABERYSTWYTH
University of Wales
A44
South
Bridge St.
Mill
St.
Park
Ystwyth Retail Pk.
Avenue
Road
Sports Ground
Road
South
Marine
Ter.
Pont Aberystwyth
To Padarn Church & Brinx Superbowl
Cemy.
Harbour
Aberystwyth Town FC
Plascrug Leisure Centre
Marina
Playing Fields
Trefechan
AFON
Road
Penparcau
PENDINAS
A487
RHEIDOL
SCALE
0 100 200 Yards
0 100 200 Metres
Afon Ystwyth
Felin-y-mor
Road

AYR

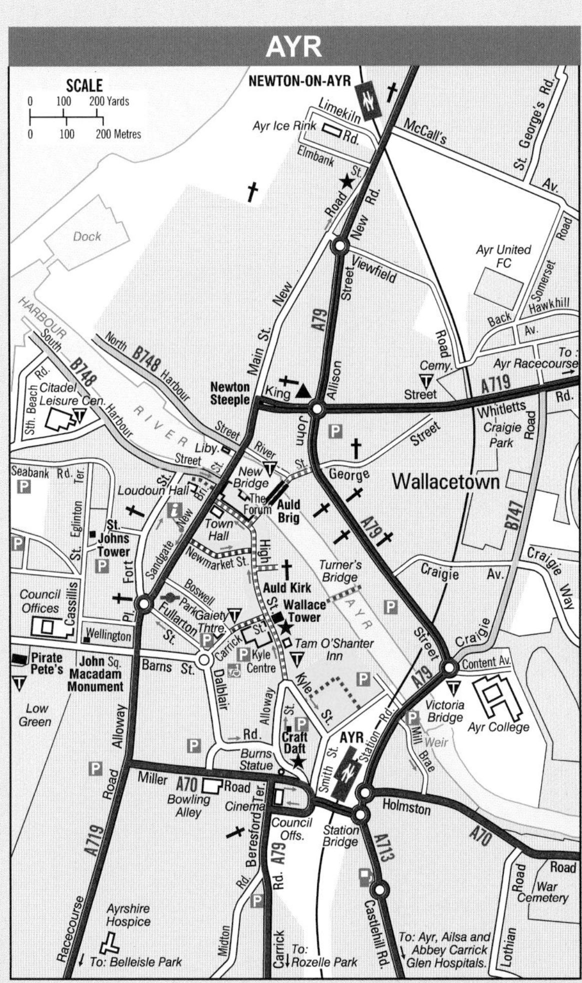
SCALE
0 100 200 Yards
0 100 200 Metres
NEWTON-ON-AYR
Limekiln
Rd.
Ayr Ice Rink
McCall's
St. George's Rd.
Elmbank
St.
Av.
Road
New
Rd.
Dock
Ayr United FC
Road
Viewfield
Street
A79
Somerset
HARBOUR
Back
Hawkhill
Av.
North
B748
Harbour
South
B748
New
Road
Cemy.
Ayr Racecourse
Rd.
Citadel Leisure Cen.
Harbour
Sth. Beach Rd.
Main St.
Newton Steeple
King
St.
A719
Whitletts
Craigie Park
Road
Allison
John
Street
Street
RIVER
Street
Liby.
River
George
Seabank Rd.
Ter.
Eglinton
New Bridge
The Forum
Auld Brig
Wallacetown
B747
Loudoun Hall
St. Johns Tower
Town Hall
Newmarket St.
High St.
A79
Craigie
Av.
Craigie Way
Turner's Bridge
Fort
Sandgate
Auld Kirk
Wallace Tower
Council Offices
Cassillis
Boswell
Park
Fullarton
Gaiety Thtre
Carrick St.
Kyle Centre
Tam O'Shanter Inn
AYR
St.
Craigie
Content Av.
Wellington
Pirate Pete's
John Sq.
Macadam Monument
Barns
St.
Dalblair
Alloway
Kyle
St.
Street
A79
Victoria Bridge
Ayr College
Low Green
Alloway
Rd.
Craft Daft
Burns Statue
Station Rd.
Mill Brae
Weir
Miller
A70
Road
Bowling Alley
Cinema
Smith St.
AYR
Holmston
A70
Road
Road
Ter.
Council Offs.
Station Bridge
A713
War Cemetery
A719
Beresford
Rd.
A79
Rd.
Ayrshire Hospice
Racecourse
To: Belleisle Park
Midton
Carrick
To: Rozelle Park
Castlehill Rd.
To: Ayr, Ailsa and Abbey Carrick Glen Hospitals.
Lothian

BATH

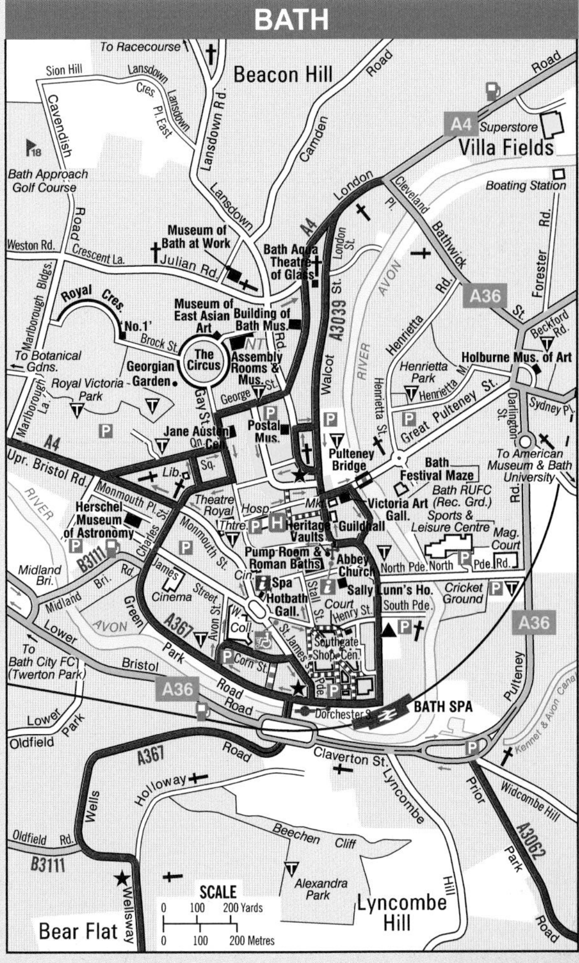
To Racecourse
Sion Hill
Lansdown Cres.
Lansdown Pl. East
Beacon Hill
Road
Lansdown Rd.
Camden
Cavendish
Bath Approach Golf Course
A4
Superstore
Villa Fields
Boating Station
Lansdown
London
Road
Cleveland Pl.
Museum of Bath at Work
Weston Rd.
Crescent La.
Julian Rd.
Bath Aqua Theatre of Glass
A4
London St.
Bathwick
Forester Rd.
Marlborough Bldgs.
Royal Cres.
No.1
Museum of East Asian Art
Building of Bath Mus.
Rd.
Walcot
A3039
St.
AVON
A36
St.
Rd.
To Botanical Gdns.
Brock St.
The Circus
Assembly Rooms & Mus.
RIVER
Henrietta
Beckford Rd.
Georgian Garden
Royal Victoria Park
Gay St.
George
Henrietta Park
Henrietta M.
Holburne Mus. of Art
Marlborough La.
Postal Mus.
Great Pulteney St.
Sydney Pl.
Darlington
A4
Jane Austen Cen.
Pulteney Bridge
To American Museum & Bath University
Upr. Bristol Rd.
Lib.
Sq.
Bath Festival Maze
Monmouth Pl.
Theatre Royal
Hosp.
Victoria Art Gall.
Bath RUFC (Rec. Grd.)
Herschel Museum of Astronomy
Thtre
Heritage Vaults
Guildhall
Sports & Leisure Centre
RIVER
Monmouth St.
Pump Room & Roman Baths
Abbey Church
Mag. Court
Charles
B3111
Pde. Rd.
North Pde. North
Midland Bri.
Bri.
Rd.
James St.
Cin.
Spa
Sally Lunn's Ho.
Cricket Ground
Cinema
Street
Hotbath Gall.
Court
South Pde.
Midland
Green
Henry St.
AVON
Coll.
A367
Avon St.
St. James
Southgate Shop. Cen.
A36
Lower
Bristol
To Bath City FC (Twerton Park)
Park
Corn St.
Road
A36
Road
Dorchester St.
BATH SPA
Lower
Oldfield
Park
A367
Road
Claverton St.
Kennet & Avon Canal
Lyncombe
Prior
Widcombe Hill
Holloway
Wells
Oldfield
Rd.
Beechen
Cliff
A3062
Park
B3111
Alexandra Park
Hill
Lyncombe Hill
SCALE
0 100 200 Yards
0 100 200 Metres
Bear Flat
Wellsway
Road

BEDFORD

BLACKPOOL

BIRMINGHAM (CITY CENTRE)

SCALE
0 100 200 Yards ¼ Mile
0 100 200 300 400 Metres

JEWELLERY QUARTER
Jewellery Quarter Museum
A38(M)
To: Alexander Stadium & Aston Villa FC
B4100
B4114
A4540
Cemetery
School of Jewellery (University)
Warstone Lane
Hockley Centre
University of Central England
Aston University
Nechells Green
A47
St. Pauls
Constitution Hill
RC Cathedral
Dental Hosp.
Children's Hosp.
Sports Centre
To City Hospital
A457
Camden St.
Spring Hill
RBSA Gall.
Graham St. Sikh Temple
Telecom Tower
Mag. Cts.
Central Hall
The Rockface
B4114
Imax Theatre
Millennium Point
Thinktank
B4132
Summer Hill Rd.
B4284
Sandpits Parade
Chest Clinic
SNOW HILL
Crown Ct.
Curzon St.
Ladywood
National Indoor Arena
Museum & Art Gallery
Cathedral
Martineau Pl.
Hall of Memory
Adrian Boult Hall
Town Hall
Birmingham Canal
National Sea Life Cen.
ICC and Symphony Hall
Theatre
BIRMINGHAM NEW ST.
The Pavilions
MOOR ST.
B4100
Bullring Shop. Cen.
The Pallasades
Fazeley Studios
Brindley Place
Ikon Gallery
Crescent Theatre
Gas St. Basin
A38
Mailbox
BBC Birmingham Public Space
Carlton TV
Theatres
Digbeth
Digbeth College
Coach Station
Bordesley
B4100
Register Office
Hippodrome
Arcadian Cen.
Back to Backs
Megabowl
Wholesale Market
Deritend
Bowlplex
Cinema
Fiveways Shopping Centre
To Birmingham City FC
A456
Edgbaston Centre
B4284
Islington Row
Five Ways
FIVE WAYS
Lee Bank
Sports Ground
To Botanical Gardens
A4540
A38
To Edgbaston Cricket Ground
BORDESLEY
River Rea
Camp Hill
B4100

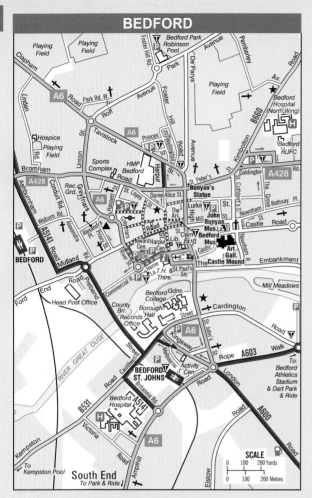

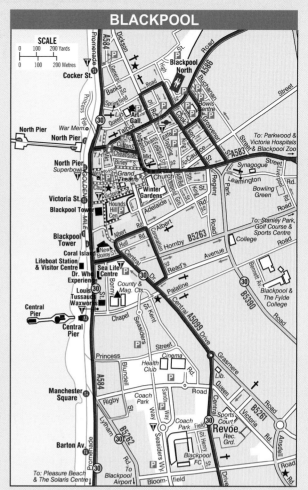

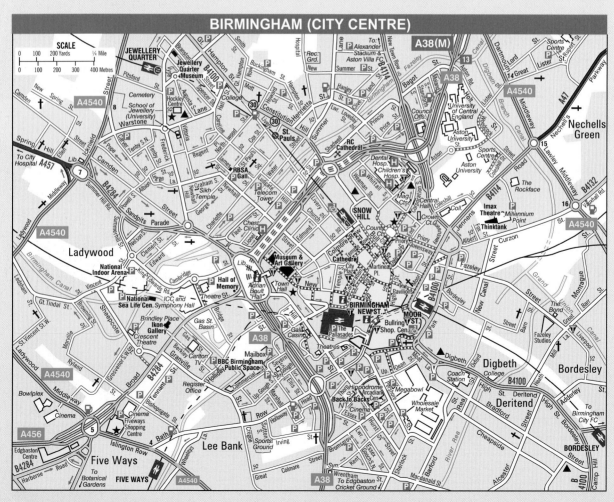

BRIGHTON and HOVE

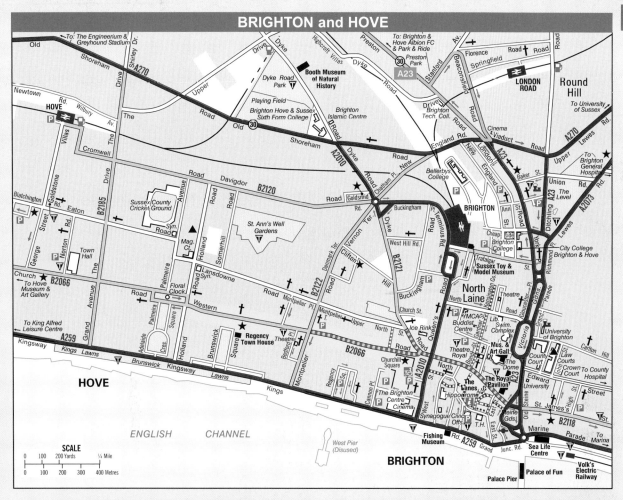

SCALE

0 100 200 Yards ¼ Mile
0 100 200 300 400 Metres

ENGLISH   CHANNEL

HOVE

West Pier
(Disused)

BRIGHTON

Palace Pier   Palace of Fun   Volk's Electric Railway

BRISTOL

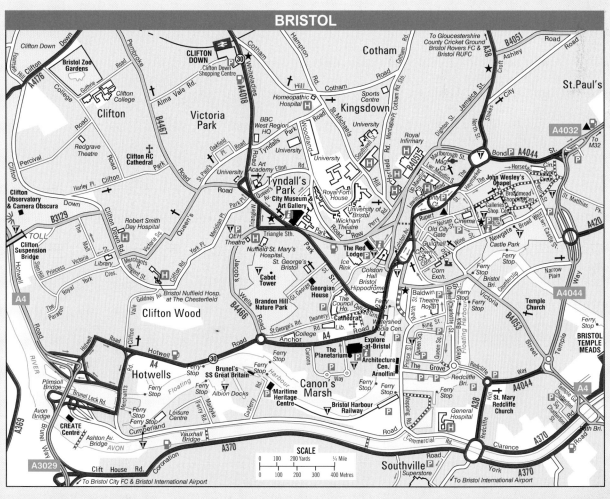

SCALE

0 100 200 Yards ¼ Mile
0 100 200 300 400 Metres

BOURNEMOUTH

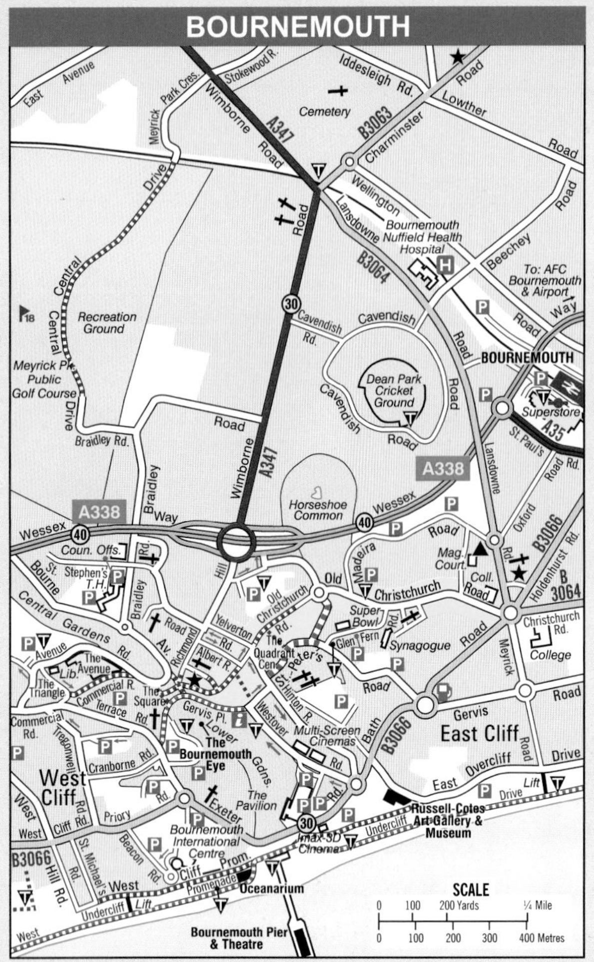
Cemetery
Recreation Ground
Meyrick Pk. Public Golf Course
Bournemouth Nuffield Health Hospital
To: AFC Bournemouth & Airport
BOURNEMOUTH
Dean Park Cricket Ground
Superstore
Horseshoe Common
Coun. Offs.
St. Stephen's T.H.
Super Bowl
Synagogue
Mag. Court
Coll.
Christchurch Rd. College
The Quadrant Cen.
The Triangle
The Square
The Bournemouth Eye
Multi-Screen Cinemas
East Cliff
West Cliff
The Pavilion
Bournemouth International Centre
Imax-3D Cinema
Russell-Cotes Art Gallery & Museum
Oceanarium
Bournemouth Pier & Theatre
A338
A347
A35
B3063
B3064
B3066
Wessex Way
Wimborne Road
Charminster Road
Lansdowne
Christchurch Road
Old Christchurch Rd.
Holdenhurst Rd.
Bath Rd.
Exeter Rd.
Priory Rd.
Undercliff Drive
Overcliff Drive
SCALE
0 100 200 Yards ¼ Mile
0 100 200 300 400 Metres

BRADFORD

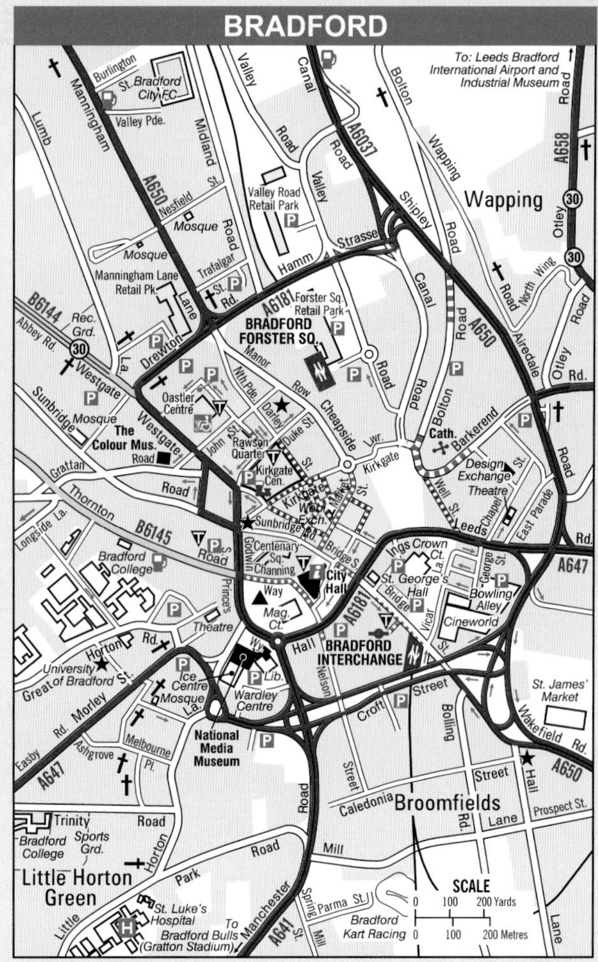
To: Leeds Bradford International Airport and Industrial Museum
Wapping
St. Bradford City F.C.
Valley Pde.
Valley Road Retail Park
Mosque
Manningham Lane Retail Pk.
Forster Sq. Retail Park
BRADFORD FORSTER SQ.
Oastler Centre
The Colour Mus.
Rawson Quarter
Kirkgate Cen.
Wool Exch.
Cath.
Design Exchange Theatre
Bradford College
Centenary Sq.
Channing Way
City Hall
St. George's Hall
Bowling Alley
Cineworld
Theatre
Mag. Ct.
University of Bradford
Ice Centre
Mosque
Lib.
Wardley Centre
BRADFORD INTERCHANGE
St. James' Market
National Media Museum
Broomfields
Trinity Bradford College
Sports Grd.
Little Horton Green
St. Luke's Hospital
To Bradford Bulls (Gratton Stadium)
Bradford Kart Racing
A650
A6037
A6181
A647
A641
A658
B6144
B6145
Manningham Lane
Canal Road
Thornton Road
Manchester Road
Wakefield Rd.
SCALE
0 100 200 Yards
0 100 200 Metres

CAERNARFON

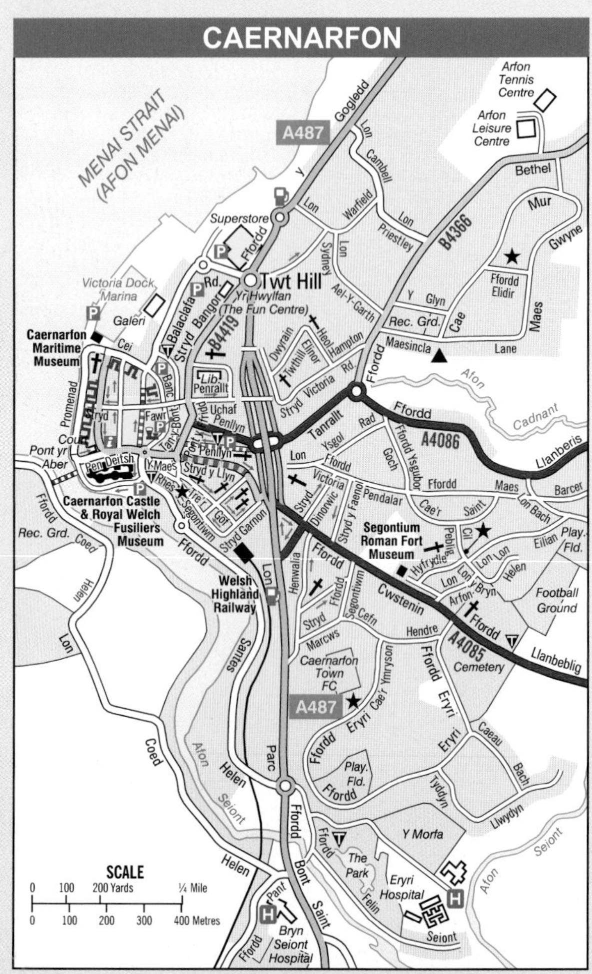
MENAI STRAIT (AFON MENAI)
Arfon Tennis Centre
Arfon Leisure Centre
Superstore
Victoria Dock Marina
Twt Hill
Yr Hwylfan (The Fun Centre)
Caernarfon Maritime Museum
Ffordd Elidir
Rec. Grd.
Lib.
Penllyn
Caernarfon Castle & Royal Welch Fusiliers Museum
Segontium Roman Fort Museum
Welsh Highland Railway
Play. Fld.
Football Ground
Caernarfon Town FC
Cemetery
Y Morfa
The Park
Eryri Hospital
Bryn Seiont Hospital
Afon Cadnant
Afon Seiont
A487
A4086
A4085
B4366
B4419
Llanberis
Llanbeblig
Ffordd Bangor
Cwstenin
Lon Parc
SCALE
0 100 200 Yards ¼ Mile
0 100 200 300 400 Metres

CANTERBURY

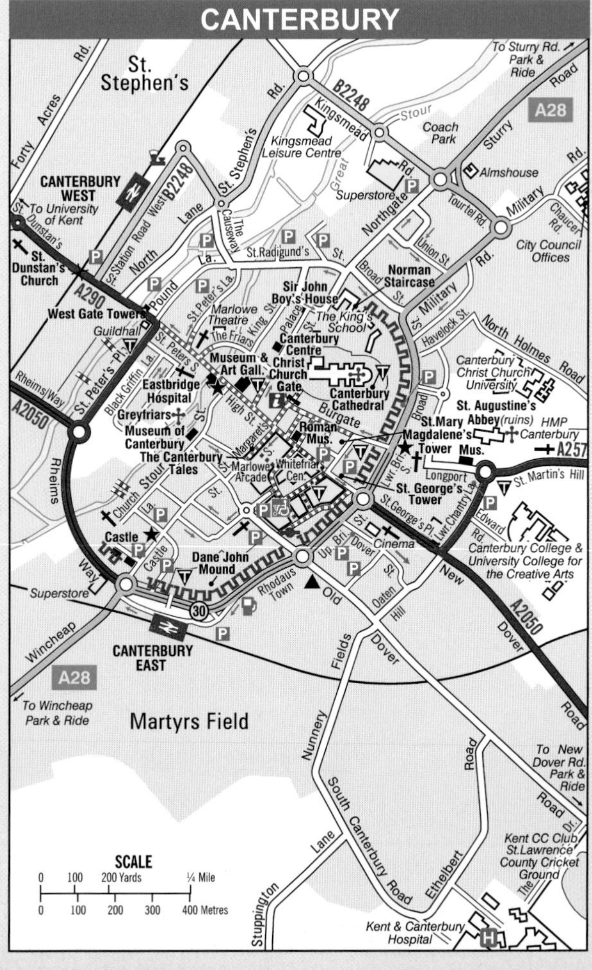
St. Stephen's
To Sturry Rd. Park & Ride
Kingsmead Leisure Centre
Coach Park
Almshouse
CANTERBURY WEST
To University of Kent
St. Dunstan's Church
City Council Offices
West Gate Towers
Guildhall
Marlowe Theatre
Sir John Boy's House
The King's School
Norman Staircase
Canterbury Centre
Museum & Art Gall.
Christ Church Gate
Canterbury Cathedral
Eastbridge Hospital
Greyfriars
Museum of Canterbury
The Canterbury Tales
Roman Mus.
Marlowe Arcade
Whitefriars Cen.
Canterbury Christ Church University
St. Augustine's Abbey (ruins)
HMP Canterbury
St. Mary Magdalene's Tower
Mus.
St. George's Tower
Cinema
Castle
Dane John Mound
Superstore
CANTERBURY EAST
Canterbury College & University College for the Creative Arts
To Wincheap Park & Ride
Martyrs Field
To New Dover Rd. Park & Ride
Kent CC Club St. Lawrence County Cricket Ground
Kent & Canterbury Hospital
A28
A290
A2050
A257
B2248
Rheims Way
Wincheap
Dover Road
Old Dover Rd.
Nunnery Fields
South Canterbury Road
North Holmes Road
SCALE
0 100 200 Yards ¼ Mile
0 100 200 300 400 Metres

CAMBRIDGE

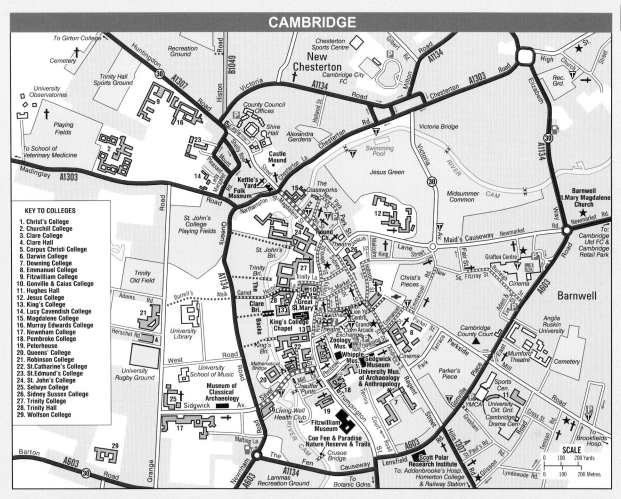

KEY TO COLLEGES
1. Christ's College
2. Churchill College
3. Clare College
4. Clare Hall
5. Corpus Christi College
6. Darwin College
7. Downing College
8. Emmanuel College
9. Fitzwilliam College
10. Gonville & Caius College
11. Hughes Hall
12. Jesus College
13. King's College
14. Lucy Cavendish College
15. Magdalene College
16. Murray Edwards College
17. Newnham College
18. Pembroke College
19. Peterhouse
20. Queens' College
21. Robinson College
22. St.Catharine's College
23. St.Edmund's College
24. St John's College
25. Selwyn College
26. Sidney Sussex College
27. Trinity College
28. Trinity Hall
29. Wolfson College

CARDIFF (CAERDYDD)

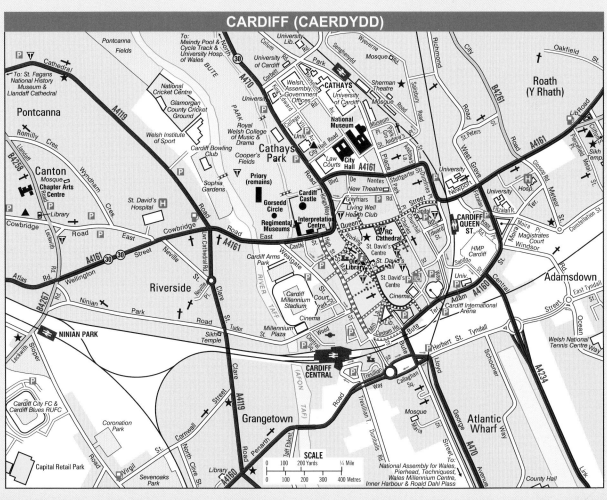

CARLISLE

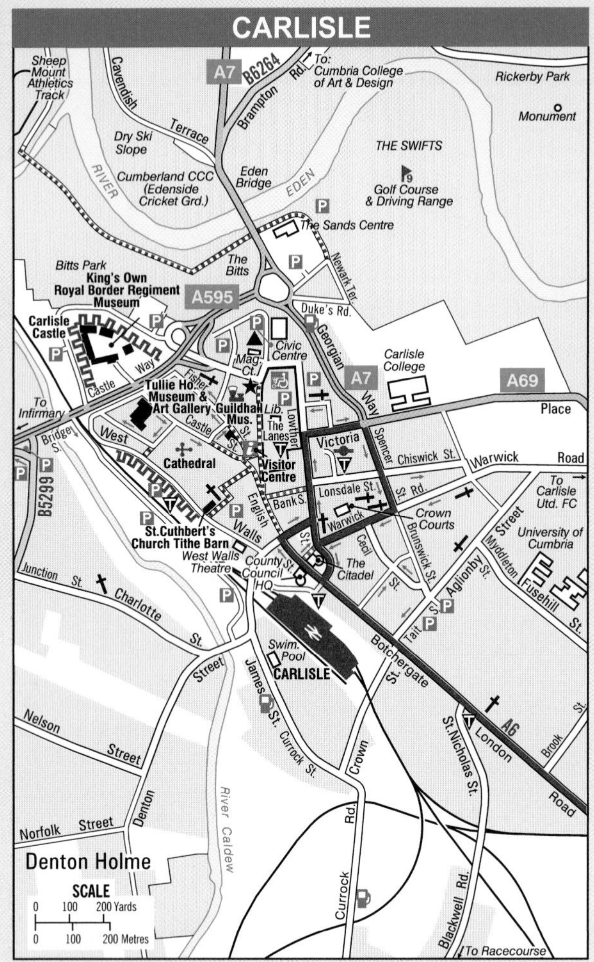

Sheep Mount Athletics Track
A7
B6264
To: Cumbria College of Art & Design
Rickerby Park
Monument
Dry Ski Slope
THE SWIFTS
Cumberland CCC (Edenside Cricket Grd.)
Eden Bridge
Golf Course & Driving Range
The Sands Centre
Bitts Park
The Bitts
King's Own Royal Border Regiment Museum
A595
Carlisle Castle
Duke's Rd.
Civic Centre
Carlisle College
Tullie House Museum & Art Gallery
Guildhall Mus.
A69
To Infirmary
Victoria
Cathedral
Visitor Centre
Chiswick St.
Warwick Road
Lonsdale St.
Crown Courts
To Carlisle Utd. FC
University of Cumbria
St.Cuthbert's Church Tithe Barn
West Walls Theatre
County Council HQ
The Citadel
Junction St.
Charlotte St.
Swim. Pool
CARLISLE
Botchergate
London Road
A6
Nelson Street
Norfolk Street
Denton Holme
River Caldew
Currock Rd.
Blackwell Rd.
To Racecourse
B5299
SCALE
0 100 200 Yards
0 100 200 Metres

CHELTENHAM

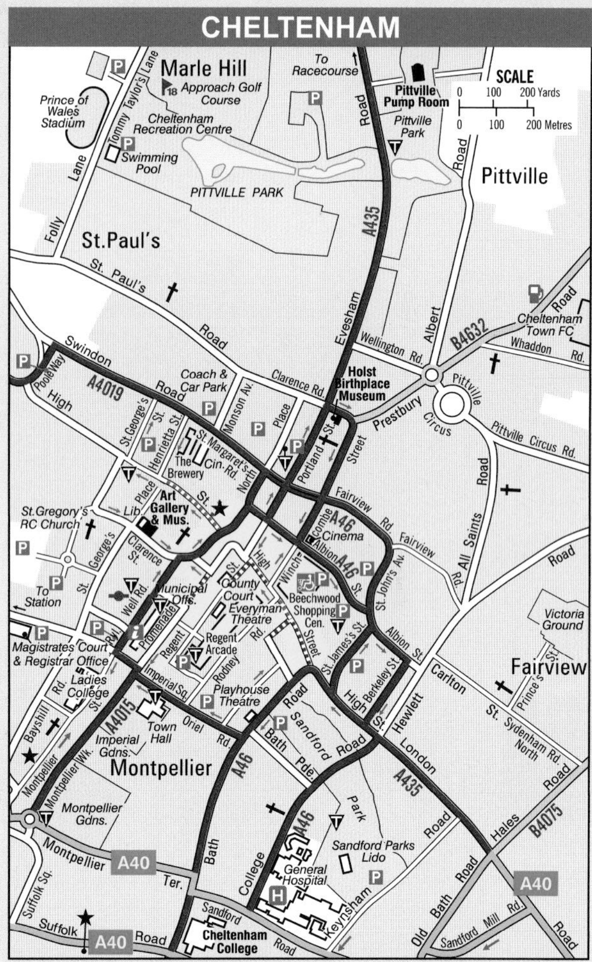

Marle Hill
Approach Golf Course
To Racecourse
Pittville Pump Room
SCALE
0 100 200 Yards
0 100 200 Metres
Prince of Wales Stadium
Cheltenham Recreation Centre
Pittville Park
Swimming Pool
Pittville
PITTVILLE PARK
St.Paul's
A435
Evesham Road
Cheltenham Town FC
Whaddon Rd.
B4632
Swindon Road
A4019
Coach & Car Park
Clarence Rd.
Holst Birthplace Museum
Prestbury
Pittville Circus
The Brewery
Art Gallery & Mus.
St.Gregory's RC Church
Cinema
A46
Fairview
All Saints Rd.
To Station
Municipal Offs.
County Court
Everyman Theatre
Beechwood Shopping Cen.
Regent Arcade
Victoria Ground
Magistrates Court & Registrar Office
Ladies College
Imperial Sq.
Playhouse Theatre
Town Hall
Imperial Gdns.
Montpellier
Sandford Park
A435
Montpellier Gdns.
A40
Sandford Parks Lido
General Hospital
B4075
Cheltenham College
Suffolk Road

CHESTER

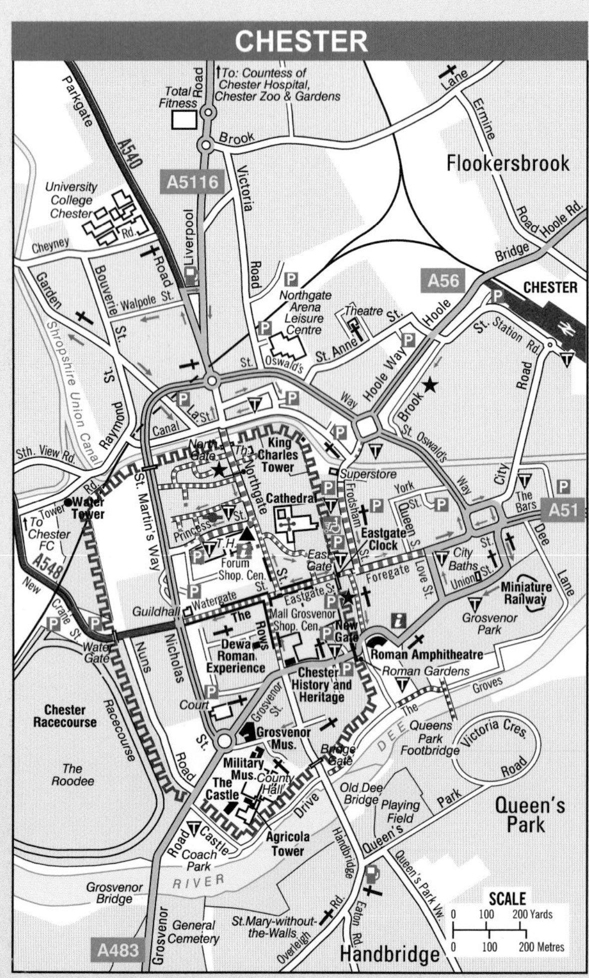

To: Countess of Chester Hospital, Chester Zoo & Gardens
Total Fitness
Parkgate
A540
Brook
A5116
Flookersbrook
University College Chester
Hoole Rd.
Northgate Arena Leisure Centre
A56
CHESTER
Shropshire Union Canal
King Charles Tower
Superstore
Water Tower
Cathedral
To Chester FC
A548
Eastgate Clock
The Bars
A51
Forum Shop. Cen.
City Baths
Miniature Railway
Grosvenor Park
The Rows
Dewa Roman Experience
Roman Amphitheatre
Roman Gardens
Chester History and Heritage
Chester Racecourse
The Roodee
Grosvenor Mus.
Queens Park Footbridge
Military Mus.
The Castle
County Hall
Agricola Tower
Old Dee Bridge
Playing Field
Queen's Park
Coach Park
RIVER DEE
Grosvenor Bridge
General Cemetery
St.Mary-without-the-Walls
Handbridge
A483
SCALE
0 100 200 Yards
0 100 200 Metres

COVENTRY

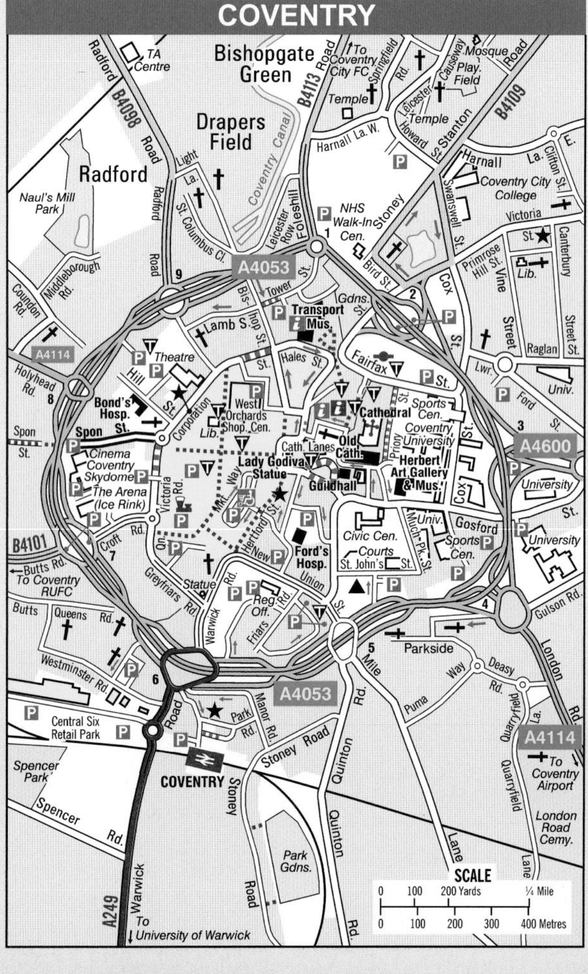

TA Centre
Bishopgate Green
To Coventry City FC
Mosque
Play. Field
Temple
Drapers Field
Radford
Coventry Canal
Coventry City College
Naul's Mill Park
NHS Walk-In Cen.
A4053
Transport Mus.
A4114
Theatre
Bond's Hosp.
West Orchards Shop. Cen.
Cathedral
Sports Cen.
Coventry University
Cinema Coventry Skydome
The Arena (Ice Rink)
Lady Godiva Statue
Old Cath.
Guildhall
Herbert Art Gallery & Mus.
A4600
University
B4101
To Coventry RUFC
Civic Cen.
Courts
Ford's Hosp.
Gosford Sports Cen.
Reg. Off.
Parkside
Central Six Retail Park
A4114
To Coventry Airport
London Road Cemy.
COVENTRY
Spencer Park
Park Gdns.
A249
To University of Warwick
SCALE
0 100 200 Yards ¼ Mile
0 100 200 300 400 Metres

DERBY

DUMFRIES

DOVER

To: Buckland Hospital & Dover Ath FC
Superstores
A256
Tower Hamlets
Castleton Retail Pk.
Charlton Centre
Maison Dieu (Town Hall)
Connaught Park
Bleriot Memorial
A2
Langdon Cliffs Picnic Site
Gateway to the White Cliffs
NT
TOLL
Dover Castle
PWRR & Queen's Regt. Mus.
Hellfire Corner & Underground Hospital
The Pharos
St. Mary-in-Castro Saxon Church
Car Ferry Terminal
Dover College
Pencester Gds.
Old St. James Church Ruins
Moat's Bulwark
Secret Wartime Tunnels
EASTERN DOCKS
DOVER PRIORY
Roman Painted House
Dover Leisure Centre
Dover Mus.
Bureau de Change
Dover Discovery Centre & Lib.
Captain Webb Memorial
C S Rolls Statue
To The Women's Land Army Musem
B2011
Clarendon
Drop Redoubt
Western Heights
Dunkirk Memorial
Sea Sports Centre
OUTER HARBOUR
Boulogne 1hr. 45mins.
Calais 1hr. 10mins.
Dieppe 4hrs. 15mins.
Dunkirk 2hrs.
Grand Shaft
Knights Templar Church (remains of)
WESTERN DOCKS
Prince of Wales Pier
Southern Breakwater
Aycliff
A20
To Shakespeare Cliff
Old Folkestone Road
INNER HARBOUR
Cruise Liner Terminal
Admiralty Pier
SCALE
0 100 200 Yards ¼ Mile
0 100 200 300 400 Metres

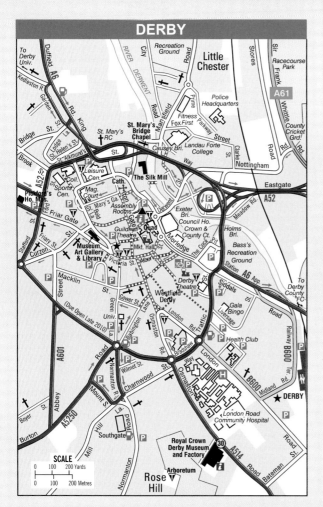

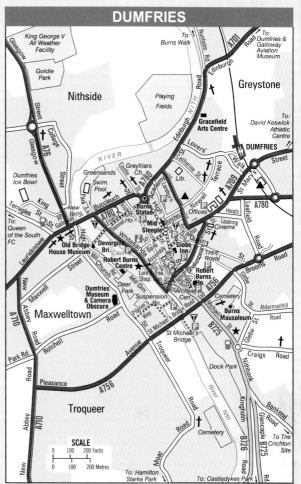

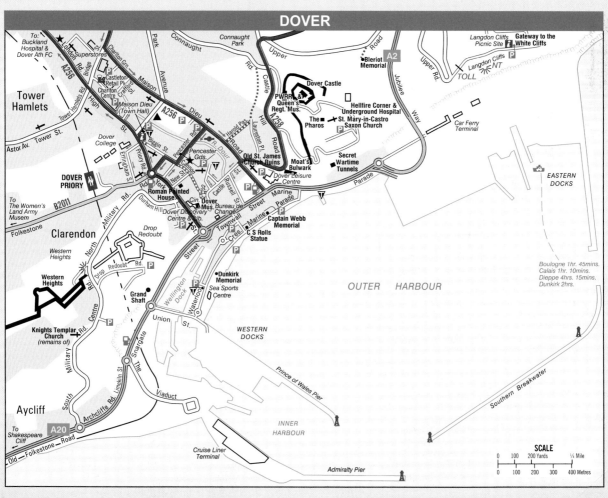

DUNDEE

DURHAM

EDINBURGH

SCALE
0 100 200 Yards ¼ Mile
0 100 200 300 400 Metres

Stockbridge
To Royal Botanic Garden
Football Ground
Cricket Ground
Broughton
McDonald Rd.
Hibernian FC
Raeburn Pl.
B900
Henderson Row
Patriothall Gallery
Great King Street
Drummond Place
London St.
Montgomery
Norton Park
To Meadowbank Sports Centre
Royal Terrace Gardens
B1350
Abbeyhill
A1
New Town
The Scottish Gallery
Open Eye Gallery
Scottish National Portrait Gallery
St. Mary's RC Cathedral
Picardy Pl.
Omni Centre
Edinburgh Playhouse
To Scottish National Gallery of Modern Art
Moray Place
Heriot Queen Street
St. James Centre
St. Andrew Sq.
Register House
Calton Hill
Regent Gardens
National Monument
Calton
City Observatory
Nelson Monument
Dean Bri.
Queen Street
Thistle
St. Andrew's House
Burns Monument
Holyrood Abbey (remains)
The Queen's Gall.
Palace of Holyroodhouse
The Georgian House
Assembly Rooms
Princes Mall
EDINBURGH WAVERLEY
City Council
West Register House
Charlotte Square
Scott Mon.
Fruitmarket Gall.
The People's Story
Canongate Kirk
Scottish Parliament
No. 28 Charlotte Square
Princes St.
Floral Clock
Academy
National Gallery
The Dungeon
Stills Gallery
Mus. on the Mound
City Art Centre
John Knox Ho.
The Netherbow
Museum of Edinburgh
Canongate
Our Dynamic Earth
Trams for Edinburgh Due open Mid. 2012
Open Air Theatre
West Princes Street Gardens
Camera Obscura
Tartan Weaving Mill & Exhibition
Gladstone's Land
The Writer's Mus.
St. Giles Cathedral
Parliament House
Museum of Childhood
Holyrood
St. Mary's Episcopal Cathedral
Edinburgh Castle
Nat. War Mem. & Museum
Scotch Whisky Experience
National Library
Central Library
Museum
Gallery
Shandwick Pl.
Traverse Theatre
Usher Hall
Ryl. Lyceum Theatre
Greyfriars Bobby
Greyfriars Tolbooth & Highland Kirk
National Museum of Scotland
University
Pleasance Theatre
Holyrood Park
Conference Centre
Cinema
Morrison St.
Bread St.
Old Town
Museum of Fire
George Heriot's Coll. School
Festival Theatre
Crags Sports Centre
Salisbury Crags
Arthur's Seat
To: Murrayfield Rugby Ground & Airport
Lauriston
Reid Concert Hall
Mus. of Instruments
George Sq.
Mosque
Leisure Centre
Princess Alexandra Eye Pavilion
Edinburgh Dental Institute
South Side
Edinburgh University
George Sq. Theatre
To Heart of Midlothian FC
Fountainbridge
Cameo Cinema
The Meadows
St. Leonards
King's Theatre
West Meadow Park
East Meadow Park
Union Canal
Viewforth
Melville Drive
A700
The Queen's Hall
To Royal Infirmary
To Royal Commonwealth Pool
A702
Queen's Drive

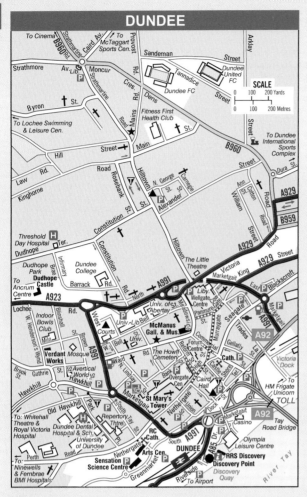

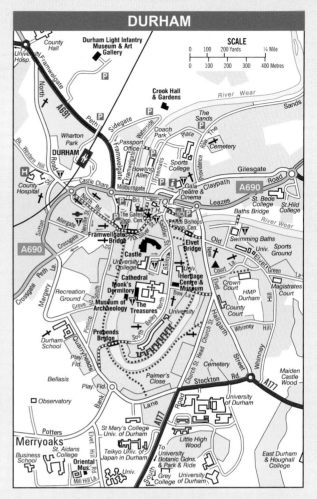

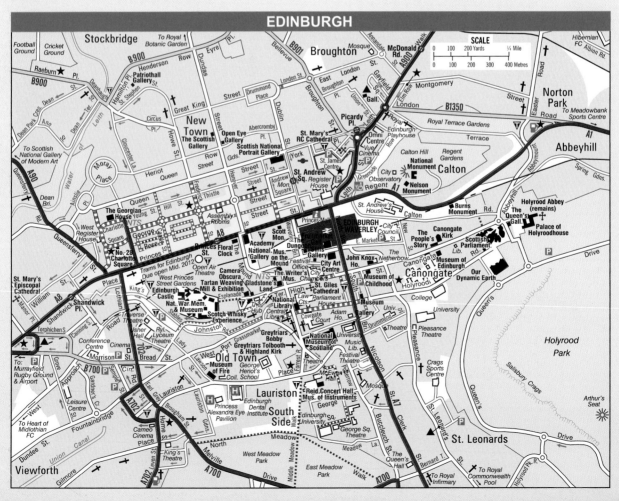

EXETER

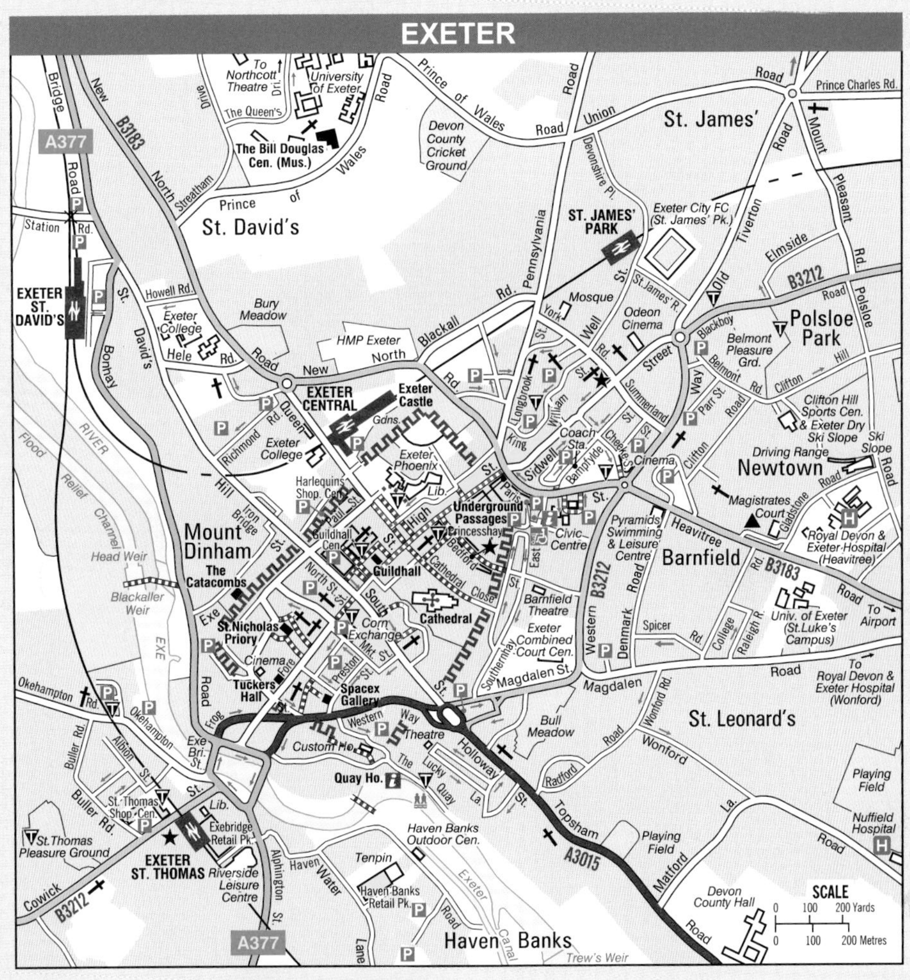

St. David's
St. James'
Polsloe Park
Newtown
Mount Dinham
Barnfield
St. Leonard's
Haven Banks
EXETER ST. DAVID'S
EXETER CENTRAL
EXETER ST. THOMAS
ST. JAMES' PARK
Exeter City FC (St. James' Pk.)
University of Exeter
The Bill Douglas Cen. (Mus.)
Devon County Cricket Ground
HMP Exeter
Exeter Castle
Exeter Phoenix
Harlequins Shop. Cen.
Underground Passages
Princesshay
Civic Centre
Guildhall
Guildhall Cen.
The Catacombs
St. Nicholas Priory
Cathedral
Corn Exchange
Tuckers Hall
Spacex Gallery
Custom Ho.
Quay Ho.
Barnfield Theatre
Exeter Combined Court Cen.
Pyramids Swimming & Leisure Centre
Magistrates Court
Royal Devon & Exeter Hospital (Heavitree)
Univ. of Exeter (St.Luke's Campus)
Royal Devon & Exeter Hospital (Wonford)
Nuffield Hospital
Playing Field
Devon County Hall
Haven Banks Outdoor Cen.
Tenpin
Haven Banks Retail Pk.
Exebridge Retail Pk.
Riverside Leisure Centre
St.Thomas Pleasure Ground
St. Thomas Shop. Cen.
Bury Meadow
Bull Meadow
Head Weir
Blackaller Weir
Trew's Weir
Clifton Hill Sports Cen. & Exeter Dry Ski Slope
Driving Range
Belmont Pleasure Grd.
Odeon Cinema
Mosque
Coach Sta.
A377
B3183
B3212
A3015
SCALE
0 100 200 Yards
0 100 200 Metres

EASTBOURNE

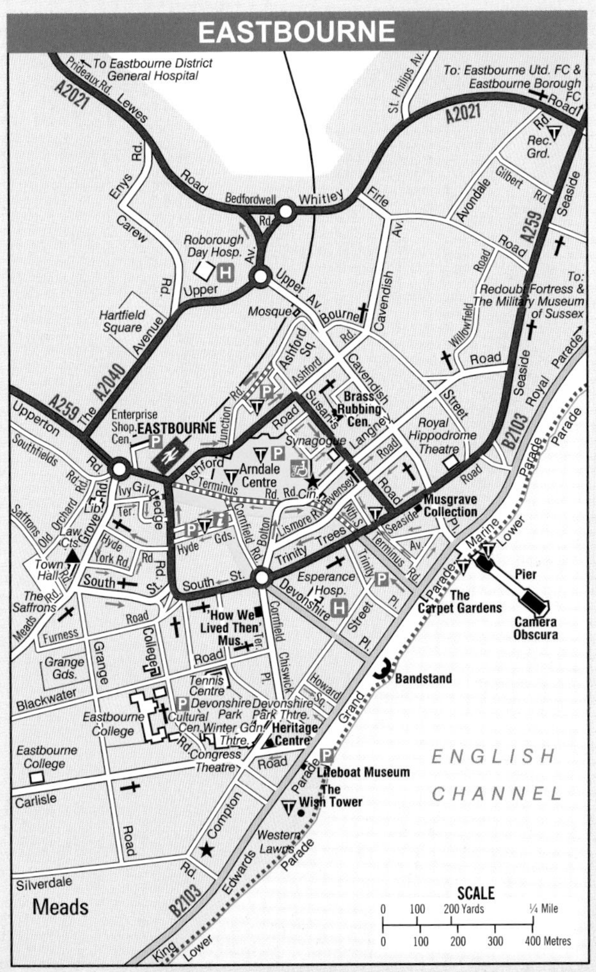

To Eastbourne District General Hospital
To: Eastbourne Utd. FC & Eastbourne Borough FC
Roborough Day Hosp.
Hartfield Square
EASTBOURNE
Enterprise Shop. Cen.
Arndale Centre
Brass Rubbing Cen.
Royal Hippodrome Theatre
Musgrave Collection
Esperance Hosp.
'How We Lived Then' Mus.
Pier
Camera Obscura
The Carpet Gardens
Bandstand
Devonshire Park Thtre.
Winter Gdn. Thtre.
Heritage Centre
Congress Theatre
Eastbourne College
Lifeboat Museum
The Wish Tower
Western Lawns
Town Hall
Meads
To: Redoubt Fortress & The Military Museum of Sussex
ENGLISH CHANNEL
A2021
A259
A2040
B2103
SCALE
0 100 200 Yards ¼ Mile
0 100 200 300 400 Metres

FOLKESTONE

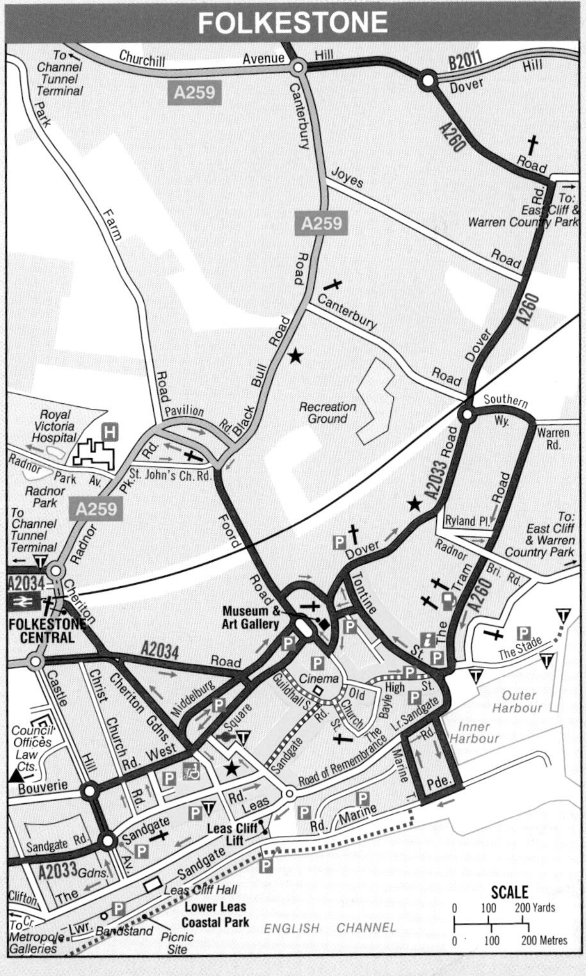

To Channel Tunnel Terminal
To: East Cliff & Warren Country Park
Recreation Ground
Royal Victoria Hospital
FOLKESTONE CENTRAL
Museum & Art Gallery
Cinema
Council Offices
Law Cts.
Leas Cliff Lift
Leas Cliff Hall
Lower Leas Coastal Park
Bandstand
Picnic Site
To Metropole Galleries
Outer Harbour
Inner Harbour
ENGLISH CHANNEL
A259
A260
A2033
A2034
B2011
SCALE
0 100 200 Yards
0 100 200 Metres

GLASGOW

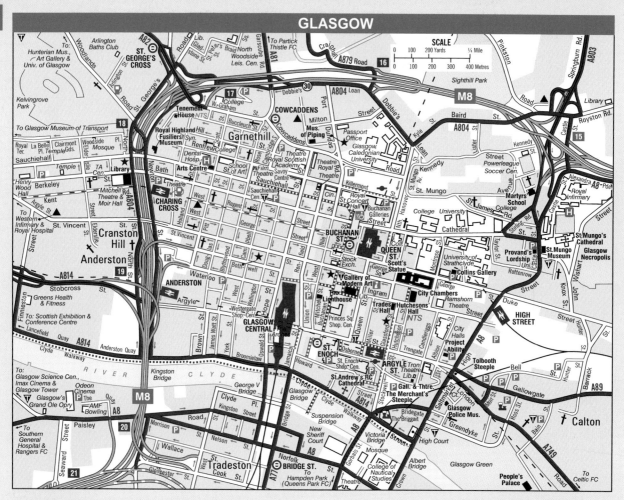

SCALE
0   100   200 Yards   ¼ Mile
0   100   200   300   400 Metres

GLOUCESTER

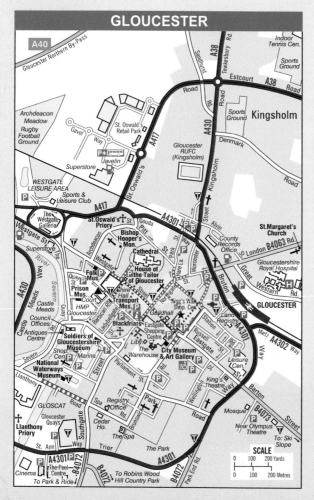

SCALE
0   100   200 Yards
0   100   200 Metres

GREAT YARMOUTH

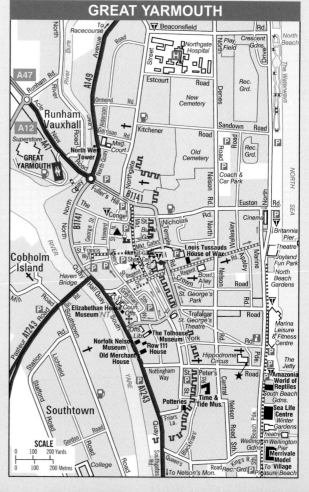

SCALE
0   100   200 Yards
0   100   200 Metres

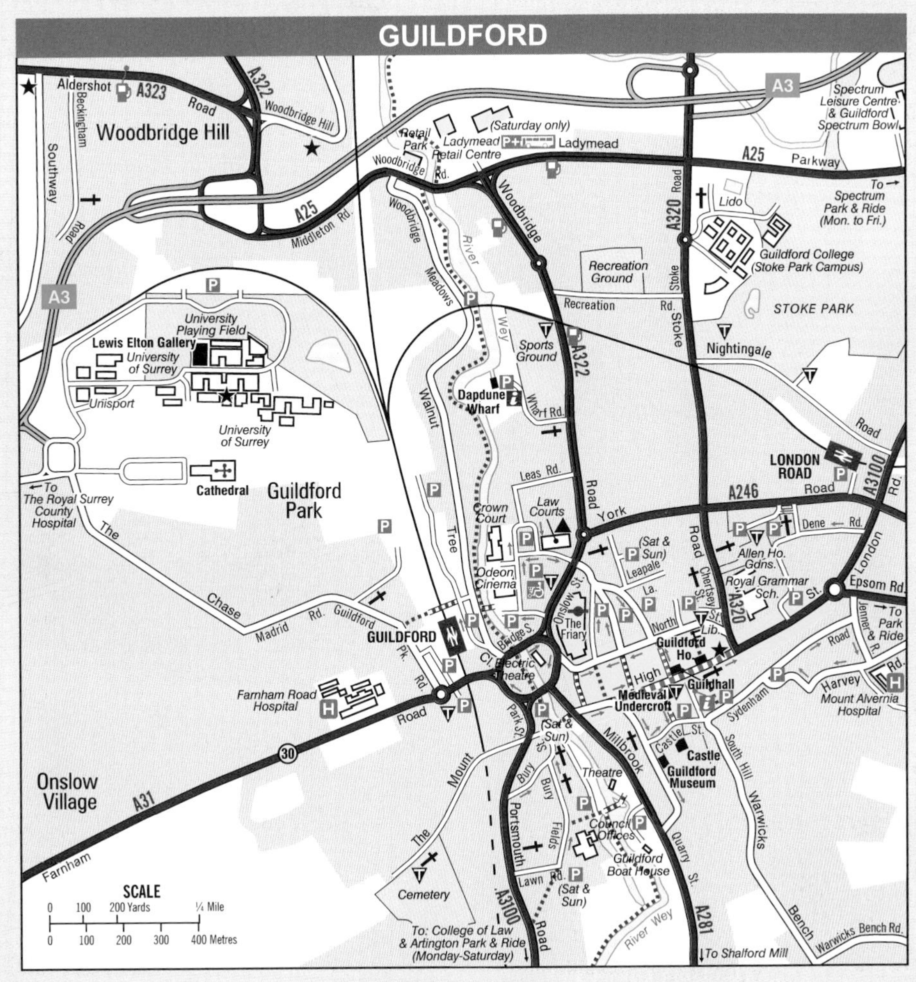

Aldershot ★ A323 Road
Woodbridge Hill
Beckingham
Woodbridge Hill
Southway
A25
A322
Woodbridge Hill
Middleton Rd.
Woodbridge
Retail Park
(Saturday only)
Ladymead Retail Centre P+R Ladymead
A25
A320
Lido
A25 Parkway
Spectrum Leisure Centre & Guildford Spectrum Bowl
A3
To Spectrum Park & Ride (Mon. to Fri.)
A3
River Wey
Meadows
Recreation Ground
Recreation Rd.
Stoke Road
Guildford College (Stoke Park Campus)
STOKE PARK
Nightingale
A320
P
University Playing Field
Lewis Elton Gallery
University of Surrey
Unisport
University of Surrey
Walnut Tree
Dapdune Wharf
Wharf Rd.
Sports Ground
Leas Rd.
York Road
Stoke Road
A246
London
LONDON ROAD
A3100
Epsom Rd.
To Park & Ride
To The Royal Surrey County Hospital
The Chase
Cathedral
Guildford Park
P
Madrid Rd. Guildford
Crown Court
Law Courts
Leapale
Allen Ho. Gdns.
Royal Grammar Sch.
A320
Charter
Jenner Rd.
Harvey Rd.
Mount Alvernia Hospital
GUILDFORD
Electric Theatre
Odeon Cinema
The Friary
North St.
High
Guildford Ho.
Guildhall
Sydenham
Farnham Road Hospital
Farnham Road Hospital H
Farnham Road
Mount
Bury St.
Portsmouth Road
Park St.
Millbrook
Medieval Undercroft
Castle St.
South Hill
Warwicks
Castle
Guildford Museum
Quarry St.
Onslow Village
A31
Farnham
Theatre
Fields
Council Offices
Guildford Boat House
Lawn Rd.
Bench Rd.
Warwicks Bench Rd.
Cemetery
River Wey
A3100
A281
To Shalford Mill
To College of Law & Artington Park & Ride (Monday-Saturday)

SCALE
0 100 200 Yards ¼ Mile
0 100 200 300 400 Metres

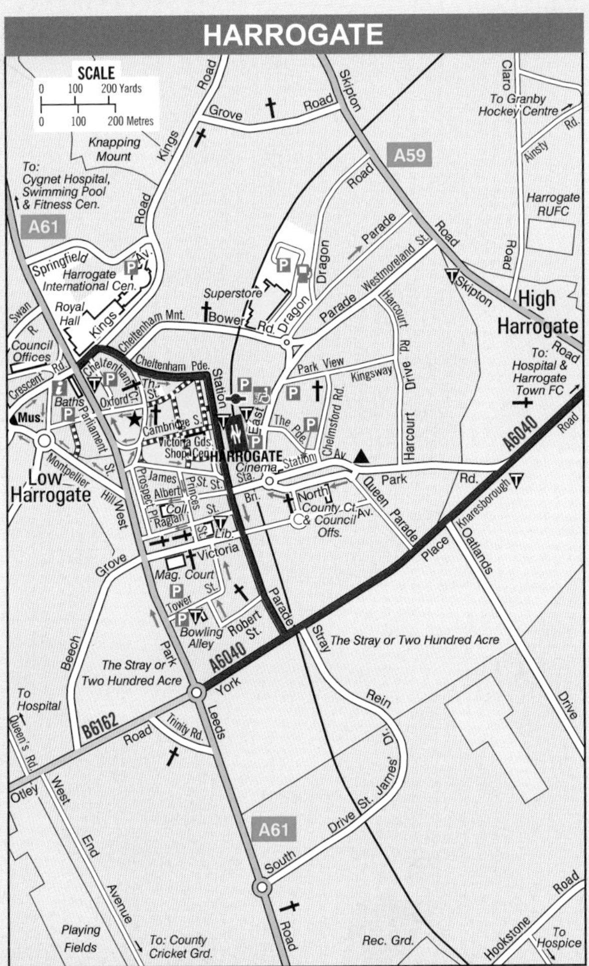

SCALE
0 100 200 Yards
0 100 200 Metres
Grove Road
Kings Road
Knapping Mount
A59
Claro Road
To Granby Hockey Centre
To: Cygnet Hospital, Swimming Pool & Fitness Cen.
A61
Springfield
Harrogate International Cen.
Royal Hall
Kings Road
Council Offices
Cheltenham Mnt.
Cheltenham Pde.
Superstore
Bower Rd.
Dragon Parade
Dragon Road
Westmoreland St.
Harcourt Rd.
Skipton Road
Harrogate RUFC
Skipton Road
High Harrogate
Mus.
Baths
Oxford St.
Crescent Rd.
Parliament St.
Cambridge St.
Park View
Kingsway
Chelmsford Rd.
Harcourt Dr.
To Hospital & Harrogate Town FC
A6040
Low Harrogate
Montpellier Hill
Prospect
James St.
St. Albans
HARROGATE
Cinema
The Pde.
Station
Bn.
North County Ct. & Council Offs.
Park
Knaresborough Rd.
A6040
Victoria
Mag. Court
Tower
Oatlands Drive
Beech Grove
West Park
Bowling Alley
Robert St.
Stray
Parade
The Stray or Two Hundred Acre
The Stray or Two Hundred Acre
To Hospital
B6162
Queen's Rd.
Otley Road
West End Avenue
Drive
St. James
A6040
York Place
Rein
Leeds Road
Trinity Rd.
A61
Playing Fields
South
Hookstone
Rec. Grd.
To County Cricket Grd.
To Hospice

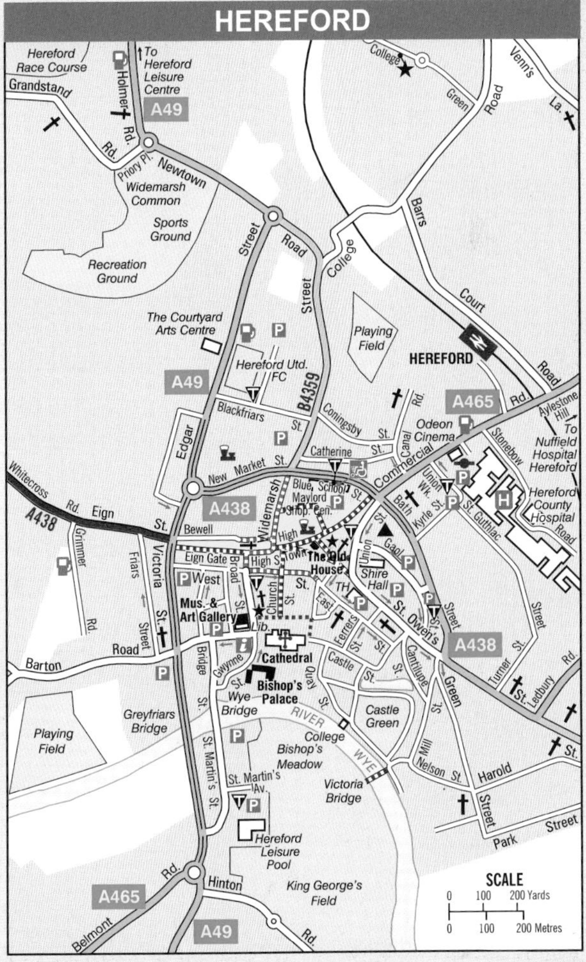

Hereford Race Course
Grandstand
Holmer Rd.
To Hereford Leisure Centre
A49
College Road
Venns La.
Priory Pk.
Newtown
Widemarsh Common
Sports Ground
Recreation Ground
Station Road
Barrs Court Road
The Courtyard Arts Centre
Playing Field
HEREFORD
A49
Hereford Utd. FC
Edgar St.
B4359
Blackfriars
Conningsby St.
Catherine St.
Commercial Road
A465
Odeon Cinema
Stonebow
To Nuffield Hospital Hereford
Hereford County Hospital
H
Whitecross Rd.
A438
Eign St.
Grimmer
New Market
Widemarsh St.
Blueschool St.
Maylord
St. Owen St.
Kyrle St.
Gaol St.
Victoria St.
Friars St.
Bewell St.
Eign Gate
High Town
West St.
The Old House
Shire Hall
Green
Commercial Street
St. Peter's St.
Mus. & Art Gallery
Church St.
King St.
Cathedral
Bishop's Palace
Cathedral
Gwynne St.
Bridge St.
Castle St.
Castle Green
A438
Turner St.
St. Ledbury Rd.
Greyfriars Bridge
Wye Bridge
RIVER WYE
College
Bishop's Meadow
Victoria Bridge
Nelson St.
Harold St.
Park Street
Barton Road
Playing Field
St. Martin's St.
St. Martin's Av.
King George's Field
Hereford Leisure Pool
A465
Hinton Rd.
Belmont Rd.
A49

SCALE
0 100 200 Yards
0 100 200 Metres

INVERNESS

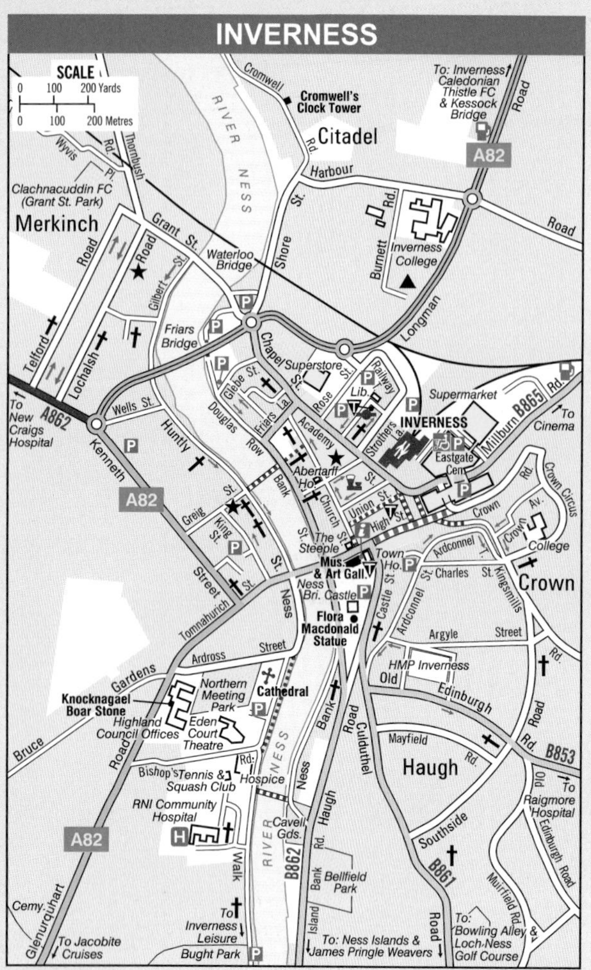

SCALE
0 100 200 Yards
0 100 200 Metres
Cromwell's Clock Tower
Citadel
To: Inverness Caledonian Thistle FC & Kessock Bridge
A82
Clachnacuddin FC (Grant St. Park)
Merkinch
Harbour
Waterloo Bridge
Inverness College
Friars Bridge
Superstore
Supermarket
INVERNESS
Eastgate Cen.
To New Craigs Hospital
A862
To Cinema
Abertarff Ho.
The Steeple
Mus. & Art Gall.
Town Ho.
Ness Bri.
Castle
Flora Macdonald Statue
Crown
College
HMP Inverness
Knocknagael Boar Stone
Northern Meeting Park
Highland Council Offices
Eden Court Theatre
Cathedral
Bishop's Tennis & Squash Club
Hospice
RNI Community Hospital
Cavell Gds.
Haugh
Bellfield Park
To Raigmore Hospital
To Jacobite Cruises
To Inverness Leisure
Bught Park
To: Ness Islands & James Pringle Weavers
To: Bowling Alley & Loch Ness Golf Course
A82
B862
B861
B853
B865

IPSWICH

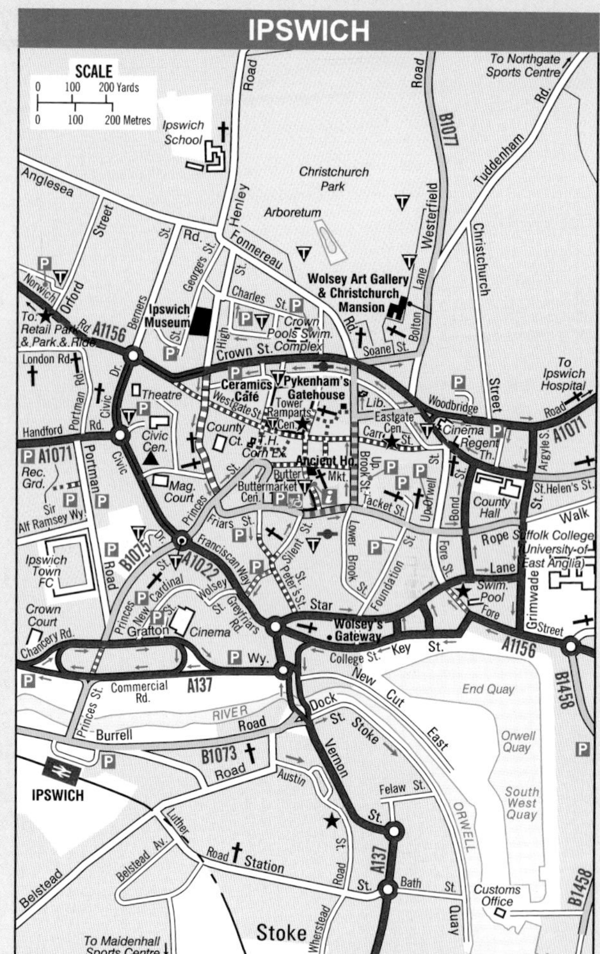

SCALE
0 100 200 Yards
0 100 200 Metres
Ipswich School
To Northgate Sports Centre
Christchurch Park
Arboretum
Wolsey Art Gallery & Christchurch Mansion
Ipswich Museum
Crown Pools Swim. Complex
To: Retail Park & Park & Ride
A1156
To Ipswich Hospital
Theatre
Ceramics Café
Pykenham's Gatehouse
Tower Ramparts Cen.
Civic Cen.
County Ct.
Corn Ex.
Ancient Ho.
Buttermarket Cen.
Cinema
Regent Th.
County Hall
Suffolk College
University of East Anglia
A1071
Rec. Grd.
Sir Alf Ramsey Wy.
Ipswich Town FC
Mag. Court
Crown Court
Grafton
Cinema
Swim. Pool
Wolsey's Gateway
A1022
A137
Commercial Rd.
RIVER
End Quay
Orwell Quay
South West Quay
IPSWICH
B1073
Station
Customs Office
To Maidenhall Sports Centre
Stoke
A1156
B1458
B1077

KILMARNOCK

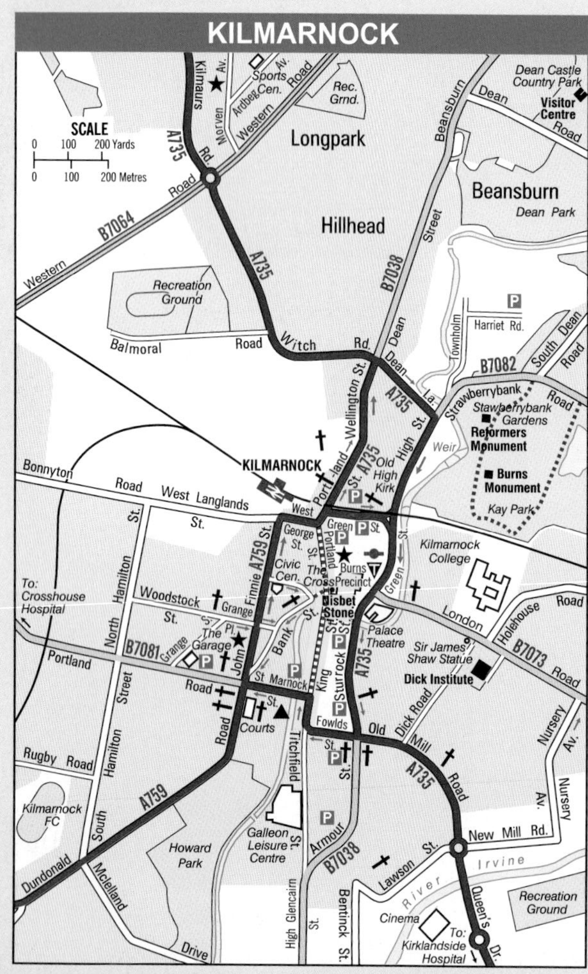

SCALE
0 100 200 Yards
0 100 200 Metres
Sports Cen.
Rec. Grnd.
Dean Castle Country Park
Visitor Centre
Longpark
Beansburn
Dean Park
Hillhead
A735
B7064
Recreation Ground
B7038
B7082
Strawberrybank Gardens
Reformers Monument
Burns Monument
Kay Park
KILMARNOCK
Kilmarnock College
To: Crosshouse Hospital
Civic Cen.
The Cross
Burns Precinct
Nisbet Stone
The Garage
Palace Theatre
Sir James Shaw Statue
Dick Institute
Courts
B7081
B7073
Kilmarnock FC
A759
Howard Park
Galleon Leisure Centre
Recreation Ground
Cinema
To: Kirklandside Hospital

LINCOLN

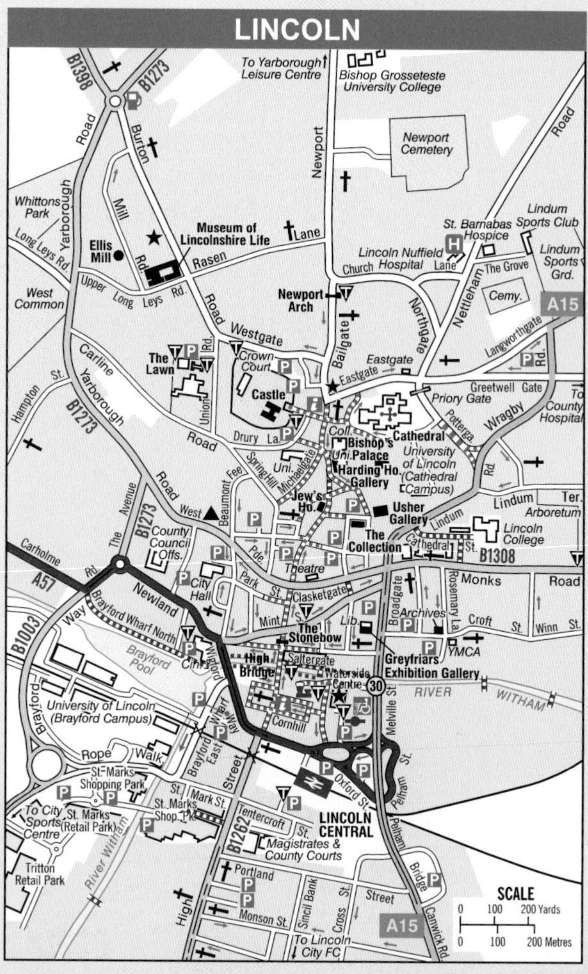

To Yarborough Leisure Centre
Bishop Grosseteste University College
B1398
B1273
Newport Cemetery
Whittons Park
Ellis Mill
Museum of Lincolnshire Life
Lindum Sports Club
St. Barnabas Hospice
Lincoln Nuffield Hospital
Lindum Sports Grd.
West Common
Newport Arch
Cemy.
A15
The Lawn
Crown Court
Castle
Priory Gate
To County Hospital
Cathedral
Bishop's Palace
Uni.
Harding Ho. Gallery
University of Lincoln (Cathedral Campus)
Jew's Ho.
Usher Gallery
The Collection
Lincoln College
County Council Offs.
A57
Theatre
B1308
City Hall
Archives
YMCA
The Stonebow
High Bridge
Greyfriars Exhibition Gallery
Waterside Centre
Brayford Pool
University of Lincoln (Brayford Campus)
RIVER WITHAM
St. Marks Shopping Park
To City Sports Centre
Tritton Retail Park
LINCOLN CENTRAL
Magistrates & County Courts
To Lincoln City FC
A15
SCALE
0 100 200 Yards
0 100 200 Metres

KINGSTON upon HULL

LEEDS

SCALE
0 100 200 Yards ¼ Mile
0 100 200 300 400 Metres

University of Leeds
Woodhouse
Little London
A58
Clay Pit La.
Street
Sheepscar St. South
Roseville Rd.
New Town
A58(M)
Clarendon Rd.
College
Hyde Ter.
Clarendon Way
Theatre
Metropolitan University
Arena (Prop.)
Skinner
Grafton St.
Leeds College
Lane
Lincoln Green Road
To St.James's University Hospital & Thackray Medical Museum
Yorkshire Television Studios
Burley
St. John's Rd.
Hosp.
Dental Hosp.
General Infirmary (Clarendon Wing)
Civic Hall
Portland Cres.
Merrion Way
Lovell Park
Byron St.
Leeds College
Mabgate
Studio Rd.
Kendal Lane
Little Woodhouse
Leeds City Museum
Bowl. Alley
North St.
A61
Beckett St.
Kirkstall A65
General Infirmary
Millennium Sq.
Theatre
Merrion Cen.
Belgrave St.
Merrion St.
Trafalgar St.
Regent St.
Nippet La.
To Yorkshire County Cricket Grd. (Headingley), Leeds RLFC & RUFC
Park Lane College
Hanover Wy.
Mag. Ct.
Crown Cts.
Town Hall
Lib. City Art Gal.
RC Cathedral
The Light
St. John's Centre
The Headrow
Theatre
A64(M)
Burmantofts St.
Park Road
Lane
Marlborough St.
Park Sq.
Cts.
Bedford
The Core
City Varieties
Templar St.
Lady La.
Bridge
DSS Offices
A64
Leeds & Liverpool Canal
West St.
Greek St.
Albion Pl.
Union St.
West Yorkshire Playhouse
BBC Studio
River Aire
Wellington
St. Paul's St.
Park Place
York Place
Infirmary St.
Quebec St.
Bond St.
Commercial St.
Leeds Shopping Plaza
Trinity St.
Kirkgate
George St.
Kirkgate Market
Shannon
Upper Accommodation
Armley
A647
Road
A58
Northern St.
Aire St.
City Sq.
Boar La.
Vicar Lane
Briggate
Corn Exchange
Kirkgate
York St.
Marsh Lane
Canal St.
LEEDS
The Calls
Swinegate
Dock St.
Kendell St.
Bowman La.
A653
Richmond St.
New Wortley
Wellington Rd.
Globe Rd.
Granary Wharf Shopping Centre
Neville St.
Sovereign St.
Waterloo St.
Armouries Way
Royal Armouries Museum
Rec. Grd.
Ellerby La.
Recreation Ground
B6154
Lane
Meadow Lane
Crown Point
A61
Cavalier Hill
Marshall St.
David St.
Camp Field
Great Wilson St.
Kidacre St.
Hunslet Rd.
Bull St.
Chadwick St.
Clarence Dock
Clarence Dr.
RIVER AIRE
Whitehall
Holbeck La.
Water Lane
Bridge Rd.
Manor Road
Victoria Rd.
Meadow Rd.
A653 La.
Crown Point Retail Park
A653
Black Bull St.
Armouries Rd.
Carlisle Rd.
Sayner Rd.
A58
Gelderd Rd.
Sydenham St.
Domestic St.
Holbeck
Sweet Street
Nineveh Rd.
Bowling Alley
Dewsbury Rd.
Butterley St.
Road
A639
Leeds Museum Discovery Centre
Indoor Karting
A62
Domestic Road
Street
Jack La.
Leathley
Pottery Field
Sth. Accomodation Rd.
Road
A61
Atkinson St.
A643
To Leeds United FC (Elland Road)
Street
M621

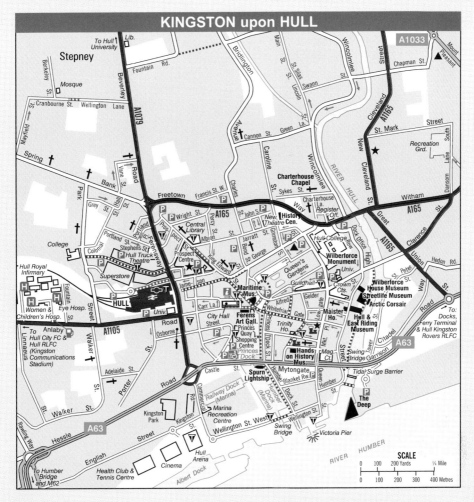

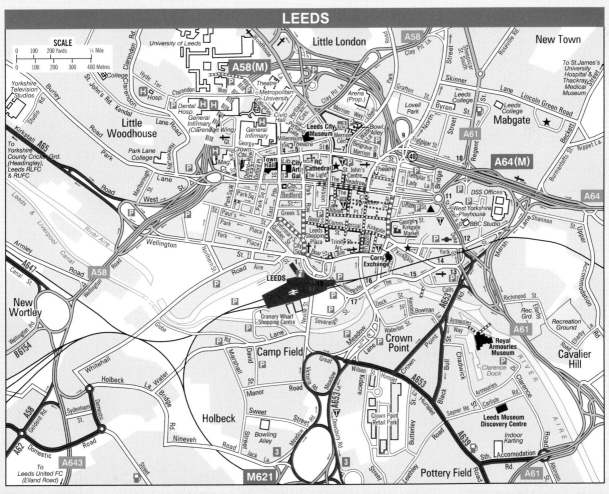

LEICESTER

LIVERPOOL

The Mega Centre
Recreation Ground
To Liverpool FC & Everton FC
Ferry Terminal
Vauxhall
Liverpool Community College
Kingsway (Mersey Tunnel) TOLL
Superstore
Princes Half Tide Dock
Thurston Billiard & Snooker Mus.
Football Pitch
Liverpool John Moores University
University College
Islington
Whitley Gardens
Grant Gardens
Douglas I.O.M. 2hrs. 30mins. (Fast Ferry)
Princes Dock
MOORFIELDS
Walker Art Gallery
Mus.
Lib.
St. George's Hall
Theatre
LIME ST.
Royal Liverpool University Hospital
Liverpool University Dental Hospital
Superstore
Western Approaches
Town Hall
Municipal Offs.
National Conservation Cen.
Royal Ct. Th.
St. John's Cen.
Liverpool Playhouse
Clayton Sq. Shop. Cen.
Central Shop. Cen.
University of Liverpool
Victoria Gallery & Museum
Seacombe Ferry 7-8mins.
RIVER MERSEY
Royal Liver Bldg.
JAMES ST.
Cavern Walks
Odeon Cinema
The Bluecoat
CENTRAL
Liverpool One
University
Liverpool Metropolitan Cathedral
University of Liverpool
Sports Cen.
Museum of Liverpool (due open 2011)
City Law Courts
Chavasse Park
Open Eye Gallery
FACT
YMCA
John Moores University
Everyman Theatre
University Art Gallery
Canning Dock
International Slavery Museum
Merseyside Maritime Museum
Tate Liverpool
Edward Pav.
Salthouse Dock
Albert Dock
Atlantic Pav.
The Colonnades
The Beatles Story
Britannia Pav.
TV Studio
Queensway (Mersey Tunnel) TOLL
Woodside Ferry
Mersey Railway Tunnel
Wapping Basin
Duke's Dock
Echo Arena & Convention Centre
Liverpool Community College
Unity Theatre
Philharmonic Hall
Mus.
Cathedral
Liverpool Women's Hosp.
A565
A5036
A5038
A59
A5053
A580
A57
A5047
B5340
A5049
A5039
A5048
A561

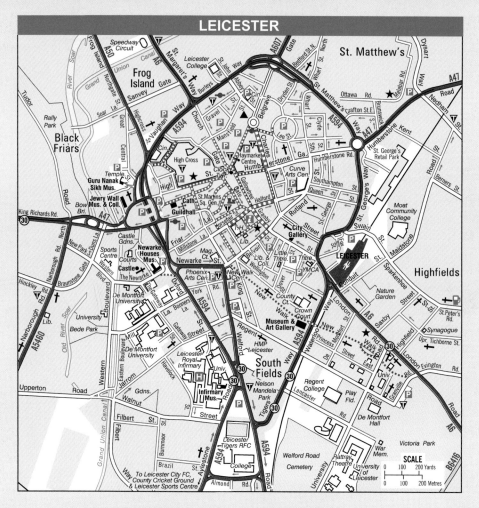

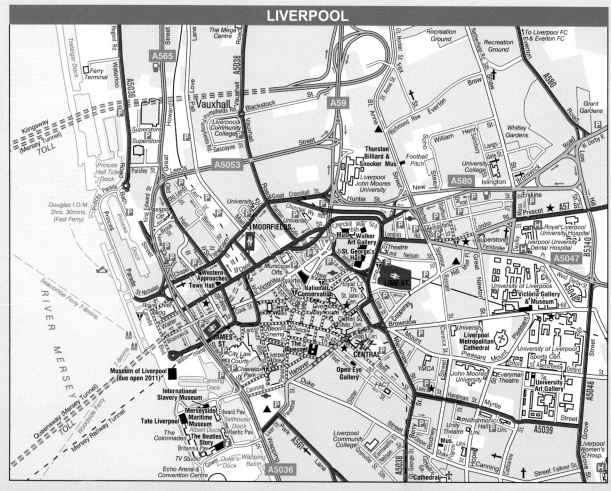

LUTON

MIDDLESBROUGH

MANCHESTER (CITY CENTRE)

MANCHESTER VICTORIA · MEN Arena · Chetham's Liby. · National Football Museum (Open 2011) · Cathedral · Shudehill · Arndale Centre · Piccadilly Gds. · MANCHESTER PICCADILLY · SALFORD CENTRAL · SALFORD CRESCENT · SALFORD · University of Salford · Salford Museum & Art Gallery · Salford RC Cathedral · People's History Mus. · John Rylands Liby. · Town Hall · Art Gallery · St. Peter's Sq. · Mus. of Science & Industry · Castlefield · G-Mex · DEANSGATE · OXFORD RD. · University of Manchester · Manchester Met. Univ. · Knott Mill · Gaythorne · Ordsall · Cornbrook · St. Georges · New Windsor · Wallness

SCALE: 0 100 200 Yards ¼ Mile; 0 100 200 300 400 Metres

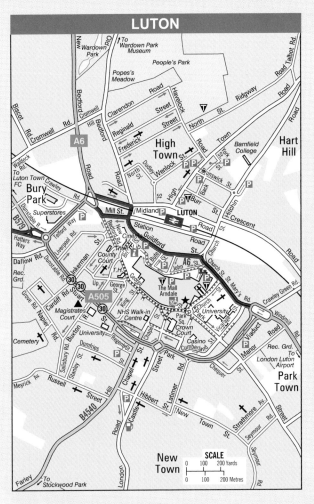

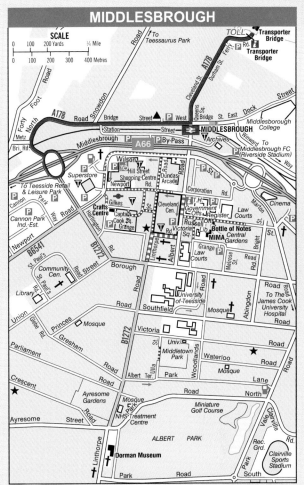

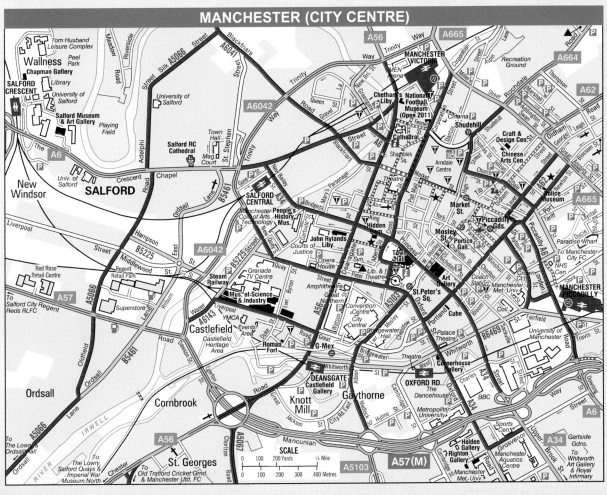

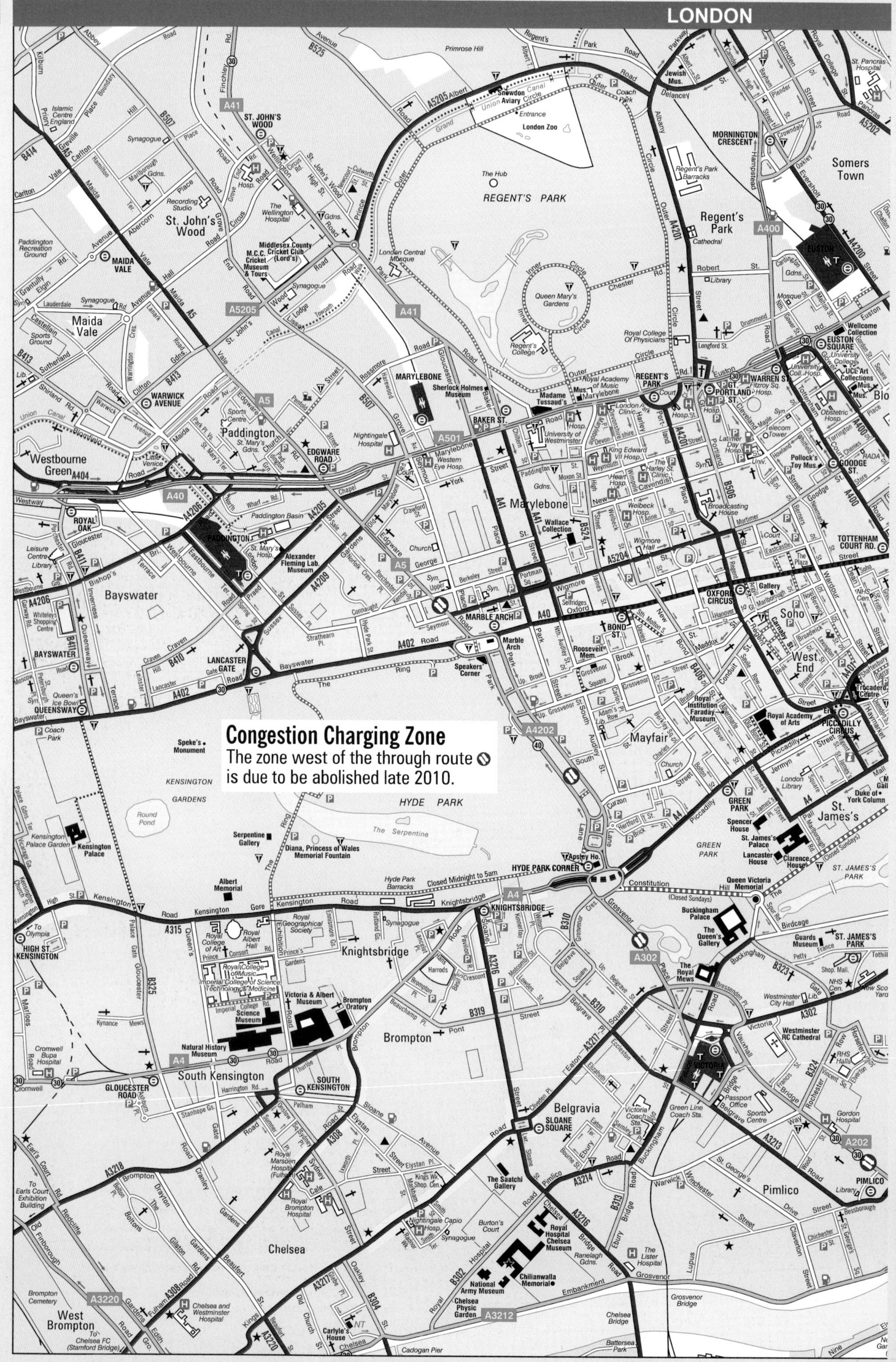

Congestion Charging Zone
The zone west of the through route ⊙
is due to be abolished late 2010.

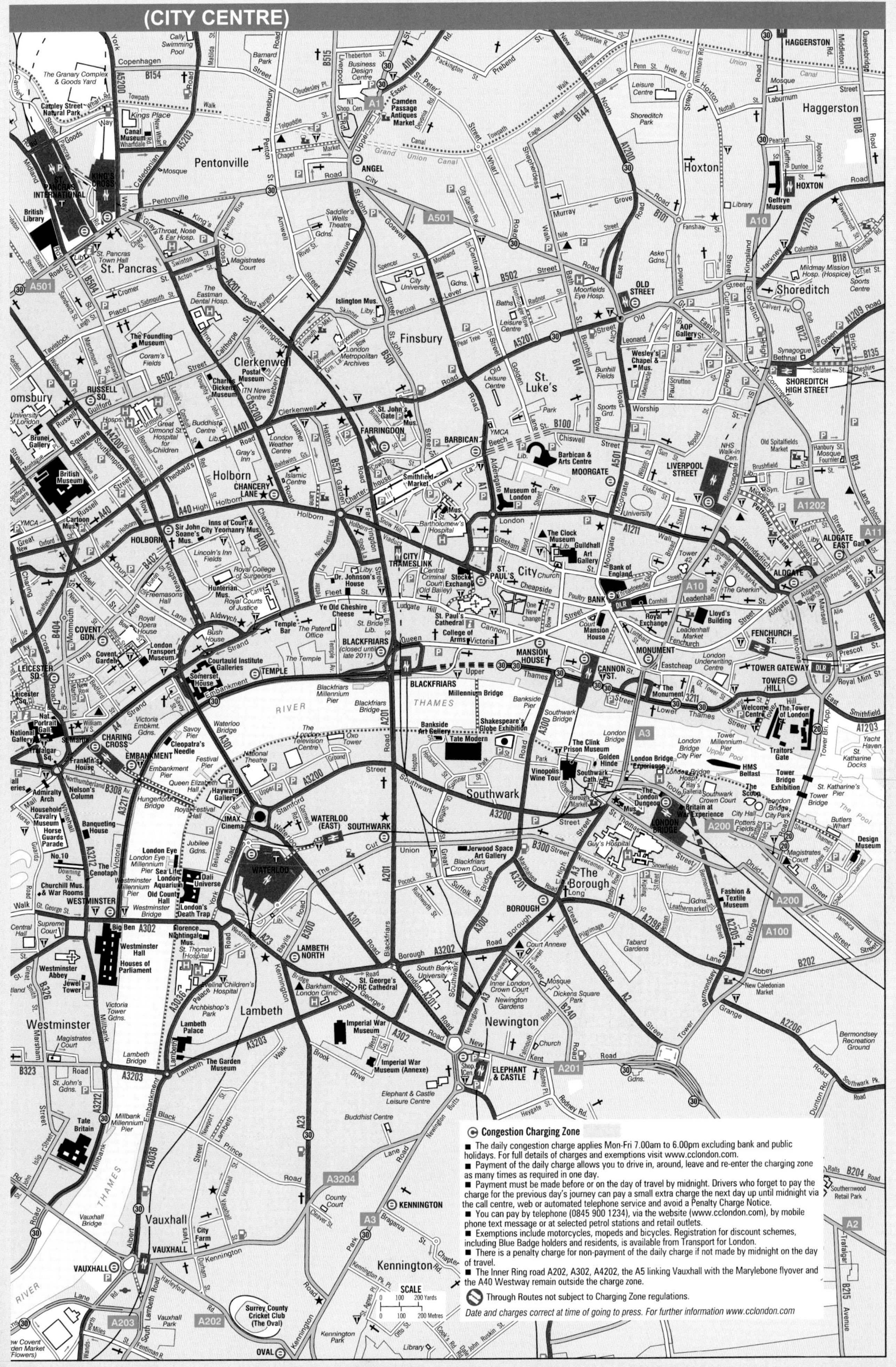

The Congestion Charging Zone

- The daily congestion charge applies Mon-Fri 7.00am to 6.00pm excluding bank and public holidays. For full details of charges and exemptions visit www.cclondon.com.
- Payment of the daily charge allows you to drive in, around, leave and re-enter the charging zone as many times as required in one day.
- Payment must be made before or on the day of travel by midnight. Drivers who forget to pay the charge for the previous day's journey can pay a small extra charge the next day up until midnight via the call centre, web or automated telephone service and avoid a Penalty Charge Notice.
- You can pay by telephone (0845 900 1234), via the website (www.cclondon.com), by mobile phone text message or at selected petrol stations and retail outlets.
- Exemptions include motorcycles, mopeds and bicycles. Registration for discount schemes, including Blue Badge holders and residents, is available from Transport for London.
- There is a penalty charge for non-payment of the daily charge if not made by midnight on the day of travel.
- The Inner Ring road A202, A302, A4202, the A5 linking Vauxhall with the Marylebone flyover and the A40 Westway remain outside the charge zone.

⊘ Through Routes not subject to Charging Zone regulations.

Date and charges correct at time of going to press. For further information www.cclondon.com

SCALE
0   100   200 Yards
0   100   200 Metres

MEDWAY TOWNS

STROOD
Strood Pier
Bridge Reach
Canal
Rochester Bridge
To Civic Cen.
ROCHESTER
Coach Park
Esplanade
Guildhall Museum
Castle
Corporation
Six Poor Travellers Ho.
Cathedral
Boley Hill
A2
Street
The Vines
Vines La.
St. Margaret's
Restoration House
Crow La.
Lib.
High St.
ROCHESTER
East Row
King Edward Rd.
Union St.
Victoria St.
King St.
Star Hill
Medway Little Theatre
Watts Av.
Foord St.
Troy Town
Delce Rd.
New Rd.
City Way
A229
B2097
Langley Rd.
Cossack St.
Cecil Road
Cemetery
Maidstone Road
Catherine St.
To: Rochester Airport, M2 Junc. 3 & Buckmore Park
Henley Business Park
Enterprise Business Estate
Medway City Estate
Neptune Close
Central Business Park
Neptune Business Park
Lake
Frindsbury Peninsula
Meridian Park
Sir Thomas Longley Road
Lime House Reach
Riverside Estate
Blue Boar Pier
RIVER MEDWAY
Ship Pier
Chatham Reach
St. Bartholomew's Hosp.
New Road
UCA Rochester
Fort Pitt Hill
Victoria Gdns.
CHATHAM
Albany T.
New Cut
Ordnance Ter.
Hill's Ter.
Road
A230
Maidstone Road
Holcombe Rd.
Jenkins Dale
SCALE
0 100 200 Yards ¼ Mile
0 100 200 300 400 Metres
Kent Police Museum
Historic Dockyard
Dock Road
A2310
Road
Wood St.
To: Medway Tunnel, Cinema, Dickens World & Dockside Outlet Centre
Brompton
War Memorial
Pasley Rd.
Royal School of Military Engineering
Khyber Road
Lower Lines
Medway Rd.
To The Strand
Arthur Rd.
Royal Engineers Museum
Prince Arthur Park
Prince Arthur Road
B2004
Indoor Bowling Cen.
Jumpers Rebound Cen.
Black Lion Leisure Cen.
Mansion Row
High St.
Garden St.
Garrison Sports Stadium
Sally Port
Brompton Road
Inner Lines
Sports Ground
Port Gardens
Bastion
A231
Cricket Ground
Mill Rd.
High St.
To: Station & Gillingham FC
Library
GILLINGHAM
Canterbury St.
Paget St.
Medway Civic HQ
Dock Road
A231
Fort Amherst
Maxwell
Kings
Great Lines
Library
Riverside Gardens
The Brook Theatre
Council Offs.
Sun Pier
County Ct.
Medway St.
Town Hall Gdns.
Magistrates Court
War Memorial
Pentagon Centre
Brook Pumping Mus.
Central Theatre
CHATHAM
Cross St.
Manor Rd.
High St.
Best St.
Old Rd.
Brook
The Brook
Street
Theatre Road
High Street
A2
Marlborough Road
York Av.
Medway Maritime Hospital
Windmill Road
Byron Rd.
Otway T.
Magpie Hall Rd.
Luton Rd.
Chatham Hill
Salisbury Rd.
Listmas Rd.
Castle R.
Upper Luton Rd.
Beacon Rd.
To Ski Centre
To Ice Bowl
30

MILTON KEYNES

McConnell Dr.
Grafton Street V6
Bradwell Towermill
Bradville
Saxon
Stantonbury Leisure Centre
Theatre
Way H3
B4034
Marlborough
Neath Hill
V9 Way
H4
Willen Park
Brickhill
Peace Pagoda & Garden
Tongwell
M1
A509
Pineham
14
Portway
H5
A5130
Milton Keynes Museum
Blue Bridge
Way H2
A422
Linford Wood
Downhead Park
Overstreet
A509
Miller's Way
Bancroft
Monks Way H3
Downs Barn
Leisure Club
V10
V11
Northfield
Stacey Bushes
Concrete Cows
Loughton
Grafton
Heelands
Dansteed
Portway
Gulliver's Theme Park
Willen Lake
Street Way
V5
Great Monks
Bradwell Abbey Chapel
Youth Hostel
Bradwell
Conniburrow
Boulvd.
Newlands
Gulliver's Dinosaur & Farm Park
Health Club
Fox Milne
A4146
Broughton
H4 Way
Campbell Park
Boulevard
Overgate
Tongwell
H6
Bradwell Abbey
City Discovery Centre
Bradwell Common
Conniburrow Boulvd.
Milton Keynes Gallery
Shopping Cen.
Open Air Theatre
Childs Way
Brickhill St.
V11 Street
H3
Road
Bradwell Common Boulvd.
Portway
Street
Civic Offs.
Lib.
Theatre
V8
H6
Pattison La.
Woolstone
Middleton
Broughton Rd.
A5
Great Monks Street
Wymbush
Rooksley
Daytona International Karting Circuit
V6
Portway
Witan
Central Milton Keynes
Xscape
County Court
Silbury
Council Offs.
Springfield
Grand Union Canal
Newport Rd.
Oakgrove
Milton Keynes Village
Leisure Centre
Claridge Dr.
Way
V10
H7
Two Mile Ash
Bradwell
National Badminton Centre
Health Club
Gate
Springfield Blvd.
River Ouzel
Chaffron
To Kingston Gymnastics Centre
Watling
Lodge Lake
Rd.
Midsummer
Avebury
Saxon
Fishermead Way
H7
Lane
Monkston Park
Monkston H8
Great Holm
Portway
Loughton
MILTON KEYNES
Leisure Plaza
Gate
Childs
Grafton
Eaglestone
Newport Valley
Picnic Site
Woughton on the Green
Ouzel or Lovat
Way
A421
Dansteed
Crownhill Crematorium & Cemetery
Bradwell
Leys Rd
Loughton Manor Equestrian Centre
H6
Retail Pk
Winterhill
Oldbrook
Woughton Leisure Centre
General Hospital
Marina
Park
Road
Brickhill
Kents Hill
The Open University
Crownhill
Fulmer
H5
Shenley Leisure Centre
Street V4
Davy
Teardrops Lake
Chaffron
Leadenhall
Milton Keynes College
Saxon BMI Clinic
H8
Standing
Way
Shenley Church End
Shenley Road
Knowlhill
Av.
Watling
H7
Skill Centre
Jonathans
Garraways
Coffee Hall
Netherfield
Street
Walton Lake
Woughton Park
Walton Hall
H9
Groveway
St.
Brickhill
V10
Portway
The National Bowl
Tinkers Bridge
Walton
Shenley Lodge
Bleak Hall
Beanhill
Street
H9
V8
Simpson
Road
Shenley Wood
Childs
Street V3
Chaffron
Elfield Park
St.
Furzton Lake
Standing
Street V6
Groveway
B4034
Ashland
Simpson
Walton Park
St.
SCALE
0 ¼ ½ ¾ 1 Mile
0 0.5 1 1.5 Kilometres
Furzton
A421
Redmoor
V4
MK Dons FC
V7
A5
Caldecote Lake
Bletcham Way
H10

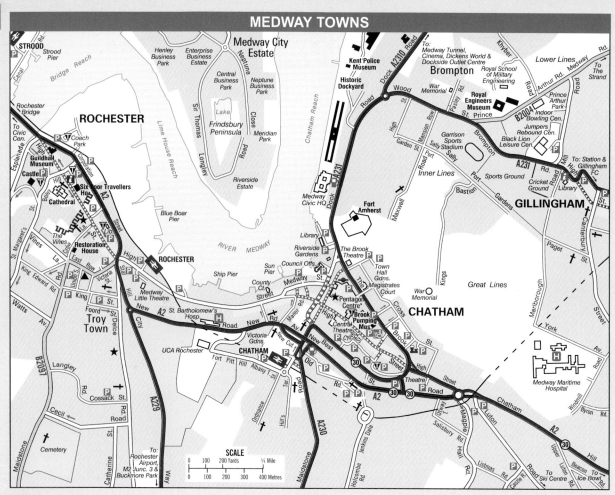

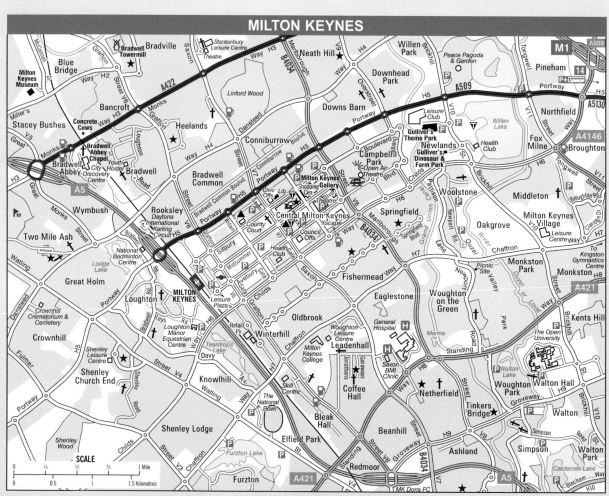

NORWICH

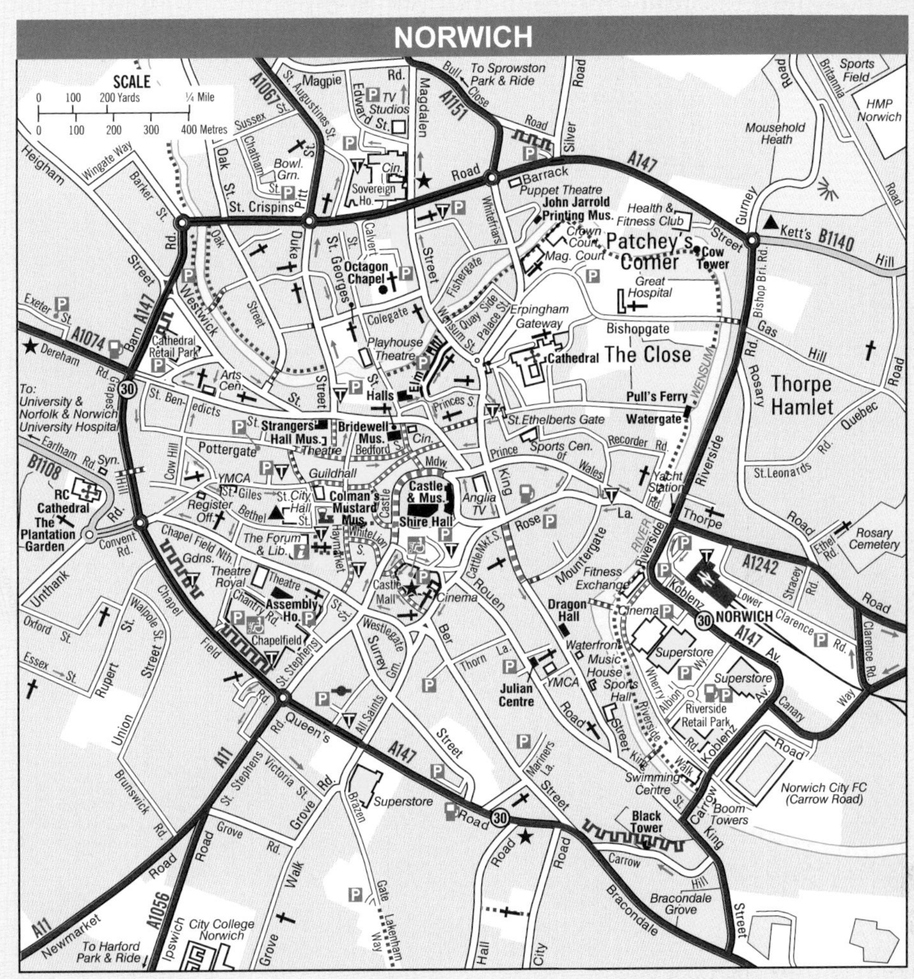
SCALE
0 100 200 Yards ¼ Mile
0 100 200 300 400 Metres
Magpie
Rd.
To Sprowston Park & Ride
Bull Close
Magdalen
St. Augustines St.
TV Studios
Edward St.
Sussex St.
Oak St.
Chatham St.
Bowl. Grn.
Sovereign Ho.
Cin.
Road
Silver Road
Sports Field
HMP Norwich
Mousehold Heath
Heigham
Wingate Way
Barker St.
St. Crispins
Pitt St.
Duke St.
Barrack
Puppet Theatre
John Jarrold Printing Mus.
Whitefriars
Health & Fitness Club
Gurney Rd.
Kett's B1140
Hill
Crown Court
Patchey's Corner
Cow Tower
Mag. Court
Great Hospital
Bishop Bri. Rd.
Octagon Chapel
Calvert St.
St. Georges St.
Colegate
Fishergate
Quay Side
Palace St.
Wensum St.
Erpingham Gateway
Bishopgate
Gas Hill
Westwick
Exeter St.
A1074
Dereham Rd.
Barn Rd.
A147
Cathedral Retail Park
Playhouse Theatre
Elm Hill
Cathedral
The Close
Rosary Rd.
Thorpe Hamlet
Arts Cen.
Halls
Princes St.
Pull's Ferry
Watergate
Quebec Rd.
To: University & Norfolk & Norwich University Hospital
St. Benedicts St.
Strangers Hall Mus.
Bridewell Mus.
Theatre
Bedford St.
Cin.
St.Ethelberts Gate
Recorder Rd.
Sports Cen.
Prince of Wales Rd.
Riverside
St.Leonards Rd.
Earlham Rd.
Syn.
Pottergate
Guildhall
Mdw.
B1108
Cow Hill
YMCA
St. Giles
St. City Hall
Colman's Mustard Mus.
Castle & Mus.
Shire Hall
Anglia TV
King St.
Yacht Station
Thorpe
RC Cathedral
The Plantation Garden
Register Off.
Bethel St.
The Forum & Lib.
Haymarket
White Lion St.
Rose La.
Mountergate
River Wensum
Road
Ethel Rd.
Rosary Cemetery
Convent Rd.
Chapel Field Nth.
Gdns.
Theatre Royal
Theatre
Assembly Ho.
Chantry Rd.
Castle Mall
Cinema
Cattle Mkt. St.
Rouen Rd.
Fitness Exchange
Cinema
A1242
Koblenz
Lower Clarence Rd.
NORWICH
Stracey Rd.
Road
Unthank Rd.
Walpole St.
Chapel Field
Chapelfield
St. Stephens St.
Westlegate
Surrey St.
Ber St.
Dragon Hall
Waterfront Music House
Sports Hall
Superstore
Wherry Rd.
Albion Way
Superstore
Clarence Rd.
Way
Oxford St.
Essex St.
Rupert St.
Union St.
Queen's Rd.
All Saints Grn.
Thorn La.
Julian Centre
YMCA
Riverside Retail Park
Canary Way
Street
Brunswick Rd.
A11
St. Stephens Rd.
Victoria St.
A147
Superstore
Mariners La.
Road
Norwich City FC (Carrow Road)
Grove Rd.
Grove Walk
Brazen Gate
Road
Black Tower
Swimming Centre
Carrow Rd.
Boom Towers
King St.
Carrow Hill
A1056
Bracondale Grove
Bracondale
Lakenham Way
Hall Rd.
City Rd.
City College Norwich
A11
Newmarket Rd.
To Harford Park & Ride
Ipswich Rd.
Grove Rd.
Street

NEWCASTLE upon TYNE

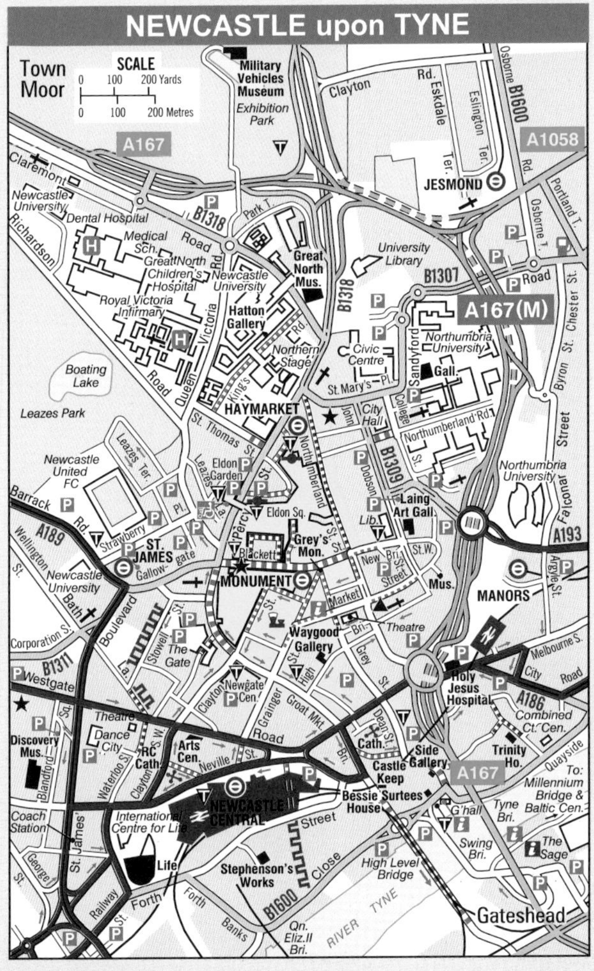
Town Moor
SCALE
0 100 200 Yards
0 100 200 Metres
Military Vehicles Museum
Exhibition Park
Clayton Rd.
Eskdale Ter.
Eslington Ter.
Osborne B1600
A1058
A167
JESMOND
Claremont Rd.
Newcastle University
Dental Hospital
Richardson Rd.
B1318
Park Ter.
Osborne Ter.
Portland Ter.
Medical Sch.
Great North Children's Hospital
Royal Victoria Infirmary
Newcastle University
Great North Mus.
University Library
B1307
Road
A167(M)
Hatton Gallery
Victoria Rd.
Northern Stage
Civic Centre
Northumbria University
Gall.
Sandyford Rd.
Chester St.
Byron St.
Boating Lake
Queen Victoria Rd.
HAYMARKET
St. Mary's Pl.
John Dobson St.
City Hall
College St.
Northumberland Rd.
Leazes Park
St. Thomas St.
Leazes Ter.
B1309
Northumbria University
Street
Newcastle United FC
Eldon Garden
Northumberland St.
Laing Art Gall.
Barrack Rd.
Strawberry Pl.
Eldon Sq.
Percy St.
Grey's Mon.
Lib.
A193
Falconar St.
A189
ST. JAMES
Gallowgate
Blackett St.
New Bri. St.
St.W.
Wellington St.
Newcastle University
MONUMENT
Market St.
Mus.
MANORS
Argyle St.
Bath La.
Boulevard
Stowell St.
The Gate
Waygood Gallery
Grey St.
Theatre
Melbourne St.
Corporation St.
B1311
Westgate Rd.
Holy Jesus Hospital
City Road
Clayton St.
Newgate Cen.
Groat Mkt.
A186
Combined Ct. Cen.
Theatre
Dance City
Arts Cen.
Grainger St.
Road
Cath.
Dean St.
Side Gallery
Trinity Ho.
Quayside
Discovery Mus.
RC Cath.
Neville St.
Castle Keep
A167
Blandford St.
Waterloo St.
NEWCASTLE CENTRAL
Bessie Surtees House
To: Millennium Bridge & Baltic Cen.
Coach Station
International Centre for Life
Street
G'hall
Tyne Bri.
Life
St. James
George St.
Stephenson's Works
Close
High Level Bridge
Swing Bri.
The Sage
Railway St.
Forth St.
Forth Banks
B1600
River Tyne
Gateshead
Qn. Eliz.II Bri.

NEWPORT (CASNEWYDD)

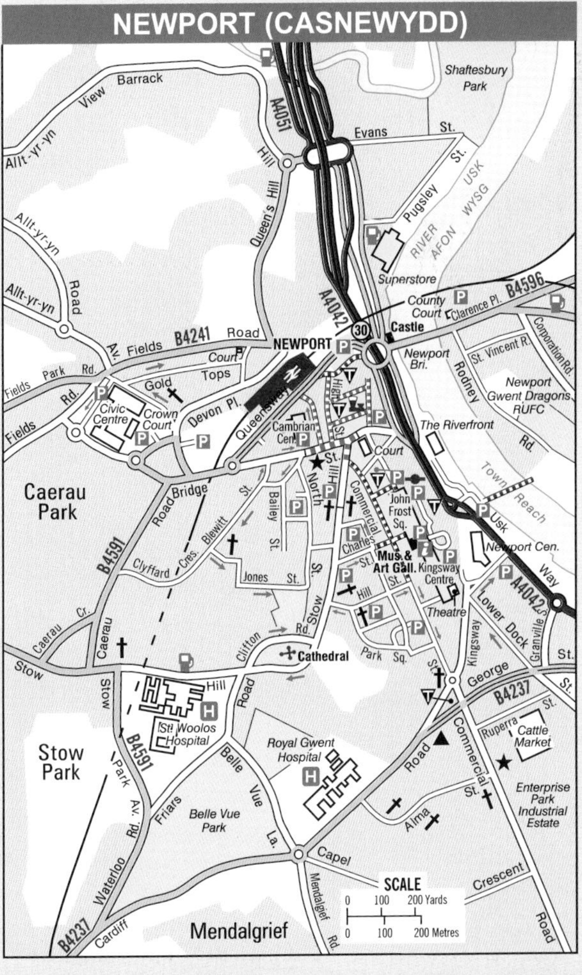
Barrack View
Shaftesbury Park
A4051
Evans St.
Allt-yr-yn
Pugsley St.
River Usk
Afon Wysg
Allt-yr-yn
Queen's Hill
Allt-yr-yn Road
Superstore
County Court
Clarence Pl.
B4596
A4042
Fields Rd.
B4241 Road
Castle
Corporation Rd.
NEWPORT
Newport Bri.
St. Vincent Rd.
Fields Park Rd.
Court
Tops
Rodney Rd.
Newport Gwent Dragons RUFC
Gold Tops
Civic Centre
Crown Court
Devon Pl.
Queensway
Cambrian Cen.
The Riverfront
Court
Rd.
Town Reach
Caerau Park
Bridge St.
Bailey St.
North St.
High St.
Commercial St.
John Frost Sq.
Usk Way
B4591
Blewitt St.
Clyffard Cres.
Jones St.
Stow Hill
Charles St.
Mus. & Art Gall.
Kingsway Centre
Newport Cen.
Lower Dock St.
A4042
Caerau Cr.
Caerau Rd.
Clifton Rd.
Cathedral
Theatre
Park Sq.
Kingsway
Granville St.
Stow Hill
Hill
Road
St. Woolos Hospital
George St.
B4237
Stow Park
B4591
Park Av.
Belle Vue
Royal Gwent Hospital
Road
Commercial Rd.
Ruperra St.
Cattle Market
Enterprise Park Industrial Estate
Friars Rd.
Belle Vue Park
Alma St.
Waterloo Rd.
Capel Cres.
Crescent
B4237
Cardiff Rd.
Mendalgief Rd.
Mendalgrief
SCALE
0 100 200 Yards
0 100 200 Metres
Road

NOTTINGHAM

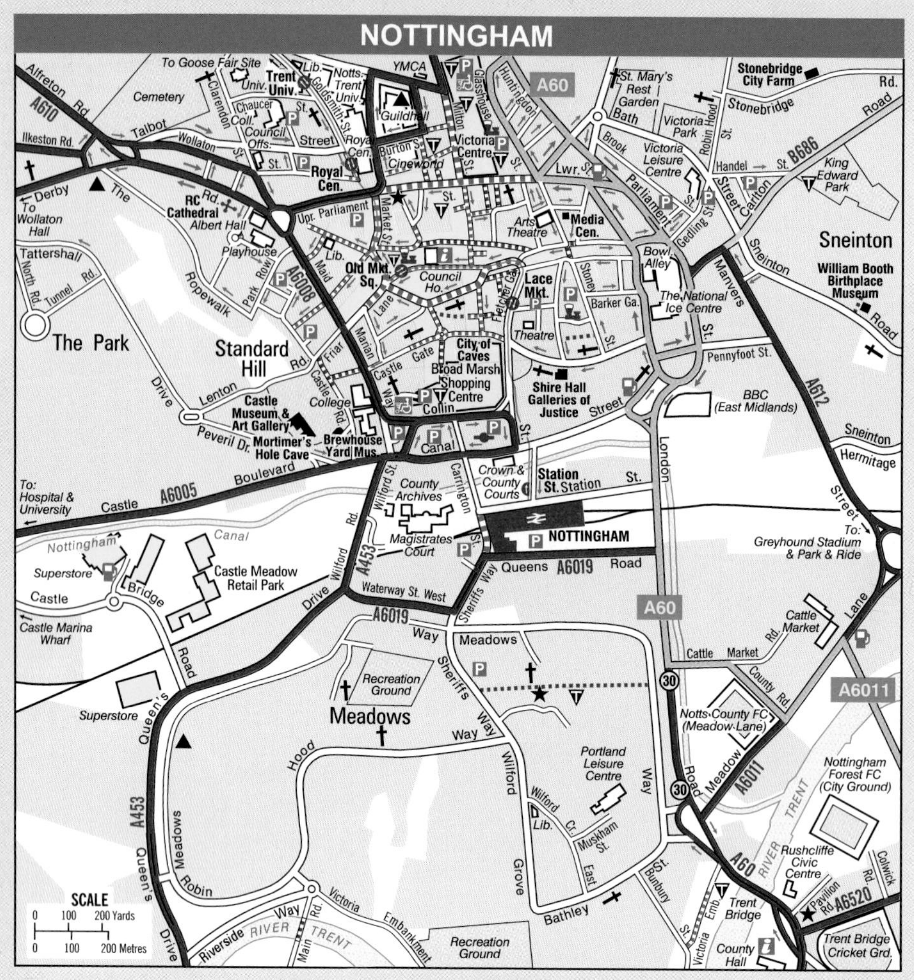

To Goose Fair Site
Trent Univ.
YMCA
A60
St. Mary's Rest Garden
Stonebridge City Farm
Cemetery
Alfreton Rd.
A610
Ilkeston Rd.
Talbot
Wollaton
Chaucer
Council Offs.
Royal Cen.
Guildhall
Cineworld
Victoria Centre
Victoria Park
Victoria Leisure Centre
Stonebridge
Handel St.
B686
King Edward Park
Derby
To Wollaton Hall
RC Cathedral
Albert Hall
Playhouse
Upr. Parliament
Arts Theatre
Media Cen.
Parliament
Sneinton
William Booth Birthplace Museum
Tattershall
North Rd.
Tunnel Rd.
The Park
Ropewalk
Standard Hill
A6008
Old Mkt. Sq.
Council Ho.
Lace Mkt.
Barker Ga.
The National Ice Centre
Manvers St.
Theatre
City of Caves
Broad Marsh Shopping Centre
Shire Hall Galleries of Justice
Pennyfoot St.
BBC (East Midlands)
A612
Castle Museum & Art Gallery
Mortimer's Hole Cave
Brewhouse Yard Mus.
Peveril Dr.
Lenton
Drive
Canal
Sneinton Hermitage
To: Hospital & University
Castle
A6005
Boulevard
County Archives
Carrington St.
Crown & County Courts
Station St. Station
London Rd.
Nottingham Canal
Magistrates Court
NOTTINGHAM
To: Greyhound Stadium & Park & Ride
Superstore
Castle Meadow Retail Park
Castle Bridge Road
A453
Wilford Rd.
Queens A6019 Road
Waterway St. West
Castle Marina Wharf
A6019 Way
Meadows
Sheriffs Way
A60
Cattle Market
Cattle Market Rd.
County Rd.
Lane
A6011
Recreation Ground
Meadows
Notts County FC (Meadow Lane)
Nottingham Forest FC (City Ground)
Queen's Drive
Hood
Portland Leisure Centre
Wilford Grove
Meadow
River Trent
Lib.
Muskham St.
East
Rushcliffe Civic Centre
Colwick Rd.
Meadows Way
Robin Hood
Bathley
Bunbury St.
Trent Bridge
Pavilion Rd.
A6520
SCALE
0 100 200 Yards
0 100 200 Metres
Riverside Way
River Trent
Victoria Embankment
Main Rd.
Recreation Ground
County Hall
Trent Bridge Cricket Grd.

NORTHAMPTON

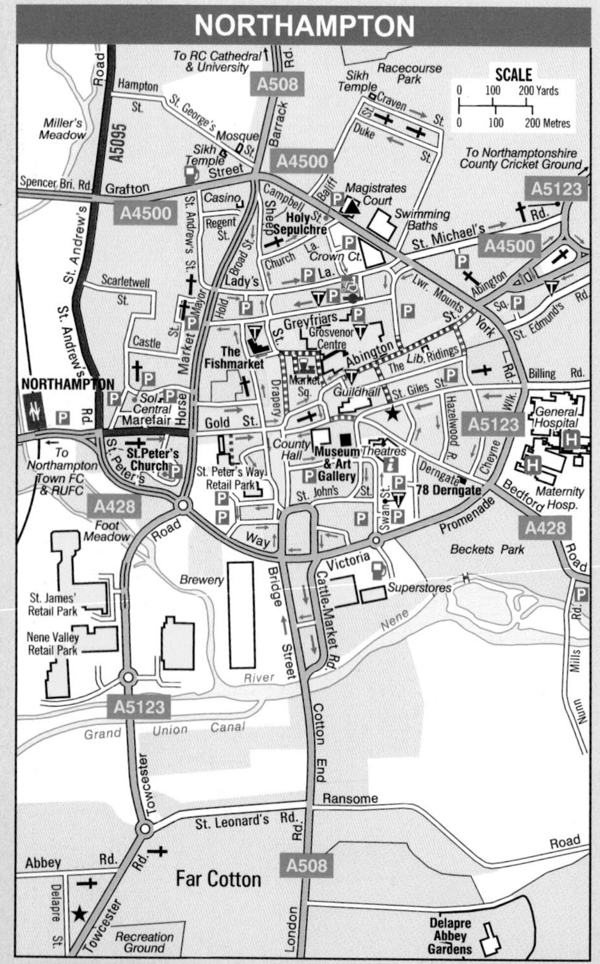

To RC Cathedral & University
Barrack Rd.
A508
Hampton St.
St. George's St.
Sikh Temple
Racecourse Park
SCALE
0 100 200 Yards
0 100 200 Metres
Miller's Meadow
A5095
Craven St.
Duke St.
Mosque
To Northamptonshire County Cricket Ground
Spencer Bri. Rd.
Grafton Street
A4500
Magistrates Court
A5123
Casino
Holy Sepulchre
Swimming Baths
St. Michael's Rd.
Regent St.
St. Andrew's Rd.
Crown Ct.
Church La.
Abington
Scarletwell St.
Lady's La.
Lwr. Mounts
St. Edmund's Rd.
Castle St.
Greyfriars
Grosvenor Centre
The Fishmarket
Abington St.
The Ridings
NORTHAMPTON
Sol Central
Guildhall
St. Giles St.
Billing Rd.
Marefair
Gold St.
Hazelwood R.
General Hospital
To Northampton Town FC & RUFC
St. Peter's Church
County Hall
Museum & Art Gallery
Theatres
St. Peter's Way Retail Park
St. John's
78 Derngate
Derngate
Bedford Rd.
Maternity Hosp.
A428
Foot Meadow
Way
Victoria
Promenade
Beckets Park
Brewery
Superstores
Nene
St. James' Retail Park
Nene Valley Retail Park
River
Bridge Street
Cattle Market Rd.
Mills Rd.
A5123
Grand Union Canal
Nunn Mills Rd.
Cotton End
Ransome Road
St. Leonard's Rd.
Towcester Rd.
Abbey Rd.
Far Cotton
A508
Delapre St.
Recreation Ground
London Rd.
Delapre Abbey Gardens

OBAN

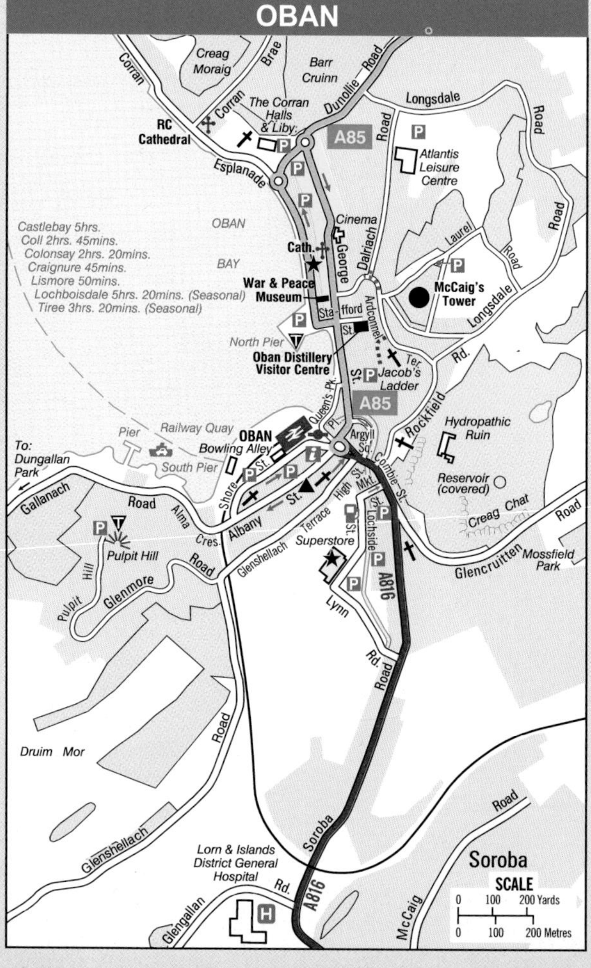

Corran Brae
Creag Moraig
Barr Cruinn
Dunollie Road
Longsdale Road
RC Cathedral
The Corran Halls & Liby.
A85
Atlantis Leisure Centre
Esplanade
Castlebay 5hrs.
Coll 2hrs. 45mins.
Colonsay 2hrs. 20mins.
Craignure 45mins.
Lismore 50mins.
Lochboisdale 5hrs. 20mins. (Seasonal)
Tiree 3hrs. 20mins. (Seasonal)
OBAN BAY
Cinema
Cath.
George St.
Dalriach
Laurel Road
McCaig's Tower
Longsdale
War & Peace Museum
Stafford St.
Ardconnel Ter.
North Pier
Oban Distillery Visitor Centre
Jacob's Ladder
A85
Rockfield Rd.
Hydropathic Ruin
Railway Quay
Pier
OBAN
Bowling Alley
South Pier
Argyll Sq.
Combie St.
To: Dungallan Park
Gallanach Road
Shore St.
Albany St.
Alma Cres.
Reservoir (covered)
Creag Chat
Pulpit Hill
Glenshellach Terrace
Superstore
Lochside St.
Glencruitten Road
Mossfield Park
Glenmore Road
Pulpit Hill
Lynn Rd.
A816
Druim Mor
Soroba Road
Glenshellach
Lorn & Islands District General Hospital
Glengallan Rd.
Soroba
McCaig Road
SCALE
0 100 200 Yards
0 100 200 Metres

OXFORD

KEY TO COLLEGES

1. All Souls College
2. Balliol College
3. Blackfriars
4. Brasenose College
5. Campion Hall
6. Christ Church
7. Corpus Christi College
8. Examination Schools
9. Exeter College
10. Green Templeton College
11. Harris Manchester College & Chapel
12. Hertford College
13. Jesus College
14. Keble College
15. Kellogg College
16. Lady Margaret Hall
17. Linacre College
18. Lincoln College
19. Magdalen College
20. Mansfield College
21. Merton College
22. New College
23. Nuffield College
24. Oriel College
25. Pembroke College
26. Queen's College, The
27. Regents Park College
28. St. Anne's College
29. St. Antony's College
30. St. Benet's Hall
31. St. Catherine's College
32. St. Cross College
33. St. Edmund Hall
34. St. Hilda's College
35. St. John's College
36. St. Peter's College
37. St. Stephen's House
38. Somerville College
39. Trinity College
40. University College
41. Wadham College
42. Worcester College
43. Wycliffe Hall

Waltham Manor
Norham Manor
Jericho
New Osney
To Pear Tree Park & Ride
To: St. Hugh's Coll. & Wolfson Coll.
English Centre
Oxford University Cricket Club (The Parks)
University Parks
Radcliffe Observatory Quarter (Under Const.)
Pitt Rivers Museum
University Museum of Natural History
Oxford University Press
Ruskin College
Synagogue
Cricket Ground
Ashmolean Mus.
OXFORD
Old Bodleian Liby.
Bridge of Sighs
Radcliffe Camera
Carfax Tower
Modern Art Oxford
Mus. of Oxford
Castle
County Hall
Westgate Centre
Oxford & Cherwell Valley College
Cathedral
Bate Collection
Botanic Garden
Deer Park
Science Oxford
Headington Hill Park
OBU Centre for Sport
To: Thornhill Park & Ride & Oxford Brookes University
To Warneford Hospital
To Seacourt Park & Ride
Christ Church Meadow
Folly Bridge
Oxford University Sports Complex
Rugby Football Ground
Hospices
To Redbridge Park & Ride and Oxford United FC
Ckt. Grd.
Ice Rink
Crown & County Courts

SCALE
0 100 200 Yards ¼ Mile
0 100 200 300 400 Metres

PAISLEY

PERTH

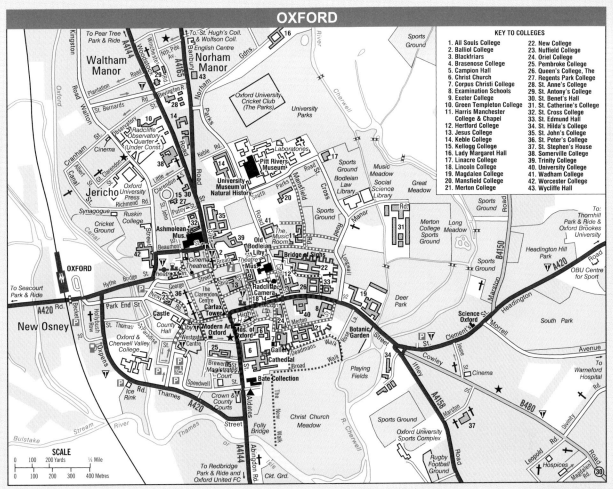

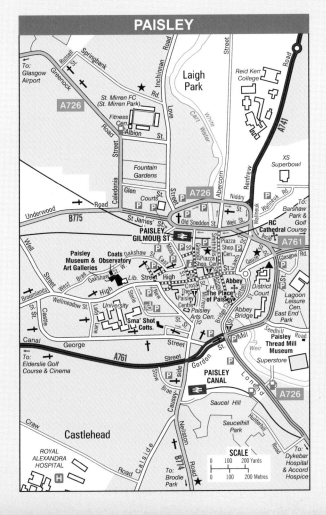

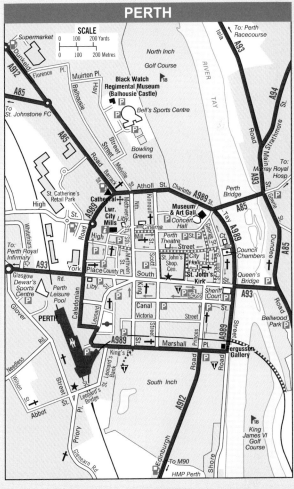

PLYMOUTH

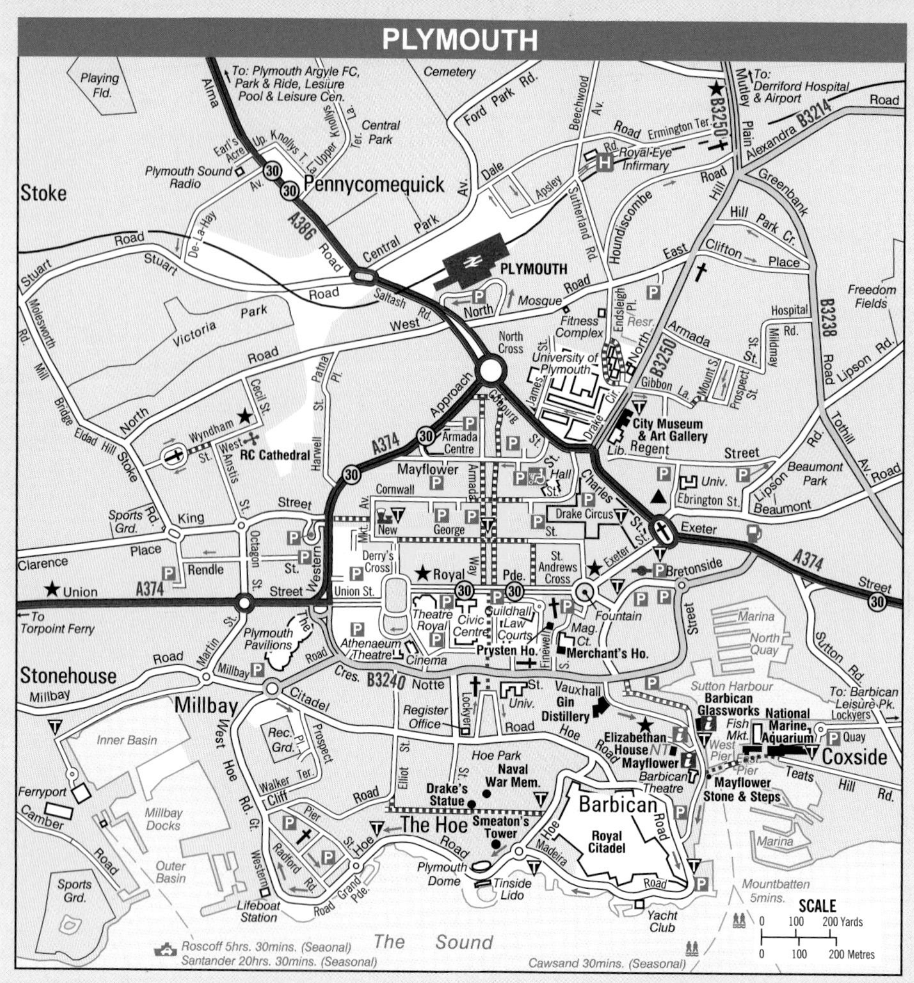
To: Plymouth Argyle FC, Park & Ride, Lesiure Pool & Leisure Cen.
To: Derriford Hospital & Airport
Playing Fld.
Cemetery
Central Park
Stoke
Pennycomequick
Plymouth Sound Radio
PLYMOUTH
Royal Eye Infirmary
Freedom Fields
North Cross
Fitness Complex
University of Plymouth
City Museum & Art Gallery
RC Cathedral
Armada Centre
Mayflower
Drake Circus
St. Andrews Cross
Derry's Cross
Theatre Royal
Civic Centre
Guildhall
Law Courts
Prysten Ho.
Merchant's Ho.
Union
To Torpoint Ferry
Stonehouse
Plymouth Pavilions
Athenaeum Theatre
Cinema
Millbay
Register Office
Univ.
Vauxhall Gin Distillery
Sutton Harbour
Barbican Glassworks
National Marine Aquarium
Coxside
To: Barbican Leisure Pk.
Elizabethan House
Mayflower
Barbican Theatre
Mayflower Stone & Steps
Hoe Park
Naval War Mem.
Drake's Statue
Smeaton's Tower
The Hoe
Barbican
Royal Citadel
Inner Basin
Ferryport
Millbay Docks
Outer Basin
Sports Grd.
Lifeboat Station
Plymouth Dome
Tinside Lido
Yacht Club
Mountbatten 5mins.
The Sound
Roscoff 5hrs. 30mins. (Seasonal)
Santander 20hrs. 30mins. (Seasonal)
Cawsand 30mins. (Seasonal)
SCALE
0 100 200 Yards
0 100 200 Metres

PETERBOROUGH

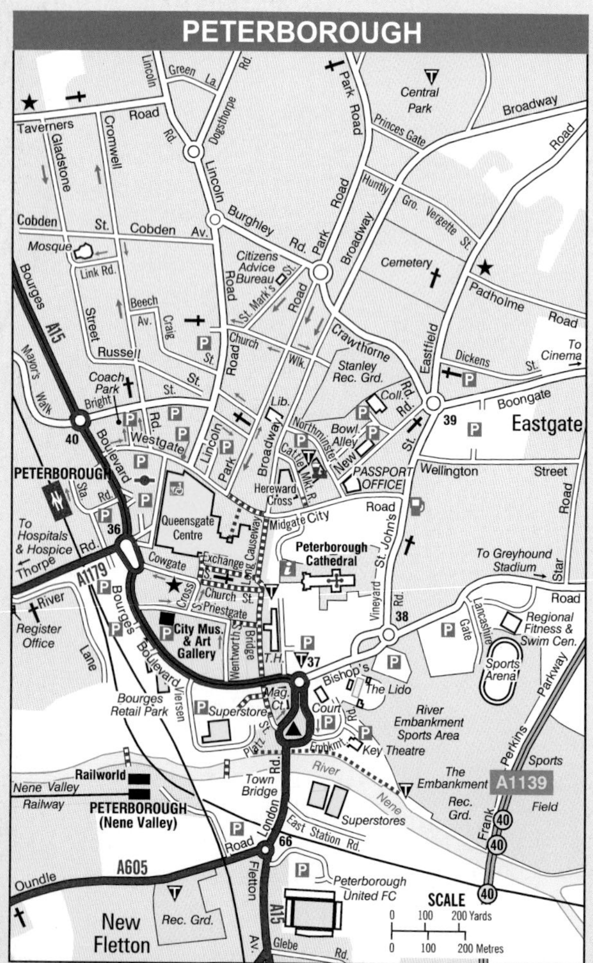
Central Park
Broadway
Cemetery
Citizens Advice Bureau
Stanley Rec. Grd.
To Cinema
Eastgate
Coach Park
PETERBOROUGH
To Hospitals & Hospice
Queensgate Centre
Hereward Cross
PASSPORT OFFICE
Peterborough Cathedral
To Greyhound Stadium
City Mus. & Art Gallery
Register Office
Bourges Retail Park
Superstore
The Lido
River Embankment Sports Area
Regional Fitness & Swim Cen.
Sports Arena
Key Theatre
The Embankment
Railworld
Nene Valley Railway
PETERBOROUGH (Nene Valley)
Town Bridge
Superstores
Rec. Grd.
Peterborough United FC
New Fletton
SCALE
0 100 200 Yards
0 100 200 Metres

PRESTON

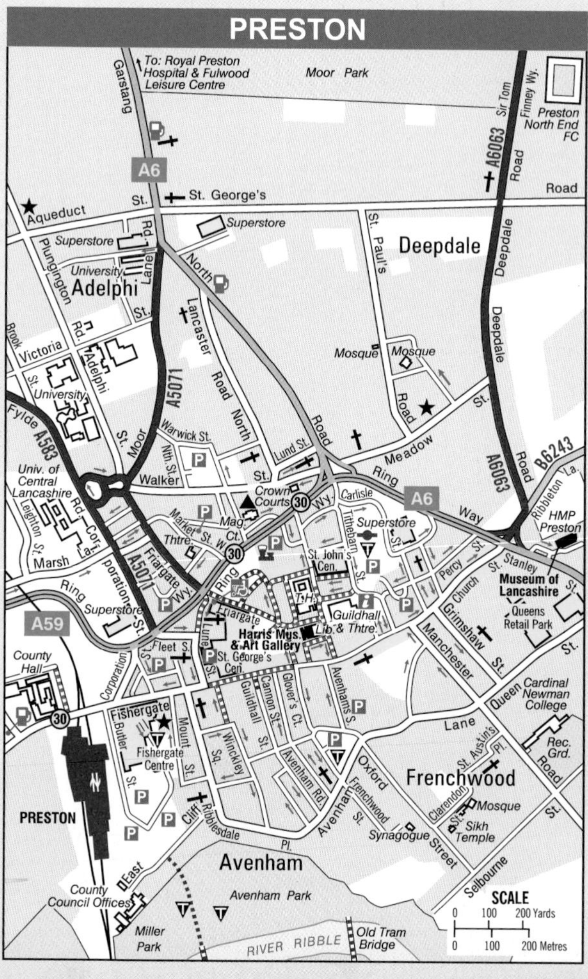
To: Royal Preston Hospital & Fulwood Leisure Centre
Moor Park
Preston North End FC
Aqueduct
Superstore
University
Adelphi
Deepdale
Mosque
University
Univ. of Central Lancashire
Crown Courts
Museum of Lancashire
HMP Preston
Queens Retail Park
Cardinal Newman College
County Hall
Harris Mus. & Art Gallery
Guildhall & Thtre
Fishergate Centre
PRESTON
Frenchwood
Sikh Temple
Synagogue
Avenham
Avenham Park
County Council Offices
Miller Park
RIVER RIBBLE
Old Tram Bridge
SCALE
0 100 200 Yards
0 100 200 Metres

PORTSMOUTH

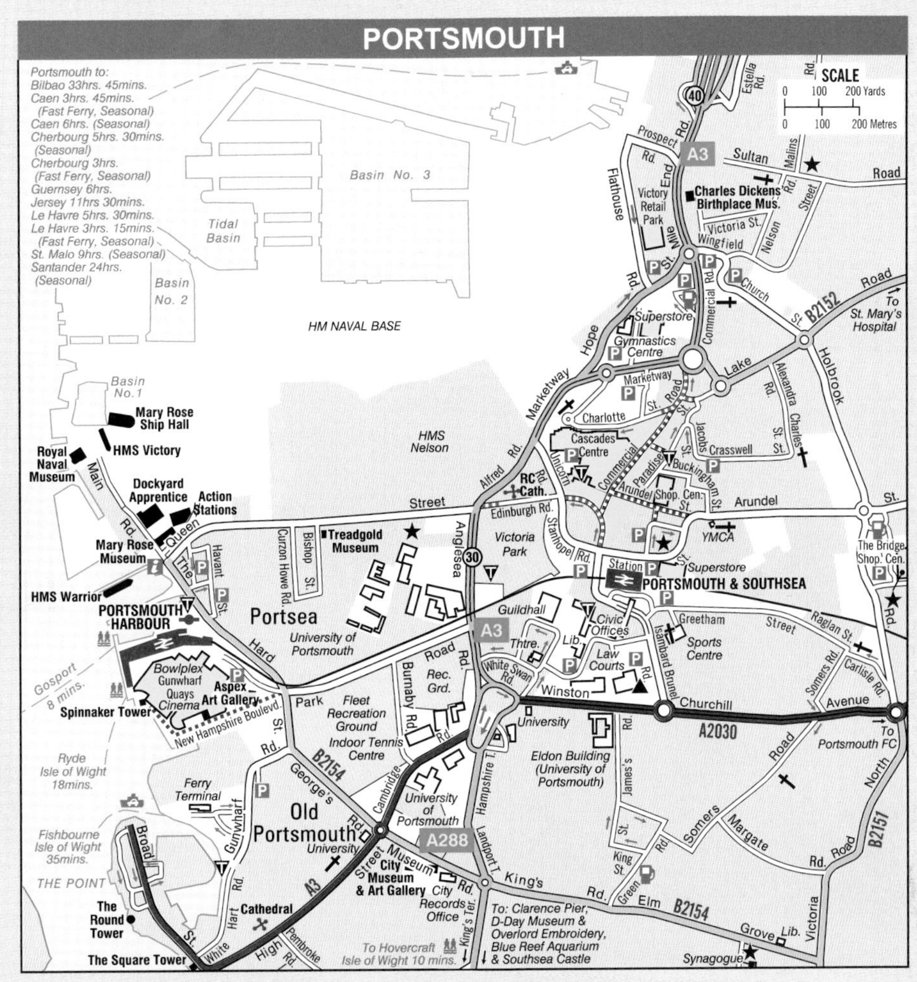

Portsmouth to:
Bilbao 33hrs. 45mins.
Caen 3hrs. 45mins.
(Fast Ferry, Seasonal)
Caen 6hrs. (Seasonal)
Cherbourg 5hrs. 30mins.
(Seasonal)
Cherbourg 3hrs.
(Fast Ferry, Seasonal)
Guernsey 6hrs.
Jersey 11hrs 30mins.
Le Havre 5hrs. 30mins.
Le Havre 3hrs. 15mins.
(Fast Ferry, Seasonal)
St. Malo 9hrs. (Seasonal)
Santander 24hrs.
(Seasonal)

SCALE

READING

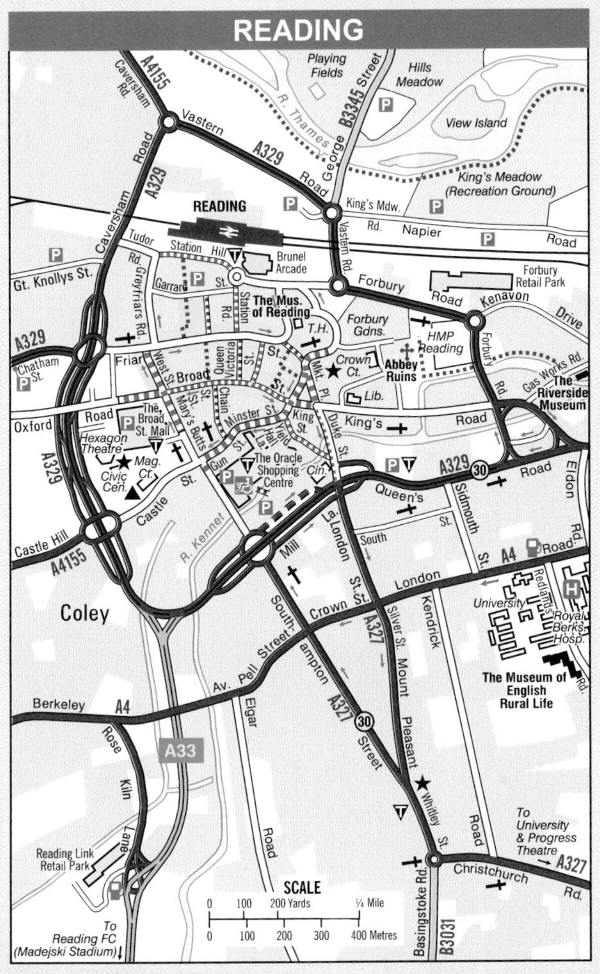

SCALE

ST ANDREWS

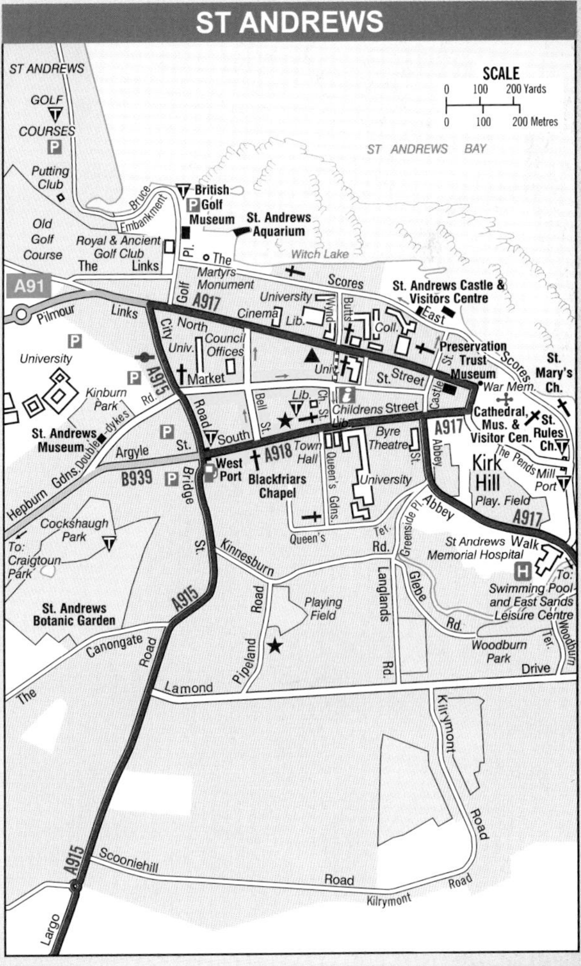

SCALE

SALISBURY

SHREWSBURY

SHEFFIELD

SCALE
0 100 200 Yards
0 100 200 Metres

Infirmary Rd.
To Sheffield Wednesday FC
Penistone Rd.
Kelham Island Museum
Mowbray
B6074 St.
Pitsmoor Rd.
Chatham St.
To Concord Sports Centre
A6135
Hill
Carlisle B6082 St.
Spital
Savile A6109 St.
Street
A6178
Rd.
Attercliffe
To Don Valley Stadium & Meadowhall Shop. Cen.
Howard
Albert Ter. Rd.
Infirmary
Lib.
Healthy Living Centre
Upperthorpe
A61
Ball
Green
Lane
Alma
Street
Upperthorpe
Road
Watery La.
Shalesmoor
Addy
Road
Meadow
Hoyle St.
A61
Shalesmoor
Bridge
Nursery
Johnson
Stanley St.
RIVER
Wicker
DON
B6073
Effingham St.
Effingham
Sussex St.
Rd.
Sheffield & Tinsley Canal
Derek Dooley Way
A61
Rd.
Barber
Recreation Ground
Bellefield St.
Road
Street
Gibraltar
Corporation
Law Courts
Blonk
Furnival
Parkway
Bernard Rd.
Crookesmoor
Rd.
Fawcett St.
St. Philip's
Scotland
Fire Police Museum
St.
Mag. Ct.
Bank St.
40
Crookesmoor
Road
Crookes Valley Rd.
Netherthorpe Rd.
Street
Hollis
Croft
Lenter
A61
Hyde Park
A57
Crookes Valley Park
Winter St.
Weston
Street
Research Centre
Hawley St.
Castle Sq.
Fitzalan Sq.
Ponds Forge
Broad St.
University of Sheffield
Harcourt
Mushroom
Bolsover St.
Netherthorpe
Solly
Broad
B6539
Lane
Bailey St.
Campo
Cath.
La.
High St.
Gate
Park Hill
University of Sheffield
Rockingham
Turner Museum of Glass
Church
Cathedral
Cutlers' Hall
RC Cath.
The Crucible
Ponds Forge International Sports Cen.
Northumberland
Weston Park Museum
Weston Park
Hill
University of Sheffield
Portobello
Tripper
St.
City Hall
Shop Cen.
Fountain Prect.
Thtre.
Pond St.
Duke
B6070
B6071
Street
Bernard
Brook
Bank
Univ. Road
Portobello
Univ. of Sheffield
West
West St.
Carver
City Hall
Surrey St.
Ponds Hill
A57
Western
Rd.
Clarkson
Children's Hosp.
Octagon Cen.
Glossop Rd.
Brunswick
Upr. Hanover St.
Fitzwilliam
Eldon
The Forum
Winter Gdn.
Town Hall
Millennium Galleries
Theatre
Graves Gallery
Archway Cen.
A61
Sheffield Station/ Sheffield Hallam University
Playing Fields
Whitham
Weston Park Hospital
Dental Hosp.
Road
Drama Studio
Wilkinson St.
Devonshire
Victoria Hall
Cambridge St.
Millennium Sq.
Arundel
Registry Office
Hallam University
Sheaf St.
SHEFFIELD
Swimming Pool
Royal Hallamshire Hospital
Broomspring
La.
Wellington
Street
Pinstone
Arundel
Charles St.
Talbot St.
Lib.
Glossop
B6547
Univ.
Dorset
Street
Hanover
The Moor
St.
Gate
Furnival
Site Gallery
Cinema
Norfolk
City Street
Rd.
Swimming Pool
Road
Broomfield
Cres.
Matilda
Suffolk
Monument Grounds
Rd.
Newbould La.
B6069
Broomsgrove
Collegiate
Road
Broomhall St.
William
A61
Department of Education & Skills
Eyre
Sidney St.
Street
Shrewsbury
Clay Wood
Road
College
Granville Rd. Sheffield District College
A6135
Clarkehouse
Clarkegrove Rd.
Broomhall
Sunnybank Nature Reserve
Young St.
St. Mary's
Way
South
La.
Jessop St.
Retail Park
Road
Road
Farm
Granville
Goals Soccer Centre
Road
Road
Southgrove
Sheffield Hallam University
Collegiate Cres.
Road
Road
Superstore
Gate
St. Mary's Rd.
Sheffield Ice Sports Centre
The Sheffield College
Park
Sheffield Botanical Gardens
A625
Summerfield
Cemetery Rd.
London Rd.
B6388
Highfield
Bramall A621 La.
Clough
Sheffield United FC
Shoreham
Charlotte Rd.
Queens
A61
East Bank
Norfolk
Rd.
Ecclesall
Norfolk Park

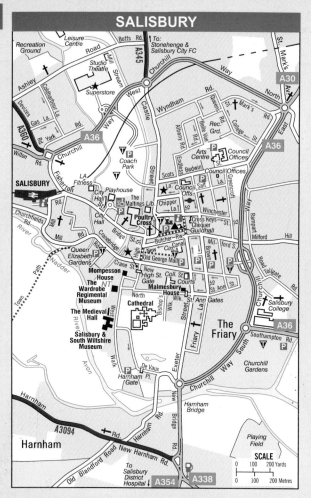

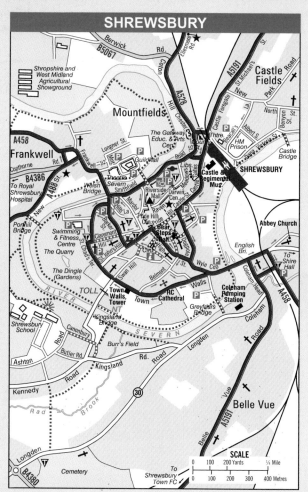

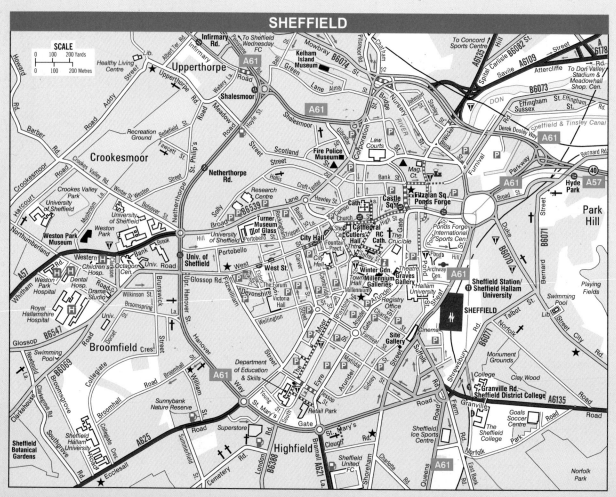

SOUTHAMPTON

SCALE
0 100 200 Yards ¼ Mile
0 100 200 300 400 Metres

Newtown
Hill
Polygon
Bedford Place
St. Mary's
Northam
Millbank
Fourposts
SOUTHAMPTON
Nichols Town
Belvidere
Peartree Green
Chapel
Crosshouse
Itchen
WOOLSTON
Woolston
Ocean Village
RIVER ITCHEN
RIVER TEST
Southampton FC (St. Mary's Stadium)
Southampton City College
West Quay Shopping Centre
Bargate
Tudor Ho. Mus.
Medieval Merchant's House
Maritime Museum
Museum of Archaeology
Hall of Aviation
Royal Pier (Closed)
City Cruise Terminal
Hythe 12mins.
West Cowes 22mins. (Fast Ferry)
East Cowes 55mins.
To: QEII Cruise Terminal
To: National Oceanography Centre
To: County Cricket Ground
To: University

STIRLING

STOKE-ON-TRENT

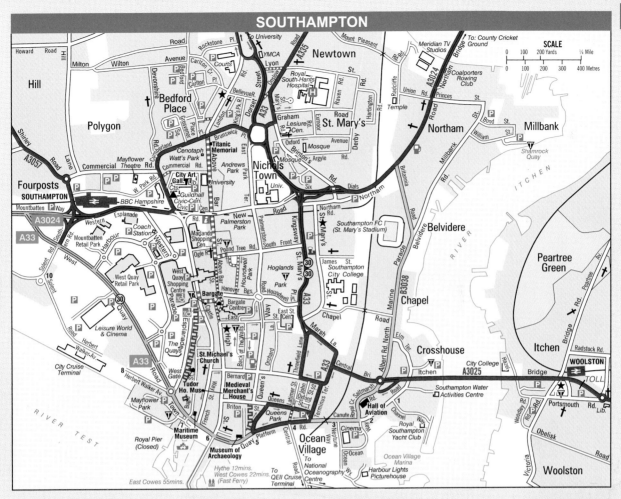

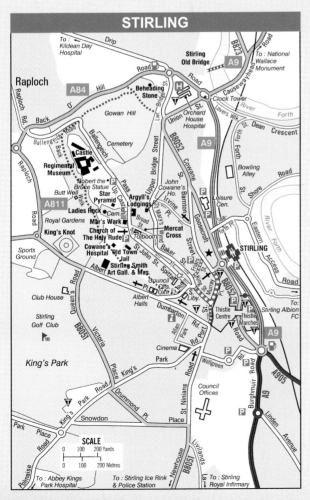

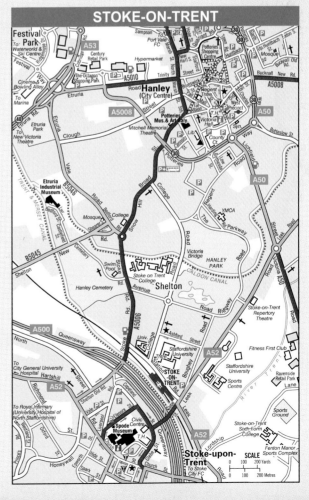

STRATFORD upon AVON

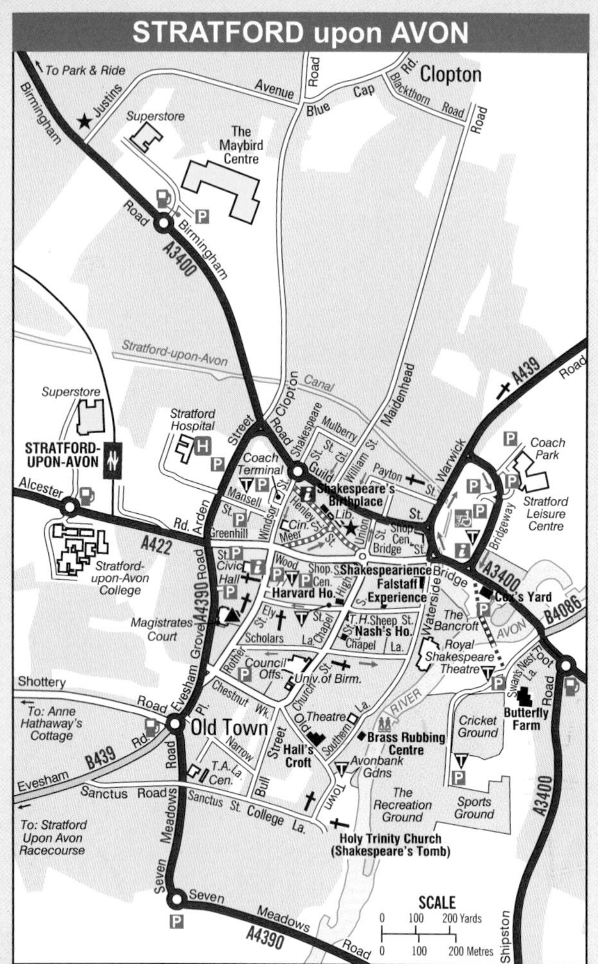

SUNDERLAND

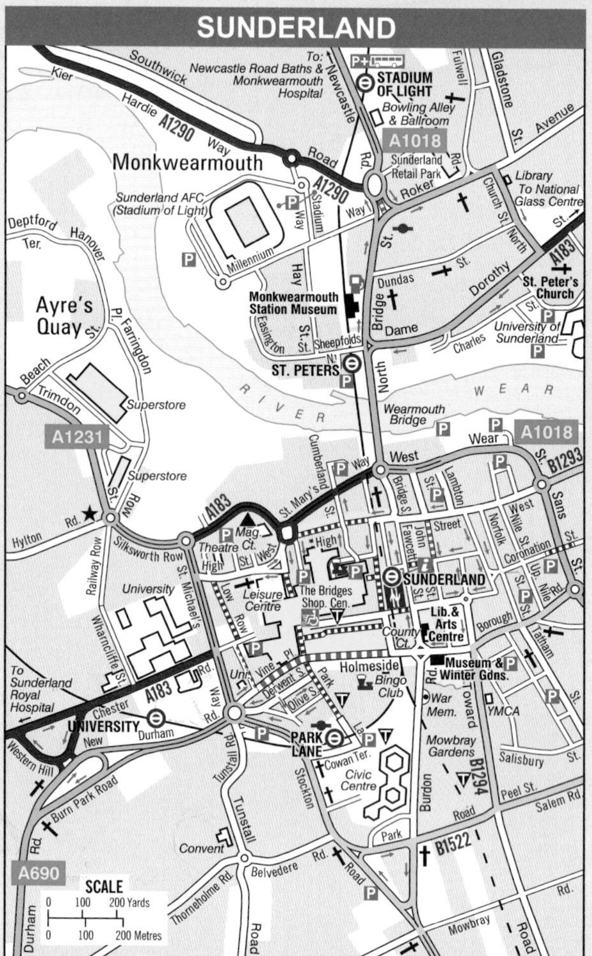

SWANSEA (ABERTAWE)

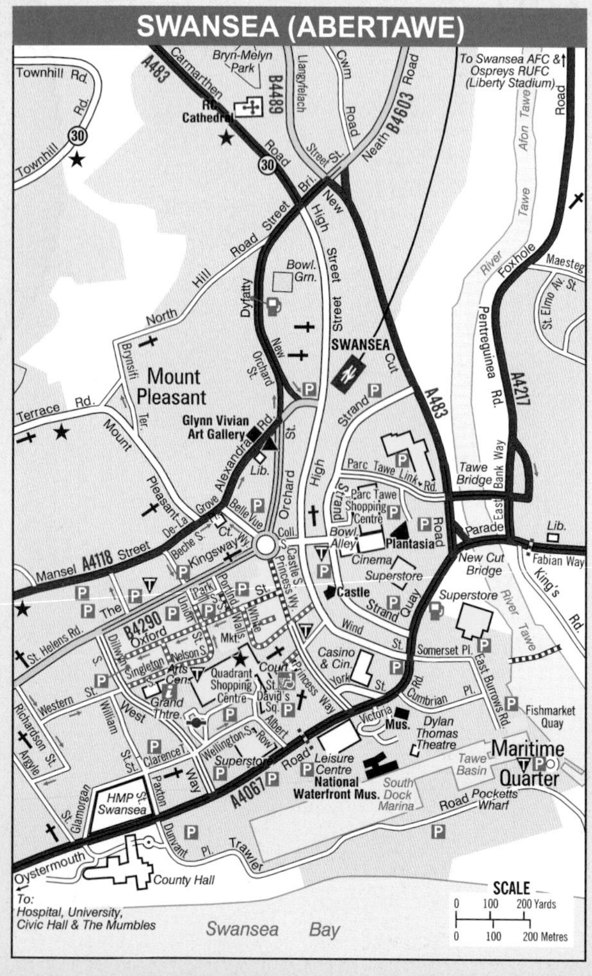

SWINDON

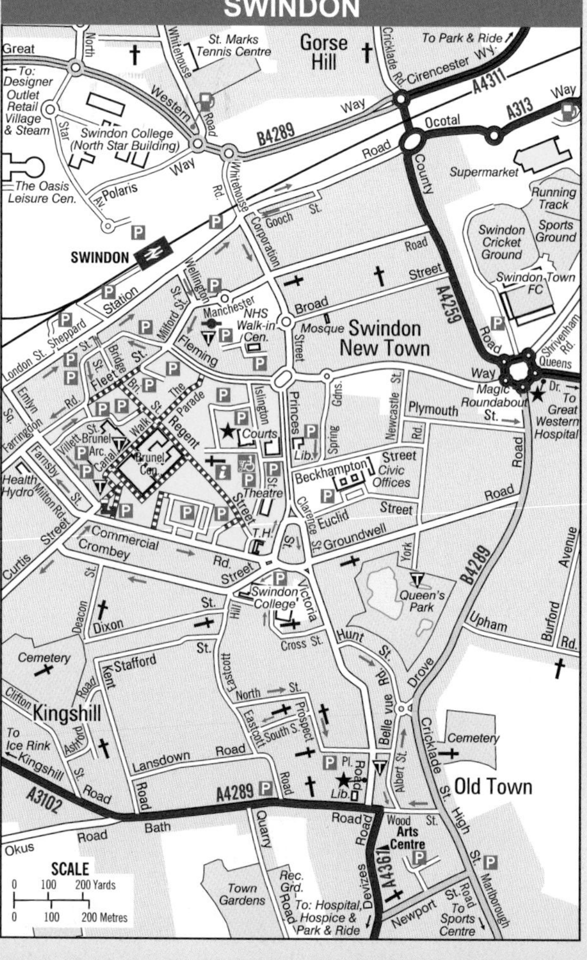

TAUNTON

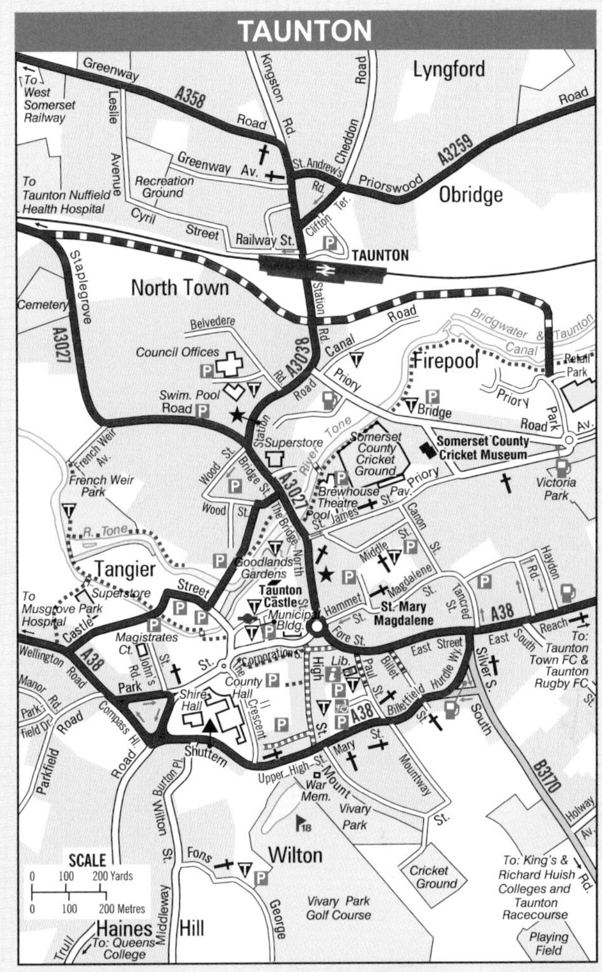

Lyngford
Obridge
North Town
Firepool
Tangier
Wilton
Haines Hill
TAUNTON
Greenway
A358
A3259
A3038
A3027
A38
B3170
To West Somerset Railway
To Taunton Nuffield Health Hospital
Recreation Ground
Railway St.
Cemetery
Council Offices
Swim. Pool
Superstore
Somerset County Cricket Ground
Somerset County Cricket Museum
Brewhouse Theatre
French Weir Park
Goodlands Gardens
Taunton Castle
Municip. Bldg.
St. Mary Magdalene
Victoria Park
To Musgrove Park Hospital
Magistrates Ct.
County Hall
Shire Hall
Shuttern
War Mem.
Vivary Park
Vivary Park Golf Course
Cricket Ground
To: Taunton Town FC & Taunton Rugby FC
To: King's & Richard Huish Colleges and Taunton Racecourse
To: Queens College
Playing Field
Bridgwater & Taunton Canal
Retail Park
SCALE
0 100 200 Yards
0 100 200 Metres

WINCHESTER

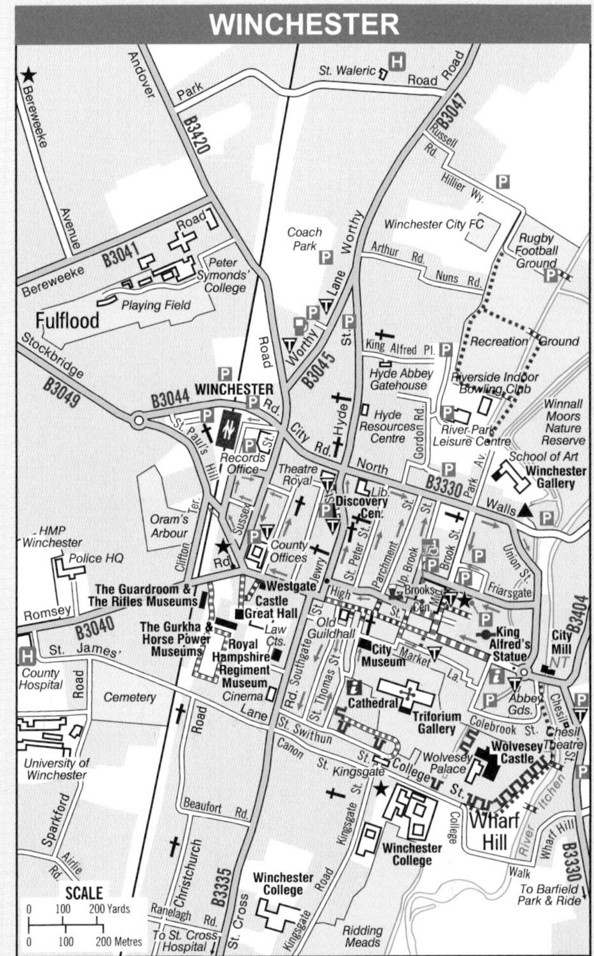

Fulflood
WINCHESTER
Wharf Hill
B3420
B3041
B3049
B3044
B3045
B3047
B3330
B3040
B3335
B3404
St. Waleric
Winchester City FC
Rugby Football Ground
Peter Symonds' College
Playing Field
Coach Park
Recreation Ground
Hyde Abbey Gatehouse
Riverside Indoor Bowling Club
Hyde Resources Centre
River Park Leisure Centre
Winnall Moors Nature Reserve
School of Art
Winchester Gallery
Records Office
Theatre Royal
Discovery Cen.
Oram's Arbour
HMP Winchester
Police HQ
County Offices
Westgate
Castle
Great Hall
The Guardroom & The Rifles Museums
The Gurkha & Horse Power Museums
Royal Hampshire Regiment Museum
Law Cts.
Old Guildhall
City Museum
King Alfred's Statue
City Mill
Cathedral
Triforium Gallery
Abbey Gds.
Theatre
Wolvesey Castle
Wolvesey Palace
County Hospital
Cemetery
University of Winchester
Winchester College
Ridding Meads
To St. Cross Hospital
To Barfield Park & Ride
SCALE
0 100 200 Yards
0 100 200 Metres

WINDSOR

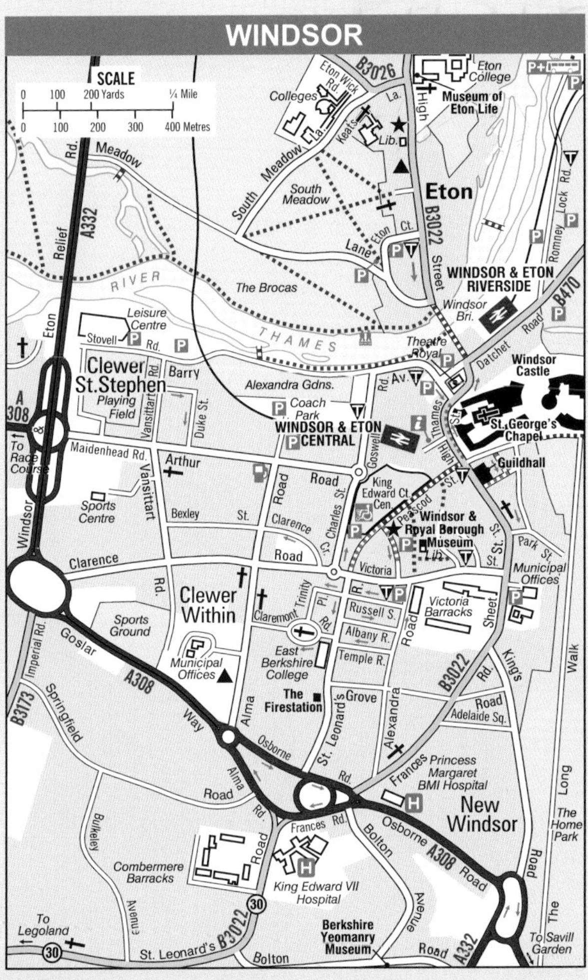

SCALE
0 100 200 Yards ¼ Mile
0 100 200 300 400 Metres
Eton
Eton College
Museum of Eton Life
Colleges
South Meadow
The Brocas
River Thames
WINDSOR & ETON RIVERSIDE
Windsor Bri.
Leisure Centre
Clewer St.Stephen
Playing Field
Alexandra Gdns.
Coach Park
Theatre Royal
Windsor Castle
St. George's Chapel
WINDSOR & ETON CENTRAL
Guildhall
King Edward Ct. Cen.
Windsor & Royal Borough Museum
Municipal Offices
Sports Centre
Clewer Within
Sports Ground
Victoria Barracks
East Berkshire College
The Firestation
Municipal Offices
Princess Margaret BMI Hospital
New Windsor
The Home Park
Combermere Barracks
King Edward VII Hospital
Berkshire Yeomanry Museum
To Legoland
To Savill Garden
To Race Course
A332
A308
B3026
B3022
B470
B3173

WOLVERHAMPTON

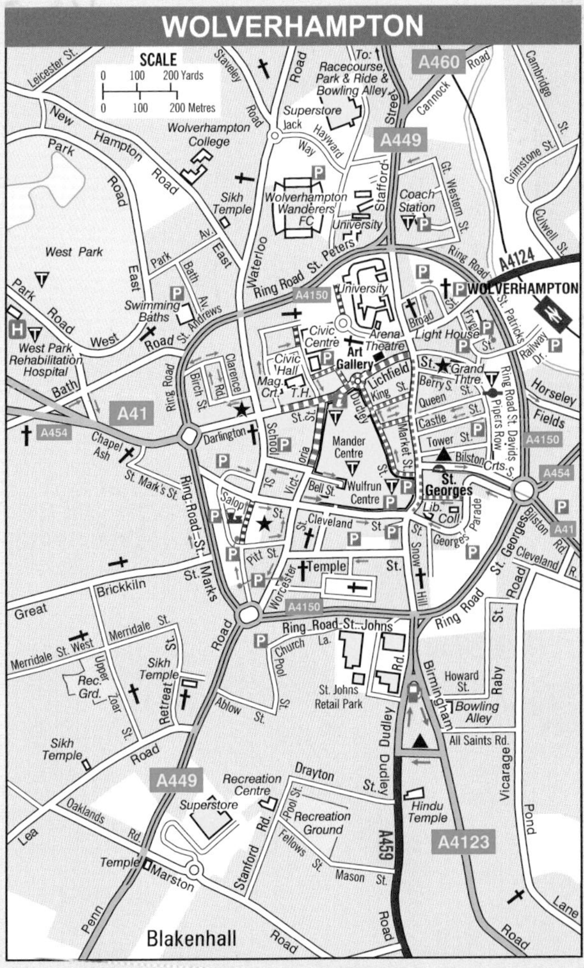

SCALE
0 100 200 Yards
0 100 200 Metres
To: Racecourse, Park & Ride & Bowling Alley
A460
A449
A4124
A4150
A41
A454
A4123
A459
Superstore
Wolverhampton College
Wolverhampton Wanderers FC
Coach Station
University
Sikh Temple
West Park
Swimming Baths
West Park Rehabilitation Hospital
WOLVERHAMPTON
Civic Centre
Art Gallery
Arena Theatre
Light House
Civic Hall
Grand Thtre.
Mander Centre
Wulfrun Centre
St. Georges
Lib. Coll
Temple
Ring Road St. Johns
St. Johns Retail Park
Howard St.
Bowling Alley
All Saints Rd.
Hindu Temple
Rec. Grd.
Sikh Temple
Recreation Centre
Superstore
Recreation Ground
Blakenhall

WORCESTER

WREXHAM (WRECSAM)

YORK

To Rawcliffe Bar Park & Ride
York City FC/ Kitkat Crescent
York Hospital
Wigginton Rd.
To York Nuffield Health Hospital
Huntington Rd.
Dodsworth Av.
To Monks Cross Park & Ride
Heworth Golf Course
Malton Rd.
Stockton La.
Clifton
End
Burton Stone La.
Grosvenor
Crescent
Ter.
Rd.
Bootham Park Hospital
Haxby Rd.
Heworth Road
Green
A1036
Clifton Bridge
Water End
Clifton
A19 Rd.
Bootham
Grosvenor
Sports Ground
Coach Park
B1363
Lowther
Townend St.
Penley's Grove Street
Huntington Rd.
Foss
Play. Field
Clarence St.
York St. John University
Lord Mayor's Walk
St. John's St.
Heworth
Parade
East
Glen Gardens
Melrosegate
Sports Ground
Bootham
Bootham Rw.
Gillygate
Treasurer's House NT
York Minster
Richard III Mus.
Monkgate
Superstore
Hawthorn Gro.
Layerthorpe
Hallfield Rd.
Marygate
York Art Gallery
King's Manor
Purey Cust Nuffield Hosp.
St. William's Coll.
Ogleforth
Deangate
St. Maurice's Rd.
River Foss
Bank
Frederic St.
Yorkshire Museum Gardens
Lib.
Theatre Royal
Monk Bar
Merchant Taylors Hall
Layerthorpe
Leeman
Stonegate
Low Petergate
Goodramgate
Peasholme Green
James St.
Play. Fields
RIVER
Museum St.
Barley Hall
Foss
National Railway Museum
Road
Lendal Bridge
Lendal
Baths
Coney St.
Shambles
The Stonebow
DIG
Foss Islands
York Model Railway
Station Rd.
Guildhall
Cinema
St. Nicholas Fields
B1227
Station
Merchant Adventurers' Hall
Red Tower
Islands
Tanner Row
North St.
Market St.
Navigation
YORK
Toft Green
Ouse Bri.
Bridge St.
Coppergate
Jorvik Viking Centre
Brewery
Micklegate
Trinity La.
St.
Opera Ho.
Dungeon Theatre
Castlegate
Fairfax House
Walmgate
Road
Bull La.
Micklegate Bar Museum
Bishophill Snr.
Skeldergate
Law Courts
Brass Rubbing Cen.
Reg. Mus.
Clifford's Tower
Castle Museum
Piccadilly
George St.
Walmgate Bar
Lawrence Street
Street
Melrosegate
Queen St.
Blossom St.
Lwr. Priory S.
Cromwell Rd.
Crown Court
Raindale Watermill
Fishergate Tower
Barbican Road
Nunnery La.
Baile Hill
Skeldergate Bridge
Paragon St.
Hull Rd.
A1079
Holgate
A59
Road
Bar Convent Museum
Bishopgate St.
York Barbican Centre
To Grimston Bar Park & Ride
Dalton Ter.
Mount
Scarcroft
Lane
Road
Clementhorpe
Terry
Fawcett St.
Kent St.
Heslington
Green Dykes La.
Road
University Rd.
Play. Fields
The Vale
A1036
Vine St.
Caravan Park
Road
OUSE
Fishergate
Cemetery
A19
Cemetery
Clementhorpe
Av.
Bishopthorpe
Rowntree Park
Terry Av.
Road
Mount
To Askham Bar Park & Ride
Racecourse
To McArthur Glen Park & Ride
SCALE
0 100 200 Yards ¼ Mile
0 100 200 300 400 Metres
To University

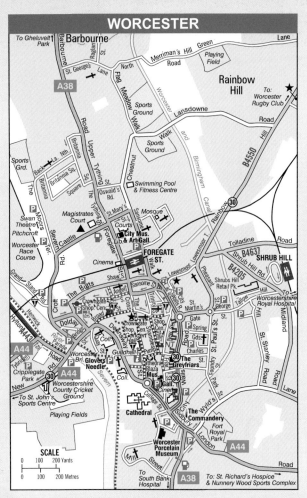

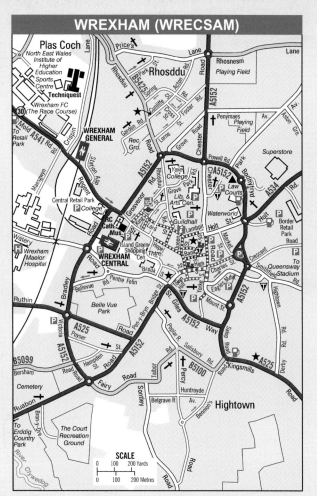

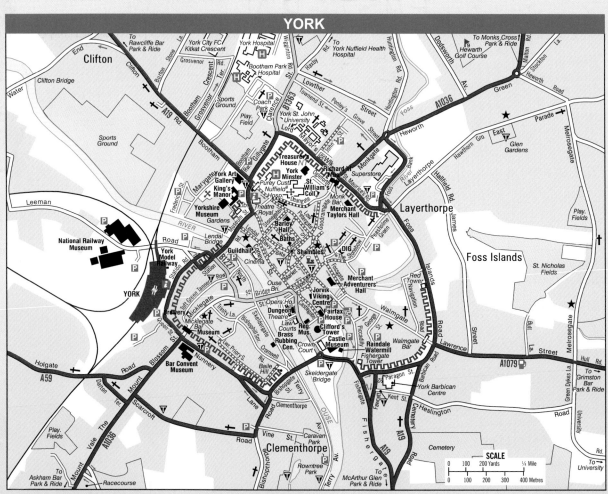

HARWICH

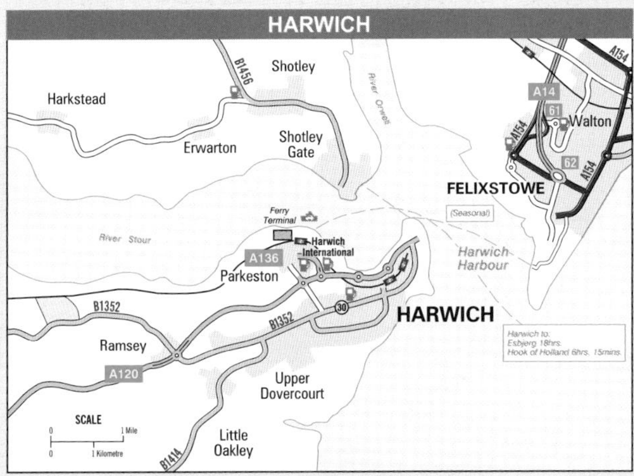

KINGSTON UPON HULL

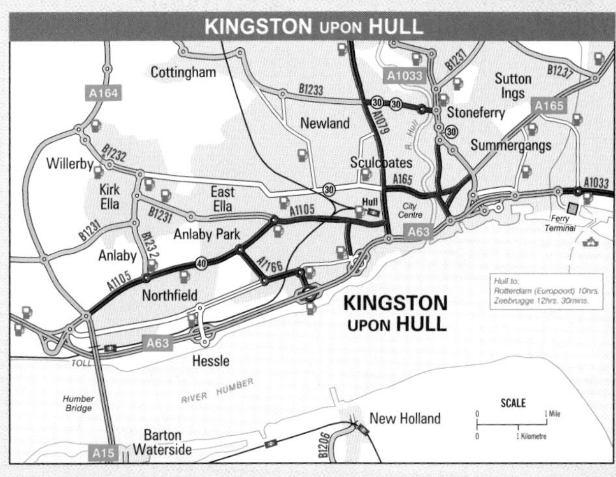

NEWCASTLE UPON TYNE

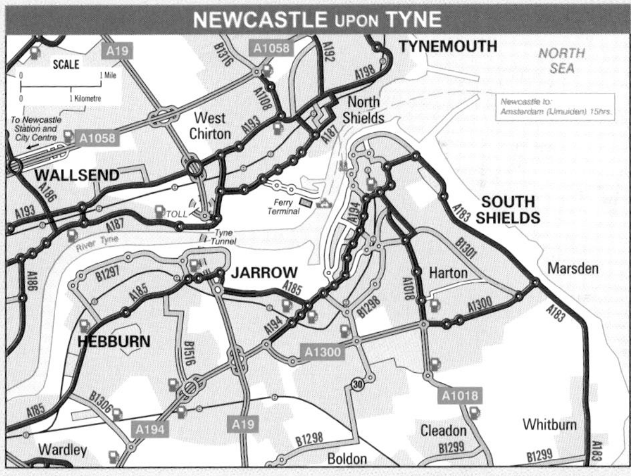

NEWHAVEN

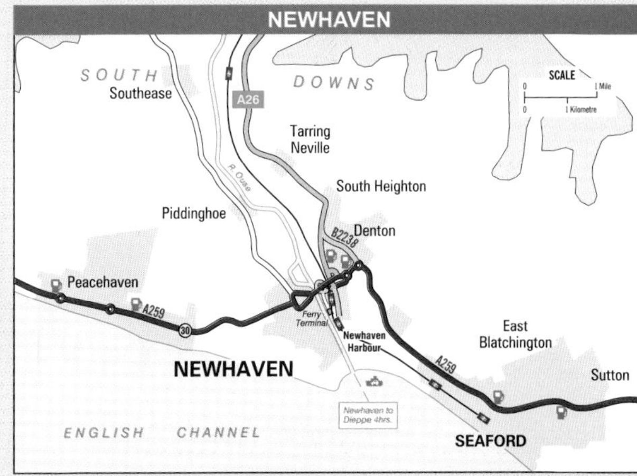

PEMBROKE DOCK (DOC PENFRO)

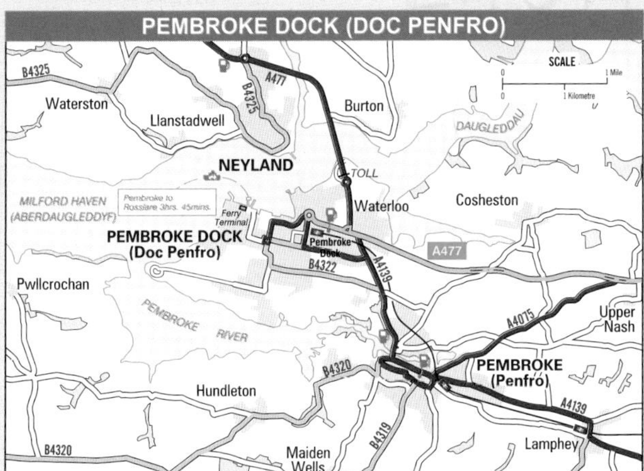

POOLE

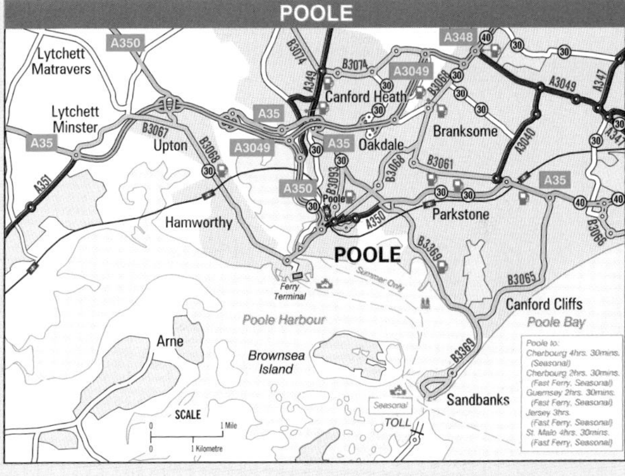

PORTSMOUTH

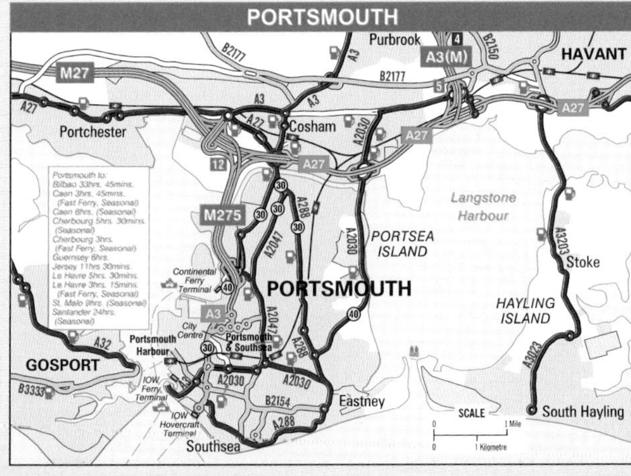

WEYMOUTH

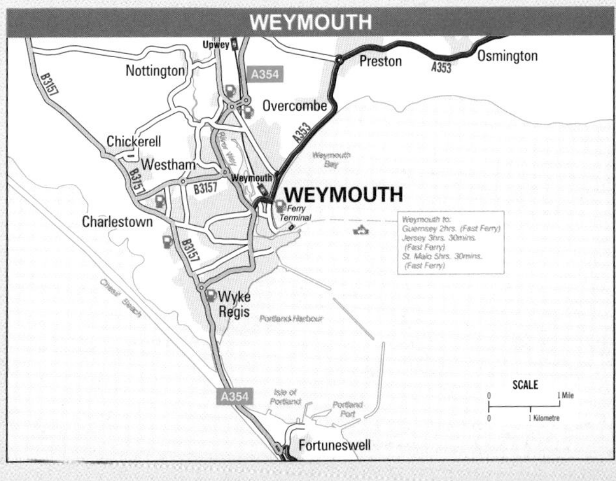

BIRMINGHAM INTERNATIONAL

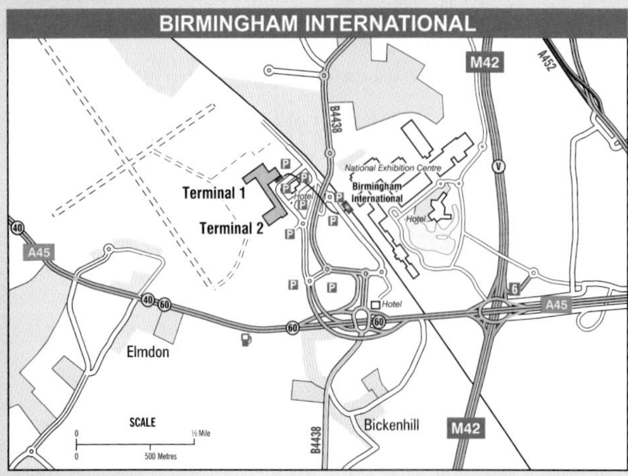

EAST MIDLANDS

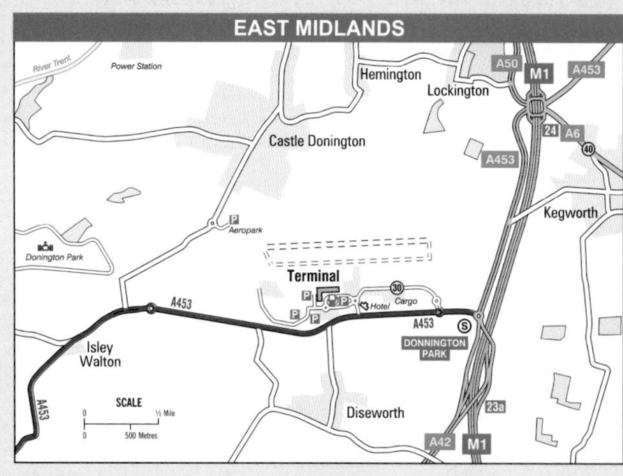

GLASGOW

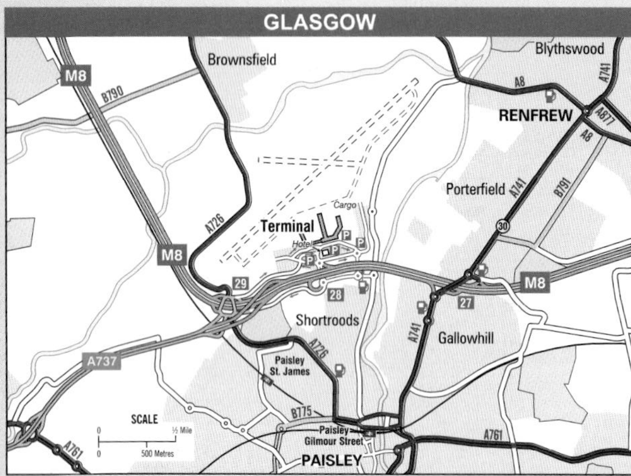

LONDON GATWICK

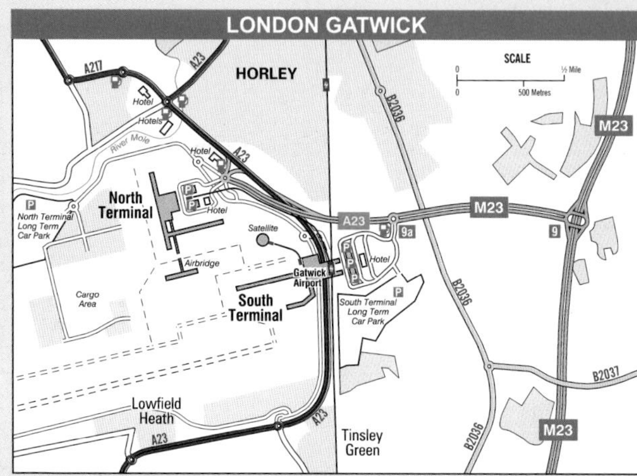

LONDON HEATHROW

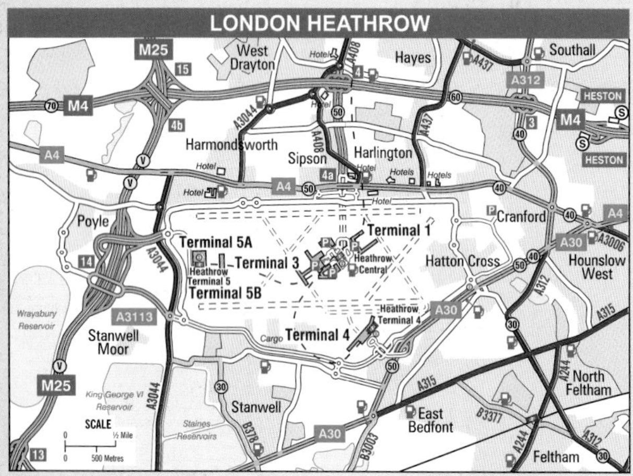

LONDON LUTON

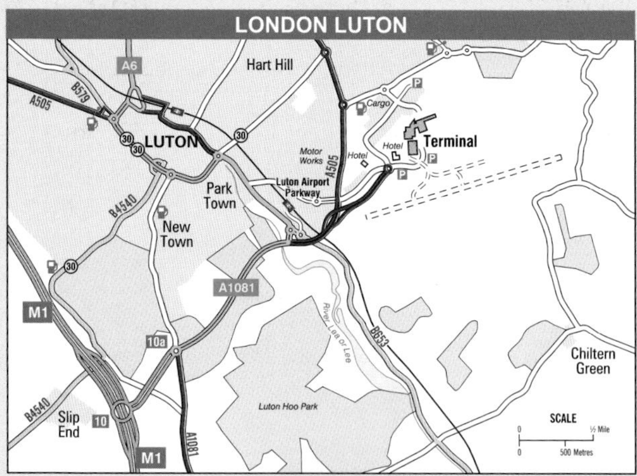

LONDON STANSTED

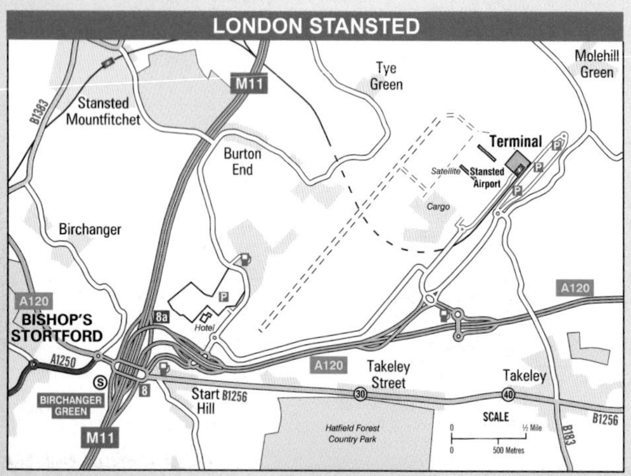

MANCHESTER INTERNATIONAL

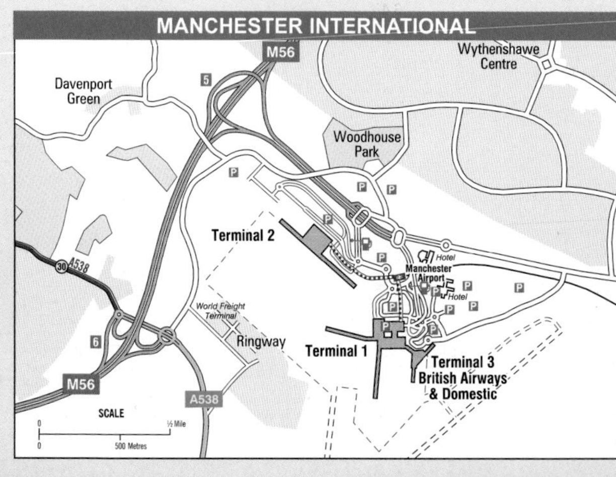

INDEX TO CITIES, TOWNS, VILLAGES, HAMLETS, LOCATIONS, AIRPORTS & PORTS

(1) A strict alphabetical order is used e.g. An Dùnan follows Andreas but precedes Andwell.

(2) The map reference given refers to the actual map square in which the town spot or built-up area is located and not to the place name.

(3) Major towns, selected airports and ports are shown in bold, i.e. **Aberdeen.** *Aber* . . . 3G **153** & **187** Where they appear on a Town Plan a second page reference is given.

(4) Where two or more places of the same name occur in the same County or Unitary Authority, the nearest large town is also given; e.g. Achiemore. *High* . . . 2D **166** (nr. Durness) indicates that Achiemore is located in square 2D on page **166** and is situated near Durness in the Unitary Authority of Highland.

(5) Only one reference is given although due to page overlaps the place may appear on more than one page.

COUNTIES and UNITARY AUTHORITIES with the abbreviations used in this index

Aberdeen : *Aber*
Aberdeenshire : *Abers*
Angus : *Ang*
Argyll & Bute : *Arg*
Bath & N E Somerset : *Bath*
Bedford : *Bed*
Blackburn with Darwen : *Bkbn*
Blackpool : *Bkpl*
Blaenau Gwent : *Blae*
Bournemouth : *Bour*
Bracknell Forest : *Brac*
Bridgend : *B'end*
Brighton & Hove : *Brig*
Bristol : *Bris*
Buckinghamshire : *Buck*
Caerphilly : *Cphy*
Cambridgeshire : *Cambs*
Cardiff : *Card*
Carmarthenshire : *Carm*
Central Bedfordshire : *C Beds*
Ceredigion : *Cdgn*
Cheshire East : *Ches E*
Cheshire West & Chester : *Ches W*
Clackmannanshire : *Clac*
Conwy : *Cnwy*
Cornwall : *Corn*
Cumbria : *Cumb*
Darlington : *Darl*
Denbighshire : *Den*
Derby : *Derb*
Derbyshire : *Derbs*
Devon : *Devn*
Dorset : *Dors*
Dumfries & Galloway : *Dum*
Dundee : *D'dee*
Durham : *Dur*
East Ayrshire : *E Ayr*
East Dunbartonshire : *E Dun*
East Lothian : *E Lot*
East Renfrewshire : *E Ren*
East Riding of Yorkshire : *E Yor*
East Sussex : *E Sus*
Edinburgh : *Edin*
Essex : *Essx*
Falkirk : *Falk*
Fife : *Fife*
Flintshire : *Flin*
Glasgow : *Glas*
Gloucestershire : *Glos*
Greater London : *G Lon*
Greater Manchester : *G Man*
Gwynedd : *Gwyn*
Halton : *Hal*
Hampshire : *Hants*
Hartlepool : *Hart*
Herefordshire : *Here*
Hertfordshire : *Herts*
Highland : *High*
Inverclyde : *Inv*
Isle of Anglesey : *IOA*
Isle of Man : *IOM*
Isle of Wight : *IOW*
Isles of Scilly : *IOS*
Kent : *Kent*
Kingston upon Hull : *Hull*
Lancashire : *Lanc*
Leicester : *Leic*
Leicestershire : *Leics*
Lincolnshire : *Linc*
Luton : *Lutn*
Medway : *Medw*
Merseyside : *Mers*
Merthyr Tydfil : *Mer T*
Middlesbrough : *Midd*
Midlothian : *Midl*
Milton Keynes : *Mil*
Monmouthshire : *Mon*
Moray : *Mor*
Neath Port Talbot : *Neat*
Newport : *Newp*
Norfolk : *Norf*
Northamptonshire : *Nptn*
North Ayrshire : *N Ayr*
North East Lincolnshire : *NE Lin*
North Lanarkshire : *N Lan*
North Lincolnshire : *N Lin*
North Somerset : *N Som*
Northumberland : *Nmbd*
North Yorkshire : *N Yor*
Nottingham : *Nott*
Nottinghamshire : *Notts*
Orkney : *Orkn*
Oxfordshire : *Oxon*
Pembrokeshire : *Pemb*
Perth & Kinross : *Per*
Peterborough : *Pet*
Plymouth : *Plym*
Poole : *Pool*
Portsmouth : *Port*
Powys : *Powy*
Reading : *Read*
Redcar & Cleveland : *Red C*
Renfrewshire : *Ren*
Rhondda Cynon Taff : *Rhon*
Rutland : *Rut*
Scottish Borders : *Bord*
Shetland : *Shet*
Shropshire : *Shrp*
Slough : *Slo*
Somerset : *Som*
Southampton : *Sotn*
South Ayrshire : *S Ayr*
Southend-on-Sea : *S'end*
South Gloucestershire : *S Glo*
South Lanarkshire : *S Lan*
South Yorkshire : *S Yor*
Staffordshire : *Staf*
Stirling : *Stir*
Stockton-on-Tees : *Stoc T*
Stoke-on-Trent : *Stoke*
Suffolk : *Suff*
Surrey : *Surr*
Swansea : *Swan*
Swindon : *Swin*
Telford & Wrekin : *Telf*
Thurrock : *Thur*
Torbay : *Torb*
Torfaen : *Torf*
Tyne & Wear : *Tyne*
Vale of Glamorgan, The : *V Glam*
Warrington : *Warr*
Warwickshire : *Warw*
West Berkshire : *W Ber*
West Dunbartonshire : *W Dun*
Western Isles : *W Isl*
West Lothian : *W Lot*
West Midlands : *W Mid*
West Sussex : *W Sus*
West Yorkshire : *W Yor*
Wiltshire : *Wilts*
Windsor & Maidenhead : *Wind*
Wokingham : *Wok*
Worcestershire : *Worc*
Wrexham : *Wrex*
York : *York*

INDEX

A

Abbas Combe. *Som* 4C **22**
Abberley. *Worc* 4B **60**
Abberley Common. *Worc* 4B **60**
Abberton. *Essx* 4D **54**
Abberton. *Worc* 5D **61**
Abberwick. *Nmbd* 3F **121**
Abbess Roding. *Essx* 4F **53**
Abbey. *Devn* 1E **13**
Abbey-cwm-hir. *Powy* 3C **58**
Abbeydale. *S Yor* 2H **85**
Abbeydale Park. *S Yor* 2H **85**
Abbey Dore. *Here* 2G **47**
Abbey Gate. *Devn* 3F **13**
Abbey Hulton. *Stoke* 1D **72**
Abbey St Bathans. *Bord* 3D **130**
Abbeystead. *Lanc* 4E **97**
Abbeytown. *Cumb* 4C **112**
Abbey Village. *Lanc* 2E **91**
Abbey Wood. *G Lon* 3F **39**
Abbots Ann. *Hants* 2B **24**
Abbots Bickington. *Devn* 1D **11**
Abbots Bromley. *Staf* 3E **73**
Abbotsbury. *Dors* 4A **14**
Abbotsham. *Devn* 4E **19**
Abbotskerswell. *Devn* 2E **9**
Abbots Langley. *Herts* 5A **52**
Abbots Leigh. *N Som* 4A **34**
Abbotsley. *Cambs* 5B **64**
Abbots Morton. *Worc* 5E **61**
Abbots Ripton. *Cambs* 3B **64**
Abbot's Salford. *Warw* 5E **61**
Abbotstone. *Hants* 3D **24**
Abbots Worthy. *Hants* 3C **24**
Abcott. *Shrp* 3F **59**
Abdon. *Shrp* 2H **59**
Abenhall. *Glos* 4B **48**
Aber. *Cdgn* 1E **45**
Aberaeron. *Cdgn* 4D **56**
Aberafan. *Neat* 3G **31**
Aberaman. *Rhon* 5D **46**
Aberangell. *Powy* 4H **69**
Aberarad. *Carm* 1H **43**
Aberarder. *High* 1A **150**
Aberargie. *Per* 2D **136**
Aberarth. *Cdgn* 4D **57**
Aberavon. *Neat* 3G **31**
Aber-banc. *Cdgn* 1D **44**
Aberbargoed. *Cphy* 2E **33**
Aberbechan. *Powy* 1D **58**
Aberbeeg. *Blae* 5F **47**
Aberbowlan. *Carm* 2G **45**
Aberbran. *Powy* 3C **46**
Abercanaid. *Mer T* 5D **46**
Abercarn. *Cphy* 2F **33**
Abercastle. *Pemb* 1C **42**
Abercegir. *Powy* 5H **69**
Aberchalder. *High* 3F **149**
Aberchirder. *Abers* 3D **160**
Abercorn. *W Lot* 2D **129**
Abercraf. *Powy* 4B **46**
Abercregan. *Neat* 2B **32**
Abercrombie. *Fife* 3H **137**
Abercwmboi. *Rhon* 2D **32**
Abercych. *Pemb* 1C **44**
Abercynon. *Rhon* 2D **32**
Aber-Cywarch. *Gwyn* 4A **70**
Aberdalgie. *Per* 1C **136**
Aberdar. *Rhon* 5C **46**
Aberdare. *Rhon* 5C **46**
Aberdaron. *Gwyn* 3A **68**
Aberdaugleddau. *Pemb* 4D **42**
Aberdeen. *Aber* 3G **153** & **187**
Aberdeen (Dyce) Airport. *Aber* 2F **153**
Aberdesach. *Gwyn* 5D **80**
Aberdour. *Fife* 1E **129**
Aberdovey. *Gwyn* 1F **57**
Aberdulais. *Neat* 5A **46**
Aberdyfi. *Gwyn* 1F **57**
Aberedw. *Powy* 1D **46**
Abereiddy. *Pemb* 1B **42**
Abererch. *Gwyn* 2C **68**
Aberfan. *Mer T* 5D **46**
Aberfeldy. *Per* 4F **143**
Aberffraw. *IOA* 4C **80**
Aberffrwd. *Cdgn* 3F **57**
Aberford. *W Yor* 1E **93**
Aberfoyle. *Stir* 3E **135**
Abergarw. *B'end* 3C **32**
Abergarwed. *Neat* 5B **46**
Abergavenny. *Mon* 4G **47**
Abergele. *Cnwy* 3B **82**
Aber-Giar. *Carm* 1F **45**
Abergorlech. *Carm* 2F **45**
Abergwaun. *Pemb* 1D **42**
Abergwesyn. *Powy* 5A **58**
Abergwili. *Carm* 3E **45**
Abergwynfi. *Neat* 2B **32**
Abergwyngregyn. *Gwyn* 3F **81**
Abergynolwyn. *Gwyn* 5F **69**
Aberhafesp. *Powy* 1C **58**
Aberhonddu. *Powy* 3D **46**
Aberhosan. *Powy* 1H **57**
Aberkenfig. *B'end* 3B **32**
Aberlady. *E Lot* 2A **130**
Aberlemno. *Ang* 3E **145**
Aberllefenni. *Gwyn* 5G **69**
Abermaw. *Gwyn* 4F **69**
Abermeurig. *Cdgn* 5E **57**
Aber-miwl. *Powy* 1D **58**
Abermule. *Powy* 1D **58**
Abernant. *Carm* 2H **43**
Abernant. *Rhon* 5D **46**
Abernethy. *Per* 2D **136**
Abernyte. *Per* 5B **144**
Aber-oer. *Wrex* 1E **71**
Aberpennar. *Rhon* 2D **32**
Aberporth. *Cdgn* 5B **56**
Aberriw. *Powy* 5D **70**
Abersoch. *Gwyn* 3C **68**
Abersychan. *Torf* 5F **47**
Abertawe. *Swan* 3F **31** & **Swansea 212**
Aberteifi. *Cdgn* 1B **44**
Aberthin. *V Glam* 4D **32**
Abertillery. *Blae* 5F **47**
Abertridwr. *Cphy* 3E **32**
Abertridwr. *Powy* 4C **70**
Abertyleri. *Blae* 5F **47**
Abertysswg. *Cphy* 5E **47**
Aberuthven. *Per* 2B **136**
Aber Village. *Powy* 3E **46**
Aberyscir. *Powy* 3D **46**
Aberystwyth. *Cdgn* 2E **57** & **187**
Abhainn Suidhe. *W Isl* 7C **171**
Abingdon. *Oxon* 2C **36**
Abinger Common. *Surr* 1C **26**
Abinger Hammer. *Surr* 1B **26**
Abington. *S Lan* 2B **118**
Abington Pigotts. *Cambs* 1D **52**
Ab Kettleby. *Leics* 3E **74**
Ab Lench. *Worc* 5E **61**
Ablington. *Glos* 5G **49**
Ablington. *Wilts* 2G **23**
Abney. *Derbs* 3F **85**
Aboyne. *Abers* 4C **152**
Abram. *G Man* 4D **90**
Abriachan. *High* 5H **157**
Abridge. *Essx* 1F **39**
Abronhill. *N Lan* 2A **128**
Abson. *S Glo* 4C **34**
Abthorpe. *Nptn* 1E **51**
Abune-the-Hill. *Orkn* 5B **172**
Aby. *Linc* 3D **88**
Acairseid. *W Isl* 8C **170**
Acaster Malbis. *York* 5H **99**
Acaster Selby. *N Yor* 5H **99**
Accott. *Devn* 3G **19**
Accrington. *Lanc* 2F **91**
Acha. *Arg* 3C **138**
Achachork. *High* 4D **155**
Achadh a' Chuirn. *High* 1E **147**
Achahoish. *Arg* 2F **125**
Achaleven. *Arg* 5D **140**
Achalleder. *Arg* 4H **141**
Acha Mor. *W Isl* 5F **171**
Achanalt. *High* 2E **157**
Achandunie. *High* 1A **158**
Ach' an Todhair. *High* 1E **141**
Achany. *High* 3C **164**
Achaphubuil. *High* 1E **141**
Acharacle. *High* 2A **140**
Acharn. *Ang* 1B **144**
Acharn. *Per* 4E **143**
Acharole. *High* 3E **169**
Achateny. *High* 2G **139**
Achavanich. *High* 4D **169**
Achdalieu. *High* 1E **141**
Achduart. *High* 3E **163**
Achentoul. *High* 5A **168**
Achfary. *High* 5C **166**
Achfrish. *High* 2C **164**
Achgarve. *High* 4C **162**
Achiemore. *High* 2D **166** (nr. Durness)
Achiemore. *High* 3A **168** (nr. Thurso)
A'Chill. *High* 3A **146**
Achiltibuie. *High* 3E **163**
Achina. *High* 2H **167**
Achinahuagh. *High* 2F **167**
Achindarroch. *High* 3E **141**
Achinduich. *High* 3C **164**
Achinduin. *Arg* 5C **140**
Achininver. *High* 2F **167**
Achintee. *High* 4B **156**
Achintraid. *High* 5H **155**
Achleck. *Arg* 4F **139**
Achlorachan. *High* 3F **157**
Achluachrach. *High* 5E **149**
Achlyness. *High* 3C **166**
Achmelvich. *High* 1E **163**
Achmony. *High* 5H **157**
Achmore. *High* 5A **156** (nr. Stromeferry)
Achmore. *High* 4E **163** (nr. Ullapool)
Achnacarnin. *High* 1E **163**
Achnacarry. *High* 5D **148**
Achnaclerach. *High* 2G **157**
Achnacloich. *High* 3D **147**
Ach na Cloiche. *High* 3D **147**
Achnaconeran. *High* 2G **149**
Achnacroish. *Arg* 4C **140**
Achnafalnich. *Arg* 1B **134**
Achnagarron. *High* 1A **158**
Achnaha. *High* 2F **139**
Achnahanat. *High* 4C **164**
Achnahannet. *High* 1D **151**
Achnairn. *High* 2C **164**
Achnamara. *Arg* 1F **125**
Achnanellan. *High* 5C **148**
Achnangoul. *Arg* 3H **133**
Achnasheen. *High* 3D **156**
Achnashellach. *High* 4C **156**
Achosnich. *High* 2F **139**
Achow. *High* 5E **169**
Achranich. *High* 4B **140**
Achreamie. *High* 2C **168**
Achriabhach. *High* 2F **141**
Achriesgill. *High* 3C **166**
Achrimsdale. *High* 3G **165**
Achscrabster. *High* 2C **168**
Achtoty. *High* 2G **167**
Achurch. *Nptn* 2H **63**
Achuvoldrach. *High* 3F **167**
Achvaich. *High* 4E **164**
Achvoan. *High* 3E **165**
Ackergill. *High* 3F **169**
Ackergillshore. *High* 3F **169**
Acklam. *Midd* 3B **106**
Acklam. *N Yor* 3B **100**
Ackleton. *Shrp* 1B **60**
Acklington. *Nmbd* 4G **121**
Ackton. *W Yor* 2E **93**
Ackworth Moor Top. *W Yor* 3E **93**
Acle. *Norf* 4G **79**
Acocks Green. *W Mid* 2F **61**
Acol. *Kent* 4H **41**
Acomb. *Nmbd* 3C **114**
Acomb. *York* 4H **99**
Aconbury. *Here* 2A **48**
Acre. *G Man* 4H **91**
Acre. *Lanc* 2F **91**
Acrefair. *Wrex* 1E **71**
Acrise. *Kent* 1F **29**
Acton. *Ches E* 5A **84**
Acton. *Dors* 5E **15**
Acton. *G Lon* 2C **38**
Acton. *Shrp* 2F **59**
Acton. *Staf* 1C **72**
Acton. *Suff* 1B **54**
Acton. *Worc* 4C **60**
Acton. *Wrex* 5F **83**
Acton Beauchamp. *Here* 5A **60**
Acton Bridge. *Ches W* 3H **83**
Acton Burnell. *Shrp* 5H **71**
Acton Green. *Here* 5A **60**
Acton Pigott. *Shrp* 5H **71**
Acton Round. *Shrp* 1A **60**
Acton Scott. *Shrp* 2G **59**
Acton Trussell. *Staf* 4D **72**
Acton Turville. *S Glo* 3D **34**
Adabroc. *W Isl* 1H **171**
Adam's Hill. *Worc* 3D **60**
Adbaston. *Staf* 3B **72**
Adber. *Dors* 4B **22**
Adderbury. *Oxon* 2C **50**
Adderley. *Shrp* 2A **72**
Adderstone. *Nmbd* 1F **121**
Addiewell. *W Lot* 3C **128**
Addingham. *W Yor* 5C **98**
Addington. *Buck* 3F **51**
Addington. *G Lon* 4E **39**
Addington. *Kent* 5A **40**
Addinston. *Bord* 4B **130**
Addiscombe. *G Lon* 4E **39**
Addlestone. *Surr* 4B **38**
Addlethorpe. *Linc* 4E **89**
Adeney. *Telf* 4B **72**
Adfa. *Powy* 5C **70**
Adforton. *Here* 3G **59**
Adgestone. *IOW* 4D **16**
Adisham. *Kent* 5G **41**
Adlestrop. *Glos* 3H **49**
Adlingfleet. *E Yor* 2B **94**
Adlington. *Ches E* 2D **84**
Adlington. *Lanc* 3E **90**
Admaston. *Staf* 3E **73**
Admaston. *Telf* 4A **72**
Admington. *Warw* 1G **49**
Adpar. *Cdgn* 1D **44**
Adsborough. *Som* 4F **21**
Adstock. *Buck* 2F **51**
Adstone. *Nptn* 5C **62**
Adversane. *W Sus* 3B **26**
Advie. *High* 5F **159**
Adwalton. *W Yor* 2C **92**
Adwell. *Oxon* 2E **37**
Adwick le Street. *S Yor* 4F **93**
Adwick upon Dearne. *S Yor* 4E **93**
Adziel. *Abers* 3G **161**
Ae. *Dum* 1A **112**
Affleck. *Abers* 1F **153**
Affpuddle. *Dors* 3D **14**
Affric Lodge. *High* 1D **148**
Afon-wen. *Flin* 3D **82**
Agglethorpe. *N Yor* 1C **98**
Aglionby. *Cumb* 4F **113**
Aigburth. *Mers* 2F **83**
Aiginis. *W Isl* 4G **171**
Aike. *E Yor* 5E **101**
Aikers. *Orkn* 8D **172**
Aiketgate. *Cumb* 5F **113**
Aikhead. *Cumb* 5D **112**
Aikton. *Cumb* 4D **112**
Ailey. *Here* 1G **47**
Ailsworth. *Pet* 1A **64**
Ainderby Quernhow. *N Yor* 1F **99**
Ainderby Steeple. *N Yor* 5A **106**
Aingers Green. *Essx* 3E **54**
Ainsdale. *Mers* 3B **90**
Ainsdale-on-Sea. *Mers* 3B **90**
Ainstable. *Cumb* 5G **113**
Ainsworth. *G Man* 3F **91**
Ainthorpe. *N Yor* 4E **107**
Aintree. *Mers* 1F **83**
Aird. *Arg* 3E **133**
Aird. *Dum* 3F **109**
Aird. *High* 1G **155** (nr. Port Henderson)
Aird. *High* 3D **147** (nr. Tarskavaig)
Aird. *W Isl* 3C **170** (on Benbecula)
Aird. *W Isl* 4H **171** (on Isle of Lewis)
Àird a Bhasair. *High* 3E **147**
Aird a Mhachair. *W Isl* 4C **170**
Aird a Mhulaidh. *W Isl* 6D **171**
Aird Asaig. *W Isl* 7D **171**
Aird Dhail. *W Isl* 1G **171**
Airdens. *High* 4D **164**
Airdeny. *Arg* 1G **133**
Aird Mhidhinis. *W Isl* 8C **170**
Aird Mhighe. *W Isl* 8D **171** (nr. Ceann a Bhaigh)
Aird Mhighe. *W Isl* 9C **171** (nr. Fionnsabhagh)
Aird Mhor. *W Isl* 8C **170** (on Barra)
Aird Mhor. *W Isl* 4D **170** (on South Uist)
Airdrie. *N Lan* 3A **128**
Aird Shleibhe. *W Isl* 9D **171**
Aird, The. *High* 3D **154**
Aird Thunga. *W Isl* 4G **171**
Aird Uig. *W Isl* 4C **171**
Airedale. *W Yor* 2E **93**
Airidh a Bhruaich. *W Isl* 6E **171**
Airies. *Dum* 3E **109**
Airmyn. *E Yor* 2H **93**
Airntully. *Per* 5H **143**
Airor. *High* 3F **147**
Airth. *Falk* 1C **128**
Airton. *N Yor* 4B **98**
Aisby. *Linc* 1F **87** (nr. Gainsborough)
Aisby. *Linc* 2H **75** (nr. Grantham)
Aisgernis. *W Isl* 6C **170**
Aish. *Devn* 2C **8** (nr. Buckfastleigh)
Aish. *Devn* 3E **9** (nr. Totnes)
Aisholt. *Som* 3E **21**
Aiskew. *N Yor* 1E **99**
Aislaby. *N Yor* 1B **100** (nr. Pickering)
Aislaby. *N Yor* 4F **107** (nr. Whitby)
Aislaby. *Stoc T* 3B **106**
Aisthorpe. *Linc* 2G **87**
Aith. *Shet* 2H **173** (on Fetlar)
Aith. *Shet* 6E **173** (on Mainland)
Aithsetter. *Shet* 8F **173**

A-Z Great Britain Road Atlas 217

Ashby Parva—Ballygrant

Ashby Parva. Leics 2C 62
Ashby Puerorum. Linc 3C 88
Ashby St Ledgars. Nptn 4C 62
Ashby St Mary. Norf 5F 79
Ashchurch. Glos 2E 49
Ashcombe. Devn 5C 12
Ashcott. Som 3H 21
Ashdon. Essx 1F 53
Ashe. Hants 1D 24
Asheldham. Essx 5C 54
Ashen. Essx 1H 53
Ashendon. Buck 4F 51
Ashey. IOW 4D 16
Ashfield. Hants 1B 16
Ashfield. Here 3A 48
Ashfield. Shrp 2H 59
Ashfield. Stir 3G 135
Ashfield. Suff 4E 66
Ashfield Green. Suff 3E 67
Ashfold Crossways. W Sus 3D 26
Ashford. Devn 3F 19 (nr. Barnstaple)
Ashford. Devn 4C 8 (nr. Kingsbridge)
Ashford. Hants 1G 15
Ashford. Kent 1E 28
Ashford. Surr 3B 38
Ashford Bowdler. Shrp 3H 59
Ashford Carbonel. Shrp 3H 59
Ashford Hill. Hants 5D 36
Ashford in the Water. Derbs 4F 85
Ashgill. S Lan 5A 128
Ash Green. Warw 2H 61
Ashgrove. Mor 2G 159
Ashill. Devn 1D 12
Ashill. Norf 5A 78
Ashill. Som 1G 13
Ashingdon. Essx 1C 40
Ashington. Nmbd 1F 115
Ashington. W Sus 4C 26
Ashkirk. Bord 2G 119
Ashlett. Hants 2C 16
Ashleworth. Glos 3D 48
Ashley. Cambs 4F 65
Ashley. Ches E 2B 84
Ashley. Dors 2G 15
Ashley. Glos 2E 35
Ashley. Hants 3A 16 (nr. New Milton)
Ashley. Hants 3B 24 (nr. Winchester)
Ashley. Kent 1H 29
Ashley. Nptn 1E 63
Ashley. Staf 2B 72
Ashley. Wilts 5D 34
Ashley Green. Buck 5H 51
Ashley Heath. Dors 2G 15
Ashley Heath. Staf 2B 72
Ashley Moor. Here 4G 59
Ash Magna. Shrp 2H 71
Ashmanhaugh. Norf 3F 79
Ashmansworth. Hants 1C 24
Ashmansworthy. Devn 1D 10
Ashmead Green. Glos 2C 34
Ashmill. Devn 3D 11 (nr. Holsworthy)
Ash Mill. Devn 4A 20 (nr. South Molton)
Ashmore. Dors 1E 15
Ashmore Green. W Ber 5D 36
Ashorne. Warw 5H 61
Ashover. Derbs 4A 86
Ashow. Warw 3H 61
Ash Parva. Shrp 2H 71
Ashperton. Here 1B 48
Ashprington. Devn 3E 9
Ash Priors. Som 4E 21
Ashreigney. Devn 1G 11
Ash Street. Suff 1D 54
Ashtead. Surr 5C 38
Ash Thomas. Devn 1D 12
Ashton. Corn 4D 4
Ashton. Here 4H 59
Ashton. Inv 2D 126
Ashton. Nptn 2H 63 (nr. Oundle)
Ashton. Nptn 1F 51 (nr. Roade)
Ashton. Pet 5A 76
Ashton Common. Wilts 1E 23
Ashton Hayes. Ches W 4H 83
Ashton-in-Makerfield. G Man 4D 90
Ashton Keynes. Wilts 2F 35
Ashton under Hill. Worc 2E 49
Ashton-under-Lyne. G Man 1D 84
Ashton upon Mersey. G Man 1B 84
Ashurst. Hants 1B 16
Ashurst. Kent 2G 27
Ashurst. Lanc 4C 90
Ashurst. W Sus 4C 26
Ashurstwood. W Sus 2F 27
Ash Vale. Surr 1G 25
Ashwater. Devn 3D 11
Ashwell. Herts 2C 52
Ashwell. Rut 4F 75
Ashwellthorpe. Norf 1D 66
Ashwick. Som 2B 22
Ashwicken. Norf 4G 77
Ashwood. Staf 2C 60
Askam in Furness. Cumb 2B 96
Askern. S Yor 3F 93
Askerswell. Dors 3A 14
Askett. Buck 5G 51
Askham. Cumb 2G 103
Askham. Notts 3E 87
Askham Bryan. York 5H 99
Askham Richard. York 5H 99
Askrigg. N Yor 5C 104
Askwith. N Yor 5D 98
Aslackby. Linc 2H 75
Aslacton. Norf 1D 66
Aslockton. Notts 1E 75
Aspatria. Cumb 5C 112
Aspenden. Herts 3D 52
Asperton. Linc 2B 76
Aspley Guise. C Beds 2H 51
Aspley Heath. C Beds 2H 51
Aspull. G Man 4E 90
Asselby. E Yor 2H 93
Assington. Suff 2C 54
Assington Green. Suff 5G 65
Astbury. Ches E 4C 84
Astcote. Nptn 5D 62
Asterby. Linc 3B 88
Asterley. Shrp 5F 71
Asterton. Shrp 1F 59
Asthall. Oxon 4A 50
Asthall Leigh. Oxon 4B 50
Astle. High 4E 165
Astley. G Man 4F 91
Astley. Shrp 4H 71
Astley. Warw 2H 61
Astley. Worc 4B 60
Astley Abbotts. Shrp 1B 60
Astley Bridge. G Man 3F 91
Astley Cross. Worc 4C 60
Aston. Ches E 1A 72
Aston. Ches W 3H 83
Aston. Derbs 2F 85
Aston. Flin 4F 83
Aston. Here 4G 59
Aston. Herts 3C 52
Aston. Oxon 5B 50
Aston. Shrp 1C 60 (nr. Bridgnorth)
Aston. Shrp 3H 71 (nr. Wem)
Aston. S Yor 2B 86
Aston. Staf 1B 72
Aston. Telf 5A 72
Aston. W Mid 1E 61
Aston. Wok 3F 37
Aston Abbotts. Buck 3G 51
Aston Botterell. Shrp 2A 60
Aston-by-Stone. Staf 2D 72
Aston Cantlow. Warw 5F 61
Aston Clinton. Buck 4G 51
Aston Crews. Here 3B 48
Aston Cross. Glos 2E 49
Aston End. Herts 3C 52
Aston Eyre. Shrp 1A 60
Aston Fields. Worc 4D 60
Aston Flamville. Leics 1B 62
Aston Ingham. Here 3B 48
Aston juxta Mondrum. Ches E 5A 84
Astonlane. Shrp 1A 60
Aston le Walls. Nptn 5B 62
Aston Magna. Glos 2G 49
Aston Munslow. Shrp 2H 59
Aston on Carrant. Glos 2E 49
Aston on Clun. Shrp 2F 59
Aston-on-Trent. Derbs 3B 74
Aston Pigott. Shrp 5F 71
Aston Rogers. Shrp 5F 71
Aston Rowant. Oxon 2F 37
Aston Sandford. Buck 5F 51
Aston Somerville. Worc 2F 49
Aston Subedge. Glos 1G 49
Aston Tirrold. Oxon 3D 36
Aston Upthorpe. Oxon 3D 36
Astrop. Nptn 2D 50
Astwick. C Beds 2C 52
Astwood. Mil 1H 51
Astwood Bank. Worc 4E 61
Aswarby. Linc 2H 75
Aswardby. Linc 3C 88
Atcham. Shrp 5H 71
Atch Lench. Worc 5E 61
Athelhampton. Dors 3C 14
Athelington. Suff 3E 66
Athelney. Som 4G 21
Athelstaneford. E Lot 2B 130
Atherfield Green. IOW 5C 16
Atherington. Devn 4F 19
Atherington. W Sus 5B 26
Athersley. S Yor 4D 92
Atherstone. Warw 1H 61
Atherstone on Stour. Warw 5G 61
Atherton. G Man 4E 91
Ath-Tharracail. High 2A 140
Atlow. Derbs 1G 73
Attadale. High 5B 156
Attenborough. Notts 2C 74
Atterby. Linc 1G 87
Atterley. Shrp 1A 60
Attleborough. Norf 1C 66
Attleborough. Warw 1A 62
Attlebridge. Norf 4D 78
Atwick. E Yor 4F 101
Atworth. Wilts 5D 34
Auberrow. Here 1H 47
Aubourn. Linc 4G 87
Aucharnie. Abers 4D 160
Auchattie. Abers 4D 152
Auchavan. Ang 2A 144
Auchbreck. Mor 1G 151
Auchenback. E Ren 4G 127
Auchenblae. Abers 1G 145
Auchenbrack. Dum 5G 117
Auchenbreck. Arg 1B 126
Auchencairn. Dum 4E 111 (nr. Dalbeattie)
Auchencairn. Dum 1A 112 (nr. Dumfries)
Auchencarroch. W Dun 1F 127
Auchencrow. Bord 3E 131
Auchendennan. W Dun 1E 127
Auchendinny. Midl 3F 129
Auchengray. S Lan 4C 128
Auchenhalrig. Mor 2A 160
Auchenheath. S Lan 5B 128
Auchenlochan. Arg 2A 126
Auchenmade. N Ayr 5E 127
Auchenmalg. Dum 4H 109
Auchentiber. N Ayr 5E 127
Auchenvennel. Arg 1D 126
Auchindrain. Arg 3H 133
Auchininna. Abers 4D 160
Auchinleck. Dum 2B 110
Auchinleck. E Ayr 2E 117
Auchinloch. N Lan 2H 127
Auchinstarry. N Lan 2A 128
Auchleven. Abers 1D 152
Auchlochan. S Lan 1H 117
Auchlunachan. High 5F 163
Auchmillan. E Ayr 2E 117
Auchmithie. Ang 4F 145
Auchmuirbridge. Per 3E 136
Auchmull. Ang 1E 145
Auchnacree. Ang 4G 161
Auchnafree. Per 5F 143
Auchnagallin. High 5E 159
Auchnagatt. Abers 4G 161
Aucholzie. Abers 4H 151
Auchreddie. Abers 4F 161
Auchterarder. Per 2B 136
Auchteraw. High 3F 149
Auchterderran. Fife 4E 136
Auchterhouse. Ang 5C 144
Auchtermuchty. Fife 2E 137
Auchterneed. High 3G 157
Auchtertool. Fife 4E 136
Auchtertyre. High 1G 147
Auchtubh. Stir 1E 135
Auckengill. High 2F 169
Auckley. S Yor 4G 93
Audenshaw. G Man 1D 84
Audlem. Ches E 1A 72
Audley. Staf 5B 84
Audley End. Essx 2F 53
Audmore. Staf 3C 72
Auds. Abers 2D 160
Aughton. E Yor 1H 93
Aughton. Lanc 3E 97 (nr. Lancaster)
Aughton. Lanc 4B 90 (nr. Ormskirk)
Aughton. S Yor 2B 86
Aughton. Wilts 1H 23
Aughton Park. Lanc 4C 90
Auldearn. High 3D 158
Aulden. Here 5G 59
Auldgirth. Dum 1G 111
Auldhouse. S Lan 4H 127
Ault a' chruinn. High 1B 148
Aultbea. High 5C 162
Aultdearg. High 2E 157
Aultgrishan. High 5B 162
Aultguish Inn. High 1F 157
Ault Hucknall. Derbs 4B 86
Aultibea. High 1H 165
Aultiphurst. High 2A 168
Aultivullin. High 2A 168
Aultmore. Mor 3B 160
Aultnamain Inn. High 5D 164
Aunby. Linc 4H 75
Aunsby. Linc 2H 75
Aust. S Glo 3A 34
Austerfield. S Yor 1D 86
Austin Fen. Linc 1C 88
Austrey. Warw 5G 73
Austwick. N Yor 3G 97
Authorpe. Linc 2D 88
Authorpe Row. Linc 3E 89
Avebury. Wilts 5G 35
Avebury Trusloe. Wilts 5F 35
Aveley. Thur 2G 39
Avening. Glos 2D 35
Averham. Notts 5E 87
Aveton Gifford. Devn 4C 8
Avielochan. High 2D 150
Aviemore. High 2C 150
Avington. Hants 3D 24
Avoch. High 3B 158
Avon. Hants 3G 15
Avonbridge. Falk 2C 128
Avon Dassett. Warw 5B 62
Avonmouth. Bris 4A 34
Avonwick. Devn 3D 8
Awbridge. Hants 4B 24
Awliscombe. Devn 2E 13
Awre. Glos 5C 48
Awsworth. Notts 1B 74
Axbridge. Som 1H 21
Axford. Hants 2E 24
Axford. Wilts 5H 35
Axminster. Devn 3F 13
Axmouth. Devn 3F 13
Aycliffe Village. Dur 2F 105
Aydon. Nmbd 3D 114
Aykley Heads. Dur 5F 115
Aylburton. Glos 5B 48
Aylburton Common. Glos 5B 48
Ayle. Nmbd 5A 114
Aylesbeare. Devn 3D 12
Aylesbury. Buck 4G 51
Aylesby. NE Lin 4F 95
Aylescott. Devn 1G 11
Aylesford. Kent 5B 40
Aylesham. Kent 5G 41
Aylestone. Leic 5C 74
Aylmerton. Norf 2D 78
Aylsham. Norf 3D 78
Aylton. Here 2B 48
Aylworth. Glos 3G 49
Aymestrey. Here 4G 59
Aynho. Nptn 2D 50
Ayot Green. Herts 4C 52
Ayot St Lawrence. Herts 4B 52
Ayot St Peter. Herts 4C 52
Ayr. S Ayr 2C 116 & 187
Ayres of Selivoe. Shet 7D 173
Ayreville. Torb 2E 9
Aysgarth. N Yor 1C 98
Ayshford. Devn 1D 12
Ayside. Cumb 1C 96
Ayston. Rut 5F 75
Ayton. Bord 3F 131
Aywick. Shet 3G 173
Azerley. N Yor 2E 99

B

Babbacombe. Torb 2F 9
Babbinswood. Shrp 3F 71
Babb's Green. Herts 4D 53
Babcary. Som 4A 22
Babel. Carm 2B 46
Babell. Flin 3D 82
Babingley. Norf 3F 77
Bablock Hythe. Oxon 5C 50
Babraham. Cambs 5E 65
Babworth. Notts 2D 86
Bac. W Isl 3G 171
Bachau. IOA 2D 80
Bacheldre. Powy 1E 59
Bachymbyd Fawr. Den 4C 82
Backaland. Orkn 4E 172
Backaskaill. Orkn 2D 172
Backbarrow. Cumb 1C 96
Backe. Carm 3G 43
Backfolds. Abers 3H 161
Backford. Ches W 3G 83
Backhill. Abers 5E 161
Backhill of Clackriach. Abers 4G 161
Backies. High 3F 165
Backmuir of New Gilston. Fife 3G 137
Back of Keppoch. High 5E 147
Back Street. Suff 5G 65
Backwell. N Som 5H 33
Backworth. Tyne 2G 115
Bacon End. Essx 4G 53
Baconsthorpe. Norf 2D 78
Bacton. Here 2G 47
Bacton. Norf 2F 79
Bacton. Suff 4C 66
Bacton Green. Norf 2F 79
Bacup. Lanc 2G 91
Badachonacher. High 1A 158
Badachro. High 1G 155
Badanloch Lodge. High 5H 167
Badavanich. High 3D 156
Badbury. Swin 3G 35
Badby. Nptn 5C 62
Badcall. High 3C 166
Badcaul. High 4E 163
Baddeley Green. Stoke 5D 84
Baddesley Clinton. W Mid 3G 61
Baddesley Ensor. Warw 1G 61
Baddidarach. High 1E 163
Baddoch. Abers 5F 151
Badenscallie. High 3E 163
Badenscoth. Abers 5E 160
Badentarbat. High 2E 163
Badgall. Corn 4C 10
Badgers Mount. Kent 4F 39
Badgeworth. Glos 4E 49
Badgworth. Som 1G 21
Badicaul. High 1F 147
Badingham. Suff 4F 67
Badlesmere. Kent 5E 40
Badlipster. High 4E 169
Badluarach. High 4D 163
Badminton. S Glo 3D 34
Badnaban. High 1E 163
Badnabay. High 4C 166
Badnagie. High 5D 168
Badnellan. High 3F 165
Badninish. High 4E 165
Badrallach. High 4E 163
Badsey. Worc 1F 49
Badshot Lea. Surr 2G 25
Badsworth. W Yor 3E 93
Badwell Ash. Suff 4B 66
Bae Cinmel. Cnwy 2B 82
Bae Colwyn. Cnwy 3A 82
Bae Penrhyn. Cnwy 2H 81
Bagby. N Yor 1G 99
Bag Enderby. Linc 3C 88
Bagendon. Glos 5F 49
Bagginswood. Shrp 2A 60
Baggrave. Leics 5D 74
Bàgh a Chàise. W Isl 1E 170
Bàgh a' Chaisteil. W Isl 9B 170
Bagham. Kent 5E 41
Baghasdal. W Isl 7C 170
Bagh Mor. W Isl 3D 170
Bagh Shiarabhagh. W Isl 8C 170
Bagillt. Flin 3E 83
Baginton. Warw 3H 61
Baglan. Neat 2A 32
Bagley. Shrp 3G 71
Bagley. Som 2H 21
Bagnall. Staf 5D 84
Bagnor. W Ber 5C 36
Bagshot. Surr 4A 38
Bagshot. Wilts 5B 36
Bagstone. S Glo 3B 34
Bagthorpe. Norf 2G 77
Bagthorpe. Notts 5B 86
Bagworth. Leics 5B 74
Bagwy Llydiart. Here 3H 47
Baildon. W Yor 1B 92
Baildon Green. W Yor 1B 92
Baile. W Isl 1E 170
Baile Ailein. W Isl 5E 171
Baile an Truiseil. W Isl 2F 171
Baile Boidheach. Arg 2F 125
Baile Glas. W Isl 3D 170
Bailemeonach. Arg 4A 140
Baile Mhanaich. W Isl 3C 170
Baile Mhartainn. W Isl 1C 170
Baile MhicPhail. W Isl 1D 170
Baile Mor. Arg 2A 132
Baile Mor. W Isl 2C 170
Baile nan Cailleach. W Isl 3C 170
Baile Raghaill. W Isl 2C 170
Bailey Green. Hants 4E 25
Baileyhead. Cumb 1G 113
Bailiesward. Abers 5B 160
Bail' Iochdrach. W Isl 3D 170
Baillieston. Glas 3H 127
Bailrigg. Lanc 4D 97
Bail' Uachdraich. W Isl 2D 170
Bail Ur Tholastaidh. W Isl 3H 171
Bainbridge. N Yor 5C 104
Bainsford. Falk 1B 128
Bainshole. Abers 5D 160
Bainton. E Yor 4D 100
Bainton. Oxon 3D 50
Bainton. Pet 5H 75
Baintown. Fife 3F 137
Baker Street. Thur 2H 39
Bakewell. Derbs 4G 85
Bala. Gwyn 2B 70
Balachuirn. High 4E 155
Balbeg. High 5G 157 (nr. Cannich)
Balbeg. High 1G 149 (nr. Loch Ness)
Balbeggie. Per 1D 136
Balblair. High 4C 164 (nr. Bonar Bridge)
Balblair. High 2B 158 (nr. Invergordon)
Balblair. High 4H 157 (nr. Inverness)
Balby. S Yor 4F 93
Balcathie. Ang 5F 145
Balchladich. High 1E 163
Balchraggan. High 4H 157
Balchrick. High 3B 166
Balcombe. W Sus 2E 27
Balcombe Lane. W Sus 2E 27
Balcurvie. Fife 3F 137
Baldersby. N Yor 2F 99
Baldersby St James. N Yor 2F 99
Balderstone. Lanc 1E 91
Balderton. Ches W 4F 83
Balderton. Notts 5F 87
Baldinnie. Fife 2G 137
Baldock. Herts 2C 52
Baldrine. IOM 3D 108
Baldslow. E Sus 4C 28
Baldwin. IOM 3C 108
Baldwinholme. Cumb 4E 113
Baldwin's Gate. Staf 2B 72
Bale. Norf 2C 78
Balearn. Abers 3H 161
Balemartine. Arg 4A 138
Balephetrish. Arg 4B 138
Balephuil. Arg 4A 138
Balerno. Edin 3E 129
Balevullin. Arg 4A 138
Balfield. Ang 2E 145
Balfour. Orkn 6D 172
Balfron. Stir 1G 127
Balgaveny. Abers 4D 160
Balgonar. Fife 4C 136
Balgowan. High 4A 150
Balgown. High 2C 154
Balgrochan. E Dun 2H 127
Balgy. High 3H 155
Balhalgardy. Abers 1E 153
Baliasta. Shet 1H 173
Baligill. High 2A 168
Balintore. Ang 3B 144
Balintore. High 1C 158
Balintraid. High 1B 158
Balk. N Yor 1G 99
Balkeerie. Ang 4C 144
Balkholme. E Yor 2A 94
Ball. Shrp 3F 71
Ballabeg. IOM 4B 108
Ballacannell. IOM 3D 108
Ballacarnane Beg. IOM 3C 108
Ballachulish. High 3E 141
Ballagyr. IOM 3B 108
Ballajora. IOM 2D 108
Ballaleigh. IOM 3C 108
Ballamodha. IOM 4B 108
Ballantrae. S Ayr 1F 109
Ballards Gore. Essx 1D 40
Ballasalla. IOM 4B 108 (nr. Castletown)
Ballasalla. IOM 2C 108 (nr. Kirk Michael)
Ballater. Abers 4A 152
Ballaugh. IOM 2C 108
Ballencrieff. E Lot 2A 130
Ballencrieff Toll. W Lot 2C 128
Ballentoul. Per 2F 143
Ball Hill. Hants 5C 36
Ballidon. Derbs 5G 85
Balliemore. Arg 1B 126 (nr. Dunoon)
Balliemore. Arg 1F 133 (nr. Oban)
Ballieward. High 5E 159
Ballig. IOM 3B 108
Ballimore. Stir 2E 135
Ballingdon. Suff 1B 54
Ballinger Common. Buck 5H 51
Ballingham. Here 2A 48
Ballingry. Fife 4D 136
Ballinluig. Per 3G 143
Ballintuim. Per 3A 144
Balliveolan. Arg 4C 140
Balloan. High 3C 164
Balloch. High 4B 158
Balloch. N Lan 2A 128
Balloch. Per 2H 135
Balloch. W Dun 1E 127
Ballochan. Abers 4C 152
Ballochgoy. Arg 3B 126
Ballochmyle. E Ayr 2E 117
Ballochroy. Arg 4F 125
Balls Cross. W Sus 3A 26
Ball's Green. E Sus 2F 27
Ballygown. Arg 4F 139
Ballygrant. Arg 3B 124

Ballymichael—Bellingdon

Ballymichael. *N Ayr* 2D **122**
Balmacara. *High* 1G **147**
Balmaclellan. *Dum* 2D **110**
Balmacqueen. *High* 1D **154**
Balmaha. *Stir* 4D **134**
Balmalcolm. *Fife* 3F **137**
Balmalloch. *N Lan* 2A **128**
Balmeanach. *High* 5E **155**
Balmedie. *Abers* 2G **153**
Balmerino. *Fife* 1F **137**
Balmerlawn. *Hants* 2B **16**
Balmore. *E Dun* 2H **127**
Balmore. *High* 4B **154**
Balmuir. *Ang* 5D **144**
Balmullo. *Fife* 1G **137**
Balmurrie. *Dum* 3H **109**
Balnaboth. *Ang* 2C **144**
Balnabruaich. *High* 1B **158**
Balnabruich. *High* 5D **168**
Balnacoil. *High* 2F **165**
Balnacra. *High* 4B **156**
Balnacroft. *Abers* 4G **151**
Balnageith. *Mor* 3E **159**
Balnaglaic. *High* 5G **157**
Balnagrantach. *High* 5G **157**
Balnaguard. *Per* 3G **143**
Balnahard. *Arg* 4B **132**
Balnain. *High* 5G **157**
Balnakeil. *High* 2D **166**
Balnaknock. *High* 2D **154**
Balnamoon. *Abers* 3G **161**
Balnamoon. *Ang* 2E **145**
Balnapaling. *High* 2B **158**
Balornock. *Glas* 3H **127**
Balquhidder. *Stir* 1E **135**
Balsall. *W Mid* 3G **61**
Balsall Common. *W Mid* 3G **61**
Balscote. *Oxon* 1B **50**
Balsham. *Cambs* 5E **65**
Balstonia. *Thur* 2A **40**
Baltasound. *Shet* 1H **173**
Balterley. *Staf* 5B **84**
Baltersan. *Dum* 3B **110**
Balthangie. *Abers* 3F **161**
Baltonsborough. *Som* 3A **22**
Balvaird. *High* 3H **157**
Balvaird. *Per* 2D **136**
Balvenie. *Mor* 4H **159**
Balvicar. *Arg* 2E **133**
Balvraid. *High* 2G **147**
Balvraid Lodge. *High* 5C **158**
Bamber Bridge. *Lanc* 2D **90**
Bamber's Green. *Essx* 3F **53**
Bamburgh. *Nmbd* 1F **121**
Bamford. *Derbs* 2G **85**
Bamfurlong. *G Man* 4D **90**
Bampton. *Cumb* 3G **103**
Bampton. *Devn* 4C **20**
Bampton. *Oxon* 5B **50**
Bampton Grange. *Cumb* 3G **103**
Banavie. *High* 1F **141**
Banbury. *Oxon* 1C **50**
Bancffosfelen. *Carm* 4E **45**
Banchory. *Abers* 4D **152**
Banchory-Devenick. *Abers* 3G **153**
Bancycapel. *Carm* 4E **45**
Bancyfelin. *Carm* 3H **43**
Banc-y-ffordd. *Carm* 2E **45**
Banff. *Abers* 2D **160**
Bangor. *Gwyn* 3E **81**
Bangor-is-y-coed. *Wrex* 1F **71**
Bangors. *Corn* 3C **10**
Bangor's Green. *Lanc* 4B **90**
Banham. *Norf* 2C **66**
Bank. *Hants* 2A **16**
Bankend. *Dum* 3B **112**
Bankfoot. *Per* 5H **143**
Bankglen. *E Ayr* 3E **117**
Bankhead. *Aber* 2F **153**
Bankhead. *Abers* 3D **152**
Bankhead. *S Lan* 5B **128**
Bankland. *Som* 4G **21**
Bank Newton. *N Yor* 4B **98**
Banknock. *Falk* 2A **128**
Banks. *Cumb* 3G **113**
Banks. *Lanc* 2B **90**
Bankshill. *Dum* 1C **112**
Bank Street. *Worc* 4A **60**
Bank, The. *Ches E* 5C **84**
Bank, The. *Shrp* 1A **60**
Bank Top. *Lanc* 4D **90**
Banners Gate. *W Mid* 1E **61**
Banningham. *Norf* 3E **78**
Banniskirk. *High* 3D **168**
Bannister Green. *Essx* 3G **53**
Bannockburn. *Stir* 4H **135**
Banstead. *Surr* 5D **38**
Bantham. *Devn* 4C **8**
Banton. *N Lan* 2A **128**
Banwell. *N Som* 1G **21**
Banyard's Green. *Suff* 3F **67**
Bapchild. *Kent* 4D **40**
Bapton. *Wilts* 3E **23**
Barabhas. *W Isl* 2F **171**
Barabhas Iarach. *W Isl* 3F **171**
Baramore. *High* 1A **140**
Barassie. *S Ayr* 1C **116**
Baravullin. *Arg* 4D **140**
Barbaraville. *High* 1B **158**
Barber Booth. *Derbs* 2F **85**
Barber Green. *Cumb* 1C **96**
Barbhas Uarach. *W Isl* 2F **171**
Barbieston. *S Ayr* 3D **116**
Barbon. *Cumb* 1F **97**
Barbourne. *Worc* 5C **60**
Barbridge. *Ches E* 5A **84**
Barbrook. *Devn* 2H **19**
Barby. *Nptn* 3C **62**
Barby Nortoft. *Nptn* 3C **62**
Barcaldine. *Arg* 4D **140**
Barcheston. *Warw* 1A **50**
Barclose. *Cumb* 3F **113**
Barcombe. *E Sus* 4F **27**
Barcombe Cross. *E Sus* 4F **27**
Barden. *N Yor* 5E **105**
Barden Scale. *N Yor* 4C **98**
Bardfield End Green. *Essx* 2G **53**
Bardfield Saling. *Essx* 3G **53**
Bardister. *Shet* 4E **173**
Bardnabeinne. *High* 4E **164**
Bardney. *Linc* 4A **88**
Bardon. *Leics* 4B **74**
Bardon Mill. *Nmbd* 3A **114**
Bardowie. *E Dun* 2G **127**
Bardrainney. *Inv* 2E **127**
Bardsea. *Cumb* 2C **96**
Bardsey. *W Yor* 5F **99**
Bardsley. *G Man* 4H **91**
Bardwell. *Suff* 3B **66**
Bare. *Lanc* 3D **96**
Barelees. *Nmbd* 1C **120**
Barewood. *Here* 5F **59**
Barford. *Hants* 3G **25**
Barford. *Norf* 5D **78**
Barford. *Warw* 4G **61**
Barford St John. *Oxon* 2C **50**
Barford St Martin. *Wilts* 3F **23**
Barford St Michael. *Oxon* 2C **50**
Barfrestone. *Kent* 5G **41**
Bargeddie. *N Lan* 3A **128**
Bargod. *Cphy* 2E **33**
Bargoed. *Cphy* 2E **33**
Bargrennan. *Dum* 2A **110**
Barham. *Cambs* 3A **64**
Barham. *Kent* 5G **41**
Barham. *Suff* 5D **66**
Barharrow. *Dum* 4D **110**
Bar Hill. *Cambs* 4C **64**
Barholm. *Linc* 4H **75**
Barkby. *Leics* 4D **74**
Barkestone-le-Vale. *Leics* 2E **75**
Barkham. *Wok* 5F **37**
Barking. *G Lon* 2F **39**
Barking. *Suff* 5C **66**
Barkingside. *G Lon* 2F **39**
Barking Tye. *Suff* 5C **66**
Barkisland. *W Yor* 3A **92**
Barkston. *Linc* 1G **75**
Barkston Ash. *N Yor* 1E **93**
Barkway. *Herts* 2D **53**
Barlanark. *Glas* 3H **127**
Barlaston. *Staf* 2C **72**
Barlavington. *W Sus* 4A **26**
Barlborough. *Derbs* 3B **86**
Barlby. *N Yor* 1G **93**
Barlestone. *Leics* 5B **74**
Barley. *Herts* 2D **53**
Barley. *Lanc* 5H **97**
Barley Mow. *Tyne* 4F **115**
Barleythorpe. *Rut* 5F **75**
Barling. *Essx* 2D **40**
Barlings. *Linc* 3H **87**
Barlow. *Derbs* 3H **85**
Barlow. *N Yor* 2G **93**
Barlow. *Tyne* 3E **115**
Barmby Moor. *E Yor* 5B **100**
Barmby on the Marsh. *E Yor* 2G **93**
Barmer. *Norf* 2H **77**
Barming. *Kent* 5B **40**
Barming Heath. *Kent* 5B **40**
Barmoor. *Nmbd* 1E **121**
Barmouth. *Gwyn* 4F **69**
Barmpton. *Darl* 3A **106**
Barmston. *E Yor* 4F **101**
Barmulloch. *Glas* 3H **127**
Barnack. *Pet* 5H **75**
Barnacle. *Warw* 2A **62**
Barnard Castle. *Dur* 3D **104**
Barnard Gate. *Oxon* 4C **50**
Barnardiston. *Suff* 1H **53**
Barnbarroch. *Dum* 4F **111**
Barnburgh. *S Yor* 4E **93**
Barnby. *Suff* 2G **67**
Barnby Dun. *S Yor* 4G **93**
Barnby in the Willows. *Notts* 5F **87**
Barnby Moor. *Notts* 2D **86**
Barnes. *G Lon* 3D **38**
Barnes Street. *Kent* 1H **27**
Barnet. *G Lon* 1D **38**
Barnetby le Wold. *N Lin* 4D **94**
Barney. *Norf* 2B **78**
Barnham. *Suff* 3A **66**
Barnham. *W Sus* 5A **26**
Barnham Broom. *Norf* 5C **78**
Barnhead. *Ang* 3F **145**
Barnhill. *D'dee* 5D **145**
Barnhill. *Mor* 3F **159**
Barnhill. *Per* 1D **136**
Barnhills. *Dum* 2E **109**
Barningham. *Dur* 3D **105**
Barningham. *Suff* 3B **66**
Barnoldby le Beck. *NE Lin* 4F **95**
Barnoldswick. *Lanc* 5A **98**
Barns Green. *W Sus* 3C **26**
Barnsley. *Glos* 5F **49**
Barnsley. *Shrp* 1B **60**
Barnsley. *S Yor* 4D **92**
Barnstaple. *Devn* 3F **19**
Barnston. *Essx* 4G **53**
Barnston. *Mers* 2E **83**
Barnstone. *Notts* 2E **75**
Barnt Green. *Worc* 3E **61**
Barnton. *Ches W* 3A **84**
Barnwell. *Cambs* 5D **64**
Barnwell. *Nptn* 2H **63**
Barnwood. *Glos* 4D **48**
Barons Cross. *Here* 5G **59**
Barony, The. *Orkn* 5B **172**
Barr. *Dum* 4G **117**
Barr. *S Ayr* 5B **116**
Barra Airport. *W Isl* 8C **170**
Barrachan. *Dum* 5A **110**
Barraglom. *W Isl* 4D **171**
Barrahormid. *Arg* 1F **125**
Barrapol. *Arg* 4A **138**
Barrasford. *Nmbd* 2C **114**
Barravullin. *Arg* 3F **133**
Barregarrow. *IOM* 3C **108**
Barrhead. *E Ren* 4G **127**
Barrhill. *S Ayr* 1H **109**
Barri. *V Glam* 5E **32**
Barrington. *Cambs* 1D **53**
Barrington. *Som* 1G **13**
Barripper. *Corn* 3D **4**
Barrmill. *N Ayr* 4E **127**
Barrock. *High* 1E **169**
Barrow. *Lanc* 1F **91**
Barrow. *Rut* 4F **75**
Barrow. *Shrp* 5A **72**
Barrow. *Som* 3C **22**
Barrow. *Suff* 4G **65**
Barroway Drove. *Norf* 5E **77**
Barrow Bridge. *G Man* 3E **91**
Barrowburn. *Nmbd* 3C **120**
Barrowby. *Linc* 2F **75**
Barrowcliff. *N Yor* 1E **101**
Barrow Common. *N Som* 5A **34**
Barrowden. *Rut* 5G **75**
Barrowford. *Lanc* 1G **91**
Barrow Gurney. *N Som* 5A **34**
Barrow Haven. *N Lin* 2D **94**
Barrow Hill. *Derbs* 3B **86**
Barrow-in-Furness. *Cumb* 3B **96**
Barrow Nook. *Lanc* 4C **90**
Barrows Green. *Cumb* 1E **97**
Barrow's Green. *Hal* 2H **83**
Barrow Street. *Wilts* 3D **22**
Barrow upon Humber. *N Lin* 2D **94**
Barrow upon Soar. *Leics* 4C **74**
Barrow upon Trent. *Derbs* 3A **74**
Barry. *Ang* 5E **145**
Barry. *V Glam* 5E **32**
Barry Island. *V Glam* 5E **32**
Barsby. *Leics* 4D **74**
Barsham. *Suff* 2F **67**
Barston. *W Mid* 3G **61**
Bartestree. *Here* 1A **48**
Barthol Chapel. *Abers* 5F **161**
Bartholomew Green. *Essx* 3H **53**
Barthomley. *Ches E* 5B **84**
Bartley. *Hants* 1B **16**
Bartley Green. *W Mid* 2E **61**
Bartlow. *Cambs* 1F **53**
Barton. *Cambs* 5D **64**
Barton. *Ches W* 5G **83**
Barton. *Cumb* 2F **103**
Barton. *Glos* 3F **49**
Barton. *IOW* 4D **16**
Barton. *Lanc* 4B **90**
(nr. Ormskirk)
Barton. *Lanc* 1D **90**
(nr. Preston)
Barton. *N Som* 1G **21**
Barton. *N Yor* 4F **105**
Barton. *Oxon* 5D **50**
Barton. *Torb* 2F **9**
Barton. *Warw* 5F **61**
Barton Bendish. *Norf* 5G **77**
Barton Gate. *Staf* 4F **73**
Barton Green. *Staf* 4F **73**
Barton Hartsthorn. *Buck* 2E **51**
Barton Hill. *N Yor* 3B **100**
Barton in Fabis. *Notts* 2C **74**
Barton in the Beans. *Leics* 5A **74**
Barton-le-Clay. *C Beds* 2A **52**
Barton-le-Street. *N Yor* 2B **100**
Barton-le-Willows. *N Yor* 3B **100**
Barton Mills. *Suff* 3G **65**
Barton on Sea. *Hants* 3H **15**
Barton-on-the-Heath. *Warw* 2A **50**
Barton St David. *Som* 3A **22**
Barton Seagrave. *Nptn* 3F **63**
Barton Stacey. *Hants* 2C **24**
Barton Town. *Devn* 2G **19**
Barton Turf. *Norf* 3F **79**
Barton-under-Needwood. *Staf* 4F **73**
Barton-upon-Humber. *N Lin* 2D **94**
Barton Waterside. *N Lin* 2D **94**
Barugh Green. *S Yor* 4D **92**
Barway. *Cambs* 3E **65**
Barwell. *Leics* 1B **62**
Barwick. *Herts* 4D **53**
Barwick. *Som* 1A **14**
Barwick in Elmet. *W Yor* 1D **93**
Baschurch. *Shrp* 3G **71**
Bascote. *Warw* 4B **62**
Basford Green. *Staf* 5D **85**
Bashall Eaves. *Lanc* 5F **97**
Bashall Town. *Lanc* 5G **97**
Bashley. *Hants* 3H **15**
Basildon. *Essx* 2B **40**
Basingstoke. *Hants* 1E **25**
Baslow. *Derbs* 3G **85**
Bason Bridge. *Som* 2G **21**
Bassaleg. *Newp* 3F **33**
Bassendean. *Bord* 5C **130**
Bassenthwaite. *Cumb* 1D **102**
Bassett. *Sotn* 1C **16**
Bassingbourn. *Cambs* 1D **52**
Bassingfield. *Notts* 2D **74**
Bassingham. *Linc* 5G **87**
Bassingthorpe. *Linc* 3G **75**
Bassus Green. *Herts* 3D **52**
Basta. *Shet* 2G **173**
Baston. *Linc* 4A **76**
Bastonford. *Worc* 5C **60**
Bastwick. *Norf* 4G **79**
Batchley. *Worc* 4E **61**
Batchworth. *Herts* 1B **38**
Batcombe. *Dors* 2B **14**
Batcombe. *Som* 3B **22**
Bate Heath. *Ches E* 3A **84**
Bath. *Bath* 5C **34** & **187**
Bathampton. *Bath* 5C **34**
Bathealton. *Som* 4D **20**
Batheaston. *Bath* 5C **34**
Bathford. *Bath* 5C **34**
Bathgate. *W Lot* 3C **128**
Bathley. *Notts* 5E **87**
Bathpool. *Corn* 5C **10**
Bathpool. *Som* 4F **21**
Bathville. *W Lot* 3C **128**
Bathway. *Som* 1A **22**
Batley. *W Yor* 2C **92**
Batsford. *Glos* 2G **49**
Batson. *Devn* 5D **8**
Battersby. *N Yor* 4C **106**
Battersea. *G Lon* 3D **39**
Battisborough Cross. *Devn* 4C **8**
Battisford. *Suff* 5C **66**
Battisford Tye. *Suff* 5C **66**
Battle. *E Sus* 4B **28**
Battle. *Powy* 2D **46**
Battleborough. *Som* 1G **21**
Battledown. *Glos* 3E **49**
Battlefield. *Shrp* 4H **71**
Battlesbridge. *Essx* 1B **40**
Battlesden. *C Beds* 3H **51**
Battlesea Green. *Suff* 3E **66**
Battleton. *Som* 4C **20**
Battramsley. *Hants* 3B **16**
Batt's Corner. *Surr* 2G **25**
Bauds of Cullen. *Mor* 2B **160**
Baugh. *Arg* 4B **138**
Baughton. *Worc* 1D **49**
Baughurst. *Hants* 5D **36**
Baulking. *Oxon* 2B **36**
Baumber. *Linc* 3B **88**
Baunton. *Glos* 5F **49**
Baverstock. *Wilts* 3F **23**
Bawburgh. *Norf* 5D **78**
Bawdeswell. *Norf* 3C **78**
Bawdrip. *Som* 3G **21**
Bawdsey. *Suff* 1G **55**
Bawdsey Manor. *Suff* 2G **55**
Bawsey. *Norf* 4F **77**
Bawtry. *S Yor* 1D **86**
Baxenden. *Lanc* 2F **91**
Baxterley. *Warw* 1G **61**
Baxter's Green. *Suff* 5G **65**
Baybridge. *Hants* 4D **24**
Baybridge. *Nmbd* 4C **114**
Baycliff. *Cumb* 2B **96**
Baydon. *Wilts* 4A **36**
Bayford. *Herts* 5D **52**
Bayford. *Som* 4C **22**
Bayles. *Cumb* 5A **114**
Baylham. *Suff* 5D **66**
Baynard's Green. *Oxon* 3D **50**
Bayston Hill. *Shrp* 5G **71**
Baythorn End. *Essx* 1H **53**
Baythorpe. *Linc* 1B **76**
Bayton. *Worc* 3A **60**
Bayton Common. *Worc* 3B **60**
Bayworth. *Oxon* 5D **50**
Beach. *S Glo* 4C **34**
Beachampton. *Buck* 2F **51**
Beachamwell. *Norf* 5G **77**
Beachley. *Glos* 2A **34**
Beacon. *Devn* 2E **13**
Beacon End. *Essx* 3C **54**
Beacon Hill. *Surr* 3G **25**
Beacon's Bottom. *Buck* 2F **37**
Beaconsfield. *Buck* 1A **38**
Beacontree. *G Lon* 2F **39**
Beacrabhaicg. *W Isl* 8D **171**
Beadlam. *N Yor* 1A **100**
Beadnell. *Nmbd* 2G **121**
Beaford. *Devn* 1F **11**
Beal. *Nmbd* 5G **131**
Beal. *N Yor* 2F **93**
Bealsmill. *Corn* 5D **10**
Beam Hill. *Staf* 3G **73**
Beamhurst. *Staf* 2E **73**
Beaminster. *Dors* 2H **13**
Beamish. *Dur* 4F **115**
Beamond End. *Buck* 1A **38**
Beamsley. *N Yor* 4C **98**
Bean. *Kent* 3G **39**
Beanacre. *Wilts* 5E **35**
Beanley. *Nmbd* 3E **121**
Beanshanger. *Nptn* 2F **51**
Beaquoy. *Orkn* 5C **172**
Beardwood. *Bkbn* 2E **91**
Beare Green. *Surr* 1C **26**
Bearley. *Warw* 4F **61**
Bearpark. *Dur* 5F **115**
Bearsbridge. *Nmbd* 4A **114**
Bearsden. *E Dun* 2G **127**
Bearsted. *Kent* 5B **40**
Bearstone. *Shrp* 2B **72**
Bearwood. *Pool* 3F **15**
Bearwood. *W Mid* 2E **61**
Beattock. *Dum* 4C **118**
Beauchamp Roding. *Essx* 5F **53**
Beauchief. *S Yor* 2H **85**
Beaufort. *Blae* 4E **47**
Beaulieu. *Hants* 2B **16**
Beauly. *High* 4H **157**
Beaumaris. *IOA* 3F **81**
Beaumont. *Cumb* 4E **113**
Beaumont. *Essx* 3E **55**
Beaumont Hill. *Darl* 3F **105**
Beaumont Leys. *Leic* 5C **74**
Beausale. *Warw* 3G **61**
Beauvale. *Notts* 1B **74**
Beauworth. *Hants* 4D **24**
Beaworthy. *Devn* 3E **11**
Beazley End. *Essx* 3H **53**
Bebington. *Mers* 2F **83**
Bebside. *Nmbd* 1F **115**
Beccles. *Suff* 2G **67**
Becconsall. *Lanc* 2C **90**
Beckbury. *Shrp* 5B **72**
Beckenham. *G Lon* 4E **39**
Beckermet. *Cumb* 4B **102**
Beckett End. *Norf* 1G **65**
Beckfoot. *Cumb* 1A **96**
(nr. Broughton in Furness)
Beck Foot. *Cumb* 5H **103**
(nr. Kendal)
Beckfoot. *Cumb* 4C **102**
(nr. Seascale)
Beckfoot. *Cumb* 5B **112**
(nr. Silloth)
Beckford. *Worc* 2E **49**
Beckhampton. *Wilts* 5F **35**
Beck Hole. *N Yor* 4F **107**
Beckingham. *Linc* 5F **87**
Beckingham. *Notts* 1E **87**
Beckington. *Som* 1D **22**
Beckley. *E Sus* 3C **28**
Beckley. *Hants* 3H **15**
Beckley. *Oxon* 4D **50**
Beck Row. *Suff* 3F **65**
Beck Side. *Cumb* 1C **96**
(nr. Cartmel)
Beckside. *Cumb* 1F **97**
(nr. Sedbergh)
Beck Side. *Cumb* 1B **96**
(nr. Ulverston)
Beckton. *G Lon* 2F **39**
Beckwithshaw. *N Yor* 4E **99**
Becontree. *G Lon* 2F **39**
Bedale. *N Yor* 1E **99**
Bedburn. *Dur* 1E **105**
Bedchester. *Dors* 1D **14**
Beddau. *Rhon* 3D **32**
Beddgelert. *Gwyn* 1E **69**
Beddingham. *E Sus* 5F **27**
Beddington. *G Lon* 4D **39**
Bedfield. *Suff* 4E **66**
Bedford. *Bed* 1A **52** & **188**
Bedford. *G Man* 4E **91**
Bedham. *W Sus* 3B **26**
Bedhampton. *Hants* 2F **17**
Bedingfield. *Suff* 4D **66**
Bedingham Green. *Norf* 1E **67**
Bedlam. *N Yor* 3E **99**
Bedlar's Green. *Essx* 4F **53**
Bedlington. *Nmbd* 1F **115**
Bedlinog. *Mer T* 5D **46**
Bedminster. *Bris* 4A **34**
Bedmond. *Herts* 5A **52**
Bednall. *Staf* 4D **72**
Bedrule. *Bord* 3A **120**
Bedstone. *Shrp* 3F **59**
Bedwas. *Cphy* 3E **33**
Bedwellty. *Cphy* 5E **47**
Bedworth. *Warw* 2A **62**
Beeby. *Leics* 5D **74**
Beech. *Hants* 3E **25**
Beech. *Staf* 2C **72**
Beechcliffe. *W Yor* 5C **98**
Beech Hill. *W Ber* 5E **37**
Beechingstoke. *Wilts* 1F **23**
Beedon. *W Ber* 4C **36**
Beeford. *E Yor* 4F **101**
Beeley. *Derbs* 4G **85**
Beelsby. *NE Lin* 4F **95**
Beenham. *W Ber* 5D **36**
Beeny. *Corn* 3B **10**
Beer. *Devn* 4F **13**
Beer. *Som* 3H **21**
Beercrocombe. *Som* 4G **21**
Beer Hackett. *Dors* 1B **14**
Beesands. *Devn* 4E **9**
Beesby. *Linc* 2D **88**
Beeson. *Devn* 4E **9**
Beeston. *C Beds* 1B **52**
Beeston. *Ches W* 5H **83**
Beeston. *Norf* 4B **78**
Beeston. *Notts* 2C **74**
Beeston. *W Yor* 1C **92**
Beeston Regis. *Norf* 1D **78**
Beeswing. *Dum* 3F **111**
Beetham. *Cumb* 2D **97**
Beetham. *Som* 1F **13**
Beetley. *Norf* 4B **78**
Beffcote. *Staf* 4C **72**
Began. *Card* 3F **33**
Begbroke. *Oxon* 4C **50**
Begdale. *Cambs* 5D **76**
Begelly. *Pemb* 4F **43**
Beggar Hill. *Essx* 5G **53**
Beggar's Bush. *Powy* 4E **59**
Beggearn Huish. *Som* 3D **20**
Beguildy. *Powy* 3D **58**
Beighton. *Norf* 5F **79**
Beighton. *S Yor* 2B **86**
Beighton Hill. *Derbs* 5G **85**
Beinn Casgro. *W Isl* 5G **171**
Beith. *N Ayr* 4E **127**
Bekesbourne. *Kent* 5F **41**
Belaugh. *Norf* 4E **79**
Belbroughton. *Worc* 3D **60**
Belchalwell. *Dors* 2C **14**
Belchalwell Street. *Dors* 2C **14**
Belchamp Otten. *Essx* 1B **54**
Belchamp St Paul. *Essx* 1A **54**
Belchamp Walter. *Essx* 1B **54**
Belchford. *Linc* 3B **88**
Belfatton. *Abers* 3H **161**
Belford. *Nmbd* 1F **121**
Belgrano. *Cnwy* 3B **82**
Belhaven. *E Lot* 2C **130**
Belhelvie. *Abers* 2G **153**
Belhinnie. *Abers* 1B **152**
Bellabeg. *Abers* 2A **152**
Belladrum. *High* 4H **157**
Bellamore. *S Ayr* 1H **109**
Bellanoch. *Arg* 4F **133**
Bell Busk. *N Yor* 4B **98**
Belleau. *Linc* 3D **88**
Belleheiglash. *Mor* 5F **159**
Bell End. *Worc* 3D **60**
Bellerby. *N Yor* 5E **105**
Bellerby Camp. *N Yor* 5D **105**
Bellever. *Devn* 5G **11**
Belle Vue. *Cumb* 1C **102**
Belle Vue. *Shrp* 4G **71**
Bellfield. *S Lan* 1H **117**
Belliehill. *Ang* 2E **145**
Bellingdon. *Buck* 5H **51**

Bellingham. Nmbd 1B 114
Bellmount. Norf 3E 77
Bellochantuy. Arg 2A 122
Bellsbank. E Ayr 4D 117
Bell's Cross. Suff 5D 66
Bellshill. N Lan 4A 128
Bellshill. Nmbd 1F 121
Bellside. N Lan 4B 128
Bellspool. Bord 1D 118
Bellsquarry. W Lot 3D 128
Bells Yew Green. E Sus 2H 27
Belmaduthy. High 3A 158
Belmesthorpe. Rut 4H 75
Belmont. Bkbn 3E 91
Belmont. Shet 1G 173
Belmont. S Ayr 3C 116
Belnacraig. Abers 2A 152
Belnie. Linc 2B 76
Belowda. Corn 2D 6
Belper. Derbs 1A 74
Belper Lane End. Derbs 1H 73
Belph. Derbs 3C 86
Belsay. Nmbd 2E 115
Belsford. Devn 3D 8
Belsize. Herts 5A 52
Belstead. Suff 1E 55
Belston. S Ayr 2C 116
Belstone. Devn 3G 11
Belstone Corner. Devn 3G 11
Belthorn. Lanc 2F 91
Beltinge. Kent 4F 41
Beltoft. N Lin 4B 94
Belton. Leics 3B 74
Belton. Linc 2G 75
Belton. Norf 5G 79
Belton. N Lin 4A 94
Belton-in-Rutland. Rut 5F 75
Beltring. Kent 1A 28
Belts of Collonach. Abers 4D 152
Belvedere. G Lon 3F 39
Belvoir. Leics 2F 75
Bembridge. IOW 4E 17
Bemersyde. Bord 1H 119
Bemerton. Wilts 3G 23
Bempton. E Yor 2F 101
Benacre. Suff 2H 67
Ben Alder Lodge. High 1C 142
Ben Armine Lodge. High 2E 164
Benbecula Airport. W Isl 3C 170
Benbuie. Dum 5G 117
Benchill. G Man 2C 84
Benderloch. Arg 5D 140
Bendish. Herts 3B 52
Bendronaig Lodge. High 5C 156
Benenden. Kent 2C 28
Benera. High 1G 147
Benfieldside. Dur 4D 115
Bengate. Norf 3F 79
Bengeworth. Worc 1F 49
Bengrove. Glos 2E 49
Benhall Green. Suff 4F 67
Benholm. Abers 2H 145
Benington. Herts 3C 52
Benington. Linc 1C 76
Benington Sea End. Linc 1D 76
Benllech. IOA 2E 81
Benmore Lodge. High 2H 163
Bennacott. Corn 3D 10
Bennah. Devn 4B 12
Bennecarngan. N Ayr 3D 122
Bennethead. Cumb 2F 103
Benningbrough. N Yor 4H 99
Benniworth. Linc 2B 88
Benover. Kent 1B 28
Benson. Oxon 2E 36
Benston. Shet 6F 173
Benstonhall. Orkn 4E 172
Bent. Abers 1F 145
Benthall. Shrp 5A 72
Bentham. Glos 4E 49
Benthoul. Aber 3F 153
Bentlawnt. Shrp 5F 71
Bentley. E Yor 1D 94
Bentley. Hants 2F 25
Bentley. S Yor 4F 93
Bentley. Suff 2E 54
Bentley. Warw 1G 61
Bentley. W Mid 1D 61
Bentley Heath. Herts 1D 38
Bentley Heath. W Mid 3F 61
Bentpath. Dum 5F 119
Bents. W Lot 3C 128
Bentworth. Hants 2E 25
Benvie. D'dee 5C 144
Benville. Dors 2A 14
Benwell. Tyne 3F 115
Benwick. Cambs 1C 64
Beoley. Worc 4E 61
Beoraidbeg. High 4E 147
Bepton. W Sus 1G 17
Berden. Essx 3E 53
Bere Alston. Devn 2A 8
Bere Ferrers. Devn 2A 8
Berepper. Corn 4D 4
Bere Regis. Dors 3D 14
Bergh Apton. Norf 5F 79
Berinsfield. Oxon 2D 36
Berkeley. Glos 2B 34
Berkhamsted. Herts 5H 51
Berkley. Som 2D 22
Berkswell. W Mid 3G 61
Bermondsey. G Lon 3E 39
Bernice. Arg 4A 134
Bernisdale. High 3D 154
Berrick Salome. Oxon 2E 36
Berriedale. High 1H 165
Berrier. Cumb 2F 103
Berriew. Powy 5D 70
Berrington. Nmbd 5G 131
Berrington. Shrp 5H 71
Berrington. Worc 4H 59
Berrington Green. Worc 4H 59
Berrington Law. Nmbd 5F 131
Berrow. Som 1G 21
Berrow Green. Worc 5B 60
Berry Cross. Devn 1E 11
Berry Down Cross. Devn 2F 19
Berry Hill. Glos 4A 48
Berry Hill. Pemb 1A 44
Berryhillock. Mor 2C 160
Berrynarbor. Devn 2F 19
Berry Pomeroy. Devn 2E 9
Berryscaur. Dum 5D 118
Berry's Green. G Lon 5F 39
Bersham. Wrex 1F 71
Berthengam. Flin 3D 82
Berwick. E Sus 5G 27
Berwick Bassett. Wilts 4G 35
Berwick Hill. Nmbd 2E 115
Berwick St James. Wilts 3F 23
Berwick St John. Wilts 4E 23
Berwick St Leonard. Wilts 3E 23
Berwick-upon-Tweed. Nmbd 4G 131
Berwyn. Den 1D 70
Bescaby. Leics 3F 75
Bescar. Lanc 3B 90
Besford. Worc 1E 49
Bessacarr. S Yor 4G 93
Bessels Leigh. Oxon 5C 50
Bessingby. E Yor 3F 101
Bessingham. Norf 2D 78
Best Beech Hill. E Sus 2H 27
Besthorpe. Norf 1C 66
Besthorpe. Notts 4F 87
Bestwood Village. Notts 1C 74
Beswick. E Yor 5E 101
Betchworth. Surr 5D 38
Bethania. Cdgn 4E 57
Bethania. Gwyn 1G 69 (nr. Blaenau Ffestiniog)
Bethania. Gwyn 5F 81 (nr. Caernarfon)
Bethel. Gwyn 2B 70 (nr. Bala)
Bethel. Gwyn 4E 81 (nr. Caernarfon)
Bethel. IOA 3C 80
Bethersden. Kent 1D 28
Bethesda. Gwyn 4F 81
Bethesda. Pemb 3E 43
Bethlehem. Carm 3G 45
Bethnal Green. G Lon 2E 39
Betishill. N Lan 3A 128
Betley. Staf 1B 72
Betsham. Kent 3H 39
Betteshanger. Kent 5H 41
Bettiscombe. Dors 3H 13
Bettisfield. Wrex 2G 71
Betton. Shrp 2A 72
Betton Strange. Shrp 5H 71
Bettws. B'end 3C 32
Bettws. Newp 2F 33
Bettws Bledrws. Cdgn 5E 57
Bettws Cedewain. Powy 1D 58
Bettws Gwerfil Goch. Den 1C 70
Bettws Ifan. Cdgn 1D 44
Bettws Newydd. Mon 5G 47
Bettyhill. High 2H 167
Betws. Carm 4G 45
Betws Garmon. Gwyn 5E 81
Betws-y-Coed. Cnwy 5G 81
Betws-yn-Rhos. Cnwy 3B 82
Beulah. Cdgn 1C 44
Beulah. Powy 5B 58
Beul an Atha. Arg 3B 124
Bevendean. Brig 5E 27
Bevercotes. Notts 3E 86
Beverley. E Yor 1D 94
Beverston. Glos 2D 34
Bevington. Glos 2B 34
Bewaldeth. Cumb 1D 102
Bewcastle. Cumb 2G 113
Bewdley. Worc 3B 60
Bewerley. N Yor 3D 98
Bewholme. E Yor 4F 101
Bexfield. Norf 3C 78
Bexhill. E Sus 5B 28
Bexley. G Lon 3F 39
Bexleyheath. G Lon 3F 39
Bexleyhill. W Sus 3A 26
Bexwell. Norf 5F 77
Beyton. Suff 4B 66
Bhalton. W Isl 4C 171
Bhatarsaigh. W Isl 9B 170
Bibbington. Derbs 3E 85
Bibury. Glos 5G 49
Bicester. Oxon 3D 50
Bickenhall. Som 1F 13
Bickenhill. W Mid 2F 61
Bicker. Linc 2B 76
Bicker Bar. Linc 2B 76
Bicker Gauntlet. Linc 2B 76
Bickershaw. G Man 4E 91
Bickerstaffe. Lanc 4C 90
Bickerton. Ches E 5H 83
Bickerton. Nmbd 4D 121
Bickerton. N Yor 4G 99
Bickford. Staf 4C 72
Bickington. Devn 3F 19 (nr. Barnstaple)
Bickington. Devn 5B 12 (nr. Newton Abbot)
Bickleigh. Devn 2B 8 (nr. Plymouth)
Bickleigh. Devn 2C 12 (nr. Tiverton)
Bickleton. Devn 3F 19
Bickley. N Yor 5G 107
Bickley Moss. Ches W 1H 71
Bickmarsh. Warw 5F 61
Bicknacre. Essx 5A 54
Bicknoller. Som 3E 20
Bicknor. Kent 5C 40
Bickton. Hants 1G 15
Bicton. Here 4G 59
Bicton. Shrp 2E 59 (nr. Bishop's Castle)
Bicton. Shrp 4G 71 (nr. Shrewsbury)
Bicton Heath. Shrp 4G 71
Bidborough. Kent 1G 27
Biddenden. Kent 2C 28
Biddenden Green. Kent 1C 28
Biddenham. Bed 1A 52
Biddestone. Wilts 4D 34
Biddisham. Som 1G 21
Biddlesden. Buck 1E 51
Biddlestone. Nmbd 4D 120
Biddulph. Staf 5C 84
Biddulph Moor. Staf 5D 84
Bideford. Devn 4E 19
Bidford-on-Avon. Warw 5E 61
Bidlake. Devn 4F 11
Bidston. Mers 2E 83
Bielby. E Yor 5B 100
Bieldside. Aber 3F 153
Bierley. IOW 5D 16
Bierley. W Yor 1B 92
Bierton. Buck 4G 51
Bigbury. Devn 4C 8
Bigbury-on-Sea. Devn 4C 8
Bigby. Linc 4D 94
Biggar. Cumb 3A 96
Biggar. S Lan 1C 118
Biggin. Derbs 5F 85 (nr. Hartington)
Biggin. Derbs 1G 73 (nr. Hulland)
Biggin. N Yor 1F 93
Biggings. Shet 5C 173
Biggin Hill. G Lon 5F 39
Biggleswade. C Beds 1B 52
Bighouse. High 2A 168
Bighton. Hants 3E 24
Biglands. Cumb 4D 112
Bignor. W Sus 4A 26
Bigrigg. Cumb 3B 102
Big Sand. High 1G 155
Bigton. Shet 9E 173
Bilberry. Corn 2E 6
Bilborough. Nott 1C 74
Bilbrook. Som 2D 20
Bilbrook. Staf 5C 72
Bilbrough. N Yor 5H 99
Bilbster. High 3E 169
Bilby. Notts 2D 86
Bildershaw. Dur 2F 105
Bildeston. Suff 1C 54
Billericay. Essx 1A 40
Billesdon. Leics 5E 74
Billesley. Warw 5F 61
Billingborough. Linc 2A 76
Billinge. Mers 4D 90
Billingford. Norf 3C 78 (nr. Dereham)
Billingford. Norf 3D 66 (nr. Diss)
Billingham. Stoc T 2B 106
Billinghay. Linc 5A 88
Billingley. S Yor 4E 93
Billingshurst. W Sus 3B 26
Billingsley. Shrp 2B 60
Billington. C Beds 3H 51
Billington. Lanc 1F 91
Billington. Staf 3C 72
Billockby. Norf 4G 79
Billy Row. Dur 1E 105
Bilsborrow. Lanc 5E 97
Bilsby. Linc 3D 88
Bilsham. W Sus 5A 26
Bilsington. Kent 2E 29
Bilson Green. Glos 4B 48
Bilsthorpe. Notts 4D 86
Bilston. Midl 3F 129
Bilston. W Mid 1D 60
Bilstone. Leics 5A 74
Bilting. Kent 1E 29
Bilton. E Yor 1E 95
Bilton. Nmbd 3G 121
Bilton. N Yor 4E 99
Bilton. Warw 3B 62
Bilton in Ainsty. N Yor 5G 99
Bimbister. Orkn 6C 172
Binbrook. Linc 1B 88
Binchester. Dur 1F 105
Bincombe. Dors 4B 14
Bindal. High 5G 165
Binegar. Som 2B 22
Bines Green. W Sus 4C 26
Binfield. Brac 4G 37
Binfield Heath. Oxon 4F 37
Bingfield. Nmbd 2C 114
Bingham. Notts 1E 74
Bingham's Melcombe. Dors 2C 14
Bingley. W Yor 1B 92
Bings Heath. Shrp 4H 71
Binham. Norf 2B 78
Binley. Hants 1C 24
Binley. W Mid 3A 62
Binnegar. Dors 4D 15
Binniehill. Falk 2B 128
Binsoe. N Yor 2E 99
Binstead. IOW 3D 16
Binstead. W Sus 5A 26
Binsted. Hants 2F 25
Binton. Warw 5F 61
Bintree. Norf 3C 78
Binweston. Shrp 5F 71
Birch. Essx 4C 54
Birchall. Staf 5D 85
Bircham Newton. Norf 2G 77
Bircham Tofts. Norf 2G 77
Birchanger. Essx 3F 53
Birchburn. N Ayr 3D 122
Birch Cross. Staf 2F 73
Bircher. Here 4G 59
Birch Green. Essx 4C 54
Birchgrove. Card 4E 33
Birchgrove. Swan 3G 31
Birch Heath. Ches W 4H 83
Birch Hill. Ches W 3H 83
Birchill. Devn 2G 13
Birchington. Kent 4G 41
Birch Langley. G Man 4G 91
Birchley Heath. Warw 1G 61
Birchmoor. Warw 5G 73
Birchmoor Green. C Beds 2H 51
Birchover. Derbs 4G 85
Birch Vale. Derbs 2E 85
Birchview. Mor 5F 159
Birchwood. Linc 4G 87
Birchwood. Som 1F 13
Birchwood. Warr 1A 84
Bircotes. Notts 1D 86
Birdbrook. Essx 1H 53
Birdham. W Sus 2G 17
Birdingbury. Warw 4B 62
Birdlip. Glos 4E 49
Birdsall. N Yor 3C 100
Birds Edge. W Yor 4C 92
Birds Green. Essx 5F 53
Birdsgreen. Shrp 2B 60
Birdsmoorgate. Dors 2G 13
Birdston. E Dun 2H 127
Birdwell. S Yor 4D 92
Birdwood. Glos 4C 48
Birgham. Bord 1B 120
Birichen. High 4E 165
Birkby. Cumb 1B 102
Birkby. N Yor 4A 106
Birkdale. Mers 3B 90
Birkenhead. Mers 2F 83
Birkenhills. Abers 4E 161
Birkenshaw. N Lan 3H 127
Birkenshaw. W Yor 2C 92
Birkhall. Abers 4H 151
Birkhill. Ang 5C 144
Birkholme. Linc 3G 75
Birkin. N Yor 2F 93
Birley. Here 5G 59
Birling. Kent 4A 40
Birling. Nmbd 4G 121
Birling Gap. E Sus 5G 27
Birlingham. Worc 1E 49
Birmingham. W Mid 2E 61 & 188
Birmingham International Airport. W Mid 2F 61 & 216
Birnam. Per 4H 143
Birsay. Orkn 5B 172
Birse. Abers 4C 152
Birsemore. Abers 4C 152
Birstall. Leics 5C 74
Birstall. W Yor 2C 92
Birstall Smithies. W Yor 2C 92
Birstwith. N Yor 4E 99
Birthorpe. Linc 2A 76
Birtle. Lanc 3G 91
Birtley. Here 4F 59
Birtley. Nmbd 2B 114
Birtley. Tyne 4F 115
Birtsmorton. Worc 2D 48
Birts Street. Worc 2C 48
Bisbrooke. Rut 1F 63
Bisham. Wind 3G 37
Bishampton. Worc 5D 61
Bish Mill. Devn 4H 19
Bishop Auckland. Dur 2F 105
Bishopbridge. Linc 1H 87
Bishopbriggs. E Dun 2H 127
Bishop Burton. E Yor 1C 94
Bishopdown. Wilts 3G 23
Bishop Middleham. Dur 1A 106
Bishopmill. Mor 2G 159
Bishop Monkton. N Yor 3F 99
Bishop Norton. Linc 1G 87
Bishopsbourne. Kent 5F 41
Bishops Cannings. Wilts 5F 35
Bishop's Castle. Shrp 2F 59
Bishop's Caundle. Dors 1B 14
Bishop's Cleeve. Glos 3E 49
Bishop's Down. Dors 1B 14
Bishop's Frome. Here 1B 48
Bishop's Green. Essx 4G 53
Bishop's Green. Hants 5D 36
Bishop's Hull. Som 4F 21
Bishop's Itchington. Warw 5A 62
Bishops Lydeard. Som 4E 21
Bishop's Norton. Glos 3D 48
Bishop's Nympton. Devn 4A 20
Bishop's Offley. Staf 3B 72
Bishop's Stortford. Herts 3E 53
Bishops Sutton. Hants 3E 24
Bishop's Tachbrook. Warw 4H 61
Bishop's Tawton. Devn 3F 19
Bishopsteignton. Devn 5C 12
Bishopstoke. Hants 1C 16
Bishopston. Swan 4E 31
Bishopstone. Buck 4G 51
Bishopstone. E Sus 5F 27
Bishopstone. Here 1H 47
Bishopstone. Swin 3H 35
Bishopstone. Wilts 4F 23
Bishopstrow. Wilts 2D 23
Bishop Sutton. Bath 1A 22
Bishop's Waltham. Hants 1D 16
Bishopswood. Som 1F 13
Bishops Wood. Staf 5C 72
Bishopsworth. Bris 5A 34
Bishop Thornton. N Yor 3E 99
Bishopthorpe. York 5H 99
Bishopton. Darl 2A 106
Bishopton. Dum 5B 110
Bishopton. N Yor 2F 99
Bishopton. Ren 2F 127
Bishopton. Warw 5F 61
Bishop Wilton. E Yor 4B 100
Bishton. Newp 3G 33
Bishton. Staf 3E 73
Bisley. Glos 5E 49
Bisley. Surr 5A 38
Bispham. Bkpl 5C 96
Bispham Green. Lanc 3C 90
Bissoe. Corn 4B 6
Bisterne. Hants 2G 15
Bisterne Close. Hants 2H 15
Bitchfield. Linc 3G 75
Bittadon. Devn 2F 19
Bittaford. Devn 3C 8
Bittering. Norf 4B 78
Bitterley. Shrp 3H 59
Bitterne. Sotn 1C 16
Bitteswell. Leics 2C 62
Bitton. S Glo 5B 34
Bix. Oxon 3F 37
Bixter. Shet 6E 173
Blaby. Leics 1C 62
Blackawton. Devn 3E 9
Black Bank. Cambs 2E 65
Black Barn. Linc 3D 76
Blackborough. Devn 2D 12
Blackborough. Norf 4F 77
Blackborough End. Norf 4F 77
Black Bourton. Oxon 5A 50
Blackboys. E Sus 3G 27
Blackbrook. Derbs 1H 73
Blackbrook. Mers 1H 83
Blackbrook. Staf 2B 72
Blackbrook. Surr 1C 26
Blackburn. Abers 2F 153
Blackburn. Bkbn 2E 91
Blackburn. W Lot 3C 128
Black Callerton. Tyne 3E 115
Black Carr. Norf 1C 66
Black Clauchrie. S Ayr 1H 109
Black Corries. High 3G 141
Black Crofts. Arg 5D 140
Black Cross. Corn 2D 6
Blackden Heath. Ches E 3B 84
Blackditch. Oxon 5C 50
Blackdog. Abers 2G 153
Black Dog. Devn 2B 12
Blackdown. Dors 2G 13
Blackdyke. Cumb 4C 112
Blacker Hill. S Yor 4D 92
Blackfen. G Lon 3F 39
Blackfield. Hants 2C 16
Blackford. Cumb 3E 113
Blackford. Per 3A 136
Blackford. Shrp 2H 59
Blackford. Som 2H 21 (nr. Burnham-on-Sea)
Blackford. Som 4B 22 (nr. Wincanton)
Blackfordby. Leics 4H 73
Blackgang. IOW 5C 16
Blackhall. Edin 2F 129
Blackhall. Ren 3F 127
Blackhall Colliery. Dur 1B 106
Blackhall Mill. Tyne 4E 115
Blackhall Rocks. Dur 1B 106
Blackham. E Sus 2F 27
Blackheath. Essx 3D 54
Blackheath. G Lon 3E 39
Blackheath. Suff 3G 67
Blackheath. Surr 1B 26
Blackheath. W Mid 2D 61
Black Heddon. Nmbd 2D 115
Blackhill. Abers 4H 161
Blackhill. High 3C 154
Black Hill. Warw 5G 61
Blackhills. Abers 2G 161
Blackhills. High 3D 158
Blackjack. Linc 2B 76
Blackland. Wilts 5F 35
Black Lane. G Man 4F 91
Blackleach. Lanc 1C 90
Blackley. G Man 4G 91
Blackley. W Yor 3B 92
Blacklunans. Per 2A 144
Blackmill. B'end 3C 32
Blackmoor. G Man 4E 91
Blackmoor. Hants 3F 25
Blackmoor Gate. Devn 2G 19
Blackmore. Essx 5G 53
Blackmore End. Essx 2H 53
Blackmore End. Herts 4B 52
Black Mount. Arg 4G 141
Blackness. Falk 2D 128
Blacknest. Hants 2F 25
Blackney. Dors 3H 13
Blacknoll. Dors 4D 14
Black Notley. Essx 3A 54
Blacko. Lanc 5A 98
Black Pill. Swan 3F 31
Blackpool. Bkpl 1B 90 & 188
Blackpool. Devn 4E 9
Blackpool Airport. Lanc 1B 90
Blackpool Corner. Devn 3G 13
Blackpool Gate. Cumb 2G 113
Blackridge. W Lot 3C 128
Blackrock. Arg 3B 124
Blackrock. Mon 4F 47
Blackrod. G Man 3E 90
Blackshaw. Dum 3B 112
Blackshaw Head. W Yor 2H 91
Blacksmith's Green. Suff 4D 66
Blacksnape. Bkbn 2F 91
Blackstone. W Sus 4D 26
Black Street. Suff 2H 67
Black Tar. Pemb 4D 43
Blackthorn. Oxon 4E 50
Blackthorpe. Suff 4B 66
Blacktoft. E Yor 2B 94
Blacktop. Aber 3F 153
Black Torrington. Devn 2E 11
Blacktown. Newp 3F 33
Blackwall Tunnel. G Lon 2E 39
Blackwater. Corn 4B 6
Blackwater. Hants 1G 25
Blackwater. IOW 4D 16
Blackwater. Som 1F 13
Blackwaterfoot. N Ayr 3C 122
Blackwell. Darl 3F 105

Blackwell—Bradley

Blackwell. *Derbs* 5B **86**
(nr. Alfreton)
Blackwell. *Derbs* 3F **85**
(nr. Buxton)
Blackwell. *Som* 4D **20**
Blackwell. *Warw* 1H **49**
Blackwell. *Worc* 3D **61**
Blackwood. *Cphy* 2E **33**
Blackwood. *Dum* 1G **111**
Blackwood. *S Lan* 5A **128**
Blackwood Hill. *Staf* 5D **84**
Blacon. *Ches W* 4F **83**
Bladnoch. *Dum* 4B **110**
Bladon. *Oxon* 4C **50**
Blaenannerch. *Cdgn* 1C **44**
Blaenau Dolwyddelan. *Cnwy* 5F **81**
Blaenau Ffestiniog. *Gwyn* 1G **69**
Blaenavon. *Torf* 5F **47**
Blaenawey. *Mon* 4F **47**
Blaen Celyn. *Cdgn* 5C **56**
Blaen Clydach. *Rhon* 2C **32**
Blaendulais. *Neat* 5B **46**
Blaenffos. *Pemb* 1F **43**
Blaengarw. *B'end* 2C **32**
Blaen-geuffordd. *Cdgn* 2F **57**
Blaengwrach. *Neat* 5B **46**
Blaengwynfi. *Neat* 2B **32**
Blaenllechau. *Rhon* 2D **32**
Blaenpennal. *Cdgn* 4F **57**
Blaenplwyf. *Cdgn* 3E **57**
Blaenporth. *Cdgn* 1C **44**
Blaenrhondda. *Rhon* 2C **32**
Blaenwaun. *Carm* 2G **43**
Blaen-y-coed. *Carm* 2H **43**
Blaenycwm. *Rhon* 2C **32**
Blagdon. *N Som* 1A **22**
Blagdon. *Torb* 2E **9**
Blagdon Hill. *Som* 1F **13**
Blagill. *Cumb* 5A **114**
Blaguegate. *Lanc* 4C **90**
Blaich. *High* 1E **141**
Blain. *High* 2A **140**
Blaina. *Blae* 5F **47**
Blair Atholl. *Per* 2F **143**
Blair Drummond. *Stir* 4G **135**
Blairgowrie. *Per* 4A **144**
Blairhall. *Fife* 1D **128**
Blairingone. *Per* 4B **136**
Blairlogie. *Stir* 4H **135**
Blairmore. *Abers* 5B **160**
Blairmore. *Arg* 1C **126**
Blairmore. *High* 3B **166**
Blairquhanan. *W Dun* 1F **127**
Blaisdon. *Glos* 4C **48**
Blakebrook. *Worc* 3C **60**
Blakedown. *Worc* 3C **60**
Blake End. *Essx* 3H **53**
Blakemere. *Here* 1G **47**
Blakeney. *Glos* 5B **48**
Blakeney. *Norf* 1C **78**
Blakenhall. *Ches E* 1B **72**
Blakenhall. *W Mid* 1C **60**
Blakeshall. *Worc* 2C **60**
Blakesley. *Nptn* 5D **62**
Blanchland. *Nmbd* 4C **114**
Blandford Camp. *Dors* 2E **15**
Blandford Forum. *Dors* 2D **15**
Blandford St Mary. *Dors* 2D **15**
Bland Hill. *N Yor* 4E **98**
Blandy. *High* 3G **167**
Blanefield. *Stir* 2G **127**
Blankney. *Linc* 4H **87**
Blantyre. *S Lan* 4H **127**
Blarmachfoldach. *High* 2E **141**
Blarnalearoch. *High* 4F **163**
Blashford. *Hants* 2G **15**
Blaston. *Leics* 1F **63**
Blatchbridge. *Som* 2C **22**
Blathaisbhal. *W Isl* 1D **170**
Blatherwycke. *Nptn* 1G **63**
Blawith. *Cumb* 1B **96**
Blaxhall. *Suff* 5F **67**
Blaxton. *S Yor* 4G **93**
Blaydon. *Tyne* 3E **115**
Bleadney. *Som* 2H **21**
Bleadon. *N Som* 1G **21**
Blean. *Kent* 4F **41**
Bleasby. *Linc* 2A **88**
Bleasby. *Notts* 1E **74**
Bleasby Moor. *Linc* 2A **88**
Blebocraigs. *Fife* 2G **137**
Bleddfa. *Powy* 4E **58**
Bledington. *Glos* 3H **49**
Bledlow. *Buck* 5F **51**
Bledlow Ridge. *Buck* 2F **37**
Blencarn. *Cumb* 1H **103**
Blencogo. *Cumb* 5C **112**
Blendworth. *Hants* 1F **17**
Blenheim. *Oxon* 5D **50**
Blennerhasset. *Cumb* 5C **112**
Bletchingdon. *Oxon* 4D **50**
Bletchingley. *Surr* 5E **39**
Bletchley. *Mil* 2G **51**
Bletchley. *Shrp* 2A **72**
Bletherston. *Pemb* 2E **43**
Bletsoe. *Bed* 5H **63**
Blewbury. *Oxon* 3D **36**
Blickling. *Norf* 3D **78**
Blidworth. *Notts* 5C **86**
Blindburn. *Nmbd* 3C **120**
Blindcrake. *Cumb* 1C **102**
Blindley Heath. *Surr* 1E **27**
Blindmoor. *Som* 1F **13**
Blisland. *Corn* 5A **10**
Blissford. *Hants* 1G **15**
Bliss Gate. *Worc* 3B **60**
Blists Hill. *Telf* 5A **72**
Blisworth. *Nptn* 5E **63**
Blithbury. *Staf* 3E **73**
Blitterlees. *Cumb* 4C **112**
Blockley. *Glos* 2G **49**
Blofield. *Norf* 5F **79**
Blofield Heath. *Norf* 4F **79**
Blo' Norton. *Norf* 3C **66**
Bloomfield. *Bord* 2H **119**
Blore. *Staf* 1F **73**
Blount's Green. *Staf* 2E **73**
Bloxham. *Oxon* 2C **50**
Bloxholm. *Linc* 5H **87**
Bloxwich. *W Mid* 5E **73**
Bloxworth. *Dors* 3D **15**
Blubberhouses. *N Yor* 4D **98**
Blue Anchor. *Som* 2D **20**
Blue Anchor. *Swan* 3E **31**
Blue Bell Hill. *Kent* 4B **40**
Blue Row. *Essx* 4D **54**
Bluetown. *Kent* 5D **40**
Blundeston. *Suff* 1H **67**
Blunham. *C Beds* 5A **64**
Blunsdon St Andrew. *Swin* 3G **35**
Bluntington. *Worc* 3C **60**
Bluntisham. *Cambs* 3C **64**
Blunts. *Corn* 2H **7**
Blurton. *Stoke* 1C **72**
Blyborough. *Linc* 1G **87**
Blyford. *Suff* 3G **67**
Blymhill. *Staf* 4C **72**
Blymhill Lawns. *Staf* 4C **72**
Blyth. *Nmbd* 1G **115**
Blyth. *Notts* 2D **86**
Blyth. *Bord* 5E **129**
Blyth Bank. *Bord* 5E **129**
Blyth Bridge. *Bord* 5E **129**
Blythburgh. *Suff* 3G **67**
Blythe Bridge. *Staf* 1D **72**
Blythe Marsh. *Staf* 1D **72**
Blythe, The. *Staf* 3E **73**
Blyton. *Linc* 1F **87**
Boarhills. *Fife* 2H **137**
Boarhunt. *Hants* 2E **16**
Boarshead. *E Sus* 2G **27**
Boar's Head. *G Man* 4D **90**
Boars Hill. *Oxon* 5C **50**
Boarstall. *Buck* 4E **51**
Boasley Cross. *Devn* 3E **11**
Boath. *High* 1H **157**
Boat of Garten. *High* 2D **150**
Bobbing. *Kent* 4C **40**
Bobbington. *Staf* 1C **60**
Bobbingworth. *Essx* 5F **53**
Bocaddon. *Corn* 3F **7**
Bocking. *Essx* 3A **54**
Bocking Churchstreet. *Essx* 3A **54**
Boddam. *Abers* 4H **161**
Boddam. *Shet* 10E **173**
Boddington. *Glos* 3D **49**
Bodedern. *IOA* 2C **80**
Bodelwyddan. *Den* 3C **82**
Bodenham. *Here* 5H **59**
Bodenham. *Wilts* 4G **23**
Bodewryd. *IOA* 1C **80**
Bodfari. *Den* 3C **82**
Bodffordd. *IOA* 3D **80**
Bodham. *Norf* 1D **78**
Bodiam. *E Sus* 3B **28**
Bodicote. *Oxon* 2C **50**
Bodieve. *Corn* 1D **6**
Bodinnick. *Corn* 3F **7**
Bodle Street Green. *E Sus* 4A **28**
Bodmin. *Corn* 2E **7**
Bodnant. *Cnwy* 3H **81**
Bodney. *Norf* 1H **65**
Bodorgan. *IOA* 4C **80**
Bodrane. *Corn* 2G **7**
Bodsham. *Kent* 1F **29**
Boduan. *Gwyn* 2C **68**
Bodymoor Heath. *Warw* 1F **61**
Bogallan. *High* 3A **158**
Bogbrae Croft. *Abers* 5H **161**
Bogend. *S Ayr* 1C **116**
Boghall. *Midl* 3F **129**
Boghall. *W Lot* 3C **128**
Boghead. *S Lan* 5A **128**
Bogindollo. *Ang* 3D **144**
Bogmoor. *Mor* 2A **160**
Bogniebrae. *Abers* 4C **160**
Bognor Regis. *W Sus* 3H **17**
Bograxie. *Abers* 2E **152**
Bogside. *N Lan* 4B **128**
Bog, The. *Shrp* 1F **59**
Bogton. *Abers* 3D **160**
Bogue. *Dum* 1D **110**
Bohenie. *High* 5E **149**
Bohortha. *Corn* 5C **6**
Boirseam. *W Isl* 9C **171**
Bokiddick. *Corn* 2E **7**
Bolam. *Dur* 2E **105**
Bolam. *Nmbd* 1D **115**
Bolberry. *Devn* 5C **8**
Bold Heath. *Mers* 2H **83**
Boldon. *Tyne* 3G **115**
Boldon Colliery. *Tyne* 3G **115**
Boldre. *Hants* 3B **16**
Boldron. *Dur* 3D **104**
Bole. *Notts* 2E **87**
Bolehall. *Staf* 5G **73**
Bolehill. *Derbs* 5G **85**
Bolenowe. *Corn* 5A **6**
Boleside. *Bord* 1G **119**
Bolham. *Devn* 1C **12**
Bolham Water. *Devn* 1E **13**
Bolingey. *Corn* 3B **6**
Bollington. *Ches E* 3D **84**
Bolney. *W Sus* 3D **26**
Bolnhurst. *Bed* 5H **63**
Bolshan. *Ang* 3F **145**
Bolsover. *Derbs* 3B **86**
Bolsterstone. *S Yor* 1G **85**
Bolstone. *Here* 2A **48**
Boltachan. *Per* 3F **143**
Boltby. *N Yor* 1G **99**
Bolton. *Cumb* 2H **103**
Bolton. *E Lot* 2B **130**
Bolton. *E Yor* 4B **100**
Bolton. *G Man* 4F **91**
Bolton. *Nmbd* 3F **121**
Bolton Abbey. *N Yor* 4C **98**
Bolton-by-Bowland. *Lanc* 5G **97**
Boltonfellend. *Cumb* 3F **113**
Boltongate. *Cumb* 5D **112**
Bolton Green. *Lanc* 3D **90**
Bolton-le-Sands. *Lanc* 3D **97**
Bolton Low Houses. *Cumb* 5D **112**
Bolton New Houses. *Cumb* 5D **112**
Bolton-on-Swale. *N Yor* 5F **105**
Bolton Percy. *N Yor* 5H **99**
Bolton Town End. *Lanc* 3D **97**
Bolton upon Dearne. *S Yor* 4E **93**
Bolton Wood Lane. *Cumb* 5D **112**
Bolventor. *Corn* 5B **10**
Bomarsund. *Nmbd* 1F **115**
Bomere Heath. *Shrp* 4G **71**
Bonar Bridge. *High* 4D **164**
Bonawe. *Arg* 5E **141**
Bonby. *N Lin* 3D **94**
Boncath. *Pemb* 1G **43**
Bonchester Bridge. *Bord* 3H **119**
Bonchurch. *IOW* 5D **16**
Bond End. *Staf* 4F **73**
Bondleigh. *Devn* 2G **11**
Bonds. *Lanc* 5D **97**
Bonehill. *Devn* 5H **11**
Bonehill. *Staf* 5F **73**
Bo'ness. *Falk* 1C **128**
Boney Hay. *Staf* 4E **73**
Bonham. *Wilts* 3C **22**
Bonhill. *W Dun* 2E **127**
Boningale. *Shrp* 5C **72**
Bonjedward. *Bord* 2A **120**
Bonkle. *N Lan* 4B **128**
Bonnington. *Ang* 5E **145**
Bonnington. *Edin* 3E **129**
Bonnington. *Kent* 2E **29**
Bonnybank. *Fife* 3F **137**
Bonnybridge. *Falk* 1B **128**
Bonnykelly. *Abers* 3F **161**
Bonnyrigg. *Midl* 3G **129**
Bonnyton. *Ang* 5C **144**
Bonnytown. *Fife* 2H **137**
Bonsall. *Derbs* 5G **85**
Bont. *Mon* 4G **47**
Bontddu. *Gwyn* 4F **69**
Bont Dolgadfan. *Powy* 5A **70**
Bontgoch. *Cdgn* 2F **57**
Bonthorpe. *Linc* 3D **89**
Bontnewydd. *Cdgn* 4F **57**
Bont-newydd. *Cnwy* 3C **82**
Bontnewydd. *Gwyn* 4D **81**
(nr. Caernarfon)
Bont Newydd. *Gwyn* 1G **69**
(nr. Llan Ffestiniog)
Bontuchel. *Den* 5C **82**
Bonvilston. *V Glam* 4D **32**
Bon-y-maen. *Swan* 3F **31**
Booker. *Buck* 2G **37**
Booley. *Shrp* 3H **71**
Boorley Green. *Hants* 1D **16**
Boosbeck. *Red C* 3D **106**
Boot. *Cumb* 4C **102**
Booth. *W Yor* 2A **92**
Boothby Graffoe. *Linc* 5G **87**
Boothby Pagnell. *Linc* 2G **75**
Booth Green. *Ches E* 2D **84**
Booth of Toft. *Shet* 4F **173**
Boothstown. *G Man* 4F **91**
Boothville. *Nptn* 4E **63**
Booth Wood. *W Yor* 3A **92**
Bootle. *Cumb* 1A **96**
Bootle. *Mers* 1F **83**
Booton. *Norf* 3D **78**
Booze. *N Yor* 4D **104**
Boquhan. *Stir* 1G **127**
Boraston. *Shrp* 3A **60**
Borden. *Kent* 4C **40**
Borden. *W Sus* 4G **25**
Bordlands. *Bord* 5E **129**
Bordley. *N Yor* 3B **98**
Bordon. *Hants* 3G **25**
Boreham. *Essx* 5A **54**
Boreham. *Wilts* 2D **23**
Boreham Street. *E Sus* 4A **28**
Borehamwood. *Herts* 1C **38**
Boreland. *Dum* 5D **118**
Boreston. *Devn* 3D **8**
Borestone Brae. *Stir* 4H **135**
Boreton. *Shrp* 5H **71**
Borgh. *W Isl* 8B **170**
(on Barra)
Borgh. *W Isl* 3C **170**
(on Benbecula)
Borgh. *W Isl* 1E **170**
(on Berneray)
Borgh. *W Isl* 2G **171**
(on Isle of Lewis)
Borghasdal. *W Isl* 9C **171**
Borghastan. *W Isl* 3D **171**
Borgh na Sgiotaig. *High* 1C **154**
Borgie. *High* 3G **167**
Borgue. *Dum* 5D **110**
Borgue. *High* 1H **165**
Borley. *Essx* 1B **54**
Borley Green. *Essx* 1B **54**
Borley Green. *Suff* 4B **66**
Borlum. *High* 1H **149**
Bornais. *W Isl* 6C **170**
Bornesketaig. *High* 1C **154**
Boroughbridge. *N Yor* 3F **99**
Borough Green. *Kent* 5H **39**
Borras Head. *Wrex* 5F **83**
Borreraig. *High* 3A **154**
Borrobol Lodge. *High* 1F **165**
Borrodale. *High* 4A **154**
Borrowash. *Derb* 2B **74**
Borrowby. *N Yor* 1G **99**
(nr. Northallerton)
Borrowby. *N Yor* 3E **107**
(nr. Whitby)
Borrowston. *High* 4F **169**
Borrowstonehill. *Orkn* 7D **172**
Borrowstoun. *Falk* 1C **128**
Borstal. *Medw* 4B **40**
Borth. *Cdgn* 2F **57**
Borthwick. *Midl* 4G **129**
Borth-y-Gest. *Gwyn* 2E **69**
Borve. *High* 4D **154**
Borwick. *Lanc* 2E **97**
Bosbury. *Here* 1B **48**
Boscastle. *Corn* 3A **10**
Boscombe. *Bour* 3G **15**
Boscombe. *Wilts* 3H **23**
Boscoppa. *Corn* 3E **7**
Bosham. *W Sus* 2G **17**
Bosherston. *Pemb* 5D **42**
Bosley. *Ches E* 4D **84**
Bossall. *N Yor* 3B **100**
Bossiney. *Corn* 4A **10**
Bossingham. *Kent* 1F **29**
Bossington. *Som* 2B **20**
Bostadh. *W Isl* 3D **171**
Bostock Green. *Ches W* 4A **84**
Boston. *Linc* 1C **76**
Boston Spa. *W Yor* 5G **99**
Boswarthen. *Corn* 3B **4**
Boswinger. *Corn* 4D **6**
Botallack. *Corn* 3A **4**
Botany Bay. *G Lon* 1D **39**
Botcheston. *Leics* 5B **74**
Botesdale. *Suff* 3C **66**
Bothal. *Nmbd* 1F **115**
Bothampstead. *W Ber* 4D **36**
Bothamsall. *Notts* 3D **86**
Bothel. *Cumb* 1C **102**
Bothenhampton. *Dors* 3H **13**
Bothwell. *S Lan* 4H **127**
Botley. *Buck* 5H **51**
Botley. *Hants* 1D **16**
Botley. *Oxon* 5C **50**
Botloe's Green. *Glos* 3C **48**
Botolph Claydon. *Buck* 3F **51**
Botolphs. *W Sus* 5C **26**
Bottacks. *High* 2G **157**
Bottesford. *Leics* 2F **75**
Bottesford. *N Lin* 4B **94**
Bottisham. *Cambs* 4E **65**
Bottlesford. *Wilts* 1G **23**
Bottomcraig. *Fife* 1F **137**
Bottom o' th' Moor. *G Man* 3E **91**
Botton. *N Yor* 4D **107**
Botton Head. *Lanc* 3F **97**
Bottreaux Mill. *Devn* 4B **20**
Botusfleming. *Corn* 2A **8**
Botwnnog. *Gwyn* 2B **68**
Bough Beech. *Kent* 1F **27**
Boughrood. *Powy* 2E **47**
Boughspring. *Glos* 2A **34**
Boughton. *Norf* 5F **77**
Boughton. *Nptn* 4E **63**
Boughton. *Notts* 4D **86**
Boughton Aluph. *Kent* 1E **29**
Boughton Green. *Kent* 5B **40**
Boughton Lees. *Kent* 1E **28**
Boughton Malherbe. *Kent* 1C **28**
Boughton Monchelsea. *Kent* 5B **40**
Boughton under Blean. *Kent* 5E **41**
Boulby. *Red C* 3E **107**
Bouldnor. *IOW* 4B **16**
Bouldon. *Shrp* 2H **59**
Boulmer. *Nmbd* 3G **121**
Boulston. *Pemb* 3D **42**
Boultham. *Linc* 4G **87**
Boulton. *Derb* 2A **74**
Boundary. *Staf* 1D **73**
Bounds. *Here* 2B **48**
Bourn. *Cambs* 5C **64**
Bournbrook. *W Mid* 2E **61**
Bourne. *Linc* 3H **75**
Bourne End. *Bed* 4H **63**
Bourne End. *Buck* 3G **37**
Bourne End. *C Beds* 1H **51**
Bourne End. *Herts* 5A **52**
Bournemouth. *Bour* 3F **15** & **190**
Bournemouth Airport. *Dors* 3G **15**
Bournes Green. *Glos* 5E **49**
Bournes Green. *S'end* 2D **40**
Bourne, The. *Surr* 2G **25**
Bournheath. *Worc* 3D **60**
Bournmoor. *Dur* 4G **115**
Bournville. *W Mid* 2E **61**
Bourton. *Dors* 3C **22**
Bourton. *N Som* 5G **33**
Bourton. *Oxon* 3H **35**
Bourton. *Shrp* 1H **59**
Bourton. *Wilts* 5F **35**
Bourton on Dunsmore. *Warw* 3B **62**
Bourton-on-the-Hill. *Glos* 2G **49**
Bourton-on-the-Water. *Glos* 3G **49**
Bousd. *Arg* 2D **138**
Bousta. *Shet* 6D **173**
Boustead Hill. *Cumb* 4D **112**
Bouth. *Cumb* 1C **96**
Bouthwaite. *N Yor* 2D **98**
Boveney. *Buck* 3A **38**
Boveridge. *Dors* 1F **15**
Boverton. *V Glam* 5C **32**
Bovey Tracey. *Devn* 5B **12**
Bovingdon. *Herts* 5A **52**
Bovingdon Green. *Buck* 3G **37**
Bovinger. *Essx* 5F **53**
Bovington Camp. *Dors* 4D **14**
Bow. *Devn* 2H **11**
Bowbank. *Dur* 2C **104**
Bow Brickhill. *Mil* 2H **51**
Bowbridge. *Glos* 5D **48**
Bowburn. *Dur* 1A **106**
Bowcombe. *IOW* 4C **16**
Bowd. *Devn* 4E **12**
Bowden. *Devn* 4E **9**
Bowden. *Bord* 1H **119**
Bowden Hill. *Wilts* 5E **35**
Bowdens. *Som* 4H **21**
Bowdon. *G Man* 2B **84**
Bower. *Nmbd* 1A **114**
Bowerchalke. *Wilts* 4F **23**
Bowerhill. *Wilts* 5E **35**
Bower Hinton. *Som* 1H **13**
Bowermadden. *High* 2E **169**
Bowers. *Staf* 2C **72**
Bowers Gifford. *Essx* 2B **40**
Bowershall. *Fife* 4C **136**
Bowertower. *High* 2E **169**
Bowes. *Dur* 3C **104**
Bowgreave. *Lanc* 5D **97**
Bowhousebog. *N Lan* 4B **128**
Bowithick. *Corn* 4B **10**
Bowland Bridge. *Cumb* 1D **96**
Bowlees. *Dur* 2C **104**
Bowley. *Here* 5H **59**
Bowlhead Green. *Surr* 2A **26**
Bowling. *W Dun* 2F **127**
Bowling. *W Yor* 1B **92**
Bowling Bank. *Wrex* 1F **71**
Bowling Green. *Worc* 5C **60**
Bowlish. *Som* 2B **22**
Bowmanstead. *Cumb* 5E **102**
Bowmore. *Arg* 4B **124**
Bowness-on-Solway. *Cumb* 3D **112**
Bowness-on-Windermere.
Cumb 5F **103**
Bow of Fife. *Fife* 2F **137**
Bowriefauld. *Ang* 4E **145**
Bowscale. *Cumb* 1E **103**
Bowsden. *Nmbd* 5F **131**
Bowside Lodge. *High* 2A **168**
Bowston. *Cumb* 5F **103**
Bow Street. *Cdgn* 2F **57**
Bowthorpe. *Norf* 5D **78**
Box. *Glos* 5D **48**
Box. *Wilts* 5D **34**
Boxbush. *Glos* 3B **48**
Box End. *Bed* 1A **52**
Boxford. *Suff* 1C **54**
Boxford. *W Ber* 4C **36**
Boxgrove. *W Sus* 5A **26**
Boxley. *Kent* 5B **40**
Boxmoor. *Herts* 5A **52**
Box's Shop. *Corn* 2C **10**
Boxted. *Essx* 2C **54**
Boxted. *Suff* 5H **65**
Boxted Cross. *Essx* 2D **54**
Boxworth. *Cambs* 4C **64**
Boxworth End. *Cambs* 4C **64**
Boyden End. *Suff* 5G **65**
Boyden Gate. *Kent* 4G **41**
Boylestone. *Derbs* 2F **73**
Boylestonfield. *Derbs* 2F **73**
Boyndlie. *Abers* 2D **160**
Boynton. *E Yor* 3F **101**
Boys Hill. *Dors* 1B **14**
Boythorpe. *Derbs* 4A **86**
Boyton. *Corn* 3D **10**
Boyton. *Suff* 1G **55**
Boyton. *Wilts* 3E **23**
Boyton Cross. *Essx* 5G **53**
Boyton End. *Essx* 2G **53**
Boyton End. *Suff* 1H **53**
Bozeat. *Nptn* 5G **63**
Braaid. *IOM* 4C **108**
Braal Castle. *High* 2D **168**
Brabling Green. *Suff* 4E **67**
Brabourne. *Kent* 1F **29**
Brabourne Lees. *Kent* 1E **29**
Brabster. *High* 2F **169**
Bracadale. *High* 5C **154**
Bracara. *High* 4F **147**
Braceborough. *Linc* 4H **75**
Bracebridge. *Linc* 4G **87**
Bracebridge Heath. *Linc* 4G **87**
Braceby. *Linc* 2H **75**
Bracewell. *Lanc* 5A **98**
Brackenfield. *Derbs* 5A **86**
Brackenlands. *Cumb* 5D **112**
Brackenthwaite. *Cumb* 5D **112**
Brackenthwaite. *N Yor* 4E **99**
Brackla. *B'end* 4C **32**
Brackla. *High* 3C **158**
Bracklesham. *W Sus* 3G **17**
Brackletter. *High* 5D **148**
Brackley. *Nptn* 2D **50**
Brackley Hatch. *Nptn* 1E **51**
Brackloch. *High* 1F **163**
Bracknell. *Brac* 5G **37**
Braco. *Per* 3H **135**
Bracobrae. *Mor* 3C **160**
Bracon. *N Lin* 4A **94**
Bracon Ash. *Norf* 1D **66**
Bradbourne. *Derbs* 5G **85**
Bradbury. *Dur* 2A **106**
Bradda. *IOM* 4A **108**
Bradden. *Nptn* 1E **51**
Bradenham. *Buck* 2G **37**
Bradenham. *Norf* 5B **78**
Bradenstoke. *Wilts* 4F **35**
Bradfield. *Essx* 2E **55**
Bradfield. *Norf* 2E **79**
Bradfield. *W Ber* 4E **36**
Bradfield Combust. *Suff* 5A **66**
Bradfield Green. *Ches E* 5A **84**
Bradfield Heath. *Essx* 3E **55**
Bradfield St Clare. *Suff* 5B **66**
Bradfield St George. *Suff* 4B **66**
Bradford. *Derbs* 4G **85**
Bradford. *Devn* 2E **11**
Bradford. *Nmbd* 1F **121**
Bradford. *W Yor* 1B **92** & **190**
Bradford Abbas. *Dors* 1A **14**
Bradford Barton. *Devn* 1B **12**
Bradford Leigh. *Wilts* 5D **34**
Bradford-on-Avon. *Wilts* 5D **34**
Bradford-on-Tone. *Som* 4E **21**
Bradford Peverell. *Dors* 3B **14**
Bradiford. *Devn* 3F **19**
Brading. *IOW* 4E **16**
Bradley. *Ches W* 3H **83**
Bradley. *Derbs* 1G **73**
Bradley. *Glos* 2C **34**

Bradley—Brompton

Bradley. *Hants* 2E **25**
Bradley. *NE Lin* 4F **95**
Bradley. *N Yor* 1C **98**
Bradley. *Staf* 4C **72**
Bradley. *W Mid* 1D **60**
Bradley. *W Yor* 2B **92**
Bradley. *Wrex* 5F **83**
Bradley Cross. *Som* 1H **21**
Bradley Green. *Ches W* 1H **71**
Bradley Green. *Som* 3F **21**
Bradley Green. *Warw* 5G **73**
Bradley Green. *Worc* 4D **61**
Bradley in the Moors. *Staf* 1E **73**
Bradley Mount. *Ches E* 3D **84**
Bradley Stoke. *S Glo* 3B **34**
Bradlow. *Here* 2C **48**
Bradmore. *Notts* 2C **74**
Bradmore. *W Mid* 1C **60**
Bradninch. *Devn* 2D **12**
Bradnop. *Staf* 5E **85**
Bradpole. *Dors* 3H **13**
Bradshaw. *G Man* 3F **91**
Bradstone. *Devn* 4D **11**
Bradwall Green. *Ches E* 4B **84**
Bradway. *S Yor* 2H **85**
Bradwell. *Derbs* 2F **85**
Bradwell. *Essx* 3B **54**
Bradwell. *Mil* 2G **51**
Bradwell. *Norf* 5H **79**
Bradwell-on-Sea. *Essx* 5D **54**
Bradwell Waterside. *Essx* 5C **54**
Bradworthy. *Devn* 1D **10**
Brae. *High* 5C **162**
Brae. *Shet* 5E **173**
Braeantra. *High* 1H **157**
Braefield. *High* 5G **157**
Braefindon. *High* 3A **158**
Braegrum. *Per* 1C **136**
Braehead. *Ang* 3F **145**
Braehead. *Dum* 4B **110**
Braehead. *Mor* 4G **159**
Braehead. *Orkn* 3D **172**
Braehead. *S Lan* 1H **117**
(nr. Coalburn)
Braehead. *S Lan* 4C **128**
(nr. Forth)
Braehoulland. *Shet* 4D **173**
Braemar. *Abers* 4F **151**
Braemore. *High* 5C **168**
(nr. Dunbeath)
Braemore. *High* 1D **156**
(nr. Ullapool)
Brae of Achnahaird. *High* 2E **163**
Brae Roy Lodge. *High* 4F **149**
Braeside. *Abers* 5G **161**
Braeside. *Inv* 2D **126**
Braes of Coul. *Ang* 3B **144**
Braeswick. *Orkn* 4F **172**
Braetongue. *High* 3F **167**
Braeval. *Stir* 3E **135**
Braevallich. *Arg* 3G **133**
Braewick. *Shet* 6E **173**
Brafferton. *Darl* 2F **105**
Brafferton. *N Yor* 2G **99**
Brafield-on-the-Green. *Nptn* 5F **63**
Bragar. *W Isl* 3E **171**
Bragbury End. *Herts* 3C **52**
Bragleenbeg. *Arg* 1G **133**
Braichmelyn. *Gwyn* 4F **81**
Braides. *Lanc* 4D **96**
Braidwood. *S Lan* 5B **128**
Braigo. *Arg* 3A **124**
Brailsford. *Derbs* 1G **73**
Braintree. *Essx* 3A **54**
Braiseworth. *Suff* 3D **66**
Braishfield. *Hants* 4B **24**
Braithwaite. *Cumb* 2D **102**
Braithwaite. *S Yor* 3G **93**
Braithwaite. *W Yor* 5C **98**
Braithwell. *S Yor* 1C **86**
Brakefield Green. *Norf* 5C **78**
Bramber. *W Sus* 4C **26**
Brambledown. *Kent* 3D **40**
Brambridge. *Hants* 4C **24**
Bramcote. *Notts* 2C **74**
Bramcote. *Warw* 2B **62**
Bramdean. *Hants* 4E **24**
Bramerton. *Norf* 5E **79**
Bramfield. *Herts* 4C **52**
Bramfield. *Suff* 3F **67**
Bramford. *Suff* 1E **54**
Bramhall. *G Man* 2C **84**
Bramham. *W Yor* 5G **99**
Bramhope. *W Yor* 5E **99**
Bramley. *Hants* 1E **25**
Bramley. *S Yor* 1B **86**
Bramley. *Surr* 1B **26**
Bramley. *W Yor* 1C **92**
Bramley Green. *Hants* 1E **25**
Bramley Head. *N Yor* 4D **98**
Bramley Vale. *Derbs* 4B **86**
Bramling. *Kent* 5G **41**
Brampford Speke. *Devn* 3C **12**
Brampton. *Cambs* 3B **64**
Brampton. *Cumb* 2H **103**
(nr. Appleby-in-Westmorland)
Brampton. *Cumb* 3G **113**
(nr. Carlisle)
Brampton. *Linc* 3F **87**
Brampton. *Norf* 3E **78**
Brampton. *S Yor* 4E **93**
Brampton. *Suff* 2G **67**
Brampton Abbotts. *Here* 3B **48**
Brampton Ash. *Nptn* 2E **63**
Brampton Bryan. *Here* 3F **59**
Brampton en le Morthen. *S Yor* 2B **86**
Bramshall. *Staf* 2E **73**
Bramshaw. *Hants* 1A **16**
Bramshill. *Hants* 5F **37**
Bramshott. *Hants* 3G **25**
Branault. *High* 2G **139**
Brancaster. *Norf* 1G **77**
Brancaster Staithe. *Norf* 1G **77**
Brancepeth. *Dur* 1F **105**
Branch End. *Nmbd* 3D **114**
Branchill. *Mor* 3E **159**
Brand End. *Linc* 1C **76**
Branderburgh. *Mor* 1G **159**
Brandesburton. *E Yor* 5F **101**
Brandeston. *Suff* 4E **67**
Brand Green. *Glos* 3C **48**
Brandhill. *Shrp* 3G **59**
Brandis Corner. *Devn* 2E **11**
Brandish Street. *Som* 2C **20**
Brandiston. *Norf* 3D **78**
Brandon. *Dur* 1F **105**
Brandon. *Linc* 1G **75**
Brandon. *Nmbd* 3E **121**
Brandon. *Suff* 2G **65**
Brandon. *Warw* 3B **62**
Brandon Bank. *Cambs* 2F **65**
Brandon Creek. *Norf* 1F **65**
Brandon Parva. *Norf* 5C **78**
Brandsby. *N Yor* 2H **99**
Brandy Wharf. *Linc* 1H **87**
Brane. *Corn* 4B **4**
Bran End. *Essx* 3G **53**
Branksome. *Pool* 3F **15**
Bransbury. *Hants* 2C **24**
Bransby. *Linc* 3G **87**
Branscombe. *Devn* 4E **13**
Bransford. *Worc* 5B **60**
Bransgore. *Hants* 3G **15**
Bransholme. *Hull* 1D **94**
Bransley. *Shrp* 3A **60**
Branston. *Leics* 3F **75**
Branston. *Linc* 4H **87**
Branston. *Staf* 3G **73**
Branston Booths. *Linc* 4H **87**
Branstone. *IOW* 4D **16**
Bransty. *Cumb* 3A **102**
Brant Broughton. *Linc* 5G **87**
Brantham. *Suff* 2E **54**
Branthwaite. *Cumb* 1D **102**
(nr. Caldbeck)
Branthwaite. *Cumb* 2B **102**
(nr. Workington)
Brantingham. *E Yor* 2C **94**
Branton. *Nmbd* 3E **121**
Branton. *S Yor* 4G **93**
Branton Green. *N Yor* 3G **99**
Branxholme. *Bord* 3G **119**
Branxton. *Nmbd* 1C **120**
Brassington. *Derbs* 5G **85**
Brasted. *Kent* 5F **39**
Brasted Chart. *Kent* 5F **39**
Brathens. *Abers* 4D **152**
Bratoft. *Linc* 4D **88**
Brattleby. *Linc* 2G **87**
Bratton. *Som* 2C **20**
Bratton. *Telf* 4A **72**
Bratton. *Wilts* 1E **23**
Bratton Clovelly. *Devn* 3E **11**
Bratton Fleming. *Devn* 3G **19**
Bratton Seymour. *Som* 4B **22**
Braughing. *Herts* 3D **53**
Braulen Lodge. *High* 5E **157**
Braunston. *Nptn* 4C **62**
Braunstone Town. *Leic* 5C **74**
Braunston-in-Rutland. *Rut* 5F **75**
Braunton. *Devn* 3E **19**
Brawby. *N Yor* 2B **100**
Brawl. *High* 2A **168**
Brawlbin. *High* 3C **168**
Bray. *Wind* 3A **38**
Braybrooke. *Nptn* 2E **63**
Brayford. *Devn* 3G **19**
Bray Shop. *Corn* 5D **10**
Braystones. *Cumb* 4B **102**
Brayton. *N Yor* 1G **93**
Bray Wick. *Wind* 4G **37**
Brazacott. *Corn* 3C **10**
Brea. *Corn* 4A **6**
Breach. *W Sus* 2F **17**
Breachwood Green. *Herts* 3B **52**
Breacleit. *W Isl* 4D **171**
Breaden Heath. *Shrp* 2G **71**
Breadsall. *Derbs* 1A **74**
Breadstone. *Glos* 5C **48**
Breage. *Corn* 4D **4**
Breakachy. *High* 4G **157**
Breakish. *High* 1E **147**
Bream. *Glos* 5B **48**
Breamore. *Hants* 1G **15**
Bream's Meend. *Glos* 5B **48**
Brean. *Som* 1F **21**
Breanais. *W Isl* 5B **171**
Brearton. *N Yor* 3F **99**
Breascleit. *W Isl* 4E **171**
Breaston. *Derbs* 2B **74**
Brecais Àrd. *High* 1E **147**
Brecais Iosal. *High* 1E **147**
Brechfa. *Carm* 2F **45**
Brechin. *Ang* 3F **145**
Breckles. *Norf* 1B **66**
Brecon. *Powy* 3D **46**
Bredbury. *G Man* 1D **84**
Brede. *E Sus* 4C **28**
Bredenbury. *Here* 5A **60**
Breden's Norton. *Worc* 2E **49**
Bredfield. *Suff* 5E **67**
Bredgar. *Kent* 4C **40**
Bredhurst. *Kent* 4B **40**
Bredicot. *Worc* 5D **60**
Bredon. *Worc* 2E **49**
Bredwardine. *Here* 1G **47**
Breedon on the Hill. *Leics* 3B **74**
Breibhig. *W Isl* 9B **170**
(on Barra)
Breibhig. *W Isl* 4G **171**
(on Isle of Lewis)
Breich. *W Lot* 3C **128**
Breightmet. *G Man* 3F **91**
Breighton. *E Yor* 1H **93**
Breinton. *Here* 2H **47**
Breinton Common. *Here* 2H **47**
Breiwick. *Shet* 7F **173**
Brelston Green. *Here* 3A **48**
Bremhill. *Wilts* 4E **35**
Brenachie. *High* 1B **158**
Brenchley. *Kent* 1A **28**
Brendon. *Devn* 2A **20**
Brent Cross. *G Lon* 2D **38**
Brent Eleigh. *Suff* 1C **54**
Brentford. *G Lon* 3C **38**
Brentingby. *Leics* 4E **75**
Brent Knoll. *Som* 1G **21**
Brent Pelham. *Herts* 2E **53**
Brentwood. *Essx* 1H **39**
Brenzett. *Kent* 3E **28**
Brereton. *Staf* 4E **73**
Brereton Cross. *Staf* 4E **73**
Brereton Green. *Ches E* 4B **84**
Brereton Heath. *Ches E* 4C **84**
Bressingham. *Norf* 2C **66**
Bretby. *Derbs* 3G **73**
Bretford. *Warw* 3B **62**
Bretforton. *Worc* 1F **49**
Bretherdale Head. *Cumb* 4G **103**
Bretherton. *Lanc* 2C **90**
Brettabister. *Shet* 6F **173**
Brettenham. *Norf* 2B **66**
Brettenham. *Suff* 5B **66**
Bretton. *Flin* 4F **83**
Bretton. *Pet* 5A **76**
Brewer Street. *Surr* 5E **39**
Brewlands Bridge. *Ang* 2A **144**
Brewood. *Staf* 5C **72**
Briantspuddle. *Dors* 3D **14**
Bricket Wood. *Herts* 5B **52**
Bricklehampton. *Worc* 1E **49**
Bride. *IOM* 1D **108**
Bridekirk. *Cumb* 1C **102**
Bridell. *Pemb* 1B **44**
Bridestowe. *Devn* 4F **11**
Brideswell. *Abers* 5C **160**
Bridford. *Devn* 4B **12**
Bridfordmills. *Devn* 4B **12**
Bridge. *Corn* 4A **6**
Bridge. *Kent* 5F **41**
Bridge. *Som* 2G **13**
Bridge End. *Bed* 5H **63**
Bridge End. *Cumb* 5D **102**
Bridge End. *Linc* 2A **76**
Bridge End. *Shet* 8E **173**
Bridgefoot. *Ang* 5C **144**
Bridgefoot. *Cumb* 2B **102**
Bridge Green. *Essx* 2E **53**
Bridgehampton. *Som* 4A **22**
Bridge Hewick. *N Yor* 2F **99**
Bridgehill. *Dur* 4D **115**
Bridgemary. *Hants* 2D **16**
Bridgemere. *Ches E* 1B **72**
Bridgemont. *Derbs* 2E **85**
Bridgend. *Abers* 5C **160**
(nr. Huntly)
Bridgend. *Abers* 5H **161**
(nr. Peterhead)
Bridgend. *Ang* 2E **145**
(nr. Brechin)
Bridgend. *Ang* 4C **144**
(nr. Kirriemuir)
Bridgend. *Arg* 4F **133**
(nr. Lochgilphead)
Bridgend. *Arg* 3B **124**
(on Islay)
Bridgend. *B'end* 3C **32**
Bridgend. *Cumb* 3F **103**
Bridgend. *Devn* 4B **8**
Bridgend. *Fife* 2F **137**
Bridgend. *High* 3F **157**
Bridgend. *Mor* 5A **160**
Bridgend. *Per* 1D **136**
Bridgend. *W Lot* 2D **128**
Bridgend of Lintrathen.
Ang 3B **144**
Bridgeness. *Falk* 1D **128**
Bridge of Alford. *Abers* 2C **152**
Bridge of Allan. *Stir* 4G **135**
Bridge of Avon. *Mor* 5F **159**
Bridge of Awe. *Arg* 1H **133**
Bridge of Balgie. *Per* 4C **142**
Bridge of Brown. *High* 1F **151**
Bridge of Cally. *Per* 3A **144**
Bridge of Canny. *Abers* 4D **152**
Bridge of Dee. *Dum* 3E **111**
Bridge of Don. *Aber* 2G **153**
Bridge of Dun. *Ang* 3F **145**
Bridge of Dye. *Abers* 5D **152**
Bridge of Earn. *Per* 2D **136**
Bridge of Ericht. *Per* 3C **142**
Bridge of Feugh. *Abers* 4E **152**
Bridge of Forss. *High* 2C **168**
Bridge of Gairn. *Abers* 4A **152**
Bridge of Gaur. *Per* 3C **142**
Bridge of Muchalls. *Abers* 4F **153**
Bridge of Oich. *High* 3F **149**
Bridge of Orchy. *Arg* 5H **141**
Bridge of Walls. *Shet* 6D **173**
Bridge of Weir. *Ren* 3E **127**
Bridge Reeve. *Devn* 1G **11**
Bridgerule. *Devn* 2C **10**
Bridge Sollers. *Here* 1H **47**
Bridge Street. *Suff* 1B **54**
Bridgetown. *Devn* 2E **9**
Bridgetown. *Som* 3C **20**
Bridge Town. *Warw* 5G **61**
Bridge Trafford. *Ches W* 3G **83**
Bridgeyate. *S Glo* 4B **34**
Bridgham. *Norf* 2B **66**
Bridgnorth. *Shrp* 1B **60**
Bridgtown. *Staf* 5D **73**
Bridgwater. *Som* 3G **21**
Bridister. *Shet* 6D **173**
Bridlington. *E Yor* 3F **101**
Bridport. *Dors* 3H **13**
Bridstow. *Here* 3A **48**
Brierfield. *Lanc* 1G **91**
Brierley. *Glos* 4B **48**
Brierley. *Here* 5G **59**
Brierley. *S Yor* 3E **93**
Brierley Hill. *W Mid* 2D **60**
Brierton. *Hart* 1B **106**
Briestfield. *W Yor* 3C **92**
Brigg. *N Lin* 4D **94**
Briggate. *Norf* 3F **79**
Briggswath. *N Yor* 4F **107**
Brigham. *Cumb* 1B **102**
Brigham. *E Yor* 4E **101**
Brighouse. *W Yor* 2B **92**
Brighstone. *IOW* 4C **16**
Brightgate. *Derbs* 5G **85**
Brighthampton. *Oxon* 5B **50**
Brightholmlee. *S Yor* 1G **85**
Brightley. *Devn* 3G **11**
Brightling. *E Sus* 3A **28**
Brightlingsea. *Essx* 4D **54**
Brighton. *Brig* 5E **27** & **189**
Brighton. *Corn* 3D **6**
Brighton Hill. *Hants* 2E **24**
Brightons. *Falk* 2C **128**
Brightwalton. *W Ber* 4C **36**
Brightwalton Green. *W Ber* 4C **36**
Brightwell. *Suff* 1F **55**
Brightwell Baldwin. *Oxon* 2E **37**
Brightwell-cum-Sotwell.
Oxon 2D **36**
Brigmerston. *Wilts* 2G **23**
Brignall. *Dur* 3D **104**
Brig o'Turk. *Stir* 3E **135**
Brigsley. *NE Lin* 4F **95**
Brigsteer. *Cumb* 1D **97**
Brigstock. *Nptn* 2G **63**
Brill. *Buck* 4E **51**
Brill. *Corn* 4E **5**
Brilley. *Here* 1F **47**
Brimaston. *Pemb* 2D **42**
Brimfield. *Here* 4H **59**
Brimington. *Derbs* 3B **86**
Brimley. *Devn* 5B **12**
Brimpsfield. *Glos* 4E **49**
Brimpton. *W Ber* 5D **36**
Brims. *Orkn* 9B **172**
Brimscombe. *Glos* 5D **48**
Brimstage. *Mers* 2F **83**
Brincliffe. *S Yor* 2H **85**
Brind. *E Yor* 1H **93**
Brindister. *Shet* 8F **173**
Brindle. *Lanc* 2E **90**
Brindley Ford. *Stoke* 5C **84**
Brineton. *Staf* 4C **72**
Bringhurst. *Leics* 1F **63**
Brington. *Cambs* 3H **63**
Brinian. *Orkn* 5D **172**
Briningham. *Norf* 2C **78**
Brinkhill. *Linc* 3C **88**
Brinkley. *Cambs* 5F **65**
Brinklow. *Warw* 3B **62**
Brinkworth. *Wilts* 3F **35**
Brinscall. *Lanc* 2E **91**
Brinscombe. *Som* 1H **21**
Brinsley. *Notts* 1B **74**
Brinsty Common. *Here* 5A **60**
Brinsworth. *S Yor* 2B **86**
Brinton. *Norf* 2C **78**
Brisco. *Cumb* 4F **113**
Brisley. *Norf* 3B **78**
Brislington. *Bris* 4B **34**
Brissenden Green. *Kent* 2D **28**
Bristol. *Bris* 4A **34** & **189**
Bristol International Airport.
N Som 5A **34**
Briston. *Norf* 2C **78**
Britannia. *Lanc* 2G **91**
Britford. *Wilts* 4G **23**
Brithdir. *Cphy* 5E **47**
Brithdir. *Cdgn* 1D **44**
Brithdir. *Gwyn* 4G **69**
Briton Ferry. *Neat* 3G **31**
Britwell Salome. *Oxon* 2E **37**
Brixham. *Torb* 3F **9**
Brixton. *Devn* 3B **8**
Brixton. *G Lon* 3E **39**
Brixton Deverill. *Wilts* 3D **22**
Brixworth. *Nptn* 3E **63**
Brize Norton. *Oxon* 5B **50**
Broad Alley. *Worc* 4C **60**
Broad Blunsdon. *Swin* 2G **35**
Broadbottom. *G Man* 1D **85**
Broadbridge. *W Sus* 2G **17**
Broadbridge Heath. *W Sus* 2C **26**
Broad Campden. *Glos* 2G **49**
Broad Chalke. *Wilts* 4F **23**
Broadclyst. *Devn* 3C **12**
Broadfield. *Inv* 2E **127**
Broadfield. *Pemb* 4F **43**
Broadfield. *W Sus* 2D **26**
Broadford. *High* 1E **147**
Broadford Bridge. *W Sus* 3B **26**
Broad Green. *Cambs* 5F **65**
Broad Green. *C Beds* 1H **51**
Broad Green. *Worc* 3D **61**
(nr. Bromsgrove)
Broad Green. *Worc* 5B **60**
(nr. Worcester)
Broadhaven. *High* 3F **169**
Broad Haven. *Pemb* 3C **42**
Broadheath. *G Man* 2B **84**
Broad Heath. *Staf* 3C **72**
Broadheath. *Worc* 4A **60**
Broadhembury. *Devn* 2E **12**
Broadhempston. *Devn* 2E **9**
Broad Hill. *Cambs* 3E **65**
Broad Hinton. *Wilts* 4G **35**
Broadholm. *Derbs* 1A **74**
Broadholme. *Linc* 3F **87**
Broadlay. *Carm* 5D **44**
Broad Laying. *Hants* 5C **36**
Broadley. *Lanc* 3G **91**
Broadley. *Mor* 2A **160**
Broadley Common. *Essx* 5E **53**
Broad Marston. *Worc* 1G **49**
Broadmayne. *Dors* 4C **14**
Broadmere. *Hants* 2E **24**
Broadmoor. *Pemb* 4E **43**
Broad Oak. *Carm* 3F **45**
Broad Oak. *Cumb* 5C **102**
Broad Oak. *Devn* 3D **12**
Broadoak. *Dors* 3H **13**
(nr. Bridport)
Broad Oak. *Dors* 1C **14**
(nr. Sturminster Newton)
Broad Oak. *E Sus* 4C **28**
(nr. Hastings)
Broad Oak. *E Sus* 3H **27**
(nr. Heathfield)
Broadoak. *Glos* 4B **48**
Broadoak. *Hants* 1C **16**
Broad Oak. *Here* 3H **47**
Broad Oak. *Kent* 4F **41**
Broadrashes. *Mor* 3B **160**
Broadsea. *Abers* 2G **161**
Broad's Green. *Essx* 4G **53**
Broadshard. *Som* 1H **13**
Broadstairs. *Kent* 4H **41**
Broadstone. *Pool* 3F **15**
Broadstone. *Shrp* 2H **59**
Broad Street. *E Sus* 4C **28**
Broad Street. *Kent* 1F **29**
(nr. Ashford)
Broad Street. *Kent* 5C **40**
(nr. Maidstone)
Broad Street Green. *Essx* 5B **54**
Broad, The. *Here* 4G **59**
Broad Town. *Wilts* 4F **35**
Broadwas. *Worc* 5B **60**
Broadwath. *Cumb* 4F **113**
Broadway. *Carm* 5D **45**
(nr. Kidwelly)
Broadway. *Carm* 3G **43**
(nr. Laugharne)
Broadway. *Pemb* 3C **42**
Broadway. *Som* 1G **13**
Broadway. *Suff* 3F **67**
Broadway. *Worc* 2G **49**
Broadwell. *Glos* 4A **48**
(nr. Cinderford)
Broadwell. *Glos* 3H **49**
(nr. Stow-on-the-Wold)
Broadwell. *Oxon* 5A **50**
Broadwell. *Warw* 4B **62**
Broadwell House. *Nmbd* 4C **114**
Broadwey. *Dors* 4B **14**
Broadwindsor. *Dors* 2H **13**
Broadwoodkelly. *Devn* 2G **11**
Broadwoodwidger. *Devn* 4E **11**
Broallan. *High* 4G **157**
Brobury. *Here* 1G **47**
Brochel. *High* 4E **155**
Brockamin. *Worc* 5B **60**
Brockbridge. *Hants* 1E **16**
Brockdish. *Norf* 3E **66**
Brockencote. *Worc* 3C **60**
Brockenhurst. *Hants* 2A **16**
Brocketsbrae. *S Lan* 1H **117**
Brockford Street. *Suff* 4D **66**
Brockhall. *Nptn* 4D **62**
Brockham. *Surr* 1C **26**
Brockhampton. *Glos* 3E **49**
(nr. Bishop's Cleeve)
Brockhampton. *Glos* 3F **49**
(nr. Sevenhampton)
Brockhampton. *Here* 2A **48**
Brockhill. *Bord* 2F **119**
Brockholes. *W Yor* 3B **92**
Brockhouse. *S Yor* 2C **86**
Brockhurst. *Hants* 2D **16**
Brocklesby. *Linc* 3E **95**
Brockley. *N Som* 5H **33**
Brockley Corner. *Suff* 3H **65**
Brockley Green. *Suff* 1H **53**
(nr. Bury St Edmunds)
Brockley Green. *Suff* 5H **65**
(nr. Haverhill)
Brockleymoor. *Cumb* 1F **103**
Brockmoor. *W Mid* 2C **60**
Brockton. *Shrp* 2F **59**
(nr. Bishop's Castle)
Brockton. *Shrp* 5B **72**
(nr. Madeley)
Brockton. *Shrp* 1H **59**
(nr. Much Wenlock)
Brockton. *Shrp* 5F **71**
(nr. Pontesbury)
Brockton. *Staf* 2C **72**
Brockton. *Telf* 4B **72**
Brockweir. *Glos* 5A **48**
Brockworth. *Glos* 4D **49**
Brocton. *Staf* 4D **72**
Brodick. *N Ayr* 2E **123**
Brodie. *Mor* 3D **159**
Brodiesord. *Abers* 3C **160**
Brodsworth. *S Yor* 4F **93**
Brogaig. *High* 2D **154**
Brogborough. *C Beds* 2H **51**
Brokenborough. *Wilts* 3E **35**
Broken Cross. *Ches E* 3C **84**
Bromborough. *Mers* 2F **83**
Bromdon. *Shrp* 2A **60**
Brome. *Suff* 3D **66**
Brome Street. *Suff* 3D **66**
Bromeswell. *Suff* 5F **67**
Bromfield. *Cumb* 5C **112**
Bromfield. *Shrp* 3G **59**
Bromford. *W Mid* 1F **61**
Bromham. *Bed* 5H **63**
Bromham. *Wilts* 5E **35**
Bromley. *G Lon* 4F **39**
Bromley. *Herts* 3E **53**
Bromley. *Shrp* 1B **60**
Bromley Cross. *G Man* 3F **91**
Bromley Green. *Kent* 2D **28**
Bromley Wood. *Staf* 3F **73**
Brompton. *Medw* 4B **40**

Brompton—Burton Lazars

Brompton. *N Yor* 5A **106**
(nr. Northallerton)
Brompton. *N Yor* 1D **100**
(nr. Scarborough)
Brompton. *Shrp* 5H **71**
Brompton-on-Swale. *N Yor* 5F **105**
Brompton Ralph. *Som* 3D **20**
Brompton Regis. *Som* 3C **20**
Bromsash. *Here* 3B **48**
Bromsberrow. *Glos* 2C **48**
Bromsberrow Heath. *Glos* 2C **48**
Bromsgrove. *Worc* 3D **60**
Bromstead Heath. *Staf* 4B **72**
Bromyard. *Here* 5A **60**
Bromyard Downs. *Here* 5A **60**
Bronaber. *Gwyn* 2G **69**
Broncroft. *Shrp* 2H **59**
Brongest. *Cdgn* 1D **44**
Brongwyn. *Cdgn* 1C **44**
Bronington. *Wrex* 2G **71**
Bronllys. *Powy* 2E **47**
Bronnant. *Cdgn* 4F **57**
Bronwydd Arms. *Carm* 3E **45**
Bronydd. *Powy* 1F **47**
Bronygarth. *Shrp* 2E **71**
Brook. *Carm* 4G **43**
Brook. *Devn* 5E **11**
Brook. *Hants* 1A **16**
(nr. Cadnam)
Brook. *Hants* 4B **24**
(nr. Romsey)
Brook. *IOW* 4B **16**
Brook. *Kent* 1E **29**
Brook. *Surr* 1B **26**
(nr. Guildford)
Brook. *Surr* 2A **26**
(nr. Haslemere)
Brooke. *Norf* 1E **67**
Brooke. *Rut* 5F **75**
Brookend. *Glos* 5B **48**
Brook End. *Worc* 1D **48**
Brookfield. *Lanc* 1D **90**
Brookfield. *Ren* 3F **127**
Brookhouse. *Lanc* 3E **97**
Brookhouse Green. *Ches E* 4C **84**
Brookhouses. *Staf* 1D **73**
Brookhurst. *Mers* 2F **83**
Brookland. *Kent* 3D **28**
Brooklands. *G Man* 1B **84**
Brooklands. *Shrp* 1H **71**
Brookmans Park. *Herts* 5C **52**
Brooks. *Powy* 1D **58**
Brooksby. *Leics* 4D **74**
Brooks Green. *W Sus* 3C **26**
Brook Street. *Essx* 1G **39**
Brook Street. *Kent* 2D **28**
Brook Street. *W Sus* 3E **27**
Brookthorpe. *Glos* 4D **48**
Brookville. *Norf* 1G **65**
Brookwood. *Surr* 5A **38**
Broom. *C Beds* 1B **52**
Broom. *Fife* 3F **137**
Broom. *Warw* 5E **61**
Broome. *Norf* 1F **67**
Broome. *Shrp* 1H **59**
(nr. Cardington)
Broome. *Shrp* 2G **59**
(nr. Craven Arms)
Broome. *Worc* 3D **60**
Broomedge. *Warr* 2B **84**
Broomend. *Abers* 2E **153**
Broome Park. *Nmbd* 3F **121**
Broomer's Corner. *W Sus* 3C **26**
Broomfield. *Abers* 5G **161**
Broomfield. *Essx* 4H **53**
Broomfield. *Kent* 4F **41**
(nr. Herne Bay)
Broomfield. *Kent* 5C **40**
(nr. Maidstone)
Broomfield. *Som* 3F **21**
Broomfleet. *E Yor* 2B **94**
Broom Green. *Norf* 3B **78**
Broomhall. *Ches E* 1A **72**
Broomhall. *Wind* 4A **38**
Broomhaugh. *Nmbd* 3D **114**
Broomhill. *Bris* 4B **34**
Broom Hill. *Dors* 2F **15**
Broomhill. *High* 1D **151**
(nr. Grantown-on-Spey)
Broomhill. *High* 1B **158**
(nr. Invergordon)
Broomhill. *Norf* 5F **77**
Broomhill. *S Yor* 4E **93**
Broom Hill. *Worc* 3D **60**
Broomhillbank. *Dum* 5D **118**
Broomholm. *Norf* 2F **79**
Broomlands. *Dum* 4C **118**
Broomley. *Nmbd* 3D **114**
Broom of Moy. *Mor* 3E **159**
Broompark. *Dur* 5F **115**
Broom's Green. *Glos* 2C **48**
Brora. *High* 3G **165**
Broseley. *Shrp* 5A **72**
Brotherhouse Bar. *Linc* 4B **76**
Brotheridge Green. *Worc* 1D **48**
Brotherlee. *Dur* 1C **104**
Brothertoft. *Linc* 1B **76**
Brotherton. *N Yor* 2E **93**
Brotton. *Red C* 2D **107**
Broubster. *High* 2C **168**
Brough. *Cumb* 3A **104**
Brough. *Derbs* 2F **85**
Brough. *E Yor* 2C **94**
Brough. *High* 1E **169**
Brough. *Notts* 5F **87**
Brough. *Orkn* 6C **172**
(nr. Finstown)
Brough. *Orkn* 9D **172**
(nr. St Margaret's Hope)
Brough. *Shet* 6F **173**
(nr. Benston)
Brough. *Shet* 4F **173**
(nr. Booth of Toft)
Brough. *Shet* 7G **173**
(on Bressay)
Brough. *Shet* 5G **173**
(on Whalsay)
Broughall. *Shrp* 1H **71**
Brougham. *Cumb* 2G **103**
Brough Lodge. *Shet* 2G **173**
Brough Sowerby. *Cumb* 3A **104**
Broughton. *Cambs* 3B **64**
Broughton. *Flin* 4F **83**
Broughton. *Hants* 3B **24**
Broughton. *Lanc* 1D **90**
Broughton. *Mil* 2G **51**
Broughton. *Nptn* 3F **63**
Broughton. *N Lin* 4C **94**
Broughton. *N Yor* 2B **100**
(nr. Malton)
Broughton. *N Yor* 4B **98**
(nr. Skipton)
Broughton. *Orkn* 3D **172**
Broughton. *Oxon* 2C **50**
Broughton. *Bord* 1D **118**
Broughton. *Staf* 2B **72**
Broughton. *V Glam* 4C **32**
Broughton Astley. *Leics* 1C **62**
Broughton Beck. *Cumb* 1B **96**
Broughton Cross. *Cumb* 1B **102**
Broughton Gifford. *Wilts* 5D **35**
Broughton Green. *Worc* 4D **60**
Broughton Hackett. *Worc* 5D **60**
Broughton in Furness.
Cumb 1B **96**
Broughton Mills. *Cumb* 5D **102**
Broughton Moor. *Cumb* 1B **102**
Broughton Park. *G Man* 4G **91**
Broughton Poggs. *Oxon* 5H **49**
Broughtown. *Orkn* 3F **172**
Broughty Ferry. *D'dee* 5D **144**
Browland. *Shet* 6D **173**
Brownber. *Cumb* 4A **104**
Brownbread Street. *E Sus* 4A **28**
Brown Candover. *Hants* 3D **24**
Brown Edge. *Lanc* 3B **90**
Brown Edge. *Staf* 5D **84**
Brownhill. *Bkbn* 1E **91**
Brownhill. *Shrp* 3G **71**
Brownhills. *Shrp* 2A **72**
Brownhills. *W Mid* 5E **73**
Brown Knowl. *Ches W* 5G **83**
Brownlow. *Ches E* 4C **84**
Brownlow Heath. *Ches E* 4C **84**
Brown's Green. *W Mid* 1E **61**
Brownshill. *Glos* 5D **49**
Brownston. *Devn* 3C **8**
Brownstone. *Devn* 2A **12**
Browston Green. *Norf* 5G **79**
Broxa. *N Yor* 5G **107**
Broxbourne. *Herts* 5D **52**
Broxburn. *E Lot* 2C **130**
Broxburn. *W Lot* 2D **129**
Broxholme. *Linc* 3G **87**
Broxted. *Essx* 3F **53**
Broxton. *Ches W* 5G **83**
Broxwood. *Here* 5F **59**
Broyle Side. *E Sus* 4F **27**
Brù. *W Isl* 3F **171**
Bruach Mairi. *W Isl* 4G **171**
Bruairnis. *W Isl* 8C **170**
Bruan. *High* 5F **169**
Bruar Lodge. *Per* 1F **143**
Brucehill. *W Dun* 2E **127**
Brucklay. *Abers* 3G **161**
Bruera. *Ches W* 4G **83**
Bruern Abbey. *Oxon* 3A **50**
Bruichladdich. *Arg* 3A **124**
Bruisyard. *Suff* 4F **67**
Bruisyard Street. *Suff* 4F **67**
Brumby. *N Lin* 4B **94**
Brund. *Staf* 4F **85**
Brundall. *Norf* 5F **79**
Brundish. *Norf* 1F **67**
Brundish. *Suff* 4E **67**
Brundish Street. *Suff* 3E **67**
Brunery. *High* 1B **140**
Brunswick Village. *Tyne* 2F **115**
Brunthwaite. *W Yor* 5C **98**
Bruntingthorpe. *Leics* 1D **62**
Brunton. *Fife* 1F **137**
Brunton. *Nmbd* 2G **121**
Brunton. *Wilts* 1H **23**
Brushford. *Devn* 2G **11**
Brushford. *Som* 4C **20**
Brusta. *W Isl* 1E **170**
Bruton. *Som* 3B **22**
Bryanston. *Dors* 2D **15**
Bryant's Bottom. *Buck* 2G **37**
Brydekirk. *Dum* 2C **112**
Brymbo. *Cnwy* 3H **81**
Brymbo. *Wrex* 5E **83**
Brympton D'Evercy. *Som* 1A **14**
Bryn. *Carm* 5F **45**
Bryn. *G Man* 4D **90**
Bryn. *Neat* 2B **32**
Bryn. *Shrp* 2E **59**
Brynamman. *Carm* 4H **45**
Brynberian. *Pemb* 1F **43**
Brynbryddan. *Neat* 2A **32**
Bryncae. *Rhon* 3C **32**
Bryncethin. *B'end* 3C **32**
Bryncir. *Gwyn* 1D **69**
Bryn-coch. *Neat* 3G **31**
Bryncroes. *Gwyn* 2B **68**
Bryncrug. *Gwyn* 5F **69**
Bryn Du. *IOA* 3C **80**
Bryn Eden. *Gwyn* 3G **69**
Bryneglwys. *Den* 1D **70**
Bryn Eglwys. *Gwyn* 4F **81**
Brynford. *Flin* 3D **82**
Bryn Gates. *G Man* 4D **90**
Bryn Golau. *Rhon* 3D **32**
Bryngwran. *IOA* 3C **80**
Bryngwyn. *Mon* 5G **47**
Bryngwyn. *Powy* 1E **47**
Bryn-henllan. *Pemb* 1E **43**
Brynhoffnant. *Cdgn* 5C **56**
Bryn-llwyn. *Flin* 2C **82**
Brynllywarch. *Powy* 2D **58**
Bryn-mawr. *Blae* 4E **47**
Bryn-mawr. *Gwyn* 2B **68**
Brynmenyn. *B'end* 3C **32**
Brynmill. *Swan* 3F **31**
Brynna. *Rhon* 3C **32**
Brynrefail. *Gwyn* 4E **81**
Brynrefail. *IOA* 2D **81**
Brynsadler. *Rhon* 3D **32**
Bryn-Saith Marchog. *Den* 5C **82**
Brynsiencyn. *IOA* 4D **81**
Brynteg. *IOA* 2D **81**
Brynteg. *Wrex* 5F **83**
Brynygwenyn. *Mon* 4G **47**
Bryn-y-maen. *Cnwy* 3H **81**
Buaile nam Bodach. *W Isl* 8C **170**
Bualintur. *High* 1C **146**
Bubbenhall. *Warw* 3A **62**
Bubwith. *E Yor* 1H **93**
Buccleuch. *Bord* 3F **119**
Buchanan Smithy. *Stir* 1F **127**
Buchanhaven. *Abers* 4H **161**
Buchanty. *Per* 1B **136**
Buchany. *Stir* 3G **135**
Buchley. *E Dun* 2G **127**
Buchlyvie. *Stir* 4E **135**
Buckabank. *Cumb* 5E **113**
Buckden. *Cambs* 4A **64**
Buckden. *N Yor* 2B **98**
Buckenham. *Norf* 5F **79**
Buckerell. *Devn* 2E **13**
Buckfast. *Devn* 2D **8**
Buckfastleigh. *Devn* 2D **8**
Buckhaven. *Fife* 4F **137**
Buckholm. *Bord* 1G **119**
Buckholt. *Here* 4A **48**
Buckhorn Weston. *Dors* 4C **22**
Buckhurst Hill. *Essx* 1F **39**
Buckie. *Mor* 2B **160**
Buckingham. *Buck* 2E **51**
Buckland. *Buck* 4G **51**
Buckland. *Glos* 2F **49**
Buckland. *Here* 5H **59**
Buckland. *Herts* 2D **52**
Buckland. *Kent* 1H **29**
Buckland. *Oxon* 2B **36**
Buckland. *Surr* 5D **38**
Buckland Brewer. *Devn* 4E **19**
Buckland Common. *Buck* 5H **51**
Buckland Dinham. *Som* 1C **22**
Buckland Filleigh. *Devn* 2E **11**
Buckland in the Moor. *Devn* 5H **11**
Buckland Monachorum.
Devn 2A **8**
Buckland Newton. *Dors* 2B **14**
Buckland Ripers. *Dors* 4B **14**
Buckland St Mary. *Som* 1F **13**
Buckland-tout-Saints. *Devn* 4D **8**
Bucklebury. *W Ber* 4D **36**
Bucklegate. *Linc* 2C **76**
Buckleigh. *Devn* 4E **19**
Bucklers Hard. *Hants* 3C **16**
Bucklesham. *Suff* 1F **55**
Buckley. *Flin* 4E **83**
Buckley Green. *Warw* 4F **61**
Buckley Hill. *Mers* 1F **83**
Bucklow Hill. *Ches E* 2B **84**
Buckminster. *Leics* 3F **75**
Bucknall. *Linc* 4A **88**
Bucknall. *Stoke* 1D **72**
Bucknell. *Oxon* 3D **50**
Bucknell. *Shrp* 3F **59**
Buckpool. *Mor* 2B **160**
Bucksburn. *Aber* 3F **153**
Buck's Cross. *Devn* 4D **18**
Bucks Green. *W Sus* 2B **26**
Buckshaw Village. *Lanc* 2D **90**
Bucks Hill. *Herts* 5A **52**
Bucks Horn Oak. *Hants* 2G **25**
Buck's Mills. *Devn* 4D **18**
Buckton. *E Yor* 2F **101**
Buckton. *Here* 3F **59**
Buckton. *Nmbd* 1E **121**
Buckton Vale. *G Man* 4H **91**
Buckworth. *Cambs* 3A **64**
Budby. *Notts* 4D **86**
Bude. *Corn* 2C **10**
Budge's Shop. *Corn* 3H **7**
Budlake. *Devn* 2C **12**
Budle. *Nmbd* 1F **121**
Budleigh Salterton. *Devn* 4D **12**
Budock Water. *Corn* 5B **6**
Buerton. *Ches E* 1A **72**
Buffler's Holt. *Buck* 2E **51**
Bugbrooke. *Nptn* 5D **62**
Buglawton. *Ches E* 4C **84**
Bugle. *Corn* 3E **6**
Bugthorpe. *E Yor* 4B **100**
Buildwas. *Shrp* 5A **72**
Builth Road. *Powy* 5C **58**
Builth Wells. *Powy* 5C **58**
Bulbourne. *Herts* 4H **51**
Bulby. *Linc* 3H **75**
Bulcote. *Notts* 1D **74**
Buldoo. *High* 2B **168**
Bulford. *Wilts* 2G **23**
Bulford Camp. *Wilts* 2G **23**
Bulkeley. *Ches E* 5H **83**
Bulkington. *Warw* 2A **62**
Bulkington. *Wilts* 1E **23**
Bulkworthy. *Devn* 1D **11**
Bullamoor. *N Yor* 5A **106**
Bull Bay. *IOA* 1D **80**
Bullbridge. *Derbs* 5A **86**
Bullgill. *Cumb* 1B **102**
Bull Hill. *Hants* 3B **16**
Bullinghope. *Here* 2A **48**
Bull's Green. *Herts* 4C **52**
Bullwood. *Arg* 2C **126**
Bulmer. *Essx* 1B **54**
Bulmer. *N Yor* 3A **100**
Bulmer Tye. *Essx* 2B **54**
Bulphan. *Thur* 2H **39**
Bulverhythe. *E Sus* 5B **28**
Bulwark. *Abers* 4G **161**
Bulwell. *Nott* 1C **74**
Bulwick. *Nptn* 1G **63**
Bumble's Green. *Essx* 5E **53**
Bun Abhainn Eadarra. *W Isl* 7D **171**
Bunacaimb. *High* 5E **147**
Bun a' Mhuillinn. *W Isl* 7C **170**
Bunarkaig. *High* 5D **148**
Bunbury. *Ches E* 5H **83**
Bunchrew. *High* 4A **158**
Bundalloch. *High* 1A **148**
Buness. *Shet* 1H **173**
Bunessan. *Arg* 1A **132**
Bungay. *Suff* 2F **67**
Bunkegivie. *High* 2H **149**
Bunker's Hill. *Cambs* 5D **76**
Bunkers Hill. *Linc* 5B **88**
Bunker's Hill. *Norf* 5H **79**
Bunloit. *High* 1H **149**
Bunnahabhain. *Arg* 2C **124**
Bunny. *Notts* 3C **74**
Bunoich. *High* 3F **149**
Bunree. *High* 2E **141**
Bunroy. *High* 5E **149**
Buntait. *High* 5F **157**
Buntingford. *Herts* 3D **52**
Buntings Green. *Essx* 2B **54**
Bunwell. *Norf* 1D **66**
Burbage. *Derbs* 3E **85**
Burbage. *Leics* 1B **62**
Burbage. *Wilts* 5H **35**
Burcher. *Here* 4F **59**
Burchett's Green. *Wind* 3G **37**
Burcombe. *Wilts* 3F **23**
Burcot. *Oxon* 2D **36**
Burcote. *Shrp* 1B **60**
Burcott. *Buck* 3G **51**
Burcott. *Som* 2A **22**
Burdale. *N Yor* 3C **100**
Burdrop. *Oxon* 2B **50**
Bures. *Suff* 2C **54**
Burford. *Oxon* 4A **50**
Burford. *Shrp* 4H **59**
Burf, The. *Worc* 4C **60**
Burg. *Arg* 4E **139**
Burgate Great Green. *Suff* 3C **66**
Burgate Little Green. *Suff* 3C **66**
Burgess Hill. *W Sus* 4E **27**
Burgh. *Suff* 5E **67**
Burgh by Sands. *Cumb* 4E **113**
Burgh Castle. *Norf* 5G **79**
Burghclere. *Hants* 5C **36**
Burghead. *Mor* 2F **159**
Burghfield. *W Ber* 5E **37**
Burghfield Common. *W Ber* 5E **37**
Burghfield Hill. *W Ber* 5E **37**
Burgh Heath. *Surr* 5D **38**
Burghill. *Here* 1H **47**
Burgh le Marsh. *Linc* 4E **89**
Burgh Muir. *Abers* 2E **153**
Burgh next Aylsham. *Norf* 3E **78**
Burgh on Bain. *Linc* 2B **88**
Burgh St Margaret. *Norf* 4G **79**
Burgh St Peter. *Norf* 1G **67**
Burghwallis. *S Yor* 3F **93**
Burgie. *Mor* 3E **159**
Burham. *Kent* 4B **40**
Buriton. *Hants* 4F **25**
Burland. *Ches E* 5A **84**
Burland. *Shet* 8E **173**
Burlawn. *Corn* 2D **6**
Burleigh. *Brac* 3A **38**
Burleigh. *Glos* 5D **48**
Burlescombe. *Devn* 1D **12**
Burleston. *Dors* 3C **14**
Burlestone. *Devn* 4E **9**
Burley. *Hants* 2H **15**
Burley. *Rut* 4F **75**
Burley. *W Yor* 1C **92**
Burley Gate. *Here* 1A **48**
Burley in Wharfedale. *W Yor* 5D **98**
Burley Street. *Hants* 2H **15**
Burley Woodhead. *W Yor* 5D **98**
Burlingjobb. *Powy* 5E **59**
Burlton. *Shrp* 3G **71**
Burmantofts. *W Yor* 1D **92**
Burmarsh. *Kent* 2F **29**
Burmington. *Warw* 2A **50**
Burn. *N Yor* 2F **93**
Burnage. *G Man* 1C **84**
Burnaston. *Derbs* 2G **73**
Burnbanks. *Cumb* 3G **103**
Burnby. *E Yor* 5C **100**
Burncross. *S Yor* 1H **85**
Burneside. *Cumb* 5G **103**
Burness. *Orkn* 3F **172**
Burneston. *N Yor* 1F **99**
Burnett. *Bath* 5B **34**
Burnfoot. *E Ayr* 4D **116**
Burnfoot. *Per* 3B **136**
Burnfoot. *Bord* 3H **119**
(nr. Hawick)
Burnfoot. *Bord* 3G **119**
(nr. Roberton)
Burngreave. *S Yor* 2A **86**
Burnham. *Buck* 2A **38**
Burnham. *N Lin* 3D **94**
Burnham Deepdale. *Norf* 1H **77**
Burnham Green. *Herts* 4C **52**
Burnham Market. *Norf* 1H **77**
Burnham Norton. *Norf* 1H **77**
Burnham-on-Crouch. *Essx* 1D **40**
Burnham-on-Sea. *Som* 2G **21**
Burnham Overy Staithe.
Norf 1H **77**
Burnham Overy Town. *Norf* 1H **77**
Burnham Thorpe. *Norf* 1A **78**
Burnhaven. *Abers* 4H **161**
Burnhead. *Dum* 5A **118**
Burnhervie. *Abers* 2E **153**
Burnhill Green. *Staf* 5B **72**
Burnhope. *Dur* 5E **115**
Burnhouse. *N Ayr* 4E **127**
Burniston. *N Yor* 5H **107**
Burnlee. *W Yor* 4B **92**
Burnley. *Lanc* 1G **91**
Burnleydam. *Ches E* 1A **72**
Burnmouth. *Bord* 3F **131**
Burn Naze. *Lanc* 5C **96**
Burn of Cambus. *Stir* 3G **135**
Burnopfield. *Dur* 4E **115**
Burnsall. *N Yor* 3C **98**
Burnside. *Ang* 3E **145**
Burnside. *E Ayr* 3E **117**
Burnside. *Per* 3D **136**
Burnside. *Shet* 4D **173**
Burnside. *S Lan* 4H **127**
Burnside. *W Lot* 2D **129**
(nr. Broxburn)
Burnside. *W Lot* 2D **128**
(nr. Winchburgh)
Burntcommon. *Surr* 5B **38**
Burntheath. *Derbs* 2G **73**
Burnt Heath. *Essx* 3D **54**
Burnt Hill. *W Ber* 4D **36**
Burnt Houses. *Dur* 2E **105**
Burntisland. *Fife* 1F **129**
Burnt Oak. *G Lon* 1D **38**
Burnton. *E Ayr* 4D **117**
Burntstalk. *Norf* 2G **77**
Burntwood. *Staf* 5E **73**
Burntwood Green. *Staf* 5E **73**
Burnt Yates. *N Yor* 3E **99**
Burnwynd. *Edin* 3E **129**
Burpham. *Surr* 5B **38**
Burpham. *W Sus* 5B **26**
Burradon. *Nmbd* 4D **121**
Burradon. *Tyne* 2F **115**
Burrafirth. *Shet* 1H **173**
Burragarth. *Shet* 1G **173**
Burras. *Corn* 5A **6**
Burraton. *Corn* 3A **8**
Burravoe. *Shet* 3E **173**
(nr. North Roe)
Burravoe. *Shet* 5E **173**
(on Mainland)
Burravoe. *Shet* 4G **173**
(on Yell)
Burray Village. *Orkn* 8D **172**
Burrells. *Cumb* 3H **103**
Burrelton. *Per* 5A **144**
Burridge. *Devn* 2G **13**
Burridge. *Hants* 1D **16**
Burrigill. *High* 5E **169**
Burrill. *N Yor* 1E **99**
Burringham. *N Lin* 4B **94**
Burrington. *Devn* 1G **11**
Burrington. *Here* 3G **59**
Burrington. *N Som* 1H **21**
Burrough End. *Cambs* 5F **65**
Burrough Green. *Cambs* 5F **65**
Burrough on the Hill. *Leics* 4E **75**
Burroughston. *Orkn* 5E **172**
Burrow. *Devn* 4D **12**
Burrow. *Som* 2C **20**
Burrowbridge. *Som* 4G **21**
Burrowhill. *Surr* 4A **38**
Burry. *Swan* 3D **30**
Burry Green. *Swan* 3D **30**
Burry Port. *Carm* 5E **45**
Burscough. *Lanc* 3C **90**
Burscough Bridge. *Lanc* 3C **90**
Bursea. *E Yor* 1B **94**
Burshill. *E Yor* 5E **101**
Bursledon. *Hants* 2C **16**
Burslem. *Stoke* 1C **72**
Burstall. *Suff* 1D **54**
Burstock. *Dors* 2H **13**
Burston. *Devn* 2H **11**
Burston. *Norf* 2D **66**
Burston. *Staf* 2D **72**
Burstow. *Surr* 1E **27**
Burstwick. *E Yor* 2F **95**
Burtersett. *N Yor* 1A **98**
Burtholme. *Cumb* 3G **113**
Burthorpe. *Suff* 4G **65**
Burthwaite. *Cumb* 5F **113**
Burtle. *Som* 2H **21**
Burtoft. *Linc* 2B **76**
Burton. *Ches W* 4H **83**
(nr. Kelsall)
Burton. *Ches W* 3F **83**
(nr. Neston)
Burton. *Dors* 3G **15**
(nr. Christchurch)
Burton. *Dors* 3B **14**
(nr. Dorchester)
Burton. *Nmbd* 1F **121**
Burton. *Pemb* 4D **43**
Burton. *Som* 2E **21**
Burton. *Wilts* 4D **34**
(nr. Chippenham)
Burton. *Wilts* 3D **22**
(nr. Warminster)
Burton. *Wrex* 5F **83**
Burton Agnes. *E Yor* 3F **101**
Burton Bradstock. *Dors* 4H **13**
Burton-by-Lincoln. *Linc* 3G **87**
Burton Coggles. *Linc* 3G **75**
Burton Constable. *E Yor* 1E **95**
Burton Corner. *Linc* 1C **76**
Burton End. *Cambs* 1G **53**
Burton End. *Essx* 3F **53**
Burton Fleming. *E Yor* 2E **101**
Burton Green. *W Mid* 3G **61**
Burton Green. *Wrex* 5F **83**
Burton Hastings. *Warw* 2B **62**
Burton-in-Kendal. *Cumb* 2E **97**
Burton in Lonsdale. *N Yor* 2F **97**
Burton Joyce. *Notts* 1D **74**
Burton Latimer. *Nptn* 3G **63**
Burton Lazars. *Leics* 4E **75**

Burton Leonard—Carrow Hill

Burton Leonard. *N Yor* 3F 99
Burton on the Wolds. *Leics* 3C 74
Burton Overy. *Leics* 1D 62
Burton Pedwardine. *Linc* 1A 76
Burton Pidsea. *E Yor* 1F 95
Burton Salmon. *N Yor* 2E 93
Burton's Green. *Essx* 3B 54
Burton Stather. *N Lin* 3B 94
Burton upon Stather. *N Lin* 3B 94
Burton upon Trent. *Staf* 3G 73
Burton Wolds. *Leics* 3D 74
Burtonwood. *Warr* 1H 83
Burwardsley. *Ches W* 5H 83
Burwarton. *Shrp* 2A 60
Burwash. *E Sus* 3A 28
Burwash Common. *E Sus* 3H 27
Burwash Weald. *E Sus* 3A 28
Burwell. *Cambs* 4E 65
Burwell. *Linc* 3C 88
Burwen. *IOA* 1D 80
Burwick. *Orkn* 9D 172
Bury. *Cambs* 2B 64
Bury. *G Man* 3G 91
Bury. *Som* 4C 20
Bury. *W Sus* 4B 26
Bury End. *Worc* 2F 49
Bury Green. *Herts* 3E 53
Bury Hill. *S Glo* 3C 34
Bury St Edmunds. *Suff* 4A 66
Burythorpe. *N Yor* 3B 100
Busbridge. *Surr* 1A 26
Busby. *E Ren* 4G 127
Busby. *Per* 1C 136
Buscot. *Oxon* 2H 35
Bush. *Corn* 2C 10
Bush Bank. *Here* 5G 59
Bushbury. *W Mid* 5D 72
Bushby. *Leics* 5D 74
Bushey. *Dors* 4E 15
Bushey. *Herts* 1C 38
Bushey Heath. *Herts* 1C 38
Bush Green. *Norf* 1C 66
(nr. Attleborough)
Bush Green. *Norf* 2E 66
(nr. Harleston)
Bush Green. *Suff* 5B 66
Bushley. *Worc* 2D 48
Bushley Green. *Worc* 2D 48
Bushmead. *Bed* 4A 64
Bushmoor. *Shrp* 2G 59
Bushton. *Wilts* 4F 35
Bushy Common. *Norf* 4B 78
Busk. *Cumb* 5H 113
Buslingthorpe. *Linc* 2H 87
Bussage. *Glos* 5D 49
Bussex. *Som* 3G 21
Busta. *Shet* 5E 173
Bustard Green. *Essx* 3G 53
Butcher's Cross. *E Sus* 3G 27
Butcombe. *N Som* 5A 34
Bute Town. *Cphy* 5E 46
Butleigh. *Som* 3A 22
Butleigh Wootton. *Som* 3A 22
Butlers Marston. *Warw* 5H 61
Butley. *Suff* 5F 67
Butley High Corner. *Suff* 1G 55
Butlocks Heath. *Hants* 2C 16
Butterburn. *Cumb* 2H 113
Buttercrambe. *N Yor* 4B 100
Butterknowle. *Dur* 2E 105
Butterleigh. *Devn* 2C 12
Buttermere. *Cumb* 3C 102
Buttermere. *Wilts* 5B 36
Buttershaw. *W Yor* 2B 92
Butterstone. *Per* 4H 143
Butterton. *Staf* 5E 85
(nr. Leek)
Butterton. *Staf* 1C 72
(nr. Stoke-on-Trent)
Butterwick. *Dur* 2A 106
Butterwick. *Linc* 1C 76
Butterwick. *N Yor* 2B 100
(nr. Malton)
Butterwick. *N Yor* 2D 101
(nr. Weaverthorpe)
Butteryhaugh. *Nmbd* 5A 120
Butt Green. *Ches E* 5A 84
Buttington. *Powy* 5E 71
Buttonbridge. *Shrp* 3B 60
Buttonoak. *Shrp* 3B 60
Buttsash. *Hants* 2C 16
Butt's Green. *Essx* 5A 54
Butt Yeats. *Lanc* 3E 97
Buxhall. *Suff* 5C 66
Buxted. *E Sus* 3F 27
Buxton. *Derbs* 3E 85
Buxton. *Norf* 3E 79
Buxworth. *Derbs* 2E 85
Bwcle. *Flin* 4E 83
Bwlch. *Powy* 3E 47
Bwlchderwin. *Gwyn* 1D 68
Bwlchgwyn. *Wrex* 5E 83
Bwlch-Llan. *Cdgn* 5E 57
Bwlchnewydd. *Carm* 3D 44
Bwlchtocyn. *Gwyn* 3C 68
Bwlch-y-cibau. *Powy* 4D 70
Bwlchyddar. *Powy* 3D 70
Bwlch-y-fadfa. *Cdgn* 1E 45
Bwlch-y-ffridd. *Powy* 1C 58
Bwlch y Garreg. *Powy* 1C 58
Bwlch-y-groes. *Pemb* 1G 43
Bwlch-yr-haiarn. *Cnwy* 5G 81
Bwlch-y-sarnau. *Powy* 3C 58
Bybrook. *Kent* 1E 28
Byermoor. *Tyne* 4E 115
Byers Garth. *Dur* 5G 115
Byers Green. *Dur* 1F 105
Byfield. *Nptn* 5C 62
Byfleet. *Surr* 4B 38
Byford. *Here* 1G 47
Bygrave. *Herts* 2C 52
Byker. *Tyne* 3F 115
Byland Abbey. *N Yor* 2H 99
Bylchau. *Cnwy* 4B 82
Byley. *Ches W* 4B 84
Bynea. *Carm* 3E 31
Byram. *N Yor* 2E 93
Byrness. *Nmbd* 4B 120
Bystock. *Devn* 4D 12
Bythorn. *Cambs* 3H 63
Byton. *Here* 4F 59
Bywell. *Nmbd* 3D 114
Byworth. *W Sus* 3A 26

C

Cabharstadh. *W Isl* 6F 171
Cabourne. *Linc* 4E 95
Cabrach. *Arg* 3C 124
Cabrach. *Mor* 1A 152
Cabus. *Lanc* 5D 97
Cadbury. *Devn* 2C 12
Cadder. *E Dun* 2H 127
Caddington. *C Beds* 4A 52
Caddonfoot. *Bord* 1G 119
Cadeby. *Leics* 5B 74
Cadeby. *S Yor* 4F 93
Cadeleigh. *Devn* 2C 12
Cade Street. *E Sus* 3H 27
Cadgwith. *Corn* 5E 5
Cadham. *Fife* 3E 137
Cadishead. *G Man* 1B 84
Cadle. *Swan* 3F 31
Cadley. *Lanc* 1D 90
Cadley. *Wilts* 1H 23
(nr. Ludgershall)
Cadley. *Wilts* 5H 35
(nr. Marlborough)
Cadmore End. *Buck* 2F 37
Cadnam. *Hants* 1A 16
Cadney. *N Lin* 4D 94
Cadole. *Flin* 4E 82
Cadoxton-Juxta-Neath. *Neat* 2A 32
Cadwell. *Herts* 2B 52
Cadwst. *Den* 2C 70
Cadzow. *S Lan* 4A 128
Caeathro. *Gwyn* 4E 81
Caehopkin. *Powy* 4B 46
Caenby. *Linc* 2H 87
Caenn-na-Cleithe. *W Isl* 8D 171
Caerau. *B'end* 2B 32
Caerau. *Card* 4E 33
Cae'r-bont. *Powy* 4B 46
Cae'r-bryn. *Carm* 4F 45
Caerdeon. *Gwyn* 4F 69
Caerdydd. *Card* 4E 33 & **Cardiff** 191
Caerfarchell. *Pemb* 2B 42
Caerffili. *Cphy* 3E 33
Caerfyrddin. *Carm* 4E 45
Caergeiliog. *IOA* 3C 80
Caergwrle. *Flin* 5F 83
Caergybi. *IOA* 2B 80
Caerlaverock. *Per* 2A 136
Caerleon. *Newp* 2G 33
Caerlleon. *Carm* 2G 43
Caerllion. *Newp* 2G 33
Caernarfon. *Gwyn* 4D 81 & 190
Caerphilly. *Cphy* 3E 33
Caersws. *Powy* 1C 58
Caerwedros. *Cdgn* 5C 56
Caerwent. *Mon* 2H 33
Caerwys. *Flin* 3D 82
Caim. *IOA* 2F 81
Caio. *Carm* 2G 45
Cairinis. *W Isl* 2D 170
Cairisiadar. *W Isl* 4D 171
Cairminis. *W Isl* 9C 171
Cairnbaan. *Arg* 4F 133
Cairnbulg. *Abers* 2H 161
Cairncross. *Ang* 1D 145
Cairndow. *Arg* 2A 134
Cairness. *Abers* 2H 161
Cairneyhill. *Fife* 1D 128
Cairngarroch. *Dum* 5F 109
Cairnhill. *Abers* 5D 160
Cairnie. *Abers* 4B 160
Cairnorrie. *Abers* 4F 161
Cairnryan. *Dum* 3F 109
Cairston. *Orkn* 6B 172
Caister-on-Sea. *Norf* 4H 79
Caistor. *Linc* 4E 95
Caistor St Edmund. *Norf* 5E 79
Caistron. *Nmbd* 4D 121
Cakebole. *Worc* 3C 60
Calais Street. *Suff* 1C 54
Calanais. *W Isl* 4E 171
Calbost. *W Isl* 6G 171
Calbourne. *IOW* 4C 16
Calceby. *Linc* 3C 88
Calcot. *Glos* 4F 49
Calcot Row. *W Ber* 4E 37
Calcott. *Kent* 4F 41
Calcott. *Shrp* 4G 71
Caldback. *Shet* 1H 173
Caldbeck. *Cumb* 1E 102
Caldbergh. *N Yor* 1C 98
Caldecote. *Cambs* 5C 64
(nr. Cambridge)
Caldecote. *Cambs* 2A 64
(nr. Peterborough)
Caldecote. *Herts* 2C 52
Caldecote. *Warw* 1A 62
Caldecott. *Nptn* 4G 63
Caldecott. *Oxon* 2C 36
Caldecott. *Rut* 1F 63
Calderbank. *N Lan* 3A 128
Calder Bridge. *Cumb* 4B 102
Calderbrook. *G Man* 3H 91
Caldercruix. *N Lan* 3B 128
Calder Grove. *W Yor* 3D 92
Calder Mains. *High* 3C 168
Caldermill. *S Lan* 5H 127
Calder Vale. *Lanc* 5E 97
Calderwood. *S Lan* 4H 127
Caldescote. *Nptn* 5D 62
Caldicot. *Mon* 3H 33
Caldwell. *N Yor* 3E 105
Caldy. *Mers* 2E 83
Calebrack. *Cumb* 1E 103
Caledfwlch. *Carm* 3G 45
Calford Green. *Suff* 1G 53
Calfsound. *Orkn* 4E 172
Calgary. *Arg* 3E 139
Califer. *Mor* 3E 159
California. *Cambs* 2E 65
California. *Falk* 2C 128
California. *Norf* 4H 79
California. *Suff* 1E 55
Calke. *Derbs* 3A 74
Callakille. *High* 3F 155
Callaly. *Nmbd* 4E 121
Callander. *Stir* 3F 135
Callaughton. *Shrp* 1A 60
Callendoun. *Arg* 1E 127
Callestick. *Corn* 3B 6
Calligarry. *High* 3E 147
Callington. *Corn* 2H 7
Callingwood. *Staf* 3F 73
Callow. *Here* 2H 47
Callowell. *Glos* 5D 48
Callow End. *Worc* 1D 48
Callow Hill. *Wilts* 3F 35
Callow Hill. *Worc* 3B 60
(nr. Bewdley)
Callow Hill. *Worc* 4E 61
(nr. Redditch)
Calmore. *Hants* 1B 16
Calmsden. *Glos* 5F 49
Calne. *Wilts* 4E 35
Calow. *Derbs* 3B 86
Calshot. *Hants* 2C 16
Calstock. *Corn* 2A 8
Calstone Wellington. *Wilts* 5F 35
Calthorpe. *Norf* 2D 78
Calthorpe Street. *Norf* 3G 79
Calthwaite. *Cumb* 5F 113
Calton. *N Yor* 4B 98
Calton. *Staf* 5F 85
Calveley. *Ches E* 5H 83
Calver. *Derbs* 3G 85
Calverhall. *Shrp* 2A 72
Calverleigh. *Devn* 1C 12
Calverley. *W Yor* 1C 92
Calvert. *Buck* 3E 51
Calverton. *Mil* 2F 51
Calverton. *Notts* 1D 74
Calvine. *Per* 2F 143
Calvo. *Cumb* 4C 112
Cam. *Glos* 2C 34
Camaghael. *High* 1F 141
Camas-luinie. *High* 1B 148
Camasnacroise. *High* 3C 140
Camastianavaig. *High* 5E 155
Camasunary. *High* 2D 146
Camault Muir. *High* 4H 157
Camb. *Shet* 2G 173
Camber. *E Sus* 4D 28
Camberley. *Surr* 5G 37
Camberwell. *G Lon* 3E 39
Camblesforth. *N Yor* 2G 93
Cambo. *Nmbd* 1D 114
Cambois. *Nmbd* 1G 115
Camborne. *Corn* 3D 4
Cambourne. *Cambs* 5C 64
Cambridge. *Cambs* 5D 64 & 191
Cambridge. *Glos* 5C 48
Cambrose. *Corn* 4A 6
Cambus. *Clac* 4A 136
Cambusbarron. *Stir* 4G 135
Cambuskenneth. *Stir* 4H 135
Cambuslang. *S Lan* 3H 127
Cambusnethan. *N Lan* 4B 128
Cambus o'May. *Abers* 4B 152
Camden Town. *G Lon* 2D 39
Cameley. *Bath* 1B 22
Camelford. *Corn* 4B 10
Camelon. *Falk* 1B 128
Camelsdale. *Surr* 2A 26
Camer's Green. *Worc* 2C 48
Camerton. *Bath* 1B 22
Camerton. *Cumb* 1B 102
Camerton. *E Yor* 2F 95
Camghouran. *Per* 3C 142
Cammachmore. *Abers* 4G 153
Cammeringham. *Linc* 2G 87
Camore. *High* 4E 165
Campbelton. *N Ayr* 4C 126
Campbeltown. *Arg* 3B 122
Campbeltown Airport. *Arg* 3A 122
Cample. *Dum* 5B 118
Campmuir. *Per* 5B 144
Campsall. *S Yor* 3F 93
Campsea Ashe. *Suff* 5F 67
Camps End. *Cambs* 1G 53
Camp, The. *Glos* 5E 49
Campton. *C Beds* 2B 52
Camptoun. *E Lot* 2B 130
Camptown. *Bord* 3A 120
Camrose. *Pemb* 2D 42
Camserney. *Per* 4F 143
Camster. *High* 4E 169
Camus Croise. *High* 2E 147
Camuscross. *High* 2E 147
Camusdarach. *High* 4E 147
Camusnagaul. *High* 1E 141
(nr. Fort William)
Camusnagaul. *High* 5E 163
(nr. Little Loch Broom)
Camusteel. *High* 4G 155
Camusterrach. *High* 4G 155
Camusvrachan. *Per* 4D 142
Canada. *Hants* 1A 16
Canadia. *E Sus* 4B 28
Canaston Bridge. *Pemb* 3E 43
Candlesby. *Linc* 4D 88
Candle Street. *Suff* 3C 66
Candy Mill. *S Lan* 5D 128
Cane End. *Oxon* 4E 37
Canewdon. *Essx* 1C 40
Canford Cliffs. *Pool* 4F 15
Canford Heath. *Pool* 3F 15
Canford Magna. *Pool* 3F 15
Cangate. *Norf* 3F 79
Canham's Green. *Suff* 4C 66
Canholes. *Derbs* 3E 85
Canisbay. *High* 1F 169
Canley. *W Mid* 3H 61
Cann. *Dors* 4D 22
Cann Common. *Dors* 4D 23
Cannich. *High* 5F 157
Cannington. *Som* 3F 21
Cannock. *Staf* 4D 73
Cannock Wood. *Staf* 4E 73
Canonbie. *Dum* 2E 113
Canon Bridge. *Here* 1H 47
Canon Frome. *Here* 1B 48
Canon Pyon. *Here* 1H 47
Canons Ashby. *Nptn* 5C 62
Canonstown. *Corn* 3C 4
Canterbury. *Kent* 5F 41 & 190
Cantley. *Norf* 5F 79
Cantley. *S Yor* 4G 93
Cantlop. *Shrp* 5H 71
Canton. *Card* 4E 33
Cantray. *High* 4B 158
Cantraybruich. *High* 4B 158
Cantraywood. *High* 4B 158
Cantsdam. *Fife* 4D 136
Cantsfield. *Lanc* 2F 97
Canvey Island. *Essx* 2B 40
Canwick. *Linc* 4G 87
Canworthy Water. *Corn* 3C 10
Caol. *High* 1F 141
Caolas. *W Isl* 9B 170
Caolas Liubharsaigh. *W Isl* 4D 170
Caolas Scalpaigh. *W Isl* 8E 171
Caolas Stocinis. *W Isl* 8D 171
Caoles. *Arg* 4B 138
Caol Ila. *Arg* 3C 124
Caol Loch Ailse. *High* 1F 147
Caol Reatha. *High* 1F 147
Capel. *Kent* 1H 27
Capel. *Surr* 1C 26
Capel Bangor. *Cdgn* 2F 57
Capel Betws Lleucu. *Cdgn* 5F 57
Capel Coch. *IOA* 2D 80
Capel Curig. *Cnwy* 5G 81
Capel Cynon. *Cdgn* 1D 45
Capel Dewi. *Carm* 3E 45
Capel Dewi. *Cdgn* 2F 57
(nr. Aberystwyth)
Capel Dewi. *Cdgn* 1E 45
(nr. Llandysul)
Capel Garmon. *Cnwy* 5H 81
Capel Green. *Suff* 1G 55
Capel Gwyn. *IOA* 3C 80
Capel Gwynfe. *Carm* 3H 45
Capel Hendre. *Carm* 4F 45
Capel Isaac. *Carm* 3F 45
Capel Iwan. *Carm* 1G 43
Capel-le-Ferne. *Kent* 2G 29
Capel Llanilterne. *Card* 4D 32
Capel Mawr. *IOA* 3D 80
Capel Newydd. *Pemb* 1G 43
Capel St Andrew. *Suff* 1G 55
Capel St Mary. *Suff* 2D 54
Capel Seion. *Carm* 4F 45
Capel Seion. *Cdgn* 3F 57
Capel Uchaf. *Gwyn* 1D 68
Capel-y-ffin. *Powy* 2F 47
Capenhurst. *Ches W* 3F 83
Capernwray. *Lanc* 2E 97
Capheaton. *Nmbd* 1D 114
Cappercleuch. *Bord* 2E 119
Capplegill. *Dum* 4D 118
Capton. *Devn* 3E 9
Capton. *Som* 3D 20
Caputh. *Per* 5H 143
Caradon Town. *Corn* 5C 10
Carbis Bay. *Corn* 3C 4
Carbost. *High* 5C 154
(nr. Loch Harport)
Carbost. *High* 4D 154
(nr. Portree)
Carbrook. *S Yor* 2A 86
Carbrooke. *Norf* 5B 78
Carburton. *Notts* 3D 86
Carcluie. *S Ayr* 3C 116
Car Colston. *Notts* 1E 74
Carcroft. *S Yor* 3F 93
Cardenden. *Fife* 4E 136
Cardeston. *Shrp* 4F 71
Cardewlees. *Cumb* 4E 113
Cardiff. *Card* 4E 33 & 191
Cardiff International Airport.
V Glam 5D 32
Cardigan. *Cdgn* 1B 44
Cardinal's Green. *Cambs* 1G 53
Cardington. *Bed* 1A 52
Cardington. *Shrp* 1H 59
Cardinham. *Corn* 2F 7
Cardno. *Abers* 2G 161
Cardow. *Mor* 4F 159
Cardross. *Arg* 2E 127
Cardurnock. *Cumb* 4C 112
Careby. *Linc* 4H 75
Careston. *Ang* 2E 145
Carew. *Pemb* 4E 43
Carew Cheriton. *Pemb* 4E 43
Carew Newton. *Pemb* 4E 43
Carey. *Here* 2A 48
Carfin. *N Lan* 4A 128
Carfrae. *Bord* 4B 130
Cargate Green. *Norf* 4F 79
Cargenbridge. *Dum* 2G 111
Cargill. *Per* 5A 144
Cargo. *Cumb* 4E 113
Cargreen. *Corn* 2A 8
Carham. *Nmbd* 1B 120
Carhampton. *Som* 2D 20
Carharrack. *Corn* 4B 6
Carie. *Per* 3D 142
(nr. Loch Rannah)
Carie. *Per* 5D 142
(nr. Loch Tay)
Carisbrooke. *IOW* 4C 16
Cark. *Cumb* 2C 96
Carkeel. *Corn* 2A 8
Carlabhagh. *W Isl* 3E 171
Carland Cross. *Corn* 3C 6
Carlbury. *Darl* 3F 105
Carlby. *Linc* 4H 75
Carlecotes. *S Yor* 4B 92
Carleen. *Corn* 4D 4
Carlesmoor. *N Yor* 2D 98
Carleton. *Cumb* 4F 113
(nr. Carlisle)
Carleton. *Cumb* 4B 102
(nr. Egremont)
Carleton. *Cumb* 2G 103
(nr. Penrith)
Carleton. *Lanc* 1B 90
Carleton. *N Yor* 5B 98
Carleton. *W Yor* 2E 93
Carleton Forehoe. *Norf* 5C 78
Carleton Rode. *Norf* 1D 66
Carleton St Peter. *Norf* 5F 79
Carlidnack. *Corn* 4E 5
Carlingcott. *Bath* 1B 22
Carlin How. *Red C* 3E 107
Carlisle. *Cumb* 4F 113 & 192
Carloonan. *Arg* 2H 133
Carlops. *Bord* 4E 129
Carlton. *Bed* 5G 63
Carlton. *Cambs* 5F 65
Carlton. *Leics* 5A 74
Carlton. *N Yor* 1A 100
(nr. Helmsley)
Carlton. *N Yor* 1C 98
(nr. Middleham)
Carlton. *N Yor* 2G 93
(nr. Selby)
Carlton. *Notts* 1D 74
Carlton. *S Yor* 3D 92
Carlton. *Stoc T* 2A 106
Carlton. *Suff* 4F 67
Carlton. *W Yor* 2D 92
Carlton Colville. *Suff* 1H 67
Carlton Curlieu. *Leics* 1D 62
Carlton Husthwaite. *N Yor* 2G 99
Carlton in Cleveland. *N Yor* 4C 106
Carlton in Lindrick. *Notts* 2C 86
Carlton-le-Moorland. *Linc* 5G 87
Carlton Miniott. *N Yor* 1F 99
Carlton-on-Trent. *Notts* 4F 87
Carlton Scroop. *Linc* 1G 75
Carluke. *S Lan* 4B 128
Carlyon Bay. *Corn* 3E 7
Carmarthen. *Carm* 4E 45
Carmel. *Carm* 4F 45
Carmel. *Flin* 3D 82
Carmel. *Gwyn* 5D 81
Carmel. *IOA* 2C 80
Carmichael. *S Lan* 1B 118
Carmunnock. *Glas* 4H 127
Carmyle. *S Lan* 3H 127
Carmyllie. *Ang* 4E 145
Carnaby. *E Yor* 3F 101
Carnach. *High* 1C 148
(nr. Lochcarron)
Carnach. *High* 4E 163
(nr. Ullapool)
Carnach. *Mor* 4E 159
Carnach. *W Isl* 8E 171
Carnachy. *High* 3H 167
Carnain. *Arg* 3B 124
Carnais. *W Isl* 4C 171
Carnan. *Arg* 4B 138
Carnan. *W Isl* 4C 170
Carnbee. *Fife* 3H 137
Carnbo. *Per* 3C 136
Carn Brea Village. *Corn* 4A 6
Carndu. *High* 1A 148
Carne. *Corn* 5D 6
Carnell. *S Ayr* 1D 116
Carnforth. *Lanc* 2E 97
Carn-gorm. *High* 1B 148
Carnhedryn. *Pemb* 2B 42
Carnhell Green. *Corn* 3D 4
Carnie. *Abers* 3F 153
Carnkie. *Corn* 5B 6
(nr. Falmouth)
Carnkie. *Corn* 5A 6
(nr. Redruth)
Carnkief. *Corn* 3B 6
Carno. *Powy* 1B 58
Carnock. *Fife* 1D 128
Carnon Downs. *Corn* 4B 6
Carnoustie. *Ang* 5E 145
Carntyne. *Glas* 3H 127
Carnwath. *S Lan* 5C 128
Carnyorth. *Corn* 3A 4
Carol Green. *W Mid* 3G 61
Carpalla. *Corn* 3D 6
Carperby. *N Yor* 1C 98
Carradale. *Arg* 2C 122
Carragraich. *W Isl* 8D 171
Carrbridge. *High* 1D 150
Carr Cross. *Lanc* 3B 90
Carreglefn. *IOA* 2C 80
Carrhouse. *N Lin* 4A 94
Carrick Castle. *Arg* 4A 134
Carrick Ho. *Orkn* 4E 172
Carriden. *Falk* 1D 128
Carrington. *G Man* 1B 84
Carrington. *Linc* 5C 88
Carrington. *Midl* 3G 129
Carrog. *Cnwy* 1G 69
Carrog. *Den* 1D 70
Carron. *Falk* 1B 128
Carron. *Mor* 4G 159
Carronbridge. *Dum* 5A 118
Carronshore. *Falk* 1B 128
Carrow Hill. *Mon* 2H 33

Carr Shield—Chicksands

Carr Shield. Nmbd 5B 114
Carrutherstown. Dum 2C 112
Carr Vale. Derbs 4B 86
Carrville. Dur 5G 115
Carrycoats Hall. Nmbd 2C 114
Carsaig. Arg 1C 132
Carscreugh. Dum 3H 109
Carsegowan. Dum 4B 110
Carse House. Arg 3F 125
Carseriggan. Dum 3A 110
Carsethorn. Dum 4A 112
Carshalton. G Lon 4D 38
Carsington. Derbs 5G 85
Carskiey. Arg 5A 122
Carsluith. Dum 4B 110
Carsphairn. Dum 5E 117
Carstairs. S Lan 5C 128
Carstairs Junction. S Lan 5C 128
Cartbridge. Surr 5B 38
Carterhaugh. Ang 4D 144
Carter's Clay. Hants 4B 24
Carterton. Oxon 5A 50
Carterway Heads. Nmbd 4D 114
Carthew. Corn 3E 6
Carthorpe. N Yor 1F 99
Cartington. Nmbd 4E 121
Cartland. S Lan 5B 128
Cartmel. Cumb 2C 96
Cartmel Fell. Cumb 1D 96
Cartworth. W Yor 4B 92
Carwath. Cumb 5E 112
Carway. Carm 5E 45
Carwinley. Cumb 2F 113
Cascob. Powy 4E 59
Cas-gwent. Mon 2A 34
Cash Feus. Fife 3E 136
Cashlie. Per 4B 142
Cashmoor. Dors 1E 15
Cas-Mael. Pemb 2E 43
Casnewydd. Newp 3G 33 & **Newport 205**
Cassington. Oxon 4C 50
Cassop. Dur 1A 106
Castell. Cnwy 4G 81
Castell. Den 4D 82
Castell Hendre. Pemb 2E 43
Castell-nedd. Neat 2A 32
Castell Newydd Emlyn. Carm 1D 44
Castell-y-bwch. Torf 2F 33
Casterton. Cumb 2F 97
Castle. Som 2A 22
Castle Acre. Norf 4H 77
Castle Ashby. Nptn 5F 63
Castlebay. W Isl 9B 170
Castle Bolton. N Yor 5D 104
Castle Bromwich. W Mid 2F 61
Castle Bytham. Linc 4G 75
Castlebythe. Pemb 2E 43
Castle Caereinion. Powy 5D 70
Castle Camps. Cambs 1G 53
Castle Carrock. Cumb 4G 113
Castlecary. N Lan 2A 128
Castle Cary. Som 3B 22
Castle Combe. Wilts 4D 34
Castlecraig. High 2C 158
Castle Donington. Leics 3B 74
Castle Douglas. Dum 3E 111
Castle Eaton. Swin 2G 35
Castle Eden. Dur 1B 106
Castleford. W Yor 2E 93
Castle Frome. Here 1B 48
Castle Green. Surr 4A 38
Castle Green. Warw 3G 61
Castle Gresley. Derbs 4G 73
Castle Heaton. Nmbd 5F 131
Castle Hedingham. Essx 2A 54
Castle Hill. Kent 1A 28
Castlehill. Per 5B 144
Castlehill. S Lan 4B 128
Castle Hill. Suff 1E 55
Castlehill. W Dun 2E 127
Castle Kennedy. Dum 4G 109
Castle Lachlan. Arg 4H 133
Castlemartin. Pemb 5D 42
Castlemilk. Glas 4H 127
Castlemorris. Pemb 1D 42
Castlemorton. Worc 2C 48
Castle O'er. Dum 5E 119
Castle Park. N Yor 3F 107
Castlerigg. Cumb 2D 102
Castle Rising. Norf 3F 77
Castleside. Dur 5D 115
Castlethorpe. Mil 1F 51
Castleton. Abers 4F 151
Castleton. Arg 1G 125
Castleton. Derbs 2F 85
Castleton. G Man 3G 91
Castleton. Mor 1F 151
Castleton. Newp 3F 33
Castleton. N Yor 4D 107
Castleton. Per 2B 136
Castletown. Cumb 1G 103
Castletown. Dors 5B 14
Castletown. High 2D 169
Castletown. IOM 5B 108
Castletown. Tyne 4G 115
Castley. N Yor 5E 99
Caston. Norf 1B 66
Castor. Pet 1A 64
Caswell. Swan 4E 31
Catacol. N Ayr 5H 125
Catbrook. Mon 5A 48
Catchems End. Worc 3B 60
Catchgate. Dur 4E 115
Catcleugh. Nmbd 4B 120
Catcliffe. S Yor 2B 86
Catcott. Som 3G 21
Caterham. Surr 5E 39
Catfield. Norf 3F 79
Catfield Common. Norf 3F 79
Catfirth. Shet 6F 173
Catford. G Lon 3E 39
Catforth. Lanc 1C 90
Cathcart. Glas 3G 127
Cathedine. Powy 3E 47
Catherine-de-Barnes. W Mid 2F 61
Catherington. Hants 1E 17
Catherston Leweston. Dors 3G 13
Catherton. Shrp 3A 60
Catisfield. Hants 2D 16
Catlodge. High 4A 150
Catlowdy. Cumb 2F 113
Catmore. W Ber 3C 36
Caton. Devn 5A 12
Caton. Lanc 3E 97
Catrine. E Ayr 2E 117
Cat's Ash. Newp 2G 33
Catsfield. E Sus 4B 28
Catsgore. Som 4A 22
Catshill. Worc 3D 60
Cattal. N Yor 4G 99
Cattawade. Suff 2E 54
Catterall. Lanc 5D 97
Catterick. N Yor 5F 105
Catterick Bridge. N Yor 5F 105
Catterick Garrison. N Yor 5E 105
Catterlen. Cumb 1F 103
Catterline. Abers 1H 145
Catterton. N Yor 5H 99
Catteshall. Surr 1A 26
Catthorpe. Leics 3C 62
Cattistock. Dors 3A 14
Catton. Nmbd 4B 114
Catton. N Yor 2F 99
Catton Hall. Derbs 4G 73
Catwick. E Yor 5F 101
Catworth. Cambs 3H 63
Caudle Green. Glos 4E 49
Caulcott. Oxon 3D 50
Cauldhame. Stir 4F 135
Cauldmill. Bord 3H 119
Cauldon. Staf 1E 73
Cauldon Lowe. Staf 1E 73
Cauldwell. Derbs 4G 73
Cauldwells. Abers 3E 161
Caulkerbush. Dum 4G 111
Caulside. Dum 1F 113
Caunsall. Worc 2C 60
Caunton. Notts 4E 87
Causewayend. S Lan 1C 118
Causewayhead. Stir 4H 135
Causey Park. Nmbd 5F 121
Caute. Devn 1E 11
Cautley. Cumb 5H 103
Cavendish. Suff 1B 54
Cavendish Bridge. Derbs 2B 74
Cavenham. Suff 4G 65
Caversfield. Oxon 3D 50
Caversham. Read 4F 37
Caversham Heights. Read 4E 37
Caverswall. Staf 1D 72
Cawdor. High 4C 158
Cawkwell. Linc 2B 88
Cawood. N Yor 1F 93
Cawsand. Corn 3A 8
Cawston. Norf 3D 78
Cawston. Warw 3B 62
Cawthorne. N Yor 1B 100
Cawthorne. S Yor 4C 92
Cawthorpe. Linc 3H 75
Cawton. N Yor 2A 100
Caxton. Cambs 5C 64
Caynham. Shrp 3H 59
Caythorpe. Linc 1G 75
Caythorpe. Notts 1D 74
Cayton. N Yor 1E 101
Ceallan. W Isl 3D 170
Ceann a Bhàigh. W Isl 9C 171 (on Harris)
Ceann a Bhaigh. W Isl 2C 170 (on North Uist)
Ceann a Bhaigh. W Isl 8E 171 (on Scalpay)
Ceann a Bhaigh. W Isl 8D 171 (on South Harris)
Ceannacroc Lodge. High 2E 149
Ceann a Deas Loch Baghasdail. W Isl 7C 170
Ceann an Leothaid. High 5E 147
Ceann a Tuath Loch Baghasdail. W Isl 6C 170
Ceann Loch Ailleart. High 5F 147
Ceann Loch Muideirt. High 1B 140
Ceann Shiphoirt. W Isl 6E 171
Ceann Tarabhaigh. W Isl 6E 171
Cearsiadar. W Isl 5F 171
Ceathramh Meadhanach. W Isl 1C 170
Cefn Berain. Cnwy 4B 82
Cefn-brith. Cnwy 5B 82
Cefn-bryn-brain. Carm 4H 45
Cefn Bychan. Cphy 2F 33
Cefn-bychan. Flin 4D 82
Cefncaeau. Carm 3E 31
Cefn Canol. Powy 2E 71
Cefn Coch. Powy 5C 70 (nr. Llanfair Caereinion)
Cefn-coch. Powy 3D 70 (nr. Llanrhaeadr-ym-Mochnant)
Cefn-coed-y-cymmer. Mer T 5D 46
Cefn Cribwr. B'end 3B 32
Cefn-ddwysarn. Gwyn 2B 70
Cefn Einion. Shrp 2E 59
Cefneithin. Carm 4F 45
Cefn Glas. B'end 3B 32
Cefngorwydd. Powy 1C 46
Cefn Llwyd. Cdgn 2F 57
Cefn-mawr. Wrex 1E 71
Cefn-y-bedd. Flin 5F 83
Cefn-y-coed. Powy 1D 58
Cefn-y-pant. Carm 2F 43
Cegidfa. Powy 4E 70
Ceinewydd. Cdgn 5C 56
Cellan. Cdgn 1G 45
Cellardyke. Fife 3H 137
Cellarhead. Staf 1D 72
Cemaes. IOA 1C 80
Cemmaes. Powy 5H 69
Cemmaes Road. Powy 5H 69
Cenarth. Carm 1C 44
Cenin. Gwyn 1D 68
Ceos. W Isl 5F 171
Ceres. Fife 2G 137
Ceri. Powy 2D 58
Cerist. Powy 2B 58
Cerne Abbas. Dors 2B 14
Cerney Wick. Glos 2F 35
Cerrigceinwen. IOA 3D 80
Cerrigydrudion. Cnwy 1B 70
Cess. Norf 4G 79
Cessford. Bord 2B 120
Ceunant. Gwyn 4E 81
Chaceley. Glos 2D 48
Chacewater. Corn 4B 6
Chackmore. Buck 2E 51
Chacombe. Nptn 1C 50
Chadderton. G Man 4H 91
Chaddesden. Derb 2A 74
Chaddesden Common. Derb 2A 74
Chaddesley Corbett. Worc 3C 60
Chaddlehanger. Devn 5E 11
Chaddleworth. W Ber 4C 36
Chadlington. Oxon 3B 50
Chadshunt. Warw 5H 61
Chadstone. Nptn 5F 63
Chad Valley. W Mid 2E 61
Chadwell. Leics 3E 75
Chadwell. Shrp 4B 72
Chadwell Heath. G Lon 2F 39
Chadwell St Mary. Thur 3H 39
Chadwick End. W Mid 3G 61
Chadwick Green. Mers 1H 83
Chaffcombe. Som 1G 13
Chafford Hundred. Thur 3H 39
Chagford. Devn 4H 11
Chailey. E Sus 4E 27
Chainbridge. Cambs 5D 76
Chain Bridge. Linc 1C 76
Chainhurst. Kent 1B 28
Chalbury. Dors 2F 15
Chalbury Common. Dors 2F 15
Chaldon. Surr 5E 39
Chaldon Herring. Dors 4C 14
Chale. IOW 5C 16
Chale Green. IOW 5C 16
Chalfont Common. Buck 1B 38
Chalfont St Giles. Buck 1A 38
Chalfont St Peter. Buck 2B 38
Chalford. Glos 5D 49
Chalgrove. Oxon 2E 37
Chalk. Kent 3A 40
Chalk End. Essx 4G 53
Chalk Hill. Glos 3G 49
Challaborough. Devn 4C 8
Challacombe. Devn 2G 19
Challister. Shet 5G 173
Challoch. Dum 3A 110
Challock. Kent 5E 40
Chalton. C Beds 5A 64 (nr. Bedford)
Chalton. C Beds 3A 52 (nr. Luton)
Chalton. Hants 1F 17
Chalvington. E Sus 5G 27
Champany. Falk 2D 128
Chance Inn. Fife 2F 137
Chancery. Cdgn 3E 57
Chandler's Cross. Herts 1B 38
Chandler's Cross. Worc 2C 48
Chandler's Ford. Hants 4C 24
Chanlockfoot. Dum 4G 117
Channel's End. Bed 5A 64
Channel Tunnel. Kent 2F 29
Channerwick. Shet 9F 173
Chantry. Som 2C 22
Chantry. Suff 1E 55
Chapel. Cumb 1D 102
Chapel. Fife 4E 137
Chapel Allerton. Som 1H 21
Chapel Allerton. W Yor 1D 92
Chapel Amble. Corn 1D 6
Chapel Brampton. Nptn 4E 63
Chapelbridge. Cambs 1B 64
Chapel Chorlton. Staf 2C 72
Chapel Cleeve. Som 2D 20
Chapel End. C Beds 1A 52
Chapel-en-le-Frith. Derbs 2E 85
Chapelfield. Abers 2G 145
Chapelgate. Linc 3D 76
Chapel Green. Warw 2G 61 (nr. Coventry)
Chapel Green. Warw 4B 62 (nr. Southam)
Chapel Haddlesey. N Yor 2F 93
Chapelhall. N Lan 3A 128
Chapel Hill. Abers 5H 161
Chapel Hill. Linc 5B 88
Chapel Hill. Mon 5A 48
Chapelhill. Per 1E 136 (nr. Glencarse)
Chapelhill. Per 5H 143 (nr. Harrietfield)
Chapelknowe. Dum 2E 112
Chapel Lawn. Shrp 3F 59
Chapel le Dale. N Yor 2G 97
Chapel Milton. Derbs 2E 85
Chapel of Garioch. Abers 1E 152
Chapel Row. W Ber 5D 36
Chapels. Cumb 1B 96
Chapel St Leonards. Linc 3E 89
Chapel Stile. Cumb 4E 102
Chapelthorne. W Yor 3D 92
Chapelton. Ang 4F 145
Chapelton. Devn 4F 19
Chapelton. High 2D 150 (nr. Grantown-on-Spey)
Chapelton. High 3H 157 (nr. Inverness)
Chapelton. S Lan 5H 127
Chapeltown. Bkbn 3F 91
Chapel Town. Corn 3C 6
Chapeltown. Mor 1G 151
Chapeltown. S Yor 1H 85
Chapmanslade. Wilts 2D 22
Chapmans Well. Devn 3D 10
Chapmore End. Herts 4D 52
Chappel. Essx 3B 54
Chard. Som 2G 13
Chard Junction. Dors 2G 13
Chardstock. Devn 2G 13
Charfield. S Glo 2C 34
Charing. Kent 1D 28
Charing Heath. Kent 1D 28
Charing Hill. Kent 5D 40
Charingworth. Glos 2H 49
Charlbury. Oxon 4B 50
Charlcombe. Bath 5C 34
Charlcutt. Wilts 4E 35
Charlecote. Warw 5G 61
Charles. Devn 3G 19
Charlesfield. Dum 3C 112
Charleshill. Surr 2G 25
Charleston. Ang 4C 144
Charleston. Ren 3F 127
Charlestown. Aber 3G 153
Charlestown. Abers 2H 161
Charlestown. Corn 3E 7
Charlestown. Dors 5B 14
Charlestown. Fife 1D 128
Charlestown. G Man 4G 91
Charlestown. High 1H 155 (nr. Gairloch)
Charlestown. High 4A 158 (nr. Inverness)
Charlestown. W Yor 2H 91
Charlestown of Aberlour. Mor 4G 159
Charles Tye. Suff 5C 66
Charlesworth. Derbs 1E 85
Charlton. G Lon 3F 39
Charlton. Hants 2B 24
Charlton. Herts 3B 52
Charlton. Nptn 2D 50
Charlton. Nmbd 1B 114
Charlton. Oxon 3C 36
Charlton. Som 1B 22 (nr. Radstock)
Charlton. Som 2B 22 (nr. Shepton Mallet)
Charlton. Som 4F 21 (nr. Taunton)
Charlton. Telf 4H 71
Charlton. W Sus 1G 17
Charlton. Wilts 3E 35 (nr. Malmesbury)
Charlton. Wilts 1G 23 (nr. Pewsey)
Charlton. Wilts 4G 23 (nr. Salisbury)
Charlton. Wilts 4E 23 (nr. Shaftesbury)
Charlton. Worc 1F 49 (nr. Evesham)
Charlton. Worc 3C 60 (nr. Stourport-on-Severn)
Charlton Abbots. Glos 3F 49
Charlton Adam. Som 4A 22
Charlton Down. Dors 3B 14
Charlton Horethorne. Som 4B 22
Charlton Kings. Glos 3E 49
Charlton Mackrell. Som 4A 22
Charlton Marshall. Dors 2E 15
Charlton Musgrove. Som 4C 22
Charlton-on-Otmoor. Oxon 4D 50
Charlton on the Hill. Dors 2D 15
Charlwood. Hants 3E 25
Charlwood. Surr 1D 26
Charlynch. Som 3F 21
Charminster. Dors 3B 14
Charmouth. Dors 3G 13
Charndon. Buck 3E 51
Charney Bassett. Oxon 2B 36
Charnock Green. Lanc 3D 90
Charnock Richard. Lanc 3D 90
Charsfield. Suff 5E 67
Chart Corner. Kent 5B 40
Charter Alley. Hants 1D 24
Charterhouse. Som 1H 21
Charterville Allotments. Oxon 4B 50
Chartham. Kent 5F 41
Chartham Hatch. Kent 5F 41
Chartridge. Buck 5H 51
Chart Sutton. Kent 5B 40
Chart, The. Kent 5F 39
Charvil. Wok 4F 37
Charwelton. Nptn 5C 62
Chase Terrace. Staf 5E 73
Chasetown. Staf 5E 73
Chastleton. Oxon 3H 49
Chasty. Devn 2D 10
Chatburn. Lanc 5G 97
Chatcull. Staf 2B 72
Chatham. Medw 4B 40 & **Medway 204**
Chatham Green. Essx 4H 53
Chathill. Nmbd 2F 121
Chatley. Worc 4C 60
Chattenden. Medw 3B 40
Chatteris. Cambs 2C 64
Chattisham. Suff 1D 54
Chatton. Nmbd 2E 121
Chatwall. Shrp 1H 59
Chaulden. Herts 5A 52
Chaul End. C Beds 3A 52
Chawleigh. Devn 1H 11
Chawley. Oxon 5C 50
Chawston. Bed 5A 64
Chawton. Hants 3F 25
Chaxhill. Glos 4C 48
Cheadle. G Man 2C 84
Cheadle. Staf 1E 73
Cheadle Hulme. G Man 2C 84
Cheam. Surr 4D 38
Cheapside. Wind 4A 38
Chearsley. Buck 4F 51
Chebsey. Staf 3C 72
Checkendon. Oxon 3E 37
Checkley. Ches E 1B 72
Checkley. Here 2A 48
Checkley. Staf 2E 73
Chedburgh. Suff 5G 65
Cheddar. Som 1H 21
Cheddington. Buck 4H 51
Cheddleton. Staf 5D 84
Cheddon Fitzpaine. Som 4F 21
Chedglow. Wilts 2E 35
Chedgrave. Norf 1F 67
Chedington. Dors 2H 13
Chediston. Suff 3F 67
Chediston Green. Suff 3F 67
Chedworth. Glos 4F 49
Chedzoy. Som 3G 21
Cheeseman's Green. Kent 2E 29
Cheetham Hill. G Man 4G 91
Cheglinch. Devn 2F 19
Cheldon. Devn 1H 11
Chelford. Ches E 3C 84
Chellaston. Derb 2A 74
Chellington. Bed 5G 63
Chelmarsh. Shrp 2B 60
Chelmick. Shrp 1G 59
Chelmondiston. Suff 2F 55
Chelmorton. Derbs 4F 85
Chelmsford. Essx 5H 53
Chelsea. G Lon 3D 39
Chelsfield. G Lon 4F 39
Chelsham. Surr 5E 39
Chelston. Som 4E 21
Chelsworth. Suff 1C 54
Cheltenham. Glos 3E 49 & 192
Chelveston. Nptn 4G 63
Chelvey. N Som 5H 33
Chelwood. Bath 5B 34
Chelwood Common. E Sus 3F 27
Chelwood Gate. E Sus 3F 27
Chelworth. Wilts 2E 35
Chelworth Lower Green. Wilts 2F 35
Chelworth Upper Green. Wilts 2F 35
Chelynch. Som 2B 22
Cheney Longville. Shrp 2G 59
Chenies. Buck 1B 38
Chepstow. Mon 2A 34
Chequerfield. W Yor 2E 93
Chequers Corner. Norf 5D 77
Cherhill. Wilts 4F 35
Cherington. Glos 2E 35
Cherington. Warw 2A 50
Cheriton. Devn 2H 19
Cheriton. Hants 4D 24
Cheriton. Kent 2G 29
Cheriton. Pemb 5D 43
Cheriton. Swan 3D 30
Cheriton Bishop. Devn 3A 12
Cheriton Cross. Devn 3A 12
Cheriton Fitzpaine. Devn 2B 12
Cherrington. Telf 3A 72
Cherrybank. Per 1D 136
Cherry Burton. E Yor 5D 101
Cherry Green. Herts 3D 52
Cherry Hinton. Cambs 5D 65
Cherry Willingham. Linc 3H 87
Chertsey. Surr 4B 38
Cheselbourne. Dors 3C 14
Chesham. Buck 5H 51
Chesham. G Man 3G 91
Chesham Bois. Buck 1A 38
Cheshunt. Herts 5D 52
Cheslyn Hay. Staf 5D 73
Chessetts Wood. Warw 3F 61
Chessington. G Lon 4C 38
Chester. Ches W 4G 83 & 192
Chesterblade. Som 2B 22
Chesterfield. Derbs 3A 86
Chesterfield. Staf 5F 73
Chesterhope. Nmbd 1C 114
Chester-le-Street. Dur 4F 115
Chester Moor. Dur 5F 115
Chesters. Bord 3A 120
Chesterton. Cambs 4D 64 (nr. Cambridge)
Chesterton. Cambs 1A 64 (nr. Peterborough)
Chesterton. Glos 5F 49
Chesterton. Oxon 3D 50
Chesterton. Shrp 1B 60
Chesterton. Staf 1C 72
Chesterton Green. Warw 5H 61
Chesterwood. Nmbd 3B 114
Chestfield. Kent 4F 41
Cheston. Devn 3C 8
Cheswardine. Shrp 2B 72
Cheswell. Telf 4B 72
Cheswick. Nmbd 5G 131
Cheswick Green. W Mid 3F 61
Chetnole. Dors 2B 14
Chettiscombe. Devn 1C 12
Chettisham. Cambs 2E 65
Chettle. Dors 1E 15
Chetton. Shrp 1A 60
Chetwode. Buck 3E 51
Chetwynd Aston. Telf 4B 72
Cheveley. Cambs 4F 65
Chevening. Kent 5F 39
Chevington. Suff 5G 65
Chevithorne. Devn 1C 12
Chew Magna. Bath 5A 34
Chew Moor. G Man 4E 91
Chew Stoke. Bath 5A 34
Chewton Keynsham. Bath 5B 34
Chewton Mendip. Som 1A 22
Chichacott. Devn 3G 11
Chicheley. Mil 1H 51
Chichester. W Sus 2G 17
Chickerell. Dors 4B 14
Chickering. Suff 3E 66
Chicklade. Wilts 3E 23
Chicksands. C Beds 2B 52

Clyst St Mary—Coton Hill

Clyst St Mary. *Devn* 3C 12
Clyth. *High* 5E 169
Cnip. *W Isl* 4C 171
Cnoc Amhlaigh. *W Isl* 4H 171
Cnwcau. *Pemb* 1C 44
Cnwch Coch. *Cdgn* 3F 57
Coad's Green. *Corn* 5C 10
Coal Aston. *Derbs* 3A 86
Coalbrookdale. *Telf* 5A 72
Coalbrookvale. *Blae* 5F 47
Coalburn. *S Lan* 1H 117
Coalburns. *Tyne* 3E 115
Coalcleugh. *Nmbd* 5B 114
Coaley. *Glos* 5C 48
Coalford. *Abers* 4F 153
Coalhall. *E Ayr* 3D 116
Coalhill. *Essx* 1B 40
Coalpit Heath. *S Glo* 3B 34
Coal Pool. *W Mid* 5E 73
Coalport. *Telf* 5B 72
Coalsnaughton. *Clac* 4B 136
Coaltown of Balgonie. *Fife* 4F 137
Coaltown of Wemyss. *Fife* 4F 137
Coalville. *Leics* 4B 74
Coalway. *Glos* 4A 48
Coanwood. *Nmbd* 4H 113
Coat. *Som* 4H 21
Coatbridge. *N Lan* 3A 128
Coatdyke. *N Lan* 3A 128
Coate. *Swin* 3G 35
Coate. *Wilts* 5F 35
Coates. *Cambs* 1C 64
Coates. *Glos* 5E 49
Coates. *Linc* 2G 87
Coates. *W Sus* 4A 26
Coatham. *Red C* 2C 106
Coatham Mundeville. *Darl* 2F 105
Cobbaton. *Devn* 4G 19
Coberley. *Glos* 4E 49
Cobhall Common. *Here* 2H 47
Cobham. *Kent* 4A 40
Cobham. *Surr* 4C 38
Cobnash. *Here* 4G 59
Coburg. *Devn* 5B 12
Cockayne. *N Yor* 5D 106
Cockayne Hatley. *C Beds* 1C 52
Cock Bank. *Wrex* 1F 71
Cock Bridge. *Abers* 3G 151
Cockburnspath. *Bord* 2D 130
Cock Clarks. *Essx* 5B 54
Cockenzie and Port Seton. *E Lot* 2H 129
Cockerham. *Lanc* 4D 96
Cockermouth. *Cumb* 1C 102
Cockernhoe. *Herts* 3B 52
Cockfield. *Dur* 2E 105
Cockfield. *Suff* 5B 66
Cockfosters. *G Lon* 1D 39
Cock Gate. *Here* 4G 59
Cock Green. *Essx* 4G 53
Cocking. *W Sus* 1G 17
Cocking Causeway. *W Sus* 1G 17
Cockington. *Torb* 2F 9
Cocklake. *Som* 2H 21
Cocklaw. *Abers* 4H 161
Cocklaw. *Nmbd* 2C 114
Cockley Beck. *Cumb* 4D 102
Cockley Cley. *Norf* 5G 77
Cockmuir. *Abers* 3G 161
Cockpole Green. *Wind* 3G 37
Cockshutford. *Shrp* 2H 59
Cockshutt. *Shrp* 3G 71
Cockthorpe. *Norf* 1B 78
Cockwood. *Devn* 4C 12
Cockyard. *Derbs* 3E 85
Cockyard. *Here* 2H 47
Codda. *Corn* 5B 10
Coddenham. *Suff* 5D 66
Coddenham Green. *Suff* 5D 66
Coddington. *Ches W* 5G 83
Coddington. *Here* 1C 48
Coddington. *Notts* 5F 87
Codford St Mary. *Wilts* 3E 23
Codford St Peter. *Wilts* 3E 23
Codicote. *Herts* 4C 52
Codmore Hill. *W Sus* 3B 26
Codnor. *Derbs* 1B 74
Codrington. *S Glo* 4C 34
Codsall. *Staf* 5C 72
Codsall Wood. *Staf* 5C 72
Coed Duon. *Cphy* 2E 33
Coedely. *Rhon* 3D 32
Coedglasson. *Powy* 4C 58
Coedkernew. *Newp* 3F 33
Coed Morgan. *Mon* 4G 47
Coedpoeth. *Wrex* 5E 83
Coedway. *Powy* 4F 71
Coed-y-bryn. *Cdgn* 1D 44
Coed-y-paen. *Mon* 2G 33
Coed-yr-ynys. *Powy* 3E 47
Coed Ystumgwern. *Gwyn* 3E 69
Coelbren. *Powy* 4B 46
Coffinswell. *Devn* 2E 9
Cofton Hackett. *Worc* 3E 61
Cogan. *V Glam* 4E 33
Cogenhoe. *Nptn* 4F 63
Cogges. *Oxon* 5B 50
Coggeshall. *Essx* 3B 54
Coggeshall Hamlet. *Essx* 3B 54
Coggins Mill. *E Sus* 3G 27
Coignafearn Lodge. *High* 2A 150
Coig Peighinnean. *W Isl* 1H 171
Coig Peighinnean Bhuirgh. *W Isl* 2G 171
Coilleag. *W Isl* 7C 170
Coilliemore. *High* 1A 158
Coillore. *High* 5C 154
Coire an Fhuarain. *W Isl* 4E 171
Coity. *B'end* 3C 32
Cokhay Green. *Derbs* 3G 73
Col. *W Isl* 3G 171
Colaboll. *High* 2C 164
Colan. *Corn* 2C 6
Colaton Raleigh. *Devn* 4D 12
Colbost. *High* 4B 154
Colburn. *N Yor* 5E 105
Colby. *Cumb* 2H 103
Colby. *IOM* 4B 108
Colby. *Norf* 2E 78
Colchester. *Essx* 3D 54
Cold Ash. *W Ber* 5D 36
Cold Ashby. *Nptn* 3D 62
Cold Ashton. *S Glo* 4C 34
Cold Aston. *Glos* 4G 49
Coldbackie. *High* 3G 167
Cold Blow. *Pemb* 3F 43
Cold Brayfield. *Mil* 5G 63
Cold Cotes. *N Yor* 2G 97
Coldean. *Brig* 5E 27
Coldeast. *Devn* 5B 12
Colden. *W Yor* 2H 91
Colden Common. *Hants* 4C 24
Coldfair Green. *Suff* 4G 67
Coldham. *Cambs* 5D 76
Coldham. *Staf* 5C 72
Cold Hanworth. *Linc* 2H 87
Coldharbour. *Corn* 4B 6
Cold Harbour. *Dors* 3E 15
Coldharbour. *Glos* 5A 48
Coldharbour. *Kent* 5G 39
Coldharbour. *Surr* 1C 26
Cold Hatton. *Telf* 3A 72
Cold Hatton Heath. *Telf* 3A 72
Cold Hesledon. *Dur* 5H 115
Cold Hiendley. *W Yor* 3D 92
Cold Higham. *Nptn* 5D 62
Coldingham. *Bord* 3F 131
Cold Kirby. *N Yor* 1H 99
Coldmeece. *Staf* 2C 72
Cold Northcott. *Corn* 4C 10
Cold Norton. *Essx* 5B 54
Cold Overton. *Leics* 4F 75
Coldrain. *Per* 3C 136
Coldred. *Kent* 1G 29
Coldridge. *Devn* 2G 11
Cold Row. *Lanc* 5C 96
Coldstream. *Bord* 5E 131
Coldwaltham. *W Sus* 4B 26
Coldwell. *Here* 2H 47
Coldwells. *Abers* 5H 161
Coldwells Croft. *Abers* 1C 152
Cole. *Shet* 5E 173
Cole. *Som* 3B 22
Colebatch. *Shrp* 2F 59
Colebrook. *Devn* 2D 12
Colebrooke. *Devn* 2A 12
Coleburn. *Mor* 3G 159
Coleby. *Linc* 4G 87
Coleby. *N Lin* 3B 94
Cole End. *Warw* 2G 61
Coleford. *Devn* 2A 12
Coleford. *Glos* 4A 48
Coleford. *Som* 2B 22
Colegate End. *Norf* 2D 66
Cole Green. *Herts* 4C 52
Cole Henley. *Hants* 1C 24
Colehill. *Dors* 2F 15
Coleman Green. *Herts* 4B 52
Coleman's Hatch. *E Sus* 2F 27
Colemere. *Shrp* 2G 71
Colemore. *Hants* 3F 25
Colemore Green. *Shrp* 1B 60
Coleorton. *Leics* 4B 74
Colerne. *Wilts* 4D 34
Colesbourne. *Glos* 4E 49
Colesden. *Bed* 5A 64
Coles Green. *Worc* 5B 60
Coleshill. *Buck* 1A 38
Coleshill. *Oxon* 2H 35
Coleshill. *Warw* 2G 61
Colestocks. *Devn* 2D 12
Colethrop. *Glos* 4D 48
Coley. *Bath* 1A 22
Colgate. *W Sus* 2D 26
Colinsburgh. *Fife* 3G 137
Colinton. *Edin* 3F 129
Colintraive. *Arg* 2B 126
Colkirk. *Norf* 3B 78
Collace. *Per* 5B 144
Collam. *W Isl* 8D 171
Collaton. *Devn* 5D 8
Collaton St Mary. *Torb* 2E 9
College of Roseisle. *Mor* 2F 159
Collessie. *Fife* 2E 137
Collier Row. *G Lon* 1F 39
Colliers End. *Herts* 3D 52
Collier Street. *Kent* 1B 28
Colliery Row. *Tyne* 5G 115
Collieston. *Abers* 1H 153
Collin. *Dum* 2B 112
Collingbourne Ducis. *Wilts* 1H 23
Collingbourne Kingston. *Wilts* 1H 23
Collingham. *Notts* 4F 87
Collingham. *W Yor* 5F 99
Collingtree. *Nptn* 5E 63
Collins Green. *Warr* 1H 83
Collins Green. *Worc* 5B 60
Colliston. *Ang* 4F 145
Colliton. *Devn* 2D 12
Collydean. *Fife* 3E 137
Collyweston. *Nptn* 5G 75
Colmonell. *S Ayr* 1G 109
Colmworth. *Bed* 5A 64
Colnbrook. *Slo* 3B 38
Colne. *Cambs* 3C 64
Colne. *Lanc* 5A 98
Colne Engaine. *Essx* 2B 54
Colney. *Norf* 5D 78
Colney Heath. *Herts* 5C 52
Colney Street. *Herts* 5B 52
Coln Rogers. *Glos* 5F 49
Coln St Aldwyns. *Glos* 5G 49
Coln St Dennis. *Glos* 4F 49
Colpitts Grange. *Nmbd* 4C 114
Colpy. *Abers* 5D 160
Colscott. *Devn* 1D 10
Colsterdale. *N Yor* 1D 98
Colsterworth. *Linc* 3G 75
Colston Bassett. *Notts* 2D 74
Colstoun House. *E Lot* 2B 130
Coltfield. *Mor* 2F 159
Colthouse. *Cumb* 5E 103
Coltishall. *Norf* 4E 79
Coltness. *N Lan* 4A 128
Colton. *Cumb* 1C 96
Colton. *Norf* 5D 78
Colton. *N Yor* 5H 99
Colton. *Staf* 3E 73
Colton. *W Yor* 1D 92
Colt's Hill. *Kent* 1H 27
Col Uarach. *W Isl* 4G 171
Colvend. *Dum* 4F 111
Colvister. *Shet* 2G 173
Colwall Green. *Here* 1C 48
Colwall Stone. *Here* 1C 48
Colwell. *Nmbd* 2C 114
Colwich. *Staf* 3E 73
Colwick. *Notts* 1D 74
Colwinston. *V Glam* 4C 32
Colworth. *W Sus* 5A 26
Colwyn Bay. *Cnwy* 3A 82
Colyford. *Devn* 3F 13
Colyton. *Devn* 3F 13
Combe. *Devn* 2D 8
Combe. *Here* 4F 59
Combe. *Oxon* 4C 50
Combe. *W Ber* 5B 36
Combe Almer. *Dors* 3E 15
Combebow. *Devn* 4E 11
Combe Common. *Surr* 2A 26
Combe Down. *Bath* 5C 34
Combe Fishacre. *Devn* 2E 9
Combe Florey. *Som* 3E 21
Combe Hay. *Bath* 1C 22
Combeinteignhead. *Devn* 5C 12
Combe Martin. *Devn* 2F 19
Combe Moor. *Here* 4F 59
Combe Raleigh. *Devn* 2E 13
Comberbach. *Ches W* 3A 84
Comberford. *Staf* 5F 73
Comberton. *Cambs* 5C 64
Comberton. *Here* 4G 59
Combe St Nicholas. *Som* 1G 13
Combpyne. *Devn* 3F 13
Combridge. *Staf* 2E 73
Combrook. *Warw* 5H 61
Combs. *Derbs* 3E 85
Combs. *Suff* 5C 66
Combs Ford. *Suff* 5C 66
Combwich. *Som* 2F 21
Comers. *Abers* 3D 152
Comhampton. *Worc* 4C 60
Comins Coch. *Cdgn* 2F 57
Comley. *Shrp* 1G 59
Commercial End. *Cambs* 4E 65
Commins. *Powy* 3D 70
Commins Coch. *Powy* 5H 69
Commondale. *N Yor* 3D 106
Common End. *Cumb* 2B 102
Common Hill. *Here* 2A 48
Common Moor. *Corn* 2G 7
Common Platt. *Wilts* 3G 35
Commonside. *Ches W* 3H 83
Common Side. *Derbs* 3H 85 (nr. Chesterfield)
Commonside. *Derbs* 1G 73 (nr. Derby)
Common, The. *Wilts* 3H 23 (nr. Salisbury)
Common, The. *Wilts* 3F 35 (nr. Swindon)
Compstall. *G Man* 1D 84
Compton. *Devn* 2E 9
Compton. *Hants* 4C 24
Compton. *Staf* 2C 60
Compton. *Surr* 1A 26
Compton. *W Ber* 3D 36
Compton. *W Sus* 1F 17
Compton. *Wilts* 1G 23
Compton Abbas. *Dors* 1D 14
Compton Abdale. *Glos* 4F 49
Compton Bassett. *Wilts* 4F 35
Compton Beauchamp. *Oxon* 3A 36
Compton Bishop. *Som* 1G 21
Compton Chamberlayne. *Wilts* 4F 23
Compton Dando. *Bath* 5B 34
Compton Dundon. *Som* 3H 21
Compton Greenfield. *S Glo* 3A 34
Compton Martin. *Bath* 1A 22
Compton Pauncefoot. *Som* 4B 22
Compton Valence. *Dors* 3A 14
Comrie. *Fife* 1D 128
Comrie. *Per* 1G 135
Conaglen. *High* 2E 141
Conchra. *Arg* 1B 126
Conchra. *High* 1A 148
Conder Green. *Lanc* 4D 96
Conderton. *Worc* 2E 49
Condicote. *Glos* 3G 49
Condorrat. *N Lan* 2A 128
Condover. *Shrp* 5G 71
Coneyhurst Common. *W Sus* 3C 26
Coneysthorpe. *N Yor* 2B 100
Coneythorpe. *N Yor* 4F 99
Coney Weston. *Suff* 3B 66
Conford. *Hants* 3G 25
Congdon's Shop. *Corn* 5C 10
Congerstone. *Leics* 5A 74
Congham. *Norf* 3G 77
Congleton. *Ches E* 4C 84
Congl-y-wal. *Gwyn* 1G 69
Congresbury. *N Som* 5H 33
Congreve. *Staf* 4D 72
Conham. *S Glo* 4B 34
Conicaval. *Mor* 3D 159
Coningsby. *Linc* 5B 88
Conington. *Cambs* 4C 64 (nr. Fenstanton)
Conington. *Cambs* 2A 64 (nr. Sawtry)
Conisbrough. *S Yor* 1C 86
Conisby. *Arg* 3A 124
Conisholme. *Linc* 1D 88
Coniston. *Cumb* 5E 102
Coniston. *E Yor* 1E 95
Coniston Cold. *N Yor* 4B 98
Conistone. *N Yor* 3B 98
Connah's Quay. *Flin* 4E 83
Connel. *Arg* 5D 140
Connel Park. *E Ayr* 3F 117
Connista. *High* 1D 154
Connor Downs. *Corn* 3C 4
Conock. *Wilts* 1F 23
Conon Bridge. *High* 3H 157
Cononley. *N Yor* 5B 98
Cononsyth. *Ang* 4E 145
Conordan. *High* 5E 155
Consall. *Staf* 1D 73
Consett. *Dur* 4E 115
Constable Burton. *N Yor* 5E 105
Constantine. *Corn* 4E 5
Constantine Bay. *Corn* 1C 6
Contin. *High* 3G 157
Contullich. *High* 1A 158
Conwy. *Cnwy* 3G 81
Conyer. *Kent* 4D 40
Conyer's Green. *Suff* 4A 66
Cooden. *E Sus* 5B 28
Cooil. *IOM* 4C 108
Cookbury. *Devn* 2E 11
Cookbury Wick. *Devn* 2D 11
Cookham. *Wind* 3G 37
Cookham Dean. *Wind* 3G 37
Cookham Rise. *Wind* 3G 37
Cookhill. *Worc* 5E 61
Cookley. *Suff* 3F 67
Cookley. *Worc* 2C 60
Cookley Green. *Oxon* 2E 37
Cookney. *Abers* 4F 153
Cooksbridge. *E Sus* 4F 27
Cooksey Corner. *Worc* 4D 60
Cooksey Green. *Worc* 4D 60
Cookshill. *Staf* 1D 72
Cooksmill Green. *Essx* 5G 53
Coolham. *W Sus* 3C 26
Cooling. *Medw* 3B 40
Cooling Street. *Medw* 3B 40
Coombe. *Corn* 1C 10 (nr. Bude)
Coombe. *Corn* 3D 6 (nr. St Austell)
Coombe. *Corn* 4C 6 (nr. Truro)
Coombe. *Devn* 3E 12 (nr. Sidmouth)
Coombe. *Devn* 5C 12 (nr. Teignmouth)
Coombe. *Glos* 2C 34
Coombe. *Hants* 4E 25
Coombe. *Wilts* 1G 23
Coombe Bissett. *Wilts* 4G 23
Coombe Hill. *Glos* 3D 49
Coombe Keynes. *Dors* 4D 14
Coombes. *W Sus* 5C 26
Coombe Street. *Som* 3C 22
Coopersale Common. *Essx* 5E 53
Coopersale Street. *Essx* 5E 53
Cooper's Corner. *Kent* 1F 27
Cooper Street. *Kent* 5H 41
Cootham. *W Sus* 4B 26
Copalder Corner. *Cambs* 1C 64
Copdock. *Suff* 1E 54
Copford. *Essx* 3C 54
Copford Green. *Essx* 3C 54
Copgrove. *N Yor* 3F 99
Copister. *Shet* 4F 173
Cople. *Bed* 1B 52
Copley. *Dur* 2D 105
Coplow Dale. *Derbs* 3F 85
Copmanthorpe. *York* 5H 99
Copp. *Lanc* 1C 90
Coppathorne. *Corn* 2C 10
Coppenhall. *Ches E* 5B 84
Coppenhall. *Staf* 4D 72
Coppenhall Moss. *Ches E* 5B 84
Copperhouse. *Corn* 3C 4
Coppicegate. *Shrp* 2B 60
Coppingford. *Cambs* 2A 64
Copplestone. *Devn* 2A 12
Coppull. *Lanc* 3D 90
Coppull Moor. *Lanc* 3D 90
Copsale. *W Sus* 3C 26
Copster Green. *Lanc* 1E 91
Copston Magna. *Warw* 2B 62
Copt Green. *Warw* 4F 61
Copthall Green. *Essx* 5E 53
Copt Heath. *W Mid* 3F 61
Copt Hewick. *N Yor* 2F 99
Copthill. *Dur* 5B 114
Copthorne. *W Sus* 2E 27
Coptiviney. *Shrp* 2G 71
Copy's Green. *Norf* 2B 78
Copythorne. *Hants* 1B 16
Corbridge. *Nmbd* 3C 114
Corby. *Nptn* 2F 63
Corby Glen. *Linc* 3H 75
Cordon. *N Ayr* 2E 123
Coreley. *Shrp* 3A 60
Corfe. *Som* 1F 13
Corfe Castle. *Dors* 4E 15
Corfe Mullen. *Dors* 3E 15
Corfton. *Shrp* 2G 59
Corgarff. *Abers* 3G 151
Corhampton. *Hants* 4E 24
Corlae. *Dum* 5F 117
Corlannau. *Neat* 2A 32
Corley. *Warw* 2H 61
Corley Ash. *Warw* 2G 61
Corley Moor. *Warw* 2G 61
Cormiston. *S Lan* 1C 118
Cornaa. *IOM* 3D 108
Cornaigbeg. *Arg* 4A 138
Cornaigmore. *Arg* 2D 138 (on Coll)
Cornaigmore. *Arg* 4A 138 (on Tiree)
Corner Row. *Lanc* 1C 90
Corney. *Cumb* 5C 102
Cornforth. *Dur* 1A 106
Cornhill. *Abers* 3C 160
Cornhill. *High* 4C 164
Cornhill-on-Tweed. *Nmbd* 1C 120
Cornholme. *W Yor* 2H 91
Cornish Hall End. *Essx* 2G 53
Cornquoy. *Orkn* 7E 172
Cornriggs. *Dur* 5B 114
Cornsay. *Dur* 5E 115
Cornsay Colliery. *Dur* 5E 115
Corntown. *High* 3H 157
Corntown. *V Glam* 4C 32
Cornwell. *Oxon* 3A 50
Cornwood. *Devn* 3C 8
Cornworthy. *Devn* 3E 9
Corpach. *High* 1E 141
Corpusty. *Norf* 3D 78
Corra. *Dum* 3F 111
Corran. *High* 2E 141 (nr. Arnisdale)
Corran. *High* 3A 148 (nr. Fort William)
Corrany. *IOM* 3D 108
Corribeg. *High* 1D 141
Corrie. *N Ayr* 5B 126
Corrie Common. *Dum* 1D 112
Corriecravie. *N Ayr* 3D 122
Corriekinloch. *High* 1A 164
Corriemoillie. *High* 2F 157
Corrievarkie Lodge. *Per* 1C 142
Corrievorrie. *High* 1B 150
Corrigall. *Orkn* 6C 172
Corrimony. *High* 5F 157
Corringham. *Linc* 1F 87
Corringham. *Thur* 2B 40
Corris. *Gwyn* 5G 69
Corris Uchaf. *Gwyn* 5G 69
Corrour Shooting Lodge. *High* 2B 142
Corry. *High* 1E 147
Corrybrough. *High* 1C 150
Corrygills. *N Ayr* 2E 123
Corry of Ardnagrask. *High* 4H 157
Corsback. *High* 1E 169 (nr. Dunnet)
Corsback. *High* 3E 169 (nr. Halkirk)
Corscombe. *Dors* 2A 14
Corse. *Abers* 4D 160
Corse. *Glos* 3C 48
Corsehill. *Abers* 3G 161
Corse Lawn. *Worc* 2D 48
Corse of Kinnoir. *Abers* 4C 160
Corsham. *Wilts* 4D 34
Corsley. *Wilts* 2D 22
Corsley Heath. *Wilts* 2D 22
Corsock. *Dum* 2E 111
Corston. *Bath* 5B 34
Corston. *Wilts* 3E 35
Corstorphine. *Edin* 2F 129
Cortachy. *Ang* 3C 144
Corton. *Suff* 1H 67
Corton. *Wilts* 2E 23
Corton Denham. *Som* 4B 22
Corwar House. *S Ayr* 1H 109
Corwen. *Den* 1C 70
Coryates. *Dors* 4B 14
Coryton. *Devn* 4E 11
Coryton. *Thur* 2B 40
Cosby. *Leics* 1C 62
Coscote. *Oxon* 3D 36
Coseley. *W Mid* 1D 60
Cosgrove. *Nptn* 1F 51
Cosham. *Port* 2E 17
Cosheston. *Pemb* 4E 43
Coskills. *N Lin* 3D 94
Cosmeston. *V Glam* 5E 33
Cossall. *Notts* 1B 74
Cossington. *Leics* 4D 74
Cossington. *Som* 2G 21
Costa. *Orkn* 5C 172
Costessey. *Norf* 4D 78
Costock. *Notts* 3C 74
Coston. *Leics* 3F 75
Coston. *Norf* 5C 78
Cote. *Oxon* 5B 50
Cotebrook. *Ches W* 4H 83
Cotehill. *Cumb* 4F 113
Cotes. *Cumb* 1D 97
Cotes. *Leics* 3C 74
Cotes. *Staf* 2C 72
Cotesbach. *Leics* 2C 62
Cotes Heath. *Staf* 2C 72
Cotford St Luke. *Som* 4E 21
Cotgrave. *Notts* 2D 74
Cothall. *Abers* 2F 153
Cotham. *Notts* 1E 75
Cothelstone. *Som* 3E 21
Cotheridge. *Worc* 5B 60
Cotherstone. *Dur* 3D 104
Cothill. *Oxon* 2C 36
Cotland. *Mon* 5A 48
Cotleigh. *Devn* 2F 13
Cotmanhay. *Derbs* 1B 74
Coton. *Cambs* 5D 64
Coton. *Nptn* 3D 62
Coton. *Staf* 3C 72 (nr. Gnosall)
Coton. *Staf* 2D 73 (nr. Stone)
Coton. *Staf* 5F 73 (nr. Tamworth)
Coton Clanford. *Staf* 3C 72
Coton Hayes. *Staf* 2D 73
Coton Hill. *Shrp* 4G 71

Deopham. *Norf* 5C **78**
Deopham Green. *Norf* 1C **66**
Depden. *Suff* 5G **65**
Depden Green. *Suff* 5G **65**
Deptford. *G Lon* 3E **39**
Deptford. *Wilts* 3F **23**
Derby. *Derb* 2A **74** & **193**
Derbyhaven. *IOM* 5B **108**
Derculich. *Per* 3F **143**
Dereham. *Norf* 4B **78**
Deri. *Cphy* 5E **47**
Derril. *Devn* 2D **10**
Derringstone. *Kent* 1G **29**
Derrington. *Shrp* 1A **60**
Derrington. *Staf* 3C **72**
Derriton. *Devn* 2D **10**
Derryguaig. *Arg* 5F **139**
Derry Hill. *Wilts* 4E **35**
Derrythorpe. *N Lin* 4B **94**
Dersingham. *Norf* 2F **77**
Dervaig. *Arg* 3F **139**
Derwen. *Den* 5C **82**
Derwen Gam. *Cdgn* 5D **56**
Derwenlas. *Powy* 1G **57**
Desborough. *Nptn* 2F **63**
Desford. *Leics* 5B **74**
Detchant. *Nmbd* 1E **121**
Dethick. *Derbs* 5H **85**
Detling. *Kent* 5B **40**
Deuchar. *Ang* 2D **144**
Deuddwr. *Powy* 4E **71**
Devauden. *Mon* 2H **33**
Devil's Bridge. *Cdgn* 3G **57**
Devitts Green. *Warw* 1G **61**
Devizes. *Wilts* 5F **35**
Devonport. *Plym* 3A **8**
Devonside. *Clac* 4B **136**
Devoran. *Corn* 5B **6**
Dewartown. *Midl* 3G **129**
Dewlish. *Dors* 3C **14**
Dewsbury. *W Yor* 2C **92**
Dewshall Court. *Here* 2H **47**
Dexbeer. *Devn* 2C **10**
Dhoon. *IOM* 3D **108**
Dhoor. *IOM* 2D **108**
Dhowin. *IOM* 1D **108**
Dial Green. *W Sus* 3A **26**
Dial Post. *W Sus* 4C **26**
Dibberford. *Dors* 2H **13**
Dibden. *Hants* 2C **16**
Dibden Purlieu. *Hants* 2C **16**
Dickleburgh. *Norf* 2D **66**
Didbrook. *Glos* 2F **49**
Didcot. *Oxon* 2D **36**
Diddington. *Cambs* 4A **64**
Diddlebury. *Shrp* 2H **59**
Didley. *Here* 2H **47**
Didling. *W Sus* 1G **17**
Didmarton. *Glos* 3D **34**
Didsbury. *G Man* 1C **84**
Didworthy. *Devn* 2C **8**
Digby. *Linc* 5H **87**
Digg. *High* 2D **154**
Diggle. *G Man* 4A **92**
Digmoor. *Lanc* 4C **90**
Digswell. *Herts* 4C **52**
Dihewyd. *Cdgn* 5D **57**
Dilham. *Norf* 3F **79**
Dilhorne. *Staf* 1D **72**
Dillarburn. *S Lan* 5B **128**
Dillington. *Cambs* 4A **64**
Dilston. *Nmbd* 3C **114**
Dilton Marsh. *Wilts* 2D **22**
Dilwyn. *Here* 5G **59**
Dimmer. *Som* 3B **22**
Dimple. *G Man* 3F **91**
Dinas. *Carm* 1G **43**
Dinas. *Gwyn* 5D **81** (nr. Caernarfon)
Dinas. *Gwyn* 2B **68** (nr. Tudweiliog)
Dinas Cross. *Pemb* 1E **43**
Dinas Dinlle. *Gwyn* 5D **80**
Dinas Mawddwy. *Gwyn* 4A **70**
Dinas Powys. *V Glam* 4E **33**
Dinbych. *Den* 4C **82**
Dinbych-y-Pysgod. *Pemb* 4F **43**
Dinckley. *Lanc* 1E **91**
Dinder. *Som* 2A **22**
Dinedor. *Here* 2A **48**
Dinedor Cross. *Here* 2A **48**
Dingestow. *Mon* 4H **47**
Dingle. *Mers* 2F **83**
Dingleden. *Kent* 2C **28**
Dingleton. *Bord* 1H **119**
Dingley. *Nptn* 2E **63**
Dingwall. *High* 3H **157**
Dinmael. *Cnwy* 1C **70**
Dinnet. *Abers* 4B **152**
Dinnington. *Som* 1H **13**
Dinnington. *S Yor* 2C **86**
Dinnington. *Tyne* 2F **115**
Dinorwic. *Gwyn* 4E **81**
Dinton. *Buck* 4F **51**
Dinton. *Wilts* 3F **23**
Dinworthy. *Devn* 1D **10**
Dipley. *Hants* 1F **25**
Dippen. *Arg* 2B **122**
Dippenhall. *Surr* 2G **25**
Dippertown. *Devn* 4E **11**
Dippin. *N Ayr* 3E **123**
Dipple. *S Ayr* 4B **116**
Diptford. *Devn* 3D **8**
Dipton. *Dur* 4E **115**
Dirleton. *E Lot* 1B **130**
Dirt Pot. *Nmbd* 5B **114**
Discoed. *Powy* 4E **59**
Diseworth. *Leics* 3B **74**
Dishes. *Orkn* 5F **172**
Dishforth. *N Yor* 2F **99**
Disley. *Ches E* 2D **85**
Diss. *Norf* 3D **66**
Disserth. *Powy* 5C **58**
Distington. *Cumb* 2B **102**
Ditchampton. *Wilts* 3F **23**
Ditcheat. *Som* 3B **22**
Ditchingham. *Norf* 1F **67**
Ditchling. *E Sus* 4E **27**
Ditteridge. *Wilts* 5D **34**
Dittisham. *Devn* 3E **9**
Ditton. *Hal* 2G **83**
Ditton. *Kent* 5B **40**
Ditton Green. *Cambs* 5F **65**
Ditton Priors. *Shrp* 2A **60**
Divach. *High* 1G **149**
Dixonfield. *High* 2D **168**
Dixton. *Glos* 2E **49**
Dixton. *Mon* 4A **48**
Dizzard. *Corn* 3B **10**
Dobcross. *G Man* 4H **91**
Dobs Hill. *Flin* 4F **83**
Dobson's Bridge. *Shrp* 2G **71**
Dobwalls. *Corn* 2G **7**
Doccombe. *Devn* 4A **12**
Dochgarroch. *High* 4A **158**
Docking. *Norf* 2G **77**
Docklow. *Here* 5H **59**
Dockray. *Cumb* 2E **103**
Doc Penfro. *Pemb* 4D **42** & **215**
Dodbrooke. *Devn* 4D **8**
Doddenham. *Worc* 5B **60**
Doddinghurst. *Essx* 1G **39**
Doddington. *Cambs* 1C **64**
Doddington. *Kent* 5D **40**
Doddington. *Linc* 4G **87**
Doddington. *Nmbd* 1D **121**
Doddington. *Shrp* 3A **60**
Doddiscombsleigh. *Devn* 4B **12**
Doddshill. *Norf* 2G **77**
Dodford. *Nptn* 4D **62**
Dodford. *Worc* 3D **60**
Dodington. *Som* 2E **21**
Dodington. *S Glo* 4C **34**
Dodleston. *Ches W* 4F **83**
Dods Leigh. *Staf* 2E **73**
Dodworth. *S Yor* 4D **92**
Doe Lea. *Derbs* 4B **86**
Dogdyke. *Linc* 5B **88**
Dogmersfield. *Hants* 1F **25**
Dogsthorpe. *Pet* 5B **76**
Dog Village. *Devn* 3C **12**
Dolanog. *Powy* 4C **70**
Dolau. *Powy* 4D **58**
Dolau. *Rhon* 3D **32**
Dolbenmaen. *Gwyn* 1E **69**
Doley. *Staf* 3B **72**
Dol-fach. *Powy* 5B **70** (nr. Llanbrynmair)
Dolfach. *Powy* 3B **58** (nr. Llanidloes)
Dolfor. *Powy* 2D **58**
Dolgarrog. *Cnwy* 4G **81**
Dolgellau. *Gwyn* 4G **69**
Dolgoch. *Gwyn* 5F **69**
Dol-gran. *Carm* 2E **45**
Dolhelfa. *Powy* 3B **58**
Doll. *High* 3F **165**
Dollar. *Clac* 4B **136**
Dolley Green. *Powy* 4E **59**
Dollwen. *Cdgn* 2F **57**
Dolphin. *Flin* 3D **82**
Dolphingstone. *E Lot* 2G **129**
Dolphinholme. *Lanc* 4E **97**
Dolphinton. *S Lan* 5E **129**
Dolton. *Devn* 1F **11**
Dolwen. *Cnwy* 3A **82**
Dolwyddelan. *Cnwy* 5G **81**
Dol-y-Bont. *Cdgn* 2F **57**
Dolyhir. *Powy* 5E **59**
Domgay. *Powy* 4E **71**
Doncaster. *S Yor* 4F **93**
Donhead St Andrew. *Wilts* 4E **23**
Donhead St Mary. *Wilts* 4E **23**
Doniford. *Som* 2D **20**
Donington. *Linc* 2B **76**
Donington. *Shrp* 5C **72**
Donington Eaudike. *Linc* 2B **76**
Donington le Heath. *Leics* 4B **74**
Donington on Bain. *Linc* 2B **88**
Donington South Ing. *Linc* 2B **76**
Donisthorpe. *Leics* 4H **73**
Donkey Street. *Kent* 2F **29**
Donkey Town. *Surr* 4A **38**
Donna Nook. *Linc* 1D **88**
Donnington. *Glos* 3G **49**
Donnington. *Here* 2C **48**
Donnington. *Shrp* 5H **71**
Donnington. *Telf* 4B **72**
Donnington. *W Ber* 5C **36**
Donnington. *W Sus* 2G **17**
Donyatt. *Som* 1G **13**
Doomsday Green. *W Sus* 2C **26**
Doonfoot. *S Ayr* 3C **116**
Doonholm. *S Ayr* 3C **116**
Dorback Lodge. *High* 2E **151**
Dorchester. *Dors* 3B **14**
Dorchester on Thames. *Oxon* 2D **36**
Dordon. *Warw* 5G **73**
Dore. *S Yor* 2H **85**
Dores. *High* 5H **157**
Dorking. *Surr* 1C **26**
Dorking Tye. *Suff* 2C **54**
Dormansland. *Surr* 1F **27**
Dormans Park. *Surr* 1E **27**
Dormanstown. *Red C* 2C **106**
Dormington. *Here* 1A **48**
Dormston. *Worc* 5D **61**
Dorn. *Glos* 2H **49**
Dorney. *Buck* 3A **38**
Dornie. *High* 1A **148**
Dornoch. *High* 5E **165**
Dornock. *Dum* 3D **112**
Dorrery. *High* 3C **168**
Dorridge. *W Mid* 3F **61**
Dorrington. *Linc* 5H **87**
Dorrington. *Shrp* 5G **71**
Dorsington. *Warw* 1G **49**
Dorstone. *Here* 1G **47**
Dorton. *Buck* 4E **51**
Dotham. *IOA* 3C **80**
Dottery. *Dors* 3H **13**
Doublebois. *Corn* 2F **7**
Dougarie. *N Ayr* 2C **122**
Doughton. *Glos* 2D **35**
Douglas. *IOM* 4C **108**
Douglas. *S Lan* 1H **117**
Douglastown. *Ang* 4D **144**
Douglas Water. *S Lan* 1A **118**
Doulting. *Som* 2B **22**
Dounby. *Orkn* 5B **172**
Doune. *High* 3C **150** (nr. Kingussie)
Doune. *High* 3B **164** (nr. Lairg)
Doune. *Stir* 3G **135**
Dounie. *High* 4C **164** (nr. Bonar Bridge)
Dounie. *High* 5D **164** (nr. Tain)
Dounreay. *High* 2B **168**
Doura. *N Ayr* 5E **127**
Dousland. *Devn* 2B **8**
Dovaston. *Shrp* 3F **71**
Dove Holes. *Derbs* 3E **85**
Dovenby. *Cumb* 1B **102**
Dover. *Kent* 1H **29** & **193**
Dovercourt. *Essx* 2F **55**
Doverdale. *Worc* 4C **60**
Doveridge. *Derbs* 2F **73**
Doversgreen. *Surr* 1D **26**
Dowally. *Per* 4H **143**
Dowbridge. *Lanc* 1C **90**
Dowdeswell. *Glos* 4F **49**
Dowlais. *Mer T* 5D **46**
Dowland. *Devn* 1F **11**
Dowlands. *Devn* 3F **13**
Dowles. *Worc* 3B **60**
Dowlesgreen. *Wok* 5G **37**
Dowlish Wake. *Som* 1G **13**
Downall Green. *Mers* 4D **90**
Down Ampney. *Glos* 2F **35**
Downderry. *Corn* 3H **7** (nr. Looe)
Downderry. *Corn* 3D **6** (nr. St Austell)
Downe. *G Lon* 4F **39**
Downend. *IOW* 4D **16**
Downend. *S Glo* 4B **34**
Downend. *W Ber* 4C **36**
Down Field. *Cambs* 3F **65**
Downfield. *D'dee* 5C **144**
Downgate. *Corn* 5D **10** (nr. Kelly Bray)
Downgate. *Corn* 5C **10** (nr. Upton Cross)
Downham. *Essx* 1B **40**
Downham. *Lanc* 5G **97**
Downham. *Nmbd* 1C **120**
Downham Market. *Norf* 5F **77**
Down Hatherley. *Glos* 3D **48**
Downhead. *Som* 2B **22** (nr. Frome)
Downhead. *Som* 4A **22** (nr. Yeovil)
Downholland Cross. *Lanc* 4B **90**
Downholme. *N Yor* 5E **105**
Downies. *Abers* 4G **153**
Downley. *Buck* 2G **37**
Down St Mary. *Devn* 2H **11**
Downside. *Som* 1B **22** (nr. Chilcompton)
Downside. *Som* 2B **22** (nr. Shepton Mallet)
Downside. *Surr* 5C **38**
Down, The. *Shrp* 1A **60**
Down Thomas. *Devn* 3B **8**
Downton. *Hants* 3A **16**
Downton. *Wilts* 4G **23**
Downton on the Rock. *Here* 3G **59**
Dowsby. *Linc* 3A **76**
Dowsdale. *Linc* 4B **76**
Dowthwaitehead. *Cumb* 2E **103**
Doxey. *Staf* 3D **72**
Doxford. *Nmbd* 2F **121**
Doynton. *S Glo* 4C **34**
Drabblegate. *Norf* 3E **78**
Draethen. *Cphy* 3F **33**
Draffan. *S Lan* 5A **128**
Dragonby. *N Lin* 3C **94**
Dragons Green. *W Sus* 3C **26**
Drakelow. *Worc* 2C **60**
Drakemyre. *N Ayr* 4D **126**
Drakes Broughton. *Worc* 1E **49**
Drakes Cross. *Worc* 3E **61**
Drakewalls. *Corn* 5E **11**
Draughton. *Nptn* 3E **63**
Draughton. *N Yor* 4C **98**
Drax. *N Yor* 2G **93**
Draycot. *Oxon* 5E **51**
Draycote. *Warw* 4B **62**
Draycot Foliat. *Swin* 4G **35**
Draycott. *Derbs* 2B **74**
Draycott. *Glos* 2G **49**
Draycott. *Shrp* 1C **60**
Draycott. *Som* 1H **21** (nr. Cheddar)
Draycott. *Som* 4A **22** (nr. Yeovil)
Draycott. *Worc* 1D **48**
Draycott in the Clay. *Staf* 3F **73**
Draycott in the Moors. *Staf* 1D **73**
Drayford. *Devn* 1A **12**
Drayton. *Leics* 1F **63**
Drayton. *Linc* 2B **76**
Drayton. *Norf* 4D **78**
Drayton. *Nptn* 4C **62**
Drayton. *Oxon* 2C **36** (nr. Abingdon)
Drayton. *Oxon* 1C **50** (nr. Banbury)
Drayton. *Port* 2E **17**
Drayton. *Som* 4H **21**
Drayton. *Warw* 5F **61**
Drayton. *Worc* 3D **60**
Drayton Bassett. *Staf* 5F **73**
Drayton Beauchamp. *Buck* 4H **51**
Drayton Parslow. *Buck* 3G **51**
Drayton St Leonard. *Oxon* 2D **36**
Drebley. *N Yor* 4C **98**
Dreenhill. *Pemb* 3D **42**
Drefach. *Carm* 4F **45** (nr. Meidrim)
Drefach. *Carm* 2D **44** (nr. Newcastle Emlyn)
Drefach. *Carm* 2G **43** (nr. Tumble)
Drefach. *Cdgn* 1E **45**
Dreghorn. *N Ayr* 1C **116**
Drellingore. *Kent* 1G **29**
Drem. *E Lot* 2B **130**
Dreumasdal. *W Isl* 5C **170**
Drewsteignton. *Devn* 3H **11**
Drewston. *Devn* 4H **11**
Driby. *Linc* 3C **88**
Driffield. *E Yor* 4E **101**
Driffield. *Glos* 2F **35**
Drift. *Corn* 4B **4**
Drigg. *Cumb* 5B **102**
Drighlington. *W Yor* 2C **92**
Drimnin. *High* 3G **139**
Drimpton. *Dors* 2H **13**
Dringhoe. *E Yor* 4F **101**
Drinisiadar. *W Isl* 8D **171**
Drinkstone. *Suff* 4B **66**
Drinkstone Green. *Suff* 4B **66**
Drointon. *Staf* 3E **73**
Droitwich Spa. *Worc* 4C **60**
Droman. *High* 3B **166**
Dron. *Per* 2D **136**
Dronfield. *Derbs* 3A **86**
Dronfield Woodhouse. *Derbs* 3H **85**
Drongan. *E Ayr* 3D **116**
Dronley. *Ang* 5C **144**
Droop. *Dors* 2C **14**
Drope. *V Glam* 4E **32**
Droxford. *Hants* 1E **16**
Droylsden. *G Man* 1C **84**
Druggers End. *Worc* 2C **48**
Druid. *Den* 1C **70**
Druid's Heath. *W Mid* 5E **73**
Druidston. *Pemb* 3C **42**
Druim. *High* 3D **158**
Druimarbin. *High* 1E **141**
Druim Fhearna. *High* 2E **147**
Druimindarroch. *High* 5E **147**
Druim Saighdinis. *W Isl* 2D **170**
Drum. *Per* 3C **136**
Drumbeg. *High* 5B **166**
Drumblade. *Abers* 4C **160**
Drumbuie. *Dum* 1C **110**
Drumbuie. *High* 5G **155**
Drumburgh. *Cumb* 4D **112**
Drumburn. *Dum* 3A **112**
Drumchapel. *Glas* 2G **127**
Drumchardine. *High* 4H **157**
Drumchork. *High* 5C **162**
Drumclog. *S Lan* 1F **117**
Drumeldrie. *Fife* 3G **137**
Drumelzier. *Bord* 1D **118**
Drumfearn. *High* 2E **147**
Drumgask. *High* 4A **150**
Drumgelloch. *N Lan* 3A **128**
Drumgley. *Ang* 3D **144**
Drumguish. *High* 4B **150**
Drumin. *Mor* 5F **159**
Drumindorsair. *High* 4G **157**
Drumlamford House. *S Ayr* 2H **109**
Drumlasie. *Abers* 3D **152**
Drumlemble. *Arg* 4A **122**
Drumlithie. *Abers* 5E **153**
Drummoddie. *Dum* 5A **110**
Drummond. *High* 2A **158**
Drummore. *Dum* 5E **109**
Drummuir. *Mor* 4A **160**
Drumnadrochit. *High* 5H **157**
Drumnagorrach. *Mor* 3C **160**
Drumoak. *Abers* 4E **153**
Drumrunie. *High* 3F **163**
Drumry. *W Dun* 2G **127**
Drums. *Abers* 1G **153**
Drumsleet. *Dum* 2G **111**
Drumsmittal. *High* 4A **158**
Drums of Park. *Abers* 3C **160**
Drumsturdy. *Ang* 5D **145**
Drumtochty Castle. *Abers* 5D **152**
Drumuie. *High* 4D **154**
Drumuillie. *High* 1D **150**
Drumvaich. *Stir* 3F **135**
Drumwhindle. *Abers* 5G **161**
Drunkendub. *Ang* 4F **145**
Drury. *Flin* 4E **83**
Drury Square. *Norf* 4B **78**
Drybeck. *Cumb* 3H **103**
Drybridge. *Mor* 2B **160**
Drybridge. *N Ayr* 1C **116**
Drybrook. *Glos* 4B **48**
Drybrook. *Here* 4A **48**
Dryburgh. *Bord* 1H **119**
Dry Doddington. *Linc* 1F **75**
Dry Drayton. *Cambs* 4C **64**
Drym. *Corn* 3D **4**
Drymen. *Stir* 1F **127**
Drymuir. *Abers* 4G **161**
Drynachan Lodge. *High* 5C **158**
Drynie Park. *High* 3H **157**
Drynoch. *High* 5D **154**
Dry Sandford. *Oxon* 5C **50**
Dryslwyn. *Carm* 3F **45**
Dry Street. *Essx* 2A **40**
Dryton. *Shrp* 5H **71**
Dubford. *Abers* 2E **161**
Dubiton. *Abers* 3D **160**
Dubton. *Ang* 3E **145**
Duchally. *High* 2A **164**
Duck End. *Essx* 3G **53**
Duckington. *Ches W* 5G **83**
Ducklington. *Oxon* 5B **50**
Duckmanton. *Derbs* 3B **86**
Duck Street. *Hants* 2B **24**
Dudbridge. *Glos* 5D **48**
Duddenhoe End. *Essx* 2E **53**
Duddingston. *Edin* 2F **129**
Duddington. *Nptn* 5G **75**
Duddleswell. *E Sus* 3F **27**
Duddo. *Nmbd* 5F **131**
Duddon. *Ches W* 4H **83**
Duddon Bridge. *Cumb* 1A **96**
Dudleston. *Shrp* 2F **71**
Dudleston Heath. *Shrp* 2F **71**
Dudley. *Tyne* 2F **115**
Dudley. *W Mid* 2D **60**
Dudston. *Shrp* 1E **59**
Dudwells. *Pemb* 2D **42**
Duffield. *Derbs* 1H **73**
Duffryn. *Neat* 2B **32**
Dufftown. *Mor* 4H **159**
Duffus. *Mor* 2F **159**
Dufton. *Cumb* 2H **103**
Duggleby. *N Yor* 3C **100**
Duirinish. *High* 5G **155**
Duisdalemore. *High* 2E **147**
Duisdeil Mòr. *High* 2E **147**
Duisky. *High* 1E **141**
Dukesfield. *Nmbd* 4C **114**
Dukestown. *Blae* 5E **47**
Dukinfield. *G Man* 1D **84**
Dulas. *IOA* 2D **81**
Dulcote. *Som* 2A **22**
Dulford. *Devn* 2D **12**
Dull. *Per* 4F **143**
Dullatur. *N Lan* 2A **128**
Dullingham. *Cambs* 5F **65**
Dullingham Ley. *Cambs* 5F **65**
Dulnain Bridge. *High* 1D **151**
Duloe. *Bed* 4A **64**
Duloe. *Corn* 3G **7**
Dulverton. *Som* 4C **20**
Dulwich. *G Lon* 3E **39**
Dumbarton. *W Dun* 2F **127**
Dumbleton. *Glos* 2F **49**
Dumfin. *Arg* 1E **127**
Dumfries. *Dum* 2A **112** & **193**
Dumgoyne. *Stir* 1G **127**
Dummer. *Hants* 2D **24**
Dumpford. *W Sus* 4G **25**
Dun. *Ang* 2F **145**
Dunagoil. *Arg* 4B **126**
Dunalastair. *Per* 3E **142**
Dunan. *High* 1D **147**
Dunball. *Som* 2G **21**
Dunbar. *E Lot* 2C **130**
Dunbeath. *High* 5D **168**
Dunbeg. *Arg* 5C **140**
Dunblane. *Stir* 3G **135**
Dunbog. *Fife* 2E **137**
Dunbridge. *Hants* 4B **24**
Duncanston. *Abers* 1C **152**
Duncanston. *High* 3H **157**
Dun Charlabhaigh. *W Isl* 3D **171**
Dunchideock. *Devn* 4B **12**
Dunchurch. *Warw* 3B **62**
Duncote. *Nptn* 5D **62**
Duncow. *Dum* 1A **112**
Duncrievie. *Per* 3D **136**
Duncton. *W Sus* 4A **26**
Dundee. *D'dee* 5D **144** & **194**
Dundee Airport. *D'dee* 1F **137**
Dundon. *Som* 3H **21**
Dundonald. *S Ayr* 1C **116**
Dundonnell. *High* 5E **163**
Dundraw. *Cumb* 5D **112**
Dundreggan. *High* 2F **149**
Dundrennan. *Dum* 5E **111**
Dundridge. *Hants* 1D **16**
Dundry. *N Som* 5A **34**
Dunecht. *Abers* 3E **153**
Dunfermline. *Fife* 1D **129**
Dunford Bridge. *S Yor* 4B **92**
Dungate. *Kent* 5D **40**
Dunge. *Wilts* 1D **23**
Dungeness. *Kent* 4E **29**
Dungworth. *S Yor* 2G **85**
Dunham-on-the-Hill. *Ches W* 3G **83**
Dunham-on-Trent. *Notts* 3F **87**
Dunhampton. *Worc* 4C **60**
Dunham Town. *G Man* 2B **84**
Dunham Woodhouses. *G Man* 2B **84**
Dunholme. *Linc* 3H **87**
Dunino. *Fife* 2H **137**
Dunipace. *Falk* 1B **128**
Dunira. *Per* 1G **135**
Dunkeld. *Per* 4H **143**
Dunkerton. *Bath* 1C **22**
Dunkeswell. *Devn* 2E **13**
Dunkeswick. *N Yor* 5F **99**
Dunkirk. *Kent* 5E **41**
Dunkirk. *S Glo* 3C **34**
Dunkirk. *Staf* 5C **84**
Dunkirk. *Wilts* 5E **35**
Dunk's Green. *Kent* 5H **39**
Dunlappie. *Ang* 2E **145**
Dunley. *Hants* 1C **24**
Dunley. *Worc* 4B **60**
Dunlichity Lodge. *High* 5A **158**
Dunlop. *E Ayr* 5F **127**
Dunmaglass Lodge. *High* 1H **149**
Dunmore. *Arg* 3F **125**
Dunmore. *Falk* 1B **128**

Dunmore—Ebford

Dunmore. *High* 4H 157
Dunnet. *High* 1E 169
Dunnichen. *Ang* 4E 145
Dunning. *Per* 2C 136
Dunnington. *E Yor* 4F 101
Dunnington. *Warw* 5E 61
Dunnington. *York* 4A 100
Dunnockshaw. *Lanc* 2G 91
Dunoon. *Arg* 2C 126
Dunphail. *Mor* 4E 159
Dunragit. *Dum* 4G 109
Dunrostan. *Arg* 1F 125
Duns. *Bord* 4D 130
Dunsby. *Linc* 3A 76
Dunscar. *G Man* 3F 91
Dunscore. *Dum* 1F 111
Dunscroft. *S Yor* 4G 93
Dunsdale. *Red C* 3D 106
Dunsden Green. *Oxon* 4F 37
Dunsfold. *Surr* 2B 26
Dunsford. *Devn* 4B 12
Dunshalt. *Fife* 2E 137
Dunshillock. *Abers* 4G 161
Dunsley. *N Yor* 3F 107
Dunsley. *Staf* 2C 60
Dunsmore. *Buck* 5G 51
Dunsop Bridge. *Lanc* 4F 97
Dunstable. *C Beds* 3A 52
Dunstal. *Staf* 3E 73
Dunstall. *Staf* 3F 73
Dunstall Green. *Suff* 4G 65
Dunstall Hill. *W Mid* 1D 60
Dunstan. *Nmbd* 3G 121
Dunster. *Som* 2C 20
Duns Tew. *Oxon* 3C 50
Dunston. *Linc* 4H 87
Dunston. *Norf* 5E 79
Dunston. *Staf* 4D 72
Dunston. *Tyne* 3F 115
Dunstone. *Devn* 3B 8
Dunston Heath. *Staf* 4D 72
Dunsville. *S Yor* 4G 93
Dunswell. *E Yor* 1D 94
Dunsyre. *S Lan* 5D 128
Dunterton. *Devn* 5D 11
Duntisbourne Abbots. *Glos* 5E 49
Duntisbourne Leer. *Glos* 5E 49
Duntisbourne Rouse. *Glos* 5E 49
Duntish. *Dors* 2B 14
Duntocher. *W Dun* 2F 127
Dunton. *Buck* 3G 51
Dunton. *C Beds* 1C 52
Dunton. *Norf* 2A 78
Dunton Bassett. *Leics* 1C 62
Dunton Green. *Kent* 5G 39
Dunton Patch. *Norf* 2A 78
Duntulm. *High* 1D 154
Dunure. *S Ayr* 3B 116
Dunvant. *Swan* 3E 31
Dunvegan. *High* 4B 154
Dunwich. *Suff* 3G 67
Dunwood. *Staf* 5D 84
Durdar. *Cumb* 4F 113
Durgates. *E Sus* 2H 27
Durham. *Dur* 5F 115 & 194
Durham Tees Valley Airport. *Darl* 3A 106
Durisdeer. *Dum* 4A 118
Durisdeermill. *Dum* 4A 118
Durkar. *W Yor* 3D 92
Durleigh. *Som* 3F 21
Durley. *Hants* 1D 16
Durley. *Wilts* 5H 35
Durley Street. *Hants* 1D 16
Durlow Common. *Here* 2B 48
Durnamuck. *High* 4E 163
Durness. *High* 2E 166
Durno. *Abers* 1E 152
Durns Town. *Hants* 3A 16
Duror. *High* 3D 141
Durran. *Arg* 3G 133
Durran. *High* 2D 169
Durrant Green. *Kent* 2C 28
Durrants. *Hants* 1F 17
Durrington. *W Sus* 5C 26
Durrington. *Wilts* 2G 23
Dursley. *Glos* 2C 34
Dursley Cross. *Glos* 4B 48
Durston. *Som* 4F 21
Durweston. *Dors* 2D 14
Dury. *Shet* 6F 173
Duston. *Nptn* 4E 62
Duthil. *High* 1D 150
Dutlas. *Powy* 3E 58
Duton Hill. *Essx* 3G 53
Dutson. *Corn* 4D 10
Dutton. *Ches W* 3H 83
Duxford. *Cambs* 1E 53
Duxford. *Oxon* 2B 36
Dwygyfylchi. *Cnwy* 3G 81
Dwyran. *IOA* 4D 80
Dyce. *Aber* 2F 153
Dyffryn. *B'end* 2B 32
Dyffryn. *Carm* 2H 43
Dyffryn. *Pemb* 1D 42
Dyffryn. *V Glam* 4D 32
Dyffryn Ardudwy. *Gwyn* 3E 69
Dyffryn Castell. *Cdgn* 2G 57
Dyffryn Ceidrych. *Carm* 3H 45
Dyffryn Cellwen. *Neat* 5B 46
Dyke. *Linc* 3A 76
Dyke. *Mor* 3D 159
Dykehead. *Ang* 2C 144
Dykehead. *N Lan* 3B 128
Dykehead. *Stir* 4E 135
Dykend. *Ang* 3B 144
Dykesfield. *Cumb* 4E 112
Dylife. *Powy* 1A 58
Dymchurch. *Kent* 3F 29
Dymock. *Glos* 2C 48
Dyrham. *S Glo* 4C 34
Dysart. *Fife* 4F 137
Dyserth. *Den* 3C 82

E

Eachwick. *Nmbd* 2E 115
Eadar Dha Fhadhail. *W Isl* 4C 171
Eagland Hill. *Lanc* 5D 96
Eagle. *Linc* 4F 87
Eagle Barnsdale. *Linc* 4F 87
Eagle Moor. *Linc* 4F 87
Eaglescliffe. *Stoc T* 3B 106
Eaglesfield. *Cumb* 2B 102
Eaglesfield. *Dum* 2D 112
Eaglesham. *E Ren* 4G 127
Eaglethorpe. *Nptn* 1H 63
Eagley. *G Man* 3F 91
Eairy. *IOM* 4B 108
Eakley Lanes. *Mil* 5F 63
Eakring. *Notts* 4D 86
Ealand. *N Lin* 3A 94
Ealing. *G Lon* 2C 38
Eallabus. *Arg* 3B 124
Eals. *Nmbd* 4H 113
Eamont Bridge. *Cumb* 2G 103
Earby. *Lanc* 5B 98
Earcroft. *Bkbn* 2E 91
Eardington. *Shrp* 1B 60
Eardisland. *Here* 5G 59
Eardisley. *Here* 1G 47
Eardiston. *Shrp* 3F 71
Eardiston. *Worc* 4A 60
Earith. *Cambs* 3C 64
Earlais. *High* 2C 154
Earle. *Nmbd* 2D 121
Earlesfield. *Linc* 2G 75
Earlestown. *Mers* 1H 83
Earley. *Wok* 4F 37
Earlham. *Norf* 5D 78
Earlish. *High* 2C 154
Earls Barton. *Nptn* 4F 63
Earls Colne. *Essx* 3B 54
Earls Common. *Worc* 5D 60
Earl's Croome. *Worc* 1D 48
Earlsdon. *W Mid* 3H 61
Earlsferry. *Fife* 3G 137
Earlsford. *Abers* 5F 161
Earl's Green. *Suff* 4C 66
Earlsheaton. *W Yor* 2C 92
Earl Shilton. *Leics* 1B 62
Earl Soham. *Suff* 4E 67
Earl Sterndale. *Derbs* 4E 85
Earlston. *E Ayr* 1D 116
Earlston. *Bord* 1H 119
Earl Stonham. *Suff* 5D 66
Earlstoun. *Dum* 1D 110
Earlswood. *Mon* 2H 33
Earlswood. *Warw* 3F 61
Earlyvale. *Bord* 4F 129
Earnley. *W Sus* 3G 17
Earsairidh. *W Isl* 9C 170
Earsdon. *Tyne* 2G 115
Earsham. *Norf* 2F 67
Earsham Street. *Suff* 3E 67
Earswick. *York* 4A 100
Eartham. *W Sus* 5A 26
Earthcott Green. *S Glo* 3B 34
Easby. *N Yor* 4C 106
(nr. Great Ayton)
Easby. *N Yor* 4E 105
(nr. Richmond)
Easdale. *Arg* 2E 133
Easebourne. *W Sus* 4G 25
Easenhall. *Warw* 3B 62
Eashing. *Surr* 1A 26
Easington. *Buck* 4E 51
Easington. *Dur* 5H 115
Easington. *E Yor* 3G 95
Easington. *Nmbd* 1F 121
Easington. *Oxon* 2C 50
(nr. Banbury)
Easington. *Oxon* 2E 37
(nr. Watlington)
Easington. *Red C* 3E 107
Easington Colliery. *Dur* 5H 115
Easington Lane. *Tyne* 5G 115
Easingwold. *N Yor* 3H 99
Easole Street. *Kent* 5G 41
Eassie. *Ang* 4C 144
Eassie and Nevay. *Ang* 4C 144
East Aberthaw. *V Glam* 5D 32
Eastacombe. *Devn* 4F 19
Eastacott. *Devn* 4G 19
East Allington. *Devn* 4D 8
East Anstey. *Devn* 4B 20
East Anton. *Hants* 2B 24
East Appleton. *N Yor* 5F 105
East Ardsley. *W Yor* 2D 92
East Ashley. *Devn* 1G 11
East Ashling. *W Sus* 2G 17
East Aston. *Hants* 2C 24
East Ayton. *N Yor* 1D 101
East Barkwith. *Linc* 2A 88
East Barnby. *N Yor* 3F 107
East Barnet. *G Lon* 1D 39
East Barns. *E Lot* 2D 130
East Barsham. *Norf* 2B 78
East Beach. *W Sus* 3G 17
East Beckham. *Norf* 1D 78
East Bedfont. *G Lon* 3B 38
East Bennan. *N Ayr* 3D 123
East Bergholt. *Suff* 2D 54
East Bierley. *W Yor* 2B 92
East Blatchington. *E Sus* 5F 27
East Bliney. *Norf* 4B 78
East Bloxworth. *Dors* 3D 15
East Boldre. *Hants* 2B 16
East Bolton. *Nmbd* 3F 121
Eastbourne. *Darl* 3F 105
Eastbourne. *E Sus* 5H 27 & 195
East Brent. *Som* 1G 21
East Bridge. *Suff* 4G 67
East Bridgford. *Notts* 1D 74
East Briscoe. *Dur* 3C 104
East Buckland. *Devn* 3G 19
(nr. Barnstaple)
East Buckland. *Devn* 4C 8
(nr. Thurlestone)
East Budleigh. *Devn* 4D 12
Eastburn. *W Yor* 5C 98
East Burnham. *Buck* 2A 38
East Burrafirth. *Shet* 6E 173
East Burton. *Dors* 4D 14
Eastbury. *Herts* 1B 38
Eastbury. *W Ber* 4B 36
East Butsfield. *Dur* 5E 115
East Butterleigh. *Devn* 2C 12
East Butterwick. *N Lin* 4B 94
Eastby. *N Yor* 4C 98
East Calder. *W Lot* 3D 129
East Carleton. *Norf* 5D 78
East Carlton. *Nptn* 2F 63
East Carlton. *W Yor* 5E 98
East Chaldon. *Dors* 4C 14
East Challow. *Oxon* 3B 36
East Charleton. *Devn* 4D 8
East Chelborough. *Dors* 2A 14
East Chiltington. *E Sus* 4E 27
East Chinnock. *Som* 1H 13
East Chisenbury. *Wilts* 1G 23
Eastchurch. *Kent* 3D 40
East Clandon. *Surr* 5B 38
East Claydon. *Buck* 3F 51
East Clevedon. *N Som* 4H 33
East Clyne. *High* 3F 165
East Clyth. *High* 5E 169
East Coker. *Som* 1A 14
Eastcombe. *Glos* 5D 49
East Combe. *Som* 3E 21
East Common. *N Yor* 1G 93
East Compton. *Som* 2B 22
East Cornworthy. *Devn* 3E 9
Eastcote. *G Lon* 2C 38
Eastcote. *Nptn* 5D 62
Eastcote. *W Mid* 3F 61
Eastcott. *Corn* 1C 10
Eastcott. *Wilts* 1F 23
East Cottingwith. *E Yor* 5B 100
East Coulston. *Wilts* 1E 23
Eastcourt. *Wilts* 5H 35
(nr. Pewsey)
Eastcourt. *Wilts* 2E 35
(nr. Tetbury)
East Cowes. *IOW* 3D 16
East Cowick. *E Yor* 2G 93
East Cowton. *N Yor* 4A 106
East Cramlington. *Nmbd* 2F 115
East Cranmore. *Som* 2B 22
East Creech. *Dors* 4E 15
East Croachy. *High* 1A 150
East Dean. *E Sus* 5G 27
East Dean. *Glos* 3B 48
East Dean. *Hants* 4A 24
East Dean. *W Sus* 4A 26
East Down. *Devn* 2G 19
East Drayton. *Notts* 3E 87
East Dundry. *N Som* 5A 34
East Ella. *Hull* 2D 94
East End. *Cambs* 3C 64
East End. *Dors* 3E 15
East End. *E Yor* 4F 101
(nr. Ulrome)
East End. *E Yor* 2F 95
(nr. Withernsea)
East End. *Hants* 3B 16
(nr. Lymington)
East End. *Hants* 5C 36
(nr. Newbury)
East End. *Herts* 3E 53
East End. *Kent* 3D 40
(nr. Minster)
East End. *Kent* 2C 28
(nr. Tenterden)
East End. *N Som* 4H 33
East End. *Oxon* 4B 50
East End. *Som* 1A 22
East End. *Suff* 2E 54
Easter Ardross. *High* 1A 158
Easter Balgedie. *Per* 3D 136
Easter Balmoral. *Abers* 4G 151
Easter Brae. *High* 2A 158
Easter Buckieburn. *Stir* 1A 128
Easter Bush. *Midl* 3F 129
Easter Compton. *S Glo* 3A 34
Easter Fearn. *High* 5D 164
Easter Galcantray. *High* 4C 158
Eastergate. *W Sus* 5A 26
Easterhouse. *Glas* 3H 127
Easter Howgate. *Midl* 3F 129
Easter Kinkell. *High* 3H 157
Easter Lednathie. *Ang* 2C 144
Easter Ogil. *Ang* 2D 144
Easter Ord. *Abers* 3F 153
Easter Quarff. *Shet* 8F 173
Easter Rhynd. *Per* 2D 136
Easter Skeld. *Shet* 7E 173
Easter Suddie. *High* 3A 158
Easterton. *Wilts* 1F 23
Eastertown. *Som* 1G 21
Easter Tulloch. *Abers* 1G 145
East Everleigh. *Wilts* 1H 23
East Farleigh. *Kent* 5B 40
East Farndon. *Nptn* 2E 62
East Ferry. *Linc* 1F 87
Eastfield. *N Lan* 3B 128
(nr. Caldercruix)
Eastfield. *N Lan* 3B 128
(nr. Harthill)
Eastfield. *N Yor* 1E 101
Eastfield. *S Lan* 3H 127
Eastfield Hall. *Nmbd* 4G 121
East Fortune. *E Lot* 2B 130
East Garforth. *W Yor* 1E 93
East Garston. *W Ber* 4B 36
Eastgate. *Dur* 1C 104
Eastgate. *Norf* 3D 78
East Ginge. *Oxon* 3C 36
East Gores. *Essx* 3B 54
East Goscote. *Leics* 4D 74
East Grafton. *Wilts* 5A 36
East Green. *Suff* 5F 65
East Grimstead. *Wilts* 4H 23
East Grinstead. *W Sus* 2E 27
East Guldeford. *E Sus* 3D 28
East Haddon. *Nptn* 4D 62
East Hagbourne. *Oxon* 3D 36
East Halton. *N Lin* 2E 95
East Ham. *G Lon* 2F 39
Eastham. *Mers* 2F 83
Eastham. *Worc* 4A 60
Eastham Ferry. *Mers* 2F 83
Easthampstead. *Brac* 5G 37
Easthampton. *Here* 4G 59
East Hanney. *Oxon* 2C 36
East Hanningfield. *Essx* 5A 54
East Hardwick. *W Yor* 3E 93
East Harling. *Norf* 2B 66
East Harlsey. *N Yor* 5B 106
East Harnham. *Wilts* 4G 23
East Harptree. *Bath* 1A 22
East Hartford. *Nmbd* 2F 115
East Harting. *W Sus* 1G 17
East Hatch. *Wilts* 4E 23
East Hatley. *Cambs* 5B 64
Easthaugh. *Norf* 4C 78
East Hauxwell. *N Yor* 5E 105
East Haven. *Ang* 5E 145
Eastheath. *Wok* 5G 37
East Heckington. *Linc* 1A 76
East Hedleyhope. *Dur* 5E 115
East Helmsdale. *High* 2H 165
East Hendred. *Oxon* 3C 36
East Heslerton. *N Yor* 2D 100
East Hoathly. *E Sus* 4G 27
East Holme. *Dors* 4D 15
Easthope. *Shrp* 1H 59
Easthorpe. *Essx* 3C 54
Easthorpe. *Leics* 2F 75
East Horrington. *Som* 2A 22
East Horsley. *Surr* 5B 38
East Horton. *Nmbd* 1E 121
Easthouses. *Midl* 3G 129
East Howe. *Bour* 3F 15
East Huntspill. *Som* 2G 21
East Hyde. *C Beds* 4B 52
East Ilsley. *W Ber* 3C 36
Eastington. *Devn* 2H 11
Eastington. *Glos* 4G 49
(nr. Northleach)
Eastington. *Glos* 5C 48
(nr. Stonehouse)
East Keal. *Linc* 4C 88
East Kennett. *Wilts* 5G 35
East Keswick. *W Yor* 5F 99
East Kilbride. *S Lan* 4H 127
East Kirkby. *Linc* 4C 88
East Knapton. *N Yor* 2C 100
East Knighton. *Dors* 4D 14
East Knowstone. *Devn* 4B 20
East Knoyle. *Wilts* 3D 23
East Kyloe. *Nmbd* 1E 121
East Lambrook. *Som* 1H 13
East Langdon. *Kent* 1H 29
East Langton. *Leics* 1E 63
East Langwell. *High* 3E 164
East Lavant. *W Sus* 2G 17
East Lavington. *W Sus* 4A 26
East Layton. *N Yor* 4E 105
Eastleach Martin. *Glos* 5H 49
Eastleach Turville. *Glos* 5G 49
East Leake. *Notts* 3C 74
East Learmouth. *Nmbd* 1C 120
Eastleigh. *Devn* 4E 19
(nr. Bideford)
East Leigh. *Devn* 2H 11
(nr. Crediton)
East Leigh. *Devn* 3C 8
(nr. Modbury)
Eastleigh. *Hants* 1C 16
East Lexham. *Norf* 4A 78
East Lilburn. *Nmbd* 2E 121
Eastling. *Kent* 5D 40
East Linton. *E Lot* 2B 130
East Liss. *Hants* 4F 25
East Lockinge. *Oxon* 3C 36
East Looe. *Corn* 3G 7
East Lound. *N Lin* 1E 87
East Lulworth. *Dors* 4D 14
East Lutton. *N Yor* 3D 100
East Lydford. *Som* 3A 22
East Lyng. *Som* 4G 21
East Mains. *Abers* 4D 152
East Malling. *Kent* 5B 40
East Marden. *W Sus* 1G 17
East Markham. *Notts* 3E 87
East Marton. *N Yor* 4B 98
East Meon. *Hants* 4E 25
East Mersea. *Essx* 4D 54
East Mey. *High* 1F 169
East Midlands Airport. *Leics* 3B 74 & 216
East Molesey. *Surr* 4C 38
Eastmoor. *Norf* 5G 77
East Morden. *Dors* 3E 15
East Morton. *W Yor* 5D 98
East Ness. *N Yor* 2A 100
East Newton. *E Yor* 1F 95
East Newton. *N Yor* 2A 100
Eastney. *Port* 3E 17
Eastnor. *Here* 2C 48
East Norton. *Leics* 5E 75
East Nynehead. *Som* 4E 21
East Oakley. *Hants* 1D 24
Eastoft. *N Lin* 3B 94
East Ogwell. *Devn* 5B 12
Easton. *Cambs* 3A 64
Easton. *Cumb* 4D 112
(nr. Burgh by Sands)
Easton. *Cumb* 2F 113
(nr. Longtown)
Easton. *Devn* 4H 11
Easton. *Dors* 5B 14
Easton. *Hants* 3D 24
Easton. *Linc* 3G 75
Easton. *Norf* 4D 78
Easton. *Som* 2A 22
Easton. *Suff* 5E 67
Easton. *Wilts* 4D 35
Easton Grey. *Wilts* 3D 35
Easton-in-Gordano. *N Som* 4A 34
Easton Maudit. *Nptn* 5F 63
Easton on the Hill. *Nptn* 5H 75
Easton Royal. *Wilts* 5H 35
East Orchard. *Dors* 1D 14
East Ord. *Nmbd* 4F 131
East Panson. *Devn* 3D 10
East Peckham. *Kent* 1A 28
East Pennard. *Som* 3A 22
East Perry. *Cambs* 4A 64
East Pitcorthie. *Fife* 3H 137
East Portlemouth. *Devn* 5D 8
East Prawle. *Devn* 5D 9
East Preston. *W Sus* 5B 26
East Putford. *Devn* 1D 10
East Quantoxhead. *Som* 2E 21
East Rainton. *Tyne* 5G 115
East Ravendale. *NE Lin* 1B 88
East Raynham. *Norf* 3A 78
Eastrea. *Cambs* 1B 64
East Rhidorroch Lodge. *High* 4G 163
Eastriggs. *Dum* 3D 112
East Rigton. *W Yor* 5F 99
Eastrington. *E Yor* 1A 94
East Rounton. *N Yor* 4B 106
East Row. *N Yor* 3F 107
East Rudham. *Norf* 3H 77
East Runton. *Norf* 1D 78
East Ruston. *Norf* 3F 79
Eastry. *Kent* 5H 41
East Saltoun. *E Lot* 3A 130
East Shaws. *Dur* 3D 105
East Shefford. *W Ber* 4B 36
Eastshore. *Shet* 10E 173
East Sleekburn. *Nmbd* 1F 115
East Somerton. *Norf* 4G 79
East Stockwith. *Linc* 1E 87
East Stoke. *Dors* 4D 14
East Stoke. *Notts* 1E 75
East Stoke. *Som* 1H 13
East Stour. *Dors* 4D 22
East Stourmouth. *Kent* 4G 41
East Stowford. *Devn* 4G 19
East Stratton. *Hants* 2D 24
East Studdal. *Kent* 1H 29
East Taphouse. *Corn* 2F 7
East-the-Water. *Devn* 4E 19
East Thirston. *Nmbd* 5F 121
East Tilbury. *Thur* 3A 40
East Tisted. *Hants* 3F 25
East Torrington. *Linc* 2A 88
East Tuddenham. *Norf* 4C 78
East Tytherley. *Hants* 4A 24
East Tytherton. *Wilts* 4E 35
East Village. *Devn* 2B 12
Eastville. *Linc* 5D 88
East Wall. *Shrp* 1H 59
East Walton. *Norf* 4G 77
East Week. *Devn* 3G 11
Eastwell. *Leics* 3E 75
East Wellow. *Hants* 4B 24
East Wemyss. *Fife* 4F 137
East Whitburn. *W Lot* 3C 128
Eastwick. *Herts* 4E 53
Eastwick. *Shet* 4E 173
East Williamston. *Pemb* 4E 43
East Winch. *Norf* 4F 77
East Winterslow. *Wilts* 3H 23
East Wittering. *W Sus* 3F 17
East Witton. *N Yor* 1D 98
Eastwood. *Notts* 1B 74
Eastwood. *S'end* 2C 40
East Woodburn. *Nmbd* 1C 114
Eastwood End. *Cambs* 1D 64
East Woodhay. *Hants* 5C 36
East Woodlands. *Som* 2C 22
East Worldham. *Hants* 3F 25
East Worlington. *Devn* 1A 12
East Wretham. *Norf* 1B 66
East Youlstone. *Devn* 1C 10
Eathorpe. *Warw* 4A 62
Eaton. *Ches E* 4C 84
Eaton. *Ches W* 4H 83
Eaton. *Leics* 3E 75
Eaton. *Norf* 2F 77
(nr. Heacham)
Eaton. *Norf* 5E 78
(nr. Norwich)
Eaton. *Notts* 3E 86
Eaton. *Oxon* 5C 50
Eaton. *Shrp* 2F 59
(nr. Bishop's Castle)
Eaton. *Shrp* 1H 59
(nr. Church Stretton)
Eaton Bishop. *Here* 2H 47
Eaton Bray. *C Beds* 3H 51
Eaton Constantine. *Shrp* 5H 71
Eaton Hastings. *Oxon* 2A 36
Eaton Socon. *Cambs* 5A 64
Eaton upon Tern. *Shrp* 3A 72
Eau Brink. *Norf* 4E 77
Eaves Green. *W Mid* 2G 61
Ebberley Hill. *Devn* 1F 11
Ebberston. *N Yor* 1C 100
Ebbesbourne Wake. *Wilts* 4E 23
Ebblake. *Dors* 2G 15
Ebbsfleet. *Kent* 3H 39
Ebbw Vale. *Blae* 5E 47
Ebchester. *Dur* 4E 115
Ebford. *Devn* 4C 12

Ebley—Falmer

Ebley. *Glos* 5D **48**
Ebnal. *Ches W* 1G **71**
Ebrington. *Glos* 1G **49**
Ecchinswell. *Hants* 1D **24**
Ecclefechan. *Dum* 2C **112**
Eccles. *G Man* 1B **84**
Eccles. *Kent* 4B **40**
Eccles. *Bord* 5D **130**
Ecclesall. *S Yor* 2H **85**
Ecclesfield. *S Yor* 1A **86**
Eccles Green. *Here* 1G **47**
Eccleshall. *Staf* 3C **72**
Eccleshill. *W Yor* 1B **92**
Ecclesmachan. *W Lot* 2D **128**
Eccles on Sea. *Norf* 3G **79**
Eccles Road. *Norf* 1C **66**
Eccleston. *Ches W* 4G **83**
Eccleston. *Lanc* 3D **90**
Eccleston. *Mers* 1G **83**
Eccup. *W Yor* 5E **99**
Echt. *Abers* 3E **153**
Eckford. *Bord* 2B **120**
Eckington. *Derbs* 3B **86**
Eckington. *Worc* 1E **49**
Ecton. *Nptn* 4F **63**
Edale. *Derbs* 2F **85**
Eday Airport. *Orkn* 4E **172**
Edburton. *W Sus* 4D **26**
Edderside. *Cumb* 5C **112**
Edderton. *High* 5E **164**
Eddington. *Kent* 4F **41**
Eddington. *W Ber* 5B **36**
Eddleston. *Bord* 5F **129**
Eddlewood. *S Lan* 4A **128**
Edenbridge. *Kent* 1F **27**
Edendonich. *Arg* 1A **134**
Edenfield. *Lanc* 3G **91**
Edenhall. *Cumb* 1G **103**
Edenham. *Linc* 3H **75**
Edensor. *Derbs* 4G **85**
Edentaggart. *Arg* 4C **134**
Edenthorpe. *S Yor* 4G **93**
Eden Vale. *Dur* 1B **106**
Edern. *Gwyn* 2B **68**
Edgarley. *Som* 3A **22**
Edgbaston. *W Mid* 2E **61**
Edgcott. *Buck* 3E **51**
Edgcott. *Som* 3B **20**
Edge. *Glos* 5D **48**
Edge. *Shrp* 5F **71**
Edgebolton. *Shrp* 3H **71**
Edge End. *Glos* 4A **48**
Edgefield. *Norf* 2C **78**
Edgefield Street. *Norf* 2C **78**
Edge Green. *Ches W* 5G **83**
Edgehead. *Midl* 3G **129**
Edgeley. *Shrp* 1H **71**
Edgeside. *Lanc* 2G **91**
Edgeworth. *Glos* 5E **49**
Edgiock. *Worc* 4E **61**
Edgmond. *Telf* 4B **72**
Edgmond Marsh. *Telf* 3B **72**
Edgton. *Shrp* 2F **59**
Edgware. *G Lon* 1C **38**
Edgworth. *Bkbn* 3F **91**
Edinbane. *High* 3C **154**
Edinburgh. *Edin* 2F **129** & **194**
Edinburgh Airport. *Edin* 2E **129**
Edingale. *Staf* 4G **73**
Edingley. *Notts* 5D **86**
Edingthorpe. *Norf* 2F **79**
Edington. *Som* 3G **21**
Edington. *Wilts* 1E **23**
Edingworth. *Som* 1G **21**
Edistone. *Devn* 4C **18**
Edithmead. *Som* 2G **21**
Edith Weston. *Rut* 5G **75**
Edlaston. *Derbs* 1F **73**
Edlesborough. *Buck* 4H **51**
Edlingham. *Nmbd* 4F **121**
Edlington. *Linc* 3B **88**
Edmondsham. *Dors* 1F **15**
Edmondsley. *Dur* 5F **115**
Edmondthorpe. *Leics* 4F **75**
Edmonstone. *Orkn* 5E **172**
Edmonton. *Corn* 1D **6**
Edmonton. *G Lon* 1E **39**
Edmundbyers. *Dur* 4D **114**
Ednam. *Bord* 1B **120**
Ednaston. *Derbs* 1G **73**
Edney Common. *Essx* 5G **53**
Edrom. *Bord* 4E **131**
Edstaston. *Shrp* 2H **71**
Edstone. *Warw* 4F **61**
Edwalton. *Notts* 2D **74**
Edwardstone. *Suff* 1C **54**
Edwardsville. *Mer T* 2D **32**
Edwinsford. *Carm* 2G **45**
Edwinstowe. *Notts* 4D **86**
Edworth. *C Beds* 1C **52**
Edwyn Ralph. *Here* 5A **60**
Edzell. *Ang* 2F **145**
Efail-fach. *Neat* 2A **32**
Efail Isaf. *Rhon* 3D **32**
Efailnewydd. *Gwyn* 2C **68**
Efail-rhyd. *Powy* 3D **70**
Efailwen. *Carm* 2F **43**
Efenechtyd. *Den* 5D **82**
Effingham. *Surr* 5C **38**
Effingham Common. *Surr* 5C **38**
Effirth. *Shet* 6E **173**
Efflinch. *Staf* 4F **73**
Efford. *Devn* 2B **12**
Efstigarth. *Shet* 2F **173**
Egbury. *Hants* 1C **24**
Egdon. *Worc* 5D **60**
Egerton. *G Man* 3F **91**
Egerton. *Kent* 1D **28**
Egerton Forstal. *Kent* 1C **28**
Eggborough. *N Yor* 2F **93**
Eggbuckland. *Plym* 3A **8**
Eggesford. *Devn* 1G **11**
Eggington. *C Beds* 3H **51**
Egginton. *Derbs* 3G **73**
Egglescliffe. *Stoc T* 3B **106**
Eggleston. *Dur* 2C **104**
Egham. *Surr* 3B **38**
Egham Hythe. *Surr* 3B **38**
Egleton. *Rut* 5F **75**
Eglingham. *Nmbd* 3F **121**
Egloshayle. *Corn* 5A **10**
Egloskerry. *Corn* 4C **10**
Eglwysbach. *Cnwy* 3H **81**
Eglwys Brewis. *V Glam* 5D **32**
Eglwys Fach. *Cdgn* 1F **57**
Eglwyswrw. *Pemb* 1F **43**
Egmanton. *Notts* 4E **87**
Egremont. *Cumb* 3B **102**
Egremont. *Mers* 1F **83**
Egton. *N Yor* 4F **107**
Egton Bridge. *N Yor* 4F **107**
Egypt. *Buck* 2A **38**
Egypt. *Hants* 2C **24**
Eight Ash Green. *Essx* 3C **54**
Eight Mile Burn. *Midl* 4E **129**
Eignaig. *High* 4B **140**
Eilanreach. *High* 2G **147**
Eildon. *Bord* 1H **119**
Eileanach Lodge. *High* 2H **157**
Eilean Fhlodaigh. *W Isl* 3D **170**
Eilean Iarmain. *High* 2F **147**
Einacleit. *W Isl* 5D **171**
Eisgein. *W Isl* 6F **171**
Eisingrug. *Gwyn* 2F **69**
Elan Village. *Powy* 4B **58**
Elberton. *S Glo* 3B **34**
Elbridge. *W Sus* 5A **26**
Elburton. *Plym* 3B **8**
Elcho. *Per* 1D **136**
Elcombe. *Swin* 3G **35**
Elcot. *W Ber* 5B **36**
Eldernell. *Cambs* 1C **64**
Eldersfield. *Worc* 2D **48**
Elderslie. *Ren* 3F **127**
Elder Street. *Essx* 2F **53**
Eldon. *Dur* 2F **105**
Eldroth. *N Yor* 3G **97**
Eldwick. *W Yor* 5D **98**
Elfhowe. *Cumb* 5F **103**
Elford. *Nmbd* 1F **121**
Elford. *Staf* 4F **73**
Elford Closes. *Cambs* 3D **65**
Elgin. *Mor* 2G **159**
Elgol. *High* 2D **146**
Elham. *Kent* 1F **29**
Elie. *Fife* 3G **137**
Eling. *Hants* 1B **16**
Eling. *W Ber* 4D **36**
Elishaw. *Nmbd* 5C **120**
Elizafield. *Dum* 2B **112**
Elkesley. *Notts* 3D **86**
Elkington. *Nptn* 3D **62**
Elkins Green. *Essx* 5G **53**
Elkstone. *Glos* 4E **49**
Ellan. *High* 1C **150**
Elland. *W Yor* 2B **92**
Ellary. *Arg* 2F **125**
Ellastone. *Staf* 1F **73**
Ellbridge. *Corn* 2A **8**
Ellel. *Lanc* 4D **97**
Ellemford. *Bord* 3D **130**
Ellenabeich. *Arg* 2E **133**
Ellenborough. *Cumb* 1B **102**
Ellenbrook. *Herts* 5C **52**
Ellenhall. *Staf* 3C **72**
Ellen's Green. *Surr* 2B **26**
Ellerbec. *N Yor* 5B **106**
Ellerburn. *N Yor* 1C **100**
Ellerby. *N Yor* 3E **107**
Ellerdine. *Telf* 3A **72**
Ellerdine Heath. *Telf* 3A **72**
Ellerhayes. *Devn* 2C **12**
Elleric. *Arg* 4E **141**
Ellerker. *E Yor* 2C **94**
Ellerton. *E Yor* 1H **93**
Ellerton. *N Yor* 5F **105**
Ellerton. *Shrp* 3B **72**
Ellesborough. *Buck* 5G **51**
Ellesmere. *Shrp* 2F **71**
Ellesmere Port. *Ches W* 3G **83**
Ellingham. *Hants* 2G **15**
Ellingham. *Norf* 1F **67**
Ellingham. *Nmbd* 2F **121**
Ellingstring. *N Yor* 1D **98**
Ellington. *Cambs* 3A **64**
Ellington. *Nmbd* 5G **121**
Ellington Thorpe. *Cambs* 3A **64**
Elliot. *Ang* 5F **145**
Ellisfield. *Hants* 2E **25**
Ellishadder. *High* 2E **155**
Ellistown. *Leics* 4B **74**
Ellon. *Abers* 5G **161**
Ellonby. *Cumb* 1F **103**
Ellough. *Suff* 2G **67**
Elloughton. *E Yor* 2C **94**
Ellwood. *Glos* 5A **48**
Elm. *Cambs* 5D **76**
Elmbridge. *Glos* 4D **48**
Elmbridge. *Worc* 4D **60**
Elmdon. *Essx* 2E **53**
Elmdon. *W Mid* 2F **61**
Elmdon Heath. *W Mid* 2F **61**
Elmesthorpe. *Leics* 1B **62**
Elmfield. *IOW* 3D **16**
Elm Hill. *Dors* 4D **22**
Elmhurst. *Staf* 4F **73**
Elmley Castle. *Worc* 1E **49**
Elmley Lovett. *Worc* 4C **60**
Elmore. *Glos* 4C **48**
Elmore Back. *Glos* 4C **48**
Elm Park. *G Lon* 2G **39**
Elmscott. *Devn* 4C **18**
Elmsett. *Suff* 1D **54**
Elmstead. *Essx* 3D **54**
Elmstead Heath. *Essx* 3D **54**
Elmstead Market. *Essx* 3D **54**
Elmsted. *Kent* 1F **29**
Elmstone. *Kent* 4G **41**
Elmstone Hardwicke. *Glos* 3E **49**
Elmswell. *E Yor* 4D **101**
Elmswell. *Suff* 4B **66**
Elmton. *Derbs* 3C **86**
Elphin. *High* 2G **163**
Elphinstone. *E Lot* 2G **129**
Elrick. *Abers* 3F **153**
Elrick. *Mor* 1B **152**
Elrig. *Dum* 5A **110**
Elsdon. *Nmbd* 5D **120**
Elsecar. *S Yor* 1A **86**
Elsenham. *Essx* 3F **53**
Elsfield. *Oxon* 4D **50**
Elsham. *N Lin* 3D **94**
Elsing. *Norf* 4C **78**
Elslack. *N Yor* 5B **98**
Elsrickle. *S Lan* 5D **128**
Elstead. *Surr* 1A **26**
Elsted. *W Sus* 1G **17**
Elsted Marsh. *W Sus* 4G **25**
Elsthorpe. *Linc* 3H **75**
Elstob. *Dur* 2A **106**
Elston. *Devn* 2A **12**
Elston. *Lanc* 1E **90**
Elston. *Notts* 1E **75**
Elston. *Wilts* 2F **23**
Elstone. *Devn* 1G **11**
Elstow. *Bed* 1A **52**
Elstree. *Herts* 1C **38**
Elstronwick. *E Yor* 1F **95**
Elswick. *Lanc* 1C **90**
Elswick. *Tyne* 3F **115**
Elsworth. *Cambs* 4C **64**
Elterwater. *Cumb* 4E **103**
Eltham. *G Lon* 3F **39**
Eltisley. *Cambs* 5B **64**
Elton. *Cambs* 1H **63**
Elton. *Ches W* 3G **83**
Elton. *Derbs* 4G **85**
Elton. *Glos* 4C **48**
Elton. *G Man* 3F **91**
Elton. *Here* 3G **59**
Elton. *Notts* 2E **75**
Elton. *Stoc T* 3B **106**
Elton Green. *Ches W* 3G **83**
Eltringham. *Nmbd* 3D **115**
Elvanfoot. *S Lan* 3B **118**
Elvaston. *Derbs* 2B **74**
Elveden. *Suff* 3H **65**
Elvetham Heath. *Hants* 1F **25**
Elvingston. *E Lot* 2A **130**
Elvington. *Kent* 5G **41**
Elvington. *York* 5B **100**
Elwick. *Hart* 1B **106**
Elwick. *Nmbd* 1F **121**
Elworth. *Ches E* 4B **84**
Elworth. *Dors* 4A **14**
Elworthy. *Som* 3D **20**
Ely. *Cambs* 2E **65**
Ely. *Card* 4E **33**
Emberton. *Mil* 1G **51**
Embleton. *Cumb* 1C **102**
Embleton. *Dur* 2B **106**
Embleton. *Nmbd* 2G **121**
Embo. *High* 4F **165**
Emborough. *Som* 1B **22**
Embo Street. *High* 4F **165**
Embsay. *N Yor* 4C **98**
Emery Down. *Hants* 2A **16**
Emley. *W Yor* 3C **92**
Emmbrook. *Wok* 5F **37**
Emmer Green. *Read* 4F **37**
Emmington. *Oxon* 5F **51**
Emneth. *Norf* 5D **77**
Emneth Hungate. *Norf* 5E **77**
Empingham. *Rut* 5G **75**
Empshott. *Hants* 3F **25**
Emsworth. *Hants* 2F **17**
Enborne. *W Ber* 5C **36**
Enborne Row. *W Ber* 5C **36**
Enchmarsh. *Shrp* 1H **59**
Enderby. *Leics* 1C **62**
Endmoor. *Cumb* 1E **97**
Endon. *Staf* 5D **84**
Endon Bank. *Staf* 5D **84**
Enfield. *G Lon* 1E **39**
Enfield Wash. *G Lon* 1E **39**
Enford. *Wilts* 1G **23**
Engine Common. *S Glo* 3B **34**
Englefield. *W Ber* 4E **36**
Englefield Green. *Surr* 3A **38**
Engleseabrook. *Ches E* 5B **84**
English Bicknor. *Glos* 4A **48**
Englishcombe. *Bath* 5C **34**
English Frankton. *Shrp* 3G **71**
Enham Alamein. *Hants* 2B **24**
Enmore. *Som* 3F **21**
Ennerdale Bridge. *Cumb* 3B **102**
Enniscaven. *Corn* 3D **6**
Enoch. *Dum* 4A **118**
Enochdhu. *Per* 2H **143**
Ensay. *Arg* 4E **139**
Ensbury. *Bour* 3F **15**
Ensdon. *Shrp* 4G **71**
Ensis. *Devn* 4F **19**
Enson. *Staf* 3D **72**
Enstone. *Oxon* 3B **50**
Enterkinfoot. *Dum* 4A **118**
Enville. *Staf* 2C **60**
Eolaigearraidh. *W Isl* 8C **170**
Eorabus. *Arg* 1A **132**
Eoropaidh. *W Isl* 1H **171**
Epney. *Glos* 4C **48**
Epperstone. *Notts* 1D **74**
Epping. *Essx* 5E **53**
Epping Green. *Essx* 5E **53**
Epping Green. *Herts* 5C **52**
Epping Upland. *Essx* 5E **53**
Eppleby. *N Yor* 3E **105**
Eppleworth. *E Yor* 1D **94**
Epsom. *Surr* 4D **38**
Epwell. *Oxon* 1B **50**
Epworth. *N Lin* 4A **94**
Epworth Turbary. *N Lin* 4A **94**
Erbistock. *Wrex* 1F **71**
Erbusaig. *High* 1F **147**
Erchless Castle. *High* 4G **157**
Erdington. *W Mid* 1F **61**
Eredine. *Arg* 3G **133**
Eriboll. *High* 3E **167**
Ericstane. *Dum* 3C **118**
Eridge Green. *E Sus* 2G **27**
Erines. *Arg* 2G **125**
Eriswell. *Suff* 3G **65**
Erith. *G Lon* 3G **39**
Erlestoke. *Wilts* 1E **23**
Ermine. *Linc* 3G **87**
Ermington. *Devn* 3C **8**
Ernesettle. *Plym* 3A **8**
Erpingham. *Norf* 2D **78**
Erriottwood. *Kent* 5D **40**
Errogie. *High* 1H **149**
Errol. *Per* 1E **137**
Errol Station. *Per* 1E **137**
Erskine. *Ren* 2F **127**
Erskine Bridge. *Ren* 2F **127**
Ervie. *Dum* 3F **109**
Erwarton. *Suff* 2F **55**
Erwood. *Powy* 1D **46**
Eryholme. *N Yor* 4A **106**
Eryrys. *Den* 5E **82**
Escalls. *Corn* 4A **4**
Escomb. *Dur* 1E **105**
Escrick. *N Yor* 5A **100**
Esgair. *Carm* 3D **45**
(nr. Carmarthen)
Esgair. *Carm* 3G **43**
(nr. St Clears)
Esgairgeiliog. *Powy* 5G **69**
Esh. *Dur* 5E **115**
Esher. *Surr* 4C **38**
Esholt. *W Yor* 5D **98**
Eshott. *Nmbd* 5G **121**
Eshton. *N Yor* 4B **98**
Esh Winning. *Dur* 5E **115**
Eskadale. *High* 5G **157**
Eskbank. *Midl* 3G **129**
Eskdale Green. *Cumb* 4C **102**
Eskdalemuir. *Dum* 5E **119**
Eskham. *Linc* 1C **88**
Esknish. *Arg* 3B **124**
Esk Valley. *N Yor* 4F **107**
Eslington Hall. *Nmbd* 3E **121**
Espley Hall. *Nmbd* 5F **121**
Esprick. *Lanc* 1C **90**
Essendine. *Rut* 4H **75**
Essendon. *Herts* 5C **52**
Essich. *High* 5A **158**
Essington. *Staf* 5D **72**
Eston. *Red C* 3C **106**
Estover. *Plym* 3B **8**
Eswick. *Shet* 6F **173**
Etal. *Nmbd* 1D **120**
Etchilhampton. *Wilts* 5F **35**
Etchingham. *E Sus* 3B **28**
Etchinghill. *Kent* 2F **29**
Etchinghill. *Staf* 4E **73**
Etherley Dene. *Dur* 2E **105**
Ethie Haven. *Ang* 4F **145**
Etling Green. *Norf* 4C **78**
Etloe. *Glos* 5B **48**
Eton. *Wind* 3A **38**
Eton Wick. *Wind* 3A **38**
Etteridge. *High* 4A **150**
Ettersgill. *Dur* 2B **104**
Ettiley Heath. *Ches E* 4B **84**
Ettington. *Warw* 1A **50**
Etton. *E Yor* 5D **101**
Etton. *Pet* 5A **76**
Ettrick. *Bord* 3E **119**
Ettrickbridge. *Bord* 2F **119**
Etwall. *Derbs* 2G **73**
Eudon Burnell. *Shrp* 2B **60**
Eudon George. *Shrp* 2A **60**
Euston. *Suff* 3A **66**
Euxton. *Lanc* 3D **90**
Evanstown. *B'end* 3C **32**
Evanton. *High* 2A **158**
Evedon. *Linc* 1H **75**
Evelix. *High* 4E **165**
Evendine. *Here* 1C **48**
Evenjobb. *Powy* 4E **59**
Evenley. *Nptn* 2D **50**
Evenlode. *Glos* 3H **49**
Even Swindon. *Swin* 3G **35**
Evenwood. *Dur* 2E **105**
Evenwood Gate. *Dur* 2E **105**
Everbay. *Orkn* 5F **172**
Evercreech. *Som* 3B **22**
Everdon. *Nptn* 5C **62**
Everingham. *E Yor* 5C **100**
Everleigh. *Wilts* 1H **23**
Everley. *N Yor* 1D **100**
Eversholt. *C Beds* 2H **51**
Evershot. *Dors* 2A **14**
Eversley. *Hants* 5F **37**
Eversley Centre. *Hants* 5F **37**
Eversley Cross. *Hants* 5F **37**
Everthorpe. *E Yor* 1C **94**
Everton. *C Beds* 5B **64**
Everton. *Hants* 3A **16**
Everton. *Mers* 1F **83**
Everton. *Notts* 1D **86**
Evertown. *Dum* 2E **113**
Evesbatch. *Here* 1B **48**
Evesham. *Worc* 1F **49**
Evington. *Leic* 5D **74**
Ewden Village. *S Yor* 1G **85**
Ewdness. *Shrp* 1B **60**
Ewell. *Surr* 4D **38**
Ewell Minnis. *Kent* 1G **29**
Ewelme. *Oxon* 2E **37**
Ewen. *Glos* 2F **35**
Ewenny. *V Glam* 4C **32**
Ewerby. *Linc* 1A **76**
Ewes. *Dum* 5F **119**
Ewesley. *Nmbd* 5E **121**
Ewhurst. *Surr* 1B **26**
Ewhurst Green. *E Sus* 3B **28**
Ewhurst Green. *Surr* 2B **26**
Ewlo. *Flin* 4F **83**
Ewloe. *Flin* 4F **83**
Ewood Bridge. *Lanc* 2F **91**
Eworthy. *Devn* 3E **11**
Ewshot. *Hants* 1G **25**
Ewyas Harold. *Here* 3G **47**
Exbourne. *Devn* 2G **11**
Exbury. *Hants* 2C **16**
Exceat. *E Sus* 5G **27**
Exebridge. *Som* 4C **20**
Exelby. *N Yor* 1E **99**
Exeter. *Devn* 3C **12** & **195**
Exeter International Airport. *Devn* 3D **12**
Exford. *Som* 3B **20**
Exfords Green. *Shrp* 5G **71**
Exhall. *Warw* 5F **61**
Exlade Street. *Oxon* 3E **37**
Exminster. *Devn* 4C **12**
Exmouth. *Devn* 4D **12**
Exnaboe. *Shet* 10E **173**
Exning. *Suff* 4F **65**
Exton. *Devn* 4C **12**
Exton. *Hants* 4E **24**
Exton. *Rut* 4G **75**
Exton. *Som* 3C **20**
Exwick. *Devn* 3C **12**
Eyam. *Derbs* 3G **85**
Eydon. *Nptn* 5C **62**
Eye. *Here* 4G **59**
Eye. *Pet* 5B **76**
Eye. *Suff* 3D **66**
Eye Green. *Pet* 5B **76**
Eyemouth. *Bord* 3F **131**
Eyeworth. *C Beds* 1C **52**
Eyhorne Street. *Kent* 5C **40**
Eyke. *Suff* 5F **67**
Eynesbury. *Cambs* 5A **64**
Eynort. *High* 1B **146**
Eynsford. *Kent* 4G **39**
Eynsham. *Oxon* 5C **50**
Eyre. *High* 3D **154**
(on Isle of Skye)
Eyre. *High* 5E **155**
(on Raasay)
Eythorne. *Kent* 1G **29**
Eyton. *Here* 4G **59**
Eyton. *Shrp* 2F **59**
(nr. Bishop's Castle)
Eyton. *Shrp* 4F **71**
(nr. Shrewsbury)
Eyton. *Wrex* 1F **71**
Eyton on Severn. *Shrp* 5H **71**
Eyton upon the Weald Moors. *Telf* 4A **72**

F

Faccombe. *Hants* 1B **24**
Faceby. *N Yor* 4B **106**
Faddiley. *Ches E* 5H **83**
Fadmoor. *N Yor* 1A **100**
Fagwyr. *Swan* 5G **45**
Faichem. *High* 3E **149**
Faifley. *W Dun* 2G **127**
Fail. *S Ayr* 2D **116**
Failand. *N Som* 4A **34**
Failford. *S Ayr* 2D **116**
Failsworth. *G Man* 4H **91**
Fairbourne. *Gwyn* 4F **69**
Fairbourne Heath. *Kent* 5C **40**
Fairburn. *N Yor* 2E **93**
Fairfield. *Derbs* 3E **85**
Fairfield. *Kent* 3D **28**
Fairfield. *Worc* 3D **60**
(nr. Bromsgrove)
Fairfield. *Worc* 1F **49**
(nr. Evesham)
Fairford. *Glos* 5G **49**
Fair Green. *Norf* 4F **77**
Fair Hill. *Cumb* 1G **103**
Fairhill. *S Lan* 4A **128**
Fair Isle Airport. *Shet* 1B **172**
Fairlands. *Surr* 5A **38**
Fairlie. *N Ayr* 4D **126**
Fairlight. *E Sus* 4C **28**
Fairlight Cove. *E Sus* 4C **28**
Fairmile. *Devn* 3D **12**
Fairmile. *Surr* 4C **38**
Fairmilehead. *Edin* 3F **129**
Fair Oak. *Devn* 1D **12**
Fair Oak. *Hants* 1C **16**
(nr. Eastleigh)
Fair Oak. *Hants* 5D **36**
(nr. Kingsclere)
Fairoak. *Staf* 2B **72**
Fair Oak Green. *Hants* 5E **37**
Fairseat. *Kent* 4H **39**
Fairstead. *Essx* 4A **54**
Fairstead. *Norf* 4F **77**
Fairwarp. *E Sus* 3F **27**
Fairwater. *Card* 4E **33**
Fairy Cross. *Devn* 4E **19**
Fakenham. *Norf* 3B **78**
Fakenham Magna. *Suff* 3B **66**
Fala. *Midl* 3H **129**
Fala Dam. *Midl* 3H **129**
Falcon. *Here* 2B **48**
Faldingworth. *Linc* 2H **87**
Falfield. *S Glo* 2B **34**
Falkenham. *Suff* 2F **55**
Falkirk. *Falk* 2B **128**
Falkland. *Fife* 3E **137**
Fallin. *Stir* 4H **135**
Fallowfield. *G Man* 1C **84**
Falmer. *E Sus* 5E **27**

Forneth. Per 4H 143
Fornham All Saints. Suff 4H 65
Fornham St Martin. Suff 4A 66
Forres. Mor 3E 159
Forrestfield. N Lan 3B 128
Forrest Lodge. Dum 1C 110
Forsbrook. Staf 1D 72
Forse. High 5E 169
Forsinard. High 4A 168
Forss. High 2C 168
Forstal, The. Kent 2E 29
Forston. Dors 3B 14
Fort Augustus. High 3F 149
Forteviot. Per 2C 136
Fort George. High 3B 158
Forth. S Lan 4C 128
Forthampton. Glos 2D 48
Forthay. Glos 2C 34
Forth Road Bridge. Fife 2E 129
Fortingall. Per 4E 143
Fort Matilda. Inv 2D 126
Forton. Hants 2C 24
Forton. Lanc 4D 97
Forton. Shrp 4G 71
Forton. Som 2G 13
Forton. Staf 3B 72
Forton Heath. Shrp 4G 71
Fortrie. Abers 4D 160
Fortrose. High 3B 158
Fortuneswell. Dors 5B 14
Fort William. High 1F 141
Forty Green. Buck 1A 38
Forty Hill. G Lon 1E 39
Forward Green. Suff 5C 66
Fosbury. Wilts 1B 24
Foscot. Oxon 3H 49
Fosdyke. Linc 2C 76
Foss. Per 3E 143
Fossebridge. Glos 4F 49
Foster Street. Essx 5E 53
Foston. Derbs 2F 73
Foston. Leics 1D 62
Foston. Linc 1F 75
Foston. N Yor 3A 100
Foston on the Wolds. E Yor 4F 101
Fotherby. Linc 1C 88
Fothergill. Cumb 1B 102
Fotheringhay. Nptn 1H 63
Foubister. Orkn 7E 172
Foula Airport. Shet 8A 173
Foul Anchor. Cambs 4D 76
Foulbridge. Cumb 5F 113
Foulden. Norf 1G 65
Foulden. Bord 4F 131
Foul Mile. E Sus 4H 27
Foulridge. Lanc 5A 98
Foulsham. Norf 3C 78
Fountainhall. Bord 5H 129
Four Alls, The. Shrp 2A 72
Four Ashes. Staf 5D 72 (nr. Cannock)
Four Ashes. Staf 2C 60 (nr. Kinver)
Four Ashes. Suff 3C 66
Four Crosses. Powy 5C 70 (nr. Llanerfyl)
Four Crosses. Powy 4E 71 (nr. Llanymynech)
Four Crosses. Staf 5D 72
Four Elms. Kent 1F 27
Four Forks. Som 3F 21
Four Gotes. Cambs 4D 76
Four Lane End. S Yor 4C 92
Four Lane Ends. Lanc 4E 97
Four Lanes. Corn 5A 6
Fourlanes End. Ches E 5B 84
Four Marks. Hants 3E 25
Four Mile Bridge. IOA 3B 80
Four Oaks. E Sus 3C 28
Four Oaks. Glos 3B 48
Four Oaks. W Mid 2G 61
Four Roads. Carm 5E 45
Four Roads. IOM 5B 108
Fourstones. Nmbd 3B 114
Four Throws. Kent 3B 28
Fovant. Wilts 4F 23
Foveran. Abers 1G 153
Fowey. Corn 3F 7
Fowlershill. Abers 2G 153
Fowley Common. Warr 1A 84
Fowlis. Ang 5C 144
Fowlis Wester. Per 1B 136
Fowlmere. Cambs 1E 53
Fownhope. Here 2A 48
Foxcombe Hill. Oxon 5C 50
Fox Corner. Surr 5A 38
Foxcote. Glos 4F 49
Foxcote. Som 1C 22
Foxdale. IOM 4B 108
Foxearth. Essx 1B 54
Foxfield. Cumb 1B 96
Foxham. Wilts 4E 35
Fox Hatch. Essx 1G 39
Foxhole. Corn 3D 6
Foxholes. N Yor 2E 101
Foxhunt Green. E Sus 4G 27
Fox Lane. Hants 1G 25
Foxlediate. Worc 4E 61
Foxley. Norf 3C 78
Foxley. Nptn 5D 62
Foxley. Wilts 3D 35
Fox Street. Essx 3D 54
Foxt. Staf 1E 73
Foxton. Cambs 1E 53
Foxton. Dur 2A 106
Foxton. Leics 2D 62
Foxton. N Yor 5B 106
Foxup. N Yor 2A 98
Foxwist Green. Ches W 4A 84
Foxwood. Shrp 3A 60
Foy. Here 3A 48
Foyers. High 1G 149
Foynesfield. High 3C 158
Fraddam. Corn 3C 4
Fraddon. Corn 3D 6
Fradley. Staf 4F 73
Fradley South. Staf 4F 73
Fradswell. Staf 2D 73
Fraisthorpe. E Yor 3F 101
Framfield. E Sus 3F 27
Framingham Earl. Norf 5E 79
Framingham Pigot. Norf 5E 79
Framlingham. Suff 4E 67
Frampton. Dors 3B 14
Frampton. Linc 2C 76
Frampton Cotterell. S Glo 3B 34
Frampton Mansell. Glos 5E 49
Frampton on Severn. Glos 5C 48
Frampton West End. Linc 1B 76
Framsden. Suff 5D 66
Framwellgate Moor. Dur 5F 115
Franche. Worc 3C 60
Frandley. Ches W 3A 84
Frankby. Mers 2E 83
Frankfort. Norf 3F 79
Frankley. Worc 2D 61
Frank's Bridge. Powy 5D 58
Frankton. Warw 3B 62
Frankwell. Shrp 4G 71
Frant. E Sus 2G 27
Fraserburgh. Abers 2G 161
Frating Green. Essx 3D 54
Fratton. Port 2E 17
Freathy. Corn 3A 8
Freckenham. Suff 3F 65
Freckleton. Lanc 2C 90
Freeby. Leics 3F 75
Freefolk Priors. Hants 2C 24
Freehay. Staf 1E 73
Freeland. Oxon 4C 50
Freester. Shet 6F 173
Freethorpe. Norf 5G 79
Freiston. Linc 1C 76
Freiston Shore. Linc 1C 76
Fremington. Devn 3F 19
Fremington. N Yor 5D 104
Frenchbeer. Devn 4G 11
French Street. Kent 5F 39
Frenich. Stir 3D 134
Frensham. Surr 2G 25
Frenze. Norf 2D 66
Fresgoe. High 2B 168
Freshfield. Mers 4A 90
Freshford. Bath 5C 34
Freshwater. IOW 4B 16
Freshwater Bay. IOW 4B 16
Freshwater East. Pemb 5E 43
Fressingfield. Suff 3E 67
Freston. Suff 2E 55
Freswick. High 2F 169
Fretherne. Glos 5C 48
Frettenham. Norf 4E 79
Freuchie. Fife 3E 137
Freystrop. Pemb 3D 42
Friar's Gate. E Sus 2F 27
Friar Waddon. Dors 4B 14
Friday Bridge. Cambs 5D 76
Friday Street. E Sus 5H 27
Friday Street. Surr 1C 26
Fridaythorpe. E Yor 4C 100
Friden. Derbs 4F 85
Friern Barnet. G Lon 1D 39
Friesthorpe. Linc 2H 87
Frieston. Linc 1G 75
Frieth. Buck 2F 37
Friezeland. Notts 5B 86
Frilford. Oxon 2C 36
Frilsham. W Ber 4D 36
Frimley. Surr 1G 25
Frimley Green. Surr 1G 25
Frindsbury. Medw 4B 40
Fring. Norf 2G 77
Fringford. Oxon 3E 50
Frinsted. Kent 5C 40
Frinton-on-Sea. Essx 4F 55
Friockheim. Ang 4E 145
Friog. Gwyn 4F 69
Frisby. Linc 4D 88
Frisby on the Wreake. Leics 4D 74
Friskney. Linc 5D 88
Friskney Eaudyke. Linc 5D 88
Friston. E Sus 5G 27
Friston. Suff 4G 67
Fritchley. Derbs 5A 86
Fritham. Hants 1H 15
Frith Bank. Linc 1C 76
Frith Common. Worc 4A 60
Frithelstock. Devn 1E 11
Frithelstock Stone. Devn 1E 11
Frithsden. Herts 5A 52
Frithville. Linc 5C 88
Frittenden. Kent 1C 28
Frittiscombe. Devn 4E 9
Fritton. Norf 5G 79 (nr. Great Yarmouth)
Fritton. Norf 1E 67 (nr. Long Stratton)
Fritwell. Oxon 3D 50
Frizinghall. W Yor 1B 92
Frizington. Cumb 3B 102
Frobost. W Isl 6C 170
Frocester. Glos 5C 48
Frochas. Powy 5D 70
Frodesley. Shrp 5H 71
Frodingham. N Lin 3C 94
Frodsham. Ches W 3H 83
Froggat. Derbs 3G 85
Froghall. Staf 1E 73
Frogham. Hants 1G 15
Frogham. Kent 5G 41
Frogmore. Devn 4D 8
Frogmore. Hants 5G 37
Frogmore. Herts 5B 52
Frognall. Linc 4A 76
Frogshall. Norf 2E 79
Frogwell. Corn 2H 7
Frolesworth. Leics 1C 62
Frome. Som 2C 22
Fromefield. Som 2C 22
Frome St Quintin. Dors 2A 14
Fromes Hill. Here 1B 48
Fron. Carm 2A 46
Fron. Gwyn 5E 81 (nr. Caernarfon)
Fron. Gwyn 2C 68 (nr. Pwllheli)
Fron. Powy 4C 58 (nr. Llandrindod Wells)
Fron. Powy 1D 58 (nr. Newtown)
Fron. Powy 5E 71 (nr. Welshpool)
Froncysyllte. Wrex 1E 71
Frongoch. Gwyn 2B 70
Fron Isaf. Wrex 1E 71
Fronoleu. Gwyn 2G 69
Frosterley. Dur 1D 104
Frotoft. Orkn 5D 172
Froxfield. C Beds 2H 51
Froxfield. Wilts 5A 36
Froxfield Green. Hants 4F 25
Fryern Hill. Hants 4C 24
Fryerning. Essx 5G 53
Fryton. N Yor 2A 100
Fugglestone St Peter. Wilts 3G 23
Fulbeck. Linc 5G 87
Fulbourn. Cambs 5E 65
Fulbrook. Oxon 4A 50
Fulflood. Hants 3C 24
Fulford. Som 4F 21
Fulford. Staf 2D 72
Fulford. York 5A 100
Fulham. G Lon 3D 38
Fulking. W Sus 4D 26
Fuller's Moor. Ches W 5G 83
Fuller Street. Essx 4H 53
Fullerton. Hants 3B 24
Fulletby. Linc 3B 88
Full Sutton. E Yor 4B 100
Fullwood. E Ayr 4F 127
Fulmer. Buck 2A 38
Fulmodestone. Norf 2B 78
Fulnetby. Linc 3H 87
Fulney. Linc 3B 76
Fulstow. Linc 1C 88
Fulthorpe. Stoc T 2B 106
Fulwell. Tyne 4G 115
Fulwood. Lanc 1D 90
Fulwood. Notts 5B 86
Fulwood. Som 1F 13
Fulwood. S Yor 2G 85
Fundenhall. Norf 1D 66
Funtington. W Sus 2G 17
Funtley. Hants 2D 16
Funzie. Shet 2H 173
Furley. Devn 2F 13
Furnace. Arg 3H 133
Furnace. Carm 5F 45
Furnace. Cdgn 1F 57
Furner's Green. E Sus 3F 27
Furness Vale. Derbs 2E 85
Furneux Pelham. Herts 3E 53
Furzebrook. Dors 4E 15
Furzehill. Devn 2H 19
Furzehill. Dors 2F 15
Furzeley Corner. Hants 1E 17
Furzey Lodge. Hants 2B 16
Furzley. Hants 1A 16
Fyfield. Essx 5F 53
Fyfield. Glos 5H 49
Fyfield. Hants 2A 24
Fyfield. Oxon 2C 36
Fyfield. Wilts 5G 35
Fylde, The. Lanc 1B 90
Fylingthorpe. N Yor 4G 107
Fyning. W Sus 4G 25
Fyvie. Abers 5E 161

G

Gabhsann bho Dheas. W Isl 2G 171
Gabhsann bho Thuath. W Isl 2G 171
Gabroc Hill. E Ayr 4F 127
Gadbrook. Surr 1D 26
Gaddesby. Leics 4D 74
Gadfa. IOA 2D 80
Gadgirth. S Ayr 2D 116
Gaer. Powy 3E 47
Gaerwen. IOA 3D 81
Gagingwell. Oxon 3C 50
Gaick Lodge. High 5B 150
Gailey. Staf 4D 72
Gainford. Dur 3E 105
Gainsborough. Linc 1F 87
Gainsborough. Suff 1E 55
Gainsford End. Essx 2H 53
Gairletter. Arg 1C 126
Gairloch. Abers 3E 153
Gairloch. High 1H 155
Gairlochy. High 5D 148
Gairney Bank. Per 4D 136
Gairnshiel Lodge. Abers 3G 151
Gaisgill. Cumb 4H 103
Gaitsgill. Cumb 5E 113
Galashiels. Bord 1G 119
Galgate. Lanc 4D 97
Galhampton. Som 4B 22
Gallatown. Fife 4E 137
Galley Common. Warw 1H 61
Galleyend. Essx 5H 53
Galleywood. Essx 5H 53
Gallin. Per 4C 142
Gallowfauld. Ang 4D 144
Gallowhill. E Dun 2H 127
Gallowhill. Per 5A 144
Gallowhill. Ren 3F 127
Gallowhills. Abers 3H 161
Gallows Green. Staf 1E 73
Gallows Green. Worc 4D 60
Gallowstree Common. Oxon 3E 37
Galltair. High 1G 147
Gallt Melyd. Den 2C 82
Galmington. Som 4F 21
Galmisdale. High 5C 146
Galmpton. Devn 4C 8
Galmpton. Torb 3E 9
Galmpton Warborough. Torb 3E 9
Galphay. N Yor 2E 99
Galston. E Ayr 1D 117
Galton. Dors 4C 14
Galtrigill. High 3A 154
Gamblesby. Cumb 1H 103
Gamelsby. Cumb 4D 112
Gamesley. Derbs 1E 85
Gamlingay. Cambs 5B 64
Gamlingay Cinques. Cambs 5B 64
Gamlingay Great Heath. C Beds 5B 64
Gammaton. Devn 4E 19
Gammersgill. N Yor 1C 98
Gamston. Notts 2D 74 (nr. Nottingham)
Gamston. Notts 3E 86 (nr. Retford)
Ganarew. Here 4A 48
Ganavan. Arg 5C 140
Ganborough. Glos 3G 49
Gang. Corn 2H 7
Ganllwyd. Gwyn 3G 69
Gannochy. Ang 1E 145
Gannochy. Per 1D 136
Gansclet. High 4F 169
Ganstead. E Yor 1E 95
Ganthorpe. N Yor 2A 100
Ganton. N Yor 2D 101
Gants Hill. G Lon 2F 39
Gappah. Devn 5B 12
Garafad. High 2D 155
Garboldisham. Norf 2C 66
Garden City. Flin 4F 83
Gardeners Green. Wok 5G 37
Gardenstown. Abers 2F 161
Garden Village. S Yor 1G 85
Garden Village. Swan 3E 31
Garderhouse. Shet 7E 173
Gardham. E Yor 5D 100
Gardie. Shet 5C 173 (on Papa Stour)
Gardie. Shet 1H 173 (on Unst)
Gardie Ho. Shet 7F 173
Gare Hill. Som 2C 22
Garelochhead. Arg 4B 134
Garford. Oxon 2C 36
Garforth. W Yor 1E 93
Gargrave. N Yor 4B 98
Gargunnock. Stir 4G 135
Garleffin. S Ayr 1F 109
Garlieston. Dum 5B 110
Garlinge Green. Kent 5F 41
Garlogie. Abers 3E 153
Garmelow. Staf 3B 72
Garmond. Abers 3F 161
Garmondsway. Dur 1A 106
Garmony. Arg 4A 140
Garmouth. Mor 2H 159
Garmston. Shrp 5A 72
Garnant. Carm 4G 45
Garndiffaith. Torf 5F 47
Garndolbenmaen. Gwyn 1D 69
Garnett Bridge. Cumb 5G 103
Garnfadryn. Gwyn 2B 68
Garnkirk. N Lan 3H 127
Garnlydan. Blae 4E 47
Garnsgate. Linc 3D 76
Garnswllt. Swan 5G 45
Garn-yr-erw. Torf 4F 47
Garrabost. W Isl 4H 171
Garrallan. E Ayr 3E 117
Garras. Corn 4E 5
Garreg. Gwyn 1F 69
Garrigill. Cumb 5A 114
Garriston. N Yor 5E 105
Garrogie Lodge. High 2H 149
Garros. High 2D 155
Garrow. Per 4F 143
Garsdale. Cumb 1G 97
Garsdale Head. Cumb 5A 104
Garsdon. Wilts 3E 35
Garshall Green. Staf 2D 72
Garsington. Oxon 5D 50
Garstang. Lanc 5D 97
Garston. Mers 2G 83
Garswood. Mers 1H 83
Gartcosh. N Lan 3H 127
Garth. B'end 2B 32
Garth. Cdgn 2F 57
Garth. Gwyn 2E 69
Garth. IOM 4C 108
Garth. Powy 1C 46 (nr. Builth Wells)
Garth. Powy 3E 59 (nr. Knighton)
Garth. Shet 6D 173 (nr. Sandness)
Garth. Shet 6F 173 (nr. Skellister)
Garth. Wrex 1E 71
Garthamlock. Glas 3H 127
Garthbrengy. Powy 2D 46
Gartheli. Cdgn 5E 57
Garthmyl. Powy 1D 58
Garthorpe. Leics 3F 75
Garthorpe. N Lin 3B 94
Garth Owen. Powy 1D 58
Garth Row. Cumb 5G 103
Gartly. Abers 5C 160
Gartmore. Stir 4E 135
Gartness. N Lan 3A 128
Gartness. Stir 1G 127
Gartocharn. W Dun 1F 127
Garton. E Yor 1F 95
Garton-on-the-Wolds. E Yor 4D 101
Gartsherrie. N Lan 3A 128
Gartymore. High 2H 165
Garvald. E Lot 2B 130
Garvamore. High 4H 149
Garvard. Arg 4A 132
Garvault. High 5H 167
Garve. High 2F 157
Garvestone. Norf 5C 78
Garvie. Arg 4H 133
Garvock. Abers 1G 145
Garvock. Inv 2D 126
Garway. Here 3H 47
Garway Common. Here 3H 47
Garway Hill. Here 3H 47
Garwick. Linc 1A 76
Gaskan. High 1C 140
Gasper. Wilts 3C 22
Gastard. Wilts 5D 35
Gasthorpe. Norf 2B 66
Gatcombe. IOW 4C 16
Gateacre. Mers 2G 83
Gatebeck. Cumb 1E 97
Gate Burton. Linc 2F 87
Gateforth. N Yor 2F 93
Gatehead. E Ayr 1C 116
Gate Helmsley. N Yor 4A 100
Gatehouse. Nmbd 1A 114
Gatehouse of Fleet. Dum 4D 110
Gatelawbridge. Dum 5B 118
Gateley. Norf 3B 78
Gatenby. N Yor 1F 99
Gatesgarth. Cumb 3C 102
Gateshead. Tyne 3F 115
Gatesheath. Ches W 4G 83
Gateside. Ang 4D 144 (nr. Forfar)
Gateside. Ang 4C 144 (nr. Kirriemuir)
Gateside. Fife 3D 136
Gateside. N Ayr 4E 127
Gathurst. G Man 4D 90
Gatley. G Man 2C 84
Gatton. Surr 5D 39
Gattonside. Bord 1H 119
Gatwick (London) Airport. W Sus 1D 27 & 216
Gaufron. Powy 4B 58
Gaulby. Leics 5D 74
Gauldry. Fife 1F 137
Gaultree. Norf 5D 77
Gaunt's Common. Dors 2F 15
Gaunt's Earthcott. S Glo 3B 34
Gautby. Linc 3A 88
Gavinton. Bord 4D 130
Gawber. S Yor 4D 92
Gawcott. Buck 2E 51
Gawsworth. Ches E 4C 84
Gawthorpe. W Yor 2C 92
Gawthrop. Cumb 1F 97
Gawthwaite. Cumb 1B 96
Gay Bowers. Essx 5A 54
Gaydon. Warw 5A 62
Gayfield. Orkn 2D 172
Gayhurst. Mil 1G 51
Gayle. N Yor 1A 98
Gayles. N Yor 4E 105
Gay Street. W Sus 3B 26
Gayton. Mers 2E 83
Gayton. Norf 4G 77
Gayton. Nptn 5E 62
Gayton. Staf 3D 73
Gayton le Marsh. Linc 2D 88
Gayton le Wold. Linc 2B 88
Gayton Thorpe. Norf 4G 77
Gaywood. Norf 3F 77
Gazeley. Suff 4G 65
Geanies. High 1C 158
Gearraidh Bhailteas. W Isl 6C 170
Gearraidh Bhaird. W Isl 6F 171
Gearraidh ma Monadh. W Isl 7C 170
Gearraidh na h-Aibhne. W Isl 4E 171
Geary. High 2B 154
Geddes. High 3C 158
Gedding. Suff 5B 66
Geddington. Nptn 2F 63
Gedintailor. High 5E 155
Gedling. Notts 1D 74
Gedney. Linc 3D 76
Gedney Broadgate. Linc 3D 76
Gedney Drove End. Linc 3D 76
Gedney Dyke. Linc 3D 76
Gedney Hill. Linc 4C 76
Gee Cross. G Man 1D 84
Geeston. Rut 5G 75
Geilston. Arg 2E 127
Geirinis. W Isl 4C 170
Geise. High 2D 168
Geisiadar. W Isl 4D 171
Gelder Shiel. Abers 5G 151
Geldeston. Norf 1F 67
Gell. Cnwy 4A 82
Gelli. Pemb 3E 43
Gelli. Rhon 2C 32
Gellifor. Den 4D 82
Gelligaer. Cphy 2E 33
Gellilydan. Gwyn 2F 69
Gellinudd. Neat 5H 45
Gellyburn. Per 5H 143
Gellywen. Carm 2G 43
Gelston. Dum 4E 111
Gelston. Linc 1G 75
Gembling. E Yor 4F 101
Geneva. Cdgn 5D 56
Gentleshaw. Staf 4E 73
Geocrab. W Isl 8D 171
George Green. Buck 2A 38
Georgeham. Devn 3E 19
George Nympton. Devn 4H 19
Georgetown. Blae 5E 47
Georgetown. Ren 3F 127
Georth. Orkn 5C 172

Gerlan—Great Bromley

Gerlan. *Gwyn* 4F 81
Germansweek. *Devn* 3E 11
Germoe. *Corn* 4C 4
Gerrans. *Corn* 5C 6
Gerrard's Bromley. *Staf* 2B 72
Gerrards Cross. *Buck* 2A 38
Gerston. *High* 3D 168
Gestingthorpe. *Essx* 2B 54
Gethsemane. *Pemb* 1A 44
Geuffordd. *Powy* 4E 70
Gibraltar. *Buck* 4F 51
Gibraltar. *Linc* 5E 89
Gibraltar. *Suff* 5D 66
Gibsmere. *Notts* 1E 74
Giddeahall. *Wilts* 4D 34
Gidea Park. *G Lon* 2G 39
Gidleigh. *Devn* 4G 11
Giffnock. *E Ren* 4G 127
Gifford. *E Lot* 3B 130
Giffordtown. *Fife* 2E 137
Giggetty. *Staf* 1C 60
Giggleswick. *N Yor* 3H 97
Gignog. *Pemb* 2C 42
Gilberdyke. *E Yor* 2B 94
Gilbert's End. *Worc* 1D 48
Gilbert's Green. *Warw* 3F 61
Gilchriston. *E Lot* 3A 130
Gilcrux. *Cumb* 1C 102
Gildersome. *W Yor* 2C 92
Gildingwells. *S Yor* 2C 86
Gilesgate Moor. *Dur* 5F 115
Gileston. *V Glam* 5D 32
Gilfach. *Cphy* 2E 33
Gilfach Goch. *Rhon* 2C 32
Gilfachreda. *Cdgn* 5D 56
Gillamoor. *N Yor* 5D 107
Gillan. *Corn* 4E 5
Gillar's Green. *Mers* 1G 83
Gillen. *High* 3B 154
Gilling East. *N Yor* 2A 100
Gillingham. *Dors* 4D 22
Gillingham. *Medw* 4B 40 & Medway 204
Gillingham. *Norf* 1G 67
Gilling West. *N Yor* 4E 105
Gillock. *High* 3E 169
Gillow Heath. *Staf* 5C 84
Gills. *High* 1F 169
Gill's Green. *Kent* 2B 28
Gilmanscleuch. *Bord* 2F 119
Gilmerton. *Edin* 3F 129
Gilmerton. *Per* 1A 136
Gilmonby. *Dur* 3C 104
Gilmorton. *Leics* 2C 62
Gilsland. *Nmbd* 3H 113
Gilsland Spa. *Cumb* 3H 113
Gilston. *Midl* 4H 129
Giltbrook. *Notts* 1B 74
Gilwern. *Mon* 4F 47
Gimingham. *Norf* 2E 79
Giosla. *W Isl* 5D 171
Gipping. *Suff* 4C 66
Gipsey Bridge. *Linc* 1B 76
Gipton. *W Yor* 1D 92
Girdle Toll. *N Ayr* 5E 127
Girlsta. *Shet* 6F 173
Girsby. *N Yor* 4A 106
Girthon. *Dum* 4D 110
Girton. *Cambs* 4D 64
Girton. *Notts* 4F 87
Girvan. *S Ayr* 5A 116
Gisburn. *Lanc* 5H 97
Gisleham. *Suff* 2H 67
Gislingham. *Suff* 3C 66
Gissing. *Norf* 2D 66
Gittisham. *Devn* 3E 13
Gladestry. *Powy* 5E 59
Gladsmuir. *E Lot* 2A 130
Glaichbea. *High* 5H 157
Glais. *Swan* 5H 45
Glaisdale. *N Yor* 4E 107
Glame. *High* 4E 155
Glamis. *Ang* 4C 144
Glamisdale. *High* 5C 146
Glanaman. *Carm* 4G 45
Glan-Conwy. *Cnwy* 5H 81
Glandford. *Norf* 1C 78
Glan Duar. *Carm* 1F 45
Glandwr. *Blae* 5F 47
Glandwr. *Pemb* 2F 43
Glan-Dwyfach. *Gwyn* 1D 69
Glandy Cross. *Carm* 2F 43
Glandyfi. *Cdgn* 1F 57
Glangrwyney. *Powy* 4F 47
Glanmule. *Powy* 1D 58
Glanrhyd. *Gwyn* 2B 68
Glanrhyd. *Pemb* 1B 44 (nr. Cardigan)
Glan-rhyd. *Pemb* 1F 43 (nr. Crymych)
Glan-rhyd. *Powy* 5A 46
Glanton. *Nmbd* 3E 121
Glanton Pyke. *Nmbd* 3E 121
Glanvilles Wootton. *Dors* 2B 14
Glan-y-don. *Flin* 3D 82
Glan-y-nant. *Powy* 2B 58
Glan-yr-afon. *Gwyn* 1C 70
Glan-yr-afon. *IOA* 2F 81
Glan-yr-afon. *Powy* 5C 70
Glan-y-wern. *Gwyn* 2F 69
Glapthorn. *Nptn* 1H 63
Glapwell. *Derbs* 4B 86
Glas Aird. *Arg* 4A 132
Glas-allt Shiel. *Abers* 5G 151
Glasbury. *Powy* 2E 47
Glaschoil. *Mor* 5E 159
Glascoed. *Den* 3B 82
Glascoed. *Mon* 5G 47
Glascote. *Staf* 5G 73
Glascwm. *Powy* 5D 58
Glasfryn. *Cnwy* 5B 82
Glasgow. *Glas* 3G 127 & 196
Glasgow Airport. *Ren* 3F 127 & 216
Glasgow Prestwick International Airport. *S Ayr* 2C 116
Glashvin. *High* 2D 154
Glasinfryn. *Gwyn* 4E 81
Glas na Cardaich. *High* 4E 147
Glasnacardoch. *High* 4E 147
Glasnakille. *High* 2D 146
Glaspwll. *Cdgn* 1G 57
Glassburn. *High* 5F 157
Glassenbury. *Kent* 2B 28
Glasserton. *Dum* 5B 110
Glassford. *S Lan* 5A 128
Glassgreen. *Mor* 2G 159
Glasshouse. *Glos* 3C 48
Glasshouses. *N Yor* 3D 98
Glasson. *Cumb* 3D 112
Glasson. *Lanc* 4D 96
Glassonby. *Cumb* 1G 103
Glasterlaw. *Ang* 3E 145
Glaston. *Rut* 5F 75
Glastonbury. *Som* 3H 21
Glatton. *Cambs* 2A 64
Glazebrook. *Warr* 1A 84
Glazebury. *Warr* 1A 84
Glazeley. *Shrp* 2B 60
Gleadless. *S Yor* 2A 86
Gleadsmoss. *Ches E* 4C 84
Gleann Dail bho Dheas. *W Isl* 7C 170
Gleann Tholastaidh. *W Isl* 3H 171
Gleann Uige. *High* 1A 140
Gleaston. *Cumb* 2B 96
Glecknabae. *Arg* 3B 126
Gledrid. *Shrp* 2E 71
Gleiniant. *Powy* 1B 58
Glemsford. *Suff* 1B 54
Glen. *Dum* 4C 110
Glenancross. *High* 4E 147
Glen Audlyn. *IOM* 2D 108
Glenbarr. *Arg* 2A 122
Glenbeg. *High* 2G 139
Glen Bernisdale. *High* 4D 154
Glenbervie. *Abers* 5E 153
Glenboig. *N Lan* 3A 128
Glenborrodale. *High* 2A 140
Glenbranter. *Arg* 4A 134
Glenbreck. *Bord* 2C 118
Glenbrein Lodge. *High* 2G 149
Glenbrittle. *High* 1C 146
Glenbuchat Lodge. *Abers* 2H 151
Glenbuck. *E Ayr* 2G 117
Glenburn. *Ren* 3F 127
Glencalvie Lodge. *High* 5B 164
Glencaple. *Dum* 3A 112
Glencarron Lodge. *High* 3C 156
Glencarse. *Per* 1D 136
Glencassley Castle. *High* 3B 164
Glencat. *Abers* 4C 152
Glencoe. *High* 3F 141
Glen Cottage. *High* 5E 147
Glencraig. *Fife* 4D 136
Glendale. *High* 4A 154
Glendevon. *Per* 3B 136
Glendoebeg. *High* 3G 149
Glendoick. *Per* 1E 136
Glendoune. *S Ayr* 5A 116
Glenduckie. *Fife* 2E 137
Gleneagles. *Per* 3B 136
Glenegedale. *Arg* 4B 124
Glenegedale Lots. *Arg* 4B 124
Glenelg. *High* 2G 147
Glenernie. *Mor* 4E 159
Glenesslin. *Dum* 1F 111
Glenfarg. *Per* 2D 136
Glenfarquhar Lodge. *Abers* 5E 152
Glenferness Mains. *High* 4D 158
Glenfeshie Lodge. *High* 4C 150
Glenfiddich Lodge. *Mor* 5H 159
Glenfield. *Leics* 5C 74
Glenfinnan. *High* 5B 148
Glenfintaig Lodge. *High* 5E 149
Glenfoot. *Per* 2D 136
Glenfyne Lodge. *Arg* 2B 134
Glengap. *Dum* 4D 110
Glengarnock. *N Ayr* 4E 126
Glengolly. *High* 2D 168
Glengorm Castle. *Arg* 3F 139
Glengrasco. *High* 4D 154
Glenhead Farm. *Ang* 2B 144
Glenholm. *Bord* 1D 118
Glen House. *Bord* 1E 119
Glenhurich. *High* 2C 140
Glenkerry. *Bord* 3E 119
Glenkiln. *Dum* 2F 111
Glenkindie. *Abers* 2B 152
Glenkinglass Lodge. *Arg* 5F 141
Glenkirk. *Bord* 2C 118
Glenlean. *Arg* 1B 126
Glenlee. *Dum* 1D 110
Glenleraig. *High* 5B 166
Glenlichorn. *Per* 2G 135
Glenlivet. *Mor* 1F 151
Glenlochar. *Dum* 3E 111
Glenlochsie Lodge. *Per* 1H 143
Glenluce. *Dum* 4G 109
Glenmarskie. *High* 3F 157
Glenmassan. *Arg* 1C 126
Glenmavis. *N Lan* 3A 128
Glen Maye. *IOM* 4B 108
Glenmazeran Lodge. *High* 1B 150
Glenmidge. *Dum* 1F 111
Glen Mona. *IOM* 3D 108
Glenmore. *High* 2G 139 (nr. Glenborrodale)
Glenmore. *High* 3D 151 (nr. Kingussie)
Glenmore. *High* 4D 154 (on Isle of Skye)
Glenmoy. *Ang* 2D 144
Glennoe. *Arg* 5E 141
Glen of Coachford. *Abers* 4B 160
Glenogil. *Ang* 2D 144
Glen Parva. *Leics* 1C 62
Glenprosen Village. *Ang* 2C 144
Glenree. *N Ayr* 3D 122
Glenridding. *Cumb* 3E 103
Glenrosa. *N Ayr* 2E 123
Glenrothes. *Fife* 3E 137
Glensanda. *High* 4C 140
Glensaugh. *Abers* 1F 145
Glenshero Lodge. *High* 4H 149
Glensluain. *Arg* 4H 133
Glenstockadale. *Dum* 3F 109
Glenstriven. *Arg* 2B 126
Glen Tanar House. *Abers* 4B 152
Glentham. *Linc* 1H 87
Glenton. *Abers* 1D 152
Glentress. *Bord* 1E 119
Glentromie Lodge. *High* 4B 150
Glentrool Lodge. *Dum* 1B 110
Glentrool Village. *Dum* 2A 110
Glentruim House. *High* 4A 150
Glentworth. *Linc* 2G 87
Glenuig. *High* 1A 140
Glen Village. *Falk* 2B 128
Glen Vine. *IOM* 4C 108
Glenwhilly. *Dum* 2G 109
Glenzierfoot. *Dum* 2E 113
Glespin. *S Lan* 2H 117
Gletness. *Shet* 6F 173
Glewstone. *Here* 3A 48
Glib Cheois. *W Isl* 5F 171
Glinton. *Pet* 5A 76
Glooston. *Leics* 1E 63
Glossop. *Derbs* 1E 85
Gloster Hill. *Nmbd* 4G 121
Gloucester. *Glos* 4D 48 & 196
Gloucestershire Airport. *Glos* 3D 49
Gloup. *Shet* 1G 173
Glusburn. *N Yor* 5C 98
Glutt Lodge. *High* 5B 168
Glutton Bridge. *Staf* 4E 85
Gluvian. *Corn* 2D 6
Glympton. *Oxon* 3C 50
Glyn. *Cnwy* 3A 82
Glynarthen. *Cdgn* 1D 44
Glynbrochan. *Powy* 2B 58
Glyn Ceiriog. *Wrex* 2E 70
Glyncoch. *Rhon* 2D 32
Glyncorrwg. *Neat* 2B 32
Glynde. *E Sus* 5F 27
Glyndebourne. *E Sus* 4F 27
Glyndyfrdwy. *Den* 1D 70
Glyn Ebwy. *Blae* 5E 47
Glynllan. *B'end* 3C 32
Glyn-neath. *Neat* 5B 46
Glynogwr. *B'end* 3C 32
Glyntaff. *Rhon* 3D 32
Glyntawe. *Powy* 4B 46
Glynteg. *Carm* 2D 44
Gnosall. *Staf* 3C 72
Gnosall Heath. *Staf* 3C 72
Goadby. *Leics* 1E 63
Goadby Marwood. *Leics* 3E 75
Goatacre. *Wilts* 4F 35
Goathill. *Dors* 1B 14
Goathland. *N Yor* 4F 107
Goathurst. *Som* 3F 21
Goathurst Common. *Kent* 5F 39
Goat Lees. *Kent* 1E 28
Gobernuisgach Lodge. *High* 4E 167
Gobernuisgeach. *High* 5B 168
Gobhaig. *W Isl* 7C 171
Gobowen. *Shrp* 2F 71
Godalming. *Surr* 1A 26
Goddard's Corner. *Suff* 4E 67
Goddard's Green. *Kent* 2C 28 (nr. Benenden)
Goddard's Green. *Kent* 2B 28 (nr. Cranbrook)
Goddards Green. *W Sus* 3D 27
Godford Cross. *Devn* 2E 13
Godleybrook. *Staf* 1D 73
Godmanchester. *Cambs* 3B 64
Godmanstone. *Dors* 3B 14
Godmersham. *Kent* 5E 41
Godolphin Cross. *Corn* 3D 4
Godre'r-graig. *Neat* 5A 46
Godshill. *Hants* 1G 15
Godshill. *IOW* 4D 16
Godstone. *Staf* 2E 73
Godstone. *Surr* 5E 39
Goetre. *Mon* 5G 47
Goff's Oak. *Herts* 5D 52
Gogar. *Edin* 2E 129
Goginan. *Cdgn* 2F 57
Golan. *Gwyn* 1E 69
Golant. *Corn* 3F 7
Golberdon. *Corn* 5D 10
Golborne. *G Man* 1A 84
Golcar. *W Yor* 3A 92
Goldcliff. *Newp* 3G 33
Golden Cross. *E Sus* 4G 27
Golden Green. *Kent* 1H 27
Golden Grove. *Carm* 4F 45
Golden Grove. *N Yor* 4F 107
Golden Hill. *Pemb* 2D 43
Goldenhill. *Stoke* 5C 84
Golden Pot. *Hants* 2F 25
Golden Valley. *Glos* 3E 49
Golders Green. *G Lon* 2D 38
Goldhanger. *Essx* 5C 54
Gold Hill. *Norf* 1E 65
Golding. *Shrp* 5H 71
Goldington. *Bed* 5H 63
Goldsborough. *N Yor* 4F 99 (nr. Harrogate)
Goldsborough. *N Yor* 3F 107 (nr. Whitby)
Goldsithney. *Corn* 3C 4
Goldstone. *Kent* 4G 41
Goldstone. *Shrp* 3B 72
Goldthorpe. *S Yor* 4E 93
Goldworthy. *Devn* 4D 19
Golfa. *Powy* 3D 70
Gollanfield. *High* 3C 158
Gollinglith Foot. *N Yor* 1D 98
Golsoncott. *Som* 3D 20
Golspie. *High* 4F 165
Gomeldon. *Wilts* 3G 23
Gomersal. *W Yor* 2C 92
Gometra House. *Arg* 4E 139
Gomshall. *Surr* 1B 26
Gonalston. *Notts* 1D 74
Gonerby Hill Foot. *Linc* 2G 75
Gonfirth. *Shet* 5E 173
Gonnabarn. *Corn* 3D 6
Good Easter. *Essx* 4G 53
Gooderstone. *Norf* 5G 77
Goodleigh. *Devn* 3G 19
Goodmanham. *E Yor* 5C 100
Goodmayes. *G Lon* 2F 39
Goodnestone. *Kent* 5G 41 (nr. Aylesham)
Goodnestone. *Kent* 4E 41 (nr. Faversham)
Goodrich. *Here* 4A 48
Goodrington. *Torb* 3E 9
Goodshaw. *Lanc* 2G 91
Goodshaw Fold. *Lanc* 2G 91
Goodstone. *Devn* 5A 12
Goodwick. *Pemb* 1D 42
Goodworth Clatford. *Hants* 2B 24
Goole. *E Yor* 2H 93
Goom's Hill. *Worc* 5E 61
Goonbell. *Corn* 4B 6
Goonhavern. *Corn* 3B 6
Goonvrea. *Corn* 4B 6
Goose Green. *Cumb* 1E 97
Goose Green. *S Glo* 3C 34
Gooseham. *Corn* 1C 10
Goosewell. *Plym* 3B 8
Goosey. *Oxon* 2B 36
Goosnargh. *Lanc* 1D 90
Goostrey. *Ches E* 3B 84
Gorcott Hill. *Warw* 4E 61
Gord. *Shet* 9F 173
Gordon. *Bord* 5C 130
Gordonbush. *High* 3F 165
Gordonstown. *Abers* 3C 160 (nr. Cornhill)
Gordonstown. *Abers* 5E 160 (nr. Fyvie)
Gorebridge. *Midl* 3G 129
Gorefield. *Cambs* 4D 76
Gores. *Wilts* 1G 23
Gorgie. *Edin* 2F 129
Goring. *Oxon* 3E 36
Goring-by-Sea. *W Sus* 5C 26
Goring Heath. *Oxon* 4E 37
Gorleston-on-Sea. *Norf* 5H 79
Gornalwood. *W Mid* 1D 60
Gorran Churchtown. *Corn* 4D 6
Gorran Haven. *Corn* 4E 6
Gorran High Lanes. *Corn* 4D 6
Gors. *Cdgn* 3F 57
Gorsedd. *Flin* 3D 82
Gorseinon. *Swan* 3E 31
Gorseness. *Orkn* 6D 172
Gorseybank. *Derbs* 5G 85
Gorsgoch. *Cdgn* 5D 57
Gorslas. *Carm* 4F 45
Gorsley. *Glos* 3B 48
Gorsley Common. *Here* 3B 48
Gorstan. *High* 2F 157
Gorstella. *Ches W* 4F 83
Gorsty Common. *Here* 2H 47
Gorsty Hill. *Staf* 3E 73
Gortantaoid. *Arg* 2B 124
Gorteneorn. *High* 2A 140
Gortenfern. *High* 2A 140
Gorton. *G Man* 1C 84
Gosbeck. *Suff* 5D 66
Gosberton. *Linc* 2B 76
Gosberton Clough. *Linc* 3A 76
Goseley Dale. *Derbs* 3H 73
Gosfield. *Essx* 3A 54
Gosford. *Oxon* 4D 50
Gosforth. *Cumb* 4B 102
Gosforth. *Tyne* 3F 115
Gosmore. *Herts* 3B 52
Gospel End Village. *Staf* 1C 60
Gosport. *Hants* 2E 16
Gossabrough. *Shet* 3G 173
Gossington. *Glos* 5C 48
Gossops Green. *W Sus* 2D 26
Goswick. *Nmbd* 5G 131
Gotham. *Notts* 2C 74
Gotherington. *Glos* 3E 49
Gott. *Arg* 4B 138
Gott. *Shet* 7F 173
Goudhurst. *Kent* 2B 28
Goulceby. *Linc* 3B 88
Gourdon. *Abers* 1H 145
Gourock. *Inv* 2D 126
Govan. *Glas* 3G 127
Govanhill. *Glas* 3G 127
Goverton. *Notts* 1E 74
Goveton. *Devn* 4D 8
Govilon. *Mon* 4F 47
Gowanhill. *Abers* 2H 161
Gowdall. *E Yor* 2G 93
Gowerton. *Swan* 3E 31
Gowkhall. *Fife* 1D 128
Gowthorpe. *E Yor* 4B 100
Goxhill. *E Yor* 5F 101
Goxhill. *N Lin* 2E 94
Goxhill Haven. *N Lin* 2E 94
Goytre. *Neat* 3A 32
Grabhair. *W Isl* 6F 171
Graby. *Linc* 3H 75
Graffham. *W Sus* 4A 26
Grafham. *Cambs* 4A 64
Grafham. *Surr* 1B 26
Grafton. *Here* 2H 47
Grafton. *N Yor* 3G 99
Grafton. *Oxon* 5A 50
Grafton. *Shrp* 4G 71
Grafton. *Worc* 2E 49 (nr. Evesham)
Grafton. *Worc* 4H 59 (nr. Leominster)
Grafton Flyford. *Worc* 5D 60
Grafton Regis. *Nptn* 1F 51
Grafton Underwood. *Nptn* 2G 63
Grafty Green. *Kent* 1C 28
Graianrhyd. *Den* 5E 82
Graig. *Carm* 5E 45
Graig. *Cnwy* 3H 81
Graig. *Den* 3C 82
Graig-fechan. *Den* 5D 82
Graig Penllyn. *V Glam* 4C 32
Grain. *Medw* 3C 40
Grainsby. *Linc* 1B 88
Grainthorpe. *Linc* 1C 88
Grainthorpe Fen. *Linc* 1C 88
Graiselound. *N Lin* 1E 87
Gramasdail. *W Isl* 3D 170
Grampound. *Corn* 4D 6
Grampound Road. *Corn* 3D 6
Granborough. *Buck* 3F 51
Granby. *Notts* 2E 75
Grandborough. *Warw* 4B 62
Grandpont. *Oxon* 5D 50
Grandtully. *Per* 3G 143
Grange. *Cumb* 3D 102
Grange. *E Ayr* 1D 116
Grange. *Here* 3G 59
Grange. *Mers* 2E 83
Grange. *Per* 1E 137
Grange Crossroads. *Mor* 3B 160
Grange Hill. *G Lon* 1F 39
Grangemill. *Derbs* 5G 85
Grange Moor. *W Yor* 3C 92
Grangemouth. *Falk* 1C 128
Grange of Lindores. *Fife* 2E 137
Grange-over-Sands. *Cumb* 2D 96
Grangepans. *Falk* 1D 128
Grange, The. *N Yor* 5C 106
Grangetown. *Card* 4E 33
Grangetown. *Red C* 2C 106
Grange Villa. *Dur* 4F 115
Granish. *High* 2C 150
Gransmoor. *E Yor* 4F 101
Granston. *Pemb* 1C 42
Grantchester. *Cambs* 5D 64
Grantham. *Linc* 2G 75
Grantley. *N Yor* 3E 99
Grantlodge. *Abers* 2E 152
Granton. *Edin* 2F 129
Grantown-on-Spey. *High* 1E 151
Grantshouse. *Bord* 3E 130
Grappenhall. *Warr* 2A 84
Grasby. *Linc* 4D 94
Grasmere. *Cumb* 4E 103
Grasscroft. *G Man* 4H 91
Grassendale. *Mers* 2F 83
Grassgarth. *Cumb* 5E 113
Grassholme. *Dur* 2C 104
Grassington. *N Yor* 3C 98
Grassmoor. *Derbs* 4B 86
Grassthorpe. *Notts* 4E 87
Grateley. *Hants* 2A 24
Gratton. *Devn* 1D 11
Gratton. *Staf* 5D 84
Gratwich. *Staf* 2E 73
Graveley. *Cambs* 4B 64
Graveley. *Herts* 3C 52
Gravelhill. *Shrp* 4G 71
Gravel Hole. *G Man* 4H 91
Gravelly Hill. *W Mid* 1F 61
Graven. *Shet* 4F 173
Graveney. *Kent* 4E 41
Gravesend. *Kent* 3H 39
Grayingham. *Linc* 1G 87
Grayrigg. *Cumb* 5G 103
Grays. *Thur* 3H 39
Grayshott. *Hants* 3G 25
Grayson Green. *Cumb* 2A 102
Grayswood. *Surr* 2A 26
Graythorp. *Hart* 2C 106
Grazeley. *Wok* 5E 37
Grealin. *High* 2E 155
Greasbrough. *S Yor* 1B 86
Greasby. *Mers* 2E 83
Great Abington. *Cambs* 1F 53
Great Addington. *Nptn* 3G 63
Great Alne. *Warw* 5F 61
Great Altcar. *Lanc* 4B 90
Great Amwell. *Herts* 4D 52
Great Asby. *Cumb* 3H 103
Great Ashfield. *Suff* 4B 66
Great Ayton. *N Yor* 3C 106
Great Baddow. *Essx* 5H 53
Great Bardfield. *Essx* 2G 53
Great Barford. *Bed* 5A 64
Great Barr. *W Mid* 1E 61
Great Barrington. *Glos* 4H 49
Great Barrow. *Ches W* 4G 83
Great Barton. *Suff* 4A 66
Great Barugh. *N Yor* 2B 100
Great Bavington. *Nmbd* 1C 114
Great Bealings. *Suff* 1F 55
Great Bedwyn. *Wilts* 5A 36
Great Bentley. *Essx* 3E 54
Great Billing. *Nptn* 4F 63
Great Bircham. *Norf* 2G 77
Great Blakenham. *Suff* 5D 66
Great Blencow. *Cumb* 1F 103
Great Bolas. *Telf* 3A 72
Great Bookham. *Surr* 5C 38
Great Bosullow. *Corn* 3B 4
Great Bourton. *Oxon* 1C 50
Great Bowden. *Leics* 2E 63
Great Bradley. *Suff* 5F 65
Great Braxted. *Essx* 4B 54
Great Bricett. *Suff* 5C 66
Great Brickhill. *Buck* 2H 51
Great Bridgeford. *Staf* 3C 72
Great Brington. *Nptn* 4D 62
Great Bromley. *Essx* 3D 54

Great Broughton—Halfway

Great Broughton. *Cumb* 1B 102
Great Broughton. *N Yor* 4C 106
Great Budworth. *Ches W* 3A 84
Great Burdon. *Darl* 3A 106
Great Burstead. *Essx* 1A 40
Great Busby. *N Yor* 4C 106
Great Canfield. *Essx* 4F 53
Great Carlton. *Linc* 2D 88
Great Casterton. *Rut* 5H 75
Great Chalfield. *Wilts* 5D 34
Great Chart. *Kent* 1D 28
Great Chatwell. *Staf* 4B 72
Great Chesterford. *Essx* 1F 53
Great Cheverell. *Wilts* 1E 23
Great Chilton. *Dur* 1F 105
Great Chishill. *Cambs* 2E 53
Great Clacton. *Essx* 4E 55
Great Cliff. *W Yor* 3D 92
Great Clifton. *Cumb* 2B 102
Great Coates. *NE Lin* 3F 95
Great Comberton. *Worc* 1E 49
Great Corby. *Cumb* 4F 113
Great Cornard. *Suff* 1B 54
Great Cowden. *E Yor* 5G 101
Great Coxwell. *Oxon* 2A 36
Great Crakehall. *N Yor* 1E 99
Great Cransley. *Nptn* 3F 63
Great Cressingham. *Norf* 5H 77
Great Crosby. *Mers* 1F 83
Great Cubley. *Derbs* 2F 73
Great Dalby. *Leics* 4E 75
Great Doddington. *Nptn* 4F 63
Great Doward. *Here* 4A 48
Great Dunham. *Norf* 4A 78
Great Dunmow. *Essx* 3G 53
Great Durnford. *Wilts* 3G 23
Great Easton. *Essx* 3G 53
Great Easton. *Leics* 1F 63
Great Eccleston. *Lanc* 5D 96
Great Edstone. *N Yor* 1B 100
Great Ellingham. *Norf* 1C 66
Great Elm. *Som* 2C 22
Great Eppleton. *Tyne* 5G 115
Great Eversden. *Cambs* 5C 64
Great Fencote. *N Yor* 5F 105
Great Finborough. *Suff* 5C 66
Greatford. *Linc* 4H 75
Great Fransham. *Norf* 4A 78
Great Gaddesden. *Herts* 4A 52
Great Gate. *Staf* 1E 73
Great Gidding. *Cambs* 2A 64
Great Givendale. *E Yor* 4C 100
Great Glemham. *Suff* 4F 67
Great Glen. *Leics* 1D 62
Great Gonerby. *Linc* 2G 75
Great Gransden. *Cambs* 5B 64
Great Green. *Norf* 2E 67
Great Green. *Suff* 5B 66 (nr. Lavenham)
Great Green. *Suff* 3D 66 (nr. Palgrave)
Great Habton. *N Yor* 2B 100
Great Hale. *Linc* 1A 76
Great Hallingbury. *Essx* 4F 53
Greatham. *Hants* 3F 25
Greatham. *Hart* 2B 106
Greatham. *W Sus* 4B 26
Great Hampden. *Buck* 5G 51
Great Harrowden. *Nptn* 3F 63
Great Harwood. *Lanc* 1F 91
Great Haseley. *Oxon* 5E 51
Great Hatfield. *E Yor* 5F 101
Great Haywood. *Staf* 3D 73
Great Heath. *W Mid* 2H 61
Great Heck. *N Yor* 2F 93
Great Henny. *Essx* 2B 54
Great Hinton. *Wilts* 1E 23
Great Hockham. *Norf* 1B 66
Great Holland. *Essx* 4F 55
Great Horkesley. *Essx* 2C 54
Great Hormead. *Herts* 2E 53
Great Horton. *W Yor* 1B 92
Great Horwood. *Buck* 2F 51
Great Houghton. *Nptn* 5E 63
Great Houghton. *S Yor* 4E 93
Great Hucklow. *Derbs* 3F 85
Great Kelk. *E Yor* 4F 101
Great Kendale. *E Yor* 3E 101
Great Kimble. *Buck* 5G 51
Great Kingshill. *Buck* 2G 37
Great Langdale. *Cumb* 4D 102
Great Langton. *N Yor* 5F 105
Great Leighs. *Essx* 4H 53
Great Limber. *Linc* 4E 95
Great Linford. *Mil* 1G 51
Great Livermere. *Suff* 3A 66
Great Longstone. *Derbs* 3G 85
Great Lumley. *Dur* 5F 115
Great Lyth. *Shrp* 5G 71
Great Malvern. *Worc* 1C 48
Great Maplestead. *Essx* 2B 54
Great Marton. *Bkpl* 1B 90
Great Massingham. *Norf* 3G 77
Great Melton. *Norf* 5D 78
Great Milton. *Oxon* 5E 51
Great Missenden. *Buck* 5G 51
Great Mitton. *Lanc* 1F 91
Great Mongeham. *Kent* 5H 41
Great Moulton. *Norf* 1D 66
Great Munden. *Herts* 3D 52
Great Musgrave. *Cumb* 3A 104
Great Ness. *Shrp* 4F 71
Great Notley. *Essx* 3H 53
Great Oak. *Mon* 5G 47
Great Oakley. *Essx* 3E 55
Great Oakley. *Nptn* 2F 63
Great Offley. *Herts* 3B 52
Great Ormside. *Cumb* 3A 104
Great Orton. *Cumb* 4E 113
Great Ouseburn. *N Yor* 3G 99
Great Oxendon. *Nptn* 2E 63
Great Oxney Green. *Essx* 5G 53
Great Parndon. *Essx* 5E 53
Great Paxton. *Cambs* 4B 64
Great Plumpton. *Lanc* 1B 90
Great Plumstead. *Norf* 4F 79
Great Ponton. *Linc* 2G 75
Great Potheridge. *Devn* 1F 11
Great Preston. *W Yor* 2E 93
Great Raveley. *Cambs* 2B 64
Great Rissington. *Glos* 4G 49
Great Rollright. *Oxon* 2B 50
Great Ryburgh. *Norf* 3B 78
Great Ryle. *Nmbd* 3E 121
Great Ryton. *Shrp* 5G 71
Great Saling. *Essx* 3G 53
Great Salkeld. *Cumb* 1G 103
Great Sampford. *Essx* 2G 53
Great Sankey. *Warr* 2H 83
Great Saredon. *Staf* 5D 72
Great Saxham. *Suff* 4G 65
Great Shefford. *W Ber* 4B 36
Great Shelford. *Cambs* 5D 64
Great Shoddesden. *Hants* 2A 24
Great Smeaton. *N Yor* 4A 106
Great Snoring. *Norf* 2B 78
Great Somerford. *Wilts* 3E 35
Great Stainton. *Darl* 2A 106
Great Stambridge. *Essx* 1C 40
Great Staughton. *Cambs* 4A 64
Great Steeping. *Linc* 4D 88
Great Stonar. *Kent* 5H 41
Greatstone-on-Sea. *Kent* 3E 29
Great Strickland. *Cumb* 2G 103
Great Stukeley. *Cambs* 3B 64
Great Sturton. *Linc* 3B 88
Great Sutton. *Ches W* 3F 83
Great Sutton. *Shrp* 2H 59
Great Swinburne. *Nmbd* 2C 114
Great Tew. *Oxon* 3B 50
Great Tey. *Essx* 3B 54
Great Thirkleby. *N Yor* 2G 99
Great Thorness. *IOW* 3C 16
Great Thurlow. *Suff* 5F 65
Great Torr. *Devn* 4C 8
Great Torrington. *Devn* 1E 11
Great Tosson. *Nmbd* 4E 121
Great Totham North. *Essx* 4B 54
Great Totham South. *Essx* 4B 54
Great Tows. *Linc* 1B 88
Great Urswick. *Cumb* 2B 96
Great Wakering. *Essx* 2D 40
Great Waldingfield. *Suff* 1C 54
Great Walsingham. *Norf* 2B 78
Great Waltham. *Essx* 4G 53
Great Warley. *Essx* 1G 39
Great Washbourne. *Glos* 2E 49
Great Wenham. *Suff* 2D 54
Great Whelnetham. *Suff* 5A 66
Great Whittington. *Nmbd* 2D 114
Great Wigborough. *Essx* 4C 54
Great Wilbraham. *Cambs* 5E 65
Great Wilne. *Derbs* 2B 74
Great Wishford. *Wilts* 3F 23
Great Witchingham. *Norf* 3D 78
Great Witcombe. *Glos* 4E 49
Great Witley. *Worc* 4B 60
Great Wolford. *Warw* 2H 49
Greatworth. *Nptn* 1D 50
Great Wratting. *Suff* 1G 53
Great Wymondley. *Herts* 3C 52
Great Wyrley. *Staf* 5D 73
Great Wytheford. *Shrp* 4H 71
Great Yarmouth. *Norf* 5H 79 & 196
Great Yeldham. *Essx* 2A 54
Grebby. *Linc* 4D 88
Greeba Castle. *IOM* 3C 108
Greenbank. *Shet* 1G 173
Greenbottom. *Corn* 4B 6
Greenburn. *W Lot* 3C 128
Greencroft. *Dur* 4E 115
Greencroft Park. *Dur* 5E 115
Greendown. *Som* 1A 22
Greendykes. *Nmbd* 2E 121
Green End. *Bed* 1A 52 (nr. Bedford)
Green End. *Bed* 4A 64 (nr. St Neots)
Green End. *Herts* 2D 52 (nr. Buntingford)
Green End. *Herts* 3D 52 (nr. Stevenage)
Green End. *N Yor* 4F 107
Green End. *Warw* 2G 61
Greenfield. *Arg* 4B 134
Greenfield. *C Beds* 2A 52
Greenfield. *Flin* 3D 82
Greenfield. *G Man* 4H 91
Greenfield. *Oxon* 2F 37
Greenfoot. *N Lan* 3A 128
Greenford. *G Lon* 2C 38
Greengairs. *N Lan* 2A 128
Greengate. *Norf* 4C 78
Greengill. *Cumb* 1C 102
Greenhalgh. *Lanc* 1C 90
Greenham. *Dors* 2H 13
Greenham. *Som* 4D 20
Greenham. *W Ber* 5C 36
Green Hammerton. *N Yor* 4G 99
Greenhaugh. *Nmbd* 1A 114
Greenhead. *Nmbd* 3H 113
Green Heath. *Staf* 4D 73
Greenhill. *Dum* 2C 112
Greenhill. *Falk* 2B 128
Greenhill. *Kent* 4F 41
Greenhill. *S Yor* 2H 85
Greenhill. *Worc* 3C 60
Greenhills. *N Ayr* 4E 127
Greenhithe. *Kent* 3G 39
Greenholm. *E Ayr* 1E 117
Greenhow Hill. *N Yor* 3D 98
Greenigoe. *Orkn* 7D 172
Greenland. *High* 2E 169
Greenland Mains. *High* 2E 169
Greenlands. *Worc* 4E 61
Green Lane. *Shrp* 3A 72
Green Lane. *Warw* 4E 61
Greenlaw. *Bord* 5D 130
Greenlea. *Dum* 2B 112
Greenloaning. *Per* 3H 135
Greenmount. *G Man* 3F 91
Greenmow. *Shet* 9F 173
Greenock. *Inv* 2D 126
Greenock Mains. *E Ayr* 2F 117
Greenodd. *Cumb* 1C 96
Green Ore. *Som* 1A 22
Greenrow. *Cumb* 4C 112
Greens. *Abers* 4F 161
Greensgate. *Norf* 4D 78
Greenside. *Tyne* 3E 115
Greensidehill. *Nmbd* 3D 121
Greens Norton. *Nptn* 1E 51
Greenstead Green. *Essx* 3B 54
Greensted Green. *Essx* 5F 53
Green Street. *Herts* 1C 38
Green Street. *Suff* 3D 66
Green Street Green. *G Lon* 4F 39
Green Street Green. *Kent* 3G 39
Greenstreet Green. *Suff* 1D 54
Green, The. *Cumb* 1A 96
Green, The. *Wilts* 3D 22
Green Tye. *Herts* 4E 53
Greenwall. *Orkn* 7E 172
Greenway. *Pemb* 2E 43
Greenway. *V Glam* 4D 32
Greenwell. *Cumb* 4G 113
Greenwich. *G Lon* 3E 39
Greet. *Glos* 2F 49
Greete. *Shrp* 3H 59
Greetham. *Linc* 3C 88
Greetham. *Rut* 4G 75
Greetland. *W Yor* 2A 92
Gregson Lane. *Lanc* 2D 90
Grein. *W Isl* 8B 170
Greinetobht. *W Isl* 1D 170
Greinton. *Som* 3H 21
Gremista. *Shet* 7F 173
Grenaby. *IOM* 4B 108
Grendon. *Nptn* 4F 63
Grendon. *Warw* 1G 61
Grendon Common. *Warw* 1G 61
Grendon Green. *Here* 5H 59
Grendon Underwood. *Buck* 3E 51
Grenofen. *Devn* 5E 11
Grenoside. *S Yor* 1H 85
Greosabhagh. *W Isl* 8D 171
Gresford. *Wrex* 5F 83
Gresham. *Norf* 2D 78
Greshornish. *High* 3C 154
Gressenhall. *Norf* 4B 78
Gressingham. *Lanc* 2E 97
Greta Bridge. *Dur* 3D 105
Gretna. *Dum* 3E 112
Gretna Green. *Dum* 3E 112
Gretton. *Glos* 2F 49
Gretton. *Nptn* 1G 63
Gretton. *Shrp* 1H 59
Grewelthorpe. *N Yor* 2E 99
Greygarth. *N Yor* 2D 98
Grey Green. *N Lin* 4A 94
Greylake. *Som* 3G 21
Greysouthen. *Cumb* 2B 102
Greystoke. *Cumb* 1F 103
Greystoke Gill. *Cumb* 2F 103
Greystone. *Ang* 4E 145
Greystones. *S Yor* 2H 85
Greywell. *Hants* 1F 25
Griais. *W Isl* 3G 171
Grianan. *W Isl* 4G 171
Gribthorpe. *E Yor* 1A 94
Gribun. *Arg* 5F 139
Griff. *Warw* 2A 62
Griffithstown. *Torf* 2F 33
Griffydam. *Leics* 4B 74
Griggs Green. *Hants* 3G 25
Grimbister. *Orkn* 6C 172
Grimeford Village. *Lanc* 3E 90
Grimeston. *Orkn* 6C 172
Grimethorpe. *S Yor* 4E 93
Griminis. *W Isl* 3C 170 (on Benbecula)
Griminis. *W Isl* 1C 170 (on North Uist)
Grimister. *Shet* 2F 173
Grimley. *Worc* 4C 60
Grimness. *Orkn* 8D 172
Grimoldby. *Linc* 2C 88
Grimpo. *Shrp* 3F 71
Grimsargh. *Lanc* 1D 90
Grimsbury. *Oxon* 1C 50
Grimsby. *NE Lin* 3F 95
Grimscote. *Nptn* 5D 62
Grimscott. *Corn* 2C 10
Grimshaw. *Bkbn* 2F 91
Grimshaw Green. *Lanc* 3C 90
Grimsthorpe. *Linc* 3H 75
Grimston. *E Yor* 1F 95
Grimston. *Leics* 3D 74
Grimston. *Norf* 3G 77
Grimston. *York* 4A 100
Grimstone. *Dors* 3B 14
Grimstone End. *Suff* 4B 66
Grinacombe Moor. *Devn* 3E 11
Grindale. *E Yor* 2F 101
Grindhill. *Devn* 3E 11
Grindiscol. *Shet* 8F 173
Grindle. *Shrp* 5B 72
Grindleford. *Derbs* 3G 85
Grindleton. *Lanc* 5G 97
Grindley. *Staf* 3E 73
Grindley Brook. *Shrp* 1H 71
Grindlow. *Derbs* 3F 85
Grindon. *Nmbd* 5F 131
Grindon. *Staf* 5E 85
Gringley on the Hill. *Notts* 1E 87
Grinsdale. *Cumb* 4E 113
Grinshill. *Shrp* 3H 71
Grinton. *N Yor* 5D 104
Griomsidar. *W Isl* 5G 171
Grishipoll. *Arg* 3C 138
Grisling Common. *E Sus* 3F 27
Gristhorpe. *N Yor* 1E 101
Griston. *Norf* 1B 66
Gritley. *Orkn* 7E 172
Grittenham. *Wilts* 3F 35
Grittleton. *Wilts* 4D 34
Grizebeck. *Cumb* 1B 96
Grizedale. *Cumb* 5E 103
Grobister. *Orkn* 5F 172
Grobsness. *Shet* 5E 173
Groby. *Leics* 5C 74
Groes. *Cnwy* 4C 82
Groes. *Neat* 3A 32
Groes-faen. *Rhon* 3D 32
Groesffordd. *Gwyn* 2B 68
Groesffordd. *Powy* 3D 46
Groeslon. *Gwyn* 5D 81
Groes-lwyd. *Powy* 4E 70
Groes-wen. *Cphy* 3E 33
Grogport. *Arg* 5G 125
Groigearraidh. *W Isl* 4C 170
Gromford. *Suff* 5F 67
Gronant. *Flin* 2C 82
Groombridge. *E Sus* 2G 27
Grosmont. *Mon* 3H 47
Grosmont. *N Yor* 4F 107
Groton. *Suff* 1C 54
Grove. *Dors* 5C 14
Grove. *Kent* 4G 41
Grove. *Notts* 3E 87
Grove. *Oxon* 2B 36
Grovehill. *E Yor* 1D 94
Grove Park. *G Lon* 3F 39
Grovesend. *Swan* 5F 45
Grove, The. *Dum* 2A 112
Grove, The. *Worc* 1D 48
Grub Street. *Staf* 3B 72
Grudie. *High* 2F 157
Gruids. *High* 3C 164
Gruinard House. *High* 4D 162
Gruinart. *Arg* 3A 124
Grulinbeg. *Arg* 3A 124
Gruline. *Arg* 4G 139
Grummore. *High* 5G 167
Grundisburgh. *Suff* 5E 66
Gruting. *Shet* 7D 173
Grutness. *Shet* 10F 173
Gualachulain. *High* 4F 141
Gualin House. *High* 3D 166
Guardbridge. *Fife* 2G 137
Guarlford. *Worc* 1D 48
Guay. *Per* 4H 143
Gubblecote. *Herts* 4H 51
Guestling Green. *E Sus* 4C 28
Guestling Thorn. *E Sus* 4C 28
Guestwick. *Norf* 3C 78
Guestwick Green. *Norf* 3C 78
Guide. *Bkbn* 2F 91
Guide Post. *Nmbd* 1F 115
Guilden Down. *Shrp* 2F 59
Guilden Morden. *Cambs* 1C 52
Guilden Sutton. *Ches W* 4G 83
Guildford. *Surr* 1A 26 & 197
Guildtown. *Per* 5A 144
Guilsborough. *Nptn* 3D 62
Guilsfield. *Powy* 4E 70
Guineaford. *Devn* 3F 19
Guisborough. *Red C* 3D 106
Guiseley. *W Yor* 5D 98
Guist. *Norf* 3B 78
Guiting Power. *Glos* 3F 49
Gulberwick. *Shet* 8F 173
Gullane. *E Lot* 1A 130
Gulling Green. *Suff* 5H 65
Gulval. *Corn* 3B 4
Gumfreston. *Pemb* 4F 43
Gumley. *Leics* 1D 62
Gunby. *E Yor* 1H 93
Gunby. *Linc* 3G 75
Gundleton. *Hants* 3E 24
Gun Green. *Kent* 2B 28
Gun Hill. *E Sus* 4G 27
Gunn. *Devn* 3G 19
Gunnerside. *N Yor* 5C 104
Gunnerton. *Nmbd* 2C 114
Gunness. *N Lin* 3B 94
Gunnislake. *Corn* 5E 11
Gunnista. *Shet* 7F 173
Gunsgreenhill. *Bord* 3F 131
Gunstone. *Staf* 5C 72
Gunthorpe. *Norf* 2C 78
Gunthorpe. *N Lin* 1F 87
Gunthorpe. *Notts* 1D 74
Gunthorpe. *Pet* 5A 76
Gunville. *IOW* 4C 16
Gupworthy. *Som* 3C 20
Gurnard. *IOW* 3C 16
Gurney Slade. *Som* 2B 22
Gurnos. *Powy* 5A 46
Gussage All Saints. *Dors* 1F 15
Gussage St Andrew. *Dors* 1E 15
Gussage St Michael. *Dors* 1E 15
Guston. *Kent* 1H 29
Gutcher. *Shet* 2G 173
Guthram Gowt. *Linc* 3A 76
Guthrie. *Ang* 3E 145
Guyhirn. *Cambs* 5D 76
Guyhirn Gull. *Cambs* 5C 76
Guy's Head. *Linc* 3D 77
Guy's Marsh. *Dors* 4D 22
Guyzance. *Nmbd* 4G 121
Gwaelod-y-garth. *Card* 3E 32
Gwaenynog Bach. *Den* 4C 82
Gwaenysgor. *Flin* 2C 82
Gwalchmai. *IOA* 3C 80
Gwastad. *Pemb* 2E 43
Gwaun-Cae-Gurwen. *Neat* 4H 45
Gwaun-y-bara. *Cphy* 3E 33
Gwbert. *Cdgn* 1B 44
Gweek. *Corn* 4E 5
Gwehelog. *Mon* 5G 47
Gwenddwr. *Powy* 1D 46
Gwennap. *Corn* 4B 6
Gwenter. *Corn* 5E 5
Gwernaffield. *Flin* 4E 82
Gwernesney. *Mon* 5H 47
Gwernogle. *Carm* 2F 45
Gwern-y-go. *Powy* 1E 58
Gwernymynydd. *Flin* 4E 82
Gwersyllt. *Wrex* 5F 83
Gwespyr. *Flin* 2D 82
Gwinear. *Corn* 3C 4
Gwithian. *Corn* 2C 4
Gwredog. *IOA* 2D 80
Gwyddelwern. *Den* 1C 70
Gwyddgrug. *Carm* 2E 45
Gwynfryn. *Wrex* 5E 83
Gwystre. *Powy* 4C 58
Gwytherin. *Cnwy* 4A 82
Gyfelia. *Wrex* 1F 71
Gyffin. *Cnwy* 3G 81

H

Haa of Houlland. *Shet* 1G 173
Habberley. *Shrp* 5F 71
Habblesthorpe. *Notts* 2E 87
Habergham. *Lanc* 1G 91
Habin. *W Sus* 4G 25
Habrough. *NE Lin* 3E 95
Haceby. *Linc* 2H 75
Hacheston. *Suff* 5F 67
Hackenthorpe. *S Yor* 2B 86
Hackford. *Norf* 5C 78
Hackforth. *N Yor* 5F 105
Hackland. *Orkn* 5C 172
Hackleton. *Nptn* 5F 63
Hackness. *N Yor* 5G 107
Hackness. *Orkn* 8C 172
Hackney. *G Lon* 2E 39
Hackthorn. *Linc* 2G 87
Hackthorpe. *Cumb* 2G 103
Haclait. *W Isl* 4D 170
Haconby. *Linc* 3A 76
Hadden. *Bord* 1B 120
Haddenham. *Buck* 5F 51
Haddenham. *Cambs* 3D 64
Haddenham End. *Cambs* 3D 64
Haddington. *E Lot* 2B 130
Haddington. *Linc* 4G 87
Haddiscoe. *Norf* 1G 67
Haddo. *Abers* 5F 161
Haddon. *Cambs* 1A 64
Hademore. *Staf* 5F 73
Hadfield. *Derbs* 1E 85
Hadham Cross. *Herts* 4E 53
Hadham Ford. *Herts* 3E 53
Hadleigh. *Essx* 2C 40
Hadleigh. *Suff* 1D 54
Hadleigh Heath. *Suff* 1C 54
Hadley. *Telf* 4A 72
Hadley. *Worc* 4C 60
Hadley End. *Staf* 3F 73
Hadley Wood. *G Lon* 1D 38
Hadlow. *Kent* 1H 27
Hadlow Down. *E Sus* 3G 27
Hadnall. *Shrp* 3H 71
Hadstock. *Essx* 1F 53
Hadston. *Nmbd* 5G 121
Hady. *Derbs* 3A 86
Hadzor. *Worc* 4D 60
Haffenden Quarter. *Kent* 1C 28
Haggate. *Lanc* 1G 91
Haggbeck. *Cumb* 2F 113
Haggersta. *Shet* 7E 173
Haggerston. *Nmbd* 5G 131
Haggrister. *Shet* 4E 173
Hagley. *Here* 1A 48
Hagley. *Worc* 2D 60
Hagnaby. *Linc* 4C 88
Hagworthingham. *Linc* 4C 88
Haigh. *G Man* 4E 90
Haigh Moor. *W Yor* 2C 92
Haighton Green. *Lanc* 1D 90
Haile. *Cumb* 4B 102
Hailes. *Glos* 2F 49
Hailey. *Herts* 4D 52
Hailey. *Oxon* 4B 50
Hailsham. *E Sus* 5G 27
Hail Weston. *Cambs* 4A 64
Hainault. *G Lon* 1F 39
Hainford. *Norf* 4E 78
Hainton. *Linc* 2A 88
Hainworth. *W Yor* 1A 92
Haisthorpe. *E Yor* 3F 101
Hakin. *Pemb* 4C 42
Halam. *Notts* 5D 86
Halbeath. *Fife* 1E 129
Halberton. *Devn* 1D 12
Halcro. *High* 2E 169
Hale. *Cumb* 2E 97
Hale. *G Man* 2B 84
Hale. *Hal* 2G 83
Hale. *Hants* 1G 15
Hale. *Surr* 2G 25
Hale Bank. *Hal* 2G 83
Halebarns. *G Man* 2B 84
Hales. *Norf* 1F 67
Hales. *Staf* 2B 72
Halesgate. *Linc* 3C 76
Hales Green. *Derbs* 1F 73
Halesowen. *W Mid* 2D 60
Hale Street. *Kent* 1A 28
Halesworth. *Suff* 3F 67
Halewood. *Mers* 2G 83
Halford. *Devn* 5B 12
Halford. *Shrp* 2G 59
Halford. *Warw* 1A 50
Halfpenny. *Cumb* 1E 97
Halfpenny Furze. *Carm* 3G 43
Halfpenny Green. *Shrp* 1C 60
Halfway. *Carm* 2G 45
Halfway. *Powy* 2B 46

Halfway—Haye

Halfway. *S Yor* 2B 86
Halfway. *W Ber* 5C 36
Halfway House. *Shrp* 4F 71
Halfway Houses. *Kent* 3D 40
Halgabron. *Corn* 4A 10
Halifax. *W Yor* 2A 92
Halistra. *High* 3B 154
Halket. *E Ayr* 4F 127
Halkirk. *High* 3D 168
Halkyn. *Flin* 3E 82
Hall. *E Ren* 4F 127
Hallam Fields. *Derbs* 1B 74
Halland. *E Sus* 4G 27
Hallands, The. *N Lin* 2D 94
Hallaton. *Leics* 1E 63
Hallatrow. *Bath* 1B 22
Hallbank. *Cumb* 5H 103
Hallbankgate. *Cumb* 4G 113
Hall Dunnerdale. *Cumb* 5D 102
Hallen. *S Glo* 3A 34
Hall End. *Bed* 1A 52
Hallgarth. *Dur* 5G 115
Hall Green. *Ches E* 5C 84
Hall Green. *Norf* 2D 66
Hall Green. *W Mid* 2F 61
Hall Green. *W Yor* 3D 92
Hall Green. *Wrex* 1G 71
Halliburton. *Bord* 5C 130
Hallin. *High* 3B 154
Halling. *Medw* 4B 40
Hallington. *Linc* 2C 88
Hallington. *Nmbd* 2C 114
Halloughton. *Notts* 5D 86
Hallow. *Worc* 5C 60
Hallow Heath. *Worc* 5C 60
Hallowsgate. *Ches W* 4H 83
Hallsands. *Devn* 5E 9
Hall's Green. *Herts* 3C 52
Hallspill. *Devn* 4E 19
Hallthwaites. *Cumb* 1A 96
Hall Waberthwaite. *Cumb* 5C 102
Hallwood Green. *Glos* 2B 48
Hallworthy. *Corn* 4B 10
Hallyne. *Bord* 5E 129
Halmer End. *Staf* 1C 72
Halmond's Frome. *Here* 1B 48
Halmore. *Glos* 5B 48
Halnaker. *W Sus* 5A 26
Halsall. *Lanc* 3B 90
Halse. *Nptn* 1D 50
Halse. *Som* 4E 21
Halsetown. *Corn* 3C 4
Halsham. *E Yor* 2F 95
Halsinger. *Devn* 3F 19
Halstead. *Essx* 2B 54
Halstead. *Kent* 4F 39
Halstead. *Leics* 5E 75
Halstock. *Dors* 2A 14
Halstow. *Devn* 3B 12
Halsway. *Som* 3E 21
Haltcliff Bridge. *Cumb* 1E 103
Haltham. *Linc* 4B 88
Haltoft End. *Linc* 1C 76
Halton. *Buck* 5G 51
Halton. *Hal* 2H 83
Halton. *Lanc* 3E 97
Halton. *Nmbd* 3C 114
Halton. *W Yor* 1D 92
Halton. *Wrex* 2F 71
Halton East. *N Yor* 4C 98
Halton Fenside. *Linc* 4D 88
Halton Gill. *N Yor* 2A 98
Halton Holegate. *Linc* 4D 88
Halton Lea Gate. *Nmbd* 4H 113
Halton Moor. *W Yor* 1D 92
Halton Shields. *Nmbd* 3D 114
Halton West. *N Yor* 4H 97
Haltwhistle. *Nmbd* 3A 114
Halvergate. *Norf* 5G 79
Halwell. *Devn* 3D 9
Halwill. *Devn* 3E 11
Halwill Junction. *Devn* 3E 11
Ham. *Devn* 2F 13
Ham. *Glos* 2B 34
Ham. *G Lon* 3C 38
Ham. *High* 1E 169
Ham. *Kent* 5H 41
Ham. *Plym* 3A 8
Ham. *Shet* 8A 173
Ham. *Som* 1F 13
(nr. Ilminster)
Ham. *Som* 4F 21
(nr. Taunton)
Ham. *Som* 4E 21
(nr. Wellington)
Ham. *Wilts* 5B 36
Hambleden. *Buck* 3F 37
Hambledon. *Hants* 1E 17
Hambledon. *Surr* 2A 26
Hamble-le-Rice. *Hants* 2C 16
Hambleton. *Lanc* 5C 96
Hambleton. *N Yor* 1F 93
Hambridge. *Som* 4G 21
Hambrook. *S Glo* 4B 34
Hambrook. *W Sus* 2F 17
Ham Common. *Dors* 4D 22
Hameringham. *Linc* 4C 88
Hamerton. *Cambs* 3A 64
Ham Green. *Here* 1C 48
Ham Green. *Kent* 4C 40
Ham Green. *N Som* 4A 34
Ham Green. *Worc* 4E 61
Ham Hill. *Kent* 4A 40
Hamilton. *Leics* 5D 74
Hamilton. *S Lan* 4A 128
Hamister. *Shet* 5G 173
Hammer. *W Sus* 3G 25
Hammersmith. *G Lon* 3D 38
Hammerwich. *Staf* 5E 73
Hammerwood. *E Sus* 2F 27
Hammill. *Kent* 5G 41
Hammond Street. *Herts* 5D 52
Hammoon. *Dors* 1D 14
Hamnavoe. *Shet* 3D 173
(nr. Braehoulland)
Hamnavoe. *Shet* 8E 173
(nr. Burland)
Hamnavoe. *Shet* 4F 173
(nr. Lunna)
Hamnavoe. *Shet* 3F 173
(on Yell)
Hamp. *Som* 3G 21
Hampden Park. *E Sus* 5H 27
Hampen. *Glos* 3F 49
Hamperden End. *Essx* 2F 53
Hamperley. *Shrp* 2G 59
Hampnett. *Glos* 4F 49
Hampole. *S Yor* 3F 93
Hampreston. *Dors* 3F 15
Hampstead. *G Lon* 2D 38
Hampstead Norreys. *W Ber* 4D 36
Hampsthwaite. *N Yor* 4E 99
Hampton. *Devn* 3F 13
Hampton. *G Lon* 3C 38
Hampton. *Kent* 4F 41
Hampton. *Shrp* 2B 60
Hampton. *Swin* 2G 35
Hampton. *Worc* 1F 49
Hampton Bishop. *Here* 2A 48
Hampton Fields. *Glos* 2D 35
Hampton Hargate. *Pet* 1A 64
Hampton Heath. *Ches W* 1H 71
Hampton in Arden. *W Mid* 2G 61
Hampton Loade. *Shrp* 2B 60
Hampton Lovett. *Worc* 4C 60
Hampton Lucy. *Warw* 5G 61
Hampton Magna. *Warw* 4G 61
Hampton on the Hill. *Warw* 4G 61
Hampton Poyle. *Oxon* 4D 50
Hampton Wick. *G Lon* 4C 38
Hamptworth. *Wilts* 1H 15
Hamrow. *Norf* 3B 78
Hamsey. *E Sus* 4F 27
Hamsey Green. *Surr* 5E 39
Hamstall Ridware. *Staf* 4F 73
Hamstead. *IOW* 3C 16
Hamstead. *W Mid* 1E 61
Hamstead Marshall. *W Ber* 5C 36
Hamsterley. *Dur* 4E 115
(nr. Consett)
Hamsterley. *Dur* 1E 105
(nr. Wolsingham)
Hamsterley Mill. *Dur* 4E 115
Hamstreet. *Kent* 2E 28
Ham Street. *Som* 3A 22
Hamworthy. *Pool* 3E 15
Hanbury. *Staf* 3F 73
Hanbury. *Worc* 4D 60
Hanbury Woodend. *Staf* 3F 73
Hanby. *Linc* 2H 75
Hanchurch. *Staf* 1C 72
Hand and Pen. *Devn* 3D 12
Handbridge. *Ches W* 4G 83
Handcross. *W Sus* 3D 26
Handforth. *Ches E* 2C 84
Handley. *Ches W* 5G 83
Handley. *Derbs* 4A 86
Handsacre. *Staf* 4E 73
Handsworth. *S Yor* 2B 86
Handsworth. *W Mid* 1E 61
Handy Cross. *Buck* 2G 37
Hanford. *Dors* 1D 14
Hanford. *Stoke* 1C 72
Hangersley. *Hants* 2G 15
Hanging Houghton. *Nptn* 3E 63
Hanging Langford. *Wilts* 3F 23
Hangleton. *Brig* 5D 26
Hangleton. *W Sus* 5B 26
Hanham. *S Glo* 4B 34
Hanham Green. *S Glo* 4B 34
Hankelow. *Ches E* 1A 72
Hankerton. *Wilts* 2E 35
Hankham. *E Sus* 5H 27
Hanley. *Stoke* 1C 72 & **Stoke** 211
Hanley Castle. *Worc* 1D 48
Hanley Childe. *Worc* 4A 60
Hanley Swan. *Worc* 1D 48
Hanley William. *Worc* 4A 60
Hanlith. *N Yor* 3B 98
Hanmer. *Wrex* 2G 71
Hannaborough. *Devn* 2F 11
Hannaford. *Devn* 4G 19
Hannah. *Linc* 3E 89
Hannington. *Hants* 1D 24
Hannington. *Nptn* 3F 63
Hannington. *Swin* 2G 35
Hannington Wick. *Swin* 2G 35
Hanscombe End. *C Beds* 2B 52
Hanslope. *Mil* 1G 51
Hanthorpe. *Linc* 3H 75
Hanwell. *G Lon* 2C 38
Hanwell. *Oxon* 1C 50
Hanwood. *Shrp* 5G 71
Hanworth. *G Lon* 3C 38
Hanworth. *Norf* 2D 78
Happas. *Ang* 4D 144
Happendon. *S Lan* 1A 118
Happisburgh. *Norf* 2F 79
Happisburgh Common.
Norf 3F 79
Hapsford. *Ches W* 3G 83
Hapton. *Lanc* 1F 91
Hapton. *Norf* 1D 66
Harberton. *Devn* 3D 9
Harbertonford. *Devn* 3D 9
Harbledown. *Kent* 5F 41
Harborne. *W Mid* 2E 61
Harborough Magna. *Warw* 3B 62
Harbottle. *Nmbd* 4D 120
Harbourneford. *Devn* 2D 8
Harbours Hill. *Worc* 4D 60
Harbridge. *Hants* 1G 15
Harbury. *Warw* 4A 62
Harby. *Leics* 2E 75
Harby. *Notts* 3F 87
Harcombe. *Devn* 3E 13
Harcombe Bottom. *Devn* 3G 13
Harcourt. *Corn* 5C 6
Harden. *W Yor* 1A 92
Hardenhuish. *Wilts* 4E 35
Hardgate. *Abers* 3E 153
Hardgate. *Dum* 3F 111
Hardham. *W Sus* 4B 26
Hardingham. *Norf* 5C 78
Hardingstone. *Nptn* 5E 63
Hardings Wood. *Ches E* 5C 84
Hardington. *Som* 1C 22
Hardington Mandeville.
Som 1A 14
Hardington Marsh. *Som* 2A 14
Hardington Moor. *Som* 1A 14
Hardley. *Hants* 2C 16
Hardley Street. *Norf* 5F 79
Hardmead. *Mil* 1H 51
Hardraw. *N Yor* 5B 104
Hardstoft. *Derbs* 4B 86
Hardway. *Hants* 2E 16
Hardway. *Som* 3C 22
Hardwick. *Buck* 4G 51
Hardwick. *Cambs* 5C 64
Hardwick. *Norf* 2E 66
Hardwick. *Nptn* 4F 63
Hardwick. *Oxon* 3D 50
(nr. Bicester)
Hardwick. *Oxon* 5B 50
(nr. Witney)
Hardwick. *Shrp* 1F 59
Hardwick. *S Yor* 2B 86
Hardwick. *Stoc T* 2B 106
Hardwick. *W Mid* 1E 61
Hardwicke. *Glos* 3E 49
(nr. Cheltenham)
Hardwicke. *Glos* 4C 48
(nr. Gloucester)
Hardwicke. *Here* 1F 47
Hardwick Village. *Notts* 3D 86
Hardy's Green. *Essx* 3C 54
Hare. *Som* 1F 13
Hareby. *Linc* 4C 88
Hareden. *Lanc* 4F 97
Harefield. *G Lon* 1B 38
Hare Green. *Essx* 3D 54
Hare Hatch. *Wok* 4G 37
Harehill. *Derbs* 2F 73
Harehills. *W Yor* 1D 92
Harehope. *Nmbd* 2E 121
Harelaw. *Dum* 2F 113
Harelaw. *Dur* 4E 115
Hareplain. *Kent* 2C 28
Haresceugh. *Cumb* 5H 113
Harescombe. *Glos* 4D 48
Haresfield. *Glos* 4D 48
Haresfinch. *Mers* 1H 83
Hareshaw. *N Lan* 3B 128
Hare Street. *Essx* 5E 53
Hare Street. *Herts* 3D 53
Harewood. *W Yor* 5F 99
Harewood End. *Here* 3A 48
Harford. *Devn* 3C 8
Hargate. *Norf* 1D 66
Hargatewall. *Derbs* 3F 85
Hargrave. *Ches W* 4G 83
Hargrave. *Nptn* 3H 63
Hargrave. *Suff* 5G 65
Harker. *Cumb* 3E 113
Harkland. *Shet* 3F 173
Harkstead. *Suff* 2E 55
Harlaston. *Staf* 4G 73
Harlaxton. *Linc* 2F 75
Harlech. *Gwyn* 2E 69
Harlequin. *Notts* 2D 74
Harlescott. *Shrp* 4H 71
Harleston. *Devn* 4D 9
Harleston. *Norf* 2E 67
Harleston. *Suff* 4C 66
Harlestone. *Nptn* 4E 62
Harley. *Shrp* 5H 71
Harley. *S Yor* 1A 86
Harling Road. *Norf* 2B 66
Harlington. *C Beds* 2A 52
Harlington. *G Lon* 3B 38
Harlington. *S Yor* 4E 93
Harlosh. *High* 4B 154
Harlow. *Essx* 4E 53
Harlow Hill. *Nmbd* 3D 115
Harlsey Castle. *N Yor* 5B 106
Harlthorpe. *E Yor* 1H 93
Harlton. *Cambs* 5C 64
Harlyn. *Corn* 1C 6
Harman's Cross. *Dors* 4E 15
Harmby. *N Yor* 1D 98
Harmer Green. *Herts* 4C 52
Harmer Hill. *Shrp* 3G 71
Harmondsworth. *G Lon* 3B 38
Harmston. *Linc* 4G 87
Harnage. *Shrp* 5H 71
Harnham. *Nmbd* 1D 115
Harnhill. *Glos* 5F 49
Harold Hill. *G Lon* 1G 39
Haroldston West. *Pemb* 3C 42
Haroldswick. *Shet* 1H 173
Harold Wood. *G Lon* 1G 39
Harome. *N Yor* 1A 100
Harpenden. *Herts* 4B 52
Harpford. *Devn* 3D 12
Harpham. *E Yor* 3E 101
Harpley. *Norf* 3G 77
Harpley. *Worc* 4A 60
Harpole. *Nptn* 4D 62
Harpsdale. *High* 3D 168
Harpsden. *Oxon* 3F 37
Harpswell. *Linc* 2G 87
Harpurhey. *G Man* 4G 91
Harpur Hill. *Derbs* 3E 85
Harraby. *Cumb* 4F 113
Harracott. *Devn* 4F 19
Harrapool. *High* 1E 147
Harrapul. *High* 1E 147
Harrietfield. *Per* 1B 136
Harrietsham. *Kent* 5C 40
Harrington. *Cumb* 2A 102
Harrington. *Linc* 3C 88
Harrington. *Nptn* 2E 63
Harringworth. *Nptn* 1G 63
Harriseahead. *Staf* 5C 84
Harriston. *Cumb* 5C 112
Harrogate. *N Yor* 4F 99 & 197
Harrold. *Bed* 5G 63
Harrop Dale. *G Man* 4A 92
Harrow. *G Lon* 2C 38
Harrowbarrow. *Corn* 2H 7
Harrowden. *Bed* 1A 52
Harrowgate Hill. *Darl* 3F 105
Harrow on the Hill. *G Lon* 2C 38
Harrow Weald. *G Lon* 1C 38
Harry Stoke. *S Glo* 4B 34
Harston. *Cambs* 5D 64
Harston. *Leics* 2F 75
Harswell. *E Yor* 5C 100
Hart. *Hart* 1B 106
Hartburn. *Nmbd* 1D 115
Hartburn. *Stoc T* 3B 106
Hartest. *Suff* 5H 65
Hartfield. *E Sus* 2F 27
Hartford. *Cambs* 3B 64
Hartford. *Ches W* 3A 84
Hartford. *Som* 4C 20
Hartfordbridge. *Hants* 1F 25
Hartford End. *Essx* 4G 53
Harthill. *Ches W* 5H 83
Harthill. *N Lan* 3C 128
Harthill. *S Yor* 2B 86
Hartington. *Derbs* 4F 85
Hartland. *Devn* 4C 18
Hartland Quay. *Devn* 4C 18
Hartle. *Worc* 3D 60
Hartlebury. *Worc* 3C 60
Hartlepool. *Hart* 1C 106
Hartley. *Cumb* 4A 104
Hartley. *Kent* 2B 28
(nr. Cranbrook)
Hartley. *Kent* 4H 39
(nr. Dartford)
Hartley. *Nmbd* 2G 115
Hartley Green. *Staf* 2D 73
Hartley Mauditt. *Hants* 3F 25
Hartley Wespall. *Hants* 1E 25
Hartley Wintney. *Hants* 1F 25
Hartlip. *Kent* 4C 40
Hartmount. *High* 1B 158
Hartoft End. *N Yor* 5E 107
Harton. *N Yor* 3B 100
Harton. *Shrp* 2G 59
Harton. *Tyne* 3G 115
Hartpury. *Glos* 3C 48
Hartshead. *W Yor* 2B 92
Hartshill. *Warw* 1H 61
Hartshorne. *Derbs* 3H 73
Hartsop. *Cumb* 3F 103
Hart Station. *Hart* 1B 106
Hartswell. *Som* 4D 20
Hartwell. *Nptn* 5E 63
Hartwood. *Lanc* 3D 90
Hartwood. *N Lan* 4B 128
Harvel. *Kent* 4A 40
Harvington. *Worc* 1F 49
(nr. Evesham)
Harvington. *Worc* 3C 60
(nr. Kidderminster)
Harwell. *Oxon* 3C 36
Harwich. *Essx* 2F 55 & 215
Harwood. *Dur* 1B 104
Harwood. *G Man* 3F 91
Harwood Dale. *N Yor* 5G 107
Harworth. *Notts* 1D 86
Hascombe. *Surr* 2A 26
Haselbech. *Nptn* 3E 62
Haselbury Plucknett. *Som* 1H 13
Haseley. *Warw* 4G 61
Haselor. *Warw* 5F 61
Hasfield. *Glos* 3D 48
Hasguard. *Pemb* 4C 42
Haskayne. *Lanc* 4B 90
Hasketon. *Suff* 5E 67
Hasland. *Derbs* 4A 86
Haslemere. *Surr* 2A 26
Haslingden. *Lanc* 2F 91
Haslingden Grane. *Lanc* 2F 91
Haslingfield. *Cambs* 5D 64
Haslington. *Ches E* 5B 84
Hassall. *Ches E* 5B 84
Hassall Green. *Ches E* 5B 84
Hassell Street. *Kent* 1E 29
Hassendean. *Bord* 2H 119
Hassingham. *Norf* 5F 79
Hassness. *Cumb* 3C 102
Hassocks. *W Sus* 4E 27
Hassop. *Derbs* 3G 85
Haste Hill. *Surr* 2A 26
Haster. *High* 3F 169
Hasthorpe. *Linc* 4D 89
Hastigrow. *High* 2E 169
Hastingleigh. *Kent* 1E 29
Hastings. *E Sus* 5C 28
Hastingwood. *Essx* 5E 53
Hastoe. *Herts* 5H 51
Haston. *Shrp* 3H 71
Haswell. *Dur* 5G 115
Haswell Plough. *Dur* 5G 115
Hatch. *C Beds* 1B 52
Hatch Beauchamp. *Som* 4G 21
Hatch End. *G Lon* 1C 38
Hatch Green. *Som* 1G 13
Hatching Green. *Herts* 4B 52
Hatchmere. *Ches W* 3H 83
Hatch Warren. *Hants* 2E 24
Hatcliffe. *NE Lin* 4F 95
Hatfield. *Here* 5H 59
Hatfield. *Herts* 5C 52
Hatfield. *S Yor* 4G 93
Hatfield. *Worc* 5C 60
Hatfield Broad Oak. *Essx* 4F 53
Hatfield Garden Village. *Herts* 5C 52
Hatfield Heath. *Essx* 4F 53
Hatfield Hyde. *Herts* 4C 52
Hatfield Peverel. *Essx* 4A 54
Hatfield Woodhouse. *S Yor* 4G 93
Hatford. *Oxon* 2B 36
Hatherden. *Hants* 1B 24
Hatherleigh. *Devn* 2F 11
Hathern. *Leics* 3C 74
Hatherop. *Glos* 5G 49
Hathersage. *Derbs* 2G 85
Hathersage Booths. *Derbs* 2G 85
Hatherton. *Ches E* 1A 72
Hatherton. *Staf* 4D 72
Hatley St George. *Cambs* 5B 64
Hatt. *Corn* 2H 7
Hattersley. *G Man* 1D 85
Hattingley. *Hants* 3E 25
Hatton. *Abers* 5H 161
Hatton. *Derbs* 2G 73
Hatton. *G Lon* 3B 38
Hatton. *Linc* 3A 88
Hatton. *Shrp* 1G 59
Hatton. *Warr* 2H 83
Hatton. *Warw* 4G 61
Hattoncrook. *Abers* 1F 153
Hatton Heath. *Ches W* 4G 83
Hatton of Fintray. *Abers* 2F 153
Haugh. *E Ayr* 2D 117
Haugh. *Linc* 3D 88
Haugham. *Linc* 2C 88
Haugh Head. *Nmbd* 2E 121
Haughley. *Suff* 4C 66
Haughley Green. *Suff* 4C 66
Haugh of Ballechin. *Per* 3G 143
Haugh of Glass. *Mor* 5B 160
Haugh of Urr. *Dum* 3F 111
Haughton. *Notts* 3D 86
Haughton. *Shrp* 1A 60
(nr. Bridgnorth)
Haughton. *Shrp* 3F 71
(nr. Oswestry)
Haughton. *Shrp* 5B 72
(nr. Shifnal)
Haughton. *Shrp* 4H 71
(nr. Shrewsbury)
Haughton. *Staf* 3C 72
Haughton Green. *G Man* 1D 84
Haughton le Skerne. *Darl* 3A 106
Haughton Moss. *Ches E* 5H 83
Haultwick. *Herts* 3D 52
Haunn. *Arg* 4E 139
Haunn. *W Isl* 7C 170
Haunton. *Staf* 4G 73
Hauxton. *Cambs* 5D 64
Havannah. *Ches E* 4C 84
Havant. *Hants* 2F 17
Haven. *Here* 5G 59
Haven Bank. *Linc* 5B 88
Havenside. *E Yor* 2E 95
Havenstreet. *IOW* 3D 16
Haven, The. *W Sus* 2B 26
Havercroft. *W Yor* 3D 93
Haverfordwest. *Pemb* 3D 42
Haverhill. *Suff* 1G 53
Haverigg. *Cumb* 2A 96
Havering-atte-Bower. *G Lon* 1G 39
Havering's Grove. *Essx* 1A 40
Haversham. *Mil* 1G 51
Haverthwaite. *Cumb* 1C 96
Haverton Hill. *Stoc T* 2B 106
Havyatt. *Som* 3A 22
Hawarden. *Flin* 4F 83
Hawcoat. *Cumb* 2B 96
Hawcross. *Glos* 2C 48
Hawen. *Cdgn* 1D 44
Hawes. *N Yor* 1A 98
Hawes Green. *Norf* 1E 67
Hawick. *Bord* 3H 119
Hawkchurch. *Devn* 2G 13
Hawkedon. *Suff* 5G 65
Hawkenbury. *Kent* 1C 28
Hawkeridge. *Wilts* 1D 22
Hawkerland. *Devn* 4D 12
Hawkesbury. *S Glo* 3C 34
Hawkesbury Upton. *S Glo* 3C 34
Hawkes End. *W Mid* 2G 61
Hawk Green. *G Man* 2D 84
Hawkhurst. *Kent* 2B 28
Hawkhurst Common. *E Sus* 4G 27
Hawkinge. *Kent* 1G 29
Hawkley. *Hants* 4F 25
Hawkridge. *Som* 3B 20
Hawksdale. *Cumb* 5E 113
Hawkshaw. *G Man* 3F 91
Hawkshead. *Cumb* 5E 103
Hawkshead Hill. *Cumb* 5E 103
Hawkswick. *N Yor* 2B 98
Hawksworth. *Notts* 1E 75
Hawksworth. *W Yor* 5D 98
Hawkwell. *Essx* 1C 40
Hawley. *Hants* 1G 25
Hawley. *Kent* 3G 39
Hawling. *Glos* 3F 49
Hawnby. *N Yor* 1H 99
Haworth. *W Yor* 1A 92
Hawstead. *Suff* 5A 66
Hawthorn. *Dur* 5H 115
Hawthorn Hill. *Brac* 4G 37
Hawthorn Hill. *Linc* 5B 88
Hawthorpe. *Linc* 3H 75
Hawton. *Notts* 5E 87
Haxby. *York* 4A 100
Haxey. *N Lin* 1E 87
Haybridge. *Shrp* 3A 60
Haybridge. *Som* 2A 22
Haydock. *Mers* 1H 83
Haydon. *Bath* 1B 22
Haydon. *Dors* 1B 14
Haydon. *Som* 4F 21
Haydon Bridge. *Nmbd* 3B 114
Haydon Wick. *Swin* 3G 35
Haye. *Corn* 2H 7

Hayes—Highstreet Green

Hayes. G Lon 4F 39
(nr. Bromley)
Hayes. G Lon 2B 38
(nr. Uxbridge)
Hayfield. Derbs 2E 85
Hay Green. Norf 4E 77
Hayhill. E Ayr 3D 116
Haylands. IOW 3D 16
Hayle. Corn 3C 4
Hayley Green. W Mid 2D 60
Hayling Island. Hants 3F 17
Hayne. Devn 2B 12
Haynes. C Beds 1A 52
Haynes West End. C Beds 1A 52
Hay-on-Wye. Powy 1F 47
Hayscastle. Pemb 2C 42
Hayscastle Cross. Pemb 2D 42
Haysden. Kent 1G 27
Hayshead. Ang 4F 145
Hay Street. Herts 3D 53
Hayton. Aber 3G 153
Hayton. Cumb 5C 112
(nr. Aspatria)
Hayton. Cumb 4G 113
(nr. Brampton)
Hayton. E Yor 5C 100
Hayton. Notts 2E 87
Hayton's Bent. Shrp 2H 59
Haytor Vale. Devn 5A 12
Haytown. Devn 1D 11
Haywards Heath. W Sus 3E 27
Haywood. S Lan 4C 128
Hazelbank. S Lan 5B 128
Hazelbury Bryan. Dors 2C 14
Hazeleigh. Essx 5B 54
Hazeley. Hants 1F 25
Hazel Grove. G Man 2D 84
Hazelhead. S Yor 4B 92
Hazelslade. Staf 4E 73
Hazel Street. Kent 2A 28
Hazelton Walls. Fife 1F 137
Hazelwood. Derbs 1H 73
Hazlemere. Buck 2G 37
Hazler. Shrp 1G 59
Hazlerigg. Tyne 2F 115
Hazles. Staf 1E 73
Hazleton. Glos 4F 49
Hazon. Nmbd 4F 121
Heacham. Norf 2F 77
Headbourne Worthy. Hants 3C 24
Headcorn. Kent 1C 28
Headingley. W Yor 1C 92
Headington. Oxon 5D 50
Headlam. Dur 3E 105
Headless Cross. Worc 4E 61
Headley. Hants 3G 25
(nr. Haslemere)
Headley. Hants 5D 36
(nr. Kingsclere)
Headley. Surr 5D 38
Headley Down. Hants 3G 25
Headley Heath. Worc 3E 61
Headley Park. Bris 5A 34
Head of Muir. Falk 1B 128
Headon. Notts 3E 87
Heads Nook. Cumb 4F 113
Heage. Derbs 5A 86
Healaugh. N Yor 5D 104
(nr. Grinton)
Healaugh. N Yor 5H 99
(nr. York)
Heald Green. G Man 2C 84
Heale. Devn 2G 19
Healey. G Man 3G 91
Healey. Nmbd 4D 114
Healey. N Yor 1D 98
Healeyfield. Dur 5D 114
Healey Hall. Nmbd 4D 114
Healing. NE Lin 3F 95
Heamoor. Corn 3B 4
Heanish. Arg 4B 138
Heanor. Derbs 1B 74
Heanton Punchardon. Devn 3F 19
Heapham. Linc 2F 87
Heartsease. Powy 4D 58
Heasley Mill. Devn 3H 19
Heaste. High 2E 147
Heath. Derbs 4B 86
Heath and Reach. C Beds 3H 51
Heath Common. W Sus 4C 26
Heathcote. Derbs 4F 85
Heath Cross. Devn 3H 11
Heathencote. Nptn 1F 51
Heath End. Derbs 3A 74
Heath End. Hants 5D 36
Heath End. W Mid 5E 73
Heather. Leics 4A 74
Heatherfield. High 4D 155
Heatherton. Derb 2H 73
Heathfield. Cambs 1E 53
Heathfield. Cumb 5C 112
Heathfield. Devn 5B 12
Heathfield. E Sus 3G 27
Heathfield. Ren 3E 126
Heathfield. Som 3E 21
(nr. Lydeard St Lawrence)
Heathfield. Som 4E 21
(nr. Norton Fitzwarren)
Heath Green. Worc 3E 61
Heathhall. Dum 2A 112
Heath Hayes. Staf 4E 73
Heath Hill. Shrp 4B 72
Heath House. Som 2H 21
Heathrow (London) Airport.
G Lon 3B 38 & 216
Heathstock. Devn 2F 13
Heath, The. Norf 3E 79
(nr. Buxton)
Heath, The. Norf 3B 78
(nr. Fakenham)
Heath, The. Norf 3D 78
(nr. Hevingham)
Heath, The. Staf 2E 73
Heath, The. Suff 2E 55
Heathton. Shrp 1C 60
Heathtop. Derbs 2F 73
Heath Town. W Mid 1D 60
Heatley. G Man 2B 84
Heatley. Staf 3E 73
Heaton. Lanc 3D 96
Heaton. Staf 4D 84
Heaton. Tyne 3F 115
Heaton. W Yor 1B 92
Heaton Moor. G Man 1C 84
Heaton's Bridge. Lanc 3C 90
Heaverham. Kent 5G 39
Heavitree. Devn 3C 12
Hebburn. Tyne 3G 115
Hebden. N Yor 3C 98
Hebden Bridge. W Yor 2H 91
Hebden Green. Ches W 4A 84
Hebing End. Herts 3D 52
Hebron. Carm 2F 43
Hebron. Nmbd 1E 115
Heck. Dum 1B 112
Heckdyke. Notts 1E 87
Heckfield. Hants 5F 37
Heckfield Green. Suff 3D 66
Heckfordbridge. Essx 3C 54
Heckington. Linc 1A 76
Heckmondwike. W Yor 2C 92
Heddington. Wilts 5E 35
Heddle. Orkn 6C 172
Heddon. Devn 4G 19
Heddon-on-the-Wall. Nmbd 3E 115
Hedenham. Norf 1F 67
Hedge End. Hants 1C 16
Hedgerley. Buck 2A 38
Hedging. Som 4G 21
Hedley on the Hill. Nmbd 4D 115
Hednesford. Staf 4E 73
Hedon. E Yor 2E 95
Hegdon Hill. Here 5H 59
Heglibister. Shet 6E 173
Heighington. Darl 2F 105
Heighington. Linc 4H 87
Heightington. Worc 3B 60
Heights of Brae. High 2H 157
Heights of Fodderty. High 2H 157
Heights of Kinlochewe. High 2C 156
Heiton. Bord 1B 120
Hele. Devn 5H 11
(nr. Ashburton)
Hele. Devn 2C 12
(nr. Exeter)
Hele. Devn 3D 10
(nr. Holsworthy)
Hele. Devn 2F 19
(nr. Ilfracombe)
Hele. Torb 2F 9
Helensburgh. Arg 1D 126
Helford. Corn 4E 5
Helhoughton. Norf 3A 78
Helions Bumpstead. Essx 1G 53
Helland. Corn 5A 10
Helland. Som 4G 21
Hellandbridge. Corn 5A 10
Hellesdon. Norf 4E 78
Hellesveor. Corn 2C 4
Hellidon. Nptn 5C 62
Hellifield. N Yor 4A 98
Hellingly. E Sus 4G 27
Hellington. Norf 5F 79
Hellister. Shet 7E 173
Helmdon. Nptn 1D 50
Helmingham. Suff 5D 66
Helmington Row. Dur 1E 105
Helmsdale. High 2H 165
Helmshore. Lanc 2F 91
Helmsley. N Yor 1A 100
Helperby. N Yor 3G 99
Helperthorpe. N Yor 2D 100
Helpringham. Linc 1A 76
Helpston. Pet 5A 76
Helsby. Ches W 3G 83
Helsey. Linc 3E 89
Helston. Corn 4D 4
Helstone. Corn 4A 10
Helton. Cumb 2G 103
Helwith. N Yor 4D 105
Helwith Bridge. N Yor 3H 97
Helygain. Flin 3E 82
Hemblington. Norf 4F 79
Hemel Hempstead. Herts 5A 52
Hemerdon. Devn 3B 8
Hemingbrough. N Yor 1G 93
Hemingby. Linc 3B 88
Hemingfield. S Yor 4D 93
Hemingford Abbots. Cambs 3B 64
Hemingford Grey. Cambs 3B 64
Hemingstone. Suff 5D 66
Hemington. Leics 3B 74
Hemington. Nptn 2H 63
Hemington. Som 1C 22
Hemley. Suff 1F 55
Hemlington. Midd 3B 106
Hempholme. E Yor 4E 101
Hempnall. Norf 1E 67
Hempnall Green. Norf 1E 67
Hempriggs. High 4F 169
Hemp's Green. Essx 3C 54
Hempstead. Essx 2G 53
Hempstead. Medw 4B 40
Hempstead. Norf 2D 78
(nr. Holt)
Hempstead. Norf 3G 79
(nr. Stalham)
Hempsted. Glos 4D 48
Hempton. Norf 3B 78
Hempton. Oxon 2C 50
Hemsby. Norf 4G 79
Hemswell. Linc 1G 87
Hemswell Cliff. Linc 2G 87
Hemsworth. Dors 2E 15
Hemsworth. W Yor 3E 93
Hem, The. Shrp 5B 72
Hemyock. Devn 1E 13
Henallt. Carm 3E 45
Henbury. Bris 4A 34
Henbury. Ches E 3C 84
Hendomen. Powy 1E 58
Hendon. G Lon 2D 38
Hendon. Tyne 4H 115
Hendra. Corn 3D 6
Hendre. B'end 3C 32
Hendreforgan. Rhon 3C 32
Hendy. Carm 5F 45
Heneglwys. IOA 3D 80
Henfeddau Fawr. Pemb 1G 43
Henfield. S Glo 4B 34
Henfield. W Sus 4D 26
Henford. Devn 3D 10
Hengoed. Cphy 2E 33
Hengoed. Shrp 2E 71
Hengrave. Suff 4H 65
Henham. Essx 3F 53
Heniarth. Powy 5D 70
Henlade. Som 4F 21
Henley. Dors 2B 14
Henley. Shrp 2G 59
(nr. Church Stretton)
Henley. Shrp 3H 59
(nr. Ludlow)
Henley. Som 3H 21
Henley. Suff 5D 66
Henley. W Sus 4G 25
Henley-in-Arden. Warw 4F 61
Henley-on-Thames. Oxon 3F 37
Henley's Down. E Sus 4B 28
Henley Street. Kent 4A 40
Henllan. Cdgn 1D 44
Henllan. Den 4C 82
Henllan. Mon 3F 47
Henllan Amgoed. Carm 3F 43
Henllys. Torf 2F 33
Henlow. C Beds 2B 52
Hennock. Devn 4B 12
Henny Street. Essx 2B 54
Henryd. Cnwy 3G 81
Henry's Moat. Pemb 2E 43
Hensall. N Yor 2F 93
Henshaw. Nmbd 3A 114
Hensingham. Cumb 3A 102
Henstead. Suff 2G 67
Hensting. Hants 4C 24
Henstridge. Som 1C 14
Henstridge Ash. Som 4C 22
Henstridge Bowden. Som 4B 22
Henstridge Marsh. Som 4C 22
Henton. Oxon 5F 51
Henton. Som 2H 21
Henwood. Corn 5C 10
Heogan. Shet 7F 173
Heol Senni. Powy 3C 46
Heol-y-Cyw. B'end 3C 32
Hepburn. Nmbd 2E 121
Hepple. Nmbd 4D 121
Hepscott. Nmbd 1F 115
Heptonstall. W Yor 2H 91
Hepworth. Suff 3B 66
Hepworth. W Yor 4B 92
Herbrandston. Pemb 4C 42
Hereford. Here 2A 48 & 197
Heribusta. High 1D 154
Heriot. Bord 4H 129
Hermiston. Edin 2E 129
Hermitage. Dors 2B 14
Hermitage. Bord 5H 119
Hermitage. W Ber 4D 36
Hermitage. W Sus 2F 17
Hermon. Carm 3G 45
(nr. Llandeilo)
Hermon. Carm 2D 44
(nr. Newcastle Emlyn)
Hermon. IOA 4C 80
Hermon. Pemb 1G 43
Herne. Kent 4F 41
Herne Bay. Kent 4F 41
Herne Common. Kent 4F 41
Herne Pound. Kent 5A 40
Herner. Devn 4F 19
Hernhill. Kent 4E 41
Herodsfoot. Corn 2G 7
Heronden. Kent 5G 41
Herongate. Essx 1H 39
Heronsford. S Ayr 1G 109
Heronsgate. Herts 1B 38
Heron's Ghyll. E Sus 3F 27
Herra. Shet 2H 173
Herriard. Hants 2E 25
Herringfleet. Suff 1G 67
Herringswell. Suff 4G 65
Herrington. Tyne 4G 115
Hersden. Kent 4G 41
Hersham. Corn 2C 10
Hersham. Surr 4C 38
Herstmonceux. E Sus 4H 27
Herston. Dors 5F 15
Herston. Orkn 8D 172
Hertford. Herts 4D 52
Hertford Heath. Herts 4D 52
Hertingfordbury. Herts 4D 52
Hesketh. Lanc 2C 90
Hesketh Bank. Lanc 2C 90
Hesketh Lane. Lanc 5F 97
Hesket Newmarket. Cumb 1E 103
Heskin Green. Lanc 3D 90
Hesleden. Dur 1B 106
Hesleyside. Nmbd 1B 114
Heslington. York 4A 100
Hessay. York 4H 99
Hessenford. Corn 3H 7
Hessett. Suff 4B 66
Hessilhead. N Ayr 4E 127
Hessle. Hull 2D 94
Hestaford. Shet 6D 173
Hest Bank. Lanc 3D 96
Hester's Way. Glos 3E 49
Hestinsetter. Shet 7D 173
Heston. G Lon 3C 38
Hestwall. Orkn 6B 172
Heswall. Mers 2E 83
Hethe. Oxon 3D 50
Hethelpit Cross. Glos 3C 48
Hethersett. Norf 5D 78
Hethersgill. Cumb 3F 113
Hetherside. Cumb 3F 113
Hethpool. Nmbd 2C 120
Hett. Dur 1F 105
Hetton. N Yor 4B 98
Hetton-le-Hole. Tyne 5G 115
Hetton Steads. Nmbd 1E 121
Heugh. Nmbd 2D 115
Heugh-head. Abers 2A 152
Heveningham. Suff 3F 67
Hever. Kent 1F 27
Heversham. Cumb 1D 97
Hevingham. Norf 3D 78
Hewas Water. Corn 4D 6
Hewelsfield. Glos 5A 48
Hewish. N Som 5G 33
Hewish. Som 2H 13
Hewood. Dors 2G 13
Heworth. York 4A 100
Hexham. Nmbd 3C 114
Hextable. Kent 3G 39
Hexton. Herts 2B 52
Hexworthy. Devn 5G 11
Heybridge. Essx 1H 39
(nr. Brentwood)
Heybridge. Essx 5B 54
(nr. Maldon)
Heybridge Basin. Essx 5B 54
Heybrook Bay. Devn 4A 8
Heydon. Cambs 1E 53
Heydon. Norf 3D 78
Heydour. Linc 2H 75
Heylipol. Arg 4A 138
Heyop. Powy 3E 59
Heysham. Lanc 3D 96
Heyshott. W Sus 1G 17
Heytesbury. Wilts 2E 23
Heythrop. Oxon 3B 50
Heywood. G Man 3G 91
Heywood. Wilts 1D 22
Hibaldstow. N Lin 4C 94
Hickleton. S Yor 4E 93
Hickling. Norf 3G 79
Hickling. Notts 3D 74
Hickling Green. Norf 3G 79
Hickling Heath. Norf 3G 79
Hickstead. W Sus 3D 26
Hidcote Bartrim. Glos 1G 49
Hidcote Boyce. Glos 1G 49
Higford. Shrp 5B 72
High Ackworth. W Yor 3E 93
Higham. Derbs 5A 86
Higham. Kent 3B 40
Higham. Lanc 1G 91
Higham. S Yor 4D 92
Higham. Suff 2D 54
(nr. Ipswich)
Higham. Suff 4G 65
(nr. Newmarket)
Higham Dykes. Nmbd 2E 115
Higham Ferrers. Nptn 4G 63
Higham Gobion. C Beds 2B 52
Higham on the Hill. Leics 1A 62
Highampton. Devn 2E 11
Higham Wood. Kent 1G 27
High Angerton. Nmbd 1D 115
High Auldgirth. Dum 1G 111
High Bankhill. Cumb 5G 113
High Banton. N Lan 1A 128
High Barnet. G Lon 1D 38
High Beech. Essx 1F 39
High Bentham. N Yor 3F 97
High Bickington. Devn 4G 19
High Biggins. Cumb 2F 97
High Birkwith. N Yor 2H 97
High Blantyre. S Lan 4H 127
High Bonnybridge. Falk 2B 128
High Borrans. Cumb 4F 103
High Bradfield. S Yor 1G 85
High Bray. Devn 3G 19
Highbridge. Cumb 5E 113
Highbridge. High 5D 148
Highbridge. Som 2G 21
Highbrook. W Sus 2E 27
High Brooms. Kent 1G 27
High Bullen. Devn 4F 19
Highburton. W Yor 3B 92
Highbury. Som 2B 22
High Buston. Nmbd 4G 121
High Callerton. Nmbd 2E 115
High Carlingill. Cumb 4H 103
High Catton. E Yor 4B 100
High Church. Nmbd 1E 115
Highclere. Hants 5C 36
Highcliffe. Dors 3H 15
High Cogges. Oxon 5B 50
High Common. Norf 5B 78
High Coniscliffe. Darl 3F 105
High Crosby. Cumb 4F 113
High Cross. Hants 4F 25
High Cross. Herts 4D 52
High Dougarie. N Ayr 2C 122
High Easter. Essx 4G 53
High Eggborough. N Yor 2F 93
High Ellington. N Yor 1D 98
Higher Alham. Som 2B 22
Higher Ansty. Dors 2C 14
Higher Ashton. Devn 4B 12
Higher Ballam. Lanc 1B 90
Higher Bartle. Lanc 1D 90
Higher Bockhampton. Dors 3C 14
Higher Bojewyan. Corn 3A 4
High Ercall. Telf 4H 71
Higher Cheriton. Devn 2E 12
Higher Clovelly. Devn 4D 18
Higher Compton. Plym 3A 8
Higher Dean. Devn 2D 8
Higher Dinting. Derbs 1E 85
Higher Dunstone. Devn 5H 11
Higher End. G Man 4D 90
Higher Gabwell. Devn 2F 9
Higher Halstock Leigh. Dors 2A 14
Higher Heysham. Lanc 3D 96
Higher Hurdsfield. Ches E 3D 84
Higher Kingcombe. Dors 3A 14
Higher Kinnerton. Flin 4F 83
Higher Melcombe. Dors 2C 14
Higher Penwortham. Lanc 2D 90
Higher Porthpean. Corn 3E 7
Higher Poynton. Ches E 2D 84
Higher Shotton. Flin 4F 83
Higher Shurlach. Ches W 3A 84
Higher Slade. Devn 2F 19
Higher Tale. Devn 2D 12
Highertown. Corn 4C 6
Higher Town. IOS 1B 4
Higher Town. Som 2C 20
Higher Vexford. Som 3E 20
Higher Walton. Lanc 2D 90
Higher Walton. Warr 2H 83
Higher Whatcombe. Dors 2D 14
Higher Wheelton. Lanc 2E 90
Higher Whiteleigh. Corn 3C 10
Higher Whitley. Ches W 3A 84
Higher Wincham. Ches W 3A 84
Higher Wraxall. Dors 2A 14
Higher Wych. Wrex 1G 71
Higher Yalberton. Torb 3E 9
High Etherley. Dur 2E 105
High Ferry. Linc 1C 76
Highfield. E Yor 1H 93
Highfield. N Ayr 4E 126
Highfield. Tyne 4E 115
Highfields Caldecote. Cambs 5C 64
High Garrett. Essx 3A 54
Highgate. G Lon 2D 39
Highgate. N Ayr 4E 127
Highgate. Powy 1D 58
High Grange. Dur 1E 105
High Green. Cumb 4F 103
High Green. Norf 5D 78
High Green. Shrp 2B 60
High Green. S Yor 1H 85
High Green. W Yor 3B 92
High Green. Worc 1D 49
Highgreen Manor. Nmbd 5C 120
High Halden. Kent 2C 28
High Halstow. Medw 3B 40
High Ham. Som 3H 21
High Harrington. Cumb 2B 102
High Haswell. Dur 5G 115
High Hatton. Shrp 3A 72
High Hawkser. N Yor 4G 107
High Hesket. Cumb 5F 113
High Hesleden. Dur 1B 106
High Hoyland. S Yor 3C 92
High Hunsley. E Yor 1C 94
High Hurstwood. E Sus 3F 27
High Hutton. N Yor 3B 100
High Ireby. Cumb 1D 102
High Keil. Arg 5A 122
High Kelling. Norf 1D 78
High Kilburn. N Yor 2H 99
High Knipe. Cumb 3G 103
High Lands. Dur 2E 105
Highlands, The. Shrp 2A 60
Highlane. Ches E 4C 84
Highlane. Derbs 2B 86
High Lane. G Man 2D 84
High Lane. Here 4A 60
High Laver. Essx 5F 53
Highlaws. Cumb 5C 112
Highleadon. Glos 3C 48
High Legh. Ches E 2A 84
Highleigh. W Sus 3G 17
High Leven. Stoc T 3B 106
Highley. Shrp 2B 60
High Littleton. Bath 1B 22
High Longthwaite. Cumb 5D 112
High Lorton. Cumb 2C 102
High Marishes. N Yor 2C 100
High Marnham. Notts 3F 87
High Melton. S Yor 4F 93
High Mickley. Nmbd 3D 115
Highmoor. Cumb 5D 112
High Moor. Lanc 3D 90
Highmoor. Oxon 3F 37
Highmoor Hill. Mon 3H 33
High Mowthorpe. N Yor 3C 100
Highnam. Glos 4C 48
High Newport. Tyne 4G 115
High Newton. Cumb 1D 96
High Newton-by-the-Sea.
Nmbd 2G 121
High Nibthwaite. Cumb 1B 96
High Offley. Staf 3B 72
High Ongar. Essx 5F 53
High Onn. Staf 4C 72
High Orchard. Glos 4D 48
High Park. Mers 3B 90
High Roding. Essx 4G 53
High Row. Cumb 1E 103
High Salvington. W Sus 5C 26
High Scales. Cumb 5C 112
High Shaw. N Yor 5B 104
High Shincliffe. Dur 5F 115
High Side. Cumb 1D 102
High Spen. Tyne 3E 115
Highsted. Kent 4D 40
High Stoop. Dur 5E 115
High Street. Corn 3D 6
High Street. Suff 5G 67
(nr. Aldeburgh)
High Street. Suff 2F 67
(nr. Bungay)
High Street. Suff 3G 67
(nr. Yoxford)
Highstreet Green. Essx 2A 54
High Street Green. Suff 5C 66
Highstreet Green. Surr 2A 26

Hightae—Horton Cross

Hightae. Dum 2B 112
High Throston. Hart 1B 106
Hightown. Ches E 4C 84
Hightown. Mers 4A 90
High Town. Staf 4D 73
Hightown Green. Suff 5B 66
High Toynton. Linc 4B 88
High Trewhitt. Nmbd 4E 121
High Valleyfield. Fife 1D 128
Highway. Here 1H 47
Highweek. Devn 5B 12
High Westwood. Dur 4E 115
Highwood. Staf 2E 73
Highwood. Worc 4A 60
High Worsall. N Yor 4A 106
Highworth. Swin 2H 35
High Wray. Cumb 5E 103
High Wych. Herts 4E 53
High Wycombe. Buck 2G 37
Hilborough. Norf 5H 77
Hilcott. Wilts 1G 23
Hildenborough. Kent 1G 27
Hildersham. Cambs 1F 53
Hilderstone. Staf 2D 72
Hilderthorpe. E Yor 3F 101
Hilfield. Dors 2B 14
Hilgay. Norf 1F 65
Hill. S Glo 2B 34
Hill. Warw 4B 62
Hill. Worc 1E 49
Hillam. N Yor 2F 93
Hillbeck. Cumb 3A 104
Hillberry. IOM 4C 108
Hillborough. Kent 4G 41
Hillbourne. Pool 3F 15
Hillbrae. Abers 4D 160
(nr. Aberchirder)
Hillbrae. Abers 1E 153
(nr. Inverurie)
Hillbrae. Abers 5F 161
(nr. Methlick)
Hill Brow. Hants 4F 25
Hillbutts. Dors 2E 15
Hillclifflane. Derbs 1G 73
Hillcommon. Som 4E 21
Hill Deverill. Wilts 2D 22
Hilldyke. Linc 1C 76
Hill End. Dur 1D 104
Hillend. Fife 1E 129
(nr. Inverkeithing)
Hill End. Fife 4C 136
(nr. Saline)
Hillend. N Lan 3B 128
Hill End. N Yor 4C 98
Hillend. Shrp 1C 60
Hillend. Swan 3D 30
Hillersland. Glos 4A 48
Hillerton. Devn 3H 11
Hillesden. Buck 3E 51
Hillesley. Glos 3C 34
Hillfarrance. Som 4E 21
Hill Furze. Worc 1E 49
Hill Gate. Here 3H 47
Hill Green. Essx 2E 53
Hillgreen. W Ber 4C 36
Hillhead. Abers 5C 160
Hill Head. Hants 2D 16
Hillhead. S Ayr 3D 116
Hillhead. Torb 3F 9
Hillhead of Auchentumb. Abers 3G 161
Hilliard's Cross. Staf 4F 73
Hilliclay. High 2D 168
Hillingdon. G Lon 2B 38
Hillington. Norf 3G 77
Hillington. Ren 3G 127
Hillmorton. Warw 3C 62
Hill of Beath. Fife 4D 136
Hill of Fearn. High 1C 158
Hill of Fiddes. Abers 1G 153
Hill of Keillor. Ang 4B 144
Hill of Overbrae. Abers 2F 161
Hill Ridware. Staf 4E 73
Hillsborough. S Yor 1H 85
Hillside. Abers 4G 153
Hillside. Ang 2G 145
Hillside. Devn 2D 8
Hillside. Hants 1F 25
Hillside. Mers 3B 90
Hillside. Orkn 5C 172
Hillside. Shet 5F 173
Hillside. Shrp 2A 60
Hill Side. W Yor 3B 92
Hillside. Worc 4B 60
Hillside of Prieston. Ang 5C 144
Hill Somersal. Derbs 2F 73
Hillstown. Derbs 4B 86
Hillstreet. Hants 1B 16
Hillswick. Shet 4D 173
Hill, The. Cumb 1A 96
Hill Top. Dur 2C 104
(nr. Barnard Castle)
Hill Top. Dur 5F 115
(nr. Durham)
Hill Top. Dur 4E 115
(nr. Stanley)
Hill Top. Hants 2C 16
Hill View. Dors 3E 15
Hillwell. Shet 10E 173
Hill Wootton. Warw 4H 61
Hillyland. Per 1C 136
Hilmarton. Wilts 4F 35
Hilperton. Wilts 1D 22
Hilperton Marsh. Wilts 1D 22
Hilsea. Port 2E 17
Hilston. E Yor 1F 95
Hiltingbury. Hants 4C 24
Hilton. Cambs 4B 64
Hilton. Cumb 2A 104
Hilton. Derbs 2G 73
Hilton. Dors 2C 14
Hilton. Dur 2E 105
Hilton. High 5E 165
Hilton. Shrp 1B 60
Hilton. Staf 5E 73
Hilton. Stoc T 3B 106
Hilton of Cadboll. High 1C 158
Himbleton. Worc 5D 60
Himley. Staf 1C 60
Hincaster. Cumb 1E 97
Hinchcliffe Mill. W Yor 4B 92
Hinchwick. Glos 2G 49
Hinckley. Leics 1B 62
Hinderclay. Suff 3C 66
Hinderwell. N Yor 3E 107
Hindford. Shrp 2F 71
Hindhead. Surr 3G 25
Hindley. G Man 4E 90
Hindley. Nmbd 4D 114
Hindley Green. G Man 4E 91
Hindlip. Worc 5C 60
Hindolveston. Norf 3C 78
Hindon. Wilts 3E 23
Hindringham. Norf 2B 78
Hingham. Norf 5C 78
Hinksford. Staf 2C 60
Hinstock. Shrp 3A 72
Hintlesham. Suff 1D 54
Hinton. Hants 3H 15
Hinton. Here 2G 47
Hinton. Nptn 5C 62
Hinton. Shrp 5G 71
Hinton. S Glo 4C 34
Hinton Ampner. Hants 4D 24
Hinton Blewett. Bath 1A 22
Hinton Charterhouse. Bath 1C 22
Hinton-in-the-Hedges. Nptn 2D 50
Hinton Martell. Dors 2F 15
Hinton on the Green. Worc 1F 49
Hinton Parva. Swin 3H 35
Hinton St George. Som 1H 13
Hinton St Mary. Dors 1C 14
Hinton Waldrist. Oxon 2B 36
Hints. Shrp 3A 60
Hints. Staf 5F 73
Hinwick. Bed 4G 63
Hinxhill. Kent 1E 29
Hinxton. Cambs 1E 53
Hinxworth. Herts 1C 52
Hipley. Hants 1E 16
Hipperholme. W Yor 2B 92
Hipsburn. Nmbd 3G 121
Hipswell. N Yor 5E 105
Hiraeth. Carm 2F 43
Hirn. Abers 3E 153
Hirnant. Powy 3C 70
Hirst. N Lan 3B 128
Hirst. Nmbd 1F 115
Hirst Courtney. N Yor 2G 93
Hirwaen. Den 4D 82
Hirwaun. Rhon 5C 46
Hiscott. Devn 4F 19
Histon. Cambs 4D 64
Hitcham. Suff 5B 66
Hitchin. Herts 3B 52
Hittisleigh. Devn 3H 11
Hittisleigh Barton. Devn 3H 11
Hive. E Yor 1B 94
Hixon. Staf 3E 73
Hoaden. Kent 5G 41
Hoar Cross. Staf 3F 73
Hoarwithy. Here 3A 48
Hoath. Kent 4G 41
Hobarris. Shrp 3F 59
Hobbister. Orkn 7C 172
Hobbles Green. Suff 5G 65
Hobbs Cross. Essx 1F 39
Hobkirk. Bord 3H 119
Hobson. Dur 4E 115
Hoby. Leics 4D 74
Hockering. Norf 4C 78
Hockering Heath. Norf 4C 78
Hockerton. Notts 5E 86
Hockley. Essx 1C 40
Hockley. Staf 5G 73
Hockley. W Mid 3G 61
Hockley Heath. W Mid 3F 61
Hockliffe. C Beds 3H 51
Hockwold cum Wilton. Norf 2G 65
Hockworthy. Devn 1D 12
Hoddesdon. Herts 5D 52
Hoddlesden. Bkbn 2F 91
Hoddomcross. Dum 2C 112
Hodgeston. Pemb 5E 43
Hodley. Powy 1D 58
Hodnet. Shrp 3A 72
Hodsoll Street. Kent 4H 39
Hodson. Swin 3G 35
Hodthorpe. Derbs 3C 86
Hoe. Norf 4B 78
Hoe Gate. Hants 1E 17
Hoe, The. Plym 3A 8
Hoff. Cumb 3H 103
Hoffleet Stow. Linc 2B 76
Hogaland. Shet 4E 173
Hogben's Hill. Kent 5E 41
Hoggard's Green. Suff 5A 66
Hoggeston. Buck 3G 51
Hoggrill's End. Warw 1G 61
Hogha Gearraidh. W Isl 1C 170
Hoghton. Lanc 2E 90
Hoghton Bottoms. Lanc 2E 91
Hognaston. Derbs 5G 85
Hogsthorpe. Linc 3E 89
Hogstock. Dors 2E 15
Holbeach. Linc 3C 76
Holbeach Bank. Linc 3C 76
Holbeach Clough. Linc 3C 76
Holbeach Drove. Linc 4C 76
Holbeach Hurn. Linc 3C 76
Holbeach St Johns. Linc 4C 76
Holbeach St Marks. Linc 2C 76
Holbeach St Matthew. Linc 2D 76
Holbeck. Notts 3C 86
Holbeck. W Yor 1C 92
Holbeck Woodhouse. Notts 3C 86
Holberrow Green. Worc 5E 61
Holbeton. Devn 3C 8
Holborn. G Lon 2E 39
Holbrook. Derbs 1A 74
Holbrook. S Yor 2B 86
Holbrook. Suff 2E 55
Holburn. Nmbd 1E 121
Holbury. Hants 2C 16
Holcombe. Devn 5C 12
Holcombe. G Man 3F 91
Holcombe. Som 2B 22
Holcombe Brook. G Man 3F 91
Holcombe Rogus. Devn 1D 12
Holcot. Nptn 4E 63
Holden. Lanc 5G 97
Holdenby. Nptn 4D 62
Holder's Green. Essx 3G 53
Holdgate. Shrp 2H 59
Holdingham. Linc 1H 75
Holditch. Dors 2G 13
Holemoor. Devn 2E 11
Hole Street. W Sus 4C 26
Holford. Som 2E 21
Holker. Cumb 2C 96
Holkham. Norf 1A 78
Hollacombe. Devn 2D 11
Holland. Orkn 2D 172
(on Papa Westray)
Holland. Orkn 5F 172
(on Stronsay)
Holland Fen. Linc 1B 76
Holland Lees. Lanc 4D 90
Holland-on-Sea. Essx 4F 55
Holland Park. W Mid 5E 73
Hollandstoun. Orkn 2G 172
Hollesley. Suff 1G 55
Hollinfare. Warr 1A 84
Hollingbourne. Kent 5C 40
Hollingbury. Brig 5E 27
Hollingdon. Buck 3G 51
Hollingrove. E Sus 3A 28
Hollington. Derbs 1G 73
Hollington. E Sus 4B 28
Hollington. Staf 2E 73
Hollington Grove. Derbs 2G 73
Hollingworth. G Man 1E 85
Hollins. Derbs 3H 85
Hollins. G Man 4G 91
(nr. Bury)
Hollins. G Man 4G 91
(nr. Middleton)
Hollinsclough. Staf 4E 85
Hollinswood. Telf 5A 72
Hollinthorpe. W Yor 1D 93
Hollinwood. G Man 4H 91
Hollinwood. Shrp 2H 71
Hollocombe. Devn 1G 11
Holloway. Derbs 5H 85
Hollow Court. Worc 5D 61
Hollowell. Nptn 3D 62
Hollow Meadows. S Yor 2G 85
Hollows. Dum 2E 113
Hollybush. Cphy 5E 47
Hollybush. E Ayr 3C 116
Hollybush. Worc 2C 48
Holly End. Norf 5D 77
Holly Hill. N Yor 4E 105
Hollyhurst. Ches E 1H 71
Hollym. E Yor 2G 95
Hollywood. Staf 2D 72
Hollywood. Worc 3E 61
Holmacott. Devn 4F 19
Holmbridge. W Yor 4B 92
Holmbury St Mary. Surr 1C 26
Holmbush. Corn 3E 7
Holmcroft. Staf 3D 72
Holme. Cambs 2A 64
Holme. Cumb 2E 97
Holme. N Lin 4C 94
Holme. N Yor 1F 99
Holme. Notts 5F 87
Holme. W Yor 4B 92
Holmebridge. Dors 4D 15
Holme Chapel. Lanc 2G 91
Holme Hale. Norf 5A 78
Holme Lacy. Here 2A 48
Holme Marsh. Here 5F 59
Holmend. Dum 4C 118
Holme next the Sea. Norf 1G 77
Holme-on-Spalding-Moor. E Yor 1B 94
Holme on the Wolds. E Yor 5D 100
Holme Pierrepont. Notts 2D 74
Holmer. Here 1A 48
Holmer Green. Buck 1A 38
Holmes. Lanc 3C 90
Holme St Cuthbert. Cumb 5C 112
Holmes Chapel. Ches E 4B 84
Holmesfield. Derbs 3H 85
Holmeswood. Lanc 3C 90
Holmewood. Derbs 4B 86
Holmfirth. W Yor 4B 92
Holmhead. E Ayr 2E 117
Holmisdale. High 4A 154
Holm of Drumlanrig. Dum 5H 117
Holmpton. E Yor 2G 95
Holmrook. Cumb 5B 102
Holmsgarth. Shet 7F 173
Holmside. Dur 5F 115
Holmwrangle. Cumb 5G 113
Holne. Devn 2D 8
Holsworthy. Devn 2D 10
Holsworthy Beacon. Devn 2D 10
Holt. Dors 2F 15
Holt. Norf 2C 78
Holt. Wilts 5D 34
Holt. Worc 4C 60
Holt. Wrex 5G 83
Holtby. York 4A 100
Holt End. Hants 3E 25
Holt End. Worc 4E 61
Holt Fleet. Worc 4C 60
Holt Green. Lanc 4B 90
Holt Heath. Dors 2F 15
Holt Heath. Worc 4C 60
Holton. Oxon 5E 50
Holton. Som 4B 22
Holton. Suff 3F 67
Holton cum Beckering. Linc 2A 88
Holton Heath. Dors 3E 15
Holton le Clay. Linc 4F 95
Holton le Moor. Linc 1H 87
Holton St Mary. Suff 2D 54
Holt Pound. Hants 2G 25
Holtsmere End. Herts 4A 52
Holtye. E Sus 2F 27
Holwell. Dors 1C 14
Holwell. Herts 2B 52
Holwell. Leics 3E 75
Holwell. Oxon 5H 49
Holwell. Som 2C 22
Holwick. Dur 2C 104
Holworth. Dors 4C 14
Holybourne. Hants 2F 25
Holy City. Devn 2G 13
Holy Cross. Worc 3D 60
Holyfield. Essx 5D 53
Holyhead. IOA 2B 80
Holy Island. Nmbd 5H 131
Holymoorside. Derbs 4H 85
Holyport. Wind 4G 37
Holystone. Nmbd 4D 120
Holytown. N Lan 3A 128
Holywell. Cambs 3C 64
Holywell. Corn 3B 6
Holywell. Dors 2A 14
Holywell. Flin 3D 82
Holywell. Glos 2C 34
Holywell. Nmbd 2G 115
Holywell. Warw 4F 61
Holywell Green. W Yor 3A 92
Holywell Lake. Som 4E 20
Holywell Row. Suff 3G 65
Holywood. Dum 1G 111
Homer. Shrp 5A 72
Homer Green. Mers 4B 90
Homersfield. Suff 2E 67
Hom Green. Here 3A 48
Homington. Wilts 4G 23
Honeyborough. Pemb 4D 42
Honeybourne. Worc 1G 49
Honeychurch. Devn 2G 11
Honeydon. Bed 5A 64
Honey Hill. Kent 4F 41
Honey Street. Wilts 5G 35
Honey Tye. Suff 2C 54
Honeywick. C Beds 3H 51
Honiley. Warw 3G 61
Honing. Norf 3F 79
Honingham. Norf 4D 78
Honington. Linc 1G 75
Honington. Suff 3B 66
Honington. Warw 1A 50
Honiton. Devn 2E 13
Honley. W Yor 3B 92
Honnington. Telf 4B 72
Hoo. Suff 5E 67
Hoobrook. Worc 3C 60
Hood Green. S Yor 4D 92
Hooe. E Sus 5A 28
Hooe. Plym 3B 8
Hooe Common. E Sus 4A 28
Hoohill. Bkpl 1B 90
Hook. Cambs 1D 64
Hook. E Yor 2A 94
Hook. G Lon 4C 38
Hook. Hants 1F 25
(nr. Basingstoke)
Hook. Hants 2D 16
(nr. Fareham)
Hook. Pemb 3D 43
Hook. Wilts 3F 35
Hook-a-Gate. Shrp 5G 71
Hook Bank. Worc 1D 48
Hooke. Dors 2A 14
Hooker Gate. Tyne 4E 115
Hookgate. Staf 2B 72
Hook Green. Kent 2A 28
(nr. Lamberhurst)
Hook Green. Kent 3H 39
(nr. Longfield)
Hook Green. Kent 4H 39
(nr. Meopham)
Hook Norton. Oxon 2B 50
Hook's Cross. Herts 3C 52
Hook Street. Glos 2B 34
Hookway. Devn 3B 12
Hookwood. Surr 1D 26
Hoole. Ches W 4G 83
Hooley. Surr 5D 39
Hooley Bridge. G Man 3G 91
Hooley Brow. G Man 3G 91
Hoo St Werburgh. Medw 3B 40
Hooton. Ches W 3F 83
Hooton Levitt. S Yor 1C 86
Hooton Pagnell. S Yor 4E 93
Hooton Roberts. S Yor 1B 86
Hoove. Shet 7E 173
Hope. Derbs 2F 85
Hope. Flin 5F 83
Hope. High 2E 167
Hope. Powy 5E 71
Hope. Shrp 5F 71
Hope. Staf 5F 85
Hope Bagot. Shrp 3H 59
Hope Bowdler. Shrp 1G 59
Hopedale. Staf 5F 85
Hope Green. Ches E 2D 84
Hopeman. Mor 2F 159
Hope Mansell. Here 4B 48
Hopesay. Shrp 2F 59
Hope's Green. Essx 2B 40
Hopetown. W Yor 2D 93
Hope under Dinmore. Here 5H 59
Hopley's Green. Here 5F 59
Hopperton. N Yor 4G 99
Hop Pole. Linc 4A 76
Hopstone. Shrp 1B 60
Hopton. Derbs 5G 85
Hopton. Powy 1E 59
Hopton. Shrp 3F 71
(nr. Oswestry)
Hopton. Shrp 3H 71
(nr. Wem)
Hopton. Staf 3D 72
Hopton. Suff 3B 66
Hopton Cangeford. Shrp 2H 59
Hopton Castle. Shrp 3F 59
Hoptonheath. Shrp 3F 59
Hopton Heath. Staf 3D 72
Hopton on Sea. Norf 5H 79
Hopton Wafers. Shrp 3A 60
Hopwas. Staf 5F 73
Hopwood. Worc 3E 61
Horam. E Sus 4G 27
Horbling. Linc 2A 76
Horbury. W Yor 3C 92
Horcott. Glos 5G 49
Horden. Dur 5H 115
Horderley. Shrp 2G 59
Hordle. Hants 3A 16
Hordley. Shrp 2F 71
Horeb. Carm 3F 45
(nr. Brechfa)
Horeb. Carm 5E 45
(nr. Llanelli)
Horeb. Cdgn 1D 45
Horfield. Bris 4B 34
Horgabost. W Isl 8C 171
Horham. Suff 3E 66
Horkesley Heath. Essx 3C 54
Horkstow. N Lin 3C 94
Horley. Oxon 1C 50
Horley. Surr 1D 27
Horn Ash. Dors 2G 13
Hornblotton Green. Som 3A 22
Hornby. Lanc 3E 97
Hornby. N Yor 4A 106
(nr. Appleton Wiske)
Hornby. N Yor 5F 105
(nr. Catterick Garrison)
Horncastle. Linc 4B 88
Hornchurch. G Lon 2G 39
Horncliffe. Nmbd 5F 131
Horndean. Hants 1E 17
Horndean. Bord 5E 131
Horndon. Devn 4F 11
Horndon on the Hill. Thur 2A 40
Horne. Surr 1E 27
Horner. Som 2C 20
Horning. Norf 4F 79
Horninghold. Leics 1F 63
Horninglow. Staf 3G 73
Horningsea. Cambs 4D 65
Horningsham. Wilts 2D 22
Horningtoft. Norf 3B 78
Hornsbury. Som 1G 13
Hornsby. Cumb 4G 113
Hornsbygate. Cumb 4G 113
Horns Corner. Kent 3B 28
Horns Cross. Devn 4D 19
Hornsea. E Yor 5G 101
Hornsea Burton. E Yor 5G 101
Hornsey. G Lon 2E 39
Hornton. Oxon 1B 50
Horpit. Swin 3H 35
Horrabridge. Devn 2B 8
Horringer. Suff 4H 65
Horringford. IOW 4D 16
Horrocks Fold. G Man 3F 91
Horrocksford. Lanc 5G 97
Horsbrugh Ford. Bord 1E 119
Horsebridge. Devn 5E 11
Horsebridge. Hants 3B 24
Horse Bridge. Staf 5D 84
Horsebrook. Staf 4C 72
Horsecastle. N Som 5H 33
Horsehay. Telf 5A 72
Horseheath. Cambs 1G 53
Horsehouse. N Yor 1C 98
Horsell. Surr 5A 38
Horseman's Green. Wrex 1G 71
Horsenden. Buck 5F 51
Horseway. Cambs 2D 64
Horsey. Norf 3G 79
Horsey. Som 3G 21
Horsford. Norf 4D 78
Horsforth. W Yor 1C 92
Horsham. W Sus 2C 26
Horsham. Worc 5B 60
Horsham St Faith. Norf 4E 78
Horsington. Linc 4A 88
Horsington. Som 4C 22
Horsley. Derbs 1A 74
Horsley. Glos 2D 34
Horsley. Nmbd 3D 115
(nr. Prudhoe)
Horsley. Nmbd 5C 120
(nr. Rochester)
Horsley Cross. Essx 3E 54
Horsleycross Street. Essx 3E 54
Horsleyhill. Bord 3H 119
Horsleyhope. Dur 5D 114
Horsley Woodhouse. Derbs 1A 74
Horsmonden. Kent 1A 28
Horspath. Oxon 5D 50
Horstead. Norf 4E 79
Horsted Keynes. W Sus 3E 27
Horton. Buck 4H 51
Horton. Dors 2F 15
Horton. Lanc 4A 98
Horton. Nptn 5F 63
Horton. Shrp 2G 71
Horton. Som 1G 13
Horton. S Glo 3C 34
Horton. Staf 5D 84
Horton. Swan 4D 30
Horton. Wilts 5F 35
Horton. Wind 3B 38
Horton Cross. Som 1G 13

Horton-cum-Studley—Islibhig

Horton-cum-Studley. Oxon 4D 50
Horton Grange. Nmbd 2F 115
Horton Green. Ches W 1G 71
Horton Heath. Hants 1C 16
Horton in Ribblesdale. N Yor 2H 97
Horton Kirby. Kent 4G 39
Hortonwood. Telf 4A 72
Horwich. G Man 3E 91
Horwich End. Derbs 2E 85
Horwood. Devn 4F 19
Hoscar. Lanc 3C 90
Hose. Leics 3E 75
Hosh. Per 1A 136
Hosta. W Isl 1C 170
Hoswick. Shet 9F 173
Hotham. E Yor 1B 94
Hothfield. Kent 1D 28
Hoton. Leics 3C 74
Houbie. Shet 2H 173
Hough. Arg 4A 138
Hough. Ches E 5B 84 (nr. Crewe)
Hough. Ches E 3C 84 (nr. Wilmslow)
Hougham. Linc 1F 75
Hough Green. Hal 2G 83
Hough-on-the-Hill. Linc 1G 75
Houghton. Cambs 3B 64
Houghton. Cumb 4F 113
Houghton. Hants 3B 24
Houghton. Nmbd 3E 115
Houghton. Pemb 4D 43
Houghton. W Sus 4B 26
Houghton Bank. Darl 2F 105
Houghton Conquest. C Beds 1A 52
Houghton Green. E Sus 3D 28
Houghton-le-Side. Darl 2F 105
Houghton-le-Spring. Tyne 5G 115
Houghton on the Hill. Leics 5D 74
Houghton Regis. C Beds 3A 52
Houghton St Giles. Norf 2B 78
Houlland. Shet 6E 173 (on Mainland)
Houlland. Shet 4G 173 (on Yell)
Houlsyke. N Yor 4E 107
Hound. Hants 2C 16
Hound Green. Hants 1F 25
Houndslow. Bord 5C 130
Houndsmoor. Som 4E 21
Houndwood. Bord 3E 131
Hounsdown. Hants 1B 16
Hounslow. G Lon 3C 38
Housabister. Shet 6F 173
Housay. Shet 4H 173
Househill. High 3C 158
Housetter. Shet 3E 173
Houss. Shet 8E 173
Houston. Ren 3F 127
Housty. High 5D 168
Houton. Orkn 7C 172
Hove. Brig 5D 27 & 189
Hoveringham. Notts 1E 74
Hoveton. Norf 4F 79
Hovingham. N Yor 2A 100
How. Cumb 4G 113
How Caple. Here 2B 48
Howden. E Yor 2H 93
Howden-le-Wear. Dur 1E 105
Howe. High 2F 169
Howe. Norf 5E 79
Howe. N Yor 1F 99
Howe Green. Essx 5H 53 (nr. Chelmsford)
Howegreen. Essx 5B 54 (nr. Maldon)
Howe Green. Warw 2H 61
Howell. Linc 1A 76
How End. C Beds 1A 52
Howe of Teuchar. Abers 4E 161
Howes. Dum 3C 112
Howe Street. Essx 4G 53 (nr. Chelmsford)
Howe Street. Essx 2G 53 (nr. Finchingfield)
Howe, The. Cumb 1D 96
Howe, The. IOM 5A 108
Howey. Powy 5C 58
Howgate. Midl 4F 129
Howgill. Lanc 5H 97
Howgill. N Yor 4C 98
How Green. Kent 1F 27
How Hill. Norf 4F 79
Howick. Nmbd 3G 121
Howle. Telf 3A 72
Howle Hill. Here 3B 48
Howleigh. Som 1F 13
Howlett End. Essx 2F 53
Howley. Som 2F 13
Howley. Warr 2A 84
Hownam. Bord 3B 120
Howsham. N Lin 4D 94
Howsham. N Yor 3B 100
Howtel. Nmbd 1C 120
Howt Green. Kent 4C 40
Howton. Here 3H 47
Howwood. Ren 3E 127
Hoxne. Suff 3D 66
Hoylake. Mers 2E 82
Hoyland. S Yor 4D 92
Hoylandswaine. S Yor 4C 92
Hoyle. W Sus 4A 26
Hubberholme. N Yor 2B 98
Hubberston. Pemb 4C 42
Hubbert's Bridge. Linc 1B 76
Huby. N Yor 5E 99 (nr. Harrogate)
Huby. N Yor 3H 99 (nr. York)
Huccaby. Devn 5G 11
Hucclecote. Glos 4D 48
Hucking. Kent 5C 40
Hucknall. Notts 1C 74
Huddersfield. W Yor 3B 92
Huddington. Worc 5D 60
Huddlesford. Staf 5F 73
Hudswell. N Yor 4E 105
Huggate. E Yor 4C 100
Hugglescote. Leics 4B 74
Hughenden Valley. Buck 2G 37
Hughley. Shrp 1H 59
Hughton. High 4G 157
Hugh Town. IOS 1B 4
Hugus. Corn 4B 6
Huish. Devn 1F 11
Huish. Wilts 5G 35
Huish Champflower. Som 4D 20
Huish Episcopi. Som 4H 21
Huisinis. W Isl 6B 171
Hulcote. Nptn 5E 62
Hulcott. Buck 4G 51
Hulham. Devn 4D 12
Hull. Hull 2D 94 & 199
Hulland. Derbs 1G 73
Hulland Moss. Derbs 1G 73
Hulland Ward. Derbs 1G 73
Hullavington. Wilts 3D 35
Hullbridge. Essx 1C 40
Hulme. G Man 1C 84
Hulme. Staf 1D 72
Hulme End. Staf 5F 85
Hulme Walfield. Ches E 4C 84
Hulverstone. IOW 4B 16
Hulver Street. Suff 2G 67
Humber. Devn 5C 12
Humber. Here 5H 59
Humber Bridge. N Lin 2D 94
Humberside International Airport. N Lin 3D 94
Humberston. NE Lin 4G 95
Humberstone. Leic 5D 74
Humbie. E Lot 3A 130
Humbleton. E Yor 1F 95
Humbleton. Nmbd 2D 121
Humby. Linc 2H 75
Hume. Bord 5D 130
Humshaugh. Nmbd 2C 114
Huna. High 1F 169
Huncoat. Lanc 1F 91
Huncote. Leics 1C 62
Hundall. Derbs 3A 86
Hunderthwaite. Dur 2C 104
Hundleby. Linc 4C 88
Hundle Houses. Linc 5B 88
Hundleton. Pemb 4D 42
Hundon. Suff 1H 53
Hundred Acres. Hants 1D 16
Hundred House. Powy 5D 58
Hundred, The. Here 4H 59
Hungarton. Leics 5D 74
Hungerford. Hants 1G 15
Hungerford. Shrp 2H 59
Hungerford. Som 2D 20
Hungerford. W Ber 5B 36
Hungerford Newtown. W Ber 4B 36
Hunger Hill. G Man 4E 91
Hungerton. Linc 2F 75
Hungladder. High 1C 154
Hungryhatton. Shrp 3A 72
Hunmanby. N Yor 2E 101
Hunmanby Sands. N Yor 2F 101
Hunningham. Warw 4A 62
Hunnington. Worc 2D 60
Hunny Hill. IOW 4C 16
Hunsdon. Herts 4E 53
Hunsdonbury. Herts 4E 53
Hunsingore. N Yor 4G 99
Hunslet. W Yor 1D 92
Hunslet Carr. W Yor 2D 92
Hunsonby. Cumb 1G 103
Hunspow. High 1E 169
Hunstanton. Norf 1F 77
Hunstanworth. Dur 5C 114
Hunston. Suff 4B 66
Hunston. W Sus 2G 17
Hunstrete. Bath 5B 34
Hunt End. Worc 4E 61
Hunterfield. Midl 3G 129
Hunters Forstal. Kent 4F 41
Hunter's Quay. Arg 2C 126
Huntham. Som 4G 21
Hunthill Lodge. Ang 1D 144
Huntingdon. Cambs 3B 64
Huntingfield. Suff 3F 67
Huntingford. Wilts 3D 22
Huntington. Ches W 4G 83
Huntington. E Lot 2A 130
Huntington. Here 5E 59
Huntington. Staf 4D 72
Huntington. Telf 5A 72
Huntington. York 4A 100
Huntingtower. Per 1C 136
Huntley. Glos 4C 48
Huntley. Staf 1E 73
Huntly. Abers 4C 160
Huntlywood. Bord 5C 130
Hunton. Hants 3C 24
Hunton. Kent 1B 28
Hunton. N Yor 5E 105
Hunton Bridge. Herts 5A 52
Hunt's Corner. Norf 2C 66
Huntscott. Som 2C 20
Hunt's Cross. Mers 2G 83
Hunts Green. Warw 1F 61
Huntsham. Devn 4D 20
Huntshaw. Devn 4F 19
Huntspill. Som 2G 21
Huntstile. Som 3F 21
Huntstrete. Bath 5B 34
Huntworth. Som 3G 21
Hunwick. Dur 1E 105
Hunworth. Norf 2C 78
Hurcott. Som 1G 13 (nr. Ilminster)
Hurcott. Som 4A 22 (nr. Somerton)
Hurdcott. Wilts 3G 23
Hurdley. Powy 1E 59
Hurdsfield. Ches E 3D 84
Hurlet. Glas 3G 127
Hurley. Warw 1G 61
Hurley. Wind 3G 37
Hurlford. E Ayr 1D 116
Hurliness. Orkn 9B 172
Hurlston Green. Lanc 3B 90
Hurn. Dors 3G 15
Hursey. Dors 2H 13
Hursley. Hants 4C 24
Hurst. G Man 4H 91
Hurst. N Yor 4D 104
Hurst. Som 1H 13
Hurst. Wok 4F 37
Hurstbourne Priors. Hants 2C 24
Hurstbourne Tarrant. Hants 1B 24
Hurst Green. Ches E 1H 71
Hurst Green. E Sus 3B 28
Hurst Green. Essx 4D 54
Hurst Green. Lanc 1E 91
Hurst Green. Surr 5E 39
Hurstley. Here 1G 47
Hurstpierpoint. W Sus 4D 27
Hurstway Common. Here 1F 47
Hurst Wickham. W Sus 4D 27
Hurstwood. Lanc 1G 91
Hurtmore. Surr 1A 26
Hurworth-on-Tees. Darl 3A 106
Hurworth Place. Darl 3F 105
Hury. Dur 3C 104
Husbands Bosworth. Leics 2D 62
Husborne Crawley. C Beds 2H 51
Husthwaite. N Yor 2H 99
Hutcherleigh. Devn 3D 9
Hut Green. N Yor 2F 93
Huthwaite. Notts 5B 86
Huttoft. Linc 3E 89
Hutton. Cumb 2F 103
Hutton. E Yor 4E 101
Hutton. Essx 1H 39
Hutton. Lanc 2C 90
Hutton. N Som 1G 21
Hutton. Bord 4F 131
Hutton Bonville. N Yor 4A 106
Hutton Buscel. N Yor 1D 100
Hutton Conyers. N Yor 2F 99
Hutton Cranswick. E Yor 4E 101
Hutton End. Cumb 1F 103
Hutton Gate. Red C 3C 106
Hutton Henry. Dur 1B 106
Hutton-le-Hole. N Yor 1B 100
Hutton Magna. Dur 3E 105
Hutton Mulgrave. N Yor 4F 107
Hutton Roof. Cumb 2E 97 (nr. Kirkby Lonsdale)
Hutton Roof. Cumb 1E 103 (nr. Penrith)
Hutton Rudby. N Yor 4B 106
Huttons Ambo. N Yor 3B 100
Hutton Sessay. N Yor 2G 99
Hutton Village. Red C 3D 106
Hutton Wandesley. N Yor 4H 99
Huxham. Devn 3C 12
Huxham Green. Som 3A 22
Huxley. Ches W 4H 83
Huxter. Shet 6C 173 (on Mainland)
Huxter. Shet 5G 173 (on Whalsay)
Huyton. Mers 1G 83
Hwlffordd. Pemb 3D 42
Hycemoor. Cumb 1A 96
Hyde. Glos 5D 49 (nr. Stroud)
Hyde. Glos 3F 49 (nr. Winchcombe)
Hyde. G Man 1D 84
Hyde Heath. Buck 5H 51
Hyde Lea. Staf 3D 72
Hyde Park. S Yor 4F 93
Hydestile. Surr 1A 26
Hyndford Bridge. S Lan 5C 128
Hynish. Arg 5A 138
Hyssington. Powy 1F 59
Hythe. Hants 2C 16
Hythe. Kent 2F 29
Hythe End. Wind 3B 38
Hythie. Abers 3H 161
Hyton. Cumb 1A 96

I

Ianstown. Mor 2B 160
Iarsiadar. W Isl 4D 171
Ibberton. Dors 2C 14
Ible. Derbs 5G 85
Ibrox. Glas 3G 127
Ibsley. Hants 2G 15
Ibstock. Leics 4B 74
Ibstone. Buck 2F 37
Ibthorpe. Hants 1B 24
Iburndale. N Yor 4F 107
Ibworth. Hants 1D 24
Icelton. N Som 5G 33
Ichrachan. Arg 5E 141
Ickburgh. Norf 1H 65
Ickenham. G Lon 2B 38
Ickford. Buck 5E 51
Ickham. Kent 5G 41
Ickleford. Herts 2B 52
Icklesham. E Sus 4C 28
Ickleton. Cambs 1E 53
Icklingham. Suff 3G 65
Ickwell. C Beds 1B 52
Icomb. Glos 3H 49
Idbury. Oxon 3H 49
Iddesleigh. Devn 2F 11
Ide. Devn 3B 12
Ideford. Devn 5B 12
Ide Hill. Kent 5F 39
Iden. E Sus 3D 28
Iden Green. Kent 2C 28 (nr. Benenden)
Iden Green. Kent 2B 28 (nr. Goudhurst)
Idle. W Yor 1B 92
Idless. Corn 4C 6
Idlicote. Warw 1A 50
Idmiston. Wilts 3G 23
Idole. Carm 4E 45
Idridgehay. Derbs 1G 73
Idrigill. High 2C 154
Idstone. Oxon 3A 36
Iffley. Oxon 5D 50
Ifield. W Sus 2D 26
Ifieldwood. W Sus 2D 26
Ifold. W Sus 2B 26
Iford. E Sus 5F 27
Ifton Heath. Shrp 2F 71
Ightfield. Shrp 2H 71
Ightham. Kent 5G 39
Iken. Suff 5G 67
Ilam. Staf 5F 85
Ilchester. Som 4A 22
Ilderton. Nmbd 2E 121
Ilford. G Lon 2F 39
Ilford. Som 1G 13
Ilfracombe. Devn 2F 19
Ilkeston. Derbs 1B 74
Ilketshall St Andrew. Suff 2F 67
Ilketshall St Lawrence. Suff 2F 67
Ilketshall St Margaret. Suff 2F 67
Ilkley. W Yor 5D 98
Illand. Corn 5C 10
Illey. W Mid 2D 61
Illidge Green. Ches E 4B 84
Illington. Norf 2B 66
Illingworth. W Yor 2A 92
Illogan. Corn 4A 6
Illogan Highway. Corn 4A 6
Illston on the Hill. Leics 1E 62
Ilmer. Buck 5F 51
Ilmington. Warw 1H 49
Ilminster. Som 1G 13
Ilsington. Devn 5A 12
Ilsington. Dors 3C 14
Ilston. Swan 3E 31
Ilton. N Yor 2D 98
Ilton. Som 1G 13
Imachar. N Ayr 5G 125
Imber. Wilts 2E 23
Immingham. NE Lin 3E 95
Immingham Dock. NE Lin 3E 95
Impington. Cambs 4D 64
Ince. Ches W 3G 83
Ince Blundell. Mers 4B 90
Ince-in-Makerfield. G Man 4D 90
Inchbae Lodge. High 2G 157
Inchbare. Ang 2F 145
Inchberry. Mor 3H 159
Inchbraoch. Ang 3G 145
Inchbrook. Glos 5D 48
Incheril. High 2C 156
Inchinnan. Ren 3F 127
Inchlaggan. High 3D 148
Inchmichael. Per 1E 137
Inchnadamph. High 1G 163
Inchree. High 2E 141
Inchture. Per 1E 137
Inchyra. Per 1D 136
Indian Queens. Corn 3D 6
Ingatestone. Essx 1H 39
Ingbirchworth. S Yor 4C 92
Ingestre. Staf 3D 73
Ingham. Linc 2G 87
Ingham. Norf 3F 79
Ingham. Suff 3A 66
Ingham Corner. Norf 3F 79
Ingleborough. Norf 4D 76
Ingleby. Derbs 3H 73
Ingleby Arncliffe. N Yor 4B 106
Ingleby Barwick. Stoc T 3B 106
Ingleby Greenhow. N Yor 4C 106
Ingleigh Green. Devn 2G 11
Inglemire. Hull 1D 94
Inglesbatch. Bath 5C 34
Ingleton. Dur 2E 105
Ingleton. N Yor 2F 97
Inglewhite. Lanc 5E 97
Ingoe. Nmbd 2D 114
Ingol. Lanc 1D 90
Ingoldisthorpe. Norf 2F 77
Ingoldmells. Linc 4E 89
Ingoldsby. Linc 2H 75
Ingon. Warw 5G 61
Ingram. Nmbd 3E 121
Ingrave. Essx 1H 39
Ingrow. W Yor 1A 92
Ings. Cumb 5F 103
Ingst. S Glo 3A 34
Ingthorpe. Rut 5G 75
Ingworth. Norf 3D 78
Inkberrow. Worc 5E 61
Inkford. Worc 3E 61
Inkpen. W Ber 5B 36
Inkstack. High 1E 169
Innellan. Arg 3C 126
Inner Hope. Devn 5C 8
Innerleith. Fife 2E 137
Innerleithen. Bord 1F 119
Innerleven. Fife 3F 137
Innermessan. Dum 3F 109
Innerwick. E Lot 2D 130
Innerwick. Per 4C 142
Innsworth. Glos 3D 48
Insch. Abers 1D 152
Insh. High 3C 150
Inshegra. High 3C 166
Inshore. High 1D 166
Inskip. Lanc 1C 90
Instow. Devn 3E 19
Intwood. Norf 5D 78
Inver. Abers 4G 151
Inver. High 5F 165
Inver. Per 4H 143
Inverailort. High 5F 147
Inveralligin. High 3H 155
Inverallochy. Abers 2H 161
Inveramsay. Abers 1E 153
Inveran. High 4C 164
Inveraray. Arg 3H 133
Inverarish. High 5E 155
Inverarity. Ang 4D 144
Inverarnan. Arg 2C 134
Inverarnie. High 5A 158
Inverbeg. Arg 4C 134
Inverbervie. Abers 1H 145
Inverboyndie. Abers 2D 160
Invercassley. High 3B 164
Invercharnan. High 4F 141
Inverchoran. High 3E 157
Invercreran. Arg 4E 141
Inverdruie. High 2D 150
Inverebrie. Abers 5G 161
Invereck. Arg 1C 126
Inveresk. E Lot 2G 129
Inveresragan. Arg 5D 141
Inverey. Abers 5E 151
Inverfarigaig. High 1H 149
Invergarry. High 3F 149
Invergeldie. Per 1G 135
Invergordon. High 2B 158
Invergowrie. Per 5C 144
Inverguseran. High 3F 147
Inverharroch. Mor 5A 160
Inverie. High 3F 147
Inverinan. Arg 2G 133
Inverinate. High 1B 148
Inverkeilor. Ang 4F 145
Inverkeithing. Fife 1E 129
Inverkeithny. Abers 4D 160
Inverkip. Inv 2D 126
Inverkirkaig. High 2E 163
Inverlael. High 5F 163
Inverliever Lodge. Arg 3F 133
Inverliver. Arg 5E 141
Inverloch. High 1F 141
Inverlochlarig. Stir 2D 134
Inverlussa. Arg 1E 125
Inver Mallie. High 5D 148
Invermarkie. Abers 5B 160
Invermoriston. High 2G 149
Invernaver. High 2H 167
Inverneil House. Arg 1G 125
Inverness. High 4A 158 & 198
Inverness Airport. High 3B 158
Invernettie. Abers 4H 161
Inverpolly Lodge. High 2E 163
Inverquhomery. Abers 4H 161
Inverroy. High 5E 149
Inversanda. High 3D 140
Invershiel. High 2B 148
Invershin. High 4C 164
Invershore. High 5E 169
Inversnaid. Stir 3C 134
Inverugie. Abers 4H 161
Inveruglas. Arg 3C 134
Inverurie. Abers 1E 153
Invervar. Per 4D 142
Inverythan. Abers 4E 161
Inwardleigh. Devn 3F 11
Inworth. Essx 4B 54
Iochdar. W Isl 4C 170
Iping. W Sus 4G 25
Ipplepen. Devn 2E 9
Ipsden. Oxon 3E 37
Ipstones. Staf 1E 73
Ipswich. Suff 1E 55 & 198
Irby. Mers 2E 83
Irby in the Marsh. Linc 4D 88
Irby upon Humber. NE Lin 4E 95
Irchester. Nptn 4G 63
Ireby. Cumb 1D 102
Ireby. Lanc 2F 97
Ireland. Shet 9E 173
Ireleth. Cumb 2B 96
Ireshopeburn. Dur 1B 104
Ireton Wood. Derbs 1G 73
Irlam. G Man 1B 84
Irnham. Linc 3H 75
Iron Acton. S Glo 3B 34
Iron Bridge. Cambs 1D 65
Ironbridge. Telf 5A 72
Iron Cross. Warw 5E 61
Ironville. Derbs 5B 86
Irstead. Norf 3F 79
Irthington. Cumb 3F 113
Irthlingborough. Nptn 3G 63
Irton. N Yor 1E 101
Irvine. N Ayr 1C 116
Irvine Mains. N Ayr 1C 116
Isabella Pit. Nmbd 1G 115
Isauld. High 2B 168
Isbister. Orkn 6C 172
Isbister. Shet 2E 173 (on Mainland)
Isbister. Shet 5G 173 (on Whalsay)
Isfield. E Sus 4F 27
Isham. Nptn 3F 63
Island Carr. N Lin 4C 94
Islay Airport. Arg 4B 124
Isle Abbotts. Som 4G 21
Isle Brewers. Som 4G 21
Isleham. Cambs 3F 65
Isle of Man Airport. IOM 5B 108
Isle of Thanet. Kent 4H 41
Isle of Whithorn. Dum 5B 110
Isleornsay. High 2F 147
Islesburgh. Shet 5E 173
Isles of Scilly (St Mary's) Airport. IOS 1B 4
Islesteps. Dum 2A 112
Isleworth. G Lon 3C 38
Isley Walton. Leics 3B 74
Islibhig. W Isl 5B 171

Islington—Kingston

Islington. *G Lon* 2E 39
Islington. *Telf* 3B 72
Islip. *Nptn* 3G 63
Islip. *Oxon* 4D 50
Islwyn. *Cphy* 2F 33
Istead Rise. *Kent* 4H 39
Itchen. *Sotn* 1C 16
Itchen Abbas. *Hants* 3D 24
Itchen Stoke. *Hants* 3D 24
Itchingfield. *W Sus* 3C 26
Itchington. *S Glo* 3B 34
Itlaw. *Abers* 3D 160
Itteringham. *Norf* 2D 78
Itteringham Common. *Norf* 3D 78
Itton. *Devn* 3G 11
Itton Common. *Mon* 2H 33
Ivegill. *Cumb* 5F 113
Ivelet. *N Yor* 5C 104
Iverchaolain. *Arg* 2B 126
Iver Heath. *Buck* 2B 38
Iveston. *Dur* 4E 115
Ivetsey Bank. *Staf* 4C 72
Ivinghoe. *Buck* 4H 51
Ivinghoe Aston. *Buck* 4H 51
Ivington. *Here* 5G 59
Ivington Green. *Here* 5G 59
Ivybridge. *Devn* 3C 8
Ivychurch. *Kent* 3E 29
Ivy Hatch. *Kent* 5G 39
Ivy Todd. *Norf* 5A 78
Iwade. *Kent* 4D 40
Iwerne Courtney. *Dors* 1D 14
Iwerne Minster. *Dors* 1D 14
Ixworth. *Suff* 3B 66
Ixworth Thorpe. *Suff* 3B 66

J

Jackfield. *Shrp* 5A 72
Jack Hill. *N Yor* 4E 98
Jacksdale. *Notts* 5B 86
Jackton. *S Lan* 4G 127
Jacobstow. *Corn* 3B 10
Jacobstowe. *Devn* 2F 11
Jacobswell. *Surr* 5A 38
Jameston. *Pemb* 5E 43
Jamestown. *Dum* 5F 119
Jamestown. *Fife* 1E 129
Jamestown. *High* 3G 157
Jamestown. *W Dun* 1E 127
Janetstown. *High* 2C 168 (nr. Thurso)
Janetstown. *High* 3F 169 (nr. Wick)
Jarrow. *Tyne* 3G 115
Jarvis Brook. *E Sus* 3G 27
Jasper's Green. *Essx* 3H 53
Jaywick. *Essx* 4E 55
Jedburgh. *Bord* 2A 120
Jeffreyston. *Pemb* 4E 43
Jemimaville. *High* 2B 158
Jenkins Park. *High* 3F 149
Jersey Marine. *Neat* 3G 31
Jesmond. *Tyne* 3F 115
Jevington. *E Sus* 5G 27
Jingle Street. *Mon* 4H 47
Jockey End. *Herts* 4A 52
Jodrell Bank. *Ches E* 3B 84
Johnby. *Cumb* 1F 103
John o' Gaunts. *W Yor* 2D 92
John o' Groats. *High* 1F 169
John's Cross. *E Sus* 3B 28
Johnshaven. *Abers* 2G 145
Johnson Street. *Norf* 4F 79
Johnston. *Pemb* 3D 42
Johnstone. *Ren* 3F 127
Johnstonebridge. *Dum* 5C 118
Johnstown. *Carm* 4D 45
Johnstown. *Wrex* 1F 71
Joppa. *Edin* 2G 129
Joppa. *S Ayr* 3D 116
Jordan Green. *Norf* 3C 78
Jordans. *Buck* 1A 38
Jordanston. *Pemb* 1D 42
Jump. *S Yor* 4D 93
Jumpers Common. *Dors* 3G 15
Juniper. *Nmbd* 4C 114
Juniper Green. *Edin* 3E 129
Jurby East. *IOM* 2C 108
Jurby West. *IOM* 2C 108
Jury's Gap. *E Sus* 4D 28

K

Kaber. *Cumb* 3A 104
Kaimend. *S Lan* 5C 128
Kaimes. *Edin* 3F 129
Kaimrig End. *Bord* 5D 129
Kames. *Arg* 2A 126
Kames. *E Ayr* 2F 117
Kea. *Corn* 4C 6
Keadby. *N Lin* 3B 94
Keal Cotes. *Linc* 4C 88
Kearsley. *G Man* 4F 91
Kearsney. *Kent* 1G 29
Kearstwick. *Cumb* 1F 97
Kearton. *N Yor* 5C 104
Kearvaig. *High* 1C 166
Keasden. *N Yor* 3G 97
Keason. *Corn* 2H 7
Keckwick. *Hal* 2H 83
Keddington. *Linc* 2C 88
Keddington Corner. *Linc* 2C 88
Kedington. *Suff* 1H 53
Kedleston. *Derbs* 1H 73
Kedlock Feus. *Fife* 2F 137
Keelby. *Linc* 3E 95
Keele. *Staf* 1C 72
Keeley Green. *Bed* 1A 52
Keeston. *Pemb* 3D 42
Keevil. *Wilts* 1E 23
Kegworth. *Leics* 3B 74
Kehelland. *Corn* 2D 4
Keig. *Abers* 2D 152
Keighley. *W Yor* 5C 98
Keilarsbrae. *Clac* 4A 136
Keillmore. *Arg* 1E 125
Keillor. *Per* 4B 144
Keillour. *Per* 1B 136
Keills. *Arg* 3C 124
Keiloch. *Abers* 4F 151
Keils. *Arg* 3D 124
Keinton Mandeville. *Som* 3A 22
Keir Mill. *Dum* 5A 118
Keirsleywell Row. *Nmbd* 4A 114
Keisby. *Linc* 3H 75
Keisley. *Cumb* 2A 104
Keiss. *High* 2F 169
Keith. *Mor* 3B 160
Keith Inch. *Abers* 4H 161
Kelbrook. *Lanc* 5B 98
Kelby. *Linc* 1H 75
Keld. *Cumb* 3G 103
Keld. *N Yor* 4B 104
Keldholme. *N Yor* 1B 100
Kelfield. *N Lin* 4B 94
Kelfield. *N Yor* 1F 93
Kelham. *Notts* 5E 87
Kellacott. *Devn* 4E 11
Kellan. *Arg* 4G 139
Kellas. *Ang* 5D 144
Kellas. *Mor* 3F 159
Kellaton. *Devn* 5E 9
Kelleth. *Cumb* 4H 103
Kelling. *Norf* 1C 78
Kellingley. *N Yor* 2F 93
Kellington. *N Yor* 2F 93
Kelloe. *Dur* 1A 106
Kelloholm. *Dum* 3G 117
Kells. *Cumb* 3A 102
Kelly. *Devn* 4D 11
Kelly Bray. *Corn* 5D 10
Kelmarsh. *Nptn* 3E 63
Kelmscott. *Oxon* 2A 36
Kelsale. *Suff* 4F 67
Kelsall. *Ches W* 4H 83
Kelshall. *Herts* 2D 52
Kelsick. *Cumb* 4C 112
Kelso. *Bord* 1B 120
Kelstedge. *Derbs* 4H 85
Kelstern. *Linc* 1B 88
Kelsterton. *Flin* 3E 83
Kelston. *Bath* 5C 34
Keltneyburn. *Per* 4E 143
Kelton. *Dum* 2A 112
Kelton Hill. *Dum* 4E 111
Kelty. *Fife* 4D 136
Kelvedon. *Essx* 4B 54
Kelvedon Hatch. *Essx* 1G 39
Kelvinside. *Glas* 3G 127
Kelynack. *Corn* 3A 4
Kemback. *Fife* 2G 137
Kemberton. *Shrp* 5B 72
Kemble. *Glos* 2E 35
Kemerton. *Worc* 2E 49
Kemeys Commander. *Mon* 5G 47
Kemnay. *Abers* 2E 153
Kempe's Corner. *Kent* 1E 29
Kempley. *Glos* 3B 48
Kempley Green. *Glos* 3B 48
Kempsey. *Worc* 1D 48
Kempsford. *Glos* 2G 35
Kemps Green. *Warw* 3F 61
Kempshott. *Hants* 1E 24
Kempston. *Bed* 1A 52
Kempston Hardwick. *Bed* 1A 52
Kempton. *Shrp* 2F 59
Kemp Town. *Brig* 5E 27
Kemsing. *Kent* 5G 39
Kemsley. *Kent* 4D 40
Kenardington. *Kent* 2D 28
Kenchester. *Here* 1H 47
Kencot. *Oxon* 5A 50
Kendal. *Cumb* 5G 103
Kendleshire. *S Glo* 4B 34
Kendray. *S Yor* 4D 92
Kenfig. *B'end* 3B 32
Kenfig Hill. *B'end* 3B 32
Kengharair. *Arg* 4F 139
Kenidjack. *Corn* 3A 4
Kenilworth. *Warw* 3G 61
Kenknock. *Stir* 5B 142
Kenley. *G Lon* 5E 39
Kenley. *Shrp* 5H 71
Kenmore. *High* 3G 155
Kenmore. *Per* 4E 143
Kenn. *Devn* 4C 12
Kenn. *N Som* 5H 33
Kennacraig. *Arg* 3G 125
Kenneggy Downs. *Corn* 4C 4
Kennerleigh. *Devn* 2B 12
Kennet. *Clac* 4B 136
Kennethmont. *Abers* 1C 152
Kennett. *Cambs* 4G 65
Kennford. *Devn* 4C 12
Kenninghall. *Norf* 2C 66
Kennington. *Kent* 1E 29
Kennington. *Oxon* 5D 50
Kennoway. *Fife* 3F 137
Kennyhill. *Suff* 3F 65
Kennythorpe. *N Yor* 3B 100
Kenovay. *Arg* 4A 138
Kensaleyre. *High* 3D 154
Kensington. *G Lon* 3D 38
Kenstone. *Shrp* 3H 71
Kensworth. *C Beds* 4A 52
Kensworth Common. *C Beds* 4A 52
Kentallen. *High* 3E 141
Kentchurch. *Here* 3H 47
Kentford. *Suff* 4G 65
Kent International Airport. *Kent* 4H 41
Kentisbeare. *Devn* 2D 12
Kentisbury. *Devn* 2G 19
Kentisbury Ford. *Devn* 2G 19
Kentmere. *Cumb* 4F 103
Kenton. *Devn* 4C 12
Kenton. *G Lon* 2C 38
Kenton. *Suff* 4D 66
Kenton Bankfoot. *Tyne* 3F 115
Kentra. *High* 2A 140
Kentrigg. *Cumb* 5G 103
Kents Bank. *Cumb* 2C 96
Kent's Green. *Glos* 3C 48
Kent's Oak. *Hants* 4B 24
Kent Street. *E Sus* 4B 28
Kent Street. *Kent* 5A 40
Kent Street. *W Sus* 3D 26
Kenwick. *Shrp* 2G 71
Kenwyn. *Corn* 4C 6
Kenyon. *Warr* 1A 84
Keoldale. *High* 2D 166
Keppoch. *High* 1B 148
Kepwick. *N Yor* 5B 106
Keresley. *W Mid* 2H 61
Keresley Newland. *Warw* 2H 61
Keristal. *IOM* 4C 108
Kerne Bridge. *Here* 4A 48
Kerridge. *Ches E* 3D 84
Kerris. *Corn* 4B 4
Kerrow. *High* 5F 157
Kerry. *Powy* 2D 58
Kerrycroy. *Arg* 3C 126
Kerry's Gate. *Here* 2G 47
Kersall. *Notts* 4E 86
Kersbrook. *Devn* 4D 12
Kerse. *Ren* 4E 127
Kersey. *Suff* 1D 54
Kershopefoot. *Cumb* 1F 113
Kersoe. *Worc* 2E 49
Kerswell. *Devn* 2D 12
Kerswell Green. *Worc* 1D 48
Kesgrave. *Suff* 1F 55
Kessingland. *Suff* 2H 67
Kessingland Beach. *Suff* 2H 67
Kestle. *Corn* 4D 6
Kestle Mill. *Corn* 3C 6
Keston. *G Lon* 4F 39
Keswick. *Cumb* 2D 102
Keswick. *Norf* 2F 79 (nr. North Walsham)
Keswick. *Norf* 5E 78 (nr. Norwich)
Ketsby. *Linc* 3C 88
Kettering. *Nptn* 3F 63
Ketteringham. *Norf* 5D 78
Kettins. *Per* 5B 144
Kettlebaston. *Suff* 5B 66
Kettlebridge. *Fife* 3F 137
Kettlebrook. *Staf* 5G 73
Kettleburgh. *Suff* 4E 67
Kettleholm. *Dum* 2C 112
Kettleness. *N Yor* 3F 107
Kettleshulme. *Ches E* 3D 85
Kettlesing. *N Yor* 4E 99
Kettlesing Bottom. *N Yor* 4E 99
Kettlestone. *Norf* 2B 78
Kettlethorpe. *Linc* 3F 87
Kettletoft. *Orkn* 4F 172
Kettlewell. *N Yor* 2B 98
Ketton. *Rut* 5G 75
Kew. *G Lon* 3C 38
Kewaigue. *IOM* 4C 108
Kewstoke. *N Som* 5G 33
Kexbrough. *S Yor* 4D 92
Kexby. *Linc* 2F 87
Kexby. *York* 4B 100
Keyford. *Som* 2C 22
Key Green. *Ches E* 4C 84
Key Green. *N Yor* 4F 107
Keyham. *Leics* 5D 74
Keyhaven. *Hants* 3B 16
Keyhead. *Abers* 3H 161
Keyingham. *E Yor* 2F 95
Keymer. *W Sus* 4E 27
Keynsham. *Bath* 5B 34
Keysoe. *Bed* 4H 63
Keysoe Row. *Bed* 4H 63
Key's Toft. *Linc* 5D 89
Keyston. *Cambs* 3H 63
Key Street. *Kent* 4C 40
Keyworth. *Notts* 2D 74
Kibblesworth. *Tyne* 4F 115
Kibworth Beauchamp. *Leics* 1D 62
Kibworth Harcourt. *Leics* 1D 62
Kidbrooke. *G Lon* 3F 39
Kidburngill. *Cumb* 2B 102
Kiddemore Green. *Staf* 5C 72
Kidderminster. *Worc* 3C 60
Kiddington. *Oxon* 3C 50
Kidd's Moor. *Norf* 5D 78
Kidlington. *Oxon* 4C 50
Kidmore End. *Oxon* 4E 37
Kidnal. *Ches W* 1G 71
Kidsgrove. *Staf* 5C 84
Kidstones. *N Yor* 1B 98
Kidwelly. *Carm* 5E 45
Kiel Crofts. *Arg* 5D 140
Kielder. *Nmbd* 5A 120
Kilbagie. *Fife* 4B 136
Kilbarchan. *Ren* 3F 127
Kilbeg. *High* 3E 147
Kilberry. *Arg* 3F 125
Kilbirnie. *N Ayr* 4E 126
Kilbride. *Arg* 1F 133
Kilbride. *High* 1D 147
Kilbucho Place. *Bord* 1C 118
Kilburn. *Derbs* 1A 74
Kilburn. *G Lon* 2D 38
Kilburn. *N Yor* 2H 99
Kilby. *Leics* 1D 62
Kilchattan. *Arg* 4A 132 (on Colonsay)
Kilchattan. *Arg* 4C 126 (on Isle of Bute)
Kilchattan Bay. *Arg* 4B 126
Kilchenzie. *Arg* 3A 122
Kilcheran. *Arg* 5C 140
Kilchiaran. *Arg* 3A 124
Kilchoan. *High* 1G 147 (nr. Inverie)
Kilchoan. *High* 2F 139 (nr. Tobermory)
Kilchoman. *Arg* 3A 124
Kilchrenan. *Arg* 1H 133
Kilconquhar. *Fife* 3G 137
Kilcot. *Glos* 3B 48
Kilcoy. *High* 3H 157
Kilcreggan. *Arg* 1D 126
Kildale. *N Yor* 4D 106
Kildary. *High* 1B 158
Kildermorie Lodge. *High* 1H 157
Kildonan. *Dum* 4F 109
Kildonan. *High* 1G 165 (nr. Helmsdale)
Kildonan. *High* 3C 154 (on Isle of Skye)
Kildonan. *N Ayr* 3E 123
Kildonnan. *High* 5C 146
Kildrummy. *Abers* 2B 152
Kildwick. *N Yor* 5C 98
Kilfillan. *Dum* 4H 109
Kilfinan. *Arg* 2H 125
Kilfinnan. *High* 4E 149
Kilgetty. *Pemb* 4F 43
Kilgour. *Fife* 3E 136
Kilgrammie. *S Ayr* 4B 116
Kilham. *E Yor* 3E 101
Kilham. *Nmbd* 1C 120
Kilkenneth. *Arg* 4A 138
Kilkhampton. *Corn* 1C 10
Killamarsh. *Derbs* 2B 86
Killandrist. *Arg* 4C 140
Killay. *Swan* 3F 31
Killean. *Arg* 5E 125
Killearn. *Stir* 1G 127
Killellan. *Arg* 4A 122
Killen. *High* 3A 158
Killerby. *Darl* 3E 105
Killichonan. *Per* 3C 142
Killiechronan. *Arg* 4G 139
Killiecrankie. *Per* 2G 143
Killilan. *High* 5B 156
Killimster. *High* 3F 169
Killin. *Stir* 5C 142
Killinghall. *N Yor* 4E 99
Killinghurst. *Surr* 2A 26
Killington. *Cumb* 1F 97
Killingworth. *Tyne* 2F 115
Killin Lodge. *High* 3H 149
Killinochonoch. *Arg* 4F 133
Killochyett. *Bord* 5A 130
Killundine. *High* 4G 139
Kilmacolm. *Inv* 3E 127
Kilmahog. *Stir* 3F 135
Kilmahumaig. *Arg* 4E 133
Kilmalieu. *High* 3C 140
Kilmaluag. *High* 1D 154
Kilmany. *Fife* 1F 137
Kilmarie. *High* 2D 146
Kilmarnock. *E Ayr* 1D 116 & 198
Kilmaron. *Fife* 2F 137
Kilmartin. *Arg* 4F 133
Kilmaurs. *E Ayr* 5F 127
Kilmelford. *Arg* 2F 133
Kilmeny. *Arg* 3B 124
Kilmersdon. *Som* 1B 22
Kilmeston. *Hants* 4D 24
Kilmichael Glassary. *Arg* 4F 133
Kilmichael of Inverlussa. *Arg* 1F 125
Kilmington. *Devn* 3F 13
Kilmington. *Wilts* 3C 22
Kilmoluag. *Arg* 4A 138
Kilmorack. *High* 4G 157
Kilmore. *Arg* 1F 133
Kilmore. *High* 3E 147
Kilmory. *Arg* 2F 125
Kilmory. *High* 1G 139 (nr. Kilchoan)
Kilmory. *High* 3B 146 (on Rùm)
Kilmory. *N Ayr* 3D 122
Kilmory Lodge. *Arg* 3E 132
Kilmote. *High* 2G 165
Kilmuir. *High* 4B 154 (nr. Dunvegan)
Kilmuir. *High* 1B 158 (nr. Invergordon)
Kilmuir. *High* 4A 158 (nr. Inverness)
Kilmuir. *High* 1C 154 (nr. Uig)
Kilmun. *Arg* 1C 126
Kilnave. *Arg* 2A 124
Kilncadzow. *S Lan* 5B 128
Kilndown. *Kent* 2B 28
Kiln Green. *Here* 4B 48
Kiln Green. *Wind* 4G 37
Kilnhill. *Cumb* 1D 102
Kilnhurst. *S Yor* 1B 86
Kilninian. *Arg* 4E 139
Kilninver. *Arg* 1F 133
Kiln Pit Hill. *Nmbd* 4D 114
Kilnsea. *E Yor* 3H 95
Kilnsey. *N Yor* 3B 98
Kilnwick. *E Yor* 5D 101
Kiloran. *Arg* 4A 132
Kilpatrick. *N Ayr* 3D 122
Kilpeck. *Here* 2H 47
Kilpin. *E Yor* 2A 94
Kilpin Pike. *E Yor* 2A 94
Kilrenny. *Fife* 3H 137
Kilsby. *Nptn* 3C 62
Kilspindie. *Per* 1E 136
Kilsyth. *N Lan* 2A 128
Kiltarlity. *High* 4H 157
Kilton. *Som* 2E 21
Kilton Thorpe. *Red C* 3D 107
Kilvaxter. *High* 2C 154
Kilve. *Som* 2E 21
Kilvington. *Notts* 1F 75
Kilwinning. *N Ayr* 5D 126
Kimberley. *Norf* 5C 78
Kimberley. *Notts* 1B 74
Kimblesworth. *Dur* 5F 115
Kimble Wick. *Buck* 5G 51
Kimbolton. *Cambs* 4H 63
Kimbolton. *Here* 4H 59
Kimcote. *Leics* 2C 62
Kimmeridge. *Dors* 5E 15
Kimmerston. *Nmbd* 1D 120
Kimpton. *Hants* 2A 24
Kimpton. *Herts* 4B 52
Kinbeachie. *High* 2A 158
Kinbrace. *High* 5A 168
Kinbuck. *Stir* 3G 135
Kincaple. *Fife* 2G 137
Kincardine. *Fife* 1C 128
Kincardine. *High* 5D 164
Kincardine Bridge. *Fife* 1C 128
Kincardine O'Neil. *Abers* 4C 152
Kinchrackine. *Arg* 1A 134
Kincorth. *Aber* 3G 153
Kincraig. *High* 3C 150
Kincraigie. *Per* 4G 143
Kindallachan. *Per* 3G 143
Kineton. *Glos* 3F 49
Kineton. *Warw* 5H 61
Kinfauns. *Per* 1D 136
Kingairloch. *High* 3C 140
Kingarth. *Arg* 4B 126
Kingcoed. *Mon* 5H 47
Kingerby. *Linc* 1H 87
Kingham. *Oxon* 3A 50
Kingholm Quay. *Dum* 2A 112
Kinghorn. *Fife* 1F 129
Kingie. *High* 3D 148
Kinglassie. *Fife* 4E 137
Kingledores. *Bord* 2D 118
Kingodie. *Per* 1F 137
King o' Muirs. *Clac* 4A 136
King's Acre. *Here* 1H 47
Kingsand. *Corn* 3A 8
Kingsash. *Buck* 5G 51
Kingsbarns. *Fife* 2H 137
Kingsbridge. *Devn* 4D 8 (nr. Salcombe)
Kingsbridge. *Som* 3C 20 (nr. Luxborough)
King's Bromley. *Staf* 4F 73
Kingsburgh. *High* 3C 154
Kingsbury. *G Lon* 2C 38
Kingsbury. *Warw* 1G 61
Kingsbury Episcopi. *Som* 4H 21
Kings Caple. *Here* 3A 48
Kingscavil. *W Lot* 2D 128
Kingsclere. *Hants* 1D 24
King's Cliffe. *Nptn* 1H 63
Kingscote. *Glos* 2D 34
Kingscott. *Devn* 1F 11
Kings Coughton. *Warw* 5E 61
Kingscross. *N Ayr* 3E 123
Kingsdon. *Som* 4A 22
Kingsdown. *Kent* 1H 29
Kingsdown. *Swin* 3G 35
Kingsdown. *Wilts* 5D 34
Kingseat. *Fife* 4D 136
Kingsey. *Buck* 5F 51
Kingsfold. *Lanc* 2D 90
Kingsfold. *W Sus* 2C 26
Kingsford. *E Ayr* 5F 127
Kingsford. *Worc* 2C 60
Kingsforth. *N Lin* 3D 94
Kingsgate. *Kent* 3H 41
King's Green. *Glos* 2C 48
Kingshall Street. *Suff* 4B 66
Kingsheanton. *Devn* 3F 19
King's Heath. *W Mid* 2E 61
Kings Hill. *Kent* 5A 40
Kingsholm. *Glos* 4D 48
Kingshouse. *High* 3G 141
Kingshouse. *Stir* 1E 135
Kingshurst. *W Mid* 2F 61
Kingskerswell. *Devn* 2E 9
Kingskettle. *Fife* 3F 137
Kingsland. *Here* 4G 59
Kingsland. *IOA* 2B 80
Kings Langley. *Herts* 5A 52
Kingsley. *Ches W* 3H 83
Kingsley. *Hants* 3F 25
Kingsley. *Staf* 1E 73
Kingsley Green. *W Sus* 3G 25
Kingsley Holt. *Staf* 1E 73
King's Lynn. *Norf* 3F 77
King's Meaburn. *Cumb* 2H 103
Kings Moss. *Mers* 4D 90
Kingsmuir. *Ang* 4D 145
Kingsmuir. *Fife* 3H 137
Kings Muir. *Bord* 1E 119
King's Newnham. *Warw* 3B 62
Kings Newton. *Derbs* 3A 74
Kingsnorth. *Kent* 2E 28
Kingsnorth. *Medw* 3C 40
King's Norton. *Leics* 5D 74
King's Norton. *W Mid* 3E 61
King's Nympton. *Devn* 1G 11
King's Pyon. *Here* 5G 59
Kings Ripton. *Cambs* 3B 64
King's Somborne. *Hants* 3B 24
King's Stag. *Dors* 1C 14
King's Stanley. *Glos* 5D 48
King's Sutton. *Nptn* 2C 50
Kingstanding. *W Mid* 1E 61
Kingsteignton. *Devn* 5B 12
Kingsteps. *High* 3D 158
King Sterndale. *Derbs* 3E 85
King's Thorn. *Here* 2A 48
Kingsthorpe. *Nptn* 4E 63
Kingston. *Cambs* 5C 64

Kingston—Laneham

Kingston. *Devn* 4C 8
Kingston. *Dors* 2C 14 (nr. Sturminster Newton)
Kingston. *Dors* 5E 15 (nr. Swanage)
Kingston. *E Lot* 1B 130
Kingston. *Hants* 2G 15
Kingston. *IOW* 4C 16
Kingston. *Kent* 5F 41
Kingston. *Mor* 2H 159
Kingston. *W Sus* 5B 26
Kingston Bagpuize. *Oxon* 2C 36
Kingston Blount. *Oxon* 2F 37
Kingston by Sea. *W Sus* 5D 26
Kingston Deverill. *Wilts* 3D 22
Kingstone. *Here* 2H 47
Kingstone. *Som* 1G 13
Kingstone. *Staf* 3E 73
Kingston Lisle. *Oxon* 3B 36
Kingston Maurward. *Dors* 3C 14
Kingston near Lewes. *E Sus* 5E 27
Kingston on Soar. *Notts* 3C 74
Kingston Russell. *Dors* 3A 14
Kingston St Mary. *Som* 4F 21
Kingston Seymour. *N Som* 5H 33
Kingston Stert. *Oxon* 5F 51
Kingston upon Hull. *Hull* 2D 94 & 199
Kingston upon Thames. *G Lon* 4C 38
King's Walden. *Herts* 3B 52
Kingswear. *Devn* 3E 9
Kingswells. *Aber* 3F 153
Kingswinford. *W Mid* 2C 60
Kingswood. *Buck* 4E 51
Kingswood. *Glos* 2C 34
Kingswood. *Here* 5E 59
Kingswood. *Kent* 5C 40
Kingswood. *Per* 5H 143
Kingswood. *Powy* 5E 71
Kingswood. *Som* 3E 20
Kingswood. *S Glo* 4B 34
Kingswood. *Surr* 5D 38
Kingswood. *Warw* 3F 61
Kingswood Common. *Staf* 5C 72
Kings Worthy. *Hants* 3C 24
Kingthorpe. *Linc* 3A 88
Kington. *Here* 5F 59
Kington. *S Glo* 2B 34
Kington. *Worc* 5D 61
Kington Langley. *Wilts* 4E 35
Kington Magna. *Dors* 4C 22
Kington St Michael. *Wilts* 4E 35
Kingussie. *High* 3B 150
Kingweston. *Som* 3A 22
Kinharrachie. *Abers* 5G 161
Kinhrive. *High* 1B 158
Kinkell Bridge. *Per* 2B 136
Kinknockie. *Abers* 4H 161
Kinkry Hill. *Cumb* 2G 113
Kinlet. *Shrp* 2B 60
Kinloch. *High* 5D 166 (nr. Loch More)
Kinloch. *High* 3A 140 (nr. Lochaline)
Kinloch. *High* 4C 146 (on Rùm)
Kinloch. *Per* 4A 144
Kinlochard. *Stir* 3D 134
Kinlochbervie. *High* 3C 166
Kinlocheil. *High* 1D 141
Kinlochewe. *High* 2C 156
Kinloch Hourn. *High* 3B 148
Kinloch Laggan. *High* 5H 149
Kinlochleven. *High* 2F 141
Kinloch Lodge. *High* 3F 167
Kinlochmoidart. *High* 1B 140
Kinlochmore. *High* 2F 141
Kinloch Rannoch. *Per* 3D 142
Kinlochspelve. *Arg* 1D 132
Kinloid. *High* 5E 147
Kinloss. *Mor* 2E 159
Kinmel Bay. *Cnwy* 2B 82
Kinmuck. *Abers* 2F 153
Kinnadie. *Abers* 4G 161
Kinnaird. *Per* 1E 137
Kinneff. *Abers* 1H 145
Kinnelhead. *Dum* 4C 118
Kinnell. *Ang* 3F 145
Kinnerley. *Shrp* 3F 71
Kinnernie. *Abers* 2E 152
Kinnersley. *Here* 1G 47
Kinnersley. *Worc* 1D 48
Kinnerton. *Powy* 4E 59
Kinnerton. *Shrp* 1F 59
Kinnesswood. *Per* 3D 136
Kinninvie. *Dur* 2D 104
Kinnordy. *Ang* 3C 144
Kinoulton. *Notts* 2D 74
Kinross. *Per* 3D 136
Kinrossie. *Per* 5A 144
Kinsbourne Green. *Herts* 4B 52
Kinsey Heath. *Ches E* 1A 72
Kinsham. *Here* 4F 59
Kinsham. *Worc* 2E 49
Kinsley. *W Yor* 3E 93
Kinson. *Bour* 3F 15
Kintbury. *W Ber* 5B 36
Kintessack. *Mor* 2E 159
Kintillo. *Per* 2D 136
Kinton. *Here* 3G 59
Kinton. *Shrp* 4F 71
Kintore. *Abers* 2E 153
Kintour. *Arg* 4C 124
Kintra. *Arg* 2B 132
Kintraw. *Arg* 3F 133
Kinveachy. *High* 2D 150
Kinver. *Staf* 2C 60
Kinwarton. *Warw* 5F 61
Kiplingcotes. *E Yor* 5D 100
Kippax. *W Yor* 1E 93
Kippen. *Stir* 4F 135
Kippford. *Dum* 4F 111
Kipping's Cross. *Kent* 1H 27
Kirbister. *Orkn* 7C 172 (nr. Hobbister)
Kirbister. *Orkn* 6B 172 (nr. Quholm)
Kirbuster. *Orkn* 5F 172
Kirby Bedon. *Norf* 5E 79
Kirby Bellars. *Leics* 4E 74
Kirby Cane. *Norf* 1F 67
Kirby Cross. *Essx* 3F 55
Kirby Fields. *Leics* 5C 74
Kirby Grindalythe. *N Yor* 3D 100
Kirby Hill. *N Yor* 4E 105 (nr. Richmond)
Kirby Hill. *N Yor* 3F 99 (nr. Ripon)
Kirby Knowle. *N Yor* 1G 99
Kirby-le-Soken. *Essx* 3F 55
Kirby Misperton. *N Yor* 2B 100
Kirby Muxloe. *Leics* 5C 74
Kirby Row. *Norf* 1F 67
Kirby Sigston. *N Yor* 5B 106
Kirby Underdale. *E Yor* 4C 100
Kirby Wiske. *N Yor* 1F 99
Kirdford. *W Sus* 3B 26
Kirk. *High* 3E 169
Kirkabister. *Shet* 8F 173 (on Bressay)
Kirkabister. *Shet* 6F 173 (on Mainland)
Kirkandrews. *Dum* 5D 110
Kirkandrews-on-Eden. *Cumb* 4E 113
Kirkapol. *Arg* 4B 138
Kirkbampton. *Cumb* 4E 112
Kirkbean. *Dum* 4A 112
Kirk Bramwith. *S Yor* 3G 93
Kirkbride. *Cumb* 4D 112
Kirkbridge. *N Yor* 5F 105
Kirkbuddo. *Ang* 4E 145
Kirkburn. *E Yor* 4D 101
Kirkburton. *W Yor* 3B 92
Kirkby. *Linc* 1H 87
Kirkby. *Mers* 1G 83
Kirkby. *N Yor* 4C 106
Kirkby Fenside. *Linc* 4C 88
Kirkby Fleetham. *N Yor* 5F 105
Kirkby Green. *Linc* 5H 87
Kirkby-in-Ashfield. *Notts* 5C 86
Kirkby Industrial Estate. *Mers* 1G 83
Kirkby-in-Furness. *Cumb* 1A 96
Kirkby la Thorpe. *Linc* 1A 76
Kirkby Lonsdale. *Cumb* 2F 97
Kirkby Malham. *N Yor* 3A 98
Kirkby Mallory. *Leics* 5B 74
Kirkby Malzeard. *N Yor* 2E 99
Kirkby Mills. *N Yor* 1B 100
Kirkbymoorside. *N Yor* 1A 100
Kirkby on Bain. *Linc* 4B 88
Kirkby Overblow. *N Yor* 5F 99
Kirkby Stephen. *Cumb* 4A 104
Kirkby Thore. *Cumb* 2H 103
Kirkby Underwood. *Linc* 3H 75
Kirkby Wharfe. *N Yor* 5H 99
Kirkcaldy. *Fife* 4E 137
Kirkcambeck. *Cumb* 3G 113
Kirkcolm. *Dum* 3F 109
Kirkconnel. *Dum* 3G 117
Kirkconnell. *Dum* 3A 112
Kirkcowan. *Dum* 3A 110
Kirkcudbright. *Dum* 4D 111
Kirkdale. *Mers* 1F 83
Kirk Deighton. *N Yor* 4F 99
Kirk Ella. *E Yor* 2D 94
Kirkfieldbank. *S Lan* 5B 128
Kirkforthar Feus. *Fife* 3E 137
Kirkgunzeon. *Dum* 3F 111
Kirk Hallam. *Derbs* 1B 74
Kirkham. *Lanc* 1C 90
Kirkham. *N Yor* 3B 100
Kirkhamgate. *W Yor* 2C 92
Kirk Hammerton. *N Yor* 4G 99
Kirkharle. *Nmbd* 1D 114
Kirkheaton. *Nmbd* 2D 114
Kirkheaton. *W Yor* 3B 92
Kirkhill. *Ang* 2F 145
Kirkhill. *High* 4H 157
Kirkhope. *S Lan* 4B 118
Kirkhouse. *Bord* 1F 119
Kirkibost. *High* 2D 146
Kirkinch. *Ang* 4C 144
Kirkinner. *Dum* 4B 110
Kirkintilloch. *E Dun* 2H 127
Kirk Ireton. *Derbs* 5G 85
Kirkland. *Cumb* 3B 102 (nr. Cleator Moor)
Kirkland. *Cumb* 1H 103 (nr. Penrith)
Kirkland. *Cumb* 5D 112 (nr. Wigton)
Kirkland. *Dum* 3G 117 (nr. Kirkconnel)
Kirkland. *Dum* 5H 117 (nr. Moniaive)
Kirkland Guards. *Cumb* 5C 112
Kirk Langley. *Derbs* 2G 73
Kirklauchline. *Dum* 4F 109
Kirkleatham. *Red C* 2C 106
Kirklevington. *Stoc T* 4B 106
Kirkley. *Suff* 1H 67
Kirklington. *N Yor* 1F 99
Kirklington. *Notts* 5D 86
Kirklinton. *Cumb* 3F 113
Kirkliston. *Edin* 2E 129
Kirkmabreck. *Dum* 4B 110
Kirkmaiden. *Dum* 5E 109
Kirk Merrington. *Dur* 1F 105
Kirk Michael. *IOM* 2C 108
Kirkmichael. *Per* 2H 143
Kirkmichael. *S Ayr* 4C 116
Kirkmuirhill. *S Lan* 5A 128
Kirknewton. *Nmbd* 1D 120
Kirknewton. *W Lot* 3E 129
Kirkney. *Abers* 5C 160
Kirk of Shotts. *N Lan* 3B 128
Kirkoswald. *Cumb* 5G 113
Kirkoswald. *S Ayr* 4B 116
Kirkpatrick. *Dum* 5B 118
Kirkpatrick Durham. *Dum* 2E 111
Kirkpatrick-Fleming. *Dum* 2D 112
Kirk Sandall. *S Yor* 4G 93
Kirksanton. *Cumb* 1A 96
Kirk Smeaton. *N Yor* 3F 93
Kirkstall. *W Yor* 1C 92
Kirkstile. *Dum* 5F 119
Kirkstyle. *High* 1F 169
Kirkthorpe. *W Yor* 2D 92
Kirkton. *Abers* 2D 152 (nr. Alford)
Kirkton. *Abers* 1D 152 (nr. Insch)
Kirkton. *Abers* 4F 161 (nr. Turriff)
Kirkton. *Ang* 5D 144 (nr. Dundee)
Kirkton. *Ang* 4D 144 (nr. Forfar)
Kirkton. *Ang* 5B 152 (nr. Tarfside)
Kirkton. *Dum* 1A 112
Kirkton. *Fife* 1F 137
Kirkton. *High* 4E 165 (nr. Golspie)
Kirkton. *High* 1G 147 (nr. Kyle of Lochalsh)
Kirkton. *High* 4B 156 (nr. Lochcarron)
Kirkton. *Bord* 3H 119
Kirkton. *S Lan* 2B 118
Kirktonhill. *W Dun* 2E 127
Kirkton Manor. *Bord* 1E 118
Kirkton of Airlie. *Ang* 3C 144
Kirkton of Auchterhouse. *Ang* 5C 144
Kirkton of Bourtie. *Abers* 1F 153
Kirkton of Collace. *Per* 5A 144
Kirkton of Craig. *Ang* 3G 145
Kirkton of Culsalmond. *Abers* 5D 160
Kirkton of Durris. *Abers* 4E 153
Kirkton of Glenbuchat. *Abers* 2A 152
Kirkton of Glenisla. *Ang* 2B 144
Kirkton of Kingoldrum. *Ang* 3C 144
Kirkton of Largo. *Fife* 3G 137
Kirkton of Lethendy. *Per* 4A 144
Kirkton of Logie Buchan. *Abers* 1G 153
Kirkton of Maryculter. *Abers* 4F 153
Kirkton of Menmuir. *Ang* 2E 145
Kirkton of Monikie. *Ang* 5E 145
Kirkton of Oyne. *Abers* 1D 152
Kirkton of Rayne. *Abers* 5D 160
Kirkton of Skene. *Abers* 3F 153
Kirktown. *Abers* 2G 161 (nr. Fraserburgh)
Kirktown. *Abers* 3H 161 (nr. Peterhead)
Kirktown of Alvah. *Abers* 2D 160
Kirktown of Auchterless. *Abers* 4E 160
Kirktown of Deskford. *Mor* 2C 160
Kirktown of Fetteresso. *Abers* 5F 153
Kirktown of Mortlach. *Mor* 5H 159
Kirktown of Slains. *Abers* 1H 153
Kirkurd. *Bord* 5E 129
Kirkwall. *Orkn* 6D 172
Kirkwall Airport. *Orkn* 7D 172
Kirkwhelpington. *Nmbd* 1C 114
Kirk Yetholm. *Bord* 2C 120
Kirmington. *N Lin* 3E 94
Kirmond le Mire. *Linc* 1A 88
Kirn. *Arg* 2C 126
Kirriemuir. *Ang* 3C 144
Kirstead Green. *Norf* 1E 67
Kirtlebridge. *Dum* 2D 112
Kirtleton. *Dum* 2D 112
Kirtling. *Cambs* 5F 65
Kirtling Green. *Cambs* 5F 65
Kirtlington. *Oxon* 4D 50
Kirtomy. *High* 2H 167
Kirton. *Linc* 2C 76
Kirton. *Notts* 4D 86
Kirton. *Suff* 2F 55
Kirton End. *Linc* 1B 76
Kirton Holme. *Linc* 1B 76
Kirton in Lindsey. *N Lin* 1G 87
Kishorn. *High* 4H 155
Kislingbury. *Nptn* 5D 62
Kite Hill. *IOW* 3D 16
Kites Hardwick. *Warw* 4B 62
Kittisford. *Som* 4D 20
Kittle. *Swan* 4E 31
Kittybrewster. *Aber* 3G 153
Kitwood. *Hants* 3E 25
Kivernoll. *Here* 2H 47
Kiveton Park. *S Yor* 2B 86
Knaith. *Linc* 2F 87
Knaith Park. *Linc* 2F 87
Knaphill. *Surr* 5A 38
Knapp. *Hants* 4C 24
Knapp. *Per* 5B 144
Knapp. *Som* 4G 21
Knapperfield. *High* 3E 169
Knapton. *Norf* 2F 79
Knapton. *York* 4H 99
Knapton Green. *Here* 5G 59
Knapwell. *Cambs* 4C 64
Knaresborough. *N Yor* 4F 99
Knarsdale. *Nmbd* 4H 113
Knatts Valley. *Kent* 4G 39
Knaven. *Abers* 4F 161
Knayton. *N Yor* 1G 99
Knebworth. *Herts* 3C 52
Knedlington. *E Yor* 2H 93
Kneesall. *Notts* 4E 86
Kneesworth. *Cambs* 1D 52
Kneeton. *Notts* 1E 74
Knelston. *Swan* 4D 30
Knenhall. *Staf* 2D 72
Knightacott. *Devn* 3G 19
Knightcote. *Warw* 5B 62
Knightcott. *N Som* 1G 21
Knightley. *Staf* 3C 72
Knightley Dale. *Staf* 3C 72
Knightlow Hill. *Warw* 3B 62
Knighton. *Devn* 4B 8
Knighton. *Dors* 1B 14
Knighton. *Leic* 5D 74
Knighton. *Powy* 3E 59
Knighton. *Som* 2E 21
Knighton. *Staf* 3B 72
Knighton. *Wilts* 4A 36
Knighton. *Worc* 5E 61
Knighton Common. *Worc* 3A 60
Knight's End. *Cambs* 1D 64
Knightswood. *Glas* 3G 127
Knightwick. *Worc* 5B 60
Knill. *Here* 4E 59
Knipton. *Leics* 2F 75
Knitsley. *Dur* 5E 115
Kniveton. *Derbs* 5G 85
Knock. *Arg* 5G 139
Knock. *Cumb* 2H 103
Knock. *Mor* 3C 160
Knockally. *High* 5D 168
Knockan. *Arg* 1B 132
Knockan. *High* 2G 163
Knockandhu. *Mor* 1G 151
Knockando. *Mor* 4F 159
Knockarthur. *High* 3E 165
Knockbain. *High* 3A 158
Knockbreck. *High* 2B 154
Knockdee. *High* 2D 168
Knockdolian. *S Ayr* 1G 109
Knockdon. *S Ayr* 3C 116
Knockdown. *Glos* 3D 34
Knockenbaird. *Abers* 1D 152
Knockenkelly. *N Ayr* 3E 123
Knockentiber. *E Ayr* 1C 116
Knockfarrel. *High* 3H 157
Knockglass. *High* 2C 168
Knockholt. *Kent* 5F 39
Knockholt Pound. *Kent* 5F 39
Knockie Lodge. *High* 2G 149
Knockin. *Shrp* 3F 71
Knockinlaw. *E Ayr* 1D 116
Knockinnon. *High* 5D 169
Knockrome. *Arg* 2D 124
Knocksharry. *IOM* 3B 108
Knockshinnoch. *E Ayr* 3D 116
Knockvennie. *Dum* 2E 111
Knockvologan. *Arg* 3B 132
Knodishall. *Suff* 4G 67
Knole. *Som* 4H 21
Knollbury. *Mon* 3H 33
Knolls Green. *Ches E* 3C 84
Knolton. *Wrex* 2F 71
Knook. *Wilts* 2E 23
Knossington. *Leics* 5F 75
Knott. *High* 3C 154
Knott End-on-Sea. *Lanc* 5C 96
Knotting. *Bed* 4H 63
Knotting Green. *Bed* 4H 63
Knottingley. *W Yor* 2E 93
Knotts. *Cumb* 2F 103
Knotty Ash. *Mers* 1G 83
Knotty Green. *Buck* 1A 38
Knowbury. *Shrp* 3H 59
Knowe. *Dum* 2A 110
Knowefield. *Cumb* 4F 113
Knowehead. *Dum* 5F 117
Knowes. *E Lot* 2C 130
Knowesgate. *Nmbd* 1C 114
Knoweside. *S Ayr* 3B 116
Knowle. *Bris* 4A 34
Knowle. *Devn* 3E 19 (nr. Braunton)
Knowle. *Devn* 4D 12 (nr. Budleigh Salterton)
Knowle. *Devn* 2A 12 (nr. Crediton)
Knowle. *Shrp* 3H 59
Knowle. *W Mid* 3F 61
Knowle Green. *Lanc* 1E 91
Knowle St Giles. *Som* 1G 13
Knowles of Elrick. *Abers* 3D 160
Knowle Village. *Hants* 2D 16
Knowl Hill. *Wind* 4G 37
Knowlton. *Kent* 5G 41
Knowsley. *Mers* 1G 83
Knowstone. *Devn* 4B 20
Knucklas. *Powy* 3E 59
Knuston. *Nptn* 4G 63
Knutsford. *Ches E* 3B 84
Knypersley. *Staf* 5C 84
Krumlin. *W Yor* 3A 92
Kuggar. *Corn* 5E 5
Kyleakin. *High* 1F 147
Kyle of Lochalsh. *High* 1F 147
Kylerhea. *High* 1F 147
Kylesku. *High* 5C 166
Kyles Lodge. *W Isl* 9B 171
Kylesmorar. *High* 4G 147
Kylestrome. *High* 5C 166
Kymin. *Mon* 4A 48
Kynaston. *Here* 2B 48
Kynaston. *Shrp* 3F 71
Kynnersley. *Telf* 4A 72
Kyre Green. *Worc* 4A 60
Kyre Park. *Worc* 4A 60
Kyrewood. *Worc* 4A 60

L

Labost. *W Isl* 3E 171
Lacasaidh. *W Isl* 5F 171
Lacasdail. *W Isl* 4G 171
Laceby. *NE Lin* 4F 95
Lacey Green. *Buck* 5G 51
Lach Dennis. *Ches W* 3B 84
Lache. *Ches W* 4F 83
Lackford. *Suff* 3G 65
Lacock. *Wilts* 5E 35
Ladbroke. *Warw* 5B 62
Laddingford. *Kent* 1A 28
Lade Bank. *Linc* 5C 88
Ladock. *Corn* 3C 6
Lady. *Orkn* 3F 172
Ladybank. *Fife* 2F 137
Ladycross. *Corn* 4D 10
Lady Green. *Mers* 4B 90
Lady Hall. *Cumb* 1A 96
Ladykirk. *Bord* 5E 131
Ladysford. *Abers* 2G 161
Ladywood. *W Mid* 2E 61
Ladywood. *Worc* 4C 60
Laga. *High* 2A 140
Lagavulin. *Arg* 5C 124
Lagg. *Arg* 2D 125
Lagg. *N Ayr* 3D 122
Laggan. *Arg* 4A 124
Laggan. *High* 4E 149 (nr. Fort Augustus)
Laggan. *High* 4A 150 (nr. Newtonmore)
Laggan. *Mor* 5H 159
Lagganlia. *High* 3C 150
Lagganulva. *Arg* 4F 139
Laglingarten. *Arg* 3A 134
Lagness. *W Sus* 2G 17
Laid. *High* 3E 166
Laide. *High* 4D 162
Laigh Fenwick. *E Ayr* 5F 127
Laindon. *Essx* 2A 40
Lairg. *High* 3C 164
Lairg Muir. *High* 3C 164
Laithes. *Cumb* 1F 103
Laithkirk. *Dur* 2C 104
Lake. *Devn* 3F 19
Lake. *IOW* 4D 16
Lake. *Wilts* 3G 23
Lakenham. *Norf* 5E 79
Lakenheath. *Suff* 2G 65
Lakesend. *Norf* 1E 65
Lakeside. *Cumb* 1C 96
Laleham. *Surr* 4B 38
Laleston. *B'end* 3B 32
Lamancha. *Bord* 4F 129
Lamarsh. *Essx* 2B 54
Lamas. *Norf* 3E 79
Lamb Corner. *Essx* 2D 54
Lambden. *Bord* 5D 130
Lamberhead Green. *G Man* 4D 90
Lamberhurst. *Kent* 2A 28
Lamberhurst Quarter. *Kent* 2A 28
Lamberton. *Bord* 4F 131
Lambeth. *G Lon* 3E 39
Lambfell Moar. *IOM* 3B 108
Lambhill. *Glas* 3G 127
Lambley. *Nmbd* 4H 113
Lambley. *Notts* 1D 74
Lambourn. *W Ber* 4B 36
Lambourne End. *Essx* 1F 39
Lambourn Woodlands. *W Ber* 4B 36
Lambrook. *Som* 4F 21
Lambs Green. *Dors* 3E 15
Lambs Green. *W Sus* 2D 26
Lambston. *Pemb* 3D 42
Lamellion. *Corn* 2G 7
Lamerton. *Devn* 5E 11
Lamesley. *Tyne* 4F 115
Laminess. *Orkn* 4F 172
Lamington. *High* 1B 158
Lamington. *S Lan* 1B 118
Lamlash. *N Ayr* 2E 123
Lamonby. *Cumb* 1F 103
Lamorick. *Corn* 2E 7
Lamorna. *Corn* 4B 4
Lamorran. *Corn* 4C 6
Lampeter. *Cdgn* 1F 45
Lampeter Velfrey. *Pemb* 3F 43
Lamphey. *Pemb* 4E 43
Lamplugh. *Cumb* 2B 102
Lamport. *Nptn* 3E 63
Lamyatt. *Som* 3B 22
Lana. *Devn* 3D 10 (nr. Ashwater)
Lana. *Devn* 2D 10 (nr. Holsworthy)
Lanark. *S Lan* 5B 128
Lanarth. *Corn* 4E 5
Lancaster. *Lanc* 3D 97
Lanchester. *Dur* 5E 115
Lancing. *W Sus* 5C 26
Landbeach. *Cambs* 4D 64
Landcross. *Devn* 4E 19
Landerberry. *Abers* 3E 153
Landford. *Wilts* 1A 16
Land Gate. *G Man* 4D 90
Landhallow. *High* 5D 169
Landimore. *Swan* 3D 30
Landkey. *Devn* 3F 19
Landkey Newland. *Devn* 3F 19
Landore. *Swan* 3F 31
Landport. *Port* 2E 17
Landrake. *Corn* 2H 7
Landscove. *Devn* 2D 9
Land's End (St Just) Airport. *Corn* 4A 4
Landshipping. *Pemb* 3F 43
Landulph. *Corn* 2A 8
Landywood. *Staf* 5D 73
Lane. *Corn* 2C 6
Laneast. *Corn* 4C 10
Lane Bottom. *Lanc* 1G 91
Lane End. *Buck* 2G 37
Lane End. *Cumb* 5C 102
Lane End. *Hants* 4D 24
Lane End. *IOW* 4E 17
Lane End. *Wilts* 2D 22
Lane Ends. *Derbs* 2G 73
Lane Ends. *Dur* 1E 105
Lane Ends. *Lanc* 4G 97
Laneham. *Notts* 3F 87

Lintmill—Llangadfan

Lintmill. Mor 2C 160
Linton. Cambs 1F 53
Linton. Derbs 4G 73
Linton. Here 3B 48
Linton. Kent 5B 40
Linton. N Yor 3B 98
Linton. Bord 2B 120
Linton. W Yor 5F 99
Linton Colliery. Nmbd 5G 121
Linton Hill. Here 3B 48
Linton-on-Ouse. N Yor 3G 99
Lintzford. Tyne 4E 115
Lintzgarth. Dur 5C 114
Linwood. Hants 2G 15
Linwood. Linc 2A 88
Linwood. Ren 3F 127
Lionacleit. W Isl 4C 170
Lionacro. High 2C 154
Lionacuidhe. W Isl 4C 170
Lional. W Isl 1H 171
Liphook. Hants 3G 25
Lipley. Shrp 2B 72
Lipyeate. Som 1B 22
Liquo. N Lan 4B 128
Liscard. Mers 1F 83
Liscombe. Som 3B 20
Liskeard. Corn 2G 7
Lisle Court. Hants 3B 16
Liss. Hants 4F 25
Lissett. E Yor 4F 101
Liss Forest. Hants 4F 25
Lissington. Linc 2A 88
Liston. Essx 1B 54
Lisvane. Card 3E 33
Liswerry. Newp 3G 33
Litcham. Norf 4A 78
Litchard. B'end 3C 32
Litchborough. Nptn 5D 62
Litchfield. Hants 1C 24
Litherland. Mers 1F 83
Litlington. Cambs 1D 52
Litlington. E Sus 5G 27
Littemill. Nmbd 3G 121
Litterty. Abers 3E 161
Little Abington. Cambs 1F 53
Little Addington. Nptn 3G 63
Little Airmyn. N Yor 2H 93
Little Alne. Warw 4F 61
Little Ardo. Abers 5F 161
Little Asby. Cumb 4H 103
Little Aston. Staf 5E 73
Little Atherfield. IOW 4C 16
Little Ayton. N Yor 3C 106
Little Baddow. Essx 5A 54
Little Badminton. S Glo 3D 34
Little Ballinluig. Per 3G 143
Little Bampton. Cumb 4D 112
Little Bardfield. Essx 2G 53
Little Barford. Bed 5A 64
Little Barningham. Norf 2D 78
Little Barrington. Glos 4H 49
Little Barrow. Ches W 4G 83
Little Barugh. N Yor 2B 100
Little Bavington. Nmbd 2C 114
Little Bealings. Suff 1F 55
Littlebeck. Cumb 3H 103
Little Bedwyn. Wilts 5A 36
Little Bentley. Essx 3E 54
Little Berkhamsted. Herts 5C 52
Little Billing. Nptn 4F 63
Little Billington. C Beds 3H 51
Little Birch. Here 2A 48
Little Bispham. Bkpl 5C 96
Little Blakenham. Suff 1E 54
Little Blencow. Cumb 1F 103
Little Bognor. W Sus 3B 26
Little Bolas. Shrp 3A 72
Little Bollington. Ches E 2B 84
Little Bookham. Surr 5C 38
Littleborough. Devn 1B 12
Littleborough. G Man 3H 91
Littleborough. Notts 2F 87
Littlebourne. Kent 5G 41
Little Bourton. Oxon 1C 50
Little Bowden. Leics 2E 63
Little Bradley. Suff 5F 65
Little Brampton. Shrp 2F 59
Little Brechin. Ang 2E 145
Littlebredy. Dors 4A 14
Little Brickhill. Mil 2H 51
Little Bridgeford. Staf 3C 72
Little Brington. Nptn 4D 62
Little Bromley. Essx 3D 54
Little Broughton. Cumb 1B 102
Little Budworth. Ches W 4H 83
Little Burstead. Essx 1A 40
Little Burton. E Yor 5F 101
Littlebury. Essx 2F 53
Littlebury Green. Essx 2E 53
Little Bytham. Linc 4H 75
Little Canfield. Essx 3F 53
Little Canford. Dors 3F 15
Little Carlton. Linc 2C 88
Little Carlton. Notts 5E 87
Little Casterton. Rut 5H 75
Little Catwick. E Yor 5F 101
Little Catworth. Cambs 3A 64
Little Cawthorpe. Linc 2C 88
Little Chalfont. Buck 1A 38
Little Chart. Kent 1D 28
Little Chesterford. Essx 1F 53
Little Cheverell. Wilts 1E 23
Little Chishill. Cambs 2E 53
Little Clacton. Essx 4E 55
Little Clanfield. Oxon 5A 50
Little Clifton. Cumb 2B 102
Little Coates. NE Lin 4F 95
Little Comberton. Worc 1E 49
Little Common. E Sus 5B 28
Little Compton. Warw 2A 50
Little Cornard. Suff 2B 54
Littlecote. Buck 3G 51
Littlecott. Wilts 1G 23
Little Cowarne. Here 5A 60
Little Coxwell. Oxon 2A 36
Little Crakehall. N Yor 5F 105
Little Crawley. Mil 1H 51
Little Creich. High 5D 164
Little Cressingham. Norf 5A 78
Little Crosby. Mers 4B 90
Little Crosthwaite. Cumb 2D 102
Little Cubley. Derbs 2F 73
Little Dalby. Leics 4E 75
Little Dawley. Telf 5A 72
Littledean. Glos 4B 48
Little Dens. Abers 4H 161
Little Dewchurch. Here 2A 48
Little Ditton. Cambs 5F 65
Little Down. Hants 1B 24
Little Downham. Cambs 2E 65
Little Drayton. Shrp 2A 72
Little Driffield. E Yor 4E 101
Little Dunham. Norf 4A 78
Little Dunkeld. Per 4H 143
Little Dunmow. Essx 3G 53
Little Easton. Essx 3G 53
Little Eaton. Derbs 1A 74
Little Eccleston. Lanc 5D 96
Little Ellingham. Norf 1C 66
Little Elm. Som 2C 22
Little End. Essx 5F 53
Little Everdon. Nptn 5C 62
Little Eversden. Cambs 5C 64
Little Faringdon. Oxon 5H 49
Little Fencote. N Yor 5F 105
Little Fenton. N Yor 1F 93
Littleferry. High 4F 165
Little Fransham. Norf 4B 78
Little Gaddesden. Herts 4H 51
Little Garway. Here 3H 47
Little Gidding. Cambs 2A 64
Little Glemham. Suff 5F 67
Little Glenshee. Per 5G 143
Little Gransden. Cambs 5B 64
Little Green. Suff 3C 66
Little Green. Wrex 1G 71
Little Grimsby. Linc 1C 88
Little Habton. N Yor 2B 100
Little Hadham. Herts 3E 53
Little Hale. Linc 1A 76
Little Hallingbury. Essx 4E 53
Littleham. Devn 4E 19
(nr. Bideford)
Littleham. Devn 4D 12
(nr. Exmouth)
Little Hampden. Buck 5G 51
Littlehampton. W Sus 5B 26
Little Haresfield. Glos 5D 48
Little Harrowden. Nptn 3F 63
Little Haseley. Oxon 5E 51
Little Hatfield. E Yor 5F 101
Little Hautbois. Norf 3E 79
Little Haven. Pemb 3C 42
Little Hay. Staf 5F 73
Little Hayfield. Derbs 2E 85
Little Haywood. Staf 3E 73
Little Heath. W Mid 2H 61
Little Heck. N Yor 2F 93
Littlehempston. Devn 2E 9
Little Herbert's. Glos 3E 49
Little Hereford. Here 4H 59
Little Horkesley. Essx 2C 54
Little Hormead. Herts 3E 53
Little Horsted. E Sus 4F 27
Little Horton. W Yor 1B 92
Little Horwood. Buck 2F 51
Little Houghton. Nptn 5F 63
Littlehoughton. Nmbd 3G 121
Little Houghton. S Yor 4E 93
Little Hucklow. Derbs 3F 85
Little Hulton. G Man 4F 91
Little Ingestre. Staf 3D 73
Little Irchester. Nptn 4G 63
Little Kelk. E Yor 3E 101
Little Kimble. Buck 5G 51
Little Kineton. Warw 5H 61
Little Kingshill. Buck 2G 37
Little Langdale. Cumb 4E 102
Little Langford. Wilts 3F 23
Little Laver. Essx 5F 53
Little Lawford. Warw 3B 62
Little Leigh. Ches W 3A 84
Little Leighs. Essx 4H 53
Little Leven. E Yor 5E 101
Little Lever. G Man 4F 91
Little Linford. Mil 1G 51
Little London. Buck 4E 51
Little London. E Sus 4G 27
Little London. Hants 2B 24
(nr. Andover)
Little London. Hants 1E 24
(nr. Basingstoke)
Little London. Linc 3D 76
(nr. Long Sutton)
Little London. Linc 3B 76
(nr. Spalding)
Little London. Norf 2E 79
(nr. North Walsham)
Little London. Norf 1G 65
(nr. Northwold)
Little London. Norf 2D 78
(nr. Saxthorpe)
Little London. Norf 1F 65
(nr. Southery)
Little London. Powy 2C 58
Little Longstone. Derbs 3F 85
Little Malvern. Worc 1C 48
Little Maplestead. Essx 2B 54
Little Marcle. Here 2B 48
Little Marlow. Buck 3G 37
Little Massingham. Norf 3G 77
Little Melton. Norf 5D 78
Littlemill. Abers 4H 151
Littlemill. E Ayr 3D 116
Littlemill. High 4D 158
Little Mill. Mon 5G 47
Little Milton. Oxon 5E 50
Little Missenden. Buck 1A 38
Littlemoor. Derbs 4A 86
Littlemoor. Dors 4B 14
Littlemore. Oxon 5D 50
Little Mountain. Flin 4E 83
Little Musgrave. Cumb 3A 104
Little Ness. Shrp 4G 71
Little Neston. Ches W 3F 83
Little Newcastle. Pemb 2D 43
Little Newsham. Dur 3E 105
Little Oakley. Essx 3F 55
Little Oakley. Nptn 2F 63
Little Onn. Staf 4C 72
Little Ormside. Cumb 3A 104
Little Orton. Cumb 4E 113
Little Orton. Leics 5H 73
Little Ouse. Norf 2F 65
Little Ouseburn. N Yor 3G 99
Littleover. Derb 2H 73
Little Packington. Warw 2G 61
Little Paxton. Cambs 4A 64
Little Petherick. Corn 1D 6
Little Plumpton. Lanc 1B 90
Little Plumstead. Norf 4F 79
Little Ponton. Linc 2G 75
Littleport. Cambs 2E 65
Little Posbrook. Hants 2D 16
Little Potheridge. Devn 1F 11
Little Preston. Nptn 5C 62
Little Raveley. Cambs 3B 64
Little Reynoldston. Swan 4D 31
Little Ribston. N Yor 4F 99
Little Rissington. Glos 4G 49
Little Rogart. High 3E 165
Little Rollright. Oxon 2A 50
Little Ryburgh. Norf 3B 78
Little Ryle. Nmbd 3E 121
Little Ryton. Shrp 5G 71
Little Salkeld. Cumb 1G 103
Little Sampford. Essx 2G 53
Little Sandhurst. Brac 5G 37
Little Saredon. Staf 5D 72
Little Saxham. Suff 4G 65
Little Scatwell. High 3F 157
Little Shelford. Cambs 5D 64
Little Shoddesden. Hants 2A 24
Little Singleton. Lanc 1B 90
Little Smeaton. N Yor 3F 93
Little Snoring. Norf 2B 78
Little Sodbury. S Glo 3C 34
Little Somborne. Hants 3B 24
Little Somerford. Wilts 3E 35
Little Soudley. Shrp 3B 72
Little Stainforth. N Yor 3H 97
Little Stainton. Darl 2A 106
Little Stanney. Ches W 3G 83
Little Staughton. Bed 4A 64
Little Steeping. Linc 4D 88
Littlester. Shet 3G 173
Little Stoke. Staf 2D 72
Littlestone-on-Sea. Kent 3E 29
Little Stonham. Suff 4D 66
Little Stretton. Leics 5D 74
Little Stretton. Shrp 1G 59
Little Strickland. Cumb 3G 103
Little Stukeley. Cambs 3B 64
Little Sugnall. Staf 2C 72
Little Sutton. Ches W 3F 83
Little Sutton. Linc 3D 76
Little Swinburne. Nmbd 2C 114
Little Tew. Oxon 3B 50
Little Tey. Essx 3B 54
Little Thetford. Cambs 3E 65
Little Thirkleby. N Yor 2G 99
Little Thornton. Lanc 5C 96
Littlethorpe. Leics 1C 62
Littlethorpe. N Yor 3F 99
Little Thorpe. W Yor 2B 92
Little Thurlow. Suff 5F 65
Little Thurrock. Thur 3H 39
Littleton. Ches W 4G 83
Littleton. Hants 3C 24
Littleton. Som 3H 21
Littleton. Surr 1A 26
(nr. Guildford)
Littleton. Surr 4B 38
(nr. Staines)
Littleton Drew. Wilts 3D 34
Littleton Pannell. Wilts 1E 23
Littleton-upon-Severn. S Glo 3A 34
Little Torboll. High 4E 165
Little Torrington. Devn 1E 11
Little Totham. Essx 4B 54
Little Town. Cumb 3D 102
Littletown. Dur 5G 115
Littletown. High 5E 165
Little Town. Lanc 1E 91
Little Twycross. Leics 5H 73
Little Urswick. Cumb 2B 96
Little Wakering. Essx 2D 40
Little Walden. Essx 1F 53
Little Waldingfield. Suff 1C 54
Little Walsingham. Norf 2B 78
Little Waltham. Essx 4H 53
Little Warley. Essx 1H 39
Little Washbourne. Glos 2E 49
Little Weighton. E Yor 1C 94
Little Wenham. Suff 2D 54
Little Wenlock. Telf 5A 72
Little Whelnetham. Suff 5A 66
Little Whittingham Green. Suff 3E 67
Littlewick Green. Wind 4G 37
Little Wilbraham. Cambs 5E 65
Littlewindsor. Dors 2H 13
Little Wisbeach. Linc 2A 76
Little Witcombe. Glos 4E 49
Little Witley. Worc 4B 60
Little Wittenham. Oxon 2D 36
Little Wolford. Warw 2A 50
Littleworth. Bed 1A 52
Littleworth. Glos 2G 49
Littleworth. Oxon 2B 36
Littleworth. Staf 4E 73
(nr. Cannock)
Littleworth. Staf 3B 72
(nr. Eccleshall)
Littleworth. Staf 3D 72
(nr. Stafford)
Littleworth. W Sus 3C 26
Littleworth. Worc 4D 61
(nr. Redditch)
Littleworth. Worc 1D 49
(nr. Worcester)
Little Wratting. Suff 1G 53
Little Wymington. Nptn 4G 63
Little Wymondley. Herts 3C 52
Little Wyrley. Staf 5E 73
Little Yeldham. Essx 2A 54
Littley Green. Essx 4G 53
Litton. Derbs 3F 85
Litton. N Yor 2B 98
Litton. Som 1A 22
Litton Cheney. Dors 3A 14
Liurbost. W Isl 5F 171
Liverpool. Mers 1F 83 & 200
Liverpool John Lennon Airport.
Mers 2G 83
Liversedge. W Yor 2B 92
Liverton. Devn 5B 12
Liverton. Red C 3E 107
Liverton Mines. Red C 3E 107
Livingston. W Lot 3D 128
Livingston Village. W Lot 3D 128
Lixwm. Flin 3D 82
Lizard. Corn 5E 5
Llaingoch. IOA 2B 80
Llaithddu. Powy 2C 58
Llampha. V Glam 4C 32
Llan. Powy 5A 70
Llanaber. Gwyn 4F 69
Llanaelhaearn. Gwyn 1C 68
Llanaeron. Cdgn 4D 57
Llanafan. Cdgn 3F 57
Llanafan-fawr. Powy 5B 58
Llanafan-fechan. Powy 5B 58
Llanallgo. IOA 2D 81
Llanandras. Powy 4F 59
Llananno. Powy 3C 58
Llanarmon. Gwyn 2D 68
Llanarmon Dyffryn Ceiriog.
Wrex 2D 70
Llanarmon-yn-Ial. Den 5D 82
Llanarth. Cdgn 5D 56
Llanarth. Mon 4G 47
Llanarthne. Carm 3F 45
Llanasa. Flin 2D 82
Llanbabo. IOA 2C 80
Llanbadarn Fawr. Cdgn 2F 57
Llanbadarn Fynydd. Powy 3C 58
Llanbadarn-y-garreg. Powy 1E 46
Llanbadoc. Mon 5G 47
Llanbadrig. IOA 1C 80
Llanbeder. Newp 2G 33
Llanbedr. Gwyn 3E 69
Llanbedr. Powy 3F 47
(nr. Crickhowell)
Llanbedr. Powy 1E 47
(nr. Hay-on-Wye)
Llanbedr-Dyffryn-Clwyd. Den 5D 82
Llanbedrgoch. IOA 2E 81
Llanbedrog. Gwyn 2C 68
Llanbedr Pont Steffan. Cdgn 1F 45
Llanbedr-y-cennin. Cnwy 4G 81
Llanberis. Gwyn 4E 81
Llanbethery. V Glam 5D 32
Llanbister. Powy 3D 58
Llanblethian. V Glam 4C 32
Llanboidy. Carm 2G 43
Llanbradach. Cphy 2E 33
Llanbrynmair. Powy 5A 70
Llanbydderi. V Glam 5D 32
Llancadle. V Glam 5D 32
Llancarfan. V Glam 4D 32
Llancatal. V Glam 5D 32
Llancayo. Mon 5G 47
Llancloudy. Here 3H 47
Llancoch. Powy 3E 58
Llancynfelyn. Cdgn 1F 57
Llandaff. Card 4E 33
Llandanwg. Gwyn 3E 69
Llandarcy. Neat 3G 31
Llandawke. Carm 3G 43
Llanddaniel-Fab. IOA 3D 81
Llanddarog. Carm 4F 45
Llanddeiniol. Cdgn 3E 57
Llanddeiniolen. Gwyn 4E 81
Llandderfel. Gwyn 2B 70
Llanddeusant. Carm 3A 46
Llanddeusant. IOA 2C 80
Llanddew. Powy 2D 46
Llanddewi. Swan 4D 30
Llanddewi Brefi. Cdgn 5F 57
Llanddewi'r Cwm. Powy 1D 46
Llanddewi Rhydderch. Mon 4G 47
Llanddewi Velfrey. Pemb 3F 43
Llanddewi Ystradenni. Powy 4D 58
Llanddoged. Cnwy 4H 81
Llanddona. IOA 3E 81
Llanddowror. Carm 3G 43
Llanddulas. Cnwy 3B 82
Llanddwywe. Gwyn 3E 69
Llanddyfnan. IOA 3E 81
Llandecwyn. Gwyn 2F 69
Llandefaelog Fach. Powy 2D 46
Llandefaelog-tre'r-graig. Powy 2E 47
Llandefalle. Powy 2E 46
Llandegai. Gwyn 3E 81
Llandegfan. IOA 3E 81
Llandegla. Den 5D 82
Llandegley. Powy 4D 58
Llandegveth. Mon 2G 33
Llandeilo. Carm 3G 45
Llandeilo Graban. Powy 1D 46
Llandeilo'r Fan. Powy 2B 46
Llandeloy. Pemb 2C 42
Llandenny. Mon 5H 47
Llandevaud. Newp 2H 33
Llandevenny. Mon 3G 33
Llandilo. Pemb 2F 43
Llandinabo. Here 3A 48
Llandinam. Powy 2C 58
Llandissilio. Pemb 2F 43
Llandogo. Mon 5A 48
Llandough. V Glam 4C 32
(nr. Cowbridge)
Llandough. V Glam 4E 33
(nr. Penarth)
Llandovery. Carm 2A 46
Llandow. V Glam 4C 32
Llandre. Cdgn 2F 57
Llandrillo. Den 2C 70
Llandrillo-yn-Rhos. Cnwy 2H 81
Llandrindod. Powy 4C 58
Llandrindod Wells. Powy 4C 58
Llandrinio. Powy 4E 71
Llandsadwrn. Carm 2G 45
Llandudno. Cnwy 2G 81
Llandudno Junction. Cnwy 3G 81
Llandudoch. Pemb 1B 44
Llandw. V Glam 4C 32
Llandwrog. Gwyn 5D 80
Llandybie. Carm 4G 45
Llandyfaelog. Carm 4E 45
Llandyfan. Carm 4G 45
Llandyfriog. Cdgn 1D 44
Llandyfrydog. IOA 2D 80
Llandygwydd. Cdgn 1C 44
Llandynan. Den 1D 70
Llandyrnog. Den 4D 82
Llandysilio. Powy 4E 71
Llandyssil. Powy 1D 58
Llandysul. Cdgn 1E 45
Llanedeyrn. Card 3F 33
Llaneglwys. Powy 2D 46
Llanegryn. Gwyn 5F 69
Llanegwad. Carm 3F 45
Llaneilian. IOA 1D 80
Llanelian-yn-Rhos. Cnwy 3A 82
Llanelidan. Den 5D 82
Llanelieu. Powy 2E 47
Llanellen. Mon 4G 47
Llanelli. Carm 3E 31
Llanelltyd. Gwyn 4G 69
Llanelly. Mon 4F 47
Llanelly Hill. Mon 4F 47
Llanelwedd. Powy 5C 58
Llanelwy. Den 3C 82
Llanenddwyn. Gwyn 3E 69
Llanengan. Gwyn 3B 68
Llanerch. Powy 1F 59
Llanerchymedd. IOA 2D 80
Llanerfyl. Powy 5C 70
Llaneuddog. IOA 2D 80
Llanfachraeth. IOA 2C 80
Llanfaelog. IOA 3C 80
Llanfaelrhys. Gwyn 3B 68
Llanfaenor. Mon 4H 47
Llanfaes. IOA 3F 81
Llanfaes. Powy 3D 46
Llanfaethlu. IOA 2C 80
Llanfaglan. Gwyn 4D 80
Llanfair. Gwyn 3E 69
Llanfair. Here 1F 47
Llanfair Caereinion. Powy 5D 70
Llanfair Clydogau. Cdgn 5F 57
Llanfair Dyffryn Clwyd. Den 5D 82
Llanfairfechan. Cnwy 3F 81
Llanfair-Nant-Gwyn. Pemb 1F 43
Llanfair Pwllgwyngyll. IOA 3E 81
Llanfair Talhaiarn. Cnwy 3B 82
Llanfair Waterdine. Shrp 3E 59
Llanfair-ym-Muallt. Powy 5C 58
Llanfairyneubwll. IOA 3C 80
Llanfairynghornwy. IOA 1C 80
Llanfallteg. Carm 3F 43
Llanfallteg West. Carm 3F 43
Llanfaredd. Powy 5C 58
Llanfarian. Cdgn 3E 57
Llanfechain. Powy 3D 70
Llanfechell. IOA 1C 80
Llanfechreth. Gwyn 3G 69
Llanfendigaid. Gwyn 5E 69
Llanferres. Den 4D 82
Llan Ffestiniog. Gwyn 1G 69
Llanfflewyn. IOA 2C 80
Llanfihangel Glyn Myfyr. Cnwy 1B 70
Llanfihangel Nant Bran. Powy 2C 46
Llanfihangel-Nant-Melan. Powy 5D 58
Llanfihangel Rhydithon. Powy 4D 58
Llanfihangel Rogiet. Mon 3H 33
Llanfihangel Tal-y-llyn. Powy 3E 46
Llanfihangel-uwch-Gwili. Carm 3E 45
Llanfihangel-yng-Ngwynfa.
Powy 4C 70
Llanfihangel yn Nhowyn. IOA 3C 80
Llanfihangel-y-pennant. Gwyn 1E 69
(nr. Golan)
Llanfihangel-y-pennant. Gwyn 5F 69
(nr. Tywyn)
Llanfilo. Powy 2E 46
Llanfinhangel-ar-Arth. Carm 2E 45
Llanfinhangel-y-Creuddyn.
Cdgn 3F 57
Llanfinhangel-y-traethau.
Gwyn 2E 69
Llanfleiddan. V Glam 4C 32
Llanfoist. Mon 4F 47
Llanfor. Gwyn 2B 70
Llanfrechfa. Torf 2G 33
Llanfrothen. Gwyn 1F 69
Llanfrynach. Powy 3D 46
Llanfwrog. Den 5D 82
Llanfwrog. IOA 2C 80
Llanfyllin. Powy 4D 70
Llanfynydd. Carm 3F 45
Llanfynydd. Flin 5E 83
Llanfyrnach. Pemb 1G 43
Llangadfan. Powy 4C 70

Llangadog—Lower Foxdale

Llangadog. *Carm* 3H **45** (nr. Llandovery)
Llangadog. *Carm* 5E **45** (nr. Llanelli)
Llangadwaladr. *IOA* 4C **80**
Llangadwaladr. *Powy* 2D **70**
Llangaffo. *IOA* 4D **80**
Llangain. *Carm* 4D **45**
Llangammarch Wells. *Powy* 1C **46**
Llangan. *V Glam* 4C **32**
Llangarron. *Here* 3A **48**
Llangasty-Talyllyn. *Powy* 3E **47**
Llangathen. *Carm* 3F **45**
Llangattock. *Powy* 4F **47**
Llangattock Lingoed. *Mon* 3G **47**
Llangattock-Vibon-Avel. *Mon* 4H **47**
Llangedwyn. *Powy* 3D **70**
Llangefni. *IOA* 3D **80**
Llangeinor. *B'end* 3C **32**
Llangeitho. *Cdgn* 5F **57**
Llangeler. *Carm* 2D **44**
Llangelynin. *Gwyn* 5E **69**
Llangendeirne. *Carm* 4E **45**
Llangennech. *Carm* 5F **45**
Llangennith. *Swan* 3D **30**
Llangenny. *Powy* 4F **47**
Llangernyw. *Cnwy* 4A **82**
Llangian. *Gwyn* 3B **68**
Llangiwg. *Neat* 5H **45**
Llangloffan. *Pemb* 1D **42**
Llanglydwen. *Carm* 2F **43**
Llangoed. *IOA* 3F **81**
Llangoedmor. *Cdgn* 1B **44**
Llangollen. *Den* 1E **70**
Llangolman. *Pemb* 2F **43**
Llangorse. *Powy* 3E **47**
Llangorwen. *Cdgn* 2F **57**
Llangovan. *Mon* 5H **47**
Llangower. *Gwyn* 2B **70**
Llangranog. *Cdgn* 5C **56**
Llangristiolus. *IOA* 3D **80**
Llangrove. *Here* 4A **48**
Llangua. *Mon* 3G **47**
Llangunllo. *Powy* 3E **58**
Llangunnor. *Carm* 3E **45**
Llangurig. *Powy* 3B **58**
Llangwm. *Cnwy* 1B **70**
Llangwm. *Mon* 5H **47**
Llangwm. *Pemb* 4D **43**
Llangwm-isaf. *Mon* 5H **47**
Llangwnnadl. *Gwyn* 2B **68**
Llangwyfan. *Den* 4D **82**
Llangwyfan-isaf. *IOA* 4C **80**
Llangwyllog. *IOA* 3D **80**
Llangwyryfon. *Cdgn* 3E **57**
Llangybi. *Cdgn* 5F **57**
Llangybi. *Gwyn* 1D **68**
Llangybi. *Mon* 2G **33**
Llangyfelach. *Swan* 3F **31**
Llangynhafal. *Den* 4D **82**
Llangynidr. *Powy* 4E **47**
Llangynin. *Carm* 3G **43**
Llangynog. *Carm* 3H **43**
Llangynog. *Powy* 3C **70**
Llangynwyd. *B'end* 3B **32**
Llanhamlach. *Powy* 3D **46**
Llanharan. *Rhon* 3D **32**
Llanharry. *Rhon* 3D **32**
Llanhennock. *Mon* 2G **33**
Llanhilleth. *Blae* 5F **47**
Llanidloes. *Powy* 2B **58**
Llaniestyn. *Gwyn* 2B **68**
Llanigon. *Powy* 1F **47**
Llanilar. *Cdgn* 3F **57**
Llanilid. *Rhon* 3C **32**
Llanilltud Fawr. *V Glam* 5C **32**
Llanishen. *Card* 3E **33**
Llanishen. *Mon* 5H **47**
Llanllawddog. *Carm* 3E **45**
Llanllechid. *Gwyn* 4F **81**
Llanllowell. *Mon* 2G **33**
Llanllugan. *Powy* 5C **70**
Llanllwch. *Carm* 4D **45**
Llanllwchaiarn. *Powy* 1D **58**
Llanllwni. *Carm* 2E **45**
Llanllyfni. *Gwyn* 5D **80**
Llanmadoc. *Swan* 3D **30**
Llanmaes. *V Glam* 5C **32**
Llanmartin. *Newp* 3G **33**
Llanmerwig. *Powy* 1D **58**
Llanmihangel. *V Glam* 4C **32**
Llan-mill. *Pemb* 3F **43**
Llanmiloe. *Carm* 4G **43**
Llanmorlais. *Swan* 3E **31**
Llannefydd. *Cnwy* 3B **82**
Llannon. *Carm* 5F **45**
Llan-non. *Cdgn* 4E **57**
Llannor. *Gwyn* 2C **68**
Llanpumsaint. *Carm* 3E **45**
Llanrhaeadr. *Den* 4C **82**
Llanrhaeadr-ym-Mochnant. *Powy* 3D **70**
Llanrhidian. *Swan* 3D **31**
Llanrhos. *Cnwy* 2G **81**
Llanrhyddlad. *IOA* 2C **80**
Llanrhystud. *Cdgn* 4E **57**
Llanrian. *Pemb* 1C **42**
Llanrothal. *Here* 4H **47**
Llanrug. *Gwyn* 4E **81**
Llanrumney. *Card* 3F **33**
Llanrwst. *Cnwy* 4G **81**
Llansadurnen. *Carm* 3G **43**
Llansadwrn. *IOA* 3E **81**
Llansaint. *Carm* 5D **45**
Llansamlet. *Swan* 3F **31**
Llansanffraid Glan Conwy. *Cnwy* 3H **81**
Llansannan. *Cnwy* 4B **82**
Llansannor. *V Glam* 4C **32**
Llansantffraed. *Cdgn* 4E **57**
Llansantffraed. *Powy* 3E **46**
Llansantffraed Cwmdeuddwr. *Powy* 4B **58**
Llansantffraed in Elwel. *Powy* 5C **58**
Llansantffraid-ym-Mechain. *Powy* 3E **70**
Llansawel. *Carm* 2G **45**
Llansawel. *Neat* 3G **31**
Llansilin. *Powy* 3E **70**
Llansoy. *Mon* 5H **47**
Llanspyddid. *Powy* 3D **46**
Llanstadwell. *Pemb* 4D **42**
Llansteffan. *Carm* 3H **43**
Llanstephan. *Powy* 1E **46**
Llantarnam. *Torf* 2F **33**
Llanteg. *Pemb* 3F **43**
Llanthony. *Mon* 3F **47**
Llantilio Crossenny. *Mon* 4G **47**
Llantilio Pertholey. *Mon* 4G **47**
Llantood. *Pemb* 1B **44**
Llantrisant. *Mon* 2G **33**
Llantrisant. *Rhon* 3D **32**
Llantrithyd. *V Glam* 4D **32**
Llantwit Fardre. *Rhon* 3D **32**
Llantwit Major. *V Glam* 5C **32**
Llanuwchllyn. *Gwyn* 2A **70**
Llanvaches. *Newp* 2H **33**
Llanvair Discoed. *Mon* 2H **33**
Llanvapley. *Mon* 4G **47**
Llanvetherine. *Mon* 4G **47**
Llanveynoe. *Here* 2G **47**
Llanvihangel Crucorney. *Mon* 3G **47**
Llanvihangel Gobion. *Mon* 5G **47**
Llanvihangel Ystern-Llewern. *Mon* 4H **47**
Llanwarne. *Here* 3A **48**
Llanwddyn. *Powy* 4C **70**
Llanwenarth. *Mon* 4F **47**
Llanwenog. *Cdgn* 1E **45**
Llanwern. *Newp* 3G **33**
Llanwinio. *Carm* 2G **43**
Llanwnda. *Gwyn* 5D **81**
Llanwnda. *Pemb* 1D **42**
Llanwnnen. *Cdgn* 1F **45**
Llanwnog. *Powy* 1C **58**
Llanwrda. *Carm* 2H **45**
Llanwrin. *Powy* 5G **69**
Llanwrthwl. *Powy* 4B **58**
Llanwrtud. *Powy* 1B **46**
Llanwrtyd. *Powy* 1B **46**
Llanwrtyd Wells. *Powy* 1B **46**
Llanwyddelan. *Powy* 5C **70**
Llanyblodwel. *Shrp* 3E **71**
Llanybri. *Carm* 3H **43**
Llanybydder. *Carm* 1F **45**
Llanycefn. *Pemb* 2E **43**
Llanychaer. *Pemb* 1D **43**
Llanycil. *Gwyn* 2B **70**
Llanymawddwy. *Gwyn* 4B **70**
Llanymddyfri. *Carm* 2A **46**
Llanymynech. *Shrp* 3E **71**
Llanynghenedl. *IOA* 2C **80**
Llanynys. *Den* 4D **82**
Llan-y-pwll. *Wrex* 5F **83**
Llanyrafon. *Torf* 2G **33**
Llanyre. *Powy* 4C **58**
Llanystumdwy. *Gwyn* 2D **68**
Llanywern. *Powy* 3E **46**
Llawhaden. *Pemb* 3E **43**
Llawndy. *Flin* 2D **82**
Llawnt. *Shrp* 2E **71**
Llawr Dref. *Gwyn* 3B **68**
Llawryglyn. *Powy* 1B **58**
Llay. *Wrex* 5F **83**
Llechfaen. *Powy* 3D **46**
Llechryd. *Cphy* 5E **46**
Llechryd. *Cdgn* 1C **44**
Llechrydau. *Wrex* 2E **71**
Lledrod. *Cdgn* 3F **57**
Llethrid. *Swan* 3E **31**
Llidiad-Nenog. *Carm* 2F **45**
Llidiardau. *Gwyn* 2A **70**
Llidiart y Parc. *Den* 1D **70**
Llithfaen. *Gwyn* 1C **68**
Lloc. *Flin* 3D **82**
Llong. *Flin* 4E **83**
Llowes. *Powy* 1E **47**
Lloyney. *Powy* 3E **59**
Llundain-fach. *Cdgn* 5E **57**
Llwydcoed. *Rhon* 5C **46**
Llwyncelyn. *Cdgn* 5D **56**
Llwyncelyn. *Swan* 5G **45**
Llwyndaffydd. *Cdgn* 5C **56**
Llwynderw. *Powy* 5E **70**
Llwyn-du. *Mon* 4F **47**
Llwyngwril. *Gwyn* 5E **69**
Llwynhendy. *Carm* 3E **31**
Llwynmawr. *Wrex* 2E **71**
Llwyn-on Village. *Mer T* 4D **46**
Llwyn-teg. *Carm* 5F **45**
Llwyn-y-brain. *Carm* 3F **43**
Llwynygog. *Powy* 1A **58**
Llwyn-y-groes. *Cdgn* 5E **57**
Llwynypia. *Rhon* 2C **32**
Llynclys. *Shrp* 3E **71**
Llynfaes. *IOA* 3D **80**
Llysfaen. *Cnwy* 3A **82**
Llyswen. *Powy* 2E **47**
Llysworney. *V Glam* 4C **32**
Llys-y-fran. *Pemb* 2E **43**
Llywel. *Powy* 2B **46**
Llywernog. *Cdgn* 2G **57**
Loan. *Falk* 2C **128**
Loanend. *Nmbd* 4F **131**
Loanhead. *Midl* 3F **129**
Loaningfoot. *Dum* 4A **112**
Loanreoch. *High* 1A **158**
Loans. *S Ayr* 1C **116**
Loansdean. *Nmbd* 1F **115**
Lobb. *Devn* 3E **19**
Lobhillcross. *Devn* 4E **11**
Lochaber. *Mor* 3E **159**
Loch a Charnain. *W Isl* 4D **170**
Loch a Ghainmhich. *W Isl* 5E **171**
Lochailort. *High* 5F **147**
Lochaline. *High* 4A **140**
Lochans. *Dum* 4F **109**
Locharbriggs. *Dum* 1A **112**
Lochardil. *High* 4A **158**
Lochassynt Lodge. *High* 1F **163**
Lochavich. *Arg* 2G **133**
Lochawe. *Arg* 1A **134**
Loch Baghasdail. *W Isl* 7C **170**
Lochboisdale. *W Isl* 7C **170**
Lochbuie. *Arg* 1D **132**
Lochcarron. *High* 5A **156**
Loch Choire Lodge. *High* 5G **167**
Lochdochart House. *Stir* 1D **134**
Lochdon. *Arg* 5B **140**
Lochearnhead. *Stir* 1E **135**
Lochee. *D'dee* 5C **144**
Lochend. *High* 5H **157** (nr. Inverness)
Lochend. *High* 2E **169** (nr. Thurso)
Locherben. *Dum* 5B **118**
Loch Euphort. *W Isl* 2D **170**
Lochfoot. *Dum* 2F **111**
Lochgair. *Arg* 4G **133**
Lochgarthside. *High* 2H **149**
Lochgelly. *Fife* 4D **136**
Lochgilphead. *Arg* 1G **125**
Lochgoilhead. *Arg* 3A **134**
Loch Head. *Dum* 5A **110**
Lochhill. *Mor* 2G **159**
Lochindorb Lodge. *High* 5D **158**
Lochinver. *High* 1E **163**
Lochlane. *Per* 1H **135**
Loch Loyal Lodge. *High* 4G **167**
Lochluichart. *High* 2F **157**
Lochmaben. *Dum* 1B **112**
Lochmaddy. *W Isl* 2E **170**
Loch nam Madadh. *W Isl* 2E **170**
Lochore. *Fife* 4D **136**
Lochportain. *W Isl* 1E **170**
Lochranza. *N Ayr* 4H **125**
Loch Sgioport. *W Isl* 5D **170**
Lochside. *Abers* 2G **145**
Lochside. *High* 5A **168** (nr. Achentoul)
Lochside. *High* 3C **158** (nr. Nairn)
Lochslin. *High* 5F **165**
Lochstack Lodge. *High* 4C **166**
Lochton. *Abers* 4E **153**
Lochty. *Fife* 3H **137**
Lochuisge. *High* 3B **140**
Lochussie. *High* 3G **157**
Lochwinnoch. *Ren* 4E **127**
Lochyside. *High* 1F **141**
Lockengate. *Corn* 2E **7**
Lockerbie. *Dum* 1C **112**
Lockeridge. *Wilts* 5G **35**
Lockerley. *Hants* 4A **24**
Lockhills. *Cumb* 5G **113**
Locking. *N Som* 1G **21**
Lockington. *E Yor* 5D **101**
Lockington. *Leics* 3B **74**
Lockleywood. *Shrp* 3A **72**
Locksgreen. *IOW* 3C **16**
Locks Heath. *Hants* 2D **16**
Lockton. *N Yor* 5F **107**
Loddington. *Leics* 5E **75**
Loddington. *Nptn* 3F **63**
Loddiswell. *Devn* 4D **8**
Loddon. *Norf* 1F **67**
Lode. *Cambs* 4E **65**
Loders. *Dors* 3H **13**
Lodsworth. *W Sus* 3A **26**
Lofthouse. *N Yor* 2D **98**
Lofthouse. *W Yor* 2D **92**
Lofthouse Gate. *W Yor* 2D **92**
Loftus. *Red C* 3E **107**
Logan. *E Ayr* 2E **117**
Loganlea. *W Lot* 3C **128**
Logaston. *Here* 5F **59**
Loggerheads. *Staf* 2B **72**
Loggie. *High* 4F **163**
Logie. *Ang* 2F **145**
Logie. *Fife* 1G **137**
Logie. *Mor* 3E **159**
Logie Coldstone. *Abers* 3B **152**
Logie Pert. *Ang* 2F **145**
Logierait. *Per* 3G **143**
Login. *Carm* 2F **43**
Lolworth. *Cambs* 4C **64**
Lonbain. *High* 3F **155**
Londesborough. *E Yor* 5C **100**
London. *G Lon* 2E **39** & **202-203**
London Apprentice. *Corn* 3E **6**
London Ashford (Lydd) Airport. *Kent* 3E **29**
London City Airport. *G Lon* 2F **39**
London Colney. *Herts* 5B **52**
Londonderry. *N Yor* 1F **99**
London Gatwick Airport. *W Sus* 1D **27** & **216**
London Heathrow Airport. *G Lon* 3B **38** & **216**
London Luton Airport. *Lutn* 3B **52** & **216**
London Southend Airport. *Essx* 2C **40**
London Stansted Airport. *Essx* 3F **53** & **216**
Londonthorpe. *Linc* 2G **75**
Londubh. *High* 5C **162**
Lone. *High* 4D **166**
Lonemore. *High* 5E **165** (nr. Dornoch)
Lonemore. *High* 1G **155** (nr. Gairloch)
Long Ashton. *N Som* 4A **34**
Long Bank. *Worc* 3B **60**
Longbar. *N Ayr* 4E **127**
Long Bennington. *Linc* 1F **75**
Longbenton. *Tyne* 3F **115**
Longborough. *Glos* 3G **49**
Long Bredy. *Dors* 3A **14**
Longbridge. *Warw* 4G **61**
Longbridge. *W Mid* 3E **61**
Longbridge Deverill. *Wilts* 2D **22**
Long Buckby. *Nptn* 4D **62**
Long Buckby Wharf. *Nptn* 4D **62**
Longburgh. *Cumb* 4E **112**
Longburton. *Dors* 1B **14**
Long Clawson. *Leics* 3E **74**
Longcliffe. *Derbs* 5G **85**
Long Common. *Hants* 1D **16**
Long Compton. *Staf* 3C **72**
Long Compton. *Warw* 2A **50**
Longcot. *Oxon* 2A **36**
Long Crendon. *Buck* 5E **51**
Long Crichel. *Dors* 1E **15**
Longcroft. *Cumb* 4D **112**
Longcroft. *Falk* 2A **128**
Longcross. *Surr* 4A **38**
Longdale. *Cumb* 4H **103**
Longdales. *Cumb* 5G **113**
Longden. *Shrp* 5G **71**
Longden Common. *Shrp* 5G **71**
Long Ditton. *Surr* 4C **38**
Longdon. *Staf* 4E **73**
Longdon. *Worc* 2D **48**
Longdon Green. *Staf* 4E **73**
Longdon on Tern. *Telf* 4A **72**
Longdown. *Devn* 3B **12**
Longdowns. *Corn* 5B **6**
Long Drax. *N Yor* 2G **93**
Long Duckmanton. *Derbs* 3B **86**
Long Eaton. *Derbs* 2B **74**
Longfield. *Kent* 4H **39**
Longfield. *Shet* 10E **173**
Longfield Hill. *Kent* 4H **39**
Longford. *Derbs* 2G **73**
Longford. *Glos* 3D **48**
Longford. *G Lon* 3B **38**
Longford. *Shrp* 2A **72**
Longford. *Telf* 4B **72**
Longford. *W Mid* 2H **61**
Longforgan. *Per* 1F **137**
Longformacus. *Bord* 4C **130**
Longframlington. *Nmbd* 4F **121**
Long Gardens. *Essx* 2B **54**
Long Green. *Ches W* 3G **83**
Long Green. *Worc* 2D **48**
Longham. *Dors* 3F **15**
Longham. *Norf* 4B **78**
Long Hanborough. *Oxon* 4C **50**
Longhedge. *Wilts* 2D **22**
Longhill. *Abers* 3H **161**
Longhirst. *Nmbd* 1F **115**
Longhope. *Glos* 4B **48**
Longhope. *Orkn* 8C **172**
Longhorsley. *Nmbd* 5F **121**
Longhoughton. *Nmbd* 3G **121**
Long Itchington. *Warw* 4B **62**
Longlands. *Cumb* 1D **102**
Longlane. *Derbs* 2G **73**
Long Lane. *Telf* 4A **72**
Longlane. *W Ber* 4C **36**
Long Lawford. *Warw* 3B **62**
Long Lease. *N Yor* 4G **107**
Longley Green. *Worc* 5B **60**
Long Load. *Som* 4H **21**
Longmanhill. *Abers* 2E **161**
Long Marston. *Herts* 4G **51**
Long Marston. *N Yor* 4H **99**
Long Marston. *Warw* 1G **49**
Long Marton. *Cumb* 2H **103**
Long Meadow. *Cambs* 4E **65**
Long Meadowend. *Shrp* 2G **59**
Long Melford. *Suff* 1B **54**
Longmoor Camp. *Hants* 3F **25**
Longmorn. *Mor* 3G **159**
Longmoss. *Ches E* 3C **84**
Long Newnton. *Glos* 2E **35**
Longnewton. *Bord* 2H **119**
Long Newton. *Stoc T* 3A **106**
Longney. *Glos* 4C **48**
Longniddry. *E Lot* 2H **129**
Longnor. *Shrp* 5G **71**
Longnor. *Staf* 4E **85** (nr. Leek)
Longnor. *Staf* 4C **72** (nr. Stafford)
Longparish. *Hants* 2C **24**
Longpark. *Cumb* 3F **113**
Long Preston. *N Yor* 4H **97**
Longridge. *Lanc* 1E **90**
Longridge. *Staf* 4D **72**
Longridge. *W Lot* 3C **128**
Longriggend. *N Lan* 2B **128**
Long Riston. *E Yor* 5F **101**
Long Rock. *Corn* 3C **4**
Longsdon. *Staf* 5D **84**
Longshaw. *G Man* 4D **90**
Longshaw. *Staf* 1E **73**
Longside. *Abers* 4H **161**
Longslow. *Shrp* 2A **72**
Longstanton. *Cambs* 4C **64**
Longstock. *Hants* 3B **24**
Longstowe. *Cambs* 5C **64**
Long Stratton. *Norf* 1D **66**
Long Street. *Mil* 1F **51**
Longstreet. *Wilts* 1G **23**
Long Sutton. *Hants* 2F **25**
Long Sutton. *Linc* 3D **76**
Long Sutton. *Som* 4H **21**
Longthorpe. *Pet* 1A **64**
Long Thurlow. *Suff* 4C **66**
Longthwaite. *Cumb* 2F **103**
Longton. *Lanc* 2C **90**
Longton. *Stoke* 1D **72**
Longtown. *Cumb* 3E **113**
Longtown. *Here* 3G **47**
Longville in the Dale. *Shrp* 1H **59**
Long Whatton. *Leics* 3B **74**
Longwick. *Buck* 5F **51**
Long Wittenham. *Oxon* 2D **36**
Longwitton. *Nmbd* 1D **115**
Longworth. *Oxon* 2B **36**
Longyester. *E Lot* 3B **130**
Lonmore. *High* 4B **154**
Looe. *Corn* 3G **7**
Loose. *Kent* 5B **40**
Loosegate. *Linc* 3C **76**
Loosley Row. *Buck* 5G **51**
Lopcombe Corner. *Wilts* 3A **24**
Lopen. *Som* 1H **13**
Loppington. *Shrp* 3G **71**
Lorbottle. *Nmbd* 4E **121**
Lorbottle Hall. *Nmbd* 4E **121**
Lordington. *W Sus* 2F **17**
Loscoe. *Derbs* 1B **74**
Loscombe. *Dors* 3A **14**
Losgaintir. *W Isl* 8C **171**
Lossiemouth. *Mor* 2G **159**
Lossit. *Arg* 4A **124**
Lostock Gralam. *Ches W* 3A **84**
Lostock Green. *Ches W* 3A **84**
Lostock Hall. *Lanc* 2D **90**
Lostock Junction. *G Man* 4E **91**
Lostwithiel. *Corn* 3F **7**
Lothbeg. *High* 2G **165**
Lothersdale. *N Yor* 5B **98**
Lothianbridge. *Midl* 3G **129**
Lothianburn. *Edin* 3F **129**
Lothmore. *High* 2G **165**
Lottisham. *Som* 3A **22**
Loudwater. *Buck* 1A **38**
Loughborough. *Leics* 4C **74**
Loughor. *Swan* 3E **31**
Loughton. *Essx* 1F **39**
Loughton. *Mil* 2G **51**
Loughton. *Shrp* 2A **60**
Lound. *Linc* 4H **75**
Lound. *Notts* 2D **86**
Lound. *Suff* 1H **67**
Lount. *Leics* 4A **74**
Louth. *Linc* 2C **88**
Love Clough. *Lanc* 2G **91**
Lovedean. *Hants* 1E **17**
Lover. *Wilts* 4H **23**
Loversall. *S Yor* 1C **86**
Loves Green. *Essx* 5G **53**
Loveston. *Pemb* 4E **43**
Lovington. *Som* 3A **22**
Low Ackworth. *W Yor* 3E **93**
Low Angerton. *Nmbd* 1D **115**
Low Ardwell. *Dum* 5F **109**
Low Ballochdoan. *S Ayr* 2F **109**
Lowbands. *Glos* 2C **48**
Low Barlings. *Linc* 3H **87**
Low Bell End. *N Yor* 5E **107**
Low Bentham. *N Yor* 3F **97**
Low Borrowbridge. *Cumb* 4H **103**
Low Bradfield. *S Yor* 1G **85**
Low Bradley. *N Yor* 5C **98**
Low Braithwaite. *Cumb* 5F **113**
Low Brunton. *Nmbd* 2C **114**
Low Burnham. *N Lin* 4A **94**
Lowca. *Cumb* 2A **102**
Low Catton. *E Yor* 4B **100**
Low Coniscliffe. *Darl* 3F **105**
Low Coylton. *S Ayr* 3D **116**
Low Crosby. *Cumb* 4F **113**
Low Dalby. *N Yor* 1C **100**
Lowdham. *Notts* 1D **74**
Low Dinsdale. *Darl* 3A **106**
Lowe. *Shrp* 2G **71**
Low Ellington. *N Yor* 1E **98**
Lower Amble. *Corn* 1D **6**
Lower Ansty. *Dors* 2C **14**
Lower Arboll. *High* 5F **165**
Lower Arncott. *Oxon* 4E **50**
Lower Ashton. *Devn* 4B **12**
Lower Assendon. *Oxon* 3F **37**
Lower Auchenreath. *Mor* 2A **160**
Lower Badcall. *High* 4B **166**
Lower Ballam. *Lanc* 1B **90**
Lower Basildon. *W Ber* 4E **36**
Lower Beeding. *W Sus* 3D **26**
Lower Benefield. *Nptn* 2G **63**
Lower Bentley. *Worc* 4D **61**
Lower Beobridge. *Shrp* 1B **60**
Lower Bockhampton. *Dors* 3C **14**
Lower Boddington. *Nptn* 5B **62**
Lower Bordean. *Hants* 4E **25**
Lower Brailes. *Warw* 2B **50**
Lower Breakish. *High* 1E **147**
Lower Broadheath. *Worc* 5C **60**
Lower Brynamman. *Neat* 4H **45**
Lower Bullingham. *Here* 2A **48**
Lower Bullington. *Hants* 2C **24**
Lower Burgate. *Hants* 1G **15**
Lower Cam. *Glos* 5C **48**
Lower Catesby. *Nptn* 5C **62**
Lower Chapel. *Powy* 2D **46**
Lower Cheriton. *Devn* 2E **12**
Lower Chicksgrove. *Wilts* 3E **23**
Lower Chute. *Wilts* 1B **24**
Lower Clopton. *Warw* 5F **61**
Lower Common. *Hants* 2E **25**
Lower Cumberworth. *W Yor* 4C **92**
Lower Darwen. *Bkbn* 2E **91**
Lower Dean. *Bed* 4H **63**
Lower Dean. *Devn* 2D **8**
Lower Diabaig. *High* 2G **155**
Lower Dicker. *E Sus* 4G **27**
Lower Dounreay. *High* 2B **168**
Lower Down. *Shrp* 2F **59**
Lower Dunsforth. *N Yor* 3G **99**
Lower East Carleton. *Norf* 5D **78**
Lower Egleton. *Here* 1B **48**
Lower Ellastone. *Derbs* 1F **73**
Lower End. *Nptn* 4F **63**
Lower Everleigh. *Wilts* 1G **23**
Lower Eype. *Dors* 3H **13**
Lower Failand. *N Som* 4A **34**
Lower Faintree. *Shrp* 2A **60**
Lower Farringdon. *Hants* 3F **25**
Lower Foxdale. *IOM* 4B **108**

Lower Frankton—Mariansleigh

Lower Frankton. *Shrp* 2F **71**
Lower Froyle. *Hants* 2F **25**
Lower Gabwell. *Devn* 2F **9**
Lower Gledfield. *High* 4C **164**
Lower Godney. *Som* 2H **21**
Lower Gravenhurst. *C Beds* 2B **52**
Lower Green. *Essx* 2E **53**
Lower Green. *Norf* 2B **78**
Lower Green. *Staf* 5D **72**
Lower Green. *W Ber* 5B **36**
Lower Halstow. *Kent* 4C **40**
Lower Hardres. *Kent* 5F **41**
Lower Hardwick. *Here* 5G **59**
Lower Hartshay. *Derbs* 5A **86**
Lower Hawthwaite. *Cumb* 1B **96**
Lower Hayton. *Shrp* 2H **59**
Lower Hergest. *Here* 5E **59**
Lower Heyford. *Oxon* 3C **50**
Lower Heysham. *Lanc* 3D **96**
Lower Higham. *Kent* 3B **40**
Lower Holbrook. *Suff* 2E **55**
Lower Holditch. *Dors* 2G **13**
Lower Hordley. *Shrp* 3F **71**
Lower Horncroft. *W Sus* 4B **26**
Lower Horsebridge. *E Sus* 4G **27**
Lower Kilcott. *Glos* 3C **34**
Lower Killeyan. *Arg* 5A **124**
Lower Kingcombe. *Dors* 3A **14**
Lower Kingswood. *Surr* 5D **38**
Lower Kinnerton. *Ches W* 4F **83**
Lower Langford. *N Som* 5H **33**
Lower Largo. *Fife* 3G **137**
Lower Layham. *Suff* 1D **54**
Lower Ledwyche. *Shrp* 3H **59**
Lower Leigh. *Staf* 2E **73**
Lower Lemington. *Glos* 2H **49**
Lower Lenie. *High* 1H **149**
Lower Ley. *Glos* 4C **48**
Lower Llanfadog. *Powy* 4B **58**
Lower Lode. *Glos* 2D **49**
Lower Lovacott. *Devn* 4F **19**
Lower Loxhore. *Devn* 3G **19**
Lower Loxley. *Staf* 2E **73**
Lower Lydbrook. *Glos* 4A **48**
Lower Lye. *Here* 4G **59**
Lower Machen. *Newp* 3F **33**
Lower Maes-coed. *Here* 2G **47**
Lower Meend. *Glos* 5A **48**
Lower Milovaig. *High* 3A **154**
Lower Moor. *Worc* 1E **49**
Lower Morton. *S Glo* 2B **34**
Lower Mountain. *Flin* 5F **83**
Lower Nazeing. *Essx* 5D **53**
Lower Nyland. *Dors* 4C **22**
Lower Oakfield. *Fife* 4D **136**
Lower Oddington. *Glos* 3H **49**
Lower Ollach. *High* 5E **155**
Lower Penarth. *V Glam* 5E **33**
Lower Penn. *Staf* 1C **60**
Lower Pennington. *Hants* 3B **16**
Lower Peover. *Ches W* 3B **84**
Lower Pitkerrie. *High* 1C **158**
Lower Place. *G Man* 3H **91**
Lower Quinton. *Warw* 1G **49**
Lower Rainham. *Medw* 4C **40**
Lower Raydon. *Suff* 2D **54**
Lower Seagry. *Wilts* 3E **35**
Lower Shelton. *C Beds* 1H **51**
Lower Shiplake. *Oxon* 4F **37**
Lower Shuckburgh. *Warw* 4B **62**
Lower Skelty. *Swan* 3F **31**
Lower Slade. *Devn* 2F **19**
Lower Slaughter. *Glos* 3G **49**
Lower Soudley. *Glos* 4B **48**
Lower Stanton St Quintin. *Wilts* 3E **35**
Lower Stoke. *Medw* 3C **40**
Lower Stondon. *C Beds* 2B **52**
Lower Stonnall. *Staf* 5E **73**
Lower Stow Bedon. *Norf* 1B **66**
Lower Street. *Norf* 2E **79**
Lower Strensham. *Worc* 1E **49**
Lower Sundon. *C Beds* 3A **52**
Lower Swanwick. *Hants* 2C **16**
Lower Swell. *Glos* 3G **49**
Lower Tale. *Devn* 2D **12**
Lower Tean. *Staf* 2E **73**
Lower Thurlton. *Norf* 1G **67**
Lower Thurnham. *Lanc* 4D **96**
Lower Thurvaston. *Derbs* 2G **73**
Lowertown. *Corn* 4D **4**
Lower Town. *Devn* 5H **11**
Lower Town. *Here* 1B **48**
Lower Town. *IOS* 1B **4**
Lowertown. *Orkn* 8D **172**
Lower Town. *Pemb* 1D **42**
Lower Tysoe. *Warw* 1B **50**
Lower Upham. *Hants* 1D **16**
Lower Upnor. *Medw* 3B **40**
Lower Vexford. *Som* 3E **20**
Lower Walton. *Warr* 2A **84**
Lower Wear. *Devn* 4C **12**
Lower Weare. *Som* 1H **21**
Lower Welson. *Here* 5E **59**
Lower Whatcombe. *Dors* 2D **14**
Lower Whitley. *Ches W* 3A **84**
Lower Wield. *Hants* 2E **25**
Lower Winchendon. *Buck* 4F **51**
Lower Withington. *Ches E* 4C **84**
Lower Woodend. *Buck* 3G **37**
Lower Woodford. *Wilts* 3G **23**
Lower Wraxall. *Dors* 2A **14**
Lower Wych. *Ches W* 1G **71**
Lower Wyche. *Worc* 1C **48**
Lowesby. *Leics* 5E **74**
Lowestoft. *Suff* 1H **67**
Loweswater. *Cumb* 2C **102**
Low Etherley. *Dur* 2E **105**
Lowfield Heath. *W Sus* 1D **26**
Lowford. *Hants* 1C **16**
Low Fulney. *Linc* 3B **76**
Low Gate. *Nmbd* 3C **114**
Lowgill. *Cumb* 5H **103**
Lowgill. *Lanc* 3F **97**
Low Grantley. *N Yor* 2E **99**
Low Green. *N Yor* 4E **98**
Low Habberley. *Worc* 3C **60**
Low Ham. *Som* 4H **21**
Low Hameringham. *Linc* 4C **88**
Low Hawkser. *N Yor* 4G **107**
Low Hesket. *Cumb* 5F **113**
Low Hesleyhurst. *Nmbd* 5E **121**
Lowick. *Cumb* 1B **96**
Lowick. *Nptn* 2G **63**
Lowick. *Nmbd* 1E **121**
Lowick Bridge. *Cumb* 1B **96**
Lowick Green. *Cumb* 1B **96**
Low Knipe. *Cumb* 3G **103**
Low Leighton. *Derbs* 2E **85**
Low Lorton. *Cumb* 2C **102**
Low Marishes. *N Yor* 2C **100**
Low Marnham. *Notts* 4F **87**
Low Mill. *N Yor* 5D **106**
Low Moor. *Lanc* 5G **97**
Low Moor. *W Yor* 2B **92**
Low Moorsley. *Tyne* 5G **115**
Low Newton-by-the-Sea. *Nmbd* 2G **121**
Lownie Moor. *Ang* 4D **145**
Lowood. *Bord* 1H **119**
Low Row. *Cumb* 3G **113** (nr. Brampton)
Low Row. *Cumb* 5C **112** (nr. Wigton)
Low Row. *N Yor* 5C **104**
Lowsonford. *Warw* 4F **61**
Low Street. *Norf* 5C **78**
Lowther. *Cumb* 2G **103**
Lowthorpe. *E Yor* 3E **101**
Lowton. *Devn* 2G **11**
Lowton. *G Man* 1A **84**
Lowton. *Som* 1E **13**
Lowton Common. *G Man* 1A **84**
Low Torry. *Fife* 1D **128**
Low Toynton. *Linc* 3B **88**
Low Valleyfield. *Fife* 1C **128**
Low Westwood. *Dur* 4E **115**
Low Whinnow. *Cumb* 4E **112**
Low Wood. *Cumb* 1C **96**
Low Worsall. *N Yor* 4A **106**
Low Wray. *Cumb* 4E **103**
Loxbeare. *Devn* 1C **12**
Loxhill. *Surr* 2B **26**
Loxhore. *Devn* 3G **19**
Loxley. *S Yor* 2H **85**
Loxley. *Warw* 5G **61**
Loxley Green. *Staf* 2E **73**
Loxton. *N Som* 1G **21**
Loxwood. *W Sus* 2B **26**
Lubcroy. *High* 3A **164**
Lubenham. *Leics* 2E **62**
Lubinvullin. *High* 2F **167**
Luccombe. *Som* 2C **20**
Luccombe Village. *IOW* 4D **16**
Lucker. *Nmbd* 1F **121**
Luckett. *Corn* 5D **11**
Luckington. *Wilts* 3D **34**
Lucklawhill. *Fife* 1G **137**
Luckwell Bridge. *Som* 3C **20**
Lucton. *Here* 4G **59**
Ludag. *W Isl* 7C **170**
Ludborough. *Linc* 1B **88**
Ludchurch. *Pemb* 3F **43**
Luddenden. *W Yor* 2A **92**
Luddenden Foot. *W Yor* 2A **92**
Luddenham. *Kent* 4D **40**
Ludderburn. *Cumb* 5F **103**
Luddesdown. *Kent* 4A **40**
Luddington. *N Lin* 3B **94**
Luddington. *Warw* 5F **61**
Luddington in the Brook. *Nptn* 2A **64**
Ludford. *Linc* 2A **88**
Ludford. *Shrp* 3H **59**
Ludgershall. *Buck* 4E **51**
Ludgershall. *Wilts* 1A **24**
Ludgvan. *Corn* 3C **4**
Ludham. *Norf* 4F **79**
Ludlow. *Shrp* 3H **59**
Ludstone. *Shrp* 1C **60**
Ludwell. *Wilts* 4E **23**
Ludworth. *Dur* 5G **115**
Luffenhall. *Herts* 3C **52**
Luffincott. *Devn* 3D **10**
Lugar. *E Ayr* 2E **117**
Luggate Burn. *E Lot* 2C **130**
Lugg Green. *Here* 4G **59**
Luggiebank. *N Lan* 2A **128**
Lugton. *E Ayr* 4F **127**
Lugwardine. *Here* 1A **48**
Luib. *High* 1D **146**
Luib. *Stir* 1D **135**
Lulham. *Here* 1H **47**
Lullington. *Derbs* 4G **73**
Lullington. *Som* 1C **22**
Lulsgate Bottom. *N Som* 5A **34**
Lulsley. *Worc* 5B **60**
Lulworth Camp. *Dors* 4D **14**
Lumb. *Lanc* 2G **91**
Lumb. *W Yor* 2A **92**
Lumby. *N Yor* 1E **93**
Lumphanan. *Abers* 3C **152**
Lumphinnans. *Fife* 4D **136**
Lumsdaine. *Bord* 3E **131**
Lumsden. *Abers* 1B **152**
Lunan. *Ang* 3F **145**
Lunanhead. *Ang* 3D **145**
Luncarty. *Per* 1C **136**
Lund. *E Yor* 5D **100**
Lund. *N Yor* 1G **93**
Lundie. *Ang* 5B **144**
Lundin Links. *Fife* 3G **137**
Lundy Green. *Norf* 1E **67**
Lunna. *Shet* 5F **173**
Lunning. *Shet* 5G **173**
Lunnon. *Swan* 4E **31**
Lunsford. *Kent* 5B **40**
Lunsford's Cross. *E Sus* 4B **28**
Lunt. *Mers* 4B **90**
Luppitt. *Devn* 2E **13**
Lupridge. *Devn* 3D **8**
Lupset. *W Yor* 3D **92**
Lupton. *Cumb* 1E **97**
Lurgashall. *W Sus* 3A **26**
Lurley. *Devn* 1C **12**
Lusby. *Linc* 4C **88**
Luscombe. *Devn* 3D **9**
Luson. *Devn* 4C **8**
Luss. *Arg* 4C **134**
Lussagiven. *Arg* 1E **125**
Lusta. *High* 3B **154**
Lustleigh. *Devn* 4A **12**
Luston. *Here* 4G **59**
Luthermuir. *Abers* 2F **145**
Luthrie. *Fife* 2F **137**
Lutley. *Staf* 2C **60**
Luton. *Devn* 2D **12** (nr. Honiton)
Luton. *Devn* 5C **12** (nr. Teignmouth)
Luton. *Lutn* 3A **52** & **201**
Luton (London) Airport. *Lutn* 3B **52** & **216**
Lutterworth. *Leics* 2C **62**
Lutton. *Devn* 3B **8** (nr. Ivybridge)
Lutton. *Devn* 2C **8** (nr. South Brent)
Lutton. *Linc* 3D **76**
Lutton. *Nptn* 2A **64**
Lutton Gowts. *Linc* 3D **76**
Lutworthy. *Devn* 1A **12**
Luxborough. *Som* 3C **20**
Luxley. *Glos* 3B **48**
Luxulyan. *Corn* 3E **7**
Lybster. *High* 5E **169**
Lydbury North. *Shrp* 2F **59**
Lydcott. *Devn* 3G **19**
Lydd. *Kent* 3E **29**
Lydden. *Kent* 1G **29** (nr. Dover)
Lydden. *Kent* 4H **41** (nr. Margate)
Lyddington. *Rut* 1F **63**
Lydd (London Ashford) Airport. *Kent* 3E **29**
Lydd-on-Sea. *Kent* 3E **29**
Lydeard St Lawrence. *Som* 3E **21**
Lyde Green. *Hants* 1F **25**
Lydford. *Devn* 4F **11**
Lydford Fair Place. *Som* 3A **22**
Lydgate. *G Man* 4H **91**
Lydgate. *W Yor* 2H **91**
Lydham. *Shrp* 1F **59**
Lydiard Millicent. *Wilts* 3F **35**
Lydiate. *Mers* 4B **90**
Lydiate Ash. *Worc* 3D **61**
Lydlinch. *Dors* 1C **14**
Lydmarsh. *Som* 2G **13**
Lydney. *Glos* 5B **48**
Lydstep. *Pemb* 5E **43**
Lye. *W Mid* 2D **60**
Lye Green. *Buck* 5H **51**
Lye Green. *E Sus* 2G **27**
Lye Head. *Worc* 3B **60**
Lye, The. *Shrp* 1A **60**
Lyford. *Oxon* 2B **36**
Lyham. *Nmbd* 1E **121**
Lylestone. *N Ayr* 5E **127**
Lymbridge Green. *Kent* 1F **29**
Lyme Regis. *Dors* 3G **13**
Lyminge. *Kent* 1F **29**
Lymington. *Hants* 3B **16**
Lyminster. *W Sus* 5B **26**
Lymm. *Warr* 2A **84**
Lymore. *Hants* 3A **16**
Lympne. *Kent* 2F **29**
Lympsham. *Som* 1G **21**
Lympstone. *Devn* 4C **12**
Lynaberack Lodge. *High* 4B **150**
Lynbridge. *Devn* 2H **19**
Lynch. *Som* 2C **20**
Lynchat. *High* 3B **150**
Lynch Green. *Norf* 5D **78**
Lyndhurst. *Hants* 2B **16**
Lyndon. *Rut* 5G **75**
Lyne. *Bord* 5F **129**
Lyne. *Surr* 4B **38**
Lyneal. *Shrp* 2G **71**
Lyne Down. *Here* 2B **48**
Lyneham. *Oxon* 3A **50**
Lyneham. *Wilts* 4F **35**
Lyneholmeford. *Cumb* 2G **113**
Lynemouth. *Nmbd* 5G **121**
Lyne of Gorthleck. *High* 1H **149**
Lyne of Skene. *Abers* 2E **153**
Lynesack. *Dur* 2D **105**
Lyness. *Orkn* 8C **172**
Lyng. *Norf* 4C **78**
Lyngate. *Norf* 2E **79** (nr. North Walsham)
Lyngate. *Norf* 3F **79** (nr. Worstead)
Lynmouth. *Devn* 2H **19**
Lynn. *Staf* 5E **73**
Lynn. *Telf* 4B **72**
Lynsted. *Kent* 4D **40**
Lynstone. *Corn* 2C **10**
Lynton. *Devn* 2H **19**
Lynwilg. *High* 2C **150**
Lyon's Gate. *Dors* 2B **14**
Lyonshall. *Here* 5F **59**
Lytchett Matravers. *Dors* 3E **15**
Lytchett Minster. *Dors* 3E **15**
Lyth. *High* 2E **169**
Lytham. *Lanc* 2B **90**
Lytham St Anne's. *Lanc* 2B **90**
Lythe. *N Yor* 3F **107**
Lythes. *Orkn* 9D **172**
Lythmore. *High* 2C **168**

M

Mabe Burnthouse. *Corn* 5B **6**
Mabie. *Dum* 2A **112**
Mablethorpe. *Linc* 2E **89**
Macbiehill. *Bord* 4E **129**
Macclesfield. *Ches E* 3D **84**
Macclesfield Forest. *Ches E* 3D **85**
Macduff. *Abers* 2E **160**
Machan. *S Lan* 4A **128**
Macharioch. *Arg* 5B **122**
Machen. *Cphy* 3F **33**
Machrie. *N Ayr* 2C **122**
Machrihanish. *Arg* 3A **122**
Machroes. *Gwyn* 3C **68**
Machynlleth. *Powy* 5G **69**
Mackerye End. *Herts* 4B **52**
Mackworth. *Derb* 2H **73**
Macmerry. *E Lot* 2H **129**
Maddaford. *Devn* 3F **11**
Madderty. *Per* 1B **136**
Maddington. *Wilts* 2F **23**
Maddiston. *Falk* 2C **128**
Madehurst. *W Sus* 4A **26**
Madeley. *Staf* 1B **72**
Madeley. *Telf* 5A **72**
Madeley Heath. *Staf* 1B **72**
Madeley Heath. *Worc* 3D **60**
Madford. *Devn* 1E **13**
Madingley. *Cambs* 4C **64**
Madley. *Here* 2H **47**
Madresfield. *Worc* 1D **48**
Madron. *Corn* 3B **4**
Maenaddwyn. *IOA* 2D **80**
Maenclochog. *Pemb* 2E **43**
Maendy. *V Glam* 4D **32**
Maenporth. *Corn* 4E **5**
Maentwrog. *Gwyn* 1F **69**
Maen-y-groes. *Cdgn* 5C **56**
Maer. *Staf* 2B **72**
Maerdy. *Carm* 3G **45**
Maerdy. *Cnwy* 1C **70**
Maerdy. *Rhon* 2C **32**
Maesbrook. *Shrp* 3E **71**
Maesbury. *Shrp* 3F **71**
Maesbury Marsh. *Shrp* 3F **71**
Maes-glas. *Flin* 3D **82**
Maesgwyn-Isaf. *Powy* 4D **70**
Maeshafn. *Den* 4E **82**
Maes Llyn. *Cdgn* 1D **44**
Maesmynis. *Powy* 1D **46**
Maesteg. *B'end* 2B **32**
Maestir. *Cdgn* 1F **45**
Maesybont. *Carm* 4F **45**
Maesycrugiau. *Carm* 1E **45**
Maesycwmmer. *Cphy* 2E **33**
Maesyrhandir. *Powy* 1C **58**
Magdalen Laver. *Essx* 5F **53**
Maggieknockater. *Mor* 4H **159**
Magham Down. *E Sus* 4H **27**
Maghull. *Mers* 4B **90**
Magna Park. *Leics* 2C **62**
Magor. *Mon* 3H **33**
Magpie Green. *Suff* 3C **66**
Magwyr. *Mon* 3H **33**
Maidenbower. *W Sus* 2D **27**
Maiden Bradley. *Wilts* 3D **22**
Maidencombe. *Torb* 2F **9**
Maidenhayne. *Devn* 3F **13**
Maidenhead. *Wind* 3G **37**
Maiden Law. *Dur* 5E **115**
Maiden Newton. *Dors* 3A **14**
Maidens. *S Ayr* 4B **116**
Maiden's Green. *Brac* 4G **37**
Maidensgrove. *Oxon* 3F **37**
Maidenwell. *Corn* 5B **10**
Maidenwell. *Linc* 3C **88**
Maiden Wells. *Pemb* 5D **42**
Maidford. *Nptn* 5D **62**
Maids Moreton. *Buck* 2F **51**
Maidstone. *Kent* 5B **40**
Maidwell. *Nptn* 3E **63**
Mail. *Shet* 9F **173**
Maindee. *Newp* 3G **33**
Mainsforth. *Dur* 1A **106**
Mains of Auchindachy. *Mor* 4B **160**
Mains of Auchnagatt. *Abers* 4G **161**
Mains of Drum. *Abers* 4F **153**
Mains of Edingight. *Mor* 3C **160**
Mainsriddle. *Dum* 4G **111**
Mainstone. *Shrp* 2E **59**
Maisemore. *Glos* 3D **48**
Major's Green. *Worc* 3F **61**
Makeney. *Derbs* 1A **74**
Makerstoun. *Bord* 1A **120**
Malacleit. *W Isl* 1C **170**
Malaig. *High* 4E **147**
Malaig Bheag. *High* 4E **147**
Malborough. *Devn* 5D **8**
Malcoff. *Derbs* 2E **85**
Malcolmburn. *Mor* 3A **160**
Malden Rushett. *G Lon* 4C **38**
Maldon. *Essx* 5B **54**
Malham. *N Yor* 3B **98**
Maligar. *High* 2D **155**
Malinslee. *Telf* 5A **72**
Mallaig. *High* 4E **147**
Malleny Mills. *Edin* 3E **129**
Mallows Green. *Essx* 3E **53**
Malltraeth. *IOA* 4D **80**
Mallwyd. *Gwyn* 4A **70**
Malmesbury. *Wilts* 3E **35**
Malmsmead. *Devn* 2A **20**
Malpas. *Ches W* 1G **71**
Malpas. *Corn* 4C **6**
Malpas. *Newp* 2F **33**
Malswick. *Glos* 3C **48**
Maltby. *S Yor* 1C **86**
Maltby. *Stoc T* 3B **106**
Maltby le Marsh. *Linc* 2D **88**
Malt Lane. *Arg* 3H **133**
Maltman's Hill. *Kent* 1D **28**
Malton. *N Yor* 2B **100**
Malvern Link. *Worc* 1C **48**
Malvern Wells. *Worc* 1C **48**
Mamble. *Worc* 3A **60**
Mamhilad. *Mon* 5G **47**
Manaccan. *Corn* 4E **5**
Manafon. *Powy* 5D **70**
Manais. *W Isl* 9D **171**
Manaton. *Devn* 4A **12**
Manby. *Linc* 2C **88**
Mancetter. *Warw* 1H **61**
Manchester. *G Man* 1C **84** & **201**
Manchester International Airport. *G Man* 2C **84** & **216**
Mancot. *Flin* 4F **83**
Manea. *Cambs* 2D **65**
Maney. *W Mid* 1F **61**
Manfield. *N Yor* 3F **105**
Mangotsfield. *S Glo* 4B **34**
Mangurstadh. *W Isl* 4C **171**
Mankinholes. *W Yor* 2H **91**
Manley. *Ches W* 3H **83**
Manmoel. *Cphy* 5E **47**
Mannal. *Arg* 4A **138**
Mannerston. *Falk* 2D **128**
Manningford Bohune. *Wilts* 1G **23**
Manningford Bruce. *Wilts* 1G **23**
Manningham. *W Yor* 1B **92**
Mannings Heath. *W Sus* 3D **26**
Mannington. *Dors* 2F **15**
Manningtree. *Essx* 2E **54**
Mannofield. *Aber* 3G **153**
Manorbier. *Pemb* 5E **43**
Manorbier Newton. *Pemb* 5E **43**
Manorowen. *Pemb* 1D **42**
Manor Park. *G Lon* 2F **39**
Mansell Gamage. *Here* 1G **47**
Mansell Lacy. *Here* 1H **47**
Mansergh. *Cumb* 1F **97**
Mansewood. *Glas* 3G **127**
Mansfield. *E Ayr* 3F **117**
Mansfield. *Notts* 4C **86**
Mansfield Woodhouse. *Notts* 4C **86**
Mansriggs. *Cumb* 1B **96**
Manston. *Dors* 1D **14**
Manston. *Kent* 4H **41**
Manston. *W Yor* 1D **92**
Manswood. *Dors* 2E **15**
Manthorpe. *Linc* 4H **75** (nr. Bourne)
Manthorpe. *Linc* 2G **75** (nr. Grantham)
Manton. *N Lin* 4C **94**
Manton. *Notts* 3C **86**
Manton. *Rut* 5F **75**
Manton. *Wilts* 5G **35**
Manuden. *Essx* 3E **53**
Maperton. *Som* 4B **22**
Maplebeck. *Notts* 4E **86**
Maple Cross. *Herts* 1B **38**
Mapledurham. *Oxon* 4E **37**
Mapledurwell. *Hants* 1E **25**
Maplehurst. *W Sus* 3C **26**
Maplescombe. *Kent* 4G **39**
Mapperley. *Derbs* 1B **74**
Mapperley. *Notts* 1C **74**
Mapperley Park. *Notts* 1C **74**
Mapperton. *Dors* 3A **14** (nr. Beaminster)
Mapperton. *Dors* 3E **15** (nr. Poole)
Mappleborough Green. *Warw* 4E **61**
Mappleton. *Derbs* 1F **73**
Mappleton. *E Yor* 5G **101**
Mapplewell. *S Yor* 4D **92**
Mappowder. *Dors* 2C **14**
Maraig. *W Isl* 7E **171**
Marazion. *Corn* 3C **4**
Marbhig. *W Isl* 6G **171**
Marbury. *Ches E* 1H **71**
March. *Cambs* 1D **64**
Marcham. *Oxon* 2C **36**
Marchamley. *Shrp* 3H **71**
Marchington. *Staf* 2F **73**
Marchington Woodlands. *Staf* 3F **73**
Marchwiel. *Wrex* 1F **71**
Marchwood. *Hants* 1B **16**
Marcross. *V Glam* 5C **32**
Marden. *Here* 1A **48**
Marden. *Kent* 1B **28**
Marden. *Wilts* 1F **23**
Marden Beech. *Kent* 1B **28**
Marden Thorn. *Kent* 1B **28**
Mardu. *Shrp* 2E **59**
Mardy. *Mon* 4G **47**
Marefield. *Leics* 5E **75**
Mareham le Fen. *Linc* 4B **88**
Mareham on the Hill. *Linc* 4B **88**
Marehay. *Derbs* 1A **74**
Marehill. *W Sus* 4B **26**
Maresfield. *E Sus* 3F **27**
Marfleet. *Hull* 2E **95**
Marford. *Wrex* 5F **83**
Margam. *Neat* 3A **32**
Margaret Marsh. *Dors* 1D **14**
Margaret Roding. *Essx* 4F **53**
Margaretting. *Essx* 5G **53**
Margaretting Tye. *Essx* 5G **53**
Margate. *Kent* 3H **41**
Margery. *Surr* 5D **38**
Margnaheglish. *N Ayr* 2E **123**
Marham. *Norf* 5G **77**
Marhamchurch. *Corn* 2C **10**
Marholm. *Pet* 5A **76**
Marian Cwm. *Den* 3C **82**
Mariandyrys. *IOA* 2F **81**
Marian-glas. *IOA* 2E **81**
Mariansleigh. *Devn* 4H **19**

Marian-y-de. *Gwyn* 2C 68
Marine Town. *Kent* 3D 40
Marion-y-mor. *Gwyn* 2C 68
Marishader. *High* 2D 155
Marjoriebanks. *Dum* 1B 112
Mark. *Dum* 4G 109
Mark. *Som* 2G 21
Markbeech. *Kent* 1F 27
Markby. *Linc* 3D 89
Mark Causeway. *Som* 2G 21
Mark Cross. *E Sus* 2G 27
Markeaton. *Derb* 2H 73
Market Bosworth. *Leics* 5B 74
Market Deeping. *Linc* 4A 76
Market Drayton. *Shrp* 2A 72
Market End. *Warw* 2H 61
Market Harborough. *Leics* 2E 63
Markethill. *Per* 5B 144
Market Lavington. *Wilts* 1F 23
Market Overton. *Rut* 4F 75
Market Rasen. *Linc* 2A 88
Market Stainton. *Linc* 2B 88
Market Weighton. *E Yor* 5C 100
Market Weston. *Suff* 3B 66
Markfield. *Leics* 4B 74
Markham. *Cphy* 5E 47
Markinch. *Fife* 3E 137
Markington. *N Yor* 3E 99
Marksbury. *Bath* 5B 34
Mark's Corner. *IOW* 3C 16
Marks Tey. *Essx* 3C 54
Markwell. *Corn* 3H 7
Markyate. *Herts* 4A 52
Marlborough. *Wilts* 5G 35
Marlcliff. *Warw* 5E 61
Marldon. *Devn* 2E 9
Marle Green. *E Sus* 4G 27
Marlesford. *Suff* 5F 67
Marley Green. *Ches E* 1H 71
Marley Hill. *Tyne* 4F 115
Marlingford. *Norf* 5D 78
Marloes. *Pemb* 4B 42
Marlow. *Buck* 3G 37
Marlow. *Here* 3G 59
Marlow Bottom. *Buck* 3G 37
Marlow Common. *Buck* 3G 37
Marlpit Hill. *Kent* 1F 27
Marlpits. *E Sus* 3F 27
Marlpool. *Derbs* 1B 74
Marnhull. *Dors* 1C 14
Marnoch. *Abers* 3C 160
Marnock. *N Lan* 3A 128
Marple. *G Man* 2D 84
Marr. *S Yor* 4F 93
Marrel. *High* 2H 165
Marrick. *N Yor* 5D 105
Marrister. *Shet* 5G 173
Marros. *Carm* 4G 43
Marsden. *Tyne* 3G 115
Marsden. *W Yor* 3A 92
Marsett. *N Yor* 1B 98
Marsh. *Buck* 5G 51
Marsh. *Devn* 1F 13
Marshall Meadows. *Nmbd* 4F 131
Marshalsea. *Dors* 2G 13
Marshalswick. *Herts* 5B 52
Marsham. *Norf* 3D 78
Marshaw. *Lanc* 4E 97
Marsh Baldon. *Oxon* 2D 36
Marsh Benham. *W Ber* 5C 36
Marshborough. *Kent* 5H 41
Marshbrook. *Shrp* 2G 59
Marshbury. *Essx* 4G 53
Marshchapel. *Linc* 1C 88
Marshfield. *Newp* 3F 33
Marshfield. *S Glo* 4C 34
Marshgate. *Corn* 3B 10
Marsh Gibbon. *Buck* 3E 51
Marsh Green. *Devn* 3D 12
Marsh Green. *Kent* 1F 27
Marsh Green. *Staf* 5C 84
Marsh Green. *Telf* 4A 72
Marsh Lane. *Derbs* 3B 86
Marshside. *Kent* 4G 41
Marshside. *Mers* 3B 90
Marsh Side. *Norf* 1G 77
Marsh Street. *Som* 2C 20
Marsh, The. *Powy* 1F 59
Marsh, The. *Shrp* 3A 72
Marshwood. *Dors* 3G 13
Marske. *N Yor* 4E 105
Marske-by-the-Sea. *Red C* 2D 106
Marston. *Ches W* 3A 84
Marston. *Here* 5F 59
Marston. *Linc* 1F 75
Marston. *Oxon* 5D 50
Marston. *Staf* 3D 72
(nr. Stafford)
Marston. *Staf* 4C 72
(nr. Wheaton Aston)
Marston. *Warw* 1G 61
Marston. *Wilts* 1E 23
Marston Doles. *Warw* 5B 62
Marston Green. *W Mid* 2F 61
Marston Hill. *Glos* 2G 35
Marston Jabbett. *Warw* 2A 62
Marston Magna. *Som* 4A 22
Marston Meysey. *Wilts* 2G 35
Marston Montgomery. *Derbs* 2F 73
Marston Moretaine. *C Beds* 1H 51
Marston on Dove. *Derbs* 3G 73
Marston St Lawrence.
Nptn 1D 50
Marston Stannett. *Here* 5H 59
Marston Trussell. *Nptn* 2D 62
Marstow. *Here* 4A 48
Marsworth. *Buck* 4H 51
Marten. *Wilts* 5A 36
Marthall. *Ches E* 3C 84
Martham. *Norf* 4G 79
Marthwaite. *Cumb* 5H 103
Martin. *Hants* 1F 15
Martin. *Kent* 1H 29
Martin. *Linc* 4B 88
(nr. Horncastle)
Martin. *Linc* 5A 88
(nr. Metheringham)
Martindale. *Cumb* 3F 103
Martin Dales. *Linc* 4A 88
Martin Drove End. *Hants* 4F 23
Martinhoe. *Devn* 2G 19
Martinhoe Cross. *Devn* 2G 19
Martin Hussingtree. *Worc* 4C 60
Martin Mill. *Kent* 1H 29
Martinscroft. *Warr* 2A 84
Martin's Moss. *Ches E* 4C 84
Martinstown. *Dors* 4B 14
Martlesham. *Suff* 1F 55
Martlesham Heath. *Suff* 1F 55
Martletwy. *Pemb* 3E 43
Martley. *Worc* 5B 60
Martock. *Som* 1H 13
Marton. *Ches E* 4C 84
Marton. *Cumb* 2B 96
Marton. *E Yor* 3G 101
(nr. Bridlington)
Marton. *E Yor* 1E 95
(nr. Hull)
Marton. *Linc* 2F 87
Marton. *Midd* 3C 106
Marton. *N Yor* 3G 99
(nr. Boroughbridge)
Marton. *N Yor* 1B 100
(nr. Pickering)
Marton. *Shrp* 3G 71
(nr. Myddle)
Marton. *Shrp* 5E 71
(nr. Worthen)
Marton. *Warw* 4B 62
Marton Abbey. *N Yor* 3H 99
Marton-le-Moor. *N Yor* 2F 99
Martyr's Green. *Surr* 5B 38
Martyr Worthy. *Hants* 3D 24
Marwick. *Orkn* 5B 172
Marwood. *Devn* 3F 19
Marybank. *High* 3G 157
(nr. Dingwall)
Marybank. *High* 1B 158
(nr. Invergordon)
Maryburgh. *High* 3H 157
Maryfield. *Corn* 3A 8
Maryhill. *Glas* 3G 127
Marykirk. *Abers* 2F 145
Marylebone. *G Lon* 2D 39
Marylebone. *G Man* 4D 90
Marypark. *Mor* 5F 159
Maryport. *Cumb* 1B 102
Maryport. *Dum* 5E 109
Marystow. *Devn* 4E 11
Mary Tavy. *Devn* 5F 11
Maryton. *Ang* 3C 144
(nr. Kirriemuir)
Maryton. *Ang* 3F 145
(nr. Montrose)
Marywell. *Abers* 4C 152
Marywell. *Ang* 4F 145
Masham. *N Yor* 1E 98
Mashbury. *Essx* 4G 53
Masongill. *N Yor* 2F 97
Masons Lodge. *Abers* 3F 153
Mastin Moor. *Derbs* 3B 86
Mastrick. *Aber* 3G 153
Matching. *Essx* 4F 53
Matching Green. *Essx* 4F 53
Matching Tye. *Essx* 4F 53
Matfen. *Nmbd* 2D 114
Matfield. *Kent* 1A 28
Mathern. *Mon* 2A 34
Mathon. *Here* 1C 48
Mathry. *Pemb* 1C 42
Matlaske. *Norf* 2D 78
Matlock. *Derbs* 4G 85
Matlock Bath. *Derbs* 5G 85
Matterdale End. *Cumb* 2E 103
Mattersey. *Notts* 2D 86
Mattersey Thorpe. *Notts* 2D 86
Mattingley. *Hants* 1F 25
Mattishall. *Norf* 4C 78
Mattishall Burgh. *Norf* 4C 78
Mauchline. *E Ayr* 2D 117
Maud. *Abers* 4G 161
Maudlin. *Corn* 2E 7
Maugersbury. *Glos* 3G 49
Maughold. *IOM* 2D 108
Maulden. *C Beds* 2A 52
Maulds Meaburn. *Cumb* 3H 103
Maunby. *N Yor* 1F 99
Maund Bryan. *Here* 5H 59
Mautby. *Norf* 4G 79
Mavesyn Ridware. *Staf* 4E 73
Mavis Enderby. *Linc* 4C 88
Mawbray. *Cumb* 5B 112
Mawdesley. *Lanc* 3C 90
Mawdlam. *B'end* 3B 32
Mawgan. *Corn* 4E 5
Mawgan Porth. *Corn* 2C 6
Maw Green. *Ches E* 5B 84
Mawla. *Corn* 4B 6
Mawnan. *Corn* 4E 5
Mawnan Smith. *Corn* 4E 5
Mawsley Village. *Nptn* 3F 63
Mawthorpe. *Linc* 3D 88
Maxey. *Pet* 5A 76
Maxstoke. *Warw* 2G 61
Maxted Street. *Kent* 1F 29
Maxton. *Kent* 1G 29
Maxton. *Bord* 1A 120
Maxwellheugh. *Bord* 1B 120
Maxwelltown. *Dum* 2A 112
Maxworthy. *Corn* 3C 10
Mayals. *Swan* 4F 31
Maybole. *S Ayr* 4C 116
Maybush. *Sotn* 1B 16
Mayes Green. *Surr* 2C 26
Mayfield. *E Sus* 3G 27
Mayfield. *Midl* 3G 129
Mayfield. *Per* 1C 136
Mayfield. *Staf* 1F 73
Mayford. *Surr* 5A 38
Mayhill. *Swan* 3F 31
Mayland. *Essx* 5C 54
Maylandsea. *Essx* 5C 54
Maynard's Green. *E Sus* 4G 27
Maypole. *IOS* 1B 4
Maypole. *Kent* 4G 41
Maypole. *Mon* 4H 47
Maypole Green. *Norf* 1G 67
Maypole Green. *Suff* 5B 66
Mayshill. *S Glo* 3B 34
Maywick. *Shet* 9E 173
Mead. *Devn* 1C 10
Meadgate. *Bath* 1B 22
Meadle. *Buck* 5G 51
Meadowbank. *Ches W* 4A 84
Meadowfield. *Dur* 1F 105
Meadow Green. *Here* 5B 60
Meadowmill. *E Lot* 2H 129
Meadows. *Nott* 2C 74
Meadowtown. *Shrp* 5F 71
Meadwell. *Devn* 4E 11
Mealabost. *W Isl* 2G 171
(nr. Borgh)
Mealabost. *W Isl* 4G 171
(nr. Stornoway)
Mealasta. *W Isl* 5B 171
Meal Bank. *Cumb* 5G 103
Mealrigg. *Cumb* 5C 112
Mealsgate. *Cumb* 5D 112
Meanwood. *W Yor* 1C 92
Mearbeck. *N Yor* 3H 97
Meare. *Som* 2H 21
Meare Green. *Som* 4F 21
(nr. Curry Mallet)
Meare Green. *Som* 4G 21
(nr. Stoke St Gregory)
Mears Ashby. *Nptn* 4F 63
Measham. *Leics* 4H 73
Meath Green. *Surr* 1D 27
Meathop. *Cumb* 1D 96
Meaux. *E Yor* 1D 94
Meavy. *Devn* 2B 8
Medbourne. *Leics* 1E 63
Medburn. *Nmbd* 2E 115
Meddon. *Devn* 1C 10
Meden Vale. *Notts* 4C 86
Medlam. *Linc* 5C 88
Medlicott. *Shrp* 1G 59
Medmenham. *Buck* 3G 37
Medomsley. *Dur* 4E 115
Medstead. *Hants* 3E 25
Medway Towns. *Medw* 4B 40
Meerbrook. *Staf* 4D 85
Meer End. *W Mid* 3G 61
Meers Bridge. *Linc* 2D 89
Meesden. *Herts* 2E 53
Meeson. *Telf* 3A 72
Meeth. *Devn* 2F 11
Meeting Green. *Suff* 5G 65
Meeting House Hill. *Norf* 3F 79
Meidrim. *Carm* 2G 43
Meifod. *Powy* 4D 70
Meigle. *Per* 4B 144
Meikle Earnock. *S Lan* 4A 128
Meikle Kilchattan Butts. *Arg* 4B 126
Meikleour. *Per* 5A 144
Meikle Tarty. *Abers* 1G 153
Meikle Wartle. *Abers* 5E 160
Meinciau. *Carm* 4E 45
Meir. *Stoke* 1D 72
Meir Heath. *Staf* 1D 72
Melbourn. *Cambs* 1D 53
Melbourne. *Derbs* 3A 74
Melbourne. *E Yor* 5B 100
Melbury Abbas. *Dors* 4D 23
Melbury Bubb. *Dors* 2A 14
Melbury Osmond. *Dors* 2A 14
Melbury Sampford. *Dors* 2A 14
Melby. *Shet* 6C 173
Melchbourne. *Bed* 4H 63
Melcombe Bingham. *Dors* 2C 14
Melcombe Regis. *Dors* 4B 14
Meldon. *Devn* 3F 11
Meldon. *Nmbd* 1E 115
Meldreth. *Cambs* 1D 53
Melfort. *Arg* 2F 133
Melgarve. *High* 4G 149
Meliden. *Den* 2C 82
Melinbyrhedyn. *Powy* 1H 57
Melincourt. *Neat* 5B 46
Melin-y-coed. *Cnwy* 4H 81
Melin-y-ddol. *Powy* 5C 70
Melin-y-wig. *Den* 1C 70
Melkington. *Nmbd* 5E 131
Melkinthorpe. *Cumb* 2G 103
Melkridge. *Nmbd* 3A 114
Melksham. *Wilts* 5E 35
Mellangaun. *High* 5C 162
Melldalloch. *Arg* 2H 125
Mellguards. *Cumb* 5F 113
Melling. *Lanc* 2E 97
Melling. *Mers* 4B 90
Melling Mount. *Mers* 4C 90
Mellis. *Suff* 3C 66
Mellon Charles. *High* 4C 162
Mellon Udrigle. *High* 4C 162
Mellor. *G Man* 2D 85
Mellor. *Lanc* 1E 91
Mellor Brook. *Lanc* 1E 91
Mells. *Som* 2C 22
Melmerby. *Cumb* 1H 103
Melmerby. *N Yor* 1C 98
(nr. Middleham)
Melmerby. *N Yor* 2F 99
(nr. Ripon)
Melplash. *Dors* 3H 13
Melrose. *Bord* 1H 119
Melsetter. *Orkn* 9B 172
Melsonby. *N Yor* 4E 105
Meltham. *W Yor* 3A 92
Meltham Mills. *W Yor* 3B 92
Melton. *E Yor* 2C 94
Melton. *Suff* 5E 67
Meltonby. *E Yor* 4B 100
Melton Constable. *Norf* 2C 78
Melton Mowbray. *Leics* 4E 75
Melton Ross. *N Lin* 3D 94
Melvaig. *High* 5B 162
Melverley. *Shrp* 4F 71
Melverley Green. *Shrp* 4F 71
Melvich. *High* 2A 168
Membury. *Devn* 2F 13
Memsie. *Abers* 2G 161
Memus. *Ang* 3D 144
Menabilly. *Corn* 3E 7
Menai Bridge. *IOA* 3E 81
Mendham. *Suff* 2E 67
Mendlesham. *Suff* 4D 66
Mendlesham Green. *Suff* 4C 66
Menethorpe. *N Yor* 3B 100
Menheniot. *Corn* 2G 7
Menithwood. *Worc* 4B 60
Menna. *Corn* 3D 6
Mennock. *Dum* 4H 117
Menston. *W Yor* 5D 98
Menstrie. *Clac* 4H 135
Menthorpe. *N Yor* 1H 93
Mentmore. *Buck* 4H 51
Meole Brace. *Shrp* 4G 71
Meols. *Mers* 2E 83
Meon. *Hants* 2D 16
Meonstoke. *Hants* 4E 24
Meopham. *Kent* 4H 39
Meopham Green. *Kent* 4H 39
Meopham Station. *Kent* 4H 39
Mepal. *Cambs* 2D 64
Meppershall. *C Beds* 2B 52
Merbach. *Here* 1G 47
Mercaston. *Derbs* 1G 73
Merchiston. *Edin* 2F 129
Mere. *Ches E* 2B 84
Mere. *Wilts* 3D 22
Mere Brow. *Lanc* 3C 90
Mereclough. *Lanc* 1G 91
Mere Green. *W Mid* 1F 61
Mere Green. *Worc* 4D 60
Mere Heath. *Ches W* 3A 84
Mereside. *Bkpl* 1B 90
Meretown. *Staf* 3B 72
Mereworth. *Kent* 5A 40
Meriden. *W Mid* 2G 61
Merkadale. *High* 5C 154
Merkland. *S Ayr* 5B 116
Merkland Lodge. *High* 1A 164
Merley. *Pool* 3F 15
Merlin's Bridge. *Pemb* 3D 42
Merridge. *Som* 3F 21
Merrington. *Shrp* 3G 71
Merrion. *Pemb* 5D 42
Merriott. *Som* 1H 13
Merrivale. *Devn* 5F 11
Merrow. *Surr* 5B 38
Merrybent. *Darl* 3F 105
Merry Lees. *Leics* 5B 74
Merrymeet. *Corn* 2G 7
Mersham. *Kent* 2E 29
Merstham. *Surr* 5D 39
Merston. *W Sus* 2G 17
Merstone. *IOW* 4D 16
Merther. *Corn* 4C 6
Merthyr. *Carm* 3D 44
Merthyr Cynog. *Powy* 2C 46
Merthyr Dyfan. *V Glam* 4E 32
Merthyr Mawr. *B'end* 4B 32
Merthyr Tudful. *Mer T* 5D 46
Merthyr Tydfil. *Mer T* 5D 46
Merthyr Vale. *Mer T* 5D 46
Merton. *Devn* 1F 11
Merton. *G Lon* 4D 38
Merton. *Norf* 1B 66
Merton. *Oxon* 4D 50
Meshaw. *Devn* 1A 12
Messing. *Essx* 4B 54
Messingham. *N Lin* 4B 94
Metcombe. *Devn* 3D 12
Metfield. *Suff* 2E 67
Metherell. *Corn* 2A 8
Metheringham. *Linc* 4H 87
Methil. *Fife* 4F 137
Methilhill. *Fife* 4F 137
Methley. *W Yor* 2D 93
Methley Junction. *W Yor* 2D 93
Methlick. *Abers* 5F 161
Methven. *Per* 1C 136
Methwold. *Norf* 1G 65
Methwold Hythe. *Norf* 1G 65
Mettingham. *Suff* 1F 67
Metton. *Norf* 2D 78
Mevagissey. *Corn* 4E 6
Mexborough. *S Yor* 4E 93
Mey. *High* 1E 169
Meysey Hampton. *Glos* 2G 35
Miabhag. *W Isl* 8D 171
(nr. Tarbert)
Miabhaig. *W Isl* 7C 171
(nr. Cliasmol)
Miabhaig. *W Isl* 4D 171
(nr. Timsgearraidh)
Mial. *High* 1G 155
Michaelchurch. *Here* 3A 48
Michaelchurch Escley. *Here* 2G 47
Michaelchurch-on-Arrow. *Powy* 5E 59
Michaelston-le-Pit. *V Glam* 4E 33
Michaelston-y-Fedw. *Newp* 3F 33
Michaelstow. *Corn* 5A 10
Michelcombe. *Devn* 2C 8
Micheldever. *Hants* 3D 24
Micheldever Station. *Hants* 2D 24
Michelmersh. *Hants* 4B 24
Mickfield. *Suff* 4D 66
Micklebring. *S Yor* 1C 86
Mickleby. *N Yor* 3F 107
Micklefield. *W Yor* 1E 93
Micklefield Green. *Herts* 1B 38
Mickleham. *Surr* 5C 38
Mickleover. *Derb* 2H 73
Micklethwaite. *Cumb* 4D 112
Micklethwaite. *W Yor* 5D 98
Mickleton. *Dur* 2C 104
Mickleton. *Glos* 1G 49
Mickletown. *W Yor* 2D 93
Mickle Trafford. *Ches W* 4G 83
Mickley. *N Yor* 2E 99
Mickley Green. *Suff* 5H 65
Mickley Square. *Nmbd* 3D 115
Mid Ardlaw. *Abers* 2G 161
Midbea. *Orkn* 3D 172
Mid Beltie. *Abers* 3D 152
Mid Calder. *W Lot* 3D 129
Mid Clyth. *High* 5E 169
Middle Assendon. *Oxon* 3F 37
Middle Aston. *Oxon* 3C 50
Middle Barton. *Oxon* 3C 50
Middlebie. *Dum* 2D 112
Middle Chinnock. *Som* 1H 13
Middle Claydon. *Buck* 3F 51
Middlecliffe. *S Yor* 4E 93
Middlecott. *Devn* 4H 11
Middle Drums. *Ang* 3E 145
Middle Duntisbourne. *Glos* 5E 49
Middle Essie. *Abers* 3H 161
Middleforth Green. *Lanc* 2D 90
Middleham. *N Yor* 1D 98
Middle Handley. *Derbs* 3B 86
Middle Harling. *Norf* 2B 66
Middlehope. *Shrp* 2G 59
Middle Littleton. *Worc* 1F 49
Middle Maes-coed. *Here* 2G 47
Middlemarsh. *Dors* 2B 14
Middle Marwood. *Devn* 3F 19
Middle Mayfield. *Staf* 1F 73
Middlemoor. *Devn* 5E 11
Middlemuir. *Abers* 4F 161
(nr. New Deer)
Middlemuir. *Abers* 3G 161
(nr. Strichen)
Middle Rainton. *Tyne* 5G 115
Middle Rasen. *Linc* 2H 87
Middlesbrough. *Midd* 3B 106 & 201
Middlesceugh. *Cumb* 5E 113
Middleshaw. *Cumb* 1E 97
Middlesmoor. *N Yor* 2C 98
Middles, The. *Dur* 4F 115
Middlestone. *Dur* 1F 105
Middlestone Moor. *Dur* 1F 105
Middle Stoughton. *Som* 2H 21
Middlestown. *W Yor* 3C 92
Middle Street. *Glos* 5C 48
Middle Taphouse. *Corn* 2F 7
Middleton. *Ang* 4E 145
Middleton. *Arg* 4A 138
Middleton. *Cumb* 1F 97
Middleton. *Derbs* 4F 85
(nr. Bakewell)
Middleton. *Derbs* 5G 85
(nr. Wirksworth)
Middleton. *Essx* 2B 54
Middleton. *G Man* 4G 91
Middleton. *Hants* 2C 24
Middleton. *Hart* 1C 106
Middleton. *Here* 4H 59
Middleton. *IOW* 4B 16
Middleton. *Lanc* 4D 96
Middleton. *Midl* 4G 129
Middleton. *Norf* 4F 77
Middleton. *Nptn* 1F 63
Middleton. *Nmbd* 1F 121
(nr. Belford)
Middleton. *Nmbd* 1D 114
(nr. Morpeth)
Middleton. *N Yor* 5D 98
(nr. Ilkley)
Middleton. *N Yor* 1B 100
(nr. Pickering)
Middleton. *Per* 3D 136
Middleton. *Shrp* 3H 59
(nr. Ludlow)
Middleton. *Shrp* 3F 71
(nr. Oswestry)
Middleton. *Suff* 4G 67
Middleton. *Swan* 4D 30
Middleton. *Warw* 1F 61
Middleton. *W Yor* 2D 92
Middleton Cheney. *Nptn* 1D 50
Middleton Green. *Staf* 2D 73
Middleton Hall. *Nmbd* 2D 121
Middleton-in-Teesdale. *Dur* 2C 104
Middleton One Row. *Darl* 3A 106
Middleton-on-Leven. *N Yor* 4B 106
Middleton-on-Sea. *W Sus* 5A 26
Middleton on the Hill. *Here* 4H 59
Middleton-on-the-Wolds.
E Yor 5D 100
Middleton Priors. *Shrp* 1A 60
Middleton Quernhow. *N Yor* 2F 99
Middleton St George. *Darl* 3A 106
Middleton Scriven. *Shrp* 2A 60
Middleton Stoney. *Oxon* 3D 50
Middleton Tyas. *N Yor* 4F 105
Middletown. *Cumb* 4A 102
Middle Town. *IOS* 1B 4
Middletown. *Powy* 4F 71
Middle Tysoe. *Warw* 1B 50
Middle Wallop. *Hants* 3A 24
Middlewich. *Ches E* 4B 84
Middle Winterslow. *Wilts* 3H 23
Middlewood. *Corn* 5C 10
Middlewood. *S Yor* 1H 85
Middle Woodford. *Wilts* 3G 23
Middlewood Green. *Suff* 4C 66
Middleyard. *Glos* 5D 48
Middlezoy. *Som* 3G 21
Middridge. *Dur* 2F 105
Midelney. *Som* 4H 21
Midfield. *High* 2F 167
Midford. *Bath* 5C 34

Moulton—New Hutton

Moulton. N Yor 4F 105
Moulton. Suff 4F 65
Moulton. V Glam 4D 32
Moulton Chapel. Linc 4B 76
Moulton Eugate. Linc 4B 76
Moulton St Mary. Norf 5F 79
Moulton Seas End. Linc 3C 76
Mount. Corn 2F 7 (nr. Bodmin)
Mount. Corn 3B 6 (nr. Newquay)
Mountain Ash. Rhon 2D 32
Mountain Cross. Bord 5E 129
Mountain Street. Kent 5E 41
Mountain Water. Pemb 2D 42
Mount Ambrose. Corn 4B 6
Mountbenger. Bord 2F 119
Mountblow. W Dun 2F 127
Mount Bures. Essx 2C 54
Mountfield. E Sus 3B 28
Mountgerald. High 2H 157
Mount Hawke. Corn 4B 6
Mount High. High 2A 158
Mountjoy. Corn 2C 6
Mount Lothian. Midl 4F 129
Mountnessing. Essx 1H 39
Mounton. Mon 2A 34
Mount Pleasant. Buck 2E 51
Mount Pleasant. Ches E 5C 84
Mount Pleasant. Derbs 1H 73 (nr. Derby)
Mount Pleasant. Derbs 4G 73 (nr. Swadlincote)
Mount Pleasant. E Sus 4F 27
Mount Pleasant. Fife 2E 137
Mount Pleasant. Hants 3A 16
Mount Pleasant. Norf 1B 66
Mount Skippett. Oxon 4B 50
Mountsorrel. Leics 4C 74
Mount Stuart. Arg 4C 126
Mousehole. Corn 4B 4
Mouswald. Dum 2B 112
Mow Cop. Ches E 5C 84
Mowden. Darl 3F 105
Mowhaugh. Bord 2C 120
Mowmacre Hill. Leic 5C 74
Mowsley. Leics 2D 62
Moy. High 5B 158
Moylgrove. Pemb 1B 44
Moy Lodge. High 5G 149
Muasdale. Arg 5E 125
Muchalls. Abers 4G 153
Much Birch. Here 2A 48
Much Cowarne. Here 1B 48
Much Dewchurch. Here 2H 47
Muchelney. Som 4H 21
Muchelney Ham. Som 4H 21
Much Hadham. Herts 4E 53
Much Hoole. Lanc 2C 90
Muchlarnick. Corn 3G 7
Much Marcle. Here 2B 48
Muchrachd. High 5E 157
Much Wenlock. Shrp 1A 60
Mucking. Thur 2A 40
Muckle Breck. Shet 5G 173
Muckleford. Dors 3B 14
Mucklestone. Staf 2B 72
Muckleton. Norf 2H 77
Muckleton. Shrp 3H 71
Muckley. Shrp 1A 60
Muckley Corner. Staf 5E 73
Muckton. Linc 2C 88
Mudale. High 5F 167
Muddiford. Devn 3F 19
Mudeford. Dors 3G 15
Mudford. Som 1A 14
Mudgley. Som 2H 21
Mugdock. Stir 2G 127
Mugeary. High 5D 154
Muggington. Derbs 1G 73
Muggintonlane End. Derbs 1G 73
Muggleswick. Dur 4D 114
Mugswell. Surr 5D 38
Muie. High 3D 164
Muirden. Abers 3E 160
Muirdrum. Ang 5E 145
Muiredge. Per 1E 137
Muirend. Glas 3G 127
Muirhead. Ang 5C 144
Muirhead. Fife 3E 137
Muirhead. N Lan 3H 127
Muirhouses. Falk 1D 128
Muirkirk. E Ayr 2F 117
Muir of Alford. Abers 2C 152
Muir of Fairburn. High 3G 157
Muir of Fowlis. Abers 2C 152
Muir of Miltonduff. Mor 3F 159
Muir of Ord. High 3H 157
Muir of Tarradale. High 3H 157
Muirshearlich. High 5D 148
Muirtack. Abers 5G 161
Muirton. High 2B 158
Muirton. Per 1D 136
Muirton of Ardblair. Per 4A 144
Muirtown. Per 2B 136
Muiryfold. Abers 3E 161
Muker. N Yor 5C 104
Mulbarton. Norf 5D 78
Mulben. Mor 3A 160
Mulindry. Arg 4B 124
Mulla. Shet 5F 173
Mullach Charlabhaigh. W Isl 3E 171
Mullacott. Devn 2F 19
Mullion. Corn 5D 5
Mullion Cove. Corn 5D 4
Mumbles. Swan 4F 31
Mumby. Linc 3E 89
Munderfield Row. Here 5A 60
Munderfield Stocks. Here 5A 60
Mundesley. Norf 2F 79
Mundford. Norf 1H 65
Mundham. Norf 1F 67
Mundon. Essx 5B 54
Munerigie. High 3E 149
Muness. Shet 1H 173
Mungasdale. High 4D 162
Mungrisdale. Cumb 1E 103
Munlochy. High 3A 158
Munsley. Here 1B 48
Munslow. Shrp 2H 59
Murchington. Devn 4G 11
Murcot. Worc 1F 49
Murcott. Oxon 4D 50
Murdishaw. Hal 2H 83
Murieston. W Lot 3D 128
Murkle. High 2D 168
Murlaggan. High 4C 148
Murra. Orkn 7B 172
Murrayfield. Edin 2F 129
Murray, The. S Lan 4H 127
Murrell Green. Hants 1F 25
Murroes. Ang 5D 144
Murrow. Cambs 5C 76
Mursley. Buck 3G 51
Murthly. Per 5H 143
Murton. Cumb 2A 104
Murton. Dur 5G 115
Murton. Nmbd 5F 131
Murton. Swan 4E 31
Murton. York 4A 100
Musbury. Devn 3F 13
Muscoates. N Yor 1A 100
Muscott. Nptn 4D 62
Musselburgh. E Lot 2G 129
Muston. Leics 2F 75
Muston. N Yor 2E 101
Mustow Green. Worc 3C 60
Muswell Hill. G Lon 2D 39
Mutehill. Dum 5D 111
Mutford. Suff 2G 67
Muthill. Per 2A 136
Mutterton. Devn 2D 12
Muxton. Telf 4B 72
Mwmbwls. Swan 4F 31
Mybster. High 3D 168
Myddfai. Carm 2A 46
Myddle. Shrp 3G 71
Mydroilyn. Cdgn 5D 56
Myerscough. Lanc 1C 90
Mylor Bridge. Corn 5C 6
Mylor Churchtown. Corn 5C 6
Mynachlog-ddu. Pemb 1F 43
Mynydd-bach. Mon 2H 33
Mynydd Isa. Flin 4E 83
Mynyddislwyn. Cphy 2E 33
Mynydd Llandegai. Gwyn 4F 81
Mynydd Mechell. IOA 1C 80
Mynydd-y-briw. Powy 3D 70
Mynyddygarreg. Carm 5E 45
Mynytho. Gwyn 2C 68
Myrebird. Abers 4E 153
Myrelandhorn. High 3E 169
Mytchett. Surr 1G 25
Mythe, The. Glos 2D 49
Mytholmroyd. W Yor 2A 92
Myton-on-Swale. N Yor 3G 99
Mytton. Shrp 4G 71

N

Naast. High 5C 162
Na Buirgh. W Isl 8C 171
Naburn. York 5H 99
Nab Wood. W Yor 1B 92
Nackington. Kent 5F 41
Nacton. Suff 1F 55
Nafferton. E Yor 4E 101
Na Gearrannan. W Isl 3D 171
Nailbridge. Glos 4B 48
Nailsbourne. Som 4F 21
Nailsea. N Som 4H 33
Nailstone. Leics 5B 74
Nailsworth. Glos 2D 34
Nairn. High 3C 158
Nalderswood. Surr 1D 26
Nancegollan. Corn 3D 4
Nancekuke. Corn 4A 6
Nancledra. Corn 3B 4
Nangreaves. G Man 3G 91
Nanhyfer. Pemb 1E 43
Nannerch. Flin 4D 82
Nanpantan. Leics 4C 74
Nanpean. Corn 3D 6
Nanstallon. Corn 2E 7
Nant-ddu. Powy 4D 46
Nanternis. Cdgn 5C 56
Nantgaredig. Carm 3E 45
Nantgarw. Rhon 3E 33
Nant Glas. Powy 4B 58
Nantglyn. Den 4C 82
Nantgwyn. Powy 3B 58
Nantlle. Gwyn 5E 81
Nantmawr. Shrp 3E 71
Nantmel. Powy 4C 58
Nantmor. Gwyn 1F 69
Nant Peris. Gwyn 5F 81
Nantwich. Ches E 5A 84
Nant-y-bai. Carm 1A 46
Nant-y-bwch. Blae 4E 47
Nant-y-Derry. Mon 5G 47
Nant-y-dugoed. Powy 4B 70
Nant-y-felin. Cnwy 3F 81
Nantyffyllon. B'end 2B 32
Nantyglo. Blae 4E 47
Nant-y-meichiaid. Powy 4D 70
Nant-y-moel. B'end 2C 32
Nant-y-Pandy. Cnwy 3F 81
Naphill. Buck 2G 37
Nappa. Lanc 4A 98
Napton on the Hill. Warw 4B 62
Narberth. Pemb 3F 43
Narberth Bridge. Pemb 3F 43
Narborough. Leics 1C 62
Narborough. Norf 4G 77
Narkurs. Corn 3H 7
Narth, The. Mon 5A 48
Narthwaite. Cumb 5A 104
Nasareth. Gwyn 1D 68
Naseby. Nptn 3D 62
Nash. Buck 2F 51
Nash. Here 4F 59
Nash. Kent 5G 41
Nash. Newp 3G 33
Nash. Shrp 3A 60
Nash Lee. Buck 5G 51
Nassington. Nptn 1H 63
Nasty. Herts 3D 52
Natcott. Devn 4C 18
Nateby. Cumb 4A 104
Nateby. Lanc 5D 96
Nately Scures. Hants 1F 25
Natland. Cumb 1E 97
Naughton. Suff 1D 54
Naunton. Glos 3G 49
Naunton. Worc 2D 49
Naunton Beauchamp. Worc 5D 60
Navenby. Linc 5G 87
Navestock Heath. Essx 1G 39
Navestock Side. Essx 1G 39
Navidale. High 2H 165
Nawton. N Yor 1A 100
Nayland. Suff 2C 54
Nazeing. Essx 5E 53
Neacroft. Hants 3G 15
Neal's Green. W Mid 2H 61
Neap House. N Lin 3B 94
Near Sawrey. Cumb 5E 103
Neasden. G Lon 2D 38
Neasham. Darl 3A 106
Neath. Neat 2A 32
Neath Abbey. Neat 3G 31
Neatishead. Norf 3F 79
Neaton. Norf 5B 78
Nebo. Cdgn 4E 57
Nebo. Cnwy 5H 81
Nebo. Gwyn 5D 81
Nebo. IOA 1D 80
Necton. Norf 5A 78
Nedd. High 5B 166
Nedderton. Nmbd 1F 115
Nedging. Suff 1D 54
Nedging Tye. Suff 1D 54
Needham. Norf 2E 67
Needham Market. Suff 5C 66
Needham Street. Suff 4G 65
Needingworth. Cambs 3C 64
Needwood. Staf 3F 73
Neen Savage. Shrp 3A 60
Neen Sollars. Shrp 3A 60
Neenton. Shrp 2A 60
Nefyn. Gwyn 1C 68
Neilston. E Ren 4F 127
Neithrop. Oxon 1C 50
Nelly Andrews Green. Powy 5E 71
Nelson. Cphy 2E 32
Nelson. Lanc 1G 91
Nelson Village. Nmbd 2F 115
Nemphlar. S Lan 5B 128
Nempnett Thrubwell. Bath 5A 34
Nene Terrace. Linc 5B 76
Nenthall. Cumb 5A 114
Nenthead. Cumb 5A 114
Nenthorn. Bord 1A 120
Nercwys. Flin 4E 83
Neribus. Arg 4A 124
Nerston. S Lan 4H 127
Nesbit. Nmbd 1D 121
Nesfield. N Yor 5C 98
Ness. Ches W 3F 83
Nesscliffe. Shrp 4F 71
Ness of Tenston. Orkn 6B 172
Neston. Ches W 3E 83
Neston. Wilts 5D 34
Netchwood. Shrp 1A 60
Nethanfoot. S Lan 5B 128
Nether Alderley. Ches E 3C 84
Netheravon. Wilts 2G 23
Nether Blainslie. Bord 5B 130
Netherbrae. Abers 3E 161
Netherbrough. Orkn 6C 172
Nether Broughton. Leics 3D 74
Netherburn. S Lan 5B 128
Nether Burrow. Lanc 2F 97
Netherbury. Dors 3H 13
Netherby. Cumb 2E 113
Nether Careston. Ang 3E 145
Nether Cerne. Dors 3B 14
Nether Compton. Dors 1A 14
Nethercote. Glos 3G 49
Nethercote. Warw 4C 62
Nethercott. Devn 3E 19
Nethercott. Oxon 3C 50
Nether Dallachy. Mor 2A 160
Nether Durdie. Per 1E 136
Nether End. Derbs 3G 85
Netherend. Glos 5A 48
Nether Exe. Devn 2C 12
Netherfield. E Sus 4B 28
Netherfield. Notts 1D 74
Nethergate. Norf 3C 78
Netherhampton. Wilts 4G 23
Nether Handley. Derbs 3B 86
Nether Haugh. S Yor 1B 86
Nether Heage. Derbs 5A 86
Nether Heyford. Nptn 5D 62
Netherhouses. Cumb 1B 96
Nether Howcleugh. Dum 3C 118
Nether Kellet. Lanc 3E 97
Nether Kinmundy. Abers 4H 161
Netherland Green. Staf 2F 73
Nether Langwith. Notts 3C 86
Netherlaw. Dum 5E 111
Netherley. Abers 4F 153
Nethermill. Dum 1B 112
Nethermills. Mor 3C 160
Nether Moor. Derbs 4A 86
Nether Padley. Derbs 3G 85
Netherplace. E Ren 4G 127
Nether Poppleton. York 4H 99
Netherseal. Derbs 4G 73
Nether Silton. N Yor 5B 106
Nether Stowey. Som 3E 21
Nether Street. Essx 4F 53
Netherstreet. Wilts 5E 35
Netherthird. E Ayr 3E 117
Netherthong. W Yor 4B 92
Netherton. Ang 3E 145
Netherton. Cumb 1B 102
Netherton. Devn 5B 12
Netherton. Hants 1B 24
Netherton. Here 3A 48
Netherton. Mers 1F 83
Netherton. N Lan 4A 128
Netherton. Nmbd 4D 121
Netherton. Per 3A 144
Netherton. Shrp 2B 60
Netherton. Stir 2G 127
Netherton. W Mid 2D 60
Netherton. W Yor 3C 92 (nr. Horbury)
Netherton. W Yor 3B 92 (nr. Huddersfield)
Netherton. Worc 1E 49
Nethertown. Cumb 4A 102
Nethertown. High 1F 169
Nethertown. Staf 4F 73
Nether Urquhart. Fife 3D 136
Nether Wallop. Hants 3B 24
Nether Wasdale. Cumb 4C 102
Nether Welton. Cumb 5E 113
Nether Westcote. Glos 3H 49
Nether Whitacre. Warw 1G 61
Netherwhitton. Nmbd 5F 121
Nether Worton. Oxon 2C 50
Nethy Bridge. High 1E 151
Netley. Hants 2C 16
Netley. Shrp 5G 71
Netley Marsh. Hants 1B 16
Nettlebed. Oxon 3F 37
Nettlebridge. Som 2B 22
Nettlecombe. Dors 3A 14
Nettlecombe. IOW 5D 16
Nettleden. Herts 4A 52
Nettleham. Linc 3H 87
Nettlestead. Kent 5A 40
Nettlestead Green. Kent 5A 40
Nettlestone. IOW 3E 16
Nettlesworth. Dur 5F 115
Nettleton. Linc 4E 94
Nettleton. Wilts 4D 34
Netton. Devn 4B 8
Netton. Wilts 3G 23
Neuadd. Carm 3H 45
Neuadd. Powy 5C 70
Neuk, The. Abers 4E 153
Nevendon. Essx 1B 40
Nevern. Pemb 1A 44
New Abbey. Dum 3A 112
New Aberdour. Abers 2F 161
New Addington. G Lon 4E 39
Newall. W Yor 5D 98
New Alresford. Hants 3D 24
New Alyth. Per 4B 144
Newark. Orkn 3G 172
Newark. Pet 5B 76
Newark-on-Trent. Notts 5E 87
New Arley. Warw 2G 61
Newarthill. N Lan 4A 128
New Ash Green. Kent 4H 39
New Balderton. Notts 5F 87
New Barn. Kent 4H 39
New Barnetby. N Lin 3D 94
Newbattle. Midl 3G 129
New Bewick. Nmbd 2E 121
Newbiggin. Cumb 2H 103 (nr. Appleby)
Newbiggin. Cumb 3B 96 (nr. Barrow-in-Furness)
Newbiggin. Cumb 5G 113 (nr. Cumrew)
Newbiggin. Cumb 2F 103 (nr. Penrith)
Newbiggin. Cumb 5B 102 (nr. Seascale)
Newbiggin. Dur 5E 115 (nr. Consett)
Newbiggin. Dur 2C 104 (nr. Holwick)
Newbiggin. Nmbd 5C 114
Newbiggin. N Yor 5C 104 (nr. Askrigg)
Newbiggin. N Yor 1F 101 (nr. Filey)
Newbiggin. N Yor 1B 98 (nr. Thoralby)
Newbiggin-by-the-Sea. Nmbd 1G 115
Newbigging. Ang 5D 145 (nr. Monikie)
Newbigging. Ang 4B 144 (nr. Newtyle)
Newbigging. Ang 5D 144 (nr. Tealing)
Newbigging. Edin 2E 129
Newbigging. S Lan 5D 128
Newbiggin-on-Lune. Cumb 4A 104
Newbold. Derbs 3A 86
Newbold. Leics 4B 74
Newbold on Avon. Warw 3B 62
Newbold on Stour. Warw 1H 49
Newbold Pacey. Warw 5G 61
Newbold Verdon. Leics 5B 74
New Bolingbroke. Linc 5C 88
Newborough. IOA 4D 80
Newborough. Pet 5B 76
Newborough. Staf 3F 73
Newbottle. Nptn 2D 50
Newbottle. Tyne 4G 115
New Boultham. Linc 3G 87
Newbourne. Suff 1F 55
New Brancepeth. Dur 5F 115
Newbridge. Cphy 2F 33
Newbridge. Cdgn 5E 57
Newbridge. Corn 3B 4
New Bridge. Dum 2G 111
Newbridge. Edin 2E 129
Newbridge. Hants 1A 16
Newbridge. IOW 4C 16
Newbridge. N Yor 1C 100
Newbridge. Pemb 1D 42
Newbridge. Wrex 1E 71
Newbridge Green. Worc 2D 48
Newbridge-on-Usk. Mon 2G 33
Newbridge on Wye. Powy 5C 58
New Brighton. Flin 4E 83
New Brighton. Hants 2F 17
New Brighton. Mers 1F 83
New Brinsley. Notts 5B 86
Newbrough. Nmbd 3B 114
New Broughton. Wrex 5F 83
New Buckenham. Norf 1C 66
Newbuildings. Devn 2A 12
Newburgh. Abers 1G 153
Newburgh. Fife 2E 137
Newburgh. Lanc 3C 90
Newburn. Tyne 3E 115
Newbury. W Ber 5C 36
Newbury. Wilts 2D 22
Newby. Cumb 2G 103
Newby. N Yor 2G 97 (nr. Ingleton)
Newby. N Yor 1E 101 (nr. Scarborough)
Newby. N Yor 3C 106 (nr. Stokesley)
Newby Bridge. Cumb 1C 96
Newby Cote. N Yor 2G 97
Newby East. Cumb 4F 113
Newby Head. Cumb 2G 103
New Byth. Abers 3F 161
Newby West. Cumb 4E 113
Newby Wiske. N Yor 1F 99
Newcastle. B'end 3B 32
Newcastle. Mon 4H 47
Newcastle. Shrp 2E 59
Newcastle Emlyn. Carm 1D 44
Newcastle International Airport. Tyne 2E 115
Newcastleton. Bord 1F 113
Newcastle-under-Lyme. Staf 1C 72
Newcastle upon Tyne. Tyne 3F 115 & 205
Newchapel. Pemb 1G 43
Newchapel. Powy 2B 58
Newchapel. Staf 5C 84
Newchapel. Surr 1E 27
New Cheriton. Hants 4D 24
Newchurch. Carm 3D 45
Newchurch. Here 5F 59
Newchurch. IOW 4D 16
Newchurch. Kent 2E 29
Newchurch. Lanc 1G 91 (nr. Nelson)
Newchurch. Lanc 2G 91 (nr. Rawtenstall)
Newchurch. Mon 2H 33
Newchurch. Powy 5E 58
Newchurch. Staf 3F 73
New Costessey. Norf 4D 78
Newcott. Devn 2F 13
New Cowper. Cumb 5C 112
Newcraighall. Edin 2G 129
New Crofton. W Yor 3D 93
New Cross. Cdgn 3F 57
New Cross. Som 1H 13
New Cumnock. E Ayr 3F 117
New Deer. Abers 4F 161
New Denham. Buck 2B 38
Newdigate. Surr 1C 26
New Duston. Nptn 4E 62
New Earswick. York 4A 100
New Edlington. S Yor 1C 86
New Elgin. Mor 2G 159
New Ellerby. E Yor 1E 95
Newell Green. Brac 4G 37
New Eltham. G Lon 3F 39
New End. Warw 4F 61
New End. Worc 5E 61
Newenden. Kent 3C 28
New England. Essx 1H 53
New England. Pet 5A 76
Newent. Glos 3C 48
New Ferry. Mers 2F 83
Newfield. Dur 4F 115 (nr. Chester-le-Street)
Newfield. Dur 1F 105 (nr. Willington)
Newfound. Hants 1D 24
New Fryston. W Yor 2E 93
New Galloway. Dum 2D 110
Newgate. Norf 1C 78
Newgate. Pemb 2C 42
Newgate Street. Herts 5D 52
New Greens. Herts 5B 52
New Grimsby. IOS 1A 4
New Hainford. Norf 4E 78
Newhall. Ches E 1A 72
Newhall. Staf 3G 73
Newham. Nmbd 2F 121
New Hartley. Nmbd 2G 115
Newhaven. Derbs 4F 85
Newhaven. E Sus 5F 27 & 215
Newhaven. Edin 2F 129
New Haw. Surr 4B 38
New Hedges. Pemb 4F 43
New Herrington. Tyne 4G 115
Newhey. G Man 3H 91
New Holkham. Norf 2A 78
New Holland. N Lin 2D 94
Newholm. N Yor 3F 107
New Houghton. Derbs 4C 86
New Houghton. Norf 3G 77
Newhouse. N Lan 3A 128
New Houses. N Yor 2H 97
New Hutton. Cumb 5G 103

New Hythe—Northorpe

New Hythe. *Kent* 5B **40**
Newick. *E Sus* 3F **27**
Newingreen. *Kent* 2F **29**
Newington. *Edin* 2F **129**
Newington. *Kent* 2F **29**
(nr. Folkestone)
Newington. *Kent* 4C **40**
(nr. Sittingbourne)
Newington. *Notts* 1D **86**
Newington. *Oxon* 2E **36**
Newington Bagpath. *Glos* 2D **34**
New Inn. *Carm* 2E **45**
New Inn. *Mon* 5H **47**
New Inn. *N Yor* 2H **97**
New Inn. *Torf* 5G **47**
New Invention. *Shrp* 3E **59**
New Kelso. *High* 4B **156**
New Lanark. *S Lan* 5B **128**
Newland. *Glos* 5A **48**
Newland. *Hull* 1D **94**
Newland. *N Yor* 2G **93**
Newland. *Som* 3B **20**
Newland. *Worc* 1C **48**
Newlandrig. *Midl* 3G **129**
Newlands. *Cumb* 1E **103**
Newlands. *Essx* 2C **40**
Newlands. *High* 4B **158**
Newlands. *Nmbd* 4D **115**
Newlands. *Notts* 4C **86**
Newlands. *Staf* 3E **73**
Newlands of Geise. *High* 2C **168**
Newlands of Tynet. *Mor* 2A **160**
Newlands Park. *IOA* 2B **80**
New Lane. *Lanc* 3C **90**
New Lane End. *Warr* 1A **84**
New Langholm. *Dum* 1E **113**
New Leake. *Linc* 5D **88**
New Leeds. *Abers* 3G **161**
New Lenton. *Nott* 2C **74**
New Longton. *Lanc* 2D **90**
Newlot. *Orkn* 6E **172**
New Luce. *Dum* 3G **109**
Newlyn. *Corn* 4B **4**
Newmachar. *Abers* 2F **153**
Newmains. *N Lan* 4B **128**
New Mains of Ury. *Abers* 5F **153**
New Malden. *G Lon* 4D **38**
Newman's Green. *Suff* 1B **54**
Newmarket. *Suff* 4F **65**
Newmarket. *W Isl* 4G **171**
New Marske. *Red C* 2D **106**
New Marton. *Shrp* 2F **71**
New Micklefield. *W Yor* 1E **93**
New Mill. *Abers* 4E **160**
New Mill. *Corn* 3B **4**
New Mill. *Herts* 4H **51**
Newmill. *Mor* 3B **160**
Newmill. *Bord* 3G **119**
New Mill. *W Yor* 4B **92**
New Mill. *Wilts* 5G **35**
Newmillerdam. *W Yor* 3D **92**
New Mills. *Corn* 3C **6**
New Mills. *Derbs* 2E **85**
Newmills. *Fife* 1D **128**
Newmills. *High* 2A **158**
New Mills. *Mon* 5A **48**
New Mills. *Powy* 5C **70**
Newmiln. *Per* 5A **144**
Newmilns. *E Ayr* 1E **117**
New Milton. *Hants* 3H **15**
New Mistley. *Essx* 2E **54**
New Moat. *Pemb* 2E **43**
Newmore. *High* 3H **157**
(nr. Dingwall)
Newmore. *High* 1A **158**
(nr. Invergordon)
Newnham. *Cambs* 5D **64**
Newnham. *Glos* 4B **48**
Newnham. *Hants* 1F **25**
Newnham. *Herts* 2C **52**
Newnham. *Kent* 5D **40**
Newnham. *Nptn* 5C **62**
Newnham. *Warw* 4F **61**
Newnham Bridge. *Worc* 4A **60**
New Ollerton. *Notts* 4D **86**
New Oscott. *W Mid* 1F **61**
Newpark. *Fife* 2G **137**
New Park. *N Yor* 4E **99**
New Pitsligo. *Abers* 3F **161**
New Polzeath. *Corn* 1D **6**
Newport. *Corn* 4D **10**
Newport. *Devn* 3F **19**
Newport. *E Yor* 1B **94**
Newport. *Essx* 2F **53**
Newport. *Glos* 2B **34**
Newport. *High* 1H **165**
Newport. *IOW* 4D **16**
Newport. *Newp* 3G **33** & **205**
Newport. *Norf* 4H **79**
Newport. *Pemb* 1E **43**
Newport. *Som* 4G **21**
Newport. *Telf* 4B **72**
Newport-on-Tay. *Fife* 1G **137**
Newport Pagnell. *Mil* 1G **51**
Newpound Common. *W Sus* 3B **26**
New Prestwick. *S Ayr* 2C **116**
New Quay. *Cdgn* 5C **56**
Newquay. *Corn* 2C **6**
Newquay Airport. *Corn* 2C **6**
New Rackheath. *Norf* 4E **79**
New Radnor. *Powy* 4E **58**
New Rent. *Cumb* 1F **103**
New Ridley. *Nmbd* 4D **114**
New Romney. *Kent* 3E **29**
New Rossington. *S Yor* 1D **86**
New Row. *Cdgn* 3G **57**
New Row. *Lanc* 1E **91**
New Row. *N Yor* 3D **106**
New Sauchie. *Clac* 4A **136**
Newsbank. *Ches E* 4C **84**
Newseat. *Abers* 5E **160**
Newsham. *Lanc* 1D **90**
Newsham. *Nmbd* 2G **115**
Newsham. *N Yor* 3E **105**
(nr. Richmond)
Newsham. *N Yor* 1F **99**
(nr. Thirsk)
New Sharlston. *W Yor* 3D **93**
Newsholme. *E Yor* 2H **93**
Newsholme. *Lanc* 4H **97**
New Shoreston. *Nmbd* 1F **121**
New Springs. *G Man* 4D **90**
Newstead. *Notts* 5C **86**
Newstead. *Bord* 1H **119**
New Stevenston. *N Lan* 4A **128**
New Street. *Here* 5F **59**
Newstreet Lane. *Shrp* 2A **72**
New Swanage. *Dors* 4F **15**
New Swannington. *Leics* 4B **74**
Newthorpe. *N Yor* 1E **93**
Newthorpe. *Notts* 1B **74**
Newton. *Arg* 4H **133**
Newton. *B'end* 4B **32**
Newton. *Cambs* 1E **53**
(nr. Cambridge)
Newton. *Cambs* 4D **76**
(nr. Wisbech)
Newton. *Ches W* 4G **83**
(nr. Chester)
Newton. *Ches W* 5H **83**
(nr. Tattenhall)
Newton. *Cumb* 2B **96**
Newton. *Derbs* 5B **86**
Newton. *Dors* 1C **14**
Newton. *Dum* 2D **112**
(nr. Annan)
Newton. *Dum* 5D **118**
(nr. Moffat)
Newton. *G Man* 1D **84**
Newton. *Here* 2G **47**
(nr. Ewyas Harold)
Newton. *Here* 5H **59**
(nr. Leominster)
Newton. *High* 2B **158**
(nr. Cromarty)
Newton. *High* 4B **158**
(nr. Inverness)
Newton. *High* 5C **166**
(nr. Kylestrome)
Newton. *High* 4F **169**
(nr. Wick)
Newton. *Lanc* 2E **97**
(nr. Carnforth)
Newton. *Lanc* 4F **97**
(nr. Clitheroe)
Newton. *Lanc* 1C **90**
(nr. Kirkham)
Newton. *Linc* 2H **75**
Newton. *Mers* 2E **83**
Newton. *Mor* 2F **159**
Newton. *Norf* 4H **77**
Newton. *Nptn* 2F **63**
Newton. *Nmbd* 3D **114**
Newton. *Notts* 1D **74**
Newton. *Bord* 2A **120**
Newton. *Shet* 8E **173**
Newton. *Shrp* 1B **60**
(nr. Bridgnorth)
Newton. *Shrp* 2G **71**
(nr. Wem)
Newton. *Som* 3E **20**
Newton. *S Lan* 3H **127**
(nr. Glasgow)
Newton. *S Lan* 1B **118**
(nr. Lanark)
Newton. *Staf* 3E **73**
Newton. *Suff* 1C **54**
Newton. *Swan* 4F **31**
Newton. *Warw* 3C **62**
Newton. *W Lot* 2D **129**
Newton. *Wilts* 4H **23**
Newton Abbot. *Devn* 5B **12**
Newtonairds. *Dum* 1F **111**
Newton Arlosh. *Cumb* 4D **112**
Newton Aycliffe. *Dur* 2F **105**
Newton Bewley. *Hart* 2B **106**
Newton Blossomville. *Mil* 5G **63**
Newton Bromswold. *Bed* 4G **63**
Newton Burgoland. *Leics* 5A **74**
Newton by Toft. *Linc* 2H **87**
Newton Ferrers. *Devn* 4B **8**
Newton Flotman. *Norf* 1E **66**
Newtongrange. *Midl* 3G **129**
Newton Green. *Mon* 2A **34**
Newton Hall. *Dur* 5F **115**
Newton Hall. *Nmbd* 3D **114**
Newton Harcourt. *Leics* 1D **62**
Newton Heath. *G Man* 4G **91**
Newtonhill. *Abers* 4G **153**
Newtonhill. *High* 4H **157**
Newton Hill. *W Yor* 2D **92**
Newton Ketton. *Darl* 2A **106**
Newton Kyme. *N Yor* 5G **99**
Newton-le-Willows. *Mers* 1H **83**
Newton-le-Willows. *N Yor* 1E **98**
Newton Longville. *Buck* 2G **51**
Newton Mearns. *E Ren* 4G **127**
Newtonmore. *High* 4B **150**
Newton Morrell. *N Yor* 4F **105**
Newton Mulgrave. *N Yor* 3E **107**
Newton of Ardtoe. *High* 1A **140**
Newton of Balcanquhal. *Per* 2D **136**
Newton of Beltrees. *Ren* 4E **127**
Newton of Falkland. *Fife* 3E **137**
Newton of Mountblairy. *Abers* 3E **160**
Newton of Pitcairns. *Per* 2C **136**
Newton-on-Ouse. *N Yor* 4H **99**
Newton-on-Rawcliffe. *N Yor* 5F **107**
Newton on the Hill. *Shrp* 3G **71**
Newton-on-the-Moor. *Nmbd* 4F **121**
Newton on Trent. *Linc* 3F **87**
Newton Poppleford. *Devn* 4D **12**
Newton Purcell. *Oxon* 2E **51**
Newton Regis. *Warw* 5G **73**
Newton Reigny. *Cumb* 1F **103**
Newton Rigg. *Cumb* 1F **103**
Newton St Cyres. *Devn* 3B **12**
Newton St Faith. *Norf* 4E **78**
Newton St Loe. *Bath* 5C **34**
Newton St Petrock. *Devn* 1E **11**
Newton Solney. *Derbs* 3G **73**
Newton Stacey. *Hants* 2C **24**
Newton Stewart. *Dum* 3B **110**
Newton Toney. *Wilts* 2H **23**
Newton Tony. *Wilts* 2H **23**
Newton Tracey. *Devn* 4F **19**
Newton under Roseberry.
Red C 3C **106**
Newton Unthank. *Leics* 5B **74**
Newton upon Ayr. *S Ayr* 2C **116**
Newton upon Derwent. *E Yor* 5B **100**
Newton Valence. *Hants* 3F **25**
Newton-with-Scales. *Lanc* 1B **90**
Newtown. *Abers* 2E **160**
Newtown. *Cambs* 4H **63**
Newtown. *Corn* 5C **10**
Newtown. *Cumb* 5B **112**
(nr. Aspatria)
Newtown. *Cumb* 3G **113**
(nr. Brampton)
Newtown. *Cumb* 2G **103**
(nr. Penrith)
Newtown. *Derbs* 2D **85**
Newtown. *Devn* 4A **20**
Newtown. *Dors* 2H **13**
(nr. Beaminster)
New Town. *Dors* 1E **15**
(nr. Sixpenny Handley)
New Town. *E Lot* 2H **129**
Newtown. *Falk* 1C **128**
Newtown. *Glos* 5B **48**
(nr. Lydney)
Newtown. *Glos* 2E **49**
(nr. Tewkesbury)
Newtown. *Hants* 1D **16**
(nr. Bishop's Waltham)
Newtown. *Hants* 1A **16**
(nr. Lyndhurst)
Newtown. *Hants* 5C **36**
(nr. Newbury)
Newtown. *Hants* 4B **24**
(nr. Romsey)
Newtown. *Hants* 2C **16**
(nr. Warsash)
Newtown. *Hants* 1E **16**
(nr. Wickham)
Newtown. *Here* 2B **48**
(nr. Ledbury)
Newtown. *Here* 2A **48**
(nr. Little Dewchurch)
Newtown. *Here* 1B **48**
(nr. Stretton Grandison)
Newtown. *High* 3F **149**
Newtown. *IOM* 4C **108**
Newtown. *IOW* 3C **16**
Newtown. *Lanc* 3D **90**
New Town. *Lutn* 3A **52**
Newtown. *Nmbd* 4E **121**
(nr. Rothbury)
Newtown. *Nmbd* 2E **121**
(nr. Wooler)
Newtown. *Pool* 3F **15**
Newtown. *Powy* 1D **58**
Newtown. *Rhon* 2D **32**
Newtown. *Shet* 3F **173**
Newtown. *Shrp* 2G **71**
Newtown. *Som* 1F **13**
Newtown. *Staf* 4D **84**
(nr. Biddulph)
Newtown. *Staf* 5D **73**
(nr. Cannock)
Newtown. *Staf* 4E **85**
(nr. Longnor)
New Town. *W Yor* 2E **93**
Newtown. *Wilts* 4E **23**
Newtown-in-St Martin. *Corn* 4E **5**
Newtown Linford. *Leics* 5C **74**
Newtown St Boswells. *Bord* 1H **119**
New Tredegar. *Cphy* 5E **47**
Newtyle. *Ang* 4B **144**
New Village. *E Yor* 1D **94**
New Village. *S Yor* 4F **93**
New Walsoken. *Cambs* 5D **76**
New Waltham. *NE Lin* 4F **95**
New Winton. *E Lot* 2H **129**
New World. *Cambs* 1C **64**
New Yatt. *Oxon* 4B **50**
Newyears Green. *G Lon* 2B **38**
New York. *Linc* 5B **88**
New York. *Tyne* 2G **115**
Nextend. *Here* 5F **59**
Neyland. *Pemb* 4D **42**
Nib Heath. *Shrp* 4G **71**
Nicholashayne. *Devn* 1E **12**
Nicholaston. *Swan* 4E **31**
Nidd. *N Yor* 3F **99**
Niddrie. *Edin* 2F **129**
Niddry. *Edin* 2D **129**
Nigg. *Aber* 3G **153**
Nigg. *High* 1C **158**
Nigg Ferry. *High* 2B **158**
Nightcott. *Som* 4B **20**
Nimmer. *Som* 1G **13**
Nine Ashes. *Essx* 5F **53**
Ninebanks. *Nmbd* 4A **114**
Nine Elms. *Swin* 3G **35**
Ninemile Bar. *Dum* 2F **111**
Nine Mile Burn. *Midl* 4E **129**
Ninfield. *E Sus* 4B **28**
Ningwood. *IOW* 4C **16**
Nisbet. *Bord* 2A **120**
Nisbet Hill. *Bord* 4D **130**
Niton. *IOW* 5D **16**
Nitshill. *E Ren* 3G **127**
Niwbwrch. *IOA* 4D **80**
Noak Hill. *G Lon* 1G **39**
Nobold. *Shrp* 4G **71**
Nobottle. *Nptn* 4D **62**
Nocton. *Linc* 4H **87**
Nogdam End. *Norf* 5F **79**
Noke. *Oxon* 4D **50**
Nolton. *Pemb* 3C **42**
Nolton Haven. *Pemb* 3C **42**
No Man's Heath. *Ches W* 1H **71**
No Man's Heath. *Warw* 5G **73**
Nomansland. *Devn* 1B **12**
Nomansland. *Wilts* 1A **16**
Noneley. *Shrp* 3G **71**
Noness. *Shet* 9F **173**
Nonikiln. *High* 1A **158**
Nonington. *Kent* 5G **41**
Nook. *Cumb* 2F **113**
(nr. Longtown)
Nook. *Cumb* 1E **97**
(nr. Milnthorpe)
Noranside. *Ang* 2D **144**
Norbreck. *Bkpl* 5C **96**
Norbridge. *Here* 1C **48**
Norbury. *Ches E* 1H **71**
Norbury. *Derbs* 1F **73**
Norbury. *Shrp* 1F **59**
Norbury. *Staf* 3B **72**
Norby. *N Yor* 1G **99**
Norby. *Shet* 6C **173**
Norcross. *Lanc* 5C **96**
Nordelph. *Norf* 5E **77**
Norden. *G Man* 3G **91**
Nordley. *Shrp* 1A **60**
Norham. *Nmbd* 5F **131**
Norland Town. *W Yor* 2A **92**
Norley. *Ches W* 3H **83**
Norleywood. *Hants* 3B **16**
Normanby. *N Lin* 3B **94**
Normanby. *N Yor* 1B **100**
Normanby. *Red C* 3C **106**
Normanby-by-Spital. *Linc* 2H **87**
Normanby le Wold. *Linc* 1A **88**
Norman Cross. *Cambs* 1A **64**
Normandy. *Surr* 5A **38**
Norman's Bay. *E Sus* 5A **28**
Norman's Green. *Devn* 2D **12**
Normanton. *Derb* 2H **73**
Normanton. *Leics* 1F **75**
Normanton. *Linc* 1G **75**
Normanton. *Notts* 5E **86**
Normanton. *W Yor* 2D **93**
Normanton le Heath. *Leics* 4A **74**
Normanton on Soar. *Notts* 3C **74**
Normanton-on-the-Wolds. *Notts* 2D **74**
Normanton on Trent. *Notts* 4E **87**
Normoss. *Lanc* 1B **90**
Norrington Common. *Wilts* 5D **35**
Norris Green. *Mers* 1F **83**
Norris Hill. *Leics* 4H **73**
Norristhorpe. *W Yor* 2C **92**
Northacre. *Norf* 1B **66**
Northall. *Buck* 3H **51**
Northallerton. *N Yor* 5A **106**
Northam. *Devn* 4E **19**
Northam. *Sotn* 1C **16**
Northampton. *Nptn* 4E **63** & **206**
North Anston. *S Yor* 2C **86**
North Ascot. *Brac* 4A **38**
North Aston. *Oxon* 3C **50**
Northaw. *Herts* 5C **52**
Northay. *Som* 1F **13**
North Baddesley. *Hants* 4B **24**
North Balfern. *Dum* 4B **110**
North Ballachulish. *High* 2E **141**
North Barrow. *Som* 4B **22**
North Barsham. *Norf* 2B **78**
Northbeck. *Linc* 1H **75**
North Benfleet. *Essx* 2B **40**
North Bersted. *W Sus* 5A **26**
North Berwick. *E Lot* 1B **130**
North Bitchburn. *Dur* 1E **105**
North Blyth. *Nmbd* 1G **115**
North Boarhunt. *Hants* 1E **16**
North Bockhampton. *Dors* 3G **15**
Northborough. *Pet* 5A **76**
Northbourne. *Kent* 5H **41**
Northbourne. *Oxon* 3D **36**
North Bovey. *Devn* 4H **11**
North Bowood. *Dors* 3H **13**
North Bradley. *Wilts* 1D **22**
North Brentor. *Devn* 4E **11**
North Brewham. *Som* 3C **22**
Northbrook. *Oxon* 3C **50**
North Brook End. *Cambs* 1C **52**
North Broomhill. *Nmbd* 4G **121**
North Buckland. *Devn* 2E **19**
North Burlingham. *Norf* 4F **79**
North Cadbury. *Som* 4B **22**
North Carlton. *Linc* 3G **87**
North Cave. *E Yor* 1B **94**
North Cerney. *Glos* 5F **49**
North Chailey. *E Sus* 3E **27**
Northchapel. *W Sus* 3A **26**
North Charford. *Hants* 1G **15**
North Charlton. *Nmbd* 2F **121**
North Cheriton. *Som* 4B **22**
North Chideock. *Dors* 3H **13**
Northchurch. *Herts* 5H **51**
North Cliffe. *E Yor* 1B **94**
North Clifton. *Notts* 3F **87**
North Close. *Dur* 1F **105**
North Cockerington. *Linc* 1C **88**
North Coker. *Som* 1A **14**
North Collafirth. *Shet* 3E **173**
North Common. *E Sus* 3E **27**
North Commonty. *Abers* 4F **161**
North Coombe. *Devn* 1B **12**
North Corbelly. *Dum* 3A **112**
North Cornelly. *B'end* 3B **32**
North Cotes. *Linc* 4G **95**
Northcott. *Devn* 3D **10**
(nr. Boyton)
Northcott. *Devn* 1D **12**
(nr. Culmstock)
Northcourt. *Oxon* 2D **36**
North Cove. *Suff* 2G **67**
North Cowton. *N Yor* 4F **105**
North Craigo. *Ang* 2F **145**
North Crawley. *Mil* 1H **51**
North Cray. *G Lon* 3F **39**
North Creake. *Norf* 2A **78**
North Curry. *Som* 4G **21**
North Dalton. *E Yor* 4D **100**
North Deighton. *N Yor* 4F **99**
North Dronley. *Ang* 5C **144**
North Duffield. *N Yor* 1G **93**
Northdyke. *Orkn* 5B **172**
Northedge. *Derbs* 4A **86**
North Elkington. *Linc* 1B **88**
North Elmham. *Norf* 3B **78**
North Elmsall. *W Yor* 3E **93**
Northend. *Buck* 2F **37**
North End. *E Yor* 1F **95**
North End. *Essx* 4G **53**
(nr. Great Dunmow)
North End. *Essx* 2A **54**
(nr. Great Yeldham)
North End. *Hants* 5C **36**
North End. *Leics* 4C **74**
North End. *Linc* 1B **76**
North End. *Norf* 1B **66**
North End. *N Som* 5H **33**
North End. *Port* 2E **17**
Northend. *Warw* 5A **62**
North End. *W Sus* 5C **26**
North End. *Wilts* 2F **35**
North Erradale. *High* 5B **162**
North Evington. *Leic* 5D **74**
North Fambridge. *Essx* 1C **40**
North Fearns. *High* 5E **155**
North Featherstone. *W Yor* 2E **93**
North Feorline. *N Ayr* 3D **122**
North Ferriby. *E Yor* 2C **94**
Northfield. *Aber* 3F **153**
Northfield. *Hull* 2D **94**
Northfield. *Som* 3F **21**
Northfield. *W Mid* 3E **61**
Northfleet. *Kent* 3H **39**
North Frodingham. *E Yor* 4F **101**
Northgate. *Linc* 3A **76**
North Gluss. *Shet* 4E **173**
North Gorley. *Hants* 1G **15**
North Green. *Norf* 2E **66**
North Green. *Suff* 4F **67**
(nr. Framlingham)
North Green. *Suff* 3F **67**
(nr. Halesworth)
North Green. *Suff* 4F **67**
(nr. Saxmundham)
North Greetwell. *Linc* 3H **87**
North Grimston. *N Yor* 3C **100**
North Halling. *Medw* 4B **40**
North Hayling. *Hants* 2F **17**
North Hazelrigg. *Nmbd* 1E **121**
North Heasley. *Devn* 3H **19**
North Heath. *W Sus* 3B **26**
North Hill. *Corn* 5C **10**
North Hinksey Village. *Oxon* 5C **50**
North Holmwood. *Surr* 1C **26**
North Huish. *Devn* 3D **8**
North Hykeham. *Linc* 4G **87**
Northiam. *E Sus* 3C **28**
Northill. *C Beds* 1B **52**
Northington. *Hants* 3D **24**
North Kelsey. *Linc* 4D **94**
North Kelsey Moor. *Linc* 4D **94**
North Kessock. *High* 4A **158**
North Killingholme. *N Lin* 3E **95**
North Kilvington. *N Yor* 1G **99**
North Kilworth. *Leics* 2D **62**
North Kyme. *Linc* 5A **88**
North Lancing. *W Sus* 5C **26**
Northlands. *Linc* 5C **88**
Northleach. *Glos* 4G **49**
North Lee. *Buck* 5G **51**
North Lees. *N Yor* 2E **99**
Northleigh. *Devn* 3G **19**
(nr. Barnstaple)
Northleigh. *Devn* 3E **13**
(nr. Honiton)
North Leigh. *Kent* 1F **29**
North Leigh. *Oxon* 4B **50**
North Leverton. *Notts* 2E **87**
Northlew. *Devn* 3F **11**
North Littleton. *Worc* 1F **49**
North Lopham. *Norf* 2C **66**
North Luffenham. *Rut* 5G **75**
North Marden. *W Sus* 1G **17**
North Marston. *Buck* 3F **51**
North Middleton. *Midl* 4G **129**
North Middleton. *Nmbd* 2E **121**
North Molton. *Devn* 4H **19**
North Moor. *N Yor* 1D **100**
Northmoor. *Oxon* 5C **50**
Northmoor Green. *Som* 3G **21**
North Moreton. *Oxon* 3D **36**
Northmuir. *Ang* 3C **144**
North Mundham. *W Sus* 2G **17**
North Murie. *Per* 1E **137**
North Muskham. *Notts* 5E **87**
North Ness. *Orkn* 8C **172**
North Newbald. *E Yor* 1C **94**
North Newington. *Oxon* 2C **50**
North Newnton. *Wilts* 1G **23**
North Newton. *Som* 3F **21**
Northney. *Hants* 2F **17**
North Nibley. *Glos* 2C **34**
North Oakley. *Hants* 1D **24**
North Ockendon. *G Lon* 2G **39**
Northolt. *G Lon* 2C **38**
Northop. *Flin* 4E **83**
Northop Hall. *Flin* 4E **83**
North Ormesby. *Midd* 3C **106**
North Ormsby. *Linc* 1B **88**
Northorpe. *Linc* 4H **75**
(nr. Bourne)
Northorpe. *Linc* 2B **76**
(nr. Donington)
Northorpe. *Linc* 1F **87**
(nr. Gainsborough)

North Otterington—Ottinge

North Otterington. *N Yor* 1F 99
Northover. *Som* 3H 21 (nr. Glastonbury)
Northover. *Som* 4A 22 (nr. Yeovil)
North Owersby. *Linc* 1H 87
Northowram. *W Yor* 2B 92
North Perrott. *Som* 2H 13
North Petherton. *Som* 3F 21
North Petherwin. *Corn* 4C 10
North Pickenham. *Norf* 5A 78
North Piddle. *Worc* 5D 60
North Poorton. *Dors* 3A 14
North Port. *Arg* 1H 133
Northport. *Dors* 4E 15
North Queensferry. *Fife* 1E 129
North Radworthy. *Devn* 3A 20
North Rauceby. *Linc* 1H 75
Northrepps. *Norf* 2E 79
North Rigton. *N Yor* 5E 99
North Rode. *Ches E* 4C 84
North Roe. *Shet* 3E 173
North Ronaldsay Airport. *Orkn* 2G 172
North Row. *Cumb* 1D 102
North Runcton. *Norf* 4F 77
North Sannox. *N Ayr* 5B 126
North Scale. *Cumb* 2A 96
North Scarle. *Linc* 4F 87
North Seaton. *Nmbd* 1F 115
North Seaton Colliery. *Nmbd* 1F 115
North Sheen. *G Lon* 3C 38
North Shian. *Arg* 4D 140
North Shields. *Tyne* 3G 115
North Shoebury. *S'end* 2D 40
North Shore. *Bkpl* 1B 90
North Side. *Cumb* 2B 102
North Skelton. *Red C* 3D 106
North Somercotes. *Linc* 1D 88
North Stainley. *N Yor* 2E 99
North Stainmore. *Cumb* 3B 104
North Stifford. *Thur* 2H 39
North Stoke. *Bath* 5C 34
North Stoke. *Oxon* 3E 36
North Stoke. *W Sus* 4B 26
Northstowe. *Cambs* 4D 64
North Street. *Hants* 3E 25
North Street. *Kent* 5E 40
North Street. *Medw* 3C 40
North Street. *W Ber* 4E 37
North Sunderland. *Nmbd* 1G 121
North Tamerton. *Corn* 3D 10
North Tawton. *Devn* 2G 11
North Thoresby. *Linc* 1B 88
North Town. *Devn* 2F 11
Northtown. *Orkn* 8D 172
North Town. *Shet* 10E 173
North Tuddenham. *Norf* 4C 78
North Walbottle. *Tyne* 3E 115
Northwall. *Orkn* 3G 172
North Walney. *Cumb* 3A 96
North Walsham. *Norf* 2E 79
North Waltham. *Hants* 2D 24
North Warnborough. *Hants* 1F 25
North Water Bridge. *Ang* 2F 145
North Watten. *High* 3E 169
Northway. *Glos* 2E 49
Northway. *Swan* 4E 31
North Weald Bassett. *Essx* 5F 53
North Weston. *N Som* 4H 33
North Weston. *Oxon* 5E 51
North Wheatley. *Notts* 2E 87
North Whilborough. *Devn* 2E 9
Northwich. *Ches W* 3A 84
North Wick. *Bath* 5A 34
Northwick. *Som* 2G 21
Northwick. *S Glo* 3A 34
North Widcombe. *Bath* 1A 22
North Willingham. *Linc* 2A 88
North Wingfield. *Derbs* 4B 86
North Witham. *Linc* 3G 75
Northwold. *Norf* 1G 65
Northwood. *Derbs* 4G 85
Northwood. *G Lon* 1B 38
Northwood. *IOW* 3C 16
Northwood. *Kent* 4H 41
Northwood. *Shrp* 2G 71
Northwood. *Stoke* 1C 72
Northwood Green. *Glos* 4C 48
North Wootton. *Dors* 1B 14
North Wootton. *Norf* 3F 77
North Wootton. *Som* 2A 22
North Wraxall. *Wilts* 4D 34
North Wroughton. *Swin* 3G 35
North Yardhope. *Nmbd* 4D 120
Norton. *Devn* 3E 9
Norton. *Glos* 3D 48
Norton. *Hal* 2H 83
Norton. *Herts* 2C 52
Norton. *IOW* 4B 16
Norton. *Mon* 3H 47
Norton. *Nptn* 4D 62
Norton. *Notts* 3C 86
Norton. *Powy* 4F 59
Norton. *Shrp* 2G 59 (nr. Ludlow)
Norton. *Shrp* 5B 72 (nr. Madeley)
Norton. *Shrp* 5H 71 (nr. Shrewsbury)
Norton. *S Yor* 3F 93 (nr. Askern)
Norton. *S Yor* 2A 86 (nr. Sheffield)
Norton. *Stoc T* 2B 106
Norton. *Suff* 4B 66
Norton. *Swan* 4F 31
Norton. *W Sus* 5A 26 (nr. Arundel)
Norton. *W Sus* 3G 17 (nr. Selsey)
Norton. *Wilts* 3D 35
Norton. *Worc* 1F 49 (nr. Evesham)
Norton. *Worc* 5C 60 (nr. Worcester)
Norton Bavant. *Wilts* 2E 23
Norton Bridge. *Staf* 2C 72
Norton Canes. *Staf* 5E 73
Norton Canon. *Here* 1G 47
Norton Corner. *Norf* 3C 78
Norton Disney. *Linc* 5F 87
Norton East. *Staf* 5E 73
Norton Ferris. *Wilts* 3C 22
Norton Fitzwarren. *Som* 4F 21
Norton Green. *IOW* 4B 16
Norton Green. *Stoke* 5D 84
Norton Hawkfield. *Bath* 5A 34
Norton Heath. *Essx* 5G 53
Norton in Hales. *Shrp* 2B 72
Norton in the Moors. *Stoke* 5C 84
Norton-Juxta-Twycross. *Leics* 5H 73
Norton-le-Clay. *N Yor* 2G 99
Norton Lindsey. *Warw* 4G 61
Norton Little Green. *Suff* 4B 66
Norton Malreward. *Bath* 5B 34
Norton Mandeville. *Essx* 5F 53
Norton-on-Derwent. *N Yor* 2B 100
Norton St Philip. *Som* 1C 22
Norton Subcourse. *Norf* 1G 67
Norton sub Hamdon. *Som* 1H 13
Norton Woodseats. *S Yor* 2A 86
Norwell. *Notts* 4E 87
Norwell Woodhouse. *Notts* 4E 87
Norwich. *Norf* 5E 79 & 205
Norwich International Airport. *Norf* 4E 79
Norwick. *Shet* 1H 173
Norwood. *Derbs* 2B 86
Norwood Green. *W Yor* 2B 92
Norwood Hill. *Surr* 1D 26
Norwood Park. *Som* 3A 22
Norwoodside. *Cambs* 1D 64
Noseley. *Leics* 1E 63
Noss. *Shet* 10E 173
Noss Mayo. *Devn* 4B 8
Nosterfield. *N Yor* 1E 99
Nostie. *High* 1A 148
Notgrove. *Glos* 3G 49
Nottage. *B'end* 4B 32
Nottingham. *Nott* 1C 74 & 206
Nottington. *Dors* 4B 14
Notton. *Dors* 3B 14
Notton. *W Yor* 3D 92
Notton. *Wilts* 5E 35
Nounsley. *Essx* 4A 54
Noutard's Green. *Worc* 4B 60
Nox. *Shrp* 4G 71
Noyadd Trefawr. *Cdgn* 1C 44
Nuffield. *Oxon* 3E 37
Nunburnholme. *E Yor* 5C 100
Nuncargate. *Notts* 5B 86
Nunclose. *Cumb* 5F 113
Nuneaton. *Warw* 1A 62
Nuneham Courtenay. *Oxon* 2D 36
Nun Monkton. *N Yor* 4H 99
Nunnerie. *S Lan* 3B 118
Nunney. *Som* 2C 22
Nunnington. *N Yor* 2A 100
Nunnykirk. *Nmbd* 5E 121
Nunsthorpe. *NE Lin* 4F 95
Nunthorpe. *Red C* 3C 106
Nunthorpe. *York* 5H 99
Nunton. *Wilts* 4G 23
Nunwick. *Nmbd* 2B 114
Nunwick. *N Yor* 2F 99
Nupend. *Glos* 5C 48
Nursling. *Hants* 1B 16
Nursted. *W Sus* 4F 25
Nursteed. *Wilts* 5F 35
Nurston. *V Glam* 5D 32
Nutbourne. *W Sus* 2F 17 (nr. Chichester)
Nutbourne. *W Sus* 4B 26 (nr. Pulborough)
Nutfield. *Surr* 5E 39
Nuthall. *Notts* 1C 74
Nuthampstead. *Herts* 2E 53
Nuthurst. *Warw* 3F 61
Nuthurst. *W Sus* 3C 26
Nutley. *E Sus* 3F 27
Nuttall. *G Man* 3F 91
Nutwell. *S Yor* 4G 93
Nybster. *High* 2F 169
Nyetimber. *W Sus* 3G 17
Nyewood. *W Sus* 4G 25
Nymet Rowland. *Devn* 2H 11
Nymet Tracey. *Devn* 2H 11
Nympsfield. *Glos* 5D 48
Nynehead. *Som* 4E 21
Nyton. *W Sus* 5A 26

O

Oadby. *Leics* 5D 74
Oad Street. *Kent* 4C 40
Oakamoor. *Staf* 1E 73
Oakbank. *Arg* 5B 140
Oakbank. *W Lot* 3D 129
Oakdale. *Cphy* 2E 33
Oakdale. *Pool* 3F 15
Oake. *Som* 4E 21
Oaken. *Staf* 5C 72
Oakenclough. *Lanc* 5E 97
Oakengates. *Telf* 4B 72
Oakenholt. *Flin* 3E 83
Oakenshaw. *Dur* 1F 105
Oakenshaw. *W Yor* 2B 92
Oakerthorpe. *Derbs* 5A 86
Oakford. *Cdgn* 5D 56
Oakford. *Devn* 4C 20
Oakfordbridge. *Devn* 4C 20
Oakgrove. *Ches E* 4D 84
Oakham. *Rut* 5F 75
Oakhanger. *Ches E* 5B 84
Oakhanger. *Hants* 3F 25
Oakhill. *Som* 2B 22
Oakington. *Cambs* 4D 64
Oaklands. *Powy* 5C 58
Oakle Street. *Glos* 4C 48
Oakley. *Bed* 5H 63
Oakley. *Buck* 4E 51
Oakley. *Fife* 1D 128
Oakley. *Hants* 1D 24
Oakley. *Suff* 3D 66
Oakley Green. *Wind* 3A 38
Oakley Park. *Powy* 2B 58
Oakmere. *Ches W* 4H 83
Oakridge. *Glos* 5E 49
Oaks. *Shrp* 5G 71
Oaksey. *Wilts* 2E 35
Oaks Green. *Derbs* 2F 73
Oakshaw Ford. *Cumb* 2G 113
Oakshott. *Hants* 4F 25
Oakthorpe. *Leics* 4H 73
Oak Tree. *Darl* 3A 106
Oakwood. *Derb* 2A 74
Oakwood. *W Yor* 1D 92
Oakwoodhill. *Surr* 2C 26
Oakworth. *W Yor* 1A 92
Oape. *High* 3B 164
Oare. *Kent* 4E 40
Oare. *Som* 2B 20
Oare. *W Ber* 4D 36
Oare. *Wilts* 5G 35
Oareford. *Som* 2B 20
Oasby. *Linc* 2H 75
Oath. *Som* 4G 21
Oathlaw. *Ang* 3D 145
Oatlands. *N Yor* 4F 99
Oban. *Arg* 1F 133 & 206
Oban. *W Isl* 7D 171
Oborne. *Dors* 1B 14
Obsdale. *High* 2A 158
Obthorpe. *Linc* 4H 75
Occlestone Green. *Ches W* 4A 84
Occold. *Suff* 3D 66
Ochiltree. *E Ayr* 2E 117
Ochtermuthill. *Per* 2H 135
Ochtertyre. *Per* 1H 135
Ockbrook. *Derbs* 2B 74
Ockeridge. *Worc* 4B 60
Ockham. *Surr* 5B 38
Ockle. *High* 1G 139
Ockley. *Surr* 1C 26
Ocle Pychard. *Here* 1A 48
Octofad. *Arg* 4A 124
Octomore. *Arg* 4A 124
Octon. *E Yor* 3E 101
Odcombe. *Som* 1A 14
Odd Down. *Bath* 5C 34
Oddingley. *Worc* 5D 60
Oddington. *Oxon* 4D 50
Oddsta. *Shet* 2G 173
Odell. *Bed* 5G 63
Odie. *Orkn* 5F 172
Odiham. *Hants* 1F 25
Odsey. *Cambs* 2C 52
Odstock. *Wilts* 4G 23
Odstone. *Leics* 5A 74
Offchurch. *Warw* 4A 62
Offenham. *Worc* 1F 49
Offenham Cross. *Worc* 1F 49
Offerton. *G Man* 2D 84
Offerton. *Tyne* 4G 115
Offham. *E Sus* 4F 27
Offham. *Kent* 5A 40
Offham. *W Sus* 5B 26
Offleyhay. *Staf* 3C 72
Offley Hoo. *Herts* 3B 52
Offleymarsh. *Staf* 3B 72
Offord Cluny. *Cambs* 4B 64
Offord D'Arcy. *Cambs* 4B 64
Offton. *Suff* 1D 54
Offwell. *Devn* 3E 13
Ogbourne Maizey. *Wilts* 4G 35
Ogbourne St Andrew. *Wilts* 4G 35
Ogbourne St George. *Wilts* 4H 35
Ogden. *G Man* 3H 91
Ogle. *Nmbd* 2E 115
Ogmore. *V Glam* 4B 32
Ogmore-by-Sea. *V Glam* 4B 32
Ogmore Vale. *B'end* 2C 32
Okeford Fitzpaine. *Dors* 1D 14
Okehampton. *Devn* 3F 11
Okehampton Camp. *Devn* 3F 11
Okraquoy. *Shet* 8F 173
Okus. *Swin* 3G 35
Old. *Nptn* 3E 63
Old Aberdeen. *Aber* 3G 153
Old Alresford. *Hants* 3D 24
Oldany. *High* 5B 166
Old Arley. *Warw* 1G 61
Old Basford. *Nott* 1C 74
Old Basing. *Hants* 1E 25
Oldberrow. *Warw* 4F 61
Old Bewick. *Nmbd* 2E 121
Old Bexley. *G Lon* 3F 39
Old Blair. *Per* 2F 143
Old Bolingbroke. *Linc* 4C 88
Oldborough. *Devn* 2A 12
Old Brampton. *Derbs* 3H 85
Old Bridge of Tilt. *Per* 2F 143
Old Bridge of Urr. *Dum* 3E 111
Old Buckenham. *Norf* 1C 66
Old Burghclere. *Hants* 1C 24
Oldbury. *Shrp* 1B 60
Oldbury. *Warw* 1H 61
Oldbury. *W Mid* 2D 61
Oldbury-on-Severn. *S Glo* 2B 34
Oldbury on the Hill. *Glos* 3D 34
Old Byland. *N Yor* 1H 99
Old Cassop. *Dur* 1A 106
Oldcastle. *Mon* 3G 47
Oldcastle Heath. *Ches W* 1G 71
Old Catton. *Norf* 4E 79
Old Clee. *NE Lin* 4F 95
Old Cleeve. *Som* 2D 20
Old Clipstone. *Notts* 4D 86
Old Colwyn. *Cnwy* 3A 82
Oldcotes. *Notts* 2C 86
Old Coulsdon. *G Lon* 5E 39
Old Dailly. *S Ayr* 5B 116
Old Dalby. *Leics* 3D 74
Old Dam. *Derbs* 3F 85
Old Deer. *Abers* 4G 161
Old Dilton. *Wilts* 2D 22
Old Down. *S Glo* 3B 34
Oldeamere. *Cambs* 1C 64
Old Edlington. *S Yor* 1C 86
Old Eldon. *Dur* 2F 105
Old Ellerby. *E Yor* 1E 95
Old Fallings. *W Mid* 5D 72
Oldfallow. *Staf* 4D 72
Old Felixstowe. *Suff* 2G 55
Oldfield. *Shrp* 2A 60
Oldfield. *Worc* 4C 60
Old Fletton. *Pet* 1A 64
Oldford. *Som* 1C 22
Old Forge. *Here* 4A 48
Old Glossop. *Derbs* 1E 85
Old Goole. *E Yor* 2H 93
Old Gore. *Here* 3B 48
Old Graitney. *Dum* 3E 112
Old Grimsby. *IOS* 1A 4
Oldhall. *High* 3E 169
Old Hall Street. *Norf* 2F 79
Oldham. *G Man* 4H 91
Oldhamstocks. *E Lot* 2D 130
Old Heathfield. *E Sus* 3G 27
Old Hill. *W Mid* 2D 60
Old Hunstanton. *Norf* 1F 77
Old Hurst. *Cambs* 3B 64
Old Hutton. *Cumb* 1E 97
Old Kea. *Corn* 4C 6
Old Kilpatrick. *W Dun* 2F 127
Old Kinnernie. *Abers* 3E 152
Old Knebworth. *Herts* 3C 52
Oldland. *S Glo* 4B 34
Old Laxey. *IOM* 3D 108
Old Leake. *Linc* 5D 88
Old Lenton. *Nott* 2C 74
Old Llanberis. *Gwyn* 5F 81
Old Malton. *N Yor* 2B 100
Oldmeldrum. *Abers* 1F 153
Old Micklefield. *W Yor* 1E 93
Old Mill. *Corn* 5D 10
Oldmixon. *N Som* 1G 21
Old Monkland. *N Lan* 3A 128
Old Newton. *Suff* 4C 66
Old Park. *Telf* 5A 72
Old Pentland. *Midl* 3F 129
Old Philpstoun. *W Lot* 2D 128
Old Quarrington. *Dur* 1A 106
Old Radnor. *Powy* 5E 59
Old Rayne. *Abers* 1D 152
Oldridge. *Devn* 3B 12
Old Romney. *Kent* 3E 29
Old Scone. *Per* 1D 136
Oldshore Beg. *High* 3B 166
Oldshoremore. *High* 3C 166
Old Snydale. *W Yor* 2E 93
Old Sodbury. *S Glo* 3C 34
Old Somerby. *Linc* 2G 75
Old Spital. *Dur* 3C 104
Oldstead. *N Yor* 1H 99
Old Stratford. *Nptn* 1F 51
Old Swan. *Mers* 1F 83
Old Swarland. *Nmbd* 4F 121
Old Tebay. *Cumb* 4H 103
Old Town. *Cumb* 5F 113
Old Town. *E Sus* 5G 27
Oldtown. *High* 5C 164
Old Town. *IOS* 1B 4
Old Town. *Nmbd* 5C 120
Oldtown of Ord. *Abers* 3D 160
Old Trafford. *G Man* 1C 84
Old Tupton. *Derbs* 4A 86
Oldwall. *Cumb* 3F 113
Oldwalls. *Swan* 3D 31
Old Warden. *C Beds* 1B 52
Oldways End. *Som* 4B 20
Old Westhall. *Abers* 1D 152
Old Weston. *Cambs* 3H 63
Oldwhat. *Abers* 3F 161
Old Windsor. *Wind* 3A 38
Old Wives Lees. *Kent* 5E 41
Old Woking. *Surr* 5B 38
Oldwood Common. *Worc* 4H 59
Old Woodstock. *Oxon* 4C 50
Olgrinmore. *High* 3C 168
Oliver's Battery. *Hants* 4C 24
Ollaberry. *Shet* 3E 173
Ollerton. *Ches E* 3B 84
Ollerton. *Notts* 4D 86
Ollerton. *Shrp* 3A 72
Olmarch. *Cdgn* 5F 57
Olmstead Green. *Cambs* 1G 53
Olney. *Mil* 5F 63
Olrig. *High* 2D 169
Olton. *W Mid* 2F 61
Olveston. *S Glo* 3B 34
Ombersley. *Worc* 4C 60
Ompton. *Notts* 4D 86
Omunsgarth. *Shet* 7E 173
Onchan. *IOM* 4D 108
Onecote. *Staf* 5E 85
Onehouse. *Suff* 5C 66
Onen. *Mon* 4H 47
Ongar Hill. *Norf* 3E 77
Ongar Street. *Here* 4F 59
Onibury. *Shrp* 3G 59
Onich. *High* 2E 141
Onllwyn. *Neat* 4B 46
Onneley. *Shrp* 1B 72
Onslow Green. *Essx* 4G 53
Onslow Village. *Surr* 1A 26
Onthank. *E Ayr* 1D 116
Openwoodgate. *Derbs* 1A 74
Opinan. *High* 1G 155 (nr. Gairloch)
Opinan. *High* 4C 162 (nr. Laide)
Orasaigh. *W Isl* 6F 171
Orbost. *High* 4B 154
Orby. *Linc* 4D 89
Orchard Hill. *Devn* 4E 19
Orchard Portman. *Som* 4F 21
Orcheston. *Wilts* 2F 23
Orcop. *Here* 3H 47
Orcop Hill. *Here* 3H 47
Ord. *High* 2E 147
Ordale. *Shet* 1H 173
Ordhead. *Abers* 2D 152
Ordie. *Abers* 3B 152
Ordiquish. *Mor* 3H 159
Ordley. *Nmbd* 4C 114
Ordsall. *Notts* 3E 86
Ore. *E Sus* 4C 28
Oreham Common. *W Sus* 4D 26
Oreton. *Shrp* 2A 60
Orford. *Linc* 1B 88
Orford. *Suff* 1H 55
Orford. *Warr* 1A 84
Organford. *Dors* 3E 15
Orgil. *Orkn* 7B 172
Orgreave. *Staf* 4F 73
Oridge Street. *Glos* 3C 48
Orlestone. *Kent* 2D 28
Orleton. *Here* 4G 59
Orleton. *Worc* 4A 60
Orleton Common. *Here* 4G 59
Orlingbury. *Nptn* 3F 63
Ormacleit. *W Isl* 5C 170
Ormathwaite. *Cumb* 2D 102
Ormesby. *Midd* 3C 106
Ormesby St Margaret. *Norf* 4G 79
Ormesby St Michael. *Norf* 4G 79
Ormiscaig. *High* 4C 162
Ormiston. *E Lot* 3H 129
Ormsaigbeg. *High* 2F 139
Ormsaigmore. *High* 2F 139
Ormsary. *Arg* 2F 125
Ormsgill. *Cumb* 2A 96
Ormskirk. *Lanc* 4C 90
Orphir. *Orkn* 7C 172
Orpington. *G Lon* 4F 39
Orrell. *Lanc* 4D 90
Orrell. *Mers* 1F 83
Orrisdale. *IOM* 2C 108
Orsett. *Thur* 2H 39
Orslow. *Staf* 4C 72
Orston. *Notts* 1E 75
Orthwaite. *Cumb* 1D 102
Orton. *Cumb* 4H 103
Orton. *Mor* 3H 159
Orton. *Nptn* 3F 63
Orton. *Staf* 1C 60
Orton Longueville. *Pet* 1A 64
Orton-on-the-Hill. *Leics* 5H 73
Orton Waterville. *Pet* 1A 64
Orton Wistow. *Pet* 1A 64
Orwell. *Cambs* 5C 64
Osbaldeston. *Lanc* 1E 91
Osbaldwick. *York* 4A 100
Osbaston. *Leics* 5B 74
Osbaston. *Shrp* 3F 71
Osbournby. *Linc* 2H 75
Osclay. *High* 5E 169
Oscroft. *Ches W* 4H 83
Ose. *High* 4C 154
Osgathorpe. *Leics* 4B 74
Osgodby. *Linc* 1H 87
Osgodby. *N Yor* 1E 101 (nr. Scarborough)
Osgodby. *N Yor* 1G 93 (nr. Selby)
Oskaig. *High* 5E 155
Oskamull. *Arg* 4F 139
Osleston. *Derbs* 2G 73
Osmaston. *Derb* 2A 74
Osmaston. *Derbs* 1G 73
Osmington. *Dors* 4C 14
Osmington Mills. *Dors* 4C 14
Osmondthorpe. *W Yor* 1D 92
Osmondwall. *Orkn* 9C 172
Osmotherley. *N Yor* 5B 106
Osnaburgh. *Fife* 2G 137
Ospisdale. *High* 5E 164
Ospringe. *Kent* 4E 40
Ossett. *W Yor* 2C 92
Ossington. *Notts* 4E 87
Ostend. *Essx* 1D 40
Ostend. *Norf* 2F 79
Osterley. *G Lon* 3C 38
Oswaldkirk. *N Yor* 2A 100
Oswaldtwistle. *Lanc* 2F 91
Oswestry. *Shrp* 3E 71
Otby. *Linc* 1A 88
Otford. *Kent* 5G 39
Otham. *Kent* 5B 40
Otherton. *Staf* 4D 72
Othery. *Som* 3G 21
Otley. *Suff* 5E 66
Otley. *W Yor* 5E 98
Otterbourne. *Hants* 4C 24
Otterburn. *Nmbd* 5C 120
Otterburn. *N Yor* 4A 98
Otterburn Camp. *Nmbd* 5C 120
Otterburn Hall. *Nmbd* 5C 120
Otter Ferry. *Arg* 1H 125
Otterford. *Som* 1F 13
Otterham. *Corn* 3B 10
Otterhampton. *Som* 2F 21
Otterham Quay. *Kent* 4C 40
Ottershaw. *Surr* 4B 38
Otterspool. *Mers* 2F 83
Otterswick. *Shet* 3G 173
Otterton. *Devn* 4D 12
Otterwood. *Hants* 2C 16
Ottery St Mary. *Devn* 3E 12
Ottinge. *Kent* 1F 29

Ottringham—Pens

Ottringham. *E Yor* 2F 95
Oughterby. *Cumb* 4D 112
Oughtershaw. *N Yor* 1A 98
Oughterside. *Cumb* 5C 112
Oughtibridge. *S Yor* 1H 85
Oughtrington. *Warr* 2A 84
Oulston. *N Yor* 2H 99
Oulton. *Cumb* 4D 112
Oulton. *Norf* 3D 78
Oulton. *Staf* 3B 72
(nr. Gnosall Heath)
Oulton. *Staf* 2D 72
(nr. Stone)
Oulton. *Suff* 1H 67
Oulton. *W Yor* 2D 92
Oulton Broad. *Suff* 1H 67
Oulton Street. *Norf* 3D 78
Oundle. *Nptn* 2H 63
Ousby. *Cumb* 1H 103
Ousdale. *High* 1H 165
Ousden. *Suff* 5G 65
Ousefleet. *E Yor* 2B 94
Ouston. *Dur* 4F 115
Ouston. *Nmbd* 4A 114
(nr. Bearsbridge)
Ouston. *Nmbd* 2D 114
(nr. Stamfordham)
Outer Hope. *Devn* 4C 8
Outertown. *Orkn* 6B 172
Outgate. *Cumb* 5E 103
Outhgill. *Cumb* 4A 104
Outlands. *Staf* 2B 72
Outlane. *W Yor* 3A 92
Out Newton. *E Yor* 2G 95
Out Rawcliffe. *Lanc* 5D 96
Outwell. *Norf* 5E 77
Outwick. *Hants* 1G 15
Outwood. *Surr* 1E 27
Outwood. *W Yor* 2D 92
Outwood. *Worc* 3D 60
Outwoods. *Leics* 4B 74
Outwoods. *Staf* 4B 72
Ouzlewell Green. *W Yor* 2D 92
Ovenden. *W Yor* 2A 92
Over. *Cambs* 3C 64
Over. *Ches W* 4A 84
Over. *Glos* 4D 48
Over. *S Glo* 3A 34
Overbister. *Orkn* 3F 172
Over Burrows. *Derbs* 2G 73
Overbury. *Worc* 2E 49
Overcombe. *Dors* 4B 14
Over Compton. *Dors* 1A 14
Over End. *Cambs* 1H 63
Over Finlarg. *Ang* 4D 144
Overgreen. *Derbs* 3H 85
Over Green. *W Mid* 1F 61
Over Haddon. *Derbs* 4G 85
Over Hulton. *G Man* 4E 91
Over Kellet. *Lanc* 2E 97
Over Kiddington. *Oxon* 3C 50
Overleigh. *Som* 3H 21
Overley. *Staf* 4F 73
Over Monnow. *Mon* 4A 48
Over Norton. *Oxon* 3B 50
Over Peover. *Ches E* 3B 84
Overpool. *Ches W* 3F 83
Overscaig. *High* 1B 164
Overseal. *Derbs* 4G 73
Over Silton. *N Yor* 5B 106
Oversland. *Kent* 5E 41
Overstone. *Nptn* 4F 63
Over Stowey. *Som* 3E 21
Overstrand. *Norf* 1E 79
Over Stratton. *Som* 1H 13
Over Street. *Wilts* 3F 23
Overthorpe. *Nptn* 1C 50
Overton. *Aber* 2F 153
Overton. *Ches W* 3H 83
Overton. *Hants* 2D 24
Overton. *High* 5E 169
Overton. *Lanc* 4D 96
Overton. *N Yor* 4H 99
Overton. *Shrp* 2A 60
(nr. Bridgnorth)
Overton. *Shrp* 3H 59
(nr. Ludlow)
Overton. *Swan* 4D 30
Overton. *W Yor* 3C 92
Overton. *Wrex* 1F 71
Overtown. *N Lan* 4B 128
Overtown. *Swin* 4G 35
Over Wallop. *Hants* 3A 24
Over Whitacre. *Warw* 1G 61
Over Worton. *Oxon* 3C 50
Oving. *Buck* 3F 51
Oving. *W Sus* 5A 26
Ovingdean. *Brig* 5E 27
Ovingham. *Nmbd* 3D 115
Ovington. *Dur* 3E 105
Ovington. *Essx* 1A 54
Ovington. *Hants* 3D 24
Ovington. *Norf* 5B 78
Ovington. *Nmbd* 3D 114
Owen's Bank. *Staf* 3G 73
Ower. *Hants* 2C 16
(nr. Holbury)
Ower. *Hants* 1B 16
(nr. Totton)
Owermoigne. *Dors* 4C 14
Owlbury. *Shrp* 1F 59
Owler Bar. *Derbs* 3G 85
Owlerton. *S Yor* 2H 85
Owlsmoor. *Brac* 5G 37
Owlswick. *Buck* 5F 51
Owmby. *Linc* 4D 94
Owmby-by-Spital. *Linc* 2H 87
Ownham. *W Ber* 4C 36
Owrytn. *Wrex* 1F 71
Owslebury. *Hants* 4D 24
Owston. *Leics* 5E 75
Owston. *S Yor* 3F 93
Owston Ferry. *N Lin* 4B 94
Owstwick. *E Yor* 1F 95
Owthorne. *E Yor* 2G 95
Owthorpe. *Notts* 2D 74
Owton Manor. *Hart* 2B 106
Oxborough. *Norf* 5G 77
Oxbridge. *Dors* 3H 13
Oxcombe. *Linc* 3C 88
Oxen End. *Essx* 3G 53
Oxenhall. *Glos* 3C 48
Oxenholme. *Cumb* 5G 103
Oxenhope. *W Yor* 1A 92
Oxen Park. *Cumb* 1C 96
Oxenpill. *Som* 2H 21
Oxenton. *Glos* 2E 49
Oxenwood. *Wilts* 1B 24
Oxford. *Oxon* 5D 50 & 207
Oxgangs. *Edin* 3F 129
Oxhey. *Herts* 1C 38
Oxhill. *Warw* 1B 50
Oxley. *W Mid* 5C 72
Oxley Green. *Essx* 4C 54
Oxley's Green. *E Sus* 3A 28
Oxlode. *Cambs* 2D 65
Oxnam. *Bord* 3B 120
Oxshott. *Surr* 4C 38
Oxspring. *S Yor* 4C 92
Oxted. *Surr* 5E 39
Oxton. *Mers* 2E 83
Oxton. *N Yor* 5H 99
Oxton. *Notts* 5D 86
Oxton. *Bord* 4A 130
Oxwich. *Swan* 4D 31
Oxwich Green. *Swan* 4D 31
Oxwick. *Norf* 3B 78
Oykel Bridge. *High* 3A 164
Oyne. *Abers* 1D 152
Oystermouth. *Swan* 4F 31
Ozleworth. *Glos* 2C 34

P

Pabail Iarach. *W Isl* 4H 171
Pabail Uarach. *W Isl* 4H 171
Pachesham. *Surr* 5C 38
Packers Hill. *Dors* 1C 14
Packington. *Leics* 4A 74
Packmoor. *Stoke* 5C 84
Packmores. *Warw* 4G 61
Packwood. *W Mid* 3F 61
Packwood Gullett. *W Mid* 3F 61
Padanaram. *Ang* 3D 144
Padbury. *Buck* 2F 51
Paddington. *G Lon* 2D 38
Paddington. *Warr* 2A 84
Paddlesworth. *Kent* 2F 29
Paddock. *Kent* 5D 40
Paddockhole. *Dum* 1D 112
Paddock Wood. *Kent* 1A 28
Paddolgreen. *Shrp* 2H 71
Padeswood. *Flin* 4E 83
Padiham. *Lanc* 1F 91
Padside. *N Yor* 4D 98
Padson. *Devn* 3F 11
Padstow. *Corn* 1D 6
Padworth. *W Ber* 5E 36
Page Bank. *Dur* 1F 105
Pagham. *W Sus* 3G 17
Paglesham Churchend. *Essx* 1D 40
Paglesham Eastend. *Essx* 1D 40
Paibeil. *W Isl* 2C 170
(on North Uist)
Paibeil. *W Isl* 8C 171
(on Taransay)
Paiblesgearraidh. *W Isl* 2C 170
Paignton. *Torb* 2E 9
Pailton. *Warw* 2B 62
Paine's Corner. *E Sus* 3H 27
Painleyhill. *Staf* 2E 73
Painscastle. *Powy* 1E 47
Painshawfield. *Nmbd* 3D 114
Painsthorpe. *E Yor* 4C 100
Painswick. *Glos* 5D 48
Painter's Forstal. *Kent* 5D 40
Painthorpe. *W Yor* 3D 92
Pairc Shiaboist. *W Isl* 3E 171
Paisley. *Ren* 3F 127 & 207
Pakefield. *Suff* 1H 67
Pakenham. *Suff* 4B 66
Pale. *Gwyn* 2B 70
Palehouse Common. *E Sus* 4F 27
Palestine. *Hants* 2A 24
Paley Street. *Wind* 4G 37
Palgowan. *Dum* 1A 110
Palgrave. *Suff* 3D 66
Pallington. *Dors* 3C 14
Palmarsh. *Kent* 2F 29
Palmer Moor. *Derbs* 2F 73
Palmers Cross. *W Mid* 5C 72
Palmerstown. *V Glam* 5E 33
Palnackie. *Dum* 4F 111
Palnure. *Dum* 3B 110
Palterton. *Derbs* 4B 86
Pamber End. *Hants* 1E 24
Pamber Green. *Hants* 1E 24
Pamber Heath. *Hants* 5E 36
Pamington. *Glos* 2E 49
Pamphill. *Dors* 2E 15
Pampisford. *Cambs* 1E 53
Panborough. *Som* 2H 21
Panbride. *Ang* 5E 145
Pancakehill. *Glos* 4F 49
Pancrasweek. *Devn* 2C 10
Pandy. *Gwyn* 3A 70
(nr. Bala)
Pandy. *Gwyn* 5F 69
(nr. Tywyn)
Pandy. *Mon* 3G 47
Pandy. *Powy* 5B 70
Pandy. *Wrex* 2D 70
Pandy Tudur. *Cnwy* 4A 82
Panfield. *Essx* 3H 53
Pangbourne. *W Ber* 4E 37
Pannal. *N Yor* 4F 99
Pannal Ash. *N Yor* 4E 99
Pannanich. *Abers* 4A 152
Pant. *Shrp* 3E 71
Pant. *Wrex* 1F 71
Pantasaph. *Flin* 3D 82
Pant Glas. *Gwyn* 1D 68
Pant-glas. *Shrp* 2E 71
Pantgwyn. *Carm* 3F 45
Pantgwyn. *Cdgn* 1C 44
Pant-lasau. *Swan* 3F 31
Panton. *Linc* 3A 88
Pant-pastynog. *Den* 4C 82
Pantperthog. *Gwyn* 5G 69
Pant-teg. *Carm* 3E 45
Pant-y-Caws. *Carm* 2F 43
Pant-y-dwr. *Powy* 3B 58
Pant-y-ffridd. *Powy* 5D 70
Pantyffynnon. *Carm* 4G 45
Pantygasseg. *Torf* 5F 47
Pant-y-llyn. *Carm* 4G 45
Pant-yr-awel. *B'end* 3C 32
Pant y Wacco. *Flin* 3D 82
Panxworth. *Norf* 4F 79
Papa Stour Airport. *Shet* 6C 173
Papa Westray Airport. *Orkn* 2D 172
Papcastle. *Cumb* 1C 102
Papigoe. *High* 3F 169
Papil. *Shet* 8E 173
Papple. *E Lot* 2B 130
Papplewick. *Notts* 5C 86
Papworth Everard. *Cambs* 4B 64
Papworth St Agnes. *Cambs* 4B 64
Par. *Corn* 3E 7
Paramour Street. *Kent* 4G 41
Parbold. *Lanc* 3C 90
Parbrook. *Som* 3A 22
Parbrook. *W Sus* 3B 26
Parc. *Gwyn* 2A 70
Parcllyn. *Cdgn* 5B 56
Parc-Seymour. *Newp* 2H 33
Pardown. *Hants* 2D 24
Pardshaw. *Cumb* 2B 102
Parham. *Suff* 4F 67
Park. *Abers* 4E 153
Park. *Arg* 4D 140
Park. *Dum* 5B 118
Park Bottom. *Corn* 4A 6
Parkburn. *Abers* 5E 161
Park Corner. *E Sus* 2G 27
Park Corner. *Oxon* 3E 37
Parkend. *Glos* 5B 48
Park End. *Nmbd* 2B 114
Parkeston. *Essx* 2F 55
Parkfield. *Corn* 2H 7
Parkgate. *Ches W* 3E 83
Parkgate. *Cumb* 5D 112
Parkgate. *Dum* 1B 112
Park Gate. *Hants* 2D 16
Parkgate. *Surr* 1D 26
Park Gate. *Worc* 3D 60
Parkhall. *W Dun* 2F 127
Parkham. *Devn* 4D 19
Parkham Ash. *Devn* 4D 18
Parkhead. *Cumb* 5E 113
Parkhead. *Glas* 3H 127
Park Hill. *Mers* 4C 90
Parkhouse. *Mon* 5H 47
Parkhurst. *IOW* 3C 16
Park Lane. *G Man* 4F 91
Park Lane. *Staf* 5C 72
Parkmill. *Swan* 4E 31
Park Mill. *W Yor* 3C 92
Parkneuk. *Abers* 1G 145
Parkside. *N Lan* 4B 128
Parkstone. *Pool* 3F 15
Park Street. *Herts* 5B 52
Park Street. *W Sus* 2C 26
Park Town. *Oxon* 5D 50
Park Village. *Nmbd* 3H 113
Parkway. *Here* 2C 48
Parley Cross. *Dors* 3F 15
Parmoor. *Buck* 3F 37
Parr. *Mers* 1H 83
Parracombe. *Devn* 2G 19
Parrog. *Pemb* 1E 43
Parsonage Green. *Essx* 4H 53
Parsonby. *Cumb* 1C 102
Parson Cross. *S Yor* 1A 86
Parson Drove. *Cambs* 5C 76
Partick. *Glas* 3G 127
Partington. *G Man* 1B 84
Partney. *Linc* 4D 88
Parton. *Cumb* 2A 102
(nr. Whitehaven)
Parton. *Cumb* 4D 112
(nr. Wigton)
Parton. *Dum* 2D 111
Partridge Green. *W Sus* 4C 26
Parwich. *Derbs* 5F 85
Passenham. *Nptn* 2F 51
Passfield. *Hants* 3G 25
Passingford Bridge. *Essx* 1G 39
Paston. *Norf* 2F 79
Pasturefields. *Staf* 3D 73
Patchacott. *Devn* 3E 11
Patcham. *Brig* 5E 27
Patchetts Green. *Herts* 1C 38
Patching. *W Sus* 5B 26
Patchole. *Devn* 2G 19
Patchway. *S Glo* 3B 34
Pateley Bridge. *N Yor* 3D 98
Pathe. *Som* 3G 21
Pathfinder Village. *Devn* 3B 12
Pathhead. *Abers* 2G 145
Pathhead. *E Ayr* 3F 117
Pathhead. *Fife* 4E 137
Pathhead. *Midl* 3G 129
Pathlow. *Warw* 5F 61
Path of Condie. *Per* 2C 136
Pathstruie. *Per* 2C 136
Patmore Heath. *Herts* 3E 53
Patna. *E Ayr* 3D 116
Patney. *Wilts* 1F 23
Patrick. *IOM* 3B 108
Patrick Brompton. *N Yor* 5F 105
Patrington. *E Yor* 2G 95
Patrington Haven. *E Yor* 2G 95
Patrixbourne. *Kent* 5F 41
Patterdale. *Cumb* 3E 103
Pattiesmuir. *Fife* 1D 129
Pattingham. *Staf* 1C 60
Pattishall. *Nptn* 5D 62
Pattiswick. *Essx* 3B 54
Patton Bridge. *Cumb* 5G 103
Paul. *Corn* 4B 4
Paulerspury. *Nptn* 1F 51
Paull. *E Yor* 2E 95
Paulton. *Bath* 1B 22
Pauperhaugh. *Nmbd* 5F 121
Pave Lane. *Telf* 4B 72
Pavenham. *Bed* 5G 63
Pawlett. *Som* 2G 21
Pawston. *Nmbd* 1C 120
Paxford. *Glos* 2G 49
Paxton. *Bord* 4F 131
Payhembury. *Devn* 2D 12
Paythorne. *Lanc* 4H 97
Payton. *Som* 4E 20
Peacehaven. *E Sus* 5F 27
Peak Dale. *Derbs* 3E 85
Peak Forest. *Derbs* 3F 85
Peak Hill. *Linc* 4B 76
Peakirk. *Pet* 5A 76
Pearsie. *Ang* 3C 144
Peasedown St John. *Bath* 1C 22
Peaseland Green. *Norf* 4C 78
Peasemore. *W Ber* 4C 36
Peasenhall. *Suff* 4F 67
Pease Pottage. *W Sus* 2D 26
Peaslake. *Surr* 1B 26
Peasley Cross. *Mers* 1H 83
Peasmarsh. *E Sus* 3C 28
Peasmarsh. *Som* 1G 13
Peasmarsh. *Surr* 1A 26
Peaston. *E Lot* 3H 129
Peastonbank. *E Lot* 3H 129
Peathill. *Abers* 2G 161
Peat Inn. *Fife* 3G 137
Peatling Magna. *Leics* 1C 62
Peatling Parva. *Leics* 2C 62
Peaton. *Arg* 1D 126
Peaton. *Shrp* 2H 59
Peats Corner. *Suff* 4D 66
Pebmarsh. *Essx* 2B 54
Pebworth. *Worc* 1G 49
Pecket Well. *W Yor* 2H 91
Peckforton. *Ches E* 5H 83
Peckham Bush. *Kent* 5A 40
Peckleton. *Leics* 5B 74
Pedair-ffordd. *Powy* 3D 70
Pedham. *Norf* 4F 79
Pedlinge. *Kent* 2F 29
Pedmore. *W Mid* 2D 60
Pedwell. *Som* 3H 21
Peebles. *Bord* 5F 129
Peel. *IOM* 3B 108
Peel. *Bord* 1G 119
Peel Common. *Hants* 2D 16
Peening Quarter. *Kent* 3C 28
Peggs Green. *Leics* 4B 74
Pegsdon. *C Beds* 2B 52
Pegswood. *Nmbd* 1F 115
Peinchorran. *High* 5E 155
Peinlich. *High* 3D 154
Pelaw. *Tyne* 3G 115
Pelcomb Bridge. *Pemb* 3D 42
Pelcomb Cross. *Pemb* 3D 42
Peldon. *Essx* 4C 54
Pelsall. *W Mid* 5E 73
Pelton. *Dur* 4F 115
Pelutho. *Cumb* 5C 112
Pelynt. *Corn* 3G 7
Pemberton. *Carm* 5F 45
Pembrey. *Carm* 5E 45
Pembridge. *Here* 5F 59
Pembroke. *Pemb* 4D 43
Pembroke Dock. *Pemb* 4D 42 & 215
Pembroke Ferry. *Pemb* 4D 43
Pembury. *Kent* 1H 27
Penallt. *Mon* 4A 48
Penally. *Pemb* 5F 43
Penalt. *Here* 3A 48
Penalum. *Pemb* 5F 43
Penare. *Corn* 4D 6
Penarth. *V Glam* 4E 33
Penbeagle. *Corn* 3C 4
Penberth. *Corn* 4B 4
Pen-bont Rhydybeddau. *Cdgn* 2F 57
Penbryn. *Cdgn* 5B 56
Pencader. *Carm* 2E 45
Pen-cae. *Cdgn* 5D 56
Pencaenewydd. *Gwyn* 1D 68
Pencaerau. *Neat* 3G 31
Pencaitland. *E Lot* 3H 129
Pencarnisiog. *IOA* 3C 80
Pencarreg. *Carm* 1F 45
Pencarrow. *Corn* 4B 10
Pencelli. *Powy* 3D 46
Pen-clawdd. *Swan* 3E 31
Pencoed. *B'end* 3C 32
Pencombe. *Here* 5H 59
Pencraig. *Here* 3A 48
Pencraig. *Powy* 3C 70
Pendeen. *Corn* 3A 4
Pendeford. *W Mid* 5D 72
Penderyn. *Rhon* 5C 46
Pendine. *Carm* 4G 43
Pendlebury. *G Man* 4F 91
Pendleton. *G Man* 1C 84
Pendleton. *Lanc* 1F 91
Pendock. *Worc* 2C 48
Pendoggett. *Corn* 5A 10
Pendomer. *Som* 1A 14
Pendoylan. *V Glam* 4D 32
Pendre. *B'end* 3C 32
Penegoes. *Powy* 5
Penelewey. *Corn* 4
Penffordd. *Pemb* 2E
Penffordd-Lâs. *Powy* 1A 5
Penfro. *Pemb* 4D 43
Pengam. *Cphy* 2E 33
Pengam. *Card* 4F 33
Penge. *G Lon* 3E 39
Pengelly. *Corn* 4A 10
Pengenffordd. *Powy* 2E 47
Pengorffwysfa. *IOA* 1D 80
Pengover Green. *Corn* 2G 7
Pengwern. *Den* 3C 82
Penhale. *Corn* 5D 5
(nr. Mullion)
Penhale. *Corn* 3D 6
(nr. St Austell)
Penhale Camp. *Corn* 3B 6
Penhallow. *Corn* 3B 6
Penhalvean. *Corn* 5B 6
Penhelig. *Gwyn* 1F 57
Penhill. *Swin* 3G 35
Penhow. *Newp* 2H 33
Penhurst. *E Sus* 4A 28
Peniarth. *Gwyn* 5F 69
Penicuik. *Midl* 3F 129
Peniel. *Carm* 3E 45
Penifiler. *High* 4D 155
Peninver. *Arg* 3B 122
Penisa'r Waun. *Gwyn* 4E 81
Penistone. *S Yor* 4C 92
Penketh. *Warr* 2H 83
Penkill. *S Ayr* 5B 116
Penkridge. *Staf* 4D 72
Penley. *Wrex* 2G 71
Penllech. *Gwyn* 2B 68
Penllergaer. *Swan* 3F 31
Pen-llyn. *IOA* 2C 80
Penmachno. *Cnwy* 5G 81
Penmaen. *Swan* 4E 31
Penmaenmawr. *Cnwy* 3G 81
Penmaenpool. *Gwyn* 4F 69
Penmaen Rhos. *Cnwy* 3A 82
Pen-marc. *V Glam* 5D 32
Penmark. *V Glam* 5D 32
Penmarth. *Corn* 5B 6
Penmon. *IOA* 2F 81
Penmorfa. *Gwyn* 1E 69
Penmynydd. *IOA* 3E 81
Penn. *Buck* 1A 38
Penn. *Dors* 3G 13
Penn. *W Mid* 1C 60
Pennal. *Gwyn* 5G 69
Pennan. *Abers* 2F 161
Pennant. *Cdgn* 4E 57
Pennant. *Den* 2C 70
Pennant. *Gwyn* 3B 70
Pennant. *Powy* 1A 58
Pennant Melangell. *Powy* 3C 70
Pennar. *Pemb* 4D 42
Pennard. *Swan* 4E 31
Pennerley. *Shrp* 1F 59
Pennington. *Cumb* 2B 96
Pennington. *G Man* 1A 84
Pennington. *Hants* 3B 16
Pennorth. *Powy* 3E 46
Penn Street. *Buck* 1A 38
Pennsylvania. *Devn* 3C 12
Pennsylvania. *S Glo* 4C 34
Penny Bridge. *Cumb* 1C 96
Pennycross. *Plym* 3A 8
Pennygate. *Norf* 3F 79
Pennyghael. *Arg* 1C 132
Penny Hill. *Linc* 3C 76
Pennylands. *Lanc* 4C 90
Pennymoor. *Devn* 1B 12
Pennyvenie. *E Ayr* 4D 117
Pennywell. *Tyne* 4G 115
Penparc. *Cdgn* 1C 44
Penparcau. *Cdgn* 2E 57
Penpedairheol. *Cphy* 2E 33
Penperlleni. *Mon* 5G 47
Penpillick. *Corn* 3E 7
Penpol. *Corn* 5C 6
Penpoll. *Corn* 3F 7
Penponds. *Corn* 3D 4
Penpont. *Corn* 5A 10
Penpont. *Dum* 5H 117
Penpont. *Powy* 3C 46
Penprysg. *B'end* 3C 32
Penquit. *Devn* 3C 8
Penrherber. *Carm* 1G 43
Penrhiw. *Pemb* 1C 44
Penrhiwceiber. *Rhon* 2D 32
Pen Rhiwfawr. *Neat* 4H 45
Penrhiw-llan. *Cdgn* 1D 44
Penrhiw-pal. *Cdgn* 1D 44
Penrhos. *Gwyn* 2C 68
Penrhos. *Here* 5F 59
Penrhos. *IOA* 2B 80
Penrhos. *Mon* 4H 47
Penrhos. *Powy* 4A 46
Penrhos Garnedd. *Gwyn* 3E 81
Penrhyn. *IOA* 1C 80
Penrhyn Bay. *Cnwy* 2H 81
Penrhyn-coch. *Cdgn* 2F 57
Penrhyndeudraeth. *Gwyn* 2F 69
Penrhyn Side. *Cnwy* 2H 81
Penrice. *Swan* 4D 31
Penrith. *Cumb* 2G 103
Penrose. *Corn* 1C 6
Penruddock. *Cumb* 2F 103
Penryn. *Corn* 5B 6
Pensarn. *Carm* 4E 45
Pen-sarn. *Gwyn* 3E 69
Pensax. *Worc* 4B 60
Pensby. *Mers* 2E 83
Penselwood. *Som* 3C 22
Pensford. *Bath* 5B 34
Pensham. *Worc* 1E 49
Penshaw. *Tyne* 4G 115
Penshurst. *Kent* 1G 27
Pensilva. *Corn* 2G 7

.2D 60	Peover Heath. *Ches E* 3B 84	Pilleth. *Powy* 4E 59	Platts Common. *S Yor* 4D 92	Ponteland. *Nmbd* 2E 115	
.2H 129	Peper Harow. *Surr* 1A 26	Pilley. *Hants* 3B 16	Platt's Heath. *Kent* 5C 40	Ponterwyd. *Cdgn* 2G 57	
.2A 12	Peplow. *Shrp* 3A 72	Pilley. *S Yor* 4D 92	Platt, The. *E Sus* 2G 27	Pontesbury. *Shrp* 5G 71	
.4H 81	Pepper Arden. *N Yor* 4F 105	Pillgwenlly. *Newp* 3G 33	Plawsworth. *Dur* 5F 115	Pontesford. *Shrp* 5G 71	
.4E 6	Perceton. *N Ayr* 5E 127	Pilling. *Lanc* 5D 96	Plaxtol. *Kent* 5H 39	Pontfadog. *Wrex* 2E 71	
.4E 81	Percyhorner. *Abers* 2G 161	Pilling Lane. *Lanc* 5C 96	Playden. *E Sus* 3D 28	Pont-faen. *Pemb* 1E 43	
.2B 6	Perham Down. *Wilts* 2A 24	Pillowell. *Glos* 5B 48	Playford. *Suff* 1F 55	Pont-faen. *Shrp* 2E 71	
.4F 43	Periton. *Som* 2C 20	Pill, The. *Mon* 3H 33	Play Hatch. *Oxon* 4F 37	Pontgarreg. *Cdgn* 5C 56	
.1B 54	Perkinsville. *Dur* 4F 115	Pilsbury. *Derbs* 4F 85	Playing Place. *Corn* 4C 6	Pont-Henri. *Carm* 5E 45	
.4G 77	Perlethorpe. *Notts* 3D 86	Pilsdon. *Dors* 3H 13	Playley Green. *Glos* 2C 48	Ponthir. *Torf* 2G 33	
...wsey. *Hants* 2B 24	Perranarworthal. *Corn* 5B 6	Pilsgate. *Pet* 5H 75	Plealey. *Shrp* 5G 71	Ponthirwaun. *Cdgn* 1C 44	
...n. *IOA* 3E 81	Perranporth. *Corn* 3B 6	Pilsley. *Derbs* 3G 85	Plean. *Stir* 1B 128	Pont-iets. *Carm* 5E 45	
... *Powy* 1E 59	Perranuthnoe. *Corn* 4C 4	Pilsley. *Derbs* ....4B 86 (nr. Bakewell)	Pleasington. *Bkbn* 2E 91	Pontllanfraith. *Cphy* 2E 33	
(nr. Church Stoke)	Perranwell. *Corn* 5B 6		Pleasley. *Derbs* 4C 86	Pontlliw. *Swan* 5G 45	
entre. *Powy* 2D 58	Perranzabuloe. *Corn* 3B 6	Pilsley. *Derbs* ....4B 86 (nr. Clay Cross)	Pledgdon Green. *Essx* 3F 53	Pont Llogel. *Powy* 4C 70	
(nr. Kerry)	Perrott's Brook. *Glos* 5F 49	Pilson Green. *Norf* 4F 79	Plenmeller. *Nmbd* 3A 114	Pontllyfni. *Gwyn* 5D 80	
Pentre. *Powy* 2C 58	Perry. *W Mid* 1E 61	Piltdown. *E Sus* 3F 27	Pleshey. *Essx* 4G 53	Pontlottyn. *Cphy* 5E 46	
(nr. Mochdre)	Perry Barr. *W Mid* 1E 61	Pilton. *Edin* 2F 129	Plockton. *High* 5H 155	Pontneddfechan. *Neat* 5C 46	
Pentre. *Rhon* 2C 32	Perry Crofts. *Staf* 5G 73	Pilton. *Nptn* 2H 63	Plocrapol. *W Isl* 8D 171	Pont-newydd. *Carm* 5E 45	
Pentre. *Shrp* 4F 71	Perry Green. *Essx* 3B 54	Pilton. *Rut* 5G 75	Ploughfield. *Here* 1G 47	Pont-newydd. *Flin* 4D 82	
Pentre. *Wrex* 2D 70	Perry Green. *Herts* 4E 53	Pilton. *Som* 2A 22	Plowden. *Shrp* 2F 59	Pontnewydd. *Torf* 2F 33	
(nr. Llanfyllin)	Perry Green. *Wilts* 3E 35	Pilton Green. *Swan* 4D 30	Ploxgreen. *Shrp* 5F 71	Ponton. *Shet* 6E 173	
Pentre. *Wrex* 1E 71	Perry Street. *Kent* 3H 39	Pimperne. *Dors* 2E 15	Pluckley. *Kent* 1D 28	Pont Pen-y-benglog. *Gwyn* 4F 81	
(nr. Rhosllanerchrugog)	Perry Street. *Som* 2G 13	Pinchbeck. *Linc* 3B 76	Plucks Gutter. *Kent* 4G 41	Pontrhydfendigaid. *Cdgn* 4G 57	
Pentrebach. *Carm* 2B 46	Perrywood. *Kent* 5E 41	Pinchbeck Bars. *Linc* 3A 76	Plumbland. *Cumb* 1C 102	Pont Rhyd-y-cyff. *B'end* 3B 32	
Pentre-bach. *Cdgn* 1F 45	Pershall. *Staf* 2C 72	Pinchbeck West. *Linc* 3B 76	Plumgarths. *Cumb* 5F 103	Pontrhydyfen. *Neat* 2A 32	
Pentrebach. *Mer T* 5D 46	Pershore. *Worc* 1E 49	Pinford End. *Suff* 5H 65	Plumley. *Ches E* 3B 84	Pont-rhyd-y-groes. *Cdgn* 3G 57	
Pentre-bach. *Powy* 2C 46	Pertenhall. *Bed* 4H 63	Pinged. *Carm* 5E 45	Plumpton. *Cumb* 1F 103	Pontrhydyrun. *Torf* 2F 33	
Pentrebach. *Swan* 5G 45	Perth. *Per* ....1D 136 & 207	Pinhoe. *Devn* 3C 12	Plumpton. *E Sus* 4E 27	Pont Rhythallt. *Gwyn* 4E 81	
Pentre Berw. *IOA* 3D 80	Perthy. *Shrp* 2F 71	Pinkerton. *E Lot* 2D 130	Plumpton. *Nptn* 1D 50	Pontrilas. *Here* 3G 47	
Pentre-bont. *Cnwy* 5G 81	Perton. *Staf* 1C 60	Pinkneys Green. *Wind* 3G 37	Plumpton Foot. *Cumb* 1F 103	Pontrilas Road. *Here* 3G 47	
Pentrecagal. *Carm* 1D 44	Pertwood. *Wilts* 3D 23	Pinley. *W Mid* 3A 62	Plumpton Green. *E Sus* 4E 27	Pontrobert. *Powy* 4D 70	
Pentre-celyn. *Den* 5D 82	Peterborough. *Pet* ....1A 64 & 208	Pinley Green. *Warw* 4G 61	Plumpton Head. *Cumb* 1G 103	Pont-rug. *Gwyn* 4E 81	
Pentre-clawdd. *Shrp* 2E 71	Peterburn. *High* 5B 162	Pinmill. *Suff* 2F 55	Plumstead. *G Lon* 3F 39	Ponts Green. *E Sus* 4A 28	
Pentreclwydau. *Neat* 5B 46	Peterchurch. *Here* 2G 47	Pinmore. *S Ayr* 5B 116	Plumstead. *Norf* 2D 78	Pontshill. *Here* 3B 48	
Pentre-cwrt. *Carm* 2D 45	Peterculter. *Aber* 3F 153	Pinner. *G Lon* 2C 38	Plumtree. *Notts* 2D 74	Pont-Sian. *Cdgn* 1E 45	
Pentre Dolau Honddu. *Powy* 1C 46	Peterhead. *Abers* 4H 161	Pins Green. *Worc* 1C 48	Plumtree Park. *Notts* 2D 74	Pontsticill. *Mer T* 4D 46	
Pentre-du. *Cnwy* 5G 81	Peterlee. *Dur* 5H 115	Pinsley Green. *Ches E* 1H 71	Plungar. *Leics* 2E 75	Pont-Walby. *Neat* 5B 46	
Pentre-dwr. *Swan* 3F 31	Petersfield. *Hants* 4F 25	Pinvin. *Worc* 1E 49	Plush. *Dors* 2C 14	Pontwelly. *Carm* 2E 45	
Pentrefelin. *Carm* 3F 45	Petersfinger. *Wilts* 4G 23	Pinwherry. *S Ayr* 1G 109	Plushabridge. *Corn* 5D 10	Pontwgan. *Cnwy* 3G 81	
Pentrefelin. *Cdgn* 1G 45	Peter's Green. *Herts* 4B 52	Pinxton. *Derbs* 5B 86	Plwmp. *Cdgn* 5C 56	Pontyates. *Carm* 5E 45	
Pentrefelin. *Cnwy* 3H 81	Peters Marland. *Devn* 1E 11	Pipe and Lyde. *Here* 1A 48	Plymouth. *Plym* ....3A 8 & 208	Pontyberem. *Carm* 4F 45	
Pentrefelin. *Gwyn* 2E 69	Peterstone Wentlooge. *Newp* 3F 33	Pipe Aston. *Here* 3G 59	Plymouth City Airport. *Plym* 3B 8	Pontybodkin. *Flin* 5E 83	
Pentrefoelas. *Cnwy* 5A 82	Peterston-super-Ely. *V Glam* 4D 32	Pipe Gate. *Shrp* 1B 72	Plympton. *Plym* 3B 8	Pontyclun. *Rhon* 3D 32	
Pentre Galar. *Pemb* 1F 43	Peterstow. *Here* 3A 48	Pipehill. *Staf* 5E 73	Plymstock. *Plym* 3B 8	Pontycymer. *B'end* 2C 32	
Pentregat. *Carm* 5C 56	Peter Tavy. *Devn* 5F 11	Piperhill. *High* 3C 158	Plymtree. *Devn* 2D 12	Pontyglazier. *Pemb* 1F 43	
Pentre Gwenlais. *Carm* 4G 45	Petertown. *Orkn* 7C 172	Pipe Ridware. *Staf* 4E 73	Pockley. *N Yor* 1A 100	Pontygwaith. *Rhon* 2D 32	
Pentre Gwynfryn. *Gwyn* 3E 69	Petham. *Kent* 5F 41	Pipers Pool. *Corn* 4C 10	Pocklington. *E Yor* 5C 100	Pont-y-pant. *Cnwy* 5G 81	
Pentre Halkyn. *Flin* 3E 82	Petherwin Gate. *Corn* 4C 10	Pipewell. *Nptn* 2F 63	Pode Hole. *Linc* 3B 76	Pontypool. *Torf* 2G 33	
Pentre Hodre. *Shrp* 3F 59	Petrockstowe. *Devn* 2F 11	Pippacott. *Devn* 3F 19	Podimore. *Som* 4A 22	Pontypridd. *Rhon* 3D 32	
Pentre-Llanrhaeadr. *Den* 4C 82	Petsoe End. *Mil* 1G 51	Pipton. *Powy* 2E 47	Podington. *Bed* 4G 63	Pontypwl. *Torf* 2G 33	
Pentre Llifior. *Powy* 1D 58	Pett. *E Sus* 4C 28	Pirbright. *Surr* 5A 38	Podmore. *Staf* 2B 72	Pontywaun. *Cphy* 2F 33	
Pentrellwyn. *IOA* 2E 81	Pettaugh. *Suff* 5D 66	Pirnmill. *N Ayr* 5G 125	Poffley End. *Oxon* 4B 50	Pooksgreen. *Hants* 1B 16	
Pentre-llwyn-llwyd. *Powy* 5B 58	Pett Bottom. *Kent* 5F 41	Pirton. *Herts* 2B 52	Point Clear. *Essx* 4D 54	Pool. *Corn* 4A 6	
Pentre-llyn-cymmer. *Cnwy* 5B 82	Petteridge. *Kent* 1A 28	Pirton. *Worc* 1D 49	Pointon. *Linc* 2A 76	Pool. *W Yor* 5E 99	
Pentre Meyrick. *V Glam* 4C 32	Petterill Green. *Cumb* 5F 113	Pisgah. *Stir* 3G 135	Pokesdown. *Bour* 3G 15	Poole. *N Yor* 2E 93	
Pentre-piod. *Gwyn* 2A 70	Pettinain. *S Lan* 5C 128	Pishill. *Oxon* 3F 37	Polapit Tamar. *Corn* 4D 10	Poole. *Pool* ....3F 15 & 215	
Pentre-poeth. *Newp* 3F 33	Pettistree. *Suff* 5E 67	Pistyll. *Gwyn* 1C 68	Polbae. *Dum* 2H 109	Poole. *Som* 4E 21	
Pentre'r Beirdd. *Powy* 4D 70	Petton. *Devn* 4D 20	Pitagowan. *Per* 2F 143	Polbain. *High* 3E 163	Poole Keynes. *Glos* 2E 35	
Pentre'r-felin. *Powy* 2C 46	Petton. *Shrp* 3G 71	Pitcairn. *Per* 3F 143	Polbathic. *Corn* 3H 7	Poolend. *Staf* 5D 84	
Pentre-ty-gwyn. *Carm* 2B 46	Petts Wood. *G Lon* 4F 39	Pitcairngreen. *Per* 1C 136	Polbeth. *W Lot* 3D 128	Poolewe. *High* 5C 162	
Pentre-uchaf. *Gwyn* 2C 68	Pettycur. *Fife* 1F 129	Pitcalnie. *High* 1C 158	Polbrock. *Corn* 2E 6	Poolfold. *Staf* 5C 84	
Pentrich. *Derbs* 5A 86	Pettywell. *Norf* 3C 78	Pitcaple. *Abers* 1E 152	Polchar. *High* 3C 150	Pool Head. *Here* 5H 59	
Pentridge. *Dors* 1F 15	Petworth. *W Sus* 3A 26	Pitchcombe. *Glos* 5D 48	Polebrook. *Nptn* 2H 63	Pool Hey. *Lanc* 3B 90	
Pen-twyn. *Cphy* 5F 47	Pevensey. *E Sus* 5A 28	Pitchcott. *Buck* 3F 51	Pole Elm. *Worc* 1D 48	Poolhill. *Glos* 3C 48	
(nr. Oakdale)	Pevensey Bay. *E Sus* 5A 28	Pitch Green. *Buck* 5F 51	Polegate. *E Sus* 5G 27	Pool o' Muckhart. *Clac* 3C 136	
Pentwyn. *Cphy* 5E 46	Pewsey. *Wilts* 5G 35	Pitch Place. *Surr* 5A 38	Pole Moor. *W Yor* 3A 92	Pool Quay. *Powy* 4E 71	
(nr. Rhymney)	Pheasants Hill. *Buck* 3F 37	Pitcombe. *Som* 3B 22	Poles. *High* 4E 165	Poolsbrook. *Derbs* 3B 86	
Pentwyn. *Card* 3F 33	Philadelphia. *Tyne* 4G 115	Pitcox. *E Lot* 2C 130	Polesworth. *Warw* 5G 73	Pool Street. *Essx* 2A 54	
Pentyrch. *Card* 3E 32	Philham. *Devn* 4C 18	Pitcur. *Per* 5B 144	Polglass. *High* 3E 163	Pootings. *Kent* 1F 27	
Pentywyn. *Carm* 4G 43	Philiphaugh. *Bord* 2G 119	Pitfichie. *Abers* 2D 152	Polgooth. *Corn* 3D 6	Pope Hill. *Pemb* 3D 42	
Penuwch. *Cdgn* 4E 57	Phillack. *Corn* 3C 4	Pitgrudy. *High* 4E 165	Poling. *W Sus* 5B 26	Pope's Hill. *Glos* 4B 48	
Penwithick. *Corn* 3E 7	Philleigh. *Corn* 5C 6	Pitkennedy. *Ang* 3E 145	Poling Corner. *W Sus* 5B 26	Popeswood. *Brac* 5G 37	
Penwyllt. *Powy* 4B 46	Philpstoun. *W Lot* 2D 128	Pitlessie. *Fife* 3F 137	Polio. *High* 1B 158	Popham. *Hants* 2D 24	
Penybanc. *Carm* 4G 45	Phocle Green. *Here* 3B 48	Pitlochry. *Per* 3G 143	Polkerris. *Corn* 3E 7	Poplar. *G Lon* 2E 39	
(nr. Ammanford)	Phoenix Green. *Hants* 1F 25	Pitmachie. *Abers* 1D 152	Polla. *High* 3D 166	Popley. *Hants* 1E 25	
Pen-y-banc. *Carm* 3G 45	Pibsbury. *Som* 4H 21	Pitmaduthy. *High* 1B 158	Pollard Street. *Norf* 2F 79	Porchfield. *IOW* 3C 16	
(nr. Llandeilo)	Pibwrlwyd. *Carm* 4E 45	Pitminster. *Som* 1F 13	Pollicott. *Buck* 4F 51	Porin. *High* 3F 157	
Pen-y-bont. *Carm* 2H 43	Pica. *Cumb* 2B 102	Pitnacree. *Per* 3G 143	Pollington. *E Yor* 3G 93	Poringland. *Norf* 5E 79	
Penybont. *Powy* 4D 58	Piccadilly. *Warw* 1G 61	Pitney. *Som* 4H 21	Polloch. *High* 2B 140	Porkellis. *Corn* 5A 6	
(nr. Llandrindod Wells)	Piccadilly Corner. *Norf* 2E 67	Pitroddie. *Per* 1E 136	Pollok. *Glas* 3G 127	Porlock. *Som* 2B 20	
Pen-y-bont. *Powy* 2E 70	Piccotts End. *Herts* 5A 52	Pitscottie. *Fife* 2G 137	Pollokshaws. *Glas* 3G 127	Porlock Weir. *Som* 2B 20	
(nr. Llanfyllin)	Pickering. *N Yor* 1B 100	Pitsea. *Essx* 2B 40	Pollokshields. *Glas* 3G 127	Portachoillan. *Arg* 4F 125	
Pen-y-Bont Ar Ogwr. *B'end* 3C 32	Picket Piece. *Hants* 2B 24	Pitsford. *Nptn* 4E 63	Polmaily. *High* 5G 157	Port Adhair Bheinn na Faoghla. *W Isl* 3C 170	
Penybontfawr. *Powy* 3C 70	Picket Post. *Hants* 2G 15	Pitsford Hill. *Som* 3E 20	Polmassick. *Corn* 4D 6	Port Ann. *Arg* 1H 125	
Penybryn. *Cphy* 2E 33	Pickford. *W Mid* 2G 61	Pitsmoor. *S Yor* 2A 86	Polmear. *Corn* 3E 7	Port Appin. *Arg* 4D 140	
Pen-y-bryn. *Pemb* 1B 44	Pickhill. *N Yor* 1F 99	Pitstone. *Buck* 4H 51	Polmont. *Falk* 2C 128	Port Asgaig. *Arg* 3C 124	
Pen-y-bryn. *Wrex* 1E 71	Picklenash. *Glos* 3C 48	Pitt. *Hants* 4C 24	Polnessan. *E Ayr* 3D 116	Port Askaig. *Arg* 3C 124	
Pen-y-cae. *Powy* 4B 46	Picklescott. *Shrp* 1G 59	Pitt Court. *Glos* 2C 34	Polnish. *High* 5F 147	Portavadie. *Arg* 3H 125	
Penycae. *Wrex* 1E 71	Pickletillem. *Fife* 1G 137	Pittentrail. *High* 3E 164	Polperro. *Corn* 3G 7	Port Bannatyne. *Arg* 3B 126	
Pen-y-cae-mawr. *Mon* 2H 33	Pickmere. *Ches E* 3A 84	Pittenweem. *Fife* 3H 137	Polruan. *Corn* 3F 7	Portbury. *N Som* 4A 34	
Penycaerau. *Gwyn* 3A 68	Pickstock. *Telf* 3B 72	Pittington. *Dur* 5G 115	Polscoe. *Corn* 2F 7	Port Carlisle. *Cumb* 3D 112	
Pen-y-cefn. *Flin* 3D 82	Pickwell. *Devn* 2E 19	Pitton. *Swan* 4D 30	Polsham. *Som* 2A 22	Port Charlotte. *Arg* 4A 124	
Pen-y-clawdd. *Mon* 5H 47	Pickwell. *Leics* 4E 75	Pitton. *Wilts* 3H 23	Polskeoch. *Dum* 4F 117	Portchester. *Hants* 2E 16	
Pen-y-coedcae. *Rhon* 3D 32	Pickworth. *Linc* 2H 75	Pittswood. *Kent* 1H 27	Polstead. *Suff* 2C 54	Port Clarence. *Stoc T* 2B 106	
Pencwm. *Pemb* 2C 42	Pickworth. *Rut* 4G 75	Pittulie. *Abers* 2G 161	Polstead Heath. *Suff* 1C 54	Port Dinorwig. *Gwyn* 4E 81	
Pen-y-Darren. *Mer T* 5D 46	Picton. *Ches W* 3G 83	Pittville. *Glos* 3E 49	Poltesco. *Corn* 5E 5	Port Driseach. *Arg* 2A 126	
Pen-y-fai. *B'end* 3B 32	Picton. *Flin* 2D 82	Pitversie. *Per* 2D 136	Poltimore. *Devn* 3C 12	Port Dundas. *Glas* 3H 127	
Penyffordd. *Flin* 4F 83	Picton. *N Yor* 4B 106	Pity Me. *Dur* 5F 115	Polton. *Midl* 3G 129	Port Ellen. *Arg* 5B 124	
(nr. Mold)	Pict's Hill. *Som* 4H 21	Pixey Green. *Suff* 3E 67	Polwarth. *Bord* 4D 130	Port Elphinstone. *Abers* 1E 153	
Pen-y-ffordd. *Flin* 2D 82	Piddinghoe. *E Sus* 5F 27	Pixley. *Here* 2B 48	Polyphant. *Corn* 4C 10	Portencalzie. *Dum* 2F 109	
(nr. Prestatyn)	Piddington. *Buck* 2G 37	Place Newton. *N Yor* 2C 100	Polzeath. *Corn* 1D 6	Portencross. *N Ayr* 5C 126	
Penyffridd. *Gwyn* 5E 81	Piddington. *Nptn* 5F 63	Plaidy. *Abers* 3E 161	Ponde. *Powy* 2E 46	Port Erin. *IOM* 5A 108	
Pen-y-garn. *Cdgn* 2F 57	Piddington. *Oxon* 4E 51	Plaidy. *Corn* 3G 7	Pondersbridge. *Cambs* 1B 64	Port Erroll. *Abers* 5H 161	
Pen-y-garnedd. *IOA* 3E 81	Piddletrenthide. *Dors* 2C 14	Plain Dealings. *Pemb* 3E 43	Ponders End. *G Lon* 1E 39	Porter's Fen Corner. *Norf* 5E 77	
Penygarnedd. *Powy* 3D 70	Pidley. *Cambs* 3C 64	Plains. *N Lan* 3A 128	Pond Street. *Essx* 2E 53	Portesham. *Dors* 4B 14	
Pen-y-graig. *Gwyn* 2B 68	Pidney. *Dors* 2C 14	Plainsfield. *Som* 3E 21	Pondtail. *Hants* 1G 25	Portessie. *Mor* 2B 160	
Penygraig. *Rhon* 2C 32	Pie Corner. *Here* 4A 60	Plaish. *Shrp* 1H 59	Ponsanooth. *Corn* 5B 6	Port e Vullen. *IOM* 2D 108	
Penygraigwen. *IOA* 2D 80	Piercebridge. *Darl* 3F 105	Plaistow. *Here* 2B 48	Ponsongath. *Corn* 5E 5	Port-Eynon. *Swan* 4D 30	
Pen-y-groes. *Carm* 4F 45	Pierowall. *Orkn* 3D 172	Plaistow. *W Sus* 2B 26	Ponsworthy. *Devn* 5H 11	Portfield. *Som* 4H 21	
Penygroes. *Gwyn* 5D 80	Pigdon. *Nmbd* 1E 115	Plaitford. *Wilts* 1A 16	Pontamman. *Carm* 4G 45	Portfield Gate. *Pemb* 3D 42	
Penygroes. *Pemb* 1F 43	Pightley. *Som* 3F 21	Plas Llwyd. *Cnwy* 3B 82	Pontantwn. *Carm* 4E 45	Port Gaverne. *Corn* 4A 10	
Pen-y-Mynydd. *Carm* 5E 45	Pikehall. *Derbs* 5F 85	Plastow Green. *Hants* 5D 36	Pontardawe. *Neat* 5H 45	Port Glasgow. *Inv* 2E 127	
Penymynydd. *Flin* 4F 83	Pikeshill. *Hants* 2A 16	Plas yn Cefn. *Den* 3C 82	Pontarddulais. *Swan* 5F 45	Portgordon. *Mor* 2A 160	
Penyrheol. *Cphy* 3E 33	Pilford. *Dors* 2F 15	Platt. *Kent* 5H 39	Pontarfynach. *Cdgn* 3G 57	Portgower. *High* 2H 165	
Penyrheol. *Mon* 4H 47	Pilham. *Linc* 1F 87	Platt Bridge. *G Man* 4E 90	Pont-ar-gothi. *Carm* 3F 45	Porth. *Corn* 2C 6	
Penyrheol. *Swan* 3E 31	Pill. *N Som* 4A 34	Platt Lane. *Shrp* 2H 71	Pont ar Hydfer. *Powy* 3B 46	Porth. *Rhon* 2D 32	
Pen-yr-Heolgerrig. *Mer T* 5D 46	Pillaton. *Corn* 2H 7		Pontarllechau. *Carm* 3H 45	Porthaethwy. *IOA* 3E 81	
Penysarn. *IOA* 1D 80	Pillaton. *Staf* 4D 72		Pontarsais. *Carm* 3E 45		
Pen-y-stryt. *Den* 5E 82	Pillerton Hersey. *Warw* 1A 50		Pontblyddyn. *Flin* 4E 83		
Penywaun. *Rhon* 5C 46	Pillerton Priors. *Warw* 1A 50		Pont Cyfyng. *Cnwy* 5G 81		
Penzance. *Corn* 3B 4			Pontdolgoch. *Powy* 1C 58		
Peopleton. *Worc* 5D 60			Pontefract. *W Yor* 2E 93		

Porthallow—Rawri

Porthallow. *Corn* 3G **7**
(nr. Looe)
Porthallow. *Corn* 4E **5**
(nr. St Keverne)
Porthalong. *High* 5C **154**
Porthcawl. *B'end* 4B **32**
Porthceri. *V Glam* 5D **32**
Porthcothan. *Corn* 1C **6**
Porthcurno. *Corn* 4A **4**
Port Henderson. *High* 1G **155**
Porthgain. *Pemb* 1C **42**
Porthgwarra. *Corn* 4A **4**
Porthill. *Shrp* 4G **71**
Porthkerry. *V Glam* 5D **32**
Porthleven. *Corn* 4D **4**
Porthllechog. *IOA* 1D **80**
Porthmadog. *Gwyn* 2E **69**
Porthmeirion. *Gwyn* 2E **69**
Porthmeor. *Corn* 3B **4**
Porth Navas. *Corn* 4E **5**
Portholland. *Corn* 4D **6**
Porthoustock. *Corn* 4F **5**
Porthtowan. *Corn* 4A **6**
Porth Tywyn. *Carm* 5E **45**
Porth-y-felin. *IOA* 2B **80**
Porthyrhyd. *Carm* 4F **45**
(nr. Carmarthen)
Porthyrhyd. *Carm* 2H **45**
(nr. Llandovery)
Porth-y-waen. *Shrp* 3E **71**
Portincaple. *Arg* 4B **134**
Portington. *E Yor* 1A **94**
Portinnisherrich. *Arg* 2G **133**
Portinscale. *Cumb* 2D **102**
Port Isaac. *Corn* 1D **6**
Portishead. *N Som* 4H **33**
Portknockie. *Mor* 2B **160**
Port Lamont. *Arg* 2B **126**
Portlethen. *Abers* 4G **153**
Portlethen Village. *Abers* 4G **153**
Portling. *Dum* 4F **111**
Port Lion. *Pemb* 4D **43**
Portloe. *Corn* 5D **6**
Port Logan. *Dum* 5F **109**
Portmahomack. *High* 5G **165**
Port Mead. *Swan* 3F **31**
Portmellon. *Corn* 4E **6**
Port Mholair. *W Isl* 4H **171**
Port Mor. *High* 1F **139**
Portmore. *Hants* 3B **16**
Port Mulgrave. *N Yor* 3E **107**
Portnacroish. *Arg* 4D **140**
Portnahaven. *Arg* 4A **124**
Portnalong. *High* 5C **154**
Portnaluchaig. *High* 5E **147**
Portnancon. *High* 2E **167**
Port Nan Giuran. *W Isl* 4H **171**
Port nan Long. *W Isl* 1D **170**
Port Nis. *W Isl* 1H **171**
Portobello. *Edin* 2G **129**
Portobello. *W Yor* 3D **92**
Port of Menteith. *Stir* 3E **135**
Porton. *Wilts* 3G **23**
Portormin. *High* 5D **168**
Portpatrick. *Dum* 4F **109**
Port Quin. *Corn* 1D **6**
Port Ramsay. *Arg* 4C **140**
Portreath. *Corn* 4A **6**
Portree. *High* 4D **155**
Port Righ. *High* 4D **155**
Port St Mary. *IOM* 5B **108**
Portscatho. *Corn* 5C **6**
Portsea. *Port* 2E **17**
Portskerra. *High* 2A **168**
Portskewett. *Mon* 3A **34**
Portslade-by-Sea. *Brig* 5D **26**
Portsmouth. *Port* 3E **17** & **209**
Portsmouth. *W Yor* 2H **91**
Port Soderick. *IOM* 4C **108**
Port Solent. *Port* 2E **17**
Portsonachan. *Arg* 1H **133**
Portsoy. *Abers* 2C **160**
Port Sunlight. *Mers* 2F **83**
Portswood. *Sotn* 1C **16**
Port Talbot. *Neat* 4G **31**
Porttannachy. *Mor* 2A **160**
Port Tennant. *Swan* 3F **31**
Portuairk. *High* 2F **139**
Portway. *Here* 1H **47**
Portway. *Worc* 3E **61**
Port Wemyss. *Arg* 4A **124**
Port William. *Dum* 5A **110**
Portwrinkle. *Corn* 3H **7**
Poslingford. *Suff* 1A **54**
Postbridge. *Devn* 5G **11**
Postcombe. *Oxon* 2F **37**
Post Green. *Dors* 3E **15**
Posthill. *Staf* 5G **73**
Postling. *Kent* 2F **29**
Postlip. *Glos* 3F **49**
Post-Mawr. *Cdgn* 5D **56**
Postwick. *Norf* 5E **79**
Potarch. *Abers* 4D **152**
Potsgrove. *C Beds* 3H **51**
Potten End. *Herts* 5A **52**
Potter Brompton. *N Yor* 2D **101**
Pottergate Street. *Norf* 1D **66**
Potterhanworth. *Linc* 4H **87**
Potterhanworth Booths. *Linc* 4H **87**
Potter Heigham. *Norf* 4G **79**
Potter Hill. *Leics* 3E **75**
Potteries, The. *Stoke* 1C **72**
Petterne. *Wilts* 1E **23**
Potterne Wick. *Wilts* 1E **23**
Potternewton. *W Yor* 1D **92**
Potters Bar. *Herts* 5C **52**
Potters Brook. *Lanc* 4D **97**
Potter's Cross. *Staf* 2C **60**
Potters Crouch. *Herts* 5B **52**
Potter Somersal. *Derbs* 2F **73**
Potterspury. *Nptn* 1F **51**
Potter Street. *Essx* 5E **53**
Potterton. *Abers* 2G **153**
Potthorpe. *Norf* 3B **78**
Pottle Street. *Wilts* 2D **22**
Potto. *N Yor* 4B **106**
Potton. *C Beds* 1C **52**
Pott Row. *Norf* 3G **77**
Pott Shrigley. *Ches E* 3D **84**
Poughill. *Corn* 2C **10**
Poughill. *Devn* 2B **12**
Poulner. *Hants* 2G **15**
Poulshot. *Wilts* 1E **23**
Poulton. *Glos* 5G **49**
Poulton-le-Fylde. *Lanc* 1B **90**
Pound Bank. *Worc* 3B **60**
Poundbury. *Dors* 3B **14**
Poundfield. *E Sus* 2G **27**
Poundgate. *E Sus* 3F **27**
Pound Green. *E Sus* 3G **27**
Pound Green. *Suff* 5G **65**
Pound Hill. *W Sus* 2D **27**
Poundland. *S Ayr* 1G **109**
Poundon. *Buck* 3E **51**
Poundsgate. *Devn* 5H **11**
Poundstock. *Corn* 3C **10**
Pound Street. *Hants* 5C **36**
Pounsley. *E Sus* 3G **27**
Powburn. *Nmbd* 3F **121**
Powderham. *Devn* 4C **12**
Powerstock. *Dors* 3A **14**
Powfoot. *Dum* 3C **112**
Powick. *Worc* 5C **60**
Powmill. *Per* 4C **136**
Poxwell. *Dors* 4C **14**
Poyle. *Slo* 3B **38**
Poynings. *W Sus* 4D **26**
Poyntington. *Dors* 4B **22**
Poynton. *Ches E* 2D **84**
Poynton. *Telf* 4H **71**
Poynton Green. *Telf* 4H **71**
Poystreet Green. *Suff* 5B **66**
Praa Sands. *Corn* 4C **4**
Pratt's Bottom. *G Lon* 4F **39**
Praze-an-Beeble. *Corn* 3D **4**
Prees. *Shrp* 2H **71**
Preesall. *Lanc* 5C **96**
Preesall Park. *Lanc* 5C **96**
Prees Green. *Shrp* 2H **71**
Prees Higher Heath. *Shrp* 2H **71**
Prendergast. *Pemb* 3D **42**
Prendwick. *Nmbd* 3E **121**
Pren-gwyn. *Cdgn* 1E **45**
Prenteg. *Gwyn* 1E **69**
Prenton. *Mers* 2F **83**
Prescot. *Mers* 1G **83**
Prescott. *Devn* 1D **12**
Prescott. *Shrp* 3G **71**
Preshute. *Wilts* 5G **35**
Pressen. *Nmbd* 1C **120**
Prestatyn. *Den* 2C **82**
Prestbury. *Ches E* 3D **84**
Prestbury. *Glos* 3E **49**
Presteigne. *Powy* 4F **59**
Presthope. *Shrp* 1H **59**
Prestleigh. *Som* 2B **22**
Preston. *Brig* 5E **27**
Preston. *Devn* 5B **12**
Preston. *Dors* 4C **14**
Preston. *E Lot* 2B **130**
(nr. East Linton)
Preston. *E Lot* 2G **129**
(nr. Prestonpans)
Preston. *E Yor* 1E **95**
Preston. *Glos* 5F **49**
Preston. *Herts* 3B **52**
Preston. *Kent* 4G **41**
(nr. Canterbury)
Preston. *Kent* 4E **40**
(nr. Faversham)
Preston. *Lanc* 2D **90** & **208**
Preston. *Nmbd* 2F **121**
Preston. *Rut* 5F **75**
Preston. *Bord* 4D **130**
Preston. *Shrp* 4H **71**
Preston. *Suff* 5B **66**
Preston. *Wilts* 4A **36**
(nr. Aldbourne)
Preston. *Wilts* 4F **35**
(nr. Lyneham)
Preston Bagot. *Warw* 4F **61**
Preston Bissett. *Buck* 3E **51**
Preston Bowyer. *Som* 4E **21**
Preston Brockhurst. *Shrp* 3H **71**
Preston Brook. *Hal* 3H **83**
Preston Candover. *Hants* 2E **24**
Preston Capes. *Nptn* 5C **62**
Preston Cross. *Glos* 2B **48**
Preston Gubbals. *Shrp* 4G **71**
Preston-le-Skerne. *Dur* 2A **106**
Preston Marsh. *Here* 1A **48**
Prestonmill. *Dum* 4A **112**
Preston on Stour. *Warw* 5G **61**
Preston on the Hill. *Hal* 2H **83**
Preston on Wye. *Here* 1G **47**
Prestonpans. *E Lot* 2G **129**
Preston Plucknett. *Som* 1A **14**
Preston-under-Scar. *N Yor* 5D **104**
Preston upon the Weald Moors. *Telf* 4A **72**
Preston Wynne. *Here* 1A **48**
Prestwich. *G Man* 4G **91**
Prestwick. *Nmbd* 2E **115**
Prestwick. *S Ayr* 2C **116**
Prestwold. *Leics* 3C **74**
Prestwood. *Buck* 5G **51**
Prestwood. *Staf* 1E **73**
Price Town. *B'end* 2C **32**
Prickwillow. *Cambs* 2E **65**
Priddy. *Som* 1A **22**
Priestcliffe. *Derbs* 3F **85**
Priesthill. *Glas* 3G **127**
Priest Hutton. *Lanc* 2E **97**
Priestland. *E Ayr* 1E **117**
Priest Weston. *Shrp* 1E **59**
Priestwood. *Brac* 4G **37**
Priestwood. *Kent* 4A **40**
Primethorpe. *Leics* 1C **62**
Primrose Green. *Norf* 4C **78**
Primrose Hill. *Derbs* 5B **86**
Primrose Hill. *Glos* 5B **48**
Primrose Hill. *Lanc* 4B **90**
Primrose Valley. *N Yor* 2F **101**
Primsidemill. *Bord* 2C **120**
Princes Gate. *Pemb* 3F **43**
Princes Risborough. *Buck* 5G **51**
Princethorpe. *Warw* 3B **62**
Princetown. *Devn* 5F **11**
Prinsted. *W Sus* 2F **17**
Prion. *Den* 4C **82**
Prior Muir. *Fife* 2H **137**
Prior's Frome. *Here* 2A **48**
Priors Halton. *Shrp* 3G **59**
Priors Hardwick. *Warw* 5B **62**
Priorslee. *Telf* 4B **72**
Priors Marston. *Warw* 5B **62**
Prior's Norton. *Glos* 3D **48**
Priory, The. *W Ber* 5B **36**
Priory Wood. *Here* 1F **47**
Priston. *Bath* 5B **34**
Pristow Green. *Norf* 2D **66**
Prittlewell. *S'end* 2C **40**
Privett. *Hants* 4E **25**
Prixford. *Devn* 3F **19**
Probus. *Corn* 4D **6**
Prospect. *Cumb* 5C **112**
Provanmill. *Glas* 3H **127**
Prudhoe. *Nmbd* 3D **115**
Publow. *Bath* 5B **34**
Puckeridge. *Herts* 3D **53**
Puckington. *Som* 1G **13**
Pucklechurch. *S Glo* 4B **34**
Puckrup. *Glos* 2D **49**
Puddinglake. *Ches W* 4B **84**
Puddington. *Ches W* 3F **83**
Puddington. *Devn* 1B **12**
Puddlebrook. *Glos* 4B **48**
Puddledock. *Norf* 1C **66**
Puddletown. *Dors* 3C **14**
Pudleston. *Here* 5H **59**
Pudsey. *W Yor* 1C **92**
Pulborough. *W Sus* 4B **26**
Puleston. *Telf* 3B **72**
Pulford. *Ches W* 5F **83**
Pulham. *Dors* 2C **14**
Pulham Market. *Norf* 2D **66**
Pulham St Mary. *Norf* 2E **66**
Pulley. *Shrp* 5G **71**
Pulloxhill. *C Beds* 2A **52**
Pulpit Hill. *Arg* 1F **133**
Pulverbatch. *Shrp* 5G **71**
Pumpherston. *W Lot* 3D **128**
Pumsaint. *Carm* 1G **45**
Puncheston. *Pemb* 2E **43**
Puncknowle. *Dors* 4A **14**
Punnett's Town. *E Sus* 3H **27**
Purbrook. *Hants* 2E **17**
Purfleet. *Thur* 3G **39**
Puriton. *Som* 2G **21**
Purleigh. *Essx* 5B **54**
Purley. *G Lon* 4E **39**
Purley on Thames. *W Ber* 4E **37**
Purlogue. *Shrp* 3E **59**
Purl's Bridge. *Cambs* 2D **65**
Purse Caundle. *Dors* 1B **14**
Purslow. *Shrp* 2F **59**
Purston Jaglin. *W Yor* 3E **93**
Purtington. *Som* 2G **13**
Purton. *Glos* 5B **48**
(nr. Lydney)
Purton. *Glos* 5B **48**
(nr. Sharpness)
Purton. *Wilts* 3F **35**
Purton Stoke. *Wilts* 2F **35**
Pury End. *Nptn* 1F **51**
Pusey. *Oxon* 2B **36**
Putley. *Here* 2B **48**
Putney. *G Lon* 3D **38**
Putsborough. *Devn* 2E **19**
Puttenham. *Herts* 4G **51**
Puttenham. *Surr* 1A **26**
Puttock End. *Essx* 1B **54**
Puttock's End. *Essx* 4F **53**
Puxey. *Dors* 1C **14**
Puxton. *N Som* 5H **33**
Pwll. *Carm* 5E **45**
Pwll. *Powy* 5D **70**
Pwllcrochan. *Pemb* 4D **42**
Pwll-glas. *Den* 5D **82**
Pwllgloyw. *Powy* 2D **46**
Pwllheli. *Gwyn* 2C **68**
Pwllmeyric. *Mon* 2A **34**
Pwlltrap. *Carm* 3G **43**
Pwll-y-glaw. *Neat* 2A **32**
Pyecombe. *W Sus* 4D **27**
Pye Corner. *Herts* 4E **53**
Pye Corner. *Newp* 3G **33**
Pye Green. *Staf* 4D **73**
Pyewipe. *NE Lin* 3F **95**
Pyle. *B'end* 3B **32**
Pyle. *IOW* 5C **16**
Pylle. *Som* 3B **22**
Pymoor. *Cambs* 2D **65**
Pymoor. *Dors* 3H **13**
Pyrford. *Surr* 5B **38**
Pyrford Village. *Surr* 5B **38**
Pyrton. *Oxon* 2E **37**
Pytchley. *Nptn* 3F **63**
Pyworthy. *Devn* 2D **10**

Q

Quabbs. *Shrp* 2E **58**
Quadring. *Linc* 2B **76**
Quadring Eaudike. *Linc* 2B **76**
Quainton. *Buck* 3F **51**
Quaking Houses. *Dur* 4E **115**
Quarley. *Hants* 2A **24**
Quarndon. *Derbs* 1H **73**
Quarndon Common. *Derbs* 1H **73**
Quarrendon. *Buck* 4G **51**
Quarrier's Village. *Inv* 3E **127**
Quarrington. *Linc* 1H **75**
Quarrington Hill. *Dur* 1A **106**
Quarry Bank. *W Mid* 2D **60**
Quarry, The. *Glos* 2C **34**
Quarrywood. *Mor* 2F **159**
Quartalehouse. *Abers* 4G **161**
Quarter. *N Ayr* 3C **126**
Quarter. *S Lan* 4A **128**
Quatford. *Shrp* 1B **60**
Quatt. *Shrp* 2B **60**
Quebec. *Dur* 5E **115**
Quedgeley. *Glos* 4D **48**
Queen Adelaide. *Cambs* 2E **65**
Queenborough. *Kent* 3D **40**
Queen Camel. *Som* 4A **22**
Queen Charlton. *Bath* 5B **34**
Queen Dart. *Devn* 1B **12**
Queenhill. *Worc* 2D **48**
Queen Oak. *Dors* 3C **22**
Queensbury. *W Yor* 2B **92**
Queensferry. *Flin* 4F **83**
Queenstown. *Bkpl* 1B **90**
Queen Street. *Kent* 1A **28**
Queenzieburn. *N Lan* 2H **127**
Quemerford. *Wilts* 5F **35**
Quendale. *Shet* 10E **173**
Quendon. *Essx* 2F **53**
Queniborough. *Leics* 4D **74**
Quenington. *Glos* 5G **49**
Quernmore. *Lanc* 3E **97**
Quethiock. *Corn* 2H **7**
Quholm. *Orkn* 6B **172**
Quick's Green. *W Ber* 4D **36**
Quidenham. *Norf* 2C **66**
Quidhampton. *Hants* 1D **24**
Quidhampton. *Wilts* 3G **23**
Quilquox. *Abers* 5G **161**
Quina Brook. *Shrp* 2H **71**
Quindry. *Orkn* 8D **172**
Quine's Hill. *IOM* 4C **108**
Quinton. *Nptn* 5E **63**
Quinton. *W Mid* 2D **61**
Quintrell Downs. *Corn* 2C **6**
Quixhill. *Staf* 1F **73**
Quoditch. *Devn* 3E **11**
Quorn. *Leics* 4C **74**
Quorndon. *Leics* 4C **74**
Quothquan. *S Lan* 1B **118**
Quoyloo. *Orkn* 5B **172**
Quoyness. *Orkn* 7B **172**
Quoys. *Shet* 5F **173**
(on Mainland)
Quoys. *Shet* 1H **173**
(on Unst)

R

Rableyheath. *Herts* 4C **52**
Raby. *Cumb* 4C **112**
Raby. *Mers* 3F **83**
Rachan Mill. *Bord* 1D **118**
Rachub. *Gwyn* 4F **81**
Rack End. *Oxon* 5C **50**
Rackenford. *Devn* 1B **12**
Rackham. *W Sus* 4B **26**
Rackheath. *Norf* 4E **79**
Racks. *Dum* 2B **112**
Rackwick. *Orkn* 8A **172**
(on Hoy)
Rackwick. *Orkn* 3D **172**
(on Westray)
Radbourne. *Derbs* 2G **73**
Radcliffe. *G Man* 4F **91**
Radcliffe. *Nmbd* 4G **121**
Radcliffe on Trent. *Notts* 2D **74**
Radclive. *Buck* 2E **51**
Radernie. *Fife* 2G **137**
Radfall. *Kent* 4F **41**
Radford. *Bath* 1B **22**
Radford. *Nott* 1C **74**
Radford. *W Mid* 2H **61**
Radford. *Worc* 5E **61**
Radford Semele. *Warw* 4H **61**
Radipole. *Dors* 4B **14**
Radlett. *Herts* 1C **38**
Radley. *Oxon* 2D **36**
Radnage. *Buck* 2F **37**
Radstock. *Bath* 1B **22**
Radstone. *Nptn* 1D **50**
Radway. *Warw* 1B **50**
Radway Green. *Ches E* 5B **84**
Radwell. *Bed* 5H **63**
Radwell. *Herts* 2C **52**
Radwinter. *Essx* 2G **53**
Radyr. *Card* 3E **33**
RAF Coltishall. *Norf* 3E **79**
Rafford. *Mor* 3E **159**
Ragdale. *Leics* 4D **74**
Ragdon. *Shrp* 1G **59**
Ragged Appleshaw. *Hants* 2B **24**
Raggra. *High* 4F **169**
Raglan. *Mon* 5H **47**
Ragnall. *Notts* 3F **87**
Raigbeg. *High* 1C **150**
Rainford. *Mers* 4C **90**
Rainford Junction. *Mers* 4C **90**
Rainham. *G Lon* 2G **39**
Rainham. *Medw* 4C **40**
Rainhill. *Mers* 1G **83**
Rainow. *Ches E* 3D **84**
Rainton. *N Yor* 2F **99**
Rainworth. *Notts* 5C **86**
Raisbeck. *Cumb* 4H **103**
Raise. *Cumb* 5A **114**
Rait. *Per* 1E **137**
Raithby. *Linc* 2C **88**
Raithby by Spilsby. *Linc* 4C **88**
Raithwaite. *N Yor* 3F **107**
Rake. *W Sus* 4G
Rake End. *Staf* 4E
Rakeway. *Staf* 1E 7
Rakewood. *G Man* 3H 9
Ralia. *High* 4B **150**
Ram Alley. *Wilts* 5H **35**
Ramasaig. *High* 4A **154**
Rame. *Corn* 4A **8**
(nr. Millbrook)
Rame. *Corn* 5B **6**
(nr. Penryn)
Ram Lane. *Kent* 1D **28**
Ramnageo. *Shet* 1H **173**
Rampisham. *Dors* 2A **14**
Rampside. *Cumb* 3B **96**
Rampton. *Cambs* 4D **64**
Rampton. *Notts* 3E **87**
Ramsbottom. *G Man* 3F **91**
Ramsburn. *Mor* 3C **160**
Ramsbury. *Wilts* 4A **36**
Ramscraigs. *High* 1H **165**
Ramsdean. *Hants* 4F **25**
Ramsdell. *Hants* 1D **24**
Ramsden. *Oxon* 4B **50**
Ramsden. *Worc* 1E **49**
Ramsden Bellhouse. *Essx* 1B **40**
Ramsden Heath. *Essx* 1B **40**
Ramsey. *Cambs* 2B **64**
Ramsey. *Essx* 2F **55**
Ramsey. *IOM* 2D **108**
Ramsey Forty Foot. *Cambs* 2C **64**
Ramsey Heights. *Cambs* 2B **64**
Ramsey Island. *Essx* 5C **54**
Ramsey Mereside. *Cambs* 2B **64**
Ramsey St Mary's. *Cambs* 2B **64**
Ramsgate. *Kent* 4H **41**
Ramsgill. *N Yor* 2D **98**
Ramshaw. *Dur* 5C **114**
Ramshorn. *Staf* 1E **73**
Ramsley. *Devn* 3G **11**
Ramsnest Common. *Surr* 2A **26**
Ramstone. *Abers* 2D **152**
Ranais. *W Isl* 5G **171**
Ranby. *Linc* 3B **88**
Ranby. *Notts* 2D **86**
Rand. *Linc* 3A **88**
Randwick. *Glos* 5D **48**
Ranfurly. *Ren* 3E **127**
Rangag. *High* 4D **168**
Rangemore. *Staf* 3F **73**
Rangeworthy. *S Glo* 3B **34**
Rankinston. *E Ayr* 3D **116**
Rank's Green. *Essx* 4H **53**
Ranmore Common. *Surr* 5C **38**
Rannoch Station. *Per* 3B **142**
Ranochan. *High* 5G **147**
Ranskill. *Notts* 2D **86**
Ranton. *Staf* 3C **72**
Ranton Green. *Staf* 3C **72**
Ranworth. *Norf* 4F **79**
Raploch. *Stir* 4G **135**
Rapness. *Orkn* 3E **172**
Rapps. *Som* 1G **13**
Rascal Moor. *E Yor* 1B **94**
Rascarrel. *Dum* 5E **111**
Rashfield. *Arg* 1C **126**
Rashwood. *Worc* 4D **60**
Raskelf. *N Yor* 2G **99**
Rassau. *Blae* 4E **47**
Rastrick. *W Yor* 2B **92**
Ratagan. *High* 2B **148**
Ratby. *Leics* 5C **74**
Ratcliffe Culey. *Leics* 1H **61**
Ratcliffe on Soar. *Notts* 3B **74**
Ratcliffe on the Wreake. *Leics* 4D **74**
Rathen. *Abers* 2H **161**
Rathillet. *Fife* 1F **137**
Rathmell. *N Yor* 4H **97**
Ratho. *Edin* 2E **129**
Ratho Station. *Edin* 2E **129**
Rathven. *Mor* 2B **160**
Ratley. *Hants* 4B **24**
Ratley. *Warw* 1B **50**
Ratlinghope. *Shrp* 1G **59**
Rattar. *High* 1E **169**
Ratten Row. *Cumb* 5E **113**
Ratten Row. *Lanc* 5D **96**
Rattery. *Devn* 2D **8**
Rattlesden. *Suff* 5B **66**
Ratton Village. *E Sus* 5G **27**
Rattray. *Abers* 3H **161**
Rattray. *Per* 4A **144**
Raughton. *Cumb* 5E **113**
Raughton Head. *Cumb* 5E **113**
Raunds. *Nptn* 3G **63**
Ravenfield. *S Yor* 1B **86**
Ravenglass. *Cumb* 5B **102**
Ravenhills Green. *Worc* 5B **60**
Raveningham. *Norf* 1F **67**
Ravenscar. *N Yor* 4G **107**
Ravensdale. *IOM* 2C **108**
Ravensden. *Bed* 5H **63**
Ravenseat. *N Yor* 4B **104**
Ravenshead. *Notts* 5C **86**
Ravensmoor. *Ches E* 5A **84**
Ravensthorpe. *Nptn* 3D **62**
Ravensthorpe. *W Yor* 2C **92**
Ravenstone. *Leics* 4B **74**
Ravenstone. *Mil* 5F **63**
Ravenstonedale. *Cumb* 4A **104**
Ravenstown. *Cumb* 2C **96**
Ravenstruther. *S Lan* 5C **128**
Ravensworth. *N Yor* 4E **105**
Raw. *N Yor* 4G **107**
Rawcliffe. *E Yor* 2G **93**
Rawcliffe. *York* 4H **99**
Rawcliffe Bridge. *E Yor* 2G **93**
Rawdon. *W Yor* 1C **92**
Rawgreen. *Nmbd* 4C **114**
Rawmarsh. *S Yor* 1B **86**
Rawnsley. *Staf* 4E **73**
Rawreth. *Essx* 1B **40**
Rawridge. *Devn* 2F **13**

Green—Rosudgeon

1A **74**
2F **91**
2D **54**
5D **120**
1C **40**
3G **13**
3H **53**
Lon 2C **38**
4E **65**
1F **91**
Read 4F **37** & **209**
Green. *Suff* 3D **66**
ng Street. *Kent* 2D **28**
adymoney. *Corn* 3F **7**
eagill. *Cumb* 3H **103**
Rea Hill. *Torb* 3F **9**
Rearquhar. *High* 4E **165**
Rearsby. *Leics* 4D **74**
Reasby. *Linc* 3H **87**
Reaseheath. *Ches E* 5A **84**
Reaster. *High* 2E **169**
Reawick. *Shet* 7E **173**
Reay. *High* 2B **168**
Rechullin. *High* 3A **156**
Reculver. *Kent* 4G **41**
Redberth. *Pemb* 4E **43**
Redbourn. *Herts* 4B **52**
Redbourne. *N Lin* 4C **94**
Redbrook. *Glos* 4A **48**
Redbrook. *Wrex* 1H **71**
Redburn. *High* 4D **158**
Redburn. *Nmbd* 3A **114**
Redcar. *Red C* 2D **106**
Redcastle. *High* 4H **157**
Redcliff Bay. *N Som* 4H **33**
Red Dial. *Cumb* 5D **112**
Redding. *Falk* 2C **128**
Reddingmuirhead. *Falk* 2C **128**
Reddings, The. *Glos* 3E **49**
Reddish. *G Man* 1C **84**
Redditch. *Worc* 4E **61**
Rede. *Suff* 5H **65**
Redenhall. *Norf* 2E **67**
Redesdale Camp. *Nmbd* 5C **120**
Redesmouth. *Nmbd* 1B **114**
Redford. *Ang* 4E **145**
Redford. *Dur* 1D **105**
Redford. *W Sus* 4G **25**
Redfordgreen. *Bord* 3F **119**
Redgate. *Corn* 2G **7**
Redgrave. *Suff* 3C **66**
Redhill. *Abers* 3E **153**
Redhill. *Herts* 2C **52**
Redhill. *N Som* 5H **33**
Redhill. *Shrp* 4B **72**
Redhill. *Surr* 5D **39**
Red Hill. *Warw* 5F **61**
Red Hill. *W Yor* 2E **93**
Redhouses. *Arg* 3B **124**
Redisham. *Suff* 2G **67**
Redland. *Bris* 4A **34**
Redland. *Orkn* 5C **172**
Redlingfield. *Suff* 3D **66**
Red Lodge. *Suff* 3F **65**
Redlynch. *Som* 3C **22**
Redlynch. *Wilts* 4H **23**
Redmain. *Cumb* 1C **102**
Redmarley. *Worc* 4B **60**
Redmarley D'Abitot. *Glos* 2C **48**
Redmarshall. *Stoc T* 2A **106**
Redmile. *Leics* 2E **75**
Redmire. *N Yor* 5D **104**
Rednal. *Shrp* 3F **71**
Redpath. *Bord* 1H **119**
Redpoint. *High* 2G **155**
Red Post. *Corn* 2C **10**
Red Rock. *G Man* 4D **90**
Red Roses. *Carm* 3G **43**
Red Row. *Nmbd* 5G **121**
Redruth. *Corn* 4B **6**
Red Street. *Staf* 5C **84**
Redvales. *G Man* 4F **91**
Red Wharf Bay. *IOA* 2E **81**
Redwick. *Newp* 3H **33**
Redwick. *S Glo* 3A **34**
Redworth. *Darl* 2F **105**
Reed. *Herts* 2D **52**
Reed End. *Herts* 2D **52**
Reedham. *Linc* 5B **88**
Reedham. *Norf* 5G **79**
Reedness. *E Yor* 2B **94**
Reeds Beck. *Linc* 4B **88**
Reemshill. *Abers* 4E **161**
Reepham. *Linc* 3H **87**
Reepham. *Norf* 3C **78**
Reeth. *N Yor* 5D **104**
Regaby. *IOM* 2D **108**
Regil. *N Som* 5A **34**
Regoul. *High* 3C **158**
Reiff. *High* 2D **162**
Reigate. *Surr* 5D **38**
Reighton. *N Yor* 2F **101**
Reilth. *Shrp* 2E **59**
Reinigeadal. *W Isl* 7E **171**
Reisque. *Abers* 1F **153**
Reiss. *High* 3F **169**
Rejerrah. *Corn* 3B **6**
Releath. *Corn* 5A **6**
Relubbus. *Corn* 3C **4**
Relugas. *Mor* 4D **159**
Remenham. *Wok* 3F **37**
Remenham Hill. *Wok* 3F **37**
Rempstone. *Notts* 3C **74**
Rendcomb. *Glos* 5F **49**
Rendham. *Suff* 4F **67**
Rendlesham. *Suff* 5F **67**
Renfrew. *Ren* 3G **127**
Renhold. *Bed* 5H **63**
Renishaw. *Derbs* 3B **86**
Rennington. *Nmbd* 3G **121**
Renton. *W Dun* 2E **127**
Renwick. *Cumb* 5G **113**
Repps. *Norf* 4G **79**
Repton. *Derbs* 3H **73**
Resaurie. *High* 4B **158**
Rescassa. *Corn* 4D **6**
Rescobie. *Ang* 3E **145**
Rescorla. *Corn* 3E **7**
(nr. Rosevean)
Rescorla. *Corn* 4D **6**
(nr. St Ewe)
Resipole. *High* 2B **140**
Resolfen. *Neat* 5B **46**
Resolis. *High* 2A **158**
Resolven. *Neat* 5B **46**
Rest and be thankful. *Arg* 3B **134**
Reston. *Bord* 3E **131**
Restrop. *Wilts* 3F **35**
Retford. *Notts* 2E **86**
Retire. *Corn* 2E **6**
Rettendon. *Essx* 1B **40**
Retyn. *Corn* 3C **6**
Revesby. *Linc* 4C **88**
Rew. *Devn* 5D **8**
Rewe. *Devn* 3C **12**
Rew Street. *IOW* 3C **16**
Rexon. *Devn* 4E **11**
Reybridge. *Wilts* 5E **35**
Reydon. *Suff* 3H **67**
Reymerston. *Norf* 5C **78**
Reynalton. *Pemb* 4E **43**
Reynoldston. *Swan* 4D **31**
Rezare. *Corn* 5D **10**
Rhadyr. *Mon* 5G **47**
Rhaeadr Gwy. *Powy* 4B **58**
Rhandirmwyn. *Carm* 1A **46**
Rhayader. *Powy* 4B **58**
Rheindown. *High* 4H **157**
Rhemore. *High* 3G **139**
Rhenetra. *High* 3D **154**
Rhewl. *Den* 1D **70**
(nr. Llangollen)
Rhewl. *Den* 4D **82**
(nr. Ruthin)
Rhewl. *Shrp* 2F **71**
Rhewl-Mostyn. *Flin* 3D **82**
Rhian. *High* 2C **164**
Rhian Breck. *High* 3C **164**
Rhicarn. *High* 1E **163**
Rhiconich. *High* 3C **166**
Rhicullen. *High* 1A **158**
Rhidorroch. *High* 4F **163**
Rhifail. *High* 4H **167**
Rhigos. *Rhon* 5C **46**
Rhilochan. *High* 3E **165**
Rhiroy. *High* 5F **163**
Rhitongue. *High* 3G **167**
Rhiw. *Gwyn* 3B **68**
Rhiwabon. *Wrex* 1F **71**
Rhiwbina. *Card* 3E **33**
Rhiwbryfdir. *Gwyn* 1F **69**
Rhiwderin. *Newp* 3F **33**
Rhiwlas. *Gwyn* 2B **70**
(nr. Bala)
Rhiwlas. *Gwyn* 4E **81**
(nr. Bangor)
Rhiwlas. *Powy* 2D **70**
Rhodes. *G Man* 4G **91**
Rhodesia. *Notts* 2C **86**
Rhodes Minnis. *Kent* 1F **29**
Rhodiad-y-Brenin. *Pemb* 2B **42**
Rhondda. *Rhon* 2C **32**
Rhonehouse. *Dum* 4E **111**
Rhoose. *V Glam* 5D **32**
Rhos. *Carm* 2D **45**
Rhos. *Neat* 5H **45**
Rhosaman. *Carm* 4H **45**
Rhoscefnhir. *IOA* 3E **81**
Rhoscolyn. *IOA* 3B **80**
Rhos Common. *Powy* 4E **71**
Rhoscrowther. *Pemb* 4D **42**
Rhos-ddu. *Gwyn* 2B **68**
Rhosdylluan. *Gwyn* 3A **70**
Rhosesmor. *Flin* 4E **82**
Rhos-fawr. *Gwyn* 2C **68**
Rhosgadfan. *Gwyn* 5E **81**
Rhosgoch. *IOA* 2D **80**
Rhosgoch. *Powy* 1E **47**
Rhos Haminiog. *Cdgn* 4E **57**
Rhos-hill. *Pemb* 1B **44**
Rhoshirwaun. *Gwyn* 3A **68**
Rhoslan. *Gwyn* 1D **69**
Rhoslefain. *Gwyn* 5E **69**
Rhosllanerchrugog. *Wrex* 1E **71**
Rhos Lligwy. *IOA* 2D **81**
Rhosmaen. *Carm* 3G **45**
Rhosmeirch. *IOA* 3D **80**
Rhosneigr. *IOA* 3C **80**
Rhos-on-Sea. *Cnwy* 2H **81**
Rhossili. *Swan* 4D **30**
Rhosson. *Pemb* 2B **42**
Rhos, The. *Pemb* 3E **43**
Rhostrenwfa. *IOA* 3D **80**
Rhostryfan. *Gwyn* 5D **81**
Rhostyllen. *Wrex* 1F **71**
Rhoswiel. *Shrp* 2E **71**
Rhosybol. *IOA* 2D **80**
Rhos-y-brithdir. *Powy* 3D **70**
Rhos-y-garth. *Cdgn* 3F **57**
Rhos-y-gwaliau. *Gwyn* 2B **70**
Rhos-y-llan. *Gwyn* 2B **68**
Rhos-y-meirch. *Powy* 4E **59**
Rhu. *Arg* 1D **126**
Rhualit. *Den* 3C **82**
Rhubadach. *Arg* 2B **126**
Rhubha Stoer. *High* 1E **163**
Rhuddall Heath. *Ches W* 4H **83**
Rhuddlan. *Cdgn* 1E **45**
Rhuddlan. *Den* 3C **82**
Rhue. *High* 4E **163**
Rhulen. *Powy* 1E **47**
Rhunahaorine. *Arg* 5F **125**
Rhuthun. *Den* 5D **82**
Rhuvoult. *High* 3C **166**
Rhyd. *Gwyn* 1F **69**
Rhydaman. *Carm* 4G **45**
Rhydargaeau. *Carm* 3E **45**
Rhydcymerau. *Carm* 2F **45**
Rhydd. *Worc* 1D **48**
Rhyd-Ddu. *Gwyn* 5E **81**
Rhydding. *Neat* 3G **31**
Rhydfudr. *Cdgn* 4E **57**
Rhydlanfair. *Cnwy* 5H **81**
Rhydlewis. *Cdgn* 1D **44**
Rhydlios. *Gwyn* 2A **68**
Rhydlydan. *Cnwy* 5A **82**
Rhyd-meirionydd. *Cdgn* 2F **57**
Rhydowen. *Cdgn* 1E **45**
Rhyd-Rosser. *Cdgn* 4E **57**
Rhydspence. *Powy* 1F **47**
Rhydtalog. *Flin* 5E **83**
Rhyd-uchaf. *Gwyn* 2B **70**
Rhydwyn. *IOA* 2C **80**
Rhyd-y-clafdy. *Gwyn* 2C **68**
Rhydycroesau. *Shrp* 2E **71**
Rhydyfelin. *Cdgn* 3E **57**
Rhydyfelin. *Rhon* 3E **32**
Rhyd-y-foel. *Cnwy* 3B **82**
Rhyd-y-fro. *Neat* 5H **45**
Rhydymain. *Gwyn* 3H **69**
Rhyd-y-meirch. *Mon* 5G **47**
Rhyd-y-meudwy. *Den* 5D **82**
Rhydymwyn. *Flin* 4E **82**
Rhyd-yr-onen. *Gwyn* 5F **69**
Rhyd-y-sarn. *Gwyn* 1F **69**
Rhyl. *Den* 2C **82**
Rhymney. *Cphy* 5E **46**
Rhymni. *Cphy* 5E **46**
Rhynd. *Per* 1D **136**
Rhynie. *Abers* 1B **152**
Ribbesford. *Worc* 3B **60**
Ribbleton. *Lanc* 1D **90**
Ribby. *Lanc* 1C **90**
Ribchester. *Lanc* 1E **91**
Riber. *Derbs* 5H **85**
Ribigill. *High* 3F **167**
Riby. *Linc* 4E **95**
Riccall. *N Yor* 1G **93**
Riccarton. *E Ayr* 1D **116**
Richards Castle. *Here* 4G **59**
Richborough Port. *Kent* 4H **41**
Richings Park. *Buck* 3B **38**
Richmond. *G Lon* 3C **38**
Richmond. *N Yor* 4E **105**
Rickarton. *Abers* 5F **153**
Rickerby. *Cumb* 4F **113**
Rickerscote. *Staf* 3D **72**
Rickford. *N Som* 1H **21**
Rickham. *Devn* 5D **8**
Rickinghall. *Suff* 3C **66**
Rickleton. *Tyne* 4F **115**
Rickling. *Essx* 2E **53**
Rickling Green. *Essx* 3F **53**
Rickmansworth. *Herts* 1B **38**
Riddings. *Derbs* 5B **86**
Riddlecombe. *Devn* 1G **11**
Riddlesden. *W Yor* 5C **98**
Ridge. *Dors* 4E **15**
Ridge. *Herts* 5C **52**
Ridge. *Wilts* 3E **23**
Ridgebourne. *Powy* 4C **58**
Ridge Lane. *Warw* 1G **61**
Ridgeway. *Derbs* 5A **86**
(nr. Alfreton)
Ridgeway. *Derbs* 2B **86**
(nr. Sheffield)
Ridgeway. *Staf* 5C **84**
Ridgeway Cross. *Here* 1C **48**
Ridgeway Moor. *Derbs* 2B **86**
Ridgewell. *Essx* 1H **53**
Ridgewood. *E Sus* 3F **27**
Ridgmont. *C Beds* 2H **51**
Ridgwardine. *Shrp* 2A **72**
Riding Mill. *Nmbd* 3D **114**
Ridley. *Kent* 4H **39**
Ridley. *Nmbd* 3A **114**
Ridlington. *Norf* 2F **79**
Ridlington. *Rut* 5F **75**
Ridsdale. *Nmbd* 1C **114**
Riemore Lodge. *Per* 4H **143**
Rievaulx. *N Yor* 1H **99**
Rift House. *Hart* 1B **106**
Rigg. *Dum* 3D **112**
Riggend. *N Lan* 2A **128**
Rigmaden Park. *Cumb* 1F **97**
Rigsby. *Linc* 3D **88**
Rigside. *S Lan* 1A **118**
Riley Green. *Lanc* 2E **90**
Rileyhill. *Staf* 4F **73**
Rilla Mill. *Corn* 5C **10**
Rillington. *N Yor* 2C **100**
Rimington. *Lanc* 5H **97**
Rimpton. *Som* 4B **22**
Rimsdale. *High* 4H **167**
Rimswell. *E Yor* 2G **95**
Ringasta. *Shet* 10E **173**
Ringford. *Dum* 4D **111**
Ringing Hill. *Leics* 4B **74**
Ringinglow. *S Yor* 2G **85**
Ringland. *Norf* 4D **78**
Ringlestone. *Kent* 5C **40**
Ringmer. *E Sus* 4F **27**
Ringmore. *Devn* 4C **8**
(nr. Kingsbridge)
Ringmore. *Devn* 5C **12**
(nr. Teignmouth)
Ring o' Bells. *Lanc* 3C **90**
Ring's End. *Cambs* 5C **76**
Ringsfield. *Suff* 2G **67**
Ringsfield Corner. *Suff* 2G **67**
Ringshall. *Buck* 4H **51**
Ringshall. *Suff* 5C **66**
Ringshall Stocks. *Suff* 5C **66**
Ringstead. *Norf* 1G **77**
Ringstead. *Nptn* 3G **63**
Ringwood. *Hants* 2G **15**
Ringwould. *Kent* 1H **29**
Rinmore. *Abers* 2B **152**
Rinnigill. *Orkn* 8C **172**
Rinsey. *Corn* 4C **4**
Riof. *W Isl* 4D **171**
Ripe. *E Sus* 4G **27**
Ripley. *Derbs* 1B **74**
Ripley. *Hants* 3G **15**
Ripley. *N Yor* 3E **99**
Ripley. *Surr* 5B **38**
Riplingham. *E Yor* 1C **94**
Riplington. *Hants* 4E **25**
Ripon. *N Yor* 2F **99**
Rippingale. *Linc* 3H **75**
Ripple. *Kent* 1H **29**
Ripple. *Worc* 2D **48**
Ripponden. *W Yor* 3A **92**
Rireavach. *High* 4E **163**
Risabus. *Arg* 5B **124**
Risbury. *Here* 5H **59**
Risby. *E Yor* 1D **94**
Risby. *N Lin* 3C **94**
Risby. *Suff* 4G **65**
Risca. *Cphy* 2F **33**
Rise. *E Yor* 5F **101**
Riseden. *E Sus* 2H **27**
Riseden. *Kent* 2B **28**
Rise End. *Derbs* 5G **85**
Risegate. *Linc* 2B **76**
Riseholme. *Linc* 3G **87**
Riseley. *Bed* 4H **63**
Riseley. *Wok* 5F **37**
Rishangles. *Suff* 4D **66**
Rishton. *Lanc* 1F **91**
Rishworth. *W Yor* 3A **92**
Risley. *Derbs* 2B **74**
Risley. *Warr* 1A **84**
Risplith. *N Yor* 3E **99**
Rispond. *High* 2E **167**
Rivar. *Wilts* 5B **36**
Rivenhall. *Essx* 4B **54**
Rivenhall End. *Essx* 4B **54**
River. *Kent* 1G **29**
River. *W Sus* 3A **26**
River Bank. *Cambs* 4E **65**
Riverhead. *Kent* 5G **39**
Rivington. *Lanc* 3E **91**
Roach Bridge. *Lanc* 2D **90**
Roachill. *Devn* 4B **20**
Roade. *Nptn* 5E **63**
Road Green. *Norf* 1E **67**
Roadhead. *Cumb* 2G **113**
Roadmeetings. *S Lan* 5B **128**
Roadside. *High* 2D **168**
Roadside of Catterline. *Abers* 1H **145**
Roadside of Kinneff. *Abers* 1H **145**
Roadwater. *Som* 3D **20**
Road Weedon. *Nptn* 5D **62**
Roag. *High* 4B **154**
Roa Island. *Cumb* 3B **96**
Roath. *Card* 4E **33**
Roberton. *Bord* 3G **119**
Roberton. *S Lan* 2B **118**
Robertsbridge. *E Sus* 3B **28**
Robertstown. *Mor* 4G **159**
Robertstown. *Rhon* 5C **46**
Roberttown. *W Yor* 2B **92**
Robeston Back. *Pemb* 3E **43**
Robeston Wathen. *Pemb* 3E **43**
Robeston West. *Pemb* 4C **42**
Robin Hood. *Lanc* 3D **90**
Robin Hood. *W Yor* 2D **92**
Robin Hood Airport Doncaster Sheffield. *S Yor* 1D **86**
Robinhood End. *Essx* 2H **53**
Robin Hood's Bay. *N Yor* 4G **107**
Roborough. *Devn* 1F **11**
(nr. Great Torrington)
Roborough. *Devn* 2B **8**
(nr. Plymouth)
Rob Roy's House. *Arg* 2A **134**
Roby Mill. *Lanc* 4D **90**
Rocester. *Staf* 2F **73**
Roch. *Pemb* 2C **42**
Rochdale. *G Man* 3G **91**
Roche. *Corn* 2D **6**
Rochester. *Medw* 4B **40** & **Medway 204**
Rochester. *Nmbd* 5C **120**
Rochford. *Essx* 1C **40**
Rock. *Corn* 1D **6**
Rock. *Nmbd* 2G **121**
Rock. *W Sus* 4C **26**
Rock. *Worc* 3B **60**
Rockbeare. *Devn* 3D **12**
Rockbourne. *Hants* 1G **15**
Rockcliffe. *Cumb* 3E **113**
Rockcliffe. *Dum* 4F **111**
Rockcliffe Cross. *Cumb* 3E **113**
Rock Ferry. *Mers* 2F **83**
Rockfield. *High* 5G **165**
Rockfield. *Mon* 4H **47**
Rockford. *Hants* 2G **15**
Rockgreen. *Shrp* 3H **59**
Rockhampton. *S Glo* 2B **34**
Rockhead. *Corn* 4A **10**
Rockingham. *Nptn* 1F **63**
Rockland All Saints. *Norf* 1B **66**
Rockland St Mary. *Norf* 5F **79**
Rockland St Peter. *Norf* 1B **66**
Rockley. *Wilts* 4G **35**
Rockwell End. *Buck* 3F **37**
Rockwell Green. *Som* 1E **13**
Rodborough. *Glos* 5D **48**
Rodbourne. *Wilts* 3E **35**
Rodd. *Here* 4F **59**
Roddam. *Nmbd* 2E **121**
Rodden. *Dors* 4B **14**
Roddenloft. *E Ayr* 2D **117**
Roddymoor. *Dur* 1E **105**
Rode. *Som* 1D **22**
Rodeheath. *Ches E* 4C **84**
(nr. Congleton)
Rode Heath. *Ches E* 5C **84**
(nr. Kidsgrove)
Roden. *Telf* 4H **71**
Rodhuish. *Som* 3D **20**
Rodington. *Telf* 4H **71**
Rodington Heath. *Telf* 4H **71**
Rodley. *Glos* 4C **48**
Rodmarton. *Glos* 2E **35**
Rodmell. *E Sus* 5F **27**
Rodmersham. *Kent* 4D **40**
Rodmersham Green. *Kent* 4D **40**
Rodney Stoke. *Som* 2H **21**
Rodsley. *Derbs* 1G **73**
Rodway. *Som* 2F **21**
Rodway. *Telf* 4A **72**
Rodwell. *Dors* 5B **14**
Roecliffe. *N Yor* 3F **99**
Roe Green. *Herts* 2D **52**
Roehampton. *G Lon* 3D **38**
Roesound. *Shet* 5E **173**
Roffey. *W Sus* 2C **26**
Rogart. *High* 3E **165**
Rogate. *W Sus* 4G **25**
Roger Ground. *Cumb* 5E **103**
Rogerstone. *Newp* 3F **33**
Roghadal. *W Isl* 9C **171**
Rogiet. *Mon* 3H **33**
Rogue's Alley. *Cambs* 5C **76**
Roke. *Oxon* 2E **37**
Rokemarsh. *Oxon* 2E **36**
Roker. *Tyne* 4H **115**
Rollesby. *Norf* 4G **79**
Rolleston. *Leics* 5E **75**
Rolleston. *Notts* 5E **87**
Rolleston on Dove. *Staf* 3G **73**
Rolston. *E Yor* 5G **101**
Rolvenden. *Kent* 2C **28**
Rolvenden Layne. *Kent* 2C **28**
Romaldkirk. *Dur* 2C **104**
Roman Bank. *Shrp* 1H **59**
Romanby. *N Yor* 5A **106**
Roman Camp. *W Lot* 2D **129**
Romannobridge. *Bord* 5E **129**
Romansleigh. *Devn* 4H **19**
Romers Common. *Worc* 4H **59**
Romesdal. *High* 3D **154**
Romford. *Dors* 2F **15**
Romford. *G Lon* 2G **39**
Romiley. *G Man* 1D **84**
Romsey. *Hants* 4B **24**
Romsley. *Shrp* 2B **60**
Romsley. *Worc* 3D **60**
Ronague. *IOM* 4B **108**
Ronaldsvoe. *Orkn* 8D **172**
Rookby. *Cumb* 3B **104**
Rookhope. *Dur* 5C **114**
Rooking. *Cumb* 3F **103**
Rookley. *IOW* 4D **16**
Rooks Bridge. *Som* 1G **21**
Rooksey Green. *Suff* 5B **66**
Rook's Nest. *Som* 3D **20**
Rookwood. *W Sus* 3F **17**
Roos. *E Yor* 1F **95**
Roosebeck. *Cumb* 3B **96**
Roosecote. *Cumb* 3B **96**
Rootfield. *High* 3H **157**
Rootham's Green. *Bed* 5A **64**
Rootpark. *S Lan* 4C **128**
Ropley. *Hants* 3E **25**
Ropley Dean. *Hants* 3E **25**
Ropsley. *Linc* 2G **75**
Rora. *Abers* 3H **161**
Rorandle. *Abers* 2D **152**
Rorrington. *Shrp* 5F **71**
Rose. *Corn* 3B **6**
Roseacre. *Lanc* 1C **90**
Rose Ash. *Devn* 4A **20**
Rosebank. *S Lan* 5B **128**
Rosebush. *Pemb* 2E **43**
Rosedale Abbey. *N Yor* 5E **107**
Roseden. *Nmbd* 2E **121**
Rose Green. *Essx* 3C **54**
Rose Green. *Suff* 1C **54**
Rosehall. *High* 3B **164**
Rosehearty. *Abers* 2G **161**
Rose Hill. *E Sus* 4F **27**
Rose Hill. *Lanc* 1G **91**
Rosehill. *Shrp* 2A **72**
(nr. Market Drayton)
Rosehill. *Shrp* 4G **71**
(nr. Shrewsbury)
Roseisle. *Mor* 2F **159**
Rosemarket. *Pemb* 4D **42**
Rosemarkie. *High* 3B **158**
Rosemary Lane. *Devn* 1E **13**
Rosemount. *Per* 4A **144**
Rosenannon. *Corn* 2D **6**
Roser's Cross. *E Sus* 3G **27**
Rosevean. *Corn* 3E **6**
Rosewell. *Midl* 3F **129**
Roseworth. *Stoc T* 2B **106**
Roseworthy. *Corn* 3D **4**
Rosgill. *Cumb* 3G **103**
Roshven. *High* 1B **140**
Roskhill. *High* 4B **154**
Roskorwell. *Corn* 4E **5**
Rosley. *Cumb* 5E **112**
Roslin. *Midl* 3F **129**
Rosliston. *Derbs* 4G **73**
Rosneath. *Arg* 1D **126**
Ross. *Dum* 5D **110**
Ross. *Nmbd* 1F **121**
Ross. *Per* 1G **135**
Ross. *Bord* 3F **131**
Rossendale. *Lanc* 2F **91**
Rossett. *Wrex* 5F **83**
Rossington. *S Yor* 1D **86**
Rosskeen. *High* 2A **158**
Rossland. *Ren* 2F **127**
Ross-on-Wye. *Here* 3B **48**
Roster. *High* 4E **169**
Rostherne. *Ches E* 2B **84**
Rostholme. *S Yor* 4F **93**
Rosthwaite. *Cumb* 3D **102**
Roston. *Derbs* 1F **73**
Rosudgeon. *Corn* 4C **4**

Rosyth—Sandf

Rosyth. *Fife* 1E 129
Rothbury. *Nmbd* 4E 121
Rotherby. *Leics* 4D 74
Rotherfield. *E Sus* 3G 27
Rotherfield Greys. *Oxon* 3F 37
Rotherfield Peppard. *Oxon* 3F 37
Rotherham. *S Yor* 1B 86
Rothersthorpe. *Nptn* 5E 62
Rotherwick. *Hants* 1F 25
Rothes. *Mor* 4G 159
Rothesay. *Arg* 3B 126
Rothienorman. *Abers* 5E 160
Rothiesholm. *Orkn* 5F 172
Rothley. *Leics* 4C 74
Rothley. *Nmbd* 1D 114
Rothwell. *Linc* 1A 88
Rothwell. *Nptn* 2F 63
Rothwell. *W Yor* 2D 92
Rothwell Haigh. *W Yor* 2D 92
Rotsea. *E Yor* 4E 101
Rottal. *Ang* 2C 144
Rotten End. *Suff* 4F 67
Rotten Row. *Norf* 4C 78
Rotten Row. *W Ber* 4D 36
Rotten Row. *W Mid* 3F 61
Rottingdean. *Brig* 5E 27
Rottington. *Cumb* 3A 102
Roud. *IOW* 4D 16
Rougham. *Norf* 3H 77
Rougham. *Suff* 4B 66
Rough Close. *Staf* 2D 72
Rough Common. *Kent* 5F 41
Roughcote. *Staf* 1D 72
Rough Haugh. *High* 4H 167
Rough Hay. *Staf* 3G 73
Roughlee. *Lanc* 5H 97
Roughley. *W Mid* 1F 61
Roughsike. *Cumb* 2G 113
Roughton. *Linc* 4B 88
Roughton. *Norf* 2E 78
Roughton. *Shrp* 1B 60
Roundbush Green. *Essx* 4F 53
Roundham. *Som* 2H 13
Roundhay. *W Yor* 1D 92
Round Hill. *Torb* 2F 9
Roundhurst Common. *W Sus* 2A 26
Round Maple. *Suff* 1C 54
Round Oak. *Shrp* 2F 59
Roundstreet Common. *W Sus* 3B 26
Roundthwaite. *Cumb* 4H 103
Roundway. *Wilts* 5F 35
Roundyhill. *Ang* 3C 144
Rousdon. *Devn* 3F 13
Rousham. *Oxon* 3C 50
Rous Lench. *Worc* 5E 61
Routh. *E Yor* 5E 101
Rout's Green. *Buck* 2F 37
Row. *Corn* 5A 10
Row. *Cumb* 1D 96 (nr. Kendal)
Row. *Cumb* 1H 103 (nr. Penrith)
Rowanburn. *Dum* 2F 113
Rowanhill. *Abers* 3H 161
Rowardennan. *Stir* 4C 134
Rowarth. *Derbs* 2E 85
Row Ash. *Hants* 1D 16
Rowberrow. *Som* 1H 21
Rowde. *Wilts* 5E 35
Rowden. *Devn* 3G 11
Rowden Hill. *Wilts* 4E 35
Rowen. *Cnwy* 3G 81
Rowfoot. *Nmbd* 3H 113
Row Green. *Essx* 3H 53
Row Heath. *Essx* 4E 55
Rowhedge. *Essx* 3D 54
Rowhook. *W Sus* 2C 26
Rowington. *Warw* 4G 61
Rowland. *Derbs* 3G 85
Rowland's Castle. *Hants* 1F 17
Rowlands Gill. *Tyne* 4E 115
Rowledge. *Surr* 2G 25
Rowley. *Dur* 5D 115
Rowley. *E Yor* 1C 94
Rowley. *Shrp* 5F 71
Rowley. *Staf* 3F 73
Rowley Hill. *W Yor* 3B 92
Rowley Regis. *W Mid* 2D 60
Rowlstone. *Here* 3G 47
Rowly. *Surr* 1B 26
Rowner. *Hants* 2D 16
Rowney Green. *Worc* 3E 61
Rownhams. *Hants* 1B 16
Rowrah. *Cumb* 3B 102
Rowsham. *Buck* 4G 51
Rowsley. *Derbs* 4G 85
Rowstock. *Oxon* 3C 36
Rowston. *Linc* 5H 87
Row, The. *Lanc* 2D 96
Rowthorne. *Derbs* 4B 86
Rowton. *Ches W* 4G 83
Rowton. *Shrp* 2G 59 (nr. Ludlow)
Rowton. *Shrp* 4F 71 (nr. Shrewsbury)
Rowton. *Telf* 4A 72
Row Town. *Surr* 4B 38
Roxburgh. *Bord* 1B 120
Roxby. *N Lin* 3C 94
Roxby. *N Yor* 3E 107
Roxton. *Bed* 5A 64
Roxwell. *Essx* 5G 53
Royal Leamington Spa. *Warw* 4H 61
Royal Oak. *Darl* 2F 105
Royal Oak. *Lanc* 4C 90
Royal Oak. *N Yor* 2F 101
Royal's Green. *Ches E* 1A 72
Royal Tunbridge Wells. *Kent* 2G 27
Roybridge. *High* 5E 149
Roydon. *Essx* 4E 53
Roydon. *Norf* 2C 66 (nr. Diss)
Roydon. *Norf* 3G 77 (nr. King's Lynn)
Roydon Hamlet. *Essx* 5E 53
Royston. *Herts* 1D 52
Royston. *S Yor* 3D 92
Royston Water. *Som* 1F 13
Royton. *G Man* 4H 91
Ruabon. *Wrex* 1F 71
Ruaig. *Arg* 4B 138
Ruan High Lanes. *Corn* 5D 6
Ruan Lanihorne. *Corn* 4C 6
Ruan Major. *Corn* 5E 5
Ruan Minor. *Corn* 5E 5
Ruarach. *High* 1B 148
Ruardean. *Glos* 4B 48
Ruardean Hill. *Glos* 4B 48
Ruardean Woodside. *Glos* 4B 48
Rubery. *W Mid* 3D 61
Ruchazie. *Glas* 3H 127
Ruckcroft. *Cumb* 5G 113
Ruckinge. *Kent* 2E 29
Ruckland. *Linc* 3C 88
Rucklers Lane. *Herts* 5A 52
Ruckley. *Shrp* 5H 71
Rudbaxton. *Pemb* 2D 42
Rudby. *N Yor* 4B 106
Ruddington. *Notts* 2C 74
Rudford. *Glos* 3C 48
Rudge. *Shrp* 1C 60
Rudge. *Wilts* 1D 22
Rudge Heath. *Shrp* 1B 60
Rudgeway. *S Glo* 3B 34
Rudgwick. *W Sus* 2B 26
Rudhall. *Here* 3B 48
Rudheath. *Ches W* 3A 84
Rudley Green. *Essx* 5B 54
Rudloe. *Wilts* 4D 34
Rudry. *Cphy* 3E 33
Rudston. *E Yor* 3E 101
Rudyard. *Staf* 5D 84
Rufford. *Lanc* 3C 90
Rufforth. *York* 4H 99
Rugby. *Warw* 3C 62
Rugeley. *Staf* 4E 73
Ruglen. *S Ayr* 4B 116
Ruilick. *High* 4H 157
Ruisaurie. *High* 4G 157
Ruishton. *Som* 4F 21
Ruisigearraidh. *W Isl* 1E 170
Ruislip. *G Lon* 2B 38
Ruislip Common. *G Lon* 2B 38
Rumbling Bridge. *Per* 4C 136
Rumburgh. *Suff* 2F 67
Rumford. *Corn* 1C 6
Rumford. *Falk* 2C 128
Rumney. *Card* 4F 33
Rumwell. *Som* 4E 21
Runcorn. *Hal* 2H 83
Runcton. *W Sus* 2G 17
Runcton Holme. *Norf* 5F 77
Rundlestone. *Devn* 5F 11
Runfold. *Surr* 2G 25
Runhall. *Norf* 5C 78
Runham. *Norf* 4G 79
Runnington. *Som* 4E 20
Runshaw Moor. *Lanc* 3D 90
Runswick. *N Yor* 3F 107
Runtaleave. *Ang* 2B 144
Runwell. *Essx* 1B 40
Ruscombe. *Wok* 4F 37
Rushall. *Here* 2B 48
Rushall. *Norf* 2D 66
Rushall. *W Mid* 5E 73
Rushall. *Wilts* 1G 23
Rushbrooke. *Suff* 4A 66
Rushbury. *Shrp* 1H 59
Rushden. *Herts* 2D 52
Rushden. *Nptn* 4G 63
Rushenden. *Kent* 3D 40
Rushford. *Devn* 5E 11
Rushford. *Suff* 2B 66
Rush Green. *Herts* 3C 52
Rushlake Green. *E Sus* 4H 27
Rushmere. *Suff* 2G 67
Rushmere St Andrew. *Suff* 1E 55
Rushmoor. *Surr* 2G 25
Rushock. *Worc* 3C 60
Rusholme. *G Man* 1C 84
Rushton. *Ches W* 4H 83
Rushton. *Nptn* 2F 63
Rushton. *Shrp* 5A 72
Rushton Spencer. *Staf* 4D 84
Rushwick. *Worc* 5C 60
Rushyford. *Dur* 2F 105
Ruskie. *Stir* 3F 135
Ruskington. *Linc* 5H 87
Rusland. *Cumb* 1C 96
Rusper. *W Sus* 2D 26
Ruspidge. *Glos* 4B 48
Russell's Water. *Oxon* 3F 37
Russel's Green. *Suff* 3E 67
Russ Hill. *Surr* 1D 26
Russland. *Orkn* 6C 172
Rusthall. *Kent* 2G 27
Rustington. *W Sus* 5B 26
Ruston. *N Yor* 1D 100
Ruston Parva. *E Yor* 3E 101
Ruswarp. *N Yor* 4F 107
Rutherglen. *S Lan* 3H 127
Ruthernbridge. *Corn* 2E 6
Ruthin. *Den* 5D 82
Ruthin. *V Glam* 4C 32
Ruthrieston. *Aber* 3G 153
Ruthven. *Abers* 4C 160
Ruthven. *Ang* 4B 144
Ruthven. *High* 5C 158 (nr. Inverness)
Ruthven. *High* 4B 150 (nr. Kingussie)
Ruthvoes. *Corn* 2D 6
Ruthwaite. *Cumb* 1D 102
Ruthwell. *Dum* 3C 112
Ruxton Green. *Here* 4A 48
Ruyton-XI-Towns. *Shrp* 3F 71
Ryal. *Nmbd* 2D 114
Ryall. *Dors* 3H 13
Ryall. *Worc* 1D 48
Ryarsh. *Kent* 5A 40
Rychraggan. *High* 5G 157
Rydal. *Cumb* 4E 103
Ryde. *IOW* 3D 16
Rye. *E Sus* 3D 28
Ryecroft Gate. *Staf* 4D 84
Ryeford. *Here* 3B 48
Rye Foreign. *E Sus* 3D 28
Rye Harbour. *E Sus* 4D 28
Ryehill. *E Yor* 2F 95
Rye Street. *Worc* 2C 48
Ryhall. *Rut* 4H 75
Ryhill. *W Yor* 3D 93
Ryhope. *Tyne* 4H 115
Ryhope Colliery. *Tyne* 4H 115
Rylands. *Notts* 2C 74
Rylstone. *N Yor* 4B 98
Ryme Intrinseca. *Dors* 1A 14
Ryther. *N Yor* 1F 93
Ryton. *Glos* 2C 48
Ryton. *N Yor* 2B 100
Ryton. *Shrp* 5B 72
Ryton. *Tyne* 3E 115
Ryton. *Warw* 2A 62
Ryton-on-Dunsmore. *Warw* 3A 62
Ryton Woodside. *Tyne* 3E 115

S

Saasaig. *High* 3E 147
Sabden. *Lanc* 1F 91
Sacombe. *Herts* 4D 52
Sacriston. *Dur* 5F 115
Sadberge. *Darl* 3A 106
Saddell. *Arg* 2B 122
Saddington. *Leics* 1D 62
Saddle Bow. *Norf* 4F 77
Saddlescombe. *W Sus* 4D 26
Saddleworth. *G Man* 4H 91
Sadgill. *Cumb* 4F 103
Saffron Walden. *Essx* 2F 53
Sageston. *Pemb* 4E 43
Saham Hills. *Norf* 5B 78
Saham Toney. *Norf* 5A 78
Saighdinis. *W Isl* 2D 170
Saighton. *Ches W* 4G 83
Sain Dunwyd. *V Glam* 5C 32
Sain Hilari. *V Glam* 4D 32
St Abbs. *Bord* 3F 131
St Agnes. *Corn* 3B 6
St Albans. *Herts* 5B 52
St Allen. *Corn* 3C 6
St Andrews. *Fife* 2H 137 & 209
St Andrews Major. *V Glam* 4E 33
St Anne's. *Lanc* 2B 90
St Ann's. *Dum* 5C 118
St Ann's Chapel. *Corn* 5E 11 (nr. Gunnislake)
St Ann's Chapel. *Devn* 4C 8 (nr. Aveton Gifford)
St Anthony. *Corn* 5C 6
St Anthony-in-Meneage. *Corn* 4E 5
St Arvans. *Mon* 2A 34
St Asaph. *Den* 3C 82
Sain Tathan. *V Glam* 5D 32
St Athan. *V Glam* 5D 32
St Austell. *Corn* 3E 6
St Bartholomew's Hill. *Wilts* 4E 23
St Bees. *Cumb* 3A 102
St Blazey. *Corn* 3E 7
St Blazey Gate. *Corn* 3E 7
St Boswells. *Bord* 1A 120
St Breock. *Corn* 1D 6
St Breward. *Corn* 5A 10
St Briavels. *Glos* 5A 48
St Brides. *Pemb* 3B 42
St Bride's Major. *V Glam* 4B 32
St Bride's Netherwent. *Mon* 3H 33
St Bride's-super-Ely. *V Glam* 4D 32
St Brides Wentlooge. *Newp* 3F 33
St Budeaux. *Plym* 3A 8
Saintbury. *Glos* 2G 49
St Buryan. *Corn* 4B 4
St Catherine. *Bath* 4C 34
St Catherines. *Arg* 3A 134
St Clears. *Carm* 3G 43
St Cleer. *Corn* 2G 7
St Clement. *Corn* 4C 6
St Clether. *Corn* 4C 10
St Colmac. *Arg* 3B 126
St Columb Major. *Corn* 2D 6
St Columb Minor. *Corn* 2C 6
St Columb Road. *Corn* 3D 6
St Combs. *Abers* 2H 161
St Cross. *Hants* 4C 24
St Cross South Elmham. *Suff* 2E 67
St Cyrus. *Abers* 2G 145
St David's. *Pemb* 2B 42
St David's. *Per* 1B 136
St Day. *Corn* 4B 6
St Dennis. *Corn* 3D 6
St Dogmaels. *Pemb* 1B 44
St Dominick. *Corn* 2H 7
St Donat's. *V Glam* 5C 32
St Edith's Marsh. *Wilts* 5E 35
St Endellion. *Corn* 1D 6
St Enoder. *Corn* 3C 6
St Erme. *Corn* 4C 6
St Erney. *Corn* 3H 7
St Erth. *Corn* 3C 4
St Erth Praze. *Corn* 3C 4
St Ervan. *Corn* 1C 6
St Eval. *Corn* 2C 6
St Ewe. *Corn* 4D 6
St Fagans. *Card* 4E 32
St Fergus. *Abers* 3H 161
St Fillans. *Per* 1F 135
St Florence. *Pemb* 4E 43
St Gennys. *Corn* 3B 10
St George. *Cnwy* 3B 82
St Georges. *N Som* 5G 33
St Georges. *V Glam* 4D 32
St George's Hill. *Surr* 4B 38
St Germans. *Corn* 3H 7
St Giles in the Wood. *Devn* 1F 11
St Giles on the Heath. *Devn* 3D 10
St Giles's Hill. *Hants* 4C 24
St Gluvias. *Corn* 5B 6
St Harmon. *Powy* 3B 58
St Helena. *Warw* 5G 73
St Helen Auckland. *Dur* 2E 105
St Helens. *Cumb* 1B 102
St Helens. *E Sus* 4C 28
St Helens. *IOW* 4E 17
St Helens. *Mers* 1G 83
St Hilary. *Corn* 3C 4
St Hilary. *V Glam* 4D 32
Saint Hill. *Devn* 2D 12
Saint Hill. *W Sus* 2E 27
St Illtyd. *Blae* 5F 47
St Ippolyts. *Herts* 3B 52
St Ishmael. *Carm* 5D 44
St Ishmael's. *Pemb* 4C 42
St Issey. *Corn* 1D 6
St Ive. *Corn* 2H 7
St Ives. *Cambs* 3C 64
St Ives. *Corn* 2C 4
St Ives. *Dors* 2G 15
St James' End. *Nptn* 4E 63
St James South Elmham. *Suff* 2F 67
St Jidgey. *Corn* 2D 6
St John. *Corn* 3A 8
St John's. *IOM* 3B 108
St Johns. *Worc* 5C 60
St John's Chapel. *Devn* 4F 19
St John's Chapel. *Dur* 1B 104
St John's Fen End. *Norf* 4E 77
St John's Hall. *Dur* 1D 104
St John's Town of Dalry. *Dum* 1D 110
St Judes. *IOM* 2C 108
St Just. *Corn* 5C 6 (nr. Falmouth)
St Just. *Corn* 3A 4 (nr. Penzance)
St Just in Roseland. *Corn* 5C 6
St Katherines. *Abers* 5E 161
St Keverne. *Corn* 4E 5
St Kew. *Corn* 5A 10
St Kew Highway. *Corn* 5A 10
St Keyne. *Corn* 2G 7
St Lawrence. *Corn* 2E 7
St Lawrence. *Essx* 5C 54
St Lawrence. *IOW* 5D 16
St Leonards. *Buck* 5H 51
St Leonards. *Dors* 2G 15
St Leonards. *E Sus* 5B 28
St Levan. *Corn* 4A 4
St Lythans. *V Glam* 4E 32
St Mabyn. *Corn* 5A 10
St Madoes. *Per* 1D 136
St Margarets. *Here* 2G 47
St Margaret's. *Herts* 4A 52 (nr. Hemel Hempstead)
St Margarets. *Herts* 4D 53 (nr. Hoddesdon)
St Margaret's. *Wilts* 5G 35
St Margaret's at Cliffe. *Kent* 1H 29
St Margaret's Hope. *Orkn* 8D 172
St Margaret South Elmham. *Suff* 2F 67
St Mark's. *IOM* 4B 108
St Martin. *Corn* 4E 5 (nr. Helston)
St Martin. *Corn* 3G 7 (nr. Looe)
St Martins. *Per* 5A 144
St Martin's. *Shrp* 2F 71
St Mary Bourne. *Hants* 1C 24
St Marychurch. *Torb* 2F 9
St Mary Church. *V Glam* 4D 32
St Mary Cray. *G Lon* 4F 39
St Mary Hill. *V Glam* 4C 32
St Mary Hoo. *Medw* 3C 40
St Mary in the Marsh. *Kent* 3E 29
St Mary's. *Orkn* 7D 172
St Mary's Bay. *Kent* 3E 29
St Maughan's Green. *Mon* 4H 47
St Mawes. *Corn* 5C 6
St Mawgan. *Corn* 2C 6
St Mellion. *Corn* 2H 7
St Mellons. *Card* 3F 33
St Merryn. *Corn* 1C 6
St Mewan. *Corn* 3D 6
St Michael Caerhays. *Corn* 4D 6
St Michael Penkevil. *Corn* 4C 6
St Michaels. *Kent* 2C 28
St Michaels. *Torb* 3E 9
St Michaels. *Worc* 4H 59
St Michael's on Wyre. *Lanc* 5D 96
St Michael South Elmham. *Suff* 2F 67
St Minver. *Corn* 1D 6
St Monans. *Fife* 3H 137
St Neot. *Corn* 2F 7
St Neots. *Cambs* 4A 64
St Newlyn East. *Corn* 3C 6
St Nicholas. *Pemb* 1D 42
St Nicholas. *V Glam* 4D 32
St Nicholas at Wade. *Kent* 4G 41
St Nicholas South Elmham. *Suff* 2F 67
St Ninians. *Stir* 4H 135
St Olaves. *Norf* 1G 67
St Osyth. *Essx* 4E 54
St Osyth Heath. *Essx* 4E 55
St Owen's Cross. *Here* 3A 48
St Paul's Cray. *G Lon* 4F 39
St Paul's Walden. *Herts* 3B 52
St Peter's. *Kent* 4H 41
St Peter The Great. *Worc* 5C 60
St Petrox. *Pemb* 5D 42
St Pinnock. *Corn* 2
St Quivox. *S Ayr* 2C 1
St Ruan. *Corn* 5E
St Stephen. *Corn* 3D
St Stephens. *Corn* 4D 10 (nr. Launceston)
St Stephens. *Corn* 3A 8 (nr. Saltash)
St Teath. *Corn* 4A 10
St Thomas. *Devn* 3C 12
St Thomas. *Swan* 3F 31
St Tudy. *Corn* 5A 10
St Twynnells. *Pemb* 5D 42
St Veep. *Corn* 3F 7
St Vigeans. *Ang* 4F 145
St Wenn. *Corn* 2D 6
St Weonards. *Here* 3H 47
St Winnolls. *Corn* 3H 7
St Winnow. *Corn* 3F 7
Salcombe. *Devn* 5D 8
Salcombe Regis. *Devn* 4E 13
Salcott. *Essx* 4C 54
Sale. *G Man* 1B 84
Saleby. *Linc* 3D 88
Sale Green. *Worc* 5D 60
Salehurst. *E Sus* 3B 28
Salem. *Carm* 3G 45
Salem. *Cdgn* 2F 57
Salem. *Gwyn* 5E 81
Salen. *Arg* 4G 139
Salen. *High* 2A 140
Salesbury. *Lanc* 1E 91
Saleway. *Worc* 5D 60
Salford. *C Beds* 2H 51
Salford. *G Man* 1C 84 & **Manchester** 201
Salford. *Oxon* 3A 50
Salford Priors. *Warw* 5E 61
Salfords. *Surr* 1D 27
Salhouse. *Norf* 4F 79
Saligo. *Arg* 3A 124
Saline. *Fife* 4C 136
Salisbury. *Wilts* 3G 23 & 210
Salkeld Dykes. *Cumb* 1G 103
Sallachan. *High* 2D 141
Sallachy. *High* 3C 164 (nr. Lairg)
Sallachy. *High* 5B 156 (nr. Stromeferry)
Salle. *Norf* 3D 78
Salmonby. *Linc* 3C 88
Salmond's Muir. *Ang* 5E 145
Salperton. *Glos* 3F 49
Salph End. *Bed* 5H 63
Salsburgh. *N Lan* 3B 128
Salt. *Staf* 3D 72
Salta. *Cumb* 5B 112
Saltaire. *W Yor* 1B 92
Saltash. *Corn* 3A 8
Saltburn. *High* 2B 158
Saltburn-by-the-Sea. *Red C* 2D 106
Saltby. *Leics* 3F 75
Saltcoats. *Cumb* 5B 102
Saltcoats. *N Ayr* 5D 126
Saltdean. *Brig* 5E 27
Salt End. *E Yor* 2E 95
Salter. *Lanc* 3F 97
Salterforth. *Lanc* 5A 98
Salters Lode. *Norf* 5E 77
Salterswall. *Ches W* 4A 84
Salterton. *Wilts* 3G 23
Saltfleet. *Linc* 1D 88
Saltfleetby All Saints. *Linc* 1D 88
Saltfleetby St Clements. *Linc* 1D 88
Saltfleetby St Peter. *Linc* 2D 88
Saltford. *Bath* 5B 34
Salthouse. *Norf* 1C 78
Saltmarshe. *E Yor* 2A 94
Saltmead. *Card* 4E 33
Saltness. *Orkn* 9B 172
Saltness. *Shet* 7D 173
Saltney. *Flin* 4F 83
Salton. *N Yor* 2B 100
Saltrens. *Devn* 4E 19
Saltwick. *Nmbd* 2E 115
Saltwood. *Kent* 2F 29
Salum. *Arg* 4B 138
Salwarpe. *Worc* 4C 60
Salwayash. *Dors* 3H 13
Samalaman. *High* 1A 140
Sambourne. *Warw* 4E 61
Sambourne. *Wilts* 2D 22
Sambrook. *Telf* 3B 72
Samhia. *W Isl* 2C 170
Samlesbury. *Lanc* 1D 90
Samlesbury Bottoms. *Lanc* 2E 90
Sampford Arundel. *Som* 1E 12
Sampford Brett. *Som* 2D 20
Sampford Courtenay. *Devn* 2G 11
Sampford Peverell. *Devn* 1D 12
Sampford Spiney. *Devn* 5F 11
Samsonlane. *Orkn* 5F 172
Samuelston. *E Lot* 2A 130
Sanaigmore. *Arg* 2A 124
Sancreed. *Corn* 4B 4
Sancton. *E Yor* 1C 94
Sand. *High* 4D 162
Sand. *Shet* 7E 173
Sand. *Som* 2H 21
Sandaig. *Arg* 4A 138
Sandaig. *High* 3F 147
Sandale. *Cumb* 5D 112
Sandal Magna. *W Yor* 3D 92
Sandavore. *High* 5C 146
Sanday Airport. *Orkn* 3F 172
Sandbach. *Ches E* 4B 84
Sandbank. *Arg* 1C 126
Sandbanks. *Pool* 4F 15
Sandend. *Abers* 2C 160
Sanderstead. *G Lon* 4E 39
Sandfields. *Neat* 3G 31
Sandford. *Cumb* 3A 104
Sandford. *Devn* 2B 12

Shenmore—Sollers Hope

Shenmore. Here 2G 47
Shennanton. Dum 3A 110
Shenstone. Staf 5F 73
Shenstone. Worc 3C 60
Shenstone Woodend. Staf 5F 73
Shenton. Leics 5A 74
Shenval. Mor 1G 151
Shepeau Stow. Linc 4C 76
Shephall. Herts 3C 52
Shepherd's Bush. G Lon 2D 38
Shepherd's Gate. Norf 4E 77
Shepherd's Green. Oxon 3F 37
Shepherd's Port. Norf 2F 77
Shepherdswell. Kent 1G 29
Shepley. W Yor 4B 92
Sheppardstown. High 4D 169
Shepperdine. S Glo 2B 34
Shepperton. Surr 4B 38
Shepreth. Cambs 1D 53
Shepshed. Leics 4B 74
Shepton Beauchamp. Som 1H 13
Shepton Mallet. Som 2B 22
Shepton Montague. Som 3B 22
Shepway. Kent 5B 40
Sheraton. Dur 1B 106
Sherborne. Bath 1A 22
Sherborne. Dors 1B 14
Sherborne. Glos 4G 49
Sherborne Causeway. Dors 4D 22
Sherborne St John. Hants 1E 24
Sherbourne. Warw 4G 61
Sherburn. Dur 5G 115
Sherburn. N Yor 2D 100
Sherburn Hill. Dur 5G 115
Sherburn in Elmet. N Yor 1E 93
Shere. Surr 1B 26
Shereford. Norf 3A 78
Sherfield English. Hants 4A 24
Sherfield on Loddon. Hants 1E 25
Sherford. Devn 4D 9
Sherford. Dors 3E 15
Sheriffhales. Shrp 4B 72
Sheriff Hutton. N Yor 3A 100
Sheriffston. Mor 2G 159
Sheringham. Norf 1D 78
Sherington. Mil 1G 51
Shermanbury. W Sus 4D 26
Shernal Green. Worc 4D 60
Shernborne. Norf 2G 77
Sherrington. Wilts 3E 23
Sherston. Wilts 3D 34
Sherwood. Nott 1C 74
Sherwood Green. Devn 4F 19
Shettleston. Glas 3H 127
Shevington. G Man 4D 90
Shevington Moor. G Man 3D 90
Shevington Vale. G Man 4D 90
Sheviock. Corn 3H 7
Shide. IOW 4D 16
Shiel Bridge. High 2B 148
Shieldaig. High 1H 155 (nr. Charlestown)
Shieldaig. High 3H 155 (nr. Torridon)
Shieldhill. Dum 1B 112
Shieldhill. Falk 2B 128
Shieldhill. S Lan 5D 128
Shieldmuir. N Lan 4A 128
Shielfoot. High 2A 140
Shielhill. Abers 3H 161
Shielhill. Ang 3D 144
Shifnal. Shrp 5B 72
Shilbottle. Nmbd 4F 121
Shilbottle Grange. Nmbd 4G 121
Shildon. Dur 2F 105
Shillford. E Ren 4F 127
Shillingford. Devn 4C 20
Shillingford. Oxon 2D 36
Shillingford St George. Devn 4C 12
Shillingstone. Dors 1D 14
Shillington. C Beds 2B 52
Shillmoor. Nmbd 4C 120
Shilton. Oxon 5A 50
Shilton. Warw 2B 62
Shilvinghampton. Dors 4B 14
Shilvington. Nmbd 1E 115
Shimpling. Norf 2D 66
Shimpling. Suff 5A 66
Shimpling Street. Suff 5A 66
Shincliffe. Dur 5F 115
Shiney Row. Tyne 4G 115
Shinfield. Wok 5F 37
Shingay. Cambs 1D 52
Shingham. Norf 5G 77
Shingle Street. Suff 1G 55
Shinner's Bridge. Devn 2D 9
Shinness. High 2C 164
Shipbourne. Kent 5G 39
Shipdham. Norf 5B 78
Shipham. Som 1H 21
Shiphay. Torb 2E 9
Shiplake. Oxon 4F 37
Shipley. Derbs 1B 74
Shipley. Nmbd 3F 121
Shipley. Shrp 1C 60
Shipley. W Sus 3C 26
Shipley. W Yor 1B 92
Shipley Bridge. Surr 1E 27
Shipmeadow. Suff 1F 67
Shippon. Oxon 2C 36
Shipston-on-Stour. Warw 1A 50
Shipton. Buck 3F 51
Shipton. Glos 4F 49
Shipton. N Yor 4H 99
Shipton. Shrp 1H 59
Shipton Bellinger. Hants 2H 23
Shipton Gorge. Dors 3H 13
Shipton Green. W Sus 3G 17
Shipton Moyne. Glos 3D 35
Shipton-on-Cherwell. Oxon 4C 50
Shiptonthorpe. E Yor 5C 100
Shipton-under-Wychwood. Oxon 4A 50
Shirburn. Oxon 2E 37
Shirdley Hill. Lanc 3B 90
Shire. Cumb 1H 103
Shirebrook. Derbs 4C 86
Shiregreen. S Yor 1A 86
Shirehampton. Bris 4A 34
Shiremoor. Tyne 2G 115
Shirenewton. Mon 2H 33
Shireoaks. Notts 2C 86
Shires Mill. Fife 1C 128
Shirkoak. Kent 2D 28
Shirland. Derbs 5A 86
Shirley. Derbs 1G 73
Shirley. Sotn 1C 16
Shirley. W Mid 3F 61
Shirleywich. Staf 3D 73
Shirl Heath. Here 5G 59
Shirrell Heath. Hants 1D 16
Shirwell. Devn 3F 19
Shiskine. N Ayr 3D 122
Shobdon. Here 4F 59
Shobnall. Staf 3G 73
Shobrooke. Devn 2B 12
Shoby. Leics 3D 74
Shocklach. Ches W 1G 71
Shoeburyness. S'end 2D 40
Sholden. Kent 5H 41
Sholing. Sotn 1C 16
Sholver. G Man 4H 91
Shoot Hill. Shrp 4G 71
Shop. Corn 1C 10 (nr. Bude)
Shop. Corn 1C 6 (nr. Padstow)
Shop. Devn 1D 11
Shopford. Cumb 2G 113
Shoreditch. G Lon 2E 39
Shoreditch. Som 4F 21
Shoreham. Kent 4G 39
Shoreham Airport. W Sus 5D 26
Shoreham-by-Sea. W Sus 5D 26
Shoresdean. Nmbd 5F 131
Shoreswood. Nmbd 5F 131
Shore, The. Fife 2E 137
Shorncote. Glos 2F 35
Shorne. Kent 3A 40
Shorne Ridgeway. Kent 3A 40
Shortacombe. Devn 4F 11
Shortbridge. E Sus 3F 27
Shortgate. E Sus 4F 27
Short Green. Norf 2C 66
Shorthampton. Oxon 3B 50
Short Heath. Leics 4H 73
Short Heath. W Mid 1E 61 (nr. Erdington)
Short Heath. W Mid 5D 73 (nr. Wednesfield)
Shortlanesend. Corn 4C 6
Shorton. Torb 2E 9
Shortstown. Bed 1A 52
Shortwood. S Glo 4B 34
Shorwell. IOW 4C 16
Shoscombe. Bath 1C 22
Shotesham. Norf 1E 67
Shotgate. Essx 1B 40
Shotley. Suff 2F 55
Shotley Bridge. Dur 4D 115
Shotleyfield. Nmbd 4D 114
Shotley Gate. Suff 2F 55
Shottenden. Kent 5E 41
Shottermill. Surr 3G 25
Shottery. Warw 5F 61
Shotteswell. Warw 1C 50
Shottisham. Suff 1G 55
Shottle. Derbs 1H 73
Shotton. Dur 1B 106 (nr. Peterlee)
Shotton. Dur 2A 106 (nr. Sedgefield)
Shotton. Flin 4E 83
Shotton. Nmbd 2F 115 (nr. Morpeth)
Shotton. Nmbd 1C 120 (nr. Town Yetholm)
Shotton Colliery. Dur 5G 115
Shotts. N Lan 3B 128
Shotwick. Ches W 3F 83
Shouldham. Norf 5F 77
Shouldham Thorpe. Norf 5F 77
Shoulton. Worc 5C 60
Shrawardine. Shrp 4F 71
Shrawley. Worc 4C 60
Shreding Green. Buck 2B 38
Shrewley. Warw 4G 61
Shrewsbury. Shrp 4G 71 & 210
Shrewton. Wilts 2F 23
Shripney. W Sus 5A 26
Shrivenham. Oxon 3H 35
Shropham. Norf 1B 66
Shroton. Dors 1D 14
Shrub End. Essx 3C 54
Shucknall. Here 1A 48
Shudy Camps. Cambs 1G 53
Shulishadermor. High 4D 155
Shulista. High 1D 154
Shurdington. Glos 4E 49
Shurlock Row. Wind 4G 37
Shurrery. High 3C 168
Shurton. Som 2F 21
Shustoke. Warw 1G 61
Shute. Devn 3F 13 (nr. Axminster)
Shute. Devn 2B 12 (nr. Crediton)
Shutford. Oxon 1B 50
Shut Heath. Staf 3C 72
Shuthonger. Glos 2D 49
Shutlanehead. Staf 1C 72
Shutlanger. Nptn 1F 51
Shutt Green. Staf 5C 72
Shuttington. Warw 5G 73
Shuttlewood. Derbs 3B 86
Shuttleworth. G Man 3G 91
Siabost. W Isl 3E 171
Siabost bho Dheas. W Isl 3E 171
Siabost bho Thuath. W Isl 3E 171
Siadar. W Isl 2F 171
Siadar Uarach. W Isl 2F 171
Sibbaldbie. Dum 1C 112
Sibbertoft. Nptn 2D 62
Sibdon Carwood. Shrp 2G 59
Sibertswold. Kent 1G 29
Sibford Ferris. Oxon 2B 50
Sibford Gower. Oxon 2B 50
Sible Hedingham. Essx 2A 54
Sibsey. Linc 5C 88
Sibsey Fen Side. Linc 5C 88
Sibson. Cambs 1H 63
Sibson. Leics 5A 74
Sibster. High 3F 169
Sibthorpe. Notts 1E 75
Sibton. Suff 4F 67
Sicklesmere. Suff 4A 66
Sicklinghall. N Yor 5F 99
Sid. Devn 4E 13
Sidbury. Devn 3E 13
Sidbury. Shrp 2A 60
Sidcot. N Som 1H 21
Sidcup. G Lon 3F 39
Siddick. Cumb 1B 102
Siddington. Ches E 3C 84
Siddington. Glos 2F 35
Side of the Moor. G Man 3F 91
Sidestrand. Norf 2E 79
Sidford. Devn 3E 13
Sidlesham. W Sus 3G 17
Sidley. E Sus 5B 28
Sidlowbridge. Surr 1D 26
Sidmouth. Devn 4E 13
Sigford. Devn 5A 12
Sigglesthorne. E Yor 5F 101
Sighthill. Edin 2E 129
Sigingstone. V Glam 4C 32
Signet. Oxon 4H 49
Silchester. Hants 5E 37
Sildinis. W Isl 6E 171
Sileby. Leics 4D 74
Silecroft. Cumb 1A 96
Silfield. Norf 1D 66
Silian. Cdgn 5E 57
Silkstone. S Yor 4C 92
Silkstone Common. S Yor 4C 92
Silksworth. Tyne 4G 115
Silk Willoughby. Linc 1H 75
Silloth. Cumb 4C 112
Sills. Nmbd 4C 120
Sillyearn. Mor 3C 160
Silpho. N Yor 5G 107
Silsden. W Yor 5C 98
Silsoe. C Beds 2A 52
Silverbank. Abers 4E 152
Silverburn. Midl 3F 129
Silverdale. Lanc 2D 96
Silverdale. Staf 1C 72
Silverdale Green. Lanc 2D 96
Silver End. Essx 4B 54
Silver End. W Mid 2D 60
Silvergate. Norf 3D 78
Silver Green. Norf 1E 67
Silverhillocks. Abers 2E 161
Silverley's Green. Suff 3E 67
Silverstone. Nptn 1E 51
Silverton. Devn 2C 12
Silverton. W Dun 2F 127
Silvington. Shrp 3A 60
Simm's Cross. Hal 2H 83
Simm's Lane End. Mers 1H 83
Simonburn. Nmbd 2B 114
Simonsbath. Som 3A 20
Simonstone. Lanc 1F 91
Simprim. Bord 5E 131
Simpson. Pemb 3C 42
Simpson Cross. Pemb 3C 42
Sinclairston. E Ayr 3D 116
Sinclairtown. Fife 4E 137
Sinderby. N Yor 1F 99
Sinderhope. Nmbd 4B 114
Sindlesham. Wok 5F 37
Sinfin. Derb 2A 74
Singleborough. Buck 2F 51
Singleton. Kent 1D 28
Singleton. Lanc 1B 90
Singleton. W Sus 1G 17
Singlewell. Kent 3A 40
Sinkhurst Green. Kent 1C 28
Sinnahard. Abers 2B 152
Sinnington. N Yor 1B 100
Sinton Green. Worc 4C 60
Sipson. G Lon 3B 38
Sirhowy. Blae 4E 47
Sisland. Norf 1F 67
Sissinghurst. Kent 2B 28
Siston. S Glo 4B 34
Sithney. Corn 4D 4
Sittingbourne. Kent 4D 40
Six Ashes. Staf 2B 60
Six Bells. Blae 5F 47
Six Hills. Leics 3D 74
Sixhills. Linc 2A 88
Six Mile Bottom. Cambs 5E 65
Sixpenny Handley. Dors 1E 15
Sizewell. Suff 4G 67
Skail. High 4H 167
Skaill. Orkn 6B 172
Skaills. Orkn 7E 172
Skares. E Ayr 3E 117
Skateraw. E Lot 2D 130
Skaw. Shet 5G 173
Skeabost. High 4D 154
Skeabrae. Orkn 5B 172
Skeeby. N Yor 4E 105
Skeffington. Leics 5E 75
Skeffling. E Yor 3G 95
Skegby. Notts 4B 86 (nr. Mansfield)
Skegby. Notts 3E 87 (nr. Tuxford)
Skegness. Linc 4E 89
Skelberry. Shet 10E 173 (nr. Boddam)
Skelberry. Shet 3E 173 (nr. Housetter)
Skelbo. High 4E 165
Skelbo Street. High 4E 165
Skelbrooke. S Yor 3F 93
Skeldyke. Linc 2C 76
Skelfhill. Bord 4G 119
Skellingthorpe. Linc 3G 87
Skellister. Shet 6F 173
Skellorn Green. Ches E 2D 84
Skellow. S Yor 3F 93
Skelmanthorpe. W Yor 3C 92
Skelmersdale. Lanc 4C 90
Skelmorlie. N Ayr 3C 126
Skelpick. High 3H 167
Skelton. Cumb 1F 103
Skelton. E Yor 2A 94
Skelton. N Yor 4D 105 (nr. Richmond)
Skelton. N Yor 3F 99 (nr. Ripon)
Skelton. Red C 3D 106
Skelton. York 4H 99
Skelton Green. Red C 3D 106
Skelwick. Orkn 3D 172
Skelwith Bridge. Cumb 4E 103
Skendleby. Linc 4D 88
Skendleby Psalter. Linc 3D 88
Skenfrith. Mon 3H 47
Skerne. E Yor 4E 101
Skeroblingarry. Arg 3B 122
Skerray. High 2G 167
Skerricha. High 3C 166
Skerries Airport. Shet 4H 173
Skerton. Lanc 3D 96
Sketchley. Leics 1B 62
Sketty. Swan 3F 31
Skewen. Neat 3G 31
Skewsby. N Yor 2A 100
Skeyton. Norf 3E 79
Skeyton Corner. Norf 3E 79
Skiall. High 2C 168
Skidbrooke. Linc 1D 88
Skidbrooke North End. Linc 1D 88
Skidby. E Yor 1D 94
Skilgate. Som 4C 20
Skillington. Linc 3F 75
Skinburness. Cumb 4C 112
Skinflats. Falk 1C 128
Skinidin. High 4B 154
Skinnet. High 2F 167
Skinningrove. Red C 2E 107
Skipness. Arg 4G 125
Skippool. Lanc 5C 96
Skiprigg. Cumb 5E 113
Skipsea. E Yor 4F 101
Skipsea Brough. E Yor 4F 101
Skipton. N Yor 4B 98
Skipton-on-Swale. N Yor 2F 99
Skipwith. N Yor 1G 93
Skirbeck. Linc 1C 76
Skirbeck Quarter. Linc 1C 76
Skirlaugh. E Yor 1E 95
Skirling. Bord 1C 118
Skirmett. Buck 2F 37
Skirpenbeck. E Yor 4B 100
Skirwith. Cumb 1H 103
Skirwith. N Yor 2G 97
Skirza. High 2F 169
Skitby. Cumb 3F 113
Skitham. Lanc 5D 96
Skittle Green. Buck 5F 51
Skroo. Shet 1B 172
Skulamus. High 1E 147
Skullomie. High 2G 167
Skyborry Green. Shrp 3E 59
Skye Green. Essx 3B 54
Skye of Curr. High 1D 151
Slack. W Yor 2H 91
Slackhall. Derbs 2E 85
Slack Head. Cumb 2D 97
Slackhead. Mor 2B 160
Slackholme End. Linc 3E 89
Slacks of Cairnbanno. Abers 4F 161
Slack, The. Dur 2E 105
Slad. Glos 5D 48
Slade. Swan 4D 31
Slade End. Oxon 2D 36
Slade Field. Cambs 2C 64
Slade Green. G Lon 3G 39
Slade Heath. Staf 5D 72
Slade Hooton. S Yor 2C 86
Sladesbridge. Corn 5A 10
Slade, The. W Ber 5D 36
Slaggyford. Nmbd 4H 113
Slaidburn. Lanc 4G 97
Slaid Hill. W Yor 5F 99
Slaithwaite. W Yor 3A 92
Slaley. Derbs 5G 85
Slaley. Nmbd 4C 114
Slamannan. Falk 2B 128
Slapton. Buck 3H 51
Slapton. Devn 4E 9
Slapton. Nptn 1E 51
Slattock. G Man 4G 91
Slaugham. W Sus 3D 26
Slaughterbridge. Corn 4B 10
Slaughterford. Wilts 4D 34
Slawston. Leics 1E 63
Sleaford. Hants 3G 25
Sleaford. Linc 1H 75
Sleagill. Cumb 3G 103
Sleap. Shrp 3G 71
Sledmere. E Yor 3D 100
Sleightholme. Dur 3C 104
Sleights. N Yor 4F 107
Slepe. Dors 3E 15
Slickly. High 2E 169
Sliddery. N Ayr 3D 122
Sligachan. High 1C 146
Slimbridge. Glos 5C 48
Slindon. Staf 2C 72
Slindon. W Sus 5A 26
Slinfold. W Sus 2C 26
Slingsby. N Yor 2A 100
Slip End. C Beds 4A 52
Slipton. Nptn 3G 63
Slitting Mill. Staf 4E 73
Slochd. High 1C 150
Slockavullin. Arg 4F 133
Sloley. Norf 3E 79
Sloncombe. Devn 4H 11
Sloothby. Linc 3D 89
Slough. Slo 2A 38
Slough Green. Som 4F 21
Slough Green. W Sus 3D 27
Sluggan. High 1C 150
Slyne. Lanc 3D 97
Smailholm. Bord 1A 120
Smallbridge. G Man 3H 91
Smallbrook. Devn 3B 12
Smallburgh. Norf 3F 79
Smallburn. E Ayr 2F 117
Smalldale. Derbs 3E 85
Small Dole. W Sus 4D 26
Smalley. Derbs 1B 74
Smallfield. Surr 1E 27
Small Heath. W Mid 2E 61
Smallholm. Dum 2C 112
Small Hythe. Kent 2C 28
Smallrice. Staf 2D 72
Smallridge. Devn 2G 13
Smallwood Hey. Lanc 5C 96
Smallworth. Norf 2C 66
Smannell. Hants 2B 24
Smardale. Cumb 4A 104
Smarden. Kent 1C 28
Smarden Bell. Kent 1C 28
Smart's Hill. Kent 1G 27
Smeatharpe. Devn 1F 13
Smeeth. Kent 2E 29
Smeeth, The. Norf 4E 77
Smeeton Westerby. Leics 1D 62
Smeircleit. W Isl 7C 170
Smerral. High 5D 168
Smestow. Staf 1C 60
Smethwick. W Mid 2E 61
Smirisary. High 1A 140
Smisby. Derbs 4H 73
Smitham Hill. Bath 1A 22
Smith End Green. Worc 5B 60
Smithfield. Cumb 3F 113
Smith Green. Lanc 4D 97
Smithies, The. Shrp 1A 60
Smithincott. Devn 1D 12
Smith's Green. Essx 3F 53
Smithstown. High 1G 155
Smithton. High 4B 158
Smithwood Green. Suff 5B 66
Smithy Bridge. G Man 3H 91
Smithy Green. Ches E 3B 84
Smithy Lane Ends. Lanc 3C 90
Smockington. Warw 2B 62
Smoogro. Orkn 7C 172
Smyth's Green. Essx 4C 54
Snaigow House. Per 4H 143
Snailbeach. Shrp 5F 71
Snailwell. Cambs 4F 65
Snainton. N Yor 1D 100
Snaith. E Yor 2G 93
Snape. N Yor 1E 99
Snape. Suff 5F 67
Snape Green. Lanc 3B 90
Snapper. Devn 3F 19
Snarestone. Leics 5H 73
Snarford. Linc 2H 87
Snargate. Kent 3D 28
Snave. Kent 3E 28
Sneachill. Worc 5D 60
Snead. Powy 1F 59
Snead Common. Worc 4B 60
Sneaton. N Yor 4F 107
Sneatonthorpe. N Yor 4G 107
Snelland. Linc 2H 87
Snelston. Derbs 1F 73
Snetterton. Norf 1B 66
Snettisham. Norf 2F 77
Snibston. Leics 4B 74
Sniseabhal. W Isl 5C 170
Snitter. Nmbd 4E 121
Snitterby. Linc 1G 87
Snitterfield. Warw 5G 61
Snitton. Shrp 3H 59
Snodhill. Here 1G 47
Snodland. Kent 4A 40
Snods Edge. Nmbd 4D 114
Snowshill. Glos 2F 49
Snow Street. Norf 2C 66
Snydale. W Yor 3E 93
Soake. Hants 1E 17
Soar. Carm 3G 45
Soar. Gwyn 2F 69
Soar. IOA 3C 80
Soar. Powy 2C 46
Soberton. Hants 1E 16
Soberton Heath. Hants 1E 16
Sockbridge. Cumb 2F 103
Sockburn. Darl 4A 106
Sodom. Den 3C 82
Sodom. Shet 5G 173
Soham. Cambs 3E 65
Soham Cotes. Cambs 3E 65
Solas. W Isl 1D 170
Soldon Cross. Devn 1D 10
Soldridge. Hants 3E 25
Solent Breezes. Hants 2D 16
Sole Street. Kent 4A 40 (nr. Meopham)
Sole Street. Kent 1E 29 (nr. Waltham)
Solihull. W Mid 3F 61
Sollers Dilwyn. Here 5G 59
Sollers Hope. Here 2B 48

Staplers—Succoth

Staplers. IOW 4D 16
Stapleton. Bris 4B 34
Stapleton. Cumb 2G 113
Stapleton. Here 4F 59
Stapleton. Leics 1B 62
Stapleton. N Yor 3F 105
Stapleton. Shrp 5G 71
Stapleton. Som 4H 21
Stapley. Som 1E 13
Staploe. Bed 4A 64
Staplow. Here 1B 48
Star. Fife 3F 137
Star. Pemb 1G 43
Starbeck. N Yor 4F 99
Starbotton. N Yor 2B 98
Starcross. Devn 4C 12
Stareton. Warw 3H 61
Starkholmes. Derbs 5H 85
Starling. G Man 3F 91
Starling's Green. Essx 2E 53
Starston. Norf 2E 67
Start. Devn 4E 9
Startforth. Dur 3D 104
Start Hill. Essx 3F 53
Startley. Wilts 3E 35
Stathe. Som 4G 21
Stathern. Leics 2E 75
Station Town. Dur 1B 106
Staughton Green. Cambs 4A 64
Staughton Highway. Cambs 4A 64
Staunton. Glos 3C 48
(nr. Cheltenham)
Staunton. Glos 4A 48
(nr. Monmouth)
Staunton in the Vale. Notts 1F 75
Staunton on Arrow. Here 4F 59
Staunton on Wye. Here 1G 47
Staveley. Cumb 5F 103
Staveley. Derbs 3B 86
Staveley. N Yor 3F 99
Staveley-in-Cartmel. Cumb 1C 96
Staverton. Devn 2D 9
Staverton. Glos 3D 49
Staverton. Nptn 4C 62
Staverton. Wilts 5D 34
Stawell. Som 3G 21
Stawley. Som 4D 20
Staxigoe. High 3F 169
Staxton. N Yor 2E 101
Staylittle. Powy 1A 58
Staynall. Lanc 5C 96
Staythorpe. Notts 5E 87
Stean. N Yor 2C 98
Stearsby. N Yor 2A 100
Steart. Som 2F 21
Stebbing. Essx 3G 53
Stebbing Green. Essx 3G 53
Stedham. W Sus 4G 25
Steel. Nmbd 4C 114
Steel Cross. E Sus 2G 27
Steelend. Fife 4C 136
Steele Road. Bord 5H 119
Steel Heath. Shrp 2H 71
Steen's Bridge. Here 5H 59
Steep. Hants 4F 25
Steep Lane. W Yor 2A 92
Steeple. Dors 4E 15
Steeple. Essx 5C 54
Steeple Ashton. Wilts 1E 23
Steeple Aston. Oxon 3C 50
Steeple Barton. Oxon 3C 50
Steeple Bumpstead. Essx 1G 53
Steeple Claydon. Buck 3E 51
Steeple Gidding. Cambs 2A 64
Steeple Langford. Wilts 3F 23
Steeple Morden. Cambs 1C 52
Steeton. W Yor 5C 98
Stein. High 3B 154
Steinmanhill. Abers 4E 161
Stelling Minnis. Kent 1F 29
Stembridge. Som 4H 21
Stemster. High 2D 169
(nr. Halkirk)
Stemster. High 2C 168
(nr. Westfield)
Stenalees. Corn 3E 6
Stenhill. Devn 1D 12
Stenhouse. Edin 2F 129
Stenhousemuir. Falk 1B 128
Stenigot. Linc 2B 88
Stenscholl. High 2D 155
Stenso. Orkn 5C 172
Stenson. Derbs 3H 73
Stenson Fields. Derbs 2H 73
Stenton. E Lot 2C 130
Stenwith. Linc 2F 75
Steòrnabhagh. W Isl 4G 171
Stepaside. Pemb 4F 43
Stepford. Dum 1F 111
Stepney. G Lon 2E 39
Steppingley. C Beds 2A 52
Stepps. N Lan 3H 127
Sterndale Moor. Derbs 4F 85
Sternfield. Suff 4F 67
Stert. Wilts 1F 23
Stetchworth. Cambs 5F 65
Stevenage. Herts 3C 52
Stevenston. N Ayr 5D 126
Stevenstone. Devn 1F 11
Steventon. Hants 2D 24
Steventon. Oxon 2C 36
Steventon End. Cambs 1G 53
Stevington. Bed 5G 63
Stewartby. Bed 1A 52
Stewarton. Arg 4A 122
Stewarton. E Ayr 5F 127
Stewkley. Buck 3G 51
Stewkley Dean. Buck 3G 51
Stewley. Som 1G 13
Stewton. Linc 2C 88
Steyning. W Sus 4C 26
Steynton. Pemb 4D 42
Stibb. Corn 1C 10
Stibbard. Norf 3B 78
Stibb Cross. Devn 1E 11
Stibb Green. Wilts 5H 35
Stibbington. Cambs 1H 63
Stichill. Bord 1B 120
Sticker. Corn 3D 6
Stickford. Linc 4C 88
Sticklepath. Devn 3G 11
Sticklinch. Som 3A 22
Stickling Green. Essx 2E 53
Stickney. Linc 5C 88
Stiffkey. Norf 1B 78
Stifford's Bridge. Here 1C 48
Stileway. Som 2H 21
Stillingfleet. N Yor 5H 99
Stillington. N Yor 3H 99
Stillington. Stoc T 2A 106
Stilton. Cambs 2A 64
Stinchcombe. Glos 2C 34
Stinsford. Dors 3C 14
Stiperstones. Shrp 5F 71
Stirchley. Telf 5B 72
Stirchley. W Mid 2E 61
Stirling. Abers 4H 161
Stirling. Stir 4G 135 & 211
Stirton. N Yor 4B 98
Stisted. Essx 3A 54
Stitchcombe. Wilts 5H 35
Stithians. Corn 5B 6
Stittenham. High 1A 158
Stivichall. W Mid 3H 61
Stixwould. Linc 4A 88
Stoak. Ches W 3G 83
Stobo. Bord 1D 118
Stobo Castle. Bord 1D 118
Stoborough. Dors 4E 15
Stoborough Green. Dors 4E 15
Stobs Castle. Bord 4H 119
Stobswood. Nmbd 5G 121
Stock. Essx 1A 40
Stockbridge. Hants 3B 24
Stockbridge. W Yor 5C 98
Stockbury. Kent 4C 40
Stockcross. W Ber 5C 36
Stockdalewath. Cumb 5E 113
Stocker's Head. Kent 5D 40
Stockerston. Leics 1F 63
Stock Green. Worc 5D 61
Stocking. Here 2B 48
Stockingford. Warw 1H 61
Stocking Green. Essx 2F 53
Stocking Pelham. Herts 3E 53
Stockland. Devn 2F 13
Stockland Bristol. Som 2F 21
Stockleigh English. Devn 2B 12
Stockleigh Pomeroy. Devn 2B 12
Stockley. Wilts 5F 35
Stocklinch. Som 1G 13
Stockport. G Man 2D 84
Stocksbridge. S Yor 1G 85
Stocksfield. Nmbd 3D 114
Stocks, The. Kent 3D 28
Stockstreet. Essx 3B 54
Stockton. Here 4H 59
Stockton. Norf 1F 67
Stockton. Shrp 1B 60
(nr. Bridgnorth)
Stockton. Shrp 5E 71
(nr. Chirbury)
Stockton. Telf 4B 72
Stockton. Warw 4B 62
Stockton. Wilts 3E 23
Stockton Brook. Staf 5D 84
Stockton Cross. Here 4H 59
Stockton Heath. Warr 2A 84
Stockton-on-Tees. Stoc T 3B 106
Stockton on Teme. Worc 4B 60
Stockton-on-the-Forest. York 4A 100
Stockwell Heath. Staf 3E 73
Stockwood. Bris 5B 34
Stock Wood. Worc 5E 61
Stodmarsh. Kent 4G 41
Stody. Norf 2C 78
Stoer. High 1E 163
Stoford. Som 1A 14
Stoford. Wilts 3F 23
Stogumber. Som 3D 20
Stogursey. Som 2F 21
Stoke. Devn 4C 18
Stoke. Hants 1C 24
(nr. Andover)
Stoke. Hants 2F 17
(nr. South Hayling)
Stoke. Medw 3C 40
Stoke. W Mid 3A 62
Stoke Abbott. Dors 2H 13
Stoke Albany. Nptn 2F 63
Stoke Ash. Suff 3D 66
Stoke Bardolph. Notts 1D 74
Stoke Bliss. Worc 4A 60
Stoke Bruerne. Nptn 1F 51
Stoke by Clare. Suff 1H 53
Stoke-by-Nayland. Suff 2C 54
Stoke Canon. Devn 3C 12
Stoke Charity. Hants 3C 24
Stoke Climsland. Corn 5D 10
Stoke Cross. Here 5A 60
Stoke D'Abernon. Surr 5C 38
Stoke Doyle. Nptn 2H 63
Stoke Dry. Rut 1F 63
Stoke Edith. Here 1B 48
Stoke Farthing. Wilts 4F 23
Stoke Ferry. Norf 1G 65
Stoke Fleming. Devn 4E 9
Stokeford. Dors 4D 14
Stoke Gabriel. Devn 3E 9
Stoke Gifford. S Glo 4B 34
Stoke Golding. Leics 1A 62
Stoke Goldington. Mil 1G 51
Stokeham. Notts 3E 87
Stoke Hammond. Buck 3G 51
Stoke Heath. Shrp 3A 72
Stoke Holy Cross. Norf 5E 79
Stokeinteignhead. Devn 5C 12
Stoke Lacy. Here 1B 48
Stoke Lyne. Oxon 3D 50
Stoke Mandeville. Buck 4G 51
Stokenchurch. Buck 2F 37
Stoke Newington. G Lon 2E 39
Stokenham. Devn 4E 9
Stoke on Tern. Shrp 3A 72
Stoke-on-Trent. Stoke 1C 72 & 211
Stoke Orchard. Glos 3E 49
Stoke Pero. Som 2B 20
Stoke Poges. Buck 2A 38
Stoke Prior. Here 5H 59
Stoke Prior. Worc 4D 60
Stoke Rivers. Devn 3G 19
Stoke Rochford. Linc 3G 75
Stoke Row. Oxon 3E 37
Stoke St Gregory. Som 4G 21
Stoke St Mary. Som 4F 21
Stoke St Michael. Som 2B 22
Stoke St Milborough. Shrp 2H 59
Stokesay. Shrp 2G 59
Stokesby. Norf 4G 79
Stokesley. N Yor 4C 106
Stoke sub Hamdon. Som 1H 13
Stoke Talmage. Oxon 2E 37
Stoke Trister. Som 4C 22
Stoke-upon-Trent. Stoke 1C 72 & 211
Stoke Wake. Dors 2C 14
Stolford. Som 2F 21
Stondon Massey. Essx 5F 53
Stone. Buck 4F 51
Stone. Glos 2B 34
Stone. Kent 3G 39
Stone. Som 3A 22
Stone. Staf 2D 72
Stone. Worc 3C 60
Stonea. Cambs 1D 64
Stoneacton. Shrp 1H 59
Stone Allerton. Som 1H 21
Ston Easton. Som 1B 22
Stonebridge. N Som 1G 21
Stonebridge. Som 2C 22
Stonebridge. Surr 1C 26
Stone Bridge Corner. Pet 5B 76
Stonebroom. Derbs 5B 86
Stonebyres. S Lan 5B 128
Stone Chair. W Yor 2B 92
Stone Cross. E Sus 5H 27
Stone Cross. Kent 2G 27
Stone-edge-Batch. N Som 4H 33
Stoneferry. Hull 1D 94
Stonefield. Arg 5D 140
Stonefield. S Lan 4H 127
Stonegate. E Sus 3A 28
Stonegate. N Yor 4E 107
Stonegrave. N Yor 2A 100
Stonehall. Worc 1D 49
Stonehaugh. Nmbd 2A 114
Stonehaven. Abers 5F 153
Stone Heath. Staf 2D 72
Stone Hill. Kent 2E 29
Stone House. Cumb 1G 97
Stonehouse. Glos 5D 48
Stonehouse. Nmbd 4H 113
Stonehouse. S Lan 5A 128
Stone in Oxney. Kent 3D 28
Stoneleigh. Warw 3H 61
Stoneley Green. Ches E 5A 84
Stonely. Cambs 4A 64
Stonepits. Worc 5E 61
Stoner Hill. Hants 4F 25
Stonesby. Leics 3F 75
Stonesfield. Oxon 4B 50
Stones Green. Essx 3E 55
Stone Street. Kent 5G 39
Stone Street. Suff 2C 54
(nr. Boxford)
Stone Street. Suff 2F 67
(nr. Halesworth)
Stonethwaite. Cumb 3D 102
Stoneyburn. W Lot 3C 128
Stoney Cross. Hants 1A 16
Stoneyford. Devn 2D 12
Stoneygate. Leic 5D 74
Stoneyhills. Essx 1D 40
Stoneykirk. Dum 4F 109
Stoney Middleton. Derbs 3G 85
Stoney Stanton. Leics 1B 62
Stoney Stoke. Som 3C 22
Stoney Stratton. Som 3B 22
Stoney Stretton. Shrp 5F 71
Stoneywood. Aber 2F 153
Stonham Aspal. Suff 5D 66
Stonnall. Staf 5E 73
Stonor. Oxon 3F 37
Stonton Wyville. Leics 1E 63
Stonybreck. Shet 1B 172
Stony Cross. Devn 4F 19
Stony Cross. Here 1C 48
(nr. Great Malvern)
Stony Cross. Here 4H 59
(nr. Leominster)
Stony Houghton. Derbs 4B 86
Stony Stratford. Mil 1F 51
Stoodleigh. Devn 3G 19
(nr. Barnstaple)
Stoodleigh. Devn 1C 12
(nr. Tiverton)
Stopham. W Sus 4B 26
Stopsley. Lutn 3B 52
Stoptide. Corn 1D 6
Storeton. Mers 2F 83
Stormontfield. Per 1D 136
Stornoway. W Isl 4G 171
Stornoway Airport. W Isl 4G 171
Storridge. Here 1C 48
Storrington. W Sus 4B 26
Storrs. Cumb 5E 103
Storth. Cumb 1D 97
Storwood. E Yor 5B 100
Stotfield. Mor 1G 159
Stotfold. C Beds 2C 52
Stottesdon. Shrp 2A 60
Stoughton. Leics 5D 74
Stoughton. Surr 5A 38
Stoughton. W Sus 1G 17
Stoul. High 4F 147
Stoulton. Worc 1E 49
Stourbridge. W Mid 2C 60
Stourpaine. Dors 2D 14
Stourport-on-Severn. Worc 3C 60
Stour Provost. Dors 4C 22
Stour Row. Dors 4D 22
Stourton. Staf 2C 60
Stourton. Warw 2A 50
Stourton. W Yor 1D 92
Stourton. Wilts 3C 22
Stourton Caundle. Dors 1C 14
Stove. Orkn 4F 172
Stove. Shet 9F 173
Stoven. Suff 2G 67
Stow. Linc 2H 75
(nr. Billingborough)
Stow. Linc 2F 87
(nr. Gainsborough)
Stow. Bord 5A 130
Stow Bardolph. Norf 5F 77
Stow Bedon. Norf 1B 66
Stowbridge. Norf 5F 77
Stow cum Quy. Cambs 4E 65
Stowe. Glos 5A 48
Stowe. Shrp 3F 59
Stowe. Staf 4F 73
Stowe-by-Chartley. Staf 3E 73
Stowell. Som 4B 22
Stowey. Bath 1A 22
Stowford. Devn 2G 19
(nr. Combe Martin)
Stowford. Devn 4D 12
(nr. Exmouth)
Stowford. Devn 4E 11
(nr. Tavistock)
Stowlangtoft. Suff 4B 66
Stow Longa. Cambs 3A 64
Stow Maries. Essx 1C 40
Stowmarket. Suff 5C 66
Stow-on-the-Wold. Glos 3G 49
Stowting. Kent 1F 29
Stowupland. Suff 5C 66
Straad. Arg 3B 126
Strachan. Abers 4D 152
Stradbroke. Suff 3E 67
Stradbrook. Wilts 1E 23
Stradishall. Suff 5G 65
Stradsett. Norf 5F 77
Stragglethorpe. Linc 5G 87
Stragglethorpe. Notts 2D 74
Straid. S Ayr 5A 116
Straight Soley. Wilts 4B 36
Straiton. Edin 3F 129
Straiton. S Ayr 4C 116
Straloch. Per 2H 143
Stramshall. Staf 2E 73
Strang. IOM 4C 108
Strangford. Here 3A 48
Stranraer. Dum 3F 109
Strata Florida. Cdgn 4G 57
Stratfield Mortimer. W Ber 5E 37
Stratfield Saye. Hants 5E 37
Stratfield Turgis. Hants 1E 25
Stratford. Glos 2D 49
Stratford. G Lon 2E 39
Stratford St Andrew. Suff 4F 67
Stratford St Mary. Suff 2D 54
Stratford sub Castle. Wilts 3G 23
Stratford Tony. Wilts 4F 23
Stratford-upon-Avon. Warw 5G 61 & 212
Strath. High 1G 155
(nr. Gairloch)
Strath. High 3E 169
(nr. Wick)
Strathan. High 4B 148
(nr. Fort William)
Strathan. High 1E 163
(nr. Lochinver)
Strathan. High 2F 167
(nr. Tongue)
Strathan Skerray. High 2G 167
Strathaven. S Lan 5A 128
Strathblane. Stir 2G 127
Strathcanaird. High 3F 163
Strathcarron. High 4B 156
Strathcoil. Arg 5A 140
Strathdon. Abers 2A 152
Strathkinness. Fife 2G 137
Strathmashie House. High 4H 149
Strathmiglo. Fife 2E 136
Strathmore Lodge. High 4D 168
Strathpeffer. High 3G 157
Strathrannoch. High 1F 157
Strathtay. Per 3G 143
Strathvaich Lodge. High 1F 157
Strathwhillan. N Ayr 2E 123
Strathy. High 1A 158
(nr. Invergordon)
Strathy. High 2A 168
(nr. Melvich)
Strathyre. Stir 2E 135
Stratton. Corn 2C 10
Stratton. Dors 3B 14
Stratton. Glos 5F 49
Stratton Audley. Oxon 3E 50
Stratton-on-the-Fosse. Som 1B 22
Stratton St Margaret. Swin 3G 35
Stratton St Michael. Norf 1E 66
Stratton Strawless. Norf 3E 78
Stravithie. Fife 2H 137
Stream. Som 3D 20
Streat. E Sus 4E 27
Streatham. G Lon 3D 39
Streatley. C Beds 3A 52
Streatley. W Ber 3D 36
Street. Corn 3C 10
Street. Lanc 4E 97
Street. N Yor 4E 107
Street. Som 2G 13
(nr. Chard)
Street. Som 3H 21
(nr. Glastonbury)
Street Ash. Som 1F 13
Street Dinas. Shrp 2F 71
Street End. Kent 5F 41
Street End. W Sus 3G 17
Street Gate. Tyne 4F 115
Streethay. Staf 4F 73
Streethouse. W Yor 3D 93
Streetlam. N Yor 5A 106
Street Lane. Derbs 1A 74
Streetly. W Mid 1E 61
Streetly End. Cambs 1G 53
Street on the Fosse. Som 3B 22
Strefford. Shrp 2G 59
Strelley. Notts 1C 74
Strensall. York 3A 100
Strensall Camp. York 4A 100
Stretcholt. Som 2F 21
Strete. Devn 4E 9
Stretford. G Man 1C 84
Stretford. Here 5H 59
Strethall. Essx 2E 53
Stretham. Cambs 3E 65
Stretton. Ches W 5G 83
Stretton. Derbs 4A 86
Stretton. Rut 4G 75
Stretton. Staf 4C 72
(nr. Brewood)
Stretton. Staf 3G 73
(nr. Burton upon Trent)
Stretton. Warr 2A 84
Stretton en le Field. Leics 4H 73
Stretton Grandison. Here 1B 48
Stretton Heath. Shrp 4F 71
Stretton-on-Dunsmore. Warw 3B 62
Stretton-on-Fosse. Warw 2H 49
Stretton Sugwas. Here 1H 47
Stretton under Fosse. Warw 2B 62
Stretton Westwood. Shrp 1H 59
Strichen. Abers 3G 161
Strines. G Man 2D 84
Stringston. Som 2E 21
Strixton. Nptn 4G 63
Stroanfreggan. Dum 5F 117
Stroat. Glos 2A 34
Stromeferry. High 5A 156
Stromemore. High 5A 156
Stromness. Orkn 7B 172
Stronachie. Per 3C 136
Stronachlachar. Stir 2D 134
Stronchreggan. High 1E 141
Strone. Arg 1C 126
Strone. High 1H 149
(nr. Drumnadrochit)
Strone. High 3B 150
(nr. Kingussie)
Stronenaba. High 5E 148
Stronganess. Shet 1G 173
Stronmilchan. Arg 1A 134
Stronsay Airport. Orkn 5F 172
Strontian. High 2C 140
Strood. Kent 2C 28
Strood. Medw 4B 40
Strood Green. Surr 1D 26
Strood Green. W Sus 3B 26
(nr. Billingshurst)
Strood Green. W Sus 2C 26
(nr. Horsham)
Strothers Dale. Nmbd 4C 114
Stroud. Glos 5D 48
Stroud. Hants 4F 25
Stroud Green. Essx 1C 40
Stroxton. Linc 2G 75
Struan. High 5C 154
Struan. Per 2F 143
Struanmore. High 5C 154
Strubby. Linc 2D 88
Strugg's Hill. Linc 2B 76
Strumpshaw. Norf 5F 79
Strutherhill. S Lan 4A 128
Struy. High 5F 157
Stryd. IOA 2B 80
Stryt-issa. Wrex 1E 71
Stuartfield. Abers 4G 161
Stubbington. Hants 2D 16
Stubbins. Lanc 3F 91
Stubble Green. Cumb 5B 102
Stubb's Cross. Kent 2D 28
Stubbs Green. Norf 1F 67
Stubhampton. Dors 1E 15
Stubton. Linc 1F 75
Stubwood. Staf 2E 73
Stuckton. Hants 1G 15
Studham. C Beds 4A 52
Studland. Dors 4F 15
Studley. Warw 4E 61
Studley. Wilts 4E 35
Studley Roger. N Yor 3E 99
Stuntney. Cambs 3E 65
Stunts Green. E Sus 4H 27
Sturbridge. Staf 2C 72
Sturgate. Linc 2F 87
Sturmer. Essx 1G 53
Sturminster Marshall. Dors 2E 15
Sturminster Newton. Dors 1C 14
Sturry. Kent 4F 41
Sturton. N Lin 4C 94
Sturton by Stow. Linc 2F 87
Sturton le Steeple. Notts 2E 87
Stuston. Suff 3D 66
Stutton. N Yor 5G 99
Stutton. Suff 2E 55
Styal. Ches E 2C 84
Stydd. Lanc 1E 91
Styrrup. Notts 1D 86
Suainebost. W Isl 1H 171
Suardail. W Isl 4G 171
Succoth. Abers 5B 160
Succoth. Arg 3B 134

Suckley—Thelbridge Barton

Suckley. *Worc* 5B **60**
Suckley Knowl. *Worc* 5B **60**
Sudborough. *Nptn* 2G **63**
Sudbourne. *Suff* 5G **67**
Sudbrook. *Linc* 1G **75**
Sudbrook. *Mon* 3A **34**
Sudbrooke. *Linc* 3H **87**
Sudbury. *Derbs* 2F **73**
Sudbury. *Suff* 1B **54**
Sudgrove. *Glos* 5E **49**
Suffield. *Norf* 2E **79**
Suffield. *N Yor* 5G **107**
Sugnall. *Staf* 2B **72**
Sugwas Pool. *Here* 1H **47**
Suisnish. *High* 5E **155**
Sulaisiadar. *W Isl* 4H **171**
Sùlaisiadar Mòr. *High* 4D **155**
Sulby. *IOM* 2C **108**
Sulgrave. *Nptn* 1D **50**
Sulham. *W Ber* 4E **37**
Sulhamstead. *W Ber* 5E **37**
Sullington. *W Sus* 4B **26**
Sullom. *Shet* 4E **173**
Sully. *V Glam* 5E **33**
Sumburgh. *Shet* 10F **173**
Sumburgh Airport. *Shet* 10E **173**
Summer Bridge. *N Yor* 3E **98**
Summercourt. *Corn* 3C **6**
Summerfield. *Norf* 2G **77**
Summergangs. *Hull* 1E **95**
Summerhill. *Aber* 3G **153**
Summerhill. *Pemb* 4F **43**
Summer Hill. *W Mid* 1D **60**
Summerhouse. *Darl* 3F **105**
Summersdale. *W Sus* 2G **17**
Summerseat. *G Man* 3F **91**
Summit. *G Man* 3H **91**
Sunbury. *Surr* 4C **38**
Sunderland. *Cumb* 1C **102**
Sunderland. *Lanc* 4D **96**
Sunderland. *Tyne* 4G **115** & **212**
Sunderland Bridge. *Dur* 1F **105**
Sundon Park. *Lutn* 3A **52**
Sundridge. *Kent* 5F **39**
Sunk Island. *E Yor* 3F **95**
Sunningdale. *Wind* 4A **38**
Sunninghill. *Wind* 4A **38**
Sunningwell. *Oxon* 5C **50**
Sunniside. *Dur* 1E **105**
Sunniside. *Tyne* 4F **115**
Sunny Bank. *Cumb* 5D **102**
Sunny Hill. *Derb* 2H **73**
Sunnyhurst. *Bkbn* 2E **91**
Sunnylaw. *Stir* 4G **135**
Sunnymead. *Oxon* 5D **50**
Sunnyside. *S Yor* 1B **86**
Sunnyside. *W Sus* 2E **27**
Sunton. *Wilts* 1H **23**
Surbiton. *G Lon* 4C **38**
Surby. *IOM* 4B **108**
Surfleet. *Linc* 3B **76**
Surfleet Seas End. *Linc* 3B **76**
Surlingham. *Norf* 5F **79**
Surrex. *Essx* 3B **54**
Sustead. *Norf* 2D **78**
Susworth. *Linc* 4B **94**
Sutcombe. *Devn* 1D **10**
Suton. *Norf* 1C **66**
Sutors of Cromarty. *High* 2C **158**
Sutterby. *Linc* 3C **88**
Sutterton. *Linc* 2B **76**
Sutterton Dowdyke. *Linc* 2B **76**
Sutton. *Buck* 3B **38**
Sutton. *Cambs* 3D **64**
Sutton. *C Beds* 1C **52**
Sutton. *E Sus* 5F **27**
Sutton. *G Lon* 4D **38**
Sutton. *Kent* 1H **29**
Sutton. *Norf* 3F **79**
Sutton. *Notts* 2E **75**
Sutton. *Oxon* 5C **50**
Sutton. *Pemb* 3D **42**
Sutton. *Pet* 1H **63**
Sutton. *Shrp* 2B **60**
(nr. Bridgnorth)
Sutton. *Shrp* 2A **72**
(nr. Market Drayton)
Sutton. *Shrp* 3F **71**
(nr. Oswestry)
Sutton. *Shrp* 4H **71**
(nr. Shrewsbury)
Sutton. *Som* 3B **22**
Sutton. *S Yor* 3F **93**
Sutton. *Staf* 3B **72**
Sutton. *Suff* 1G **55**
Sutton. *W Sus* 4A **26**
Sutton. *Worc* 4A **60**
Sutton Abinger. *Surr* 1C **26**
Sutton at Hone. *Kent* 4G **39**
Sutton Bassett. *Nptn* 1E **63**
Sutton Benger. *Wilts* 4E **35**
Sutton Bingham. *Som* 1A **14**
Sutton Bonington. *Notts* 3C **74**
Sutton Bridge. *Linc* 3D **76**
Sutton Cheney. *Leics* 5B **74**
Sutton Coldfield. *W Mid* 1F **61**
Sutton Corner. *Linc* 3D **76**
Sutton Courtenay. *Oxon* 2D **36**
Sutton Crosses. *Linc* 3D **76**
Sutton cum Lound. *Notts* 2D **86**
Sutton Gault. *Cambs* 3D **64**
Sutton Grange. *N Yor* 2E **99**
Sutton Green. *Surr* 5B **38**
Sutton Howgrave. *N Yor* 2F **99**
Sutton in Ashfield. *Notts* 5B **86**
Sutton-in-Craven. *N Yor* 5C **98**
Sutton Ings. *Hull* 1E **94**
Sutton in the Elms. *Leics* 1C **62**
Sutton Lane Ends. *Ches E* 3D **84**
Sutton Leach. *Mers* 1H **83**
Sutton Maddock. *Shrp* 5B **72**
Sutton Mallet. *Som* 3G **21**
Sutton Mandeville. *Wilts* 4E **23**
Sutton Montis. *Som* 4B **22**
Sutton-on-Hull. *Hull* 1E **94**
Sutton on Sea. *Linc* 2E **89**
Sutton-on-the-Forest. *N Yor* 3H **99**
Sutton on the Hill. *Derbs* 2G **73**
Sutton on Trent. *Notts* 4E **87**
Sutton Poyntz. *Dors* 4C **14**
Sutton St Edmund. *Linc* 4C **76**
Sutton St Edmund's Common. *Linc* 5C **76**
Sutton St James. *Linc* 4C **76**
Sutton St Michael. *Here* 1A **48**
Sutton St Nicholas. *Here* 1A **48**
Sutton Scarsdale. *Derbs* 4B **86**
Sutton Scotney. *Hants* 3C **24**
Sutton-under-Brailes. *Warw* 2B **50**
Sutton-under-Whitestonecliffe. *N Yor* 1G **99**
Sutton upon Derwent. *E Yor* 5B **100**
Sutton Valence. *Kent* 1C **28**
Sutton Veny. *Wilts* 2E **23**
Sutton Waldron. *Dors* 1D **14**
Sutton Weaver. *Ches W* 3H **83**
Swaby. *Linc* 3C **88**
Swadlincote. *Derbs* 4G **73**
Swaffham. *Norf* 5H **77**
Swaffham Bulbeck. *Cambs* 4E **65**
Swaffham Prior. *Cambs* 4E **65**
Swafield. *Norf* 2E **79**
Swainby. *N Yor* 4B **106**
Swainshill. *Here* 1H **47**
Swainsthorpe. *Norf* 5E **78**
Swainswick. *Bath* 5C **34**
Swalcliffe. *Oxon* 2B **50**
Swalecliffe. *Kent* 4F **41**
Swallow. *Linc* 4E **95**
Swallow Beck. *Linc* 4G **87**
Swallowcliffe. *Wilts* 4E **23**
Swallowfield. *Wok* 5F **37**
Swallownest. *S Yor* 2B **86**
Swampton. *Hants* 1C **24**
Swanage. *Dors* 5F **15**
Swanbister. *Orkn* 7C **172**
Swanbourne. *Buck* 3G **51**
Swanbridge. *V Glam* 5E **33**
Swan Green. *Ches W* 3B **84**
Swanland. *E Yor* 2C **94**
Swanley. *Kent* 4G **39**
Swanmore. *Hants* 1D **16**
Swannington. *Leics* 4B **74**
Swannington. *Norf* 4D **78**
Swanpool. *Linc* 3G **87**
Swanscombe. *Kent* 3G **39**
Swansea. *Swan* 3F **31** & **212**
Swansmoor. *Staf* 3E **73**
Swan Street. *Essx* 3B **54**
Swanton Abbott. *Norf* 3E **79**
Swanton Morley. *Norf* 4C **78**
Swanton Novers. *Norf* 2C **78**
Swanton Street. *Kent* 5C **40**
Swanwick. *Derbs* 5B **86**
Swanwick. *Hants* 2D **16**
Swanwick Green. *Ches E* 1H **71**
Swarby. *Linc* 1H **75**
Swardeston. *Norf* 5E **78**
Swarister. *Shet* 3G **173**
Swarkestone. *Derbs* 3A **74**
Swarland. *Nmbd* 4F **121**
Swarraton. *Hants* 3D **24**
Swartha. *W Yor* 5C **98**
Swarthmoor. *Cumb* 2B **96**
Swaton. *Linc* 2A **76**
Swavesey. *Cambs* 4C **64**
Sway. *Hants* 3A **16**
Swayfield. *Linc* 3G **75**
Swaythling. *Sotn* 1C **16**
Sweet Green. *Worc* 4A **60**
Sweetham. *Devn* 3B **12**
Sweetholme. *Cumb* 3G **103**
Sweets. *Corn* 3B **10**
Sweetshouse. *Corn* 2E **7**
Swefling. *Suff* 4F **67**
Swell. *Som* 4G **21**
Swepstone. *Leics* 4A **74**
Swerford. *Oxon* 2B **50**
Swettenham. *Ches E* 4C **84**
Swetton. *N Yor* 2D **98**
Swffryd. *Cphy* 2F **33**
Swiftsden. *E Sus* 3B **28**
Swilland. *Suff* 5D **66**
Swillington. *W Yor* 1D **93**
Swimbridge. *Devn* 4G **19**
Swimbridge Newland. *Devn* 3G **19**
Swinbrook. *Oxon* 4A **50**
Swincliffe. *N Yor* 4E **99**
Swincliffe. *W Yor* 2C **92**
Swinderby. *Linc* 4F **87**
Swindon. *Glos* 3E **49**
Swindon. *Nmbd* 5D **121**
Swindon. *Staf* 1C **60**
Swindon. *Swin* 3G **35** & **212**
Swine. *E Yor* 1E **95**
Swinefleet. *E Yor* 2A **94**
Swineford. *S Glo* 5B **34**
Swineshead. *Bed* 4H **63**
Swineshead. *Linc* 1B **76**
Swineshead Bridge. *Linc* 1B **76**
Swiney. *High* 5E **169**
Swinford. *Leics* 3C **62**
Swinford. *Oxon* 5C **50**
Swingate. *Notts* 1C **74**
Swingbrow. *Cambs* 2C **64**
Swingfield Minnis. *Kent* 1G **29**
Swingfield Street. *Kent* 1G **29**
Swingleton Green. *Suff* 1C **54**
Swinhill. *S Lan* 5A **128**
Swinhoe. *Nmbd* 2G **121**
Swinhope. *Linc* 1B **88**
Swinister. *Shet* 3E **173**
Swinithwaite. *N Yor* 1C **98**
Swinmore Common. *Here* 1B **48**
Swinscoe. *Staf* 1F **73**
Swinside Hall. *Bord* 3B **120**
Swinstead. *Linc* 3H **75**
Swinton. *G Man* 4F **91**
Swinton. *N Yor* 2B **100**
(nr. Malton)
Swinton. *N Yor* 2E **98**
(nr. Masham)
Swinton. *Bord* 5E **131**
Swinton. *S Yor* 1B **86**
Swithland. *Leics* 4C **74**
Swordale. *High* 2H **157**
Swordly. *High* 2H **167**
Sworton Heath. *Ches E* 2A **84**
Swydd-ffynnon. *Cdgn* 4F **57**
Swyffrd. *Cphy* 2F **33**
Swynnerton. *Staf* 2C **72**
Swyre. *Dors* 4A **14**
Sycharth. *Powy* 3E **70**
Sychdyn. *Flin* 4E **83**
Sychnant. *Powy* 3B **58**
Sychtyn. *Powy* 5B **70**
Syde. *Glos* 4E **49**
Sydenham. *G Lon* 3E **39**
Sydenham. *Oxon* 5F **51**
Sydenham. *Som* 3G **21**
Sydenham Damerel. *Devn* 5E **11**
Syderstone. *Norf* 2H **77**
Sydling St Nicholas. *Dors* 3B **14**
Sydmonton. *Hants* 1C **24**
Sydney. *Ches E* 5B **84**
Syerston. *Notts* 1E **75**
Syke. *G Man* 3G **91**
Sykehouse. *S Yor* 3G **93**
Sykes. *Lanc* 4F **97**
Syleham. *Suff* 3E **66**
Sylen. *Carm* 5F **45**
Sylfaen. *Powy* 5D **70**
Symbister. *Shet* 5G **173**
Symington. *S Ayr* 1C **116**
Symington. *S Lan* 1B **118**
Symondsbury. *Dors* 3H **13**
Symonds Yat. *Here* 4A **48**
Synod Inn. *Cdgn* 5D **56**
Syre. *High* 4G **167**
Syreford. *Glos* 3F **49**
Syresham. *Nptn* 1E **51**
Syston. *Leics* 4D **74**
Syston. *Linc* 1G **75**
Sytchampton. *Worc* 4C **60**
Sywell. *Nptn* 4F **63**

T

Tabost. *W Isl* 6F **171**
(nr. Cearsiadar)
Tabost. *W Isl* 1H **171**
(nr. Suainebost)
Tachbrook Mallory. *Warw* 4H **61**
Tackley. *Oxon* 3C **50**
Tacleit. *W Isl* 4D **171**
Tacolneston. *Norf* 1D **66**
Tadcaster. *N Yor* 5G **99**
Taddington. *Derbs* 3F **85**
Taddington. *Glos* 2F **49**
Taddiport. *Devn* 1E **11**
Tadley. *Hants* 5E **36**
Tadlow. *Cambs* 1C **52**
Tadmarton. *Oxon* 2B **50**
Tadwick. *Bath* 4C **34**
Tadworth. *Surr* 5D **38**
Tafarnaubach. *Blae* 4E **46**
Tafarn-y-bwlch. *Pemb* 1E **43**
Tafarn-y-Gelyn. *Den* 4D **82**
Taff's Well. *Rhon* 3E **33**
Tafolwern. *Powy* 5A **70**
Taibach. *Neat* 3A **32**
Tai-bach. *Powy* 3D **70**
Taigh a Ghearraidh. *W Isl* 1C **170**
Taigh Bhuirgh. *W Isl* 8C **171**
Tain. *High* 5E **165**
(nr. Invergordon)
Tain. *High* 2E **169**
(nr. Thurso)
Tai-Nant. *Wrex* 1E **71**
Tai'n Lon. *Gwyn* 5D **80**
Tairbeart. *W Isl* 8D **171**
Tairgwaith. *Neat* 4H **45**
Takeley. *Essx* 3F **53**
Takeley Street. *Essx* 3F **53**
Talachddu. *Powy* 2D **46**
Talacre. *Flin* 2D **82**
Talardd. *Gwyn* 3A **70**
Talaton. *Devn* 3D **12**
Talbenny. *Pemb* 3C **42**
Talbot Green. *Rhon* 3D **32**
Taleford. *Devn* 3D **12**
Talerddig. *Powy* 5B **70**
Talgarreg. *Cdgn* 5D **56**
Talgarth. *Powy* 2E **47**
Talisker. *High* 5C **154**
Talke. *Staf* 5C **84**
Talkin. *Cumb* 4G **113**
Talladale. *High* 1B **156**
Talla Linnfoots. *Bord* 2D **118**
Tallaminnock. *S Ayr* 5D **116**
Tallarn Green. *Wrex* 1G **71**
Tallentire. *Cumb* 1C **102**
Talley. *Carm* 2G **45**
Tallington. *Linc* 5H **75**
Talmine. *High* 2F **167**
Talog. *Carm* 2H **43**
Talsarn. *Carm* 3A **46**
Talsarn. *Cdgn* 5E **57**
Talsarnau. *Gwyn* 2F **69**
Talskiddy. *Corn* 2D **6**
Talwrn. *IOA* 3D **81**
Talwrn. *Wrex* 1E **71**
Tal-y-bont. *Cdgn* 2F **57**
Tal-y-Bont. *Cnwy* 4G **81**
Tal-y-bont. *Gwyn* 3F **81**
(nr. Bangor)
Tal-y-bont. *Gwyn* 3E **69**
(nr. Barmouth)
Talybont-on-Usk. *Powy* 3E **46**
Tal-y-cafn. *Cnwy* 3G **81**
Tal-y-coed. *Mon* 4H **47**
Tal-y-llyn. *Gwyn* 5G **69**
Talyllyn. *Powy* 3E **46**
Talysarn. *Gwyn* 5D **81**
Tal-y-waenydd. *Gwyn* 1F **69**
Talywain. *Torf* 5F **47**
Talywern. *Powy* 5H **69**
Tamerton Foliot. *Plym* 2A **8**
Tamworth. *Staf* 5G **73**
Tamworth Green. *Linc* 1C **76**
Tandlehill. *Ren* 3F **127**
Tandridge. *Surr* 5E **39**
Tanerdy. *Carm* 3E **45**
Tanfield. *Dur* 4E **115**
Tanfield Lea. *Dur* 4E **115**
Tangasdale. *W Isl* 8B **170**
Tang Hall. *York* 4A **100**
Tangiers. *Pemb* 3D **42**
Tangley. *Hants* 1B **24**
Tangmere. *W Sus* 5A **26**
Tangwick. *Shet* 4D **173**
Tankerness. *Orkn* 7E **172**
Tankersley. *S Yor* 1H **85**
Tankerton. *Kent* 4F **41**
Tan-lan. *Cnwy* 4G **81**
Tan-lan. *Gwyn* 1F **69**
Tannach. *High* 4F **169**
Tannadice. *Ang* 3D **145**
Tanner's Green. *Worc* 3E **61**
Tannington. *Suff* 4E **67**
Tannochside. *N Lan* 3A **128**
Tan Office Green. *Suff* 5G **65**
Tansley. *Derbs* 5H **85**
Tansley Knoll. *Derbs* 4H **85**
Tansor. *Nptn* 1H **63**
Tantobie. *Dur* 4E **115**
Tanton. *N Yor* 3C **106**
Tanvats. *Linc* 4A **88**
Tanworth-in-Arden. *Warw* 3F **61**
Tan-y-bwlch. *Gwyn* 1F **69**
Tan-y-fron. *Cnwy* 4B **82**
Tanyfron. *Wrex* 5E **83**
Tan-y-goes. *Cdgn* 1C **44**
Tanygrisiau. *Gwyn* 1F **69**
Tan-y-pistyll. *Powy* 3C **70**
Tan-yr-allt. *Den* 2C **82**
Taobh a Chaolais. *W Isl* 7C **170**
Taobh a Deas Loch Aineort. *W Isl* 6C **170**
Taobh a Ghlinne. *W Isl* 6F **171**
Taobh a Tuath Loch Aineort. *W Isl* 6C **170**
Taobh Tuath. *W Isl* 9B **171**
Taplow. *Buck* 2A **38**
Tapton. *Derbs* 3A **86**
Tarbert. *Arg* 1E **125**
(on Jura)
Tarbert. *Arg* 3G **125**
(on Kintyre)
Tarbert. *W Isl* 8D **171**
Tarbet. *Arg* 3C **134**
Tarbet. *High* 4F **147**
(nr. Mallaig)
Tarbet. *High* 4B **166**
(nr. Scourie)
Tarbock Green. *Mers* 2G **83**
Tarbolton. *S Ayr* 2D **116**
Tarbrax. *S Lan* 4D **128**
Tardebigge. *Worc* 4E **61**
Tarfside. *Ang* 1D **145**
Tarland. *Abers* 3B **152**
Tarleton. *Lanc* 2C **90**
Tarlogie. *High* 5E **165**
Tarlscough. *Lanc* 3C **90**
Tarlton. *Glos* 2E **35**
Tarnbrook. *Lanc* 4E **97**
Tarnock. *Som* 1G **21**
Tarns. *Cumb* 5C **112**
Tarporley. *Ches W* 4H **83**
Tarpots. *Essx* 2B **40**
Tarr. *Som* 3E **20**
Tarrant Crawford. *Dors* 2E **15**
Tarrant Gunville. *Dors* 1E **15**
Tarrant Hinton. *Dors* 1E **15**
Tarrant Keyneston. *Dors* 2E **15**
Tarrant Launceston. *Dors* 2E **15**
Tarrant Monkton. *Dors* 2E **15**
Tarrant Rawston. *Dors* 2E **15**
Tarrant Rushton. *Dors* 2E **15**
Tarrel. *High* 5F **165**
Tarring Neville. *E Sus* 5F **27**
Tarrington. *Here* 1B **48**
Tarsappie. *Per* 1D **136**
Tarscabhaig. *High* 3D **147**
Tarskavaig. *High* 3D **147**
Tarves. *Abers* 5F **161**
Tarvie. *High* 3G **157**
Tarvin. *Ches W* 4G **83**
Tasburgh. *Norf* 1E **66**
Tasley. *Shrp* 1A **60**
Taston. *Oxon* 3B **50**
Tatenhill. *Staf* 3G **73**
Tathall End. *Mil* 1G **51**
Tatham. *Lanc* 3F **97**
Tathwell. *Linc* 2C **88**
Tatling End. *Buck* 2B **38**
Tatsfield. *Surr* 5F **39**
Tattenhall. *Ches W* 5G **83**
Tatterford. *Norf* 3A **78**
Tattersett. *Norf* 2H **77**
Tattershall. *Linc* 5B **88**
Tattershall Bridge. *Linc* 5A **88**
Tattershall Thorpe. *Linc* 5B **88**
Tattingstone. *Suff* 2E **55**
Tattingstone White Horse. *Suff* 2E **55**
Tattle Bank. *Warw* 4F **61**
Tatworth. *Som* 2G **13**
Taunton. *Som* 4F **21** & **213**
Taverham. *Norf* 4D **78**
Taverners Green. *Essx* 4F **53**
Tavernspite. *Pemb* 3F **43**
Tavistock. *Devn* 5E **11**
Tavool House. *Arg* 1B **132**
Taw Green. *Devn* 3G **11**
Tawstock. *Devn* 4F **19**
Taxal. *Derbs* 2E **85**
Tayinloan. *Arg* 5E **125**
Taynish. *Arg* 1F **125**
Taynton. *Glos* 3C **48**
Taynton. *Oxon* 4H **49**
Taynuilt. *Arg* 5E **141**
Tayport. *Fife* 1G **137**
Tay Road Bridge. *Fife* 1G **137**
Tayvallich. *Arg* 1F **125**
Tealby. *Linc* 1A **88**
Tealing. *Ang* 5D **144**
Teams. *Tyne* 3F **115**
Teangue. *High* 3E **147**
Teanna Machair. *W Isl* 2C **170**
Tebay. *Cumb* 4H **103**
Tebworth. *C Beds* 3H **51**
Tedburn St Mary. *Devn* 3B **12**
Teddington. *Glos* 2E **49**
Teddington. *G Lon* 3C **38**
Tedsmore. *Shrp* 3F **71**
Tedstone Delamere. *Here* 5A **60**
Tedstone Wafer. *Here* 5A **60**
Teesport. *Red C* 2C **106**
Teesside. *Stoc T* 2C **106**
Teeton. *Nptn* 3D **62**
Teffont Evias. *Wilts* 3E **23**
Teffont Magna. *Wilts* 3E **23**
Tegryn. *Pemb* 1G **43**
Teigh. *Rut* 4F **75**
Teigncombe. *Devn* 4G **11**
Teigngrace. *Devn* 5B **12**
Teignmouth. *Devn* 5C **12**
Telford. *Telf* 4A **72**
Telham. *E Sus* 4B **28**
Tellisford. *Som* 1D **22**
Telscombe. *E Sus* 5F **27**
Telscombe Cliffs. *E Sus* 5E **27**
Tempar. *Per* 3D **142**
Templand. *Dum* 1B **112**
Temple. *Corn* 5B **10**
Temple. *Glas* 3G **127**
Temple. *Midl* 4G **129**
Temple Balsall. *W Mid* 3G **61**
Temple Bar. *Carm* 4F **45**
Temple Bar. *Cdgn* 5E **57**
Temple Cloud. *Bath* 1B **22**
Templecombe. *Som* 4C **22**
Temple Ewell. *Kent* 1G **29**
Temple Grafton. *Warw* 5F **61**
Temple Guiting. *Glos* 3F **49**
Templehall. *Fife* 4E **137**
Temple Hirst. *N Yor* 2G **93**
Temple Normanton. *Derbs* 4B **86**
Temple Sowerby. *Cumb* 2H **103**
Templeton. *Devn* 1B **12**
Templeton. *Pemb* 3F **43**
Templeton. *W Ber* 5B **36**
Templetown. *Dur* 5E **115**
Tempsford. *C Beds* 5A **64**
Tenandry. *Per* 2G **143**
Tenbury Wells. *Worc* 4H **59**
Tenby. *Pemb* 4F **43**
Tendring. *Essx* 3E **55**
Tendring Green. *Essx* 3E **55**
Tenga. *Arg* 4G **139**
Ten Mile Bank. *Norf* 1F **65**
Tenterden. *Kent* 2C **28**
Terfyn. *Cnwy* 3B **82**
Terhill. *Som* 3E **21**
Terling. *Essx* 4A **54**
Ternhill. *Shrp* 2A **72**
Terregles. *Dum* 2G **111**
Terrick. *Buck* 5G **51**
Terrington. *N Yor* 2A **100**
Terrington St Clement. *Norf* 3E **77**
Terrington St John. *Norf* 4E **77**
Terry's Green. *Warw* 3F **61**
Teston. *Kent* 5B **40**
Testwood. *Hants* 1B **16**
Tetbury. *Glos* 2D **35**
Tetbury Upton. *Glos* 2D **35**
Tetchill. *Shrp* 2F **71**
Tetcott. *Devn* 3D **10**
Tetford. *Linc* 3C **88**
Tetney. *Linc* 4G **95**
Tetney Lock. *Linc* 4G **95**
Tetsworth. *Oxon* 5E **51**
Tettenhall. *W Mid* 1C **60**
Teversal. *Notts* 4B **86**
Teversham. *Cambs* 5D **65**
Teviothead. *Bord* 4G **119**
Tewel. *Abers* 5F **153**
Tewin. *Herts* 4C **52**
Tewkesbury. *Glos* 2D **49**
Teynham. *Kent* 4D **40**
Teynham Street. *Kent* 4D **40**
Thackthwaite. *Cumb* 2F **103**
Thakeham. *W Sus* 4C **26**
Thame. *Oxon* 5F **51**
Thames Ditton. *Surr* 4C **38**
Thames Haven. *Thur* 2B **40**
Thamesmead. *G Lon* 2F **39**
Thamesport. *Medw* 3C **40**
Thanington Without. *Kent* 5F **41**
Thankerton. *S Lan* 1B **118**
Tharston. *Norf* 1D **66**
Thatcham. *W Ber* 5D **36**
Thatto Heath. *Mers* 1H **83**
Thaxted. *Essx* 2G **53**
Theakston. *N Yor* 1F **99**
Thealby. *N Lin* 3B **94**
Theale. *Som* 2H **21**
Theale. *W Ber* 4E **37**
Thearne. *E Yor* 1D **94**
Theberton. *Suff* 4G **67**
Theddingworth. *Leics* 2D **62**
Theddlethorpe All Saints. *Linc* 2D **88**
Theddlethorpe St Helen. *Linc* 2D **89**
Thelbridge Barton. *Devn* 1A **12**

Towans, The—Uigshader

Towans, The. Corn 3C 4
Toward. Arg 3C 126
Towcester. Nptn 1E 51
Towednack. Corn 3B 4
Tower End. Norf 4F 77
Tower Hill. Mers 4C 90
Tower Hill. W Sus 3C 26
Towersey. Oxon 5F 51
Towie. Abers 2B 152
Towiemore. Mor 4A 160
Tow Law. Dur 1E 105
Town End. Cambs 1D 64
Town End. Cumb 4F 103 (nr. Ambleside)
Town End. Cumb 2H 103 (nr. Kirkby Thore)
Town End. Cumb 1D 96 (nr. Lindale)
Town End. Cumb 1C 96 (nr. Newby Bridge)
Town End. Mers 2G 83
Townend. W Dun 2F 127
Townfield. Dur 5C 114
Towngate. Cumb 5G 113
Towngate. Linc 4A 76
Town Green. Lanc 4B 90
Town Head. Cumb 4E 103 (nr. Grasmere)
Town Head. Cumb 3H 103 (nr. Great Asby)
Townhead. Cumb 1G 103 (nr. Lazonby)
Townhead. Cumb 1B 102 (nr. Maryport)
Townhead. Cumb 1H 103 (nr. Ousby)
Townhead. Dum 5D 111
Townhead of Greenlaw. Dum 3E 111
Townhill. Fife 1E 129
Townhill. Swan 3F 31
Town Kelloe. Dur 1A 106
Town Littleworth. E Sus 4F 27
Town Row. E Sus 2G 27
Towns End. Hants 1D 24
Townsend. Herts 5B 52
Townshend. Corn 3C 4
Town Street. Suff 2G 65
Town, The. IOS 1A 4
Town Yetholm. Bord 2C 120
Towthorpe. E Yor 3C 100
Towthorpe. York 4A 100
Towton. N Yor 1E 93
Towyn. Cnwy 3B 82
Toxteth. Mers 2F 83
Toynton All Saints. Linc 4C 88
Toynton Fen Side. Linc 4C 88
Toynton St Peter. Linc 4D 88
Toy's Hill. Kent 5F 39
Trabboch. E Ayr 2D 116
Traboe. Corn 4E 5
Tradespark. High 3C 158
Tradespark. Orkn 7D 172
Trafford Park. G Man 1B 84
Trallong. Powy 3C 46
Tranent. E Lot 2H 129
Tranmere. Mers 2F 83
Trantlebeg. High 3A 168
Trantlemore. High 3A 168
Tranwell. Nmbd 1E 115
Trapp. Carm 4G 45
Traquair. Bord 1F 119
Trash Green. W Ber 5E 37
Trawden. Lanc 1H 91
Trawscoed. Powy 2D 46
Trawsfynydd. Gwyn 2G 69
Trawsgoed. Cdgn 3F 57
Treaddow. Here 3A 48
Trealaw. Rhon 2D 32
Treales. Lanc 1C 90
Trearddur. IOA 3B 80
Treaslane. High 3C 154
Treator. Corn 1D 6
Trebanog. Rhon 2D 32
Trebanos. Neat 5H 45
Trebarber. Corn 2C 6
Trebartha. Corn 5C 10
Trebarwith. Corn 4A 10
Trebetherick. Corn 1D 6
Treborough. Som 3D 20
Trebudannon. Corn 2C 6
Trebullett. Corn 5D 10
Treburley. Corn 5D 10
Treburrick. Corn 1C 6
Trebyan. Corn 2E 7
Trecastle. Powy 3B 46
Trecenydd. Cphy 3E 33
Trecott. Devn 2G 11
Trecwn. Pemb 1D 42
Trecynon. Rhon 5C 46
Tredaule. Corn 4C 10
Tredavoe. Corn 4B 4
Tredegar. Blae 5E 47
Trederwen. Powy 4E 71
Tredington. Glos 3E 49
Tredington. Warw 1A 50
Tredinnick. Corn 2F 7 (nr. Bodmin)
Tredinnick. Corn 3G 7 (nr. Looe)
Tredinnick. Corn 1D 6 (nr. Padstow)
Tredogan. V Glam 5D 32
Tredomen. Powy 2E 46
Tredunnock. Mon 2G 33
Tredustan. Powy 2E 47
Treen. Corn 4A 4 (nr. Land's End)
Treen. Corn 3B 4 (nr. St Ives)
Treeton. S Yor 2B 86
Trefaldwyn. Powy 1E 58
Trefasser. Pemb 1C 42
Trefdraeth. IOA 3D 80
Trefdraeth. Pemb 1E 43
Trefecca. Powy 2E 47
Trefechan. Mer T 5D 46
Trefeglwys. Powy 1B 58
Trefeitha. Powy 2E 46
Trefenter. Cdgn 4F 57
Treffgarne. Pemb 2D 42
Treffynnon. Flin 3D 82
Treffynnon. Pemb 2C 42
Trefil. Blae 4E 46
Trefilan. Cdgn 5E 57
Trefin. Pemb 1C 42
Treflach. Shrp 3E 71
Trefnant. Den 3C 82
Trefonen. Shrp 3E 71
Trefor. Gwyn 1C 68
Trefor. IOA 2C 80
Treforest. Rhon 3D 32
Trefrew. Corn 4B 10
Trefriw. Cnwy 4G 81
Tref-y-Clawdd. Powy 3E 59
Trefynwy. Mon 4A 48
Tregada. Corn 4D 10
Tregadillett. Corn 4D 10
Tregare. Mon 4H 47
Tregarne. Corn 4E 5
Tregaron. Cdgn 5F 57
Tregarth. Gwyn 4F 81
Tregear. Corn 3C 6
Tregeare. Corn 4C 10
Tregeiriog. Wrex 2D 70
Tregele. IOA 1C 80
Tregeseal. Corn 3A 4
Tregiskey. Corn 4E 6
Tregole. Corn 3B 10
Tregolwyn. V Glam 4C 32
Tregonetha. Corn 2D 6
Tregonhawke. Corn 3A 8
Tregony. Corn 4D 6
Tregoodwell. Corn 4B 10
Tregorrick. Corn 3E 6
Tregoss. Corn 2D 6
Tregowris. Corn 4E 5
Tregoyd. Powy 2E 47
Tregrehan Mills. Corn 3E 7
Tre-groes. Cdgn 1E 45
Tregullon. Corn 2E 7
Tregurrian. Corn 2C 6
Tregynon. Powy 1C 58
Trehafod. Rhon 2D 32
Trehan. Corn 3A 8
Treharris. Mer T 2E 32
Treherbert. Rhon 2C 32
Trehunist. Corn 2H 7
Trekenner. Corn 5D 10
Trekenning. Corn 2D 6
Treknow. Corn 4A 10
Trelales. B'end 3B 32
Trelan. Corn 5E 5
Trelash. Corn 3B 10
Trelassick. Corn 3C 6
Trelawnyd. Flin 3C 82
Trelech. Carm 1G 43
Treleddyd-fawr. Pemb 2B 42
Trelewis. Mer T 2E 32
Treligga. Corn 4A 10
Trelights. Corn 1D 6
Trelill. Corn 5A 10
Trelissick. Corn 5C 6
Trelleck. Mon 5A 48
Trelleck Grange. Mon 5H 47
Trelogan. Flin 2D 82
Trelystan. Powy 5E 71
Tremadog. Gwyn 1E 69
Tremail. Corn 4B 10
Tremain. Cdgn 1C 44
Tremaine. Corn 4C 10
Tremar. Corn 2G 7
Trematon. Corn 3H 7
Tremeirchion. Den 3C 82
Tremore. Corn 2E 6
Tremorfa. Card 4F 33
Trenance. Corn 5D 4 (nr. Helston)
Trenance. Corn 2C 6 (nr. Newquay)
Trenance. Corn 1D 6 (nr. Padstow)
Trenarren. Corn 4E 7
Trench. Telf 4A 72
Trencreek. Corn 2C 6
Trendeal. Corn 3C 6
Trenear. Corn 5A 6
Treneglos. Corn 4C 10
Trenewan. Corn 3F 7
Trengune. Corn 3B 10
Trent. Dors 1A 14
Trentham. Stoke 1C 72
Trentishoe. Devn 2G 19
Trentlock. Derbs 2B 74
Treoes. V Glam 4C 32
Treorchy. Rhon 2C 32
Treorci. Rhon 2C 32
Tre'r-ddol. Cdgn 1F 57
Tre'r llai. Powy 5E 71
Trerulefoot. Corn 3H 7
Tresaith. Cdgn 5B 56
Trescott. Staf 1C 60
Trescowe. Corn 3C 4
Tresham. Glos 2C 34
Tresigin. V Glam 4C 32
Tresillian. Corn 4C 6
Tresimwn. V Glam 4D 32
Tresinney. Corn 4B 10
Treskillard. Corn 5A 6
Treskinnick Cross. Corn 3C 10
Tresmeer. Corn 4C 10
Tresparrett. Corn 3B 10
Tresparrett Posts. Corn 3B 10
Tressady. High 3D 164
Tressait. Per 2F 143
Tresta. Shet 2H 173 (on Fetlar)
Tresta. Shet 6E 173 (on Mainland)
Treswell. Notts 3E 87
Treswithian. Corn 3D 4
Tre Taliesin. Cdgn 1F 57
Trethomas. Cphy 3E 33
Trethosa. Corn 3D 6
Trethurgy. Corn 3E 7
Tretio. Pemb 2B 42
Tretire. Here 3A 48
Tretower. Powy 3E 47
Treuddyn. Flin 5E 83
Trevadlock. Corn 5C 10
Trevalga. Corn 3A 10
Trevalyn. Wrex 5F 83
Trevance. Corn 1D 6
Trevanger. Corn 1D 6
Trevanson. Corn 1D 6
Trevarrack. Corn 3B 4
Trevarren. Corn 2D 6
Trevarrian. Corn 2C 6
Trevarrick. Corn 4D 6
Tre-vaughan. Carm 3E 45 (nr. Carmarthen)
Trevaughan. Carm 3F 43 (nr. Whitland)
Treveighan. Corn 5A 10
Trevellas. Corn 3B 6
Trevelmond. Corn 2G 7
Treverva. Corn 5B 6
Trevescan. Corn 4A 4
Trevethin. Torf 5F 47
Trevia. Corn 4A 10
Trevigro. Corn 2H 7
Trevilley. Corn 4A 4
Treviscoe. Corn 3D 6
Trevivian. Corn 4B 10
Trevone. Corn 1C 6
Trevor. Wrex 1E 71
Trevor Uchaf. Den 1E 71
Trew. Corn 4D 4
Trewalder. Corn 4A 10
Trewarlett. Corn 4D 10
Trewarmett. Corn 4A 10
Trewassa. Corn 4B 10
Treween. Corn 4C 10
Trewellard. Corn 3A 4
Trewen. Corn 4C 10
Trewennack. Corn 4D 5
Trewern. Powy 4E 71
Trewetha. Corn 5A 10
Trewidland. Corn 2G 7
Trewint. Corn 3B 10
Trewithian. Corn 5C 6
Trewoofe. Corn 4B 4
Trewoon. Corn 3D 6
Treworthal. Corn 5C 6
Trewyddel. Pemb 1B 44
Treyarnon. Corn 1C 6
Treyford. W Sus 1G 17
Triangle. Staf 5E 73
Triangle. W Yor 2A 92
Trickett's Cross. Dors 2F 15
Trimdon. Dur 1A 106
Trimdon Colliery. Dur 1A 106
Trimdon Grange. Dur 1A 106
Trimingham. Norf 2E 79
Trimley Lower Street. Suff 2F 55
Trimley St Martin. Suff 2F 55
Trimley St Mary. Suff 2F 55
Trimpley. Worc 3B 60
Trimsaran. Carm 5E 45
Trimstone. Devn 2F 19
Trinafour. Per 2E 142
Trinant. Cphy 2F 33
Tring. Herts 4H 51
Trinity. Ang 2F 145
Trinity. Edin 2F 129
Trisant. Cdgn 3G 57
Triscombe. Som 3E 21
Trislaig. High 1E 141
Trispen. Corn 3C 6
Tritlington. Nmbd 5G 121
Trochry. Per 4G 143
Troedrhiwdalar. Powy 5B 58
Troedrhiwfuwch. Cphy 5E 47
Troedrhiwgwair. Blae 5E 47
Troedyraur. Cdgn 1D 44
Troedyrhiw. Mer T 5D 46
Trondavoe. Shet 4E 173
Troon. Corn 5A 6
Troon. S Ayr 1C 116
Troqueer. Dum 2A 112
Troston. Suff 3A 66
Trottiscliffe. Kent 4H 39
Trotton. W Sus 4G 25
Troutbeck. Cumb 4F 103 (nr. Ambleside)
Troutbeck. Cumb 2E 103 (nr. Penrith)
Troutbeck Bridge. Cumb 4F 103
Troway. Derbs 3A 86
Trowbridge. Wilts 1D 22
Trowell. Notts 2B 74
Trowle Common. Wilts 1D 22
Trowley Bottom. Herts 4A 52
Trowse Newton. Norf 5E 79
Trudoxhill. Som 2C 22
Trull. Som 4F 21
Trumaisgearraidh. W Isl 1D 170
Trumpan. High 2B 154
Trumpet. Here 2B 48
Trumpington. Cambs 5D 64
Trumps Green. Surr 4A 38
Trunch. Norf 2E 79
Trunnah. Lanc 5C 96
Truro. Corn 4C 6
Trusham. Devn 4B 12
Trusley. Derbs 2G 73
Trusthorpe. Linc 2E 89
Tryfil. IOA 2D 80
Trysull. Staf 1C 60
Tubney. Oxon 2C 36
Tuckenhay. Devn 3E 9
Tuckhill. Staf 2B 60
Tuckingmill. Corn 4A 6
Tuckton. Bour 3G 15
Tuddenham. Suff 3G 65
Tuddenham St Martin. Suff 1E 55
Tudeley. Kent 1H 27
Tudhoe. Dur 1F 105
Tudhoe Grange. Dur 1F 105
Tudorville. Here 3A 48
Tudweiliog. Gwyn 2B 68
Tuesley. Surr 1A 26
Tufton. Hants 2C 24
Tufton. Pemb 2E 43
Tugby. Leics 5E 75
Tugford. Shrp 2H 59
Tughall. Nmbd 2G 121
Tulchan. Per 1B 136
Tullibardine. Per 2B 136
Tullibody. Clac 4A 136
Tullich. Arg 2H 133
Tullich. High 4B 156 (nr. Lochcarron)
Tullich. High 1C 158 (nr. Tain)
Tullich. Mor 4H 159
Tullich Muir. High 1B 158
Tulliemet. Per 3G 143
Tulloch. Abers 5F 161
Tulloch. High 4D 164 (nr. Bonar Bridge)
Tulloch. High 5F 149 (nr. Fort William)
Tulloch. High 2D 151 (nr. Grantown-on-Spey)
Tulloch. Per 1C 136
Tullochgorm. Arg 4G 133
Tullybeagles Lodge. Per 5H 143
Tullymurdoch. Per 3A 144
Tullynessle. Abers 2C 152
Tumble. Carm 4F 45
Tumbler's Green. Essx 3B 54
Tumby. Linc 4B 88
Tumby Woodside. Linc 5B 88
Tummel Bridge. Per 3E 143
Tunbridge Wells, Royal. Kent 2G 27
Tunga. W Isl 4G 171
Tungate. Norf 3E 79
Tunley. Bath 1B 22
Tunstall. E Yor 1G 95
Tunstall. Kent 4C 40
Tunstall. Lanc 2F 97
Tunstall. Norf 5G 79
Tunstall. N Yor 5F 105
Tunstall. Staf 3B 72
Tunstall. Stoke 5C 84
Tunstall. Suff 5F 67
Tunstall. Tyne 4G 115
Tunstead. Derbs 3F 85
Tunstead. Norf 3E 79
Tunstead Milton. Derbs 2E 85
Tunworth. Hants 2E 25
Tupsley. Here 1A 48
Tupton. Derbs 4A 86
Turfholm. S Lan 1H 117
Turfmoor. Devn 2F 13
Turgis Green. Hants 1E 25
Turkdean. Glos 4G 49
Turkey Island. Hants 1D 16
Tur Langton. Leics 1E 62
Turleigh. Wilts 5D 34
Turlin Moor. Pool 3E 15
Turnant. Here 3G 47
Turnastone. Here 2G 47
Turnberry. S Ayr 4B 116
Turnchapel. Plym 3A 8
Turnditch. Derbs 1G 73
Turners Hill. W Sus 2E 27
Turners Puddle. Dors 3D 14
Turnford. Herts 5D 52
Turnhouse. Edin 2E 129
Turnworth. Dors 2D 14
Turriff. Abers 4E 161
Tursdale. Dur 1A 106
Turton Bottoms. Bkbn 3F 91
Turtory. Mor 4C 160
Turves Green. W Mid 3E 61
Turvey. Bed 5G 63
Turville. Buck 2F 37
Turville Heath. Buck 2F 37
Turweston. Buck 2E 50
Tushielaw. Bord 3F 119
Tutbury. Staf 3G 73
Tutnall. Worc 3D 61
Tutsbill. Glos 2A 34
Tuttington. Norf 3E 79
Tutts Clump. W Ber 4D 36
Tutwell. Corn 5D 11
Tuxford. Notts 3E 87
Twatt. Orkn 5B 172
Twatt. Shet 6E 173
Twechar. E Dun 2A 128
Tweedale. Telf 5B 72
Tweedmouth. Nmbd 4F 131
Tweedsmuir. Bord 2C 118
Twelveheads. Corn 4B 6
Twemlow Green. Ches E 4B 84
Twenty. Linc 3A 76
Twerton. Bath 5C 34
Twickenham. G Lon 3C 38
Twigworth. Glos 3D 48
Twineham. W Sus 3D 26
Twinhoe. Bath 1C 22
Twinstead. Essx 2B 54
Twinstead Green. Essx 2B 54
Twiss Green. Warr 1A 84
Twiston. Lanc 5H 97
Twitchen. Devn 3A 20
Twitchen. Shrp 3F 59
Two Bridges. Devn 5G 11
Two Bridges. Glos 5B 48
Two Dales. Derbs 4G 85
Two Gates. Staf 5G 73
Two Mile Oak. Devn 2E 9
Twycross. Leics 5H 73
Twyford. Buck 3E 51
Twyford. Derbs 3H 73
Twyford. Dors 1D 14
Twyford. Hants 4C 24
Twyford. Leics 4E 75
Twyford. Norf 3C 78
Twyford. Wok 4F 37
Twyford Common. Here 2A 48
Twyncarno. Cphy 5E 46
Twynholm. Dum 4D 110
Twyning. Glos 2D 49
Twyning Green. Glos 2E 49
Twynllanan. Carm 3A 46
Twyn-y-Sheriff. Mon 5H 47
Twywell. Nptn 3G 63
Tyberton. Here 2G 47
Tyburn. W Mid 1F 61
Tyby. Norf 3C 78
Tycroes. Carm 4G 45
Tycrwyn. Powy 4D 70
Tyddewi. Pemb 2B 42
Tydd Gote. Linc 4D 76
Tydd St Giles. Cambs 4D 76
Tydd St Mary. Linc 4D 76
Tye. Hants 2F 17
Tye Green. Essx 3F 53 (nr. Bishop's Stortford)
Tye Green. Essx 3A 54 (nr. Braintree)
Tye Green. Essx 2F 53 (nr. Saffron Walden)
Tyersal. W Yor 1B 92
Ty Issa. Powy 3D 70
Tyldesley. G Man 4E 91
Tyle. Carm 3G 45
Tyler Hill. Kent 4F 41
Tylers Green. Buck 2G 37
Tyler's Green. Essx 5F 53
Tylorstown. Rhon 2D 32
Tylwch. Powy 2B 58
Ty-nant. Cnwy 1B 70
Tyndrum. Stir 5H 141
Tyneham. Dors 4D 15
Tynehead. Midl 4G 129
Tynemouth. Tyne 3G 115
Tyneside. Tyne 3F 115
Tyne Tunnel. Tyne 3G 115
Tynewydd. Rhon 2C 32
Tyninghame. E Lot 2C 130
Tynron. Dum 5H 117
Ty'n-y-bryn. Rhon 3D 32
Tyn-y-celyn. Wrex 2D 70
Tyn-y-cwm. Swan 5G 45
Tyn-y-ffridd. Powy 2D 70
Tynygongl. IOA 2E 81
Tynygraig. Cdgn 4F 57
Ty'n-y-groes. Cnwy 3G 81
Ty'n-yr-eithin. Cdgn 4F 57
Tyn-y-rhyd. Powy 4C 70
Tyn-y-wern. Powy 3C 70
Tyrie. Abers 2G 161
Tyringham. Mil 1G 51
Tythecott. Devn 1E 11
Tythegston. B'end 4B 32
Tytherington. Ches E 3D 84
Tytherington. Som 2C 22
Tytherington. S Glo 3B 34
Tytherington. Wilts 2E 23
Tytherleigh. Devn 2G 13
Tywardreath. Corn 3E 7
Tywardreath Highway. Corn 3E 7
Tywyn. Cnwy 3G 81
Tywyn. Gwyn 5E 69

U

Uachdar. W Isl 3D 170
Uags. High 5G 155
Ubbeston Green. Suff 3F 67
Ubley. Bath 1A 22
Uckerby. N Yor 4F 105
Uckfield. E Sus 3F 27
Uckinghall. Worc 2D 48
Uckington. Glos 3E 49
Uckington. Shrp 5H 71
Uddingston. S Lan 3H 127
Uddington. S Lan 1A 118
Udimore. E Sus 4C 28
Udny Green. Abers 1F 153
Udny Station. Abers 1G 153
Udston. S Lan 4A 128
Udstonhead. S Lan 5A 128
Uffcott. Wilts 4G 35
Uffculme. Devn 1D 12
Uffington. Linc 5H 75
Uffington. Oxon 3B 36
Uffington. Shrp 4H 71
Ufford. Pet 5H 75
Ufford. Suff 5E 67
Ufton. Warw 4A 62
Ufton Nervet. W Ber 5E 37
Ugadale. Arg 3B 122
Ugborough. Devn 3C 8
Ugford. Wilts 3F 23
Uggeshall. Suff 2G 67
Ugglebarnby. N Yor 4F 107
Ugley. Essx 3F 53
Ugley Green. Essx 3F 53
Ugthorpe. N Yor 3E 107
Uidh. W Isl 9B 170
Uig. Arg 3C 138
Uig. High 2C 154 (nr. Balgown)
Uig. High 3A 154 (nr. Dunvegan)
Uigshader. High 4D 154

Uisken—Walton

Uisken. *Arg* 2A 132
Ulbster. *High* 4F 169
Ulcat Row. *Cumb* 2F 103
Ulceby. *Linc* 3D 88
Ulceby. *N Lin* 3E 94
Ulceby Skitter. *N Lin* 3E 94
Ulcombe. *Kent* 1C 28
Uldale. *Cumb* 1D 102
Uley. *Glos* 2C 34
Ulgham. *Nmbd* 5G 121
Ullapool. *High* 4F 163
Ullenhall. *Warw* 4F 61
Ulleskelf. *N Yor* 1F 93
Ullesthorpe. *Leics* 2C 62
Ulley. *S Yor* 2B 86
Ullingswick. *Here* 1A 48
Ullinish. *High* 5C 154
Ullock. *Cumb* 2B 102
Ulpha. *Cumb* 5C 102
Ulrome. *E Yor* 4F 101
Ulsta. *Shet* 3F 173
Ulting. *Essx* 5B 54
Ulva House. *Arg* 5F 139
Ulverston. *Cumb* 2B 96
Ulwell. *Dors* 4F 15
Umberleigh. *Devn* 4G 19
Unapool. *High* 5C 166
Underbarrow. *Cumb* 5F 103
Undercliffe. *W Yor* 1B 92
Underdale. *Shrp* 4H 71
Underhoull. *Shet* 1G 173
Underriver. *Kent* 5G 39
Under Tofts. *S Yor* 2H 85
Underton. *Shrp* 1A 60
Underwood. *Newp* 3G 33
Underwood. *Notts* 5B 86
Underwood. *Plym* 3B 8
Undley. *Suff* 2F 65
Undy. *Mon* 3H 33
Union Mills. *IOM* 4C 108
Union Street. *E Sus* 2B 28
Unstone. *Derbs* 3A 86
Unstone Green. *Derbs* 3A 86
Unthank. *Cumb* 5E 113
(nr. Carlisle)
Unthank. *Cumb* 5H 113
(nr. Gamblesby)
Unthank. *Cumb* 1F 103
(nr. Penrith)
Unthank End. *Cumb* 1F 103
Upavon. *Wilts* 1G 23
Up Cerne. *Dors* 2B 14
Upchurch. *Kent* 4C 40
Upcott. *Devn* 2F 11
Upcott. *Here* 5F 59
Upend. *Cambs* 5G 65
Up Exe. *Devn* 2C 12
Upgate. *Norf* 4D 78
Upgate Street. *Norf* 1C 66
Uphall. *Dors* 2A 14
Uphall. *W Lot* 2D 128
Uphall Station. *W Lot* 2D 128
Upham. *Devn* 2B 12
Upham. *Hants* 4D 24
Uphampton. *Here* 4F 59
Uphampton. *Worc* 4C 60
Up Hatherley. *Glos* 3E 49
Uphill. *N Som* 1G 21
Up Holland. *Lanc* 4D 90
Uplawmoor. *E Ren* 4F 127
Upleadon. *Glos* 3C 48
Upleatham. *Red C* 3D 106
Uplees. *Kent* 4D 40
Uploders. *Dors* 3A 14
Uplowman. *Devn* 1D 12
Uplyme. *Devn* 3G 13
Up Marden. *W Sus* 1F 17
Upminster. *G Lon* 2G 39
Up Nately. *Hants* 1E 25
Upottery. *Devn* 2F 13
Uppat. *High* 3F 165
Upper Affcot. *Shrp* 2G 59
Upper Arley. *Worc* 2B 60
Upper Armley. *W Yor* 1C 92
Upper Arncott. *Oxon* 4E 50
Upper Astrop. *Nptn* 2D 50
Upper Badcall. *High* 4B 166
Upper Bangor. *Gwyn* 3E 81
Upper Basildon. *W Ber* 4D 36
Upper Batley. *W Yor* 2C 92
Upper Beeding. *W Sus* 4C 26
Upper Benefield. *Nptn* 2G 63
Upper Bentley. *Worc* 4D 61
Upper Bighouse. *High* 3A 168
Upper Boddam. *Abers* 5D 160
Upper Boddington. *Nptn* 5B 62
Upper Bogside. *Mor* 3G 159
Upper Booth. *Derbs* 2F 85
Upper Borth. *Cdgn* 2F 57
Upper Boyndlie. *Abers* 2G 161
Upper Brailes. *Warw* 2B 50
Upper Breinton. *Here* 1H 47
Upper Broadheath. *Worc* 5C 60
Upper Broughton. *Notts* 3D 74
Upper Brynamman. *Carm* 4H 45
Upper Bucklebury. *W Ber* 5D 36
Upper Bullington. *Hants* 2C 24
Upper Burgate. *Hants* 1G 15
Upper Caldecote. *C Beds* 1B 52
Upper Canterton. *Hants* 1A 16
Upper Catesby. *Nptn* 5C 62
Upper Chapel. *Powy* 1D 46
Upper Cheddon. *Som* 4F 21
Upper Chicksgrove. *Wilts* 4E 23
Upper Church Village. *Rhon* 3D 32
Upper Chute. *Wilts* 1A 24
Upper Clatford. *Hants* 2B 24
Upper Coberley. *Glos* 4E 49
Upper Coedcae. *Torf* 5F 47
Upper Cokeham. *W Sus* 5C 26
Upper Common. *Hants* 2E 25
Upper Cound. *Shrp* 5H 71
Upper Cudworth. *S Yor* 4D 93
Upper Cumberworth. *W Yor* 4C 92
Upper Cuttlehill. *Abers* 4B 160
Upper Cwmbran. *Torf* 2F 33
Upper Dallachy. *Mor* 2A 160
Upper Dean. *Bed* 4H 63
Upper Denby. *W Yor* 4C 92
Upper Derraid. *High* 5E 159
Upper Diabaig. *High* 2H 155
Upper Dicker. *E Sus* 5G 27
Upper Dinchope. *Shrp* 2G 59
Upper Dochcarty. *High* 2H 157
Upper Dounreay. *High* 2B 168
Upper Dovercourt. *Essx* 2F 55
Upper Dunsforth. *N Yor* 3G 99
Upper Dunsley. *Herts* 4H 51
Upper Eastern Green.
W Mid 2G 61
Upper Elkstone. *Staf* 5E 85
Upper Ellastone. *Staf* 1F 73
Upper End. *Derbs* 3E 85
Upper Enham. *Hants* 2B 24
Upper Farringdon. *Hants* 3F 25
Upper Framilode. *Glos* 4C 48
Upper Froyle. *Hants* 2F 25
Upper Gills. *High* 1F 169
Upper Glenfintaig. *High* 5E 149
Upper Godney. *Som* 2H 21
Upper Gravenhurst. *C Beds* 2B 52
Upper Green. *Essx* 2E 53
Upper Green. *W Ber* 5B 36
Upper Green. *W Yor* 2C 92
Upper Grove Common.
Here 3A 48
Upper Hackney. *Derbs* 4G 85
Upper Hale. *Surr* 2G 25
Upper Halliford. *Surr* 4B 38
Upper Halling. *Medw* 4A 40
Upper Hambleton. *Rut* 5G 75
Upper Hardres Court. *Kent* 5F 41
Upper Hardwick. *Here* 5G 59
Upper Hartfield. *E Sus* 2F 27
Upper Haugh. *S Yor* 1B 86
Upper Hayton. *Shrp* 2H 59
Upper Heath. *Shrp* 2H 59
Upper Hellesdon. *Norf* 4E 79
Upper Helmsley. *N Yor* 4A 100
Upper Hengoed. *Shrp* 2E 71
Upper Hergest. *Here* 5E 59
Upper Heyford. *Nptn* 5D 62
Upper Heyford. *Oxon* 3C 50
Upper Hill. *Here* 5G 59
Upper Hindhope. *Bord* 4B 120
Upper Hopton. *W Yor* 3B 92
Upper Horsebridge. *E Sus* 4G 27
Upper Howsell. *Worc* 1C 48
Upper Hulme. *Staf* 4E 85
Upper Inglesham. *Swin* 2H 35
Upper Kilcott. *Glos* 3C 34
Upper Killay. *Swan* 3E 31
Upper Kirkton. *Abers* 5E 161
Upper Kirkton. *N Ayr* 4C 126
Upper Knockando. *Mor* 4F 159
Upper Knockchoilum. *High* 2G 149
Upper Lambourn. *W Ber* 3B 36
Upper Langford. *N Som* 1H 21
Upper Langwith. *Derbs* 4C 86
Upper Largo. *Fife* 3G 137
Upper Latheron. *High* 5D 169
Upper Layham. *Suff* 1D 54
Upper Leigh. *Staf* 2E 73
Upper Lenie. *High* 1H 149
Upper Lochton. *Abers* 4E 152
Upper Longdon. *Staf* 4E 73
Upper Longwood. *Shrp* 5A 72
Upper Lybster. *High* 5E 169
Upper Lydbrook. *Glos* 4B 48
Upper Lye. *Here* 4F 59
Upper Maes-coed. *Here* 2G 47
Upper Midway. *Derbs* 3G 73
Uppermill. *G Man* 4H 91
Upper Millichope. *Shrp* 2H 59
Upper Milovaig. *High* 4A 154
Upper Minety. *Wilts* 2F 35
Upper Mitton. *Worc* 3C 60
Upper Nash. *Pemb* 4E 43
Upper Neepaback. *Shet* 3G 173
Upper Netchwood. *Shrp* 1A 60
Upper Nobut. *Staf* 2E 73
Upper North Dean. *Buck* 2G 37
Upper Norwood. *W Sus* 4A 26
Upper Nyland. *Dors* 4C 22
Upper Oddington. *Glos* 3H 49
Upper Ollach. *High* 5E 155
Upper Outwoods. *Staf* 3G 73
Upper Padley. *Derbs* 3G 85
Upper Pennington. *Hants* 3B 16
Upper Poppleton. *York* 4H 99
Upper Quinton. *Warw* 1G 49
Upper Rochford. *Worc* 4A 60
Upper Rusko. *Dum* 3C 110
Upper Sandaig. *High* 2F 147
Upper Sanday. *Orkn* 7E 172
Upper Sapey. *Here* 4A 60
Upper Seagry. *Wilts* 3E 35
Upper Shelton. *C Beds* 1H 51
Upper Sheringham. *Norf* 1D 78
Upper Skelmorlie. *N Ayr* 3C 126
Upper Slaughter. *Glos* 3G 49
Upper Sonachan. *Arg* 1H 133
Upper Soudley. *Glos* 4B 48
Upper Staploe. *Bed* 5A 64
Upper Stoke. *Norf* 5E 79
Upper Stondon. *C Beds* 2B 52
Upper Stowe. *Nptn* 5D 62
Upper Street. *Hants* 1G 15
Upper Street. *Norf* 4F 79
(nr. Horning)
Upper Street. *Norf* 4F 79
(nr. Hoveton)
Upper Street. *Suff* 2E 55
Upper Strensham. *Worc* 2E 49
Upper Studley. *Wilts* 1D 22
Upper Sundon. *C Beds* 3A 52
Upper Swell. *Glos* 3G 49
Upper Tankersley. *S Yor* 1H 85
Upper Tean. *Staf* 2E 73
Upperthong. *W Yor* 4B 92
Upperthorpe. *N Lin* 4A 94
Upper Thurnham. *Lanc* 4D 96
Upper Tillyrie. *Per* 3D 136
Upperton. *W Sus* 3A 26
Upper Tooting. *G Lon* 3D 38
Uppertown. *Derbs* 4H 85
(nr. Ashover)
Upper Town. *Derbs* 5G 85
(nr. Bonsall)
Upper Town. *Derbs* 5G 85
(nr. Hognaston)
Upper Town. *Here* 1A 48
Uppertown. *High* 1F 169
Upper Town. *N Som* 5A 34
Uppertown. *Nmbd* 2B 114
Uppertown. *Orkn* 8D 172
Upper Tysoe. *Warw* 1B 50
Upper Upham. *Wilts* 4H 35
Upper Upnor. *Medw* 3B 40
Upper Urquhart. *Fife* 3D 136
Upper Wardington. *Oxon* 1C 50
Upper Weald. *Mil* 2G 51
Upper Weedon. *Nptn* 5D 62
Upper Wellingham. *E Sus* 4F 27
Upper Whiston. *S Yor* 2B 86
Upper Wield. *Hants* 3E 25
Upper Winchendon. *Buck* 4F 51
Upperwood. *Derbs* 5G 85
Upper Woodford. *Wilts* 3G 23
Upper Wootton. *Hants* 1D 24
Upper Wraxall. *Wilts* 4D 34
Upper Wyche. *Here* 1C 48
Uppincott. *Devn* 2B 12
Uppingham. *Rut* 1F 63
Uppington. *Shrp* 5H 71
Upsall. *N Yor* 1G 99
Upsettlington. *Bord* 5E 131
Upshire. *Essx* 5E 53
Up Somborne. *Hants* 3B 24
Upstreet. *Kent* 4G 41
Up Sydling. *Dors* 2B 14
Upthorpe. *Suff* 3B 66
Upton. *Buck* 4F 51
Upton. *Cambs* 3A 64
Upton. *Ches W* 4G 83
Upton. *Corn* 2C 10
(nr. Bude)
Upton. *Corn* 5C 10
(nr. Liskeard)
Upton. *Cumb* 1E 102
Upton. *Devn* 2D 12
(nr. Honiton)
Upton. *Devn* 4D 8
(nr. Kingsbridge)
Upton. *Dors* 3E 15
(nr. Poole)
Upton. *Dors* 4C 14
(nr. Weymouth)
Upton. *E Yor* 4F 101
Upton. *Hants* 1B 24
(nr. Andover)
Upton. *Hants* 1B 16
(nr. Southampton)
Upton. *IOW* 3D 16
Upton. *Leics* 1A 62
Upton. *Linc* 2F 87
Upton. *Mers* 2E 83
Upton. *Norf* 4F 79
Upton. *Nptn* 4E 62
Upton. *Notts* 3E 87
(nr. Retford)
Upton. *Notts* 5E 87
(nr. Southwell)
Upton. *Oxon* 3D 36
Upton. *Pemb* 4E 43
Upton. *Pet* 5A 76
Upton. *Slo* 3A 38
Upton. *Som* 4H 21
(nr. Somerton)
Upton. *Som* 4C 20
(nr. Wiveliscombe)
Upton. *Warw* 5F 61
Upton. *W Yor* 3E 93
Upton. *Wilts* 3D 22
Upton Bishop. *Here* 3B 48
Upton Cheyney. *S Glo* 5B 34
Upton Cressett. *Shrp* 1A 60
Upton Crews. *Here* 3B 48
Upton Cross. *Corn* 5C 10
Upton End. *C Beds* 2B 52
Upton Grey. *Hants* 2E 25
Upton Heath. *Ches W* 4G 83
Upton Hellions. *Devn* 2B 12
Upton Lovell. *Wilts* 2E 23
Upton Magna. *Shrp* 4H 71
Upton Noble. *Som* 3C 22
Upton Pyne. *Devn* 3C 12
Upton St Leonards. *Glos* 4D 48
Upton Scudamore. *Wilts* 2D 22
Upton Snodsbury. *Worc* 5D 60
Upton upon Severn. *Worc* 1D 48
Upton Warren. *Worc* 4D 60
Upwaltham. *W Sus* 4A 26
Upware. *Cambs* 3E 65
Upwell. *Cambs* 5D 77
Upwey. *Dors* 4B 14
Upwick Green. *Herts* 3E 53
Upwood. *Cambs* 2B 64
Urafirth. *Shet* 4E 173
Uragaig. *Arg* 4A 132
Urchany. *High* 4C 158
Urchfont. *Wilts* 1F 23
Urdimarsh. *Here* 1A 48
Ure. *Shet* 4D 173
Ure Bank. *N Yor* 2F 99
Urgha. *W Isl* 8D 171
Urlay Nook. *Stoc T* 3B 106
Urmston. *G Man* 1B 84
Urquhart. *Mor* 2G 159
Urra. *N Yor* 4C 106
Urray. *High* 3H 157
Usan. *Ang* 3G 145
Ushaw Moor. *Dur* 5F 115
Usk. *Mon* 5G 47
Usselby. *Linc* 1H 87
Usworth. *Tyne* 4G 115
Utkinton. *Ches W* 4H 83
Uton. *Devn* 3B 12
Utterby. *Linc* 1C 88
Uttoxeter. *Staf* 2E 73
Uwchmynydd. *Gwyn* 3A 68
Uxbridge. *G Lon* 2B 38
Uyeasound. *Shet* 1G 173
Uzmaston. *Pemb* 3D 42

V

Valley. *IOA* 3B 80
Valley End. *Surr* 4A 38
Valley Truckle. *Corn* 4B 10
Valsgarth. *Shet* 1H 173
Valtos. *High* 2E 155
Van. *Powy* 2B 58
Vange. *Essx* 2B 40
Varteg. *Torf* 5F 47
Vatsetter. *Shet* 3G 173
Vatten. *High* 4B 154
Vaul. *Arg* 4B 138
Vauld,The. *Here* 1A 48
Vaynol. *Gwyn* 3E 81
Vaynor. *Mer T* 4D 46
Veensgarth. *Shet* 7F 173
Velindre. *Powy* 2E 47
Vellow. *Som* 3D 20
Velly. *Devn* 4C 18
Veness. *Orkn* 5E 172
Venhay. *Devn* 1A 12
Venn. *Devn* 4D 8
Venngreen. *Devn* 1D 11
Vennington. *Shrp* 5F 71
Venn Ottery. *Devn* 3D 12
Venn's Green. *Here* 1A 48
Venny Tedburn. *Devn* 3B 12
Venterdon. *Corn* 5D 10
Ventnor. *IOW* 5D 16
Vernham Dean. *Hants* 1B 24
Vernham Street. *Hants* 1B 24
Vernolds Common. *Shrp* 2G 59
Verwood. *Dors* 2F 15
Veryan. *Corn* 5D 6
Veryan Green. *Corn* 4D 6
Vicarage. *Devn* 4F 13
Vickerstown. *Cumb* 3A 96
Victoria. *Corn* 2D 6
Vidlin. *Shet* 5F 173
Viewpark. *N Lan* 3A 128
Vigo. *W Mid* 5E 73
Vigo Village. *Kent* 4H 39
Village Bay. *High* 3B 154
Vinehall Street. *E Sus* 3B 28
Vine's Cross. *E Sus* 4G 27
Viney Hill. *Glos* 5B 48
Virginia Water. *Surr* 4A 38
Virginstow. *Devn* 3D 11
Vobster. *Som* 2C 22
Voe. *Shet* 5F 173
(nr. Hillside)
Voe. *Shet* 3E 173
(nr. Swinister)
Vole. *Som* 2G 21
Vowchurch. *Here* 2G 47
Voxter. *Shet* 4E 173
Voy. *Orkn* 6B 172
Vulcan Village. *Warr* 1H 83

W

Wackerfield. *Dur* 2E 105
Wacton. *Norf* 1D 66
Wadbister. *Shet* 7F 173
Wadborough. *Worc* 1E 49
Wadbrook. *Devn* 2G 13
Waddesdon. *Buck* 4F 51
Waddeton. *Devn* 3E 9
Waddicar. *Mers* 1F 83
Waddingham. *Linc* 1G 87
Waddington. *Lanc* 5G 97
Waddington. *Linc* 4G 87
Waddon. *Devn* 5B 12
Wadebridge. *Corn* 1D 6
Wadeford. *Som* 1G 13
Wadenhoe. *Nptn* 2H 63
Wadesmill. *Herts* 4D 52
Wadhurst. *E Sus* 2H 27
Wadshelf. *Derbs* 3H 85
Wadsley. *S Yor* 1H 85
Wadsley Bridge. *S Yor* 1H 85
Wadswick. *Wilts* 5D 34
Wadwick. *Hants* 1C 24
Wadworth. *S Yor* 1C 86
Waen. *Den* 4C 82
(nr. Bodfari)
Waen. *Den* 4D 82
(nr. Llandyrnog)
Waen. *Den* 4B 82
(nr. Nantglyn)
Waen. *Powy* 1B 58
Waen Fach. *Powy* 4E 70
Waen Goleugoed. *Den* 3C 82
Wag. *High* 1H 165
Wainfleet All Saints. *Linc* 5D 89
Wainfleet Bank. *Linc* 5D 88
Wainfleet St Mary. *Linc* 5D 89
Wainhouse Corner. *Corn* 3B 10
Wainscott. *Medw* 3B 40
Wainstalls. *W Yor* 2A 92
Waitby. *Cumb* 4A 104
Waithe. *Linc* 4F 95
Wakefield. *W Yor* 2D 92
Wakerley. *Nptn* 1G 63
Wakes Colne. *Essx* 3B 54
Walberswick. *Suff* 3G 67
Walberton. *W Sus* 5A 26
Walbottle. *Tyne* 3E 115
Walby. *Cumb* 3F 113
Walcombe. *Som* 2A 22
Walcot. *Linc* 2H 75
Walcot. *N Lin* 2B 94
Walcot. *Swin* 3G 35
Walcot. *Telf* 4H 71
Walcot. *Warw* 5F 61
Walcote. *Leics* 2C 62
Walcot Green. *Norf* 2D 66
Walcott. *Linc* 5A 88
Walcott. *Norf* 2F 79
Walden. *N Yor* 1C 98
Walden Head. *N Yor* 1B 98
Walden Stubbs. *N Yor* 3F 93
Walderslade. *Medw* 4B 40
Walderton. *W Sus* 1F 17
Walditch. *Dors* 3H 13
Waldley. *Derbs* 2F 73
Waldridge. *Dur* 4F 115
Waldringfield. *Suff* 1F 55
Waldron. *E Sus* 4G 27
Wales. *S Yor* 2B 86
Walesby. *Linc* 1A 88
Walesby. *Notts* 3D 86
Walford. *Here* 3F 59
(nr. Leintwardine)
Walford. *Here* 3A 48
(nr. Ross-on-Wye)
Walford. *Shrp* 3G 71
Walford. *Staf* 2C 72
Walford Heath. *Shrp* 4G 71
Walgherton. *Ches E* 1A 72
Walgrave. *Nptn* 3F 63
Walhampton. *Hants* 3B 16
Walkden. *G Man* 4F 91
Walker. *Tyne* 3F 115
Walkerburn. *Bord* 1F 119
Walker Fold. *Lanc* 5F 97
Walkeringham. *Notts* 1E 87
Walkerith. *Linc* 1E 87
Walkern. *Herts* 3C 52
Walker's Green. *Here* 1A 48
Walkerton. *Fife* 3E 137
Walkerville. *N Yor* 5F 105
Walkford. *Dors* 3H 15
Walkhampton. *Devn* 2B 8
Walkington. *E Yor* 1C 94
Walkley. *S Yor* 2H 85
Walk Mill. *Lanc* 1G 91
Wall. *Corn* 3D 4
Wall. *Nmbd* 3C 114
Wall. *Staf* 5F 73
Wallaceton. *Dum* 1F 111
Wallacetown. *Shet* 6E 173
Wallacetown. *S Ayr* 2C 116
(nr. Ayr)
Wallacetown. *S Ayr* 4B 116
(nr. Dailly)
Wallands Park. *E Sus* 4F 27
Wallasey. *Mers* 1F 83
Wallaston Green. *Pemb* 4D 42
Wallbrook. *W Mid* 1D 60
Wallcrouch. *E Sus* 2A 28
Wall End. *Cumb* 1B 96
Wallend. *Medw* 3C 40
Wall Heath. *W Mid* 2C 60
Wallingford. *Oxon* 3E 36
Wallington. *G Lon* 4D 39
Wallington. *Hants* 2D 16
Wallington. *Herts* 2C 52
Wallis. *Pemb* 2E 43
Wallisdown. *Pool* 3F 15
Walliswood. *Surr* 2C 26
Wall Nook. *Dur* 5F 115
Walls. *Shet* 7D 173
Wallsend. *Tyne* 3G 115
Wallsworth. *Glos* 3D 48
Wall under Heywood.
Shrp 1H 59
Wallyford. *E Lot* 2G 129
Walmer. *Kent* 5H 41
Walmer Bridge. *Lanc* 2C 90
Walmersley. *G Man* 3G 91
Walmley. *W Mid* 1F 61
Walnut Grove. *Per* 1D 136
Walpole. *Suff* 3F 67
Walpole Cross Keys. *Norf* 4E 77
Walpole Gate. *Norf* 4E 77
Walpole Highway. *Norf* 4E 77
Walpole Marsh. *Norf* 4D 77
Walpole St Andrew. *Norf* 4E 77
Walpole St Peter. *Norf* 4E 77
Walsall. *W Mid* 1E 61
Walsall Wood. *W Mid* 5E 73
Walsden. *W Yor* 2H 91
Walsgrave on Sowe. *W Mid* 2A 62
Walsham le Willows. *Suff* 3C 66
Walshaw. *G Man* 3F 91
Walshford. *N Yor* 4G 99
Walsoken. *Cambs* 4D 76
Walston. *S Lan* 5D 128
Walsworth. *Herts* 2B 52
Walter's Ash. *Buck* 2G 37
Walterston. *V Glam* 4D 32
Walterstone. *Here* 3G 47
Waltham. *Kent* 1F 29
Waltham. *NE Lin* 4F 95
Waltham Abbey. *Essx* 5D 53
Waltham Chase. *Hants* 1D 16
Waltham Cross. *Herts* 5D 52
Waltham on the Wolds.
Leics 3F 75
Waltham St Lawrence.
Wind 4G 37
Waltham's Cross. *Essx* 2G 53
Walthamstow. *G Lon* 2E 39
Walton. *Cumb* 3G 113
Walton. *Derbs* 4A 86

Wester Shian—Whitson

Wester Shian. Per 5F 143
Wester Skeld. Shet 7D 173
Westerton. Ang 3F 145
Westerton. Dur 1F 105
Westerton. W Sus 2G 17
Westerwick. Shet 7D 173
West Farleigh. Kent 5B 40
West Farndon. Nptn 5C 62
West Felton. Shrp 3F 71
Westfield. Cumb 2A 102
Westfield. E Sus 4C 28
Westfield. High 2C 168
Westfield. Norf 5B 78
Westfield. N Lan 2A 128
Westfield. W Lot 2C 128
Westfields. Dors 2C 14
Westfields of Rattray. Per 4A 144
West Firle. E Sus 5F 27
West Fleetham. Nmbd 2F 121
Westford. Som 1E 13
West Garforth. W Yor 1D 93
Westgate. Dur 1C 104
Westgate. Norf 1B 78
Westgate. N Lin 4A 94
Westgate on Sea. Kent 3H 41
West Ginge. Oxon 3C 36
West Grafton. Wilts 5H 35
West Green. Hants 1F 25
West Grimstead. Wilts 4H 23
West Grinstead. W Sus 3C 26
West Haddlesey. N Yor 2F 93
West Haddon. Nptn 3D 62
West Hagbourne. Oxon 3D 36
West Hagley. Worc 2C 60
West Hall. Cumb 3G 113
Westhall. Suff 2G 67
West Hallam. Derbs 1B 74
Westhall Terrace. Ang 5D 144
West Halton. N Lin 2C 94
Westham. Dors 5B 14
Westham. E Sus 5H 27
West Ham. G Lon 2E 39
Westham. Som 2H 21
Westhampnett. W Sus 2G 17
West Handley. Derbs 3A 86
West Hanney. Oxon 2C 36
West Hanningfield. Essx 1B 40
West Hardwick. W Yor 3E 93
West Harnham. Wilts 4G 23
West Harptree. Bath 1A 22
West Harting. W Sus 4F 25
West Harton. Tyne 3G 115
West Hatch. Som 4F 21
Westhay. Som 2H 21
Westhead. Lanc 4C 90
West Head. Norf 5E 77
West Heath. Hants 1D 24
(nr. Basingstoke)
West Heath. Hants 1G 25
(nr. Farnborough)
West Helmsdale. High 2H 165
West Hendred. Oxon 3C 36
West Heogaland. Shet 4D 173
West Heslerton. N Yor 2D 100
West Hewish. N Som 5G 33
Westhide. Here 1A 48
Westhill. Abers 3F 153
West Hill. Devn 3D 12
West Hill. E Yor 3F 101
Westhill. High 4B 158
West Hill. N Som 4H 33
West Hill. W Sus 2E 27
West Hoathly. W Sus 2E 27
West Holme. Dors 4D 15
Westhope. Here 5G 59
Westhope. Shrp 2G 59
West Horndon. Essx 2H 39
Westhorp. Nptn 5C 62
Westhorpe. Linc 2B 76
Westhorpe. Suff 4C 66
West Horrington. Som 2A 22
West Horsley. Surr 5B 38
West Horton. Nmbd 1E 121
West Hougham. Kent 1G 29
Westhoughton. G Man 4E 91
West Houlland. Shet 6D 173
Westhouse. N Yor 2F 97
West Howe. Bour 3F 15
Westhumble. Surr 5C 38
West Huntspill. Som 2G 21
West Hyde. Herts 1B 38
West Hynish. Arg 5A 138
West Hythe. Kent 2F 29
West Ilsley. W Ber 3C 36
Westing. Shet 1G 173
West Itchenor. W Sus 2G 17
West Keal. Linc 4C 88
West Kennett. Wilts 5G 35
West Kilbride. N Ayr 5D 126
West Kingsdown. Kent 4G 39
West Kington. Wilts 4D 34
West Kirby. Mers 2E 82
West Knapton. N Yor 2C 100
West Knighton. Dors 4C 14
West Knoyle. Wilts 3D 22
West Kyloe. Nmbd 5G 131
Westlake. Devn 3C 8
West Lambrook. Som 1H 13
West Langdon. Kent 1H 29
West Langwell. High 3D 164
West Lavington. W Sus 4G 25
West Lavington. Wilts 1F 23
West Layton. N Yor 4E 105
West Leake. Notts 3C 74
West Learmouth. Nmbd 1C 120
Westleigh. Devn 4E 19
(nr. Bideford)
Westleigh. Devn 1D 12
(nr. Tiverton)
West Leigh. Devn 2G 11
(nr. Winkleigh)
Westleigh. G Man 4E 91
West Leith. Buck 4H 51
Westleton. Suff 4G 67
West Lexham. Norf 4H 77
Westley. Shrp 5F 71
Westley. Suff 4H 65
Westley Waterless. Cambs 5F 65
West Lilling. N Yor 3A 100
West Lingo. Fife 3G 137
Westlington. Buck 4F 51
Westlinton. Cumb 3E 113
West Linton. Bord 4E 129
West Littleton. S Glo 4C 34
West Looe. Corn 3G 7
West Lulworth. Dors 4D 14
West Lutton. N Yor 3D 100
West Lydford. Som 3A 22
West Lyng. Som 4G 21
West Lynn. Norf 4F 77
West Mains. Per 2B 136
West Malling. Kent 5A 40
West Malvern. Worc 1C 48
Westmancote. Worc 2E 49
West Marden. W Sus 1F 17
West Markham. Notts 3E 86
Westmarsh. Kent 4G 41
West Marsh. NE Lin 4F 95
West Marton. N Yor 4A 98
West Meon. Hants 4E 25
West Mersea. Essx 4D 54
Westmeston. E Sus 4E 27
Westmill. Herts 3D 52
(nr. Buntingford)
Westmill. Herts 2B 52
(nr. Hitchin)
West Milton. Dors 3A 14
Westminster. G Lon 3D 39
West Molesey. Surr 4C 38
West Monkton. Som 4F 21
Westmoor End. Cumb 1B 102
West Moors. Dors 2F 15
West Morden. Dors 3E 15
West Muir. Ang 2E 145
(nr. Brechin)
Westmuir. Ang 3C 144
(nr. Forfar)
West Murkle. High 2D 168
West Ness. N Yor 2A 100
Westness. Orkn 5C 172
Westnewton. Cumb 5C 112
West Newton. E Yor 1E 95
West Newton. Norf 3F 77
Westnewton. Nmbd 1D 120
West Newton. Som 4F 21
West Norwood. G Lon 3E 39
Westoe. Tyne 3G 115
West Ogwell. Devn 2E 9
Weston. Bath 5C 34
Weston. Ches E 5B 84
(nr. Crewe)
Weston. Ches E 3D 84
(nr. Macclesfield)
Weston. Devn 2E 13
(nr. Honiton)
Weston. Devn 4E 13
(nr. Sidmouth)
Weston. Dors 5B 14
(nr. Weymouth)
Weston. Dors 2A 14
(nr. Yeovil)
Weston. Hal 2H 83
Weston. Hants 4F 25
Weston. Here 5F 59
Weston. Herts 2C 52
Weston. Linc 3B 76
Weston. Nptn 1D 50
Weston. Notts 4E 87
Weston. Shrp 1H 59
(nr. Bridgnorth)
Weston. Shrp 3F 59
(nr. Knighton)
Weston. Shrp 3H 71
(nr. Wem)
Weston. S Lan 5D 128
Weston. Staf 3D 73
Weston. Suff 2G 67
Weston. W Ber 4B 36
Weston Bampfylde. Som 4B 22
Weston Beggard. Here 1A 48
Westonbirt. Glos 3D 34
Weston by Welland. Nptn 1E 63
Weston Colville. Cambs 5F 65
Westoncommon. Shrp 3G 71
Weston Coyney. Stoke 1D 72
Weston Ditch. Suff 3F 65
Weston Favell. Nptn 4E 63
Weston Green. Cambs 5F 65
Weston Green. Norf 4D 78
Weston Heath. Shrp 4B 72
Weston Hills. Linc 4B 76
Weston in Arden. Warw 2A 62
Westoning. C Beds 2A 52
Weston-in-Gordano. N Som 4H 33
Weston Jones. Staf 3B 72
Weston Longville. Norf 4D 78
Weston Lullingfields. Shrp 3G 71
Weston-on-Avon. Warw 5F 61
Weston-on-the-Green. Oxon 4D 50
Weston-on-Trent. Derbs 3B 74
Weston Patrick. Hants 2E 25
Weston Rhyn. Shrp 2E 71
Weston Subedge. Glos 1G 49
Weston-super-Mare. N Som 5G 33
Weston Town. Som 2C 22
Weston Turville. Buck 4G 51
Weston under Lizard. Staf 4C 72
Weston under Penyard. Here 3B 48
Weston under Wetherley. Warw 4A 62
Weston Underwood. Derbs 1G 73
Weston Underwood. Mil 5F 63
Westonzoyland. Som 3G 21
West Orchard. Dors 1D 14
West Overton. Wilts 5G 35
Westow. N Yor 3B 100
Westown. Per 1E 137
West Panson. Devn 3D 10
West Park. Hart 1B 106
West Parley. Dors 3F 15
West Peckham. Kent 5H 39
West Pelton. Dur 4F 115
West Pennard. Som 3A 22
West Pentire. Corn 2B 6
West Perry. Cambs 4A 64
West Pitcorthie. Fife 3H 137
West Plean. Stir 1B 128
West Poringland. Norf 5E 79
West Porlock. Som 2B 20
Westport. Som 1G 13
West Putford. Devn 1D 10
West Quantoxhead. Som 2E 20
Westra. V Glam 4E 33
West Rainton. Dur 5G 115
West Rasen. Linc 2H 87
West Ravendale. NE Lin 1B 88
Westray Airport. Orkn 2D 172
West Raynham. Norf 3A 78
Westrigg. W Lot 3C 128
West Rounton. N Yor 4B 106
West Row. Suff 3F 65
West Rudham. Norf 3H 77
West Runton. Norf 1D 78
Westruther. Bord 4C 130
Westry. Cambs 1C 64
West Saltoun. E Lot 3A 130
West Sandford. Devn 2B 12
West Sandwick. Shet 3F 173
West Scrafton. N Yor 1C 98
Westside. Orkn 5C 172
West Sleekburn. Nmbd 1F 115
West Somerton. Norf 4G 79
West Stafford. Dors 4C 14
West Stockwith. Notts 1E 87
West Stoke. W Sus 2G 17
West Stonesdale. N Yor 4B 104
West Stoughton. Som 2H 21
West Stour. Dors 4C 22
West Stourmouth. Kent 4G 41
West Stow. Suff 3H 65
West Stowell. Wilts 5G 35
West Strathan. High 2F 167
West Stratton. Hants 2D 24
West Street. Kent 5D 40
West Tanfield. N Yor 2E 99
West Taphouse. Corn 2F 7
West Tarbert. Arg 3G 125
West Thirston. Nmbd 4F 121
West Thorney. W Sus 2F 17
West Thurrock. Thur 3G 39
West Tilbury. Thur 3A 40
West Tisted. Hants 4E 25
West Tofts. Norf 1H 65
West Torrington. Linc 2A 88
West Town. Bath 5A 34
West Town. Hants 3F 17
West Town. N Som 5H 33
West Tytherley. Hants 4A 24
West Tytherton. Wilts 4E 35
West View. Hart 1C 106
Westville. Notts 1C 74
West Walton. Norf 4D 76
Westward. Cumb 5D 112
Westward Ho!. Devn 4E 19
Westwell. Kent 1D 28
Westwell. Oxon 5H 49
Westwell Leacon. Kent 1D 28
West Wellow. Hants 1A 16
West Wemyss. Fife 4F 137
Westwick. Cambs 4D 64
Westwick. Dur 3D 104
Westwick. Norf 3E 79
West Wick. N Som 5G 33
West Wickham. Cambs 1G 53
West Wickham. G Lon 4E 39
West Williamston. Pemb 4E 43
West Willoughby. Linc 1G 75
West Winch. Norf 4F 77
West Winterslow. Wilts 3H 23
West Wittering. W Sus 3F 17
West Witton. N Yor 1C 98
Westwood. Devn 3D 12
Westwood. Kent 4H 41
Westwood. Pet 1A 64
Westwood. S Lan 4H 127
Westwood. Wilts 1D 22
West Woodburn. Nmbd 1B 114
West Woodhay. W Ber 5B 36
West Woodlands. Som 2C 22
West Woodside. Cumb 5E 112
Westwoodside. N Lin 4H 93
West Worldham. Hants 3F 25
West Worlington. Devn 1A 12
West Worthing. W Sus 5C 26
West Wratting. Cambs 5F 65
West Wycombe. Buck 2G 37
West Wylam. Nmbd 3E 115
West Yatton. Wilts 4D 34
West Yell. Shet 3F 173
West Youlstone. Corn 1C 10
Wetheral. Cumb 4F 113
Wetherby. W Yor 5G 99
Wetherden. Suff 4C 66
Wetheringsett. Suff 4D 66
Wethersfield. Essx 2H 53
Wethersta. Shet 5E 173
Wetherup Street. Suff 4D 66
Wetley Rocks. Staf 1D 72
Wettenhall. Ches E 4A 84
Wetton. Staf 5F 85
Wetwang. E Yor 4D 100
Wetwood. Staf 2B 72
Wexcombe. Wilts 1A 24
Wexham Street. Buck 2A 38
Weybourne. Norf 1D 78
Weybourne. Surr 2G 25
Weybread. Suff 2E 67
Weybridge. Surr 4B 38
Weycroft. Devn 3G 13
Weydale. High 2D 168
Weyhill. Hants 2B 24
Weymouth. Dors 5B 14 & 215
Weythel. Powy 5E 59
Whaddon. Buck 2G 51
Whaddon. Cambs 1D 52
Whaddon. Glos 4D 48
Whaddon. Wilts 4G 23
Whale. Cumb 2G 103
Whaley. Derbs 3C 86
Whaley Bridge. Derbs 2E 85
Whaley Thorns. Derbs 3C 86
Whalley. Lanc 1F 91
Whalton. Nmbd 1E 115
Wham. N Yor 3G 97
Whaplode. Linc 3C 76
Whaplode Drove. Linc 4C 76
Whaplode St Catherine. Linc 3C 76
Wharfe. N Yor 3G 97
Wharles. Lanc 1C 90
Wharley End. C Beds 1H 51
Wharncliffe Side. S Yor 1G 85
Wharram-le-Street. N Yor 3C 100
Wharton. Ches W 4A 84
Wharton. Here 5H 59
Whashton. N Yor 4E 105
Whasset. Cumb 1E 97
Whatcote. Warw 1A 50
Whateley. Warw 1G 61
Whatfield. Suff 1D 54
Whatley. Som 2G 13
(nr. Chard)
Whatley. Som 2C 22
(nr. Frome)
Whatlington. E Sus 4B 28
Whatmore. Shrp 3A 60
Whatstandwell. Derbs 5H 85
Whatton. Notts 2E 75
Whauphill. Dum 5B 110
Whaw. N Yor 4C 104
Wheatacre. Norf 1G 67
Wheatcroft. Derbs 5A 86
Wheathampstead. Herts 4B 52
Wheathill. Shrp 2A 60
Wheatley. Devn 3B 12
Wheatley. Hants 2F 25
Wheatley. Oxon 5D 50
Wheatley. S Yor 4F 93
Wheatley. W Yor 2A 92
Wheatley Hill. Dur 1A 106
Wheatley Lane. Lanc 1G 91
Wheatley Park. S Yor 4F 93
Wheaton Aston. Staf 4C 72
Wheatstone Park. Staf 5C 72
Wheddon Cross. Som 3C 20
Wheelerstreet. Surr 1A 26
Wheelock. Ches E 5B 84
Wheelock Heath. Ches E 5B 84
Wheelton. Lanc 2E 90
Wheldrake. York 5A 100
Whelford. Glos 2G 35
Whelpley Hill. Buck 5H 51
Whelpo. Cumb 1E 102
Whelston. Flin 3E 82
Whenby. N Yor 3A 100
Whepstead. Suff 5H 65
Wherstead. Suff 1E 55
Wherwell. Hants 2B 24
Wheston. Derbs 3F 85
Whetsted. Kent 1A 28
Whetstone. G Lon 1D 38
Whetstone. Leics 1C 62
Whicham. Cumb 1A 96
Whichford. Warw 2B 50
Whickham. Tyne 3F 115
Whiddon. Devn 2E 11
Whiddon Down. Devn 3G 11
Whigstreet. Ang 4D 145
Whilton. Nptn 4D 62
Whimble. Devn 2D 10
Whimple. Devn 3D 12
Whimpwell Green. Norf 3F 79
Whinburgh. Norf 5C 78
Whin Lane End. Lanc 5C 96
Whinnyfold. Abers 5H 161
Whinny Hill. Stoc T 3A 106
Whippingham. IOW 3D 16
Whipsnade. C Beds 4A 52
Whipton. Devn 3C 12
Whirlow. S Yor 2H 85
Whisby. Linc 4G 87
Whissendine. Rut 4F 75
Whissonsett. Norf 3B 78
Whisterfield. Ches E 3C 84
Whistley Green. Wok 4F 37
Whiston. Mers 1G 83
Whiston. Nptn 4F 63
Whiston. S Yor 1B 86
Whiston. Staf 1E 73
(nr. Cheadle)
Whiston. Staf 4C 72
(nr. Penkridge)
Whiston Cross. Shrp 5B 72
Whiston Eaves. Staf 1E 73
Whitacre Heath. Warw 1G 61
Whitbeck. Cumb 1A 96
Whitbourne. Here 5B 60
Whitburn. Tyne 3H 115
Whitburn. W Lot 3C 128
Whitburn Colliery. Tyne 3H 115
Whitby. Ches W 3F 83
Whitby. N Yor 3F 107
Whitbyheath. Ches W 3F 83
Whitchester. Bord 4D 130
Whitchurch. Bath 5B 34
Whitchurch. Buck 3G 51
Whitchurch. Card 4E 33
Whitchurch. Devn 5E 11
Whitchurch. Hants 2C 24
Whitchurch. Here 4A 48
Whitchurch. Pemb 2C 42
Whitchurch. Shrp 1H 71
Whitchurch Canonicorum. Dors 3G 13
Whitchurch Hill. Oxon 4E 37
Whitchurch-on-Thames. Oxon 4E 37
Whitcombe. Dors 4C 14
Whitcot. Shrp 1F 59
Whitcott Keysett. Shrp 2E 59
Whiteash Green. Essx 2A 54
Whitebog. High 2B 158
Whitebridge. High 2G 149
Whitebrook. Mon 5A 48
Whitecairns. Abers 2G 153
White Chapel. Lanc 5E 97
Whitechurch. Pemb 1F 43
White Colne. Essx 3B 54
White Coppice. Lanc 3E 90
White Corries. High 3G 141
Whitecraig. E Lot 2G 129
Whitecroft. Glos 5B 48
White Cross. Corn 4D 5
(nr. Mullion)
Whitecross. Corn 1D 6
(nr. Wadebridge)
Whitecross. Falk 2C 128
White End. Worc 2C 48
Whiteface. High 5E 164
Whitefarland. N Ayr 5G 125
Whitefaulds. S Ayr 4B 116
Whitefield. Dors 3E 15
Whitefield. G Man 4G 91
Whitefield. Som 4D 20
Whiteford. Abers 1E 152
Whitegate. Ches W 4A 84
Whitehall. Devn 1E 13
Whitehall. Hants 1F 25
Whitehall. Orkn 5F 172
Whitehall. W Sus 3C 26
Whitehaven. Cumb 3A 102
Whitehaven. Shrp 3E 71
Whitehill. Hants 3F 25
Whitehill. N Ayr 4D 126
Whitehills. Abers 2D 160
Whitehills. Ang 3D 144
White Horse Common. Norf 3F 79
Whitehough. Derbs 2E 85
Whitehouse. Abers 2D 152
Whitehouse. Arg 3G 125
Whiteinch. Glas 3G 127
Whitekirk. E Lot 1B 130
White Kirkley. Dur 1D 104
White Lackington. Dors 3C 14
Whitelackington. Som 1G 13
White Ladies Aston. Worc 5D 60
White Lee. W Yor 2C 92
Whiteley. Hants 1D 16
Whiteley Bank. IOW 4D 16
Whiteley Village. Surr 4B 38
Whitemans Green. W Sus 3E 27
White Mill. Carm 3E 45
Whitemire. Mor 3D 159
Whitemoor. Corn 3D 6
Whitenap. Hants 4B 24
Whiteness. Shet 7F 173
White Notley. Essx 4A 54
Whiteoak Green. Oxon 4B 50
Whiteparish. Wilts 4H 23
White Pit. Linc 3C 88
Whiterashes. Abers 1F 153
White Rocks. Here 3H 47
White Roding. Essx 4F 53
Whiterow. High 4F 169
Whiterow. Mor 3E 159
Whiteshill. Glos 5D 48
Whiteside. Nmbd 3A 114
Whiteside. W Lot 3C 128
Whitesmith. E Sus 4G 27
Whitestaunton. Som 1F 13
Whitestone. Abers 4D 152
Whitestone. Devn 3B 12
White Stone. Here 1A 48
Whitestones. Abers 3F 161
Whitestreet Green. Suff 2C 54
Whitewall Corner. N Yor 2B 100
White Waltham. Wind 4G 37
Whiteway. Glos 4E 49
Whitewell. Lanc 5F 97
Whitewell Bottom. Lanc 2G 91
Whiteworks. Devn 5G 11
Whitewreath. Mor 3G 159
Whitfield. D'dee 5D 144
Whitfield. Kent 1H 29
Whitfield. Nptn 2E 50
Whitfield. Nmbd 4A 114
Whitfield. S Glo 2B 34
Whitford. Devn 3F 13
Whitford. Flin 3D 82
Whitgift. E Yor 2B 94
Whitgreave. Staf 3C 72
Whithorn. Dum 5B 110
Whiting Bay. N Ayr 3E 123
Whitington. Norf 1G 65
Whitkirk. W Yor 1D 92
Whitland. Carm 3G 43
Whitleigh. Plym 3A 8
Whitletts. S Ayr 2C 116
Whitley. N Yor 2F 93
Whitley. Wilts 5D 35
Whitley Bay. Tyne 2G 115
Whitley Chapel. Nmbd 4C 114
Whitley Heath. Staf 3C 72
Whitley Lower. W Yor 3C 92
Whitley Thorpe. N Yor 2F 93
Whitlock's End. W Mid 3F 61
Whitminster. Glos 5C 48
Whitmore. Dors 2F 15
Whitmore. Staf 1C 72
Whitnage. Devn 1D 12
Whitnash. Warw 4H 61
Whitney. Here 1F 47
Whitrigg. Cumb 4D 112
(nr. Kirkbride)
Whitrigg. Cumb 1D 102
(nr. Torpenhow)
Whitsbury. Hants 1G 15
Whitsome. Bord 4E 131
Whitson. Newp 3G 33

Woodland—Zouch

Woodland. *Dur* 2D **104**
Woodland Head. *Devn* 3A **12**
Woodlands. *Abers* 4E **153**
Woodlands. *Dors* 2F **15**
Woodlands. *Hants* 1B **16**
Woodlands. *Kent* 4G **39**
Woodlands. *N Yor* 4F **99**
Woodlands. *S Yor* 4F **93**
Woodlands Park. *Wind* 4G **37**
Woodlands St Mary. *W Ber* 4B **36**
Woodlane. *Shrp* 3A **72**
Woodlane. *Staf* 3F **73**
Woodleigh. *Devn* 4D **8**
Woodlesford. *W Yor* 2D **92**
Woodley. *G Man* 1D **84**
Woodley. *Wok* 4F **37**
Woodmancote. *Glos* 3E **49**
(nr. Cheltenham)
Woodmancote. *Glos* 5F **49**
(nr. Cirencester)
Woodmancote. *W Sus* 2F **17**
(nr. Chichester)
Woodmancote. *W Sus* 4D **26**
(nr. Henfield)
Woodmancote. *Worc* 1E **49**
Woodmancott. *Hants* 2D **24**
Woodmansey. *E Yor* 1D **94**
Woodmansgreen. *W Sus* 4G **25**
Woodmansterne. *Surr* 5D **39**
Woodmanton. *Devn* 4D **12**
Woodmill. *Staf* 3F **73**
Woodminton. *Wilts* 4F **23**
Woodnesborough. *Kent* 5H **41**
Woodnewton. *Nptn* 1H **63**
Woodnook. *Linc* 2G **75**
Wood Norton. *Norf* 3C **78**
Woodplumpton. *Lanc* 1D **90**
Woodrising. *Norf* 5B **78**
Woodrow. *Cumb* 5D **112**
Woodrow. *Dors* 1C **14**
(nr. Fifehead Neville)
Woodrow. *Dors* 2C **14**
(nr. Hazelbury Bryan)
Wood Row. *W Yor* 2D **93**
Woods Eaves. *Here* 1F **47**
Woodseaves. *Shrp* 2A **72**
Woodseaves. *Staf* 3B **72**
Woodsend. *Wilts* 4H **35**
Woodsetts. *S Yor* 2C **86**
Woodsford. *Dors* 3C **14**
Wood's Green. *E Sus* 2H **27**
Woodshaw. *Wilts* 3F **35**
Woodside. *Aber* 3G **153**
Woodside. *Brac* 3A **38**
Woodside. *Cumb* 1B **102**
Woodside. *Derbs* 1A **74**
Woodside. *Dum* 2B **112**
Woodside. *Dur* 2E **105**
Woodside. *Fife* 3G **137**
Woodside. *Herts* 5C **52**
Woodside. *Per* 5B **144**
Wood Stanway. *Glos* 2F **49**
Woodstock. *Oxon* 4C **50**
Woodstock Slop. *Pemb* 2E **43**
Woodston. *Pet* 1A **64**
Wood Street. *Norf* 3F **79**
Wood Street Village. *Surr* 5A **38**
Woodthorpe. *Derbs* 3B **86**
Woodthorpe. *Leics* 4C **74**
Woodthorpe. *Linc* 2D **88**
Woodthorpe. *York* 5H **99**
Woodton. *Norf* 1E **67**
Woodtown. *Devn* 4E **19**
(nr. Bideford)
Woodtown. *Devn* 4E **19**
(nr. Littleham)
Woodvale. *Mers* 3B **90**
Woodville. *Derbs* 4H **73**
Woodwalton. *Cambs* 2B **64**
Woodwick. *Orkn* 5C **172**
Woodyates. *Dors* 1F **15**
Woody Bay. *Devn* 2G **19**
Woofferton. *Shrp* 4H **59**
Wookey. *Som* 2A **22**
Wookey Hole. *Som* 2A **22**
Wool. *Dors* 4D **14**
Woolacombe. *Devn* 2E **19**
Woolage Green. *Kent* 1G **29**
Woolage Village. *Kent* 5G **41**
Woolaston. *Glos* 2A **34**
Woolavington. *Som* 2G **21**
Woolbeding. *W Sus* 4G **25**
Woolcotts. *Som* 3C **20**
Wooldale. *W Yor* 4B **92**
Wooler. *Nmbd* 2D **121**
Woolfardisworthy. *Devn* 4D **18**
(nr. Bideford)
Woolfardisworthy. *Devn* 2B **12**
(nr. Crediton)
Woolfords. *S Lan* 4D **128**
Woolgarston. *Dors* 4E **15**
Woolhampton. *W Ber* 5D **36**
Woolhope. *Here* 2B **48**
Woolland. *Dors* 2C **14**
Woollard. *Bath* 5B **34**
Woolley. *Bath* 5C **34**
Woolley. *Cambs* 3A **64**
Woolley. *Corn* 1C **10**
Woolley. *Derbs* 4A **86**
Woolley. *W Yor* 3D **92**
Woolley Green. *Wilts* 5D **34**
Woolmere Green. *Worc* 4D **60**
Woolmer Green. *Herts* 4C **52**
Woolminstone. *Som* 2H **13**
Woolpit. *Suff* 4B **66**
Woolridge. *Glos* 3D **48**
Woolscott. *Warw* 4B **62**
Woolsery. *Devn* 4D **18**
Woolsington. *Tyne* 3E **115**
Woolstaston. *Shrp* 1G **59**
Woolsthorpe By Belvoir. *Linc* 2F **75**
Woolsthorpe-by-Colsterworth.
Linc 3G **75**
Woolston. *Devn* 4D **8**
Woolston. *Shrp* 2G **59**
(nr. Church Stretton)
Woolston. *Shrp* 3F **71**
(nr. Oswestry)
Woolston. *Som* 4B **22**
(nr. Wincanton)
Woolston. *Sotn* 1C **16**
Woolston. *Warr* 1A **84**
Woolstone. *Glos* 2E **49**
Woolstone. *Oxon* 3A **36**
Woolston Green. *Devn* 2D **9**
Woolton. *Mers* 2G **83**
Woolton Hill. *Hants* 5C **36**
Woolverstone. *Suff* 2E **55**
Woolverton. *Som* 1C **22**
Woolwell. *Devn* 2B **8**
Woolwich. *G Lon* 3F **39**
Woonton. *Here* 5F **59**
(nr. Kington)
Woonton. *Here* 4H **59**
(nr. Leominster)
Wooperton. *Nmbd* 2E **121**
Woore. *Shrp* 1B **72**
Wooth. *Dors* 3H **13**
Wooton. *Shrp* 2B **60**
Wootton. *Bed* 1A **52**
Wootton. *Hants* 3H **15**
Wootton. *IOW* 3D **16**
Wootton. *Kent* 1G **29**
Wootton. *Nptn* 5E **63**
Wootton. *N Lin* 3D **94**
Wootton. *Oxon* 5C **50**
(nr. Abingdon)
Wootton. *Oxon* 4C **50**
(nr. Woodstock)
Wootton. *Shrp* 3G **59**
(nr. Ludlow)
Wootton. *Shrp* 3F **71**
(nr. Oswestry)
Wootton. *Staf* 3C **72**
(nr. Eccleshall)
Wootton. *Staf* 1F **73**
(nr. Ellastone)
Wootton Bassett. *Wilts* 3F **35**
Wootton Bridge. *IOW* 3D **16**
Wootton Common. *IOW* 3D **16**
Wootton Courtenay. *Som* 2C **20**
Wootton Fitzpaine. *Dors* 3G **13**
Wootton Rivers. *Wilts* 5G **35**
Woottons. *Staf* 2E **73**
Wootton St Lawrence. *Hants* 1D **24**
Wootton Wawen. *Warw* 4F **61**
Worcester. *Worc* 5C **60** & **214**
Worcester Park. *G Lon* 4D **38**
Wordsley. *W Mid* 2C **60**
Worfield. *Shrp* 1B **60**
Work. *Orkn* 6D **172**
Workhouse Green. *Suff* 2C **54**
Workington. *Cumb* 2A **102**
Worksop. *Notts* 3C **86**
Worlaby. *N Lin* 3D **94**
Worlds End. *Hants* 1E **17**
Worldsend. *Shrp* 1G **59**
World's End. *W Ber* 4C **36**
Worlds End. *W Mid* 2F **61**
World's End. *W Sus* 4E **27**
Worle. *N Som* 5G **33**
Worleston. *Ches E* 5A **84**
Worley. *Glos* 2D **34**
Worlingham. *Suff* 1G **67**
Worlington. *Suff* 3F **65**
Worlingworth. *Suff* 4E **67**
Wormbridge. *Here* 2H **47**
Wormegay. *Norf* 4F **77**
Wormelow Tump. *Here* 2H **47**
Wormhill. *Derbs* 3F **85**
Wormingford. *Essx* 2C **54**
Worminghall. *Buck* 5E **51**
Wormington. *Glos* 2F **49**
Worminster. *Som* 2A **22**
Wormit. *Fife* 1F **137**
Wormleighton. *Warw* 5B **62**
Wormley. *Herts* 5D **52**
Wormley. *Surr* 2A **26**
Wormshill. *Kent* 5C **40**
Wormsley. *Here* 1H **47**
Worplesdon. *Surr* 5A **38**
Worrall. *S Yor* 1H **85**
Worsbrough. *S Yor* 4D **92**
Worsley. *G Man* 4F **91**
Worstead. *Norf* 3F **79**
Worsthorne. *Lanc* 1G **91**
Worston. *Lanc* 5G **97**
Worth. *Kent* 5H **41**
Worth. *W Sus* 2E **27**
Wortham. *Suff* 3C **66**
Worthen. *Shrp* 5F **71**
Worthenbury. *Wrex* 1G **71**
Worthing. *Norf* 4B **78**
Worthing. *W Sus* 5C **26**
Worthington. *Leics* 3B **74**
Worth Matravers. *Dors* 5E **15**
Worting. *Hants* 1E **24**
Wortley. *Glos* 2C **34**
Wortley. *S Yor* 1H **85**
Wortley. *W Yor* 1C **92**
Worton. *N Yor* 5C **104**
Worton. *Wilts* 1E **23**
Wortwell. *Norf* 2E **67**
Wotherton. *Shrp* 5E **71**
Wothorpe. *Nptn* 5H **75**
Wotter. *Devn* 2B **8**
Wotton. *Glos* 4D **48**
Wotton. *Surr* 1C **26**
Wotton-under-Edge. *Glos* 2C **34**
Wotton Underwood. *Buck* 4E **51**
Wouldham. *Kent* 4B **40**
Wrabness. *Essx* 2E **55**
Wrafton. *Devn* 3E **19**
Wragby. *Linc* 3A **88**
Wragby. *W Yor* 3E **93**
Wramplingham. *Norf* 5D **78**
Wrangbrook. *W Yor* 3E **93**
Wrangle. *Linc* 5D **88**
Wrangle Lowgate. *Linc* 5D **88**
Wrangway. *Som* 1E **13**
Wrantage. *Som* 4G **21**
Wrawby. *N Lin* 4D **94**
Wraxall. *N Som* 4H **33**
Wraxall. *Som* 3B **22**
Wray. *Lanc* 3F **97**
Wraysbury. *Wind* 3B **38**
Wrayton. *Lanc* 2F **97**
Wrea Green. *Lanc* 1B **90**
Wreay. *Cumb* 5F **113**
(nr. Carlisle)
Wreay. *Cumb* 2F **103**
(nr. Penrith)
Wrecclesham. *Surr* 2G **25**
Wrecsam. *Wrex*
5F **83** & **Wrexham 214**
Wrekenton. *Tyne* 4F **115**
Wrelton. *N Yor* 1B **100**
Wrenbury. *Ches E* 1H **71**
Wreningham. *Norf* 1D **66**
Wrentham. *Suff* 2G **67**
Wrenthorpe. *W Yor* 2D **92**
Wrentnall. *Shrp* 5G **71**
Wressle. *E Yor* 1H **93**
Wressle. *N Lin* 4C **94**
Wrestlingworth. *C Beds* 1C **52**
Wretton. *Norf* 1F **65**
Wrexham. *Wrex* 5F **83** & **214**
Wrexham Industrial Estate.
Wrex 1F **71**
Wreyland. *Devn* 4A **12**
Wrickton. *Shrp* 2A **60**
Wrightlington Bar. *Lanc* 3D **90**
Wright's Green. *Essx* 4F **53**
Wrinehill. *Staf* 1B **72**
Wrington. *N Som* 5H **33**
Writtle. *Essx* 5G **53**
Wrockwardine. *Telf* 4A **72**
Wroot. *N Lin* 4H **93**
Wrotham. *Kent* 5H **39**
Wrotham Heath. *Kent* 5H **39**
Wroughton. *Swin* 3G **35**
Wroxall. *IOW* 4D **16**
Wroxall. *Warw* 3G **61**
Wroxeter. *Shrp* 5H **71**
Wroxham. *Norf* 4F **79**
Wroxton. *Oxon* 1C **50**
Wyaston. *Derbs* 1F **73**
Wyatt's Green. *Essx* 1G **39**
Wybers Wood. *NE Lin* 4F **95**
Wyberton. *Linc* 1C **76**
Wyboston. *Bed* 5A **64**
Wybunbury. *Ches E* 1A **72**
Wychbold. *Worc* 4D **60**
Wych Cross. *E Sus* 2F **27**
Wychnor. *Staf* 4F **73**
Wychnor Bridges. *Staf* 4F **73**
Wyck. *Hants* 3F **25**
Wyck Hill. *Glos* 3G **49**
Wyck Rissington. *Glos* 3G **49**
Wycliffe. *Dur* 3E **105**
Wycombe Marsh. *Buck* 2G **37**
Wyddial. *Herts* 2D **52**
Wye. *Kent* 1E **29**
Wyesham. *Mon* 4A **48**
Wyfold Grange. *Oxon* 3E **37**
Wyfordby. *Leics* 4E **75**
Wyke. *Devn* 3B **12**
Wyke. *Dors* 4C **22**
Wyke. *Shrp* 5A **72**
Wyke. *Surr* 5A **38**
Wyke. *W Yor* 2B **92**
Wyke Champflower. *Som* 3B **22**
Wykeham. *Linc* 3B **76**
Wykeham. *N Yor* 2C **100**
(nr. Malton)
Wykeham. *N Yor* 1D **100**
(nr. Scarborough)
Wyken. *Shrp* 1B **60**
Wyken. *W Mid* 2A **62**
Wyke Regis. *Dors* 5B **14**
Wyke, The. *Shrp* 5B **72**
Wykey. *Shrp* 3F **71**
Wykin. *Leics* 1B **62**
Wylam. *Nmbd* 3E **115**
Wylde Green. *W Mid* 1F **61**
Wylye. *Wilts* 3F **23**
Wymering. *Port* 2E **17**
Wymeswold. *Leics* 3D **74**
Wymington. *Bed* 4G **63**
Wymondham. *Leics* 4F **75**
Wymondham. *Norf* 5D **78**
Wyndham. *B'end* 2C **32**
Wynford Eagle. *Dors* 3A **14**
Wyng. *Orkn* 8C **172**
Wynyard Village. *Stoc T* 2B **106**
Wyre Piddle. *Worc* 1E **49**
Wysall. *Notts* 3D **74**
Wyson. *Here* 4H **59**
Wythall. *Worc* 3E **61**
Wytham. *Oxon* 5C **50**
Wythenshawe. *G Man* 2C **84**
Wythop Mill. *Cumb* 2C **102**
Wyton. *Cambs* 3B **64**
Wyton. *E Yor* 1E **95**
Wyverstone. *Suff* 4C **66**
Wyverstone Street. *Suff* 4C **66**
Wyville. *Linc* 3F **75**
Wyvis Lodge. *High* 1G **157**

Y

Yaddlethorpe. *N Lin* 4B **94**
Yafford. *IOW* 4C **16**
Yafforth. *N Yor* 5A **106**
Yalding. *Kent* 5A **40**
Yanley. *N Som* 5A **34**
Yanwath. *Cumb* 2G **103**
Yanworth. *Glos* 4F **49**
Yapham. *E Yor* 4B **100**
Yapton. *W Sus* 5A **26**
Yarburgh. *Linc* 1C **88**
Yarcombe. *Devn* 2F **13**
Yarde. *Som* 3D **20**
Yardley. *W Mid* 2F **61**
Yardley Gobion. *Nptn* 1F **51**
Yardley Hastings. *Nptn* 5F **63**
Yardley Wood. *W Mid* 2F **61**
Yardro. *Powy* 5E **58**
Yarhampton. *Worc* 4B **60**
Yarkhill. *Here* 1B **48**
Yarlet. *Staf* 3D **72**
Yarley. *Som* 2A **22**
Yarlington. *Som* 4B **22**
Yarm. *Stoc T* 3B **106**
Yarmouth. *IOW* 4B **16**
Yarnbrook. *Wilts* 1D **22**
Yarnfield. *Staf* 2C **72**
Yarnscombe. *Devn* 4F **19**
Yarnton. *Oxon* 4C **50**
Yarpole. *Here* 4G **59**
Yarrow. *Nmbd* 1A **114**
Yarrow. *Bord* 2F **119**
Yarrow. *Som* 2G **21**
Yarrow Feus. *Bord* 2F **119**
Yarrow Ford. *Bord* 1G **119**
Yarsop. *Here* 1H **47**
Yarwell. *Nptn* 1H **63**
Yate. *S Glo* 3C **34**
Yateley. *Hants* 5G **37**
Yatesbury. *Wilts* 4F **35**
Yattendon. *W Ber* 4D **36**
Yatton. *Here* 4G **59**
(nr. Leominster)
Yatton. *Here* 2B **48**
(nr. Ross-on-Wye)
Yatton. *N Som* 5H **33**
Yatton Keynell. *Wilts* 4D **34**
Yaverland. *IOW* 4E **16**
Yawl. *Devn* 3G **13**
Yaxham. *Norf* 4C **78**
Yaxley. *Cambs* 1A **64**
Yaxley. *Suff* 3D **66**
Yazor. *Here* 1H **47**
Y Bala. *Gwyn* 2B **70**
Y Bont-Faen. *V Glam* 4C **32**
Y Clun. *Neat* 5B **46**
Y Dref. *Gwyn* 2D **69**
Y Drenewydd. *Powy* 1D **58**
Yeading. *G Lon* 2C **38**
Yeadon. *W Yor* 5E **98**
Yealand Conyers. *Lanc* 2E **97**
Yealand Redmayne. *Lanc* 2E **97**
Yealmpton. *Devn* 3B **8**
Yearby. *Red C* 2D **106**
Yearngill. *Cumb* 5C **112**
Yearsett. *Here* 5B **60**
Yearsley. *N Yor* 2H **99**
Yeaton. *Shrp* 4G **71**
Yeaveley. *Derbs* 1F **73**
Yeavering. *Nmbd* 1D **120**
Yedingham. *N Yor* 2C **100**
Yeldersley Hollies. *Derbs* 1G **73**
Yelford. *Oxon* 5B **50**
Yelland. *Devn* 3E **19**
Yelling. *Cambs* 4B **64**
Yelsted. *Kent* 4C **40**
Yelvertoft. *Nptn* 3C **62**
Yelverton. *Devn* 2B **8**
Yelverton. *Norf* 5E **79**
Yenston. *Som* 4C **22**
Yeoford. *Devn* 3A **12**
Yeolmbridge. *Corn* 4D **10**
Yeo Mill. *Devn* 4B **20**
Yeovil. *Som* 1A **14**
Yeovil Marsh. *Som* 1A **14**
Yeovilton. *Som* 4A **22**
Yerbeston. *Pemb* 4E **43**
Yesnaby. *Orkn* 6B **172**
Yetlington. *Nmbd* 4E **121**
Yetminster. *Dors* 1A **14**
Yett. *N Lan* 4A **128**
Yett. *S Ayr* 2D **116**
Yettington. *Devn* 4D **12**
Yetts o' Muckhart. *Clac* 3C **136**
Y Fali. *IOA* 3B **80**
Y Felinheli. *Gwyn* 4E **81**
Y Fenni. *Mon* 4G **47**
Y Ferwig. *Cdgn* 1B **44**
Y Fflint. *Flin* 3E **83**
Y Ffor. *Gwyn* 2C **68**
Y Gelli Gandryll. *Powy* 1F **47**
Yielden. *Bed* 4H **63**
Yieldshields. *S Lan* 4B **128**
Yiewsley. *G Lon* 2B **38**
Yinstay. *Orkn* 6E **172**
Ynysboeth. *Rhon* 2D **32**
Ynysddu. *Cphy* 2E **33**
Ynysforgan. *Swan* 3F **31**
Ynyshir. *Rhon* 2D **32**
Ynyslas. *Cdgn* 1F **57**
Ynysmaerdy. *Rhon* 3D **32**
Ynysmeudwy. *Neat* 5H **45**
Ynystawe. *Swan* 5G **45**
Ynyswen. *Powy* 4B **46**
Ynys-wen. *Rhon* 2C **32**
Ynys y Barri. *V Glam* 5E **32**
Ynysybwl. *Rhon* 2D **32**
Ynysymaerdy. *Neat* 3G **31**
Yockenthwaite. *N Yor* 2B **98**
Yockleton. *Shrp* 4G **71**
Yokefleet. *E Yor* 2B **94**
Yoker. *Glas* 3G **127**
Yonder Bognie. *Abers* 4C **160**
Yonderton. *Abers* 5G **161**
York. *York* 4A **100** & **214**
Yorkletts. *Kent* 4E **41**
Yorkley. *Glos* 5B **48**
Yorton. *Shrp* 3H **71**
Yorton Heath. *Shrp* 3H **71**
Youlgreave. *Derbs* 4G **85**
Youlthorpe. *E Yor* 4B **100**
Youlton. *N Yor* 3G **99**
Young's End. *Essx* 4H **53**
Young Wood. *Linc* 3A **88**
Yoxall. *Staf* 4F **73**
Yoxford. *Suff* 4F **67**
Yr Hob. *Flin* 5F **83**
Y Rhws. *V Glam* 5D **32**
Yr Wyddgrug. *Flin* 4E **83**
Ysbyty Cynfyn. *Cdgn* 3G **57**
Ysbyty Ifan. *Cnwy* 1H **69**
Ysbyty Ystwyth. *Cdgn* 3G **57**
Ysceifiog. *Flin* 3D **82**
Yspitty. *Carm* 3E **31**
Ystalyfera. *Neat* 5A **46**
Ystrad. *Rhon* 2C **32**
Ystrad Aeron. *Cdgn* 5E **57**
Ystradfellte. *Powy* 4C **46**
Ystradffin. *Carm* 1A **46**
Ystradgynlais. *Powy* 4A **46**
Ystradmeurig. *Cdgn* 4G **57**
Ystrad Mynach. *Cphy* 2E **33**
Ystradowen. *Carm* 4A **46**
Ystradowen. *V Glam* 4D **32**
Ystumtuen. *Cdgn* 3G **57**
Ythanbank. *Abers* 5G **161**
Ythanwells. *Abers* 5D **160**
Y Trallwng. *Powy* 5E **70**
Y Tymbl. *Carm* 4A **48**
Y Waun. *Wrex* 2E **71**

Z

Zeal Monachorum. *Devn* 2H **11**
Zeals. *Wilts* 3C **22**
Zelah. *Corn* 3C **6**
Zennor. *Corn* 3B **4**
Zouch. *Notts* 3C **74**

(1) A strict alphabetical order is used e.g. Benmore Botanic Gdn. follows Ben Macdui but precedes Ben Nevis.

(2) Entries shown without a main map index reference have the name of the appropriate Town Plan and its page number; e.g. American Mus. in Britain, The (BA2 7BD) .... Bath 187
The Town Plan title is not given when this is included in the name of the Place of Interest.

(3) Entries are in italics are not named on the map but are shown with a symbol only.
Where this occurs the nearest town or village is also given, unless that name is already included in the name of the Place of Interest.

SAT NAV POSTCODES

Postcodes (in brackets) are included as a navigation aid to assist Sat Nav users and are supplied on this basis. It should be noted that postcodes have been selected by their proximity to the Place of Interest and that they may not form part of the actual postal address.
Drivers should follow the Tourist Brown Signs when available.

ABBREVIATIONS USED IN THIS INDEX

Garden : Gdn.	National : Nat
Gardens : Gdns.	Park : Pk.
Museum : Mus.	

INDEX

Cruachan Power Station—Lancaster Castle

Cruachan Power Station (PA33 1AN) 1H **133**
Culloden Battle Site (IV2 5EU) 4B **158**
Culross Palace (KY12 8JH) 1C **128**
Culzean Castle (KA19 8LE) 3B **116**
Curraghs Wildlife Pk. (IM7 5EA) 2C **108**
Cymer Abbey (LL40 2HE) 4G **69**

D

Dalemain (CA11 0HB) 2F **103**
Dales Countryside Mus. (DL8 3NT) 5B **104**
Dallas Dhu Historic Distillery (IV36 2RR) 3E **159**
Dalmeny House (EH30 9TQ) 2E **129**
Dapdune Wharf & Vis. Cen. (GU1 4PR) **Guildford 197**
Darby Houses (TF8 7DQ) 5A **72**
Dartington Crystal (EX38 7AN) 1E **11**
Dartington Hall Gdns. (TQ9 6EL) 2E **9**
Dartmoor Nat. Pk. (TQ13 9JQ) 4F **11**
Dartmoor Zoological Pk. (PL7 5DG) 3B **8**
Dartmouth Castle (TQ6 0JN) 3E **9**
Dawyck Botanic Gdn. (EH45 9JU) 1D **118**
*Deal Castle (CT14 7BA) 5H **41***
Dean Castle (KA3 1XB) 1D **116**
Dean Forest Railway (GL15 4ET) 5B **48**
Deene Pk. (NN17 3EW) 1G **63**
Deep Sea World (KY11 1JR) 1E **129**
Deep, The (HU1 4DP) **Hull 199**
Delamere Forest Pk. (CW8 2JD) 3H **83**
Delgatie Castle (AB53 5TD) 3E **161**
*Denbigh Castle (LL16 3NB) 4C **82***
Devil's Dyke (BN45 7DE) 4D **26**
Devil's Punch Bowl (GU26 6AB) 3G **25**
Dewa Roman Experience (CH1 1NL) **Chester 192**
DH Lawrence Birthplace Mus. (NG16 3AW) 1B **74**
Dickens House Mus. (CT10 1QS) 4H **41**
*Didcot Railway Centre (OX11 7NJ) 2D **36***
Dinefwr Castle (SA19 6PF) 3G **45**
Dinorwig Power Station (LL55 4UR) 5E **81**
Dinosaur Adventure Pk. (NR9 5JW) 4D **78**
Dinosaur Mus., The (DT1 1EW) 3B **14**
Dirleton Castle (EH39 5ER) 1B **130**
Discovery Mus. (Newcastle) (NE1 4JA) **205**
Discovery Point & RRS Discovery (DD1 4XA) **Dundee 194**
Dock Mus., The (LA14 2PW) 3A **96**
Doddington Hall (LN6 4RU) 4F **87**
Doddington Place Gdns. (ME9 0BB) 5D **40**
Dolaucothi Gold Mines (SA19 8RR) 2G **45**
Dolbadarn Castle (LL55 4SU) 5E **81**
Dolforwyn Castle (SY15 6JH) 1D **58**
*Dolwyddelan Castle (LL25 0JD) 5G **81***
Domestic Fowl Trust, The (WR11 7QZ) 1G **49**
Donkey Sanctuary, The (EX10 0NU) 4E **13**
*Donnington Castle (RG14 2LE) 5C **36***
Dorfold Hall (CW5 8LD) 5A **84**
Dorothy Clive Gdn. (TF9 4EU) 2B **72**
Doune Castle (FK16 6EA) 3G **135**
Dove Cottage (LA22 9SH) 4E **103**
Dove Dale (DE6 1NL) 5F **85**
Dover Castle (CT16 1HU) **193**
Down House (BR6 7JT) 4F **39**
Dozmary Pool (PL15 7TP) 5B **10**
Drayton Manor Theme Pk. (B78 3TW) 5F **73**
Drum Castle (AB31 5EY) 3E **153**
Drumlanrig Castle Gdns. (DG3 4AQ) 5A **118**
Drummond Castle Gdns. (PH5 2AA) 2H **135**
Drusillas Pk. (BN26 5QS) 5G **27**
Dryburgh Abbey (TD6 0RQ) 1H **119**
*Dryslwyn Castle (SA32 8JQ) 3F **45***
Duart Castle (PA64 6AP) 5B **140**
Dudmaston Hall (WV15 6QN) 2B **60**
Duff House Country Gallery (AB45 3SX) 2D **160**
Duffus Castle (IV30 5RH) 2F **159**
Dukeries, The (S80 3BT) 3D **86**
Dumbarton Castle (G82 1JJ) 2F **127**
Dunblane Cathedral (FK15 0AQ) 3G **135**
Duncombe Pk. (YO62 5EB) 1A **100**
*Dundonald Castle (KA2 9HD) 1C **116***
Dundrennan Abbey (DG6 4QX) 5E **111**
Dunfermline Abbey & Palace (KY12 7PE) 1D **129**
Dunfermline Abbey & Palace (KY12 7PE) 1D **129**
Dungeness Nuclear Power Station (TN29 9PP) 4E **29**
Dungeon Ghyll Force (LA22 9JY) 4D **102**
Dunge Valley Rhododendron Gdns. (SK23 7RF) 3D **85**
Dunham Massey (WA14 4SJ) 2B **84**
Dunkery Beacon (TA24 7AT) 2B **20**
Dunnet Head (KW14 8XS) 1D **169**
Dunninald (DD10 9TD) 3G **145**
Dunnottar Castle (AB39 2TL) 5F **153**
Dunrobin Castle (KW10 6SF) 3F **165**
Dunstaffnage Castle (PA37 1PZ) 5C **140**
Dunstanburgh Castle (NE66 3TG) 2G **121**
*Dunster Castle (TA24 6SL) 2C **20***
Dunvegan Castle (IV55 8WF) 4B **154**
Durdle Door (BH20 5PU) 4D **14**
Durham Castle (DH1 3RW) **194**
Durham Cathedral (DH1 3EH) **194**
Dyffryn Gdns. (CF5 6SU) 4D **32**
Dylan Thomas Boathouse, The (SA33 4SD) 3H **43**
Dyrham Pk. (SN14 8ER) 4C **34**

E

Easby Abbey (DL10 7JU) 4E **105**
East Anglian Railway Mus. (CO6 2DS) 3B **54**
East Bergholt Place Gdn. (CO7 6UP) 2D **54**
East Kent Railway (CT15 7PD) 1G **29**
East Lambrook Manor Gdns. (TA13 5HH) 1H **13**
East Lancashire Railway (BL9 0EY) 2G **91**
Eastnor Castle (HR8 1RD) 2C **48**
Easton Farm Pk. (IP13 0EQ) 5E **67**
East Riddlesden Hall (BD20 5EL) 5C **98**
East Somerset Railway (BA4 4QP) 2B **22**
Ebbsfleet Saxon Landing Site (CT12 5DL) 4H **41**
Eden Project (PL24 2SG) 3E **7**
Edinburgh Castle (EH1 2NG) **194**
Edinburgh Cathedral (EH1 1RE) **194**
Edinburgh Zoo (EH12 6TS) 2F **129**
Edzell Castle (DD9 7UE) 2E **145**
Egglestone Abbey (DL12 9TN) 3D **104**
Eilean Donan Castle (IV40 8DX) 1A **148**
Elcho Castle (PH2 8QQ) 1D **136**
Elgar Birthplace Mus. (WR2 6RH) 5C **60**
Elgin Cathedral (IV30 1EL) 2G **159**
Eltham Palace (SE9 5QE) 3F **39**
Elton Hall (PE8 6SH) 1H **63**
*Ely Cathedral (CB7 4DL) 2E **65***
Embsay & Bolton Abbey Steam Railway (BD23 6AF) 4C **98**
Emmetts Gdn. (TN14 6BA) 5F **39**
Enginuity (TF8 7DQ) 5A **72**
Erddig (LL13 0YT) 1F **71**
Escot Gdns. (EX11 1LU) 3D **12**
*Etal Castle (TD12 4TN) 1D **120***
*Eureka! The Mus. for Children, Halifax (HX1 2NE) 2A **92***
Euston Hall (IP24 2QW) 3A **66**
Ewloe Castle (CH5 3BZ) 4E **83**
Exbury Gdns. (SO45 1AZ) 2C **16**
Exeter Cathedral (EX1 1HS) **195**
Exmoor Nat. Pk. (TA22 9HL) 2A **20**
Eyam Hall (S32 5QW) 3G **85**
Eye Castle (IP23 7AP) 3D **66**
Eynsford Castle (DA4 0AA) 4G **39**

F

Fairbourne Steam Railway (LL38 2PZ) 4F **69**
Fairhaven Woodland & Water Gdn. (NR13 6DZ) 4F **79**
Falkirk Wheel (FK1 4RS) 1B **128**
Falkland Palace (KY15 7BU) 3E **137**
Falls of Glomach (IV40 8DS) 1C **148**
*Farleigh Hungerford Castle (BA2 7RS) 1D **22***
Farmland Mus. & Denny Abbey, The (CB25 9PQ) 4D **65**
Farnborough Hall (OX17 1DU) 1C **50**
Farne Islands (NE68 7SY) 1G **121**
Farnham Castle (GU9 0AG) 2G **25**
Felbrigg Hall (NR11 8PR) 2D **78**
Fell Foot Pk. (LA12 8NN) 1C **96**
Ferniehirst Castle (TD8 6NX) 3A **120**
Ffestiniog Power Station (LL41 3TP) 1F **69**
Ffestiniog Railway (LL49 9NF) 1F **69**
Ffos Las Racecourse (SA17 4DE) 5E **45**
Fiddleford Manor (DT10 2BU) 1D **14**
Finchale Priory (DH1 5SH) 5F **115**
Finchcocks (TN17 1HH) 2A **28**
Finch Foundry (EX20 2NW) 3G **11**
Fingal's Cave (PA73 6NA) 5E **138**
Finlaystone Country Estate (PA14 6TJ) 2E **127**
Firle Place (BN8 6LP) 5F **27**
Fishbourne Roman Palace (PO19 3QR) 2G **17**
Fitzwilliam Mus. (CB2 1RB) **Cambridge 191**
Flambards Experience, The (TR13 0QA) 4D **4**
Flamingo Land (YO17 6UX) 2B **100**
Fleet Air Arm Mus. (BA22 8HT) 4A **22**
*Flint Castle (CH6 5PE) 3E **83***
Floors Castle & Gdns. (TD5 7SF) 1B **120**
*Fonmon Castle (CF62 3ZN) 5D **32***
Forde Abbey (TA20 4LU) 2G **13**
Ford Green Hall (ST6 1NG) 5C **84**
Forest of Dean (GL15 4SL) 5B **48**
Fort George (IV2 7TD) 3B **158**
Forth Bridge (EH30 9TB) 2E **129**
Fountains Abbey & Studley Royal Water Gdn. (HG4 3DY) 3E **99**
Foxfield Steam Railway (ST11 9BG) 1D **72**
Foxton Staircase Locks (LE16 7RA) 2D **62**
Framlingham Castle (IP13 9BP) 4E **67**
Froghall Wharf (ST10 2HH) 1E **73**
Furness Abbey (LA13 0PG) 2B **96**
Furzey Gdns. (SO43 7GL) 1A **16**
Future World @ Goonhilly (TR12 6LQ) 4E **5**
Fyne Court Visitor Centre (TA5 2EQ) 3F **21**
Fyvie Castle (AB53 8JS) 5E **161**

G

Gainsborough Old Hall (DN21 2NB) 1F **87**
Gainsborough's House Mus. (CO10 2EU) 1B **54**
Gallery of Modern Art (G1 3AH) **Glasgow 196**
Galloway Forest Pk. (DG8 6TA) 1B **110**
Galloway House Gdns. (DG8 8HF) 5B **110**
Galloway Wildlife Conservation Pk. (DG6 4XX) 4E **111**
Garden House, The (PL20 7LQ) 2A **8**
Garden Organic Ryton (CV8 3LG) 3B **62**
Garden Organic Yalding (ME18 6EX) 1A **28**
Gardens of the Rose (AL2 3NR) 5B **52**
Gaulden Manor Gdns. (TA4 3PN) 3E **20**
Gawsworth Hall (SK11 9RN) 4C **84**
Gawthorpe Hall (BB12 8UA) 1G **91**
Geevor Tin Mine Heritage Centre (TR19 7EW) 3A **4**
George Stephenson's Birthplace (NE41 8BP) 3E **115**
Georgian House (EH2 4DR) **Edinburgh 194**
Gilbert White's House (GU34 3JH) 3F **25**
Gisborough Priory (TS14 6BU) 3D **106**
Gladstone Pottery Mus. (ST3 1PQ) 1D **72**
Gladstone's Land (EH1 2NT) **Edinburgh 194**
Glamis Castle (DD8 1QJ) 4C **144**
Glasgow Mus. of Transport (G3 8DP) **196**
Glastonbury Abbey (BA6 9EL) 3A **22**
Glastonbury Tor (BA6 8BG) 3A **22**
Glenarn Gdn. (G84 8LL) 1D **126**
Glenbuchat Castle (AB36 8TN) 2A **152**
Glencoe Gorge (PH50 4SG) 3F **141**
Glendurgan Gdn. (TR11 5JZ) 4E **5**
Glenfinnan Monument (PH37 4LT) 5B **148**
Glenluce Abbey (DG8 0LW) 4G **109**
Glenmore Forest Pk. (PH22 1QT) 3D **150**
Glenwhan Gdns. (DG9 8PH) 4G **109**
Gloucester Cathedral (GL1 2LR) **196**
Gloucestershire Warwickshire Railway (GL54 5DT) 2F **49**
Glynde Place (BN8 6SX) 5F **27**
Godinton House & Gdns. (TN23 3BP) 1D **28**
Godolphin House (TR13 9RE) 3D **4**
Goodnestone Pk. Gdns. (CT3 1PL) 5G **41**
*Goodrich Castle (HR9 6HY) 3A **48***
Goodwood House (PO18 0PX) 2G **17**
Gordale Scar (BD23 4DL) 3B **98**
Gorge, Museum of The (TF8 7NH) 5A **72**
Gosford House (EH32 0PX) 2A **130**
Grampian Transport Mus. (AB33 8AE) 2C **152**
Grasmere (LA22 9RJ) 4E **103**
Graves Gallery (S1 1XZ) **Sheffield 210**
Graythwaite Hall Gdns. (LA12 8BA) 5E **103**
Great Central Railway (LE11 1RW) 4C **74**
Great Chalfield Manor (SN12 8NH) 5D **34**
Great Comp Gdn. (TN15 8QS) 5H **39**
Great Dixter (TN31 6PH) 3C **28**
Greenbank House & Gdn. (G76 8RB) 4G **127**
Greenknowe Tower (TD3 6JL) 5C **130**
Gretna Green Old Blacksmith's Shop Centre (DG16 5EA) 3E **112**
Grey Mare's Tail Waterfall (DG10 9LH) 3D **118**
Greys Court (RG9 4PG) 3F **37**
Grimes Graves (IP26 5DE) 1H **65**
Grimspound (PL20 6TB) 4H **11**
Grimsthorpe Castle (PE10 0LZ) 3H **75**
Grizedale Forest Pk. (LA22 0QJ) 5E **103**
Groombridge Place Gdns. & Enchanted Forest (TN3 9QG) 2G **27**
Grove House & Gdns., The (IM8 3UA) 2D **108**
*Gullivers Kingdom Theme Pk., Matlock Bath (DE4 3PG) 5G **85***
Gulliver's (MK15 0DT) **Milton Keynes 204**
Gulliver's World (WA5 9YZ) 1H **83**
Gunby Hall (PE23 5SS) 4D **88**
Gwili Steam Railway (SA33 6HT) 3E **45**
Gwydir Castle (LL26 0PN) 4G **81**

H

Haddo House (AB41 7EQ) 5F **161**
Haddon Hall (DE45 1LA) 4G **85**
Hadleigh Castle (SS7 2AR) 2C **40**
Hadrian's Wall (NE47 6NN) 3A **114**
Hagley Hall (DY9 9LG) 2D **60**
Hailes Abbey (GL54 5PB) 2F **49**
Hailes Castle (EH41 3SB) 2B **130**
Hall i' th' Wood Mus. (BL1 8UA) 3F **91**
Hall Place (DA5 1PQ) 3G **39**
Hamerton Zoo Pk. (PE28 5RE) 2A **64**
Ham House (TW10 7RS) 3C **38**
Hammerwood Pk. (RH19 3QE) 2F **27**
Hampden Experience, The (G42 9AY) 3G **127**
Hampton Court Palace (KT8 9AU) 4C **38**
Hamptworth Lodge (SP5 2EA) 1H **15**
Hanbury Hall (WR9 7EA) 4D **60**
Hardknott (Mediobogdum) Roman Fort (LA20 6EQ) 4D **102**
Hardwick Hall (S44 5QJ) 4B **86**
Hardy Monument (DT2 9HY) 4B **14**
Hare Hill (SK10 4QA) 3C **84**
Harewood House (LS17 9LG) 5F **99**
*Harlech Castle (LL46 2YH) 2E **69***
Harley Gallery, The (S80 3LW) 3C **86**
Hartland Abbey (EX39 6DT) 4C **18**
Harvington Hall (DY10 4LR) 3C **60**
Harwich Redoubt (CO12 3NL) 2F **55**
Hatchlands Pk. (GU4 7RT) 5B **38**
Hatfield Forest (CM22 7TR) 4F **53**
Hatfield House (AL9 5NQ) 5C **52**
Haughley Pk. (IP14 3JY) 4C **66**
Haughmond Abbey (SY4 4RW) 4H **71**
*Haverfordwest Castle (SA61 2BW) 3D **42***
Haverfordwest Priory (SA61 1RN) 3D **42**
Hawk Conservancy, The (SP11 8DY) 2B **24**
*Head of Steam - Darlington Railway Museum (DL3 6ST) 3F **105***
Heale Gdns. (SP4 6NT) 3G **23**
Heaton Hall (M25 2SW) 4G **91**
Hedingham Castle (CO9 3DJ) 2A **54**
Heights of Abraham Country Pk. (DE4 3PD) 5G **85**
Hellen's (HR8 2LY) 2B **48**
Helmingham Hall Gdns. (IP14 6EF) 5D **66**
Helmshore Mills Textile Mus. (BB4 4NP) 2F **91**
*Helmsley Castle (YO62 5AB) 1A **100***
Helvellyn (CA12 4TP) 3E **103**
Heptonstall Mus. (HX7 7PL) 2H **91**
Hereford Cathedral (HR1 2NG) **197**
Hereford Cider Mus. (HR4 0LW) 2A **48**
Hergest Croft Gdns. (HR5 3EG) 5E **59**
Heritage Motor Centre (CV35 0BJ) 5A **62**
Hermitage Castle (TD9 0LU) 5H **119**
Herstmonceux Castle Gdns. (BN27 1RN) 4H **27**
Hestercombe Gdns. (TA2 8LG) 4F **21**
*Hever Castle (TN8 7NG) 1F **27***
Hexham Abbey (NE46 3NB) 3C **114**
Hidcote Manor Gdn. (GL55 6LR) 1G **49**
High Beeches Gdns. (RH17 6HQ) 2D **27**
Highclere Castle (RG20 9RN) 1C **24**
Highland Wildlife Pk. (PH21 1NL) 3C **150**
Hill House, The (G84 9AJ) 1D **126**
Hill of Tarvit Mansionhouse & Gdn. (KY15 5PB) 2F **137**
Hill Top (LA22 0LF) 5E **103**
Hinton Ampner (SO24 0LA) 4D **24**
Hirsel Country Pk., The (TD12 4LP) 5E **131**
Historic Dockyard Chatham, The (ME4 4TZ) **Medway 204**
HMS Victory (PO1 3LJ) **Portsmouth 209**
HMS Warrior 1860, HM Naval Base (PO1 3QX) **Portsmouth 209**
Hodnet Hall Gdns. (TF9 3NN) 3A **72**
Hoghton Tower (PR5 0SH) 2E **90**
Hog's Back (GU3 1AQ) 1A **26**
Holburne Mus. of Art, Bath (BA2 4DB) **Bath 187**
Holdenby House Gdns. (NN6 8DJ) 4D **62**
Holehird Gdns. (LA23 1NP) 4F **103**
Holker Hall (LA11 7PL) 2C **96**
Holkham Hall (NR23 1AB) 1A **78**
Hollycombe Steam Collection (GU30 7LP) 4G **25**
Holme Fen Nat. Nature Reserve (PE7 3PT) 2B **64**
Holme Pierrepont Hall (NG12 2LD) 2D **74**
Holst Birthplace Mus. (GL52 2AY) **Cheltenham 192**
Holy Jesus Hospital (NE1 2AS) **Newcastle 205**
Holyrood Abbey (EH8 8DX) **Edinburgh 194**
Hopetoun House (EH30 9SL) 2D **129**
Hop Farm, The (TN12 6PY) 1A **28**
Horton Court (BS37 6QR) 3C **34**
Houghton Hall (PE31 6UE) 3G **77**
Houghton House (MK45 2EZ) 2A **52**
Houghton Lodge Gdns. & The Hampshire Hydroponicum (SO20 6LQ) 3B **24**
House of Dun (DD10 9LQ) 3F **145**
*House of Manannan Mus., Peel (IM5 1TA) 3B **108***
House of the Binns (EH49 7NA) 1D **128**
Houses of Parliament (SW1A 0RS) **London 203**
Housesteads Roman Fort (NE47 6NN) 3A **114**
Hoveton Hall Gdns. (NR12 8RJ) 3F **79**
Hovingham Hall (YO62 4LU) 2A **100**
Howick Hall Gdns. (NE66 3LB) 3G **121**
Howletts Wild Animal Pk. (CT4 5EL) 5F **41**
Hughenden Manor (HP14 4LA) 2G **37**
Humber Bridge (HU13 0HE) 2D **94**
Hunstanton Sea Life Sanctuary (PE36 5BH) 1F **77**
Hunterian Mus. (G12 8QQ) **Glasgow 196**
Huntingtower Castle (PH1 3JL) 1C **136**
Huntly Castle (AB54 4SH) 4C **160**
Hurst Castle (SO41 0TP) 4B **16**
Hutton-in-the-Forest (CA11 9TH) 1F **103**
Hylands House & Gdn. (CM2 8WQ) 5G **53**

I

Iceni Village & Mus. (PE37 8AG) 5G **77**
Ickworth (IP29 5QE) 4H **65**
Ightham Mote (TN15 0NT) 5G **39**
*Ilam Pk. (DE6 2AZ) 5F **85***
Imperial War Mus. Duxford (CB22 4QR) 1E **53**
Imperial War Mus. London (SE1 6HZ) **203**
Imperial War Mus. North (M17 1TZ) **Manchester 201**
Inchcolm Abbey (KY3 0XR) 1E **129**
Inchmahome Priory (FK8 3RD) 3E **135**
Ingatestone Hall (CM4 9NS) 1A **40**
Inveraray Castle (PA32 8XE) 3H **133**
*Inveresk Lodge Gdn. (EH21 7TE) 2G **129***
Inverewe Gdn. (IV22 2LG) 5C **162**
*Inverlochy Castle (PH33 6TQ) 1F **141***
Inverness Mus. & Art Gallery (IV2 3EB) **198**
Iona (PA76 6SP) 2A **132**
Ironbridge Gorge (TF8 7JP) 5A **72**
Iron Bridge, The (TF8 7JP) 5A **72**
Isel Hall (CA13 0QG) 1C **102**
Isle of Man Steam Railway (IM1 4LL) 4C **108**
Isle of Wight Steam Railway (PO33 4DS) 4D **16**
*Ivinghoe Beacon (LU6 2EG) 4H **51***
Izaak Walton's Cottage (ST15 0PA) 3C **72**

J

Jackfield Tile Mus. (TF8 7ND) 5A **72**
James Brindley Mus. (ST13 8FA) 5D **85**
Jane Austen Centre, The, Bath (BA1 2NT) **Bath 187**
Jane Austen's House (GU34 1SD) 3F **25**
Jarlshof Prehistoric & Norse Settlement (ZE3 9JN) 10E **173**
Jedburgh Abbey (TD8 6JQ) 3A **120**
Jerome K. Jerome Birthplace Mus. (WS1 1PN) 1E **61**
Jervaulx Abbey (HG4 4PH) 1D **98**
JM Barrie's Birthplace (DD8 4BX) 3C **144**
Jodrell Bank Observatory Visitor Centre (SK11 9DL) 3B **84**
John Milton's Cottage (HP8 4JH) 1A **38**
Jorvik Viking Centre, York (YO1 9WT) **York 214**

K

Kedleston Hall (DE22 5JH) 1H **73**
Keighley & Worth Valley Railway (BD22 8NJ) 1A **92**
Kelburn Castle & Country Centre (KA29 0BE) 4D **126**
Keld Chapel (CA10 3QF) 3G **103**
Kelham Island Mus. (S3 8RY) **Sheffield 210**
Kellie Castle (KY10 2RF) 3H **137**
Kelmarsh Hall (NN6 9LY) 3E **63**
Kelmscott Manor (GL7 3HJ) 2A **36**
Kelso Abbey (TD5 7BB) 1B **120**
*Kendal Castle (LA9 7BN) 5G **103***
*Kenilworth Castle (CV8 1NE) 3G **61***
Kent & East Sussex Railway (TN30 6HE) 3C **28**
Kenton Vineyard (EX6 8NW) 4C **12**
Kentwell Hall (CO10 9BA) 1B **54**
Kenwood House (NW3 7JR) 2D **38**
*Keswick Mus. & Gallery (CA12 4NF) 2D **102***
Kettle's Yard House & Art Gallery (CB3 0AQ) **Cambridge 191**
Kew Gdns. (TW9 3AB) 3C **38**
*Kidwelly Castle (SA17 5BQ) 5E **45***
Kielder Castle Forest Pk. Centre (NE48 1ER) 5A **120**
Kiftsgate Court Gdns. (GL55 6LN) 1G **49**
Kilchurn Castle (PA33 1AF) 1A **134**
Kildrummy Castle (AB33 8RA) 2B **152**
Killerton (EX5 3LE) 2C **12**
Kilmartin Sculptured Stones (PA31 8RN) 4F **133**
Kilravock Castle (IV2 7PJ) 4C **158**
Kimbolton Castle (PE28 0EA) 4H **63**
Kinder Scout (S33 7ZJ) 2E **85**
King's College Chapel (CB2 1TN) **Cambridge 191**
Kingston Bagpuize House (OX13 5AX) 2C **36**
Kingston Lacy (BH21 4EA) 2E **15**
*Kingston Maurward Gdns. & Animal Pk. (DT2 8PY) 3C **14***
*Kinnaird Head Castle Lighthouse & Mus., Fraserburgh (AB43 9DP) 2G **161***
Kinnersley Castle (HR3 6QF) 1G **47**
Kinross House Gdns. (KY13 8ET) 3D **136**
*Kintail & Morvich Estate, Inverinate (IV40 8HQ) 2B **148***
*Kinver Edge (DY7 5NP) 2C **60***
Kiplin Hall (DL10 6AT) 5F **105**
Kirby Hall (NN17 3EN) 1G **63**
*Kirby Muxloe Castle (LE9 2DH) 5C **74***
Kirkham Priory (YO60 7JS) 3B **100**
Kirklees Light Railway (HD8 9XJ) 3C **92**
Kirkstall Abbey (LS5 3EH) 1C **92**
Kirkwall Cathedral (KW15 1JF) 6D **172**
*Knaresborough Castle (HG5 8BB) 4F **99***
Knebworth House (SG3 6PY) 3C **52**
Knightshayes Court (EX16 7RQ) 1C **12**
Knole (TN15 0RP) 5G **39**
Knoll Gdns. (BH21 7ND) 2F **15**
Knowsley Safari Pk. (L34 4AN) 1G **83**

L

Lacock Abbey (SN15 2LG) 5E **35**
Lady Lever Art Gallery (CH62 5EQ) 2F **83**
Laing Art Gallery (NE1 8AG) **Newcastle 205**
Lake District Nat. Pk. (LA9 7RL) 3E **103**
Lakeside & Haverthwaite Railway (LA12 8AL) 1C **96**
Lamb House (TN31 7ES) 3D **28**
Lamphey Bishop's Palace & Vis. Cen. (SA71 5NT) 4E **43**
*Lamphey Bishop's Palace & Vis. Cen. (SA71 5NT) 4E **43***
Lamport Hall (NN6 9HD) 3E **63**
*Lancaster Castle (LA1 1YJ) 3D **96***

Landmark Forest Theme Pk.—Royal Yacht Britannia

Landmark Forest Theme Pk. (PH23 3AJ) 1D 150
Land's End (TR19 7AA) 4A 4
Lanercost Priory (CA8 2HQ) 3G 113
Langdale Pikes (LA22 9JY) 4D 102
Langley Chapel (SY5 7HU) 1H 59
Langstone Court (HR9 6NR) 3A 48
Lanhydrock (PL30 5AD) 2E 7
Lappa Valley Steam Railway & Leisure Pk. (TR8 5LX) 3C 6
Larmer Tree Gdns. (SP5 5PZ) 1E 15
Laugharne Castle (SA33 4SA) 3H 43
Launceston Castle (PL15 7DR) 4D 10
Launceston Steam Railway (PL15 8DA) 4D 10
Lauriston Castle (EH4 5QD) 2F 129
Lavender Line, The (TN22 5XB) 4F 27
Lavenham Guildhall (CO10 9QZ) 1C 54
Laxey Wheel (IM4 7NL) 3D 108
Layer Marney Tower (CO5 9US) 4C 54
Leeds Castle (Kent) (ME17 1PL) 5C 40
Leeds City Mus. & Art Gallery (LS1 3AA) 199
Legoland (SL4 4AY) 3A 38
Leighton Buzzard Railway (LU7 4TN) 3H 51
Leighton Hall, Yealand Conyers (LA5 9ST) 2E 97
Leiston Abbey (IP16 4TD) 4G 67
Leith Hall (AB54 4NQ) 1C 152
Leith Hill (RH5 6LX) 1C 26
Lennoxlove House (EH41 4NZ) 2B 130
Leonardslee Gdns. (RH13 6PP) 3D 26
Levant Mine & Beam Engine (TR19 7SX) 3A 4
Levens Hall (LA8 0PD) 1D 97
Lewes Castle (BN7 1YE) 4F 27
Lichfield Cathedral (WS13 7LD) 4F 73
Life (NE1 4EP) Newcastle 205
Lightwater Valley Theme Pk. (HG4 3HT) 2E 99
Lilleshall Abbey (TF10 9HW) 4B 72
Lincoln Castle (LN1 3AA) 198
Lincoln Cathedral (LN2 1PZ) 198
Lincoln Medieval Bishops' Palace (LN2 1PU) 198
Lincolnshire Road Transport Mus. (LN6 3QT) 4G 87
Lindisfarne (TD15 2SF) 5H 131
Lindisfarne Castle (TD15 2SH) 5H 131
Lindisfarne Priory (TD15 2RX) 5H 131
Linlithgow Palace (EH49 7AL) 2D 128
Linton Zoo (CB21 4XN) 1F 53
Lion Salt Works (CW9 6ES) 3A 84
Little Clarendon (SP3 5DZ) 3F 23
Little Malvern Court (WR14 4JN) 1C 48
Little Moreton Hall (CW12 4SD) 5C 84
Liverpool Cathedral (L1 7AZ) 2F 83
Liverpool Metropolitan RC Cathedral (L3 5TQ) 200
Lizard Point (TR12 7NU) 5E 5
Llanberis Lake Railway (LL55 3HB) 4E 81
Llanerchaeron (SA48 8DG) 5D 57
Llangollen Railway (LL20 7AJ) 1D 70
Llansteffan Castle (SA33 5JX) 4D 44
Llawhaden Castle (SA67 8HL) 3E 43
Llechwedd Slate Caverns (LL41 3NB) 1G 69
Llywernog Silver-Lead Mine (SY23 3AB) 2G 57
Lochalsh Woodland Gdn. (IV40 8DN) 1F 147
Loch Doon Castle (KA6 7QE) 5D 117
Lochleven Castle (KY13 8ET) 3D 136
Loch Lomond & The Trossachs Nat. Pk. (FK8 3UA) 2D 134
Lochmaben Castle (DG11 1JE) 1B 112
Loch Ness Exhibition Centre, The (IV63 6TU) 5H 157
Locomotion: The Nat. Railway Mus. at Shildon (DL4 1PQ) 2F 105
Lodge Nature Reserve, The (SG19 2DL) 1B 52
Lodge Pk. (GL54 3PP) 4G 49
Logan Botanic Gdn. (DG9 9ND) 5F 109
Logan Fish Pond (DG9 9NF) 5F 109
London Bridge, City of London (SE1 9DD) 203
London Dungeon, The (SE1 2SZ) 203
London Eye, The (SE1 7PB) 203
London Zoo (NW1 4RY) 202
Longcross Victorian Gdns. (PL29 3TF) 1D 6
Longleat House & Safari Pk. (BA12 7NW) 2D 22
Longleat House & Safari Pk. (BA12 7NW) 2D 22
Long Mynd (SY7 8BH) 1G 59
Longthorpe Tower (PE3 6SU) 1A 64
Longtown Castle (HR2 0LE) 3G 47
Lord Leycester Hospital, Warwick (CV34 4BH) 4G 61
Loseley Pk. (GU3 1HS) 1A 26
Lost Gardens of Heligan, The (PL26 6EN) 4D 6
Lotherton Hall Mus. (LS25 3EB) 1E 93
Loudoun Castle Theme Pk. (KA4 8PE) 1E 117
Loughwood Meeting House (EX13 7DU) 3F 13
Lowry, The, Salford (M50 3AZ) Manchester 201
Ludgershall Castle (SP11 9QS) 1A 24
Ludlow Castle (SY8 1AY) 3H 59
Lullingstone Castle (DA4 0JA) 4G 39
Lullingstone Roman Villa (DA4 0JA) 4G 39
Lulworth Castle (BH20 5QS) 4D 14
Lundy Island (EX39 2LY) 2B 18
Lundy Marine Nat. Nature Reserve (EX39 2LY) 2B 18
Lyddington Bede House (LE15 9LZ) 1F 63
Lydford Castle (EX20 4BH) 4F 11
Lydford Gorge (EX20 4BH) 4F 11
Lydiard House & Pk. (SN5 3PA) 3G 35
Lydney Pk. Gdns. (GL15 6BU) 5B 48
Lyme Pk. House (SK12 2NX) 2D 84
Lytes Cary Manor (TA11 7HU) 4A 22
Lyveden New Bield (PE8 5AT) 2G 63

M

Macduff Marine Aquarium (AB44 1SL) 2E 160
MacLellan's Castle (DG6 4JD) 4D 111
Madame Tussaud's (NW1 5LR) London 202
Maeshowe Chambered Cairn (KW16 3HQ) 6C 172
Magna Science Adventure Centre (S60 1DX) 1B 86
Maiden Castle (DT2 9PP) 4B 14
Major Oak (NG21 9HN) 4D 86
Malham Cove (BD23 4DJ) 3A 98
Malham Tarn (BD24 9PU) 3A 98
Mallaig Marine World (PH41 4PX) 4E 147
Malleny Gdn. (EH14 7AF) 3E 129
Malton Roman Mus. (YO17 7LP) 2B 100
Malvern Hills (HR8 1EN) 2C 48
Manchester Art Gallery (M2 3JL) 201
Manchester United Mus. & Tour (M16 0RA) 1C 84
M & D's Theme Pk., Motherwell (ML1 3RT) 4A 128
Manderston (TD11 3PP) 4E 130
Mannington Hall Gdns. (NR11 7BB) 2D 78
Manorbier Castle (SA70 7SY) 5E 43
Manx Electric Railway (IM2 4NR) 3D 108
Manx Mus. (IM1 3LY) 4C 108
Mapledurham House (RG4 7TR) 4E 37
Marble Hill House (TW1 2NL) 3C 38
Marischal Mus. (AB10 1YS) Aberdeen 187
Markenfield Hall (HG4 3AD) 3E 99
Mar Lodge Estate (AB35 5YJ) 5F 151
Marsden Moor Estate (HD7 6DH) 3A 92
Marston Hall (NG32 2HQ) 1F 75
Martin Mere Wetland Centre (L40 0TA) 3C 90
Marwell Zoo (SO21 1JH) 4D 24
Marwood Hill Gdns. (EX31 4EB) 3F 19
Mary Arden's House (CV37 9UN) 5F 61
Mary Queen of Scots Visitor Centre (TD8 6EN) 2A 120
Mary Rose Ship & Mus. (PO1 3LX) Portsmouth 209
Max Gate (DT1 2AB) 3C 14
Megginch Castle Gdns. (PH2 7SW) 1E 137
Melbourne Hall (DE73 8EN) 3A 74
Melford Hall (CO10 9AA) 1B 54
Mellerstain (TD3 6LG) 1A 120
Melrose Abbey (TD6 9LG) 1H 119
Menai Bridge (LL59 5HH) 3E 81
Mendip Hills (BS40 7XS) 1H 21
Merriments Gdns. (TN19 7RA) 3B 28
Merseyside Maritime Mus. (L3 4AQ) Liverpool 200
Mertoun Gdns. (TD6 0EA) 1A 120
Michelham Priory (BN27 3QS) 5G 27
Middleham Castle (DL8 4QR) 1D 98
Middleton Hall (B78 2AE) 1F 61
Mid Hants Railway (SO24 9JG) 3E 25
Midland Railway Centre (DE5 3QZ) 5B 86
Mid-Norfolk Railway (NR19 1DF) 5C 78
Mid-Suffolk Light Railway (IP14 5PW) 4D 66
Millennium Coastal Pk. (SA15 2LG) 3D 31
Millennium Seed Bank (RH17 6TN) 2E 27
Miller House Mus. & Hugh Miller's Cottage (IV11 8XA) 2B 158
Milton Abbey Church (DT11 0BS) 2D 14
Milton Manor House (OX14 4EN) 2C 36
Minack Open-Air Theatre, The (TR19 6JU) 4A 4
Minsmere Nature Reserve (IP17 3BY) 4G 67
Minterne Gdns. (DT2 7AU) 2B 14
Mirehouse (CA12 4QE) 2D 102
Misarden Pk. Gdns. (GL6 7JA) 5E 49
Mistley Towers (CO11 1ET) 2E 54
Mompesson House (SP1 2EL) Salisbury 210
Monk Bretton Priory (S71 5QE) 4D 93
Monkey Sanctuary, The (PL13 1NZ) 3G 7
Monkey World (BH20 6HH) 4D 14
Monk's House (BN7 3HF) 5F 27
Monteviot House Gdn. (TD8 6UH) 2A 120
Montgomery Castle (SY15 6HN) 1E 58
Monzie Castle (PH7 4HD) 1A 136
Moreton Corbet Castle, Shawbury (SY4 4DW) 3H 71
Morwellham Quay (PL19 8JL) 2A 8
Moseley Old Hall, Featherstone (WV10 7HY) 5D 72
Motorboat Mus., The (SS16 4UH) 2B 40
Mottisfont Abbey Gdn., House & Estate (SO51 0LP) 4B 24
Mount Edgcumbe (PL10 1HZ) 3A 8
Mount Ephraim Gdns. (ME13 9TX) 4E 41
Mountfitchet Castle and Norman Village of 1066 (CM24 8SP) 3F 53
Mount Grace Priory (DL6 3JG) 5B 106
Mount Stuart & Pinetums (PA20 9LR) 4C 126
Mr Straw's House (S81 0JG) 2C 86
Muchelney Abbey (TA10 0DQ) 4H 21
Muchelney Priest's House (TA10 0DQ) 4H 21
Mull of Kintyre (PA28 6RU) 5A 122
Muncaster Castle (CA18 1RQ) 5C 102
Murton Pk. (YO19 5GH) 4A 100
Mus. of Army Flying (SO20 8DY) 3B 24
Mus. of East Anglian Life (IP14 1DL) 5C 66
Mus. of Flight (EH39 5LF) 2B 130
Mus. of Lakeland Life, Kendal (LA9 5AL) 5G 103
Mus. of Lincolnshire Life (LN1 3LY) Lincoln 198
Mus. of London (EC2Y 5HN) 203
Mus. of Science & Industry in Manchester, The (M3 4FP) 201
Mus. of Scottish Lighthouses (AB43 9DU) 2G 161
Mus. of South Yorkshire Life, Cusworth Hall (DN5 7TU) 4F 93
Mus. of The Isles (IV45 8RS) 3E 147
Mus. of the Jewellery Quarter (B18 6HA) Birmingham 188

N

Nat. Birds of Prey Centre, The (GL18 1JJ) 3C 48
Nat. Botanic Gdn. of Wales & Vis. Cen. (SA32 8HG) 4F 45
Nat. Botanic Gdn. of Wales & Vis. Cen., Llanarthne (SA32 8HG) 4F 45
Nat. Coal Mining Mus. for England, Overton (WF4 4RH) 3C 92
Nat. Coracle Centre (SA38 9JL) 1C 44
Nat. Fishing Heritage Centre, Grimsby (DN31 1UZ) 4F 95
Nat. Football Mus., The (M4 3GB) (Due open 2011) 201
Nat. Forest, The (DE12 6HZ) 4H 73
Nat. Gallery (WC2N 5DN) London 203
Nat. Gallery of Scotland (EH2 2EL) Edinburgh 194
Nat. Glass Centre (SR6 0GL) Sunderland 212
Nat. History Mus., St Fagans (CF5 6XB) Cardiff 191
Nat. Horse Racing Mus., The (CB8 8JL) 4F 65
Nat. Marine Aquarium (PL4 0LF) Plymouth 208
Nat. Maritime Mus., Greenwich (SE10 9NF) 3E 39
Nat. Maritime Mus. Cornwall, Falmouth (TR11 3QY) 5C 6
Nat. Media Mus. (BD1 1NQ) Bradford 190
Nat. Memorial Arboretum, The (DE13 7AR) 4F 73
Nat. Motorcycle Mus. (B92 0EJ) 2G 61
Nat. Motor Mus. (SO42 7ZN) 2B 16
Nat. Mus. Cardiff (CF10 3NP) 191
Nat. Mus. of Costume (DG2 8HQ) 3A 112
Nat. Mus. of Rural Life (G76 9HR) 4H 127
Nat. Mus. of Scotland (EH1 1JF) Edinburgh 194
Nat. Portrait Gallery, Marylebone (WC2H 0HE) London 203
Nat. Railway Mus., York (YO26 4XJ) York 214
Nat. Roman Legion Mus., Caerleon (NP18 1AE) 2G 33
Nat. Sea Life Centre (B1 2HL) Birmingham 188
Nat. Seal Sanctuary (TR12 6UG) 4E 5
Nat. Showcaves Centre for Wales, The (SA9 1GJ) 4B 46
Nat. Slate Mus. (LL55 4TY) 4E 81
Nat. Space Centre (LE4 5NS) 5C 74
Nat. Tramway Museum, The (DE4 5DP) 5A 86
Nat. Waterways Mus. Ellesmere Port (CH62 4EF) 3G 83
Nat. Waterways Mus. Gloucester Docks (GL1 2NS) 196
Nat. Waterways Mus. Stoke Bruerne (NN12 7SE) 5E 63
Nat. Wool Mus. (SA44 5UP) 2D 44
Natural History Mus. (SW7 5BD) London 202
Natural History Museum at Tring (HP23 6AP) 4H 51
Neath Abbey (SA10 7DW) 3G 31
Needles, The (PO39 0JH) 4A 16
Neidpath Castle (EH45 8NW) 5F 129
Nene Valley Railway (PE8 6LR) 1A 64
Ness Botanic Gdns. (CH64 4AY) 3F 83
Nether Winchendon House (HP18 0DY) 4F 51
Netley Abbey (SO31 5HB) 2C 16
New Abbey Corn Mill (DG2 8DX) 3A 112
Newark Air Mus. (NG24 2NY) 5F 87
Newark Castle (Newark-on-Trent) (NG24 1BN) 5E 87
Newark Castle (Port Glasgow) (PA14 5NH) 2E 127
Newark Pk. (GL12 7PZ) 2C 34
New Art Gallery Walsall, The (WS2 8LG) 1E 61
Newburgh Priory (YO61 4AS) 2H 99
Newby Hall & Gdns. (HG4 5AE) 3F 99
Newcastle Castle (Bridgend) (CF31 4JW) 3B 32
Newcastle upon Tyne Castle Keep (NE1 1RQ) 205
New Forest Nat. Pk. (SO43 7BD) 2H 15
Newhouse (SP5 2NX) 4H 23
New Lanark World Heritage Site Visitor Centre (ML11 9DB) 5B 128
Newquay Zoo (TR7 2LZ) 2C 6
Newstead Abbey (NG15 8NA) 5C 86
Nine Ladies Stone Circle (DE4 2LF) 4G 85
Norfolk Broads (NR3 1BQ) 5G 79
Norfolk Lavender (PE31 7JE) 2F 77
Norfolk Wildlife Centre (NR9 5PD) 4C 78
Norham Castle (TD15 2LL) 5F 131
Normanby Hall (DN15 9HU) 3B 94
North Downs (GU10 5QE) 2F 25
Northington Grange (SO24 9TG) 3D 24
North Norfolk Railway (NR26 8RA) 1D 78
North of England Open Air Mus. (DH9 0RG) 4F 115
Northumberland Nat. Pk. (NE46 1BS) 1A 114
North York Moors Nat. Pk. (YO18 8RN) 5E 107
North Yorkshire Moors Railway (YO18 7AJ) 1C 100
Norton Conyers (HG4 5EQ) 2F 99
Norton Priory Mus. (WA7 1SX) 2H 83
Norwich Castle & Mus. (NR1 3JU) 205
Norwich Castle & Mus. (NR1 3JU) 205
Norwich Cathedral (NR1 4DH) 205
Nostell Priory (WF4 1QE) 3E 93
Nottingham Transport Heritage Centre (NG11 6NZ) 2C 74
Nunney Castle (BA11 4LN) 2C 22
Nunnington Hall (YO62 5UY) 2A 100
Nymans Gdn. (RH17 6EB) 3D 26

O

Oakham Castle (LE15 6DR) 5F 75
Oakwell Hall, Birstall (WF17 9LG) 2C 92
Oakwood Theme Pk. (SA67 8DE) 3E 43
Oban Distillery (PA34 5NH) 206
Observatory Science Centre, The (BN27 1RN) 4A 28
Oceanarium (BH2 5AA) Bournemouth 190
Offa's Dyke (NP16 7NQ) 5A 48
Ogmore Castle (CF32 0QP) 4B 32
Okehampton Castle (EX20 1JA) 3F 11
Old Beaupre Castle (CF71 7LT) 4D 32
Oldbury Hill & Styants Wood, Ightham (TN15 0ET) 5G 39
Old Gorhambury House (AL3 6AH) 5B 52
Old Oswestry Hill Fort (SY10 7AA) 2E 71
Old Sarum (SP1 3SD) 3G 23
Old Wardour Castle (SP3 6RR) 4E 23
Old Winchester Hill Hill Fort (GU32 1HN) 4E 25
Orford Castle (IP12 2NF) 1H 55
Orford Ness Nat. Nature Reserve (IP12 2NU) 1H 55
Original Loch Ness Visitor Centre, The (IV63 6TU) 5H 157
Ormesby Hall (TS7 9AS) 3C 106
Osborne House (PO32 6JX) 3D 16
Osterley Pk. & House (TW7 4RB) 3C 38
Our Dynamic Earth (EH8 8AS) Edinburgh 194
Overbeck's Mus. & Gdn. (TQ8 8LW) 5D 8
Overbeck's Mus. & Gdn. (TQ8 8LW) 5D 8
Owletts (DA12 3AP) 4A 40
Owlpen Manor (GL11 5BZ) 2C 34
Oxburgh Hall (PE33 9PS) 5G 77
Oxford Christ Church Cathedral (OX1 4JF) 207
Oxwich Castle (SA3 1LU) 4D 31
Oystermouth Castle (SA3 5TA) 4F 31

P

Packwood House (B94 6AT) 3F 61
Paignton & Dartmouth Steam Railway (TQ4 6AF) 3E 9
Paignton Zoo (TQ4 7EU) 3E 9
Painshill Pk. (KT11 1JE) 5B 38
Painswick Rococo Gdn. (GL6 6TH) 4D 48
Palace of Holyroodhouse (EH8 8DX) Edinburgh 194
Papplewick Pumping Station (NG15 9AJ) 5C 86
Paradise Pk. (TR27 4HB) 3C 4
Paradise Wildlife Pk. (EN10 7QZ) 5D 52
Parcevall Hall Gdns. (BD23 6DE) 3C 98
Parham House & Gdns. (RH20 4HS) 4B 26
Pashley Manor Gdns. (TN5 7HE) 3B 28
Paul Corin's Magnificent Music Machines (PL14 4SH) 2G 7
Paultons Pk. (SO51 6AL) 1B 16
Paxton House & Country Pk. (TD15 1SZ) 4F 131
Paycocke's (CO6 1NS) 3B 54
Peak Alum Works (YO13 0NJ) 4G 107
Peak Cavern (S33 8WS) 2F 85
Peak District Nat. Pk. (DE45 1AE) 3F 85
Peak Rail (DE4 3NA) 4G 85
Peckover House & Gdn. (PE13 1JR) 5D 76
Peel Castle (IM5 1AB) 3B 108
Pembroke Castle (SA71 4LA) 4D 43
Pembrokeshire Coast Nat. Pk. (SA41 3XD) 1E 43
Pencarrow (PL30 3AG) 5A 10
Pendennis Castle (TR11 4LP) 5C 6
Penhow Castle (NP26 3AD) 2H 33
Penrhyn Castle (LL57 4HN) 3F 81
Penrith Castle (CA11 7JB) 2G 103
Penshurst Place & Gdns. (TN11 8DG) 1G 27
Peover Hall (WA16 9HW) 3B 84
Perth Mus. & Art Gallery (PH1 5LB) 207
Peterborough Cathedral (PE1 1XZ) 208
Peto Gdn. at Iford Manor, The (BA15 2BA) 1D 22
Petworth House (GU28 0AE) 3A 26
Pevensey Castle (BN24 5LE) 5H 27
Peveril Castle (S33 8WQ) 2F 85
Philipps House (SP3 5HH) 3F 23
Pickering Castle (YO18 7AX) 1C 100
Picton Castle (SA62 4AS) 3E 43
Piel Castle, Roa Island (LA13 0QN) 3B 96
Pitmedden Gdn. (AB41 7PD) 1F 153
Pitt Rivers Mus. (OX1 3PP) Oxford 207
Pittville Pump Room (GL52 3JE) Cheltenham 192
Plantasia (SA1 2AL) Swansea 212
Plas Brondanw Gdn. (LL48 6SW) 1F 69
Plas Newydd (Llanfair PG) (LL61 6DQ) 4E 81
Plas Newydd (Llangollen) (LL20 8AW) 1E 70
Plas yn Rhiw (LL53 8AB) 3B 68
Pleasurewood Hills Theme Pk. (NR32 5DZ) 1H 67
Plym Valley Railway (PL7 4NW) 3B 8
Poldark Mine (TR13 0ES) 5A 6
Polesden Lacey (RH5 6BD) 5C 38
Pollok House, Glasgow (G43 1AT) 3G 127
Pontcysyllite Aqueduct (LL20 7YS) 1E 71
Portchester Castle (PO16 9QW) 2E 17
Portland Castle (DT5 1AZ) 5B 14
Port Lympne Wild Animal Pk. (CT21 4PD) 2F 29
Portmeirion Village (LL48 6ET) 2E 69
Potteries Mus. & Art Gallery, The (ST1 3DW) Stoke 211
Powderham Castle (EX6 8JQ) 4C 12
Powis Castle (SY21 8RF) 5E 70
Prebendal Manor House, The (PE8 6QG) 1H 63
Prestongrange Mus. (EH32 9RX) 2G 129
Preston Manor (BN1 6SD) 5E 27
Preston Mill (EH40 3DS) 2B 130
Preston Tower, Chathill (NE67 5DH) 2F 121
Preston Tower, Prestonpans (EH32 9NN) 2G 129
Prideaux Place (PL28 8RP) 1D 6
Prior Pk. Landscape Gdn. (BA2 5AH) 5C 34
Provan Hall (G34 9NQ) 3H 127
Prudoe Castle (NE42 6NA) 3D 115

Q

Quantock Hills (TA4 4AP) 3E 21
Quarry Bank Mill (DL8 3SG) 2C 84
Quebec House (TN16 1TD) 5F 39
Queen Elizabeth Country Pk. (PO8 0QE) 1F 17
Queen Elizabeth Forest Pk. (FK8 3UZ) 4D 134
Quex House & Gdns. (CT7 0BH) 4H 41

R

Raby Castle (DL2 3AH) 2E 105
RAF Mus. Cosford (TF11 8UP) 5B 72
RAF Mus. Hendon (NW9 5LL) 1D 38
Raglan Castle (NP15 2BT) 5H 47
Ragley (B49 5NJ) 5E 61
Railway Age, The (CW1 2DB) 5B 84
Rammerscales House (DG11 1LD) 2B 112
Ramsey Island Nature Reserve, St Davids (SA62 6QA) 2B 42
Ravenglass & Eskdale Railway (CA18 1SW) 4C 102
Raveningham Hall Gdns. (NR14 6NS) 1F 67
Ravenscraig Castle (KY1 2AZ) 4E 137
Reculver Towers (CT6 6SX) 4G 41
Renishaw Hall (S21 3WB) 3B 86
Restoration House (ME1 1RF) Medway 204
Restormel Castle (PL22 0HN) 2F 7
Revolution House (S41 9LA) 3A 86
Rheged (CA11 0DQ) 2G 103
Rheidol Power Station & Vis. Cen. (SY23 3NF) 3G 57
Rheidol Power Station & Vis. Cen. (SY23 3NF) 3G 57
Rhossili Bay (SA3 1PR) 4D 30
RHS Garden Harlow Carr (HG3 1QB) 4E 99
RHS Garden Hyde Hall (CM3 8ET) 1B 40
RHS Garden Rosemoor (EX38 8PH) 1F 11
RHS Garden Wisley (GU23 6QB) 5B 38
Rhuddlan Castle (LL18 5AD) 3C 82
Ribchester Roman Mus. (PR3 3XS) 1E 91
Richmond Castle (DL10 4QW) 4E 105
Rievaulx Abbey (YO62 5LB) 1H 99
Rievaulx Terrace & Temples (YO62 5LJ) 1H 99
Ripley Castle (HG3 3AY) 3E 99
Ripon Cathedral (HG4 1QT) 2F 99
River & Rowing Mus. (RG9 1BF) 3F 37
Robert Burns Centre (DG2 7BE) Dumfries 193
Roche Abbey (S66 8NW) 2C 86
Rochester Castle (ME1 1SW) Medway 204
Rochester Cathedral (ME1 1SX) Medway 204
Rockbourne Roman Villa (SP6 3PG) 1G 15
Rockingham Castle (LE16 8TH) 1F 63
Rode Hall & Gdns. (ST7 3QP) 5C 84
Rodmarton Manor (GL7 6PF) 2E 35
Rokeby Pk. (DL12 9RZ) 3D 105
Rollright Stones (OX7 5QT) 2A 50
Rollright Stones (OX7 5QB) 2A 50
Rollright Stones (OX7 5QB) 2A 50
Roman Painted House (CT17 9AJ) Dover 193
Romney, Hythe & Dymchurch Railway (TN28 8PL) 3E 29
Roseberry Topping (TS9 6QX) 3D 106
Rothesay Castle (PA20 0DA) 3B 126
Rothiemurchus Visitor Centre (PH22 1QH) 2D 150
Rousham Pk. House & Gdns. (OX25 4QX) 3C 50
Royal Academy of Arts (W1J 0BD) London 202
Royal Albert Bridge (PL12 4GT) 3A 8
Royal Armouries Mus., Leeds (LS10 1LT) Leeds 199
Royal Botanic Gdn. Edinburgh (EH3 5LR) 194
Royal Botanic Gdns., Kew (TW9 3AB) 3C 38
Royal Cornwall Mus. (TR1 2SJ) 4C 6
Royal Crown Derby Mus. (DE23 8JZ) 193
Royal Navy Submarine Mus. (PO12 2AS) 3E 16
Royal Pavilion, The (BN1 1EE) Brighton & Hove 189
Royal Pump Room Mus. (HG1 2RY) Harrogate 197
Royal Shakespeare Theatre (CV37 6BB) Stratford 212
Royal Yacht Britannia (EH6 6JJ) 2F 129

Limited Interchange Motorway Junctions are shown on the maps by RED junction indicators

M1

Junction 2
Northbound: No exit, access from A1 only
Southbound: No access, exit to A1 only
Junction 4
Northbound: No exit, access from A41 only
Southbound: No access, exit to A41 only
Junction 6a
Northbound: No exit, access from M25 only
Southbound: No access, exit to M25 only
Junction 17
Northbound: No access, exit to M45 only
Southbound: No exit, access from M45 only
Junction 19
Northbound: Exit to M6 only,
access from A14 only
Southbound: Access from M6 only,
exit to A14 only
Junction 21a
Northbound: No access, exit to A46 only
Southbound: No exit, access from A46 only
Junction 24a
Northbound: Access from A50 only
Southbound: Exit to A50 only
Junction 35a
Northbound: No access, exit to A616 only
Southbound: No exit, access from A616 only
Junction 43
Northbound: Exit to M621 only
Southbound: Access from M621 only
Junction 48
Eastbound: Exit to A1(M)
Northbound only
Westbound: Access from A1(M) Southbound
only

M2

Junction 1
Eastbound: Access from A2 Eastbound only
Westbound: Exit to A2 Westbound only

M3

Junction 8
Westbound: No access, exit to A303 only
Eastbound: No exit, access from A303 only
Junction 10
Northbound: No access from A31
Southbound: No exit to A31
Junction 13
Southbound: No access from A335 to M3
leading to M27 Eastbound

M4

Junction 1
Westbound: Access from A4 Westbound only
Eastbound: Exit to A4 Eastbound only
Junction 21
Westbound: No access from M48
Eastbound: No exit to M48
Junction 23
Westbound: No exit to M48
Eastbound: No access from M48
Junction 25
Westbound: No access
Eastbound: No exit
Junction 25a
Westbound: No access
Eastbound: No exit
Junction 29
Westbound: No access, exit to A48(M) only
Eastbound: No exit, access from A48(M) only
Junction 38
Westbound: No access, exit to A48 only
Junction 39
Westbound: No exit, access from A48 only
Eastbound: No access or exit
Junction 42
Westbound: No exit to A48
Eastbound: No access from A48

M5

Junction 10
Southbound: No access, exit to A4019 only
Northbound: No exit, access from A4019 only
Junction 11a
Southbound: No exit to A417 Westbound
Junction 18a
Southbound: No exit to M49
Northbound: No access from M49

M6

Junction 3a
Eastbound: No exit to M6 TOLL
Westbound: No access from M6 TOLL
Junction 4
Northbound: No exit to M42 Northbound
No access from M42 Southbound
Southbound: No exit to M42
No access from M42 Southbound
Junction 4a
Northbound: No exit, access from M42
Southbound only
Southbound: No access, exit to M42 only
Junction 5
Northbound: No access, exit to A452 only
Southbound: No exit, access from A452 only
Junction 10a
Northbound: No access, exit to M54 only
Southbound: No exit, access from M54 only
Junction 11a
Northbound: No exit to M6 TOLL
Southbound: No access from M6 TOLL
Junction 20
Northbound: No exit to M56 Eastbound
Southbound: No access from M56 Westbound
Junction 24
Northbound: No exit, access from A58 only
Southbound: No access, exit to A58 only
Junction 25
Northbound: No access, exit to A49 only
Southbound: No exit, access from A49 only
Junction 30
Northbound: No exit, access from M61
Northbound only
Southbound: No access, exit to M61
Southbound only
Junction 31a
Northbound: No access, exit to B6242 only
Southbound: No exit, access from B6242 only
Junction 45
Northbound: No access onto A74(M)
Southbound: No exit from A74(M)

M6 TOLL

Junction T1
Northbound: No exit
Southbound: No access
Junction T2
Northbound: No access or exit
Southbound: No access
Junction T5
Northbound: No exit
Southbound: No access
Junction T7
Northbound: No access from A5
Southbound: No exit
Junction T8
Northbound: No exit to A460 Northbound
Southbound: No exit

M8

Junction 8
Westbound: No access from M73 Southbound
Eastbound: No exit to M73 Northbound
Junction 9
Westbound: No exit, access only
Eastbound: No access, exit only
Junction 13
Westbound: No exit to M80 Northbound
Eastbound: No access from M80 Southbound
Junction 14
Westbound: No exit, access only
Eastbound: No access, exit only
Junction 16
Westbound: No access, exit only
Eastbound: No exit, access only
Junction 17
Westbound: No access, exit to A82 only
Eastbound: No exit, access from A82 only
Junction 18
Westbound: No exit, access only
Junction 19
Westbound: No access from A814 Westbound
Eastbound: No exit to A814 Eastbound
Junction 20
Westbound: No exit, access only
Eastbound: No access, exit only
Junction 21
Westbound: No exit, access only
Eastbound: No access, exit only
Junction 22
Westbound: No access, exit to M77 only
Eastbound: No exit, access from M77 only

Junction 23
Westbound: No access, exit to B768 only
Eastbound: No exit, access from B768 only
Junction 25
Westbound and Eastbound:
Exit to A739 Northbound only
Access from A739 Southbound only
Junction 25a
Eastbound: Access only
Westbound: Exit only
Junction 28
Westbound: no access, exit to airport only
Eastbound: no exit, access from airport only

M9

Junction 1a
Northbound: No access, exit to M9 spur only
Southbound: No exit, access from M9 spur only
Junction 2
Northbound: No exit, access from B8046 only
Southbound: No exit, access to B8046 only
Junction 3
Northbound: No access, exit to A803 only
Southbound: No exit, access from A803 only
Junction 6
Northbound: No exit, access only
Southbound: No access, exit to A905 only
Junction 8
Northbound: No access, exit to M876 only
Southbound: No exit, access from M876 only
Junction with A90
Northbound: Exit onto A90 westbound only
Southbound: Access from A90 eastbound only

M11

Junction 4
Northbound: No exit, access from A406
Eastbound only
Southbound: No access, exit to A406
Westbound only
Junction 5
Northbound: No access, exit to A1168 only
Southbound: No exit, access from A1168 only
Junction 8a
Northbound: No access, exit only
Southbound: No exit, access only
Junction 9
Northbound: No access, exit only
Southbound: No exit, access only
Junction 13
Northbound: No access, exit only
Southbound: No exit, access only
Junction 14
Northbound: No access from A428 Eastbound
No exit to A428 Westbound
Southbound: No exit, access from A428
Eastbound only

M20

Junction 2
Eastbound: No access, exit to A20 only
(access via M26 Junction 2a)
Westbound: No exit, access only
(exit via M26 Junction 2a)
Junction 3
Eastbound: No exit, access from M26
Eastbound only
Westbound: No access, exit to M26
Westbound only
Junction 11a
Westbound: No exit to Channel Tunnel
Eastbound: No access from Channel Tunnel

M23

Junction 7
Southbound: No access from A23 Northbound
Northbound: No exit to A23 Southbound
Junction 10a
Northbound: No exit, access only
Southbound: No access, exit only

M25

Junction 5
Clockwise: No exit to M26 Eastbound
Anti-clockwise: No access from M26
Westbound

Spur to A21
Southbound: No access from M26 Westbound
Northbound: No exit to M26 Eastbound
Junction 19
Clockwise: No access exit only
Anti-clockwise: No exit access only
Junction 21
Clockwise and Anti-clockwise:
No exit to M1 Southbound
No access from M1 Northbound
Junction 31
Southbound: No exit access only
(exit via Junction 30)
Northbound: No access exit only
(access via Junction 30)

M26

Junction with M25 (M25 Junc. 5)
Westbound: No exit to M25 anti-clockwise
or spur to A21 Southbound
Eastbound: No access from M25 clockwise
or spur from A21 Northbound
Junction with M20 (M20 Junc. 3)
Eastbound: No exit to M20 Westbound
Westbound: No access from M20 Eastbound

M27

Junction 4
Eastbound and Westbound: No exit to A33
Southbound (Southampton)
No access from A33 Northbound
Junction 10
Eastbound: No exit, access from A32 only
Westbound: No access, exit to A32 only

M40

Junction 3
North-Westbound: No access,
exit to A40 only
South-Eastbound: No exit,
access from A40 only
Junction 7
South-Eastbound: No exit, access only
North-Westbound: No access, exit only
Junction 13
South-Eastbound: No access, exit only
North-Westbound: No access, exit only
Junction 14
South-Eastbound: No access, exit only
North-Westbound: No exit, access only
Junction 16
South-Eastbound: No access, exit only
North-Westbound: No exit, access only

M42

Junction 1
Eastbound: No exit
Westbound: No access
Junction 7
Northbound: No access, exit to M6 only
Southbound: No exit, access from M6
Northbound only
Junction 8
Northbound: No exit, access from M6
Southbound only
Southbound: Exit to M6 Northbound only
Access from M6 Southbound only

M45

Junction with M1 (M1 Junc. 17)
Eastbound: No exit to M1 Northbound
Westbound: No access from M1 Southbound
**Junction with A45 east
of Dunchurch**
Eastbound: No access, exit to A45 only
Westbound: No exit, access from A45
Northbound only

M48

Junction with M4 (M4 Junc. 21)
Westbound: No access from M4 Eastbound
Eastbound: No exit to M4 Westbound
Junction with M4 (M4 Junc. 23)
Westbound: No exit to M4 Eastbound
Eastbound: No access from M4 Westbound

M53

Junction 11
Southbound and Northbound: No access from
M56 Eastbound, no exit to M56 Westbound

M56

Junction 1
Westbound: No access from M60
South-Eastbound
No access from A34 Northbound
Eastbound: No exit to M60 North-Westbound
No access to A34 Southbound
Junction 2
Westbound: No access, exit to A560 only
Eastbound: No exit, access from A560 only
Junction 3
Westbound: No exit, access only
Eastbound: No access, exit only
Junction 4
Westbound: No access, exit only
Eastbound: No exit, access only
Junction 7
Westbound: No access, exit only
Junction 8
Westbound: No exit, access from A556 only
Eastbound: No access or exit
Junction 9
Westbound: No exit to M6 Southbound
Eastbound: No access from M6 Northbound
Junction 15
Westbound: No access from M53
Eastbound: No exit to M53

M57

Junction 3
Northbound: No exit, access only
Southbound: No access, exit only
Junction 5
Northbound: No exit, access from A580
Westbound only
Southbound: No access, exit to A580
Eastbound only

M58

Junction 1
Eastbound: No exit, access from A506 only
Westbound: No access, exit to A506 only

M60

Junction 2
Nth.-Eastbound: No access, exit to A560 only
Sth.-Westbound: No exit,
access from A560 only
Junction 3
Westbound: No exit to A34 Northbound
Eastbound: No access from A34 Southbound
Junction 4
Westbound: No access from A34 Southbound
No access from M56 Eastbound
Eastbound: No exit to M56 South-Westbound
No exit to A34 Northbound
Junction 5
South-Eastbound: No access from or exit to A5103 Northbound
North-Westbound: No access from or exit to A5103 Southbound
Junction 14
Eastbound: No exit to A580
No access to A580 Westbound
Westbound: No access to A580 Eastbound
No access from A580
Junction 16
Eastbound: No exit, access from A666 only
Westbound: No access, exit to A666 only
Junction 20
Eastbound: No access from A664
Westbound: No exit to A664
Junction 22
Westbound: No access from A62
Junction 25
South-Westbound:
No access from A560/A6017
Junction 26
North-Eastbound: No access or exit
Junction 27
North-Eastbound: No access, exit only
South-Westbound: No exit, access only

M61

Junctions 2 and 3
North-Westbound:
No access from A580 Eastbound
Sth.-Eastbound: No exit to A580 Westbound
Junction with M6 (M6 Junc. 30)
North-Westbound:
No exit to M6 Southbound
South-Eastbound:
No access from M6 Northbound

M62

Junction 23
Eastbound: No access, exit to A640 only
Westbound: No exit, access from A640 only

M65

Junction 9
Nth.-Eastbound: No access, exit to A679 only
Sth.-Westbound:
No exit, access from A679 only
Junction 11
North-Eastbound: No exit, access only
South-Westbound: No access, exit only

M66

Junction 1
Southbound: No exit, access from A56 only
Northbound: No access, exit to A56 only

M67

Junction 1
Eastbound: Access from A57 Eastbound only
Westbound: Exit to A57 Westbound only
Junction 1a
Eastbound: No access, exit to A6017 only
Westbound: No exit, access from A6017 only
Junction 2
Eastbound: No exit, access from A57 only
Westbound: No access, exit to A57 only

M69

Junction 2
North-Eastbound:
No exit, access from B4669 only
South-Westbound:
No access, exit to B4669 only

M73

Junction 1
Northbound: No access from A74 Eastbound
Southbound: No exit to A74 Eastbound
Junction 2
Northbound: No access from M8 Eastbound
No exit to A89 Eastbound
Southbound: No exit to M8 Westbound
No access from A89 Westbound
Junction 3
Northbound: No exit to A80 South-Westbound
Southbound:
No access from A80 North-Eastbound

M74

Junction 2
Eastbound: No exit
Westbound: No access
Junction 3
Eastbound: No access
Westbound: No exit
Junction 7
Southbound: No access, exit to A72 only
Northbound: No exit, access from A72 only
Junction 9
Southbound: No access, exit to B7078 only
Northbound: No access or exit
Junction 10
Southbound: No exit, access from B7078 only
Junction 11
Southbound: No access, exit to B7078 only
Northbound: No exit, access from B7078 only
Junction 12
Southbound: No exit, access from A70 only
Northbound: No access, exit to A70 only

M77

Junction with M8 (M8 Junc. 22)
Southbound: No access from M8 Eastbound
Northbound: No exit to M8 Westbound
Junction 4
Southbound: No access
Northbound: No exit
Junction 6
Southbound: No access from A77
Northbound: No exit to A77
Junction 7
Northbound: No access from A77
No exit to A77

M80

Junction 1
Northbound: No access from M8 Westbound
Southbound: No exit to M8 Eastbound
Junction 5
Northbound: No access from M876
Southbound: No exit to M876

M90

Junction 2a
Northbound: No access, exit to A92 only
Southbound: No exit, access from A92 only
Junction 7
Northbound: No exit, access from A91 only
Southbound: No access, exit to A91 only
Junction 8
Northbound: No access, exit to A91 only
Southbound: No exit, access from A91 only
Junction 10
Northbound: No access from A912
Exit to A912 Northbound only
Southbound: No exit to A912
Access from A912 Southbound only

M180

Junction 1
Eastbound: No access, exit only
Westbound: No exit, access from A18 only

M606

Junction 2
Northbound: No access, exit only

M621

Junction 2a
Eastbound: No exit, access only
Westbound: No access, exit only
Junction 4
Southbound: No exit
Junction 5
Northbound: No access, exit to A61 only
Southbound: No exit, access from A61 only
Junction 6
Northbound: No exit, access only
Southbound: No access, exit only
Junction 7
Westbound: No exit, access only
Eastbound: No access, exit only
Junction 8
Northbound: No access, exit only
Southbound: No exit, access only

M876

Junction with M80 (M80 Junc. 5)
North-Eastbound:
No access from M80 Southbound
South-Westbound: No exit to M80 Northbound
Junction 2
North-Eastbound: No access, exit only
South-Westbound: No exit, access only
Junction with M9 (M9 Junc. 8)
North-Eastbound: No exit to M9 Northbound
South-Westbound:
No access from M9 Southbound

A1(M) (Hertfordshire Section)

Junction 2
Southbound: No exit, access from A1001 only
Northbound: No access, exit only
Junction 3
Southbound: No access, exit only
Junction 5
Northbound: No exit, access only
Southbound: No access or exit

A1(M) (Cambridgeshire Section)

Junction 13a
Northbound: No exit to B1043
Southbound: No access from B1043
Junction 14
Northbound: No exit, access only
Southbound: No access, exit only

A1(M) (Leeds Section)

Junction 40
Southbound: Exit to A1 Southbound only
Junction 43
Northbound: Access from M1 Eastbound only
Southbound: Exit to M1 Westbound only

A1(M) (Durham Section)

Junction 57
Northbound: No access, exit to A66(M) only
Southbound: No exit, access from A66(M)
Junction 65
Northbound: Exit to A1 North-Westbound,
and to A194(M) only
Southbound: Access from A1 South-Eastbound,
and from A194(M) only

A3(M)

Junction 4
Northbound: No access, exit only
Southbound: No exit, access only

A38(M) Aston Expressway

Junction with Victoria Road, Aston
Northbound: No exit, access only
Southbound: No access, exit only

A48(M)

Junction with M4 (M4 Junc. 29)
South-Westbound: access from M4 Westbound only
North-Eastbound: exit to M4 Eastbound only
Junction 29a
South-Westbound: Exit to A48 Westbound only
North-Eastbound:
Access from A48 Eastbound only

A57(M) Mancunian Way

Junction with A34 Brook Street, Manchester
Eastbound: No access, exit to A34 Brook Street
Southbound only
Westbound: No exit, access only

A58(M) Leeds Inner Ring Road

Junction with Park Lane/ Westgate
Southbound: No access, exit only

A64(M) Leeds Inner Ring Road (Continuation of A58(M))

Junction with A58 Clay Pit Lane
Eastbound: No Access
Westbound: No exit

A66(M)

Junction with A1(M) (A1(M) Junc. 57)
South-Westbound:
Exit to A1(M) Southbound only
North-Eastbound:
Access from A1(M) Northbound only

A74(M)

Junction 18
Northbound: No access
Southbound: No exit

A167(M) Newcastle Central Motorway

Junction with Camden Street
Northbound: No exit, access only
Southbound: No access or exit

A194(M)

Junction with A1(M) (A1(M) Junc. 65) and A1 Gateshead Western By-Pass
Southbound: Exit to A1(M) only
Northbound: Access from A1(M) only

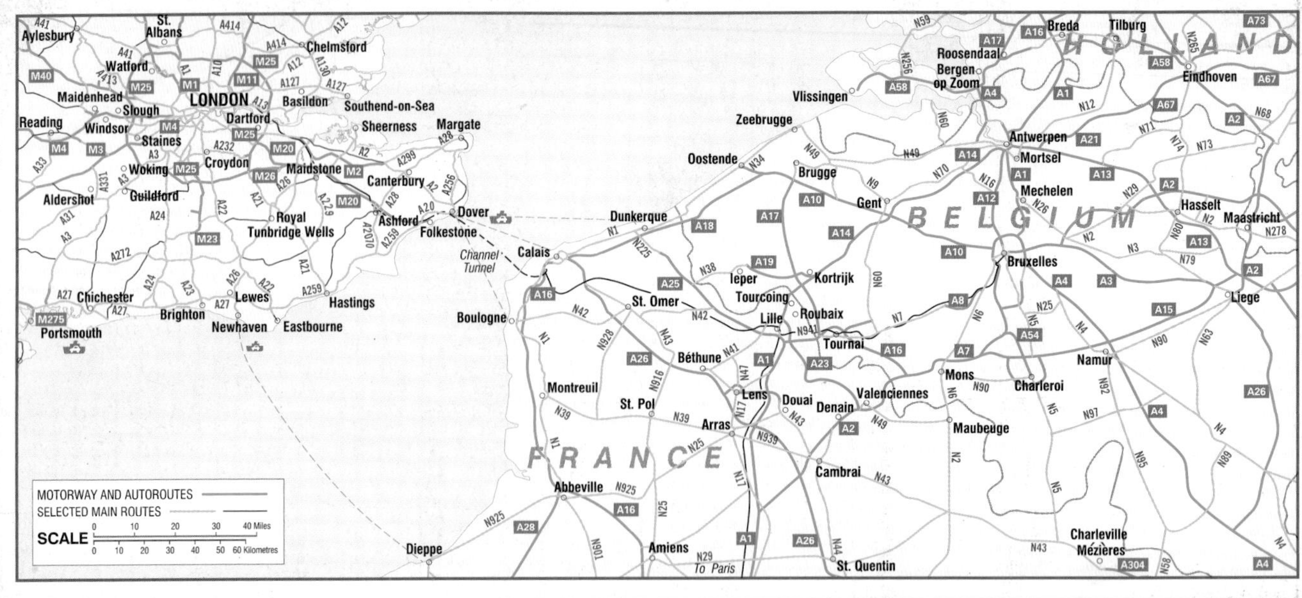

MOTORWAY AND AUTOROUTES
SELECTED MAIN ROUTES
SCALE
0   10   20   30   40 Miles
0   10 20 30 40 50 60 Kilometres

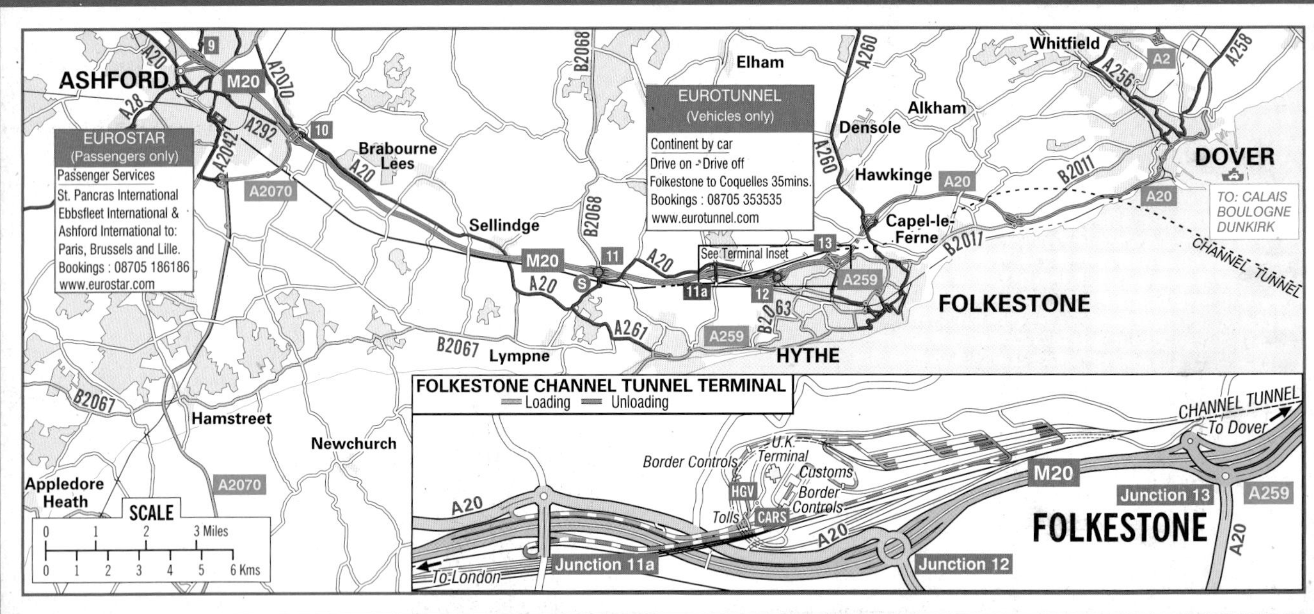

EUROSTAR
(Passengers only)
Passenger Services
St. Pancras International
Ebbsfleet International &
Ashford International to:
Paris, Brussels and Lille.
Bookings : 08705 186186
www.eurostar.com

EUROTUNNEL
(Vehicles only)
Continent by car
Drive on - Drive off
Folkestone to Coquelles 35mins.
Bookings : 08705 353535
www.eurotunnel.com

FOLKESTONE CHANNEL TUNNEL TERMINAL
— Loading — Unloading

SCALE
0   1   2   3 Miles
0   1   2   3   4   5   6 Kms

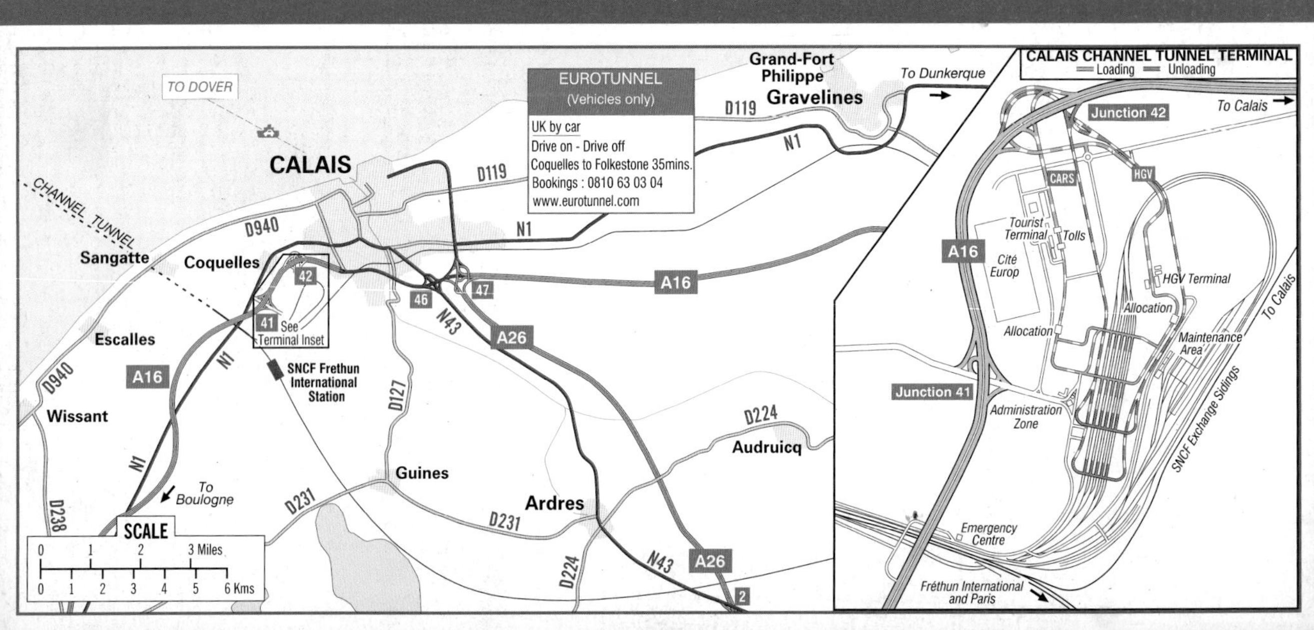

EUROTUNNEL
(Vehicles only)
UK by car
Drive on - Drive off
Coquelles to Folkestone 35mins.
Bookings : 0810 63 03 04
www.eurotunnel.com

CALAIS CHANNEL TUNNEL TERMINAL
— Loading — Unloading

SCALE
0   1   2   3 Miles
0   1   2   3   4   5   6 Kms